Justice Thurgood Marshall Dissents

Edited by Robert Dittmer

Note on the text: most italics and bold has been removed.

Note: This is only a tiny fraction of all the dissents of Justice Thurgood Marshall.

Acknowledgements

Websites (in no particular order):

www.law.cornell.edu
supreme.justia.com
caselaw.findlaw.com
public.resource.org
www.constitution.org
scholar.google.com
en.wikipedia.org

From "The Constitution Day Speech" by Franklin Delano Roosevelt (Sept 17, 1937):
"We will no longer be permitted to sacrifice each generation in turn while the law catches up with life."

From "Letting the Law Catch Up" by Deborah L. Rhode, in Stanford Law Review, vol. 44 (1992):
"[Justice Thurgood Marshall]
You do what you think is right and let the law catch up."

Table of Contents

Contents

Table of Contents 3

Maryland's maximum grant regulation is inconsistent with Social Security Act: Justice Marshall's dissent in Dandridge v. Williams (April 6, 1970) 9

AFDC benefits should not be dependent upon allowing home visits: Justice Marshall's dissent in Wyman v. James (January 12, 1971) 22

Can't use its power of contempt to prevent behavior that Congress has specifically declined to prohibit: Justice Marshall's concurrence in New York Times Co. v. United States (June 30, 1971) 28

Offset provision of 224 of the Social Security Act, 42 U.S.C. 424a, 79 Stat. 406, creates unlawful discrimination: Justice Marshall's dissent in Richardson v. Belcher (November 22, 1971) 33

Equal funding to persons under AFDC: Justice Marshall's dissent in Jefferson v. Hackney (May 30, 1972) 38

Stop-and-Frisk should be unconstitutional: Justice Marshall's dissent in Adams v. Williams (June 12, 1972) 52

The importance of the antitrust laws and competition to every citizen, including professional sports players, must not be minimized: Justice Marshall's dissent in Curt Flood v Bowie Kuhn (June 19, 1972) 57

Death penalty is cruel and unusual punishment: Justice Marshall's concurrence in Furman v. Georgia (June 29, 1972) [Appendices omitted] 62

Shouldn't deny people permission to enter country based on what they advocate: Justice Marshall's dissent in Kleindienst v. Mandel (June 29, 1972) 97

Can't prohibit adult sexual entertainment at bars: Justice Marshall's dissent in California v. LaRue (December 5, 1972) 104

Shouldn't be a fee for due process: Justice Marshall's dissent in United States v. Kras (January 10, 1973) 114

Equalize school-funding: Justice Marshall's dissent in San Antonio Independent School District v. Rodriguez (March 21, 1973) [Appendices omitted] 118

The New York Work Rules clearly exclude persons eligible for assistance under federal standards: Justice Marshall's dissent in New York Department of Social Services v. Dublino (June 21, 1973) 156

Court is mischaracterizing O'Callahan v. Parker: Justice Marshall's dissent in Gosa v. Mayden (June 25, 1973) 162

The two-felony exclusion rule violates equal protection: Justice Marshall's dissent in Marshall v. United States (January 9, 1974) 177

Bank Secrecy Act unconstitutional: Justice Marshall's dissent in California Bankers Association v. Shultz (April 1, 1974) 184

Ex-felons should have their rights restored upon release: Justice Marshall's dissent in Richardson v. Ramirez (June 24, 1974) 187

Respondents have standing: Justice Marshall's dissent in Schlesinger v. Reservists Committee to Stop the War (June 25, 1974) 205

Forced busing even without proof of intentional segregation: Justice Marshall's dissent in Milliken v. Bradley (July 25, 1974) 206

Durational residency requirements for divorce should be unconstitutional: Justice Marshall's dissent in Sosna v. Iowa (January 14, 1975).................... 226

The great discretion available to the King to dispense mercy did not incorporate into the pardoning power the royal right to invade the legislative province of assessing punishments: Justice Marshall's dissent in Schick v. Reed (December 23, 1974) 232

If we're not sure what the lower court meant, ask them: Justice Marshall's dissent in Oregon v. Hass (March 19, 1975)... 239

Sixth amendment should apply to summary courts-martial: Justice Marshall's dissent in Middendorf v. Henry (March 24, 1976) 242

Redistricting: Justice Marshall's dissent in Beer v. United States (March 30, 1976)... 255

It was an act of state: Justice Marshall's dissent in Alfred Dunhill of London, Inc. v. Republic of Cuba (May 24, 1976) 267

Material evidence shouldn't be defined narrowly: Justice Marshall's dissent in United States v. Agurs (June 24, 1976) 281

Shouldn't have to retire at 50: Justice Marshall's dissent in Massachusetts Board of Retirement v. Murgia (June 25, 1976) 286

Shouldn't inventory contents of car to be impounded without warrant: Justice Marshall's dissent in South Dakota v. Opperman (July 6, 1976) 293

Discrimination not yet eliminated: Justice Marshall's dissent in Pasadena City Board of Education v. Spangler (June 28, 1976) 300

What is perhaps most striking about the Rosebud Acts is the absence of any express provision disestablishing the Reservation: Justice Marshall's dissent in Rosebud Sioux Tribe v. Kneip (April 4, 1977) 302

The Immigration and Nationality Act of 1952 shouldn't discriminate between natural mother and natural father: Justice Marshall's dissent in Fiallo v. Bell (April 26, 1977) 314

Welfare programs should fund non-therapeutic abortions: Justice Marshall's dissent in Beal v. Doe (June 20, 1977) 326

Indian tribes enjoy the right to try and punish: Justice Marshall's dissent in Oliphant v. Suquamish Indian Tribe (March 6, 1978) 331

Shouldn't exclude aliens from public employment as state troopers: Justice Marshall's dissent in Foley v. Connelie (March 22, 1978) 331

I do not agree that the presumption should be deemed overcome in this case: Justice Marshall's concurrence and dissent in City of Los Angeles Department of Water and Power v. Manhart (April 25, 1978) 335

The Court demonstrates an attitude of callous indifference to the poor: Justice Marshall's dissent in Flagg Bros., Inc. v. Brooks (May 15, 1978) 338

Racial quotas constitutional: Justice Marshall's concurrence and dissent in Regents of the University of California v. Bakke (June 28, 1978) 340

Evidence obtained in patent violation of agency procedures shouldn't be admissible in a criminal prosecution: Justice Marshall's dissent in United States v. Caceres (April 2, 1979) 349

Some constraints on pretrial discovery are essential to ensure free speech: Justice Marshall's dissent in Herbert v. Lando (April 18, 1979) 358

Limit to burdens on pretrial detainee inmates: Justice Marshall's dissent in Bell v. Wolfish (May 14, 1979) 364

Liberty-interest in parole: Justice Marshall's dissent in Greenholtz v. Inmates of Nebraska Penal and Correctional Complex (May 29, 1979) 374

Minors should get due process, like a lawyer during questioning: Justice Marshall's dissent in Fare v. Michael C. (June 20, 1979) 387

Should need warrant for telephone numbers: Justice Marshall's dissent in Smith v. Maryland (June 20, 1979) 390

No preferences for veterans: Justice Marshall's dissent in Personnel Administrator of Massachusetts v. Feeney (June 5, 1979) 392

Racially discriminatory motivation isn't necessary ingredient of a Fifteenth Amendment violation: Justice Marshall's dissent in City of Mobile v. Bolden (April 22, 1980) 397

Speech on private property: Justice Marshall's concurrence in Pruneyard Shopping Center v. Robins (June 9, 1980) 424

Medicaid should fund abortions: Justice Marshall's dissent in Harris v. McRae (June 30, 1980) 428

Minors should be able to have abortions without their parents or anyone else knowing: Justice Marshall's dissent in H.L. v. Matheson (March 23, 1981) 435

The Commission may be obliged to hold a hearing: Justice Marshall's dissent in Federal Communications Commission v. WNCN Listeners Guild (March 24, 1981)..457

Double-celling can be cruel and unusual punishment: Justice Marshall's dissent in Rhodes v. Chapman (June 15, 1981) 467

If men have to sign up for the draft, so do women: Justice Marshall's dissent in Rostker v. Goldberg (June 25, 1981) 473

Statute criminalizing placement of hand-delivered civic association notices in letterboxes fails this test: Justice Marshall's dissent in United States Postal Service v. Council of Greenburgh Civic Associations (June 25, 1981) 491

Williams' conduct is clearly prohibited by the statute: Justice Marshall's dissent in Williams v. United States (June 29, 1982)..497

Standing: Justice Marshall's dissent in City of Los Angeles v. Lyons (April 20, 1983) 506

Murphy's failure to claim his privilege against self-incrimination did not result in the forfeiture of his rights: Justice Marshall's dissent in Minnesota v. Murphy (February 22, 1984) 523

Police should need warrant to search private land with no trespassing sign: Justice Marshall's dissent in Oliver v. United States (April 17, 1984) 538

Right to counsel should be right to effective counsel: Justice Marshall's dissent in Strickland v. Washington (May 14, 1984)..547

Preventive detention of a juvenile pursuant to 320.5(3)(b) violates the Due Process Clause: Justice Marshall's dissent in Schall v. Martin (June 4, 1984) ...556

Should be no "public safety" exception for Miranda warning: Justice Marshall's dissent in New York v. Quarles (June 12, 1984) 575

Sleeping outside in winter in a highly public place for the purpose of protesting homelessness is protected speech: Justice Marshall's dissent in Clark v. Community for Creative Nonviolence (June 29, 1984) 586

Blanket prohibition on contact visits unreasonable: Justice Marshall's dissent in Block v. Rutherford (July 3, 1984)..596

Mandatory registration for military service violates self-incrimination and equal protection: Justice Marshall's dissent in Selective Service System v. Minnesota Public Interest Research Group (July 5, 1984) 604

His occupation is maritime employment: Justice Marshall's dissent in Herb's Welding, Inc. v. Gray (March 18, 1985) 618

Distinguishing contributions from independent expenditures makes no sense: Justice Marshall's dissent in Federal Election Commission v. National Conservative Political Action Committee (March 18, 1985) 633

Court claims to be using rational-basis scrutiny, but that surely can't be the case and the court should be honest about that: Justice Marshall's dissent in City of Cleburne, Texas v. Cleburne Living Center, Inc. (July 1, 1985) 635

Have to tell jury you bribed the witness to testify: Justice Marshall's dissent in United States v. Bagley (July 2, 1985) 651

Klamath Tribe has special right to hunt and fish on certain lands: Justice Marshall's dissent in Oregon Department of Fish and Wildlife v. Klamath Indian Tribe (July 2, 1985) 666

No successive prosecutions by different States: Justice Marshall's dissent in Heath v. Alabama (December 3, 1985) 674

Court misconceives role of the grand jury and the harmless error doctrine: Justice Marshall's dissent in United States v. Mechanik (February 25, 1986) 680

No reason surviving divorced spouses who remarried could not receive the same survivor's benefits allowed to remarried widowed spouses: Justice Marshall's dissent in Bowen v. Owens (May 19, 1986) 685

Eligibility and benefit levels in the federal food stamp program may be determined on an individual basis rather than just a "household" basis: Justice Marshall's dissent in Lyng v. Castillo (June 27, 1986) 688

Shouldn't require students to pay for school-bus service: Justice Marshall's dissent in Kadrmas v. Dickinson Public Schools (June 24, 1988) 690

The "independent source" exception to the exclusionary rule doesn't justify admitting "rediscovered" evidence: Justice Marshall's dissent in Murray v. United States (June 27, 1988) 694

Can't retry someone who's already started serving their sentence: Justice Marshall's dissent in Lockhart v. Nelson (November 14, 1988) 699

Not unconstitutional for a city to allocate a portion of its contracting dollars for businesses owned or controlled only by members of minority groups: Justice Marshall's dissent in Richmond v. Croson (January 23, 1989) 704

No compulsory collection and chemical testing of railroad workers' blood and urine: Justice Marshall's dissent in Skinner v. Railway Labor Executives' Association (March 21, 1989) 725

Can't deny prisoners visits from parents, spouses, children, clergy members, and close friends: Justice Marshall's dissent in Kentucky Department of Corrections v. Thompson (May 15, 1989) 739

Can't be required to produce a child to the court if such production would be self-incriminating: Justice Marshall's dissent in Baltimore Department of Social Services v. Bouknight (February 20, 1990) 743

Evidence obtained in violation of a court ruling (like Payton v. New York) should be excluded: Justice Marshall's dissent in New York v. Harris (April 18, 1990).750

Undercover agents should also have to give Miranda warnings: Justice Marshall's dissent in Illinois v. Perkins (June 4, 1990) 757

Third Parties shouldn't be able to give consent to enter: Justice Marshall's dissent in Illinois v. Rodriguez (June 21, 1990) 762

Parental notification and 48-hour delay requirements for minors for abortions unconstitutional: Justice Marshall's concurrence and dissent in Hodgson v. Minnesota (June 25, 1990) 768

This cuts back on the principles that inform our selective-taxation precedents: Justice Marshall's dissent in Leathers v. Medlock (April 16, 1991).......................779

The Court radically redefines the content of the "abuse of the writ" doctrine: Justice Marshall's dissent in McCleskey v. Zant (April 16, 1991) 787

The court decides questions we didn't grant certiorari too, and doesn't even understand what the case is about (more than reputation): Justice Marshall's dissent in Siegert v. Gilley (May 23, 1991) 802

Consent to search car shouldn't include consent to open containers, should need another consent for that: Justice Marshall's dissent in Florida v. Luz Piedad Jimeno (May 23, 1991) 809

The suspicionless police sweep of buses violates privacy: Justice Marshall's dissent in Florida v. Bostick (June 20, 1991)...812

No victim-impact statements: Justice Marshall's dissent in Payne v. Tennessee (June 27, 1991)..819

Maryland's maximum grant regulation is inconsistent with Social Security Act: Justice Marshall's dissent in Dandridge v. Williams (April 6, 1970)

MR. JUSTICE MARSHALL, whom MR. JUSTICE BRENNAN joins, dissenting.

For the reasons stated by MR. JUSTICE DOUGLAS, to which I add some comments of my own, I believe that the Court has erroneously concluded that Maryland's maximum grant regulation is consistent with the federal statute. In my view, that regulation is fundamentally in conflict with the basic structure and purposes of the Social Security Act.

More important in the long run than this misreading of a federal statute, however, is the Court's emasculation of the Equal Protection Clause as a constitutional principle applicable to the area of social welfare administration. The Court holds today that, regardless of the arbitrariness of a classification, it must be sustained if any state goal can be imagined that is arguably furthered by its effects. This is so even though the classification's underinclusiveness or overinclusiveness clearly demonstrates that its actual basis is something other than that asserted by the State, and even though the relationship between the classification and the state interests which it purports to serve is so tenuous that it could not seriously be maintained that the classification tends to accomplish the ascribed goals.

The Court recognizes, as it must, that this case involves "the most basic economic needs of impoverished human beings," and that there is therefore a "dramatically real factual difference" between the instant case and those decisions upon which the Court relies. The acknowledgment that these dramatic differences exist is a candid recognition that the Court's decision today is wholly without precedent. I cannot subscribe to the Court's sweeping refusal to accord the Equal Protection Clause any role in this entire area of the law, and I therefore dissent from both parts of the Court's decision.

I

At the outset, it should be emphasized exactly what is involved in determining whether this maximum grant regulation is consistent with and valid under the federal law. In administering its AFDC program, Maryland has established its own standards of need, and they are not under challenge in this litigation. Indeed, the District Court specifically refused to require additional appropriations on the part of the State or to permit appellees to recover a monetary judgment against the State. At the same time, however, there is no contention, nor could there be any, that the maximum grant regulation is in any manner related to calculation of need. [1] Rather, it arbitrarily cuts across state-defined standards of need to deny any additional assistance with respect to the fifth or any succeeding child in a family. [2] In short, the regulation represents no less than the refusal of the State to give any aid whatsoever for the support of certain dependent children who meet the standards of need that the State itself has established.

Since its inception in the Social Security Act of 1935, the focus of the federal AFDC program has been to provide benefits for the support of dependent children of needy families with a view toward maintaining and strengthening family life within the family unit. As succinctly stated by the Senate Committee on Finance, "[t]he objective of the aid to dependent children program is to provide cash assistance for needy children in their own homes." [3] In meeting these objectives, moreover, Congress has provided the outlines that the AFDC plan is to follow if a State should choose to participate in the federal program. The maximum grant regulation, however, does not fall within these outlines or accord with the purposes of the Act. And the Court, by approving it, allows for a complete departure from the congressional intent.

The phrase "aid to families with dependent children," from which the AFDC program derives its name, appears in 402(a)(10) of the Act, 42 U.S.C. § 602(a)(10) (1964 ed., Supp. IV), and is defined in 42 U.S.C. § 606(b) (1964 ed., Supp. IV) as, inter alia, money payments "with respect to . . . dependent children." (Emphasis added.) Moreover, the term "dependent child" is also extensively defined in the Act. See 42 U.S.C. § 606(a) (1964 ed., Supp. IV). Nowhere in the Act is there any sanction or authority for the State to alter those definitions -- that is, to select arbitrarily from among the class of needy dependent children those whom it will aid. Yet the clear effect of the maximum grant regulation is to do just that, for the regulation creates, in effect, a class of otherwise eligible dependent children with respect to whom no assistance is granted.

It was to disapprove just such an arbitrary device to limit AFDC payments that Congress amended § 402(a)(10) in 1950 to provide that aid "shall be furnished with reasonable promptness to all eligible individuals." (Emphasis added.) Surely, as my Brother DOUGLAS demonstrates, this statutory language means at least that the State must take into account the needs of, and provide aid with respect to, all needy dependent children. Indeed, that was our assessment of the congressional design embodied in the AFDC program in King v. Smith, 392 U. S. 309, 392 U. S. 329-330, 392 U. S. 333 (1968).

The opinion of the Court attempts to avoid this reading of the statutory mandate by the conclusion that parents will see that all the children in a large family share in whatever resources are available so that all children "do receive some aid." And "[s]o long as some aid is provided to all eligible families and all eligible children, the statute itself is not violated." The Court also views sympathetically the State's contention that the "all eligible individuals" clause was designed solely to prevent discrimination against new applicants for AFDC benefits. I am unpersuaded, however, by the view that Congress simultaneously prohibited discrimination against one class of dependent children -- those in families not presently receiving benefits -- and at the same time sanctioned discrimination against another class -- those children in large families. Furthermore, the Court's interpretation would permit a State to impose a drastically reduced maximum grant limitation -- or, indeed, a uniform payment of, say, $25 per family per month -- as long as all families were subject to the rule.

Thus, merely by purporting to compute standards of need and granting some benefits to all eligible families, the State would comply with the federal law -- in spite of the fact that the needs of no or very few dependent children would thereby be taken into account in the actual assistance granted. I cannot agree that Congress intended that a State should be entitled to participate in the federally funded AFDC program under such circumstances.

Moreover, the practical consequences of the maximum grant regulation in question here confirm my view that it is invalid. Under the complicated formula for determining the extent of federal support for the AFDC program in the various States, the federal subsidy is based upon "the total number of recipients of aid to families with dependent children." 42 U.S.C. § 603(a) (1964 ed., Supp. IV). "Recipients" is defined in the same provision to include both dependent children and the eligible relative or relatives with whom they live. There is, however, no limitation upon the number of recipients per family unit for whom the federal subsidy is paid to the States. Thus, when a maximum family grant regulation is in effect, the State continues to receive a federal subsidy for each and every dependent child even though the State passes none of this subsidy on to the large families for the use of the additional dependent children.

Specifically, in Maryland, the record in this case indicates that the State spends an average of almost $40 per recipient per month. Under the federal matching formula, federal funds provide $22 of the first $32 per recipient, with anything above $32 being supplied by the State. [4] However, the Federal Government provides a maximum of $22 for every dependent child, although none of that amount is received by the needy family in the case of the fifth or sixth and succeeding children. The effect is to shift a greater proportion of the support of large families from the State to the Federal Government as the family size increases. Indeed, if the size of the family should exceed 11, the State would succeed in transferring the entire support burden for the family to the Federal Government, and even make a "profit" in the sense that it would receive more from the Federal Government with respect to the family than the $250 maximum that is actually paid to that family. It is impossible to conclude that Congress intended so incongruous a result. On the contrary, when Congress undertook to subsidize payments on behalf of each recipient -- including each dependent child -- it seems clear that Congress intended each needy dependent child to receive the use and benefit of at least the incremental amount of the federal subsidy paid on his account.

A second effect of the maximum family grant regulation further demonstrates its inconsistency with the federal program. As administered in Maryland, the regulation serves to provide a strong economic incentive to the disintegration of large families. This is so because a family subject to the maximum regulation can, merely by placing the ineligible children in the homes of other relatives, receive additional monthly payments for the support of these additional dependent children. [5] When families are receiving support that is concededly far below their bare minimum subsistence needs, the economic incentive that the maximum grant regulation provides to divide up large families can hardly be viewed as speculative or negligible. The opinion of this Court does not even dispute this effect. [6] The Court answers by saying that the family relationship "may be attenuated, but it cannot be destroyed." Yet it was just this kind of attenuation that, as the legislative history conclusively demonstrates, [7] Congress was concerned with eliminating in establishing the AFDC program. The Court's rationale takes a long step backward toward the time when persons were dependent upon the charity of their relative -- the very situation meant to be remedied by AFDC.

Despite its denial of the principle that payments should be made with regard to all eligible individuals and its conflict with the basic purposes of the Act, the Maryland regulation is nevertheless found by the Court to be consistent with the federal law because the existence of such regulations has been recognized by Congress. To bolster this view, the Court argues that the same conclusion has been reached by the department charged with administering the Act. On neither score is the Court convincing.

With regard to the position of the Secretary of HEW, about all that can be said with confidence is that we do not know his views on the validity of family maximum regulations within the federal structure. [8] The reason is simple -- he has not been asked. Thus, contrary to our admonition given today to the district courts, in considering cases in this area, that, whenever possible, they "should obtain the views of HEW in those cases where it has not set forth its views," Rosado v. Wyman, ante at 397 U. S. 407, the Government was not invited to file a brief in this case. Perhaps the reason is that this Court is fully versed in the complexities of the federal AFDC program. I am dubious, however, when the Court explicitly relies on the failure of the Secretary to disapprove the Maryland welfare scheme. For if anything at all is completely clear in this area of the law, it is that the failure of HEW to cut off funds from a state program has no meaning at all. See Rosado v. Wyman, supra, at 397 U. S. 426 (DOUGLAS, J., concurring).

Finally, the Court tells us that Congress has said that the Act permits maximum grant regulations. If it had, this part of the case would he obvious; but, of course, it has not. There is no indication Congress has focused on the family maximum, as opposed to individual or other maximums or combinations of such limiting devices. [9] And, to the extent that it could be said to have done so, as my Brother DOUGLAS fully demonstrates, it was in the context of disapproving all maximums, and ameliorating the harshness of their effects. See also Rosado v. Wyman, supra, at 397 U. S. 413-414. These slender threads of legislative comment simply cannot be woven into a conclusion of legislative sanction. Cf. Shapiro v. Thompson, 394 U. S. 618, 394 U. S. 638-640 (1969). Furthermore, it is fundamental that, in construing legislation,

"we must not he guided by a single sentence or member of a sentence, but [should] look to the provisions of the whole law, and to its object and policy."

Richards v. United States, 369 U. S. 1, 369 U. S. 11 (1962). We concluded in King v. Smith, supra, after an extensive review of the AFDC program, that Congress "intended to provide programs for the economic security and protection of all children," and did not intend "arbitrarily to leave one class of destitute children entirely without meaningful protection." 392 U.S. at 3 392 U. S. 30. (Emphasis in original.) That reasoning is likewise applicable to the instant case, in which the maximum grant regulation excludes consideration of the needs of a certain class of dependent children in large families. It is apparent, therefore, that Maryland's maximum grant regulation is not consistent with the Social Security Act, and hence appellees were entitled to the injunction they obtained against its operation.

II

Having decided that the injunction issued by the District Court was proper as a matter of statutory construction, I would affirm on that ground alone. However, the majority has, of necessity, passed on the constitutional issues. I believe that, in overruling the decision of this and every other district court that has passed on the validity of the maximum grant device, [10] the Court both reaches the wrong result and lays down an insupportable test for determining whether a State has denied its citizens the equal protection of the laws.

The Maryland AFDC program, in its basic structure, operates uniformly with regard to all needy children by taking into account the basic subsistence needs of all eligible individuals in the formulation of the standards of need for families of various sizes. However, superimposed upon this uniform system is the maximum grant regulation, the operative effect of which is to create two classes of needy children and two classes of eligible families: those small families and their members who receive payments to cover their subsistence needs and those large families who do not. [11]

This classification process effected by the maximum grant regulation produces a basic denial of equal treatment. Persons who are concededly similarly situated (dependent children and their families), are not afforded equal, or even approximately equal, treatment under the maximum grant regulation. Subsistence benefits are paid with respect to some needy dependent children; nothing is paid with respect to others. Some needy families receive full subsistence assistance as calculated by the State; the assistance paid to other families is grossly below their similarly calculated needs.

Yet, as a general principle, individuals should not be afforded different treatment by the State unless there is a relevant distinction between them, and "a statutory discrimination must be based on differences that are reasonably related to the purposes of the Act in which it is found." Morey v. Doud, 354 U. S. 457, 354 U. S. 465 (1957). See Gulf, Colorado & Santa Fe R. Co. v. Ellis, 165 U. S. 150, 165 U. S. 155 (1897). Consequently, the State may not, in the provision of important services or the distribution of governmental payments, supply benefits to some individuals while denying them to others who are similarly situated. See, e.g., Griffin v. County School Board of Prince Edward County, 377 U. S. 218 (1964).

In the instant case, the only distinction between those children with respect to whom assistance is granted and those children who are denied such assistance is the size of the family into which the child permits himself to be born. The class of individuals with respect to whom payments are actually made (the first four or five eligible dependent children in a family), is grossly underinclusive in terms of the class that the AFDC program was designed to assist, namely, all needy dependent children. Such underinclusiveness manifests "a prima facie violation of the equal protection requirement of reasonable classification," [12] compelling the State to come forward with a persuasive justification for the classification.

The Court never undertakes to inquire for such a justification; rather, it avoids the task by focusing upon the abstract dichotomy between two different approaches to equal protection problems that have been utilized by this Court.

Under the so-called "traditional test," a classification is said to be permissible under the Equal Protection Clause unless it is "without any reasonable basis." Lindsley v. Natural Carbonic Gas Co., 220 U. S. 61, 220 U. S. 78 (1911). [13] On the other hand, if the classification affects a "fundamental right," then the state interest in perpetuating the classification must be "compelling" in order to be sustained. See, e.g., Shapiro v. Thompson, supra; Harper v. Board of Elections, 383 U. S. 663 (1966); McLaughlin v. Florida, 379 U. S. 184 (1964).

This case simply defies easy characterization in terms of one or the other of these "tests." The cases relied on by the Court, in which a "mere rationality" test was actually used, e.g., Williamson v. Lee Optical Co., 348 U. S. 483 (1955), are most accurately described as involving the application of equal protection reasoning to the regulation of business interests. The extremes to which the Court has gone in dreaming up rational bases for state regulation in that area may, in many instances, be ascribed to a healthy revulsion from the Court's earlier excesses in using the Constitution to protect interests that have more than enough power to protect themselves in the legislative halls. This case, involving the literally vital interests of a powerless minority -- poor families without breadwinners -- is far removed from the area of business regulation, as the Court concedes. Why then is the standard used in those cases imposed here? We are told no more than that this case falls in "the area of economics and social welfare," with the implication that, from there, the answer is obvious.

In my view, equal protection analysis of this case is not appreciably advanced by the a priori definition of a "right," fundamental or otherwise. [14] Rather, concentration must be placed upon the character of the classification in question, the relative importance to individuals in the class discriminated against of the governmental benefit that they do not receive, and the asserted state interests in support of the classification. As we said only recently,

"In determining whether or not a state law violates the Equal Protection Clause, we must consider the facts and circumstances behind the law, the interests which the State claims to be protecting, and the interests of those who are disadvantaged by the classification."

Kramer v. Union School District, 395 U. S. 621, 395 U. S. 626 (1969), quoting Williams v. Rhodes, 393 U. S. 23, 393 U. S. 30 (1968). [15]

It is the individual interests here at stake that, as the Court concedes, most clearly distinguish this case from the "business regulation" equal protection cases. AFDC support to needy dependent children provides the stuff that sustains those children's lives: food, clothing, shelter. [16] And this Court has already recognized several times that, when a benefit, even a "gratuitous" benefit, is necessary to sustain life, stricter constitutional standards, both procedural [17] and substantive, [18] are applied to the deprivation of that benefit.

Nor is the distinction upon which the deprivation is here based -- the distinction between large and small families -- one that readily commends itself as a basis for determining which children are to have support approximating subsistence and which are not. Indeed, governmental discrimination between children on the basis of a factor over which they have no control -- the number of their brothers and sisters -- bears some resemblance to the classification between legitimate and illegitimate children which we condemned as a violation of the Equal Protection Clause in Levy v. Louisiana, 391 U. S. 68 (1968).

The asserted state interests in the maintenance of the maximum grant regulation, on the other hand, are hardly clear. In the early stages of this litigation, the State attempted to rationalize the maximum grant regulation on the theory that it was merely a device to conserve state funds, in the language of the motion to dismiss, "a legitimate way of allocating the State's limited resources available for AFDC assistance." Indeed, the initial opinion of the District Court concluded that the sole reason for the regulation, as revealed by the record, was

"to fit the total needs of the State's dependent children, as measured by the State's standards of their subsistence requirements, into an inadequate State appropriation."

297 F.Supp. at 458. The District Court quite properly rejected this asserted justification, for "[t]he saving of welfare costs cannot justify an otherwise invidious classification." Shapiro v. Thompson, supra, at 394 U. S. 633. See Goldberg v. Kelly, ante, at 397 U. S. 266.

In post-trial proceedings in the District Court, and in briefs to this court, the State apparently abandoned reliance on the fiscal justification. In its place, there have now appeared several different rationales for the maximum grant regulation, prominent among them being those relied upon by the majority -- the notions that imposition of the maximum serves as an incentive to welfare recipients to find and maintain employment, and provides a semblance of equality with persons earning a minimum wage.

With regard to the latter, Maryland has urged that the maximum grant regulation serves to maintain a rough equality between wage earning families and AFDC families, thereby increasing the political support for -- or perhaps reducing the opposition to -- the AFDC program. It is questionable whether the Court really relies on this ground, especially when, in many States, the prescribed family maximum bears no such relation to the minimum wage. [19] But the Court does not indicate that a different result might obtain in other cases. Indeed, whether elimination of the maximum would produce welfare incomes out of line with other incomes in Maryland is itself open to question on this record. [20]

It is true that government in the United States, unlike certain other countries, has not chosen to make public aid available to assist families generally in raising their children. Rather, in this case, Maryland, with the encouragement and assistance of the Federal Government, has elected to provide assistance at a subsistence level for those in particular need -- the aged, the blind, the infirm, and the unemployed and unemployable, and their children. The only question presented here is whether, having once undertaken such a program, the State may arbitrarily select from among the concededly eligible those to whom it will provide benefits. And it is too late to argue that political expediency will sustain discrimination not otherwise supportable. Cf. Cooper v. Aaron, 358 U. S. 1 (1958).

Vital to the employment incentive basis found by the Court to sustain the regulation is, of course, the supposition that an appreciable number of AFDC recipients are, in fact, employable. For it is perfectly obvious that limitations upon assistance cannot reasonably operate a a work incentive with regard to those who cannot work or who cannot be expected to work. In this connection, Maryland candidly notes that "only a very small percentage of the total universe of welfare recipients are employable." The State, however, urges us to ignore the "total universe," and to concentrate attention instead upon the heads of AFDC families. Yet the very purpose of the AFDC program since its inception has been to provide assistance for dependent children. The State's position is thus that the State may deprive certain needy children of assistance to which they would otherwise be entitled in order to provide an arguable work incentive for their parents. But the State may not wield its economic whip in this fashion when the effect is to cause a deprivation to needy dependent children in order to correct an arguable fault of their parents.

Cf. Levy v. Louisiana, supra; King v. Smith, supra, at 392 U. S. 334-336 (DOUGLAS, J., concurring); Doe v. Shapiro, 302 F.Supp. 761 (D.C. Conn.1969), appeal dismissed, 396 U. S. 488 (1970).

Even if the invitation of the State to focus upon the heads of AFDC families is accepted, the minimum rationality of the maximum grant regulation is hard to discern. The District Court found that, of Maryland's more than 32,000 AFDC families, only about 116 could be classified as having employable members, and, of these, the number to which the maximum grant regulation was applicable is not disclosed by the record. The State objects that this figure includes only families in which the father is unemployed, and fails to take account of families in which an employable mother is the head of the household. At the same time, however, the State itself has recognized that the vast proportion of these mothers are, in fact, unemployable because they are mentally or physically incapacitated, because they have no marketable skills, or, most prominently, because the best interests of the children dictate that the mother remain in the home. [21] Thus, it is clear, although the record does not disclose precise figures, that the total number of "employable" mothers is but a fraction of the total number of AFDC mothers. Furthermore, the record is silent as to what proportion of large families subject to the maximum have "employable" mothers. Indeed, one must assume that the presence of the mother in the home can be less easily dispensed with in the case of large families, particularly where small children are involved, and alternative provisions for their care are accordingly more difficult to arrange. In short, not only has the State failed to establish that there is a substantial or even a significant proportion of AFDC heads of households as to whom the maximum grant regulation arguably serves as a viable and logical work incentive, but it is also indisputable that the regulation, at best, is drastically overinclusive, since it applies with equal vigor to a very substantial number of persons who, like appellees, are completely disabled from working.

Finally, it should be noted that, to the extent there is a legitimate state interest in encouraging heads of AFDC households to find employment, application of the maximum grant regulation is also grossly underinclusive, because it singles out and affects only large families. No reason is suggested why this particular group should be carved out for the purpose of having unusually harsh "work incentives" imposed upon them. Not only has the State selected for special treatment a small group from among similarly situated families, but it has done so on a basis -- family size -- that bears no relation to the evil that the State claims the regulation was designed to correct. There is simply no indication whatever that heads of large families, as opposed to heads of small families, are particularly prone to refuse to seek or to maintain employment.

The State has presented other arguments to support the regulation. However, they are not dealt with specifically by the Court, and the reason is not difficult to discern. The Court has picked the strongest available; the others suffer from similar and greater defects. [22] Moreover, it is relevant to note that both Congress and the State have adopted other measures that deal specifically with exactly those interests the State contends are advanced by the maximum grant regulation. Thus, for example, employable AFDC recipient are required to seek employment through the congressionally established Work Incentive Program, which provide an elaborate system of counseling, training, and incentive payments for heads of AFDC families. See generally 42 U.S.C. §§ 63644 (1964 ed., Supp. IV). [23] The existence of these alternatives does not, of course, conclusively establish the invalidity of the maximum grant regulation. It is certainly relevant, however, in appraising the overall interest of the State in the maintenance of the regulation.

In the final analysis, Maryland has set up an AFDC program structured to calculate and pay the minimum standard of need to dependent children. Having set up that program, however, the State denies some of those needy children the minimum subsistence standard of living, and it does so on the wholly arbitrary basis that they happen to be members of large families. One need not speculate too far on the actual reason for the regulation, for, in the early stages of this litigation, the State virtually conceded that it set out to limit the total cost of the program along the path of least resistance. Now, however, we are told that other rationales can be manufactured to support the regulation and to sustain it against a fundamental constitutional challenge.

However, these asserted state interests, which are not insignificant in themselves, are advanced either not at all or by complete accident by the maximum grant regulation. Clearly they could be served by measures far less destructive of the individual interests at stake. Moreover, the device assertedly chosen to further them is, at one and the same time, both grossly underinclusive -- because it does not apply at all to a much larger class in an equal position -- and grossly overinclusive -- because it applies so strongly against a substantial class as to which it can rationally serve no end. Were this a case of pure business regulation, these defects would place it beyond what has heretofore seemed a borderline case, see, e.g., Railway Express Agency v. New York, 336 U. S. 106 (1949), and I do not believe that the regulation can be sustained even under the Court's "reasonableness" test.

In any event, it cannot suffice merely to invoke the spectre of the past and to recite from Lindsley v. Natural Carbonic Gas Co. and Williamson v. Lee Optical Co. to decide the case. Appellees are not a gas company or an optical dispenser; they are needy dependent children and families who are discriminated against by the State. The basis of that discrimination -- the classification of individuals into large and small families -- is too arbitrary and too unconnected to the asserted rationale, the impact on those discriminated against -- the denial of even a subsistence existence -- too great, and the supposed interests served too contrived and attenuated to meet the requirements of the Constitution. In my view, Maryland's maximum grant regulation is invalid under the Equal Protection Clause of the Fourteenth Amendment. I would affirm the judgment of the District Court.

Notes

[1] The Court is thus wrong in speaking of

"the greater ability of large families -- because of the inherent economics of scale -- to accommodate their needs to diminished per capita payments."

Those economics have already been taken into account once in calculating the standard of need. Indeed, it borders on the ludicrous to suggest that a large family is more capable of living on perhaps 50% of its standard of need than a small family is on 95%.

[2] Because of minor variations in the calculation of the subsistence needs of particular families, and because the maximum grant varies between $240 and $250 per month, depending upon the county in which a particular family resides, the cut-off point between families that receive the full subsistence allowance and those that do not is not precisely families of more than six members. In practice, it appears that the subsistence needs of a family of six members are fully met. The needs of the seventh member (i.e., the fifth or sixth child, depending upon whether one or both parents are within the assistance unit), as defined by the State, are met, if at all, only to a very small extent. In the usual situation, no payments whatever would be made with respect to any additional eligible dependent children.

[3] S.Rep. No. 165, 87th Cong., 1st Sess., 6 (1961). (Emphasis added.)

[4] More technically, the Federal Government supplies five-sixths of the overall amount spent per recipient up to $18, plus one-half of the amount from $18 to $32, to a

total of $22. See 42 U.S.C. § 603 (1964 ed., Supp. IV).

[5] For example, in the case of the appellee Mrs. Williams, if she were to place two of her children over 12 years of age with relatives, payments of $7 per month would be paid with respect to each child. Thus, a total of $408 per month, or $158 above the maximum, would be available for the support of Mrs. Williams and her eight children. Similarly, if appellees Mr. and Mrs. Cary were to place with relatives two of their children who are between the ages of 6 and 12 years, each child would be eligible to receive $65. Hence, Mr. and Mrs. Gary and their eight children would receive support in the amount of $380 per month, or some $130 above the family maximum.

[6] The State has contended that the economic incentive to the disintegration of large families that the maximum grant regulation provides is merely speculative. However, serious doubt is cast upon this view by the stipulation of facts entered in the District Court which states in part that, despite the strong desire to keep their families together, appellees in this case were having great difficulty in doing so because of the limitations on their grants.

[7] In S.Rep. No. 628, 74th Cong., 1st Sess., 17 (1935), the original goals of the AFDC program are stated as follows:

"With no income coming in, and with young children for whom provision must be made for a number of years, families without a father's support require public assistance unless they have been left with adequate means or are aided by friends and relatives. . . . Through cash grants adjusted to the needs of the family, it is possible to keep the young children with their mother in their own home, thus preventing the necessity of placing the children in institutions. This is recognized by everyone to be the least expensive, and altogether the most desirable, method for meeting the needs of these families that has yet been devised."

(Emphasis added.) See also H.R.Rep. No. 615, 74th Cong., 1st Sess., 10 (1935).

These goals remain the same today. See 42 U.S.C. § 601 (1964 ed., Supp. IV). See generally Note, Welfare's "Condition X," 6 Yale L.J. 1222, 1232-1233 (1967).

[8] In various briefs submitted both to this Court and to other courts in analogous litigation, the Secretary of HEW and the Solicitor General have taken the occasion to label family maximum grant regulations as "arbitrary," oppressive of large families, as resulting in "patently different treatment of individuals," and having received, at least inferentially, the disfavor of Congress. See, e.g., Memorandum for the United States as Amicus Curiae, Rosado v. Wyman, ante, p 397 U. S. 397; Brief of Robert H. Finch, Secretary of Health, Education, and Welfare as Amicus Curiae, Lampton v. Bonin, 299 F.Supp. 336, 304 F.Supp. 1384 (D.C.E.D.La.1969); Brief of Robert H. Finch, Jefferson v. Hackney, 304 F.Supp. 1332 (D.C.N.D.Tex.1969). Hence, the views of HEW on the precise issue presented in he instant case are, at the very best, ambiguous, and quite possibly the opposite of what the Court ascribes to it.

[9] The maximum may be expressed in terms of a flat dollar amount, as a percentage of the individual's budgetary deficit (i.e., the difference between need and

other income), or in both ways. A system of individual maximums may, or may not, be combined with a family maximum, or, alternatively, a family maximum may be imposed in the absence of individual maximums. See generally HEW, State Maximums and Other Methods of Limiting Money Payments to Recipients of the Special Types of Public Assistance, Oct.1968 (NCSS Report D-3); Sparer, Social Welfare Law Testing, 12 Prac.Law. (No. 4) 13, 21 (1966). In addition, there are differing methods by which family maximums may be related to other resources available to the family. Some States, including Maryland, subtract available resources from the state-calculated need; in other jurisdictions, available resources are subtracted from the family maximum. See, e.g., Dews v. Henry, 297 F.Supp. 587 (D.C. Ariz.1969), involving litigation with respect to the Arizona family maximum.

[10] The lower courts have been unanimous in the view that maximum grant regulations such as Maryland's are invalid. See Dews v. Henry, supra; Westberry v. Fisher, 297 F.Supp. 1109 (D.C. Me.1969); Lindsey v. Smith, 303 F.Supp. 1203 (D.C.W.D. Wash.1969); Kaiser v. Montgomery, ___ F.Supp. ___ (D.C.N.D. Cal.1969). See also Collins v. State Board of Social Welfare, 248 Iowa 369, 81 N.W.2d 4 (1957) (family maximum invalid under equal protection clause of state constitution); Metcalf v. Swank, 293 F.Supp. 268 (D.C.N.D.Ill.1968) (dictum).

[11] In theory, no payments are made with respect to needy dependent children in excess of four or five, as the case may be. In practice, of course, the excess children share in the benefits that are paid with respect to the other member of the family. The result is that support for the entire family is reduced below minimum subsistence levels. However, for purposes of equal protection analysis, it makes no difference whether the class against which the maximum grant regulation discriminates is defined as eligible dependent children in excess of the fourth or fifth, or, alternatively, as individuals in large families generally, that is, those with more than six members.

[12] Tussman & tenBroek, The Equal Protection of the Laws, 37 Calif.L.Rev. 341, 348 (1949).

[13] See generally Developments in the Law -- Equal Protection, 82 Harv.L.Rev. 1065, 1076-1087 (1969).

[14] See generally Van Alstyne, The Demise of the Right-Privilege Distinction in Constitutional Law, 81 Harv.L.Rev. 1439 (1968). Appellees do argue that their "fundamental rights" are infringed by the maximum grant regulation. They cite, for example, Skinner v. Oklahoma, 316 U. S. 535 (1942), for the proposition that the "right of procreation" is fundamental. This statement is no doubt accurate as far as it goes, but the effect of the maximum grant regulation upon the right of procreation is marginal and indirect, at best, totally unlike the compulsory sterilization law that was at issue in Skinner.

At the same time, the Court's insistence that equal protection analysis turns on the basis of a closed category of "fundamental rights" involves a curious value judgment. It is certainly difficult to believe that a person whose very survival is at stake would be comforted by the knowledge that his "fundamental" rights are preserved intact.

On the issue of whether there is a "right" to welfare assistance, see generally Graham, Public Assistance: The Right To Receive; the Obligation To Repay, 43 N.Y.U.L.Rev. 451 (1968); Harvith, Federal Equal Protection and Welfare Assistance, 31 Albany L.Rev. 210 (1967); Note, Welfare Due Process: The Maximum Grant Limitation on the Right To Survive, 3 Ga.L.Rev. 459 (1969). See also Universal Declaration of Human Rights, Art. 25.

[15] This is essentially what this Court has done in applying equal protection concepts in numerous cases, though the various aspects of the approach appear with a greater or lesser degree of clarity in particular cases. See, e.g., McLaughlin v. Florida, supra; Rinaldi v. Yeager, 384 U. S. 305 (1966); Carrington v. Rash, 380 U. S. 89 (1965); Douglas v. California, 372 U. S. 353 (1963); Skinner v. Oklahoma, supra.

For an application of this approach to several welfare questions, see Comment, Equal Protection as a Measure of Competing Interests in Welfare Litigation, 21 Me.L.Rev. 175 (1969).

[16] See also Rothstein v. Wyman, 303 F.Supp. 339, 346-347 (D.C.S.D.N.Y.1969); Harvith, supra, n. 14, 31 Albany L.Rev. at 222-226.

[17] See Sniadach v. Family Finance Corp., 395 U. S. 337, 395 U. S. 340-342 (1969) (relying on devastating impact of wage garnishment to require prior hearing as a matter of due process); Goldberg v. Kelly, ante at 397 U. S. 264:

"Thus, the crucial factor in this context -- a factor not present in the case of the blacklisted government contractor, the discharged government employee, the taxpayer denied a tax exemption, or virtually anyone else whose governmental entitlements are ended -- is that termination of aid pending resolution of a controversy over eligibility may deprive an eligible recipient of the very means by which to live while he waits."

[18] Compare Shapiro v. Thompson, supra, at 394 U. S. 627, striking down one-year residency requirement for welfare eligibility as violation of equal protection, and noting that the benefits in question are "the very means to subsist -- food, shelter, and other necessities of life," with Kirk v. Board of Regents, 273 Cal.App.2d 430, 439-440, 78 Cal.Rptr. 260, 266-267 (1969), appeal dismissed, 396 U. S. 554 (1970), upholding one-year residency requirement for tuition-free graduate education at state university, and distinguishing Shapiro on the ground that it

"involved the immediate and pressing need for preservation of life and health of persons unable to live without public assistance, and their dependent children."

These cases and those cited in n. 17, supra, suggest that, whether or not there is a constitutional "right" to subsistence (as to which see n. 14, supra), deprivations of benefits necessary for subsistence will receive closer constitutional scrutiny, under both the Due Process and Equal Protection Clauses, than will deprivations of less essential forms of governmental entitlements.

[19] See HEW Report on Money Payments to Recipients of Special Types of Public Assistance, Oct.1967, Table 4 (NCSS Report D-4).

[20] The State of Maryland has long spoken with at least two voices on the issue of the maximum grant regulation. The Department of Public Welfare has taken the position, over a number of years, that the regulation should be abolished, and has made several proposals to that effect. In so doing, the Department has taken the position that its proposals would not set welfare benefits out of line with household incomes throughout the State. See, e.g., Minutes of State Board of Public Welfare Meeting, September 26, 1958, App. 130-132.

[21] Indeed, Rule 200, § IX A(2)(b)(5) of the Manual of the Md. Dept. of Social Services prohibits the referral for employment of AFDC mothers who are needed in the home. And the unsuitability of many AFDC mothers has been well chronicled in Md. Dept. of Social Services, Profile of Caseloads, Research Report No. 5, p. 6 (1969). See also Carter, The Employment Potential of AFDC Mothers, 6 Welfare in Review, No. 4, pp. 1, 4 (1968).

[22] Thus, the State cannot single out a minuscule proportion of the total number of families in the State as in need of birth control incentives. Not only is the classification effected by the regulation totally underinclusive if this is its rationale, but it also arbitrarily punishes children for factors beyond their control, and overinclusively applies to families, like appellees', that were already large before it became necessary to seek assistance. For similar reasons, the argument that the regulation serves as a disincentive to desertion does not stand scrutiny.

[23] Likewise, the State, with the encouragement of Congress. see 42 U.S.C. §§ 602(a) (21), 610 (1964 ed., Supp. IV), has developed extensive statutory provisions to deal specifically with the problem of parental desertion. See generally Md.Ann.Code, Art. 27, §§ 88-96 (1967 Repl. Vol.). And Congress has mandated, with respect to family planning, that the States provide services to AFDC recipients with the objective of "preventing or reducing the incidence of births out of wedlock and otherwise strengthening family life." 42 U.S.C. § 602(a)(15) (1964 ed., Supp. IV).

AFDC benefits should not be dependent upon allowing home visits: Justice Marshall's dissent in Wyman v. James (January 12, 1971)

MR. JUSTICE MARSHALL, whom MR. JUSTICE BRENNAN joins, dissenting.

Although I substantially agree with its initial statement of the issue in this case, the Court's opinion goes on to imply that the appellee has refused to provide information germane to a determination of her eligibility for AFDC benefits. The record plainly shows, however, that Mrs. James offered to furnish any information that the appellants desired and to be interviewed at any place other than her home. Appellants rejected her offers and terminated her benefits solely on the ground that she refused to permit a home visit. In addition, appellants make no contention that any sort of probable cause exists to suspect appellee of welfare fraud or child abuse.

Simply stated, the issue in this case is whether a state welfare agency can require all recipients of AFDC benefits to submit to warrantless "visitations" of their homes. In answering that question, the majority dodges between constitutional issues to reach a result clearly inconsistent with the decisions of this Court. We are told that there is no search involved in this case; that, even if there were a search, it would not be unreasonable; and that, even if this were an unreasonable search, a welfare recipient waives her right to object by accepting benefits. I emphatically disagree with all three conclusions. Furthermore, I believe that binding regulations of the Department of Health, Education, and Welfare prohibit appellants from requiring the home visit.

I

The Court's assertion that this case concerns no search "in the Fourth Amendment meaning of that term" is neither "obvious" nor "simple." I should have thought that the Fourth Amendment governs all intrusions by agents of the public upon personal security, Terry v. Ohio, 392 U. S. 1, 392 U. S. 18 n. 15 (1968). As MR. JUSTICE HARLAN has said:

"[T]he Constitution protects the privacy of the home against all unreasonable intrusion of whatever character. . . . '[It applies] to all invasions on the part of the government and its employes of the sanctity of a man's home.'"

Poe v. Ullman, 367 U. S. 497, 367 U. S. 550-551 (1961) (dissenting opinion). This Court has rejected as "anomalous" the contention that only suspected criminals are protected by the Fourth Amendment, Camara v. Municipal Court, 387 U. S. 523, 387 U. S. 530 (1967). In an era of rapidly burgeoning governmental activities and their concomitant inspectors, caseworkers, and researchers, a restriction of the Fourth Amendment to "the traditional criminal law context" tramples the ancient concept that a man's home is his castle. Only last Term, we reaffirmed that this concept has lost none of its vitality, Rowan v. United States Post Office, 397 U. S. 728, 397 U. S. 738 (1970).

Even if the Fourth Amendment does not apply to each and every governmental entry into the home, the welfare visit is not some sort of purely benevolent inspection. No one questions the motives of the dedicated welfare caseworker. Of course, caseworkers seek to be friends, but the point is that they are also required to be sleuths. The majority concedes that the "visitation" is partially investigative, but claims that this investigative aspect has been given too much emphasis. Emphasis has indeed been given. Time and again, in briefs and at oral argument, appellants emphasized the need to enter AFDC homes to guard against welfare fraud and child abuse, both of which are felonies. [1] The New York statutes provide emphasis by requiring all caseworkers to report any evidence of fraud that a home visit uncovers, N.Y. Social Services Law 145. And appellants have strenuously emphasized the importance of the visit to provide evidence leading to civil forfeitures including elimination of benefits and loss of child custody.

Actually, the home visit is precisely the type of inspection proscribed by Camara and its companion case, See v. City of Seattle, 387 U. S. 541 (1967), except that the welfare visit is a more severe intrusion upon privacy and family dignity. Both the home visit and the searches in those cases may convey benefits to the householder. Fire inspectors give frequent advice concerning fire prevention, wiring capacity, and other matters, and obvious self-interest causes many to welcome the fire or safety inspection. Similarly, the welfare caseworker may provide welcome advice on home management and child care. Nonetheless, both searches may result in the imposition of civil penalties -- loss or reduction of welfare benefits or an order to upgrade a housing defect. The fact that one purpose of the visit is to provide evidence that may lead to an elimination of benefits is sufficient to grant appellee protection since Camara stated that the Fourth Amendment applies to inspections which can result in only civil violations, 387 U.S. at 387 U. S. 531. But here the case is stronger since the home visit, like many housing inspections, may lead to criminal convictions.

The Court attempts to distinguish See and Camara by telling us that those cases involved "true" and "genuine" searches. The only concrete distinction offered is that See and Camara concerned criminal prosecutions for refusal to permit the search. The Camara opinion did observe that one could be prosecuted for a refusal to allow that search; but, apart from the issue of consent, there is neither logic in, nor precedent for, the view that the ambit of the Fourth Amendment depends not on the character of the governmental intrusion but on the size of the club that the State wields against a resisting citizen. Even if the magnitude of the penalty were relevant, which sanction for resisting the search is more severe? For protecting the privacy of her home, Mrs. James lost the sole means of support for herself and her infant son. For protecting the privacy of his commercial warehouse, Mr. See received a $100 suspended fine.

Conceding for the sake of argument that someone might view the "visitation" as a search, the majority nonetheless concludes that such a search is not unreasonable. However, its mode of reaching that conclusion departs from the entire history of Fourth Amendment case law. Of course, the Fourth Amendment test is reasonableness, but, in determining whether a search is reasonable, this Court is not free merely to balance, in a totally ad hoc fashion, any number of subjective factors. An unbroken line of cases holds that, subject to a few narrowly drawn exceptions, any search without a warrant is constitutionally unreasonable, see, e.g., Agnello v. United States., 269 U. S. 20, 269 U. S. 32 (1925); Johnson v. United States, 333 U. S. 10, 333 U. S. 13-14 (1948); Chapman v. United States, 365 U. S. 610, 365 U. S. 613-615 (1961); Camara v. Municipal Court, 387 U. S. 523, 387 U. S. 528-529 (1967); Chimel v. California, 395 U. S. 752, 395 U. S. 762 (1969); Vale v. Louisiana, 399 U. S. 30, 399 U. S. 34-35 (1970). In this case, no suggestion that evidence will disappear, that a criminal will escape, or that an officer will be injured justifies the failure to obtain a warrant. Instead, the majority asserts what amounts to three state interests that allegedly render this search reasonable. None of these interests is sufficient to carve out a new exception to the warrant requirement.

First, it is argued that the home visit is justified to protect dependent children from "abuse" and "exploitation."

These are heinous crimes, but they are not confined to indigent households.

Would the majority sanction, in the absence of probable cause, compulsory visits to all American homes for the purpose of discovering child abuse? Or is this Court prepared to hold as a matter of constitutional law that a mother, merely because she is poor, is substantially more likely to injure or exploit her children? Such a categorical approach to an entire class of citizens would be dangerously at odds with the tenets of our democracy.

Second, the Court contends that caseworkers must enter the homes of AFDC beneficiaries to determine eligibility. Interestingly, federal regulations do not require the home visit. In fact, the regulations specify the recipient himself as the primary source of eligibility information, thereby rendering an inspection of the home only one of several alternative secondary sources. [2] The majority's implication that a biannual home visit somehow assures the verification of actual residence or actual physical presence in the home strains credulity in the context of urban poverty. Despite the caseworker's responsibility for dependent children, he is not even required to see the children as a part of the home visit. [3] Appellants offer scant explanation for their refusal even to attempt to utilize public records, expenditure receipts, documents such as leases, non-home interviews, personal financial records, sworn declarations, etc. -- all sources that governmental agencies regularly accept as adequate to establish eligibility for other public benefits. In this setting, it ill behooves appellants to refuse to utilize informational sources less drastic than an invasion of the privacy of the home.

We are told that the plight of Mrs. James is no different from that of a taxpayer who is required to document his right to a tax deduction, but this analogy is seriously flawed. The record shows that Mrs. James has offered to be interviewed anywhere other than her home, to answer any questions, and to provide any documentation that the welfare agency desires. The agency curtly refused all these offers and insisted on its "right" to pry into appellee's home. Tax exemptions are also governmental "bounty." A true analogy would be an Internal Revenue Service requirement that, in order to claim a dependency exemption, a taxpayer must allow a specially trained IRS agent to invade the home for the purpose of questioning the occupants and looking for evidence that the exemption is being properly utilized for the benefit of the dependent. If such a system were even proposed, the cries of constitutional outrage would be unanimous.

Appellants offer a third state interest that the Court seems to accept as partial justification for this search. We are told that the visit is designed to rehabilitate, to provide aid. This is strange doctrine indeed. A paternalistic notion that a complaining citizen's constitutional rights can be violated so long as the State is somehow helping him is alien to our Nation's philosophy. More than 40 years ago, Mr. Justice Brandeis warned:

"Experience should teach us to be most on our guard to protect liberty when the Government's purposes are beneficent."

Olmstead v. United States, 277 U. S. 438, 277 U. S. 479 (1928) (dissenting opinion).

Throughout its opinion, the majority alternates between two views of the State's interest in requiring the home visit. First we are told that the State's purpose is benevolent so that no search is involved. Next we are told that the State's need to prevent child abuse and to avoid the misappropriation of welfare funds justifies dispensing with the warrant requirement. But when all the State's purposes are considered at one time, I can only conclude that the home visit is a search and that, absent a warrant, that search is unreasonable. [4]

Although the Court does not agree with my conclusion that the home visit is an unreasonable search, its opinion suggests that, even if the visit were unreasonable, appellee has somehow waived her right to object. Surely the majority cannot believe that valid Fourth Amendment consent can be given under the threat of the loss of one's sole means of support. Nor has Mrs. James waived her rights. Had the Court squarely faced the question of whether the State can condition welfare payments on the waiver of clear constitutional rights, the answer would be plain. The decisions of this Court do not support the notion that a State can use welfare benefits as a wedge to coerce "waiver" of Fourth Amendment rights, see Reich, Midnight Welfare Searches and the Social Security Act, 72 Yale L.J. 1347, 1349-1350 (1963); Note, Rehabilitation, Investigation and the Welfare Home Visit, 79 Yale L.J. 746, 758
(1970). In Sherbert v. Verner, [5] this Court did not say, "Aid merely ceases. There is no abridgment of religious freedom." Nor did the Court say in Speiser v.Randall, [6] "The tax is simply increased. No one is compelled to relinquish First Amendment rights." As my Brother Douglas points out, the majority's statement that Mrs. James' "choice [to be searched or to lose her benefits] is entirely hers, and nothing of constitutional magnitude is involved" merely restates the issue. To MR. JUSTICE DOUGLAS' eloquent discussion of the law of unconstitutional conditions, I would add only that this Court last Term reaffirmed Sherbert and Speiser as applicable to the law of public welfare:

"Relevant constitutional restraints apply as much to the withdrawal of public assistance benefits as to disqualification for unemployment compensation . . . denial of a tax exemption . . . or . . . discharge from public employment."

Goldberg v. Kelly, 397 U. S. 254, 397 U. S. 262 (1970).

II

The Court's examination of the constitutional issues presented by this case has constrained me to respond. It would not have been necessary to reach these questions, for I believe that HEW regulations, binding on the States, prohibit the unconsented home visit. [7]

The federal Handbook of Public Assistance Administration provides:

"The [state welfare] agency especially guards against violations of legal rights and common decencies in such areas as entering a home by force, or without permission, or under false pretenses; making home visits outside of working hours, and particularly making such visits during sleeping hours. . . ."

Part IV, § 2300(a) (emphasis supplied). Although the tone of this language is descriptive, HEW requirements are Stated in terms of principles and objectives, Handbook, pt. I, § 4210(3); and appellants do not contend that this regulation is merely advisory. Instead, appellants respond with the tired assertion that consent obtained by threatening termination of benefits constitutes valid permission under this regulation. There is no reason to suspect that HEW shares this crabbed view of consent. The Handbook, itself, insists on careful scrutiny of purported consent, pt. IV, § 2400. Section 2200(a) is designed to protect the privacy of welfare recipients, and it would be somewhat ironic to adopt a construction of the regulation that provided that any person who invokes his privacy rights ceases to be a recipient.

Appellants next object that the home visit has long been a part of welfare administration, and has never been disapproved by HEW. The short answer to this is that we deal with only the unconsented home visit. The general utility and acceptance of the home visit casts little light on whether HEW might prefer not to impose the visit on unwilling recipients. Appellants also remind us that the Federal Government itself requires a limited number of home visits for sampling purposes.

However, while there may well be a special need to employ mandatory visits as a part of quality control samples, Mrs. James' home was not a part of such a sample. Furthermore, appellants admit that § 2200(a) governs the quality control program, so it is not clear that unconsented home visits are allowed even for sampling purposes. Although there appears to be no regulatory history, appellants tell us § 2200(a) merely permits a recipient to refuse a particular home visit, and does not allow him to forbid home visits altogether. I suppose that one could read such a limitation into the section, but, given the regulation's explicit language, given that HEW does not require home visits and views the visits as only one of several alternative sources of eligibility information, given HEW's concern for the privacy of its clients, and given the durable principle of this Court that doubtful questions of interpretation should be resolved in a manner which avoids constitutional questions, United States v. Delaware & Hudson Co., 213 U. S. 366, 213 U. S. 407 (1909), I would conclude that Mrs. James is protected by § 2200(a).

III

In deciding that the homes of AFDC recipients are not entitled to protection from warrantless searches by welfare caseworkers, the Court declines to follow prior case law, and employs a rationale that, if applied to the claims of all citizens, would threaten the vitality of the Fourth Amendment. This Court has occasionally pushed beyond established constitutional contours to protect the vulnerable and to further basic human values. I find no little irony in the fact that the burden of today's departure from principled adjudication is placed upon the lowly poor. Perhaps the majority has explained why a commercial warehouse deserves more protection than does this poor woman's home. I am not convinced, and therefore I must respectfully dissent.

Notes

[1] For example, appellants' Reply Brief offers two specific illustrations of the home visit's efficacy. In the first, a man was discovered in the home and benefit were terminated. In the second, child abuse was discovered.

[2] HEW Handbook of Public Assistance Administration, pt. IV, § 2200(e)(1).

[3] Appellants respond by asserting that, if the caseworker becomes suspicious concerning the child's absence, further investigation may take place. One certainly would hope that the caseworker would continue his investigation, but the fact remains that the failure to require that the child be seen undercuts the argument that the home visit is designed to protect the child's welfare and necessary to verify his presence in the home.

[4] Since the majority refuses to sanction the warrant procedure in any form, I have not discussed what standard should be required for a warrant to issue. Certainly, if one of the purposes of the welfare search is to obtain evidence of criminal conduct, that is no reason to permit less than probable cause. And because the home visit is a more severe intrusion than is the housing inspection and there are less drastic means to obtain eligibility information, I would apply the analysis of Camara and would be inclined to utilize a traditional probable cause standard.

[5] 374 U. S. 374 U.S. 398 (1963).

[6] 357 U. S. 357 U.S. 513 (1958).

[7] It is a time-honored doctrine that statutes and regulations are first examined by a reviewing court to see if constitutional questions can be avoided, Ashwander v. TVA, 297 U. S. 288, 297 U. S. 346-348 (1936) (Brandeis, J., concurring); see, e.g., Dandridge v. Willlams, 397 U. S. 471 (1970); King v. Smith, 392 U. S. 309 (1968). The court below chose not to invoke this doctrine, and litigation in this Court has emphasized the constitutional issues. However, the nonconstitutional questions were briefed by an amicus curiae and appellants responded fully in their Reply Brief. The parties may prefer a decision on constitutional grounds; but we, of course, are not bound by their litigation strategies.

Can't use its power of contempt to prevent behavior that Congress has specifically declined to prohibit: Justice Marshall's concurrence in New York Times Co. v. United States (June 30, 1971)

MR. JUSTICE MARSHALL, concurring.

The Government contends that the only issue in these cases is whether, in a suit by the United States, "the First Amendment bars a court from prohibiting a newspaper from publishing material whose disclosure would pose a 'grave and immediate danger to the security of the United States.' " Brief for the United States 7. With all due respect, I believe the ultimate issue in these cases is even more basic than the one posed by the Solicitor General. The issue is whether this Court or the Congress has the power to make law.

In these cases, there is no problem concerning the President's power to classify information as "secret" or "top secret." Congress has specifically recognized Presidential authority, which has been formally exercised in Exec.Order 10501 (1953), to classify documents and information. See, e.g., 18 U.S.C. § 798; 50 U.S.C. § 783. [1] Nor is there any issue here regarding the President's power as Chief Executive and Commander in Chief to protect national security by disciplining employees who disclose information and by taking precautions to prevent leaks.

The problem here is whether, in these particular cases, the Executive Branch has authority to invoke the equity jurisdiction of the courts to protect what it believes to be the national interest. See In re Debs, 158 U. S. 564, 158 U. S. 584 (1895). The Government argues that, in addition to the inherent power of any government to protect itself, the President's power to conduct foreign affairs and his position as Commander in Chief give him authority to impose censorship on the press to protect his ability to deal effectively with foreign nations and to conduct the military affairs of the country. Of course, it is beyond cavil that the President has broad powers by virtue of his primary responsibility for the conduct of our foreign affairs and his position as Commander in Chief. Chicago & Southern Air Lines v. Waterman S.S. Corp., 333 U. S. 103 (1948); Hirabayashi v. United States, 320 U. S. 81, 320 U. S. 93 (1943); United States v. Curtiss Wright Corp., 299 U. S. 304 (1936). [2] And, in some situations, it may be that, under whatever inherent powers the Government may have, as well as the implicit authority derived from the President's mandate to conduct foreign affairs and to act as Commander in Chief, there is a basis for the invocation of the equity jurisdiction of this Court as an aid to prevent the publication of material damaging to "national security," however that term may be defined.

It would, however, be utterly inconsistent with the concept of separation of powers for this Court to use its power of contempt to prevent behavior that Congress has specifically declined to prohibit. There would be a similar damage to the basic concept of these co-equal branches of Government if, when the Executive Branch has adequate authority granted by Congress to protect "national security," it can choose, instead, to invoke the contempt power of a court to enjoin the threatened conduct. The Constitution provides that Congress shall make laws, the President execute laws, and courts interpret laws. Youngstown Sheet & Tube Co. v. Sawyer, 343 U. S. 579 (1952). It did not provide for government by injunction in which the courts and the Executive Branch can "make law" without regard to the action of Congress. It may be more convenient for the Executive Branch if it need only convince a judge to prohibit conduct, rather than ask the Congress to pass a law, and it may be more convenient to enforce a contempt order than to seek a criminal conviction in a jury trial. Moreover, it may be considered politically wise to get a court to share the responsibility for arresting those who the Executive Branch has probable cause to believe are violating the law. But convenience and political considerations of the moment do not justify a basic departure from the principles of our system of government.

In these cases, we are not faced with a situation where Congress has failed to provide the Executive with broad power to protect the Nation from disclosure of damaging state secrets. Congress has, on several occasions, given extensive consideration to the problem of protecting the military and strategic secrets of the United States. This consideration has resulted in the enactment of statutes making it a crime to receive, disclose, communicate, withhold, and publish certain documents, photographs, instruments, appliances, and information. The bulk of these statutes is found in chapter 37 of U.S.C. Title 18, entitled Espionage and Censorship. [3] In that chapter, Congress has provided penalties ranging from a $10,000 fine to death for violating the various statutes.

Thus, it would seem that in order for this Court to issue an injunction it would require a showing that such an injunction would enhance the already exiting power of the Government to act. See Bennett v. Laman, 277 N.Y. 368, 14 N.E.2d 439 (1938). It is a traditional axiom of equity that a court of equity will not do a useless thing, just as it is a traditional axiom that equity will not enjoin the commission of a crime. See Z. Chafee & E. Re, Equity 935-954 (5th ed.1967); 1 H. Joyce, Injunctions §§ 580a (1909). Here, there has been no attempt to make such a showing. The Solicitor General does not even mention in his brief whether the Government considers that there is probable cause to believe a crime has been committed, or whether there is a conspiracy to commit future crimes.

If the Government had attempted to show that there was no effective remedy under traditional criminal law, it would have had to show that there is no arguably applicable statute. Of course, at this stage, this Court could not and cannot determine whether there has been a violation of a particular statute or decide the constitutionality of any statute. Whether a good faith prosecution could have been instituted under any statute could, however, be determined.

At least one of the many statutes in this area seems relevant to these cases. Congress has provided in 18 U.S.C. § 793(e) that whoever,

"having unauthorized possession of, access to, or control over any document, writing, code book, signal book . . . or note relating to the national defense, or information relating to the national defense which information the possessor has reason to believe could be used to the injury of the United States or to the advantage of any foreign nation, willfully communicates, delivers, transmits . . . the same to any person not entitled to receive it, or willfully retains the same and fails to deliver it to the officer or employee of the United States entitled to receive it . . . [s]hall be fined not more than $10,000 or imprisoned not more than ten years, or both."

Congress has also made it a crime to conspire to commit any of the offenses listed in 18 U.S.C. § 793(e).

It is true that Judge Gurfein found that Congress had not made it a crime to publish the items and material specified in § 793(e). He found that the words "communicates, delivers, transmits . . ." did not refer to publication of newspaper stories. And that view has some support in the legislative history, and conforms with the past practice of using the statute only to prosecute those charged with ordinary espionage. But see 103 Cong.Rec. 10449 (remarks of Sen. Humphrey). Judge Gurfein's view of the statute is not, however, the only plausible construction that could be given. See my Brother WHITE's concurring opinion.

Even if it is determined that the Government could not in good faith bring criminal prosecutions against the New York Times and the Washington Post, it is clear that Congress has specifically rejected passing legislation that would have clearly given the President the power he seeks here and made the current activity of the newspapers unlawful. When Congress specifically declines to make conduct unlawful, it is not for this Court to redecide those issues -- to overrule Congress. See Youngstown Sheet & Tube Co. v. Sawyer, 343 U. S. 579 (1952).

On at least two occasions, Congress has refused to enact legislation that would have made the conduct engaged in here unlawful and given the President the power that he seeks in this case. In 1917, during the debate over the original Espionage Act, still the basic provisions of § 793, Congress rejected a proposal to give the President in time of war or threat of war authority to directly prohibit by proclamation the publication of information relating to national defense that might be useful to the enemy. The proposal provided that:

"During any national emergency resulting from a war to which the United States is a party, or from threat of such a war, the President may, by proclamation, declare the existence of such emergency and, by proclamation, prohibit the publishing or communicating of, or the attempting to publish or communicate any information relating to the national defense which, in his judgment, is of such character that it is or might be useful to the enemy. Whoever violates any such prohibition shall be punished by a fine of not more than $10,000 or by imprisonment for not more than 10 years, or both: Provided, That nothing in this section shall be construed to limit or restrict any discussion, comment, or criticism of the acts or policies of the Government or its representatives or the publication of the same."

55 Cong.Rec. 1763. Congress rejected this proposal after war against Germany had been declared, even though many believed that there was a grave national emergency and that the threat of security leaks and espionage was serious. The Executive Branch has not gone to Congress and requested that the decision to provide such power be reconsidered. Instead, the Executive Branch comes to this Court and asks that it be granted the power Congress refused to give.

In 1957, the United States Commission on Government Security found that

"[a]irplane journals, scientific periodicals, and even the daily newspaper have featured articles containing information and other data which should have been deleted in whole or in part for security reasons."

In response to this problem, the Commission proposed that

"Congress enact legislation making it a crime for any person willfully to disclose without proper authorization, for any purpose whatever, information classified 'secret' or 'top secret,' knowing, or having reasonable grounds to believe, such information to have been so classified."

Report of Commission on Government Security 619-620 (1957). After substantial floor discussion on the proposal, it was rejected. See 103 Cong.Rec. 10447-10450. If the proposal that Sen. Cotton championed on the floor had been enacted, the publication of the documents involved here would certainly have been a crime. Congress refused, however, to make it a crime. The Government is here asking this Court to remake that decision. This Court has no such power.

Either the Government has the power under statutory grant to use traditional criminal law to protect the country or, if there is no basis for arguing that Congress has made the activity a crime, it is plain that Congress has specifically refused to grant the authority the Government seeks from this Court. In either case, this Court does not have authority to grant the requested relief. It is not for this Court to fling itself into every breach perceived by some Government official, nor is it for this Court to take on itself the burden of enacting law, especially a law that Congress has refused to pass.

I believe that the judgment of the United States Court of Appeals for the District of Columbia Circuit should be affirmed and the judgment of the United States Court of Appeals for the Second Circuit should be reversed insofar as it remands the case for further hearings.

Notes

[1] See n.3, infra.

[2] But see Kent v. Dulles, 357 U. S. 116 (1958); Youngstown Sheet & Tube Co. v. Sawyer, 343 U. S. 579 (1952).

[3] There are several other statutory provisions prohibiting and punishing the dissemination of information, the disclosure of which Congress thought sufficiently imperiled national security to warrant that result. These include 42 U.S.C. §§ 2161 through 2166, relating to the authority of the Atomic Energy Commission to classify and declassify "Restricted Data" ["Restricted Data" is a term of art employed uniquely by the Atomic Energy Act]. Specifically, 42 U.S.C. § 2162 authorizes the Atomic Energy Commission to classify certain information. Title 42 U.S.C. § 2274, subsection (a), provides penalties for a person who

"communicates, transmits, or discloses [restricted data] . . . with intent to injure the United States or with intent to secure an advantage to any foreign nation. . . ."

Subsection (b) of § 2274 provides lesser penalties for one who "communicates, transmits, or discloses" such information "with reason to believe such data will be utilized to injure the United States or to secure an advantage to any foreign nation. . . ." Other sections of Title 42 of the United States Code dealing with atomic energy prohibit and punish acquisition, removal, concealment, tampering with, alteration, mutilation, or destruction of documents incorporating "Restricted Data" and provide penalties for employees and former employees of the Atomic Energy Commission, the armed services, contractors and licensees of the Atomic Energy Commission. Title 42 U.S.C. §§ 2276, 2277. Title 50 U.S.C.App. § 781, 56 Stat. 390, prohibits the making of any sketch or other representation of military installations or any military equipment located on any military installation, as specified; and, indeed, Congress, in the National Defense Act of 1940, 54

Stat. 676, as amended, 56 Stat. 179, conferred jurisdiction on federal district courts over civil actions "to enjoin any violation" thereof. 50 U.S.C.App. § 1152(6). Title 50 U.S.C. § 783(b) makes it unlawful for any officers or employees of the United States or any corporation which is owned by the United States to communicate material which has been "classified" by the President to any person who that governmental employee knows or has reason to believe is an agent or representative of any foreign government or any Communist organization.

Offset provision of 224 of the Social Security Act, 42 U.S.C. 424a, 79 Stat. 406, creates unlawful discrimination: Justice Marshall's dissent in Richardson v. Belcher (November 22, 1971)

MR. JUSTICE MARSHALL, with whom MR. JUSTICE BRENNAN joins, dissenting.

In my view, the offset provision of 224 of the Social Security Act, 42 U.S.C. 424a, 79 Stat. 406, creates an unlawful discrimination under the Due Process Clause of the Fifth Amendment.

Before this 53-year-old appellee became disabled in March 1968, he was supporting his wife and two children on total yearly earnings of approximately $6,600. Once disabled, he could not work, but he and his family were awarded federal social security disability benefits totaling $329.70 per month. 1 Because his employer had chosen to set up a workmen's compensation fund, appellee also became entitled to workmen's compensation benefits totaling $203.60 per month. These were his only forms of disability compensation. Had appellee been allowed to keep his initial award of federal benefits, his income would have totaled nearly $6, 400 a year, somewhat less than he had earned before his disability. But because of the offset provision of 224, appellee's monthly federal payments were reduced, solely because the supplement to his federal benefits was in the form of state workmen's compensation. As a result, appellee's total yearly income was reduced to $5,146.80.

Appellee complains that the offset provision is unconstitutional because it places its severe burden on a single class of disabled persons without adequate justification. Under the challenged offset provision, federal social security disability benefits are reduced only for those persons whose disability entitles them to workmen's compensation. Other persons who receive other kinds of disability compensation - for example, private insurance benefits or tort damages - are allowed the full amount of federal social security benefits. The question here is whether workmen's compensation beneficiaries may be singled out in this way for a reduction in federal benefits.

Starting from the assumptions that federal social security insurance, like welfare assistance, is a "public benefit" in which the beneficiaries have neither contract nor property interests, and that statutory classifications affecting the basic needs of individuals are viewed no differently under the Constitution from classifications in the area of business regulation, the Court concludes that the classification here has a reasonable basis and is consistent with the Fifth Amendment. To reach today's result, the Court revitalizes Flemming v. Nestor, 363 U.S. 603 (1960), 2 and extends the doctrine of Dandridge v. Williams, 397 U.S. 471 (1970), to statutory classifications under federal law. 3 Thus, the Court today holds that Congress can take social security benefits from a disabled worker as long as it does not behave in an "arbitrary" way; classifications in the federal social security law are consistent with the Fifth Amendment if they are "rationally based and free from invidious discrimination."

In opposing this course, I adhere to my dissenting views in Dandridge v. Williams. I continue to believe that the "rational basis" test used by this Court in reviewing business regulation has no place when the Court reviews legislation providing fundamental services or distributing government funds to provide for basic human needs. In deciding whether a given classification is consistent with the requirements of the Fifth or Fourteenth Amendment, 4 we should look to "the character of the classification in question, the relative importance to individuals in the class discriminated against of the governmental benefits that they do not receive, and the asserted state [or federal] interests in support of the classification." Dandridge v. Williams, supra, at 521 (MARSHALL, J., dissenting); cf. Williams v. Rhodes, 393 U.S. 23, 30 (1968). Under this approach, it is necessary to consider more than the character of the classification and the governmental interests in support of the classification. Judges should not ignore what everyone knows, namely that legislation regulating business cannot be equated with legislation dealing with destitue î, disabled, or elderly individuals. Thus, in assessing the lawfulness of the special disadvantages suffered here by workmen's compensation beneficiaries, the Court should consider the individual interests at stake. Federal disability payments, even when supplemented by other forms of disability compensation, provide families of disabled persons with the basic means for getting by. I would require far more than a mere "rational basis" to justify a discrimination that deprives disabled persons of such support in their time of need.

It is unnecessary to elaborate further the analysis required by the principles of my Dandridge dissent. For even under the Court's "rational basis" test, the discriminatory offset provision here cannot be sustained. There simply is no reasonable basis for singling out recipients of workmen's compensation for a reduction of federal benefits, while those who receive other kinds of disability compensation are not similarly treated.

This is not to say that an offset scheme is intrinsically impermissible. Arguably, Congress has an interest in paying greater benefits to people who are relying completely on the federal social security program, and lesser benefits to people who have other sources of disability compensation. But the question here is not whether Congress has the power to prevent "duplicative" payments that might exceed previous take-home pay and might thereby discourage disabled workers from returning to work. 5 The issue is whether Congress may single out for the purpose of applying the offset only those who are receiving workmen's compensation, and exclude those who are receiving similar supplemental disability compensation from other sources. A concern about excessive combined benefits and "rehabilitation" does not explain that distinction.

What, then, is the "rational basis" for the disfavored treatment of persons receiving workmen's compensation? The majority, in its conclusory treatment of this question, appears to say that workmen's compensation "satisf[ies] a need" which is special; and, claiming to rely on "the reasoning of Congress as reflected in the legislative history," the majority finds that Congress "anticipated that a perpetuation of the duplication in benefits might lead to the erosion of the workmen's compensation programs." I cannot accept that argument as a justification for this statute. There is nothing in the Senate, House, or Conference Reports indicating that this was the basis for the legislation actually passed. 6 And I do not think that the argument is in fact rational. The statutory discrimination exceeds the maximum amount of irrationality and arbitrariness countenanced by the Fifth Amendment.

Workmen's compensation programs serve precisely the same function as other forms of disability insurance and tort damage suits. The payments assist workers in the same way, and satisfy the same need. Indeed, in appellee's home State of West Virginia, as in most States, workmen's compensation is by statute the complete functional equivalent of tort liability, since employers who participate in workmen's compensation cannot be sued for tort damages by disabled employees. W. Va. Code Ann. 23-2-6. Moreover, no distinction can be drawn on the basis of the source of the payments. In West Virginia, as in most States, workmen's compensation is financed privately, just like other forms of insurance and like tort damages. Usually the benefits are paid directly by the employer (as a self-insurer) or by the employer's insurance carriers (in which case the employer pays the premiums). See 3 A. Larson, Law of Workmen's Compensation 92.10, p. 444 (1971); W. Va. Code Ann. 23-2-1 et seq. I see no basis for singling out workmen's compensation programs for special protection or solicitude.

More pointedly, however, it defies logic to claim that 224 could to any extent protect or encourage workmen's compensation in the manner suggested by the Court. In support of its claim that 224 might discourage the erosion of workmen's compensation, the appellant relies heavily on a statement made by a representative of the Council of State Chambers of Commerce to the Senate Committee on Finance:

"A matter of equal concern is the impact of Federal disability payments on State workmen's compensation programs. Legislative proposals have been offered in several States (Colorado, Florida, Maryland, and Minnesota) to reduce workmen's compensation benefits by the amount of [social security] disability benefits payable to a disabled worker. If other States follow this direction . . . we believe it will be only a matter of time until State workmen's compensation programs are destroyed." Hearings on H. R. 6675 before the Senate Committee on Finance, 89th Cong., 1st Sess., pt. 1, p. 259.

In addition, the Government refers to the testimony of another Chamber of Commerce representative:

"Encroachment by social security is hampering efforts to improve the State workmen's compensation systems where improvements are needed. Faced with sharply rising costs and the duplication of benefits, employers in several States have supported legislative proposals to reduce workmen's compensation benefits by the amount of social security disability benefits." Id., at 252.

I am unable to see how 224 is connected to this asserted rationale. The federal offset provision provides for the reduction of federal benefits if the total of those benefits and the workmen's compensation benefits exceeds 80% of "average current earnings." However, federal benefits may not be reduced if the workmen's compensation plan provides for a reduction of its benefits in the event of an overlap. 224 (d). Thus, if a State or employers in the State want to save money, the federal statute invites them to reduce workmen's compensation benefits by means of an offset provision of their own. I do not see how it is possible to argue that the federal statute is designed to prevent States from adopting their own offset provisions. If anything, the States are encouraged to cut back on their programs. 7

Even if it were possible to believe that the challenged federal offset provision might in some way forestall States and employers from creating offset provisions in their workmen's compensation programs, I do not see how state offset provisions could to any degree "lead to the gradual weakening or atrophy of [those] programs." Ante, at 84. 8 How do offset provisions hurt a program? It is as preposterous to suggest that state offset provisions could lead to the destruction of workmen's compensation as it would be to argue that the current federal offset provision might destroy the federal social security program. Such manufactured and totally illusory concerns cannot be deemed rational.

The plain fact is that Congress passed this offset provision because it thought disabled persons should not receive excessive combined disability payments. Perhaps by oversight, 9 it arbitrarily singled out workmen's compensation benefits from the universe of disability compensations, and required that workmen's compensation alone was to be offset against federal social security. If the majority's "rational basis" test in fact is to have any meaning, Congress cannot be permitted to single out recipients of workmen's compensation for this adverse treatment. The burden of reduced federal benefits - so devastating to the families of the once-working poor - cannot be imposed arbitrarily under the Fifth Amendment. In my view, that has happened here. I dissent. 10

Notes

[î] ERRATA: "destitue" should be "destitute".

[1] The test for disability under the federal statute is a stern one. With an exception for elderly blind people, disability means "inability to engage in any substantial gainful activity by reason of any medically determinable physical or mental impairment which can be expected to result in death or which has lasted or can be expected to last for a continuous period of not less than 12 months . . . ." 42 U.S.C. 423 (d) (1) (A).

[2] Flemming was a 5-4 decision upholding a federal statute that terminated the

old-age benefits of the family of a fully eligible worker, because he was deported as a former member of the Communist Party. The case has not met with unanimous critical acclaim. See Reich, The New Property, 73 Yale L. J. 733, 768-771, 775 (1964). Prematurely, it would appear, some scholars had predicted its demise. E. g., The Supreme Court, 1969 Term, 84 Harv. L. Rev. 1, 103-104 (1970).

[3] In Dandridge, the Court held that a State's maximum grant regulation for welfare recipients did not unconstitutionally discriminate between children in large and small families. The regulation was challenged under the Equal Protection Clause of the Fourteenth Amendment.

[4] I would use essentially the same approach when statutory classifications are challenged under either Amendment. Cf. Bolling v. Sharpe, 347 U.S. 497 (1954).

[5] The offset idea has had a rocky history. As the majority notes, a prior offset provision was repealed in 1958 because Congress believed that "the danger that duplication of disability benefits might produce undesirable results [was] not of sufficient importance to justify reduction of the social security disability benefits." H. R. Rep. No. 2288, 85th Cong., 2d Sess., 13. The present offset provision was restored to the Act in 1965. It was estimated at the time that no more than 2% of the federal social security disability beneficiaries also received workmen's compensation. Hearings on H. R. 6675 before the Senate Committee on Finance, 89th Cong., 1st Sess., pt. 1, p. 152. It is perhaps plausible to reason that duplicative benefits might in some circumstances discourage rehabilitation and a return to work. It is worth noting, however, that even without the offset provision, appellee's combined benefits would not have exceeded his earnings before disability. See supra, at 88.

[6] The sole concern expressed in these documents is that Congress should prevent "excessive combined benefits." S. Rep. No. 404, 89th Cong., 1st Sess., pt. 1, p. 100; see also H. R. Conf. Rep. No. 682, 89th Cong., 1st Sess.; H. R. Rep. No. 213, 89th Cong., 1st Sess.

[7] Indeed, where they are free to do so, see 3 A. Larson, Law of Workmen's Compensation 522, Appendix A, Table 7 (1971); W. Va. Code Ann. 23-2-1, 23-2-8, individual workers are encouraged to opt out of workmen's compensation and purchase private disability insurance.

[8] It is worth noting that payments for total and permanent disability are only a small part of the total scheme of compensation of any workmen's compensation act. Benefits are also provided for medical and hospital expenses, funeral expenses, rehabilitation, specific scheduled losses, temporary disability, and other forms of loss, see, e. g., W. Va. Code Ann. 23-4-3, 23-4-4, 23-4-6, all of which are unaffected by social security.

[9] Secretary of HEW Celebrezze opposed the present offset provision, arguing that any change should await a more thorough study of the overlap problem. Hearings on H. R. 6675 before the Senate Committee on Finance, 89th Cong., 1st Sess., pt. 1, p. 146. The Committee chose not to wait.

[10] Since, in my view, the present discriminatory offset provision cannot stand, there is no need to decide finally whether Congress has the power to pass an offset provision that would qualify an already accrued interest in social security benefits. Whatever might be said about the characterization of welfare assistance as "property," see Goldberg v. Kelly, 397 U.S. 254, 262 n. 8 (1970), surely a worker who is forced to pay a social security tax on his earnings has a clearly cognizable contract interest in the benefits that justify the tax. The characterization of this interest as "noncontractual" in Flemming v. Nestor, 363 U.S. 603, 611 (1960), is, in my view, incorrect. The analogy to an annuity or insurance contract, rejected there, seems apt. Id., at 624 (Black, J., dissenting). See also Reich, The New Property, supra. Of course, as the Court says, Congress may "fix the levels of benefits under the Act or the conditions upon which they may be paid." But once Congress has fixed that level and those conditions, and a worker has contributed his tax in accord with the law, may Congress unilaterally modify the benefits in a way that defeats the expectations of beneficiaries and prospective beneficiaries? At the least, it would seem that after a worker has contributed the tax for 20 quarters, 42 U.S.C. 423 (c) (1), and his interest in the benefits has fully accrued, Congress may not unilaterally qualify that interest by introducing an offset provision not previously contemplated by the parties.

Equal funding to persons under AFDC: Justice Marshall's dissent in Jefferson v. Hackney (May 30, 1972)

MR. JUSTICE MARSHALL, with whom MR. JUSTICE BRENNAN joins, and with whom MR. JUSTICE STEWART joins as to Part I only, dissenting.

Appellants, recipients of Aid to Families With Dependent Children (AFDC) in Texas, brought this action to challenge two distinct aspects of the Texas AFDC program. First, appellants challenge the manner in which Texas arrives at the amount it will pay to persons who are needy. Second, they urge that Texas acts illegally in providing more money for persons receiving aid under other social welfare legislation than for persons receiving AFDC aid. The Court rejects both claims. I dissent.

Before proceeding to explain why I disagree with the Court, I would like to illustrate what the disputes in this case are all about. If a State is unable or unwilling to establish a level of AFDC payments to meet all the needs of all recipients, federal law permits the State to use a percentage reduction factor as a method of reducing payments in a somewhat equitable manner. Texas has adopted a system in which the percentage reduction factor is applied against the standard of need before outside income is deducted. Appellants contend that federal law requires the State to deduct outside income before the percentage reduction factor is applied. While describing the differences between the two alternatives is a Herculean task, the figures themselves are not difficult to comprehend. Footnote 6 of the Court's opinion, for example, demonstrates that the

Texas system provides less aid to a family with outside income than the alternative system. It is also immediately obvious that, under the Texas system, as soon as the family's income reaches $150, it no longer receives anything from the State, whereas, under the alternative, a family earning the same $150 would continue to receive some state funds. Hence, the Texas method of computation contracts the class of families eligible to receive state aid. Appellants contend that the characteristics of the Texas system are inconsistent with federal legislation, and that only the alternative system comports with the intent of Congress. I agree.

Appellants also claim that the percentage reduction factor employed by Texas is illegal, irrespective of the method of computing payments, because it is lower than the factor used in other social welfare programs that have participants with identical standards of need. I also agree with appellants on this point, but for slightly different reasons from those they have urged.

I

A. In considering the question whether Texas' method of computing eligibility for AFDC payments comports with the federal statute, 42 U.S.C. § 601 et seq., it is important to keep in mind the words of Mr. Justice Cardozo: "When [federal] money is spent to promote the general welfare, the concept of welfare or the opposite is shaped by Congress, not the states." Helvering v. Davis, 301 U. S. 619, 301 U. S. 645 (1937). Mr. Justice Harlan reiterated this point in Rosado v. Wyman, 397 U. S. 397, 397 U. S. 422-423 (1970), when he stated that, irrespective of the policies that a State might wish to pursue by utilizing AFDC money in one way or another, the ultimate question to be answered in each case is whether the action of the State comports with the requirements of federal law.

The Court concludes in the instant case that there is no general congressional policy violated by Texas' choice between the alternative methods of applying a percentage reduction factor to its determined standard of need, and also that no specific statutory provision prohibits Texas from choosing one alternative rather than the other. In concluding that the legislative history is inconclusive and that "what little legislative history there is on the point . . . tends to undercut appellants' theory," the Court has, in my opinion, taken only a superficial look into the history of the statute, and has ignored the intent of Congress in various sections of the AFDC legislation as interpreted by this Court in prior cases.

B. I begin by considering the impact of § 402(a)(23) of the Social Security Act of 1935, as amended, 81 Stat. 898, 42 U.S.C. § 602(a)(23), on appellants' argument. That section provides that

"(a) A State plan for aid and services to needy families with children must"
"* * * *"

"(23) provide that, by July 1, 1969, the amounts used by the State to determine the needs of individuals will have been adjusted to reflect fully changes in living costs since such amounts were established, and any maximums that the State imposes on the amount of aid paid to families will have been proportionately adjusted."

Consideration of this section must, of course, begin with Rosado v. Wyman, supra, where we examined the derivation of this section in great detail.

The relevant facts in Rosado are concisely stated in 397 U.S. at 397 U. S. 416. New York State had changed its AFDC program so that it no longer determined need on an individualized basis, but instead substituted a system fixing maximum family allowances based on the number of individuals per family. The result was a drastic reduction in overall payments. New York State welfare recipients brought the suit in Rosado, claiming that, by changing its AFDC system from an individualized grant program to a maximum grant program, New York had violated § 402(a)(23).

Despite our recognition that "[t]he background of § 402(a)(23) reveals little except that we have before us a child born of the silent union of legislative compromise," 397 U.S. at 397 U. S. 412, we determined to discover what Congress had in mind in adding the section to the preexisting AFDC legislation. We concluded that two general purposes could be ascribed to the section:

"First, to require States to face up realistically to the magnitude of the public assistance requirement and lay bare the extent to which their programs fall short of fulfilling actual need; second, to prod the States to apportion their payments on a more equitable basis."

397 U.S. at 397 U. S. 412-413. These conclusions led us to reject the holding of the District Court, 304 F.Supp. 1354, 1377, that Congress intended to prevent any reduction whatever in AFDC payments, and to reject the argument of the welfare recipients that, if payments could be reduced, § 402(a)(23) would be meaningless. We decided that

"a State may, after recomputing its standard of need, pare down payments to accommodate budgetary realities by reducing the percent of benefits paid or switching to a percent reduction system, but it may not obscure the actual standard of need."

397 U.S. at 397 U. S. 413 (emphasis in original). Far from emasculating the statute, our reading recognized that the statute had at least three specific salutary effects, and that these were the effects that Congress intended in enacting the legislation:

"It has the effect of requiring the States to recognize and accept the responsibility for those additional individuals whose income falls short of the standard of need as computed in light of economic realities and to place them among those eligible for the care and training provisions. Secondly, while it leaves the States free to effect downward adjustments in the level of benefits paid, it accomplishes within that framework the goal, however modest, of forcing a State to accept the political consequence of such a cutback and bringing to light the true extent to which actual assistance falls short of the minimum acceptable. Lastly, by imposing on those States that desire to maintain 'maximums' the requirement of an appropriate adjustment, Congress has introduced an incentive to abandon a flat 'maximum' system, thereby encouraging those States desirous of containing their welfare budget to shift to a percentage system that will more equitably apportion those funds in fact, allocated for welfare and also more accurately reflect the real measure of public assistance being given."

      Id. at 397 U. S. 413-414.

      Thus, it is clear that we based our decision in Rosado, a decision that interpreted § 402(a)(23) to permit a decrease in actual AFDC payments, largely on the conclusion that Congress wanted not to bar decreases, but to accomplish other objectives. The fact is that the Court today undermines each of those objectives and destroys the premise on which Rosado was decided.

      One specific congressional goal we saw in § 402(a)(23) was that

      "[r]ecalculation of need may serve to render eligible for benefits families which may appear under unadjusted standards marginally to have attained self-sufficiency, but which, in fact, are unable to subsist at the present cost of living."

      Memorandum for the United States as Amicus Curiae in Rosado v. Wyman, No. 540, O.T. 1969, p. 8. In other words, we read the section as expressing Congress' willingness to permit reductions in actual payments in return for the addition of more families to the rolls of AFDC recipients. Accord, Lampton v. Bonin, 304 F.Supp. 1384 (ED La.1969), vacated and remanded for reconsideration in light of Rosado, 397 U. S. 663 (1970); Alvarado v. Schmidt, 317 F.Supp. 1027 (TD Wis.1970). As I have pointed out above, the Texas system limits the number of AFDC recipients and eliminates marginal cases. This is directly contrary to the intent of Congress as we saw it in Rosado.

      A second legislative aim that we saw in the section was to force States to realize the political consequences of reducing welfare payments. It must be clear that the Texas system of administering AFDC payments effectively undermines this aim by enabling the State to maintain a constant percentage reduction factor so that the system on its face appears to contain no reductions in payments. Welfare reductions are surreptitiously accomplished by eliminating those persons who have marginal income from eligibility for AFDC payments. While the congressional intent may not be totally emasculated by this system, it is certainly not well served.

      The third and final purpose that we found that Congress had specifically in mind in enacting § 402(a)(23) was to provide an incentive to States to abandon a flat "maximum" system. Even though Texas does not now use such a system, the Court's approval of the system that Texas does use will effectively remove the incentive from the statute. A State that uses a flat maximum system was required by § 402(a)(23) to adjust the maximums upward to reflect a rise in the cost of living. Since a State that uses a percentage reduction system may avoid the strains cost of living adjustments place on the budget simply by lowering the percentage that it chooses to pay, the statute encouraged abandonment of flat maximums in favor of the more equitable percentage reductions. The Court undermines the incentive by offering States a way to circumvent the cost of living adjustments under the flat maximum system. In order to maintain the maximums without increasing expenditures, States could, under the Court's opinion, begin to use the maximum to determine AFDC eligibility, rather than the standard of need. The result of this approach would be to reduce the number of persons eligible for assistance and to reduce the grants of anyone with any outside income. Rather than serve as an incentive to States to change to a percentage reduction system, as Congress intended, § 402(a)(23) may now be a powerful incentive to States to maintain or revert to maximum grants.

The manner in which the incentive that Rosado saw in § 402(a)(23) is stifled can be illustrated by another look at the family having an income of $100 and a need of $200. Footnote 6 of the Court's opinion demonstrates that under the Texas percentage reduction system, even if the family had no income, the maximum amount of aid that the family could obtain would be $150. Let us assume that Texas maintained a maximum grant system, and that, prior to the enactment of § 402(a)(23), the maximum grant for a family with $200 need was $100. We assumed in Rosado that the following computation would be made.

Need $200
Income $100

Unmet Need $100
Maximum Grant. $100

Total Family Funds $200

Section 402(a)(23) required an increase in the standard of need and the level of maximum grants to reflect the rise in the cost of living. Assuming that a 20% increase was mandated by the rise in living costs, it is obvious that, if the number of families remained stable and if income were stable, the costs of AFDC to the State would increase by 20%. There was an incentive to change to a percentage reduction system to avoid this.

Until recently, no one thought that the State could change to the following system in order to reflect the rise in the cost of living:

New Need $240

New Maximum Grant. $120
Family Income. $100

State Aid. . . . . $ 20

To state it more simply, the maximum grant is similar to, and designed to serve the same purposes as, the percentage reduction factor. If the percentage reduction factor can be applied to need before income is subtracted, it is impossible to see why income could not be set off against maximum grants. True, Texas did not choose this alternative, but it is available under today's decision. A State can, by changing the manner in which it sets off income, absorb an increase in maximums and end up paying less. Where is the incentive now to adopt percentage reduction systems?

This illustration is much more than mere speculation as to what might happen under today's decision. The illustration represents what at least one State -- California -- has already done, or tried to do. Only very recently, the California Supreme Court struck down the State's AFDC scheme for noncompliance with the federal statute. Villa v. Hall, 6 Cal.3d 227, 490 P.2d 1148 (1971).

The California Supreme Court, having been referred to the District Court opinion in the instant case as support for California's system, took the position that neither the California nor the Texas system could stand in light of Rosado. I agree. Indeed, the United States in its Memorandum as Amicus Curiae in this case (p. 5) concedes that, if Rosado represents "a binding construction of the Act, appellants are thus entitled to prevail." The Government proceeds to argue that the question presented here was not before us in Rosado. Ibid. I must agree with appellants that the Government's argument is disingenuous, at best. See Brief for Appellants 80. The question of what § 402(a)(23) means was most certainly before us in Rosado. It was, in fact, all that was before us. In that case, we rejected the broad construction that the District Court had given the section, but we endeavored as best we could to extract some meaning from its muddled history. The United States seeks here to have us do what we explicitly said we would not do in Rosado, i.e., interpret the section in such a way that it is nothing more than a "meaningless exercise in bookkeeping.'" 397 U.S. at 397 U. S. 413. If we were not making a "binding construction" of the statute in Rosado, it is impossible for me to ascertain what we were doing. Hence, I agree with the Government that appellants are entitled to prevail.

Surprisingly enough, the Court makes even shorter shrift of Rosado than does the Government. In a footnote, the Court states that widened eligibility and the other effects that Rosado said were intended by Congress when it enacted § 402(a)(23) were merely possible effects of the statute, not necessary ones. I submit that this cavalier treatment of Rosado is completely unwarranted. Rosado was not an easy case. The absence of a clear legislative history forced us to examine the "muted strains" of the congressional voice and to struggle to "discern the theme in the cacophony of political understanding." 397 U.S. at 397 U. S. 412. Unlike the Court in this case, which simply looks to see if the legislative history is distorted enough to be ignored, the Court in Rosado carefully scrutinized every aspect of the history in order to perceive the congressional intent. That was a difficult task, but not an impossible one. The balance that we saw Congress striking in reducing payments while increasing eligibility has already been described. We relied on this balance to decide Rosado. We were not merely speculating as to the intent of Congress; we were holding that there was a specific intent that was binding in that case. That decision, in my view, is also binding here. This is my first disagreement with the majority.

C. The second provision in the AFDC legislation that I believe is relevant is § 402(a)(8) of the Social Security Act, as amended, 81 Stat. 881, 42 U.S.C. § 602(a)(8), which was added to the AFDC statute along with § 402(a)(23) in 1968. The purpose of this section is to encourage AFDC recipients to seek private employment and to end their need for public assistance. H.R.Rep. No. 544, 90th Cong., 1st Sess. (1967); S.Rep. No. 744, 90th Cong., 1st Sess. (1967). To accomplish this objective, the statute provides that all of the earned income of each dependent child receiving AFDC aid who is a full or part-time student, and a portion of the earned income of certain other relatives, will be disregarded in the State's determination of need. We only recently had occasion to consider the effect of this provision in Engelman v. Amos, 404 U. S. 23 (1971).

In Engelman, we considered a New Jersey scheme for administering AFDC funds that established income ceilings for families. When the families' incomes exceeded the ceilings, they no longer were eligible for AFDC aid. The District Court analogized Engelman to Rosado v. Wyman, supra, and determined that the State's system was inconsistent with the federal Act. 333 F.Supp. 1109. The District Court recognized that the 1968 amendments to the AFDC legislation were designed to increase eligibility for AFDC aid, not to decrease it. Because the District Court viewed § 402(a)(8) as requiring a State to disregard certain kinds of income in determining eligibility for aid, the District Court struck down the New Jersey scheme, in effect holding that New Jersey could not evade the income disregard by imposing an income ceiling not contemplated by Congress. Families that exceeded the State's income ceilings were still entitled to AFDC aid so long as their income, excluding income covered by § 402(a)(8), did not exceed the State's standard of need. The effect of the decision was to increase the class of persons eligible for AFDC aid. We affirmed the decision without even hearing argument.

Both "the New Jersey and the Texas provisions . . . appear to have been animated by the same desire. . . ." Memorandum for the United States as Amicus Curiae 11. Both seek to limit the number of AFDC recipients, and both violate the federal statute. Indeed, the very purpose of § 402(a)(8) -- to encourage people to work by permitting them to continue to draw AFDC funds -- shows that Congress wanted as many needy people as possible to be part of the program.

The Texas scheme certainly does not violate § 402(a)(8) in the way that the New Jersey scheme did, for as far as we know, Texas excludes income as required by the statute when computing eligibility. But, as the opinion of the Court indicates, the Texas system has a fault not found in New Jersey: i.e., Texas discourages recipients from earning outside income. This is why I believe that Texas violates the spirit of the federal statute.

It might be argued that Congress only sought to encourage certain AFDC recipients to earn income and only in a certain amount -- the persons and amounts specified in § 402(a)(8). This argument might be persuasive but for one fact -- Congress never had any idea that a State would attempt to employ a system such as that used by Texas. Nowhere in the legislative history is there any mention of such a system. See, e.g., House Committee on Ways and Means, Section-By-Section Analysis of H.R. 5710, 90th Cong., 1st Sess. (Comm.Print 1967). Congress was, in fact, informed by HEW that a different standard from that used by Texas was required. See Hearings on H.R. 12080 before the Senate Committee on Finance, 90th Cong., 1st Sess., pt. 1, pp. 255-266 (testimony of Wilbur Cohen). Until very recently, every indication by HEW was that the Texas system would be unlawful. In light of the state of ignorance in which Congress found itself, it is not surprising that there is no specific rejection of the Texas system in the 1968 amendments. But § 402(a)(8) and everything in the legislative history certainly indicate that Congress had a strong desire to encourage AFDC recipients to work. Because the Texas program is inconsistent with this desire, I believe it is illegal.

This is the second reason for my disagreement with the Court.

D. Another section of the statute that must be examined is § 402(a)(10) of the Social Security Act, 64 Stat. 550, as amended, 42 U.S.C. § 602(a)(10), which requires that a state AFDC plan shall

"provide . . . that all individuals wishing to make application for aid to families with dependent children shall have opportunity to do so, and that aid to families with dependent children shall be furnished with reasonable promptness to all eligible individuals."

The Court states that the primary purpose of this section was to outlaw the use of waiting lists as a means of minimizing a State's welfare expenditures. There is clearly support for this view, as the Court noted in Dandridge v. Williams, 397 U. S. 471, 397 U. S. 481 n. 12 (1970).

Before the Court in Dandridge was the question whether maximum grant limitations were inconsistent with the federal statute. The Court upheld the maximums, but said in the course of so doing: "So long as some aid is provided to all eligible families and all eligible children, the statute itself is not violated." Id. at 397 U. S. 481. This is plainly dictum, but I believe that it is well considered dictum that should be followed in this case.

It must be remembered that Dandridge and Rosado were decided on the same day. Thus, the Court assumed in Dandridge that the 1968 amendments to the AFDC legislation expanded the list of eligible recipients in the manner suggested in Rosado. The Court was also aware in Dandridge that § 402(a)(7) of the Social Security Act, as amended, 53 Stat. 1379, 42 U.S.C. § 602(a)(7), had been part of the AFDC statute since 1939. That section provides that,

"except as may be otherwise provided [in § 402(a)(8), discussed, supra] . . . the State agency shall, in determining need, take into consideration any other income and resources of any child or relative claiming aid to families with dependent children. . . ."

The Court assumed, therefore, that, in offering aid, a State would first set a standard of need and then examine the income levels of applicants for aid. Anyone whose income was less than the standard of need would be eligible for assistance, or so the Court assumed. Dandridge, of course, established that the aid that might be forthcoming did not have to equal need, and that large families could get proportionately less aid than small families. Just as in Rosado, the Court in Dandridge viewed the intent of Congress to be to aid as many needy people as possible, rather than to offer as much aid as possible to a lesser number of people. In light of this, I believe that today's decision violates the spirit of Dandridge as well as the holding of Rosado.

Moreover, in my view, § 402(a)(7) tells the States how to compute eligibility, and that section does not allow for the Texas scheme. Despite the position of the Government in this case, I find support for my reading of § 402(a)(7) in HEW's own regulations, especially 45 CFR §§ 233.20(a)(2), 233.20(a)(3)(ii), which indicate to me that income is to be subtracted from the standard of need before any determination is made as to how much aid the State will give.

Because I believe the Texas system violates § 402(a)(7), it seems to me that eligible persons are being denied aid in violation of § 402(a)(10), which requires that aid be furnished to all eligible persons promptly. For me, this case is no different from King v. Smith, 392 U. S. 309 (1968) (striking down substitute father regulation) or Townsend v. Swank, 404 U. S. 282 (1971) (striking down restriction on receipt of aid by college students). The state procedure denies eligible persons aid, and, regardless of the State's purposes, the procedure cannot stand in conflict with the federal statute.

I disagree with the Court a third time.

E. The last portion of the federal statute that I believe should be considered is that portion dealing with the social services that are available to AFDC recipients. See, e.g., 42 U.S.C. §§ 602(a)(14), (15) (assistance in family planning and child welfare services; assistance in entering the workforce and reducing the incidence of births out of wedlock); 42 U.S.C. §§ 602(a)(19), 632 (employment training programs); 42 U.S.C. § 1396a(a)(10) (medical assistance). Congress keyed all of these provisions to persons or families that were receiving aid. By limiting the number of such persons and families receiving aid, Texas has also limited the availability of these social services. At least one other court has concluded that

". . . Congress' major concern was the provision of family counseling and rehabilitation services, work incentives, and family planning programs to reduce out-of-wedlock births, for all persons in the family, in order to promote self-support and child development and to strengthen family life. . . . By making those with marginal incomes eligible for AFDC by raising the standard of need, more persons would be eligible for such services, which Congress considered vital to cut down in the long run the numbers dependent on welfare."

(Citation omitted.) Lampton v. Bonin, 304 F.Supp. at 1389. We suggested the same thing in Rosado, 397 U.S. at 397 U. S. 413. While the Court recognizes that the Texas system deprives persons with an "unmet need" of an opportunity to utilize these services (n. 10), and thus relegates these persons to perpetual dependence on welfare, the realization is apparently a source of no concern. But it was a source of tremendous concern to Congress. The value of medical assistance alone to an average Texas AFDC family is in the range of $50-$60 per month. Memorandum for the United States as Amicus Curiae 7 n. 5. Since needy families are rendered more needy by Texas' system, their ability to escape the confines of the welfare rolls is substantially impaired. At the same time, the goals of Congress as described in the preceding quotation are also impaired. There is no reason, nor any justification, for reading the statute this way. Since I believe that Congress intended that as many needy persons as possible be permitted to avail themselves of the various services provided or improved in the 1968 amendments, I again disagree with the conclusions of the Court.

F. In concluding my analysis of this aspect of Texas' percentage reduction system, I add one final note. Thus far, I have confined myself to examining the specific provisions of the AFDC legislation. In attempting to focus on each section individually in order to determine its role in the statutory scheme, something of the general flavor of the overall legislation is undoubtedly lost. That flavor, it seems to me, is to assist needy families to maintain strong family bonds and to assist needy individuals to realize their potential as unique human beings by providing them with the basic necessities of life, along with incentives and training to encourage them to work to help themselves. The Texas system negates the salutary aspects of the legislation by deterring the needy from working, by depriving the needy of social services, and by excluding some needy from any AFDC aid whatsoever. There is no conceivable reason to permit Texas to subvert the aims of Congress in this way.

II

Appellants also challenge the percentage reduction figure itself. It is agreed that Texas has established an identical standard of need for the four social welfare programs that it administers -- Old Age Assistance (OAA), Aid to the Blind (AB), Aid for the Permanently and Totally Disabled (APTD), and AFDC. But Texas provides 100% of recognized need to the aged and 95% to the disabled and the blind, while it provides only 75% to AFDC recipients. It is this disparity to which appellants also object.

A. Appellants base their primary attack on the Fourteenth Amendment; they argue that the percentage distinctions between the other welfare programs and AFDC reflect a racially discriminatory motive on the part of Texas officials. Thus, they argue that there is a violation of the Equal Protection Clause. I believe that it is unnecessary to reach the constitutional issue that appellants raise, and, therefore, I offer no opinion on its ultimate merits. I do wish to make it clear, however, that I do not subscribe in any way to the manner in which the Court treats the issue.

If I were to face this question, I would certainly have more difficulty with it than either the District Court had or than this Court seems to have. The record contains numerous statements by state officials to the effect that AFDC is funded at a lower level than the other programs because it is not a politically popular program. There is also evidence of a stigma that seemingly attaches to AFDC recipients and no others. This Court noted in King v. Smith, 392 U.S. at 392 U. S. 322, that AFDC recipients were often frowned upon by the community. The evidence also shows that 87% of the AFDC recipients in Texas are either Negro or Mexican-American. Yet both the District Court and this Court have little difficulty in concluding that the fact that AFDC is politically unpopular and the fact that AFDC recipients are disfavored by the State and its citizens have nothing whatsoever to do with the racial makeup of the program. This conclusion is neither so apparent nor so correct, in my view.

Moreover, because I find that each one of the State's reasons for treating AFDC differently from the other programs dissolves under close scrutiny, as is demonstrated infra, I am not at all certain who should bear the burden of proof on the question of racial discrimination. Nor am I sure that the "traditional" standard of review would govern the case as the Court holds. In Dandridge v. Williams, supra, on which the Court relies for the proposition that strict scrutiny of the State's action is not required, the Court never faced a question of possible racial discrimination. Percentages themselves are certainly not conclusive, but, at some point, a showing that state action has a devastating impact on the lives of minority racial groups must be relevant.

The Court reasons backwards to conclude that, because appellants have not proved racial discrimination, a less strict standard of review is necessarily tolerated. In my view, the first question that must be asked is what is the standard of review, and the second question is whether racial discrimination has been proved under the standard. It seems almost too plain for argument that the standard of review determines, in large measure, whether or not something has been proved. Whitcomb v. Chavis, 403 U. S. 124, 403 U. S. 149 (1971); Gomillion v. Lightfoot, 364 U. S. 339, (1960).

These are all complex problems, and I do not propose to resolve any of them here. It is sufficient for me to note that I believe that the constitutional issue raised by appellants need not be reached, and that, in choosing to reach it, the Court has so greatly oversimplified the issue as to distort it.

B. Appellants also challenge the distinction between programs under Title VI of the 1964 Civil Rights Act, 42 U.S.C. § 2000d:

"No person in the United States hall, on the ground of race, color, or national origin, . . . be subjected to discrimination under any program or activity receiving Federal financial assistance."

Only last Term, in Griggs v. Duke Power Co., 401 U. S. 424 (1971), we had occasion to strike down under Title VII of the 1964 Act, 42 U.S.C. § 2000e, employment practices that had a particularly harsh impact on one minority racial group and that could not be justified by business necessity. We indicated in that case that

"good intent or absence of discriminatory intent does not redeem employment procedures or testing mechanisms that operate as 'built-in headwinds' for minority groups. "

Id. at 401 U. S. 432. We said, in fact, that "Congress directed the thrust of the Act to the consequences of employment practices, not simply the motivation." Ibid. (emphasis in original). That decision even placed the burden on the employer "of showing that any given requirement must have a manifest relationship to the employment in question." Ibid.

There has been a paucity of litigation under Title VI, and I am not prepared at this point to say whether or not a similar analysis to that used in Griggs should be used in Title VI cases. This is a question of first impression in this Court, and I do not think we have to reach it in this case. I include this section only to make plain that I do not necessarily reject the argument made by appellants; I simply do not reach it.

C. This brings me to what I believe disposes of the question presented: the disparity between the various social welfare programs is not permissible under the federal statutory framework.

The four social welfare programs offered by Texas are funded in part by the Federal Government. Each program is governed by a separate statute: OAA, 42 U.S.C. § 301 et seq.; AFDC, 42 U.S.C. § 601 et seq.; AB, 42 U.S.C. § 1201 et seq.; APTD, 42 U.S.C. § 1351 et seq. No State is compelled to participate in any program, and any State that wants to participate can choose to do so in one, several, or all of the programs.

There is no doubt that States are free to choose whether or not to participate in these programs, and it is also clear that each State has considerable freedom to allocate what it wants to one or more programs by establishing different standards of need to compute eligibility for aid. Kin v. Smith, 392 U.S. at 392 U. S. 318-319. It is also true, however, that the basic aims of the four programs are identical. Indeed, when Congress first enacted the programs in 1935, it viewed them all as necessary to provide aid to families unable to obtain income from private employment. The beneficiaries of the various programs shared the basic characteristics of need and dependence. H.R.Rep. No. 615, 74th Cong., 1st Sess., 3. While the programs as they now exist go well beyond merely furnishing financial assistance as they did originally, they still maintain similar goals.

Moreover, all four programs were simultaneously amended in 1956 to provide for social and rehabilitative services to enable all needy individuals to attain the maximum economic and personal independence of which they were capable. Each program now requires a State to describe, in its plan for each social welfare program it administers, the services it offers to accomplish this objective. See 42 U.S.C. §§ 302(a)(11); 602(a)(14); 1202(a)(12); 1352(a)(11).

Congress has given the States authority to set different standards of need for different programs. But where, as here, the State concludes that the standard of need is the same for recipients of aid under the four distinct statutes, it is my opinion that Congress required that the State treat all recipients equally with respect to actual aid. In other words, as I read the federal statutes, they are designed to accomplish the same objectives, albeit for persons disadvantaged by different circumstances.

States clearly have the freedom to make a bona fide determination that blind persons have a greater need than dependent children, that adults have a higher standard of need than children, that the aged have more need than the blind, and so forth.

But, in this case, Texas made an independent determination of need, and it determined that the need of all recipients was equal. In this circumstance, I find nothing in the federal statute to enable a State to favor one group of recipients by satisfying more of its need, while at the same time denying an equally great need of another group. The purposes and objectives of the statutes are the same, those eligible for aid are suffering equally, and Congress intended that, once a State chose to participate in the programs, similarly situated persons would be treated similarly.

Everything in this record indicates that the recipients of the various forms of aid are identically situated. Although the District Court accepted the State's contentions that there are differences between AFDC children and other recipients which warranted different treatment under the federal statutes, I find each of the reasons offered totally unpersuasive.

First, Texas argues that AFDC children can be employed, whereas recipients of other benefits cannot be. Assuming arguendo that this is true, it is an argument that falls of its own weight. Whatever income the children earn is subtracted from need, or it is excluded from consideration under § 402(a)(8) to encourage self-help. Thus, income is already reflected in the computation of payments, or it is excluded in order that a specific legislative goal may be furthered. Thus, income is irrelevant in any explanation of the differences between the percentage reductions applied to the various programs. It should also be noted that a recipient's income is also taken into consideration in programs other than AFDC. See 42 U.S.C. §§ 302(a)(10)(A); 1202(a)(8); 1352(a)(8).

Second, the State maintains that AFDC families can secure help from legally responsible relatives more easily than recipients under other programs. Assuming again, for purposes of discussion, that this is true, it should be plain that any support from any relatives is subtracted from the State's grant. Moreover, appellants properly point out that recipients of aid in non-AFDC programs often have a source of aid unavailable to AFDC recipients -- the federal old age insurance, 42 U.S.C. § 201 et seq. Thus, there is no substance to this argument.

Third, Texas points to the likelihood of future employment for AFDC recipients, a likelihood that it says is nonexistent for older persons and others who receive aid. Federal law provides that a State may only consider income that is currently available in allocating funds. 45 CFR § 233.20(a)(3)(ii). This contention is therefore irrelevant.

The State makes only two other arguments. One has already been rejected. Texas urges that the purposes of the federal programs differ, but the history belies this contention. The other is that the numbers of AFDC recipients is rising, and this program should therefore bear the burden of monetary limitations. The obvious problem with this argument is that one fundamental purpose of AFDC aid is to enable people to escape the welfare rolls. But, under the Texas system, the aid is presently insufficient, people are unable to escape from dependency, and the rolls become larger. Had Texas not funded AFDC at a lower level than other programs, it is possible that the number of recipients would not have grown so large. The State's argument is a self-fulfilling prophecy on which it cannot rely to penalize AFDC recipients. Furthermore, there is nothing in the federal legislation to indicate that aid is to be reduced in a program merely because the number of beneficiaries of that program increases at a more rapid rate than in other programs. On the contrary, Congress has indicated that increased eligibility for AFDC is desirable, see 42 U.S.C. § 602(a)(23); Rosado v. Wyman, supra. It would be extreme irony if AFDC recipients were penalized by a State because their numbers grew in accordance with congressional intent.

The conclusion that I draw from the statutes is that Congress intended equal treatment for all persons similarly situated. Congress left to the States the determination of who was similarly situated by permitting States to determine levels of need. Since Texas has decided that AFDC recipients have precisely the same need as recipients of other social welfare benefits, it is my opinion that the federal legislation requires equal treatment for all.

This conclusion finds support in the legislative history of the 1950 amendments to the social welfare legislation. In those amendments, Congress made clear its intent to put AFDC recipients on a par with recipients of other welfare aid.

"Today, more than 1.1 million children under 18 years of age are receiving aid to dependent children through the State-Federal program because one or both of their parents are dead, absent from the home, or incapacitated. These children, regardless of the State in which they now live, will someday find their place in the productive activities of the Nation and, should the necessity arise, will take part in defending our Nation. Many of these children will be seriously handicapped as adults because, in childhood, they are not receiving proper and sufficient food, clothing, medical attention, and the other bare necessities of life. The national interest requires that the Federal Government provide for dependent children at least on a par with its contributions toward the support of the needy aged and blind."

S.Doc. No. 208, 80th Cong., 2d Sess., 105 (emphasis added). Congress recognized that "families with dependent children need as much in assistance payments as do aged and blind persons." Id. at 106. It concluded that sound national policy was "for the States to provide payments for aid to dependent children comparable to those for the needy aged and blind." Ibid. It is evident that Congress rejected the notion that, where AFDC recipients had the same need as other welfare beneficiaries, they should get less money. As Senator Benton said on the floor of the Senate:

"There seems no reasonable basis for such inequitable treatment of mothers and of children by the Federal Government."

"All of us with children know that it costs as much, if not more, to rear children in health, decency, and self-respect than to maintain an adult. It is surely no less important to make this investment in our future citizens than it is to provide decently for those who have retired. . . ."

96 Cong.Rec. 881-8814. In the 1950 amendments, Congress increased the federal funding of AFDC so that its beneficiaries would receive treatment equivalent to that received by beneficiaries of the other federal state social welfare legislation. Where the needs of the people receiving aid under the various programs differed, Congress recognized that the amount of aid forthcoming should also differ. But where need was determined by the State to be equal for all recipients, Congress intended that all should receive an equal amount of aid. S.Doc. No. 208, 80th Cong., 2d Sess., 108. There is absolutely no indication in any subsequent congressional action that the intent of Congress has changed.

Accordingly, I would reverse the judgment of the District Court and remand the case for formulation of relief consistent with this opinion.

Stop-and-Frisk should be unconstitutional: Justice Marshall's dissent in Adams v. Williams (June 12, 1972)

MR. JUSTICE MARSHALL, with whom MR. JUSTICE DOUGLAS joins, dissenting.

Four years have passed since we decided Terry v. Ohio, 392 U. S. 1 (1968), and its companion cases, Sibron v. New York and Peters v. New York, 392 U. S. 40 (1968). They were the first cases in which this Court explicitly recognized the concept of "stop and frisk" and squarely held that police officers may, under appropriate circumstances, stop and frisk persons suspected of criminal activity even though there is less than probable cause for an arrest. This case marks our first opportunity to give some flesh to the bones of Terry et al. Unfortunately, the flesh provided by today's decision cannot possibly be made to fit on Terry's skeletal framework.

"[T]he most basic constitutional rule in this area is that 'searches conducted outside the judicial process, without prior approval by judge or magistrate, are per se unreasonable under the Fourth Amendment -- subject only to a few specifically established and well delineated exceptions.' The exceptions are 'jealously and carefully drawn,' and there must be 'a showing by those who seek exemption . . . that the exigencies of the situation made that course imperative.' '[T]he burden is on those seeking the exemption to show the need for it.'"

Coolidge v. New Hampshire, 403 U. S. 443, 403 U. S. 454 455 (1971). In Terry, we said that.

"we do not retreat from our holdings that the police must, whenever practicable, obtain advance judicial approval of searches and seizures through the warrant procedure."

392 U.S. at 392 U. S. 20. Yet, we upheld the stop and frisk in Terry because we recognized that the realities of on-the-street law enforcement require an officer to act at times on the basis of strong evidence, short of probable cause, that criminal activity is taking place and that the criminal is armed and dangerous. Hence, Terry stands only for the proposition that police officers have a "narrowly drawn authority to . . . search for weapons" without a warrant. Id. at 392 U. S. 27.

In today's decision, the Court ignores the fact that Terry begrudgingly accepted the necessity for creating an exception from the warrant requirement of the Fourth Amendment and treats this case as if warrantless searches were the rule, rather than the "narrowly drawn" exception. This decision betrays the careful balance that Terry sought to strike between a citizen's right to privacy and his government's responsibility for effective law enforcement, and expands the concept of warrantless searches far beyond anything heretofore recognized as legitimate. I dissent.

I

A. The Court's opinion states the facts, and I repeat only those that appear to me to be relevant to the Fourth Amendment issues presented.

Respondent was sitting on the passenger side of the front seat of a car parked on the street in a "high crime area" in Bridgeport, Connecticut, at 2:15 a.m. when a police officer approached his car. During a conversation that had just taken place nearby, the officer was told by an informant that respondent had narcotics on his person and that he had a gun in his waistband. The officer saw that the motor was not running, that respondent was seated peacefully in the car, and that there was no indication that he was about to leave the scene. After the officer asked respondent to open the door, respondent rolled down his window instead, and the officer reached into the car and pulled a gun from respondent's waistband. The officer immediately placed respondent under arrest for carrying the weapon, and searched him, finding heroin in his coat. More heroin was found in a later search of the automobile. Respondent moved to suppress both the gun and the heroin prior to trial. His motion was denied, and he was convicted of possessing both items.

B. The Court erroneously attempts to describe the search for the gun as a protective search incident to a reasonable investigatory stop. But, as in Terry, Sibron and Peters, supra, there is no occasion in this case to determine whether or not police officers have a right to seize and to restrain a citizen in order to interrogate him. The facts are clear that the officer intended to make the search as soon as he approached the respondent. He asked no questions; he made no investigation; he simply searched.

There was nothing apart from the information supplied by the informant to cause the officer to search. Our inquiry must focus, therefore, as it did in Terry, on whether the officer had sufficient facts from which he could reasonably infer that respondent was not only engaging in illegal activity, but also that he was armed and dangerous. The focus falls on the informant.

The only information that the informant had previously given the officer involved homosexual conduct in the local railroad station. The following colloquy took place between respondent's counsel and the officer at the hearing on respondent's motion to suppress the evidence that had been seized from him.

"Q. Now, with respect to the information that was given you about homosexuals in the Bridgeport Police Station [sic], did that lead to an arrest? A. No."

"Q. An arrest was not made. A. No. There was no substantiating evidence."
"* * * *"

"Q. There was no substantiating evidence? A. No."

"Q. And what do you mean by that? A. I didn't have occasion to witness these individuals committing any crime of any nature."

"Q. In other words, after this person gave you the information, you checked for corroboration before you made an arrest. Is that right? A. Well, I checked to determine the possibility of homosexual activity."

"Q. And since an arrest was made, I take it you didn't find any substantiating information. A. I'm sorry counselor, you say since an arrest was made."

"Q. Was not made. Since an arrest was not made, I presume you didn't find any substantiating information. A. No. "

Q. So that, you don't recall any other specific information given you about the commission of crimes by this informant. A. No.

"Q. And you still thought this person was reliable. A. Yes. [1]"

Were we asked to determine whether the information supplied by the informant was sufficient to provide probable cause for an arrest and search, rather than a stop and frisk, there can be no doubt that we would hold that it was insufficient. This Court has squarely held that a search and seizure cannot be justified on the basis of conclusory allegations of an unnamed informant who is allegedly credible. Aguilar v. Texas, 378 U. S. 108 (1964). In the recent case of Spinelli v. United States, 393 U. S. 410 (1969), Mr. Justice Harlan made it plain beyond any doubt that, where police rely on an informant to make a search and seizure, they must know that the informant is generally trustworthy and that he has obtained his information in a reliable way. Id. at 393 U. S. 417. Since the testimony of the arresting officer in the instant case patently fails to demonstrate that the informant was known to be trustworthy, and since it is also clear that the officer had no idea of the source of the informant's "knowledge," a search and seizure would have been illegal.

Assuming, arguendo, that this case truly involves not an arrest and a search incident thereto, but a stop and frisk, [2] we must decide whether or not the information possessed by the officer justified this interference with respondent's liberty. Terry, our only case to actually uphold a stop and frisk, [3] is not directly in point, because the police officer in that case acted on the basis of his own personal observations. No informant was involved. But the rationale of Terry is still controlling, and it requires that we condemn the conduct of the police officer in encountering the respondent.

Terry did not hold that, whenever a policeman has a hunch that a citizen is engaging in criminal activity, he may engage in a stop and frisk. It held that, if police officers want to stop and frisk, they must have specific facts from which they can reasonably infer that an individual is engaged in criminal activity and is armed and dangerous. [4] It was central to our decision in Terry that the police officer acted on the basis of his own personal observations, and that he carefully scrutinized the conduct of his suspects before interfering with them in any way. When we legitimated the conduct of the officer in Terry, we did so because of the substantial reliability of the information on which the officer based his decision to act.

If the Court does not ignore the care with which we examined the knowledge possessed by the officer in Terry when he acted, then I cannot see how the actions of the officer in this case can be upheld. The Court explains what the officer knew about respondent before accosting him. But what is more significant is what he did not know. With respect to the scene generally, the officer had no idea how long respondent had been in the car, how long the car had been parked, or to whom the car belonged. With respect to the gun, [5] the officer did not know if or when the informant had ever seen the gun, or whether the gun was carried legally, as Connecticut law permitted, or illegally. [6] And with respect to the narcotics, the officer did not know what kind of narcotics respondent allegedly had, whether they were legally or illegally possessed, what the basis of the informant's knowledge was, or even whether the informant was capable of distinguishing narcotics from other substances. [7]

Unable to answer any of these questions, the officer nevertheless determined that it was necessary to intrude on respondent's liberty. I believe that his determination was totally unreasonable. As I read Terry, an officer may act on the basis of reliable information short of probable cause to make a stop, and ultimately a frisk, if necessary; but the officer may not use unreliable, unsubstantiated, conclusory hearsay to justify an invasion of liberty. Terry never meant to approve the kind of knee-jerk police reaction that we have before us in this case.

Even assuming that the officer had some legitimate reason for relying on the informant, Terry requires, before any stop and frisk is made, that the reliable information in the officer's possession demonstrate that the suspect is both armed and dangerous. [8] The fact remains that Connecticut specifically authorizes persons to carry guns so long as they have a permit. Thus, there was no reason for the officer to infer from anything that the informant said that the respondent was dangerous. His frisk was, therefore, illegal under Terry.

II

Even if I could agree with the Court that the stop and frisk in this case was proper, I could not go further and sustain the arrest and the subsequent searches. It takes probable cause to justify an arrest and search and seizure incident thereto. Probable cause means that the

"facts and circumstances before the officer are such as to warrant a man of prudence and caution in believing that the offence has been committed. . . ."

Stacey v. Emery, 97 U. S. 642, 97 U. S. 645 (1878). "[G]ood faith is not enough to constitute probable cause." Director General v. Kastenbaum, 263 U. S. 25, 263 U. S. 28 (1923).

Once the officer seized the gun from respondent, it is uncontradicted that he did not ask whether respondent had a license to carry it, or whether respondent carried it for any other legal reason under Connecticut law. Rather, the officer placed him under arrest immediately and hastened to search his person. Since Connecticut has not made it illegal for private citizens to carry guns, there is nothing in the facts of this case to warrant a man "of prudence and caution" to believe that any offense had been committed merely because respondent had a gun on his person. [9] Any implication that respondent's silence was some sort of a tacit admission of guilt would be utterly absurd.

It is simply not reasonable to expect someone to protest that he is not acting illegally before he is told that he is suspected of criminal activity. It would have been a simple matter for the officer to ask whether respondent had a permit, but he chose not to do so. In making this choice, he clearly violated the Fourth Amendment.

This case marks a departure from the mainstream of our Fourth Amendment cases. In Johnson v. United States, 333 U. S. 10 (1948), for example, the arresting officer had an informant's tip and actually smelled opium coming from a room. This Court still found the arrest unlawful. And in Spinelli v. United States, 393 U. S. 410, we found that there was no probable cause even where an informant's information was corroborated by personal observation. If there was no probable cause in those cases, I find it impossible to understand how there can be probable cause in this case.

III

MR. JUSTICE DOUGLAS was the sole dissenter in Terry. He warned of the "powerful hydraulic pressures throughout our history that bear heavily on the Court to water down constitutional guarantees. . . ." 392 U.S. at 392 U. S. 39. While I took the position then that we were not watering down rights, but were hesitantly and cautiously striking a necessary balance between the rights of American citizens to be free from government intrusion into their privacy and their government's urgent need for a narrow exception to the warrant requirement of the Fourth Amendment, today's decision demonstrates just how prescient MR. JUSTICE DOUGLAS was.

It seems that the delicate balance that Terry struck was simply too delicate, too susceptible to the "hydraulic pressures" of the day. As a result of today's decision, the balance struck in Terry is now heavily weighted in favor of the government. And the Fourth Amendment, which was included in the Bill of Rights to prevent the kind of arbitrary and oppressive police action involved herein, is dealt a serious blow. Today's decision invokes the specter of a society in which innocent citizens may be stopped, searched, and arrested at the whim of police officers who have only the slightest suspicion of improper conduct.

Notes

[1] App, 997.

[2] Terry v. Ohio, 392 U. S. 1 (1968), makes it clear that a stop and frisk is a search and seizure within the meaning of the Fourth Amendment. When I use the term stop and frisk herein, I merely intend to emphasize that it is, as Terry held, a lesser intrusion than a full-scale search and seizure.

[3] In Sibron v. New York, 392 U. S. 40 (1968), the Court held that the action of the policeman could not be justified as a stop and frisk. In Peters v. New York, 392 U. S. 40 (1968), the Court sustained the validity of a search and seizure by holding that it was incident to a legal arrest.

[4] Terry v. Ohio, 392 U.S. at 392 U. S. 29; Sibron v. New York, 392 U.S. at 392 U. S. 64.

[5] The fact that the respondent carried his gun in a high-crime area is irrelevant. In such areas, it is more probable than not that citizens would be more likely to carry weapons authorized by the State to protect themselves.

[6] See Conn.Gen.Stat.Rev. § 29-35.

[7] Connecticut permits possession of certain narcotics under specified circumstances -- e.g., pursuant to a doctor's prescription. See Conn.Gen.Stat. Rev §§ 19-443, 19-456(c), 1481.

[8] The Court virtually ignores the requirement that the suspect be dangerous, as well as armed. Other courts have followed Terry more closely. See, e.g., Commonwealth v. Bourke, 218 Pa.Super. 320, 323, 280 A.2d 425, 427 (1971); Commonwealth v. Clarke, 219 Pa.Super. 340, 343, 280 A.2d 662, 663 (1971); Finley v. People, 176 Colo. 1, 488 P.2d 883 (1971). See also State v. Goudy, 52 Haw. 497, 505, 479 P.2d 800, 805 (1971) (Abe, J., dissenting).

[9] The Court appears to rely on the fact that the existence of the gun corroborated the information supplied to the officer by the informant. It cannot be disputed that there is minimal corroboration here, but the fact remains that the officer still lacked any knowledge that respondent had done anything illegal. Since carrying a gun is not per se illegal in Connecticut, the fact that respondent carried a gun is no more relevant to probable cause than the fact that his shirt may have been blue, or that he was wearing a jacket. Moreover, the fact that the informant can identify a gun on sight does not indicate an ability to do the same with narcotics. The corroboration of this one fact is a far cry from the corroboration that the Court found sufficient to sustain an arrest in Draper v. United States, 358 U. S. 307 (1959).

The importance of the antitrust laws and competition to every citizen, including professional sports players, must not be minimized: Justice Marshall's dissent in Curt Flood v Bowie Kuhn (June 19, 1972)

MR. JUSTICE MARSHALL, with whom MR. JUSTICE BRENNAN joins, dissenting.

Petitioner was a major league baseball player from 1956, when he signed a contract with the Cincinnati Reds, until 1969, when his 12-year career with the St. Louis Cardinals, which had obtained him from the Reds, ended and he was traded to the Philadelphia Phillies. He had no notice that the Cardinals were contemplating a trade, no opportunity to indicate the teams with which he would prefer playing, and no desire to go to Philadelphia. After receiving formal notification of the trade, petitioner wrote to the Commissioner of Baseball protesting that he was not "a piece of property to be bought and sold irrespective of my wishes," 1 and urging that he had the right to consider offers from other teams than the Phillies. He requested that the Commissioner inform all of the major league teams that he was available for the 1970 season. His request was denied, and petitioner was informed that he had no choice but to play for Philadelphia or not to play at all.

To non-athletes it might appear that petitioner was virtually enslaved by the owners of major league baseball clubs who bartered among themselves for his services. But, athletes know that it was not servitude that bound petitioner to the club owners; it was the reserve system. The essence of that system is that a player is bound to the club with which he first signs a contract for the rest of his playing days. 2 He cannot escape from the club except by retiring, and he cannot prevent the club from assigning his contract to any other club.

Petitioner brought this action in the United States District Court for the Southern District of New York. He alleged, among other things, that the reserve system was an unreasonable restraint of trade in violation of federal antitrust laws. 3 The District Court thought itself bound by prior decisions of this Court and found for the respondents after a full trial. 309 F. Supp. 793 (1970). The United States Court of Appeals for the Second Circuit affirmed. 443 F.2d 264 (1971). We granted certiorari on October 19, 1971, 404 U.S. 880, in order to take a further look at the precedents relied upon by the lower courts.

This is a difficult case because we are torn between the principle of stare decisis and the knowledge that the decisions in Federal Baseball Club v. National League, 259 U.S. 200 (1922), and Toolson v. New York Yankees, Inc., 346 U.S. 356 (1953), are totally at odds with more recent and better reasoned cases.

In Federal Baseball Club, a team in the Federal League brought an antitrust action against the National and American Leagues and others. In his opinion for a unanimous Court, Mr. Justice Holmes wrote that the business being considered was "giving exhibitions of base ball, which are purely state affairs." 259 U.S., at 208 . Hence, the Court held that baseball was not within the purview of the antitrust laws. Thirty-one years later, the Court reaffirmed this decision, without reexamining it, in Toolson, a one-paragraph per curiam opinion. Like this case, Toolson involved an attack on the reserve system. The Court said:

"The business has . . . been left for thirty years to develop, on the understanding that it was not subject to existing antitrust legislation. The present cases ask us to overrule the prior decision and, with retrospective effect, hold the legislation applicable. We think that if there are evils in this field which now warrant application to it of the antitrust laws it should be by legislation." Id., at 357.

Much more time has passed since Toolson and Congress has not acted. We must now decide whether to adhere to the reasoning of Toolson - i. e., to refuse to re-examine the underlying basis of Federal Baseball Club - or to proceed with a re-examination and let the chips fall where they may.

In his answer to petitioner's complaint, the Commissioner of Baseball "admits that under present concepts of interstate commerce defendants are engaged therein." App. 40. There can be no doubt that the admission is warranted by today's reality. Since baseball is interstate commerce, if we re-examine baseball's antitrust exemption, the Court's decisions in United States v. Shubert, 348 U.S. 222 (1955), United States v. International Boxing Club, 348 U.S. 236 (1955), and Radovich v. National Football League, 352 U.S. 445 (1957), require that we bring baseball within the coverage of the antitrust laws. See also, Haywood v. National Basketball Assn., 401 U.S. 1204 (DOUGLAS, J., in chambers).

We have only recently had occasion to comment that:

"Antitrust laws in general, and the Sherman Act in particular, are the Magna Carta of free enterprise. They are as important to the preservation of economic freedom and our free-enterprise system as the Bill of Rights is to the protection of our fundamental personal freedoms. . . . Implicit in such freedom is the notion that it cannot be foreclosed with respect to one sector of the economy because certain private citizens or groups believe that such foreclosure might promote greater competition in a more important sector of the economy." United States v. Topco Associates, Inc., 405 U.S. 596, 610 (1972).

The importance of the antitrust laws to every citizen must not be minimized. They are as important to baseball players as they are to football players, lawyers, doctors, or members of any other class of workers. Baseball players cannot be denied the benefits of competition merely because club owners view other economic interests as being more important, unless Congress says so.

Has Congress acquiesced in our decisions in Federal Baseball Club and Toolson? I think not. Had the Court been consistent and treated all sports in the same way baseball was treated, Congress might have become concerned enough to take action. But, the Court was inconsistent, and baseball was isolated and distinguished from all other sports. In Toolson the Court refused to act because Congress had been silent. But the Court may have read too much into this legislative inaction.

Americans love baseball as they love all sports. Perhaps we become so enamored of athletics that we assume that they are foremost in the minds of legislators as well as fans. We must not forget, however, that there are only some 600 major league baseball players. Whatever muscle they might have been able to muster by combining forces with other athletes has been greatly impaired by the manner in which this Court has isolated them. It is this Court that has made them impotent, and this Court should correct its error.

We do not lightly overrule our prior constructions of federal statutes, but when our errors deny substantial federal rights, like the right to compete freely and effectively to the best of one's ability as guaranteed by the antitrust laws, we must admit our error and correct it. We have done so before and we should do so again here. See, e. g., Blonder-Tongue Laboratories, Inc. v. University of Illinois Foundation, 402 U.S. 313 (1971); Boys Markets, Inc. v. Retail Clerks Union, 398 U.S. 235, 241 (1970). 4

To the extent that there is concern over any reliance interests that club owners may assert, they can be satisfied by making our decision prospective only. Baseball should be covered by the antitrust laws beginning with this case and henceforth, unless Congress decides otherwise. 5

Accordingly, I would overrule Federal Baseball Club and Toolson and reverse the decision of the Court of Appeals. 6

This does not mean that petitioner would necessarily prevail, however. Lurking in the background is a hurdle of recent vintage that petitioner still must overcome. In 1966, the Major League Players Association was formed. It is the collective-bargaining representative for all major league baseball players. Respondents argue that the reserve system is now part and parcel of the collective-bargaining agreement and that because it is a mandatory subject of bargaining, the federal labor statutes are applicable, not the federal antitrust laws. 7 The lower courts did not rule on this argument, having decided the case solely on the basis of the antitrust exemption.

This Court has faced the interrelationship between the antitrust laws and the labor laws before. The decisions make several things clear. First, "benefits to organized labor cannot be utilized as a cat's-paw to pull employer's chestnuts out of the antitrust fires." United States v. Women's Sportswear Manufacturers Assn., 336 U.S. 460, 464 (1949). See also Allen Bradley Co. v. Local Union No. 3, 325 U.S. 797 (1945). Second, the very nature of a collective-bargaining agreement mandates that the parties be able to "restrain" trade to a greater degree than management could do unilaterally. United States v. Hutcheson, 312 U.S. 219 (1941); United Mine Workers v. Pennington, 381 U.S. 657 (1965); Amalgamated Meat Cutters v. Jewel Tea, 381 U.S. 676 (1965); cf., Teamsters Union v. Oliver, 358 U.S. 283 (1959). Finally, it is clear that some cases can be resolved only by examining the purposes and the competing interests of the labor and antitrust statutes and by striking a balance.

It is apparent that none of the prior cases is precisely in point. They involve union-management agreements that work to the detriment of management's competitors. In this case, petitioner urges that the reserve system works to the detriment of labor.

While there was evidence at trial concerning the collective-bargaining relationship of the parties, the issues surrounding that relationship have not been fully explored. As one commentary has suggested, this case "has been litigated with the implications for the institution of collective bargaining only dimly perceived. The labor law issues have been in the corners of the case - the courts below, for example, did not reach them - moving in and out of the shadows like an uninvited guest at a party whom one can't decide either to embrace or expel." 8

It is true that in Radovich v. National Football League, supra, the Court rejected a claim that federal labor statutes governed the relationship between a professional athlete and the professional sport. But, an examination of the briefs and record in that case indicates that the issue was not squarely faced. The issue is once again before this Court without being clearly focused. It should, therefore, be the subject of further inquiry in the District Court.

There is a surface appeal to respondents' argument that petitioner's sole remedy lies in filing a claim with the National Labor Relations Board, but this argument is premised on the notion that management and labor have agreed to accept the reserve clause. This notion is contradicted, in part, by the record in this case. Petitioner suggests that the reserve system was thrust upon the players by the owners and that the recently formed players' union has not had time to modify or eradicate it. If this is true, the question arises as to whether there would then be any exemption from the antitrust laws in this case. Petitioner also suggests that there are limits to the antitrust violations to which labor and management can agree. These limits should also be explored.

In light of these consideration, I would remand this case to the District Court for consideration of whether petitioner can state a claim under the antitrust laws despite the collective-bargaining agreement, and, if so, for a determination of whether there has been an antitrust violation in this case.

Notes

[1] Letter from Curt Flood to Bowie K. Kuhn, Dec. 24, 1969, App. 37.

[2] As MR. JUSTICE BLACKMUN points out, the reserve system is not novel. It has been employed since 1887. See Metropolitan Exhibition Co. v. Ewing, 42 F. 198, 202-204 (CC SDNY 1890). The club owners assert that it is necessary to preserve effective competition and to retain fan interest. The players do not agree and argue that the reserve system is overly restrictive. Before this lawsuit was instituted, the players refused to agree that the reserve system should be a part of the collective-bargaining contract. Instead, the owners and players agreed that the reserve system would temporarily remain in effect while they jointly investigated possible changes. Their activity along these lines has halted pending the outcome of this suit.

[3] Petitioner also alleged a violation of state antitrust laws, state civil rights laws, and of the common law, and claimed that he was forced into peonage and involuntary servitude in violation of the Thirteenth Amendment to the United States Constitution. Because I believe that federal antitrust laws govern baseball, I find that state law has been pre-empted in this area. Like the lower courts, I do not believe that there has been a violation of the Thirteenth Amendment.

[4] In the past this Court has not hesitated to change its view as to what constitutes interstate commerce. Compare United States v. Knight Co., 156 U.S. 1 (1895), with Mandeville Island Farms v. American Crystal Sugar Co., 334 U.S. 219 (1948), and United States v. Darby, 312 U.S. 100 (1941).

"The jurist concerned with `public confidence in, and acceptance of the judicial system' might well consider that, however admirable its resolute adherence to the law as it was, a decision contrary to the public sense of justice as it is, operates, so far as it is known, to diminish respect for the courts and for law itself." Szanton, Stare Decisis; A Dissenting View, 10 Hastings L. J. 394, 397 (1959).

[5] We said recently that "[i]n rare cases, decisions construing federal statutes might be denied full retroactive effect, as for instance where this Court overrules its own construction of a statute . . . ." United States v. Estate of Donnelly, 397 U.S. 286, 295 (1970). Cf. Simpson v. Union Oil Co. of California, 377 U.S. 13, 25 (1964).

[6] The lower courts did not reach the question of whether, assuming the antitrust laws apply, they have been violated. This should be considered on remand.

[7] Cf. United States v. Hutcheson, 312 U.S. 219 (1941).

[8] Jacobs & Winter, Antitrust Principles and Collective Bargaining by Athletes: Of Superstars in Peonage, 81 Yale L. J. 1, 22 (1971).

Death penalty is cruel and unusual punishment: Justice Marshall's concurrence in Furman v. Georgia (June 29, 1972) [Appendices omitted]

MR. JUSTICE MARSHALL, concurring.

The question whether the death penalty is a cruel and unusual punishment prohibited by the Eighth Amendment to the United States Constitution.[1]

In No. 69-5003, Furman was convicted of murder for shooting the father of five children when he discovered that Furman had broken into his home early one morning. Nos. 69-5030 and 69-5031 involve state convictions for forcible rape. Jackson was found guilty of rape during the course of a robbery in the victim's home. The rape was accomplished as he held the pointed ends of scissors at the victim's throat. Branch also was convicted of a rape committed in the victim's home. No weapon was utilized, but physical force and threats of physical force were employed.

The criminal acts with which we are confronted are ugly, vicious, reprehensible acts. Their sheer brutality cannot and should not be minimized. But, we are not called upon to condone the penalized conduct; we are asked only to examine the penalty imposed on each of the petitioners and to determine whether or not it violates the Eighth Amendment. The question then is not whether we condone rape or murder, for surely we do not; it is whether capital punishment is "a punishment no longer consistent with our own self-respect"[2] and, therefore, violative of the Eighth Amendment.

The elasticity of the constitutional provision under consideration presents dangers of too little or too much self-restraint.[3] Hence, we must proceed with caution to answer the question presented.[4] By first examining the historical derivation of the Eighth Amendment and the construction given it in the past by this Court, and then exploring the history and attributes of capital punishment in this country, we can answer the question presented with objectivity and a proper measure of self-restraint.

Candor is critical to such an inquiry. All relevant material must be marshaled and sorted and forthrightly examined. We must not only be precise as to the standards of judgment that we are utilizing, but exacting in examining the relevant material in light of those standards.

Candor compels me to confess that I am not oblivious to the fact that this is truly a matter of life and death. Not only does it involve the lives of these three petitioners, but those of the almost 600 other condemned men and women in this country currently awaiting execution. While this fact cannot affect our ultimate decision, it necessitates that the decision be free from any possibility of error.

I

The Eighth Amendment's ban against cruel and unusual punishments derives from English law. In 1583, John Whitgift, Archbishop of Canterbury, turned the High Commission into a permanent ecclesiastical court, and the Commission began to use torture to extract confessions from persons suspected of various offenses.[5] Sir Robert Beale protested that cruel and barbarous torture violated Magna Carta, but his protests were made in vain.[6]

Cruel punishments were not confined to those accused of crimes, but were notoriously applied with even greater relish to those who were convicted. Blackstone described in ghastly detail the myriad of inhumane forms of punishment imposed on persons found guilty of any of a large number of offenses.[7] Death, of course, was the usual result.[8]

The treason trials of 1685 - the "Bloody Assizes" - which followed an abortive rebellion by the Duke of Monmouth, marked the culmination of the parade of horrors, and most historians believe that it was this event that finally spurred the adoption of the English Bill of Rights containing the progenitor of our prohibition against cruel and unusual punishments.[9] The conduct of Lord Chief Justice Jeffreys at those trials has been described as an "insane lust for cruelty" which was "stimulated by orders from the King" (James II).[10] The assizes received wide publicity from Puritan pamphleteers and doubtless had some influence on the adoption of a cruel and unusual punishments clause. But, the legislative history of the English Bill of Rights of 1689 indicates that the assizes may not have been as critical to the adoption of the clause as is widely thought. After William and Mary of Orange crossed the channel to invade England, James II fled. Parliament was summoned into session and a committee was appointed to draft general statements containing "such things as are absolutely necessary to be considered for the better securing of our religion, laws and liberties."[11] An initial draft of the Bill of Rights prohibited "illegal" punishments, but a later draft referred to the infliction by James II of "illegal and cruel" punishments, and declared "cruel and unusual" punishments to be prohibited.[12] The use of the word "unusual" in the final draft appears to be inadvertent.

This legislative history has led at least one legal historian to conclude "that the cruel and unusual punishments clause of the Bill of Rights of 1689 was, first, an objection to the imposition of punishments that were unauthorized by statute and outside the jurisdiction of the sentencing court, and second, a reiteration of the English policy against disproportionate penalties,"[13] and not primarily a reaction to the torture of the High Commission, harsh sentences, or the assizes.

Whether the English Bill of Rights prohibition against cruel and unusual punishments is properly read as a response to excessive or illegal punishments, as a reaction to barbaric and objectionable modes of punishment, or as both, there is no doubt whatever that in borrowing the language and in including it in the Eighth Amendment, our Founding Fathers intended to outlaw torture and other cruel punishments.[14]

The precise language used in the Eighth Amendment first appeared in America on June 12, 1776, in Virginia's "Declaration of Rights,"[9] of which read: "That excessive bail ought not to be required, nor excessive fines imposed, nor cruel and unusual punishments inflicted."[15] This language was drawn verbatim from the English Bill of Rights of 1689. Other States adopted similar clauses,[16] and there is evidence in the debates of the various state conventions that were called upon to ratify the Constitution of great concern for the omission of any prohibition against torture or other cruel punishments.[17]

The Virginia Convention offers some clues as to what the Founding Fathers had in mind in prohibiting cruel and unusual punishments. At one point George Mason advocated the adoption of a Bill of Rights, and Patrick Henry concurred, stating:

"By this Constitution, some of the best barriers of human rights are thrown away. Is there not an additional reason to have a bill of rights? . . . Congress, from their general powers, may fully go into business of human legislation. They may legislate, in criminal cases, from treason to the lowest offence - petty larceny. They may define crimes and prescribe punishments. In the definition of crimes, I trust they will be directed by what wise representatives ought to be governed by. But when we come to punishments, no latitude ought to be left, nor dependence put on the virtue of representatives. What says our bill of rights? - `that excessive bail ought not to be required, nor excessive fines imposed, nor cruel and unusual punishments inflicted.' Are you not, therefore, now calling on those gentlemen who are to compose Congress, to prescribe trials and define punishments without this control? Will they find sentiments there similar to this bill of rights? You let them loose; you do more - you depart from the genius of your country. . . .

"In this business of legislation, your members of Congress will loose the restriction of not imposing excessive fines, demanding excessive bail, and inflicting cruel and unusual punishments. These are prohibited by your declaration of rights. What has distinguished our ancestors? - That they would not admit of tortures, or cruel and barbarous punishment. But Congress may introduce the practice of the civil law, in preference to that of the common law. They may introduce the practice of France, Spain, and Germany - of torturing, to extort a confession of the crime. They will say that they might as well draw examples from those countries as from Great Britain, and they will tell you that there is such a necessity of strengthening the arm of government, that they must have a criminal equity, and extort confession by torture, in order to punish with still more relentless severity. We are then lost and undone."[18]

Henry's statement indicates that he wished to insure that "relentless severity" would be prohibited by the Constitution. Other expressions with respect to the proposed Eighth Amendment by Members of the First Congress indicate that they shared Henry's view of the need for and purpose of the Cruel and Unusual Punishments Clause.[19]

Thus, the history of the clause clearly establishes that it was intended to prohibit cruel punishments. We must now turn to the case law to discover the manner in which courts have given meaning to the term "cruel."

II

This Court did not squarely face the task of interpreting the cruel and unusual punishments language for the first time until Wilkerson v. Utah, 99 U.S. 130 (1879), although the language received a cursory examination in several prior cases. See, e. g., Pervear v. Commonwealth, 5 Wall. 475 (1867). In Wilkerson, the Court unanimously upheld a sentence of public execution by shooting imposed pursuant to a conviction for premeditated murder. In his opinion for the Court, Mr. Justice Clifford wrote:

"Difficulty would attend the effort to define with exactness the extent of the constitutional provision which provides that cruel and unusual punishments shall not be inflicted; but it is safe to affirm that punishments of torture, . . . and all others in the same line of unnecessary cruelty, are forbidden by that amendment to the Constitution." 99 U.S., at 135 -136.

Thus, the Court found that unnecessary cruelty was no more permissible than torture. To determine whether the punishment under attack was unnecessarily cruel, the Court examined the history of the Utah Territory and the then-current writings on capital punishment, and compared this Nation's practices with those of other countries. It is apparent that the Court felt it could not dispose of the question simply by referring to traditional practices; instead, it felt bound to examine developing thought.

Eleven years passed before the Court again faced a challenge to a specific punishment under the Eighth Amendment. In the case of In re Kemmler, 136 U.S. 436 (1890), Chief Justice Fuller wrote an opinion for a unanimous Court upholding electrocution as a permissible mode of punishment. While the Court ostensibly held that the Eighth Amendment did not apply to the States, it is very apparent that the nature of the punishment involved was examined under the Due Process Clause of the Fourteenth Amendment. The Court held that the punishment was not objectionable. Today, Kemmler stands primarily for the proposition that a punishment is not necessarily unconstitutional simply because it is unusual, so long as the legislature has a humane purpose in selecting it.[20]

Two years later in O'Neil v. Vermont, 144 U.S. 323 (1892), the Court reaffirmed that the Eighth Amendment was not applicable to the States. O'Neil was found guilty on 307 counts of selling liquor in violation of Vermont law. A fine of $6,140 ($20 for each offense) and the costs of prosecution ($497.96) were imposed. O'Neil was committed to prison until the fine and the costs were paid; and the court provided that if they were not paid before a specified date, O'Neil was to be confined in the house of corrections for 19,914 days (approximately 54 years) at hard labor. Three Justices - Field, Harlan, and Brewer - dissented. They maintained not only that the Cruel and Unusual Punishments Clause was applicable to the States, but that in O'Neil's case it had been violated. Mr. Justice Field wrote:

"That designation [cruel and unusual], it is true, is usually applied to punishments which inflict torture, such as the rack, the thumbscrew, the iron boot, the stretching of limbs and the like, which are attended with acute pain and suffering. . . . The inhibition is directed, not only against punishments of the character mentioned, but against all punishments which by their excessive length or severity are greatly disproportioned to the offences charged. The whole inhibition is against that which is excessive . . . ." Id., at 339-340.

In Howard v. Fleming, 191 U.S. 126 (1903), the Court, in essence, followed the approach advocated by the dissenters in O'Neil. In rejecting the claim that 10-year sentences for conspiracy to defraud were cruel and unusual, the Court (per Mr. Justice Brewer) considered the nature of the crime, the purpose of the law, and the length of the sentence imposed.

The Court used the same approach seven years later in the landmark case of Weems v. United States, 217 U.S. 349 (1910). Weems, an officer of the Bureau of Coast Guard and Transportation of the United States Government of the Philippine Islands, was convicted of falsifying a "public and official document." He was sentenced to 15 years' incarceration at hard labor with chains on his ankles, to an unusual loss of his civil rights, and to perpetual surveillance. Called upon to determine whether this was a cruel and unusual punishment, the Court found that it was.[21] The Court emphasized that the Constitution was not an "ephemeral" enactment, or one "designed to meet passing occasions."[22] Recognizing that "[t]ime works changes, [and] brings into existence new conditions and purposes,"[23] the Court commented that "[i]n the application of a constitution . . . our contemplation cannot be only of what has been but of what may be."[24]

In striking down the penalty imposed on Weems, the Court examined the punishment in relation to the offense, compared the punishment to those inflicted for other crimes and to those imposed in other jurisdictions, and concluded that the punishment was excessive.[25] Justices White and Holmes dissented and argued that the cruel and unusual prohibition was meant to prohibit only those things that were objectionable at the time the Constitution was adopted.[26]

Weems is a landmark case because it represents the first time that the Court invalidated a penalty prescribed by a legislature for a particular offense. The Court made it plain beyond any reasonable doubt that excessive punishments were as objectionable as those that were inherently cruel. Thus, it is apparent that the dissenters' position in O'Neil had become the opinion of the Court in Weems.

Weems was followed by two cases that added little to our knowledge of the scope of the cruel and unusual language, Badders v. United States, 240 U.S. 391 (1916), and United States ex rel. Milwaukee Social Democratic Publishing Co. v. Burleson, 255 U.S. 407 (1921).[27] Then came another landmark case, Louisiana ex rel. Francis v. Resweber, 329 U.S. 459 (1947).

Francis had been convicted of murder and sentenced to be electrocuted. The first time the current passed through him, there was a mechanical failure and he did not die. Thereafter, Francis sought to prevent a second electrocution on the ground that it would be a cruel and unusual punishment. Eight members of the Court assumed the applicability of the Eighth Amendment to the States.[28] The Court was virtually unanimous in agreeing that "[t]he traditional humanity of modern Anglo-American law forbids the infliction of unnecessary pain,"[29] but split 5-4 on whether Francis would, under the circumstances, be forced to undergo any excessive pain. Five members of the Court treated the case like In re Kemmler and held that the legislature adopted electrocution for a humane purpose, and that its will should not be thwarted because, in its desire to reduce pain and suffering in most cases, it may have inadvertently increased suffering in one particular case.[30] The four dissenters felt that the case should be remanded for further facts.

As in Weems, the Court was concerned with excessive punishments. Resweber is perhaps most significant because the analysis of cruel and unusual punishment questions first advocated by the dissenters in O'Neil was at last firmly entrenched in the minds of an entire Court.

Trop v. Dulles, 356 U.S. 86 (1958), marked the next major cruel and unusual punishment case in this Court. Trop, a native-born American, was declared to have lost his citizenship by reason of a conviction by court-martial for wartime desertion. Writing for himself and Justices Black, DOUGLAS, and Whittaker, Chief Justice Warren concluded that loss of citizenship amounted to a cruel and unusual punishment that violated the Eighth Amendment.[31]

Emphasizing the flexibility inherent in the words "cruel and unusual," the Chief Justice wrote that "[t]he Amendment must draw its meaning from the evolving standards of decency that mark the progress of a maturing society."[32] His approach to the problem was that utilized by the Court in Weems: he scrutinized the severity of the penalty in relation to the offense, examined the practices of other civilized nations of the world, and concluded that involuntary statelessness was an excessive and, therefore, an unconstitutional punishment. Justice Frankfurter, dissenting, urged that expatriation was not punishment, and that even if it were, it was not excessive. While he criticized the conclusion arrived at by the Chief Justice, his approach to the Eighth Amendment question was identical.

Whereas in Trop a majority of the Court failed to agree on whether loss of citizenship was a cruel and unusual punishment, four years later a majority did agree in Robinson v. California, 370 U.S. 660 (1962), that a sentence of 90 days' imprisonment for violation of a California statute making it a crime to "be addicted to the use of narcotics" was cruel and unusual. MR. JUSTICE STEWART, writing the opinion of the Court, reiterated what the Court had said in Weems and what Chief Justice Warren wrote in Trop - that the cruel and unusual punishment clause was not a static concept, but one that must be continually re-examined "in the light of contemporary human knowledge."[33] The fact that the penalty under attack was only 90 days evidences the Court's willingness to carefully examine the possible excessiveness of punishment in a given case even where what is involved is a penalty that is familiar and widely accepted.[34]

We distinguished Robinson in Powell v. Texas, 392 U.S. 514 (1968), where we sustained a conviction for drunkenness in a public place and a fine of $20. Four Justices dissented on the ground that Robinson was controlling. The analysis in both cases was the same; only the conclusion as to whether or not the punishment was excessive differed. Powell marked the last time prior to today's decision that the Court has had occasion to construe the meaning of the term "cruel and unusual" punishment.

Several principles emerge from these prior cases and serve as a beacon to an enlightened decision in the instant cases.

III

Perhaps the most important principle in analyzing "cruel and unusual" punishment questions is one that is reiterated again and again in the prior opinions of the Court: i. e., the cruel and unusual language "must draw its meaning from the evolving standards of decency that mark the progress of a maturing society."[35] Thus, a penalty that was permissible at one time in our Nation's history is not necessarily permissible today.

The fact, therefore, that the Court, or individual Justices, may have in the past expressed an opinion that the death penalty is constitutional is not now binding on us. A fair reading of Wilkerson v. Utah, supra; In re Kemmler, supra; and Louisiana ex rel. Francis v. Resweber, supra, would certainly indicate an acceptance sub silentio of capital punishment as constitutionally permissible. Several Justices have also expressed their individual opinions that the death penalty is constitutional.[36] Yet, some of these same Justices and others have at times expressed concern over capital punishment.[37] There is no holding directly in point, and the very nature of the Eighth Amendment would dictate that unless a very recent decision existed, stare decisis would bow to changing values, and the question of the constitutionality of capital punishment at a given moment in history would remain open.

Faced with an open question, we must establish our standards for decision. The decisions discussed in the previous section imply that a punishment may be deemed cruel and unusual for any one of four distinct reasons.

First, there are certain punishments that inherently involve so much physical pain and suffering that civilized people cannot tolerate them - e. g., use of the rack, the thumbscrew, or other modes of torture. See O'Neil v. Vermont, 144 U.S., at 339 (Field, J., dissenting). Regardless of public sentiment with respect to imposition of one of these punishments in a particular case or at any one moment in history, the Constitution prohibits it. These are punishments that have been barred since the adoption of the Bill of Rights.

Second, there are punishments that are unusual, signifying that they were previously unknown as penalties for a given offense. Cf. United States ex rel. Milwaukee Social Democratic Publishing Co. v. Burleson, 255 U.S., at 435 (Brandeis, J., dissenting). If these punishments are intended to serve a humane purpose, they may be constitutionally permissible. In re Kemmler, 136 U.S., at 447; Louisiana ex rel. Francis v. Resweber, 329 U.S., at 464 . Prior decisions leave open the question of just how much the word "unusual" adds to the word "cruel." I have previously indicated that use of the word "unusual" in the English Bill of Rights of 1689 was inadvertent, and there is nothing in the history of the Eighth Amendment to give flesh to its intended meaning. In light of the meager history that does exist, one would suppose that an innovative punishment would probably be constitutional if no more cruel than that punishment which it superseded. We need not decide this question here, however, for capital punishment is certainly not a recent phenomenon.

Third, a penalty may be cruel and unusual because it is excessive and serves no valid legislative purpose. Weems v. United States, supra. The decisions previously discussed are replete with assertions that one of the primary functions of the cruel and unusual punishments clause is to prevent excessive or unnecessary penalties, e. g., Wilkerson v. Utah, 99 U.S., at 134; O'Neil v. Vermont, 144 U.S., at 339 -340 (Field, J., dissenting); Weems v. United States, 217 U.S., at 381; Louisiana ex rel. Francis v. Resweber, supra; these punishments are unconstitutional even though popular sentiment may favor them. Both THE CHIEF JUSTICE and MR. JUSTICE POWELL seek to ignore or to minimize this aspect of the Court's prior decisions. But, since Mr. Justice Field first suggested that "[t]he whole inhibition [of the prohibition against cruel and unusual punishments] is against that which is excessive," O'Neil v. Vermont, 144 U.S., at 340, this Court has steadfastly maintained that a penalty is unconstitutional whenever it is unnecessarily harsh or cruel. This is what the Founders of this country intended; this is what their fellow citizens believed the Eighth Amendment provided; and this was the basis for our decision in Robinson v. California, supra, for the plurality opinion by Mr. Chief Justice Warren in Trop v. Dulles, supra, and for the Court's decision in Weems v. United States, supra. See also W. Bradford, An Enquiry How Far the Punishment of Death is Necessary in Pennsylvania (1793), reprinted in 12 Am. J. Legal Hist. 122, 127 (1968). It should also be noted that the "cruel and unusual" language of the Eighth Amendment immediately follows language that prohibits excessive bail and excessive fines. The entire thrust of the Eighth Amendment is, in short, against "that which is excessive."

Fourth, where a punishment is not excessive and serves a valid legislative purpose, it still may be invalid if popular sentiment abhors it. For example, if the evidence clearly demonstrated that capital punishment served valid legislative purposes, such punishment would, nevertheless, be unconstitutional if citizens found it to be morally unacceptable. A general abhorrence on the part of the public would, in effect, equate a modern punishment with those barred since the adoption of the Eighth Amendment. There are no prior cases in this Court striking down a penalty on this ground, but the very notion of changing values requires that we recognize its existence.

It is immediately obvious, then, that since capital punishment is not a recent phenomenon, if it violates the Constitution, it does so because it is excessive or unnecessary, or because it is abhorrent to currently existing moral values.

We must proceed to the history of capital punishment in the United States.

IV

Capital punishment has been used to penalize various forms of conduct by members of society since the beginnings of civilization. Its precise origins are difficult to perceive, but there is some evidence that its roots lie in violent retaliation by members of a tribe or group, or by the tribe or group itself, against persons committing hostile acts toward group members.[38] Thus, infliction of death as a penalty for objectionable conduct appears to have its beginnings in private vengeance.[39]

As individuals gradually ceded their personal prerogatives to a sovereign power, the sovereign accepted the authority to punish wrongdoing as part of its "divine right" to rule. Individual vengeance gave way to the vengeance of the state, and capital punishment became a public function.[40] Capital punishment worked its way into the laws of various countries,[41] and was inflicted in a variety of macabre and horrific ways.[42]

It was during the reign of Henry II (1154-1189) that English law first recognized that crime was more than a personal affair between the victim and the perpetrator.[43] The early history of capital punishment in England is set forth in McGautha v. California, 402 U.S. 183, 197 -200 (1971), and need not be repeated here.

By 1500, English law recognized eight major capital crimes: treason, petty treason (killing of husband by his wife), murder, larceny, robbery, burglary, rape, and arson.[44] Tudor and Stuart kings added many more crimes to the list of those punishable by death, and by 1688 there were nearly 50.[45] George II (1727-1760) added nearly 36 more, and George III (1760-1820) increased the number by 60.[46]

By shortly after 1800, capital offenses numbered more than 200 and not only included crimes against person and property, but even some against the public peace. While England may, in retrospect, look particularly brutal, Blackstone points out that England was fairly civilized when compared to the rest of Europe.[47]

Capital punishment was not as common a penalty in the American Colonies. "The Capitall Lawes of New-England," dating from 1636, were drawn by the Massachusetts Bay Colony and are the first written expression of capital offenses known to exist in this country. These laws make the following crimes capital offenses: idolatry, witchcraft, blasphemy, murder, assault in sudden anger, sodomy, buggery, adultery, statutory rape, rape, manstealing, perjury in a capital trial, and rebellion. Each crime is accompanied by a reference to the Old Testament to indicate its source.[48] It is not known with any certainty exactly when, or even if, these laws were enacted as drafted; and, if so, just how vigorously these laws were enforced.[49] We do know that the other Colonies had a variety of laws that spanned the spectrum of severity.[50]

By the 18th century, the list of crimes became much less theocratic and much more secular. In the average colony, there were 12 capital crimes.[51] This was far fewer than existed in England, and part of the reason was that there was a scarcity of labor in the Colonies.[52] Still, there were many executions, because "[w]ith county jails inadequate and insecure, the criminal population seemed best controlled by death, mutilation, and fines."[53]

Even in the 17th century, there was some opposition to capital punishment in some of the colonies. In his "Great Act" of 1682, William Penn prescribed death only for premeditated murder and treason,[54] although his reform was not long lived.[55]

In 1776 the Philadelphia Society for Relieving Distressed Prisoners organized, and it was followed 11 years later by the Philadelphia Society for Alleviating the Miseries of Public Prisons.[56] These groups pressured for reform of all penal laws, including capital offenses. Dr. Benjamin Rush soon drafted America's first reasoned argument against capital punishment, entitled An Enquiry into the Effects of Public Punishments upon Criminals and upon Society.[57] In 1793, William Bradford, the Attorney General of Pennsylvania and later Attorney General of the United States, conducted "An Enquiry How Far the Punishment of Death is Necessary in Pennsylvania."[58] He concluded that it was doubtful whether capital punishment was at all necessary, and that until more information could be obtained, it should be immediately eliminated for all offenses except high treason and murder.[59]

The "Enquiries" of Rush and Bradford and the Pennsylvania movement toward abolition of the death penalty had little immediate impact on the practices of other States.[60] But in the early 1800's, Governors George and DeWitt Clinton and Daniel Tompkins unsuccessfully urged the New York Legislature to modify or end capital punishment. During this same period, Edward Livingston, an American lawyer who later became Secretary of State and Minister to France under President Andrew Jackson, was appointed by the Louisiana Legislature to draft a new penal code. At the center of his proposal was "the total abolition of capital punishment."[61] His Introductory Report to the System of Penal Law Prepared for the State of Louisiana[62] contained a systematic rebuttal of all arguments favoring capital punishment. Drafted in 1824, it was not published until 1833. This work was a tremendous impetus to the abolition movement for the next half century.

During the 1830's, there was a rising tide of sentiment against capital punishment. In 1834, Pennsylvania abolished public executions,[63] and two years later, The Report on Capital Punishment Made to the Maine Legislature was published. It led to a law that prohibited the executive from issuing a warrant for execution within one year after a criminal was sentenced by the courts. The totally discretionary character of the law was at odds with almost all prior practices. The "Maine Law" resulted in little enforcement of the death penalty, which was not surprising since the legislature's idea in passing the law was that the affirmative burden placed on the governor to issue a warrant one full year or more after a trial would be an effective deterrent to exercise of his power.[64] The law spread throughout New England and led to Michigan's being the first State to abolish capital punishment in 1846.[65]

Anti-capital-punishment feeling grew in the 1840's as the literature of the period pointed out the agony of the condemned man and expressed the philosophy that repentance atoned for the worst crimes, and that true repentance derived, not from fear, but from harmony with nature.[66]

By 1850, societies for abolition existed in Massachusetts, New York, Pennsylvania, Tennessee, Ohio, Alabama, Louisiana, Indiana, and Iowa.[67] New York, Massachusetts, and Pennsylvania constantly had abolition bills before their legislatures. In 1852, Rhode Island followed in the footsteps of Michigan and partially abolished capital punishment.[68] Wisconsin totally abolished the death penalty the following year.[69] Those States that did not abolish the death penalty greatly reduced its scope, and "[f]ew states outside the South had more than one or two . . . capital offenses" in addition to treason and murder.[70]

But the Civil War halted much of the abolition furor. One historian has said that "[a]fter the Civil War, men's finer sensibilities, which had once been revolted by the execution of a fellow being, seemed hardened and blunted."[71] Some of the attention previously given to abolition was diverted to prison reform. An abolitionist movement still existed, however. Maine abolished the death penalty in 1876, restored it in 1883, and abolished it again in 1887; Iowa abolished capital punishment from 1872-1878; Colorado began an erratic period of de facto abolition and revival in 1872; and Kansas also abolished it de facto in 1872, and by law in 1907.[72]

One great success of the abolitionist movement in the period from 1830-1900 was almost complete elimination of mandatory capital punishment. Before the legislatures formally gave juries discretion to refrain from imposing the death penalty, the phenomenon of "jury nullification," in which juries refused to convict in cases in which they believed that death was an inappropriate penalty, was experienced.[73] Tennessee was the first State to give juries discretion, Tenn. Laws 1837-1838, c. 29, but other States quickly followed suit. Then, Rep. Curtis of New York introduced a federal bill that ultimately became law in 1897 which reduced the number of federal capital offenses from 60 to 3 (treason, murder, and rape) and gave the jury sentencing discretion in murder and rape cases.[74]

By 1917 12 States had become abolitionist jurisdictions.[75] But, under the nervous tension of World War I, four of these States reinstituted capital punishment and promising movements in other States came grinding to a halt.[76] During the period following the First World War, the abolitionist movement never regained its momentum.

It is not easy to ascertain why the movement lost its vigor. Certainly, much attention was diverted from penal reform during the economic crisis of the depression and the exhausting years of struggle during World War II. Also, executions, which had once been frequent public spectacles, became infrequent private affairs. The manner of inflicting death changed, and the horrors of the punishment were, therefore, somewhat diminished in the minds of the general public.[77]

In recent years there has been renewed interest in modifying capital punishment. New York has moved toward abolition,[78] as have several other States.[79] In 1967, a bill was introduced in the Senate to abolish capital punishment for all federal crimes, but it died in committee.[80]

At the present time, 41 States, the District of Columbia, and other federal jurisdictions authorize the death penalty for at least one crime. It would be fruitless to attempt here to categorize the approach to capital punishment taken by the various States.[81] It is sufficient to note that murder is the crime most often punished by death, followed by kidnaping and treason.[82] Rape is a capital offense in 16 States and the federal system.[83]

The foregoing history demonstrates that capital punishment was carried from Europe to America but, once here, was tempered considerably. At times in our history, strong abolitionist movements have existed. But, they have never been completely successful, as no more than one-quarter of the States of the Union have, at any one time, abolished the death penalty. They have had partial success, however, especially in reducing the number of capital crimes, replacing mandatory death sentences with jury discretion, and developing more humane methods of conducting executions.

This is where our historical foray leads. The question now to be faced is whether American society has reached a point where abolition is not dependent on a successful grass roots movement in particular jurisdictions, but is demanded by the Eighth Amendment. To answer this question, we must first examine whether or not the death penalty is today tantamount to excessive punishment.

V

In order to assess whether or not death is an excessive or unnecessary penalty, it is necessary to consider the reasons why a legislature might select it as punishment for one or more offenses, and examine whether less severe penalties would satisfy the legitimate legislative wants as well as capital punishment. If they would, then the death penalty is unnecessary cruelty, and, therefore, unconstitutional.

There are six purposes conceivably served by capital punishment: retribution, deterrence, prevention of repetitive criminal acts, encouragement of guilty pleas and confessions, eugenics, and economy. These are considered seriatim below.

A. The concept of retribution is one of the most misunderstood in all of our criminal jurisprudence. The principal source of confusion derives from the fact that, in dealing with the concept, most people confuse the question "why do men in fact punish?" with the question "what justifies men in punishing?" 84 Men may punish for any number of reasons, but the one reason that punishment is morally good or morally justifiable is that someone has broken the law. Thus, it can correctly be said that breaking the law is the sine qua non of punishment, or, in other words, that we only tolerate punishment as it is imposed on one who deviates from the norm established by the criminal law.

The fact that the State may seek retribution against those who have broken its laws does not mean that retribution may then become the State's sole end in punishing. Our jurisprudence has always accepted deterrence in general, deterrence of individual recidivism, isolation of dangerous persons, and rehabilitation as proper goals of punishment. See Trop v. Dulles, 356 U.S., at 111 (BRENNAN, J., concurring). Retaliation, vengeance, and retribution have been roundly condemned as intolerable aspirations for a government in a free society.

Punishment as retribution has been condemned by scholars for centuries, 85 and the Eighth Amendment itself was adopted to prevent punishment from becoming synonymous with vengeance.

In Weems v. United States, 217 U.S., at 381, the Court, in the course of holding that Weems' punishment violated the Eighth Amendment, contrasted it with penalties provided for other offenses and concluded:

"[T]his contrast shows more than different exercises of legislative judgment. It is greater than that. It condemns the sentence in this case as cruel and unusual. It exhibits a difference between unrestrained power and that which is exercised under the spirit of constitutional limitations formed to establish justice. The State thereby suffers nothing and loses no power. The purpose of punishment is fulfilled, crime is repressed by penalties of just, not tormenting, severity, its repetition is prevented, and hope is given for the reformation of the criminal." (Emphasis added.)

It is plain that the view of the Weems Court was that punishment for the sake of retribution was not permissible under the Eighth Amendment. This is the only view that the Court could have taken if the "cruel and unusual" language were to be given any meaning. Retribution surely underlies the imposition of some punishment on one who commits a criminal act. But, the fact that some punishment may be imposed does not mean that any punishment is permissible. If retribution alone could serve as a justification for any particular penalty, then all penalties selected by the legislature would by definition be acceptable means for designating society's moral approbation of a particular act. The "cruel and unusual" language would thus be read out of the Constitution and the fears of Patrick Henry and the other Founding Fathers would become realities.

To preserve the integrity of the Eighth Amendment, the Court has consistently denigrated retribution as a permissible goal of punishment. 86 It is undoubtedly correct that there is a demand for vengeance on the part of many persons in a community against one who is convicted of a particularly offensive act. At times a cry is heard that morality requires vengeance to evidence society's abhorrence of the act. 87 But the Eighth Amendment is our insulation from our baser selves. The "cruel and unusual" language limits the avenues through which vengeance can be channeled. Were this not so, the language would be empty and a return to the rack and other tortures would be possible in a given case.

Mr. Justice Story wrote that the Eighth Amendment's limitation on punishment "would seem to be wholly unnecessary in a free government, since it is scarcely possible that any department of such a government should authorize or justify such atrocious conduct." 88

I would reach an opposite conclusion - that only in a free society would men recognize their inherent weaknesses and seek to compensate for them by means of a Constitution.

The history of the Eighth Amendment supports only the conclusion that retribution for its own sake is improper.

B. The most hotly contested issue regarding capital punishment is whether it is better than life imprisonment as a deterrent to crime. 89

While the contrary position has been argued, 90 it is my firm opinion that the death penalty is a more severe sanction than life imprisonment. Admittedly, there are some persons who would rather die than languish in prison for a lifetime. But, whether or not they should be able to choose death as an alternative is a far different question from that presented here - i. e., whether the State can impose death as a punishment. Death is irrevocable; life imprisonment is not. Death, of course, makes rehabilitation impossible; life imprisonment does not. In short, death has always been viewed as the ultimate sanction, and it seems perfectly reasonable to continue to view it as such. 91

It must be kept in mind, then, that the question to be considered is not simply whether capital punishment is a deterrent, but whether it is a better deterrent than life imprisonment. 92

There is no more complex problem than determining the deterrent efficacy of the death penalty. "Capital punishment has obviously failed as a deterrent when a murder is committed. We can number its failures. But we cannot number its successes. No one can ever know how many people have refrained from murder because of the fear of being hanged." 93 This is the nub of the problem and it is exacerbated by the paucity of useful data. The United States is more fortunate than most countries, however, in that it has what are generally considered to be the world's most reliable statistics. 94

The two strongest arguments in favor of capital punishment as a deterrent are both logical hypotheses devoid of evidentiary support, but persuasive nonetheless. The first proposition was best stated by Sir James Stephen in 1864:

"No other punishment deters men so effectually from committing crimes as the punishment of death. This is one of those propositions which it is difficult to prove, simply because they are in themselves more obvious than any proof can make them. It is possible to display ingenuity in arguing against it, but that is all. The whole experience of mankind is in the other direction. The threat of instant death is the one to which resort has always been made when there was an absolute necessity for producing some result. . . . No one goes to certain inevitable death except by compulsion. Put the matter the other way. Was there ever yet a criminal who, when sentenced to death and brought out to die, would refuse the offer of a commutation of his sentence for the severest secondary punishment? Surely not. Why is this? It can only be because `All that a man has will he give for his life.' In any secondary punishment, however terrible, there is hope; but death is death; its terrors cannot be described more forcibly." 95

This hypothesis relates to the use of capital punishment as a deterrent for any crime. The second proposition is that "if life imprisonment is the maximum penalty for a crime such as murder, an offender who is serving a life sentence cannot then be deterred from murdering a fellow inmate or a prison officer." 96 This hypothesis advocates a limited deterrent effect under particular circumstances.

Abolitionists attempt to disprove these hypotheses by amassing statistical evidence to demonstrate that there is no correlation between criminal activity and the existence or nonexistence of a capital sanction. Almost all of the evidence involves the crime of murder, since murder is punishable by death in more jurisdictions than are other offenses, 97 and almost 90% of all executions since 1930 have been pursuant to murder convictions. 98

Thorsten Sellin, one of the leading authorities on capital punishment, has urged that if the death penalty deters prospective murderers, the following hypotheses should be true:

"(a) Murders should be less frequent in states that have the death penalty than in those that have abolished it, other factors being equal. Comparisons of this nature must be made among states that are as alike as possible in all other respects - character of population, social and economic condition, etc. - in order not to introduce factors known to influence murder rates in a serious manner but present in only one of these states.

"(b) Murders should increase when the death penalty is abolished and should decline when it is restored.

"(c) The deterrent effect should be greatest and should therefore affect murder rates most powerfully in those communities where the crime occurred and its consequences are most strongly brought home to the population.

"(d) Law enforcement officers would be safer from murderous attacks in states that have the death penalty than in those without it." 99 (Footnote omitted.)

Sellin's evidence indicates that not one of these propositions is true. This evidence has its problems, however. One is that there are no accurate figures for capital murders; there are only figures on homicides and they, of course, include noncapital killings. 100 A second problem is that certain murders undoubtedly are misinterpreted as accidental deaths or suicides, and there is no way of estimating the number of such undetected crimes. A third problem is that not all homicides are reported. Despite these difficulties, most authorities have assumed that the proportion of capital murders in a State's or nation's homicide statistics remains reasonably constant, 101 and that the homicide statistics are therefore useful.

Sellin's statistics demonstrate that there is no correlation between the murder rate and the presence or absence of the capital sanction. He compares States that have similar characteristics and finds that irrespective of their position on capital punishment, they have similar murder rates. In the New England States, for example, there is no correlation between executions 102 and homicide rates. 103 The same is true for Midwestern States, 104 and for all others studied. Both the United Nations 105 and Great Britain 106 have acknowledged the validity of Sellin's statistics.

Sellin also concludes that abolition and/or reintroduction of the death penalty had no effect on the homicide rates of the various States involved. 107 This conclusion is borne out by others who have made similar inquiries 108 and by the experience of other countries. 109 Despite problems with the statistics, 110 Sellin's evidence has been relied upon in international studies of capital punishment. 111

Statistics also show that the deterrent effect of capital punishment is no greater in those communities where executions take place than in other communities. 112 In fact, there is some evidence that imposition of capital punishment may actually encourage crime, rather than deter it. 113 And, while police and law enforcement officers are the strongest advocates of capital punishment, 114 the evidence is overwhelming that police are no safer in communities that retain the sanction than in those that have abolished it. 115

There is also a substantial body of data showing that the existence of the death penalty has virtually no effect on the homicide rate in prisons. 116 Most of the persons sentenced to death are murderers, and murderers tend to be model prisoners. 117

In sum, the only support for the theory that capital punishment is an effective deterrent is found in the hypotheses with which we began and the occasional stories about a specific individual being deterred from doing a contemplated criminal act. 118 These claims of specific deterrence are often spurious, 119 however, and may be more than counterbalanced by the tendency of capital punishment to incite certain crimes. 120

The United Nations Committee that studied capital punishment found that "[i]t is generally agreed between the retentionists and abolitionists, whatever their opinions about the validity of comparative studies of deterrence, that the data which now exist show no correlation between the existence of capital punishment and lower rates of capital crime." 121

Despite the fact that abolitionists have not proved non-deterrence beyond a reasonable doubt, they have succeeded in showing by clear and convincing evidence that capital punishment is not necessary as a deterrent to crime in our society. This is all that they must do. We would shirk our judicial responsibilities if we failed to accept the presently existing statistics and demanded more proof. It may be that we now possess all the proof that anyone could ever hope to assemble on the subject. But, even if further proof were to be forthcoming, I believe there is more than enough evidence presently available for a decision in this case.

In 1793 William Bradford studied the utility of the death penalty in Pennsylvania and found that it probably had no deterrent effect but that more evidence was needed. 122 Edward Livingston reached a similar conclusion with respect to deterrence in 1833 upon completion of his study for Louisiana. 123 Virtually every study that has since been undertaken has reached the same result. 124

In light of the massive amount of evidence before us, I see no alternative but to conclude that capital punishment cannot be justified on the basis of its deterrent effect. 125

C. Much of what must be said about the death penalty as a device to prevent recidivism is obvious - if a murderer is executed, he cannot possibly commit another offense. The fact is, however, that murderers are extremely unlikely to commit other crimes either in prison or upon their release. 126 For the most part, they are first offenders, and when released from prison they are known to become model citizens. 127 Furthermore, most persons who commit capital crimes are not executed. With respect to those who are sentenced to die, it is critical to note that the jury is never asked to determine whether they are likely to be recidivists. In light of these facts, if capital punishment were justified purely on the basis of preventing recidivism, it would have to be considered to be excessive; no general need to obliterate all capital offenders could have been demonstrated, nor any specific need in individual cases.

D. The three final purposes which may underlie utilization of a capital sanction - encouraging guilty pleas and confessions, eugenics, and reducing state expenditures - may be dealt with quickly. If the death penalty is used to encourage guilty pleas and thus to deter suspects from exercising their rights under the Sixth Amendment to jury trials, it is unconstitutional. United States v. Jackson, 390 U.S. 570 (1968). 128 Its elimination would do little to impair the State's bargaining position in criminal cases, since life imprisonment remains a severe sanction which can be used as leverage for bargaining for pleas or confessions in exchange either for charges of lesser offenses or recommendations of leniency.

Moreover, to the extent that capital punishment is used to encourage confessions and guilty pleas, it is not being used for punishment purposes. A State that justifies capital punishment on its utility as part of the conviction process could not profess to rely on capital punishment as a deterrent. Such a State's system would be structured with twin goals only: obtaining guilty pleas and confessions and imposing imprisonment as the maximum sanction. Since life imprisonment is sufficient for bargaining purposes, the death penalty is excessive if used for the same purposes.

In light of the previous discussion on deterrence, any suggestions concerning the eugenic benefits of capital punishment are obviously meritless. 129 As I pointed out above, there is not even any attempt made to discover which capital offenders are likely to be recidivists, let alone which are positively incurable. No test or procedure presently exists by which incurables can be screened from those who would benefit from treatment. On the one hand, due process would seem to require that we have some procedure to demonstrate incurability before execution; and, on the other hand, equal protection would then seemingly require that all incurables be executed, cf. Skinner v. Oklahoma, 316 U.S. 535 (1942). In addition, the "cruel and unusual" language would require that life imprisonment, treatment, and sterilization be inadequate for eugenic purposes. More importantly, this Nation has never formally professed eugenic goals, and the history of the world does not look kindly on them. If eugenics is one of our purposes, then the legislatures should say so forthrightly and design procedures to serve this goal. Until such time, I can only conclude, as has virtually everyone else who has looked at the problem, 130 that capital punishment cannot be defended on the basis of any eugenic purposes.

As for the argument that it is cheaper to execute a capital offender than to imprison him for life, even assuming that such an argument, if true, would support a capital sanction, it is simply incorrect. A disproportionate amount of money spent on prisons is attributable to death row. 131 Condemned men are not productive members of the prison community, although they could be, 132 and executions are expensive. 133 Appeals are often automatic, and courts admittedly spend more time with death cases. 134

At trial, the selection of jurors is likely to become a costly, time-consuming problem in a capital case, 135 and defense counsel will reasonably exhaust every possible means to save his client from execution, no matter how long the trial takes.

During the period between conviction and execution, there are an inordinate number of collateral attacks on the conviction and attempts to obtain executive clemency, all of which exhaust the time, money, and effort of the State. There are also continual assertions that the condemned prisoner has gone insane. 136 Because there is a formally established policy of not executing insane persons, 137 great sums of money may be spent on detecting and curing mental illness in order to perform the execution. 138 Since no one wants the responsibility for the execution, the condemned man is likely to be passed back and forth from doctors to custodial officials to courts like a ping-pong ball. 139 The entire process is very costly.

When all is said and done, there can be no doubt that it costs more to execute a man than to keep him in prison for life. 140

E. There is but one conclusion that can be drawn from all of this - i. e., the death penalty is an excessive and unnecessary punishment that violates the Eighth Amendment. The statistical evidence is not convincing beyond all doubt, but it is persuasive. It is not improper at this point to take judicial notice of the fact that for more than 200 years men have labored to demonstrate that capital punishment serves no purpose that life imprisonment could not serve equally well. And they have done so with great success. Little, if any, evidence has been adduced to prove the contrary. The point has now been reached at which deference to the legislatures is tantamount to abdication of our judicial roles as factfinders, judges, and ultimate arbiters of the Constitution. We know that at some point the presumption of constitutionality accorded legislative acts gives way to a realistic assessment of those acts. This point comes when there is sufficient evidence available so that judges can determine, not whether the legislature acted wisely, but whether it had any rational basis whatsoever for acting. We have this evidence before us now. There is no rational basis for concluding that capital punishment is not excessive. It therefore violates the Eighth Amendment. 141

VI

In addition, even if capital punishment is not excessive, it nonetheless violates the Eighth Amendment because it is morally unacceptable to the people of the United States at this time in their history.

In judging whether or not a given penalty is morally acceptable, most courts have said that the punishment is valid unless "it shocks the conscience and sense of justice of the people." 142

Judge Frank once noted the problems inherent in the use of such a measuring stick:

"[The court,] before it reduces a sentence as `cruel and unusual,' must have reasonably good assurances that the sentence offends the `common conscience.' And, in any context, such a standard - the community's attitude - is usually an unknowable. It resembles a slithery shadow, since one can seldom learn, at all accurately, what the community, or a majority, actually feels. Even a carefully-taken `public opinion poll' would be inconclusive in a case like this." 143

While a public opinion poll obviously is of some assistance in indicating public acceptance or rejection of a specific penalty, 144 its utility cannot be very great. This is because whether or not a punishment is cruel and unusual depends, not on whether its mere mention "shocks the conscience and sense of justice of the people," but on whether people who were fully informed as to the purposes of the penalty and its liabilities would find the penalty shocking, unjust, and unacceptable. 145

In other words, the question with which we must deal is not whether a substantial proportion of American citizens would today, if polled, opine that capital punishment is barbarously cruel, but whether they would find it to be so in the light of all information presently available.

This is not to suggest that with respect to this test of unconstitutionality people are required to act rationally; they are not. With respect to this judgment, a violation of the Eighth Amendment is totally dependent on the predictable subjective, emotional reactions of informed citizens. 146

It has often been noted that American citizens know almost nothing about capital punishment. 147 Some of the conclusions arrived at in the preceding section and the supporting evidence would be critical to an informed judgment on the morality of the death penalty: e. g., that the death penalty is no more effective a deterrent than life imprisonment, that convicted murderers are rarely executed, but are usually sentenced to a term in prison; that convicted murderers usually are model prisoners, and that they almost always become law-abiding citizens upon their release from prison; that the costs of executing a capital offender exceed the costs of imprisoning him for life; that while in prison, a convict under sentence of death performs none of the useful functions that life prisoners perform; that no attempt is made in the sentencing process to ferret out likely recidivists for execution; and that the death penalty may actually stimulate criminal activity.

This information would almost surely convince the average citizen that the death penalty was unwise, but a problem arises as to whether it would convince him that the penalty was morally reprehensible. This problem arises from the fact that the public's desire for retribution, even though this is a goal that the legislature cannot constitutionally pursue as its sole justification for capital punishment, might influence the citizenry's view of the morality of capital punishment. The solution to the problem lies in the fact that no one has ever seriously advanced retribution as a legitimate goal of our society. Defenses of capital punishment are always mounted on deterrent or other similar theories. This should not be surprising. It is the people of this country who have urged in the past that prisons rehabilitate as well as isolate offenders, and it is the people who have injected a sense of purpose into our penology. I cannot believe that at this stage in our history, the American people would ever knowingly support purposeless vengeance. Thus, I believe that the great mass of citizens would conclude on the basis of the material already considered that the death penalty is immoral and therefore unconstitutional.

But, if this information needs supplementing, I believe that the following facts would serve to convince even the most hesitant of citizens to condemn death as a sanction: capital punishment is imposed discriminatorily against certain identifiable classes of people; there is evidence that innocent people have been executed before their innocence can be proved; and the death penalty wreaks havoc with our entire criminal justice system. Each of these facts is considered briefly below.

Regarding discrimination, it has been said that "[i]t is usually the poor, the illiterate, the underprivileged, the member of the minority group - the man who, because he is without means, and is defended by a court-appointed attorney - who becomes society's sacrificial lamb . . . ." 148 Indeed, a look at the bare statistics regarding executions is enough to betray much of the discrimination. A total of 3,859 persons have been executed since 1930, of whom 1,751 were white and 2,066 were Negro. 149 Of the executions, 3, 334 were for murder; 1,664 of the executed murderers were white and 1,630 were Negro; 150 455 persons, including 48 whites and 405 Negroes, were executed for rape. 151 It is immediately apparent that Negroes were executed far more often than whites in proportion to their percentage of the population. Studies indicate that while the higher rate of execution among Negroes is partially due to a higher rate of crime, there is evidence of racial discrimination. 152 Racial or other discriminations should not be surprising. In McGautha v. California, 402 U.S., at 207, this Court held "that committing to the untrammeled discretion of the jury the power to pronounce life or death in capital cases is [not] offensive to anything in the Constitution." This was an open invitation to discrimination.

There is also overwhelming evidence that the death penalty is employed against men and not women. Only 32 women have been executed since 1930, while 3,827 men have met a similar fate. 153 It is difficult to understand why women have received such favored treatment since the purposes allegedly served by capital punishment seemingly are equally applicable to both sexes. 154

It also is evident that the burden of capital punishment falls upon the poor, the ignorant, and the underprivileged members of society. 155 It is the poor, and the members of minority groups who are least able to voice their complaints against capital punishment. Their impotence leaves them victims of a sanction that the wealthier, better-represented, just-as-guilty person can escape. So long as the capital sanction is used only against the forlorn, easily forgotten members of society, legislators are content to maintain the status quo, because change would draw attention to the problem and concern might develop. Ignorance is perpetuated and apathy soon becomes its mate, and we have today's situation.

Just as Americans know little about who is executed and why, they are unaware of the potential dangers of executing an innocent man. Our "beyond a reasonable doubt" burden of proof in criminal cases is intended to protect the innocent, but we know it is not fool-proof. Various studies have shown that people whose innocence is later convincingly established are convicted and sentenced to death. 156

Proving one's innocence after a jury finding of guilt is almost impossible. While reviewing courts are willing to entertain all kinds of collateral attacks where a sentence of death is involved, they very rarely dispute the jury's interpretation of the evidence. This is, perhaps, as it should be. But, if an innocent man has been found guilty, he must then depend on the good faith of the prosecutor's office to help him establish his innocence. There is evidence, however, that prosecutors do not welcome the idea of having convictions, which they labored hard to secure, overturned, and that their cooperation is highly unlikely. 157

No matter how careful courts are, the possibility of perjured testimony, mistaken honest testimony, and human error remain all too real. 158 We have no way of judging how many innocent persons have been executed but we can be certain that there were some. Whether there were many is an open question made difficult by the loss of those who were most knowledgeable about the crime for which they were convicted. Surely there will be more as long as capital punishment remains part of our penal law.

While it is difficult to ascertain with certainty the degree to which the death penalty is discriminatorily imposed or the number of innocent persons sentenced to die, there is one conclusion about the penalty that is universally accepted - i. e., it "tends to distort the course of the criminal law." 159 As Mr. Justice Frankfurter said:

"I am strongly against capital punishment . . . . When life is at hazard in a trial, it sensationalizes the whole thing almost unwittingly; the effect on juries, the Bar, the public, the Judiciary, I regard as very bad. I think scientifically the claim of deterrence is not worth much. Whatever proof there may be in my judgment does not outweigh the social loss due to the inherent sensationalism of a trial for life." 160

The deleterious effects of the death penalty are also felt otherwise than at trial. For example, its very existence "inevitably sabotages a social or institutional program of reformation." 161 In short "[t]he presence of the death penalty as the keystone of our penal system bedevils the administration of criminal justice all the way down the line and is the stumbling block in the path of general reform and of the treatment of crime and criminals." 162

Assuming knowledge of all the facts presently available regarding capital punishment, the average citizen would, in my opinion, find it shocking to his conscience and sense of justice. 163 For this reason alone capital punishment cannot stand.

Notes

1 Certiorari was also granted in a fourth case, Aikens v. California, No. 68-5027,

but the writ was dismissed after the California Supreme Court held that capital punishment violates the State Constitution. 406 U.S. 813 . See People v. Anderson, 6 Cal. 3d 628, 493 P.2d 880, cert. denied, 406 U.S. 958 (1972). The California decision reduced by slightly more than 100 the number of persons currently awaiting execution.

2 268 Parl. Deb., H. L. (5th ser.) 703 (1965) (Lord Chancellor Gardiner).

3 Compare, e. g., Louisiana ex rel. Francis v. Resweber, 329 U.S. 459, 470 (1947) (Frankfurter, J., concurring), with F. Frankfurter, Of Law and Men 81 (1956). See In re Anderson, 69 Cal. 2d 613, 634-635, 447 P.2d 117, 131-132 (1968) (Mosk, J., concurring); cf. McGautha v. California, 402 U.S. 183, 226 (1971) (separate opinion of Black, J.); Witherspoon v. Illinois, 391 U.S. 510, 542 (1968) (WHITE, J., dissenting).

4 See generally Frankel, Book Review, 85 Harv. L. Rev. 354, 362 (1971).

5 Granucci, "Nor Cruel and Unusual Punishments Inflicted:" The Original Meaning, 57 Calif. L. Rev. 839, 848 (1969).

6 Ibid. Beale's views were conveyed from England to America and were first written into American law by the Reverend Nathaniel Ward who wrote the Body of Liberties for the Massachusetts Bay Colony. Clause 46 of that work read: "For bodilie punishments we allow amongst us none that are inhumane, Barbarous or cruel." 1 B. Schwartz, The Bill of Rights: A Documentary History 71, 77 (1971).

7 4 W. Blackstone, Commentaries *376-377. See also 1 J. Chitty, The Criminal Law 785-786 (5th ed. 1847); Sherman, ". . . Nor Cruel and Unusual Punishments Inflicted," 14 Crime & Delin. 73, 74 (1968).

8 Not content with capital punishment as a means of retribution for crimes, the English also provided for attainder ("dead in law") as the immediate and inseparable concomitant of the death sentence. The consequences of attainder were forfeiture of real and personal estates and corruption of blood. An attainted person could not inherit land or other hereditaments, nor retain those he possessed, nor transmit them by descent to any heir. Descents were also obstructed whenever posterity derived a title through one who was attained. 4 W. Blackstone, Commentaries *380-381.

9 E. g., 2 J. Story, On the Constitution 1903, p. 650 (5th ed. 1891).

10 2 G. Trevelyan, History of England 467 (1952 reissue).

11 Granucci, supra, n. 5, at 854.

12 Id., at 855.

13 Id., at 860. In reaching this conclusion, Professor Granucci relies primarily on the trial of Titus Oates as the impetus behind the adoption of the clause. Oates was a minister of the Church of England who proclaimed the existence of a plot to assassinate King Charles II. He was tried for perjury, convicted, and sentenced to a fine of 2,000 marks, life imprisonment, whippings, pillorying four times a year, and defrocking. Oates petitioned both the House of Commons and the House of Lords for release from judgment. The House of Lords rejected his petition, but a minority of its members concluded that the King's Bench had no jurisdiction to compel defrocking and that the other punishments were barbarous, inhumane, unchristian, and unauthorized by law.

The House of Commons agreed with the dissenting Lords. Id., at 857-859.

The author also relies on the dictionary definition of "cruel," which meant "severe" or "hard" in the 17th century, to support his conclusion. Ibid.

14 Most historians reach this conclusion by reading the history of the Cruel and Unusual Punishments Clause as indicating that it was a reaction to inhumane punishments. Professor Granucci reaches the same conclusion by finding that the draftsmen of the Constitution misread the British history and erroneously relied on Blackstone. Granucci, supra, n. 5, at 862-865. It is clear, however, that prior to the adoption of the Amendment there was some feeling that a safeguard against cruelty was needed and that this feeling had support in past practices. See n. 6, supra, and accompanying text.

15 Grannucci, supra, n. 5, at 840; 1 Schwartz, supra, n. 6, at 276, 278.

16 See, e. g., Delaware Declaration of Rights (1776), Maryland Declaration of Rights (1776), Massachusetts Declaration of Rights (1780), and New Hampshire Bill of Rights (1783). 1 Schwartz, supra, n. 6, at 276, 278; 279, 281; 337, 343; 374, 379.

17 See 2 J. Elliot's Debates 111 (2d ed. 1876); 3 id., at 447-481. See also, 2 Schwartz, supra, n. 6, at 629, 674, 762, 852, 968.

18 3 Elliot, supra, n. 17, at 446-448. A comment by George Mason which misinterprets a criticism leveled at himself and Patrick Henry is further evidence of the intention to prohibit torture and the like by prohibiting cruel and unusual punishments. Id., at 452.

19 1 Annals of Cong. 782-783 (1789). There is some recognition of the fact that a prohibition against cruel and unusual punishments is a flexible prohibition that may change in meaning as the mores of a society change, and that may eventually bar certain punishments not barred when the Constitution was adopted. Ibid. (remarks of Mr. Livermore of New Hampshire). There is also evidence that the general opinion at the time the Eighth Amendment was adopted was that it prohibited every punishment that was not "evidently necessary." W. Bradford, An Enquiry How Far the Punishment of Death is Necessary in Pennsylvania (1793), reprinted in 12 Am. J. Legal Hist. 122, 127 (1968).

20 The New York Court of Appeals had recognized the unusual nature of the execution, but attributed it to a legislative desire to minimize the pain of persons executed.

21 The prohibition against cruel and unusual punishments relevant to Weems was that found in the Philippine Bill of Rights. It was, however, borrowed from the Eighth Amendment to the United States Constitution and had the same meaning. 217 U.S., at 367 .

22 Id., at 373.

23 Ibid.

24 Ibid.

25 Id., at 381.

26 Id., at 389-413. Mr. Justice Black expressed a similar point of view in his

separate opinion in McGautha v. California, 402 U.S., at 226 (1971).

27 Badders was found guilty on seven counts of using the mails as part of a scheme to defraud. He was sentenced to concurrent five-year sentences and to a $1,000 fine on each count. The Court summarily rejected his claim that the sentence was a cruel and unusual punishment. In United States ex rel. Milwaukee Social Democratic Publishing Co. v. Burleson, 255 U.S. 407 (1921), the Court upheld the denial of second-class mailing privileges to a newspaper that had allegedly printed articles conveying false reports of United States conduct during the First World War with intent to cause disloyalty. Mr. Justice Brandeis dissented and indicated his belief that the "punishment" was unusual and possibly excessive under Weems v. United States, 217 U.S. 349 (1910). There is nothing in either of these cases demonstrating a departure from the approach used in Weems, or adding anything to it.

28 Mr. Justice Frankfurter was the only member of the Court unwilling to make this assumption. However, like Chief Justice Fuller in In re Kemmler, 136 U.S. 436 (1890), he examined the propriety of the punishment under the Due Process Clause of the Fourteenth Amendment. 329 U.S., at 471 . As MR. JUSTICE POWELL makes clear, Mr. Justice Frankfurter's analysis was different only in form from that of his Brethren; in substance, his test was fundamentally identical to that used by the rest of the Court.

29 Id., at 463.

30 English law required a second attempt at execution if the first attempt failed. L. Radzinowicz, A History of English Criminal Law 185-186 (1948).

31 MR. JUSTICE BRENNAN concurred and concluded that the statute authorizing deprivations of citizenship exceeded Congress' legislative powers. 356 U.S., at 114 .

32 Id., at 101.

33 370 U.S., at 666 .

34 Robinson v. California, 370 U.S. 660 (1962), removes any lingering doubts as to whether the Eighth Amendment's prohibition against cruel and unusual punishments is binding on the States. See also Powell v. Texas, 392 U.S. 514 (1968).

35 Trop v. Dulles, 356 U.S. 86, 101 (1958). See also Weems v. United States, 217 U.S., at 373; Robinson v. California, 370 U.S., at 666 . See also n. 19, supra.

36 E. g., McGautha v. California, 402 U.S., at 226 (separate opinion of Black, J.); Trop v. Dulles, supra, at 99 (Warren, C. J.), 125 (Frankfurter, J., dissenting).

37 See, e. g., Louisiana ex rel. Francis v. Resweber, 329 U.S., at 474 (Burton, J., dissenting); Trop v. Dulles, supra, at 99 (Warren, C. J.); Rudolph v. Alabama, 375 U.S. 889 (1963) (Goldberg, J., dissenting from denial of certiorari); F. Frankfurter, Of Law and Men 81 (1956).

There is no violation of the principle of stare decisis in a decision that capital punishment now violates the Eighth Amendment. The last case that implied that capital punishment was still permissible was Trop v. Dulles, supra, at 99. Not only was the implication purely dictum, but it was also made in the context of a flexible analysis that recognized that as public opinion changed, the validity of the penalty would have to be re-examined. Trop v. Dulles is nearly 15 years old now, and 15 years change many minds about many things. MR. JUSTICE POWELL suggests, however, that our recent decisions in Witherspoon v. Illinois, 391 U.S. 510 (1968), and McGautha v. California, 402 U.S. 183 (1971), imply that capital punishment is constitutionally permissible, because if they are viewed any other way they amount to little more than an academic exercise. In my view, this distorts the "rule of four" by which this Court decides which cases and which issues it will consider, and in what order. See United States v. Generes, 405 U.S. 93, 113 (1972) (DOUGLAS, J., dissenting). There are many reasons why four members of the Court might have wanted to consider the issues presented in those cases before considering the difficult question that is now before us. While I do not intend to catalogue these reasons here, it should suffice to note that I do not believe that those decisions can, in any way, fairly be used to support any inference whatever that the instant cases have already been disposed of sub silentio.

38 Ancel, The Problem of the Death Penalty, in Capital Punishment 4-5 (T. Sellin ed. 1967); G. Scott, The History of Capital Punishment 1 (1950).

39 Scott, supra, n. 38, at 1.

40 Id., at 2; Ancel, supra, n. 38, at 4-5.

41 The Code of Hammurabi is one of the first known laws to have recognized the concept of an "eye for an eye," and consequently to have accepted death as an appropriate punishment for homicide. E. Block, And May God Have Mercy . . . 13-14 (1962).

42 Scott, supra, n. 38, at 19-33.

43 Id., at 5. Prior to this time, the laws of Alfred (871-901) provided that one who willfully slayed another should die, at least under certain circumstances. 3 J. Stephen, History of the Criminal Law of England 24 (1883). But, punishment was apparently left largely to private enforcement.

44 T. Plucknett, A Concise History of the Common Law 424-454 (5th ed. 1956).

45 Introduction in H. Bedau, The Death Penalty in America 1 (1967 rev. ed.).

46 Ibid.

47 4 W. Blackstone, Commentaries *377. How many persons were actually executed for committing capital offenses is not known. See Bedau, supra, n. 45, at 3; L. Radzinowicz, A History of English Criminal Law 151, 153 (1948); Sellin, Two Myths in the History of Capital Punishment, 50 J. Crim. L. C. & P. S. 114 (1959). "Benefit of clergy" mitigated the harshness of the law somewhat. This concept arose from the struggle between church and state and originally provided that members of the clergy should be tried in ecclesiastical courts. Eventually all first offenders were entitled to "benefit of clergy." Bedau, supra, at 4.

48 G. Haskins, The Capitall Lawes of New-England, Harv. L. Sch. Bull. 10-11 (Feb. 1956).

49 Compare Haskins, supra, n. 48, with E. Powers, Crime and Punishment in Early Massachusetts, 1620-1692 (1966). See also Bedau, supra, n. 45, at 5.

50 Id., at 6.

51 Filler, Movements to Abolish the Death Penalty in the United States, 284 Annals Am. Acad. Pol. & Soc. Sci. 124 (1952).

52 Ibid.

53 Ibid. (footnotes omitted).

54 Ibid.; Bedau, supra, n. 45, at 6.

55 For an unknown reason, Pennsylvania adopted the harsher penal code of England upon William Penn's death in 1718. There was no evidence, however of an increase in crime between 1682 and 1718. Filler, supra, n. 51, at 124. In 1794, Pennsylvania eliminated capital punishment except for "murder of the first degree," which included all "willful, deliberate or premeditated" killings. The death penalty was mandatory for this crime. Pa. Stat. 1794, c. 1777. Virginia followed Pennsylvania's lead and enacted similar legislation. Other States followed suit.

56 Filler, supra, n. 51, at 124.

57 Id., at 124-125.

58 Reprinted in 12 Am. J. Legal Hist. 122 (1968).

59 His advice was in large measure followed. See n. 55, supra.

60 One scholar has noted that the early abolition movement in the United States lacked the leadership of major public figures. Bedau, supra, n. 45, at 8.

61 Ibid.; Filler, supra, n. 51, at 126-127.

62 See Scott, supra, n. 38, at 114-116.

63 Filler, supra, n. 51, at 127.

64 Davis, The Movement to Abolish Capital Punishment in America, 1787-1861, 63 Am. Hist. Rev. 23, 33 (1957).

65 Filler, supra, n. 51, at 128. Capital punishment was abolished for all crimes but treason. The law was enacted in 1846, but did not go into effect until 1847.

66 Davis, supra, n. 64, at 29-30.

67 Filler, supra, n. 51, at 129.

68 Id., at 130.

69 Ibid.

70 Bedau, supra, n. 45, at 10.

71 Davis, supra, n. 64, at 46.

72 Kansas restored it in 1935. See Appendix I to this opinion, infra, at 372.

73 See McGautha v. California, 402 U.S., at 199 .

74 Filler, supra, n. 51, at 133. See also Winston v. United States, 172 U.S. 303 (1899). More than 90% of the executions since 1930 in this country have been for offenses with a discretionary death penalty. Bedau, The Courts, the Constitution, and Capital Punishment, 1968 Utah L. Rev. 201, 204.

75 See n. 72, supra.

76 Filler, supra, n. 51, at 134.

77 Sellin, Executions in the United States, in Capital Punishment 35 (T. Sellin ed.

1967); United Nations, Department of Economic and Social Affairs, Capital Punishment, Pt. II, ◆◆ 82-85, pp. 101-102 (1968).

78 New York authorizes the death penalty only for murder of a police officer or for murder by a life term prisoner. N. Y. Penal Code 125.30 (1967).

79 See generally Bedau, supra, n. 74. Nine States do not authorize capital punishment under any circumstances: Alaska, Hawaii, Iowa, Maine, Michigan, Minnesota, Oregon, West Virginia, and Wisconsin. Puerto Rico and the Virgin Islands also have no provision for capital punishment. Bedau, supra, n. 45, at 39. Those States that severely restrict the imposition of the death penalty are: New Mexico, N. M. Stat. Ann. 40A-29-2.1 (1972); New York, N. Y. Penal Code 125.30 (1967); North Dakota, N. D. Cent. Code 12-07-01, 12-27-13 (1960); Rhode Island, R. I. Gen. Laws 11-23-2 (1970); Vermont, Vt. Stat. Ann., Tit. 13, 2303 (Supp. 1971). California is the only State in which the judiciary has declared capital punishment to be invalid. See n. 1, supra.

80 See generally Hearings on S. 1760 before the Subcommittee on Criminal Laws and Procedures of the Senate Committee on the Judiciary, 90th Cong., 2d Sess. (1968).

81 Extensive compilations of the capital crimes in particular States can be found in Bedau, supra, n. 45, at 39-52 and in the Brief for the Petitioner in No. 68-5027, App. G (Aikens v. California, 406 U.S. 813 (1972)). An attempt is made to break down capital offenses into categories in Finkel, A Survey of Capital Offenses, in Capital Punishment 22 (T. Sellin ed. 1967).

82 Bedau, supra, n. 45, at 43.

83 Ibid. See also Ralph v. Warden, 438 F.2d 786, 791-792 (CA4 1970).

[84] See Hart, Murder and the Principles of Punishment: England and the United States, 52 Nw. U. L. Rev. 433, 448 (1957); Report of Royal Commission on Capital Punishment, 1949-1953, Cmd. 8932, ◆◆ 52-53, pp. 17-18 (1953). See generally, Reichert, Capital Punishment Reconsidered, 47 Ky. L. J. 397, 399 (1959).

[85] See, e. g., C. Beccaria, On Crimes and Punishment (tr. by H. Paolucci 1963); 1 Archbold, On the Practice, Pleading, and Evidence in Criminal Cases 11-17, pp. XV-XIX (T. Waterman 7th ed. 1860).

[86] See, e. g., Rudolph v. Alabama, 375 U.S. 889 (1963) (Goldberg, J., dissenting from denial of certiorari); Trop v. Dulles, 356 U.S., at 97 (Warren, C. J.), 113 (BRENNAN, J., concurring); Morissette v. United States, 342 U.S. 246 (1952); Williams v. New York, 337 U.S. 241 (1949). In Powell v. Texas, 392 U.S., at 530, we said: "This Court has never held that anything in the Constitution requires that penal sanctions be designed solely to achieve therapeutic or rehabilitative effects . . . ." This is, of course, correct, since deterrence and isolation are clearly recognized as proper. E. g., Trop v. Dulles, supra, at 111 (BRENNAN, J., concurring). There is absolutely nothing in the language, the rationale, or the holding of Powell v. Texas that implies that retribution for its own sake is a proper legislative aim in punishing.

[87] See, e. g., Vellenga, Christianity and The Death Penalty, in Bedau, supra, n. 45, at 123-130; Hook, The Death Sentence, in Bedau, supra, at 146-154. See also

Ehrenzweig, A Psychoanalysis of the Insanity Plea - Clues to the Problems of Criminal Responsibility and Insanity in the Death Cell, 73 Yale L. J. 425, 433-439 (1964).

[88] 2 J. Story, On the Constitution 1903, p. 650 (5th ed. 1891).

[89] Note, The Death Penalty Cases, 56 Calif. L. Rev. 1268, 1275 (1968); Note, Justice or Revenge?, 60 Dick. L. Rev. 342, 343 (1956); Royal Commission, supra, n. 84, � 55, at 18.

[90] Barzun, In Favor of Capital Punishment, in Bedau, supra, n. 45, at 154, 163; Hook, supra, n. 87, at 152.

[91] See Commonwealth v. Elliott, 371 Pa. 70, 78, 89 A. 2d 782, 786 (1952) (Musmanno, J., dissenting); F. Frankfurter, Of Law and Men 101 (1956). The assertion that life imprisonment may somehow be more cruel than death is usually rejected as frivolous. Hence, I confess to surprise at finding the assertion being made in various ways in today's opinions. If there were any merit to the contention, it would do much to undercut even the retributive motive for imposing capital punishment. In any event, there is no better response to such an assertion than that of former Pennsylvania Supreme Court Justice Musmanno in his dissent in Commonwealth v. Elliott, supra, at 79-80, 89 A. 2d, at 787:

"One of the judges of the lower court indicated from the bench that a sentence of life imprisonment is not to be regarded as a lesser penalty than that of death. I challenge that statement categorically. It can be stated as a universal truth stretching from nadir to zenith that regardless of circumstances, no one wants to die. Some person may, in an instant of spiritual or physical agony express a desire for death as an anodyne from intolerable pain, but that desire is never full-hearted because there is always the reserve of realization that the silken cord of life is not broken by a mere wishing. There is no person in the actual extremity of dropping from the precipice of life who does not desperately reach for a crag of time to which to cling even for a moment against the awful eternity of silence below. With all its `slings and arrows of outrageous fortune,' life is yet sweet and death is always cruel."

Attention should also be given to the hypothesis of Sir James Stephen, quoted in the text, infra, at 347-348.

[92] See Bedau, Deterrence and the Death Penalty: A Reconsideration, 61 J. Crim. L. C. & P. S. 539, 542 (1970).

[93] Royal Commission, supra, n. 84, � 59, at 20.

[94] United Nations, supra, n. 77, � 134, at 117. The great advantage that this country has is that it can compare abolitionist and retentionist States with geographic, economic, and cultural similarities.

[95] Reprinted in Royal Commission, supra, n. 84, � 57, at 19.

[96] United Nations, supra, n. 77, � 139, at 118.

[97] See Bedau, supra, n. 45, at 43.

[98] T. Sellin, The Death Penalty, A Report for the Model Penal Code Project of the American Law Institute (ALI) 5 (1959); Morris, Thoughts on Capital Punishment, 35

Wash. L. Rev. & St. Bar J. 335, 340 (1960).

[99] Sellin, supra, n. 98, at 21.

[100] Such crimes might include lesser forms of homicide or homicide by a child or a lunatic. Id., at 22; The Laws, The Crimes, and The Executions, in Bedau, supra, n. 45, at 32, 61.

[101] Sutherland, Murder and the Death Penalty, 15 J. Crim. L. & Crim. 522 (1925); ALI, supra, n. 98, at 22; Bedau, supra, n. 45, at 73.

[102] Executions were chosen for purposes of comparison because whatever impact capital punishment had would surely be most forcefully felt where punishment was actually imposed.

[103] See Appendix II to this opinion, infra, at 373.

[104] See Appendix III to this opinion, infra, at 374.

[105] United Nations, supra, n. 77, ◆ 134, at 117.

[106] Royal Commission, supra, n. 84, at 349-351. Accord, Vold, Extent and Trend of Capital Crimes in United States, 284 Annals Am. Acad. Pol. & Soc. Sci. 1, 4 (1952).

[107] Sellin, supra, n. 98, at 34.

[108] See, e. g., Guillot, Abolition and Restoration of the Death Penalty in Missouri, in Bedau, supra, n. 45, at 351, 358-359; Cobin, Abolition and Restoration of the Death Penalty in Delaware, in Bedau, supra, at 359, 371-372.

[109] Sellin, supra, n. 98, at 38-39; Royal Commission, supra, n. 84, at 353; United Nations, supra, n. 77, ◆◆ 130-136, at 116-118.

[110] One problem is that the statistics for the 19th century are especially suspect; another is that de jure abolition may have been preceded by de facto abolition which would have distorted the figures. It should also be noted that the figures for several States reflect homicide convictions rather than homicide rates.

[111] Royal Commission, supra, n. 84, ◆ 65, at 23; 346-349; United Nations, supra, n. 77, ◆ 132, at 117.

[112] Hayner & Cranor, The Death Penalty in Washington State, 284 Annals Am. Acad. Pol. & Soc. Sci. 101 (1952); Graves, A Doctor Looks at Capital Punishment, 10 Med. Arts & Sci 137 (1956); Dann, The Deterrent Effect of Capital Punishment, Bull. 29, Friends Social Service Series, Committee on Philanthropic Labor and Philadelphia Yearly Meeting of Friends (1935); Savitz, A Study in Capital Punishment, 49 J. Crim. L. C. & P. S. 338 (1958); United Nations, supra, n. 77, ◆ 135, at 118.

[113] Graves, supra, n. 112; Hearings, supra, n. 80, at 23 (testimony of C. Duffy), 126 (statement of Dr. West); T. Reik, The Compulsion to Confess 474 (1959); McCafferty, Major Trends in the Use of Capital Punishment, 25 Fed. Prob., No. 3, p. 15 (Sept. 1961). Capital punishment may provide an outlet for suicidal impulses or a means of achieving notoriety, for example.

[114] See, e. g., Gerstein, A Prosecutor Looks at Capital Punishment, 51 J. Crim. L. C. & P. S. 252 (1960); Hoover, Statements in Favor of the Death Penalty, in Bedau,

supra, n. 45, at 130; Younger, Capital Punishment: A Sharp Medicine Reconsidered, 42 A. B. A. J. 113 (1956). But see, Symposium on Capital Punishment, District Attorneys' Assn. of State of New York, Jan. 27, 1961, 7 N. Y. L. F. 249, 267 (1961) (statement of A. Herman, head of the homicide bureau of the New York City District Attorney's office).

[115] Sellin, supra, n. 98, at 56-58; Koeninger, Capital Punishment in Texas, 1924-1968, 15 Crime & Delin. 132 (1969); Sellin, Does the Death Penalty Protect Municipal Police, in Bedau, supra, n. 45, at 284; United Nations, supra, n. 77, ◆ 136, at 118.

[116] L. Lawes, Life and Death in Sing Sing 150 (1928); McGee, Capital Punishment as Seen by a Correctional Administrator, 28 Fed. Prob., No. 2, p. 11 (June 1964); 1950 Survey of the International Penal and Penitentiary Commission, cited in Sellin, supra, n. 98, at 70-72; Sellin, Prisons Homicides, in Capital Punishment 154 (T. Sellin ed. 1967); cf. Akman, Homicides and Assaults in Canadian Prisons, in Capital Punishment, supra, at 161-168. The argument can be made that the reason for the good record of murderers is that those who are likely to be recidivists are executed. There is, however, no evidence to show that in choosing between life and death sentences juries select the lesser penalties for those persons they believe are unlikely to commit future crimes.

[117] E. g., United Nations, supra, n. 77, ◆ 144, at 119; B. Eshelman & F. Riley, Death Row Chaplain 224 (1962). This is supported also by overwhelming statistics showing an extremely low rate of recidivism for convicted murderers who are released from prison. Royal Commission, supra, n. 84, App. 15, at 486-491; Sellin, supra, n. 98, at 72-79; United Nations, supra, n. 77, ◆ 144, at 119.

[118] See, e. g., The Question of Deterrence, in Bedau, supra, n. 45, at 267.

[119] Ibid. and n. 11; Note, The Death Penalty Cases, 56 Calif. L. Rev. 1268, 1282-1283 (1968).

[120] See n. 113, supra.

[121] United Nations, supra, n. 77, ◆ 159, at 123.

[122] See nn. 58 and 59, supra, and accompanying text.

[123] See n. 62, supra, and accompanying text.

[124] Graves, A Doctor Looks at Capital Punishment, 10 Med. Arts. & Sci. 137 (1956); Royal Commission, supra, n. 84, ◆ 60, at 20-21; Schuessler, The Deterrent Influence of the Death Penalty, 284 Annals Am. Acad. Pol. & Soc. Sci. 54 (1952); United Nations, supra, n. 77, ◆ 142, at 119; M. Wolfgang, Patterns in Criminal Homicide (1958).

One would assume that if deterrence were enhanced by capital punishment, the increased deterrence would be most effective with respect to the premeditating murderer or the hired killer who plots his crime before committing it. But, such people rarely expect to be caught and usually assume that if they are caught they will either be acquitted or sentenced to prison. This is a fairly dependable assumption since a reliable estimate is that one person is executed for every 100 capital murders known to the police. Hart, Murder and the Principles of Punishment: England and the United States, 52 Nw. U. L.

Rev. 433, 444-445 (1957). For capital punishment to deter anybody it must be a certain result of a criminal act, cf. Ex parte Medley, 134 U.S. 160 (1890), and it is not. It must also follow swiftly upon completion of the offense and it cannot in our complicated due process system of justice. See, e. g., The Question of Deterrence, in Bedau, supra, n. 45, at 258, 271-272; DiSalle, Trends in the Abolition of Capital Punishment, 1969 U. Toledo L. Rev. 1, 4. It is ironic that those persons whom we would like to deter the most have the least to fear from the death penalty and recognize that fact. Sellin, Address for Canadian Society for Abolition of the Death Penalty, Feb. 7, 1965, in 8 Crim. L. Q. 36, 48 (1966); Proceedings of the Section of Criminal Law of the ABA, Aug. 24, 1959, p. 7 (M. DiSalle).

[125] In reaching this conclusion, I maintain agreement with that portion of Stephen's hypothesis that suggests that convicted criminals fear death more than they fear life imprisonment. As I stated earlier, the death penalty is a more severe sanction. The error in the hypothesis lies in its assumption that because men fear death more than imprisonment after they are convicted, they necessarily must weigh potential penalties prior to committing criminal acts and that they will conform their behavior so as to insure that, if caught, they will receive the lesser penalty. It is extremely unlikely that much thought is given to penalties before the act is committed, and even if it were, the preceding footnote explains why such thought would not lead to deterrence.

[126] See n. 117, supra.

[127] See, e. g., Royal Commission, supra, n. 84, App. 15, at 486-491.

[128] Jackson applies to the States under the criteria articulated in Duncan v. Louisiana, 391 U.S. 145, 149 (1968).

[129] See, e. g., Barzun, In Favor of Capital Punishment, in Bedau, supra, n. 45, at 154.

[130] See, e. g., Death as a Punishment, in Bedau, supra, at 214, 226-228; Caldwell, Why is the Death Penalty Retained?, 284 Annals Am. Acad. Pol. & Soc. Sci. 45, 50 (1952); Johnson, Selective Factors in Capital Punishment, 36 Social Forces 165, 169 (1957); Sellin, Capital Punishment, 25 Fed. Prob., No. 3, p. 3 (Sept. 1961). We should not be surprised at the lack of merit in the eugenic arguments. There simply is no evidence that mentally ill persons who commit capital offenses constitute a psychiatric entity distinct from other mentally disordered patients or that they do not respond as readily to treatment. Cruvant & Waldrop, The Murderer in the Mental Institution, 284 Annals Am. Acad. Pol. & Soc. Sci. 35, 43 (1952).

[131] Caldwell, supra, n. 130, at 48; McGee, supra, n. 116.

[132] McGee, supra, at 13-14; Bailey, Rehabilitation on Death Row, in Bedau, supra, n. 45, at 556.

[133] T. Thomas, This Life We Take 20 (3d ed. 1965).

[134] Stein v. New York, 346 U.S. 156, 196 (1953) (Jackson, J.); cf. Reid v. Covert, 354 U.S. 1, 77 (1957) (Harlan, J., concurring in result).

[135] See, e. g., Witherspoon v. Illinois, 391 U.S. 510 (1968).

[136] Slovenko, And the Penalty is (Sometimes) Death, 24 Antioch Review 351

(1964).

[137] See, e. g., Caritativo v. California, 357 U.S. 549 (1958).

[138] To others, as well as to the author of this opinion, this practice has seemed a strange way to spend money. See, e. g., T. Arnold, The Symbols of Government 10-13 (1935).

[139] Slovenko, supra, n. 136, at 363.

[140] B. Eshelman & F. Riley, Death Row Chaplain 226 (1962); Caldwell, supra, n. 130, at 48; McGee, supra, n. 116, at 13; Sellin, supra, n. 130, at 3 (Sept. 1961).

[141] This analysis parallels in some ways the analysis used in striking down legislation on the ground that it violates Fourteenth Amendment concepts of substantive due process. See Packer, Making the Punishment Fit the Crime, 77 Harv. L. Rev. 1071, 1074 (1964). There is one difference, however. Capital punishment is unconstitutional because it is excessive and unnecessary punishment, not because it is irrational.

The concepts of cruel and unusual punishment and substantive due process become so close as to merge when the substantive due process argument is stated in the following manner: because capital punishment deprives an individual of a fundamental right (i. e., the right to life), Johnson v. Zerbst, 304 U.S. 458, 462 (1938), the State needs a compelling interest to justify it. See Note, The Death Penalty Cases, 56 Calif. L. Rev. 1268, 1324-1354 (1968). Thus stated, the substantive due process argument reiterates what is essentially the primary purpose of the Cruel and Unusual Punishments Clause of the Eighth Amendment - i. e., punishment may not be more severe than is necessary to serve the legitimate interests of the State.

THE CHIEF JUSTICE asserts that if we hold that capital punishment is unconstitutional because it is excessive, we will next have to determine whether a 10-year prison sentence rather than a five-year sentence is also excessive, or whether a $5 fine would not do equally well as a $10 fine. He may be correct that such determinations will have to be made, but, as in these cases, those persons challenging the penalty will bear a heavy burden of demonstrating that it is excessive. These cases arise after 200 years of inquiry, 200 years of public debate and 200 years of marshaling evidence. The burden placed on those challenging capital punishment could not have been greater. I am convinced that they have met their burden. Whether a similar burden will prove too great in future cases is a question that we can resolve in time.

[142] United States v. Rosenberg, 195 F.2d 583, 608 (CA2) (Frank, J.), cert. denied, 344 U.S. 838 (1952). See also Kasper v. Brittain, 245 F.2d 92, 96 (CA6), cert. denied, 355 U.S. 834 (1957) ("shocking to the sense of justice"); People v. Morris, 80 Mich. 634, 639, 45 N. W. 591, 592 (1890) ("shock the moral sense of the people"). In Repouille v. United States, 165 F.2d 152 (CA2 1947), and Schmidt v. United States, 177 F.2d 450, 451 (CA2 1949), Judge Learned Hand wrote that the standard of "good moral character" in the Nationality Act was to be judged by "the generally accepted moral conventions current at the time." 165 F.2d, at 153. Judge Frank, who was later to author the Rosenberg opinion, in which a similar standard was adopted, dissented in Repouille

and urged that the correct standard was the "attitude of our ethical leaders." 165 F.2d, at 154. In light of Rosenberg, it is apparent that Judge Frank would require a much broader based moral approbation before striking down a punishment as cruel and unusual than he would for merely holding that conduct was evidence of bad moral character under a legislative act.

[143] United States v. Rosenberg, supra, at 608.

[144] See Repouille v. United States, supra, at 153. In Witherspoon v. Illinois, 391 U.S., at 520, the Court cited a public opinion poll that showed that 42% of the American people favored capital punishment, while 47% opposed it. But the polls have shown great fluctuation. See What Do Americans Think of the Death Penalty?, in Bedau, supra, n. 45, at 231-241.

[145] The fact that the constitutionality of capital punishment turns on the opinion of an informed citizenry undercuts the argument that since the legislature is the voice of the people, its retention of capital punishment must represent the will of the people. So few people have been executed in the past decade that capital punishment is a subject only rarely brought to the attention of the average American. Lack of exposure to the problem is likely to lead to indifference, and indifference and ignorance result in preservation of the status quo, whether or not that is desirable, or desired.

It might be argued that in choosing to remain indifferent and uninformed, citizens reflect their judgment that capital punishment is really a question of utility, not morality, and not one, therefore, of great concern. As attractive as this is on its face, it cannot be correct, because such an argument requires that the choice to remain ignorant or indifferent be a viable one. That, in turn, requires that it be a knowledgeable choice. It is therefore imperative for constitutional purposes to attempt to discern the probable opinion of an informed electorate.

[146] Cf. Packer, Making the Punishment Fit the Crime, 77 Harv. L. Rev. 1071, 1076 (1964).

[147] E. g., Gold, A Psychiatric Review of Capital Punishment, 6 J. Forensic Sci. 465, 466 (1961); A Koestler, Reflections on Hanging 164 (1957); cf. C. Duffy & A. Hirshberg, 88 Men and 2 Women 257-258 (1962).

[148] Hearings, supra, n. 80, at 11 (statement of M. DiSalle).

[149] National Prisoner Statistics No. 45, Capital Punishment 1930-1968, p. 7 (Aug. 1969).

[150] Ibid.

[151] Ibid.

[152] Alexander, The Abolition of Capital Punishment, Proceedings of the 96th Congress of Correction of the American Correctional Association, Baltimore, Md., 57 (1966); Criminal Justice: The General Aspects, in Bedau, supra, n. 45, at 405, 411-414; Bedau, Death Sentences in New Jersey, 1907-1960, 19 Rutgers L. Rev. 1, 18-21, 52-53 (1964); R. Clark, Crime in America 335 (1970); Hochkammer, The Capital Punishment Controversy, 60 J. Crim. L. C. & P. S. 360, 361-362 (1969); Johnson, The Negro and

Crime, 217 Annals Am. Acad. Pol. & Soc. Sci. 93, 95, 99 (1941); Johnson, Selective Factors in Capital Punishment, 36 Social Forces 165 (1957); United Nations, supra, n. 77, � 69, at 98; Williams, The Death Penalty and the Negro, 67 Crisis 501, 511 (1960); M. Wolfgang & B. Cohen, Crime and Race: Conceptions and Misconceptions 77, 80-81, 85-86 (1970); Wolfgang, Kelly, & Nolde, Comparison of the Executed and the Commuted Among Admissions to Death Row, 53 J. Crim. L. C. & P. S. 301 (1962). MR. JUSTICE DOUGLAS explores the discriminatory application of the death penalty at great length, ante, at 249-257.

[153] National Prisoner Statistics No. 45, Capital Punishment 1930-1968, p. 28 (Aug. 1969).

[154] Men kill between four and five times more frequently than women. See Wolfgang, A Sociological Analysis of Criminal Homicide, in Bedau, supra, n. 45, at 74, 75. Hence, it would not be irregular to see four or five times as many men executed as women. The statistics show a startlingly greater disparity, however. United Nations, supra, n. 77, � 67, at 97-98.

[155] Criminal Justice: The General Aspects, in Bedau, supra, at 405, 411; Bedau, Capital Punishment in Oregon, 1903-64, 45 Ore. L. Rev. 1 (1965); Bedau, Death Sentences in New Jersey, 1907-1960, 19 Rutgers L. Rev. 1 (1964); R. Clark, Crime in America 335 (1970); C. Duffy & A. Hirshberg, 88 Men and 2 Women 256-257 (1962); Carter & Smith, The Death Penalty in California: A Statistical and Composite Portrait, 15 Crime & Delin. 62 (1969); Hearings, supra, n. 80, at 124-125 (statement of Dr. West); Koeninger, Capital Punishment in Texas, 1924-1968, 15 Crime & Delin. 132 (1969); McGee, supra, n. 116, at 11-12.

[156] See, e. g., E. Borchard, Convicting the Innocent (1932); J. Frank & B. Frank, Not Guilty (1957); E. Gardner, Court of Last Resort (1952). These three books examine cases in which innocent persons were sentenced to die. None of the innocents was actually executed, however. Bedau has abstracted 74 cases occurring in the United States since 1893 in which a wrongful conviction for murder was alleged and usually proved "beyond doubt." In almost every case, the convictions were sustained on appeal. Bedau seriously contends that innocent persons were actually executed. Murder, Errors of Justice, and Capital Punishment, in Bedau, supra, n. 45, at 434, 438. See also Black, The Crisis in Capital Punishment, 31 Md. L. Rev. 289 (1971); Hirschberg, Wrongful Convictions, 13 Rocky Mt. L. Rev. 20 (1940); Pollak, The Errors of Justice, 284 Annals Am. Acad. Pol. & Soc. Sci. 115 (1952).

[157] E. Gardner, Court of Last Resort 178 (1952).

[158] MR. JUSTICE DOUGLAS recognized this fact when he wrote:

"One who reviews the records of criminal trials need not look long to find an instance where the issue of guilt or innocence hangs in delicate balance. A judge who denies a stay of execution in a capital case often wonders if an innocent man is going to his death. . . .

"Those doubts exist because our system of criminal justice does not work with the efficiency of a machine - errors are made and innocent as well as guilty people are sometimes punished. . . .

". . . We believe that it is better for ten guilty people to be set free than for one innocent man to be unjustly imprisoned.

"Yet the sad truth is that a cog in the machine often slips: memories fail; mistaken identifications are made; those who wield the power of life and death itself - the police officer, the witness, the prosecutor, the juror, and even the judge - become overzealous in their concern that criminals be brought to justice. And at times there is a venal combination between the police and a witness." Foreword, J. Frank & B. Frank, Not Guilty 11-12 (1957).

There has been an "incredible lag" between the development of modern scientific methods of investigation and their application to criminal cases. When modern methodology is available, prosecutors have the resources to utilize it, whereas defense counsel often may not. Lassers, Proof of Guilt in Capital Cases - An Unscience, 58 J. Crim. L. C. & P. S. 310 (1967). This increases the chances of error.

[159] Ehrmann, The Death Penalty and the Administration of Justice, 284 Annals Am. Acad. Pol. & Soc. Sci. 73, 83 (1952).

[160] F. Frankfurter, Of Law and Men 81 (1956).

[161] B. Eshelman & F. Riley, Death Row Chaplain 222 (1962).

[162] McCafferty, Major Trends in the Use of Capital Punishment, 25 Fed. Prob., No. 3, pp. 15, 21 (Sept. 1961) (quoting Dr. S. Glueck of Harvard University).

[163] MR. JUSTICE POWELL suggests that this conclusion is speculative, and he is certainly correct. But the mere recognition of this truth does not undercut the validity of the conclusion. MR. JUSTICE POWELL himself concedes that judges somehow know that certain punishments are no longer acceptable in our society; for example, he refers to branding and pillorying. Whence comes this knowledge? The answer is that it comes from our intuition as human beings that our fellow human beings no longer will tolerate such punishments.

I agree wholeheartedly with the implication in my Brother POWELL'S opinion that judges are not free to strike down penalties that they find personally offensive. But, I disagree with his suggestion that it is improper for judges to ask themselves whether a specific punishment is morally acceptable to the American public. Contrary to some current thought, judges have not lived lives isolated from a broad range of human experience. They have come into contact with many people, many ways of life, and many philosophies. They have learned to share with their fellow human beings common views of morality. If, after drawing on this experience and considering the vast range of people and views that they have encountered, judges conclude that these people would not knowingly tolerate a specific penalty in light of its costs, then this conclusion is entitled to weight. See Frankel, Book Review, 85 Harv. L. Rev. 354 (1971). Judges can find assistance in determining whether they are being objective, rather than subjective, by referring to the attitudes of the persons whom most citizens consider our "ethical leaders." See

Repouille v. United States, 165 F.2d, at 154 (Frank, J., dissenting).

I must also admit that I am confused as to the point that my Brother POWELL seeks to make regarding the underprivileged members of our society. If he is stating that this Court cannot solve all of their problems in the context of this case, or even many of them, I would agree with him. But if he is opining that it is only the poor, the ignorant, the racial minorities, and the hapless in our society who are executed; that they are executed for no real reason other than to satisfy some vague notion of society's cry for vengeance; and that knowing these things, the people of this country would not care, then I most urgently disagree.

There is too much crime, too much killing, too much hatred in this country. If the legislatures could eradicate these elements from our lives by utilizing capital punishment, then there would be a valid purpose for the sanction and the public would surely accept it. It would be constitutional. AS THE CHIEF JUSTICE and MR. JUSTICE POWELL point out, however, capital punishment has been with us a long time. What purpose has it served? The evidence is that it has served none. I cannot agree that the American people have been so hardened, so embittered that they want to take the life of one who performs even the basest criminal act knowing that the execution is nothing more than bloodlust. This has not been my experience with my fellow citizens. Rather, I have found that they earnestly desire their system of punishments to make sense in order that it can be a morally justifiable system. See generally Arnold, The Criminal Trial As a Symbol of Public Morality, in Criminal Justice In Our Time 137 (A. Howard ed. 1967).

164 R. Clark, Crime in America 336 (1970).

165 Some jurisdictions have de facto abolition; others have de jure. Id., at 330; Hearings, supra, n. 80, at 9-10 (statement of M. DiSalle). See generally Patrick, The Status of Capital Punishment: A World Perspective, 56 J. Crim. L. C. & P. S. 397 (1965); United Nations, supra, n. 77, 10-17, 63-65, at 83-85, 96-97; Brief for Petitioner in No. 68-5027, App. E (Aikens v. California, 406 U.S. 813 (1972)).

Shouldn't deny people permission to enter country based on what they advocate: Justice Marshall's dissent in Kleindienst v. Mandel (June 29, 1972)

MR. JUSTICE MARSHALL, with whom MR. JUSTICE BRENNAN joins, dissenting.

Dr. Ernest Mandel, a citizen of Belgium, is an internationally famous Marxist scholar and journalist. He was invited to our country by a group of American scholars who wished to meet him for discussion and debate. With firm plans for conferences, colloquia and lectures, the American hosts were stunned to learn that Mandel had been refused permission to enter our country. American consular officials had found Mandel "ineligible" to receive a visa under §§ 212(a)(28)(D) and (G)(v) of the Immigration and Nationality Act of 1952, 66 Stat. 185, which bars even temporary visits to the United

States by aliens who "advocate the economic, international, and governmental doctrines of world communism" or "who write or publish . . . any written or printed matter . . . advocating or teaching" such doctrines. Under § 212(d)(3), the Attorney General refused to waive inadmissibility.

I, too, am stunned to learn that a country with our proud heritage has refused Dr. Mandel temporary admission. I am convinced that Americans cannot be denied the opportunity to hear Dr. Mandel's views in person because their Government disapproves of his ideas. Therefore, I dissent from today's decision, and would affirm the judgment of the court below.

I

As the majority correctly demonstrates, in a variety of contexts, this Court has held that the First Amendment protects the right to receive information and ideas, the freedom to hear as well as the freedom to speak. The reason for this is that the First Amendment protects a process, in Justice Brandeis' words, "reason as applied through public discussion," Whitney v. California, 274 U. S. 357, 274 U. S. 375 (1927) (concurring opinion); and the right to speak and hear -- including the right to inform others and to be informed about public issues -- are inextricably part of that process. The freedom to speak and the freedom to hear are inseparable; they are two sides of the same coin. But the coin itself is the process of thought and discussion. The activity of speakers becoming listeners and listeners becoming speakers in the vital interchange of thought is the "means indispensable to the discovery and spread of political truth." Ibid.; see Terminiello v. Chicago, 337 U. S. 1, 337 U. S. 4 (1949). Its protection is "a fundamental principle of the American government." Whitney v. California, supra, at 274 U. S. 375. The First Amendment means that Government has no power to thwart the process of free discussion, to "abridge" the freedoms necessary to make that process work. See Lamont v. Postmaster General, 381 U. S. 301, 381 U. S. 308 (1965) (BRENNAN, J., concurring, with whom Goldberg and Harlan, JJ., joined).

There can be no doubt that, by denying the American appellees access to Dr. Mandel, the Government has directly prevented the free interchange of ideas guaranteed by the First Amendment. [1] It has, of course, interfered with appellees' personal rights both to hear Mandel's views and to develop and articulate their own views through interaction with Mandel. But as the court below recognized, apart from appellees' interests, there is also a "general public interest in the prevention of any stifling of political utterance." 325 F.Supp. 620, 632 (1971). And the Government has interfered with this as well. [2]

II

What is the justification for this extraordinary governmental interference with the liberty of American citizens? And by what reasoning does the Court uphold Mandel's exclusion? It is established constitutional doctrine, after all, that government may restrict First Amendment rights only if the restriction is necessary to further a compelling governmental interest. E.g., Lamont v. Postmaster General, supra, at 381 U. S. 308;

NAACP v. Button, 371 U. S. 415, 371 U. S. 438 (1963); Gibson v. Florida Legislative Investigation Committee, 372 U. S. 539, 372 U. S. 546 (1963); Shelton v. Tucker, 364 U. S. 479 (1960).

A. Today's majority apparently holds that Mandel may be excluded and Americans' First Amendment rights restricted because the Attorney General has given a "facially legitimate and bona fide reason" for refusing to waive Mandel's visa ineligibility. I do not understand the source of this unusual standard. Merely "legitimate" governmental interests cannot override constitutional rights. Moreover, the majority demands only "facial" legitimacy and good faith, by which it means that this Court will never "look behind" any reason the Attorney General gives. No citation is given for this kind of unprecedented deference to the Executive, nor can I imagine (nor am I told) the slightest justification for such a rule. [3]

Even the briefest peek behind the Attorney General's reason for refusing a waiver in this case would reveal that it is a sham. The Attorney General informed appellees' counsel that the waiver was refused because Mandel's activities on a previous American visit

"went far beyond the stated purposes of his trip . . . and represented a flagrant abuse of the opportunities afforded him to express his views in this country."

App. 68. But, as the Department of State had already conceded to appellees' counsel, Dr. Mandel

"was apparently not informed that [his previous] visa was issued only after obtaining a waiver of ineligibility, and therefore [Mandel] may not have been aware of the conditions and limitations attached to the [previous] visa issuance."

App. 22. There is no basis in the present record for concluding that Mandel's behavior on his previous visit was a "flagrant abuse" -- or even willful or knowing departure -- from visa restrictions. For good reason, the Government in this litigation has never relied on the Attorney General's reason to justify Mandel's exclusion. In these circumstances, the Attorney General's reason cannot possibly support a decision for the Government in this case. But without even remanding for a factual hearing to see if there is any support for the Attorney General's determination, the majority declares that his reason is sufficient to override appellees' First Amendment interests.

B. Even if the Attorney General had given a compelling reason for declining to grant a waiver under § 212(d)(3)(A), this would not, for me, end the case. As I understand the statutory scheme, Mandel is "ineligible" for a visa, and therefore inadmissible, solely because, within the terms of § 212(a)(28), he has advocated communist doctrine and has published writings advocating that doctrine. The waiver question under § 212(d)(3)(A) is totally secondary and dependent, since it is triggered here only by a determination of (a)(28) ineligibility. The Attorney General's refusal to grant a waiver doe not itself generate a new statutory basis for exclusion; he has no roving power to set new ad hoc standards for visa ineligibility. Rather, the Attorney General's refusal to waive ineligibility simply has the same effect as if no waiver provision existed; inadmissibility still rests on the (a)(28) determination. Thus, whether or not the Attorney General had a good reason for refusing a waiver, this Court, I think, must still face the question it tries to avoid: under our Constitution, may Mandel be declared ineligible under (a)(28)?

C. Accordingly, I turn to consider the constitutionality of the sole justification given by the Government here and below for excluding Mandel -- that he "advocates" and "publish[es] . . . printed matter . . . advocating . . . doctrines of world communism" within the term of § 212(a)(28).

Still adhering to standard First Amendment doctrine, I do not see how (a)(28) can possibly represent a compelling governmental interest that overrides appellees' interests in hearing Mandel. [4] Unlike (a)(27) or (a)(29),

(a)(28) does not claim to exclude aliens who are likely to engage in subversive activity or who represent an active and present threat to the "welfare, safety, or security of the United States." Rather, (a)(28) excludes aliens solely because they have advocated communist doctrine. Our cases make clear, however, that government has no legitimate interest in stopping the flow of ideas. It has no power to restrict the mere advocacy of communist doctrine, divorced from incitement to imminent lawless action. Noto v. United States, 367 U. S. 290, 367 U. S. 297-298 (1961); Brandenburg v. Ohio, 395 U. S. 444, 395 U. S. 447-449 (196). For those who are not sure that they have attained the final and absolute truth, all ideas, even those forcefully urged, are a contribution to the ongoing political dialogue. The First Amendment represents the view of the Framers that

"the path of safety lies in the opportunity to discuss freely supposed grievances and proposed remedies; and that the fitting remedy for evil counsels is good ones"

-- "more speech." Whitney v. California, 274 U.S. at 274 U. S. 375, 377 (Brandeis, J., concurring). If Americans want to hear about Marxist doctrine, even from advocates, government cannot intervene simply because it does not approve of the ideas. It certainly may not selectively pick and choose which ideas it will let into the country. But, as the court below put it, § 212(a)(28) is nothing more than "a mean of restraining the entry of disfavored political doctrine," 325 F.Supp. at 626, and such an enactment cannot justify the abridgment of appellees' First Amendment rights.

In saying these thing, I am merely repeating established First Amendment law. Indeed, this Court has already applied that law in a case concerning the entry of communist doctrine from foreign lands. In Lamont v. Postmaster General, 381 U. S. 301 (1965), this Court held that the right of an American addressee to receive communist political propaganda from abroad could not be fettered by requiring the addressee to request in writing its delivery from the Post Office. See id. at 381 U. S. 308 (BRENNAN, J., concurring). The burden imposed on the right to receive information in our case is far greater than in Lamont, with far less justification. In Lamont, the challenged law merely regulated the low of mail, and required the Postmaster General to forward detained mail immediately upon request by the addressee. By contract, through 212(a)(28), the Government claims absolute power to bar Mandel permanently from academic meetings in this country. Moreover, in Lamont, the Government argued that its interest was not to censor content, but rather to protect Americans from receiving unwanted mail. Here, Mandel's exclusion is not incident to a legitimate regulatory objective, but is based directly on the subject matter of his beliefs.

D. The heart of appellants' position in this case, and the basis for their distinguishing Lamont, is that the Government's power is distinctively broad and unreviewable because "[t]he regulation in question is directed at the admission of aliens." Brief for Appellant 33. Thus, in the appellants' view, this case is no different from a long line of cases holding that the power to exclude aliens is left exclusively to the "political" branches of Government, Congress, and the Executive.

These cases are not the strongest precedents in the United States Reports, and the majority's baroque approach reveals its reluctance to rely on them completely.

They include such milestones as The Chinese Exclusion Case, 130 U. S. 581 (1889), and Fong Yue Ting v. United States, 149 U. S. 698 (1893), in which this Court upheld the Government's power to exclude and expel Chinese aliens from our midst.

But none of these old cases must be "reconsidered" or overruled to strike down Dr. Mandel's exclusion, for none of them was concerned with the rights of American citizen. All of them involved only rights of the excluded aliens themselves. At least when the rights of Americas are involved, there is no basis for concluding that the power to exclude aliens is absolute.

"When Congress' exercise of one of its enumerated powers clashes with those individual liberties protected by the Bill of Rights, it is our 'delicate and difficult task' to determine whether the resulting restriction on freedom can be tolerated."

United States v. Robel, 389 U. S. 258, 389 U. S. 264 (1967). As Robel and many other cases [5] show, all governmental power even the war power, the power to maintain national security, or the power to conduct foreign affairs -- is limited by the Bill of Rights. When individual freedoms of Americans are at stake, we do not blindly defer to broad claims of the Legislative Branch or Executive Branch, but rather we consider those claims in light of the individual freedoms. This should be our approach in the present case, even though the Government urges that the question of admitting aliens may involve foreign relations and national defense policies.

The majority recognizes that the right of American citizens to hear Mandel is "implicated" in our case. There were no right of Americans involved in any of the old alien exclusion cases, and therefore their broad counsel about deference to the political branches is inapplicable. Surely a Court that can distinguish between pre-indictment and post-indictment lineups, Kirby v. Illinois, 406 U. S. 682 (1972), can distinguish between our case and cases which involve only the rights of aliens.

I do not mean to suggest that, simply because some Americans wish to hear an alien speak, they can automatically compel even his temporary admission to our country. Government may prohibit aliens from even temporary admission if exclusion is necessary to protect a compelling governmental interest. [6] Actual threats to the national security, public health needs, and genuine requirements of law enforcement are the most apparent interests that would surely be compelling. [7] But, in Dr. Mandel's case, the Government has, and claims, no such compelling interest. Mandel's visit was to be temporary. [8] His "ineligibility" for a visa was based solely on § 212(a)(28). The only governmental interest embodied in that section is the Government's desire to keep certain ideas out of circulation in this country. This is hardly a compelling governmental interest. Section (a)(28) may not be the basis for excluding an alien when Americans wish to hear him. Without any claim that Mandel "live" is an actual threat to this country, there is no difference between excluding Mandel because of his ideas and keeping his books out because of their ideas. Neither is permitted. Lamont v. Postmaster General, supra.

III

Dr. Mandel has written about his exclusion, concluding that "[i]t demonstrates a lack of confidence" on the part of our Government "in the capacity of its supporters to combat Marxism on the battleground of ideas." He observes that he

"would not be carrying any high explosives, if I had come, but only, as I did before, my revolutionary views, which are well known to the public."

And he wryly notes that,

"[i]n the nineteenth century, the British ruling class, which was sure of itself, permitted Karl Marx to live as an exile in England for almost forty years."

App. 54.

It is undisputed that Dr. Mandel's brief trip would involve nothing but a series of scholarly conferences and lectures. The progress of knowledge is an international venture. As Mandel's invitation demonstrates, individuals of differing world views have learned the ways of cooperation where governments have thus far failed. Nothing is served -- least of all our standing in the international community -- by Mandel's exclusion. In blocking his admission, the Government has departed from the basic traditions of our country, its fearless acceptance of free discussion. By now deferring to the Executive, this Court departs from its own best role as the guardian of individual liberty in the face of governmental overreaching. Principles of judicial restraint designed to allow the political branches to protect national security have no place in this case. Dr. Mandel should be permitted to make his brief visit.

I dissent.

Notes

[1] Twenty years ago, the Bulletin of the Atomic Scientists devoted an entire issue to the problem of American visa policy and its effect on the interchange of ideas between American scholars and scientists and their foreign counterparts. The general conclusion of the editors -- supported by printed statements of such men as Albert Einstein, Hans Bethe, Harold Urey, Arthur Compton, Michael Polanyi, and Raymond Aron -- was that American visa policy was hurting the continuing advance of American science and learning, and harmful to our prestige abroad. Vol. 8, No. 7, Oct.1952, pp.210-217 (statement of Special Editor Edward Shils). The detrimental effect of American visa policy

on the free exchange of ideas continues to be reported. See Comment Opening the Floodgates to Dissident Aliens, 6 Harv.Civ.Rights-Civ.Lib.L.Rev. 141, 143-149 (1970); 11 Bulletin of the Atomic Scientists, Dec. 1955, pp. 367-373.

[2] The availability to appellees of Mandel's books and taped lectures is no substitute for live, face-to-face discussion and debate, just as the availability to us of briefs and exhibits does not supplant the essential place of oral argument in this Court's work. Lengthy citations for this proposition, which the majority apparently concede, are unnecessary. I simply note that in a letter to Henrik Lorenz, accepting an invitation to lecture at the University of Leiden and to discus "the radiation problem," Albert Einstein observed that, "[i]n these unfinished things, people understand one another with difficulty unless talking face to face." Quoted in Developments in the Law -- The National Security Interest and Civil Liberties, 85 Harv.L.Rev. 1130, 1154 (1972).

[3] As Judge Frankel has taught us, even the limited requirement of facially sufficient reasons for governmental action may be significant in some contexts; but it can hardly insulate the government from subsequent challenges to the actual good faith and sufficiency of the reasons. Frankel, Bench Warrants Upon the Prosecutor's Demand: A View From the Bench, 71 Col.L.Rev. 403, 414 (1971).

[4] The majority suggests that appellees

"concede that Congress could enact a blanket prohibition against entry of all aliens falling into the class defined by §§ 212(a)(28)(D) and (G)(v), and that First Amendment rights could not override that decision."

This was certainly not the view of the court below, whose judgment the appellants alone have challenged here and appellees have moved to affirm. It is true that appellees have argued to this Court a ground of decision alternative to that argued and adopted below; but they have hardly conceded the incorrectness of what they successfully argued below. They have simply noted, at 16-17 of their brief, that, even if this Court rejects the broad decision below, there would nevertheless be a separate and narrower basis for affirmance. See Tr. of Oral Arg. 24, 226, 41-42.

[5] In United States v. Robel, 389 U. S. 258 (1967), this Court struck down a statute making it a criminal offense for any employee of a "defense facility" to remain a member of the Communist Party, in spite of Government claims that the enactment came within the "war power." In Aptheker v. Secretary of State, 378 U. S. 500 (1964), the Government unsuccessfully sought to defend the denial of passports to American members of the Communist Party, in spite of claimed threats to the national security. In Zemel v. Rusk, 381 U. S. 1 (1965), the passport restriction on travel to Cuba was upheld because individual constitutional rights were overridden by the "weightiest considerations of national security"; but the Court rejected any assumption "that simply because a statute deals with foreign relations, it can grant the Executive totally unrestricted freedom of choice." Id. at 381 U. S. 16, 381 U. S. 17. In Schneider v. Rusk, 377 U. S. 163 (1964), the Government unsuccessfully attempted to justify a statutory inequality between naturalized and native-born citizens under the foreign relations

power. And in Lamont v. Postmaster General, 381 U. S. 301 (1965), itself, as MR. JUSTICE BRENNAN noted, the Government urged that the statute was "justified by the object of avoiding the subsidization of propaganda of foreign governments which bar American propaganda"; MR. JUSTICE BRENNAN answered that the Government must act "by means and on terms which do not endanger First Amendment rights." Id. at 381 U. S. 310.

[6] I agree with the majority that courts should not inquire into such things as the "probity of the speaker's ideas." Neither should the Executive, however. Where Americans wish to hear an alien, and their claim is not a demonstrated sham, the crucial question is whether the Government's interest in excluding the alien is compelling.

[7] It goes without saying, of course, that, once he has been admitted, any alien (like any citizen) can be punished if he incites lawless acts or commits other crimes.

[8] Such "nonimmigrants" are not covered by quotas. C. Gordon & H. Rosenfield, Immigration Law and Procedure § 2.6 (1971).

Can't prohibit adult sexual entertainment at bars: Justice Marshall's dissent in California v. LaRue (December 5, 1972)

MR. JUSTICE MARSHALL, dissenting.

In my opinion, the District Court's judgment should be affirmed. The record in this case is not a pretty one, and it is possible that the State could constitutionally punish some of the activities described therein under a narrowly drawn scheme. But appellees challenge these regulations [1] on their face, rather than as applied to a specific course of conduct. [2] Cf. 405 U. S. 109, 125 Gooding v. Wilson, 405 U. S. 518 (1972). When so viewed, I think it clear that the regulations are overbroad, and therefore unconstitutional. See, e.g., Dombrowski v. Pfister, 380 U. S. 479, 380 U. S. 486 (1965). [3] Although the State's broad power to regulate the distribution of liquor and to enforce health and safety regulations is not to be doubted, that power may not be exercised in a manner that broadly stifles First Amendment freedoms. Cf. Shelton v. Tucker, 364 U. S. 479, 364 U. S. 488 (1960). Rather, as this Court has made clear, "[p]recision of regulation must be the touchstone" when First Amendment rights are implicated. NAACP v. Button, at 371 U. S. 415, 371 U. S. 438 (1963). Because I am convinced that these regulations lack the precision which our prior cases require, I must respectfully dissent.

I

It should be clear at the outset that California's regulatory scheme does not conform to the standards which we have previously enunciated for the control of obscenity. [4] Before this Court's decision in Roth v. Unite States, 354 U. S. 476 (1957), some American courts followed the rule of Regina v. Hicklin, L.R. 3 Q.B. 360 (1868), to the effect that the obscenity vel non of a piece of work could be judged by examining isolated aspects of it. See, e.g., United States v. Kennerley, 209 F. 119 (1913);

Commonwealth v. Buckley, 200 Mass. 346, 86 N.E. 910 (1909). But in Roth, we held that

"[t]he Hicklin test, judging obscenity by the effect of isolated passages upon the most susceptible persons, might well encompass material legitimately treating with sex, and so it must be rejected as unconstitutionally restrictive of the freedoms of speech and press."

354 U.S. at 354 U. S. 489. Instead, we held that the material must be "taken as a whole," ibid., and, when so viewed, must appeal to a prurient interest in sex, patently offend community standards relating to the depiction of sexual matters, and be utterly without redeeming social value. [5] See Memoirs v. Massachusetts, 383 U. S. 413, 383 U. S. 418 (1966).

Obviously, the California rules do not conform to these standards. They do not require the material to be judged as a whole, and do not speak to the necessity of proving prurient interest, offensiveness to community standards, or lack of redeeming social value. Instead of the contextual test approved in Roth and Memoirs, these regulations create a system of per se rules to be applied regardless of context: certain acts simply may not be depicted and certain parts of the body may under no circumstances be revealed. The regulations thus treat on the same level a serious movie such as "Ulysses" and a crudely made "stag film." They ban not only obviously pornographic photographs, but also great sculpture from antiquity. [6]

Roth held 15 years ago that the suppression of serious communication was too high a price to pay in order to vindicate the State's interest in controlling obscenity, and I see no reason to modify that judgment today. Indeed, even the appellants do not seriously contend that these regulations can be justified under the Roth-Memoirs test. Instead, appellants argue that California's regulations do not concern the control of pornography at all. These rules, they argue, deal with conduct, rather than with speech, and, as such, are not subject to the strict limitations of the First Amendment.

To support this proposition, appellants rely primarily on United States v. O'Brien, 391 U. S. 367 (1968), which upheld the constitutionality of legislation punishing the destruction or mutilation of Selective Service certificates. O'Brien rejected the notion that

"an apparently limitless variety of conduct can be labeled 'speech' whenever the person engaging in the conduct intends thereby to express an idea,"

and held that Government regulation of speech-related conduct is permissible

"if it is within the constitutional power of the Government; if it furthers an important or substantial governmental interest; if the governmental interest is unrelated to the suppression of free expression; and if the incidental restriction on alleged First Amendment freedoms is no greater than is essential to the furtherance of that interest."

Id. at 391 U. S. 376, 391 U. S. 377.

While I do not quarrel with these principles as stated in the abstract, their application in this case stretches them beyond the breaking point. [7] In O'Brien, the Court began its discussion by noting that the statute in question "plainly does not abridge free speech on its face." Indeed, even O'Brien himself conceded that, facially, the statute dealt "with conduct having no connection with speech." [8] Id. at 391 U. S. 375. Here, the situation is quite different. A long line of our cases makes clear that motion pictures, unlike draft card burning, are a form of expression entitled to prima facie First Amendment protection.

"It cannot be doubted that motion pictures are a significant medium for the communication of ideas. They may affect public attitudes and behavior in a variety of ways, ranging from direct espousal of a political or social doctrine to the subtle shaping of thought which characterizes all artistic expression. The importance of motion pictures as an organ of public opinion is not lessened by the fact that they are designed to entertain as well as to inform."

Joseph Burstyn, Inc. v. Wilson, 343 U. S. 495, 343 U. S. 501 (1952) (footnote omitted). See also Interstate Circuit, Inc. v. City of Dallas, 390 U. S. 676 (1968); Jacobellis v. Ohio, 378 U.S. 184 (1964); Pinkus v. Pitchess, 429 F.2d 416 (CA9 1970), aff'd by equally divided court sub nom. California v. Pinkus, 400 U.S. 922 (1970). Similarly, live performances and dance have, in recent years, been afforded broad prima facie First Amendment protection. See, e.g., Schacht v. United States, 398 U. S. 58 (1970); P.B.I.C., Inc. v. Byrne, 313 F.Supp. 757 (Mass. 1970), vacated to consider mootness, 401 U.S. 987 (1971); In re Giannini, 69 Cal.2d 563, 446 P.2d 535 (1968), cert. denied sub nom. California v. Giannini, 395 U.S. 910 (1969).

If, as these many cases hold, movies, plays, and the dance enjoy constitutional protection, it follows, ineluctably, I think, that their component parts are protected as well. It is senseless to say that a play is "speech" within the meaning of the First Amendment, but that the individual gestures of the actors are "conduct" which the State may prohibit. The State may no more allow movies while punishing the "acts" of which they are composed than it may allow newspapers while punishing the "conduct" of setting type.

Of course, I do not mean to suggest that anything which occurs upon a stage is automatically immune from state regulation. No one seriously contends, for example, that an actual murder may be legally committed so long as it is called for in the script, or that an actor may inject real heroin into his veins while evading the drug laws that apply to everyone else. But once it is recognized that movies and plays enjoy prima facie First Amendment protection, the standard for reviewing state regulation of their component parts shifts dramatically. For while

"[m]ere legislative preferences or beliefs respecting matters of public convenience may well support regulation directed at other personal activities, [they are] insufficient to justify such as diminishes the exercise of rights so vital"

as freedom of speech. Schneider v. State, 308 U. S. 147, 308 U. S. 161 (1939). Rather, in order to restrict speech, the State must show that the speech is

"used in such circumstances and [is] of such a nature as to create a clear and present danger that [it] will bring about the substantive evils that [the State] has a right to prevent."

Schenck v. United States, 249 U. S. 47, 249 U. S. 52 (1919). Cf. Brandenburg v. Ohio, 395 U. S. 444 (1969); Dennis v. United States, 341 U. S. 494 (1951). [9]

When the California regulations are measured against this stringent standard, they prove woefully inadequate. Appellants defend the rules as necessary to prevent sex crimes, drug abuse, prostitution, and a wide variety of other evils. These are precisely the same interests that have been asserted time and again before this Court as justification for laws banning frank discussion of sex, and that we have consistently rejected. In fact, the empirical link between sex-related entertainment and the criminal activity popularly associated with it has never been proved and, indeed, has now been largely discredited. See, e.g., Report of the Commission on Obscenity and Pornography 27 (1970); Cairns, Paul, & Wishner, Sex Censorship: The Assumptions of Anti-Obscenity Laws and the Empirical Evidence, 46 Minn.L.Rev. 1009 (1962). Yet even if one were to concede that such a link existed, it would hardly justify a broad-scale attack on First Amendment freedoms. The only way to stop murders and drug abuse is to punish them directly. But the State's interest in controlling material dealing with sex is secondary in nature. [10] It can control rape and prostitution by punishing those acts, rather than by punishing the speech that is one step removed from the feared harm. [11] Moreover, because First Amendment rights are at stake, the State must adopt this "less restrictive alternative" unless it can make a compelling demonstration that the protected activity and criminal conduct are so closely linked that only through regulation of one can the other be stopped. Cf. United States v. Robel, 389 U. S. 258, 389 U. S. 268 (1967). As we said in Stanley v. Georgia, 394 U. S. 557, 394 U. S. 566-567 (1969),

"if the State is only concerned about printed or filmed materials inducing antisocial conduct, we believe that, in the context of private consumption of ideas and information, we should adhere to the view that '[a]mong free men, the deterrents ordinarily to be applied to prevent crime are education and punishment for violations of the law. . . .' Whitney v. California, 274 U. S. 357, 274 U. S. 378 (1927)(Brandeis, J., concurring). . . . Given the present state of knowledge, the State may no more prohibit mere possession of obscene matter on the ground that it may lead to antisocial conduct than it may prohibit possession of chemistry books on the ground that they may lead to the manufacture of homemade spirits. [12]"

II

It should thus be evident that, under the standards previously developed by this Court, the California regulations are overbroad: they would seem to suppress not only obscenity outside the scope of the First Amendment, but also speech that is clearly protected. But California contends that these regulations do not involve suppression at all. The State claims that its rules are not regulations of obscenity, but are rather merely regulations of the sale and consumption of liquor. Appellants point out that California does not punish establishments which provide the proscribed entertainment, but only requires that they not serve alcoholic beverages on their premises. Appellants vigorously argue that such regulation falls within the State's general police power as augmented, when alcoholic beverages are involved, by the Twenty-first Amendment. [13]

I must confess that I find this argument difficult to grasp. To some extent, it seems premised on the notion that the Twenty-first Amendment authorizes the States to regulate liquor in a fashion which would otherwise be constitutionally impermissible. But the Amendment, by its terms, speaks only to state control of the importation of alcohol, and its legislative history makes clear that it was intended only to permit "dry" States to control the flow of liquor across their boundaries despite potential Commerce Clause objections. [14] See generally Seagram & Sons v. Hostetter, 384 U. S. 35 (1966); Hostetter v. Idlewild Liquor Corp., 377 U. S. 324 (1964). There is not a word in that history which indicates that Congress meant to tamper in any way with First Amendment rights. I submit that the framers of the Amendment would be astonished to discover that they had inadvertently enacted a pro tanto repealer of the rest of the Constitution. Only last Term, we held that the State's conceded power to license the distribution of intoxicating beverages did not justify use of that power in a manner that conflicted with the Equal Protection Clause. See Moose Lodge No. 107 v. Irvis, 407 U. S. 163, 407 U. S. 178-179 (1972). Cf. Wisconsin v. Constantineau, 400 U. S. 433 (1971); Hornsby v. Allen, 326 F.2d 605 (CA5 1964). I am at a loss to understand why the Twenty-first Amendment should be thought to override the First Amendment, but not the Fourteenth.

To be sure, state regulation of liquor is important, and it is deeply embedded in our history. See, e.g., Colonnade Catering Corp. v. United States, 397 U. S. 72; 397 U. S. 77 (1970). But First Amendment values are important as well. Indeed, in the past, they have been thought so important as to provide an independent restraint on every power of Government. "Freedom of press, freedom of speech, freedom of religion are in a preferred position." Murdock v. Pennsylvania, 319 U. S. 105, 319 U. S. 115 (1943). Thus, when the Government attempted to justify a limitation on freedom of association by reference to the war power, we categorically rejected the attempt. "[The] concept of national defense,'" we held,

"cannot be deemed an end in itself, justifying any exercise of legislative power designed to promote such a goal. Implicit in the term 'national defense' is the notion of defending those values and ideals which set this Nation apart. For almost two centuries, our country has taken singular pride in the democratic ideals enshrined in its Constitution, and the most cherished of those ideals have found expression in the First Amendment. It would indeed be ironic if, in the name of national defense, we would sanction the subversion of one of those liberties -- the freedom of association – which makes the defense of the Nation worthwhile."

United States v. Robel, 389 U.S. at 389 U. S. 264. Cf. New York Times Co. v. United States, 403 U. S. 713, 403 U. S. 716-717 (1971)(Black, J., concurring); Home Bldg. & Loan Assn. v. Blaisdell, 290 U. S. 398, 290 U. S. 426 (1934). If the First Amendment limits the means by which our Government can ensure its very survival, then surely it must limit the State's power to control the sale of alcoholic beverages as well.

Of course, this analysis is relevant only to the extent that California has, in fact, encroached upon First Amendment rights. Appellants argue that no such encroachment has occurred, since appellees are free to continue providing any entertainment they choose without fear of criminal penalty. Appellants suggest that this case is somehow different because all that is at stake is the "privilege" of serving liquor by the drink.

It should be clear, however, that the absence of criminal sanctions is insufficient to immunize state regulation from constitutional attack. On the contrary, "this is only the beginning, not the end, of our inquiry." Sherbert v. Verner, 374 U. S. 398, 374 U. S. 403-404 (1963). For

"[i]t is too late in the day to doubt that the liberties of religion and expression may be infringed by the denial of or placing of conditions upon a benefit or privilege."

Id. at 374 U. S. 404. As we pointed out only last Term,

"[f]or at least a quarter-century, this Court has made clear that even though a person has no 'right' to a valuable governmental benefit, and even though the government may deny him the benefit for any number of reasons, there are some reasons upon which the government may not rely. It may not deny a benefit to a person on a basis that infringes his constitutionally protected interests -- especially his interest in freedom of speech. For if the government could deny a benefit to a person because of his constitutionally protected speech or associations, his exercise of those freedoms would, in effect, be penalized and inhibited."

Perry v. Sindermann, 408 U. S. 593, 408 U. S. 597 (1972).

Thus, unconstitutional conditions on welfare benefits, [15] unemployment compensation, [16] tax exemptions, [17] public employment, [18] bar admissions, [19] and mailing privileges [20] have all been invalidated by this Court. In none of these cases were criminal penalties involved. In all of them, citizens were left free to exercise their constitutional rights so long as they were willing to give up a "gratuity" that the State had no obligation to provide. Yet, in all of them, we found that the discriminatory provision of a privilege placed too great a burden on constitutional freedoms. I therefore have some difficulty in understanding why California nightclub proprietors should be singled out and informed that they alone must sacrifice their constitutional rights before gaining the "privilege" to serve liquor.

Of course, it is true that the State may, in proper circumstances, enact a broad regulatory scheme that incidentally restricts First Amendment rights. For example, if California prohibited the sale of alcohol altogether, I do not mean to suggest that the proprietors of theaters and bookstores would be constitutionally entitled to a special dispensation. But, in that event, the classification would not be speech-related, and hence could not be rationally perceived as penalizing speech. Classifications that discriminate against the exercise of constitutional rights per se stand on an altogether different footing. They must be supported by a "compelling" governmental purpose, and must be carefully examined to insure that the purpose is unrelated to mere hostility to the right being asserted. See, e.g., Shapiro v. Thompson, 394 U. S. 618, 394 U. S. 634 (1969).

Moreover, not only is this classification speech related; it also discriminates between otherwise indistinguishable parties on the basis of the content of their speech. Thus, California nightclub owners may present live shows and movies dealing with a wide variety of topics while maintaining their licenses. But if they choose to deal with sex, they are treated quite differently. Classifications based on the content of speech have long been disfavored, and must be viewed with the gravest suspicion. See, e.g., Cox v. Louisiana, 379 U. S. 536, 379 U. S. 556-558 (1965). Whether this test is thought to derive from equal protection analysis, see Police Department of Chicago v. Mosley, 408 U. S. 92 (1972); Niemotko v. Maryland, 340 U. S. 268 (1951), or directly from the substantive constitutional provision involved, see Cox v. Louisiana, supra; Schneider v. State, 308 U. S. 147 (1939), the result is the same: any law that has "no other purpose . . . than to chill the assertion of constitutional rights by penalizing those who choose to exercise them . . . [is] patently unconstitutional." United States v. Jackson, 390 U. S. 570, 390 U. S. 581 (1968).

As argued above, the constitutionally permissible purposes asserted to justify these regulations are too remote to satisfy the Government's burden when First Amendment rights are at stake. See supra at 409 U. S. 131-133.

It may be that the Government has an interest in suppressing lewd or "indecent" speech even when it occurs in private among consenting adults. Cf. United States v. Thirty-Seven Photographs, 402 U. S. 363, 402 U. S. 376 (1971). But cf. Stanley v. Georgia, 394 U. S. 557 (1969). That interest, however, must be balanced against the overriding interest of our citizens in freedom of thought and expression. Our prior decisions on obscenity set such a balance, and hold that the Government may suppress expression treating with sex only if it meets the three-pronged Roth-Memoirs test. We have said that

"[t]he door barring federal and state intrusion into this area cannot be left ajar; it must be kept tightly closed, and opened only the slightest crack necessary to prevent encroachment upon more important interests."

Roth v. United States, 354 U.S. at 354 U. S. 488. Because I can see no reason why we should depart from that standard in this case, I must respectfully dissent.

Notes

[1]Rule 143.3(1) provides in relevant part:

"No licensee shall permit any person to perform acts of or acts which simulate: "

"(a) Sexual intercourse, masturbation, sodomy, bestiality, oral copulation, flagellation or any sexual acts which are prohibited by law."

"(b) The touching, caressing or fondling on the breast, buttocks, anus or genitals."

"(c) The displaying of the pubic hair, anus, vulva or genitals."

Rule 143.4 prohibits:

"The showing of film, still pictures, electronic reproduction, or other visual reproductions depicting: "

"(1) Acts or simulated acts of sexual intercourse, masturbation, sodomy, bestiality, oral copulation, flagellation or any sexual acts which are prohibited by law."

"(2) Any person being touched, caressed or fondled on the breast, buttocks, anus or genitals."

"(3) Scenes wherein a person displays the vulva or the anus or the genitals."

"(4) Scenes wherein artificial devices or inanimate objects are employed to depict, or drawings are employed to portray, any of the prohibited activities described above."

[2] This is not an appropriate case for application of the abstention doctrine. Since these regulations are challenged on their face for overbreadth, no purpose would be served by awaiting a state court construction of them unless the principles announced in Younger v. Harris, 401 U. S. 37 (1971), govern. See Zwickler v. Koota, 389 U. S. 241, 389 U. S. 248-250 (1967). Thus far, however, we have limited the applicability of Younger to cases where the plaintiff has an adequate remedy in a pending criminal prosecution. See Younger v. Harris, supra, at 401 U. S. 43-44. Cf. Douglas v. City of Jeannette, 319 U. S. 157 (1943). But cf. Berryhill v. Gibson, 331 F.Supp. 122, 124 (MD Ala. 1971), probable jurisdiction noted, 408 U.S. 920 (1972). The California licensing provisions are, of course, civil in nature. Cf. Hearn v. Short, 327 F.Supp. 33 (SD Tex. 1971). Moreover, the Younger doctrine has been held to "have little force in the absence of a pending state proceeding." Lake Carriers' Assn. v. MacMullan, 406 U. S. 498, 406 U. S. 509 (1972)(emphasis added). There are at present no proceedings of any kind pending against these appellees. Finally, since the Younger doctrine rests heavily on federal deference to state administration of its own statutes, see Younger v. Harris, supra, at 401 U. S. 44-45, it is waivable by the State. Cf. Hostetter v. Idlewild Liquor Corp., 377 U. S. 324, 377 U. S. 329 (1964). Appellants have nowhere mentioned the Younger doctrine in their brief before this Court, and, when the case was brought to the attention of the attorney for the appellants during oral argument, he expressly eschewed reliance on it. In the court below, appellants specifically asked for a federal decision on the validity of California's regulations and stated that they did not think the court should abstain. See 326 F.Supp. 348, 351 (CD Cal. 1971).

[3] I am startled by the majority's suggestion that the regulations are constitutional on their face even though "specific future applications of [the statute] may engender concrete problems of constitutional dimension." (Quoting with approval Seagram & Sons v. Hostetter, 384 U. S. 35, 52 (1966). Ante at 409 U. S. 119 n. 5.) Ever since Thornhill v. Alabama, 310 U. S. 88 (1940), it has been thought that statutes which trench upon First Amendment rights are facially void even if the conduct of the party challenging them could be prohibited under a more narrowly drawn scheme. See, e.g., Baggett v. Bullitt, 377 U. S. 360, 377 U. S. 366 (1964); Coates v. City of Cincinnati, 402 U. S. 611, 402 U. S. 616 (1971); NAACP v. Button, 371 U. S. 415, 371 U. S. 432-433 (1963).

Nor is it relevant that the State here "sought to prevent [bacchanalian revelries]," rather than performances by "scantily clad ballet troupe[s]." Whatever the State "sought" to do, the fact is that these regulations cover both these activities. And it should be clear that a praiseworthy legislative motive can no more rehabilitate an unconstitutional statute than an illicit motive can invalidate a proper statute.

[4] Indeed, there are some indications in the legislative history that California adopted these regulations for the specific purpose of evading those standards. Thus, Captain Robert Devin of the Los Angeles Police Department testified that the Department favored adoption of the new regulations for the following reason:

"While statutory law has been available to us to regulate what was formerly considered as antisocial behavior, the federal and state judicial system has, through a series of similar decisions, effectively emasculated law enforcement in its effort to contain and to control the growth of pornography and of obscenity and of behavior that is associated with this kind of performance."

See also testimony of Roy E. June, City Attorney of the City of Costa Mesa; testimony of Richard C. Hirsch, Office of Los Angeles County District Attorney. App. 117.

[5] I do not mean to suggest that this test need be rigidly applied in all situations. Different standards may be applicable when children are involved, see Ginsberg v. New York, 390 U. S. 629 (1968); when a consenting adult possesses putatively obscene material in his own home, see Stanley v. Georgia, 394 U. S. 557 (1969); or when the material, by the nature of its presentation, cannot be viewed as a whole, see Rabe v. Washington, 405 U. S. 313, 405 U. S. 317 n. 2 (1972) (BURGER, C.J., concurring). Similarly, I do not mean to foreclose the possibility that even the Roth-Memoirs test will ultimately be found insufficient to protect First Amendment interests when consenting adults view putatively obscene material in private. Cf. Redrup v. New York, 386 U. S. 767 (1967). But cf. United States v. Reidel, 402 U. S. 351 (1971). But I do think that, at very least, Roth-Memoirs sets an absolute limit on the kinds of speech that can be altogether read out of the First Amendment for purposes of consenting adults.

[6] Cf. Fuller, Changing Society Puts Taste to the Test, The National Observer, June 10, 1972, p. 24:

"Context is the essence of esthetic judgment. . . . There is a world of difference between Playboy and less pretentious girly magazines on the one hand, and on the other, The Nude, a picture selection from the whole history of art by that fine teacher and interpreter of civilization, Kenneth Clark. People may be just as naked in one or the other, the bodies inherently just as beautiful, but the context of the former is vulgar, of the latter, esthetic."

"The same words, the same actions, that are cheap and tawdry in one book or play may contribute to the sublimity, comic universality, or tragic power of others. For a viable theory of taste, context is all."

[7] Moreover, even if the O'Brien test were here applicable, it is far from clear that it has been satisfied. For example, most of the evils that the State alleges are caused by appellees' performances are already punishable under California law. See n. 11, infra. Since the less drastic alternative of criminal prosecution is available to punish these violations, it is hard to see how "the incidental restriction on alleged First Amendment freedoms is no greater than is essential" to further the State's interest.

[8] The Court pointed out that the statute

"does not distinguish between public and private destruction, and it does not punish only destruction engaged in for the purpose of expressing views. . . . A law prohibiting destruction of Selective Service certificates no more abridges free speech on its face than a motor vehicle law prohibiting the destruction of drivers' licenses, or a tax law prohibiting the destruction of books and records."

391 U.S. at 391 U. S. 375.

[9] Of course, the State need not meet the clear and present danger test if the material in question is obscene. See Roth v. United States, 354 U. S. 476 (1957). But, as argued above, the difficulty with California's rules is that they do not conform to the Roth test and therefore regulate material that is not obscene. See supra at 409 U. S. 126-127.

[10] This case might be different if the State asserted a primary interest in stopping the very acts performed by these dancers and actors. However, I have serious doubts whether the State may constitutionally assert an interest in regulating any sexual act between consenting adults. Cf. Griswold v. Connecticut, 381 U. S. 479 (1965). Moreover, it is unnecessary to reach that question in this case, since the State's regulations are plainly not designed to stop the acts themselves, most of which are, in fact, legal when done in private. Rather, the State punishes the acts only when done in public as part of a dramatic presentation. Cf. United States v. O'Brien, supra, at 391 U. S. 375. It must be, therefore, that the asserted state interest stems from the effect of the acts on the audience, rather than from a desire to stop the acts themselves. It should also be emphasized that this case does not present problems of an unwilling audience or of an audience composed of minors.

[11] Indeed, California already has statutes controlling virtually all of the misconduct said to flow from appellees' activities. See Calif.Penal Code § 647 (b)(Supp. 1972)(prostitution); Calif.Penal Code §§ 261, 263 (1970)(rape); Calif.Bus. & Prof.Code § 25657 (Supp. 1972)("B-Girl" activity); Calif.Health & Safety Code §§ 11500, 11501, 11721, 11910, 11912 (1964 and Supp. 1972)(sale and use of narcotics).

[12] Of course, it is true that Stanley does not govern this case, since Stanley dealt only with the private possession of obscene materials in one's own home. But in another sense, this case is stronger than Stanley. In Stanley, we held that the State's interest in the prevention of sex crimes did not justify laws restricting possession of certain materials, even though they were conceded to be obscene. It follows a fortiori that this interest is insufficient when the materials are not obscene and, indeed, are constitutionally protected.

[13] The Twenty-first Amendment, in addition to repealing the Eighteenth Amendment, provides:

"The transportation or importation into any State, Territory, or possession of the United States for delivery or use therein of intoxicating liquors, in violation of the laws thereof, is hereby prohibited."

[14] The text of the Amendment is based on the Webb-Kenyon Act, 37 Stat. 699,

which antedated prohibition. The Act was entitled "An Act Divesting intoxicating liquors of their interstate character in certain cases," and was designed to allow "dry" States to regulate the flow of alcohol across their borders. See, e.g., McCormick & Co. v. Brown, 286 U. S. 131, 286 U. S. 140-141 (1932); Clark Distilling Co. v. Western Maryland R. Co., 242 U. S. 311, 242 U. S. 324 (1917). The Twenty-first Amendment was intended to embed this principle permanently into the Constitution. As explained by its sponsor on the Senate floor,

"to assure the so-called dry States against the importation of intoxicating liquor into those States, it is proposed to write permanently into the Constitution a prohibition along that line."

"[T]he pending proposal will give the States that guarantee. When our Government was organized and the Constitution of the United States adopted, the States surrendered control over and regulation of interstate commerce. This proposal is restoring to the States, in effect, the right to regulate commerce respecting a single commodity -- namely, intoxicating liquor."

76 Cong. Rec. 4141 (remarks of Sen. Blaine).

[15] See Shapiro v. Thompson, 394 U. S. 618 (1969). But cf. Wyman v. James, 400 U. S. 309 (1971).

[16] See Sherbert v. Verner, 374 U. S. 398 (1963).

[17] See Speiser v. Randall, 357 U. S. 513 (1958).

[18] See, e.g., Pickering v. Board of Education, 391 U. S. 563 (1968); Keyishian v. Board of Regents, 385 U. S. 589 (1967); Baggett v. Bullitt, 377 U. S. 360 (1964).

[19] See, e.g., Baird v. State Bar of Arizona, 401 U. S. 1 (1971); Konigsberg v. State Bar, 353 U. S. 252 (1957); Schware v. Board of Bar Examiners, 353 U. S. 232 (1957). But cf. Law Students Civil Rights Research Council v. Wadmond, 401 U. S. 154 (1971); Konigsberg v. State Bar, 366 U. S. 36 (1961).

[20] See, e.g., Blount v. Rizzi, 400 U. S. 410 (1971); Hannegan v. Esquire Inc., 327 U. S. 146, 327 U. S. 156 (1946).

Shouldn't be a fee for due process: Justice Marshall's dissent in United States v. Kras (January 10, 1973)

MR. JUSTICE MARSHALL, dissenting.

The dissent of MR. JUSTICE STEWART, in which I have joined, makes clear the majority's failure to distinguish this case from Boddie v. Connecticut, 401 U.S. 371 (1971). I add only some comments on the extraordinary route by which the majority reaches its conclusion.

A. The majority notes that the minimum amount that appellee Kras must pay each week if he is permitted to pay the filing fees in installments is only $1.28. It says that "this much available revenue should be within his able-bodied reach." Ante, at 449.

Appellee submitted an affidavit in which he claimed that he was "unable to pay or promise to pay the filing fees, even in small installments." App. 5. This claim was supported by detailed statements of his financial condition. The affidavit was unchallenged below, but the majority does challenge it. The District Judge properly accepted the factual allegations as true. See, e. g., Poller v. Columbia Broadcasting System, 368 U.S. 464 (1962); First National Bank of Arizona v. Cities Service Co., 391 U.S. 253 (1968); 35B C. J. S., Federal Civil Procedure 1197 n. 4 (1960). The majority seems to believe that it is not restrained by the traditional notion that judges must accept unchallenged, credible affidavits as true, for it disregards the factual allegations and the inferences that necessarily follow from them. I cannot treat that notion so cavalierly. 1

Even if Kras' statement that he was unable to pay the fees was an honest mistake, surely he cannot have been mistaken in saying that he could not promise to pay the fees. The majority does not directly impugn his good faith in making that statement. Yet if he cannot promise to pay the fees, he cannot get the interim relief from creditor harassment that, the majority says, may enable him to pay the fees.

But beyond all this, I cannot agree with the majority that it is so easy for the desperately poor to save $1.92 each week over the course of six months. The 1970 Census found that over 800,000 families in the Nation had annual incomes of less than $1,000 or $19.23 a week. U.S. Bureau of Census, Current Population Reports, series P-60, No. 80; U.S. Bureau of Census, Statistical Abstract of the United States 1972, p. 323. I see no reason to require that families in such straits sacrifice over 5% of their annual income as a prerequisite to getting a discharge in bankruptcy. 2

It may be easy for some people to think that weekly savings of less than $2 are no burden. But no one who has had close contact with poor people can fail to understand how close to the margin of survival many of them are. A sudden illness, for example, may destroy whatever savings they may have accumulated, and by eliminating a sense of security may destroy the incentive to save in the future. A pack or two of cigarettes may be, for them, not a routine purchase but a luxury indulged in only rarely. The desperately poor almost never go to see a movie, which the majority seems to believe is an almost weekly activity. They have more important things to do with what little money they have - like attempting to provide some comforts for a gravely ill child, as Kras must do.

It is perfectly proper for judges to disagree about what the Constitution requires. But it is disgraceful for an interpretation of the Constitution to be premised upon unfounded assumptions about how people live.

B. The majority derives some solace from the denial of certiorari in In re Garland, 402 U.S. 966 (1971). Reliance on denial of certiorari for any proposition impairs the vitality of the discretion we exercise in controlling the cases we hear. See Brown v. Allen, 344 U.S. 443, 491 -492 (1953) (opinion of Frankfurter, J.). For all that the legal community knows, Mr. Justice Harlan did not join the dissent from denial of certiorari in that case for reasons different from those that the majority uses to distinguish this case from Boddie. Perhaps he believed that lower courts should have some time to consider the implications of Boddie. Most of the lower courts have refused to follow the First Circuit's decision in Garland, 428 F.2d 1185. See ante, at 453 n. 5 (STEWART, J., dissenting). Perhaps he thought that the record in that case made inappropriate any attempt to determine the scope of Boddie in that particular case. Or perhaps he had some other reason.

The point of our use of a discretionary writ is precisely to prohibit that kind of speculation. When we deny certiorari, no one, not even ourselves, should think that the denial indicates a view on the merits of the case. It ill serves judges of the courts throughout the country to tell them, as the majority does today, that in attempting to determine what the law is, they must read, not only the opinions of this Court, but also the thousands of cases in which we annually deny certiorari. 3

C. The majority says that "[t]he denial of access to the judicial forum in Boddie touched directly . . . on the marital relationship." It sees "no fundamental interest that is gained or lost depending on the availability of a discharge in bankruptcy." Ante, at 444, 445. If the case is to turn on distinctions between the role of courts in divorce cases and their role in bankruptcy cases, 4 I agree with MR. JUSTICE STEWART that this case and Boddie cannot be distinguished; the role of the Government in standing ready to enforce an otherwise continuing obligation is the same.

However, I would go further than MR. JUSTICE STEWART. I view the case as involving the right of access to the courts, the opportunity to be heard when one claims a legal right, and not just the right to a discharge in bankruptcy. 5 When a person raises a claim of right or entitlement under the laws, the only forum in our legal system empowered to determine that claim is a court. Kras, for example, claims that he has a right under the Bankruptcy Act to be free of any duty to pay his creditors. There is no way to determine whether he has such a right except by adjudicating his claim. 6 Failure to do so denies him access to the courts.

The legal system is, of course, not so pervasive as to preclude private resolution of disputes. But private settlements do not determine the validity of claims of right. Such questions can be authoritatively resolved only in courts. It is in that sense, I believe, that we should consider the emphasis in Boddie on the exclusiveness of the judicial forum - and give Kras his day in court.

[1] The majority also misrepresents appellee's financial condition. It says that $1.28 "is a sum less than the payments Kras makes on his couch of negligible value in storage." Ante, at 449. Nowhere in the slender record of this case can I find any statement that appellee is actually paying anything for the storage of the couch. He said only that he "owed payments of $6 per month" for storage. App. 5 (emphasis added). He also stated that he owed $6, 428.69, but I would hardly read that to mean that he was paying that much to anyone.

[2] The majority, in citing the "record of achievement" of the bankruptcy system in terminating 107, 481 no-asset cases in the fiscal year 1969, ante, at 448 n. 7, relies on spectral evidence. Because the filing fees bar relief through the bankruptcy system,

statistics showing how many people got relief through that system are unenlightening on the question of how many people could not use the system because they were too poor. I do not know how many people cannot afford to pay a $50 fee in installments. But I find nothing in the majority's opinion to convince me that due process is afforded a person who cannot receive a discharge in bankruptcy because he is too poor. Even if only one person is affected by the filing fees, he is denied due process.

[3] That one of us undertook to write a dissent, even a "pointed dissent," from the denial of certiorari should suggest, again, nothing at all about the views of any other Members of the Court on the merits of the petition. Surely each of us has seen many cases in which a colleague's dissent from the denial of certiorari pointed to an issue of great concern that we thought should be decided by this Court, but in which we did not join because we did not consider the case to be an appropriate vehicle for determination of that issue.

[4] I am intrigued by the majority's suggestion that, because the granting of a divorce impinges on "associational interests," the right to a divorce is constitutionally protected. Are we to require that state divorce laws serve compelling state interests? For example, if a State chooses to allow divorces only when one party is shown to have committed adultery, must its refusal to allow them when the parties claim irreconcilable differences be justified by some compelling state interest? I raise these questions only to suggest that the majority's focus on the relative importance in the constitutional scheme of divorce and bankruptcy is misplaced. What is involved is the importance of access to the courts, either to remove an obligation that other branches of the government stand ready to enforce, as MR. JUSTICE STEWART sees it, or to determine claims of right, as I see it.

[5] The majority suggests that no such right is involved, because Congress could have committed the administration of the Bankruptcy Act to a nonjudicial agency. Ante, at 447. I have some doubt about the proposition that a statutorily created right can be finally determined by an agency, with no method for a disappointed claimant to secure judicial review. But I have no doubt that Congress could not provide that only the well-off had the right to present their claims to the agency. As should be clear, the question is one of access to the forum empowered to determine the claim of right; it is only shorthand to call this a question of access to the courts.

[6] It might be said that the right he claims does not come into play until he has fulfilled a condition precedent by paying the filing fees. But the distinction between procedure and substance is not unknown in the law and can be drawn on to counter that argument.

Equalize school-funding: Justice Marshall's dissent in San Antonio Independent School District v. Rodriguez (March 21, 1973) [Appendices omitted]

MR. JUSTICE MARSHALL, with whom MR. JUSTICE DOUGLAS concurs, dissenting.

The Court today decides, in effect, that a State may constitutionally vary the quality of education which it offers its children in accordance with the amount of taxable wealth located in the school districts within which they reside. The majority's decision represents an abrupt departure from the mainstream of recent state and federal court decisions concerning the unconstitutionality of state educational financing schemes dependent upon taxable local wealth. 1 More unfortunately, though, the majority's holding can only be seen as a retreat from our historic commitment to equality of educational opportunity and as unsupportable acquiescence in a system which deprives children in their earliest years of the chance to reach their full potential as citizens. The Court does this despite the absence of any substantial justification for a scheme which arbitrarily channels educational resources in accordance with the fortuity of the amount of taxable wealth within each district.

In my judgment, the right of every American to an equal start in life, so far as the provision of a state service as important as education is concerned, is far too vital to permit state discrimination on grounds as tenuous as those presented by this record. Nor can I accept the notion that it is sufficient to remit these appellees to the vagaries of the political process which, contrary to the majority's suggestion, has proved singularly unsuited to the task of providing a remedy for this discrimination. 2 I, for one, am unsatisfied with the hope of an ultimate "political" solution sometime in the indefinite future while, in the meantime, countless children unjustifiably receive inferior educations that "may affect their hearts and minds in a way unlikely ever to be undone." Brown v. Board of Education, 347 U.S. 483, 494 (1954). I must therefore respectfully dissent.

I

The Court acknowledges that "substantial interdistrict disparities in school expenditures" exist in Texas, ante, at 15, and that these disparities are "largely attributable to differences in the amounts of money collected through local property taxation," ante, at 16. But instead of closely examining the seriousness of these disparities and the invidiousness of the Texas financing scheme, the Court undertakes an elaborate exploration of the efforts Texas has purportedly made to close the gaps between its districts in terms of levels of district wealth and resulting educational funding. Yet, however praiseworthy Texas' equalizing efforts, the issue in this case is not whether Texas is doing its best to ameliorate the worst features of a discriminatory scheme but, rather, whether the scheme itself is in fact unconstitutionally discriminatory in the face of the Fourteenth Amendment's guarantee of equal protection of the laws. When the Texas financing scheme is taken as a whole, I do not think it can be doubted that it produces a discriminatory impact on substantial numbers of the school-age children of the State of Texas.

A

Funds to support public education in Texas are derived from three sources: local ad valorem property taxes; the Federal Government; and the state government. 3 It is enlightening to consider these in order.

Under Texas law, the only mechanism provided the local school district for raising new, unencumbered revenues is the power to tax property located within its boundaries. 4 At the same time, the Texas financing scheme effectively restricts the use of monies raised by local property taxation to the support of public education within the boundaries of the district in which they are raised, since any such taxes must be approved by a majority of the property-taxpaying voters of the district. 5

The significance of the local property tax element of the Texas financing scheme is apparent from the fact that it provides the funds to meet some 40% of the cost of public education for Texas as a whole. 6 Yet the amount of revenue that any particular Texas district can raise is dependent on two factors - its tax rate and its amount of taxable property. The first factor is determined by the property-taxpaying voters of the district. 7 But, regardless of the enthusiasm of the local voters for public education, the second factor - the taxable property wealth of the district - necessarily restricts the district's ability to raise funds to support public education. 8 Thus, even though the voters of two Texas districts may be willing to make the same tax effort, the results for the districts will be substantially different if one is property rich while the other is property poor. The necessary effect of the Texas local property tax is, in short, to favor property-rich districts and to disfavor property-poor ones.

The seriously disparate consequences of the Texas local property tax, when that tax is considered alone, are amply illustrated by data presented to the District Court by appellees. These data included a detailed study of a sample of 110 Texas school districts 9 for the 1967-1968 school year conducted by Professor Joel S. Berke of Syracuse University's Educational Finance Policy Institute. Among other things, this study revealed that the 10 richest districts examined, each of which had more than $100,000 in taxable property per pupil, raised through local effort an average of $610 per pupil, whereas the four poorest districts studied, each of which had less than $10,000 in taxable property per pupil, were able to raise only an average of $63 per pupil. 10 And, as the Court effectively recognizes, ante, at 27, this correlation between the amount of taxable property per pupil and the amount of local revenues per pupil holds true for the 96 districts in between the richest and poorest districts. 11

It is clear, moreover, that the disparity of per-pupil revenues cannot be dismissed as the result of lack of local effort - that is, lower tax rates - by property-poor districts. To the contrary, the data presented below indicate that the poorest districts tend to have the highest tax rates and the richest districts tend to have the lowest tax rates. 12 Yet, despite the apparent extra effort being made by the poorest districts, they are unable even to begin to match the richest districts in terms of the production of local revenues. For example, the 10 richest districts studied by Professor Berke were able to produce $585 per pupil with an equalized tax rate of 31 on $100 of equalized valuation, but the four poorest districts studied, with an equalized rate of 70 on $100 of equalized valuation, were able to produce only $60 per pupil. 13 Without more, this state-imposed system of educational funding presents a serious picture of widely varying treatment of Texas school districts, and thereby of Texas schoolchildren, in terms of the amount of funds available for public education.

Nor are these funding variations corrected by the other aspects of the Texas financing scheme. The Federal Government provides funds sufficient to cover only some 10% of the total cost of public education in Texas. 14 Furthermore, while these federal funds are not distributed in Texas solely on a per-pupil basis, appellants do not here contend that they are used in such a way as to ameliorate significantly the widely varying consequences for Texas school districts and schoolchildren of the local property tax element of the state financing scheme. 15

State funds provide the remaining some 50% of the monies spent on public education in Texas. 16 Technically, they are distributed under two programs. The first is the Available School Fund, for which provision is made in the Texas Constitution. 17 The Available School Fund is composed of revenues obtained from a number of sources, including receipts from the state ad valorem property tax, one-fourth of all monies collected by the occupation tax, annual contributions by the legislature from general revenues, and the revenues derived from the Permanent School Fund. 18 For the 1970-1971 school year the Available School Fund contained $296,000,000. The Texas Constitution requires that this money be distributed annually on a per capita basis 19 to the local school districts. Obviously, such a flat grant could not alone eradicate the funding differentials attributable to the local property tax. Moreover, today the Available School Fund is in reality simply one facet of the second state financing program, the Minimum Foundation School Program, 20 since each district's annual share of the Fund is deducted from the sum to which the district is entitled under the Foundation Program. 21

The Minimum Foundation School Program provides funds for three specific purposes: professional salaries, current operating expenses, and transportation expenses. 22 The State pays, on an overall basis, for approximately 80% of the cost of the Program; the remaining 20% is distributed among the local school districts under the Local Fund Assignment. 23 Each district's share of the Local Fund Assignment is determined by a complex "economic index" which is designed to allocate a larger share of the costs to property-rich districts than to property-poor districts. 24 Each district pays its share with revenues derived from local property taxation.

The stated purpose of the Minimum Foundation School Program is to provide certain basic funding for each local Texas school district. 25 At the same time, the Program was apparently intended to improve, to some degree, the financial position of property-poor districts relative to property-rich districts, since - through the use of the economic index - an effort is made to charge a disproportionate share of the costs of the Program to rich districts. 26 It bears noting, however, that substantial criticism has been leveled at the practical effectiveness of the economic index system of local cost allocation. 27 In theory, the index is designed to ascertain the relative ability of each district to contribute to the Local Fund Assignment from local property taxes. Yet the index is not developed simply on the basis of each district's taxable wealth. It also takes into account the district's relative income from manufacturing, mining, and agriculture, its payrolls, and its scholastic population. 28 It is difficult to discern precisely how these latter factors are predictive of a district's relative ability to raise revenues through local property taxes. Thus, in 1966, one of the consultants who originally participated in the development of the Texas economic index adopted in 1949 told the Governor's Committee on Public School Education: "The Economic Index approach to evaluating local ability offers a little better measure than sheer chance, but not much." 29

Moreover, even putting aside these criticisms of the economic index as a device for achieving meaningful district wealth equalization through cost allocation, poor districts still do not necessarily receive more state aid than property-rich districts. For the standards which currently determine the amount received from the Foundation School Program by any particular district 30 favor property-rich districts. 31 Thus, focusing on the same Edgewood Independent and Alamo Heights School Districts which the majority uses for purposes of illustration, we find that in 1967-1968 property-rich Alamo Heights, 32 which raised $333 per pupil on an equalized tax rate of 85 per $100 valuation, received $225 per pupil from the Foundation School Program, while property-poor Edgewood, 33 which raised only $26 per pupil with an equalized tax rate of $1.05 per $100 valuation, received only $222 per pupil from the Foundation School Program. 34 And, more recent data, which indicate that for the 1970-1971 school year Alamo Heights received $491 per pupil from the Program while Edgewood received only $356 per pupil, hardly suggest that the wealth gap between the districts is being narrowed by the State Program. To the contrary, whereas in 1967-1968 Alamo Heights received only $3 per pupil, or about 1%, more than Edgewood in state aid, by 1970-1971 the gap had widened to a difference of $135 per pupil, or about 38%. 35 It was data of this character that prompted the District Court to observe that "the current [state aid] system tends to subsidize the rich at the expense of the poor, rather than the other way around." 36 337 F. Supp. 280, 282. And even the appellants go no further here than to venture that the Minimum Foundation School Program has "a mildly equalizing effect." 37

Despite these facts, the majority continually emphasizes how much state aid has, in recent years, been given to property-poor Texas school districts. What the Court fails to emphasize is the cruel irony of how much more state aid is being given to property-rich Texas school districts on top of their already substantial local property tax revenues. 38 Under any view, then, it is apparent that the state aid provided by the Foundation School Program fails to compensate for the large funding variations attributable to the local property tax element of the Texas financing scheme. And it is these stark differences in the treatment of Texas school districts and school children inherent in the Texas financing scheme, not the absolute amount of state aid provided to any particular school district, that are the crux of this case. There can, moreover, be no escaping the conclusion that the local property tax which is dependent upon taxable district property wealth is an essential feature of the Texas scheme for financing public education. 39

B

The appellants do not deny the disparities in educational funding caused by variations in taxable district property wealth. They do contend, however, that whatever the differences in per-pupil spending among Texas districts, there are no discriminatory consequences for the children of the disadvantaged districts. They recognize that what is at stake in this case is the quality of the public education provided Texas children in the districts in which they live. But appellants reject the suggestion that the quality of education in any particular district is determined by money - beyond some minimal level of funding which they believe to be assured every Texas district by the Minimum Foundation School Program. In their view, there is simply no denial of equal educational opportunity to any Texas schoolchildren as a result of the widely varying per-pupil spending power provided districts under the current financing scheme.

In my view, though, even an unadorned restatement of this contention is sufficient to reveal its absurdity. Authorities concerned with educational quality no doubt disagree as to the significance of variations in per-pupil spending. 40 Indeed, conflicting expert testimony was presented to the District Court in this case concerning the effect of spending variations on educational achievement. 41 We sit, however, not to resolve disputes over educational theory but to enforce our Constitution. It is an inescapable fact that if one district has more funds available per pupil than another district, the former will have greater choice in educational planning than will the latter. In this regard, I believe the question of discrimination in educational quality must be deemed to be an objective one that looks to what the State provides its children, not to what the children are able to do with what they receive. That a child forced to attend an underfunded school with poorer physical facilities, less experienced teachers, larger classes, and a narrower range of courses than a school with substantially more funds - and thus with greater choice in educational planning - may nevertheless excel is to the credit of the child, not the State, cf. Missouri ex rel. Gaines v. Canada, 305 U.S. 337, 349 (1938). Indeed, who can ever measure for such a child the opportunities lost and the talents wasted for want of a broader, more enriched education? Discrimination in the opportunity to learn that is afforded a child must be our standard.

Hence, even before this Court recognized its duty to tear down the barriers of state-enforced racial segregation in public education, it acknowledged that inequality in the educational facilities provided to students may be discriminatory state action as contemplated by the Equal Protection Clause. As a basis for striking down state-enforced segregation of a law school, the Court in Sweatt v. Painter, 339 U.S. 629, 633 -634 (1950), stated:

"[W]e cannot find substantial equality in the educational opportunities offered white and Negro law students by the State. In terms of number of the faculty, variety of courses and opportunity for specialization, size of the student body, scope of the library, availability of law review and similar activities, the [whites-only] Law School is superior. . . . It is difficult to believe that one who had a free choice between these law schools would consider the question close."

See also McLaurin v. Oklahoma State Regents for Higher Education, 339 U.S. 637 (1950). Likewise, it is difficult to believe that if the children of Texas had a free choice, they would choose to be educated in districts with fewer resources, and hence with more antiquated plants, less experienced teachers, and a less diversified curriculum. In fact, if financing variations are so insignificant to educational quality, it is difficult to understand why a number of our country's wealthiest school districts, which have no legal obligation to argue in support of the constitutionality of the Texas legislation, have nevertheless zealously pursued its cause before this Court. 42

The consequences, in terms of objective educational input, of the variations in district funding caused by the Texas financing scheme are apparent from the data introduced before the District Court. For example, in 1968-1969, 100% of the teachers in the property-rich Alamo Heights School District had college degrees. 43 By contrast, during the same school year only 80.02% of the teachers had college degrees in the property poor Edgewood Independent School District. 44 Also, in 1968-1969, approximately 47% of the teachers in the Edgewood District were on emergency teaching permits, whereas only 11% of the teachers in Alamo Heights were on such permits. 45 This is undoubtedly a reflection of the fact that the top of Edgewood's teacher salary scale was approximately 80% of Alamo Heights'. 46 And, not surprisingly, the teacher-student ratio varies significantly between the two districts. 47 In other words, as might be expected, a difference in the funds available to districts results in a difference in educational inputs available for a child's public education in Texas. For constitutional purposes, I believe this situation, which is directly attributable to the Texas financing scheme, raises a grave question of state-created discrimination in the provision of public education. Cf. Gaston County v. United States, 395 U.S. 285, 293 -294 (1969).

At the very least, in view of the substantial interdistrict disparities in funding and in resulting educational inputs shown by appellees to exist under the Texas financing scheme, the burden of proving that these disparities do not in fact affect the quality of children's education must fall upon the appellants. Cf. Hobson v. Hansen, 327 F. Supp. 844, 860-861 (DC 1971). Yet appellants made no effort in the District Court to demonstrate that educational quality is not affected by variations in funding and in resulting inputs. And, in this Court, they have argued no more than that the relationship is ambiguous. This is hardly sufficient to overcome appellees' prima facie showing of state-created discrimination between the schoolchildren of Texas with respect to objective educational opportunity.

Nor can I accept the appellants' apparent suggestion that the Texas Minimum Foundation School Program effectively eradicates any discriminatory effects otherwise resulting from the local property tax element of the Texas financing scheme. Appellants assert that, despite its imperfections, the Program "does guarantee an adequate education to every child." 48 The majority, in considering the constitutionality of the Texas financing scheme, seems to find substantial merit in this contention, for it tells us that the Foundation Program "was designed to provide an adequate minimum educational offering in every school in the State," ante, at 45, and that the Program "assur[es] a basic education for every child," ante, at 49. But I fail to understand how the constitutional problems inherent in the financing scheme are eased by the Foundation Program. Indeed, the precise thrust of the appellants' and the Court's remarks are not altogether clear to me.

The suggestion may be that the state aid received via the Foundation Program sufficiently improves the position of property-poor districts vis-a-vis property-rich districts - in terms of educational funds - to eliminate any claim of interdistrict discrimination in available educational resources which might otherwise exist if educational funding were dependent solely upon local property taxation. Certainly the Court has recognized that to demand precise equality of treatment is normally unrealistic, and thus minor differences inherent in any practical context usually will not make out a substantial equal protection claim. See, e. g., Mayer v. City of Chicago, 404 U.S. 189, 194 - 195 (1971); Draper v. Washington, 372 U.S. 487, 495 -496 (1963); Bain Peanut Co. v. Pinson, 282 U.S. 499, 501 (1931). But, as has already been seen, we are hardly presented here with some de minimis claim of discrimination resulting from the play necessary in any functioning system; to the contrary, it is clear that the Foundation Program utterly fails to ameliorate the seriously discriminatory effects of the local property tax. 49

Alternatively, the appellants and the majority may believe that the Equal Protection Clause cannot be offended by substantially unequal state treatment of persons who are similarly situated so long as the State provides everyone with some unspecified amount of education which evidently is "enough." 50 The basis for such a novel view is far from clear. It is, of course, true that the Constitution does not require precise equality in the treatment of all persons. As Mr. Justice Frankfurter explained:

"The equality at which the `equal protection' clause aims is not a disembodied equality. The Fourteenth Amendment enjoins `the equal protection of the laws,' and laws are not abstract propositions. . . . The Constitution does not require things which are different in fact or opinion to be treated in law as though they were the same." Tigner v. Texas, 310 U.S. 141, 147 (1940).

See also Douglas v. California, 372 U.S. 353, 357 (1963); Goesaert v. Cleary, 335 U.S. 464, 466 (1948). But this Court has never suggested that because some "adequate" level of benefits is provided to all, discrimination in the provision of services is therefore constitutionally excusable. The Equal Protection Clause is not addressed to the minimal sufficiency but rather to the unjustifiable inequalities of state action. It mandates nothing less than that "all persons similarly circumstanced shall be treated alike." F. S. Royster Guano Co. v. Virginia, 253 U.S. 412, 415 (1920).

Even if the Equal Protection Clause encompassed some theory of constitutional adequacy, discrimination in the provision of educational opportunity would certainly seem to be a poor candidate for its application. Neither the majority nor appellants inform us how judicially manageable standards are to be derived for determining how much education is "enough" to excuse constitutional discrimination. One would think that the majority would heed its own fervent affirmation of judicial self-restraint before undertaking the complex task of determining at large what level of education is constitutionally sufficient. Indeed, the majority's apparent reliance upon the adequacy of the educational opportunity assured by the Texas Minimum Foundation School Program seems fundamentally inconsistent with its own recognition that educational authorities are unable to agree upon what makes for educational quality, see ante, at 42-43 and n. 86 and at 47 n. 101. If, as the majority stresses, such authorities are uncertain as to the impact of various levels of funding on educational quality, I fail to see where it finds the expertise to divine that the particular levels of funding provided by the Program assure an adequate educational opportunity - much less an education substantially equivalent in quality to that which a higher level of funding might provide. Certainly appellants' mere assertion before this Court of the adequacy of the education guaranteed by the Minimum Foundation School Program cannot obscure the constitutional implications of the discrimination in educational funding and objective educational inputs resulting from the local property tax - particularly since the appellees offered substantial uncontroverted evidence before the District Court impugning the now much-touted "adequacy" of the education guaranteed by the Foundation Program. 51

In my view, then, it is inequality - not some notion of gross inadequacy - of educational opportunity that raises a question of denial of equal protection of the laws. I find any other approach to the issue unintelligible and without directing principle. Here, appellees have made a substantial showing of wide variations in educational funding and the resulting educational opportunity afforded to the schoolchildren of Texas. This discrimination is, in large measure, attributable to significant disparities in the taxable wealth of local Texas school districts. This is a sufficient showing to raise a substantial question of discriminatory state action in violation of the Equal Protection Clause. 52

C

Despite the evident discriminatory effect of the Texas financing scheme, both the appellants and the majority raise substantial questions concerning the precise character of the disadvantaged class in this case. The District Court concluded that the Texas financing scheme draws "distinction between groups of citizens depending upon the wealth of the district in which they live" and thus creates a disadvantaged class composed of persons living in property-poor districts. See 337 F. Supp., at 282. See also id., at 281. In light of the data introduced before the District Court, the conclusion that the schoolchildren of property-poor districts constitute a sufficient class for our purposes seems indisputable to me.

Appellants contend, however, that in constitutional terms this case involves nothing more than discrimination against local school districts, not against individuals, since on its face the state scheme is concerned only with the provision of funds to local districts. The result of the Texas financing scheme, appellants suggest, is merely that some local districts have more available revenues for education; others have less. In that respect, they point out, the States have broad discretion in drawing reasonable distinctions between their political subdivisions. See Griffin v. County School Board of Prince Edward County, 377 U.S. 218, 231 (1964); McGowan v. Maryland, 366 U.S. 420, 427 (1961); Salsburg v. Maryland, 346 U.S. 545, 550 -554 (1954).

But this Court has consistently recognized that where there is in fact discrimination against individual interests, the constitutional guarantee of equal protection of the laws is not inapplicable simply because the discrimination is based upon some group characteristic such as geographic location. See Gordon v. Lance, 403 U.S. 1, 4 (1971); Reynolds v. Sims, 377 U.S. 533, 565 -566 (1964); Gray v. Sanders 372 U.S. 368, 379 (1963). Texas has chosen to provide free public education for all its citizens, and it has embodied that decision in its constitution. 53 Yet, having established public education for its citizens, the State, as a direct consequence of the variations in local property wealth endemic to Texas' financing scheme, has provided some Texas schoolchildren with substantially less resources for their education than others. Thus, while on its face the Texas scheme may merely discriminate between local districts, the impact of that discrimination falls directly upon the children whose educational opportunity is dependent upon where they happen to live. Consequently, the District Court correctly concluded that the Texas financing scheme discriminates, from a constitutional perspective, between schoolchildren on the basis of the amount of taxable property located within their local districts.

In my Brother STEWART'S view, however, such a description of the discrimination inherent in this case is apparently not sufficient, for it fails to define the "kind of objectively identifiable classes" that he evidently perceives to be necessary for a claim to be "cognizable under the Equal Protection Clause," ante, at 62. He asserts that this is also the view of the majority, but he is unable to cite, nor have I been able to find, any portion of the Court's opinion which remotely suggests that there is no objectively identifiable or definable class in this case. In any event, if he means to suggest that an essential predicate to equal protection analysis is the precise identification of the particular individuals who compose the disadvantaged class, I fail to find the source from which he derives such a requirement. Certainly such precision is not analytically necessary. So long as the basis of the discrimination is clearly identified, it is possible to test it against the State's purpose for such discrimination - whatever the standard of equal protection analysis employed. 54 This is clear from our decision only last Term in Bullock v. Carter, 405 U.S. 134 (1972), where the Court, in striking down Texas' primary filing fees as violative of equal protection, found no impediment to equal protection analysis in the fact that the members of the disadvantaged class could not be readily identified. The Court recognized that the filing-fee system tended "to deny some voters the opportunity to vote for a candidate of their choosing; at the same time it gives the affluent the power to place on the ballot their own names or the names of persons they favor." Id., at 144. The Court also recognized that "[t]his disparity in voting power based on wealth cannot be described by reference to discrete and precisely defined segments of the community as is typical of inequities challenged under the Equal Protection Clause . . . ." Ibid. Nevertheless, it concluded that "we would ignore reality were we not to recognize that this system falls with unequal weight on voters . . . according to their economic status." Ibid. The nature of the classification in Bullock was clear, although the precise membership of the disadvantaged class was not. This was enough in Bullock for purposes of equal protection analysis. It is enough here.

It may be, though, that my Brother STEWART is not in fact demanding precise identification of the membership of the disadvantaged class for purposes of equal protection analysis, but is merely unable to discern with sufficient clarity the nature of the discrimination charged in this case. Indeed, the Court itself displays some uncertainty as to the exact nature of the discrimination and the resulting disadvantaged class alleged to exist in this case. See ante, at 19-20. It is, of course, essential to equal protection analysis to have a firm grasp upon the nature of the discrimination at issue. In fact, the absence of such a clear, articulable understanding of the nature of alleged discrimination in a particular instance may well suggest the absence of any real discrimination. But such is hardly the case here.

A number of theories of discrimination have, to be sure, been considered in the course of this litigation. Thus, the District Court found that in Texas the poor and minority group members tend to live in property-poor districts, suggesting discrimination on the basis of both personal wealth and race. See 337 F. Supp., at 282 and n. 3. The Court goes to great lengths to discredit the data upon which the District Court relied, and thereby its conclusion that poor people live in property-poor districts. 55 Although I have serious doubts as to the correctness of the Court's analysis in rejecting the data submitted below, 56 I have no need to join issue on these factual disputes.

I believe it is sufficient that the overarching form of discrimination in this case is between the schoolchildren of Texas on the basis of the taxable property wealth of the districts in which they happen to live. To understand both the precise nature of this discrimination and the parameters of the disadvantaged class it is sufficient to consider the constitutional principle which appellees contend is controlling in the context of educational financing. In their complaint appellees asserted that the Constitution does not permit local district wealth to be determinative of educational opportunity. 57 This is simply another way of saying, as the District Court concluded, that consistent with the guarantee of equal protection of the laws, "the quality of public education may not be a function of wealth, other than the wealth of the state as a whole." 337 F. Supp., at 284. Under such a principle, the children of a district are excessively advantaged if that district has more taxable property per pupil than the average amount of taxable property per pupil considering the State as a whole. By contrast, the children of a district are disadvantaged if that district has less taxable property per pupil than the state average. The majority attempts to disparage such a definition of the disadvantaged class as the product of an "artificially defined level" of district wealth. Ante. at 28. But such is clearly not the case, for this is the definition unmistakably dictated by the constitutional principle for which appellees have argued throughout the course of this litigation. And I do not believe that a clearer definition of either the disadvantaged class of Texas schoolchildren or the allegedly unconstitutional discrimination suffered by the members of that class under the present Texas financing scheme could be asked for, much less needed. 58 Whether this discrimination, against the schoolchildren of property-poor districts, inherent in the Texas financing scheme, is violative of the Equal Protection Clause is the question to which we must now turn.

II

To avoid having the Texas financing scheme struck down because of the interdistrict variations in taxable property wealth, the District Court determined that it was insufficient for appellants to show merely that the State's scheme was rationally related to some legitimate state purpose; rather, the discrimination inherent in the scheme had to be shown necessary to promote a "compelling state interest" in order to withstand constitutional scrutiny. The basis for this determination was twofold: first, the financing scheme divides citizens on a wealth basis, a classification which the District Court viewed as highly suspect; and second, the discriminatory scheme directly affects what it considered to be a "fundamental interest," namely, education.

This Court has repeatedly held that state discrimination which either adversely affects a "fundamental interest," see, e. g., Dunn v. Blumstein, 405 U.S. 330, 336 -342 (1972); Shapiro v. Thompson, 394 U.S. 618, 629 -631 (1969), or is based on a distinction of a suspect character, see, e. g., Graham v. Richardson, 403 U.S. 365, 372 (1971); McLaughlin v. Florida, 379 U.S. 184, 191 -192 (1964), must be carefully scrutinized to ensure that the scheme is necessary to promote a substantial, legitimate state interest. See, e. g., Dunn v. Blumstein, supra, at 342-343; Shapiro v. Thompson, supra, at 634. The majority today concludes, however, that the Texas scheme is not subject to such a strict standard of review under the Equal Protection Clause. Instead, in its view, the Texas scheme must be tested by nothing more than that lenient standard of rationality which we have traditionally applied to discriminatory state action in the context of economic and commercial matters. See, e. g., McGowan, v. Maryland, 366 U.S., at 425 -426; Morey v. Doud, 354 U.S. 457, 465 -466 (1957); F. S. Royster Guano Co. v. Virginia, 253 U.S., at 415; Lindsley v. Natural Carbonic Gas Co., 220 U.S. 61, 78 -79 (1911). By so doing, the Court avoids the telling task of searching for a substantial state interest which the Texas financing scheme, with its variations in taxable district property wealth, is necessary to further. I cannot accept such an emasculation of the Equal Protection Clause in the context of this case.

A

To begin, I must once more voice my disagreement with the Court's rigidified approach to equal protection analysis. See Dandridge v. Williams, 397 U.S. 471, 519 -521 (1970) (dissenting opinion); Richardson v. Belcher, 404 U.S. 78, 90 (1971) (dissenting opinion). The Court apparently seeks to establish today that equal protection cases fall into one of two neat categories which dictate the appropriate standard of review - strict scrutiny or mere rationality. But this Court's decisions in the field of equal protection defy such easy categorization. A principled reading of what this Court has done reveals that it has applied a spectrum of standards in reviewing discrimination allegedly violative of the Equal Protection Clause. This spectrum clearly comprehends variations in the degree of care with which the Court will scrutinize particular classifications, depending, I believe, on the constitutional and societal importance of the interest adversely affected and the recognized invidiousness of the basis upon which the particular classification is drawn. I find in fact that many of the Court's recent decisions embody the very sort of reasoned approach to equal protection analysis for which I previously argued - that is, an approach in which "concentration [is] placed upon the character of the classification in question, the relative importance to individuals in the class discriminated against of the governmental benefits that they do not receive, and the asserted state interests in support of the classification." Dandridge v. Williams, supra, at 520-521 (dissenting opinion).

I therefore cannot accept the majority's labored efforts to demonstrate that fundamental interests, which call for strict scrutiny of the challenged classification, encompass only established rights which we are somehow bound to recognize from the text of the Constitution itself. To be sure, some interests which the Court has deemed to be fundamental for purposes of equal protection analysis are themselves constitutionally protected rights. Thus, discrimination against the guaranteed right of freedom of speech has called for strict judicial scrutiny. See Police Dept. of Chicago v. Mosley, 408 U.S. 92 (1972). Further, every citizen's right to travel interstate, although nowhere expressly mentioned in the Constitution, has long been recognized as implicit in the premises underlying that document: the right "was conceived from the beginning to be a necessary concomitant of the stronger Union the Constitution created." United States v. Guest, 383 U.S. 745, 758 (1966). See also Crandall v. Nevada, 6 Wall. 35, 48 (1868). Consequently, the Court has required that a state classification affecting the constitutionally protected right to travel must be "shown to be necessary to promote a compelling governmental interest." Shapiro v. Thompson, 394 U.S., at 634 . But it will not do to suggest that the "answer" to whether an interest is fundamental for purposes of equal protection analysis is always determined by whether that interest "is a right . . . explicitly or implicitly guaranteed by the Constitution," ante, at 33-34. 59

I would like to know where the Constitution guarantees the right to procreate, Skinner v. Oklahoma, 316 U.S. 535, 541 (1942), or the right to vote in state elections, e. g., Reynolds v. Sims, 377 U.S. 533 (1964), or the right to an appeal from a criminal conviction, e. g., Griffin v. Illinois, 351 U.S. 12 (1956). These are instances in which, due to the importance of the interests at stake, the Court has displayed a strong concern with the existence of discriminatory state treatment. But the Court has never said or indicated that these are interests which independently enjoy full-blown constitutional protection.

Thus, in Buck v. Bell, 274 U.S. 200 (1927), the Court refused to recognize a substantive constitutional guarantee of the right to procreate. Nevertheless, in Skinner v. Oklahoma, supra, at 541, the Court, without impugning the continuing validity of Buck v. Bell, held that "strict scrutiny" of state discrimination affecting procreation "is essential," for "[m]arriage and procreation are fundamental to the very existence and survival of the race." Recently, in Roe v. Wade, 410 U.S. 113, 152 -154 (1973), the importance of procreation has, indeed, been explained on the basis of its intimate relationship with the constitutional right of privacy which we have recognized. Yet the limited stature thereby accorded any "right" to procreate is evident from the fact that at the same time the Court reaffirmed its initial decision in Buck v. Bell. See Roe v. Wade, supra, at 154.

Similarly, the right to vote in state elections has been recognized as a "fundamental political right," because the Court concluded very early that it is "preservative of all rights." Yick Wo v. Hopkins, 118 U.S. 356, 370 (1886); see, e. g., Reynolds v. Sims, supra, at 561-562. For this reason, "this Court has made clear that a citizen has a constitutionally protected right to participate in elections on an equal basis with other citizens in the jurisdiction." Dunn v. Blumstein, 405 U.S., at 336 (emphasis added). The final source of such protection from inequality in the provision of the state franchise is, of course, the Equal Protection Clause. Yet it is clear that whatever degree of importance has been attached to the state electoral process when unequally distributed, the right to vote in state elections has itself never been accorded the stature of an independent constitutional guarantee. 60 See Oregon v. Mitchell, 400 U.S. 112 (1970); Kramer v. Union School District, 395 U.S. 621, 626 -629 (1969); Harper v. Virginia Bd. of Elections, 383 U.S. 663, 665 (1966).

Finally, it is likewise "true that a State is not required by the Federal Constitution to provide appellate courts or a right to appellate review at all." Griffin v. Illinois, 351 U.S., at 18 . Nevertheless, discrimination adversely affecting access to an appellate process which a State has chosen to provide has been considered to require close judicial scrutiny. See, e. g., Griffin v. Illinois, supra; Douglas v. California, 372 U.S. 353 (1963). 61

The majority is, of course, correct when it suggests that the process of determining which interests are fundamental is a difficult one. But I do not think the problem is insurmountable. And I certainly do not accept the view that the process need necessarily degenerate into an unprincipled, subjective "picking-and-choosing" between various interests or that it must involve this Court in creating "substantive constitutional rights in the name of guaranteeing equal protection of the laws," ante, at 33. Although not all fundamental interests are constitutionally guaranteed, the determination of which interests are fundamental should be firmly rooted in the text of the Constitution. The task in every case should be to determine the extent to which constitutionally guaranteed rights are dependent on interests not mentioned in the Constitution. As the nexus between the specific constitutional guarantee and the nonconstitutional interest draws closer, the nonconstitutional interest becomes more fundamental and the degree of judicial scrutiny applied when the interest is infringed on a discriminatory basis must be adjusted accordingly. Thus, it cannot be denied that interests such as procreation, the exercise of the state franchise, and access to criminal appellate processes are not fully guaranteed to the citizen by our Constitution. But these interests have nonetheless been afforded special judicial consideration in the face of discrimination because they are, to some extent, interrelated with constitutional guarantees. Procreation is now understood to be important because of its interaction with the established constitutional right of privacy. The exercise of the state franchise is closely tied to basic civil and political rights inherent in the First Amendment. And access to criminal appellate processes enhances the integrity of the range of rights 62 implicit in the Fourteenth Amendment guarantee of due process of law. Only if we closely protect the related interests from state discrimination do we ultimately ensure the integrity of the constitutional guarantee itself. This is the real lesson that must be taken from our previous decisions involving interests deemed to be fundamental.

The effect of the interaction of individual interests with established constitutional guarantees upon the degree of care exercised by this Court in reviewing state discrimination affecting such interests is amply illustrated by our decision last Term in Eisenstadt v. Baird, 405 U.S. 438 (1972). In Baird, the Court struck down as violative of the Equal Protection Clause a state statute which denied unmarried persons access to contraceptive devices on the same basis as married persons. The Court purported to test the statute under its traditional standard whether there is some rational basis for the discrimination effected. Id., at 446-447. In the context of commercial regulation, the Court has indicated that the Equal Protection Clause "is offended only if the classification rests on grounds wholly irrelevant to the achievement of the State's objective." See, e. g., McGowan v. Maryland, 366 U.S., at 425; Kotch v. Board of River Port Pilot Comm'rs, 330 U.S. 552, 557 (1947). And this lenient standard is further weighted in the State's favor by the fact that "[a] statutory discrimination will not be set aside if any state of facts reasonably may be conceived [by the Court] to justify it." McGowan v. Maryland, supra, at 426. But in Baird the Court clearly did not adhere to these highly tolerant standards of traditional rational review. For although there were conceivable state interests intended to be advanced by the statute - e. g., deterrence of premarital sexual activity and regulation of the dissemination of potentially dangerous articles - the Court was not prepared to accept these interests on their face, but instead proceeded to test their substantiality by independent analysis. See 405 U.S., at 449 -454. Such close scrutiny of the State's interests was hardly characteristic of the deference shown state classifications in the context of economic interests. See, e. g., Goesaert v. Cleary, 335 U.S. 464 (1948); Kotch v. Board of River Port Pilot Comm'rs, supra. Yet I think the Court's action was entirely appropriate, for access to and use of contraceptives bears a close relationship to the individual's constitutional right of privacy. See 405 U.S., at 453 -454; id., at 463-464

(WHITE, J., concurring in result). See also Roe v. Wade, 410 U.S., at 152 -153.

A similar process of analysis with respect to the invidiousness of the basis on which a particular classification is drawn has also influenced the Court as to the appropriate degree of scrutiny to be accorded any particular case. The highly suspect character of classifications based on race, 63 nationality, 64 or alienage 65 is well established. The reasons why such classifications call for close judicial scrutiny are manifold. Certain racial and ethnic groups have frequently been recognized as "discrete and insular minorities" who are relatively powerless to protect their interests in the political process. See Graham, v. Richardson, 403 U.S., at 372; cf. United States v. Carolene Products Co., 304 U.S. 144, 152 -153, n. 4 (1938). Moreover, race, nationality, or alienage is "`in most circumstances irrelevant' to any constitutionally acceptable legislative purpose, Hirabayashi v. United States, 320 U.S. 81, 100 ." McLaughlin v. Florida, 379 U.S., at 192 . Instead, lines drawn on such bases are frequently the reflection of historic prejudices rather than legislative rationality. It may be that all of these considerations, which make for particular judicial solicitude in the face of discrimination on the basis of race, nationality, or alienage, do not coalesce - or at least not to the same degree - in other forms of discrimination. Nevertheless, these considerations have undoubtedly influenced the care with which the Court has scrutinized other forms of discrimination.

In James v. Strange, 407 U.S. 128 (1972), the Court held unconstitutional a state statute which provided for recoupment from indigent convicts of legal defense fees paid by the State. The Court found that the statute impermissibly differentiated between indigent criminals in debt to the State and civil judgment debtors, since criminal debtors were denied various protective exemptions afforded civil judgment debtors. 66 The Court suggested that in reviewing the statute under the Equal Protection Clause, it was merely applying the traditional requirement that there be "`some rationality'" in the line drawn between the different types of debtors. Id., at 140. Yet it then proceeded to scrutinize the statute with less than traditional deference and restraint. Thus, the Court recognized "that state recoupment statutes may betoken legitimate state interests" in recovering expenses and discouraging fraud. Nevertheless, MR. JUSTICE POWELL, speaking for the Court, concluded that

"these interests are not thwarted by requiring more even treatment of indigent criminal defendants with other classes of debtors to whom the statute itself repeatedly makes reference. State recoupment laws, notwithstanding the state interests they may serve, need not blight in such discriminatory fashion the hopes of indigents for self-sufficiency and self-respect." Id., at 141-142.

The Court, in short, clearly did not consider the problems of fraud and collection that the state legislature might have concluded were peculiar to indigent criminal defendants to be either sufficiently important or at least sufficiently substantiated to justify denial of the protective exemptions afforded to all civil judgment debtors, to a class composed exclusively of indigent criminal debtors.

Similarly, in Reed v. Reed, 404 U.S. 71 (1971), the Court, in striking down a state statute which gave men preference over women when persons of equal entitlement apply for assignment as an administrator of a particular estate, resorted to a more stringent standard of equal protection review than that employed in cases involving commercial matters. The Court indicated that it was testing the claim of sex discrimination by nothing more than whether the line drawn bore "a rational relationship to a state objective," which it recognized as a legitimate effort to reduce the work of probate courts in choosing between competing applications for letters of administration. Id., at 76. Accepting such a purpose, the Idaho Supreme Court had thought the classification to be sustainable on the basis that the legislature might have reasonably concluded that, as a rule, men have more experience than women in business matters relevant to the administration of an estate. 93 Idaho 511, 514, 465 P.2d 635, 638 (1970). This Court, however, concluded that "[t]o give a mandatory preference to members of either sex over members of the other, merely to accomplish the elimination of hearings on the merits, is to make the very kind of arbitrary legislative choice forbidden by the Equal Protection Clause of the Fourteenth Amendment . . . ." 404 U.S., at 76 . This Court, in other words, was unwilling to consider a theoretical and unsubstantiated basis for distinction - however reasonable it might appear - sufficient to sustain a statute discriminating on the basis of sex.

James and Reed can only be understood as instances in which the particularly invidious character of the classification caused the Court to pause and scrutinize with more than traditional care the rationality of state discrimination. Discrimination on the basis of past criminality and on the basis of sex posed for the Court the specter of forms of discrimination which it implicitly recognized to have deep social and legal roots without necessarily having any basis in actual differences. Still, the Court's sensitivity to the invidiousness of the basis for discrimination is perhaps most apparent in its decisions protecting the interests of children born out of wedlock from discriminatory state action. See Weber v. Aetna Casualty & Surety Co., 406 U.S. 164 (1972); Levy v. Louisiana, 391 U.S. 68 (1968).

In Weber, the Court struck down a portion of a state workmen's compensation statute that relegated unacknowledged illegitimate children of the deceased to a lesser status with respect to benefits than that occupied by legitimate children of the deceased. The Court acknowledged the true nature of its inquiry in cases such as these: "What legitimate state interest does the classification promote? What fundamental personal rights might the classification endanger?" Id., at 173. Embarking upon a determination of the relative substantiality of the State's justifications for the classification, the Court rejected the contention that the classifications reflected what might be presumed to have been the deceased's preference of beneficiaries as "not compelling . . . where dependency on the deceased is a prerequisite to anyone's recovery . . . ." Ibid. Likewise, it deemed the relationship between the State's interest in encouraging legitimate family relationships and the burden placed on the illegitimates too tenuous to permit the classification to stand. Ibid. A clear insight into the basis of the Court's action is provided by its conclusion:

"[I]mposing disabilities on the illegitimate child is contrary to the basic concept of our system that legal burdens should bear some relationship to individual responsibility or wrongdoing. Obviously, no child is responsible for his birth and penalizing the illegitimate child is an ineffectual - as well as an unjust - way of deterring the parent. Courts are powerless to prevent the social opprobrium suffered by these hapless children, but the Equal Protection Clause does enable us to strike down discriminatory laws relating to status of birth . . . ." Id., at 175-176.

Status of birth, like the color of one's skin, is something which the individual cannot control, and should generally be irrelevant in legislative considerations. Yet illegitimacy has long been stigmatized by our society. Hence, discrimination on the basis of birth - particularly when it affects innocent children - warrants special judicial consideration.

In summary, it seems to me inescapably clear that this Court has consistently adjusted the care with which it will review state discrimination in light of the constitutional significance of the interests affected and the invidiousness of the particular classification. In the context of economic interests, we find that discriminatory state action is almost always sustained, for such interests are generally far removed from constitutional guarantees. Moreover, "[t]he extremes to which the Court has gone in dreaming up rational bases for state regulation in that area may in many instances be ascribed to a healthy revulsion from the Court's earlier excesses in using the Constitution to protect interests that have more than enough power to protect themselves in the legislative halls." Dandridge v. Williams, 397 U.S., at 520 (dissenting opinion). But the situation differs markedly when discrimination against important individual interests with constitutional implications and against particularly disadvantaged or powerless classes is involved. The majority suggests, however, that a variable standard of review would give this Court the appearance of a "superlegislature." Ante, at 31. I cannot agree. Such an approach seems to me a part of the guarantees of our Constitution and of the historic experiences with oppression of and discrimination against discrete, powerless minorities which underlie that document. In truth, the Court itself will be open to the criticism raised by the majority so long as it continues on its present course of effectively selecting in private which cases will be afforded special consideration without acknowledging the true basis of its action. 67 Opinions such as those in Reed and James seem drawn more as efforts to shield rather than to reveal the true basis of the Court's decisions. Such obfuscated action may be appropriate to a political body such as a legislature, but it is not appropriate to this Court. Open debate of the bases for the Court's action is essential to the rationality and consistency of our decisionmaking process. Only in this way can we avoid the label of legislature and ensure the integrity of the judicial process.

Nevertheless, the majority today attempts to force this case into the same category for purposes of equal protection analysis as decisions involving discrimination affecting commercial interests. By so doing, the majority singles this case out for analytic treatment at odds with what seems to me to be the clear trend of recent decisions in this Court, and thereby ignores the constitutional importance of the interest at stake and the invidiousness of the particular classification, factors that call for far more than the lenient scrutiny of the Texas financing scheme which the majority pursues. Yet if the discrimination inherent in the Texas scheme is scrutinized with the care demanded by the interest and classification present in this case, the unconstitutionality of that scheme is unmistakable.

B

Since the Court now suggests that only interests guaranteed by the Constitution are fundamental for purposes of equal protection analysis, and since it rejects the contention that public education is fundamental, it follows that the Court concludes that public education is not constitutionally guaranteed. It is true that this Court has never deemed the provision of free public education to be required by the Constitution. Indeed, it has on occasion suggested that state-supported education is a privilege bestowed by a State on its citizens. See Missouri ex rel. Gaines v. Canada, 305 U.S., at 349 . Nevertheless, the fundamental importance of education is amply indicated by the prior decisions of this Court, by the unique status accorded public education by our society, and by the close relationship between education and some of our most basic constitutional values.

The special concern of this Court with the educational process of our country is a matter of common knowledge. Undoubtedly, this Court's most famous statement on the subject is that contained in Brown v. Board of Education, 347 U.S., at 493 :

"Today, education is perhaps the most important function of state and local governments. Compulsory school attendance laws and the great expenditures for education both demonstrate our recognition of the importance of education to our democratic society. It is required in the performance of our most basic public responsibilities, even service in the armed forces. It is the very foundation of good citizenship. Today it is a principal instrument in awakening the child to cultural values, in preparing him for later professional training, and in helping him to adjust normally to his environment. . . ."

Only last Term, the Court recognized that "[p]roviding public schools ranks at the very apex of the function of a State." Wisconsin v. Yoder, 406 U.S. 205, 213 (1972). This is clearly borne out by the fact that in 48 of our 50 States the provision of public education is mandated by the state constitution. 68 No other state function is so uniformly recognized 69 as an essential element of our society's well-being. In large measure, the explanation for the special importance attached to education must rest, as the Court recognized in Yoder, id., at 221, on the facts that "some degree of education is necessary to prepare citizens to participate effectively and intelligently in our open political system . . .," and that "education prepares individuals to be self-reliant and self-sufficient participants in society." Both facets of this observation are suggestive of the substantial relationship which education bears to guarantees of our Constitution.

Education directly affects the ability of a child to exercise his First Amendment rights, both as a source and as a receiver of information and ideas, whatever interests he may pursue in life. This Court's decision in Sweezy v. New Hampshire, 354 U.S. 234, 250 (1957), speaks of the right of students "to inquire, to study and to evaluate, to gain new maturity and understanding . . . ." Thus, we have not casually described the classroom as the "`marketplace of ideas.'" Keyishian v. Board of Regents, 385 U.S. 589, 603 (1967). The opportunity for formal education may not necessarily be the essential determinant of an individual's ability to enjoy throughout his life the rights of free speech and association guaranteed to him by the First Amendment. But such an opportunity may enhance the individual's enjoyment of those rights, not only during but also following school attendance. Thus, in the final analysis, "the pivotal position of education to success in American society and its essential role in opening up to the individual the central experiences of our culture lend it an importance that is undeniable." 70

Of particular importance is the relationship between education and the political process. "Americans regard the public schools as a most vital civic institution for the preservation of a democratic system of government." Abington School Dist. v. Schempp, 374 U.S. 203, 230 (1963) (BRENNAN, J., concurring). Education serves the essential function of instilling in our young an understanding of and appreciation for the principles and operation of our governmental processes. 71 Education may instill the interest and provide the tools necessary for political discourse and debate. Indeed, it has frequently been suggested that education is the dominant factor affecting political consciousness and participation. 72 A system of "[c]ompetition in ideas and governmental policies is at the core of our electoral process and of the First Amendment freedoms." Williams v. Rhodes, 393 U.S. 23, 32 (1968). But of most immediate and direct concern must be the demonstrated effect of education on the exercise of the franchise by the electorate. The right to vote in federal elections is conferred by Art. I, 2, and the Seventeenth Amendment of the Constitution, and access to the state franchise has been afforded special protection because it is "preservative of other basic civil and political rights," Reynolds v. Sims, 377 U.S., at 562 . Data from the Presidential Election of 1968 clearly demonstrate a direct relationship between participation in the electoral process and level of educational attainment; 73 and, as this Court recognized in Gaston County v. United States, 395 U.S. 285, 296 (1969), the quality of education offered may influence a child's decision to "enter or remain in school." It is this very sort of intimate relationship between a particular personal interest and specific constitutional guarantees that has heretofore caused the Court to attach special significance, for purposes of equal protection analysis, to individual interests such as procreation and the exercise of the state franchise. 74

While ultimately disputing little of this, the majority seeks refuge in the fact that the Court has "never presumed to possess either the ability or the authority to guarantee to the citizenry the most effective speech or the most informed electoral choice." Ante, at

36. This serves only to blur what is in fact at stake. With due respect, the issue is neither provision of the most effective speech nor of the most informed vote. Appellees do not now seek the best education Texas might provide. They do seek, however, an end to state discrimination resulting from the unequal distribution of taxable district property wealth that directly impairs the ability of some districts to provide the same educational opportunity that other districts can provide with the same or even substantially less tax effort. The issue is, in other words, one of discrimination that affects the quality of the education which Texas has chosen to provide its children; and, the precise question here is what importance should attach to education for purposes of equal protection analysis of that discrimination. As this Court held in Brown v. Board of Education, 347 U.S., at 493, the opportunity of education, "where the state has undertaken to provide it, is a right which must be made available to all on equal terms." The factors just considered, including the relationship between education and the social and political interests enshrined within the Constitution, compel us to recognize the fundamentality of education and to scrutinize with appropriate care the bases for state discrimination affecting equality of educational opportunity in Texas' school districts 75 - a conclusion which is only strengthened when we consider the character of the classification in this case.

C

The District Court found that in discriminating between Texas schoolchildren on the basis of the amount of taxable property wealth located in the district in which they live, the Texas financing scheme created a form of wealth discrimination. This Court has frequently recognized that discrimination on the basis of wealth may create a classification of a suspect character and thereby call for exacting judicial scrutiny. See e. g., Griffin v. Illinois, 351 U.S. 12 (1956); Douglas v. California, 372 U.S. 353 (1963); McDonald v. Board of Election Comm'rs of Chicago, 394 U.S. 802, 807 (1969). The majority, however, considers any wealth classification in this case to lack certain essential characteristics which it contends are common to the instances of wealth discrimination that this Court has heretofore recognized. We are told that in every prior case involving a wealth classification, the members of the disadvantaged class have "shared two distinguishing characteristics: because of their impecunity they were completely unable to pay for some desired benefit, and as a consequence, they sustained an absolute deprivation of a meaningful opportunity to enjoy that benefit." Ante, at 20. I cannot agree. The Court's distinctions may be sufficient to explain the decisions in Williams v. Illinois, 399 U.S. 235 (1970); Tate v. Short, 401 U.S. 395 (1971); and even Bullock v. Carter, 405 U.S. 134 (1972). But they are not in fact consistent with the decisions in Harper v. Virginia Bd. of Elections, 383 U.S. 663 (1966), or Griffin v. Illinois, supra, or Douglas v. California, supra.

In Harper, the Court struck down as violative of the Equal Protection Clause an annual Virginia poll tax of $1.50, payment of which by persons over the age of 21 was a prerequisite to voting in Virginia elections. In part, the Court relied on the fact that the poll tax interfered with a fundamental interest - the exercise of the state franchise. In addition, though, the Court emphasized that "[l]ines drawn on the basis of wealth or property . . . are traditionally disfavored." 383 U.S., at 668 . Under the first part of the theory announced by the majority, the disadvantaged class in Harper, in terms of a wealth analysis, should have consisted only of those too poor to afford the $1.50 necessary to vote. But the Harper Court did not see it that way. In its view, the Equal Protection Clause "bars a system which excludes [from the franchise] those unable to pay a fee to vote or who fail to pay." Ibid. (Emphasis added.) So far as the Court was concerned, the "degree of the discrimination [was] irrelevant." Ibid. Thus, the Court struck down the poll tax in toto; it did not order merely that those too poor to pay the tax be exempted; complete impecunity clearly was not determinative of the limits of the disadvantaged class, nor was it essential to make an equal protection claim.

Similarly, Griffin and Douglas refute the majority's contention that we have in the past required an absolute deprivation before subjecting wealth classifications to strict scrutiny. The Court characterizes Griffin as a case concerned simply with the denial of a transcript or an adequate substitute therefore, and Douglas as involving the denial of counsel. But in both cases the question was in fact whether "a State that [grants] appellate review can do so in a way that discriminates against some convicted defendants on account of their poverty." Griffin v. Illinois, supra, at 18 (emphasis added). In that regard, the Court concluded that inability to purchase a transcript denies "the poor an adequate appellate review accorded to all who have money enough to pay the costs in advance," ibid. (emphasis added), and that "the type of an appeal a person is afforded . . . hinges upon whether or not he can pay for the assistance of counsel," Douglas v. California, supra, at 355-356 (emphasis added). The right of appeal itself was not absolutely denied to those too poor to pay; but because of the cost of a transcript and of counsel, the appeal was a substantially less meaningful right for the poor than for the rich. 76 It was on these terms that the Court found a denial of equal protection, and those terms clearly encompassed degrees of discrimination on the basis of wealth which do not amount to outright denial of the affected right or interest. 77

This is not to say that the form of wealth classification in this case does not differ significantly from those recognized in the previous decisions of this Court. Our prior cases have dealt essentially with discrimination on the basis of personal wealth. 78 Here, by contrast, the children of the disadvantaged Texas school districts are being discriminated against not necessarily because of their personal wealth or the wealth of their families, but because of the taxable property wealth of the residents of the district in which they happen to live. The appropriate question, then, is whether the same degree of judicial solicitude and scrutiny that has previously been afforded wealth classifications is warranted here.

As the Court points out, ante, at 28-29, no previous decision has deemed the presence of just a wealth classification to be sufficient basis to call forth rigorous judicial scrutiny of allegedly discriminatory state action. Compare, e. g., Harper v. Virginia Bd. of

Elections, supra, with, e. g., James v. Valtierra, 402 U.S. 137 (1971). That wealth classifications alone have not necessarily been considered to bear the same high degree of suspectness as have classifications based on, for instance, race or alienage may be explainable on a number of grounds. The "poor" may not be seen as politically powerless as certain discrete and insular minority groups. 79 Personal poverty may entail much the same social stigma as historically attached to certain racial or ethnic groups. 80 But personal poverty is not a permanent disability; its shackles may be escaped. Perhaps most importantly, though, personal wealth may not necessarily share the general irrelevance as a basis for legislative action that race or nationality is recognized to have. While the "poor" have frequently been a legally disadvantaged group, 81 it cannot be ignored that social legislation must frequently take cognizance of the economic status of our citizens. Thus, we have generally gauged the invidiousness of wealth classifications with an awareness of the importance of the interests being affected and the relevance of personal wealth to those interests. See Harper v. Virginia Bd. of Elections, supra.

When evaluated with these considerations in mind, it seems to me that discrimination on the basis of group wealth in this case likewise calls for careful judicial scrutiny. First, it must be recognized that while local district wealth may serve other interests, 82 it bears no relationship whatsoever to the interest of Texas schoolchildren in the educational opportunity afforded them by the State of Texas. Given the importance of that interest, we must be particularly sensitive to the invidious characteristics of any form of discrimination that is not clearly intended to serve it, as opposed to some other distinct state interest. Discrimination on the basis of group wealth may not, to be sure, reflect the social stigma frequently attached to personal poverty. Nevertheless, insofar as group wealth discrimination involves wealth over which the disadvantaged individual has no significant control, 83 it represents in fact a more serious basis of discrimination than does personal wealth. For such discrimination is no reflection of the individual's characteristics or his abilities. And thus - particularly in the context of a disadvantaged class composed of children - we have previously treated discrimination on a basis which the individual cannot control as constitutionally disfavored. Cf. Weber v. Aetna Casualty & Surety Co., 406 U.S. 164 (1972); Levy v. Louisiana, 391 U.S. 68 (1968).

The disability of the disadvantaged class in this case extends as well into the political processes upon which we ordinarily rely as adequate for the protection and promotion of all interests. Here legislative reallocation of the State's property wealth must be sought in the face of inevitable opposition from significantly advantaged districts that have a strong vested interest in the preservation of the status quo, a problem not completely dissimilar to that faced by underrepresented districts prior to the Court's intervention in the process of reapportionment, 84 see Baker v. Carr, 369 U.S. 186, 191 - 192 (1962).

Nor can we ignore the extent to which, in contrast to our prior decisions, the State is responsible for the wealth discrimination in this instance. Griffin, Douglas, Williams, Tate, and our other prior cases have dealt with discrimination on the basis of indigency which was attributable to the operation of the private sector. But we have no such simple de facto wealth discrimination here. The means for financing public education in Texas are selected and specified by the State. It is the State that has created local school districts, and tied educational funding to the local property tax and thereby to local district wealth. At the same time, governmentally imposed land use controls have undoubtedly encouraged and rigidified natural trends in the allocation of particular areas for residential or commercial use, 85 and thus determined each district's amount of taxable property wealth. In short, this case, in contrast to the Court's previous wealth discrimination decisions, can only be seen as "unusual in the extent to which governmental action is the cause of the wealth classification." 86

In the final analysis, then, the invidious characteristics of the group wealth classification present in this case merely serve to emphasize the need for careful judicial scrutiny of the State's justifications for the resulting interdistrict discrimination in the educational opportunity afforded to the schoolchildren of Texas.

D

The nature of our inquiry into the justification for state discrimination is essentially the same in all equal protection cases: We must consider the substantiality of the state interests sought to be served, and we must scrutinize the reasonableness of the means by which the State has sought to advance its interest. See Police Dept. of Chicago v. Mosley, 408 U.S., at 95 . Differences in the application of this test are, in my view, a function of the constitutional importance of the interests at stake and the invidiousness of the particular classification. In terms of the asserted state interests, the Court has indicated that it will require, for instance, a "compelling," Shapiro v. Thompson, 394 U.S., at 634, or a "substantial" or "important," Dunn v. Blumstein, 405 U.S., at 343, state interest to justify discrimination affecting individual interests of constitutional significance. Whatever the differences, if any, in these descriptions of the character of the state interest necessary to sustain such discrimination, basic to each is, I believe, a concern with the legitimacy and the reality of the asserted state interests. Thus, when interests of constitutional importance are at stake, the Court does not stand ready to credit the State's classification with any conceivable legitimate purpose, 87 but demands a clear showing that there are legitimate state interests which the classification was in fact intended to serve. Beyond the question of the adequacy of the State's purpose for the classification, the Court traditionally has become increasingly sensitive to the means by which a State chooses to act as its action affects more directly interests of constitutional significance. See, e. g., United States v. Robel, 389 U.S. 258, 265 (1967); Shelton v. Tucker, 364 U.S. 479, 488 (1960). Thus, by now, "less restrictive alternatives" analysis is firmly established in equal protection jurisprudence. See Dunn v. Blumstein, supra at 343; Kramer v. Union School District, 395 U.S., at 627 . It seems to me that the range of choice we are willing to accord the State in selecting the means by which it will act, and the care with which we scrutinize the effectiveness of the means which the State selects, also must reflect the constitutional importance of the interest affected and the invidiousness of the particular classification. Here, both the nature of the interest and the classification dictate close judicial scrutiny of the purposes which Texas seeks to serve with its present educational financing scheme and of the means it has selected to serve that purpose.

The only justification offered by appellants to sustain the discrimination in educational opportunity caused by the Texas financing scheme is local educational control. Presented with this justification, the District Court concluded that "[n]ot only are defendants unable to demonstrate compelling state interests for their classifications based upon wealth, they fail even to establish a reasonable basis for these classifications." 337 F. Supp., at 284. I must agree with this conclusion.

At the outset, I do not question that local control of public education, as an abstract matter, constitutes a very substantial state interest. We observed only last Term that "[d]irect control over decisions vitally affecting the education of one's children is a need that is strongly felt in our society." Wright v. Council of the City of Emporia, 407 U.S. 451, 469 (1972). See also id., at 477-478 (BURGER, C. J., dissenting). The State's interest in local educational control - which certainly includes questions of educational funding - has deep roots in the inherent benefits of community support for public education. Consequently, true state dedication to local control would present, I think, a substantial justification to weigh against simply interdistrict variations in the treatment of a State's schoolchildren. But I need not now decide how I might ultimately strike the balance were we confronted with a situation where the State's sincere concern for local control inevitably produced educational inequality. For, on this record, it is apparent that the State's purported concern with local control is offered primarily as an excuse rather than as a justification for interdistrict inequality.

In Texas, statewide laws regulate in fact the most minute details of local public education. For example, the State prescribes required courses. 88 All textbooks must be submitted for state approval, 89 and only approved textbooks may be used. 90 The State has established the qualifications necessary for teaching in Texas public schools and the procedures for obtaining certification. 91 The State has even legislated on the length of the school day. 92 Texas' own courts have said:

"As a result of the acts of the Legislature our school system is not of mere local concern but it is statewide. While a school district is local in territorial limits, it is an integral part of the vast school system which is coextensive with the confines of the State of Texas." Treadaway v. Whitney Independent School District, 205 S. W. 2d 97, 99 Tex. Ct. Civ. App. 1947).

See also El Dorado Independent School District v. Tisdale, 3 S. W. 2d 420, 422 (Tex. Comm'n App. 1928).

Moreover, even if we accept Texas' general dedication to local control in educational matters, it is difficult to find any evidence of such dedication with respect to fiscal matters. It ignores reality to suggest - as the Court does, ante, at 49-50 - that the local property tax element of the Texas financing scheme reflects a conscious legislative effort to provide school districts with local fiscal control. If Texas had a system truly dedicated to local fiscal control, one would expect the quality of the educational opportunity provided in each district to vary with the decision of the voters in that district as to the level of sacrifice they wish to make for public education. In fact, the Texas scheme produces precisely the opposite result. Local school districts cannot choose to have the best education in the State by imposing the highest tax rate. Instead, the quality of the educational opportunity offered by any particular district is largely determined by the amount of taxable property located in the district - a factor over which local voters can exercise no control.

The study introduced in the District Court showed a direct inverse relationship between equalized taxable district property wealth and district tax effort with the result that the property-poor districts making the highest tax effort obtained the lowest per-pupil yield. 93 The implications of this situation for local choice are illustrated by again comparing the Edgewood and Alamo Heights School Districts. In 1967-1968, Edgewood, after contributing its share to the Local Fund Assignment, raised only $26 per pupil through its local property tax, whereas Alamo Heights was able to raise $333 per pupil. Since the funds received through the Minimum Foundation School Program are to be used only for minimum professional salaries, transportation costs, and operating expenses, it is not hard to see the lack of local choice - with respect to higher teacher salaries to attract more and better teachers, physical facilities, library books, and facilities, special courses, or participation in special state and federal matching funds programs - under which a property-poor district such as Edgewood is forced to labor. 94 In fact, because of the difference in taxable local property wealth, Edgewood would have to tax itself almost nine times as heavily to obtain the same yield as Alamo Heights. 95 At present, then, local control is a myth for many of the local school districts in Texas. As one district court has observed, "rather than reposing in each school district the economic power to fix its own level of per pupil expenditure, the State has so arranged the structure as to guarantee that some districts will spend low (with high taxes) while others will spend high (with low taxes)." Van Dusartz v. Hatfield, 334 F. Supp. 870, 876 (Minn. 1971).

In my judgment, any substantial degree of scrutiny of the operation of the Texas financing scheme reveals that the State has selected means wholly inappropriate to secure its purported interest in assuring its school districts local fiscal control. 96 At the same time, appellees have pointed out a variety of alternative financing schemes which may serve the State's purported interest in local control as well as, if not better than, the present scheme without the current impairment of the educational opportunity of vast numbers of Texas schoolchildren. 97 I see no need, however, to explore the practical or constitutional merits of those suggested alternatives at this time for, whatever their positive or negative features, experience with the present financing scheme impugns any suggestion that it constitutes a serious effort to provide local fiscal control. If, for the sake of local education control, this Court is to sustain interdistrict discrimination in the educational opportunity afforded Texas school children, it should require that the State present something more than the mere sham now before us.

III

In conclusion, it is essential to recognize that an end to the wide variations in taxable district property wealth inherent in the Texas financing scheme would entail none of the untoward consequences suggested by the Court or by the appellants.

First, affirmance of the District Court's decisions would hardly sound the death knell for local control of education. It would mean neither centralized decisionmaking nor federal court intervention in the operation of public schools. Clearly, this suit has nothing to do with local decisionmaking with respect to educational policy or even educational spending. It involves only a narrow aspect of local control - namely, local control over the raising of educational funds. In fact, in striking down interdistrict disparities in taxable local wealth, the District Court took the course which is most likely to make true local control over educational decisionmaking a reality for all Texas school districts.

Nor does the District Court's decision even necessarily eliminate local control of educational funding. The District Court struck down nothing more than the continued interdistrict wealth discrimination inherent in the present property tax. Both centralized and decentralized plans for educational funding not involving such interdistrict discrimination have been put forward. 98 The choice among these or other alternatives would remain with the State, not with the federal courts. In this regard, it should be evident that the degree of federal intervention in matters of local concern would be substantially less in this context than in previous decisions in which we have been asked effectively to impose a particular scheme upon the States under the guise of the Equal Protection Clause. See, e. g., Dandridge v. Williams, 397 U.S. 471 (1970); cf. Richardson v. Belcher, 404 U.S. 78 (1971).

Still, we are told that this case requires us "to condemn the State's judgment in conferring on political subdivisions the power to tax local property to supply revenues for local interest." Ante, at 40. Yet no one in the course of this entire litigation has ever questioned the constitutionality of the local property tax as a device for raising educational funds. The District Court's decision, at most, restricts the power of the State to make educational funding dependent exclusively upon local property taxation so long as there exists interdistrict disparities in taxable property wealth. But it hardly eliminates the local property tax as a source of educational funding or as a means of providing local fiscal control. 99

The Court seeks solace for its action today in the possibility of legislative reform. The Court's suggestions of legislative redress and experimentation will doubtless be of great comfort to the schoolchildren of Texas' disadvantaged districts, but considering the vested interests of wealthy school districts in the preservation of the status quo, they are worth little more. The possibility of legislative action is, in all events, no answer to this Court's duty under the Constitution to eliminate unjustified state discrimination. In this case we have been presented with an instance of such discrimination, in a particularly invidious form, against an individual interest of large constitutional and practical importance. To support the demonstrated discrimination in the provision of educational opportunity the State has offered a justification which, on analysis, takes on at best an ephemeral character. Thus, I believe that the wide disparities in taxable district property wealth inherent in the local property tax element of the Texas financing scheme render that scheme violative of the Equal Protection Clause. 100

I would therefore affirm the judgment of the District Court.

Notes

[1] See Van Dusartz v. Hatfield, 334 F. Supp. 870 (Minn. 1971); Milliken v. Green, 389 Mich. 1, 203 N. W. 2d 457 (1972), rehearing granted, Jan. 1973; Serrano v. Priest, 5 Cal. 3d 584, 487 P.2d 1241 (1971); Robinson v. Cahill, 118 N. J. Super. 223, 287 A. 2d 187, 119 N. J. Super. 40, 289 A. 2d 569 (1972); Hollins v. Shofstall, Civil No. C-253652 (Super. Ct. Maricopa County, Ariz., July 7, 1972). See also Sweetwater County Planning Com. for the Organization of School Districts v. Hinkle, 491 P.2d 1234 (Wyo. 1971), juris. relinquished, 493 P.2d 1050 (Wyo. 1972).

[2] The District Court in this case postponed decision for some two years in the hope that the Texas Legislature would remedy the gross disparities in treatment inherent in the Texas financing scheme. It was only after the legislature failed to act in its 1971 Regular Session that the District Court, apparently recognizing the lack of hope for self-initiated legislative reform, rendered its decision. See Texas Research League, Public School Finance Problems in Texas 13 (Interim Report 1972). The strong vested interest of property-rich districts in the existing property tax scheme poses a substantial barrier to self-initiated legislative reform in educational financing. See N. Y. Times, Dec. 19, 1972, p. 1, col. 1.

[3] Texas provides its school districts with extensive bonding authority to obtain capital both for the acquisition of school sites and "the construction and equipment of school buildings," Tex. Educ. Code Ann. 20.01 (1972), and for the acquisition, construction, and maintenance of "gymnasia, stadia, or other recreational facilities," id., 20.21-20.22. While such private capital provides a fourth source of revenue, it is, of course, only temporary in nature since the principal and interest of all bonds must ultimately be paid out of the receipts of the local ad valorem property tax, see id., 20.01, 20.04, except to the extent that outside revenues derived from the operation of certain facilities, such as gymnasia, are employed to repay the bonds issued thereon, see id., 20.22, 20.25.

[4] See Tex. Const., Art. 7, 3; Tex. Educ. Code Ann. 20.01-20.02. As a part of the property tax scheme, bonding authority is conferred upon the local school districts, see n. 3, supra.

[5] See Tex. Educ. Code Ann. 20.04.

[6] For the 1970-1971 school year, the precise figure was 41.1%. See Texas Research League, supra, n. 2, at 9.

[7] See Tex. Educ. Code Ann. 20.04.

Theoretically, Texas law limits the tax rate for public school maintenance, see id., 20.02, to $1.50 per $100 valuation, see id., 20.04 (d). However, it does not appear that any Texas district presently taxes itself at the highest rate allowable, although some poor districts are approaching it, see App. 174.

[8] Under Texas law local districts are allowed to employ differing bases of assessment - a fact that introduces a third variable into the local funding. See Tex. Educ. Code Ann. 20.03. But neither party has suggested that this factor is responsible for the disparities in revenues available to the various districts. Consequently, I believe we must deal with this case on the assumption that differences in local methods of assessment do not meaningfully affect the revenue-raising power of local districts relative to one another. The Court apparently admits as much. See ante, at 46. It should be noted, moreover, that the main set of data introduced before the District Court to establish the disparities at issue here was based upon "equalized taxable property" values which had been adjusted to correct for differing methods of assessment. See App. C to Affidavit of Professor Joel S. Berke.

[9] Texas has approximately 1, 200 school districts.

[10] See Appendix I, post, p. 134.

[11] See ibid. Indeed, appellants acknowledge that the relevant data from Professor Berke's affidavit show "a very positive correlation, 0.973, between market value of taxable property per pupil and state and local revenues per pupil." Reply Brief for Appellants 6 n. 9.

While the Court takes issue with much of Professor Berke's data and conclusions, ante, at 15-16, n. 38, and 25-27, I do not understand its criticism to run to the basic finding of a correlation between taxable district property per pupil and local revenues per pupil. The critique of Professor Berke's methodology upon which the Court relies, see Goldstein, Interdistrict Inequalities in School Financing: A Critical Analysis of Serrano v. Priest and its Progeny, 120 U. Pa. L. Rev. 504, 523-525, nn. 67, 71 (1972), is directed only at the suggested correlations between family income and taxable district wealth and between race and taxable district wealth. Obviously, the appellants do not question the relationship in Texas between taxable district wealth and per-pupil expenditures; and there is no basis for the Court to do so, whatever the criticisms that may be leveled at other aspects of Professor Berke's study, see infra, n. 56.

[12] See Appendix II, post, p. 135.

[13] See ibid.

[14] For the 1970-1971 school year, the precise figure was 10.9%. See Texas Research League, supra, n. 2, at 9.

[15] Appellants made such a contention before the District Court but apparently have abandoned it in this Court. Indeed, data introduced in the District Court simply belie the argument that federal funds have a significant equalizing effect. See Appendix I, post, p. 134. And, as the District Court observed, it does not follow that remedial action by

the Federal Government would excuse any unconstitutional discrimination effected by the state financing scheme. 337 F. Supp. 280, 284.

[16] For the 1970-1971 school year, the precise figure was 48%. See Texas Research League, supra, n. 2, at 9.

[17] See Tex. Const., Art. 7, 5 (Supp. 1972). See also Tex. Educ. Code Ann. 15.01 (b).

[18] See Tex. Educ. Code Ann. 15.01 (b).

The Permanent School Fund is, in essence, a public trust initially endowed with vast quantities of public land, the sale of which has provided an enormous corpus that in turn produces substantial annual revenues which are devoted exclusively to public education. See Tex. Const., Art. 7, 5 (Supp. 1972). See also 5 Report of Governor's Committee on Public School Education. The Challenge and the Chance 11 (1969) (hereinafter Governor's Committee Report).

[19] This is determined from the average daily attendance within each district for the preceding year. Tex. Educ. Code Ann. 15.01 (c).

[20] See id., 16.01-16.975.

[21] See id., 16.71 (2), 16.79.

[22] See id., 16.301-16.316, 16.45, 16.51-16.63.

[23] See id., 16.72-16.73, 16.76-16.77.

[24] See id., 16.74-16.76. The formula for calculating each district's share is described in 5 Governor's Committee Report 44-48.

[25] See Tex. Educ. Code Ann. 16.01.

[26] See 5 Governor's Committee Report 40-41.

[27] See id., at 45-67; Texas Research League, Texas Public Schools Under the Minimum Foundation Program - An Evaluation: 1949-1954, pp. 67-68 (1954).

[28] Technically, the economic index involves a two-step calculation. First, on the basis of the factors mentioned above, each Texas county's share of the Local Fund Assignment is determined. Then each county's share is divided among its school districts on the basis of their relative shares of the county's assessable wealth. See Tex. Educ. Code Ann. 16.74-16.76; 5 Governor's Committee Report 43-44; Texas Research League, Texas Public School Finance: A Majority of Exceptions 6-8 (2d Interim Report 1972).

[29] 5 Governor's Committee Report 48, quoting statement of Dr. Edgar Morphet.

[30] The extraordinarily complex standards are summarized in 5 Governor's Committee Report 41-43.

[31] The key element of the Minimum Foundation School Program is the provision of funds for professional salaries - more particularly, for teacher salaries. The Program provides each district with funds to pay its professional payroll as determined by certain state standards. See Tex. Educ. Code Ann. 16.301-16.316. If the district fails to pay its teachers at the levels determined by the state standards it receives nothing from the Program. See id., 16.301 (c). At the same time, districts are free to pay their teachers

salaries in excess of the level set by the state standards, using local revenues - that is, property tax revenue - to make up the difference, see id., 16.301 (a).

The state salary standards focus upon two factors: the educational level and the experience of the district's teachers. See id., 16.301-16.316. The higher these two factors are, the more funds the district will receive from the Foundation Program for professional salaries.

It should be apparent that the net effect of this scheme is to provide more assistance to property-rich districts than to property-poor ones. For rich districts are able to pay their teachers, out of local funds, salary increments above the state minimum levels. Thus, the rich districts are able to attract the teachers with the best education and the most experience. To complete the circle, this then means, given the state standards, that the rich districts receive more from the Foundation Program for professional salaries than do poor districts. A portion of Professor Berke's study vividly illustrates the impact of the State's standards on districts of varying wealth. See Appendix III, post, p. 136.

[32] In 1967-1968, Alamo Heights School District had $49, 478 in taxable property per pupil. See Berke Affidavit, Table VII, App. 216.

[33] In 1967-1968, Edgewood Independent School District had $5,960 in taxable property per pupil. Ibid.

[34] I fail to understand the relevance for this case of the Court's suggestion that if Alamo Heights School District, which is approximately the same physical size as Edgewood Independent School District but which has only one-fourth as many students, had the same number of students as Edgewood, the former's per-pupil expenditure would be considerably closer to the latter's. Ante, at 13 n. 33. Obviously, this is true, but it does not alter the simple fact that Edgewood does have four times as many students but not four times as much taxable property wealth. From the perspective of Edgewood's school children then - the perspective that ultimately counts here - Edgewood is clearly a much poorer district than Alamo Heights. The question here is not whether districts have equal taxable property wealth in absolute terms, but whether districts have differing taxable wealth given their respective school-age populations.

[35] In the face of these gross disparities in treatment which experience with the Texas financing scheme has revealed, I cannot accept the Court's suggestion that we are dealing here with a remedial scheme to which we should accord substantial deference because of its accomplishments rather than criticize it for its failures. Ante, at 38-39. Moreover, Texas' financing scheme is hardly remedial legislation of the type for which we have previously shown substantial tolerance. Such legislation may in fact extend the vote to "persons who otherwise would be denied it by state law," Katzenbach v. Morgan, 384 U.S. 641, 657 (1966), or it may eliminate the evils of the private bail bondsman, Schilb v. Kuebel, 404 U.S. 357 (1971). But those are instances in which a legislative body has sought to remedy problems for which it cannot be said to have been directly responsible. By contrast, public education is the function of the State in Texas, and the responsibility for any defect in the financing scheme must ultimately rest with the State. It is the State's

own scheme which has caused the funding problem, and, thus viewed, that scheme can hardly be deemed remedial.

[36] Cf. Appendix I, post, p. 134.

[37] Brief for Appellants 3.

[38] Thus, in 1967-1968, Edgewood had a total of $248 per pupil in state and local funds compared with a total of $558 per pupil for Alamo Heights. See Berke Affidavit, Table X, App. 219. For 1970-1971, the respective totals were $418 and $913. See Texas Research League, supra, n. 2, at 14.

[39] Not only does the local property tax provide approximately 40% of the funds expended on public education, but it is the only source of funds for such essential aspects of educational financing as the payment of school bonds, see n. 3, supra, and the payment of the district's share of the Local Fund Assignment, as well as for nearly all expenditures above the minimums established by the Foundation School Program.

[40] Compare, e. g., J. Coleman et al., Equality of Educational Opportunity 290-330 (1966); Jencks, The Coleman Report and the Conventional Wisdom, in On Equality of Educational Opportunity 69, 91-104 (F. Mosteller & D. Moynihan eds. 1972), with, e. g., J. Guthrie, G. Kleindorfer, H. Levin, & R. Stout, Schools and Inequality 79-90 (1971); Kiesling, Measuring a Local Government Service: A Study of School Districts in New York State, 49 Rev. Econ. & Statistics 356 (1967).

[41] Compare Berke Answers to Interrogatories 10 ("Dollar expenditures are probably the best way of measuring the quality of education afforded students . . ."), with Graham Deposition 39 ("[I]t is not just necessarily the money, no. It is how wisely you spend it"). It warrants noting that even appellants' witness, Mr. Graham, qualified the importance of money only by the requirement of wise expenditure. Quite obviously, a district which is property poor is powerless to match the education provided by a property-rich district, assuming each district allocates its funds with equal wisdom.

[42] See Brief of amici curiae, inter alia, San Marino Unified School District; Beverly Hills Unified School District; Brief of amici curiae, inter alia, Bloomfield Hills, Michigan, School District; Dearborn City, Michigan, School District; Grosse Pointe, Michigan, Public School System.

[43] Answers to Plaintiffs' Interrogatories, App. 115.

[44] Ibid. Moreover, during the same period, 37.17% of the teachers in Alamo Heights had advanced degrees, while only 14.98% of Edgewood's faculty had such degrees. See id., at 116.

[45] Id., at 117.

[46] Id., at 118.

[47] In the 1967-1968 school year, Edgewood had 22,862 students and 864 teachers, a ratio of 26.5 to 1. See id., at 110, 114. In Alamo Heights, for the same school year, there were 5, 432 students and 265 teachers for a ratio of 20.5 to 1. Ibid.

[48] Reply Brief for Appellants 17. See also, id., at 5, 15-16.

[49] Indeed, even apart from the differential treatment inherent in the local

property tax, the significant interdistrict disparities in state aid received under the Minimum Foundation School Program would seem to raise substantial equal protection questions.

[50] I find particularly strong intimations of such a view in the majority's efforts to denigrate the constitutional significance of children in property-poor districts "receiving a poorer quality education than that available to children in districts having more assessable wealth" with the assertion "that, at least where wealth is involved, the Equal Protection Clause does not require absolute equality or precisely equal advantages." Ante, at 23, 24. The Court, to be sure, restricts its remark to "wealth" discrimination. But the logical basis for such a restriction is not explained by the Court, nor is it otherwise apparent, see infra, at 117-120 and n. 77.

[51] See Answers to Interrogatories by Dr. Joel S. Berke, Ans. 17, p. 9; Ans. 48-51, pp. 22-24; Ans. 88-89, pp. 41-42; Deposition of Dr. Daniel C. Morgan, Jr., at 52-55; Affidavit of Dr. Daniel C. Morgan, Jr., App. 242-243.

[52] It is true that in two previous cases this Court has summarily affirmed district court dismissals of constitutional attacks upon other state educational financing schemes. See McInnis v. Shapiro, 293 F. Supp. 327 (ND Ill. 1968), aff'd per curiam, sub nom. McInnis v. Ogilvie, 394 U.S. 322 (1969); Burruss v. Wilkerson, 310 F. Supp. 572 (WD Va. 1969), aff'd per curiam, 397 U.S. 44 (1970). But those decisions cannot be considered dispositive of this action, for the thrust of those suits differed materially from that of the present case. In McInnis, the plaintiffs asserted that "only a financing system which apportions public funds according to the educational needs of the students satisfies the Fourteenth Amendment." 293 F. Supp., at 331. The District Court concluded that "(1) the Fourteenth Amendment does not require that public school expenditures be made only on the basis of pupils' educational needs, and (2) the lack of judicially manageable standards makes this controversy nonjustifiable." Id., at 329. The Burruss District Court dismissed that suit essentially in reliance on McInnis which it found to be "scarcely distinguishable." 310 F. Supp., at 574. This suit involves no effort to obtain an allocation of school funds that considers only educational need. The District Court ruled only that the State must remedy the discrimination resulting from the distribution of taxable local district wealth which has heretofore prevented many districts from truly exercising local fiscal control. Furthermore, the limited holding of the District Court presents none of the problems of judicial management which would exist if the federal courts were to attempt to ensure the distribution of educational funds solely on the basis of educational need, see infra, at 130-132.

[53] Tex. Const., Art. 7, 1.

[54] Problems of remedy may be another matter. If provision of the relief sought in a particular case required identification of each member of the affected class, as in the case of monetary relief, the need for clarity in defining the class is apparent. But this involves the procedural problems inherent in class action litigation, not the character of the elements essential to equal protection analysis. We are concerned here only with the

latter. Moreover, it is evident that in cases such as this, provision of appropriate relief, which takes the injunctive form, is not a serious problem since it is enough to direct the action of appropriate officials. Cf. Potts v. Flax. 313 F.2d 284, 288-290 (CA5 1963).

[55] I assume the Court would lodge the same criticism against the validity of the finding of a correlation between poor districts and racial minorities.

[56] The Court rejects the District Court's finding of a correlation between poor people and poor districts with the assertion that "there is reason to believe that the poorest families are not necessarily clustered in the poorest property districts" in Texas. Ante, at 23. In support of its conclusion the Court offers absolutely no data - which it cannot on this record - concerning the distribution of poor people in Texas to refute the data introduced below by appellees; it relies instead on a recent law review note concerned solely with the State of Connecticut, Note, A Statistical Analysis of the School Finance Decisions: On Winning Battles and Losing Wars, 81 Yale L. J. 1303 (1972). Common sense suggests that the basis for drawing a demographic conclusion with respect to a geographically large, urban-rural, industrial-agricultural State such as Texas from a geographically small, densely populated, highly industrialized State such as Connecticut is doubtful at best.

Furthermore, the article upon which the Court relies to discredit the statistical procedures employed by Professor Berke to establish the correlation between poor people and poor districts, see n. 11, supra, based its criticism primarily on the fact that only four of the 110 districts studied were in the lowest of the five categories, which were determined by relative taxable property per pupil, and most districts clustered in the middle three groups. See Goldstein, Interdistrict Inequalities in School Financing: A Critical Analysis of Serrano v. Priest and its Progeny, 120 U. Pa. L. Rev. 504, 524 n. 67 (1972). See also ante, at 26-27. But the Court fails to note that the four poorest districts in the sample had over 50,000 students which constituted 10% of the students in the entire sample. It appears, moreover, that even when the richest and the poorest categories are enlarged to include in each category 20% of the students in the sample, the correlation between district and individual wealth holds true. See Brief for the Governors of Minnesota, Maine, South Dakota, Wisconsin, and Michigan as amici Curiae 17 n. 21.

Finally, it cannot be ignored that the data introduced by appellees went unchallenged in the District Court. The majority's willingness to permit appellants to litigate the correctness of those data for the first time before this tribunal - where effective response by appellees is impossible - is both unfair and judicially unsound.

[57] Third Amended Complaint App. 23. Consistent with this theory, appellees purported to represent, among others, a class composed of "all . . . school children in independent school districts . . . who . . . have been deprived of the equal protection of the law under the Fourteenth Amendment with regard to public school education because of the low value of the property lying within the independent school districts in which they reside." Id., at 15.

[58] The degree of judicial scrutiny that this particular classification demands is

a distinct issue which I consider in Part II, C, infra.

[59] Indeed, the Court's theory would render the established concept of fundamental interests in the context of equal protection analysis superfluous, for the substantive constitutional right itself requires that this Court strictly scrutinize any asserted state interest for restricting or denying access to any particular guaranteed right, see, e. g., United States v. O'Brien, 391 U.S. 367, 377 (1968); Cox v. Louisiana, 379 U.S. 536, 545 -551 (1965).

[60] It is interesting that in its effort to reconcile the state voting rights cases with its theory of fundamentality the majority can muster nothing more than the contention that "[t]he constitutional underpinnings of the right to equal treatment in the voting process can no longer be doubted . . . ." Ante, at 34 n. 74 (emphasis added). If, by this, the Court intends to recognize a substantive constitutional "right to equal treatment in the voting process" independent of the Equal Protection Clause, the source of such a right is certainly a mystery to me.

[61] It is true that Griffin and Douglas also involved discrimination against indigents, that is, wealth discrimination. But, as the majority points out, ante, at 28-29, the Court has never deemed wealth discrimination alone to be sufficient to require strict judicial scrutiny; rather, such review of wealth classifications has been applied only where the discrimination affects an important individual interest, see, e. g., Harper v. Virginia Bd. of Elections, 383 U.S. 663 (1966). Thus, I believe Griffin and Douglas can only be understood as premised on a recognition of the fundamental importance of the criminal appellate process.

[62] See, e. g., Duncan v. Louisiana, 391 U.S. 145 (1968) (right to jury trial); Washington v. Texas, 388 U.S. 14 (1967) (right to compulsory process); Pointer v. Texas, 380 U.S. 400 (1965) (right to confront one's accusers).

[63] See, e. g., McLaughlin v. Florida, 379 U.S. 184, 191 -192 (1964); Loving v. Virginia, 388 U.S. 1, 9 (1967).

[64] See Oyama v. California, 332 U.S. 633, 644 -646 (1948); Korematsu v. United States, 323 U.S. 214, 216 (1944).

[65] See Graham v. Richardson, 403 U.S. 365, 372 (1971).

[66] The Court noted that the challenged "provision strips from indigent defendants the array of protective exemptions Kansas has erected for other civil judgment debtors, including restrictions on the amount of disposable earnings subject to garnishment, protection of the debtor from wage garnishment at times of severe personal or family sickness, and exemption from attachment and execution on a debtor's personal clothing, books, and tools of trade." 407 U.S., at 135 .

[67] See generally Gunther, The Supreme Court, 1971 Term, Foreword: In Search of Evolving Doctrine on a Changing Court: A Model for a Newer Equal Protection, 86 Harv. L. Rev. 1 (1972).

[68] See Brief of the National Education Association et al. as Amici Curiae App. A. All 48 of the 50 States which mandate public education also have compulsory-

attendance laws which require school attendance for eight years or more. Id., at 20-21.

[69] Prior to this Court's decision in Brown v. Board of Education, 347 U.S. 483 (1954), every State had a constitutional provision directing the establishment of a system of public schools. But after Brown, South Carolina repealed its constitutional provision, and Mississippi made its constitutional provision discretionary with the state legislature.

[70] Developments in the Law - Equal Protection, 82 Harv. L. Rev. 1065, 1129 (1969).

[71] The President's Commission on School Finance, Schools, People, & Money: The Need for Educational Reform 11 (1972), concluded that "[l]iterally, we cannot survive as a nation or as individuals without [education]." It further observed that:

"[I]n a democratic society, public understanding of public issues is necessary for public support. Schools generally include in their courses of instruction a wide variety of subjects related to the history, structure and principles of American government at all levels. In so doing, schools provide students with a background of knowledge which is deemed an absolute necessity for responsible citizenship." Id., at 13-14.

[72] See J. Guthrie, G. Kleindorfer, H. Levin, & R. Stout, Schools and Inequality 103-105 (1971); R. Hess & J. Torney, The Development of Political Attitudes in Children 217-218 (1967); Campbell, The Passive Citizen, in 6 Acta Sociologica, Nos. 1-2, p. 9, at 20-21 (1962).

That education is the dominant factor in influencing political participation and awareness is sufficient, I believe, to dispose of the Court's suggestion that, in all events, there is no indication that Texas is not providing all of its children with a sufficient education to enjoy the right of free speech and to participate fully in the political process. Ante, at 36-37. There is, in short, no limit on the amount of free speech or political participation that the Constitution guarantees. Moreover, it should be obvious that the political process, like most other aspects of social intercourse, is to some degree competitive. It is thus of little benefit to an individual from a property-poor district to have "enough" education if those around him have more than "enough." Cf. Sweatt v. Painter, 339 U.S. 629, 633 -634 (1950).

[73] See United States Department of Commerce, Bureau of the Census, Voting and Registration in the Election of November 1968, Current Population Reports, Series P-20, No. 192, Table 4, p. 17. See also Senate Select Committee on Equal Educational Opportunity, 92d Cong., 2d Sess., Levin, The Costs to the Nation of Inadequate Education 46-47 (Comm. Print 1972).

[74] I believe that the close nexus between education and our established constitutional values with respect to freedom of speech and participation in the political process makes this a different case from our prior decisions concerning discrimination affecting public welfare, see, e. g., Dandridge v. Williams, 397 U.S. 471 (1970), or housing, see, e. g., Lindsey v. Normet, 405 U.S. 56 (1972). There can be no question that, as the majority suggests, constitutional rights may be less meaningful for someone without enough to eat or without decent housing. Ante, at 37. But the crucial difference lies in the

closeness of the relationship. Whatever the severity of the impact of insufficient food or inadequate housing on a person's life, they have never been considered to bear the same direct and immediate relationship to constitutional concerns for free speech and for our political processes as education has long been recognized to bear. Perhaps, the best evidence of this fact is the unique status which has been accorded public education as the single public service nearly unanimously guaranteed in the constitutions of our States, see supra, at 111-112 and n. 68. Education, in terms of constitutional values, is much more analogous, in my judgment, to the right to vote in state elections than to public welfare or public housing. Indeed, it is not without significance that we have long recognized education as an essential step in providing the disadvantaged with the tools necessary to achieve economic self-sufficiency.

[75] The majority's reliance on this Court's traditional deference to legislative bodies in matters of taxation falls wide of the mark in the context of this particular case. See ante, at 40-41. The decisions on which the Court relies were simply taxpayer suits challenging the constitutionality of a tax burden in the face of exemptions or differential taxation afforded to others. See, e. g., Allied Stores of Ohio v. Bowers, 358 U.S. 522 (1959); Madden v. Kentucky, 309 U.S. 83 (1940); Carmichael v. Southern Coal & Coke Co., 301 U.S. 495 (1937); Bell's Gap R. Co. v. Pennsylvania, 134 U.S. 232 (1890). There is no question that, from the perspective of the taxpayer, the Equal Protection Clause "imposes no iron rule of equality, prohibiting the flexibility and variety that are appropriate to reasonable schemes of state taxation. The State may impose different specific taxes upon different trades and professions and may vary the rate of excise upon various products." Allied Stores of Ohio v. Bowers, supra, at 526-527. But in this case we are presented with a claim of discrimination of an entirely different nature - a claim that the revenue-producing mechanism directly discriminates against the interests of some of the intended beneficiaries; and, in contrast to the taxpayer suits, the interest adversely affected is of substantial constitutional and societal importance. Hence, a different standard of equal protection review than has been employed in the taxpayer suits is appropriate here. It is true that affirmance of the District Court decision would to some extent intrude upon the State's taxing power insofar as it would be necessary for the State to at least equalize taxable district wealth. But contrary to the suggestions of the majority, affirmance would not impose a straitjacket upon the revenue-raising powers of the State, and would certainly not spell the end of the local property tax. See infra, at 132.

[76] This does not mean that the Court has demanded precise equality in the treatment of the indigent and the person of means in the criminal process. We have never suggested, for instance, that the Equal Protection Clause requires the best lawyer money can buy for the indigent. We are hardly equipped with the objective standards which such a judgment would require. But we have pursued the goal of substantial equality of treatment in the face of clear disparities in the nature of the appellate process afforded rich versus poor. See, e. g., Draper v. Washington, 372 U.S. 487, 495 -496 (1963); cf. Coppedge v. United States, 369 U.S. 438, 447 (1962).

[77] Even if I put aside the Court's misreading of Griffin and Douglas, the Court fails to offer any reasoned constitutional basis for restricting cases involving wealth discrimination to instances in which there is an absolute deprivation of the interest affected. As I have already discussed, see supra, at 88-89, the Equal Protection Clause guarantees equality of treatment of those persons who are similarly situated; it does not merely bar some form of excessive discrimination between such persons. Outside the context of wealth discrimination, the Court's reapportionment decisions clearly indicate that relative discrimination is within the purview of the Equal Protection Clause. Thus, in Reynolds v. Sims, 377 U.S. 533, 562 -563 (1964), the Court recognized:

"It would appear extraordinary to suggest that a State could be constitutionally permitted to enact a law providing that certain of the State's voters could vote two, five, or 10 times for their legislative representatives, while voters living elsewhere could vote only once. . . . Of course, the effect of state legislative districting schemes which give the same number of representatives to unequal numbers of constituents is identical. Overweighting and overvaluation of the votes of those living here has the certain effect of dilution and undervaluation of the votes of those living there. . . . Their right to vote is simply not the same right to vote as that of those living in a favored part of the State. . . . One must be ever aware that the Constitution forbids `sophisticated as well as simple-minded modes of discrimination.'"

See also Gray v. Sanders, 372 U.S. 368, 380 -381 (1963). The Court gives no explanation why a case involving wealth discrimination should be treated any differently.

[78] But cf. Bullock v. Carter, 405 U.S. 134, 144 (1972), where prospective candidates' threatened exclusion from a primary ballot because of their inability to pay a filing fee was seen as discrimination against both the impecunious candidates and the "less affluent segment of the community" that supported such candidates but was also too poor as a group to contribute enough for the filing fees.

[79] But cf. M. Harrington, The Other America 13-17 (Penguin ed. 1963).

[80] See E. Banfield, The Unheavenly City 63, 75-76 (1970); cf. R. Lynd & H. Lynd, Middletown in Transition 450 (1937).

[81] Cf. New York v. Miln, 11 Pet. 102, 142 (1837).

[82] Theoretically, at least, it may provide a mechanism for implementing Texas' asserted interest in local educational control, see infra, at 126.

[83] True, a family may move to escape a property-poor school district, assuming it has the means to do so. But such a view would itself raise a serious constitutional question concerning an impermissible burdening of the right to travel, or, more precisely, the concomitant right to remain where one is. Cf. Shapiro v. Thompson, 394 U.S. 618, 629 -631 (1969).

[84] Indeed, the political difficulties that seriously disadvantaged districts face in securing legislative redress are augmented by the fact that little support is likely to be secured from only mildly disadvantaged districts. Cf. Gray v. Sanders, 372 U.S. 368 (1963). See also n. 2, supra.

[85] See Tex. Cities, Towns and Villages Code, Civ. Stat. Ann. 1011a-1011j (1963 and Supp. 1972-1973). See also, e. g., Skinner v. Reed, 265 S. W. 2d 850 (Tex. Ct. Civ. App. 1954); Corpus Christi v. Jones, 144 S. W. 2d 388 (Tex. Ct. Civ. App. 1940).

[86] Serrano v. Priest, 5 Cal. 3d, at 603, 487 P.2d, at 1254. See also Van Dusartz v. Hatfield, 334 F. Supp., at 875-876.

[87] Cf., e. g., Two Guys from Harrison-Allentown v. McGinley, 366 U.S. 582 (1961); McGowan v. Maryland, 366 U.S. 420 (1961); Goesaert v. Cleary, 335 U.S. 464 (1948).

[88] Tex. Educ. Code Ann. 21.101-21.117. Criminal penalties are provided for failure to teach certain required courses, Id., 4.15-4.16.

[89] Id., 12.11-12.35.

[90] Id., 12.62.

[91] Id., 13.031-13.046.

[92] Id., 21.004.

[93] See Appendix II, infra.

[94] See Affidavit of Dr. Jose Cardenas, Superintendent of Schools, Edgewood Independent School District, App. 234-238.

[95] See Appendix IV, infra.

[96] My Brother WHITE, in concluding that the Texas financing scheme runs afoul of the Equal Protection Clause, likewise finds on analysis that the means chosen by Texas - local property taxation dependent upon local taxable wealth - is completely unsuited in its present form to the achievement of the asserted goal of providing local fiscal control. Although my Brother WHITE purports to reach this result by application of that lenient standard of mere rationality traditionally applied in the context of commercial interests, it seems to me that the care with which he scrutinizes the practical effectiveness of the present local property tax as a device for affording local fiscal control reflects the application of a more stringent standard of review, a standard which at the least is influenced by the constitutional significance of the process of public education.

[97] See n. 98, infra.

[98] Centralized educational financing is, to be sure, one alternative. On analysis, though, it is clear that even centralized financing would not deprive local school districts of what has been considered to be the essence of local educational control. See Wright v. Council of the City of Emporia, 407 U.S. 451, 477 -478 (BURGER, C. J., dissenting). Central financing would leave in local hands the entire gamut of local educational policymaking - teachers, curriculum, school sites, the whole process of allocating resources among alternative educational objectives.

A second possibility is the much-discussed theory of district power equalization put forth by Professors Coons, Clune, and Sugarman in their seminal work, Private Wealth and Public Education 201-242 (1970). Such a scheme would truly reflect a dedication to local fiscal control. Under their system, each school district would receive a fixed amount of revenue per pupil for any particular level of tax effort regardless of the level of local property tax base. Appellants criticize this scheme on the rather extraordinary ground that it would encourage poorer districts to overtax themselves in order to obtain substantial revenues for education. But under the present discriminatory scheme, it is the poor districts that are already taxing themselves at the highest rates, yet are receiving the lowest returns.

District wealth reapportionment is yet another alternative which would accomplish directly essentially what district power equalization would seek to do artificially. Appellants claim that the calculations concerning state property required by such a scheme would be impossible as a practical matter. Yet Texas is already making far more complex annual calculations - involving not only local property values but also local income and other economic factors - in conjunction with the Local Fund Assignment portion of the Minimum Foundation School Program. See 5 Governor's Committee Report 43-44.

A fourth possibility would be to remove commercial, industrial, and mineral property from local tax rolls, to tax this property on a statewide basis, and to return the resulting revenues to the local districts in a fashion that would compensate for remaining variations in the local tax bases.

None of these particular alternatives are necessarily constitutionally compelled; rather, they indicate the breadth of choice which would remain to the State if the present interdistrict disparities were eliminated.

[99] See n. 98, supra.

[100] Of course, nothing in the Court's decision today should inhibit further review of state educational funding schemes under state constitutional provisions. See Milliken v. Green, 389 Mich. 1, 203 N. W. 2d 457 (1972), rehearing granted, Jan. 1973; Robinson v. Cahill, 118 N. J. Super. 223, 287 A. 2d 187, 119 N. J. Super. 40, 289 A. 2d 569 (1972); cf. Serrano v. Priest, 5 Cal. 3d 584, 487 P.2d 1241 (1971).

The New York Work Rules clearly exclude persons eligible for assistance under federal standards: Justice Marshall's dissent in New York Department of Social Services v. Dublino (June 21, 1973)

MR. JUSTICE MARSHALL, with whom MR. JUSTICE BRENNAN joins, dissenting.

Because the Court today ignores a fundamental rule for interpreting the Social Security Act, I must respectfully dissent. As we said in Townsend v. Swank, 404 U. S. 282, 404 U. S. 286 (1971),

"in the absence of congressional authorization for the exclusion clearly evidenced from the Social Security Act or its legislative history, a state eligibility standard that excludes persons eligible for assistance under federal AFDC standards violates the Social Security Act, and is therefore invalid under the Supremacy Clause."

See also King v. Smith, 392 U. S. 309 (1968); Carleson v. Remillard, 406 U. S. 598, 406 U. S. 600 (1972). The New York Work Rules fall squarely within this statement; they clearly exclude persons eligible for assistance under federal standards, and it could hardly be maintained that they did not impose additional conditions of eligibility. [1] For example, under federal standards, it is irrelevant to a determination of eligibility that a recipient has or has not filed every two weeks a certificate from the local employment office that no suitable employment opportunities are available, yet, under the Work Rules, a recipient who fails to file such a certificate is "deemed" to have refused to accept suitable employment, and so is not eligible for assistance. N.Y.Soc.Serv.Law § 131(4)(a) (Supp. 1971-1972). [2] Thus, according to the rules of interpretation we have heretofore followed, the proper inquiry is whether the Social Security Act or its legislative history clearly shows congressional authorization for state employment requirements other than those involved in WIN. [3]

The answer is that neither the Act nor its legislative history shows such an authorization. The only relevant work-related conditions of eligibility in the Act are found at 42 U.S.C. § 602(a)(19) (1970 ed., Supp. I). In addition to exempting certain persons from registration for and participation in WIN, [4] the Act permits States to disregard the needs of persons otherwise eligible for assistance who

"have refused without good cause to participate under a work incentive program . . . or . . . to accept employment in which he is able to engage."

42 U.S.C. § 602(a)(19)(F) (1970 ed., Supp. I). The Act thus makes actual refusal to participate in a WIN Program or to accept employment a permissible ground for denying assistance. In contrast, New York has adopted the none-too-subtle technique of "deeming" persons not to have accepted employment because they have not, for example, obtained a certain certificate from the local employment office every two weeks. "Deeming" is a familiar legal device to evade applicable requirements by saying that they have been satisfied when they have not, in fact, been satisfied. But the federal requirement, which the State may not alter without clear congressional authorization, [5] requires an actual refusal to participate in a WIN Program or to accept employment, not a refusal to participate in some other program or a fictitious refusal of employment. [6]

The legislative history of the Social Security Act confirms this interpretation, for whenever Congress legislated with respect to work requirements, it focused on actual refusals to accept employment or to participate in certain special programs clearly authorized by Congress. At no time has Congress authorized States to adopt other work referral programs or to make refusal to participate in such programs a condition of eligibility, even under the guise of "deeming" such a refusal a refusal to accept employment.

At its inception, the program of Aid to Dependent Children was designed to lessen somewhat the burden of supporting such children. The program provided assistance to children who had been deprived of parental support by reason of the absence of a parent. 49 Stat. 629 (1935). Assistance was provided to supply the needs of such children, thus "releas[ing the parent] from the wage-earning role." H.R.Doc. No. 81, 74th Cong., 1st Sess., 30 (1935). See also H.R.Rep. No. 615, 74th Cong., 1st Sess., 10 (1935). Thus, the program's purposes were in many ways inconsistent with a requirement that the parent leave the home to accept employment. Yet, in operation, the original program failed to provide sufficient inducement for the parent to remain at home, since the amount of assistance was measured solely by the child's needs. In order further to relieve the pressures on the parent to leave the home and accept work, Congress amended the Act in 1950 so that the aid would include payments "to meet the needs of the relative with whom any dependent child is living." 42 U.S.C. § 606(b)(1).

Until 1961, then, the sole emphasis of the Social Security Act's provisions for assistance to dependent children was on preserving the integrity of the family unit. [7]

In that year, Congress expanded the definition of dependent child to include children deprived of parental support by reason of the unemployment of a parent. 42 U.S.C. § 607. Families with two parents present could, for the first time, receive assistance, and one parent could leave the home to work without impairing the integrity of the family unit. Congress therefore required States participating in the program for aid to families with an unemployed parent to deny assistance under this provision to individuals who refused to accept bona fide offers of employment. Pub.L. 87-31, 75 Stat. 76 (1961). Refusal of actual offers of employment was clearly the contemplated condition. See S.Rep. No. 165, 87th Cong., 1st Sess., 3 (1961). Congress then developed this concept, permitting States to establish "Community Work and Training Programs" of work on public projects, Pub.L. 87-543, § 105, 76 Stat. 186, rendered inapplicable by Pub.L. 90-248, 81 Stat. 892. Refusal to accept a work assignment on such a project without good cause would be a ground for denial of public assistance. See H.R.Rep. No. 1414, 87th Cong., 2d Sess., 15 (1962).

When Congress established WIN, it did not abandon its previous policies. Recipients of public assistance could be required only to accept bona fide offers of employment or placement in specified programs. There is no indication whatsoever in the legislative history that Congress intended to permit States to deny assistance because potential recipients had refused to participate in programs not supervised by the Secretary of Labor, as WIN Programs are. The parameters of the WIN Program were designed to accommodate Congress' dual interests in guaranteeing the integrity of the family and in maximizing the potential for employment of recipients of public assistance. Without careful federal supervision, of the sort contemplated by the delegation to the Secretary of Labor to establish testing and counseling services and to require that States design employability plans, 81 Stat. 885, state work programs might upset the accommodation that Congress sought. The Work Incentive Program was thus a carefully coordinated system, whose individual parts fit into an integrated whole. It is hardly surprising that Congress did not expressly or impliedly authorize States to develop independent work programs, since the WIN Program represented Congress' recognition that such programs had to be kept under careful scrutiny if the variety of goals Congress sought to promote were to be achieved. [8] I believe that the Court seriously misconceives the purposes of the federal programs of public assistance, in its apparent belief that Congress had the sole purpose of promoting work opportunities, a purpose that precluding additional state programs would negate. Ante at 413 U. S. 418-420.

Instead, Congress has consistently indicated its desire to adopt programs that will enhance the employability of recipients of public assistance while maintaining the integrity of families receiving assistance. A work referral program can do this only if it is regulated, both as to the persons required to participate and as to the terms on which they must participate. And Congress has consistently recognized that such regulation requires close federal supervision of work programs. In my view, this course of legislation, which is not mentioned by the Court, is neither "ambiguous," "fragmentary," nor "peripheral," ante at 413 U. S. 415, 413 U. S. 416, 413 U. S. 417. No matter how it is viewed, however, one cannot fairly say that the Social Security Act or its legislative history clearly evidences congressional authorization for making participation in state work programs a condition of eligibility for public assistance. [9]

The policy of clear statement [10] in Townsend serves a useful purpose. It informs legislators that, if they wish to alter the accommodations previously arrived at in an Act of major importance, they must indicate clearly that wish, since what may appear to be minor changes of narrow scope may, in fact, have ramifications throughout the administration of the Act. A policy of clear statement insures that Congress will consider those ramifications, [11] but only if it is regularly adhered to.

Finally, it is particularly appropriate to require clear statement of authorization to impose additional conditions of eligibility for public assistance. Myths abound in this area. It is widely yet erroneously believed, for example, that recipients of public assistance have little desire to become self-supporting. See, e.g., L. Goodwin, Do the Poor Want to Work? 5, 51-52, 112 (1972). Because the recipients of public assistance generally lack substantial political influence, state legislators may find it expedient to accede to pressures generated by misconceptions. In order to lessen the possibility that erroneous beliefs will lead state legislators to single out politically unpopular recipients of assistance for harsh treatment, Congress must clearly authorize States to impose conditions of eligibility different from the federal standards. As we observed in King v. Smith, 392 U.S. at 392 U. S. 318-319, this rule leaves the States with

"considerable latitude in allocating their AFDC resources, since each State is free to set its own standard of need and to determine the level of benefits by the amount of funds it devotes to the program."

The Court today quotes this observation but misses its import. The States have latitude to adjust benefits in the two ways mentioned, but not by imposing additional conditions of eligibility. When across-the-board adjustments like those are made, legislators cannot single out especially unpopular groups for discriminatory treatment. [12]

For these reasons, I would affirm the judgment of the District Court.

Notes

[1] Appellants state that the Work Rules do not "constitute an additional condition of eligibility for public assistance." Reply Brief for Appellant N.Y. State Depts. 9. The arguments they present, however, relate entirely to the purported congressional authorization for additional conditions of this sort.

[2] The federal conditions of eligibility relating to registration for employment are found in 42 U.S.C. § 602(a)(19) (1970 ed., Supp. I).

[3] The United States, as amicus curiae, argues that the rule stated in Townsend v. Swank, 404 U. S. 282 (1971), does not fairly characterize the course of our interpretation of the Social Security Act. It relies primarily on the Court's decision in Wyman v. James, 400 U. S. 309 (1971). But, for reasons that escaped me at the time, see id. at 400 U. S. 345 n. 7, the Court did not address the statutory argument. Wyman does not, therefore, express any limitation on the rule in Townsend. Similarly, our summary affirmance in Snell v. Wyman, 393 U. S. 323 (1969), where the District Court did not have before it our opinion in King v. Smith, 392 U. S. 309 (1968), is at least offset by the summary affirmances in Carleson v. Taylor, 404 U.S. 980 (1971), Juras v. Meyers, 404 U.S. 803 (1971), and Weaver v. Doe, 404 U.S. 987 (1971).

The United States' argument from authority is weak, and its argument as a matter of logic is even weaker. The United States suggests that, while States may not narrow the class of persons eligible for assistance under federal standards, they may impose additional conditions of eligibility in pursuit of independent state policies. This distinction will not withstand analysis, for it makes decision turn on meaningless verbal tricks. One could just as easily find an independent state policy in Townsend as a narrowing of the class of eligible persons: the State might have a policy of minimizing subsidies to persons with a clear prospect of future income well above the poverty level, by denying assistance to persons attending four-year colleges while granting it to those attending vocational training schools. Such a system of subsidies would almost certainly be held constitutional under the Due Process Clause, and the position of the United States seems to be that States may impose conditions of eligibility, not squarely in conflict with federal standards, in the pursuit of some constitutional state interest.

[4] For example, no child under 16 or attending school full time need register. 42 U.S.C. § 602(a) (19)(A)(i) (1970 ed., Supp. I). I take it that the Court would find a conflict "of substance," ante at 413 U. S. 423 n. 29, between this provision and a state work requirement applicable to children under 16. For the legislative history is clear that Congress, in defining the work-related conditions of eligibility, "spell[ed] out those people we think should not be required to go to work," as Senator Long put it. 113 Cong.Rec. 32593 (1967). See also S.Rep. No. 744, 90th Cong., 1st Sess., 26. The United States' position would be, I assume, that such a provision would narrow the class of persons eligible for assistance.

[5] Appellants argue that

"the provision of section 602(a)(10) that aid be furnished 'to all eligible individuals,' when read within the context of the Social Security Act, means individuals 'eligible' under State requirements, not Federal."

Reply Brief for Appellant N.Y. State Depts. 13. We expressly rejected this argument in Townsend, 404 U.S. at 404 U. S. 286.

[6] The States may, of course, adopt procedures necessary to insure that offers of employment are transmitted to recipients of public assistance. It hardly needs extended argument, however, to show that the New York Work Rules, taken as a whole, are not necessary to do that.

[7] In 1956, Congress required States to adopt plans to provide social services to strengthen family life. Pub.L. 880, § 312, 70 Stat. 848.

[8] The original proposal for a Work Incentive Program would have permitted a State to operate Community Work and Training Programs only if a federal WIN Program were not operated in the State. H.R. 5710, 90th Cong., 1st Sess., § 204(a). Thus, either a WIN Program or a state program could operate within a State, but not both. In the final version, the preexisting authorization for Community Work and Training Programs was eliminated, and the Federal WIN Program was to be implemented in every State. Again, Congress recognized that federal and state work programs could not coexist.

The 1971 Amendments to the WIN Program, Pub.L. 92-223, 85 Stat. 802, further demonstrate Congress' desire to have federal control of work requirements. Each State must establish a "separate administrative unit" to provide social services only in connection with WIN. 42 U.S.C. § 602(a)(19)(G) (1970 ed., Supp. I). It would be anomalous for Congress to require the States to devote substantial resources to such a unit in connection with the WIN Program, and yet to permit the States to operate independent work programs using federal funds without providing the special services that Congress thought so important.

[9] It is unnecessary for me to discuss at any length the Court's analysis of the preemption problem. I note, as the Court does, ante at 413 U. S. 411 n. 9, that this case does not present the classic question of preemption, that is, does the enactment of a statute by Congress preclude state attempts to regulate the same subject? There is no question that New York may impose whatever work requirements it wishes, consistent only with constitutional limitations, when it gives public assistance solely from state funds. See ante at 413 U. S. 412. The question here relates to the conditions that Congress has placed on state programs supported by federal funds. The distinction is not without importance, for it makes inapposite the strictures in our earlier cases and relied on by the Court, against lightly interfering with state programs. Ante at 413 U. S. 413-414. For we must, of course, be cautious when we prevent a State from regulating in an area where, in the absence of congressional action, it has important interests. Holding that the Federal WIN Program is the exclusive method of imposing work requirements in conjunction with federally funded programs of public assistance would have no such impact; New York would remain free to operate public assistance programs with state funds, with

whatever work requirements it chose.

[10] See H. Hart & A. Sacks, The Legal Process 1240 (tent. ed.1958).

[11] In this connection, I cannot let pass without comment the extraordinary use the Court makes of legislative "history," in relying on exchanges on the floor of the House and Senate that occurred after the decision by the District Court in this case. Ante at 413 U. S. 416-417, n.19. Although reliance on floor exchanges has been criticized in this Court, Schwegmann Bros. v. Calvert Distillers Corp., 341 U. S. 384, 341 U. S. 395-397 (1951) (Jackson, J., concurring), there is some force to the more generally accepted proposition that such exchanges, particularly when sponsors of a bill or committee chairmen are involved, are relevant to a determination of the purpose Congress sought to achieve in enacting the bill. United States v. St. Paul, M. & M. R. Co., 247 U. S. 310, 247 U. S. 318 (1918). For legislators know how legislative history is made, and they ought to be aware of the importance of floor exchanges. If they disagree with the interpretation placed on the bill in such exchanges, they may offer amendments or vote against it. Thus, Congress, in enacting a statute, may fairly be taken to have endorsed the interpretations offered in such exchanges. None of this is true of post-enactment floor exchanges, which have no bearing on pending legislation and to which a disinterested legislator might well pay scant attention. If Senator Buckley and Representative Carey wished to have a congressional expression of intent on the issue of preemption, they were not barred from introducing legislation.

[12] That the possibility of treatment that is so discriminatory as to be unconstitutional is not insubstantial is shown by the Court's brief discussion of the jurisdiction of the District Court, ante at 413 U. S. 412 n. 11.

Court is mischaracterizing O'Callahan v. Parker: Justice Marshall's dissent in Gosa v. Mayden (June 25, 1973)

MR. JUSTICE MARSHALL, with whom MR. JUSTICE BRENNAN and MR. JUSTICE STEWART* join, dissenting.

MR. JUSTICE BLACKMUN's plurality opinion, by its efforts to establish that O'Callahan v. Parker, 395 U. S. 258 (1969), was not a decision dealing with jurisdiction in its classic form, implicitly acknowledges that, if O'Callahan were in fact, concerned with the adjudicatory power -- that is, the jurisdictional competency [1] -- of military tribunals, its holding would necessarily be fully retroactive in effect, cf. e.g., Linkletter v. Walker, 381 U. S. 618, 381 U. S. 623 (1965). The plurality now puts forth the view that O'Callahan was not concerned with the true jurisdictional competency of courts-martial, but that the decision yielded merely a new constitutional rule. This characterization of O'Callahan permits the plurality to apply in this case the three-prong test employed to judge the retroactivity of new procedural rules under Linkletter and its progeny, see, e.g., Desist v. United States, 394 U. S. 244, 394 U. S. 249 (1969); Stovall v. Denno, 388 U. S. 293, 388

U. S. 297 (1967). And, not surprisingly, application of that test leads to the conclusion that O'Callahan should have only prospective effect. With all due respect, I must dissent.

I am unable to agree with the plurality's characterization of O'Callahan. In my view, it can only be understood as a decision dealing with the constitutional limits of the military's adjudicatory power over offenses committed by servicemen. No decision could more plainly involve the limits of a tribunal's power to exercise jurisdiction over particular offenses, and thus more clearly demand retroactive application.

A

In holding that O'Callahan is to be given only prospective effect, the plurality does not reject outright the view that the decision was jurisdictional in nature. Yet it clearly does reject the contention that O'Callahan dealt with a question of true jurisdictional competency, for we are told that the decision "did announce a new constitutional principle," ante at 413 U. S. 673, and that it really "dealt with the appropriate exercise of jurisdiction by military tribunals," ante at 413 U. S. 674. The difference between a decision concerning a tribunal's jurisdictional competency -- that is, the limits of its adjudicatory power -- and "the appropriate exercise of [its] jurisdiction" is less than clear to me, at least where, as here, the question of "appropriateness" ultimately turns on the extent of Congress' constitutional authority under Art. I, § 8, cl. 14, to "make Rules for the Government and Regulation of the land and naval Forces." But whatever the nature of the distinction that the plurality now seeks to draw, it cannot, in my opinion, obscure the essential character of the decision in O'Callahan.

O'Callahan required this Court to define the class of offenses committed by servicemen that Congress, under Art. I, § 8, cl. 14, could constitutionally empower military tribunals to try. The nature of the ultimate inquiry there is plain from the question upon which the Court granted certiorari:

"'Does a court-martial, held under the Articles of War, Tit. 10, U.S.C. § 801 et seq., have jurisdiction to try a member of the Armed Forces who is charged with commission of a crime cognizable in a civilian court and having no military significance, alleged to have been committed off-post and while on leave, thus depriving him of his constitutional rights to indictment by grand jury and trial by a petit jury in a civilian court?'"

395 U.S. at 395 U. S. 261. The O'Callahan Court's discussion of this issue was consistently couched in terms of the jurisdiction of military tribunals, [2] and, in dissent, Mr. Justice Harlan, too, framed the issue presented in the unmistakable terms of "the appropriate subject matter jurisdiction of courts-martial," id. at 395 U. S. 276. Even the Court of Appeals in No. 71-6314, while ultimately holding the O'Callahan decision to be prospective only, acknowledged that the decision turned upon a determination of "lack of adjudicatory power" -- that

"O'Callahan's foundation, framework and structure deny to the legislation which breathed the breath of judicial life into the forum that tried Sgt. O'Callahan, the necessary basis in constitutional power to reach his type of case. [3]"

450 F.2d 753, 757 (CA5 1971). See also United States ex rel. Flemings v. Chafee, 458 F.2d 544, 549-550 (CA2 1972).

Despite the evident jurisdictional nature of the ultimate issue presented in O'Callahan, the plurality attempts to analogize this case to DeStefano v. Woods, 392 U. S. 631 (1968), where the Court held that the decisions in Duncan v. Louisiana, 391 U. S. 145 (1968), and Bloom v. Illinois, 391 U. S. 145 (1968), were to have only prospective effect. Duncan held that the Sixth Amendment guarantee of trial by jury in criminal cases had been made applicable to the States by the Fourteenth Amendment. And Bloom established the right to jury trial in the context of serious criminal contempt proceedings. DeStefano-like the other offspring of Linkletter that have applied the three-prong test to determine retroactivity -- involved constitutional rulings that established new procedures for the conduct of trial or for the use of evidence. But O'Callahan hardly was such a case.

The Court in O'Callahan was not setting forth procedures which the military was constitutionally required to adopt in its proceedings. Had the Court been doing so, this would certainly be a different case; the analogy to DeStefano then might well be appropriate. It is true, as the plurality now points out, that the O'Callahan Court placed considerable emphasis on the lack of jury trial in the court-martial system. But it did so only as a part of the general analytic process of determining the proper reconciliation of the competing jurisdictions of two essentially distinct [4] judicial systems, namely, the civil and military systems of justice. The Court's basic concern in this process was the preservation -- to the fullest extent possible consistent with the legitimate needs of the military -- of the fundamental civil rights guaranteed by our Constitution and Bill of Rights. Those civil rights were, in the Court's words, the "constitutional stakes in the . . . litigation." O'Callahan v. Parker, supra, at 395 U. S. 262.

Thus, the Court pointed out that one tried before a military tribunal is without the benefit of not only trial by jury, but also indictment by a grand jury. Ibid. Nor are the same rules of evidence and procedure applicable in a military proceeding, a factor affecting, for example, the defense's access to compulsory process, id. at 395 U. S. 264 n. 4. In addition, the Court was concerned with the fact that the presiding officers at courts-martial do not enjoy the independence that is thought to flow from life tenure and undiminishable salary. To the contrary, the Court recognized that

"the possibility of influence on the actions of the court-martial by the officer who convenes it, selects its members and the counsel on both sides, and who usually has direct command authority over its members is a pervasive one in military law, despite strenuous efforts to eliminate the danger."

Id. at 395 U. S. 264. In short, the Court concluded that

"[a] court-martial is not yet an independent instrument of justice but remains to a significant degree a specialized part of the overall mechanism by which military discipline is preserved,"

Id. at 395 U. S. 265.

The Court's purpose in considering these factors was not to require changes in the military system of justice, but rather to illustrate its "fundamental differences from . . . the civilian courts," id. at 395 U. S. 262, differences that compelled the Court

"'to restrict military tribunals to the narrowest jurisdiction deemed absolutely essential to maintaining discipline among troops in active service,'"

id. at 395 U. S. 265, quoting from Toth v. Quarles, 350 U. S. 11, 350 U. S. 22 (1955). As a result, the Court concluded that the "crime to be under military jurisdiction must be service-connected . . .," 395 U.S. at 395 U. S. 272, so that the power of Congress under Art. I, § 8, cl. 14, to "make Rules for the Government and Regulation of the land and naval Forces," and also the exemption from the grand jury requirement of the Fifth Amendment for "cases arising in the land or naval forces, or in the Militia, when in actual service in time of War or public danger" are not expanded to deprive servicemen unjustifiably of their civil rights. [5] The Court found that, when an offense is not service-connected, the needs of the military are not significantly implicated, and thus that the limits of Congress' constitutional power over servicemen under Art. I, § 8, cl. 14, have been passed, at least in the context of "peacetime offenses," 395 U.S. at 395 U. S. 273.

Certainly the jurisdictional nature of the O'Callahan decision is amply demonstrated by this Court's previous decision in McClaughry v. Deming, 186 U. S. 49 (1902). There, the Court was called upon to decide

"the power of an officer convening a court-martial for the trial of an officer of volunteers [reserve troops], to compose that court entirely of officers of the Regular Army."

Id. at 186 U. S. 53. The Court determined that Congress had directed by statute that volunteer officers of the Army be tried only by a court-martial composed of volunteer officers. In light of this determination, the Court concluded:

"As to the officer to be tried, there was no court, for it seems to us that it cannot be contended that men not one of whom is authorized by law to sit, but, on the contrary, all of whom are forbidden to sit, can constitute a legal court-martial because detailed to act as such court by an officer who, in making such detail, acted contrary to and in complete violation of law. Where does such a court obtain jurisdiction to perform a single official function? How does it get jurisdiction over any subject matter or over the person of any individual? The particular tribunal is a mere creature of the statute, as we have said, and must be created under its provisions."

Id. at 186 U. S. 64. In the same vein, the Court elsewhere stated:

"A court-martial is the creature of statute, and, as a body or tribunal, it must be convened and constituted in entire conformity with the provisions of the statute, or else it is without jurisdiction."

Id. at 186 U. S. 62. Because of the flaw in the composition of the court-martial, a flaw which the Court considered determinative on the issue of the court-martial's jurisdiction, the Court affirmed a lower court's issuance of a writ of habeas corpus to secure the officer's release from military custody. Significantly, this writ was issued at a time when habeas corpus clearly lay only where the court-martial had "no jurisdiction over the person of the defendant or the subject matter of the charges against him." Id. at 186 U. S. 69. [6] In O'Callahan the Court was not concerned with the composition of a particular court-martial, but with the fundamental question of the extent of Congress' constitutional power to establish court-martial jurisdiction over offenses committed by our servicemen. If the former issue goes to the jurisdiction of military tribunals, certainly the latter does.

B

With this understanding of O'Callahan, I believe, contrary to the plurality's view, that the retroactive application of our holding there is required by our prior decisions in Robinson v. Neil, 409 U. S. 505 (1973), and United States v. U.S. Coin & Currency, 401 U. S. 715, 401 U. S. 722-724 (1971). Robinson involved the retroactive application of the decision in Waller v. Florida, 397 U. S. 387 (1970), that the Fifth Amendment's guarantee, made applicable to the States through the Fourteenth Amendment, that no person should be put twice in jeopardy for the same offense barred an individual's prosecution for a single offense by both a State and a municipality of the State, that is, a legal subdivision of the State. U.S. Coin & Currency held retroactive the Court's prior determination that the Fifth Amendment privilege against compulsory self-incrimination barred the prosecution of gamblers for failure to register and to report illegal gambling proceeds for tax purposes, see Marchetti v. United States, 390 U. S. 39 (1968); Grosso v. United States, 390 U. S. 62 (1968).

In deciding whether to give retroactive effect to Waller, Marchetti, and Grosso, the Court rejected contentions that it should apply the three-prong test employed in cases such as Stovall v. Denno, 388 U. S. 293 (1967), Desist v. United States, 394 U. S. 244 (1969), and DeStefano v. Woods, 392 U. S. 631 (1968). In U.S. Coin & Currency, Mr. Justice Harlan, speaking for the Court, explained:

"Unlike some of our earlier retroactivity decisions, we are not here concerned with the implementation of a procedural rule which does not undermine the basic accuracy of the factfinding process at trial. Linkletter v. Walker, 381 U. S. 618 (1965); Tehan v. Shott, 382 U. S. 406 (1966); Johnson v. New Jersey, 384 U. S. 719 (1966); Stovall v. Denno, 388 U. S. 293 (1967). Rather, Marchetti and Grosso dealt with the kind of conduct that cannot constitutionally be punished in the first instance."

401 U.S. at 401 U. S. 723. The Robinson Court adopted essentially the same view of the Waller decision concerning the Double Jeopardy Clause and multiple prosecutions by different legal subdivisions of a single sovereign. See 409 U.S. at 409 U. S. 508. In this case, too, we are concerned not with "the implementation of a procedural rule," but with an unavoidable constitutional impediment to the prosecution of particular conduct.

In O'Callahan, as has been seen, the ultimate issue was the extent of the constitutional power that underlies the jurisdiction of military tribunals. Where an offense lies outside the limits of that power, there exists just as much of a constitutional impediment to trial by court-martial as there existed to a civilian trial in Marchetti and Grosso due to the privilege against self-incrimination or in Waller due to the Double

Jeopardy Clause. It cannot be forgotten that military tribunals are courts of limited jurisdiction. See McClaughry v. Deming, 186 U.S. at 186 U. S. 63; Ex parte Watkins, 3 Pet.193, 28 U. S. 209 (1830). They cannot exercise authority which Congress has not conferred upon them, much less authority which Congress is without constitutional power to confer. [7] It is this fundamental principle that compels retroactive application of the decision in O'Callahan.

The plurality seeks to distinguish U.S. Coin & Currency and Robinson on the grounds that the former involved a right that prevented the offender from being tried at all and the latter a right that prevented "another trial from taking place at all," ante at 413 U. S. 679, whereas the underlying issue in this case is merely which jurisdiction can try offenses committed by servicemen. But these are distinctions without meaning; they merely reflect the differences in the nature of the constitutional impediment to trial at issue in each case. The essential common thread tying these cases together is that each involved, at the least, a constitutional barrier to trial before the particular forum, regardless of the fairness of the procedures and the factfinding process of the relevant forum.

U.S. Coin & Currency swept broadly, to be sure, for it concerned a constitutional guarantee that effectively prevented any trial of the offender for the particular offense. But the nature of the Double Jeopardy Clause at issue in Robinson is such that the offender may be tried once for a particular offense by a court of a particular sovereign; it is the second prosecution for the same offense by another court of the same sovereign that that Clause clearly bars. Similarly, here, a serviceman charged with a nonservice-connected offense is subject to trial for that offense by civil tribunals, but military tribunals lack the necessary constitutional power, at least in peacetime, to try such an offense. As was true in Robinson, this case involves a constitutional barrier to adjudication of a particular offense by a particular forum, yet in neither case does it follow that the offender is constitutionally entitled to go unpunished altogether. I fail to see, therefore, why different rules from those applied only recently in Robinson should be applied in this case.

There is, of course, the additional fact that the Robinson Court left open the question whether reasonable, official reliance upon a particular rule might properly be considered "in determining retroactivity of a nonprocedural constitutional decision such as Waller." 409 U.S. at 409 U. S. 511. [8] And in this case, the plurality, in attempting to establish that O'Callahan was a "clear break with the past,'" ante at 413 U. S. 672, citing Desist v. United States, 394 U.S. at 394 U. S. 248, and should therefore be applied only prospectively, does make much of the argument that substantial, justifiable reliance was placed on pre-O'Callahan law concerning the exercise of court-martial jurisdiction over servicemen, see ante at 413 U. S. 672-673. But I seriously question the relevance of any inquiry into official reliance on prior law where, as here, the issue is jurisdictional competency. Even assuming for the moment that O'Callahan completely reinterpreted the limits of Congress' power to confer jurisdiction on courts-martial, the decision involved the authoritative construction of a constitutional provision, and no military tribunal could ever constitutionally have had more power than resided therein. But the real point is that O'Callahan did not mark a sharp, new departure from prior law.

The plurality acknowledges that O'Callahan did not involve the overruling of any prior precedent, ante at 413 U. S. 673. It is true, as the plurality indicates, that a number of prior decisions had suggested that "military status, in itself, was sufficient for the exercise of court-martial jurisdiction," ibid. Yet none of the cases upon which the plurality relies dealt, in fact, with a nonservice-connected offense committed by a serviceman in peacetime. [9] It is fair to say, in short, that, until O'Callahan, the Court had not directly faced the issue of the service-connected nature of servicemen's offenses.

More importantly, perhaps, the O'Callahan Court's efforts to define the constitutional limits of the jurisdiction of courts-martial was hardly the beginning of such efforts by the Court. O'Callahan was but one of a series of steps taken by this Court since the conclusion of the Second World War to restrict military jurisdiction to its constitutionally appropriate limits. Thus, in Toth v. Quarles, 350 U. S. 11 (1955), the Court ruled that a discharged serviceman could not be tried by a court-martial for offenses committed while a member of the Armed Forces. Subsequently, it was established that courts-martial did not have jurisdiction to try offenses committed by civilian dependents accompanying military personnel serving overseas. Kinsella v. Sinlgeton, 361 U. S. 234 (1960); Reid v. Covert, 354 U. S. 1 (1957). Finally, the Court held that civilians employed with the military overseas were not subject to court-martial jurisdiction. See Grisham v. Hagan, 361 U. S. 278 (1960); McElroy v. Guagliardo, 361 U. S. 281 (1960). This series of cases limited the reach of courts-martial to members of the Armed Forces; they did not require the Court to go on to define the breadth of offenses for which servicemen could be tried by courts-martial. Nonetheless, these cases and O'Callahan clearly were all pieces of the same cloth. Under these circumstances, I seriously doubt that retroactive application would do substantial violence to any legitimate, official reliance upon prior law [10] -- even assuming that to be a valid consideration here. [11]

II

MR. JUSTICE DOUGLAS, in his concurring opinion, contends that petitioner Gosa's case merits reargument to consider whether he should be denied relief because he failed to raise his jurisdictional objection before the court-martial that tried him. MR. JUSTICE DOUGLAS intimates that, since the jurisdiction of the military to try petitioner was not initially contested, "res judicata [may now bar] inquiry" into the question of jurisdiction, ante at 413 U. S. 689. In my opinion, such an argument is clearly untenable, and hence reargument of petitioner Gosa's case is unnecessary.

A

One of the most basic principles of our jurisprudence is that subject matter jurisdiction cannot be conferred upon a court by consent of the parties. See, e.g., American Fire & Casualty Co. v. Finn, 341 U. S. 6, 341 U. S. 17-18 (1951); Industrial

Addition Assn. v. Commissioner, 323 U. S. 310, 323 U. S. 313 (1945); People's Bank v. Calhoun, 102 U. S. 256, 102 U. S. 260-261 (1880); Cutler v. Rae, 7 How. 729, 48 U. S. 731 (1849). [12] An objection to the adjudicatory power of a tribunal may generally be raised for the first time at any stage of the litigation. [13] See, e.g., Flast v. Cohen, 392 U. S. 83, 392 U. S. 88 n. 2 (1968); United States v. Griffin, 303 U. S. 226, 303 U. S. 229 (1938); Fortier v. New Orleans National Bank, 112 U. S. 439, 112 U. S. 444 (1884). Those principles are applicable even in the context of collateral attacks upon court-martial proceedings, as is evident from this Court's decision in McClaughry v. Deming, 186 U. S. 49 (1902).

McClaughry, as previously indicated, involved a collateral attack upon the court-martial conviction of a volunteer officer who claimed that the Regular Army court-martial which had tried him had been constituted in violation of the relevant law, and therefore was without jurisdiction. The volunteer officer had failed to raise this jurisdictional objection before the court-martial, and the military contended before this Court that "his consent waived the question of invalidity," id. at 186 U. S. 66. The Court rejected his contention, saying:

"It was not a mere consent to waive some statutory provision in his favor which, if waived, permitted the court to proceed. His consent could no more give jurisdiction to the court, either over the subject matter or over his person, than if it had been composed of a like number of civilians. . . . The fundamental difficulty lies in the fact that the court was constituted in direct violation of the statute, and no consent could confer jurisdiction over the person of the defendant or over the subject matter of the accusation, because to take such jurisdiction would constitute a plain violation of law."

Ibid. See also id. at 186 U. S. 68; Givens v. Zerbst, 255 U. S. 11, 255 U. S. 20 (1921); Ver Mehren v. Sirmyer, 36 F.2d 876, 879-880 (CA8 1929). Just as the silence of the accused in McClaughry could not confer jurisdiction on a court-martial of the Regular Army that was acting in excess of its statutory authority, so here the failure of Gosa to raise his jurisdictional objection before the court-martial could not have conferred upon that tribunal authority that constitutionally could not be conferred. Consequently, his failure to object to the jurisdiction of the court-martial that tried him cannot be deemed fatal in this Court. [14]

B

Moreover, even if O'Callahan were to be treated as merely a procedural, rather than as a true jurisdictional, decision, application of the doctrine of res judicata would nonetheless be entirely inappropriate in the context of petitioner Gosa's case since that action was brought by way of a petition for federal habeas corpus. Specifically, I must vigorously disagree with the suggestion, necessarily inherent in MR. JUSTICE DOUGLAS' opinion, that the doctrine of res judicata may have some place in the law of federal habeas corpus. In the past, this Court has indicated quite explicitly to the contrary:

"At common law, the doctrine of res judicata did not extend to a decision on habeas corpus refusing to discharge the prisoner. The state courts generally have accepted that rule where not modified by statute . . .; and this Court has conformed to it, and thereby sanctioned it. . . . We regard the rule as well established in this jurisdiction."

Salinger v. Loisel, 265 U. S. 224, 265 U. S. 230 (1924). See Fay v. Noia, 372 U. S. 391, 372 U. S. 423 (1963); Darr v. Burford, 339 U. S. 200, 339 U. S. 214 (1950). Indeed, the rule was still "well established in this jurisdiction" just a few months ago. [15] See Neil v. Biggers, 409 U. S. 188, 409 U. S. 190-191 (1972). The federal courts, to be sure, are not without means for dealing with repetitious applications for habeas corpus, see, e.g., Salinger v. Loisel, supra, at 265 U. S. 231-232; 28 U.S.C. § 2244(a), (b), or with applications raising questions previously litigated in this Court, see 28 U.S.C. § 2244(c). But no such problems are presented here. Rather, a procedural problem arises in this case because petitioner Gosa failed to assert the "jurisdictional" defect, which he now raises, in seeking leave for a direct appeal to the Court of Military Appeals. This reflects, in my view, a failure on the part of Gosa to satisfy the exhaustion requirement, which is applied in the context of collateral attack on federal habeas corpus, thereby raising a substantial question whether he has waived his right to challenge the "jurisdiction" of the court-martial on habeas corpus.

The exhaustion doctrine evolved in the context of collateral attack on state criminal proceedings. See, e.g., Ex parte Hawk, 321 U. S. 114 (1944); Ex parte Royall, 117 U. S. 241 (1886). It generally requires state petitioners to utilize available state court remedies before resorting to federal habeas corpus, [16] and thus serves both to ensure the orderly functioning of state judicial processes, without disruptive federal court intervention, and to allow state courts to fulfill their roles as co-equal partners with the federal courts in the enforcement of federal law, thus often eliminating the need for federal court action, and avoiding unnecessary friction between state and federal courts. These same considerations inhere in the context of collateral attack in federal court upon the judgments of military tribunals, which constitute a judicial system -- a system with its own peculiar purposes and legal traditions -- distinct from the federal judicial system much like the independent state judicial systems. Accordingly, this Court normally has required that military petitioners exhaust all available remedies within the military justice system. See Noyd v. Bond, 395 U. S. 683, 395 U. S. 693 (1969); Gusik v. Schilder, 340 U. S. 128, 340 U. S. 131-132 (1950). [17] At the time petitioner Gosa initiated this collateral attack, he indeed had not exhausted a military remedy which was formerly available to him with respect to the claim he now asserts. But that certainly ought not to be the end of the inquiry.

In Fay v. Noia, 372 U. S. 391 (1963), the Court rejected the position that a state prisoner who had not pursued his state appellate remedies was barred from seeking federal habeas corpus because of his failure to exhaust, where the state appellate remedies were no longer available. The Court concluded, instead, that the exhaustion

"requirement refers only to a failure to exhaust state remedies still open to the applicant at the time he files his application for habeas corpus in the federal court."

Id. at 372 U. S. 399. The Court established that, where there has been a failure to resort to a state court remedy and that remedy is no longer available, the availability of federal habeas corpus would turn on whether there was a deliberate bypass of the state process. Id. at 372 U. S. 438. In determining whether such a bypass has occurred, the Court said that

"[t]he classic definition of waiver enunciated in Johnson v. Zerbst, 304 U. S. 458, 304 U. S. 464 -- 'an intentional relinquishment or abandonment of a known right or privilege' -- furnishes the controlling standard."

372 U.S. at 372 U. S. 439.

This Court has never considered the applicability of the nondeliberate bypass rule in the context of military petitioners. Fay does not speak specifically with respect to such petitioners. Nonetheless, the considerations which argue in favor of tempering the exhaustion requirement with a rule of nondeliberate bypass in the context of state petitioners are equally applicable in the context of military petitioners. Certainly, military petitioners should be encouraged to raise their constitutional claims before available military tribunals in order to ensure the orderly functioning of the system of military justice, to avoid needless federal court action, and to allow military tribunals an initial opportunity to correct their own errors. These interests are not subverted, however, by allowing a military petitioner to seek federal habeas corpus on the basis of a claim which he failed to raise before the military courts because he either was unaware of or did not otherwise willingly fail to raise that claim. As with state petitioners, the integrity of the exhaustion requirement is adequately protected by a rule prohibiting a deliberate bypass of an available military tribunal. A more stringent rule would serve only to bar presentation of valid federal claims without any countervailing justification for doing so.

On the facts of this case, I find it impossible to conclude that petitioner Gosa has waived his right to challenge the "jurisdiction" of the court-martial which convicted him of rape on the ground that the offense was not service-connected. A valid waiver requires the "intentional relinquishment . . . of a known right." [18] At the time of petitioner's 1967 application for review by the Court of Military Appeals, the substantial "jurisdictional" issue that he now raises had yet to be addressed by this Court. While O'Callahan is, to be sure, properly viewed as one further step in the ongoing process of establishing the limits of court-martial jurisdiction, see supra at 413 U. S. 705-706, I do not think it follows that we should impose a rule of waiver so strict that it requires an individual petitioner to anticipate, at the time he appeals, a particular constitutional ruling of this Court that has yet to be rendered, especially not when the protection of a number of guarantees of the Bill of Rights is at stale. Moreover, where a new constitutional rule has been established following completion of regular proceedings in the military courts, the interests served by the exhaustion requirement can be fully satisfied by requiring that the subsequently identified claim first be presented to the military courts if a means, such as post-conviction relief, [19] exists for doing so. Cf. Blair v. California, 340 F.2d 741 (CA9 1965); Pennsylvania ex rel. Raymond v. Rundle, 339 F.2d 598 (CA3 1964). Yet if it is clear that those courts would reject the claim, such post-conviction resort to the military courts would, of course, be futile, and is therefore unnecessary, see Gusik v. Schilder, 340 U.S. at 340 U. S. 132-133. This is now the case here, for, during the pendency of this action, the Court of Military Appeals, in Mercer v. Dillon, 19 U.S.C.M.A. 264, 41 C.M.R. 264 (1970), held that the "jurisdictional" principle announced in O'Callahan did not apply to cases decided before the date of the O'Callahan decision. It therefore became clear that it would be pointless to dismiss petitioner Gosa's application in order to allow him to present his claim to the military courts, [20] and, consequently, his challenge to the "jurisdiction" of the court-martial that tried him is now properly before this Court.

Since I then cannot agree with the opinion of either the plurality or MR. JUSTICE DOUGLAS, I dissent.

* MR. JUSTICE STEWART joins this opinion only as it applies to No. 71-6314. See ante this page.

Notes

[1] See generally Restatement of Judgments § 7, comments at 416 (1942)

[2] See 395 U.S. at 395 U. S. 265, 395 U. S. 267, 395 U. S. 269, 395 U. S. 272.

[3] In Relford v. Commandant, 401 U. S. 355, 401 U. S. 356 (1971), MR. JUSTICE BLACKMUN, speaking for the Court, described the O'Callahan decision as follows:

"In O'Callahan . . ., by a five-to-three vote, the Court held that a court-martial may not try a member of our armed forces charged with attempted rape of a civilian, with housebreaking, and with assault with intent to rape, when the alleged offenses were committed off-post on American territory, when the soldier was on leave, and when the charges could have been prosecuted in a civilian court."

[4] A serviceman convicted by a court-martial does, of course, ultimately have access to the federal judicial system by way of a petition for federal habeas corpus. See, e.g., Burns v. Wilson, 346 U. S. 137 (1953); Gusik v. Schilder, 340 U. S. 128 (1950).

[5] Indeed, even if the military voluntarily elected to provide servicemen on trial before courts-martial with the full panoply of procedural rights constitutionally required in civil forums, that would not affect the decision in O'Callahan. Implicit in O'Callahan is the fact that the military system of justice has never been understood to be constitutionally compelled to provide many of the procedural rights afforded by the civilian courts, and thus it would always remain free to provide only that which is constitutionally necessary. It was with an understanding of what is constitutionally required, not of what the military might elect to provide, that the scope of Congress' power under Art. I, § 8, cl. 14, had to be, and was, defined in O'Callahan, see 395 U.S. at 395 U. S. 261-262. It is this fact that perhaps best demonstrates the true jurisdictional -- as opposed to procedural -- nature of that decision.

[6] See also Developments in the Law -- Federal Habeas Corpus, 83 Harv.L.Rev. 1038, 1209 (1970). The Court moved beyond the jurisdictional limitation on collateral attacks upon court-martial convictions in Burns v. Wilson, 346 U. S. 137 (1953). See

Developments in tho Law -- Federal Habeas Corpus, supra, at 1215-1216.

[7] Cf. Restatement of Judgments § 7, comment b, pp. 42-43 (1942):

"There are many situations in which a court lacks competency to render a judgment. Thus, although a State has jurisdiction to grant a divorce of parties domiciled within the State, a decree of divorce rendered by a court which is not empowered to entertain suits for divorce is void. Similarly, a judgment rendered by a justice of the peace is void if under the law of the State such justices are not empowered to deal with the subject matter of the action; as, for example, where the action is one for tort and justices of the peace are given no power except in actions of contract. So also, where a court is given power to deal with actions involving no more than a designated amount, the statute limiting the amount is ordinarily construed not merely to make erroneous a judgment rendered by such a court in excess of its power, but to make such judgment void."

[8] In Robinson itself, the Court concluded that, in all events, there was no substantial element of reliance, since "Waller cannot be said to have marked a departure from past decisions of this Court." 409 U.S. at 409 U. S. 510.

[9] Kinsella v. Singleton, 361 U. S. 234 (1960), Reid v. Covert, 354 U. S. 1 (1957), and Ex parte Milligan, 4 Wall. 2 (1866), dealt with the exercise of military jurisdiction to try civilians, not servicemen. In each case, the Court held that the military lacked jurisdiction to try the civilians.

In Grafton v. United States, 206 U. S. 333 (1907), the Court held that a soldier who had been acquitted by a properly convened court-martial of a charge of homicide growing out of the shooting of a civilian while he was on guard duty in the Phillipine Islands could not thereafter be tried and convicted for the same offense by a civilian court of that Territory. Johnson v. Sayre, 158 U. S. 109 (1895), involved the court-martial conviction of a navy paymaster, whom the Court found to be in the naval service of the United States, for embezzling naval funds while serving on a receiving ship of the United States Navy. And in Smith v. Whitney, 116 U. S. 167 (1886), the Court was asked to order that a writ of prohibition be issued against a court-martial convened to try a naval pay inspector essentially for making various contracts not in the best interest of the Navy, for failing properly to enforce contractual agreements with the Navy, for compelling payment of illegal contractual claims against the Navy, and for failing to perform his duties and responsibilities. There can be little question that each of the offenses in Grafton, Johnson, and Smith, was "service-connected" within the meaning of O'Callahan. Contrast Relford v. Commandant, 401 U.S. at 401 U. S. 365.

Finally, Coleman v. Tennessee, 97 U. S. 509 (1879), involved the court-martial conviction of a soldier for the murder of a civilian woman. The particular circumstances of the murder are not apparent from the Court's opinion, but it is clear that the crime occurred during the Civil War, that is, during wartime, rather than during peacetime, see id. at 97 U. S. 516-517. O'Callahan did not clearly speak with respect to constitutional limits of court-martial jurisdiction during wartime, since the offense at issue there had occurred in peacetime, and the plurality does not reach the issue of wartime offenses today, although it arguably is presented in No. 71-1398, see ante at 413 U. S. 685 n. 8.

[10] With regard to the question of official reliance, it has been pointed out that, as long ago as 1955, the Departments of Justice and Defense reached an agreement that, at least federal offenses committed by servicemen off-post would fall within the jurisdiction of the Justice Department, while those committed on-post would be within the jurisdiction of the Defense Department:

"The Departments of Justice and Defense have found it desirable to establish ground rules for determining the forum for trying a serviceman charged with a civil offense in violation of both military and federal law. In general, these rules, which were established by agreement between the Departments in 1955, give to the military department concerned the responsibility of investigating and prosecuting offenses committed by persons subject to the Uniform Code of Military Justice and involving as victims only those persons or their civilian dependents residing on the military installation in question."

Duke & Vogel, The Constitution and the Standing Army: Another Problem of Court-Martial Jurisdiction, 13 Vand.L.Rev. 435, 455 (1960), citing Army Reg. 22-160, Oct. 7, 1955, implementing Memorandum of Understanding Between the Departments of Justice and Defense Relating to the Prosecution of Crimes Over Which the Two Departments have Concurrent Jurisdiction (July 19, 1955).

[11] Since the plurality opinion does not find it necessary to reach the Secretary's additional argument in No. 71-1398 that the auto theft there at issue was service-connected because the offense took place while respondent was absent without leave during wartime, I think it inappropriate for me to express any view on that additional argument at this time.

[12] See also Restatement of Judgments § 7, comment d, p. 45 (1942).

[13] Contrast n. 15, infra.

[14] MR. JUSTICE DOUGLAS would seem inclined to limit unwaivable jurisdictional flaws to instances in which an accused is "tried by a kangaroo court or by eager vigilantes . . .," ante at 413 U. S. 689-690. But the presence or absence of adjudicatory power does not turn only on the fairness of the proceeding afforded by a particular forum; rather, as McClaughry adequately illustrates, jurisdictional competency in the context of courts of limited jurisdiction such as courts-martial necessarily involves the limits of the statutory and constitutional authority that provides the legal underpinnings for such tribunals. See also Hiatt v. Brown, 339 U. S. 103, 339 U. S. 111 (1950); and n. 7, supra.

[15] For this reason, I believe that MR. JUSTICE DOUGLAS' reliance on Chicot County Drainage District v. Baxter State Bank, 308 U. S. 371 (1940), is clearly misplaced insofar as petitioner Gosa's case is concerned. Chicot County involved a question concerning the extent of indebtedness on certain municipal bonds which had previously been the subject of a federal proceeding to readjust indebtedness under the bankruptcy laws. Following the readjustment proceeding, this Court declared unconstitutional the

statute under which the proceeding had been brought, see Ashton v. Cameron County District, 298 U. S. 513 (1936). In Chicot County, this Court then held that the original decree was not open to collateral attack as void by the nonconsenting bondholders who had had notice of the original readjustment proceeding but had there lodged no objection to the court's jurisdiction.

The decision can be seen as resting simply on the doctrine of res judicata, to which the Court referred at points in its opinion, see Chicot County, supra, at 308 U. S. 374-375. The plaintiffs in the second action had had a full and fair opportunity to litigate the issue of jurisdiction in the first proceeding, but had failed to do so. At the same time, there had been substantial action taken in reliance on the readjustment plan approved in the first proceeding. New bonds had been sold to the Reconstruction Finance Corporation which had then purchased old bonds in exchange for them. Under these circumstances, it was both fair and proper to bar litigation of the jurisdiction issue in the collateral proceeding. Cf. Restatement of Judgments § 10 and comment (1942). 1,

But, as has been pointed out, the doctrine of res judicata has no place in federal habeas corpus; rigid rules restricting what questions are open to litigation on collateral attack are inappropriate in the context of judgments affecting personal liberty. There are, of course, legitimate concerns with finality in criminal proceedings -- both civilian and military -- and with the orderly functioning of independent judicial systems. But we have rules concerning exhaustion, waiver, and nonrepetitious application to protect those concerns in the context of federal habeas corpus.

More generally, Chicot County is probably most appropriately interpreted as an early decision concerning the nonretroactive application of a particular decision, namely, Ashton. Despite the Court's resort at places to the rubric of res judicata, the presence of substantial reliance on preexisting law clearly was an important consideration in the Court's decision not to allow the intervening decision in Ashton to be used to collaterally attack the original plan of readjustment. Furthermore, Chicot County was heavily relied upon by this Court when it gave the principles governing the retroactivity of new procedural constitutional rules full expression in Linkletter v. Walker, 381 U. S. 618, 381 U. S. 625-626 (1965); and the case has been cited as a retroactivity decision on a number of occasions since Linkletter, see Chevron Oil Co. v. Huson, 404 U. S. 97, 404 U. S. 106 (1971); United States v. U.S. Coin & Currency, 401 U. S. 715, 401 U. S. 742-743 (1971) (WHITE, J., dissenting); cf. United States v. Estate of Donnelly, 397 U. S. 286, 397 U. S. 293-294 (1970); id. at 397 U. S. 299-300 (DOUGLAS, J., dissenting). Viewed, then, as a precursor of the present-day retroactivity doctrine, Chicot County has no relevance for the threshold question whether Gosa is barred from raising his jurisdictional challenge on habeas corpus because he failed to present it in applying for leave to appeal to the Court of Military Appeals.

[16] This rule does not, however, entitle the state courts to more than one opportunity to consider the same claim. Thus, in Brown v. Allen, 344 U. S. 443, 344 U. S. 447 (1953), where the petitioners had presented their federal claims to the state courts on

direct review, the Court said,

"It is not necessary in such circumstances for the prisoner to ask the state for collateral relief, based on the same evidence and issues already decided by direct review. . . ."

Indeed, if the exhaustion requirement were not restricted to providing all levels of the state courts with an opportunity to hear his federal claim, it would effectively bar state prisoners from ever reaching a federal forum in States in which an unlimited number of identical applications for state post-conviction relief are permitted. The exhaustion requirement does not demand such "repetitious applications to state courts." Id. at 344 U. S. 448-449, n. 3.

[17] But see McElroy v. Guagliardo, 361 U. S. 281 (1960); Reid v. Covert, 354 U. S. 1 (1957); Toth v. Quarles, 350 U. S. 11 (1956); Noyd v. Bond, 395 U. S. 683, 395 U. S. 696 n. 8 (1969).

[18] Nothing in this Court's recent decisions in Tollett v. Henderson, 411 U. S. 258 (1973), and Davis v. United States, 411 U. S. 233 (1973), suggests that a different standard should be applied in the context of this case. Tollett involved a collateral attack upon the validity of a guilty plea in light of racial discrimination in the composition of the state grand jury that had indicted Henderson, an objection that had not been raised at the time of the entrance of the plea. Because it was clear that neither Henderson nor his counsel was aware of the claim of discrimination at the time of the plea, the Court agreed that there had been no valid waiver of the claim in traditional terms, see 411 U.S. at 411 U. S. 266, but the Court did not consider that determination dispositive in the peculiar context of a collateral attack upon a guilty plea. Rather, the Court ruled that

"[t]he focus of federal habeas inquiry is the nature of the advice and the voluntariness of the plea, not the existence as such of an antecedent constitutional infirmity,"

ibid. We, of course, do not deal here with the special problem of a collateral attack upon a guilty plea.

In Davis, the Court held that, for purposes of collateral attack, a petitioner had waived his objection to the composition of the grand jury that tried him because he had failed to raise the objection before trial as Fed.Rule Crim.Proc. 12(b)(2) expressly requires. Rule 12(b)(2) specifies that

"[d]efenses and objections based on defects in the institution of the prosecution or in the indictment . . . may be raised only by motion before trial,"

and that failure to do so "constitutes a waiver thereof." Confronted with a situation in which a specific rule provided "for the waiver of a particular kind of constitutional claim if it be not timely asserted," 411 U.S. at 411 U. S. 239-240, the Court concluded that preservation of the integrity of the Rule demanded that its standard should govern in the context of a collateral attack upon an indictment. This case, however, involves no such "express waiver provision," id. at 411 U. S. 239, and consequently the general waiver principles established by this Court's previous decisions must control.

[19] See Developments in the Law -- Federal Habeas Corpus, 83 Harv.L.Rev. 1038, 1234 (1970); cf. Noyd v. Bond, 395 U.S. at 395 U. S. 695 n. 7.

[20] In any case, while his application for habeas corpus was pending in the District Court, petitioner Gosa filed a motion to vacate his conviction and sentence, on the basis of O'Callahan, in the Court of Military Appeals. Subsequent to the denial of relief in the District Court, the Court of Military Appeals, treating petitioner's motion as a petition for reconsideration, also denied relief. It did so not on the basis that Gosa had waived the "jurisdictional" question by failing to present it on direct appeal, but on the basis of its previous decision in Mercer holding O'Callahan to be nonretroactive. 19 U.S.C.M.A. 327, 41 C.M.R. 327 (1970). Thus, in all events, it seems clear that Gosa has now adequately exhausted his military remedies, and his previous bypass can no longer be deemed a waiver of the "jurisdictional" question, see Warden v. Hayden, 387 U. S. 294, 387 U. S. 297 n. 3 (1967).

The two-felony exclusion rule violates equal protection: Justice Marshall's dissent in Marshall v. United States (January 9, 1974)

MR. JUSTICE MARSHALL, with whom MR. JUSTICE DOUGLAS and MR. JUSTICE BRENNAN concur, dissenting.

Title II of the Narcotic Addict Rehabilitation Act of 1966 authorizes treatment in lieu of prison sentence for those addicts convicted of an offense against the United States who the sentencing court has determined are "likely to be rehabilitated through treatment." 18 U.S.C. § 4253(a). Petitioner was denied treatment for his disease of narcotics addiction, even though no determination was ever made that he is not likely to be rehabilitated through treatment, because the Act excludes from consideration for the NARA program any person with two or more prior felony convictions. 18 U.S.C. § 4251(f)(4). Two courts of appeals have concluded that the two-felony exclusion, though intended by Congress to serve admittedly legitimate ends, is not a sufficiently rational means toward those ends to withstand scrutiny under equal protection principles. [1]

The Court today, while alluding to some of the statute's serious flaws, nevertheless finds it constitutional. I must respectfully dissent.

In the present case, the Court of Appeals analyzed the constitutionality of the two-felony exclusion by focusing on what it perceived to be this Court's two-tiered approach to equal protection issues. See 470 F.2d 34, 38 (1972). Under this view, classifications involving a "fundamental interest" or "suspect classification" are subject to so-called "strict scrutiny," while all other statutes are tested by a standard of minimal rationality. While the Court today neither expressly endorses nor rejects this approach, its analysis is so deferential as to confirm an earlier observation that, except in cases where the Court chooses to invoke strict scrutiny, the Equal Protection Clause has been all but emasculated. See San Antonio School Dist. v. Rodriguez, 411 U. S. 1, 411 U. S. 98 (MARSHALL, J., dissenting). [2]

At the outset, then, I must once again take issue with the Court's apparently rigid approach to equal protection issues. See, e.g., Dandridge v. Williams, 397 U. S. 471, 397 U. S. 519-530 (1970) (MARSHALL, J., dissenting); Richardson v. Belcher, 404 U. S. 78, 991 (1971) (MARSHALL, J., dissenting); San Antonio School Dist. v. Rodriguez, supra, at 411 U. S. 98-110 (MARSHALL, J., dissenting). True, as the Court of Appeals found, this case does not fit into any neat "fundamental interest" or "suspect classification" mold. Notwithstanding, I find it hard to understand why a statute which sends a man to prison and deprives him of the opportunity even to be considered for treatment for his disease of narcotics addiction, [3] while providing treatment and suspension of prison sentence to others similarly situated, should be tested under the same minimal standards of rationality that we apply to statutes regulating who can sell eyeglasses or who can own pharmacies. See Williamson v. Lee Optical Co., 348 U. S. 483 (1955); North Dakota State Bd. of Pharmacy v. Snyder's Drug Stores, Inc., ante, p. 414 U. S. 156. This case does not involve discrimination against business interests more than powerful enough to protect themselves in the legislative halls, but the very life and health of a man caught up in the spiraling web of addiction and crime.

I press my disagreement no further here, for a careful analysis of the two-felony exclusion and the ends Congress sought to achieve shows that the exclusion is a totally irrational means toward those ends. If deferential scrutiny under the equal protection guarantee is to mean more than total deference and no scrutiny, surely it must reach the statutory exclusion involved in this case.

One of Congress' primary purposes in enacting the two-felony exclusion was to limit treatment to those convicted persons considered most deserving of the special benefits provided by the new law. As the Government argues in its brief, Congress wanted to grant the benefits of treatment to those who "were primarily addicts, and only secondarily criminals." Brief for United States 6. To state the goal more precisely, Congress intended to give treatment to those addicts whose criminal activity was only a symptom or product of their addiction. The House Report recognized that "Narcotic addicts, in their desperation to obtain drugs, often turn to crime in order to obtain money to feed their addiction." H.R.Rep. No. 1486, 89th Cong., 2d Sess., 8 (1966). On the other hand, Congress knew there were others who were first of all criminals, and only secondarily addicts -- that is, persons whose criminal activity was independent of their narcotics addiction. It was thought important to preserve strict criminal penalties for such hardened criminals, rather than permit them to use the fact of their addiction to escape punishment for a crime. See 112 Cong.Rec. 11813 (1966).

The plain fact of the matter, however, is that the two-felony exclusion does not further this legislative end, as the following examples demonstrate. Defendant A, with a prior felony conviction for assault with intent to commit murder, is convicted of stealing funds from a national bank. Neither crime was in any way related to narcotics addiction.

In fact, A was not even an addict at the time he committed the crimes, but has become an addict during the pendency of his bank theft trial. Defendant B, who has two prior felony convictions for narcotics offenses, is convicted of possession of heroin for his own use. Given the above-stated legislative purpose, one would think that Defendant B, all of whose criminal activity was related to his narcotics addiction, would be eligible for NARA treatment, while Defendant A, none of whose criminal activity was so related, would not be eligible. But just the opposite is true, because of the two-felony exclusion. [4]

The problem with the statute is not, as the majority would have it, that Congress chose two felonies as the cut-off point, rather than one or three. Rather, the statute fails to achieve the legislative end of discriminating between people who are mainly addicts and those who are mainly criminals because a numerical test was used to achieve a qualitative result for which it was totally unsuited.

A second basic purpose sought to be achieved through the two-felony exclusion was to restrict NARA treatment to those persons deemed likely to be rehabilitated. But the two-felony rule, again, is not a rational means toward that end. To begin with, it must be remembered that the statute itself limits participation in the program to those persons who, after an examination in the custody of the Attorney General, are determined to be addicts "likely to be rehabilitated through treatment." The two-felony exclusion, to the extent it is justified by reference to this policy, amounts to a conclusive and irrebuttable presumption that a person with two or more felony convictions is not likely to be rehabilitated through treatment. We have only recently reiterated that "permanent irrebuttable presumptions have long been disfavored," see Vlandis v. Kline, 412 U. S. 441, 412 U. S. 446 (1973). This is particularly true where an interest as important as personal liberty is at stake. And as one would expect of medical problems in general, whether a particular individual's disease of narcotics addiction is amenable to treatment is the very kind of question which requires an individualized determination. [5]

The two-felony presumption of nonamenability to rehabilitation is also plainly contrary to fact. The Administrator of the California Youth and Adult Corrections Agency pointed out that the "two or more felonies" provision "would result in a great many persons' being excluded who might prove to be the best subjects for the program." [6] As he indicated, it was the experience of the California program, [7] upon which the federal program was modeled in large part, that

"persons who have had as many as four or five previous convictions and have grown older in years respond to the program better than some of the younger persons earlier in their careers. [8]"

Nor was any contrary evidence presented to Congress.

Another purpose of the two-felony exclusion was to weed out those violent, antisocial individuals whose participation in the program would interfere with the rehabilitation of others. But again, Congress has drawn a numerical test to achieve a qualitative result for which it is manifestly unsuited. An addict with a prior conviction for attempted murder can participate in the NARA program, while one whose prior record includes two convictions for possession of narcotic drugs cannot. [9]

It makes no sense to deem an addict a "hardened criminal" unworthy or unsuited for treatment simply because he has engaged in criminal activity which may have been the symptom or product of his addiction. Congress enacted NARA because it knew that almost all addicts are hardened criminals in this sense. Not only are they driven to rob and steal in order to obtain money to sustain their habits, but their habits themselves involve the commission of felonies every day of their lives. As the House Report stated, the purpose of the bill was

"to treat the unfortunate addict who is capable of rehabilitation to render assistance in a manner which will enable him to extricate himself from an otherwise hopeless and repetitious pattern of addiction and crime. [10]"

To deny treatment to those addicts who have been convicted of a certain number of felonies, without regard to the relationship between their addiction and the prior offenses, is, in the apt words of Congressman Ryan, like "building a sanatorium to treat tuberculosis and then refusing admittance to patients with a contagious disease." 112 Cong.Rec. 11812 (1966). [11]

It is argued that the NARA program is essentially experimental in nature, and that courts should therefore be particularly reluctant to interfere with legislative decisions. But this observation must be tempered by a realization that we are experimenting here with people's lives and health. And it can hardly be said that a program now in its seventh year of operation is still basically experimental. Only last year, Congress broadened the NARA program to include methadone maintenance as part of the available rehabilitative treatment, recognizing the many cases of addiction which, though not totally curable, can be maintained in a manner which fosters the individual's social rehabilitation and permits him to become a productive member of society. See Pub.L. No. 92-420, 86 Stat. 677; S.Rep. No. 92-1071 (1972). With the program widened in this fashion, it seems even more irrational to exclude those who might well benefit from the expanded program through the operation of broad and arbitrary exclusions that do not reasonably further any legitimate congressional purposes.

Finally, we must be mindful that the growing concern with treatment of narcotics addicts has not arisen in a legal vacuum, but has paralleled a growing awareness of the Eighth Amendment questions raised when criminal punishment is imposed for activities which are the symptom or direct product of the disease of narcotics addiction. [12] The Court today, by dicta implying that Congress may, consistent with the equal protection concept, deny NARA benefits to persons convicted of narcotics-related offenses because of two prior convictions for narcotics-related offenses, [13] only exacerbates these Eighth Amendment problems.

Mr. Justice Jackson, himself a strong opponent of substantive due process, once argued that the vitality of the Equal Protection Clause as a ground for constitutional adjudication is that it "does not disable any governmental body from dealing with the subject at hand." Rather, it merely sends the legislature back to the drawing board to draft a statute which more precisely and more evenhandedly solves the problem. See Railway Express v. New York, 336 U. S. 106, 336 U. S. 112 (1949) (concurring opinion). I would not deny Congress the right to limit the NARA program to persons whose criminal activity was a product of their addiction, to those who were likely to be rehabilitated, or to those whose presence in a treatment center would not interfere with the rehabilitation of others. But I would have Congress make a second attempt at drafting a statute which actually furthers these ends.

Notes

[1] See Watson v. United States, 141 U.S.App.D.C. 335, 439 F.2d 442 (1970); United States v. Hamilton, 149 U.S.App.D.C. 295, 462 F.2d 1190 (1972); United States v. Bishop, 469 F.2d 1337 (CA1 1972). In addition to the statute's flaws noted in this opinion, these decisions also point out other anomalies implicit in the two-felony exclusion. Under the Act, an addict who has engaged in trafficking to support his own habit would be eligible for noncriminal disposition under Tit. II, whereas a nontrafficking addict found, for the third time, in possession of narcotics for his own use would not. This result

"is curiously at odds with the Congressional preoccupation, underlying the Narcotic Addict Rehabilitation Act, with the distinction between traffickers and non-traffickers, and the reiterated purpose that"

"strict punishment . . . be meted out where required to the hardened criminal, while justice . . . be tempered with judgment and fairness in those cases where it is to the best interest of society and the individual that such a course be followed."

Watson v. United States, supra, at 349, 439 F.2d at 456. Other anomalies stem from the definition of "felony" in 18 U.S.C. § 4251(d).

"[T]wo persons who both had twice previously committed the identical crime of possession of marijuana might be treated differently under [the two-felony exclusion] simply because one committed his crime in Florida, where possession over five grams is a felony, and the other committed his in New York, where it is only a misdemeanor . . . , or because one committed both of his crimes before May 1, 1971, and the other committed them after that date, when the federal offense of marijuana possession was reduced to a misdemeanor for first offenders. . . ."

United States v: Bishop, supra, at 1345.

[2] Cf. Gunther, The Supreme Court 1971 Term, Foreword: In Search of Evolving Doctrine on a Changing Court: A Model for a Newer Equal Protection, 86 Harv.L.Rev. 1, 8 (1972).

[3] Drug addiction is specifically referred to as a "disease" in the Senate Report recommending enactment of Pub.L. No. 92-420, 86 Stat. 677, which expanded the NARA program to include methadone maintenance. See S.Rep. No. 92-1071, p. 3 (1972). The most widely accepted and authoritative definition of heroin addiction is one promulgated by the World Health Organization, which lists its characteristics as:

"(1) an overpowering desire or need to continue taking the drug and to obtain it by any means; the need can be satisfied by the drug taken initially or by another with morphine-like properties;"

"(2) a tendency to increase the dose owing to the development of tolerance;"

"(3) a psychic dependence on the effects of the drug related to a subjective and individual appreciation of those effects; and"

"(4) a physical dependence on the effects of the drug requiring its presence for maintenance of homeostasis and resulting in a definite, characteristic, and self-limited abstinence syndrome when the drug is withdrawn."

United States v. Moore, 158 U.S.App.D.C. 375, 465-466, 486 F.2d 1139, 1229-1230 (1973) (Wright, J., dissenting), quoting World Health Organization Expert Committee on Addiction-Producing Drugs, Thirteenth Report, World Health Organization Technical Report Series No. 273, p. 13 (1964). Congress has similarly defined an "addict" to include one "who is so far addicted to the use of narcotic drugs as to have lost the power of self-control with reference to his addiction." 21 U.S.C. § 802(1).

[4] Defendant A would not be excluded from the program under the statutory exclusion of "an offender who is convicted of a crime of violence," 18 U.S.C. § 4251(f)(1), since that exclusion applies only to a person convicted of a crime of violence in the same proceeding in which Tit. II is considered as an alternative to prison sentence. Thus, if one has just been convicted of a "crime of violence" as defined in § 4251(b), one is disqualified from the program under § 4251(f)(1), while if one had previously been so convicted, but is now convicted of a nonviolent crime, one would be eligible. See United States v. Bishop, 469 F.2d at 1344.

[5] Congressman Celler remarked:

"Each individual case must be scrutinized to determine whether civil commitment will be efficacious. I submit that it should not be the Congress who, at long distance, makes such determinations. In the absence of the facts of individual cases, these decisions can only be arbitrary."

See Civil Commitment and Treatment of Narcotic Addicts, Hearings on H.R. 9051, 9159, 9167, and Related Bills before Subcommittee No. 2 of the House Committee on the Judiciary, 89th Cong., 1st and 2d Sess., ser. 10, p. 55 (1965 and 1966).

[6] The Narcotic Addict Rehabilitation Act of 1966, Hearings before a Special Subcommittee of the Senate Committee on the Judiciary, 89th Cong., 2d Sess., 91 (1966).

[7] See Cal.Welf. & Inst.Code §§ 3050-3054, 3104-3107, and 3109 (1972). The California statute has no exclusion similar to the two-felony exclusion. It is also interesting to note that, while the California Act, like the federal Act, excludes persons convicted of certain crimes of violence, see id. § 3052, the statute also provides that, even in the case of an offender convicted of a crime of violence,

"the judge may request the district attorney to investigate the facts relevant to the advisability of commitment pursuant to this section. In unusual cases, wherein the interest of justice would best be served, the judge may, with the concurrence of the district attorney and defendant, order commitment notwithstanding" the "crime of violence" exclusion. Id., § 3051.

[8] Hearings, supra, n. 5, at 153.

[9] The statute's disregard of all time limits is further evidence of its arbitrary nature.

"All prior felonies are counted -- whether a joy-ride by a peer-imitating teenager or a rape committed by a 35-year-old sex deviate during the pendency of the proceedings in which sentence is about to be imposed. Any intervening period between felonies of good behavior or attempts at rehabilitation are ignored; a person is thought to harden as a criminal merely because he accumulates a fixed number of judgments, regardless of changes in his personality or personal circumstances over time."

United States v. Bishop, supra, at 1345.

[10] H.R.Rep. No. 1486, 89th Cong., 2d Sess., 5 (1966).

[11] The majority's contention, see ante at 414 U. S. 420 n. 2, that prisoners not eligible for the NARA program are not actually denied treatment because they may receive the benefits of similar programs within the Federal Bureau of Prisons is simply contrary to fact. As the Government itself indicates in its brief, treatment begins immediately upon commitment under NARA, and the offender is eligible for conditional release on parole after six months of treatment. Brief for United States 2 n. 1. Addicts not committed under NARA, however, are not placed in any rehabilitation program until about one year before their anticipated release. Ibid. Thus, an addict like petitioner, who received a 1-year sentence, will have to go many years without treatment for his disease because of his exclusion from the NARA program.

More importantly, we are told that the Bureau of Prisons does not have sufficient facilities for treatment of the approximately 5,000 federal prisoners estimated to suffer from some degree of drug dependency. In the Government's own words:

"Thus, although commitment under NARA assures treatment, a judicial recommendation for similar treatment at the time an ordinary criminal sentence is imposed does not."

Id. at 3 n. 1. Indeed, there is no indication in the record in this case that petitioner has yet received any treatment for his addiction, notwithstanding the sentencing court's recommendation of treatment.

[12] In Watson v. United States, 141 U.S.App.D.C. 335, 439 F.2d 442 (1970), it was argued that criminal punishment of an addict for possession of narcotics solely for his own use was impermissible under the Eighth Amendment, but the question was left undecided because not clearly raised before the trial court. See id. at 346, 439 F.2d at 453. Plenary consideration of the Eighth Amendment problems of convicting addicts for addiction-related offenses came in United States v. Moore, 158 U.S.App.D.C. 375, 486 F.2d 1139 (en banc), cert. denied, post, p. 980. Although the defense of addiction was rejected by a 5-4 decision, it now appears that for two members of the majority, the rejection of the Eighth Amendment defense "rested on the availability to the defendant-addict of treatment through NARA." See United States v. Harrison, 158 U.S.App.D.C. 229,

231, 485 F.2d 1008, 1010 (1973).

This Court has previously dealt with related issues in Robinson v. California, 370 U. S. 660 (1962), and Powell v. Texas, 392 U. S. 514 (1968).

[13] As the majority opinion indicates, petitioner had three prior felony convictions for burglary, forgery, and possession of a firearm, respectively, and there was no attempt to show that his prior convictions related to traffic in narcotics. In addition, there does not appear to have been any showing that petitioner's present conviction for entering a bank with intent to commit a felony was narcotics-related. Accordingly, the majority's remarks with respect to Congress' power to exclude from the NARA program persons whose prior and present offenses are addiction related or motivated purport to resolve questions not before us in this case. See ante at 414 U. S. 427-428.

Bank Secrecy Act unconstitutional: Justice Marshall's dissent in California Bankers Association v. Shultz (April 1, 1974)

MR. JUSTICE MARSHALL, dissenting.

Although I am in general agreement with the opinions of my Brothers DOUGLAS and BRENNAN, I believe it important to set forth what I view as the essential issue in these cases.

The purposes of the recordkeeping requirements of the Bank Secrecy Act are clear from the language of the legislation itself -- to require the maintenance of records which will later be available for examination by the Government in "criminal, tax, or regulatory investigations or proceedings." See 12 U.S.C. §§ 1829b(a)(2) and 1951(b). The maintenance of the records is thus but the initial step in a process whereby the Government seeks to acquire the private financial papers of the millions of individuals, businesses, and organizations that maintain accounts in banks and use negotiable instruments such as checks to carry out the financial side of their day-by-day transactions. In my view, this attempt to acquire private papers constitutes a search and seizure under the Fourth Amendment.

As this Court settled long ago in Boyd v. United States, 116 U. S. 616, 116 U. S. 622 (1886),

"a compulsory production of a man's private papers to establish a criminal charge against him . . . is within the scope of the Fourth Amendment to the Constitution. . . ."

The acquisition of records in this case, as we said of the order to produce an invoice in Boyd, may lack the "aggravating incidents of actual search and seizure, such as forcible entry into a man's house and searching amongst his papers . . .," ibid., but this cannot change its intrinsic character as a search and seizure. We do well to recall the admonishment in Boyd, id. at 116 U. S. 635:

"It may be that it is the obnoxious thing in its mildest and least repulsive form; but illegitimate and unconstitutional practices get their first footing in that way, namely, by silent approaches and slight deviations from legal modes of procedure."

By compelling an otherwise unwilling bank to photocopy the checks of its customers, the Government has as much of a hand in seizing those checks as if it had forced a private person to break into the customer's home or office and photocopy the checks there. See Byars v. United States, 273 U. S. 28 (1927). Compare Burdeau v. McDowell, 256 U. S. 465 (1921), with Lustig v. United States, 338 U. S. 74, 338 U. S. 78-79 (Frankfurter, J.). See also Corngold v. United States, 367 F.2d 1 (CA9 1966). Our Fourth Amendment jurisprudence should not be so wooden as to ignore the fact that, through microfilming and other techniques of this electronic age, illegal searches and seizures can take place without the brute force characteristic of the general warrants which raised the ire of the Founding Fathers. See Entick v. Carrington, 19 How.St.Tr. 1029 (1765); Stanford v. Texas, 379 U. S. 476, 379 U. S. 483-484 (1965). As we emphasized in Katz v. United States, 389 U. S. 347 (1967), the absence of any physical seizure of tangible property does not foreclose Fourth Amendment inquiry. Id. at 389 U. S. 352-353. The Fourth Amendment "governs not only the seizure of tangible items, but extends as well to the recording of oral statements. . . ." Id. at 389 U. S. 353. By the same logic, the Fourth Amendment should apply to the recording of checks mandated by the Act here. And such a massive and indiscriminate search and seizure, not only without a warrant but also without probable cause to believe that any evidence to be obtained is relevant to any investigation, is plainly inconsistent with the principles behind the Amendment. See Stanford v. Texas, supra, at 379 U. S. 485-486; Katz v. United States, supra, at 389 U. S. 356-359.

It is suggested that there is no seizure under the Fourth Amendment because the bank, which is required to create and maintain the record, is already a party to the transaction. See ante at 416 U. S. 52. Surely this is irrelevant to the question of whether a Government search or seizure is involved. The fact that one has disclosed private papers to the bank, for a limited purpose, within the context of a confidential customer-bank relationship, does not mean that one has waived all right to the privacy of the papers. Like the user of the pay phone in Katz v. United States, who, having paid the toll, was "entitled to assume that the words he utters into the mouthpiece will not be broadcast to the world," 389 U.S. at 389 U. S. 352, so the customer of a bank, having written or deposited a check, has a reasonable expectation that his check will be examined for bank purposes only -- to credit, debit or balance his account -- and not recorded and kept on file for several years by Government decree so that it can be available for Government scrutiny. See United States v. First Nat. Bank of Mobile, 67 F.Supp. 616 (SD Ala.1946).

The majority argues that any Fourth Amendment claim is premature, since the Act itself only affects the keeping of records, and in no way changes the law regarding acquisition of the records by the Government. I cannot agree. This attempt to bifurcate the acquisition of information into two independent and unrelated steps is wholly unrealistic. As the Government itself concedes, "banks have in the past voluntarily allowed law enforcement officials to inspect bank records without requiring the issuance of a summons." Brief for Appellees in Nos. 72-985 and 72-1196, p. 38 n.19. Indeed, the Chief of the Organized Crime and Racketeering Section of the Criminal Division of the Justice Department told a Senate Subcommittee in 1972 that access by the FBI to bank records without process occurs "with some degree of frequency." Hearings to amend the Bank Secrecy Act (S. 3814 and S. 3828) before the Subcommittee on Financial Institutions of the Senate Committee on Banking, Housing and Urban Affairs, 92d Cong., 2d Sess., 114-115 (1972).

The plain fact of the matter is that the Act's recordkeeping requirement feeds into a system of widespread informal access to bank records by Government agencies and law enforcement personnel. If these customers' Fourth Amendment claims cannot be raised now, they cannot be raised at all, for, once recorded, their checks will be readily accessible, without judicial process and without any showing of probable cause, to any of the several agencies that presently have informal access to bank records.

The Government suggests that the Act does not in any way preclude banks from refusing to allow informal access and insisting on the issuance of legal process before turning over a customer's financial records. Such a refusal, however, even if accompanied by notice to the customer with an opportunity for him to assert his constitutional claims, comes too late, for the seizure has already taken place. By virtue of the Act's recordkeeping requirement, copies of the customer's checks are already in the bank's files, and amenable to process. The seizure has already occurred, and all that remains is the transfer of the documents from the agent forced by the Government to accomplish the seizure to the Government itself. Indeed, it is ironic that, although the majority deems the bank customers' Fourth Amendment claims premature, it also intimates that, once the bank has made copies of a customer's checks, the customer no longer has standing to invoke his Fourth Amendment rights when a demand is made on the bank by the Government for the records. See ante at 416 U. S. 53. By accepting the Government's bifurcated approach to the recordkeeping requirement and the acquisition of the records, the majority engages in a hollow charade whereby Fourth Amendment claims are to be labeled premature until such time as they can be deemed too late.

Nor can I accept the majority's analysis of the First Amendment associational claims raised by the American Civil Liberties Union on behalf of its members who seek to preserve the anonymity of their financial support of the organization. The First Amendment gives organizations such as the ACLU the right to maintain in confidence the names of those who belong or contribute to the organization, absent a compelling governmental interest requiring disclosure. See NAACP v. Alabama, 357 U. S. 449 (1958). See also Lamont v. Postmaster General, 381 U. S. 301 (1965); Gibson v. Florida Legislative Investigation Comm'n, 372 U. S. 539 (1963); Louisiana ex rel. Gremillion v. NAACP, 366 U. S. 293 (1961); Shelton v. Tucker, 364 U. S. 479 (1960); Bates v. Little Rock, 361 U. S. 516 (1960); United States v. Rumley, 345 U. S. 41 (1953). It is certainly inconsistent with this long line of cases for the Government, absent any showing of need whatsoever, to require the bank with which the ACLU maintains an account to make and keep a microfilm record of all checks received by the ACLU and deposited to its account. The net result of this requirement, obviously, is an easily accessible list of all of the ACLU's contributors. And, given the widespread informal access to bank records by Government agencies, see supra at 416 U. S. 96-97, the existence of such a list surely will chill the exercise of First Amendment rights of association on the part of those who wish to have their contributions remain anonymous. The technique of examining bank accounts to investigate political organizations is, unfortunately, not rare. See, e.g., Pollard v. Roberts, 283 F.Supp. 248 (ED Ark.), aff'd per curiam, 393 U. S. 14 (1968); United States Servicemen's Fund v. Eastland, 159 U.S.App.D.C. 352. 488 F.2d 1252 (1973).

First Amendment freedoms are "delicate and vulnerable." They need breathing space to survive. NAACP v. Button, 371 U. S. 415, 371 U. S. 433 (1963). The threat of disclosure entailed in the existence of an easily accessible list of contributors may deter the exercise of First Amendment rights as potently as disclosure itself. Cf. ibid. See also United States Servicemen's Fund v. Eastland, supra, at 365-368, 488 F.2d at 1265-1268. More importantly, however slight may be the inhibition of First Amendment rights caused by the bank's maintenance of the list of contributors, the crucial factor is that the Government has shown no need, compelling or otherwise, for the maintenance of such records. Surely the fact that some may use negotiable instruments for illegal purposes cannot justify the Government's running roughshod over the First Amendment rights of the hundreds of lawful yet controversial organizations like the ACLU. Congress may well have been correct in concluding that law enforcement would be facilitated by the dragnet requirements of this Act. Those who wrote our Constitution, however, recognized more important values.

I respectfully dissent.

Ex-felons should have their rights restored upon release: Justice Marshall's dissent in Richardson v. Ramirez (June 24, 1974)

MR. JUSTICE MARSHALL, with whom MR. JUSTICE BRENNAN joins, dissenting.

The Court today holds that a State may strip ex-felons who have fully paid their debt to society of their fundamental right to vote without running afoul of the Fourteenth Amendment. This result is, in my view, based on an unsound historical analysis which already has been rejected by this Court. In straining to reach that result, I believe that the Court has also disregarded important limitations on its jurisdiction. For these reasons, I respectfully dissent.

I

A brief retracing of the procedural history of this case is necessary to a full understanding of my views. Each of the respondents, the plaintiffs below, 1 had been convicted of a felony unrelated to voting and had fully served his term of incarceration and parole. Each applied to register to vote in his respective county - Ramirez in San Luis Obispo County, Lee in Monterey County, and Gill in Stanislaus County. All three were refused registration because, under applicable provisions of the California Constitution, "no person convicted of any infamous crime . . . shall ever exercise the privileges of an elector." 2

The three named plaintiffs filed a petition for a writ of mandate in the California Supreme Court, invoking its original jurisdiction. Plaintiffs challenged the State's disenfranchisement of ex-felons as being violative of the Equal Protection Clause of the Fourteenth Amendment and sought issuance of a peremptory writ of mandate to compel their registration. The complaint labeled the suit as brought "individually and on behalf of all other persons who are ineligible to register to vote in California solely by reason of a conviction of a felony other than an election code felony" and who had fully served their terms of incarceration and parole. The complaint named, as defendants, the election officials who had refused to register them, "individually and as representatives of the class of all other County Clerks and Registrars of Voters who have the duty of determining for their respective counties whether any ex-felon will be denied the right to vote."

The three named election officials did not contest the action and represented to the state court that they would permit the named plaintiffs and all similarly situated ex-felons in their counties to register and to vote. The representative of the Secretary of State of California, also named as a defendant, has similarly agreed not to contest the suit. 3 At this point in the litigation all of the named plaintiffs had been voluntarily afforded the relief they were seeking by the election officials in their respective counties.

Subsequently, the petitioner in this Court, Viola Richardson, as County Clerk of Mendocino County, filed a motion to intervene in the proceedings before the California Supreme Court. She indicated to the court that she was being sued in a separate action in a lower state court by an ex-felon seeking to register in her county and that the decision in this case would be dispositive of the legal issue in that controversy. The State Supreme Court ordered Richardson added as a named defendant in the instant action, but did not name the ex-felon suing her as a plaintiff or named class representative herein.

In its opinion, the California Supreme Court found the case not to be moot and took the opportunity to address the merits of the Fourteenth Amendment issue. It indicated that, in its view, the ex-felon disenfranchisement provision of the California Constitution and its implementing statutes violated the Equal Protection Clause. The state court did not, however, afford the plaintiffs the relief they sought. The court denied the peremptory writ of mandate.

Although the California Supreme Court did not issue a writ ordering Richardson to register either the ex-felon suing her or any other potential elector in her county, she sought review of the state court's decision by way of writ of certiorari in this Court. The election officials in the named plaintiffs' counties did not seek review and the Secretary of State filed a memorandum opposing review by this Court.

A

There are a number of reasons why I do not believe this case is properly before us at this time. First, I am persuaded that the judgment of the California Supreme Court rests on an adequate and independent state ground.

"This Court from the time of its foundation has adhered to the principle that it will not review judgments of state courts that rest on adequate and independent state grounds. . . . Our only power over state judgments is to correct them to the extent that they incorrectly adjudge federal rights. And our power is to correct wrong judgments, not to revise opinions. We are not permitted to render an advisory opinion, and if the same judgment would be rendered by the state court after we corrected its views of federal laws, our review could amount to nothing more than an advisory opinion." Herb v. Pitcairn, 324 U.S. 117, 125 -126 (1945).

Plaintiffs sought, from the California Supreme Court, a writ of mandate compelling their registration. The state court denied that relief. The entirety of the judgment of that court is as follows:

"The alternative writ, having served its purpose, is discharged, and the petition for peremptory writ is denied." Ramirez v. Brown, 9 Cal. 3d 199, 217, 507 P.2d 1345, 1357 (1973). 4

The accompanying opinion indicates that the California court did not consider the case before it to be moot and that, in its view, the plaintiffs' assertion that the disenfranchisement provisions were unconstitutional was well taken. Since the court nonetheless denied plaintiffs the relief they sought, we can only conclude that it did so on independent state law grounds. Cf. Brockington v. Rhodes, 396 U.S. 41, 44 (1969). For example, a writ of mandate being discretionary, the state court may have declined its issuance simply because the named plaintiffs had already been registered and mandate relief seemed unnecessary. 5 There is certainly no indication that the decision to deny the writ was based on the state court's view on any federal question.

This Court creates an interesting anomaly by purporting to reverse the judgment of the California court. Since that court denied a writ of mandate to compel the registration of ex-felons, the only disposition consistent with this Court's view that the California disenfranchisement provisions are constitutional would be to affirm the judgment below. By reversing, the Court apparently directs the issuance of the peremptory writ. This anomaly demonstrates that this is a classic example of a case where "the same judgment would be rendered by the state court after we corrected its views of federal laws," Herb v. Pitcairn, supra, at 126; hence we can but offer an advisory opinion here. Whether we agree or disagree with the state court's view of the constitutionality of the challenged provisions, the judgment of the state court will necessarily remain to deny the writ of mandate.

The Court is aware of this problem and purports to resolve it by speculating that the California court may have afforded plaintiffs declaratory relief. Such speculation is totally unfounded. Neither the opinion nor the judgment of the court below even mentions declaratory relief. The plaintiffs did not seek a declaratory judgment. The

California Constitution on its face appears to bar the State Supreme Court from issuing a declaratory judgment in an original proceeding such as the one before us, since it limits that court's original jurisdiction to "proceedings for extraordinary relief in the nature of mandamus, certiorari, and prohibition." Calif. Const., Art. 6, 10 (Supp. 1974). Exclusive jurisdiction for suits seeking declaratory relief is vested, by statute, in the State Superior Courts. 6

This Court's basis for construing the judgment of the court below as affording declaratory relief is its argument that because the California Supreme Court is the highest court of the State, its observations on the constitutionality of the challenged disenfranchisement provisions are apt to be heeded by state officials. It is true that the opinion of the California court did indicate a view on the merits of the plaintiffs' constitutional claim. But this Court's power "is to correct wrong judgments, not to revise opinions." Herb v. Pitcairn, supra, at 126. One could always argue that where a state court had commented on a matter of federal law, state officials would heed those comments. To say that such comments are a "declaration of federal law" reviewable by this Court is a rationale that would reach every case in which the state court decision rests on adequate state grounds, rendering that doctrine a virtual nullity. The Court also cites two cases for the proposition that the California Supreme Court can issue a declaratory judgment in an original proceeding. But, on closer inspection, the cases cited by the Court, ante, at 41 n. 13, merely demonstrate that California courts, whose jurisdiction is not limited by any equivalent to Art. III, are free to render advisory opinions. 7 There is little doubt that many public officials would heed such an advisory opinion from the California Supreme Court and they would also heed an advisory opinion issued by this Court, but that does not free us from the constitutional limitations on our jurisdiction.

Because I believe that the judgment of the California court was based on adequate and independent state grounds, I do not think we have jurisdiction to consider any other issues presented by this case.

B

Assuming arguendo, that the California Supreme Court did grant a declaratory judgment, I still believe that we are without jurisdiction because no case or controversy is presented. The Court seems willing to concede that the claims of the named plaintiffs may well be moot. Ante, at 36. The Court, however, premises its jurisdiction on the assumption that there is a live controversy between the named petitioner in this Court and the unnamed plaintiff class members in her own county. To reach this conclusion, it is essential for the Court to conclude that this case is, in fact, a class action and that, in the circumstances of this case, it is appropriate to look to unnamed class members to determine whether there is a live controversy.

I am forced to point out that one of the crucial premises upon which the Court bases its assumption of jurisdiction - the existence of a class action - is highly speculative. I am persuaded that the California court never treated this case as a class action. As the majority notes, the case was titled a class action by its originators and the show-cause order merely tracked the language of the complaint. But the California court was, of course, not bound by that designation. In the entirety of its lengthy opinion, the California court does not once refer to this suit as a class action, to respondents as class representatives, to the existence of unnamed parties or to any other indicia of class-action status. Rather, the state court describes the case as simply "a proceeding for writ of mandate brought by three ex-felons to compel respondent election officials to register them as voters." 9 Cal. 3d, at 201, 507 P.2d, at 1346. The opinion proceeds to list the three plaintiffs and, in a footnote, to explain that the only other plaintiffs were the League of Women Voters and three nonprofit organizations which support the interests of ex-felons. The opinion describes the defendants as the election officials of San Luis Obispo, Monterey, and Stanislaus Counties and the Secretary of State "in his capacity [as] chief elections officer of California," and notes that "[u]pon application we ordered the Mendocino County clerk [the petitioner here] joined as an additional party [defendant]." Id., at 202 n. 1, 507 P.2d, at 1346 n. 1. This description of the parties plainly indicates that this suit was not treated as a class action by the state court. I think it highly inappropriate that on the basis of nothing but speculation, this case be fashioned into a class action, for the first time, in this Court.

C

Even assuming that this case is a class action, I still would not agree that it is properly before us. I do not believe that we can look beyond the named class members to find a case or controversy in the circumstances of this case. The Court seems to hold that review is not foreclosed by the possible mootness of the named plaintiffs' claim because, but for the California Supreme Court's decision, unnamed class members would still be subject to the challenged disenfranchisement, hence the case presents, as to unnamed class members, an issue capable of repetition, yet evading review. I disagree.

As the Court properly notes, a general rule of justiciability is that one may not represent a class of which he is not a part. Thus, as a general proposition, a federal court will not look to unnamed class members to establish the case-or-controversy requirement of Art. III. 8 But, the "evading review" doctrine of Southern Pacific Terminal Co. v. ICC, 219 U.S. 498, 515 (1911), as recently applied in Dunn v. Blumstein, 405 U.S. 330, 333 n. 2 (1972), provides a limited exception to the general rule - an exception necessary to insure that judicial review is not foreclosed in cases where intervening events threaten invariably to moot the named plaintiff's claim for relief.

The necessity for looking beyond the named class members in this limited category of cases is evidenced by our decision in Dunn v. Blumstein, supra, in which the Court struck down a durational residence requirement for voting. The suit had been brought to compel the registration of the named plaintiff and the members of the class he represented in order that they might participate in an election scheduled for August 6, 1970. The Federal District Court did not order preliminary relief in time for the August election and, by the time the District Court decided the case, the next election was scheduled for November 1970. By then, the named plaintiff would have met the challenged three-month requirement. The District Court, nonetheless, rejected the State's argument that the controversy over the validity of the three-month requirement was therefore moot.

By the time the appeal reached this Court, the only named plaintiff had also satisfied the one-year state residence requirement. We nonetheless reached the merits, observing that "[a]lthough appellee [the only named plaintiff] now can vote, the problem to voters posed by the Tennessee residence requirements is `"capable of repetition, yet evading review."' Moore v. Ogilvie, 394 U.S. 814, 816 (1969)." 405 U.S., at 333 n. 2. Both this Court and the District Court found that, although the named plaintiff had satisfied the challenged residence requirements and would no longer be disenfranchised thereby, the case was not moot. The challenged requirement remained applicable to unnamed class members, 9 and the issue presented was likely to evade review. Obviously the mere passage of a few months would invariably have rendered a challenge to the residence requirements by individual named plaintiffs moot - threatening virtually to foreclose judicial review.

A similar situation was presented in Roe v. Wade, 410 U.S. 113 (1973), relied on by the California court. We there held that although a woman who was not pregnant at the time the suit was filed did not have standing to challenge the constitutionality of the Texas abortion laws, a continuing controversy over the constitutionality of those laws existed as to a named plaintiff who was pregnant when the suit was filed, even though she may not have been pregnant at later stages of the appeal. We concluded that this case provided a classic example of an issue capable of repetition, yet evading review, hence the termination of the plaintiff's pregnancy while the case was on appeal did not render the case moot - even though a woman whose pregnancy has ended is no more affected by the abortion laws than one who was not pregnant at the time the suit was filed. "[T]he . . . human gestation period is so short that . . . pregnancy will come to term before the usual appellate process is complete. If that termination makes a case moot, . . . appellate review will be effectively denied." Id., at 125.

There are two common threads running through these cases - in each the challenged statute would continue to be applied, but the named plaintiff's claim would inevitably mature into mootness pending resolution of the lawsuit. In Roe, the termination of pregnancy, in Dunn, the passage of the residence requirement period, and in other voting cases, the occurrence of an election, 10 deprived the named plaintiff of a continuing controversy over the application of the challenged statute. In each instance, the mere passage of time threatened to insulate a constitutional deprivation from judicial review, and it is that danger which served as the rationale for rejecting suggestions of mootness. Where an invalid statute would thus continue to be applied simply because judicial review of a live controversy involving the named plaintiff was invariably foreclosed - the issue would be capable of repetition yet evading review.

Accordingly, the Southern Pacific doctrine requires the satisfaction of two tests in order to provide an answer to a suggestion of mootness. First, the claimed deprivation must, in fact, be "capable of repetition." This element is satisfied where, even though the named plaintiff's immediate controversy has been mooted by intervening events, either he or unnamed class members may continue to suffer the alleged constitutional deprivation in the future. The case before us clearly satisfies this first element of the Southern Pacific doctrine test. Since the California court declined to order any county clerk to register ex-felons, presumably the challenged disenfranchisement provisions could continue to be applied to unnamed class members in counties other than those in which the named plaintiffs reside. 11

Second, the issue presented must be likely to evade review, but for invocation of the Southern Pacific doctrine. It is on the "evading review" element that the Court's analysis fails. Because the claim raised in this case concerns not a time-related but rather a status-based deprivation, there is no issue evading review and no reason to look beyond the named plaintiffs. 12 This is not a situation where, by the time a case reaches this Court, it will always be too late to grant the named plaintiff relief. If and when an ex-felon is refused access to the voting rolls because of his past criminal record, an intervening election will not moot his claim for relief and the status giving rise to his disenfranchisement will not inevitably terminate pending review.

There are clearly ways in which a challenge to the California disenfranchisement provisions could reach this Court. The California Supreme Court has not issued a writ of mandate compelling the registration of any ex-felon. 13 If such a potential voter is, in fact, refused registration, a controversy suitable for resolution by this Court will be presented. The suit brought against petitioner Richardson, by an ex-felon resident of her own county, raising the same issues as those presented by this case, is presently pending in a California intermediate appellate court. 14 In that case, petitioner Richardson did, in fact, deny the plaintiff registration because he was an ex-felon. Once that case completes its passage through the state courts, it could well serve as a vehicle for our review of the California disenfranchisement provisions. That is, of course, but one example of how the issue presented here could properly reach this Court. This case does not therefore benefit from the Southern Pacific doctrine's authority to look to unnamed class members to establish a case or controversy.

That the California Supreme Court appears to have found the plaintiffs' claims not to be moot does not detract from this conclusion since "[e]ven in cases arising in the state courts, the question of mootness is a federal one which a federal court must resolve before it assumes jurisdiction." North Carolina v. Rice, 404 U.S. 244, 246 (1971). Thus, unlike the Court, I am persuaded that we can look only to the named plaintiffs to satisfy the case-or-controversy requirement of Art. III.

D

The named plaintiffs here were registered only because the clerks in their counties had voluntarily abandoned an allegedly illegal practice of disenfranchising ex-felons, and we have said that "[m]ere voluntary cessation of allegedly illegal conduct does not moot a case; if it did, the courts would be compelled to leave `[t]he defendant . . . free to return to his old ways.'. . . [But a] case might become moot if subsequent events made it absolutely clear that the allegedly wrongful behavior could not reasonably be expected to recur." United States v. Concentrated Phosphate Export Assn., 393 U.S. 199, 203 (1968); accord, United States v. W. T. Grant Co., 345 U.S. 629, 632 (1953). Accordingly, whether the named plaintiffs have a live controversy with the clerks in their own counties would depend on the likelihood of future disenfranchisement. 15 But we need not consider that question here because none of the election officials in the named plaintiffs' counties sought review in this Court and none is now before us.

The sole petitioner before this Court is Viola Richardson. None of the named plaintiffs are residents of her county. While those named plaintiffs may or may not have a live controversy with the clerks in their own counties, they surely do not have one with petitioner Richardson. While Richardson may well have a live controversy with ex-felons in her own county over the validity of the disenfranchisement laws, those ex-felons are not before this Court, and she has no dispute with the named plaintiffs. In sum, there is no controversy between the parties before this Court. Petitioner Richardson seeks to use the named plaintiffs' controversy with their own county clerks as a vehicle for this Court to issue an advisory opinion on the issue presented by the suit brought against her by an ex-felon in her own county. Such a decision would violate the "`oldest and most consistent thread in the federal law of justiciability . . . that the federal courts will not give advisory opinions.'" Flast v. Cohen, 392 U.S. 83, 96 (1968).

II

Since the Court nevertheless reaches the merits of the constitutionality of California's disenfranchisement of ex-felons, I find it necessary to register my dissent on the merits as well. The Court construes 2 of the Fourteenth Amendment as an express authorization for the States to disenfranchise former felons. Section 2 does except disenfranchisement for "participation in rebellion, or other crime" from the operation of its penalty provision. As the Court notes, however, there is little independent legislative history as to the crucial words "or other crime"; the proposed 2 went to a joint committee containing only the phrase "participation in rebellion" and emerged with "or other crime" inexplicably tacked on. 16 In its exhaustive review of the lengthy legislative history of the Fourteenth Amendment, the Court has come upon only one explanatory reference for the "other crimes" provision - a reference which is unilluminating at best. 17

The historical purpose for 2 itself is, however, relatively clear and in my view, dispositive of this case. The Republicans who controlled the 39th Congress were concerned that the additional congressional representation of the Southern States which would result from the abolition of slavery might weaken their own political dominance. 18 There were two alternatives available - either to limit southern representation, which was unacceptable on a long-term basis, 19 or to insure that southern Negroes, sympathetic to the Republican cause, would be enfranchised; but an explicit grant of suffrage to Negroes was thought politically unpalatable at the time. 20 Section 2 of the Fourteenth Amendment was the resultant compromise. It put Southern States to a choice -

enfranchise Negro voters or lose congressional representation. 21

The political motivation behind 2 was a limited one. It had little to do with the purposes of the rest of the Fourteenth Amendment. As one noted commentator explained:

"`It became a part of the Fourteenth Amendment largely through the accident of political exigency rather than through the relation which it bore to the other sections of the Amendment.'" 22 "[I]t seems quite impossible to conclude that there was a clear and deliberate understanding in the House that 2 was the sole source of national authority to protect voting rights, or that it expressly recognized the states' power to deny or abridge the right to vote." 23

It is clear that 2 was not intended and should not be construed to be a limitation on the other sections of the Fourteenth Amendment. Section 2 provides a special remedy - reduced representation - to cure a particular form of electoral abuse - the disenfranchisement of Negroes. There is no indication that the framers of the provisions intended that special penalty to be the exclusive remedy for all forms of electoral discrimination. This Court has repeatedly rejected that rationale. See Reynolds v. Sims, 377 U.S. 533 (1964); Carrington v. Rash, 380 U.S. 89 (1965).

Rather, a discrimination to which the penalty provision of 2 is inapplicable must still be judged against the Equal Protection Clause of 1 to determine whether judicial or congressional remedies should be invoked. That conclusion is compelled by this Court's holding in Oregon v. Mitchell, 400 U.S. 112 (1970). Although 2 excepts from its terms denial of the franchise not only to ex-felons but also to persons under 21 years of age, we held that the Congress, under 5, had the power to implement the Equal Protection Clause by lowering the voting age to 18 in federal elections. As MR. JUSTICE BRENNAN, joined by MR. JUSTICE WHITE, as well as myself, there observed, 2 was intended as no more "than a remedy supplementary, and in some conceivable circumstances indispensable, to other congressional and judicial remedies available under 1 and 5." 400 U.S., at 278 .

The Court's references to congressional enactments contemporaneous to the adoption of the Fourteenth Amendment, such as the Reconstruction Act and the readmission statutes, are inapposite. They do not explain the purpose for the adoption of 2 of the Fourteenth Amendment. They merely indicate that disenfranchisement for participation in crime was not uncommon in the States at the time of the adoption of the Amendment. Hence, not surprisingly, that form of disenfranchisement was excepted from the application of the special penalty provision of 2. But because Congress chose to exempt one form of electoral discrimination from the reduction-of-representation remedy provided by 2 does not necessarily imply congressional approval of this disenfranchisement. 24 By providing a special remedy for disenfranchisement of a particular class of voters in 2, Congress did not approve all election discriminations to which the 2 remedy was inapplicable, and such discriminations thus are not forever immunized from evolving standards of equal protection scrutiny. Cf. Shapiro v. Thompson, 394 U.S. 618, 638 -639 (1969). There is no basis for concluding that Congress intended by 2 to freeze the meaning of other clauses of the Fourteenth Amendment to the conception of voting rights prevalent at the time of the adoption of the Amendment. In fact, one form of disenfranchisement - one-year durational residence requirements - specifically authorized by the Reconstruction Act, one of the contemporaneous enactments upon which the Court relies to show the intendment of the framers of the Fourteenth Amendment, has already been declared unconstitutional by this Court in Dunn v. Blumstein, 405 U.S. 330 (1972).

Disenfranchisement for participation in crime, like durational residence requirements, was common at the time of the adoption of the Fourteenth Amendment. But "constitutional concepts of equal protection are not immutably frozen like insects trapped in Devonian amber." Dillenburg v. Kramer, 469 F.2d 1222, 1226 (CA9 1972). We have repeatedly observed:

"[T]he Equal Protection Clause is not shackled to the political theory of a particular era. In determining what lines are unconstitutionally discriminatory, we have never been confined to historic notions of equality, any more than we have restricted due process to a fixed catalogue of what was at a given time deemed to be the limits of fundamental rights." Harper v. Virginia Board of Elections, 383 U.S. 663, 669 (1966).

Accordingly, neither the fact that several States had ex-felon disenfranchisement laws at the time of the adoption of the Fourteenth Amendment, nor that such disenfranchisement was specifically excepted from the special remedy of 2, can serve to insulate such disenfranchisement from equal protection scrutiny.

III

In my view, the disenfranchisement of ex-felons must be measured against the requirements of the Equal Protection Clause of 1 of the Fourteenth Amendment. That analysis properly begins with the observation that because the right to vote "is of the essence of a democratic society, and any restrictions on that right strike at the heart of representative government," Reynolds v. Sims, 377 U.S., at 555, voting is a "fundamental" right. As we observed in Dunn v. Blumstein, supra, at 336:

"There is no need to repeat now the labors undertaken in earlier cases to analyze [the] right to vote and to explain in detail the judicial role in reviewing state statutes that selectively distribute the franchise. In decision after decision, this Court has made clear that a citizen has a constitutionally protected right to participate in elections on an equal basis with other citizens in the jurisdiction. See, e. g., Evans v. Cornman, 398 U.S. 419, 421 -422, 426 (1970); Kramer v. Union Free School District, 395 U.S. 621, 626 - 628 (1969); Cipriano v. City of Houma, 395 U.S. 701, 706 (1969); Harper v. Virginia Board of Elections, 383 U.S. 663, 667 (1966); Carrington v. Rash, 380 U.S. 89, 93 -94 (1965); Reynolds v. Sims, supra."

We concluded: "[I]f a challenged statute grants the right to vote to some citizens and denies the franchise to others, `the Court must determine whether the exclusions are necessary to promote a compelling state interest.'" 405 U.S., at 337 . (Emphasis in original.)

To determine that the compelling-state-interest test applies to the challenged classification is, however, to settle only a threshold question. "Compelling state interest" is merely a shorthand description of the difficult process of balancing individual and state interests that the Court must embark upon when faced with a classification touching on fundamental rights. Our other equal protection cases give content to the nature of that balance. The State has the heavy burden of showing, first, that the challenged disenfranchisement is necessary to a legitimate and substantial state interest; second, that the classification is drawn with precision - that it does not exclude too many people who should not and need not be excluded; and, third, that there are no other reasonable ways to achieve the State's goal with a lesser burden on the constitutionally protected interest. E. g., Dunn v. Blumstein, supra, at 343, 360; Kramer v. Union Free School District, 395 U.S. 621, 632 (1969); see Rosario v. Rockefeller, 410 U.S. 752, 770 (1973) (POWELL, J., dissenting); cf. Memorial Hospital v. Maricopa County, 415 U.S. 250 (1974); NAACP v. Button, 371 U.S. 415, 438 (1963); Shelton v. Tucker, 364 U.S. 479, 488 (1960).

I think it clear that the State has not met its burden of justifying the blanket disenfranchisement of former felons presented by this case. There is certainly no basis for asserting that ex-felons have any less interest in the democratic process than any other citizen. Like everyone else, their daily lives are deeply affected and changed by the decisions of government. See Kramer, supra, at 627. As the Secretary of State of California observed in his memorandum to the Court in support of respondents in this case:

"It is doubtful . . . whether the state can demonstrate either a compelling or rational policy interest in denying former felons the right to vote. The individuals involved in the present case are persons who have fully paid their debt to society. They are as much affected by the actions of government as any other citizens, and have as much of a right to participate in governmental decision-making. Furthermore, the denial of the right to vote to such persons is a hindrance to the efforts of society to rehabilitate former felons and convert them into law-abiding and productive citizens." 25

It is argued that disenfranchisement is necessary to prevent vote frauds. Although the State has a legitimate and, in fact, compelling interest in preventing election fraud, the challenged provision is not sustainable on that ground. First, the disenfranchisement provisions are patently both overinclusive and underinclusive. The provision is not limited to those who have demonstrated a marked propensity for abusing the ballot by violating election laws. Rather, it encompasses all former felons and there has been no showing that ex-felons generally are any more likely to abuse the ballot than the remainder of the population. See Dillenburg v. Kramer, 469 F.2d. at 1225. In contrast, many of those convicted of violating election laws are treated as misdemeanants and are not barred from voting at all. It seems clear that the classification here is not tailored to achieve its articulated goal, since it crudely excludes large numbers of otherwise qualified voters. See Kramer v. Union Free School District, supra, at 632; Cipriano v. City of

Houma, 395 U.S. 701, 706 (1969).

Moreover, there are means available for the State to prevent voting fraud which are far less burdensome on the constitutionally protected right to vote. As we said in Dunn, supra, at 353, the State "has at its disposal a variety of criminal laws that are more than adequate to detect and deter whatever fraud may be feared." Cf. Harman v. Forssenius, 380 U.S. 528, 543 (1965); Schneider v. State, 308 U.S. 147, 164 (1939). The California court's catalogue of that State's penal sanctions for election fraud surely demonstrates that there are adequate alternatives to disenfranchisement.

"Today . . . the Elections Code punishes at least 76 different acts as felonies, in 33 separate sections; at least 60 additional acts are punished as misdemeanors, in 40 separate sections; and 14 more acts are declared to be felony-misdemeanors. Among this plethora of offenses we take particular note, in the present connection, of the felony sanctions against fraudulent registrations (220), buying and selling of votes (12000-12008), intimidating voters by threat or bribery (29130-29135), voting twice, or fraudulently voting without being entitled to do so, or impersonating another voter (14403, 29430-29431), fraud or forgery in casting absentee ballots (14690-14692), tampering with voting machines (15280) or ballot boxes (17090-17092), forging or altering election returns (29100-29103), and so interfering `with the officers holding an election or conducting a canvass, or with the voters lawfully exercising their rights of voting at an election, as to prevent the election or canvass from being fairly held and lawfully conducted' (17093)." 9 Cal. 3d, at 215-216, 507 P.2d, at 1355-1356 (1973) (footnotes omitted).

Given the panoply of criminal offenses available to deter and to punish electoral misconduct, as well as the statutory reforms and technological changes which have transformed the electoral process in the last century, election fraud may no longer be a serious danger. 26

Another asserted purpose is to keep former felons from voting because their likely voting pattern might be subversive of the interests of an orderly society. See Green v. Board of Elections, 380 F.2d 445, 451 (CA2 1967). Support for the argument that electors can be kept from the ballot box for fear they might vote to repeal or emasculate provisions of the criminal code, is drawn primarily from this Court's decisions in Murphy v. Ramsey, 114 U.S. 15 (1885), and Davis v. Beason, 133 U.S. 333 (1890). In Murphy, the Court upheld the disenfranchisement of anyone who had ever entered into a bigamous or polygamous marriage and in Davis, the Court sanctioned, as a condition to the exercise of franchise, the requirement of an oath that the elector did not "teach, advise, counsel or encourage any person to commit the crime of bigamy or polygamy." The Court's intent was clear - "to withdraw all political influence from those who are practically hostile to" the goals of certain criminal laws. Murphy, supra, at 45; Davis, supra, at 348.

To the extent Murphy and Davis approve the doctrine that citizens can be barred from the ballot box because they would vote to change the existing criminal law, those decisions are surely of minimal continuing precedential value. We have since explicitly held that such "differences of opinion cannot justify excluding [any] group from . . . `the franchise,'" Cipriano v. City of Houma, 395 U.S., at 705 -706; see Communist Party of Indiana v. Whitcomb, 414 U.S. 441 (1974); Evans v. Cornman, 398 U.S. 419, 423 (1970).

"[I]f they are . . . residents, . . . they, as all other qualified residents, have a right to an equal opportunity for political representation. . . . `Fencing out' from the franchise a sector of the population because of the way they may vote is constitutionally impermissible." Carrington v. Rash, 380 U.S., at 94 .

See Dunn, 405 U.S., at 355 .

Although, in the last century, this Court may have justified the exclusion of voters from the electoral process for fear that they would vote to change laws considered important by a temporal majority, I have little doubt that we would not countenance such a purpose today. The process of democracy is one of change. Our laws are not frozen into immutable form, they are constantly in the process of revision in response to the needs of a changing society. The public interest, as conceived by a majority of the voting public, is constantly undergoing reexamination. This Court's holding in Davis, supra, and Murphy, supra, that a State may disenfranchise a class of voters to "withdraw all political influence from those who are practically hostile" to the existing order, strikes at the very heart of the democratic process. A temporal majority could use such a power to preserve inviolate its view of the social order simply by disenfranchising those with different views. Voters who opposed the repeal of prohibition could have disenfranchised those who advocated repeal "to prevent persons from being enabled by their votes to defeat the criminal laws of the country." Davis, supra, at 348. Today, presumably those who support the legalization of marihuana could be barred from the ballot box for much the same reason. The ballot is the democratic system's coin of the realm. To condition its exercise on support of the established order is to debase that currency beyond recognition. Rather than resurrect Davis and Murphy, I would expressly disavow any continued adherence to the dangerous notions therein expressed. 27

The public purposes asserted to be served by disenfranchisement have been found wanting in many quarters. When this suit was filed, 23 States allowed ex-felons full access to the ballot. Since that time, four more States have joined their ranks. 28 Shortly after lower federal courts sustained New York's and Florida's disenfranchisement provisions, the legislatures repealed those laws. Congress has recently provided for the restoration of felons' voting rights at the end of sentence or parole in the District of Columbia. D.C. Code 1-1102 (7) (1973). The National Conference on Uniform State Laws, 29 the American Law Institute, 30 the National Probation and Parole Association, 31 the National Advisory Commission on Criminal Justice Standards and Goals, 32 the President's Commission on Law Enforcement and the Administration of Justice, 33 the California League of Women Voters, 34 the National Democratic Party, 35 and the Secretary of State of California 36 have all strongly endorsed full suffrage rights for former felons.

The disenfranchisement of ex-felons had "its origin in the fogs and fictions of feudal jurisprudence and doubtless has been brought forward into modern statutes without fully realizing either the effect of its literal significance or the extent of its infringement upon the spirit of our system of government." Byers v. Sun Savings Bank, 41 Okla. 728, 731, 139 P. 948, 949 (1914). I think it clear that measured against the standards of this Court's modern equal protection jurisprudence, the blanket disenfranchisement of ex-felons cannot stand.

I respectfully dissent.

Notes

[1] The proceeding below was a petition for a writ of mandate in the California Supreme Court, hence the moving parties should properly be described as petitioners rather than plaintiffs. However, to avoid confusion, since the petitioners below are the respondents here and vice versa, the parties in the California court will be referred to herein simply as plaintiffs and defendants.

[2] California Const., Art. II, 1, provided, in part, that "no person convicted of any infamous crime . . . shall ever exercise the privileges of an elector in this State." Article II, 1, was repealed by referendum at the November 7, 1972, general election and was replaced by a new Art. II, 3, containing the same prohibition. The state implementing statutes include California Elections Code 310, 321, 383, 389, 390, and 14240.

[3] The Attorney General filed a separate petition for certiorari, No. 73-324, to review the judgment of the California Supreme Court. The Secretary of State filed a memorandum opposing that petition for certiorari. The petition was denied today, post, p. 904.

[4] The judgment of the California Supreme Court is by custom the final paragraph of its opinion. The alternative writ referred to is merely a show-cause order, requiring the respondent to comply with the petitioner's demand or show cause why it should not be ordered to do so.

[5] See 5 B. Witkin, Cal. Proc. 2d, Extraordinary Writs 22, pp. 3796-3797, and 123, p. 3899 (1971).

[6] Calif. Code Civ. Proc. 1060; see 15 Cal. Jur. 2d, Declaratory Relief 13; 3 B. Witkin, Cal. Proc. 2d, Pleading 705 (c), p. 2329 (1971); see, e. g., Dills v. Delira Corp., 145 Cal. App. 2d 124, 129, 302 P.2d 397, 400 (1956).

The difference between "mandamus and declaratory relief [is] that appellate courts cannot give the latter." 5 B. Witkin, Cal. Proc. 2d, Extraordinary Writs 21, p. 3796 (1971).

[7] In the first case relied on by the majority, In re William M., 3 Cal. 3d 16, 473 P.2d 737 (1970), the California Supreme Court had previously granted a writ of habeas corpus which effectively mooted the petitioner's claim for relief. The court, nonetheless, later issued an opinion on the issue posed by the case while denying further relief. In a footnote, the court observed that as a general proposition, courts should avoid advisory opinions, but, in the very next sentence, reaffirmed its inherent discretion to issue such

opinions. In the accompanying text, the court noted that it could render a decision in a moot case which would not be binding on a party before it, where the case involved issues of particular public importance. Although the court referred to its "declaratory use of habeas corpus in a number of cases," citing B. Witkin, Cal. Crim. Proc. 790 (1963), and In re Fluery, 67 Cal. 2d 600, 432 P.2d 986 (1967), the Witkin treatise refers to the court's "declaratory use of habeas corpus" and In re Fluery, supra, in particular, as examples of the "use of the writ to render a purely advisory opinion unnecessary to the determination of the particular controversy." B. Witkin, Cal. Crim. Proc., Habeas Corpus and Other Extraordinary Writs 790, p. 247 (Supp. 1967).

The second case relied on by the majority is Young v. Gnoss, 7 Cal. 3d 18, 496 P.2d 445 (1972), cited by the court below solely for the proposition that mandamus is an appropriate remedy to seek in an original proceeding. In that case, the petitioners had sought mandamus relief from the application of a state durational residence requirement for voting in order that they might vote in a June primary. The California Supreme Court, in a lengthy opinion, indicated that the challenged requirement was unconstitutional on the authority of our decision in Dunn v. Blumstein, 405 U.S. 330 (1972), but exercised its equitable discretion not to order a change in the residence requirements for the June primary because too little time remained for such a change to be implemented in an orderly fashion. Accordingly, mandamus relief was denied. The court recommended that the necessary changes in residence requirements be effected before the November election but did not so order to give the "Legislature the opportunity to address itself to the problem . . . ." 7 Cal. 3d, at 28, 496 P.2d, at 452-453. The court relied on its earlier decision in Legislature v. Reinecke, 6 Cal. 3d 595, 492 P.2d 385 (1972), where the court had expressed its views on a legislative reapportionment problem, denied a writ of mandate, and retained jurisdiction to allow the legislature an opportunity to act before providing any judicial relief.

Each of these cases involves examples of advisory opinions rather than declaratory relief. In the latter, what the California Supreme Court did was to provide some guidance to the legislature while staying its hand and not affording judicial relief for the claimed deprivation. It seems well settled that California courts have "inherent discretion" to issue such advisory opinions. See 2 B. Witkin, Cal. Proc. 2d, Actions 44, p. 920 (1970); id., 42, p. 916; 5 B. Witkin, Cal. Proc. 2d, Extraordinary Writs 117, p. 3894; cf. Kirstowsky v. Superior Court, 143 Cal. App. 2d 745, 749, 300 P.2d 163, 166 (1956).

[8] The Court has held, for example, that Art. III restricts standing to bring a class action to the actual members of the class. O'Shea v. Littleton, 414 U.S. 488 (1974). The named plaintiffs here had been disenfranchised at the time they filed suit, and there is thus no question concerning their standing to challenge the California disenfranchisement provisions.

[9] The Court distinguished its decision in Hall v. Beals, 396 U.S. 45 (1969), finding a challenge to Colorado's durational residence requirement moot, on the grounds that, in Hall, there had been an intervening change in law reducing the residence

requirements from six months to two while the case was on appeal. Accordingly, application of the six-month requirement was incapable of repetition as to the named plaintiff or any other member of his class, and, having never been disenfranchised thereby, the named plaintiff had no standing to challenge the two-month requirement.

[10] The Court has found a live controversy in other voting cases in which intervening circumstances seemed to have mooted the named plaintiff's claim for relief. Moore v. Ogilvie, 394 U.S. 814 (1969), for example, was an appeal from a decision denying relief to appellants who had unsuccessfully sought to be certified, as required by state law, as independent candidates for Presidential elector on the 1968 ballot. Appellants asserted that the Illinois certification requirement violated the State's constitutional obligation not to discriminate against voters in less populous counties. By the time their appeal reached this Court, the 1968 election had already taken place, but we held the case was not moot because "while the 1968 election is over, [the challenged burden] remains and controls future elections . . .," id., at 816; see Hall v. Beals, supra, at 49, and the short span of time between the denial of certification for candidacy and actual balloting threatens to moot all future attacks on the questioned candidacy requirements. 394 U.S., at 816 . See also Storer v. Brown, 415 U.S. 724, 737 n. 8 (1974); Rosario v. Rockefeller, 410 U.S. 752, 756 n. 5 (1973).

[11] The extent of continuing disenfranchisement is apt to be minimal. A survey conducted by the Secretary of State of California indicated that the election officials of 52 of the 58 counties in California, representing counties which contain 97.39% of the registered voters in the State, agreed with the clerks in the named plaintiffs' counties that ex-felons should not be barred from voting in their counties. Brief for Respondents 30.

[12] The Court's opinion cites our decision in Indiana Employment Security Div. v. Burney, 409 U.S. 540 (1973), for the proposition that unnamed class members may not be looked to in cases arising from the federal system, but the cases does not support that proposition. Burney concerned a constitutional challenge to the termination of unemployment insurance benefits without a prior hearing. The only named class representative received a post-termination hearing at which she obtained a reversal of the initial determination of ineligibility and full retroactive benefits. The Court remanded for consideration of mootness. The jurisdictional issue in this Court revolved around whether the case presented issues "capable of repetition, yet evading review." The Court did not have to find the alleged constitutional deprivation incapable of repetition, hence was not concerned with the problem of whether a future application to the named class representative was required. Rather, it appeared that the prior-hearing issue was not one which would evade review. But see id., at 542-546 (dissenting opinion). The Court reasoned that a post-termination hearing, afforded as a matter of course, would not invariably moot all claims for relief from members of the class. If the post-termination hearing did not result in an award of retroactive payments, as it had in the named plaintiff's case, a live and continuing controversy would be presented as to the insured's claim to the benefits allegedly wrongfully withheld pending the hearing. A case had

already come to this Court in just such a posture, and the Court had summarily affirmed the judgment of the three-judge court. Torres v. New York State Department of Labor, 405 U.S. 949 (1972), but see 410 U.S. 971 (1973) (dissenting opinion to denial of rehearing). It was a failure to satisfy the "evading review" element of the test that led the Court to remand Burney for consideration of mootness.

[13] In the absence of such an order, petitioner Richardson is under no compulsion to register ex-felons in her county nor subject to any penalty for failing to do so. See Cal. Code Civ. Proc. 1097 (1955).

[14] The suit against petitioner, Richardson v. James, 1 Civ. 32283, is presently pending in Division 3 of the Court of Appeal for the First Appellate District of California.

[15] If claims of the named plaintiffs are moot, the proper disposition of this case would seem to be to vacate the judgment of the California Supreme Court and remand for such proceedings as that court deems appropriate. Brockington v. Rhodes, 396 U.S. 41, 44 (1969).

[16] See, e. g., Note, Restoring the Ex-offender's Right to Vote: Background and Developments, 11 Am. Crim. L. Rev. 721, 746-747, n. 158 (1973).

[17] Statement of Rep. Eckley, quoted, ante, at 46.

[18] Bonfield, The Right to Vote and Judicial Enforcement of Section Two of the Fourteenth Amendment, 46 Cornell L. Q. 108, 109 (1960); H. Flack, The Adoption of the Fourteenth Amendment 98, 126 (1908); B. Kendrick, Journal of the Joint Committee of Fifteen on Reconstruction 290-291 (1914); J. James, The Framing of the Fourteenth Amendment 185 (1956); Van Alstyne, The Fourteenth Amendment, the "Right" to Vote, and the Understanding of the Thirty-ninth Congress, 1965 Sup. Ct. Rev. 33, 44 (1965).

[19] James, n. 18, supra, at 138-139.

[20] Kendrick, n. 18, supra, at 291; cf. Flack, n. 18, supra, at 111, 118.

[21] Bonfield, n. 18, supra, at 111; James, n. 18, supra, at 185; Van Alstyne, n. 18, supra, at 43-44, 58, 65.

[22] Id., at 43-44 (quoting from Mathews, Legislative and Judicial History of the Fifteenth Amendment (1909)).

[23] Id., at 65.

[24] To say that 2 of the Fourteenth Amendment is a direct limitation on the protection afforded voting rights by 1 leads to absurd results. If one accepts the premise that 2 authorizes disenfranchisement for any crime, the challenged California provision could, as the California Supreme Court has observed, require disenfranchisement for seduction under promise of marriage, or conspiracy to operate a motor vehicle without a muffler. Otsuka v. Hite, 64 Cal. 2d 596, 414 P.2d 412 (1966). Disenfranchisement extends to convictions for vagrancy in Alabama or breaking a water pipe in North Dakota, to note but two examples. Note, Disenfranchisement of Ex-felons: A Reassessment, 25 Stan. L. Rev. 845, 846 (1973). Even a jaywalking or traffic conviction could conceivably lead to disenfranchisement, since 2 does not differentiate between felonies and misdemeanors.

[25] Memorandum of the Secretary of State of California in Opposition to

Certiorari, in Class of County Clerks and Registrars of Voters of California v. Ramirez, No. 73-324.

[26] Ramirez v. Brown, 9 Cal. 3d 199, 215-216, 507 P.2d 1345, 1355-1356 (1973).

[27] The Court also notes that the disenfranchisement of ex-felons has received support in the dicta of this Court and that we have only recently affirmed without opinion the decisions of two three-judge District Courts upholding disenfranchisement provisions. Fincher v. Scott, 352 F. Supp. 117 (MDNC 1972), aff'd mem., 411 U.S. 961 (1973); Beacham v. Braterman, 300 F. Supp. 182 (SD Fla.), aff'd per curiam, 396 U.S. 12 (1969). But, dictum is not precedent and as MR. JUSTICE REHNQUIST has only recently reminded us, summary affirmances are obviously not of the same precedential value as would be an opinion of this Court treating the question on the merits. Edelman v. Jordan, 415 U.S. 651, 671 (1974). See F. Frankfurter & J. Landis, The Business of the Supreme Court at October Term, 1929, 44 Harv. L. Rev. 1, 14 (1930).

[28] The following States do not disenfranchise all former felons: Arkansas, Ark. Stat. Ann. 3-707 (Supp. 1973); Colorado, Colo. Const., Art. VII, 10, and Colo. Rev. Stat. Ann. 49-3-2 (Perm. Cum. Supp. 1971); Florida, Fla. Stat. Ann. 940.05 (1973); Hawaii, Hawaii Rev. Stat. 716-5 (Supp. 1972); Illinois, Ill. Rev. Stat., c. 46, 3-5 (1973); Indiana, Ind. Ann. Stat. 29-4804 (1969); Kansas, Kan. Stat. Ann. 22-3722 (Supp. 1973); Maine, Me. Rev. Stat. Ann., Tit. 21, 245 (1964); Massachusetts, Mass. Gen. Laws Ann., c. 51, 1 (Supp. 1974-1975) (except election code offenders); Michigan, Mich. Const., Art. II, 2, and Mich. Comp. Laws Ann. 168.10 (1970); Minnesota, Minn. Stat. 609.165 (1971); Nebraska, Neb. Rev. Stat. 29-2264 (Supp. 1972) and Neb. Rev. Stat. 83-1118 (1971); New Hampshire, N. H. Rev. Stat. Ann. 607-A:2 (Supp. 1973); New Jersey, N. J. Stat. Ann. 19:4-1 (Supp. 1974-1975) (except election code offenders); Ohio Rev. Code Ann. 2967.16 (Supp. 1972); Oregon, Ore. Rev. Stat. 137.240 and 137.250 (1973); Pennsylvania, Pa. Const., Art. VII, 1, Pa. Stat. Ann., Tit. 19 893 (1964), and Tit. 25, 3552 (1963) (except election code offenders for four years); South Dakota, S.D. Comp. Laws Ann. 24-5-2 and 23-57-7 (1969); Utah, Utah Const., Art. IV, 6 (except those convicted of treason or election code offenses); Vermont, Vt. Const., c. II, 51 (except election code offenders); Washington, Wash. Rev. Code Ann. 9.96.050 (Supp. 1972); West Virginia, 51 Op. W. Va. Atty. Gen. No. 42, p. 182 (1965) (construing W. Va. Const., Art. IV, 1); Wisconsin, Wis. Stat. Ann. 57-078 (Supp. 1974-1975); Wyoming, Wyo. Stat. Ann. 7-311 (1957).

In 1972 Montana amended its constitution to disenfranchise potential electors only while "serving a sentence for a felony." Mont. Const., Art. IV, 2; Mont. Rev. Codes Ann. 23-2701 (Supp. 1973). In 1973, New York amended its laws to allow former felons whose sentence had expired or who were released from parole to vote. N. Y. Election Law 152 (Supp. 1973-1974). Also in 1973, North Carolina amended its laws to restore all civil rights including the franchise to former felons discharged from prison or parole. N.C. Gen. Stat. 13-1 (Supp. 1973). And, in the same year, the Tennessee Legislature amended its ex-felon disenfranchisement statutes. See Tenn. Code Ann. 2-202 (Supp. 1973).

The New York ex-felon disenfranchisement provision was upheld in Green v.

Board of Elections, 380 F.2d 445 (CA2 1967), and shortly thereafter the New York Legislature repealed that law. N. Y. Election Law 152 (Supp. 1973-1974). Similarly the Florida disenfranchisement provisions were upheld in Beacham v. Braterman, 300 F. Supp. 182 (SD Fla.), aff'd per curiam, 396 U.S. 12 (1969). Subsequently, Florida statutes were amended to provide for the automatic restoration of all civil rights, including the franchise, upon the completion of sentence or release from parole or probation. Fla. Stat. Ann. 940.05 (1973).

[29] National Conference of Commissioners on Uniform State Laws, Uniform Act on Status of Convicted Persons 2-3 (1964).

[30] American Law Institute, Model Penal Code 306.3 (Proposed Official Draft 1962).

[31] National Probation and Parole Association, Standard Probation and Parole Act 12 and 27 (1955).

[32] National Advisory Commission on Criminal Justice Standards and Goals, Corrections, Standard 16.17, p. 592 (1973). The Report observed:

"Loss of citizenship rights - [including] the right to vote . . . - inhibits reformative efforts. If correction is to reintegrate an offender into free society, the offender must retain all attributes of citizenship. In addition, his respect for law and the legal system may well depend, in some measure, on his ability to participate in that system. Mandatory denials of that participation serve no legitimate public interest." Id., at 593.

[33] President's Commission on Law Enforcement and the Administration of Justice, Task Force Report: Corrections 89-90 (1967):

"[T]here seems no justification for permanently depriving all convicted felons of the vote . . . . [T]o be deprived of the right to representation in a democratic society is an important symbol. Moreover, rehabilitation might be furthered by encouraging convicted persons to participate in society by exercising the vote."

[34] California League of Women Voters, Policy Statement, Feb. 16, 1972.

[35] National Democratic Party, Party Platform 1972.

[36] Memorandum of the Secretary of State of California in Opposition to Certiorari in Class of County Clerks and Registrars of Voters of California v. Ramirez, No. 73-324.

Respondents have standing: Justice Marshall's dissent in Schlesinger v. Reservists Committee to Stop the War (June 25, 1974)

MR. JUSTICE MARSHALL, dissenting.

I agree with my Brother DOUGLAS that respondents have standing as citizens to bring this action. I cannot accept the majority's characterization of respondents' complaint as alleging only "injury in the abstract" and "`generalized grievances' about the conduct of the Government." Ante, at 217. According to their complaint, respondents are present and former members of the various Armed Forces Reserves.

"organized for the purpose of opposing the military involvement of the United States in Vietnam and of using all lawful means to end that involvement, including efforts by its members individually to persuade the Congress of the United States and all members of the Congress to take all steps necessary and appropriate to end that involvement."

The specific interest which they thus asserted, and which they alleged had been infringed by violations of the Incompatibility Clause, though doubtless widely shared, is certainly not a "general interest common to all members of the public." Ex parte Levitt, 302 U.S. 633, 634 (1937). Not all citizens desired to have the Congress take all steps necessary to terminate American involvement in Vietnam, and not all citizens who so desired sought to persuade members of Congress to that end.

Respondents nevertheless had a right under the First Amendment to attempt to persuade Congressmen to end the war in Vietnam. And respondents have alleged a right, under the Incompatibility Clause, to have their arguments considered by Congressmen not subject to a conflict of interest by virtue of their positions in the Armed Forces Reserves. Respondents' complaint therefore states, in my view, a claim of direct and concrete injury to a judicially cognizable interest. It is a sad commentary on our priorities that a litigant who contends that a violation of a federal statute has interfered with his aesthetic appreciation of natural resources can have that claim heard by a federal court, see United States v. SCRAP, 412 U.S. 669, 687 (1973), while one who contends that a violation of a specific provision of the United States Constitution has interfered with the effectiveness of expression protected by the First Amendment is turned away without a hearing on the merits of his claim.

I respectfully dissent.

Forced busing even without proof of intentional segregation: Justice Marshall's dissent in Milliken v. Bradley (July 25, 1974)

MR. JUSTICE MARSHALL, with whom MR. JUSTICE DOUGLAS, MR. JUSTICE BRENNAN, and MR. JUSTICE WHITE join, dissenting.

In Brown v. Board of Education, 347 U. S. 483 (1954), this Court held that segregation of children in public schools on the basis of race deprives minority group children of equal educational opportunities, and therefore denies them the equal protection of the laws under the Fourteenth Amendment. This Court recognized then that remedying decades of segregation in public education would not be an easy task. Subsequent events, unfortunately, have seen that prediction bear bitter fruit. But however imbedded old ways, however ingrained old prejudices, this Court has not been diverted from its appointed task of making "a living truth" of our constitutional ideal of equal justice under law. Cooper v. Aaron, 358 U. S. 1, 358 U. S. 20 (1958).

After 20 years of small, often difficult steps toward that great end, the Court today takes a giant step backwards. Notwithstanding a record showing widespread and pervasive racial segregation in the educational system provided by the State of Michigan for children in Detroit, this Court holds that the District Court was powerless to require the State to remedy its constitutional violation in any meaningful fashion. Ironically purporting to base its result on the principle that the scope of the remedy in a desegregation case should be determined by the nature and the extent of the constitutional violation, the Court's answer is to provide no remedy at all for the violation proved in this case, thereby guaranteeing that Negro children in Detroit will receive the same separate and inherently unequal education in the future as they have been unconstitutionally afforded in the past.

I cannot subscribe to this emasculation of our constitutional guarantee of equal protection of the laws, and must respectfully dissent. Our precedents, in my view, firmly establish that where, as here, state-imposed segregation has been demonstrated, it becomes the duty of the State to eliminate root and branch all vestiges of racial discrimination and to achieve the greatest possible degree of actual desegregation. I agree with both the District Court and the Court of Appeals that, under the facts of this case, this duty cannot be fulfilled unless the State of Michigan involves outlying metropolitan area school districts in its desegregation remedy. Furthermore, I perceive no basis either in law or in the practicalities of the situation justifying the State's interposition of school district boundaries as absolute barriers to the implementation of an effective desegregation remedy. Under established and frequently used Michigan procedures, school district lines are both flexible and permeable for a wide variety of purposes, and there is no reason why they must now stand in the way of meaningful desegregation relief.

The rights at issue in this case are too fundamental to be abridged on grounds as superficial as those relied on by the majority today. We deal here with the right of all of our children, whatever their race, to an equal start in life and to an equal opportunity to reach their full potential as citizens. Those children who have been denied that right in the past deserve better than to see fences thrown up to deny them that right in the future. Our Nation, I fear, will be ill-served by the Court's refusal to remedy separate and unequal education, for unless our children begin to learn together, there is little hope that our people will ever learn to live together.

I

The great irony of the Court's opinion and, in my view, its most serious analytical flaw, may be gleaned from its concluding sentence, in which the Court remands for

"prompt formulation of a decree directed to eliminating the segregation found to exist in Detroit city schools, a remedy which has been delayed since 1970."

Ante at 418 U. S. 753. The majority, however, seems to have forgotten the District Court's explicit finding that a Detroit-only decree, the only remedy permitted under today's decision, "would not accomplish desegregation."

Nowhere in the Court's opinion does the majority confront, let alone respond to, the District Court's conclusion that a remedy limited to the city of Detroit would not effectively desegregate the Detroit city schools. I, for one, find the District Court's conclusion well supported by the record, and its analysis compelled by our prior cases. Before turning to these questions, however, it is best to begin by laying to rest some mischaracterizations in the Court's opinion with respect to the basis for the District Court's decision to impose a metropolitan remedy.

The Court maintains that, while the initial focus of this lawsuit was the condition of segregation within the Detroit city schools, the District Court abruptly shifted focus in mid-course and altered its theory of the case. This new theory, in the majority's words, was "equating racial imbalance with a constitutional violation calling for a remedy." Ante at 418 U. S. 741 n.19. As the following review of the District Court's handling of the case demonstrates, however, the majority's characterization is totally inaccurate. Nowhere did the District Court indicate that racial imbalance between school districts in the Detroit metropolitan area or within the Detroit School District constituted a constitutional violation calling for inter-district relief. The focus of this case was from the beginning, and has remained, the segregated system of education in the Detroit city schools and the steps necessary to cure that condition which offends the Fourteenth Amendment.

The District Court's consideration of this case began with its finding, which the majority accepts, that the State of Michigan, through its instrumentality, the Detroit Board of Education, engaged in widespread purposeful acts of racial segregation in the Detroit School District. Without belaboring the details, it is sufficient to note that the various techniques used in Detroit were typical of methods employed to segregate students by race in areas where no statutory dual system of education has existed. See, e.g., Keyes v. School District No. 1, Denver, Colorado, 413 U. S. 189 (1973). Exacerbating the effects of extensive residential segregation between Negroes and whites, the school board consciously drew attendance zones along lines which maximized the segregation of the races in schools as well. Optional attendance zones were created for neighborhoods undergoing racial transition so as to allow whites in these areas to escape integration. Negro students in areas with overcrowded schools were transported past or away from closer white schools with available space to more distant Negro schools. Grade structures and feeder-school patterns were created and maintained in a manner which had the foreseeable and actual effect of keeping Negro and white pupils in separate schools. Schools were also constructed in locations and in sizes which ensured that they would open with predominantly one-race student bodies. In sum, the evidence adduced below showed that Negro children had been intentionally confined to an expanding core of virtually all-Negro schools immediately surrounded by a receding band of all-white schools.

Contrary to the suggestions in the Court's opinion, the basis for affording a desegregation remedy in this case was not some perceived racial imbalance either between schools within a single school district or between independent school districts. What we confront here is "a systematic program of segregation affecting a substantial portion of the students, schools . . . and facilities within the school system. . . ." Id. at 413 U. S. 201. The constitutional violation found here was not some de facto racial imbalance, but rather the purposeful, intentional, massive, de jure segregation of the Detroit city schools, which, under our decision in Keyes, forms "a predicate for a finding of the existence of a dual school system," ibid., and justifies "all-out desegregation" Id. at 413 U. S. 214.

Having found a de jure segregated public school system in operation in the city of Detroit, the District Court turned next to consider which officials and agencies should be assigned the affirmative obligation to cure the constitutional violation. The court concluded that responsibility for the segregation in the Detroit city schools rested not only with the Detroit Board of Education, but belonged to the State of Michigan itself and the state defendants in this case -- that is, the Governor of Michigan, the Attorney General, the State Board of Education, and the State Superintendent of Public Instruction. While the validity of this conclusion will merit more extensive analysis below, suffice it for now to say that it was based on three considerations. First, the evidence at trial showed that the State itself had taken actions contributing to the segregation within the Detroit schools. Second, since the Detroit Board of Education was an agency of the State of Michigan, its acts of racial discrimination were acts of the State for purposes of the Fourteenth Amendment. Finally, the District Court found that, under Michigan law and practice, the system of education was, in fact, a state school system, characterized by relatively little local control and a large degree of centralized state regulation, with respect to both educational policy and the structure and operation of school district.

Having concluded, then, that the school system in the city of Detroit was a de jure segregated system and that the State of Michigan had the affirmative duty to remedy that condition of segregation, the District Court then turned to the difficult task of devising an effective remedy. It bears repeating that the District Court's focus at this stage of the litigation remained what it had been at the beginning -- the condition of segregation within the Detroit city schools. As the District Court stated:

"From the initial ruling [on segregation] to this day, the basis of the proceedings has been and remains the violation: de jure school segregation. . . . The task before this court, therefore, is now, and . . . has always been, how to desegregate the Detroit public schools."

The District Court first considered three desegregation plans limited to the geographical boundaries of the city of Detroit. All were rejected as ineffective to desegregate the Detroit city schools. Specifically, the District Court determined that the racial composition of the Detroit student body is such that implementation of any Detroit-only plan "would clearly make the entire Detroit public school system racially identifiable as Black" and would "leave many of its schools 75 to 90 percent Black." The District Court also found that a Detroit-only plan "would change a school system which is now Black and White to one that would be perceived as Black, thereby increasing the flight of Whites from the city and the system, thereby increasing the Black student population."

Based on these findings, the District Court reasoned that "relief of segregation in the public schools of the City of Detroit cannot be accomplished within the corporate geographical limits of the city" because a Detroit-only decree "would accentuate the racial identifiability of the district as a Black school system, and would not accomplish desegregation." The District Court therefore concluded that it "must look beyond the limits of the Detroit school district for a solution to the problem of segregation in the Detroit public schools. . . ."

In seeking to define the appropriate scope of that expanded desegregation area, however, the District Court continued to maintain as its sole focus the condition shown to violate the Constitution in this case -- the segregation of the Detroit school system. As it stated, the primary question

"remains the determination of the area necessary and practicable effectively to eliminate 'root and branch' the effects of state-imposed and supported segregation and to desegregate the Detroit public schools."

There is simply no foundation in the record, then, for the majority's accusation that the only basis for the District Court's order was some desire to achieve a racial balance in the Detroit metropolitan area. [1] In fact, just the contrary is the case. In considering proposed desegregation areas, the District Court had occasion to criticize one of the State's proposals specifically because it had no basis other than its "particular racial ratio," and did not focus on "relevant factors, like eliminating racially identifiable schools [and] accomplishing maximum actual desegregation of the Detroit public schools." Similarly, in rejecting the Detroit School Board's proposed desegregation area, even though it included more all-white districts and therefore achieved a higher white-Negro ratio, the District Court commented:

"There is nothing in the record which suggests that these districts need be included in the desegregation area in order to disestablish the racial identifiabiity of the Detroit public schools. From the evidence, the primary reason for the Detroit School Board's interest in the inclusion of these school districts is not racial desegregation, but to increase the average socio-economic balance of all the schools in the abutting regions and clusters."

The Court also misstates the basis for the District Court's order by suggesting that, since the only segregation proved at trial was within the Detroit school system, any relief which extended beyond the jurisdiction of the Detroit Board of Education would be inappropriate because it would impose a remedy on outlying districts "not shown to have committed any constitutional violation." Ante at 418 U. S. 745. [2] The essential foundation of inter-district relief in this case was not to correct conditions within outlying districts which themselves engaged in purposeful segregation. Instead, inter-district relief was seen as a necessary part of any meaningful effort by the State of Michigan to remedy the state caused segregation within the city of Detroit.

Rather than consider the propriety of inter-district relief on this basis, however, the Court has conjured up a largely fictional account of what the District Court was attempting to accomplish. With all due respect, the Court, in my view, does a great disservice to the District Judge who labored long and hard with this complex litigation by accusing him of changing horses in midstream and shifting the focus of this case from the pursuit of a remedy for the condition of segregation within the Detroit school system to some unprincipled attempt to impose his own philosophy of racial balance on the entire Detroit metropolitan area. See ante at 418 U. S. 738-739. The focus of this case has always been the segregated system of education in the city of Detroit. The District Court determined that inter-district relief was necessary and appropriate only because it found that the condition of segregation within the Detroit school system could not b cured with a Detroit-only remedy. It is on this theory that the inter-district relief must stand or fall. Unlike the Court, I perceive my task to be to review the District Court's order for what it is, rather than to criticize it for what it manifestly is not.

II

As the foregoing demonstrates, the District Court's decision to expand its desegregation decree beyond the geographical limits of the city of Detroit rested in large part on its conclusions (A) that the State of Michigan was ultimately responsible for curing the condition of segregation within the Detroit city schools, and (b) that a Detroit-only remedy would not accomplish this task. In my view, both of these conclusions are well supported by the facts of this case and by this Court's precedents.

A

To begin with, the record amply supports the District Court's findings that the State of Michigan, through state officers and state agencies, had engaged in purposeful acts which created or aggravated segregation in the Detroit schools. The State Board of Education, for example, prior to 1962, exercised its authority to supervise local schoolsite selection in a manner which contributed to segregation. 484 F.2d 215, 238 (CA6 1973). Furthermore, the State's continuing authority, after 1962, to approve school building construction plans [3] had intertwined the State with site selection decisions of the Detroit Board of Education which had the purpose and effect of maintaining segregation.

The State had also stood in the way of past efforts to desegregate the Detroit city schools. In 1970, for example, the Detroit School Board had begun implementation of its own desegregation plan for its high schools, despite considerable public and official resistance. The State Legislature intervened by enacting Act 48 of the Public Acts of 1970, specifically prohibiting implementation of the desegregation plan and thereby continuing the growing segregation of the Detroit school system. Adequate desegregation of the Detroit system was also hampered by discriminatory restrictions placed by the State on the use of transportation within Detroit. While state aid for transportation was provided by statute for suburban districts, many of which were highly urbanized, aid for intra-city transportation was excepted. One of the effects of this restriction was to encourage the construction of small walk-in neighborhood schools in Detroit, thereby lending aid to the intentional policy of creating a school system which reflected, to the greatest extent feasible, extensive residential segregation. Indeed, that one of the purposes of the transportation restriction was to impede desegregation was evidenced when the Michigan Legislature amended the State Transportation Aid Act to cover intra-city transportation but expressly prohibited the allocation of funds for cross-busing of students within a school district to achieve racial balance. [4] Cf. North Carolina State Board of Education v. Swann, 402 U. S. 43 (1971).

Also significant was the State's involvement during the 1950's in the transportation of Negro high school students from the Carver School District past a closer white high school in the Oak Park District to a more distant Negro high school in the Detroit system. Certainly the District Court's finding that the State Board of Education had knowledge of this action and had given its tacit or express approval was not clearly erroneous. Given the comprehensive statutory powers of the State Board of Education over contractual arrangements between school districts in the enrollment of student on a nonresident tuition basis, including certification of the number of pupils involved in the transfer and the amount of tuition charged, over the review of transportation routes and distances, and over the disbursement of transportation funds, [5] the State Board inevitably knew and understood the significance of this discriminatory act.

Aside from the acts of purposeful segregation committed by the State Legislature and the State Board of Education, the District Court also concluded that the State was responsible for the many intentional acts of segregation committed by the Detroit Board of Education, an agency of the State. The majority is only willing to accept this finding arguendo. See ante at 418 U. S. 748. I have no doubt, however, as to its validity under the Fourteenth Amendment.

"The command of the Fourteenth Amendment," it should be recalled, "is that no state' shall deny to any person within its jurisdiction the equal protection of the laws." Cooper v. Aaron, 358 U. S. 1, 358 U. S. 16 (1958). While a State can act only through "the officers or agents by whom its powers are exerted," Ex parte Virginia, 100 U. S. 339, 100 U. S. 347 (1880), actions by an agent or officer of the State are encompassed by the Fourteenth Amendment for, "as he acts in the name and for the State, and is clothed with the State's power, his act is that of the State." Ibid. See also Cooper v. Aaron, supra; Virginia v. Rives, 100 U. S. 313, 100 U. S. 318 (1880); Shelley v. Kraemer, 334 U. S. 1, 334 U. S. 14 (1948).

Under Michigan law a "school district is an agency of the State government." School District of the City of Lansing v. State Board of Education, 367 Mich. 591, 600, 116 N.W.2d 866, 870 (1962). It is

"a legal division of territory, created by the State for educational purposes, to which the State has granted such powers as are deemed necessary to permit the district to function as a State agency."

Detroit Board of Education v. Superintendent of Public Instruction, 319 Mich.

436, 450, 29 N.W.2d 902, 908 (1947). Racial discrimination by the school district, an agency of the State, is therefore racial discrimination by the State itself, forbidden by the Fourteenth Amendment. See, e.g., Pennsylvania v. Board of Trusts, 353 U. S. 230 (1957).

We recognized only last Term in Keyes that it was the State itself which was ultimately responsible for de jure acts of segregation committed by a local school board. A deliberate policy of segregation by the local board, we held, amounted to "state-imposed segregation." 413 U.S. at 413 U. S. 200. Wherever a dual school system exists, whether compelled by state statute or created by a local board's systematic program of segregation,

"the State automatically assumes an affirmative duty 'to effectuate a transition to a racially nondiscriminatory school system' [and] to eliminate from the public schools within their school system 'all vestiges of state-imposed segregation.'"

Ibid. (emphasis added).

Vesting responsibility with the State of Michigan for Detroit's segregated schools is particularly appropriate, as Michigan, unlike some other States, operates a single state-wide system of education, rather than several separate and independent local school systems. The majority's emphasis on local governmental control and local autonomy of school districts in Michigan will come as a surprise to those with any familiarity with that State's system of education. School districts are not separate and distinct sovereign entities under Michigan law, but, rather, are "auxiliaries of the State,'" subject to its "absolute power." Attorney General of Michigan ex rel. Kies v. Lowrey, 199 U. S. 233, 199 U. S. 240 (1905). The courts of the State have repeatedly emphasized that education in Michigan is not a local governmental concern, but a state function.

"Unlike the delegation of other powers by the legislature to local governments, education is not inherently a part of the local self-government of a municipality. . . . Control of our public school system is a State matter delegated and lodged in the State legislature by the Constitution. The policy of the State has been to retain control of its school system, to be administered throughout the State under State laws by local State agencies organized with plenary powers to carry out the delegated functions given [them] by the legislature."

School District of the City of Lansing v. State Board of Education, supra at 595, 116 N.W.2d at 868. The Supreme Court of Michigan has noted the deep roots of this policy:

"It has been settled by the Ordinance of 1787, the several Constitutions adopted in this State, by its uniform course of legislation, and by the decisions of this court, that education in Michigan is a matter of State concern, that it is no part of the local self-government of a particular township or municipality. . . .

The legislature has always dictated the educational policy of the State."

In re School District No. 6, 284 Mich. 132, 145-146, 278 N.W. 792, 797 (1938).

The State's control over education is reflected in the fact that, contrary to the Court's implication, there is little or no relationship between school districts and local political units. To take the 85 outlying local school districts in the Detroit metropolitan area as examples, 17 districts lie in two counties, two in three counties. One district serves five municipalities; other suburban municipalities are fragmented into as many as six school districts. Nor is there any apparent state policy with regard to the size of school districts, as they now range from 2,000 to 285,000 students.

Centralized state control manifests itself in practice, as well as in theory. The State controls the financing of education in several ways. The legislature contributes a substantial portion of most school districts' operating budgets with funds appropriated from the State's General Fund revenues raised through state-wide taxation. [6] The State's power over the purse can be and is, in fact, used to enforce the State's powers over local districts. [7] In addition, although local districts obtain funds through local property taxation, the State has assumed the responsibility to ensure equalized property valuations throughout the State. [8] The State also establishes standards for teacher certification and teacher tenure; [9] determines part of the required curriculum; [10] sets the minimum school term; [11] approves bus routes, equipment, and drivers; [12] approves textbooks; [13] and establishes procedures for student discipline. [14] The State Superintendent of Public Instruction and the State Board of Education have the power to remove local school board members from office for neglect of their duties. [15]

Most significantly for present purposes, the State has wide-ranging powers to consolidate and merge school districts, even without the consent of the districts themselves or of the local citizenry. [16] See, e.g., Attorney General ex rel. Keis v. Lowrey, 131 Mich. 639, 92 N.W. 289 (1902), aff'd, 199 U. S. 233 (1905). Indeed, recent years have witnessed an accelerated program of school district consolidations, mergers, and annexations, many of which were state-imposed. Whereas the State had 7, 362 local districts in 1912, the number had been reduced to 1, 438 in 1964 and to 738 in 1968. [17] By June, 1972, only 608 school districts remained. Furthermore, the State has broad powers to transfer property from one district to another, again without the consent of the local school districts affected by the transfer. [18] See, e.g., School District of the City of Lansing v. State Board of Education, supra; Imlay Township District v. State Board of Education, 359 Mich. 478, 102 N.W.2d 720 (1960).

Whatever may be the history of public education in other parts of our Nation, it simply flies in the face of reality to say, as does the majority, that, in Michigan, "[n]o single tradition in public education is more deeply rooted than local control over the operation of schools. . . ." Ante at 418 U. S. 741. As the State's Supreme Court has said: "We have repeatedly held that education in this State is not a matter of local concern, but belongs to the State at large." Collins v. City of Detroit, 195 Mich. 330, 335-336, 161 N.W. 905, 907 (1917). See also Sturgis v. County of Allegan, 343 Mich. 209, 215, 72 N.W.2d 56, 59 (1955); Van Fleet v. Oltman, 244 Mich. 241, 244, 221 N.W. 299, 300 (1928); Child Welfare Society of Flint v. Kennedy School District, 220 Mich. 290, 296, 189 N.W. 1002, 1004 (1922). Indeed, a study prepared for the 1961 Michigan Constitutional Convention noted that the Michigan Constitution's articles on education had resulted in "the establishment of a state system of education in contrast to a series of local school systems." Elementary and Secondary Education and the Michigan Constitution, Michigan Constitutional Convention Studies 1 (1961).

In sum, several factors in this case coalesce to support the District Court's ruling that it was the State of Michigan itself, not simply the Detroit Board of Education, which bore the obligation of curing the condition of segregation within the Detroit city schools. The actions of the State itself directly contributed to Detroit's segregation. Under the Fourteenth Amendment, the State is ultimately responsible for the actions of its local agencies. And, finally, given the structure of Michigan's educational system, Detroit's segregation cannot be viewed as the problem of an independent and separate entity. Michigan operates a single state-wide system of education, a substantial part of which was shown to be segregated in this case.

B

What action, then, could the District Court require the State to take in order to cure Detroit's condition of segregation? Our prior cases have not minced words as to what steps responsible officials and agencies must take in order to remedy segregation in the public schools. Not only must distinctions on the basis of race be terminated for the future, but school officials are also

"clearly charged with the affirmative duty to take whatever steps might be necessary to convert to a unitary system in which racial discrimination would be eliminated root and branch."

Green v. County School Board of New Kent County, 391 U. S. 430, 391 U. S. 437-438 (1968). See also Lee v. Macon County Board of Education, 267 F.Supp. 458 (MD Ala.), aff'd sub nom. Wallace v. United States, 389 U. S. 215 (1967). Negro students are not only entitled to neutral nondiscriminatory treatment in the future. They must receive "what Brown II promised them: a school system in which all vestiges of enforced racial segregation have been eliminated." Wright v. Council of the City of Emporia, 407 U. S. 451, 407 U. S. 463 (1972). See also Swann v. Charlotte-Mecklenburg Board of Education, 402 U. S. 1, 402 U. S. 15 (1971). These remedial standards are fully applicable not only to school districts where a dual system was compelled by statute, but also where, as here, a dual system was the product of purposeful and intentional state action. See Keyes, 413 U.S. at 413 U. S. 200-201.

After examining three plans limited to the city of Detroit, the District Court correctly concluded that none would eliminate root and branch the vestiges of unconstitutional segregation. The plans' effectiveness, of course, had to be evaluated in the context of the District Court's findings as to the extent of segregation in the Detroit city schools. As indicated earlier, the most essential finding was that Negro children in Detroit had been confined by intentional acts of segregation to a growing core of Negro schools surrounded by a receding ring of white schools. [19] Thus, in 1960, of Detroit's 251 regular attendance schools, 100 were 90% or more white and 71 were 90% or more Negro. In 1970, of Detroit's 282 regular attendance schools, 69 were 90% or more white and 133 were 90% or more Negro. While in 1960, 68% of all schools were 90% or more one race, by 1970, 71.6% of the schools fell into that category. The growing core of all-Negro schools was further evidenced in total school district population figures. In 1960, the Detroit system had 46% Negro students and 54% white students, but by 1970, 64% of the students were Negro and only 36% were white. This increase in the proportion of Negro students was the highest of any major Northern city.

It was with these figures in the background that the District Court evaluated the adequacy of the three Detroit-only plans submitted by the parties. Plan A, proposed by the Detroit Board of Education, desegregated the high schools and about a fifth of the middle-level schools. It was deemed inadequate, however, because it did not desegregate elementary schools and left the middle-level schools not included in the plan more segregated than ever. Plan C, also proposed by the Detroit Board, was deemed inadequate because it too covered only some grade levels, and would leave elementary schools segregated. Plan B, the plaintiffs' plan, though requiring the transportation of 82,000 pupils and the acquisition of 900 school buses, would make little headway in rooting out the vestiges of segregation. To begin with, because of practical limitations, the District Court found that the plan would leave many of the Detroit city schools 75% to 90% Negro. More significantly, the District Court recognized that, in the context of a community which historically had a school system marked by rigid de jure segregation, the likely effect of a Detroit-only plan would be to "change a school system which is now Black and White to one that would be perceived as Black. . . ." The result of this changed perception, the District Court found, would be to increase the flight of whites from the city to the outlying suburbs, compounding the effects of the present rate of increase in the proportion of Negro students in the Detroit system. Thus, even if a plan were adopted which, at its outset, provided in every school a 65% Negro-35% white racial mix in keeping with the Negro-white proportions of the total student population, such a system would, in short order, devolve into an all-Negro system. The net result would be a continuation of the all-Negro schools which were the hallmarks of Detroit's former dual system of one-race schools.

Under our decisions, it was clearly proper for the District Court to take into account the so-called "white flight" from the city schools which would be forthcoming from any Detroit-only decree. The court's prediction of white flight was well supported by expert testimony based on past experience in other cities undergoing desegregation relief. We ourselves took the possibility of white flight into account in evaluating the effectiveness of a desegregation plan in Wright, supra, where we relied on the District Court's finding that, if the city of Emporia were allowed to withdraw from the existing system, leaving a system with a higher proportion of Negroes, it "may be anticipated that the proportion of whites in county schools may drop as those who can register in private academies.' . . . " 407 U.S. at 407 U. S. 464. One cannot ignore the white flight problem, for where legally imposed segregation has been established, the District Court has the responsibility to see to it not only that the dual system is terminated at once, but also that future events do not serve to perpetuate or reestablish segregation. See Swann, 402 U.S. at 402 U. S. 21. See also Green, 391 U.S. at 391 U. S. 438 n. 4; Monroe v. Board of Comm'rs, 391 U. S. 450, 391 U. S. 459 (1968).

We held in Swann, supra, that, where de jure segregation is shown, school authorities must make "every effort to achieve the greatest possible degree of actual desegregation." 402 U.S. at 402 U. S. 26. This is the operative standard reemphasized in Davis v. School Comm'rs of Mobile County, 402 U. S. 33, 402 U. S. 37 (1971). If these words have any meaning at all, surely it is that school authorities must, to the extent possible, take all practicable steps to ensure that Negro and white children, in fact, go to school together. This is, in the final analysis, what desegregation of the public schools is all about.

Because of the already high and rapidly increasing percentage of Negro students in the Detroit system, as well as the prospect of white flight, a Detroit-only plan simply has no hope of achieving actual desegregation. Under such a plan, white and Negro students will not go to school together. Instead, Negro children will continue to attend all-Negro schools. The very evil that Brown I was aimed at will not be cured, but will be perpetuated for the future.

Racially identifiable schools are one of the primary vestiges of state-imposed segregation which an effective desegregation decree must attempt to eliminate. In Swann, supra, for example, we held that "[t]he district judge or school authorities . . . will thus necessarily be concerned with the elimination of one-race schools." 402 U.S. at 402 U. S. 26. There is "a presumption," we stated, "against schools that are substantially disproportionate in their racial composition." Ibid. And in evaluating the effectiveness of desegregation plans in prior cases, we ourselves have considered the extent to which they discontinued racially identifiable schools. See, e.g., Green v. County School Board of New Kent County, supra; Wright v. Council of the City of Emporia, supra. For a principal end of any desegregation remedy is to ensure that it is no longer "possible to identify a white school' or a `Negro school.'" Swann, supra, at 402 U. S. 18. The evil to be remedied in the dismantling of a dual system is the "[r]acial identification of the system's schools." Green, 391 U.S. at 391 U. S. 435. The goal is a system without white schools or Negro schools a system with "just schools." Id. at 391 U. S. 442. A school authority's remedial plan or a district court's remedial decree is to be judged by its effectiveness in achieving this end. See Swann, supra, at 402 U. S. 25; Davis, supra, at 402 U. S. 37; Green, supra, at 391 U. S. 439.

We cautioned in Swann, of course, that the dismantling of a segregated school system does not mandate any particular racial balance. 402 U.S. at 402 U. S. 24. We also concluded that a remedy under which there would remain a small number of racially identifiable schools was only presumptively inadequate and might be justified. Id. at 402 U. S. 26. But this is a totally different case

The flaw of a Detroit-only decree is not that it does not reach some ideal degree of racial balance or mixing. It simply does not promise to achieve actual desegregation at all.

It is one thing to have a system where a small number of students remain in racially identifiable schools. It is something else entirely to have a system where all students continue to attend such schools.

The continued racial identifiability of the Detroit schools under a Detroit-only remedy is not simply a reflection of their high percentage of Negro students.

What is or is not a racially identifiable vestige of de jure segregation must necessarily depend on several factors. Cf. Keyes, 413 U.S. at 413 U. S. 196. Foremost among these should be the relationship between the schools in question and the neighboring community. For these purposes, the city of Detroit and its surrounding suburbs must be viewed as a single community. Detroit is closely connected to its suburbs in many ways, and the metropolitan area is viewed as a single cohesive unit by its residents. About 40% of the residents of the two suburban counties included in the desegregation plan work in Wayne County, in which Detroit is situated. Many residents of the city work in the suburbs. The three counties participate in a wide variety of cooperative governmental ventures on a metropolitan-wide basis, including a metropolitan transit system, park authority, water and sewer system, and council of governments. The Federal Government has classified the tri-county area as a Standard Metropolitan Statistical Area, indicating that it is an area of "economic and social integration." United States v. Connecticut National Bank, ante at 418 U. S. 670.

Under a Detroit-only decree, Detroit's schools will clearly remain racially identifiable in comparison with neighboring schools in the metropolitan community. Schools with 65% and more Negro students will stand in sharp and obvious contrast to schools in neighboring districts with less than 2% Negro enrollment. Negro students will continue to perceive their schools as segregated educational facilities, and this perception will only be increased when whites react to a Detroit-only decree by fleeing to the suburbs to avoid integration. School district lines, however innocently drawn, will surely be perceived as fences to separate the races when, under a Detroit-only decree, white parents withdraw their children from the Detroit city schools and move to the suburbs in order to continue them in all-white schools. The message of this action will not escape the Negro children in the city of Detroit. See Wright, 407 U.S. at 407 U. S. 466. It will be of scant significance to Negro children who have for years been confined by de jure acts of segregation to a growing core of all-Negro schools surrounded by a ring of all-white schools that the new dividing line between the races is the school district boundary.

Nor can it be said that the State is free from any responsibility for the disparity between the racial makeup of Detroit and its surrounding suburbs. The State's creation, through de jure acts of segregation, of a growing core of all-Negro schools inevitably acted as a magnet to attract Negroes to the areas served by such schools and to deter them from settling either in other areas of the city or in the suburbs. By the same token, the growing core of all-Negro schools inevitably helped drive whites to other areas of the city or to the suburbs. As we recognized in Swann:

"People gravitate toward school facilities, just as schools are located in response to the needs of people. The location of schools may thus influence the patterns of residential development of a metropolitan area and have important impact on composition of inner-city neighborhoods. . . . [Action taken] to maintain the separation of the races with a minimum departure from the formal principles of 'neighborhood zoning' . . . does more than simply influence the short-run composition of the student body. . . . It may well promote segregated residential patterns which, when combined with 'neighborhood zoning,' further lock the school system into the mold of separation of the races. Upon a proper showing, a district court may consider this in fashioning a remedy."

402 U.S. at 402 U. S. 20-21. See also Keyes, 413 U.S. at 413 U. S. 202. The rippling effects on residential patterns caused by purposeful acts of segregation do not automatically subside at the school district border. With rare exceptions, these effects naturally spread through all the residential neighborhoods within a metropolitan area. See id. at 413 U. S. 202-203.

The State must also bear part of the blame for the white flight to the suburbs which would be forthcoming from a Detroit-only decree and would render such a remedy ineffective. Having created a system where white and Negroes were intentionally kept apart so that they could not become accustomed to learning together, the State is responsible for the fact that many whites will react to the dismantling of that segregated system by attempting to flee to the suburbs. Indeed, by limiting the District Court to a Detroit-only remedy and allowing that flight to the suburbs to succeed, the Court today allows the State to profit from its own wrong and to perpetuate for years to come the separation of the races it achieved in the past by purposeful state action.

The majority asserts, however, that involvement of outlying districts would do violence to the accepted principle that "the nature of the violation determines the scope of the remedy." Swann, supra, at 402 U. S. 16. See ante at 418 U. S. 744-745. Not only is the majority's attempt to find in this single phrase the answer to the complex and difficult questions presented in this case hopelessly simplistic, but, more important, the Court reads these words in a manner which perverts their obvious meaning. The nature of a violation determines the scope of the remedy simply because the function of any remedy is to cure the violation to which it is addressed. In school segregation cases, as in other equitable causes, a remedy which effectively cures the violation is what is required. See Green, 391 U.S. at 3 U. S. 439; Davis, 402 U.S. at 402 U. S. 37. No more is necessary, but we can tolerate no less. To read this principle as barring a district court from imposing the only effective remedy for past segregation and remitting the court to a patently ineffective alternative is, in my view, to turn a simple common sense rule into a cruel and meaningless paradox. Ironically, by ruling out an inter-district remedy, the only relief which promises to cure segregation in the Detroit public schools, the majority flouts the very principle on which it purports to rely.

Nor should it be of any significance that the suburban school districts were not shown to have themselves taken any direct action to promote segregation of the races Given the State's broad powers over local school districts, it was well within the State's powers to require those districts surrounding the Detroit school district to participate in a metropolitan remedy. The State's duty should be no different here than in cases where it is shown that certain of a State's voting districts are malapportioned in violation of the Fourteenth Amendment. See Reynolds v. Sims, 377 U. S. 533 (1964). Overrepresented electoral districts are required to participate in reapportionment although their only "participation" in the violation was to do nothing about it. Similarly, electoral districts which themselves meet representation standards must frequently be redrawn as part of a remedy for other over- and under-inclusive districts. No finding of fault on the part of each electoral district and no finding of a discriminatory effect on each district is a prerequisite to its involvement in the constitutionally required remedy. By the same logic, no finding of fault on the part of the suburban school districts in this case and no finding of a discriminatory effect on each district should be a prerequisite to their involvement in the constitutionally required remedy.

It is the State, after all, which bears the responsibility under Brown of affording a nondiscriminatory system of education. The State, of course, is ordinarily free to choose any decentralized framework for education it wishes, so long as it fulfills that Fourteenth Amendment obligation. But the State should no more be allowed to hide behind its delegation and compartmentalization of school districts to avoid its constitutional obligations to its children than it could hide behind its political subdivisions to avoid its obligations to its voters. Reynolds v. Sims, supra, at 377 U. S. 575. See also Gomillion v. Lightfoot, 364 U. S. 339 (1960).

It is a hollow remedy indeed where, "after supposed desegregation,' the schools remained segregated in fact." Hobson v. Hansen, 269 F.Supp. 401, 495 (DDC 1967). We must do better than "`substitute . . . one segregated school system for another segregated school system.'" Wright, 407 U.S. at 407 U. S. 456. To suggest, as does the majority, that a Detroit-only plan somehow remedies the effects of de jure segregation of the races is, in my view, to make a solemn mockery of Brown I's holding that separate educational facilities are inherently unequal and of Swann's unequivocal mandate that the answer to de jure segregation is the greatest possible degree of actual desegregation.

III

One final set of problems remains to be considered. We recognized in Brown II, and have reemphasized ever since, that, in fashioning relief in desegregation cases,

"the courts will be guided by equitable principles. Traditionally, equity has been characterized by a practical flexibility in shaping its remedies and by a facility for adjusting and reconciling public and private needs."

Brown II, 349 U.S. at 349 U. S. 300. See also Swann, supra.

Though not resting its holding on this point, the majority suggests that various equitable considerations militate against inter-district relief. The Court, for example, refers to financing and administrative problems, the logistical problems attending large-scale transportation of students, and the prospect of the District Court's becoming a "de facto legislative authority'" and "`school superintendent' for the entire area." Ante at 418

U. S. 743-744. The entangling web of problems woven by the Court, however, appears on further consideration to be constructed of the flimsiest of threads.

I deal first with the last of the problems posed by the Court -- the specter of the District Court qua "school superintendent" and "legislative authority" -- for analysis of this problem helps put the other issues in proper perspective. Our cases, of course, make clear that the initial responsibility for devising an adequate desegregation plan belongs with school authorities, not with the District Court. The court's primary role is to review the adequacy of the school authorities' efforts and to substitute is own plan only if and to the extent they default. See Swann, 402 U.S. at 402 U. S. 16; Green, 391 U.S. at 391 U. S. 439. Contrary to the majority's suggestions, the District Judge in this case consistently adhered to these procedures, and there is every indication that he would have continued to do so. After finding de jure segregation, the court ordered the parties to submit proposed Detroit-only plans. The state defendants were also ordered to submit a proposed metropolitan plan extending beyond Detroit's boundaries. As the District Court stated, "the State defendants . . . bear the initial burden of coming forward with a proposal that promises to work." The state defendants defaulted in this obligation, however.

Rather than submit a complete plan, the State Board of Education submitted six proposals, none of which was, in fact, a desegregation plan. It was only upon this default that the District Court began to take steps to develop its own plan. Even then, the District Court maximized school authority participation by appointing a panel representing both plaintiffs and defendants to develop a plan. Pet. App. 99a-100a. Furthermore, the District Court still left the state defendants the initial responsibility for developing both interim and final financial and administrative arrangements to implement inter-district relief. Id. at 104a-105a. The Court of Appeals further protected the interests of local school authorities by ensuring that the outlying suburban districts could fully participate in the proceedings to develop a metropolitan remedy.

These processes have not been allowed to run their course. No final desegregation plan has been proposed by the panel of experts, let alone approved by the District Court. We do not know in any detail how many students will be transported to effect a metropolitan remedy, and we do not know how long or how far they will have to travel. No recommendations have yet been submitted by the state defendants on financial and administrative arrangements. In sum, the practicality of a final metropolitan plan is simply not before us at the present time. Since the State and the panel of expert have not yet had an opportunity to come up with a workable remedy, there is no foundation for the majority's suggestion of the impracticality of inter-district relief. Furthermore, there is no basis whatever for assuming that the District Court will inevitably be forced to assume the role of legislature or school superintendent. [20]

Were we to hold that it was its constitutional duty to do so, there is every indication that the State of Michigan would fulfill its obligation and develop a plan which is workable, administrable, financially sound, and, most important, in the best interest of quality education for all of the children in the Detroit metropolitan area.

Since the Court chooses, however, to speculate on the feasibility of a metropolitan plan, I feel constrained to comment on the problem areas it has targeted. To begin with, the majority's questions concerning the practicality of consolidation of school districts need not give us pause. The State clearly has the power, under existing law, to effect a consolidation if it is ultimately determined that this offers the best prospect for a workable and stable desegregation plan. See supra at 418 U. S. 796-797. And given the 1,000 or so consolidations of school districts which have taken place in the past, it is hard to believe that the State has not already devised means of solving most, if not all, of the practical problems which the Court suggests consolidation would entail.

Furthermore, the majority ignores long-established Michigan procedures under which school districts may enter into contractual agreements to educate their pupils in other districts using state or local funds to finance nonresident education. [21] Such agreements could form an easily administrable framework for inter-district relief short of outright consolidation of the school districts. The District Court found that inter-district procedures like these were frequently used to provide special educational services for handicapped children, and extensive statutory provision is also made for their use in vocational education. [22] Surely if school districts are willing to engage in inter-district programs to help those unfortunate children crippled by physical or mental handicaps, school districts can be required to participate in an inter-district program to help those children in the city of Detroit whose educations and very futures have been crippled by purposeful state segregation.

Although the majority gives this last matter only fleeting reference, it is plain that one of the basic emotional and legal issues underlying these cases concerns the propriety of transportation of students to achieve desegregation. While others may have retreated from its standards, see, e.g., Keyes, 413 U.S. at 413 U. S. 217 (POWELL, J., concurring in part and dissenting in part), I continue to adhere to the guidelines set forth in Swann on this issue. See 402 U.S. at 402 U. S. 231. And though no final desegregation plan is presently before us, to the extent the outline of such a plan is now visible, it is clear that the transportation it would entail will be fully consistent with these guidelines.

First of all, the metropolitan plan would not involve the busing of substantially more students than already ride buses. The District Court found that, state-wide, 35-40% of all students already arrive at school on a bus. In those school districts in the tri-county Detroit metropolitan area eligible for state reimbursement of transportation costs, 42%-52% of all students rode buses to school. In the tri-county areas as a whole, approximately 300,000 pupils arrived at school on some type of bus, with about 60,000 of these apparently using regular public transit. In comparison, the desegregation plan, according to its present rough outline, would involve the transportation of 310,000 students, about 40% of the population within the desegregation area.

With respect to distance and amount of time traveled, 17 of the outlying school districts involved in the plan are contiguous to the Detroit district. The rest are all within

8 miles of the Detroit city limits. The trial court, in defining the desegregation area, placed a ceiling of 40 minutes one way on the amount of travel time, and many students will obviously travel for far shorter periods. As to distance, the average state-wide bus trip is 82 miles one way, and, in some parts of the tri-county area, students already travel for one and a quarter hours or more each way. In sum, with regard to both the number of students transported and the time and distances involved, the outlined desegregation plan "compares favorably with the transportation plan previously operated. . . ." Swann, supra, at 402 U. S. 30.

As far as economics are concerned, a metropolitan remedy would actually be more sensible than a Detroit-only remedy. Because of prior transportation aid restrictions, see supra at 418 U. S. 791, Detroit largely relied on public transport, at student expense, for those students who lived too far away to walk to school. Since no inventory of school buses existed, a Detroit-only plan was estimated to require the purchase of 900 buses to effectuate the necessary transportation. The tri-county area, in contrast, already has an inventory of 1,800 buses, many of which are now underutilized. Since increased utilization of the existing inventory can take up much of the increase in transportation involved in the inter-district remedy, the District Court found that only 350 additional buses would probably be needed, almost two-thirds fewer than a Detroit-only remedy. Other features of an inter-district remedy bespeak its practicality, such as the possibility of pairing up Negro schools near Detroit's boundary with nearby white schools on the other side of the present school district line.

Some disruption, of course, is the inevitable product of any desegregation decree, whether it operates within one district or on an inter-district basis. As we said in Swann, however:

"Absent a constitutional violation, there would be no basis for judicially ordering assignment of students on a racial basis. All things being equal, with no history of discrimination, it might well be desirable to assign pupils to schools nearest their homes. But all things are not equal in a system that has been deliberately constructed and maintained to enforce racial segregation. The remedy for such segregation may be administratively awkward, inconvenient, and even bizarre in some situations, and may impose burdens on some; but all awkwardness and inconvenience cannot be avoided. . . ."

402 U.S. at 402 U. S. 28.

Desegregation is not and was never expected to be an easy task. Racial attitudes ingrained in our Nation's childhood and adolescence are not quickly thrown aside in its middle years. But just as the inconvenience of some cannot be allowed to stand in the way of the rights of others, so public opposition, no matter how strident, cannot be permitted to divert this Court from the enforcement of the constitutional principles at issue in this case. Today's holding, I fear, is more a reflection of a perceived public mood that we have gone far enough in enforcing the Constitution's guarantee of equal justice than it is the product of neutral principle of law. In the short run, it may seem to be the easier course to allow our great metropolitan areas to be divided up each into two cities -- one white, the other black -- but it is a course, I predict, our people will ultimately regret. I dissent.

Notes

[1] Contrary to the Court's characterization, the use of racial ratios in this case in no way differed from that, in Swann v. Charlotte-Mecklenburg Board of Education, 402 U. S. 1 (1971). Here, as there, mathematical ratios were used simply as "a starting point in the process of shaping a remedy, rather than an inflexible requirement." Id. at 402 U. S. 25. It may be expected that a final desegregation plan in this case would deviate from a pure mathematical approach. Indeed, the District Court's most recent order appointing a panel of experts to draft an inter-district plan requires only that the plan be designed "to achieve the greatest degree of actual desegregation . . . [w]ithin the limitations of reasonable travel time and distance factors." 345 F.Supp. 914, 918 (ED Mich.1972). Cf. 402 U.S. at 402 U. S. 23.

[2] It does not appear that even the majority places any real weight on this consideration, since it recognizes that inter-district relief would be proper where a constitutional violation within one district produces a significant segregative effect in another district, see ante at 418 U. S. 744-745, thus allowing inter-district relief to touch districts which have not themselves violated the Constitution

[3] See Mich.Comp.Laws § 388.851 (1970).

[4] See § 388.1179.

[5] See §§ 388.629 and 340.600.

[6] See § 388.611. The State contributed an average of 34% of the operating budgets of the 54 school districts included in the original proposed desegregation area. In 11 of these districts, state contributions exceeded 50% of the operating budgets.

[7] See, e.g., id. § 340.575. See also 1949-1950 Report of the Attorney General 104 (Roth); Vol. 1, 1955 Report of the Attorney General 561 (Kavanagh); 1961-1962 Report of the Attorney General 533 (Kelley).

[8] See Mich.Comp.Laws §§ 211.34 and 340.681.

[9] § 340.569.

[10] §§ 257.811(c), 340.361, 340.781, 340.782, 388.371.

[11] § 340.575.

[12] § 388.1171.

[13] § 340.887(1).

[14] Op.Atty.Gen. No. 4705 (July 7, 1970), 1969-1970 Report of the Attorney General 156 (Kelley).

[15] See Mich.Comp.Laws § 340.253.

[16] See generally §§ 340.401-340.415 (consolidations), 340.431340.449 (annexations).

[17] See 1 Michigan Senate Journal, 1968, p. 423.

[18] See generally Mich.Comp.Laws §§ 340.461-340.468

[19] Despite MR. JUSTICE STEWART's claim to the contrary, ante at 418 U. S.

756 n. 2, of his concurring opinion, the record fully supports my statement that Negro students were intentionally confined to a core of Negro schools within the city of Detroit. See, e.g., supra at 418 U. S. 784-785, 418 U. S. 790-792. Indeed, MR. JUSTICE STEWART acknowledges that intentional acts of segregation by the State have separated white and Negro students within the city, and that the resulting core of all-Negro schools has grown to encompass most of the city. In suggesting that my approval of an inter-district remedy rests on a further conclusion that the State or its political subdivisions have been responsible for the increasing percentage of Negro students in Detroit, my Brother STEWART misconceives the thrust of this dissent. In light of the high concentration of Negro students in Detroit, the District Judge's finding that a Detroit-only remedy cannot effectively cure the constitutional violation within the city should be enough to support the choice of an inter-district remedy. Whether state action is responsible for the growth of the core of all-Negro schools in Detroit is, in my view, quite irrelevant.

The difficulty with MR. JUSTICE STEWART's position is that he, like the Court, confuses the inquiry required to determine whether there has been a substantive constitutional violation with that necessary to formulate an appropriate remedy once a constitutional violation has been shown. While a finding of state action is, of course, a prerequisite to finding a violation, we have never held that, after unconstitutional state action has been shown, the District Court, at the remedial stage, must engage in a second inquiry to determine whether additional state action exists to justify a particular remedy. Rather, once a constitutional violation has been shown, the District Court is duty-bound to formulate an effective remedy and, in so doing, the court is entitled -- indeed, it is required -- to consider all the factual circumstances relevant to the framing of an effective decree. Thus, in Swann v. Charlotte-Mecklenburg Board of Education, we held that the District Court must take into account the existence of extensive residential segregation in determining whether a racially neutral "neighborhood school" attendance plan was an adequate desegregation remedy, regardless of whether this residential segregation was caused by state action. So here, the District Court was required to consider the facts that the Detroit school system was already predominantly Negro, and would likely become all-Negro upon issuance of a Detroit-only decree in framing an effective desegregation remedy, regardless of state responsibility for this situation.

[20] In fact, the District Court remarked

"that this court's task is to enforce constitutional rights, not to act as a schoolmaster; the court's task is to protect the constitutional rights here found violated with as little intrusion into the education process as possible. The court's objective is to establish the minimum constitutional framework within which the system of public schools may operate now and hereafter in a racially unified, nondiscriminatory fashion. Within that framework the body politic, educators, parents, and, most particularly, the children must be given the maximum opportunity to experiment and secure a high quality, and equal, educational opportunity."

Pet. App. 82a.

[21] See, e.g., Mich.Comp.Laws §§ 340.69, 340.121(d), 340.359, 340.582, 340.582a, 340.590.

[22] See id. §§ 340.330-340.330u

Durational residency requirements for divorce should be unconstitutional: Justice Marshall's dissent in Sosna v. Iowa (January 14, 1975)

MR. JUSTICE MARSHALL, with whom MR. JUSTICE BRENNAN joins, dissenting.

The Court today departs sharply from the course we have followed in analyzing durational residency requirements since Shapiro v. Thompson, 394 U. S. 618 (1969). Because I think the principles set out in that case and its progeny compel reversal here, I respectfully dissent.

As we have made clear in Shapiro and subsequent cases, any classification that penalizes exercise of the constitutional right to travel is invalid unless it is justified by a compelling governmental interest. As recently as last Term we held that the right to travel requires that States provide the same vital governmental benefits and privileges to recent immigrants that they do to longtime residents. Memorial Hospital v. Maricopa County, 415 U. S. 250, 415 U. S. 261 (1974). Although we recognized that not all durational residency requirements are penalties upon the exercise of the right to travel interstate, [1] we held that free medical aid, like voting, see Dunn v. Blumstein, 405 U. S. 330 (1972), and welfare assistance, see Shapiro v. Thompson, supra, was of such fundamental importance that the State could not constitutionally condition its receipt upon long-term residence. After examining Arizona's justifications for restricting the availability of free medical services, we concluded that the State had failed to show that, in pursuing legitimate objectives, it had chosen means that did not impinge unnecessarily upon constitutionally protected interests.

The Court's failure to address the instant case in these terms suggests a new distaste for the mode of analysis we have applied to this corner of equal protection law. In its stead, the Court has employed what appears to be an ad hoc balancing test, under which the State's putative interest in ensuring that its divorce petitioners establish some roots in Iowa is said to justify the one-year residency requirement. I am concerned not only about the disposition of this case, but also about the implications of the majority's analysis for other divorce statutes and for durational residency requirement cases in general.

I

The Court omits altogether what should be the first inquiry: whether the right to obtain a divorce is of sufficient importance that its denial to recent immigrants constitutes a penalty on interstate travel. In my view, it clearly meets that standard. The previous decisions of this Court make it plain that the right of marital association is one of the most basic rights conferred on the individual by the State. The interests associated with marriage and divorce have repeatedly been accorded particular deference, and the right to marry has been termed "one of the vital personal rights essential to the orderly pursuit of happiness by free men." Loving v. Virginia, 388 U. S. 1, 388 U. S. 12 (1967). In Boddie v. Connecticut, 401 U. S. 371 (1971), we recognized that the right to seek dissolution of the marital relationship was closely related to the right to marry, as both involve the voluntary adjustment of the same fundamental human relationship. Id. at 401 U. S. 383. Without further laboring the point, I think it is clear beyond cavil that the right to seek dissolution of the marital relationship is of such fundamental importance that denial of this right to the class of recent interstate travelers penalizes interstate travel within the meaning of Shapiro, Dunn, and Maricopa County.

II

Having determined that the interest in obtaining a divorce is of substantial social importance, I would scrutinize Iowa's durational residency requirement to determine whether it constitutes a reasonable means of furthering important interests asserted by the State. The Court, however, has not only declined to apply the "compelling interest" test to this case, it has conjured up possible justifications for the State's restriction in a manner much more akin to the lenient standard we have in the past applied in analyzing equal protection challenges to business regulations. See McGowan v. Maryland, 366 U. S. 420, 366 U. S. 425-428 (1961); Kotch v. Board of River Port Pilot Comm'rs, 330 U. S. 552, 330 U. S. 557 (1947); but see Johnson v. Robison, 415 U. S. 361, 415 U. S. 376 (1974). I continue to be of the view that the "rational basis" test has no place in equal protection analysis when important individual interests with constitutional implications are at stake, See San Antonio School District v. Rodriguez, 411 U.S. 1, 411 U. S. 109 (1973) (MARSHALL, J., dissenting); Dandridge v. Williams, 397 U. S. 471, 397 U. S. 520-522 (1970) (MARSHALL, J., dissenting). But whatever the ultimate resting point of the current readjustments in equal protection analysis, the Court has clearly directed that the proper standard to apply to cases in which state statutes have penalized the exercise of the right to interstate travel is the "compelling interest" test. Shapiro v. Thompson, 394 U.S. at 394 U. S. 634, 394 U. S. 638; Oregon v. Mitchell, 400 U. S. 112, 400 U. S. 238 (1970) (opinion of BRENNAN, WHITE and MARSHALL, JJ.); Dunn v. Blumstein, 405 U.S. at 405 U. S. 342-343; Memorial Hospital v. Maricopa County, 415 U.S. at 415 U. S. 262-263.

The Court proposes three defenses for the Iowa statute: first, the residency requirement merely delays receipt of the benefit in question -- it does not deprive the applicant of the benefit altogether; second, since significant social consequences may follow from the conferral of a divorce, the State may legitimately regulate the divorce process; and third, the State has interests both in protecting itself from use as a "divorce mill" and in protecting its judgments from possible collateral attack in other States. In my view, the first two defenses provide no significant support for the statute in question here. Only the third has any real force.

A

With the first justification, the Court seeks to distinguish the Shapiro, Dunn, and Maricopa County cases. Yet the distinction the Court draws seems to me specious. Iowa's residency requirement, the Court says, merely forestalls access to the courts; applicants seeking welfare payments, medical aid, and the right to vote, on the other hand, suffer unrecoverable losses throughout the waiting period. This analysis, however, ignores the severity of the deprivation suffered by the divorce petitioner who is forced to wait a year for relief. See Stanley v. Illinois, 405 U. S. 645, 405 U. S. 647 (1972). The injury accompanying that delay is not directly measurable in money terms like the loss of welfare benefits, but it cannot reasonably be argued that, when the year has elapsed, the petitioner is made whole. The year's wait prevents remarriage and locks both partners into what may be an intolerable, destructive relationship. Even applying the Court's argument on its own terms, I fail to see how the Maricopa County case can be distinguished. A potential patient may well need treatment for a single ailment. Under Arizona statutes, he would have had to wait a year before he could be treated. Yet the majority's analysis would suggest that Mr. Evaro's claim for nonemergency medical aid is not cognizable because he would "eventually qualify for the same sort of [service]," ante at 419 U. S. 406. The Court cannot mean that Mrs. Sosna has not suffered any injury by being foreclosed from seeking a divorce in Iowa for a year. It must instead mean that it does not regard that deprivation as being very severe. [2]

B

I find the majority's second argument no more persuasive. The Court forgoes reliance on the usual justifications for durational residency requirements -- budgetary considerations and administrative convenience, see Shapiro, 394 U.S. at 394 U. S. 627-638; Maricopa County, 415 U.S. at 415 U. S. 262-269. Indeed, it would be hard to make a persuasive argument that either of these interests is significantly implicated in this case. In their place, the majority invokes a more amorphous justification -- the magnitude of the interests affected and resolved by a divorce proceeding. Certainly the stakes in a divorce are weighty both for the individuals directly involved in the adjudication and for others immediately affected by it. The critical importance of the divorce process, however, weakens the argument for a long residency requirement, rather than strengthens it. The impact of the divorce decree only underscores the necessity that the State's regulation be evenhanded. [3]

It is not enough to recite the State's traditionally exclusive responsibility for regulating family law matters; some tangible interference with the State's regulatory scheme must be shown. Yet, in this case, I fail to see how any legitimate objective of Iowa's divorce regulations would be frustrated by granting equal access to new state residents. [4] To draw on an analogy, the States have great interests in the local voting process and wide latitude in regulating that process. Yet one regulation that the States may not impose is an unduly long residency requirement. Dunn v. Blumstein, 405 U. S. 330 (1972). To remark, as the Court does, that, because of the consequences riding on a divorce decree "Iowa may insist that one seeking to initiate such a proceeding have the modicum of attachment to the State required here" is not to make an argument, but merely to state the result.

C

The Court's third justification seems to me the only one that warrants close consideration. Iowa has a legitimate interest in protecting itself against invasion by those seeking quick divorces in a forum with relatively lax divorce laws, and it may have some interest in avoiding collateral attacks on its decree in other States. [5] These interests, however, would adequately be protected by a simple requirement of domicile -- physical presence plus intent to remain -- which would remove the rigid one-year barrier while permitting the State to restrict the availability of its divorce process to citizens who are genuinely its own. [6]

The majority notes that, in Williams v. North Carolina, 325 U. S. 226 (1945), the Court held that for ex parte divorces one State's finding of domicile could, under limited circumstances, be challenged in the' courts of another. From this, the majority concludes that, since Iowa's findings of domicile might be subject to collateral attack elsewhere, it should be permitted to cushion its findings with a one-year residency requirement.

For several reasons, the year's waiting period seems to me neither necessary nor much of a cushion. First, the Williams opinion was not aimed at States seeking to avoid becoming divorce mills. Quite the opposite, it was rather plainly directed at States that had cultivated a "quickie divorce" reputation by playing fast and loose with findings of domicile. See id. at 325 U. S. 236-237; id. at 325 U. S. 241 (Murphy, J., concurring). If Iowa wishes to avoid becoming a haven for divorce seekers, it is inconceivable that its good faith determinations of domicile would not meet the rather lenient full faith and credit standards set out in Williams.

A second problem with the majority's argument on this score is that Williams applies only to ex parte divorces. This Court has held that, if both spouses were before the divorcing court, a foreign State cannot recognize a collateral challenge that would not be permissible in the divorcing State. Sherrer v. Sherrer, 334 U. S. 343 (1948); Coe v. Coe, 334 U. S. 378 (1948); Johnson v. Muelberger, 340 U. S. 581 (1951); Cook v. Cook, 342 U. S. 126 (1951). Therefore, the Iowa statute sweeps too broadly even as a defense to possible collateral attacks, since it imposes a one-year requirement whenever the respondent does not reside in the State, regardless of whether the proceeding is ex parte. [7]

Third, even a one-year period does not provide complete protection against collateral attack. It merely makes it somewhat less likely that a second State will be able to find "cogent evidence" that Iowa's determination of domicile was incorrect. But if the Iowa court has erroneously determined the question of domicile, the year's residence will do nothing to preclude collateral attack under Williams.

Finally, in one sense, the year's residency requirement may technically increase, rather than reduce, the exposure of Iowa's decrees to collateral attack. Iowa appears to be among the States that have interpreted their divorce residency requirements as being of jurisdictional import. [8] Since a State's divorce decree is subject to collateral challenge in a foreign forum for any jurisdictional flaw that would void it in the State's own courts, New York ex rel. Halvey v. Halvey, 330 U. S. 610 (1947), the residency requirement exposes Iowa divorce proceedings to attack both for failure to prove domicile and for failure to prove one year's residence. If nothing else, this casts doubt on the majority's speculation that Iowa's residency requirement may have been intended as a statutory shield for its divorce decrees. In sum, concerns about the need for a long residency requirement to defray collateral attacks on state judgments seem more fanciful than real. If, as the majority assumes, Iowa is interested in assuring itself that its divorce petitioners are legitimately Iowa citizens, requiring petitioners to provide convincing evidence of bona fide domicile should be more than adequate to the task. [9]

III

I conclude that the course Iowa has chosen in restricting access to its divorce courts unduly interferes with the right to "migrate, resettle, find a new job, and start a new life." Shapiro v. Thompson, 394 U.S. at 394 U. S. 629. I would reverse the judgment of the District Court and remand for entry of an order granting relief if the court finds that there is a continuing controversy in this case. See Steffel v. Thompson, 415 U. S. 452 (1974); Johnson v. New York State Education Dept., 409 U. S. 75, 409 U. S. 79 n. 7 (1972) (MARSHALL, J., concurring).

Notes

[1] Memorial Hospital v. Maricopa County, 415 U.S. at 415 U. S. 256-259; see also Shapiro v. Thompson, 394 U.S. at 394 U. S. 638 n. 21.

[2] The majority also relies on its "mere delay" distinction to dispose of Boddie v. Connecticut, 401 U. S. 371 (1971), see ante at 419 U. S. 410. Yet even though the majority in Boddie relied on due process, rather than equal protection, I am fully convinced that, if the Connecticut statute in question in that case had required indigents to wait a year for a divorce, the statute would still have been constitutionally infirm, see 401 U.S. at 401 U. S. 383-386 (DOUGLAS, J., concurring in result), a point the Court implicitly rejects today.

[3] The majority identifies marital status, property rights, and custody and support arrangements as the important concerns commonly resolved by divorce proceedings. But by declining to exercise divorce jurisdiction over its new citizens, Iowa does not avoid affecting these weighty social concerns; instead, it freezes them in an unsatisfactory state that it would not require its long-time residents to endure.

[4] A durational requirement such as Iowa's 90-day conciliation period would not, of course, be subject to an equal protection challenge, as it is required uniformly of all divorce petitioners.

[5] Appellees do not rely on these factors to support the Iowa statute. In their brief, appellees argue that the legislature's determination to impose a one-year residency requirement was reasonable "in the light of the interest of the State of Iowa in a dissolution proceeding." Brief for Appellees 8. The full faith and credit argument is

mentioned only in the middle of a long quotation from another court's opinion, id. at 9. This is hardly sufficient to meet the requirement of a "clear showing that the burden imposed is necessary to protect a compelling and substantial governmental interest." Oregon v. Mitchell, 400 U. S. 112, 400 U. S. 238 (1970) (opinion of BRENNAN, WHITE, and MARSHALL, JJ.); Sherbert v. Verner, 374 U. S. 398, 374 U. S. 406-409 (1963).

[6] The availability of a less restrictive alternative such as a domicile requirement weighs heavily in testing a challenged state regulation against the "compelling interest" standard. See Shapiro v. Thompson, 394 U.S. at 394 U. S. 638; Dunn v. Blumstein, 405 U. S. 330, 405 U. S. 342, 405 U. S. 350-352 (1972); Memorial Hospital v. Maricopa County, 415 U.S. at 415 U. S. 267; Shelton v. Tucker, 364 U. S. 479, 364 U. S. 488 (1960). Since the Iowa courts have, in effect, interpreted the residency statute to require proof of domicile as well as one year's residence, see Korsrud v. Korsrud, 242 Iowa 178, 45 N.W.2d 848 (1951); Julson v. Julson, 255 Iowa 301, 122 N.W.2d 329 (1963), a shift to a "pure" domicile test would impose no new burden on the State's factfinding process.

[7] This problem could be cured in large part if the State waived its year's residency requirement whenever the respondent agreed to consent to the court's jurisdiction.

[8] See Hinds v. Hinds, 1 Iowa 36 (1855); Williamson v. Williamson, 179 Iowa 489, 495, 161 N.W. 482, 485 (1917); Korsrud v. Korsrud, supra; Schaefer v. Schaefer, 245 Iowa 1343, 1350, 66 N.W.2d 428, 433 (1954); cf. White v. White, 138 Conn.1, 81 A.2d 450 (1951); Wyman v. Wyman, 212 N.W.2d 368 (Minn.1973); Camp v. Camp, 21 Misc.2d 908, 189 N.Y.S.2d 561 (1959) (construing Florida law). While the Williams case establishes that collateral attack can always be mounted against the divorcing State's finding of domicile, other States have provided that failure to meet the durational residency requirement is not jurisdictional, and thus does not provide an independent basis for collateral attack, see, e.g., Schreiner v. Schreiner, 502 S.W.2d 840 (Tex.Ct. Civ.App. 1973); Hammond v. Hammond, 45 Wash.2d 855, 278 P.2d 387 (1954) (construing Idaho law).

[9] The majority argues that, since most States require a year's residence for divorce, Iowa gains refuge from the risk of collateral attack in the understanding solicitude of States with similar laws. Of course, absent unusual circumstances, a judgment by this Court striking down the Iowa statute would similarly affect the other States with one- and two-year residency requirements. For the same reason, the risk of subjecting Iowa to an invasion of divorce seekers seems minimal. If long residency requirements are held unconstitutional, Iowa will not stand conspicuously alone without a residency requirement "defense." Moreover, its 90-day conciliation period, required of all divorce petitioners in the State, would still serve to discourage peripatetic divorce seekers who are looking for the quickest possible adjudication.

The great discretion available to the King to dispense mercy did not incorporate into the pardoning power the royal right to invade the legislative province of assessing punishments: Justice Marshall's dissent in Schick v. Reed (December 23, 1974)

MR. JUSTICE MARSHALL, with whom MR. JUSTICE DOUGLAS and MR. JUSTICE BRENNAN join, dissenting.

The Court today denies petitioner relief from the no-parole condition of his commuted death sentence, paying only lip service to our intervening decision in Furman v. Georgia, 408 U. S. 238 (1972). Because I believe the retrospective application of Furman requires us to vacate petitioner's sentence and substitute the only lawful alternative -- life with the opportunity for parole, I respectfully dissent.

I

The Court misconstrues petitioner's retroactivity argument. Schick does not dispute the constitutional validity of the death penalty in 1954 under then-existing case law. Nor does he contend that he was under sentence of death [1] in 1972 when the decision issued in Furman, invalidating "the imposition and carrying out" of discretionary death sentences. Id. at 408 U. S. 239. Rather, he argues that the retroactive application of Furman to his no-parole commutation is required because the imposition of the death sentence was the indispensable vehicle through which he became subject to his present sentence. In other words, the no-parole condition could not now exist had the court-martial before which Schick was tried not imposed the death penalty.

The relationship between the death sentence and the condition is clear. Article 118 of the Uniform Code of Military Justice (UCMJ) [2] authorizes only two sentences for the crime of premeditated murder: death or life imprisonment which entails at least the possibility of parole. Confinement without possibility of parole is unknown to military law; [3] it is not and has never been authorized for any UCMJ offense, 10 U.S.C. §§ 877-934; Manual for Courts-Martial, 34 Fed.Reg. 10502 (1969). In short, the penal restriction of the commutation was a creature of Presidential clemency made possible only through the court-martial's imposition of the death sentence.

The retroactivity of Furman is equally unclouded. The Court "[has] not hesitated" to give full retroactive effect to the Furman decision. Robinson v. Neil, 409 U. S. 505, 409 U. S. 508 (1973). See Stewart v. Massachusetts, 408 U. S. 845 (1972); Marks v. Louisiana, 408 U.S. 933 (1972); Walker v. Georgia, 408 U.S. 936 (1972). The per curiam decision struck down both "the imposition and the carrying out" of discretionary death sentences as cruel and unusual punishment in violation of the Eighth Amendment. 408 U.S. at 408 U. S. 239. The opinion specifically held that the "judgment . . . is . . . reversed insofar as it leaves undisturbed the death sentence imposed. . . ." Id. at 408 U. S. 240. The retroactive application of Furman results in more than the simple enjoining of execution; it nullifies the very act of sentencing. In effect, a post-Furman court must ensure a prisoner the same treatment that he would have been afforded had the death penalty not been imposed initially. [4]

The full retroactivity of a constitutional ruling is aimed at the eradication of all adverse consequences of prior violations of that rule. We have recognized the importance of erasing "root and branch" the adverse legal consequences, both direct and indirect, of prior constitutional violations. See, e.g., McConnell v. Rhay, 393 U. S. 2, 393 U. S. 3 (1968); Linkletter v. Walker, 381 U. S. 618, 381 U. S. 639 (1965). The effective operation of this procedure was demonstrated in the decisions on the right to counsel in state felony trials. See Pickelsimer v. Wainwright, 375 U. S. 2 (1963); Kitchens v. Smith, 401 U. S. 847 (1971); Burgett v. Texas, 389 U. S. 109 (1967); United States v. Tucker, 404 U. S. 443 (1972).

Since Furman is fully retroactive petitioner's case should be simple to resolve. The terms of Art. 118 of the UCMJ provide that a person convicted of premeditated murder "shall suffer death or imprisonment for life as a court-martial may direct." A death sentence was imposed by the court-martial and affirmed by the Board of Review and the United States Court of Military Appeals, 7 U.S.C.M.A. 419, 22 C.M.R. 209 (1956). The death sentence so imposed was declared unconstitutional by Furman and is therefore null and void as a matter of law. The only legal alternative -- simple life imprisonment -- must be substituted. Concomitantly, the adverse consequence of the death sentence -- the no-parole condition of petitioner's 1960 commutation -- must also be voided, as it exceeds the lawful alternative punishment that should have been imposed. Petitioner should now be subject to treatment as a person sentenced to life imprisonment on the date of his original sentence and eligible for parole. [5]

The Court today suggests that petitioner cannot claim any benefit from Furman because no death penalty was pending against him at the time of the decision. The 1960 commutation is touted as the panacea for the constitutional defects of petitioner's original sentence. Unfortunately, such is not the case.

The imposition of the death sentence was the indispensable vehicle through which petitioner became subject to his present sentence. The commutation of the sentence did not cure the constitutional disabilities of the punishment. A noted expert on the subject of Presidential clemency states:

"Unlike a pardon, a commutation does not absolve the beneficiary from most of the legal consequences of an offense. [6]"

Although petitioner is not under direct threat of the death sentence,

"he has suffered and continues to suffer enhanced punishment -- the loss of his statutory right to be considered for parole -- as a result of an illegally imposed death sentence. [7]"

The full retrospective application of Furman requires the eradication of this vestige of the prior constitutional violation. If petitioner had been granted stays of execution until Furman was decided, there is no doubt that his sentence would have to be vacated and a life sentence imposed instead. The situation should be no different simply because the Chief Executive commuted his sentence -- in effect granting a permanent stay of execution. Nullification of the no-parole provision would relieve petitioner of this unconstitutional burden and clear the way for lawful resentencing with eligibility for parole.

II

Since the majority devotes its opinion to a discussion of the scope of Presidential power, I am compelled to comment. I have no quarrel with the proposition that the source of the President's commutation power is found in Art. II, § 2, cl. 1, of the Constitution, which authorizes the President to grant reprieves and pardons for offenses against the United States except for cases of impeachment. Biddle v. Perovich, 274 U. S. 480 (1927). Commutation is defined as the substitution of a lesser type of punishment for the punishment actually imposed at trial. [8]

The issue here is whether the President's expansion of an unencumbered life term by addition of a condition proscribing Schick's eligibility for parole went beyond the authority conferred by Art. II. Article 118 of the UCMJ and the implementing court-martial regulations prescribe mandatory adjudication of either death or life imprisonment for the crime of premeditated murder. 10 U.S.C. § 918; 34 Fed.Reg. 10704. I take issue with the Court's conclusion that annexation of the "no-parole condition . . . does not offend the Constitution." Ante at 419 U. S. 267. In my view, the President's action exceeded the limits of the Art. II pardon power. In commuting a sentence under Art. II, the Chief Executive is not imbued with the constitutional power to create unauthorized punishments.

The congressionally prescribed limits of punishment mark the boundaries within which the Executive must exercise his authority. [9] By virtue of the pardon power, the Executive may abstain from enforcing a judgment by judicial authorities; he may not, under the aegis of that power, engage in lawmaking or adjudication. Cf. United States v. Benz, 282 U. S. 304, 282 U. S. 311 (1931) (an act of clemency is an exercise of executive power which abridges the enforcement of the judgment, but does not alter it qua judgment); United States ex rel. Brazier v. Commissioner of Immigration, 5 F.2d 162 (CA2 1924) (pardon power does not embrace right to bar congressionally prescribed deportation of prisoners).

While the clemency function of the Executive in the federal criminal justice system [10] is consistent with the separation of powers, the attachment of punitive conditions to grants of clemency is not. Prescribing punishment is a prerogative reserved for the lawmaking branch of government, the legislature. As a consequence, President Eisenhower's addition to Schick's commutation of a condition that did not coincide with punishment prescribed by the legislature for any military crime, [11] much less this specific offense, was a usurpation of a legislative function. While the exercise of the pardon power was proper, the imposition of this penal condition was not embraced by that power. [12]

The Court today advances the antecedent English pardon power and prior holdings of this Court in support of the legality of the no-parole condition. Neither body of law has established an Executive right to define extra-legislative punishments. [13] Nor does the historical status of the pardon power in England or analysis of prior nonpenal conditions supply any relevance here.

A

The English annals offer dubious support to the Court. The majority opinion recounts in copious detail the historical evolution of the pardon power in England. Ante at 419 U. S. 260-262. See also Ex parte Wells, 18 How. 307, 59 U. S. 309-313 (1856). The references to English statutes and cases are no more than dictum; as the Court itself admonishes, "the [pardon] power flows from the Constitution alone." Ante at 419 U. S. 266. Accordingly, the primary resource for analyzing the scope of Art. II is our own republican system of government. See Grosjean v. American Press Co., 297 U. S. 233, 297 U. S. 248-249 (1936). The separation of powers doctrine does not vest the Chief Executive with an unrestrained clemency power, supra at 419 U. S. 274-275, but views his functions as distinct from the other coordinate branches. Ante at 419 U. S. 262-264. The references to the early American experience are not dispositive. [14]

Indeed, history recounts that even the pardon power of the King to "annex [a condition] to his bounty" was subject to statutory limitation. 4 W. Blackstone, Commentaries *401. As noted in the Wells case:

"The sovereign of England, with all the prerogatives of the crown, in granting a conditional pardon, cannot substitute a punishment which the law does not authorize."

18 How. at 59 U. S. 323 (McLean, J., dissenting). Even the authority quoted by Blackstone in support of the proposition, 2 W. Hawkins, Pleas of the Crown 547 (8th ed. 1824), does not actually support the suggestion of unlimited power in the King. In fact, the conditions discussed were either imposed pursuant to statute or of a nonpunitive nature. See Coles Case, Moore K.B. 466, 72 Eng.Rep. 700 (1597); E. Coke, A Commentary upon Littleton 274b (19th ed. 1832). The Court acknowledges instances in which statutory authority placed restrictions on the monarch's power. Ante at 419 U. S. 260. The critical role of statutes in the imposition of the condition of banishment on pardons of convicted felons was recognized in a letter addressed to a member of the House of Lords:

"There is hardly anything to be found respecting conditional pardons in the old English law-books; but the authority of the Crown to grant a conditional pardon in capital cases is . . . recognized in statute 5 Geo. 4, c. 84, s. 2. . . ."

W. Forsyth, Cases and Opinions on Constitutional Law 460 (1869).

The King's prerogative was thus not as broad as the majority's reading of Blackstone indicates. The great discretion available to the King to dispense mercy did not incorporate into the pardoning power the royal right to invade the legislative province of assessing punishments.

B

Contrary to the Court's suggestion, limitation of Executive action to the statutory framework is not undermined by earlier decisions of this Court. In Biddle v. Perovich, 274 U. S. 480, 483 [argument of counsel -- omitted] (1927), the Solicitor General expressly noted that "[a] commutation is the substitution of a milder punishment known to the law for the one inflicted by the court." Mr. Justice Holmes, writing for a unanimous Court, concluded on a related matter that consent to commutation was unnecessary since, "[b]y common understanding, imprisonment for life is a less penalty than death." Id. at 274 U. S. 487. The Court held that the "only question is whether the substituted punishment was authorized by law. . . ." Ibid. While Holmes' specific reference is to the law of the Constitution, he then proceeds with a discussion of the statutory sanctions. Commutation to life imprisonment without any opportunity for parole would penalize the prisoner here beyond the terms of the UCMJ sanctions.

The requirement that the substituted sentence be one provided by law is not hampered by Ex parte Wells, supra, in which this Court upheld conditional commutation from a death sentence to a simple life term. The validity of mitigation of a sentence without depriving the prisoner of any additional rights is not inconsistent with rejection of unauthorized penal conditions. In Wells, the Court acknowledged that limitations on the pardon power mandated its exercise "according to law; that is, as it had been used in England, and these States." 18 How. at 59 U. S. 310. Although the Wells Court was not faced with the question whether all possible conditions were in the ambit of Art. II, it addressed the specific limitation on penal conditions attached to commutations:

"So, conditional pardons by the king do not permit transportation or exile as a commutable punishment, unless the same has been provided for by legislation."

Id. at 59 U. S. 313. The remaining cases on which the Court relies to sustain the condition offer minimal support and are easily distinguished. [15]

In conclusion, I note that, where a President chooses to exercise his clemency power, he should be mindful that

"[t]he punishment appropriate for the diverse federal offenses is a matter for the discretion of Congress, subject only to constitutional limitations, more particularly the Eighth Amendment."

Bell v. United States, 349 U. S. 81, 349 U. S. 82 (1955). See Ex parte United States, 242 U. S. 27, 242 U. S. 42 (1916). The Congress has not delegated such authority to the President. I do not challenge the right of the President to issue pardons on nonpenal conditions, but, where the Executive elects to exercise the Presidential power for commutation the clear import of the Constitution mandates that the lesser punishment imposed be sanctioned by the legislature. [16]

In sum, the no-parole condition is constitutionally defective in the face of the retrospective application of Furman and the extra-legal nature of the Executive action. I would nullify the condition, and direct the lower court to remand the case for resentencing to the only alternative available life with the opportunity for parole -- and its attendant benefits.

Notes

[1] But see 419 U. S. infra.

[2] Article 118, 10 U.S.C. § 918, reads:

"Any person subject to this code who, without justification or excuse, unlawfully kills a human being, when he -- "

"(1) has a premeditated design to kill;"

"* * * *"

"shall suffer death or imprisonment for life as a court-martial may direct."

May 5, 1950, c. 169, § 1, 64 Stat. 140.

[3] Military prisoners incarcerated in federal penitentiaries are governed by the same parole statutes and regulations applicable to all federal prisoners. Under the federal parole eligibility statute, 18 U.S.C. §§ 4202-4203 (1970 ed. and Supp. II), petitioner, an inmate for 20 years at Lewisburg, now has satisfied the 15-year prerequisite for parole consideration. See 10 U.S.C. § 858. Likewise, if Schick had been confined in a military facility he would now be eligible for parole under 10 U.S.C. §§ 952-953.

[4] Where only one alternative punishment is available to the trial court, that punishment has been automatically imposed either by the appellate court itself, e.g., State v. Johnson, 31 Ohio St.2d 106, 285 N.E.2d 751 (1972); Commonwealth v. Bradley, 449 Pa.19, 295 A.2d 842 (1972); Anderson v. State, 267 So.2d 8, 10 (Fla.1972); or by the trial judge on direction from the appellate court, e.g., Capler v. State, 268 So.2d 338 (Miss.1972); State v. Square, 263 La. 291, 268 So.2d 229 (1972); Garcia v. State, 501 P.2d 1128 (Okla.Crim.1972).

[5] Nothing in Furman suggests that it is inapplicable to the military. The per curiam carves out no exceptions to the prohibition against discretionary death sentences. The opinions of the five-member majority recognize no basis for excluding the members of the Armed Forces from protection against this form of punishment. Even the list of four capital punishment statutes not affected by the Court's decision, provided by my Brother STEWART, does not include the federal military statutes. 408 U. S. 238, 408 U. S. 307 (1972). Even more persuasive is the language of my Brother POWELL in dissent which states that "numerous provisions of . . . the Uniform Code of Military Justice are also voided." Id. at 408 U. S. 417-418.

Beyond the language of Furman the Court has made clear in Trop v. Dulles, 356 U. S. 86 (1958), that the Eighth Amendment is applicable to the military. While the Court divided on the penal nature of the statute which provided additional sanctions for servicemen convicted of wartime desertion, there was no disagreement on the application of the Amendment.

I would also note that the UCMJ, enacted in 1950, has by decision and practice incorporated the Bill of Rights and afforded its protection to the members of the Armed Forces. See, e.g., United States v. Tempia, 16 U.S.C.M.A. 629, 634, 37 C.M.R. 249, 254 (1967); United States v. Jacoby, 11 U.S.C.M.A. 428, 43031, 29 C.M.R. 244, 246-247 (1960); United States v. Jobe, 10 U.S.C.M.A. 276, 279, 27 C.M.R. 350, 353 (1959).

The fact that a court-martial, rather than a jury imposes the death sentence is irrelevant. In my view, the penalty is equally severe, and, in my view, equally offensive to the Eighth Amendment for that reason, see Furman v. Georgia, 408 U.S. at 408 U. S. 314-374 (MARSHALL, J., concurring). Moreover, the potential for abuse and discrimination with which my Brethren were concerned in Furman is as evident here as in the civilian courts.

[6] W. Humbert, The Pardoning Power of the President 27 (1941).

[7] 157 U.S.App.D.C. 263, 270, 483 F.2d 1266, 1273 (1973) (Wright, J., dissenting).

[8] Although pardon and commutation emanate from the same source, they represent clearly distinct forms of clemency. Whereas commutation is a substitution of a milder form of punishment, pardon is an act of public conscience that relieves the recipient of all the legal consequences of the conviction. See, e.g., United States ex rel. Brazier v. Commissioner of Immigration, 5 F.2d 162 (CA2 1924); Chapman v. Scott, 10 F.2d 156, 159 (Conn.1925), aff'd, 10 F.2d 690 (CA2), cert. denied, 270 U.S. 657 (1926); Note, Executive Clemency in Capital Cases, 39 N.Y.U.L.Rev. 136, 138 (1964); Humbert, supra, n. 6, at 27; Black's Law Dictionary 351, 1268-1269 (4th ed.1968).

[9] Indeed, Mr. Chief Justice Marshall expanded on the notion of separation of powers, stating:

"[T]he power of punishment is vested in the legislative . . . department. It is the legislature . . . which is to define a crime, and ordain its punishment."

United States v. Wiltberger, 5 Wheat. 76, 18 U. S. 95 (1820).

[10] Article 71(a) of the UCMJ, 10 U.S.C. § 871(a), outlines the Presidential role in the review of military convictions.

With the exception of premeditated murder and felony murder the UCMJ authorizes punishment at the discretion of the court-martial. Thus, in the majority of cases the President would not be limited to only two alternatives but could commute to any lesser sentence than that imposed by the court-martial consistent with the statutory authorization. It is only in the face of the mandate of Art. 118, limiting the alternatives to death or life imprisonment with the possibility of parole, that the restriction to the statutory alternatives may appear at first blush unduly Draconian.

[11] As already indicated, confinement without opportunity for parole is unknown to military law. See text accompanying n. 3, supra. Moreover, the only federal law recognition of this punishment in a civilian context is found in the very limited no-parole provisions dealing with continuing narcotics enterprises. 21 U.S.C. § 848. Guided by the special nature of drug offenses and drug offenders the Congress enacted this narrow exception to universal eligibility for parole. See H.R.Rep. No. 2388, 84th Cong., 2d Sess., 4, 8, 11, 64 (1956).

[12] The Court cites Ex porte Wells, 18 How. 307 (1856), and an opinion of Attorney General Brownell, 41 Op.Atty.Gen. 251 (1955), in support of the statement that

"Presidents . . . have [frequently] exercised the power to pardon or commute sentences upon conditions that are not specifically authorized by statute."

Ante at 419 U. S. 266. Wells involved the simple substitution of the lesser penalty of life imprisonment for death; no separate punitive condition was attached to the Executive action. A legal opinion from the Attorney General supplies reasoned interpretations but hardly bears the force of law.

[13] The King's pardon power, from which the President's Art. II power derives, also was subject historically to statutory limitations. See Ex parte Wells, supra, at 59 U. S. 312-313; id. at 59 U. S. 322 (McLean, J., dissenting).

[14] With few exceptions conditional pardons were not granted by state governors except where authorized by law, Ex parte Wells, supra, at 59 U. S. 322 (McLean, J., dissenting). The Court's references to the Framers' writings on the pardon power fail to take account of the separation of powers doctrine so fervently embraced by the constitutional drafters. National Mutual Ins. Co. v. Tidewater Transfer Co., 337 U. S. 582 (1949); The Federalist No. 47 (J. Madison) (J. Cooke ed.1961); E. Corwin, The President: Office and Powers 140 (1940). In fact, Corwin notes:

"[T]he President is not authorized to add to sentences imposed by the courts [pursuant to legislative direction] -- he may only mitigate them. . . ."

Ibid. (emphasis in original).

[15] United States v. Wilson, 7 Pet. 150 (1833), turned on the technical question of whether a pardon must be pleaded and only referred in dictum to the possibility that the President could condition a pardon. In Ex parte Garland, 4 Wall. 333 (1867), and Ex parte Grossman, 267 U. S. 87 (1925), the Court focused on the discretionary aspect of the pardon power which is here unchallenged. The emphasis was on the right of the President to grant a pardon to any criminal, for any offense, at any time. The question of conditional action was raised in only a tangential manner.

[16] The Court likens the no-parole condition to "sanctions imposed by legislatures such as mandatory minimum sentences. . . ." The similarity is all too close, in my view. Indeed, it is precisely because the President has invaded the legislative domain that the condition must fail.

If we're not sure what the lower court meant, ask them: Justice Marshall's dissent in Oregon v. Hass (March 19, 1975)

MR. JUSTICE MARSHALL, with whom MR. JUSTICE BRENNAN joins, dissenting.

While I agree with my Brother BRENNAN that on the merits the judgment of the Oregon Supreme Court was correct, I think it appropriate to add a word about this Court's increasingly common practice of reviewing state-court decisions upholding constitutional claims in criminal cases. See Michigan v. Mosley, 51 Mich. App. 105, 214 N. W. 2d 564 (1974), cert. granted, 419 U.S. 1119 (1975); Michigan v. Payne, 412 U.S. 47 (1973); Wisconsin v. Yoder, 406 U.S. 205 (1972); California v. Byers, 402 U.S. 424 (1971); California v. Green, 399 U.S. 149 (1970).

In my view, we have too often rushed to correct state courts in their view of federal constitutional questions without sufficiently considering the risk that we will be drawn into rendering a purely advisory opinion. Plainly, if the Oregon Supreme Court had expressly decided that Hass' statement was inadmissible as a matter of state as well as federal law, this Court could not upset that judgment. See Jankovich v. Indiana Toll Road Comm'n, 379 U.S. 487 (1965); Minnesota v. National Tea Co., 309 U.S. 551 (1940); Fox Film Corp. v. Muller, 296 U.S. 207 (1935). The sound policy behind this rule was well articulated by Mr. Justice Jackson in Herb v. Pitcairn, 324 U.S. 117 (1945):

"This Court from the time of its foundation has adhered to the principle that it will not review judgments of state courts that rest on adequate and independent state grounds. The reason is so obvious that it has rarely been thought to warrant statement. It is found in the partitioning of power between the state and federal judicial systems and in the limitations of our own jurisdiction. Our only power over state judgments is to correct them to the extent that they incorrectly adjudge federal rights. And our power is to correct wrong judgments, not to revise opinions. We are not permitted to render an advisory opinion, and if the same judgment would be rendered by the state court after we corrected its views of federal laws, our review could amount to nothing more than an advisory opinion." Id., at 125-126 (citations omitted).

Where we have been unable to say with certainty that the judgment rested solely on federal law grounds, we have refused to rule on the federal issue in the case; the proper course is then either to dismiss the writ as improvidently granted or to remand the case to the state court to clarify the basis of its decision. California v. Krivda, 409 U.S. 33 (1972); Mental Hygiene Dept. v. Kirchner, 380 U.S. 194 (1965). Of course, it may often be unclear whether a state court has relied in part on state law in reaching its decision. As the Court said in Herb v. Pitcairn, supra, however, where the answer does not appear "of record" and is not "clear and decisive,"

"it seems consistent with the respect due the highest courts of states of the Union that they be asked rather than told what they have intended. If this imposes an unwelcome burden it should be mitigated by the knowledge that it is to protect their jurisdiction from unwitting interference as well as to protect our own from unwitting renunciation." 324 U.S., at 128 .

From a perusal of the Oregon Supreme Court's opinion it is evident that these exacting standards were not met in this case. The Constitution of Oregon contains an independent prohibition against compulsory self-incrimination, and there is a distinct possibility that the state court intended to express its view of state as well as federal constitutional law. The majority flatly states that the case was decided below solely on federal constitutional grounds, but I am not so certain. Although the state court did not expressly cite state law in support of its judgment, its opinion suggests that it may well have considered the matter one of state as well as federal law. The court stated that it had initially viewed the issue of the case as whether it should overrule one of its prior precedents in light of this Court's opinion in Harris v. New York, 401 U.S. 222 (1971). It concluded that it was not required to consider whether to overrule the earlier state case, however, since upon examination it determined that Harris did not reach this fact situation. In view of the court's suggestion that the federal constitutional rule in Harris would be regarded as merely a persuasive authority even if it were deemed to be squarely in conflict with the state rule, it seems quite possible that the state court intended its decision to rest at least in part on independent state grounds. In any event, I agree with Mr. Justice Jackson that state courts should be "asked rather than told what they have intended."

In addition to the importance of avoiding jurisdictional difficulties, it seems much the better policy to permit the state court the freedom to strike its own balance between individual rights and police practices, at least where the state court's ruling violates no constitutional prohibitions. It is peculiarly within the competence of the highest court of a State to determine that in its jurisdiction the police should be subject to more stringent rules than are required as a federal constitutional minimum.

The Oregon court's decision in this case was not premised on a reluctant adherence to what it deemed federal law to require, but was based on its independent conclusion that admitting evidence such as that held admissible today will encourage police misconduct in violation of the right against compulsory self-incrimination. This is precisely the setting in which it seems most likely that the state court would apply the State's self-incrimination clause to lessen what it perceives as an intolerable risk of abuse. Accordingly, in my view the Court should not review a state-court decision reversing a conviction unless it is quite clear that the state court has resolved all applicable state-law questions adversely to the defendant and that it feels compelled by its view of the federal constitutional issue to reverse the conviction at hand.

Even if the majority is correct that the Oregon Supreme Court did not intend to express a view of state as well as federal law, this Court should, at the very least, remand the case for such further proceedings as the state court deems appropriate. I can see absolutely no reason for departing from the usual course of remanding the case to permit the state court to consider any other claims, including the possible applicability of state law to the issue treated here. See Michigan v. Payne, 412 U.S., at 57; California v. Byers, 402 U.S., at 434; California v. Green, 399 U.S., at 168 -170; C. Wright, Federal Courts 488 (2d ed. 1970); cf. Georgia Railway & Electric Co. v. Decatur, 297 U.S. 620, 623 (1936). Surely the majority does not mean to suggest that the Oregon Supreme Court is foreclosed from considering the respondent's state-law claims or even ruling sua sponte that the statement in question is not admissible as a matter of state law. If so, then I should think this unprecedented assumption of authority will be as much a surprise to the Supreme Court of Oregon as it is to me.

I dissent.

Sixth amendment should apply to summary courts-martial: Justice Marshall's dissent in Middendorf v. Henry (March 24, 1976)

MR. JUSTICE MARSHALL, with whom MR. JUSTICE BRENNAN joins, dissenting.

We only recently held that, absent a waiver, "no person may be imprisoned for any offense, whether classified as petty, misdemeanor, or felony, unless he was represented by counsel at his trial." Argersinger v. Hamlin, 407 U.S. 25, 37 (1972). Today the Court refuses to apply Argersinger's holding to defendants in summary court-martial proceedings. Assuming for purposes of its opinion that the Sixth Amendment applies to courts-martial in general, the Court holds that, because of their special characteristics, summary courts-martial in particular are simply not "criminal prosecutions" within the meaning of the Sixth Amendment, and that the right to counsel is therefore inapplicable to them. I dissent.

I

Preliminarily, summary courts-martial aside, it is clear to me that a citizen does not surrender all right to appointed counsel when he enters the military. It is inconceivable, for example, that this Court could conclude that a defendant in a general court-martial proceeding, where sentences as severe as life imprisonment may be imposed, is not entitled to the same protection our Constitution affords a civilian defendant facing even a day's imprisonment. See Argersinger v. Hamlin, supra. Surely those sworn to risk their lives to defend the Constitution should derive some benefit from the right to counsel, a right that has become even more firmly entrenched in our jurisprudence over the past several generations. See Gideon v. Wainwright, 372 U.S. 335 (1963); Powell v. Alabama, 287 U.S. 45 (1932).

The only question that might arise is whether the general guarantee of counsel to court-martial defendants is to be placed under the Fifth Amendment or under the Sixth Amendment. It is my conviction that it is a Sixth Amendment guarantee. That Amendment provides an explicit guarantee of counsel "in all criminal prosecutions." Since, as we recently observed, courts-martial are "convened to adjudicate charges of criminal violations of military law," Parisi v. Davidson, 405 U.S. 34, 42 (1972), it would seem that courts-martial are criminal prosecutions and that the Sixth Amendment therefore applies on its face.

There is legitimate dispute among scholars, it is true, about whether the Framers expressly intended the Sixth Amendment right to counsel to apply to the military. See ante, at 33-34, and n. 12. 1 While the historical evidence is somewhat ambiguous, my reading of the sources suggests that the Sixth Amendment right to counsel was intended by the Framers to apply to courts-martial. But even if the historical evidence plainly showed to the contrary - and its certainly does not - that would not be determinative of the contemporary scope of the Sixth Amendment. As Mr. Chief Justice Hughes observed:

"If by the statement that what the Constitution meant at the time of its adoption it means to-day, it is intended to say that the great clauses of the Constitution must be confined to the interpretation which the framers, with the conditions and outlook of their time, would have placed upon them, the statement carries its own refutation." Home Bldg. & Loan Assn. v. Blaisdell, 290 U.S. 398, 442 -443 (1934).

Application of the Sixth Amendment right to counsel to the military follows logically and naturally from the modern right-to-counsel decisions, in which the right has been held fully applicable in every case in which a defendant faced conviction of a criminal offense and potential incarceration. 2 See, e. g., Argersinger v. Hamlin, supra; Gideon v. Wainwright, supra. The due process right to counsel, usually applied on a case-by-case basis, extends a qualified right to counsel to persons not involved in criminal proceedings, see Gagnon v. Scarpelli, 411 U.S. 778 (1973), but has not been viewed as a replacement for the Sixth Amendment right to counsel in situations in which a defendant stands to be convicted of a criminal offense.

In short, it is my belief that the Sixth Amendment demands that court-martial defendants ordinarily be accorded counsel. 3 Only if the special characteristics of summary courts-martial in particular deprive them of the status of "criminal prosecutions" is the Sixth Amendment inapplicable in the cases before us today. It is, of course, this proposition to which the major part of the Court's opinion is addressed and to which I now turn.

II

The Court's conclusion that summary courts-martial are not "criminal prosecutions" is, on its face, a surprising one. No less than in the case of other courts-martial, summary courts-martial are directed at adjudicating "charges of criminal violations of military law," and conviction at a summary court-martial can lead to confinement for one month. Nevertheless, the Court finds its conclusion mandated by a combination of four factors: 4 the limitations on the punishment that can be meted out by a summary court-martial, the nature of the offenses for which a defendant can be tried, the nature of the summary court-martial proceeding itself, and "the distinctive nature of military life and discipline." Ante, at 42 n. 19. I am totally unpersuaded that these considerations - or any others - whether taken singly or in combination, justify denying to summary court-martial defendants the right to the assistance of counsel, "one of the safeguards of the Sixth Amendment deemed necessary to insure fundamental human rights of life and liberty." Johnson v. Zerbst, 304 U.S. 458, 462 (1938).

A

It is of course true, as the Court states, that a summary court-martial may not adjudge confinement in excess of one month. Manual for Courts-Martial § 16b (1969) (MCM). 5 But Argersinger itself held the length of confinement to be wholly irrelevant in determining the applicability of the right to counsel. Aware that "the prospect of imprisonment for however short a time will seldom be viewed by the accused as a trivial or `petty' matter," Baldwin v. New York, 399 U.S. 66, 73 (1970) (plurality opinion), we held in Argersinger that the fact of confinement, not its duration, is determinative of the right to counsel. Insofar as the Court today uses the 30-day ceiling on a summary court-martial defendant's sentence as support for its holding, it is not so much finding Argersinger "inapplicable" as rejecting the very basis of Argersinger's holding. 6

B

In further support of its holding, the Court observes that "[m]uch of the conduct proscribed by the military is not `criminal' conduct in the civilian sense of the word," ante, at 38, and intimates that conviction for many offenses normally tried at summary court-martial would have no consequences "beyond the immediate punishment meted out by the military." Ante, at 39. The Court's observations are both misleading and irrelevant.

While the summary court-martial is generally designed to deal with relatively minor offenses, see MCM § 79, as a statutory matter the summary proceeding can be used to try any noncapital offense triable by general or special court-martial. Art. 20, UCMJ, 10 U.S.C. 820. 7 See United States v. Moore, 5 U.S. C. M. A. 687, 697, 18 C. M. R. 311, 321 (1955). And while the offense for which most of the plaintiffs here were tried - unauthorized absence - has no common-law counterpart, a substantial proportion of the offenses actually tried by summary court-martial are offenses, such as larceny and assault, that would also constitute criminal offenses if committed by a civilian. 8 Indeed, one of the servicemen in these cases was charged with assault. It is therefore misleading to suggest, as the Court does, that there is a fundamental difference between the type of conduct chargeable at summary court-martial and the type of conduct deemed criminal in the civilian sector.

The Court's further implication that a summary court-martial conviction has no consequences beyond "the immediate punishment" ante, at 39, is also inaccurate. One of the central distinctions between Art. 15 nonjudicial punishment and a summary court-martial conviction is that the latter is regarded as a criminal conviction. 9 And that criminal conviction has collateral consequences both in military and civilian life. As the Army itself has readily acknowledged:

"Conviction by [any] court-martial creates a criminal record which will color consideration of any subsequent misconduct by the soldier. A noncommissioned officer may survive one summary court-martial without reduction being effected, but it is unlikely that, with one conviction on his record, he will survive a second trial and retain his status. A conviction of an officer by any court-martial could have a devastating aftereffect upon his career. It could be described in some cases as a sentence to a passover on a promotion list and may serve as a basis for initiation of administrative elimination action.

"For any man, the fact of a criminal conviction on his record is a handicap in civilian life. It may interfere with his job opportunities; it may be counted against him if he has difficulty with a civilian law enforcement agency; and in general he tends to be a marked man." 10

The MCM itself belies any claim that no significant consequences beyond immediate punishment attach to a summary court-martial conviction. Paragraph 127c of the MCM establishes a comprehensive scheme by which an offender is made subject to increased punishment if he has a record of previous convictions - even if all of those previous convictions were by summary court-martial.

It is therefore wholly unrealistic to suggest that the impact of a summary court-martial conviction lies exclusively in the immediate punishment that is meted out. 11 Summary court-martial convictions carry with them a potential of stigma, injury to career, and increased punishment for future offenses in the same way as do convictions after civilian criminal trials and convictions after general and special courts-martial.

Quite apart from their flimsy factual basis, the Court's observations as to both the nature of the offenses tried at summary court-martial and the lack of collateral consequences of convictions have already been determined by Argersinger to be irrelevant to the applicability of the Sixth Amendment's right to counsel. Argersinger teaches that the right to counsel is triggered by the potential of confinement, regardless of how trivial or petty the offense may seem. See 407 U.S., at 37 . Logic itself would therefore preclude the suggestion that the right to counsel, activated by the potential of confinement, is deactivated by the absence of collateral consequences of conviction.

C

The nature of the summary court-martial proceeding - the proceeding's nonadversary nature and, relatedly, the protective functions of its presiding officer - is a third factor which, according to the Court, helps to make unnecessary the provision of counsel to the accused. Again, the Court's reliance is without substantial foundation.

The Court characterizes summary courts-martial as "nonadversary," but offers little explanation as to how that characterization advances the contention that the right to counsel is inapplicable. If the Court's argument is simply that furnishing counsel will transform the proceeding into an adversary proceeding, it is no argument at all, but simply an observation. The argument must be either that there is something peculiar about the goal of the summary court-martial proceeding that makes the right to counsel inapplicable, or that there are elements in the conduct of the proceeding itself that render counsel unnecessary.

To the extent that the Court's characterization of summary courts-martial as "nonadversary" is meant to convey something about the goal or purpose of the proceeding, it is totally unpersuasive. In this sense the summary court-martial proceeding is far less "nonadversary" than the juvenile delinquency proceedings to which we held the right to counsel applicable in In re Gault, 387 U.S. 1 (1967). The Court in Gault did not dispute that the proper purpose of the juvenile justice system is rehabilitative rather than punitive, that all parties to a juvenile delinquency proceeding might be striving for an adjudication and disposition that is in "the best interests of the child," and that the traditional notion of the "kindly juvenile judge" is a highly appropriate one. See id., at 27. Yet the Court in Gault confronted the reality that, however beneficial the goal of delinquency proceedings, they have as their potential result the confinement of an individual in an institution. Ibid. This factor mandated that accused juvenile offenders be entitled to the representation of counsel. 12

As distinguished from the situation in Gault, summary courts-martial have no special rehabilitative purpose; rather, their central immediate purpose is to discipline those who have violated the UCMJ. 13 If the goals of juvenile delinquency proceedings are an insufficient justification for the denial of counsel, it follows a fortiori that the goals of the summary court-martial are similarly insufficient.

The second possible meaning conveyed by characterizing the summary court-martial as "nonadversary" - the presence of elements in the conduct of the proceeding itself which render independent counsel unnecessary - is reflected in the Court's observation that the "function of the presiding officer is quite different from that of any participant in a civilian trial." Ante, at 41. It is the responsibility of the presiding officer to act as judge, jury, prosecutor, and defense counsel combined. The Court intimates that the presiding officer's duty to advise the accused of his rights and his ability to help the accused assemble facts, examine witnesses, and cross-examine his accusers make defense counsel unnecessary, particularly in light of the absence of a formal prosecutor in the proceeding. I find this argument unpersuasive. In Powell v. Alabama, 287 U.S. 45 (1932), we rejected the notion that a judge could "effectively discharge the obligations of counsel for the accused," largely because a judge "cannot . . . participate in those necessary conferences between counsel and accused which sometimes partake of the inviolable character of the confessional." Id., at 61.

It is true that in Powell the unrepresented defendant was opposed by a traditional prosecutor. But in Gault, supra, there was no prosecutor; the only participants in the delinquency proceedings were the juvenile, his mother, the probation officers, and the judge. All participants were presumably interested in the welfare of the juvenile. Yet we held that no matter how protective the judge or the other participants might have been, the juvenile was entitled to independent counsel.

The irreconcilable conflict among the roles of the summary court-martial presiding officer inevitably prevents him from functioning effectively as a substitute for defense counsel. For instance, a defendant has a right to remain silent and not testify at his court-martial. See Art. 31, UCMJ, 10 U.S.C. 831; MCM § 53h. An intelligent decision whether to exercise that right requires consultation as to whether testifying would hurt or help his case and inevitably involves the sharing of confidences with counsel. Full consultation cannot possibly take place when "defense counsel" is also playing the role of judge and prosecutor. The defense counsel who also serves as prosecutor and judge is effectively unavailable for many of the "necessary conferences between counsel and accused," Powell v. Alabama, supra, at 61, as well as for the making and implementation of critical tactical and strategic trial decisions. As helpful as the presiding officer might be to the defendant, his inconsistent roles bar him from being an adequate substitute for independent defense counsel.

In sum, there is nothing about the assertedly "non-adversary" nature of the summary court-martial - either in terms of its goals or alternative safeguards - that renders unnecessary the assistance of counsel.

D

Finally, the Court draws on notions of military necessity to justify its conclusion that the right to counsel is inapplicable to summary court-martial proceedings. Concerns for discipline and obedience will on occasion, it is true, justify imposing restrictions on the military that would be unconstitutional in a civilian context. See Parker v. Levy, 417 U.S. 733, 758 (1974). But denials of traditional rights to any group should not be approved without examination, especially when the group comprises members of the military, who are engaged in an endeavor of national service, frequently fraught with both danger and sacrifice. After such examination, I am persuaded that the denial of the right to counsel at summary courts-martial cannot be justified by military necessity.

The substance of the asserted justification here is that discipline, efficiency, and morale demand the utilization of an expeditious disciplinary procedure for relatively minor offenses. It would seem, however, that Art. 15 nonjudicial punishment - which can be speedily imposed by a commander, but which does not carry with it the stigma of a criminal conviction - provides just such a procedure. 14 Indeed, the 1962 amendments to Art. 15, 10 U.S.C. 815, greatly expanded the availability of nonjudicial punishment and resulted in a sharp decrease in the utilization of the summary court-martial. 15 There is, therefore, no pressing need to have a streamlined summary court-martial proceeding in order to supply an expeditious disciplinary procedure. Moreover, it is by no means clear that guaranteeing counsel to summary court-martial defendants would result in significantly longer time periods from preferral of charges to punishment than fairly conducted proceedings in the absence of counsel; 16 any timesaving that is now enjoyed might well result from the presiding officer's being something less than an adequate substitute for independent defense counsel.

It is especially difficult to accept the federal parties' claim of "military necessity" in view of the fact that well before our decision in Argersinger, each of the services allowed summary court-martial defendants to retain counsel at their own expense. 17 Given this fact, the federal parties' argument is reduced to a contention that only those defendants who cannot afford to retain counsel must, as a matter of "military necessity," be denied counsel at summary court-martial proceedings. Sustaining that contention means a defeat for those very principles of equality and justice that the military is sworn to defend; the most fundamental notions of fairness are subverted when the rights of the poor alone are sacrificed to the cause of "military necessity."

It is also significant that the United States Court of Military Appeals (USCMA), a body with recognized expertise in dealing with military problems, 18 has applied Argersinger to summary courts-martial without giving any hint that military necessity posed a problem. United States v. Alderman, 22 U.S.C. M. A. 298, 46 C. M. R. 298 (1973). 19 Indeed, Judge Duncan of that court explicitly noted that "the record contains no evidence which convinces me that application of the Argersinger rule should not be followed in our system because of military necessity." Id., at 303, 46 C. M. R., at 303 (concurring in part and dissenting in part). 20 And even before Alderman was decided, both the Air Force and the Army applied Argersinger to summary courts-martial 21 rather than advancing the theoretically available "military necessity" argument. See United States v. Priest, 21 U.S.C. M. A. 564, 45 C. M. R. 338 (1972). That they did so leads me to doubt whether even the military was then of the opinion that military necessity dictated the denial of counsel.

Virtually ignoring all the factors that cast doubt on the military-necessity justification, the Court defers to an asserted congressional judgment that "counsel should not be provided in summary courts-martial." Ante, at 43. While Congress' evaluation of military necessity is clearly entitled to deference, it would be a departure from our position in the past to suggest that the Court need not come to its own conclusion as to the validity of any argument based on military necessity. See, e. g., United States v. Robel, 389 U.S. 258, 264 (1967); Parker v. Levy, 417 U.S. 733 (1974); cf. New York Times Co. v. United States, 403 U.S. 713 (1971). But regardless of what weight is properly accorded a clear congressional determination of military necessity, there has been no such determination in this case.

The only congressional action referred to by the Court is Congress' refusal in 1956 and 1968 to abolish summary courts-martial altogether and its concurrent extending of the serviceman's opportunity to reject trial by summary court-martial. The Court refers to that action as evidence that Congress has considered "in some depth" the matter whether counsel is required in summary courts-martial. Ante, at 45 n. 21. But there is no evidence offered of any detailed congressional consideration of the specific question of the feasibility of providing counsel at summary courts-martial. And, more importantly, there is no indication that Congress made a judgment that military necessity requires the denial of the constitutional right to counsel to summary court-martial defendants.

If Congress' lack of discussion of military necessity is not enough to throw substantial doubt on the Court's inferences, the timing of the congressional action cited by the Court should certainly do so. All that action occurred substantially before our decision in Argersinger. Thus, even if we assume that Congress' decision to retain the summary court-martial represents a considered conclusion that "counsel should not be provided," that judgment was made at a time when even civilian defendants subject to prison terms of less than six months had no recognized constitutional right to counsel. There would, therefore, have been little reason for Congress in 1956 or 1968 to undertake the detailed consideration necessary to make a finding of "military necessity" before concluding that counsel need not be provided to summary court-martial defendants.

In sum, there is simply no indication that Congress ever made a clear determination that "military necessity" precludes applying the Sixth Amendment's right to counsel to summary court-martial proceedings. Indeed, the Court characterizes the congressional determination in the vaguest of terms, and never expressly claims that Congress made a determination of military necessity. Thus, I can only read the Court's opinion as a grant of almost total deference to any Act of Congress dealing with the military.

III

The Court rejects even the limited holding of the Court of Appeals that the provision of counsel in summary court-martial proceedings should be evaluated as a matter of due process on the basis of the accused's defense in any particular case. The Court explains that summary court-martial defendants can have counsel appointed by refusing trial by summary court-martial and then proceeding to trial by special court-martial - the acknowledged consequence of which is exposure to greater possible penalties. Given my conviction that a summary court-martial is a criminal prosecution under the Sixth Amendment, it is unnecessary for me to deal in detail with this due process question. 22 In the event, however, that the special court-martial option may be offered as additional support for the Court's treatment of the Sixth Amendment issue, I shall briefly assess its significance.

The Court analogizes the decision whether to expose oneself to special court-martial with counsel or to proceed by summary court-martial without counsel to the decision faced by a civilian defendant whether to proceed to trial or plead guilty to a lesser included offense. According to the Court, the right given up by such a civilian defendant is "not only his right to counsel but his right to any trial at all." Ante, at 47. The analogy is a flawed one. The civilian defendant who pleads guilty necessarily gives up whatever rights he might thereafter have been accorded to enable him to protect a claim of innocence; the conditions on his pleading guilty are logically mandated ones. By contrast, the condition on the military defendant's opting to be tried by summary court-martial - i. e., the denial of counsel - is an imposed one, and must therefore be viewed with suspicion.

Indeed, the force of the Court's analogy is entirely dissipated by the fact that a civilian defendant who pleads guilty forfeits only so much of his right to counsel as is a necessary consequence of his plea. He is fully entitled to counsel in the process leading up to the plea - including negotiations with the Government as to the possibility of a plea and the actual decision to plead. The defendant is also entitled to counsel in any sentencing proceeding that might follow the making of his plea. I have no doubt that a scheme in which the acceptance of guilty pleas was conditioned on a full abandonment of the right to counsel would be unconstitutional.

By contrast, the Court today approves the denial of counsel to the summary court-martial defendant at all stages and for all purposes - including, at least as regards sailors and marines, 23 the very decision whether to reject trial by summary court-martial. And if the accused opts for the summary court-martial - the Court's parallel to the accepted guilty plea - he has no right to counsel either at the adjudicative or sentencing phase of the proceeding. 24

Conditioning the provision of counsel on a defendant's subjecting himself to the risk of additional punishment suffers from the same defect as the scheme disapproved by the Court in United States v. Jackson, 390 U.S. 570 (1968), in which the right to a trial by jury was conditioned on a defendant's subjecting himself to the possibility of capital punishment. If the Court's analysis is correct as applied to the Sixth Amendment, then Argersinger's guarantee of counsel for the trial of any offense carrying with it the potential of imprisonment could be reduced to a nullity; a State could constitutionally establish two levels of imprisonment for the same offense - a lower tier for defendants who are willing to proceed to trial without counsel, and a higher one for those who insist on having the assistance of counsel. 25 It is inconceivable to me that the Sixth Amendment would tolerate such a result.

IV

The right to counsel has been termed "the most pervasive" 26 of all the rights accorded an accused. As a result of the Court's action today, of all accused persons protected by the United States Constitution - federal defendants and state defendants, juveniles and adults, civilians and soldiers - only those enlisted men 27 tried by summary court-martial can be imprisoned without having been accorded the right to counsel. I would have expected that such a result would have been based on justifications far more substantial than those relied on by the Court. I respectfully dissent.

Notes

[1] Those who argue that the Framers did intend the Sixth Amendment right to counsel to apply point both to congressional proceedings which seem to assume the right's applicability, see Henderson, Courts-Martial and the Constitution: The Original Understanding, 71 Harv. L. Rev. 293, 303-315 (1957), and materials cited therein, and to the fact that it was traditional in the late 18th century to allow an accused serviceman legal assistance. Id., at 318. Those who take the opposite position point, inter alia, to contemporary treatises, see Wiener, Courts-Martial and the Bill of Rights: The Original Practice I, 72 Harv. L. Rev. 1, 23-26 (1958), and materials cited therein, to the lack of mention of any right to counsel in the first military codes under the Constitution, id., at 22-23, and to the fact that any counsel who did appear in military proceedings was allowed only a limited role. Id., at 27-32.

[2] In any given case, whether there is a Sixth Amendment right to trial by jury is, of course, not at all determinative of whether there is a Sixth Amendment right to counsel. Indeed, in Argersinger itself we stated that "[w]e reject, therefore, the premise that since prosecutions for crimes punishable by imprisonment for less than six months may be tried without a jury, they may also be tried without a lawyer." 407 U.S. 25, 30 -31 (1972). Compare id., at 37, with Duncan v. Louisiana, 391 U.S. 145, 159 (1968).

This Court has indicated that the Fifth Amendment's express exemption of the military from the requirement of indictment by grand jury also exempts the military "inferentially, from the [Sixth Amendment] right to trial by jury." O'Callahan v. Parker, 395 U.S. 258, 261 (1969). But there is no reason to assume that the same inferences from the Fifth Amendment exemption should be drawn with regard to the Sixth Amendment right to counsel. Not even the federal parties suggest that the settling of the jury-trial issue with regard to the military has ipso facto settled all other Sixth Amendment issues as well.

[3] Even if a pure due process analysis were to be used, however, counsel, to my mind, would still be required for courts-martial. Many of the factors analyzed below in a Sixth Amendment context, see Part II, infra, are fully relevant to a due process analysis. See Gagnon v. Scarpelli, 411 U.S. 778 (1973); Morrissey v. Brewer, 408 U.S. 471 (1972). And, while Gagnon adopts a case-by-case approach to the right to counsel in probation revocation proceedings, the fact that in courts-martial we are dealing with a trial which can result in a criminal conviction mandates that counsel be made available in every case. See Gagnon, supra, at 789 n. 12.

[4] The Court looks to our analysis in Gagnon v. Scarpelli, supra, as support in the distinctions it draws between "criminal prosecutions" under the Sixth Amendment and summary courts-martial. I find that reliance questionable, to say the least.

The Court intimates, ante, at 35, that our holding in Gagnon that a probation revocation hearing is not part of a criminal prosecution was based on factors relating to the manner in which such hearings are conducted - factors such as the absence of a prosecutor and the informality of the proceedings. This, however, is an inaccurate reflection of what we said in Gagnon. Gagnon's conclusion, stated early in the opinion, 411 U.S., at 782, that a probation revocation hearing is "not a stage of a criminal prosecution" was not at all dependent on the manner in which such proceedings are conducted. Rather, it was held to follow from the conclusion in Morrissey v. Brewer, supra, that revocation of parole was not part of a criminal prosecution, with the following analysis in Morrissey held to be determinative:

"`Parole arises after the end of the criminal prosecution, including imposition of sentence. . . . Revocation deprives an individual, not of the absolute liberty to which every citizen is entitled, but only of the conditional liberty properly dependent on observance of special parole restrictions.' [408 U.S.], at 480." 411 U.S., at 781 .

The manner in which the hearing was conducted was simply not a factor in our conclusion that such a hearing is not part of a "criminal prosecution." Only after we reached this conclusion did we refer to the manner in which the hearing was conducted in considering the secondary question whether the right to appointed counsel was nevertheless required as a matter of due process. Thus, even assuming there are "parallels" between the manner in which probation-revocation hearings are conducted and the manner in which summary courts-martial are conducted, ante, at 41-42, Gagnon lends no support to the conclusion that summary courts-martial are not "criminal prosecutions" within the meaning of the Sixth Amendment.

[5] The MCM was prescribed by Executive Order of September 11, 1968, to supplement the Uniform Code of Military Justice (UCMJ).

[6] The Court attempts to evade Argersinger's clear mandate by relying on our decisions in Gagnon v. Scarpelli, supra, and In re Gault, 387 U.S. 1 (1967). As for Gagnon,

I have already observed, supra, n. 4, that it lends no support to the Court's Sixth Amendment analysis in this case. As for Gault, it is true that we have held that juvenile delinquency proceedings, even though they might result in confinement, are not "criminal prosecutions" under the Sixth Amendment. McKeiver v. Pennsylvania, 403 U.S. 528 (1971); see id., at 553 (opinion of BRENNAN, J.). However, that conclusion was undoubtedly based on the predominantly rehabilitative purpose of the juvenile justice system, a factor which, as shown infra, at 61, is manifestly not present in the summary court-martial context. And, while Gault did not apply the Sixth Amendment, it did, of course, hold a due process right to counsel applicable to all juvenile delinquency proceedings which pose a threat of confinement.

[7] Of course the punishment ceilings imposed by 10 U.S.C. 820 on summary courts-martial are applicable no matter what offense is being tried. But the "popular opprobrium" resulting from conviction of a serious crime - a factor in which the Court places considerable stock, ante, at 39 - is likely to be severe whatever the magnitude of the punishment; that "popular opprobrium" could, of course, have significant "practical effect," ante, at 40 n. 17, on a serviceman's future.

[8] See 10 U.S.C. 921, 928. Figures supplied by the federal parties indicate that in 1973, 14% of the summary courts-martial conducted by the Navy were for "nonmilitary offenses." Brief for Federal Parties 33; see also Fidell, The Summary Court-Martial: A Proposal, 8 Harv. J. Legis, 571, 599 n. 121 (1971). See also Joint Hearings on Military Justice before the Subcommittee on Constitutional Rights of the Senate Committee on the Judiciary and a Special Subcommittee of the Senate Committee on Armed Services, 89th Cong., 2d Sess., 1056 (1966) (hereinafter cited as 1966 Hearings).

[9] In Senate testimony, the Judge Advocate General of the Navy observed that a serviceman convicted by a summary court-martial as opposed to one punished under Art. 15, "begins to acquire a record of convictions." 1966 Hearings 33. See also Subcommittee on Constitutional Rights of the Senate Committee on the Judiciary, Summary - Report of Hearings on the Constitutional Rights of Military Personnel, 88th Cong., 1st Sess., 35 (1963).

[10] Hearings on Constitutional Rights of Military Personnel before the Subcommittee on Constitutional Rights of the Senate Committee on the Judiciary, 87th Cong., 2d Sess., 838 (1962).

[11] See also Fidell, supra, n. 8, at 594-596; Feld, The Court Martial Sentence: Fair or Foul, 39 Va. L. Rev. 319, 322 (1953).

[12] The Court intimates that our decision in Gault might have been different had Gerald Gault been faced with a period of confinement significantly less than three years in duration. Ante, at 46 n. 22. However, our opinion contained no hint of any such limitation and held the right to counsel applicable whenever a juvenile is faced with proceedings "which may result in commitment to an institution in which the juvenile's freedom is curtailed." 387 U.S., at 41 .

[13] In general, "a military trial is marked by the age-old manifest destiny of

retributive justice. . . . `[M]ilitary law has always been and continues to be primarily an instrument of discipline, not justice.' Glasser, Justice and Captain Levy, 12 Columbia Forum 46, 49 (1969)." O'Callahan v. Parker, 395 U.S. 258, 266 (1969).

[14] Differences have been advanced to distinguish the punishment that can be imposed under Art. 15 from the "confinement" that can result from a summary court-martial. See United States v. Shamel, 22 U.S.C. M. A. 361, 47 C. M. R. 116 (1973) (Quinn, J.).

[15] Between 1962 and 1969, the number of summary courts-martial per year in the Armed Services dropped from 85,166 to 28, 281, and their percentage of the total military caseload dropped from 64% to 26%. Fidell, supra, n. 8, at 573. "The chief explanation for this phenomenon lies in the expansion of nonjudicial punishment powers accomplished in 1963." Id., at 572.

[16] While, according to the federal parties to these cases, the average time period between preferral of charges and final review in summary courts-martial has increased by 13 days since the United States Court of Military Appeals applied Argersinger to the military in United States v. Alderman, 22 U.S.C. M. A. 298, 46 C. M. R. 298 (1973), Supp. Mem. for Federal Parties 3-4, the parties themselves concede that "it is not possible to ascribe the changed experience . . . exclusively to the injection of counsel into summary court proceedings." Ibid. Nothing is offered by the federal parties to indicate that the average time of the summary court-martial proceeding itself has been lengthened as a result of providing counsel to defendants.

[17] See 1966 Hearings 34 (testimony of Brig. Gen. Kenneth J. Hodson, Asst. Judge Adv. Gen. for Military Justice, Department of the Army); 38 (testimony of Maj. Gen. R. W. Manss, Judge Adv. Gen. of the Air Force); 39 (testimony of Rear Adm. Wilfred A. Hearn, Judge Adv. Gen. of the Navy); 626 (letter of June 7, 1965, to the Chairman of the Senate Committee on Armed Services from the Acting General Counsel of the Department of the Treasury).

Indeed, while acknowledging that "[t]here is no provision either in law or regulation for the appointment of counsel before a summary court-martial," the Department of the Treasury indicated, six years before Argersinger was decided, that "it is Treasury Department policy [in the Coast Guard] that military counsel for a summary court-martial will be supplied upon request if reasonably available." Id., at 627.

Moreover, the following question-and-answer exchange took place in 1966 by letter between the Senate Subcommittee on Constitutional Rights and the Navy Judge Advocate General Corps:

"Question: Are defendants permitted by official Defense Department or service policy or regulation to have counsel assist them in summary courts?

"Answer: . . . [A]lthough the right to individual representation is not extended to an accused before a summary court-martial by policy or regulation, the general practice in the naval service is to accord such representation on the request of the accused.

. . . . .

"Question: . . . If a man requests the appointment of counsel, legal or otherwise, is it the practice to grant such requests?

"Answer: Yes, dependent upon the reasonable availability of the requested counsel." Id., at 939.

[18] See Schlesinger v. Councilman, 420 U.S. 738, 758 (1975); Noyd v. Bond, 395 U.S. 683, 694 (1969).

[19] The decisions of the USCMA are final. 10 U.S.C. 876. It is indeed ironic that the federal parties - statutorily barred from appealing Alderman - have now secured its rejection through this lawsuit, originally brought in federal court by servicemen seeking the very protections later accorded them by Alderman.

[20] See also Daigle v. Warner, 490 F.2d 358 (1974), cert. pending, No. 73-6642, in which the Court of Appeals for the Ninth Circuit noted that "[w]hile the Navy argues with some vigor that naval discipline will suffer severely if appointed counsel are required [in summary courts-martial], there is scant support for this in the record." Id., at 366.

The Court, relying on previously stated views of Judge Quinn, one of the members of the Alderman majority, and on Judge Quinn's failure in his Alderman opinion to explicitly mention the military-necessity argument, declines to view Alderman as a rejection of that argument. I disagree. In United States v. Priest, 21 U.S.C. M. A. 564, 45 C. M. R. 338 (1972) - decided only 10 months before Alderman - the USCMA had recognized, albeit in another context, that military necessity may affect the application of traditional constitutional rights to members of the military, and the parties in Alderman briefed the military-necessity argument in great detail. Judge Quinn concurred in the Priest opinion. These factors, plus Judge Duncan's explicit reference to the argument, lead me to read Alderman as a rejection of the military-necessity argument.

[21] United States v. Alderman, supra, at 303, 46 C. M. R., at 303 (Duncan, J., concurring in part and dissenting in part).

[22] It does seem to me, however, that the serviceman's "option" of subjecting himself to the possibility of a special court-martial lends little support to the Court's due process analysis. We held in In re Gault, 387 U.S. 1 (1967) - a decision left unmentioned in the Court's treatment of the Fifth Amendment question - that, as a matter of due process accused offenders have an absolute right to counsel at juvenile delinquency proceedings. Surely that holding would be no different in the case of a juvenile given the opportunity "voluntarily" to subject himself to adult criminal proceedings, in which he would have counsel, but at which he would be subject to harsher punishment.

[23] Neither the UCMJ nor the MCM contains any indication that a serviceman must be provided with counsel to assist him in making his determination as to whether to consent or object to trial by summary court-martial. While internal Army guidelines do appear to allow consultation with counsel in making this determination, see Military Justice Handbook, Guide for Summary Court-Martial Trial Procedure 3-3 to 3-5, Department of the Army Pamphlet No. 27-7 (1973). Navy guidelines contain no such

provision.

[24] Assuming the "option scheme" presents the serviceman with any sort of realistic choice, its availability also substantially undercuts the federal parties' military-necessity argument. See supra, at 63-69. The federal parties argue that as a matter of "military necessity" minor offenses must be disposed of at summary court-martial proceedings without giving defendants the benefit of counsel. Yet, under the option scheme any serviceman can be assured of counsel simply by rejecting trial by summary court-martial. Thus the scheme itself could render unattainable a goal which is claimed to be a matter of military necessity.

[25] While we sustained the Kentucky two-tier system against due process and double jeopardy attacks in Colten v. Kentucky, 407 U.S. 104 (1972), we were careful to note that under that system a defendant "cannot, and will not, face the realistic threat of a prison sentence in the inferior court without having the help of counsel." Id., at 119.

[26] Schaefer, Federalism and State Criminal Procedure, 70 Harv. L. Rev. 1, 8 (1956).

[27] Officers are not subject to summary courts-martial. 10 U.S.C. 820.

Redistricting: Justice Marshall's dissent in Beer v. United States (March 30, 1976)

MR. JUSTICE MARSHALL, with whom MR. JUSTICE BRENNAN joins, dissenting.

Over the past 10 years, the Court has, again and again, read the jurisdiction of § 5 of the Voting Rights Act of 1965, 79 Stat. 439, as amended, 89 Stat. 402, 404, 42 U.S.C. § 1973c (1970 ed., Supp. V), expansively so as "to give the Act the broadest possible scope," and to reach "any state enactment which altered the election law of a covered State in even a minor way." Allen v. State Board of Elections, 393 U. S. 544, 393 U. S. 567, 566 (1969). See also Georgia v. United States, 411 U. S. 526 (1973); Perkins v. Matthews, 400 U. S. 379 (1971); South Carolina v. Katzenbach, 383 U. S. 301 (1966). While we have settled the contours of § 5's jurisdiction, however, we have yet to devote much attention to defining § 5's substantive force within those bounds. Thus, we are faced today for the first time with the question of § 5's substantive application to a redistricting plan. Essentially, we must answer one question: when does a redistricting plan have the effect of "abridging" the right to vote on account of race or color?

The Court never answers this question. Instead, it produces a convoluted construction of the statute that transforms the single question suggested by § 5 into three questions, and then provides precious little guidance in answering any of them.

Under the Court's reading of § 5, we cannot reach the abridgment question unless we have first determined that a proposed redistricting plan would "lead to a retrogression in the position of racial minorities," ante at 425 U. S. 141, in comparison to their position under the existing plan. The Court's conclusion that § 5 demands this preliminary inquiry is simply wrong; it finds no support in the language of the statute and disserves the legislative purposes behind § 5.

Implicitly admitting as much, the Court adds another question, this one to be asked if the proposed plan is not "retrogressive": whether "the new apportionment itself so discriminates on the basis of race or color as to violate the Constitution." Ante at 425 U. S. 141. This addition does much -- in theory, at least -- to salvage the Court's test, since our decisions make clear that the proper test of abridgment under § 5 is essentially the constitutional inquiry.

Still, I cannot accept the Court's awkward construction. Not only is the Court's multiple step inquiry unduly cumbersome and an unnecessary burden to place upon the Attorney General and the District Court for the District of Columbia, but the Court dilutes the meaning of unconstitutionality in this context to the point that the congressional purposes in § 5 are no longer served, and the sacred guarantees of the Fourteenth and Fifteenth Amendments emerge badly battered. And, in the process, the Court approves a blatantly discriminatory districting plan for the city of New Orleans. I dissent.

I

A

The Fifteenth Amendment provides:

"The right of citizens of the United States to vote shall not be denied or abridged by the United States or by any State on account of race, color, or previous condition of servitude."

U.S.Const., Amdt. 15, § 1. Although the Amendment is self-enforcing, litigation to secure the rights it guarantees proved time-consuming and ineffective, while the will of those who resisted its command was strong and unwavering. Finally Congress decided to intervene. In 1965, it enacted the Voting Rights Act, designed "to rid the country of racial discrimination in voting." South Carolina v. Katzenbach, 383 U.S. at 383 U. S. 315. See also id. at 383 U. S. 308-315. The Act proclaims that its purpose is "to enforce the fifteenth amendment to the Constitution . . .," 79 Stat. 437; the heart of its enforcement mechanism is § 5. In language that tracks that of the Fifteenth Amendment, § 5 declares that no State covered by the Act shall enforce any plan with respect to voting different from that in effect on November 1, 1964, unless the Attorney General or a three-judge District Court in the District of Columbia declares that such plan

"does not have the purpose and will not have the effect of denying or abridging the right to vote on account of race or color. . . ."

42 U.S.C. § 1973c (1970 ed., Supp. V). [1]

While the substantive reach of § 5 is somewhat broader than that of the Fifteenth Amendment in at least one regard -- the burden of proof is shifted from discriminate to discriminator [2] -- § 5 is undoubtedly tied to the standards of the Constitution. [3] Thus, it is questionable whether the "purpose and effect" language states anything more than the constitutional standard, [4] and it is clear that the "denying or abridging" phrase does no more than directly adopt the language of the Fifteenth Amendment.

In justifying its convoluted construction of § 5, however, the Court never deals with the fact that, by its plain language, § 5 does no more than adopt, or arguably expand, [5] the constitutional standard. Since it has never been held, or even suggested, that the constitutional standard requires an inquiry into whether a redistricting plan is "ameliorative" or "retrogressive," a fortiori there is no basis for so reading § 5. While the Court attempts to provide a basis by relying on the asserted purpose of § 5 -- to preserve present Negro voting strength [6] -- it is wholly unsuccessful. What superficial credibility the argument musters is achieved by ignoring not only the statutory language, but also at least three other purposes behind § 5. [7]

Thus, the legislative history of the Voting Rights Act makes clear, and the Court assiduously ignores, that § 5 was designed to preclude new districting plans that "perpetuate discrimination," [8] to prevent covered jurisdiction from "circumventing the guarantees of the 15th amendment" by switching to new, and discriminatory, districting plans the moment litigants appear on the verge of having an existing one declared unconstitutional, [9] and promptly to end discrimination in voting by pressuring covered jurisdictions to remove all vestiges of discrimination from their enactments before submitting them for preclearance. [10] None of these purposes is furthered by an inquiry into whether a proposed districting plan is "ameliorative" or "retrogressive." Indeed, the statement of these purposes is alone sufficient to demonstrate the error of the Court's construction.

All the purposes of the statute are met, however, by the inquiry § 5's language plainly contemplates: whether, in absolute terms, the covered jurisdiction can show that its proposed plan meets the constitutional standard. Because it is consistent with both the statutory language and the legislative purposes, this is the proper construction of the provision. Thus, it is the effect of the plan itself, rather than the effect of the change in plans, that should be at issue in a § 5 proceeding. [11]

Ultimately, the Court admits as much by adding an inquiry into whether the proposed plan, even if "ameliorative," is constitutional. After this admission, I cannot understand why the Court bothers at all with its preliminary inquiry into the nature of the change of plans, since the inquiry not only adds nothing, but will, I fear, prove to be a time-consuming distraction from the important business of assessing the constitutionality of the proposed plan. [12] Except for this unnecessary step, however, the Court's final reading of the statute, on its face, no more than duplicates my own. [13] Nonetheless, I still do not accept the Court's approach. After properly returning the constitutional inquiry to the § 5 proceeding, the Court inexplicably tosses off the question in a footnote, and never undertakes the analysis that both our constitutional cases and our § 5 cases have demanded. [14] This ultimate denigration of the constitutional standard is a result far short of the promise Congress held out in enacting, and reenacting, the Voting Rights Act, and it is one in which I cannot join.

B

The proper test in § 5 redistricting cases is preordained by our prior cases, which are ignored today by the Court. As suggested above, we have repeatedly recognized the relevance of constitutional standards to the proper construction of § 5. Thus, we have held that, in passing that provision, "Congress intended to adopt the concept of voting articulated in Reynolds v. Sims, 377 U. S. 533 (1964), and protect Negroes against a dilution of their voting power.'" Perkins v. Matthews, 400 U.S. at 400 U. S. 390, quoting Allen v. State Board of Elections, 393 U.S. at 393 U. S. 588 (opinion of Harlan, J.). See also Georgia v. United States, 411 U.S. at 411 U. S. 532-533; Allen v. State Board of Elections, supra at 393 U. S. 565-566, 393 U. S. 569. [15] In the Fourteenth Amendment Reynolds line of cases, we have made clear that dilution of voting power refers to resulting voting strength that is something less than potential (i.e., proportional) power, not to a reduction of existing power. White v. Regester, 412 U. S. 755, 412 U. S. 765-766 (1973); Whitcomb v. Chavis, 403 U. S. 124, 403 U. S. 19 (1971). Nonetheless, we have also acknowledged that a showing of less than proportional representation of Negroes by Negro-elected representatives is not alone sufficient to prove unconstitutional dilution:

"To sustain such claims [of dilution], it is not enough that the racial group allegedly discriminated against has not had legislative seats in proportion to its voting potential. The plaintiffs' burden is to produce evidence to support findings that the political processes leading to nomination and election were not equally open to participation by the group in question -- that its members had less opportunity than did other residents in the district to participate in the political processes and to elect legislators of their choice."

White v. Regester, supra at 412 U. S. 765-766. See also Whitcomb v. Chavis, supra at 403 U. S. 149. [16]

It is this constitutionally based concept of dilution that we have held to govern in § 5 proceedings. The concept may be readily transferred to the § 5 context simply by adjusting for the shifted burden of proof. Thus, if the proposed redistricting plan underrepresents minority group members, the burden is on the covered jurisdiction to show that "the political processes leading to nomination and election were . . . equally open to participation by the group in question." [17] If the jurisdiction cannot make such a showing, then the proposed plan must be rejected, unless compelling reasons for its adoption can be demonstrated. [18]

II

Application of these standards to the case before us is straightforward. Preliminarily, while I agree with the Court that the two at-large seats on the New Orleans City Council are not themselves before the Court for approval, and cannot serve as an independent basis for the rejection of Plan II, I do not think Plan II should be assessed without regard to the seven-member council it is designed to fill. Proportional representation of Negroes among the five district seats on the council does not assure Negroes proportional representation on the entire council when, as the District Court found, the two at-large seats will be occupied by white-elected members.

The Court's approach of focusing only on the five districts would allow covered municipalities to conceal discriminatory changes by making them a step at a time, and sending one two- or three-district alteration after another to the Attorney General for approval. If nothing beyond the districts actually before him could be considered, discriminatory effects could be camouflaged and the prophylactic purposes of the Act readily evaded. [19]

Thus, the District Court correctly began by considering the seven-member council and a districting plan that, given New Orleans' long history of racial bloc voting, [20] allows Negroes the expectation of no more than one seat (14 of the council), if that, in a city with a 34.5% Negro voting population. Manifestly, the plan serves to underrepresent the Negro voting population. The District Court then, properly, turned to consider whether Negroes are excluded from full participation in the political processes in New Orleans. The court found considerable evidence of both past and present exclusion, none of which is seriously contested here. [21]

The court found that Louisiana's majority vote requirement and "anti-single-shot" requirement operate, as a practical matter, to defeat Negroes in any district in which they do not constitute a majority, [22] that residual effects of Louisiana's long history of racial discrimination not only in voting, but also in public schools, public assemblies, public recreational facilities, public transportation, housing, and employment, remain; and that city officeholders have generally been unresponsive to the needs of the Negro community. The court looked to the many tactics that, until recently, had been employed with remarkable success to keep Negroes from voting in the State. See Louisiana v. United States, 380 U. S. 145, 380 U. S. 147-150 (1965). And the court found that Negro access to the political process is even further narrowed by the fact that candidates in the all-important Democratic primary run on tickets. For a city council candidate to win nomination, which is tantamount to victory in the general election, it is critical to be placed on the ticket of the winning, always white, mayoral candidate. Negro candidates for city council, however, have never been placed on such a ticket. Indeed, no Negro has ever been elected to the city council, and the court found that, on the rare occasions when a Negro has been elected to any office in the city, it has been because of the support of white candidates or of the white political organization, not because of the power of the Negro electorate. These findings plainly support the District Court's conclusion that the political processes of New Orleans are not open to Negroes on an equal basis with whites.

Since Negroes are underrepresented by Plan II and have been denied equal access to the political processes in New Orleans, Plan II infringes upon constitutionally protected rights, and only a compelling justification can save the plan. The very nature of the Negro community in New Orleans and the manner of its distortion by Plan II immediately place the city's explanations in a suspect light. The Negro community is not dispersed, but rather is collected in a concentrated curving band that runs roughly east-west. The districts in Plan II run north-south, and divide the Negro community into five parts. Counsel for intervenor Jackson vividly described the effect of this division at oral argument:

"You can walk from Jefferson Parish throughout the city for eight or ten miles through the St. Bernard Parish line and not see a white face along that band, that black belt, that parallels the river in a curve fashion throughout the city. White people live in the very wealthy sections of town out by the lake and along St. Charles Avenue to the river. The rest is left over for blacks, and these are heavy concentrations, and that plan devised by the City Council slices up that population like so many pieces of bologna. . . ."

Tr. of Oral Arg. 30. As Jonathan A. Eckert, the council staff member primarily responsible for drafting Plan II, conceded in the District Court, the "inevitable result" of Plan II's north-south orientation is "to have districts in which blacks are generally in the minority, or, at the most, in a bare majority." 2 App. 346.

New Orleans relies on seven goals that it claims mandate a north-south scheme such as Plan II. The city's own belief in this conclusion is questionable in light of Mr. Eckert's testimony in the District Court that he and his staff had drafted at least two east-west plans that satisfied them. 1 App. 336-337. In any case, however, the asserted goals, whether taken alone or in combination, do not establish a compelling justification for the plan. One claimed purpose is to prevent dilution of the vote of minority groups. Plan II plainly does not achieve this goal. Two other asserted aims are to achieve substantial numerical equality among the five districts and to keep the resultant districts compact and contiguous. Both aims can be accomplished by any number of east-west plans as well. Three more proffered justifications are to preserve ward and precinct lines, natural boundaries, and man-made boundaries. But there are findings that ward lines cannot be observed in any case because of one-person, one-vote restrictions, and that precincts are sufficiently small that their integrity can be honored in east-west districts. This latter fact minimizes any adverse effects of violating natural and man-made boundaries, except to the extent that they divide communities of different social or economic interests. And Plan II only erratically keeps such communities intact.

It is only the seventh of the proffered goals that, if compelling, mandates a north-south scheme: keeping incumbents apart in the new districts so that they will not have to run against one another for reelection. [23] Four of the five district councilmen live in an east-west line along the lake in the northern part of the city. East-west districts would place all four in the same one or two districts, 1 App. 125, 232, 235, and north-south lines are therefore necessary if these councilmen are to remain apart. 2 App 344. While the desire to keep incumbents in separate districts may have merit in some contexts, it surely cannot stand alone to justify the substantial dilution of minority voting rights found here.

Thus, the city has failed to show an acceptable justification for the racially dilutive effect of Plan II. Accordingly, the District Court correctly concluded that appellants failed to demonstrate that Plan II would not have the effect of abridging the right to vote on account of race, and correctly denied the requested declaratory judgment. [24]

Notes

[1] Section 5 actually requires that "any voting qualification or prerequisite to voting, or standard, practice, or procedure with respect to voting" different from that in effect on November 1, 1964, be approved by the Attorney General or the District Court for the District of Columbia. 42 U.S.C. § 1973c (1970 ed., Supp. V). We have held that a redistricting plan is a "standard, practice, or procedure with respect to voting" within the meaning of § 5. Georgia v. United States, 411 U. S. 526 (1973).

[2] We upheld the validity of the shifted burden of proof in South Carolina v. Katzenbach, 383 U. S. 301, 383 U. S. 335 (1966).

[3] "The Act suspends new voting regulations pending scrutiny by federal authorities to determine whether their use would violate the Fifteenth Amendment." Id. at 383 U. S. 334.

[4] The Court's decisions relating to the relevance of purpose and/or effect analysis in testing the constitutionality of legislative enactments are somewhat less than a seamless web. The possible theoretical approaches are three: (1) purpose alone is the test of unconstitutionality, and effect is irrelevant, or relevant only insofar as it sheds light on purpose; (2) effect alone is the test, and purpose is irrelevant; and (3) purpose or effect, either alone or in combination, is sufficient to show unconstitutionality. At various times in recent years, the Court has seemed to adopt each of these approaches.

In the two Fifteenth Amendment redistricting cases, Wright v. Rockefeller, 376 U. S. 52 (1964), and Gomillion v. Lightfoot, 364 U. S. 339 (1960), the Court suggested that legislative purpose alone is determinative, although language in both cases may be isolated that seems to approve some inquiry into effect insofar as it elucidates purpose. See 376 U.S. at 376 U. S. 52; 364 U.S. at 364 U. S. 341. See also 376 U.S. at 376 U. S. 73-74 (Goldberg, J., dissenting). McGowan v. Maryland, 366 U. S. 420, 366 U. S. 453 (1961), an equal protection-First Amendment case, expressly states that effect is of relevance in imputing an improper purpose, but that legislation is invalidated only for having such a purpose. And City of Richmond v. United States, 422 U. S. 358, 422 U. S. 378-379 (1975), suggests that bad purpose may invalidate a law under the Fifteenth Amendment even if there is no unconstitutional effect at all.

Completely contrary to these cases are those that hold that legislative purpose is wholly irrelevant to the constitutionality of legislation -- indeed, that purpose may not be examined at all -- and that a statute may be invalidated only if it has an unconstitutional effect. Palmer v. Thompson, 403 U. S. 217, 403 U. S. 224-225 (1971), and United States v. O'Brien, 391 U. S. 367, 391 U. S. 384-385 (1968), both vigorously attack purpose analysis and assert that Gomillion was decided as it was only because the statute in question had an unlawful effect.

Between these two positions are the cases that hold that either an impermissible purpose or an impermissible effect may alone be sufficient to invalidate a law. Board of Education v. Allen, 392 U. S. 236, 392 U. S. 243 (1968); Abington School District v.

Schempp, 374 U. S. 203, 374 U. S. 222 (1963). While there is no need here to synthesize these three positions and the various cases, if indeed a synthesis is possible, it should be clear that the language of purpose and effect selected by Congress for use in § 5 is not necessarily an expansion of the constitutional standard. Congress did no more than adopt the third of the tests that the Court itself has juggled over the years, see generally Ely, Legislative and Administrative Motivation in Constitutional Law, 79 Yale L.J. 1205 (1970).

[5] We have recognized that § 5 of the Fourteenth Amendment gives Congress the power to expand the substantive reach of that Amendment. Katzenbach v. Morgan, 384 U. S. 641 (1966). Undoubtedly, § 2 of the Fifteenth Amendment, under which the Voting Rights Act was enacted, confers similar power upon Congress with respect to the substantive reach of the Fifteenth Amendment. Thus, to the extent, if any, that analysis for purpose or for effect is not independently required for resolution of the constitutional question, see n. 4, supra, Congress may be said to have expanded the constitutional inquiry in § 5 of the Voting Rights Act. Insofar as redistricting legislation is concerned, however, I believe a showing of purpose or of effect is alone sufficient to demonstrate unconstitutionality, and so I believe that, in this context, Congress enacted no more than the constitutional standard. Evaluation of the purpose of a legislative enactment is just too ambiguous a task to be the sole tool of constitutional analysis. See Palmer v. Thompson, supra at 403 U. S. 224-225; United States v. O'Brien, supra, at 391 U. S. 384-385. Therefore, a demonstration of effect ordinarily should suffice. If, of course, purpose may conclusively be shown, it too should be sufficient to demonstrate a statute's unconstitutionality.

[6] While the Court does quote language that suggests some of the other purposes that I see in the statute, ante at 425 U. S. 140, when it comes to giving substantive content to § 5, the Court relies solely on the purpose suggested in the text.

It may be that this single purpose looms so large to the Court because it thinks it would be counterproductive to bar enforcement of a proposed plan, even if discriminatory, that is at all less discriminatory than the preexisting plan, which would otherwise remain frozen in effect. While this argument has superficial appeal, it is ultimately unrealistic, because it will be a rare jurisdiction that can retain its preexisting apportionment after the rejection of a modification by the Attorney General or District Court. Jurisdictions do not undertake redistricting without reason. In this case, for instance, the New Orleans City Charter requires redistricting every 10 years. If the plan before us now were disapproved, New Orleans would have to produce a new one or amend its charter. In other cases, redistricting will have been constitutionally compelled by our one-person, one-vote decisions. Reynolds v. Sims, 377 U. S. 533 (1964). The virtual necessity of prompt redistricting argues strongly in favor of rejecting "ameliorative" but still discriminatory redistricting plans. The jurisdictions will eventually have to return with a nondiscriminatory plan.

[7] Equally unsuccessful is the Court's attempt to paint the "ameliorative"

changes in this case as dramatic. Negroes constitute 45% of the population of New Orleans and 34.5% of the city's registered voters. Under the 1961 redistricting plan currently in effect in New Orleans, that population is distributed as follows:

Population Registered Voters

District % Negro % Negro

A 31.6 22.7

B 62.2 50.2

C 40.2 24.6

D 43.7 36.3

E 49.4 42.8

App. 621. Under Plan II, which is at issue in this lawsuit, the same population is distributed in this manner:

Population Registered Voters

District % Negro % Negro

A 29.1 22.6

B 64.1 52.6

C 35.8 23.3

D 43.5 36.8

E 50.6 43.2

App. 624.

Thus, the positive change that convinces the Court that no inquiry into possible "abridgment" is necessary is the change from a majority of registered voters in District B of 50.2% (which the Court fails to mention) to what the Court calls a "clear" majority (although the Court has no idea what percentage of registered Negro voters actually vote) in that district of 52.6%. The Court also emphasizes that now Negroes constitute a majority of the population in two districts, whereas, under the existing plan, they are a majority in only one district. This beneficial change is accomplished by the shift from a minority of 49.4% of the population in District E to a majority in that district of 50.6%.

[8] H.R.Rep. No. 91-397, pp. 6-7 (1969). See also H.R.Rep. No. 439, 89th Cong., 1st Sess., 111 (1965); S.Rep. No. 162, 89th Cong., 1st Sess., pt. 3, pp. 8, 12 (1965); South Carolina v. Katzenbach, 383 U.S. at 383 U. S. 315-316, 383 U. S. 335.

[9] S.Rep. No. 94-295, p. 15 (1975). See also H.R.Rep. No. 439, supra at 10-11. It is for this reason that the existing plan remains "frozen" in effect while the proposed plan is submitted for approval. Thus, any constitutional litigation may proceed without interruption, unless the new plan is itself found to be nondiscriminatory and is substituted. See H.R.Rep. No. 94-196, p. 58 (1975). Either way, the litigant obtains the relief he seeks -- a nondiscriminatory apportionment.

[10] The pressure of having proposed plans judged by rigorous standards and the fear of litigation over new plans were thought to encourage covered jurisdictions to end all discrimination in voting.

"The preclearance procedure -- and this is critical -- serves psychologically to control the proliferation of discriminatory laws and practices because each change must first be federally reviewed. Thus section 5 serves to prevent discrimination before it starts."

115 Cong.Rec. 38486 (1969) (remarks of Rep. McCulloch). See also id. at 38517 (remarks of Rep. Anderson); U.S. Commission on Civil Rights, The Voting Rights Act: Ten Years After, pp. 30-31 (1975).

The Act's limited term is proof that Congress intended to secure prompt, and not gradual, relief. Originally, the Act was intended to be in effect for only five years. While it has been twice extended, each extension was also for only a few years: five more years in 1970, and seven more years in 1975. Thus, it cannot be argued that the Act contemplated slow forward movement, which the Court's construction sanctifies, rather than a quick remedial "fix."

[11] While I read "abridge" in both § 5 and the Fifteenth Amendment as primarily involving an absolute assessment of dilution of Negro voting power from its potential, I do not hold that recognition of a relative change is absolutely irrelevant to this determination. For instance, it may often be useful to glean some indication of purpose from a minority's relative position under the existing and proposed plans. Moreover, there will be circumstances -- annexations, for example -- where dilution can fairly be measured only in comparison to the prior scheme. See City of Richmond v. United States, 422 U.S. at 422 U. S. 378. Cf. Gomillion v. Lightfoot, 364 U. S. 339 (1960).

[12] Today the Court finds it simple to conclude that Plan II is "ameliorative," but it will not always be so easy to determine whether a new plan increases or decreases Negro voting power relative to the prior plan. To the contrary, I believe the Court's test will prove unduly difficult of application and excessively demanding of judicial energies.

For instance, the Court today finds that an increase in the size of the Negro majority in one district, with a concomitant increased likelihood of electing a delegate, conclusively shows that Plan II is ameliorative. Will that always be so? Is it not as common for minorities to be gerrymandered into the same district as into separate ones? Is an increase in the size of an existing majority ameliorative or retrogressive? When the size of the majority increases in one district, Negro voting strength necessarily declines elsewhere. Is that decline retrogressive? Assuming that the shift from a 50.2% to a 52.6% majority in District B in this case is ameliorative, and is not outweighed by the simultaneous decrease in Negro voting strength in Districts A and C, when would an increase become retrogressive? As soon as the majority becomes "safe"? When the majority is achieved by dividing preexisting concentrations of Negro voters?

Moreover, the Court implies, ante at 425 U. S. 139 n. 11, by its attempt to harmonize its holding today with City of Richmond v. United States, supra, that this preliminary inquiry into the nature of the change is the proper approach to all § 5 cases. The Court's test will prove even more difficult of application outside the redistricting context. Some changes just do not lend themselves to comparison in positive or negative terms; others will always seem negative -- or positive -- no matter how good or bad the result. For instance, when a city goes from an appointed town manager to an elected council form of government, can the change ever be termed retrogressive, even if the new council is elected at large and Negroes are a minority? Or where a jurisdiction in which Negroes are a substantial minority switches from at-large to ward voting, can that change ever constitute a negative change, no matter how badly the wards are gerrymandered?

I realize, of course, that determining the ultimate question of "abridgment" may involve answering questions similar to those I have posed above, and that those questions will be just as difficult to answer. My point, however, is exactly that the inquiry is a difficult one, and that there is no reason substantially to compound that complexity by posing an unnecessary and equally complex preliminary inquiry.

[13] As I understand it, the Court views the constitutional inquiry as part of the § 5 inquiry. See ante at 425 U. S. 141. Thus, the burden of proof on constitutional issues, as on all § 5 issues, is on the covered jurisdiction. Although the Court's treatment of the point is ambiguous, I read its observation that "[t]he United States has made no claim" that Plan II is unconstitutional, ante at 425 U. S. 142 n. 14, as indicating only that it is for the United States to raise the issue of unconstitutionality in the § 5 proceeding, and not as suggesting that, once the issue is raised, the United States must prove the claim as well. Any other reading would frustrate still another legislative purpose. The Act freezes the existing plan and places the burden of proof on the covered jurisdiction to justify the proposed plan expressly in order "to shift the advantage of time and inertia from the perpetrators of the evil to its victims." South Carolina v. Katzenbach, 383 U.S. at 383 U. S. 328. See also H.R.Rep. No. 94-196, p. 58 (1975). I do not understand the Court, in bringing the constitutional issue in through the back door, to eliminate the primary procedural advantage to the United States of the § 5 proceeding.

[14] The Court's treatment of the constitutional questions is all the more puzzling if it intends to confine its constitutional analysis to those seats brought before the District Court in the § 5 proceeding. In this case, the Court holds that it may avoid looking at the two at-large seats on the New Orleans City Council in deciding the § 5 claim, but see infra at 425 U. S. 158-159, and its exclusion of those seats appears to extend to its ultimate constitutional inquiry as well. Yet it is obvious that an independent constitutional challenge to Plan II would also include a challenge to the at-large seats, and that such a broadened attack would be considerably more difficult to reject than the question the Court evidently considers. The change in focus caused by an expanded challenge both accentuates the dilution of the Negro vote in New Orleans, see n.19, infra and necessitates recognition of the particularly dilutive effects of at-large districting schemes. See White v. Regester, 412 U. S. 755 (1973). If the Court has ignored these factors in finding Plan II constitutional, it has engaged in no more than a time-consuming hypothetical

adjudication, for its holding will surely not bar a future constitutional challenge to the entire scheme.

[15] Because I read § 5 as incorporating the standards of the Fifteenth Amendment, see nn. 4-5, supra, I read these cases as holding, implicitly, that the Fourteenth and Fifteenth Amendments mandate the same test for assessing the validity, on racial grounds, of legislative apportionments. Since a person whose right to vote is denied or abridged on account of race is likewise denied equal protection of the laws, borrowing from the developed corpus of Fourteenth Amendment law is entirely appropriate.

Seeking another source for a § 5 test is particularly appropriate given the scarcity of Fifteenth Amendment case law. Wright v. Rockefeller, 376 U. S. 52 (1964), and Gomillion v. Lightfoot, 364 U. S. 339 (1960), the only relevant Fifteenth Amendment cases, predate not only the Voting Rights Act, its incorporation of the language of the Fifteenth Amendment, and our cases construing that incorporation, but also all the Fourteenth Amendment developments discussed in the text. For these reasons, and because neither case states a general test, Wright and Gomillion are of no help at all in formulating a test for § 5 cases.

[16] The Court refers to the cited page for the proposition that members of a minority group have no federal right "to be represented in legislative bodies in proportion to their number in the general population." Ante at 425 U. S. 136-137, n. 8. Whitcomb v. Chavis stands for no such proposition. The language the Court refers to is substantively identical to that quoted in the text and supports only the notion that there is no right to proportional representation absent evidence of denial of access to the political process.

[17] The cases make clear that the inquiry is not meant to be limited to the ability of the minority group to participate in the voting plan under attack, but also includes sweeping analysis of the minority group's past and present treatment by the jurisdiction before the court. White v. Regester, 412 U.S. at 412 U. S. 766-767; Whitcomb v. Chavis, 403 U.S. at 403 U. S. 149-153.

[18] For instance, a city with a 20% Negro population and a five-member council elected in wards might be able to justify the placement of only 20% minority population in each district, despite a history of denial of access to the political process, by showing that the minority population was perfectly distributed throughout the municipality so that the creation of a Negro-majority ward was an impossibility. On the other hand, again assuming a history of denial of access to the political process, such a plan could not survive attack if the 20% Negro population of each ward were achieved by dividing five ways a concentrated bloc of Negro voters located in the center of the city.

[19] This effect is clear in this case, where Negroes constitute 34.5% of the New Orleans electorate. Out of seven seats, Negroes should reasonably expect to control at least two. In considering only five seats, the Court suggests -- properly, given its self-imposed limitation -- that Negroes should have an expectancy of only one seat. Ante at 425 U. S. 137 n. 8. If only two of the five districts were before us, and assuming a 34.5%

minority share of the voting population in those districts, the Court could properly conclude that Negroes could lay claim to neither of the two seats. Thus, under the Court's approach, the smaller the number of seats that the city may present for consideration, the grosser the discrimination that may be numerically tolerated.

[20] The tendency to racial bloc voting in New Orleans is a finding of fact by the District Court that is not challenged here. Such voting was encouraged until 1964 by a Louisiana statute, declared unconstitutional in Anderson v. Martin, 375 U. S. 399 (1964), that required the race of each candidate to be printed on the ballots used in all elections within the State.

[21] Appellants challenge the propriety of looking at this evidence in assessing the effect of Plan II, not its accuracy.

[22] The majority vote requirement is a rule that the winner of an election must have a majority of the vote. Thus, in a race involving three or more candidates, a plurality of voters cannot elect their candidate. If no candidate wins a majority, there is a run-off election.

The "anti-single-shot" rule is a requirement that, in a multimember district, the voter must vote for as many candidates as there are seats to be filled. Thus, although the voter may be interested in only one of the candidates, he must vote for others as well.

[23] The city asserts that its seventh goal is to retain "historic and traditional councilmanic district boundaries" so as to "preserve continuity within the electorate." Brief for Appellants 229. In fact, the record is conclusive that the goal was purely to keep incumbents apart. 1 App. 206-207; 2 App. 344, 557.

[24] While the Court today finds that the District Court erred in finding a discriminatory effect, it does not address the issue not reached by the District Court: whether Plan II was drafted with a discriminatory purpose. Of course, this question remains on remand. See City of Richmond v. United States, 422 U.S. at 422 U. S. 378-379.

It was an act of state: Justice Marshall's dissent in Alfred Dunhill of London, Inc. v. Republic of Cuba (May 24, 1976)

MR. JUSTICE MARSHALL, with whom MR. JUSTICE BRENNAN, MR. JUSTICE STEWART, and MR. JUSTICE BLACKMUN join, dissenting.

The act of state doctrine commits the courts of this country not to sit in judgment on the acts of a foreign government performed within its own territory. [1] Under any realistic view of the facts of this case, the interventors' retention of and refusal to return funds paid to them by Dunhill constitute an act of state, and no affirmative recovery by Dunhill can rest on the invalidity of that conduct. The Court of Appeals so concluded, and I would affirm its judgment.

As of September 15, 1960, when the Cuban Government "intervened," or nationalized, five Cuban-owned cigar manufacturers, petitioner Dunhill had received some $148,600 worth of cigars for which it had not yet paid. In the period between intervention and February, 1961, Dunhill took delivery of an additional $93,000 worth of shipments. Both the District Court and the Court of Appeals concluded that the intervention was to be given full legal effect with respect to the property of Cuban nationals located in Cuba, and that the interventors were therefore entitled to payment for post-intervention shipments. F. Palicio y Compania, S.A. v. Brush, 256 F.Supp. 481, 486-490 (SDNY 1966), aff'd, 375 F.2d 1011 (CA2), cert. denied sub nom. Brush v. Republic of Cuba, 389 U.S. 830 (1967). It is quite clear that that result was correct, and that it would have been no different had the intervened firms been owned by United States citizens. Banco Nacional de Cuba v. Sabbatino, 376 U. S. 398 (1964).

Since the date of intervention, the interventors have taken the position that they were also entitled to receive the amounts due to the intervened firms for reintervention shipments -- in the case of Dunhill, $148,600. And throughout this litigation, respondents, the interventors [2] and the Republic of Cuba, have insisted that the act of state doctrine requires our courts to give full legal effect to the intervention decree insofar as it purported to nationalize the accounts receivable of the intervened firms. Both the District Court and the Court of Appeals held, however, that the accounts receivable involved here had their situs in New York, that the act of state doctrine did not apply, and that the attempted confiscation was ineffective. Menendez v. Faber, Coe & Greg, Inc., 345 F.Supp. 527, 536-540 (SDNY 1972); Menendez v. Saks & Co., 485 F.2d 1355, 1364-1365 (CA2 19,73). In a separate petition for certiorari, which the Court, today denies, [3] and in the course of its presentation in this case, respondents have pursued their contention that the initial intervention should be recognized as having reached the pre-intervention accounts receivable. But that is not the respondents' sole contention, and it is not necessary for us to consider it here. For, as the Court of Appeals recognized, the act of state question took on a wholly different light when Dunhill paid the amount due for pre-intervention shipments to the interventors in Cuba. [4]

The Court of Appeals held that Dunhill's claim for return of the monies paid to the interventors for pre-intervention shipments sounds in quasi-contract; it arises, the court observed, not from Dunhill's contractual obligation to the owners, which is situated in New York, but from the interventors' receipt, appropriation, and refusal to return the funds, all of which have occurred apart from the contract and in Cuba. If the interventors' course of conduct is itself an act of state, therefore, there can be no doubt that the act of state doctrine applies.

The interventors have not taken any discrete, overt action for which to claim the status of an act of state. Rather, they have received and long retained the money paid to them for pre-intervention shipments, and they have ignored Dunhill's demands for its return. The Court declines to view this course of conduct as reflecting an exercise of sovereign power to retain the funds at issue after they arrived in Cuba, explaining in part:

"No statute, decree, order, or resolution of the Cuban Government itself was offered in evidence indicating that Cuba had repudiated her obligations in general or any class thereof or that she had as a sovereign matter determined to confiscate the amounts due [Dunhill and the other] foreign importers."

Ante at 425 U. S. 695.

I do not understand the Court to suggest, however, that the act of state doctrine can be triggered only by a "statute, decree, order, or resolution" of a foreign government, or that the presence of an act of state can only be demonstrated by some affirmative action by the foreign sovereign. While it is true that an act of state generally takes the form of an executive or legislative step formalized in a decree or measure, see, e.g., Banco Nacional de Cuba v. Sabbatino, 376 U. S. 398, 376 U. S. 403-405, n. 7 (1964); Eastern States Petroleum Co. v. Asiatic Petroleum Corp., 28 F.Supp. 279 (SDNY 1939), that is only because duly constituted governments generally act through formal means. When they do not, their acts are no less the acts of a state, and the doctrine, being a practical one, is no less applicable. Thus, in Underhill v. Hernandez, 168 U. S. 250 (1897), where the plaintiff sought recovery for his detention in Venezuela by reason of the then revolutionary forces' refusal to grant him a passport out of Ciudad Bolivar, the Court held that the act of state doctrine "must necessarily extend to the agents of governments ruling by paramount force as [a] matter of fact." Id. at 168 U. S. 252. The cases of Oetjen v. Central Leather Co., 246 U. S. 297 (1918), and Ricaud v. American Metal Co., 246 U. S. 304 (1918), are further illustrations of the practical approach the Court has always taken in determining whether an act of state is present. In each case, the plaintiff claimed title to goods purchased from Mexican sellers but confiscated by generals of the Constitutionalist Carranza forces before delivery to the plaintiffs. The Generals, Villa and Pereyra respectively, had sold the goods to intermediate purchasers for the furtherance of the revolution, and the goods thereafter came into the United States in the possession of the defendant assignees. The Court held that the seizures in question must be viewed as the action, in time of civil war, of a duly commissioned agent of the prevailing Mexican Government, and could not be subjected to the scrutiny of another sovereign's courts.

These cases demonstrate not only that an act of state need not be formalized in any particular manner, but also that it need not take the form of active, rather than passive, conduct. Had General Villa come accidentally into possession of the hides sought to be replevied in Oetjen, instead of seizing them, and then simply refused the plaintiff's demand for possession, the result could not have been any different. Indeed, so far as the report of the Underhill case reveals, the plaintiff, in seeking recovery for his detention, challenged no more than General Hernandez' refusal to do anything when he demanded his passport.

That a foreign sovereign has issued no formal decree and performed no "affirmative" act is not fatal, then, to an act of state claim. If the foreign state has exercised a sovereign power either to act or to refrain from acting, there is an act of state. In a case very similar to this one, the New York Court of Appeals held that the Cuban bank's dishonoring of tax exemption certificates, the redemption of which had been suspended by a decision of the Cuban Currency Stabilization Fund, was an act of state. French v. Banco Nacional de Cuba, 23 N.Y.2d 46, 242 N.E.2d 704 (1968). The act of state, the court wrote, "was the defendant's refusal to perform; the currency regulations, though equally the product of an act of state, were simply the justification for the refusal." [5]

The Court, I take it, does not dispute that a refusal to act constitutes an act of state when shown to reflect the exercise of sovereign power. Rather, the Court finds no exercise of sovereign power to retain the funds at issue after they arrived in Cuba. Refusal to repay, the Court suggests, does not necessarily reflect anything more than the interventors' initial contention, rejected by the District Court and the Court of Appeals, that the September 15, 1960, intervention decree operated to seize the accounts receivable of the intervened firms. And the Court is unwilling

"to infer from the fact that Cuba seized the assets of the cigar business from Cuban nationals that they must necessarily . . . have made a later discriminatory and confiscatory seizure of money belonging to the United States companies."

Ante at 425 U. S. 692 n. 8.

As I have already indicated, however, the respondents' position has not been, and need not be, limited to the contention that the September 15 decree operated to seize the pre-intervention accounts receivable. Counsel for the interventors and the Republic of Cuba stated at trial, in his brief to this Court, and again in his oral argument in this Court:

"[U]nder the act of state doctrine the Cuban government, in accepting, expropriating, seizing, nationalizing, whatever other words you want, to take this money, has done so pursuant to a regulation, a law, a decree of the government of Cuba, and therefore the courts of this state will not look into the matter nor will the federal court."

"Now, I am not talking about the extraterritorial effect of an act of state. I am talking about a territorial effect, namely, the seizure or the acceptance or the appropriation of this money when it got down to Cuba. We are not now concerned with whether they expropriated debts on September 15th. The question is what happened on October 1st, and October 15th and on November 8th and December 12th, when the money came down. And at that time, the Cuban government took this money and, under the act of state doctrine, it belongs to the Cuban government."

Tr. 854-856; Brief for Respondents in Reply to Brief for United States as Amicus Curiae 5 n. 3; Tr. of Oral Rearg. 38. This statement confirms that, while Cuba's retention of and refusal to return the funds once they arrived in Cuba was "pursuant to" the September 15 decree, it was without regard to whether that decree would, in the eyes of a United States court, have entitled the interventors to collect the accounts receivable in the first place. [6] And while the Court appears to suggest that Cuba would be more hesitant to seize money belonging to United States companies than it would be to seize property belonging to Cuban nationals, the fact is that, in this case Cuba has made known its intent to retain the funds in question even if a United States court declares the funds to have been taken from Dunhill, rather than from the former owners. Speaking once again on behalf of his client, the Republic of Cuba, counsel has announced Cuba's "refusal to acquiesce in the quasi-contractual obligation [to Dunhill] sought to be imposed by a foreign court." Brief for Respondents in Reply to Brief for United States as Amicus Curiae. [7]

The above-quoted statements of counsel are not themselves acts of state. But as authoritative representations of the position of counsel's clients, the interventors and the Republic of Cuba, with respect to the monies in their possession, these statements do serve to confirm that the continued retention of those monies has been undertaken as an exercise of sovereign power. [8]

II

MR. JUSTICE WHITE advances a contention, not adopted by the Court, that, even if the Cuban Government "had purported to exercise sovereign power to confiscate" the monies at issue, ante at 425 U. S. 695, the act of state doctrine is inapplicable because of the "purely commercial" nature of the confiscation. While I am prompted to make several observations on the suggested rationale for a broad "commercial act" exception to the act of state doctrine, ultimately there is no need to consider whether, and under what circumstances, an exception for commercial acts might be appropriate. It will suffice to say that no such exception is appropriate in this case.

A

I note at the outset that the commercial act exception to the act of state doctrine is supported by the Department of State. In its most recent Bernstein letter, [9] the Department has expressed the opinion that the conduct of foreign policy would suffer no embarrassment if the Court declined to apply the act of state doctrine to this case, if it declined to apply the doctrine to commercial cases in general, or, indeed, if it overruled Banco Nacional de Cuba v. Sabbatino, 376 U. S. 398 (1964). MR. JUSTICE WHITE quite properly does not rely specifically upon the views of the Department; six Members of the Court in First Nat. City Bank v. Banco Nacional de Cuba, 406 U. S. 759 (1972) (hereinafter Citibank), disapproved finally the so-called Bernstein exception to the act of state doctrine, thus minimizing the significance of any letter from the Department of State. Id. at 406 U. S. 773 (Douglas, J., concurring in result); ibid. (POWELL, J., concurring in judgment); id. at 406 U. S. 776-777 (BRENNAN, J., dissenting). Whether the act of state question in this case is viewed as being confined to a single dispute or as extending to a broad class of disputes, the task of defining the role of the Judiciary is for this Court, not the Executive Branch. [10]

B

In concluding that the act of state doctrine should not apply to the purely commercial acts of sovereign nations, MR JUSTICE WHITE relies heavily upon the widespread acceptance of the "restrictive theory" of sovereign immunity, which declines to extend immunity to foreign governments acting in a "private," or commercial, capacity. The restrictive theory of sovereign immunity has not been adopted by this Court, but even if we assume that it is the law in this country, it does not follow that there should be a commercial act exception to the act of state doctrine.

It is true, of course, that a particular litigant's claim may be as effectively defeated by application of the act of state doctrine as by a foreign government's invocation of sovereign immunity. But the doctrines of sovereign immunity and act of state, while related, differ fundamentally in their focus and in their operation. Sovereign immunity accords a defendant exemption from suit by virtue of its status. By contrast, the act of state doctrine exempts no one from the process of the court. Equally applicable whether a sovereign nation is a party or not, the act of state doctrine merely tells a court what law to apply to a case; it "concerns the limits for determining the validity of an otherwise applicable rule of law." Sabbatino, 376 U.S. at 376 U. S. 438. [11] In the absence of "unambiguous agreement regarding controlling . . . principles" of international law, id. at 376 U. S. 428, the act of state doctrine commands that the acts of a sovereign nation committed in its own territory be accorded presumptive validity.

The act of state doctrine, "although it shares with the immunity doctrine a respect for sovereign states,' serves important policies entirely independent of that rule." Citibank, supra at 406 U. S. 795 (BRENNAN, J., dissenting), quoting Sabbatino, supra at 376 U. S. 438. The act of state doctrine is not mandated by the text of the Constitution, but it does have " 'constitutional' underpinnings." Sabbatino, supra at 376 U. S. 423.

"It arises out of the basic relationships between branches of government in a system of separation of powers. It concerns the competency of dissimilar institutions to make and implement particular kinds of decisions in the area of international relations. The doctrine as formulated in past decisions expresses the strong sense of the Judicial Branch that its engagement in the task of passing on the validity of foreign acts of state may hinder, rather than further, this country's pursuit of goals both for itself and for the community of nations as a whole in the international sphere."

Ibid. [12] MR. JUSTICE BRENNAN has observed, the act of state doctrine reflects the notion that the validity of an act of a foreign sovereign is, under some circumstances, a "political question" not cognizable in our courts. The circumstances indicating the existence of a "political question" in Sabbatino included, as MR. JUSTICE BRENNAN summarized,

"the absence of consensus on the applicable international rules, the unavailability of standards from a treaty or other agreement, the existence and recognition of the Cuban Government, the sensitivity of the issues to national concerns, and the power of the Executive alone to effect a fair remedy for all United States citizens who have been harmed."

Citibank, supra at 406 U. S. 788; see Sabbatino, supra at 376 U. S. 427-437.

The doctrine of sovereign immunity, concerned only with the status of a party to a lawsuit, does not focus on the other circumstances just mentioned; it is simply not designed to be responsive to the particular considerations underlying the act of state doctrine. Whatever exceptions there may be to sovereign immunity ought not be transferred automatically, therefore, to the act of state doctrine. [13]

C

I question the wisdom of attempting the articulation of any broad exception to the act of state doctrine within the confines of a single case. The Court in Sabbatino, aware of the variety of situations presenting act of state questions and the complexity of the relevant considerations, eschewed any inflexible rule in favor of a case-by-case approach. 376 U.S. at 376 U. S. 428. The carving out of broad exceptions to the doctrine is fundamentally at odds with the careful case-by-case approach adopted in Sabbatino.

Indeed, it is difficult to discern the precise scope of the "commercial act" exception contemplated by MR. JUSTICE WHITE. [14] In the final analysis, however, it is unnecessary to consider whether the exception would be responsive to the concerns underlying the act of state doctrine in every case to which it might apply. [15] If the exception covers this case, it is unresponsive.

Cuba's retention of and refusal to repay the funds at issue in this case took place against the background of the intervention, or nationalization, of the businesses and assets of five cigar manufacturers. As I have already indicated, the seizure and retention of the Dunhill funds were pursuant to the initial intervention decree. For all practical purposes, the seizure of the funds once they arrived in Cuba is indistinguishable from the seizure of the remainder of the cigar manufacturers' businesses. The seizure of the funds, like the initial seizures on September 15, reflected a purpose to exert sovereign power to its territorial limits in order to effectuate the intervention of ongoing cigar manufacturing businesses. It matters not that the funds have been determined by a United States court in this case to have belonged to Dunhill, rather than the cigar manufacturers. What does matter is that Cuba retained the money in the course of its program of expropriating what it viewed as part and parcel of the businesses. [16]

The applicability of the act of state doctrine in these circumstances is controlled by Sabbatino itself. As the Court there noted:

"There are few if any issues in international law today on which opinion seems to be so divided as the limitations on a state's power to expropriate the property of aliens."

376 U.S. at 376 U. S. 428. Indeed, the absence of any suggestion that Cuba's intervention program was discriminatory against United States citizens [17] renders the lack of consensus as to applicable principles of law even more apparent here than in Sabbatino. See Citibank at 406 U. S. 785 (BRENNAN, J., dissenting). And unless one takes the position that the amount of money or the value of property seized materially affects the sensitivity of the issues, we are guided in this case by the following observation in Sabbatino:

"It is difficult to imagine the courts of this country embarking on adjudication in an area which touches more sensitively the practical and ideological goals of the various members of the community of nations."

376 U.S. at 376 U. S. 430 (footnote omitted). Regardless, then, of whether the presence of consensus as to controlling legal principles, or any other circumstances, would render the act of state doctrine inapplicable to some, or even most, acts that could be characterized as "purely commercial," the doctrine is fully applicable in this case.

III

Since, in my view, the retention of and refusal to repay the funds at issue constitute an act of state that would ordinarily preclude an affirmative judgment against Cuba and the interventors, it is necessary for me to proceed to the second question on which we granted certiorari -- whether Dunhill may nonetheless secure an affirmative judgment in the peculiar circumstances of this case.

A

A brief recapitulation of the facts is necessary to understand Dunhill's contention that it is entitled to an affirmative recovery in spite of the presence of an act of state. Dunhill was one of three importers that had at the time of the intervention received cigars for which it had not yet paid. During the three months following intervention, each of the importers paid the interventors the amounts due for pre-intervention shipments. And in the period between intervention and February, 1961, each of the importers took delivery of additional shipments, for which payment was not made.

This suit stems from nine suits brought against the importers by the former owners of the five intervened firms, inter alia, to restrain payment to anyone else for goods manufactured by their firms or bearing their mark, and to recover for all such goods that the importers had already received. The interventors brought suit in the names of the intervened firms to enjoin the former owners' counsel from pursuing the nine actions in the firms' names, and to substitute their own attorneys for those of the former owners in the same nine suits. The District Court ruled as a preliminary matter that the interventors and not the former owners were entitled to sue for payment for the post-intervention shipments. F. Palicio y Compania, S.A. v. Brush, 256 F.Supp. 481 (SDNY 1966), aff'd, 375 F.2d 1011 (CA2), cert. denied sub nom. Brush v. Republic of Cuba, 389 U.S. 830 (1967). The original nine actions were then consolidated for trial, with the interventors pursuing their claim for payments for post-intervention shipments, and both the former owners and the interventors pursuing their claims to the payments for pre-intervention shipments.

The District Court concluded that the former owners, not the interventors, were entitled to payment for pre-intervention shipments. Under its view that the interventors' refusal to return the monies paid for pre-intervention shipments did not involve an act of state, the District Court set off that amount ($477,000) against the amount owed by the importers to the interventors for post-intervention shipments ($700,000). Menendez v. Faber, Coe & Gregg, Inc., 345 F.Supp. 527 (SDNY 1972). Alone among the importers, Dunhill had paid the interventors more for pre-intervention shipments ($148,000) than it owed for post-intervention shipments ($93,000). Accordingly the District Court directed that an "affirmative judgment" be entered in Dunhill's favor. [18]

The Court of Appeals found an act of state in Cuba's retention of the monies paid for pre-intervention shipments. It interpreted the various views expressed in Citibank as indicating that this Court would nevertheless uphold the importers' counterclaims up to the limits of the respective claims asserted against them by the interventors. But the court reversed the judgment of the District Court insofar as it granted Dunhill affirmative recovery. Menendez v. Saks & Co., 485 F.2d 1355 (CA2 1973). The second question on which we granted certiorari is whether, if Cuba's conduct constitutes an act of state, Dunhill may nonetheless assert its full counterclaim in the circumstances of this case, where the counterclaim exceeds Cuba's claim against it but is less than the amount owed to Cuba by the importers as a group.

B

The Court in Citibank held that the act of state doctrine does not necessarily bar a defendant from litigating the merits of a limited counterclaim against a foreign state suing in the courts of this country, Petitioner there was an American bank whose branches in Cuba had been nationalized. The bank responded by selling the collateral securing its loan of $10 million to the respondent Banco Nacional de Cuba, an instrumentality of the state. Banco Nacional then sued for the excess proceeds realized from the sale, and First National counterclaimed for an equal amount in damages resulting from the expropriation of its property. For various reasons asserted in three separate opinions, a bare majority of the Court allowed prosecution of the counterclaim, limited as it was to the amount recoverable against First National.

Because we are concerned here only with the status of a counterclaim in excess of a foreign state's principal claim, the precise question the Court addressed in Citibank -- whether a counterclaim limited by the amount of the foreign state's claim may be barred by the act of state doctrine -- does not cover the present situation. [19] The approach adopted in MR. JUSTICE BRENNAN's dissent in Citibank, which would have barred a counterclaim limited by the amount of a foreign state's claim, would be sufficient, a fortiori, to bar Dunhill's excessive counterclaim. But even putting that approach aside, the judgment of the Court of Appeals denying affirmative relief to Dunhill should be affirmed.

An affirmative judgment for the excess of a counterclaim over a foreign state's principal claim is indistinguishable in any important respect from an ordinary affirmative judgment. In this case, the situation is precisely as it would be if Cuba had voluntarily recognized the validity of Dunhill's claim in an amount equal to its on, the parties had agreed extrajudicially to consider the claims as canceling each other out pro tanto, and Dunhill had then sued Cuba for the unsettled remainder of its claim. The courts would then be presented with an unadorned suit against a foreign sovereign, barred by the act of state doctrine. [20] But an affirmative judgment offends the policy of judicial abstention from interference in international relations to an equal degree, whether it is founded upon a naked suit against a foreign state or an excessive counterclaim. [21]

Dunhill contends, however, that the nature of the act of state question is affected by the fortuity that its counterclaim, while exceeding Cuba's principal claim against it, is for a lesser amount than the sum of the judgments entered in favor of Cuba against the three importers whose cases were consolidated for trial. This contention suffers from two fatal flaws.

First, the actions against Dunhill and the other importers were not merged; they were simply consolidated for trial in the interest of economy. [22] The interventors, as substituted plaintiffs in the actions originally filed by the owners, asserted separate causes of action against each importer; no single transaction involved or gave rise to a claim against more than one importer. The actions thus did not lose their separate identities because of the consolidation. [23] In these circumstances, a ruling allowing for a counterclaim on the theory that it does not exceed the foreign state's total judgments against those parties that happen to be before the District Court would be capricious indeed. The limitation on counterclaims would then be determined by the presence or absence of actions suitable for consolidation at a particular time in a particular court, [24] and upon their outcomes.

In any event, it has become quite clear that execution of Dunhill's affirmative judgment against the judgment debts that the other importers owe to the interventors would be prohibited by the Cuban Assets Control Regulations, 31 CFR pt. 515 (1975), promulgated by the Treasury Department's Office of Foreign Assets Control pursuant to the Trading With the Enemy Act, 50 U.S.C. App. § 5. The regulations prohibit, except as authorized by the Secretary, all transactions involving property in which Cuba has an interest, direct or indirect, including "the levy of or under any judgment, decree, attachment, execution, or other judicial or administrative process or order." [25] This scheme by which the Executive has frozen Cuban assets in the United States is designed to preserve a fund for the ultimate, orderly satisfaction of claims against Cuba by American nationals if diplomatic alternatives prove unavailing. See Citibank, 406 U.S. at 406 U. S. 794 (BRENNAN, J., dissenting). In furtherance of this policy, the Treasury Department has stated that it will refuse "to authorize a judgment creditor of Cuba to execute against assets of Cuba which have been frozen" under the regulations. [26] An affirmative judgment in favor of Dunhill could not, therefore, be satisfied out of the other importers' judgment debts to Cuba, which are frozen for the benefit of all creditors or for such other disposition as future diplomatic negotiations direct. [27] To allow entry of an affirmative judgment against Cuba in these circumstances would thus mark a significant departure from our consistent policy of avoiding potential interference with the executive channels through which our Nation deals with others, while securing to Dunhill only the very speculative prospect of obtaining a preference over other United States claimants should national policy on the subject of Cuban assets change in the future.

IV

In conclusion, I would hold that the course of conduct undertaken by the interventors with respect to payments made for pre-intervention shipments constitutes an act of state, and that Dunhill is not entitled to an affirmative judgment on its counterclaim relating to those payments. I would affirm the judgment of the Court of Appeals.

Notes

[1] The classic American formulation of the doctrine, see Banco Nacional de Cuba

v. Sabbatino, 376 U. S. 398, 376 U. S. 416 (1964), appears in Underhill v. Hernandez, 168 U. S. 250, 168 U. S. 252 (1897):

"Every sovereign State is bound to respect the independence of every other sovereign State, and the courts of one country will not sit in judgment on the acts of the government of another done within its own territory. Redress of grievances by reason of such acts must be obtained through the means open to be availed of by sovereign powers as between themselves."

[2] Actually only one of the interventors is a party in this Court; he has apparently been designated as the single interventor for the five intervened tobacco companies. For the sake of convenience, I shall continue to refer to "the interventors."

[3] Republic of Cuba v. Saks & Co., No. 73-1287, post, p. 991.

[4] Payment was made to collecting banks that had previously acted as agents for the former owners. The District Court expressly found that

"the importers [including Dunhill] well knew that, following intervention, the collecting banks were acting as agents for the interventors and not the [former] owners, and also knew that the payments they were making to the collecting banks were ultimately received by the interventors in Cuba."

345 F.Supp. at 542. These findings were sustained by the Court of Appeals. 485 F.2d at 1367-1368.

[5] The quoted statement appears in the concurring opinion of Judge Hopkins, 23 N.Y.2d at 66, 242 N.E.2d at 717, which was joined by the same majority that subscribed to the opinion of Chief Judge Fuld, in which the court held: "[T]he breach of contract, of which the plaintiff complains, resulted from, and, indeed, itself constitutes, an act of state." Id. at 53, 242 N.E.2d at 709.

[6] In another brief filed in this Court, respondents' counsel observed:

"It matters not that the interventor may be wrong in the eyes of the United States court [in claiming that the September 15 decree nationalized the pre-intervention accounts receivable]. . . . Since the monies taken by the interventor were in Cuba, and he was a representative of the sovereign, it can hardly be denied that his conduct amounted to 'a taking of property within its own territory by a foreign sovereign government.' [Banco Nacional de Cuba v. Sabbatino, 376 U.S. at 376 U. S. 428.]"

Brief for Respondents 18.

[7] The Court acknowledges that this statement reflects an alternative contention by respondents that, assuming the ineffectiveness of the September 15 decree in reaching the pre-intervention accounts receivable and the existence of a quasi-contractual obligation to return the monies at issue to Dunhill, their repudiation of that obligation was an act of state. Ante at 425 U. S. 692 n. 8. But the Court emphasizes the fact that respondents have not admitted the existence of an obligation to Dunhill, and concludes that it remains unclear whether respondents have determined to retain the monies even if a United States court declares the obligation to exist. The very fact that respondents are making the alternative argument referred to herein, however, should remove any doubt

as to their intentions.

[8] Compania Espanola de Navegacion Maritima v. The Navemar, 303 U. S. 68 (1938), is not to the contrary. That was a suit in admiralty by the alleged owner of a Spanish merchant vessel to recover possession. The Spanish Ambassador sought leave to intervene as a claimant and produced an

"affidavit of the Spanish Acting Consul General suggesting that, when the suit was brought the vessel was the property of the Republic of Spain, by virtue of a decree of attachment promulgated by the President of the Republic, appropriating the vessel to the public use, and that it was then in the possession of the Spanish Government."

Id. at 303 U. S. 70. The District Court, we held, "was not bound . . . to accept the allegations of the suggestion as conclusive" on the question of possession, id. at 303 U. S. 75, where there was no proof whatever that the foreign sovereign had ever held possession and no claim that "the alleged seizure [of the vessel] by the members of the crew was an act of or in behalf of the Spanish Government." Id. at 303 U. S. 72.

By contrast, in the present case it is settled that the interventors received the payments for pre-intervention shipments on behalf of the Cuban Government, Menendez v. Faber, Coe & Gregg Inc., 345 F.Supp. at 532, and any lingering doubt that their retention was by virtue of a claim of right was dispelled by counsel for Cuba and the interventors at trial. Had possession been established in The Navemar, and the decree of appropriation been in doubt, the case would be in point, but, in fact, the contrary was true and the case is inapposite.

It was in response to the suggestion that The Navemar case controlled this one that counsel for respondents made the statement, relied upon by the Court, ante at 425 U. S. 692 n. 8:

"The statement of an ambassador, like the statement of a lawyer, is not proof of anything. It is merely an assertion made by the representative of a sovereign as to the position taken by that sovereign in litigation."

Brief for Respondent 17 n. 8. In this case, unlike in The Navemar case, it is precisely the position of the foreign sovereign with respect to property in its possession that is significant.

[9] The appellation "Bernstein letter" stems from the case Bernstein v. N. V. Nederlandsche-Amerikaansche, 210 F.2d 375 (CA2 1954).

[10] It is noteworthy that, while the Department of State now takes the position that Sabbatino can be overruled without embarrassment to the conduct of foreign policy, the result in Sabbatino had been urged by the Solicitor General at the time. See Brief for United States as Amicus Curiae in Sabbatino, O.T. 1963, No. 16.

[11] See also R. Falk, The Role of Domestic Courts in the International Legal Order 9102 (1964); Henkin, Act of State Today: Recollections in Tranquility, 6 Col.J.Transnat'l L. 175, 178-180, 187-188 (1967).

[12] While Sabbatino found the act of state doctrine to reflect the "distribution of functions between the judicial and political branches of the Government," 376 U.S. at 376

U. S. 427-428, it has also been suggested that a doctrine of deference based upon the absence of consensus as to controlling principles of international law allocates legal competence among nations in a manner that promotes the growth of international law. See generally R. Falk, The Status of Law in International Society 403-442 (1970); R. Falk, The Role of Domestic Courts in the International Legal Order 64-138 (1964). Whether considerations of its contribution to the development of international law provide a basis for the act of state doctrine independent of the notion of separation of powers is a question that the Court has not addressed and that we need not consider. It is worth noting, however, that the Sabbatino Court was sensitive to the fact that a court's invalidation of a foreign sovereign's acts on the basis of principles of international law that are not the subject of "unambiguous agreement," 376 U.S. at 376 U. S. 428, is unlikely to be regarded as impartial. Id. at 376 U. S. 434-435. In the area of state responsibility for expropriations, the Court viewed the potential contribution of United States courts to the growth of international law as "highly conjectural," id. at 376 U. S. 434, and concluded that "progress toward the goal of establishing the rule of law among nations [is] best served by maintaining intact the act of state doctrine." Id. at 376 U. S. 437.

[13] At least one commentator has proposed discarding the doctrine of sovereign immunity (except with respect to diplomatic and military activity), while retaining the nonreviewability accorded by the act of state doctrine to official acts of a sovereign performed within its territory. R. Falk, The Role of Domestic Courts in the International Legal Order 139-145, 164-169 (1964).

[14] The precise contours of the restrictive theory of sovereign immunity, on which the commercial act exception is based, are themselves unclear. See, e.g., Victory Transport, Inc. v. Comisaria General, 336 F.2d 354, 359-360 (CA2 1964); Falk, The Immunity of Foreign Sovereigns in U.S. Courts -- Proposed Legislation, 6 N.Y.U.J. Int'l L. & Pol. 473, 477 (1973); Lauterpacht, The Problem of Jurisdictional Immunities of Foreign States, 28 Brit.Y.B. of Int'l L. 220, 222-226 (1951).

[15] The general observation that

"more discernible rules of international law have emerged with regard to the commercial dealings of private parties in the international market"

than with regard to "exercises of governmental powers," ante at 425 U. S. 704, does not, however, approach he finding of "unambiguous agreement regarding controlling legal principles" contemplated by Sabbatino. 376 U.S. at 376 U. S. 428.

[16] Quite apart from the significance that may be attached to the label, I find it difficult to accept MR. JUSTICE WHITE's characterization of the course of conduct involved here as "purely commercial."

[17] Under its view of the case as a run-of-the-mill commercial case, Dunhill does assert that the retention of the monies constitutes a discriminatory taking -- the notion evidently being that Cuba has not generally repudiated its commercial debts. Supplemental Brief for Petitioner 117. But there has been no claim that Cuba has retained

only those pre-intervention shipment payments made by United States citizens, or that the intervention program was in any other sense discriminatory.

[18] This was done by entry of judgment for the interventors against Dunhill for $93,000 and in favor of Dunhill against the interventors for $148,000.

[19] Whether Citibank's approval of a setoff is applicable to the facts of this litigation is questioned in the petition in Republic of Cuba v. Saks & Co., No. 73-1287.

[20] The bar of sovereign immunity, which yields to the extent of a counterclaim against a sovereign plaintiff and no further, National City Bank v. Republic of China, 348 U. S. 356 (1955), would be absolute quite apart from the availability of the act of state defense, unless the restrictive theory of sovereign immunity is followed and the case is considered purely commercial.

[21] When this case was initially briefed and argued, Dunhill attempted to distinguish an excessive counterclaim from a simple principal claim on the ground that the former was covered by the Bernstein letter in Citibank, in which the State Department advised the Court that foreign policy considerations did not require application of the act of state doctrine "to bar consideration of a defendant's counterclaim . . . in [that] or like cases." 406 U.S. at 406 U. S. 764. The letter in Citibank provided little support for Dunhill, since it contained several qualifications to its determination that the act of state doctrine need not be applied, one of which was that "the amount of the relief to be granted is limited to the amount of the foreign state's claim." Banco Nacional de Cuba v. First Nat. City Bank, 442 F.2d 530, 537 (CA2 1971). Since the State Department has now made known its view that the act of state doctrine need not be applied in this case, it is no longer necessary for Dunhill to rely on the letter in Citibank. But, as I have already noted, the significance of any views expressed by the State Department is minimal after Citibank.

[22] "[C]onsolidation is permitted as a matter of convenience and economy in administration, but does not merge the suits into a single cause, or change the rights of the parties, or make those who are parties in one suit parties in another."

Johnson v. Manhattan R. Co., 289 U. S. 479, 289 U. S. 496-497 (1933) (footnote omitted).

[23] See 9 C. Wright & A. Miller, Federal Practice and Procedure § 232, pp. 254-256 (1971).

[24] We are informed that the interventors had pending at least four other cases against tobacco importers in the District Court at the time the present cases were tried. See Brief for Respondents 26. The reason they were not consolidated with the present case is not a matter of record here.

[25] Title 31 CFR § 515.201(b) (1975) prohibits all transactions and transfers that "involve property in which [Cuba], or any national thereof, has at any time on or since [July 8, 1963] had any interest of any nature whatsoever, direct or indirect."

"Transfer" is defined to mean any act or transaction the purpose, intent, or effect of which is to "create, surrender, release, transfer, or alter, directly or indirectly, any right, remedy, power, privilege, or interest with respect to any property," including execution of a judgment. § 515.310. Property is defined to include a judgment. § 515.311. Discharge of a judgment debt on behalf of Cuba, even if by execution of a judgment against Cuba, would thus be prohibited.

[26] After certiorari was granted in this case, counsel for respondents corresponded with the Acting Director of the Office of Foreign Assets Control, stating:

"Dunhill had assumed that, if it secured a judgment against Cuba, it could execute that judgment against money owing to Cuba from other creditors and it had, in fact, attempted to attach funds owing to Cuba by Faber, Coe & Gregg, another cigar importer whose claim is likewise in litigation. . . ."

"It would be helpful if you would confirm my understanding that, generally speaking, you will not issue a license to permit a judgment creditor of Cuba to execute against assets of Cuba which have been frozen pursuant to the Foreign Assets Control regulations. . . ."

The Acting Director responded by a letter confirming this understanding of the licensing policy. Both letters appear in Brief for Respondents, App. B.

[27] Execution of an affirmative judgment would, of course, be barred whether the basis for that judgment was the presence of other parties with judgment debts to Cuba, the absence of a sovereign act, or the application of a commercial act exception to the act of state doctrine. The point is particularly appropriate, however, in response to the contention that the presence of other parties with judgment debts to Cuba justifies an affirmative judgment in this case; this contention proceeds on the assumption that the policies behind the act of state doctrine would otherwise bar affirmative recovery by Dunhill, and permits affirmative recovery only because of the purported unfairness that would result if Cuba's debt to Dunhill were not deducted from its recovery from the other importers. As has been shown, granting an affirmative judgment to Dunhill in this way would not affect the fairness of the disposition, since execution of the judgment would be barred by the Treasury Department's freezing of Cuban assets for the benefit of all American nationals with claims against Cuba.

Material evidence shouldn't be defined narrowly: Justice Marshall's dissent in United States v. Agurs (June 24, 1976)

MR. JUSTICE MARSHALL, with whom MR. JUSTICE BRENNAN joins, dissenting.

The Court today holds that the prosecutor's constitutional duty to provide exculpatory evidence to the defense is not limited to cases in which the defense makes a request for such evidence. But once having recognized the existence of a duty to volunteer exculpatory evidence, the Court so narrowly defines the category of "material" evidence embraced by the duty as to deprive it of all meaningful content.

In considering the appropriate standard of materiality governing the prosecutor's obligation to volunteer exculpatory evidence, the Court observes:

"[T]he fact that such evidence was available to the prosecutor and not submitted to the defense places it in a different category than if it had simply been discovered from a neutral source after trial. For that reason, the defendant should not have to satisfy the severe burden of demonstrating that newly discovered evidence probably would have resulted in acquittal [the standard generally applied to a motion under Fed.Rule Crim.Proc. 33 based on newly discovered evidence [1]]. If the standard applied to the usual motion for a new trial based on newly discovered evidence were the same when the evidence was in the State's possession as when it was found in a neutral source, there would be no special significance to the prosecutor's obligation to serve the cause of justice."

Ante at 427 U. S. 111 (footnote omitted). I agree completely.

The Court, however, seemingly forgets these precautionary words when it comes time to state the proper standard of materiality to be applied in cases involving neither the knowing use of perjury nor a specific defense request for an item of information. In such cases, the prosecutor commits constitutional error, the Court holds, "if the omitted evidence creates a reasonable doubt that did not otherwise exist." Ante at 427 U. S. 112. As the Court's subsequent discussion makes clear, the defendant challenging the prosecutor's failure to disclose evidence is entitled to relief, in the Court's view, only if the withheld evidence actually creates a reasonable doubt as to guilt in the judge's mind. The burden thus imposed on the defendant is at least as "severe" as, if not more "severe" than, [2] the burden he generally faces on a Rule 33 motion. Surely if a judge is able to say that evidence actually creates a reasonable doubt as to guilt in his mind (the Court's standard), he would also conclude that the evidence "probably would have resulted in acquittal" (the general Rule 33 standard). In short, in spite of its own salutary precaution, the Court treats the case in which the prosecutor withholds evidence no differently from the case in which evidence is newly discovered from a neutral source. The "prosecutor's obligation to serve the cause of justice" is reduced to a status, to borrow the Court's words, of "no special significance." Ante at 427 U. S. 111.

Our overriding concern in cases such as the one before us is the defendant's right to a fair trial. One of the most basic elements of fairness in a criminal trial is that available evidence tending to show innocence, as well as that tending to show guilt, be fully aired before the jury; more particularly, it is that the State in its zeal to convict a defendant not suppress evidence that might exonerate him. See Moore v. Illinois, 408 U. S. 786, 408 U. S. 810 (1972) (opinion of MARSHALL, J.). This fundamental notion of fairness does not pose any irreconcilable conflict for the prosecutor, for as the Court reminds us, the prosecutor "must always be faithful to his client's overriding interest that justice shall be done.'" Ante at 427 U. S. 111. No interest of the State is served, and no duty of the prosecutor advanced, by the suppression of evidence favorable to the defendant. On the contrary, the prosecutor fulfills his most basic responsibility when he fully airs all the relevant evidence at his command.

I recognize, of course, that the exculpatory value to the defense of an item of information will often not be apparent to the prosecutor in advance of trial. And while the general obligation to disclose exculpatory information no doubt continues during the trial, giving rise to a duty to disclose information whose significance becomes apparent as the case progresses, even a conscientious prosecutor will fail to appreciate the significance of some items of information. See United States v. Keogh, 391 F.2d 138, 147 (CA2 1968). I agree with the Court that these considerations, as well as the general interest in finality of judgments, preclude the granting of a new trial in every case in which the prosecutor has failed to disclose evidence of some value to the defense. But surely these considerations do not require the rigid rule the Court intends to be applied to all but a relatively small number of such cases.

Under today's ruling, if the prosecution has not made knowing use of perjury, and if the defense has not made a specific request for an item of information, the defendant is entitled to a new trial only if the withheld evidence actually creates a reasonable doubt as to guilt in the judge's mind. With all respect, this rule is completely at odds with the overriding interest in assuring that evidence tending to show innocence is brought to the jury's attention. The rule creates little, if any, incentive for the prosecutor conscientiously to determine whether his files contain evidence helpful to the defense. Indeed, the rule reinforces the natural tendency of the prosecutor to overlook evidence favorable to the defense, and creates an incentive for the prosecutor to resolve close questions of disclosure in favor of concealment.

More fundamentally, the Court's rule usurps the function of the jury as the trier of fact in a criminal case. The Court's rule explicitly establishes the judge as the trier of fact with respect to evidence withheld by the prosecution. The defendant's fate is sealed so long as the evidence does not create a reasonable doubt as to guilt in the judge's mind, regardless of whether the evidence is such that reasonable men could disagree as to its import -- regardless, in other words, of how "close" the case may be. [3]

The Court asserts that this harsh standard of materiality is the standard that "courts appear to have applied in actual cases although the standard has been phrased in different language." Ante at 427 U. S. 113 (footnote omitted). There is no basis for this assertion. None of the cases cited by the Court in support of its statement suggests that a judgment of conviction should be sustained so long as the judge remains convinced beyond a reasonable doubt of the defendant's guilt. [4] The prevailing view in the federal courts of the standard of materiality for cases involving neither a specific request for information nor other indications of deliberate misconduct -- a standard with which the cases cited by the Court are fully consistent -- is quite different. It is essentially the following: if there is a significant chance that the withheld evidence, developed by skilled counsel, would have induced a reasonable doubt in the minds of enough jurors to avoid a conviction, then the judgment of conviction must be set aside. [5] This standard, unlike the Court's, reflects a recognition that the determination must be in terms of the impact of an item of evidence on the jury, and that this determination cannot always be made with certainty. [6]

The Court approves -- but only for a limited category of cases -- a standard virtually identical to the one I have described as reflecting the prevailing view. In cases in which

"the undisclosed evidence demonstrates that the prosecution's case includes perjured testimony and that the prosecution knew, or should have known, of the perjury,"

ante at 427 U. S. 103, the judgment of conviction must be set aside "if there is any reasonable likelihood that the false testimony could have affected the judgment of the jury." Ibid. This lesser burden on the defendant is appropriate, the Court states, primarily because the withholding of evidence contradicting testimony offered by witnesses called by the prosecution "involve[s] a corruption of the truth-seeking function of the trial process." Ante at 427 U. S. 104. But surely the truth-seeking process is corrupted by the withholding of evidence favorable to the defense, regardless of whether the evidence is directly contradictory to evidence offered by the prosecution. An example offered by Mr. Justice Fortas serves to illustrate the point.

"[L]et us assume that the State possesses information that blood was found on the victim, and that this blood is of a type which does not match that of the accused or of the victim. Let us assume that no related testimony was offered by the State."

Giles v. Maryland, 386 U. S. 66, 386 U. S. 100 (1967) (concurring in judgment). The suppression of the information unquestionably corrupts the truthseeking process, and the burden on the defendant in establishing his entitlement to a new trial ought be no different from the burden he would face if related testimony had been elicited by the prosecution. See id. at 386 U. S. 99-101.

The Court derives its "reasonable likelihood" standard for cases involving perjury from cases such as Napue v. Illinois, 360 U. S. 264 (1959), and Giglio v. United States, 405 U. S. 150 (1972). But surely the results in those cases, and the standards applied, would have been no different if perjury had not been involved. In Napue and Giglio, coconspirators testifying against the defendants testified falsely, in response to questioning by defense counsel, that they had not received promises from the prosecution. The prosecution failed to disclose that promises had, in fact, been made. The corruption of the truthseeking process stemmed from the suppression of evidence affecting the overall credibility of the witnesses, see Napue, supra at 360 U. S. 269; Giglio, supra at 405 U. S. 154, and that corruption would have been present whether or not defense counsel had elicited statements from the witnesses denying that promises had been made.

It may be that, contrary to the Court's insistence, its treatment of perjury cases reflects simply a desire to deter deliberate prosecutorial misconduct. But if that were the case, we might reasonably expect a rule imposing a lower threshold of materiality than the Court imposes -- perhaps a harmless error standard. And we would certainly expect the rule to apply to a broader category of misconduct than the failure to disclose evidence that contradicts testimony offered by witnesses called by the prosecution. For the prosecutor is guilty of misconduct when he deliberately suppresses evidence that is clearly relevant and favorable to the defense, regardless, once again, of whether the evidence relates directly to testimony given in the course of the Government's case.

This case, however, does not involve deliberate prosecutorial misconduct. Leaving open the question whether a different rule might appropriately be applied in cases involving deliberate misconduct, [7] I would hold that the defendant in this case had the burden of demonstrating that there is a significant chance that the withheld evidence, developed by skilled counsel, would have induced a reasonable doubt in the minds of enough jurors to avoid a conviction. This is essentially the standard applied by the Court of Appeals, and I would affirm its judgment.

Notes

[1] The burden generally imposed upon such a motion has also been described as a burden of demonstrating that the newly discovered evidence would probably produce a different verdict in the event of a retrial. See, e.g., United States v. Kahn, 472 F.2d 272, 287 (CA2 1973); United States v. Rodriguez, 437 F.2d 940, 912 (CA5 1971); United States v. Curran, 465 F.2d 260, 264 (CA7 1972).

[2] See United States v. Keogh, 391 F.2d 138, 148 (CA2 1968), in which Judge Friendly implies that the standard the Court adopts is more severe than the standard the Court rejects.

[3] To emphasize the harshness of the Court's rule, the defendant's fate is determined finally by the judge only if the judge does not entertain a reasonable doubt as to guilt. If evidence withheld by the prosecution does create a reasonable doubt as to guilt in the judge's mind, that does not end the case -- rather, the defendant (one might more accurately say the prosecution) is "entitled" to have the case decided by a jury.

[4] In Stout v. Cupp, 426 F.2d 881 (CA9 1970), a habeas proceeding, the court simply quoted the District Court's finding that, if the suppressed evidence had been introduced, "the jury would not have reached a different result." Id. at 883. There is no indication that the quoted language was intended as anything more than a finding of fact, which would, quite obviously, dispose of the defendant's claim under any standard that might be suggested. In Peterson v. United States, 411 F.2d. 1074 (CA8 1969), the court appeared to require a showing that the withheld evidence "was material' and would have aided the defense." Id. at 1079. The court in Lessard v. Dickson, 394 F.2d 88 (CA9 1968), found it determinative that the withheld evidence "could hardly be regarded as being able to have much force against the inexorable array of incriminating circumstances with which [the defendant] was surrounded." Id. at 91. The jury, the court noted, would not have been "likely to have had any [difficulty]" with the argument defense counsel would have made with the withheld evidence. Id. at 92. Finally, United States v. Tomaiolo, 378 F.2d 26 (CA2 1967), required the defendant to show that the evidence was "material and of some substantial use to the defendant." Id. at 28.

[5] See, e.g., United States v. Morell, 524 F.2d 550, 553 (CA2 1975); Oden v. Wolff, 522 F.2d 816, 822 (CA8 1975); Woodcock v. Amaral, 511 F.2d 985, 991 (CA1 1974); United States v. Miller, 499 F.2d 736, 744 (CA10 1974); Shuler v. Wainwright, 491 F.2d 1213, 1223 (CA5 1974); United States v. Kahn, 472 F.2d at 287; Clarke v. Burke, 440 F.2d 853, 855 (CA7 1971); Hamric v. Bailey, 386 F.2d 390, 393 (CA4 1967).

[6] That there is a significant difference between the Court's standards and what has been described as the prevailing view is made clear by Judge Friendly, writing for the court in United States v. Miller, 411 F.2d 825 (CA2 1969). After stating the court's conclusion that a new trial was required because of the Government's failure to disclose to the defense the pretrial hypnosis of its principal witness, Judge Friendly observed:

"We have reached this conclusion with some reluctance, particularly in light of the considered belief of the able and conscientious district judge, who has lived with this case for years, that review of the record in light of all the defense new trial motions left him 'convinced of the correctness of the jury's verdict.' We, who also have had no small exposure to the facts, are by no means convinced otherwise. The test, however, is not how the newly discovered evidence concerning the hypnosis would affect the trial judge or ourselves but whether, with the Government's case against [the defendant] already subject to serious attack, there was a significant chance that this added item, developed by skilled counsel as it would have been, could have induced a reasonable doubt in the minds of enough jurors to avoid a conviction. We cannot conscientiously say there was not."

Id. at 832 (footnote omitted).

[7] It is the presence of deliberate prosecutorial misconduct and a desire to deter such misconduct, presumably, that leads the Court to recognize a rule more readily permitting new trials in cases involving a specific defense request for information. The significance of the defense request, the Court states, is simply that it gives the prosecutor notice of what is important to the defense; once such notice is received, the failure to disclose is "seldom, if ever, excusable." Ante at 427 U. S. 106. It would seem to follow that, if an item of information is of such obvious importance to the defense that it could not have escaped the prosecutor's attention, its suppression should be treated in the same manner as if there had been a specific request. This is precisely the approach taken by some courts. See, e.g., United States v. Morell, 524 F.2d at 553; United States v. Miller, 499 F.2d at 744; United States v. Kahn, 472 F.2d at 287; United States v. Keogh, 391 F.2d at 146-147.

Shouldn't have to retire at 50: Justice Marshall's dissent in Massachusetts Board of Retirement v. Murgia (June 25, 1976)

MR. JUSTICE MARSHALL, dissenting.

Today the Court holds that it is permissible for the Commonwealth of

Massachusetts to declare that members of its state police force who have been proved medically fit for service are nonetheless legislatively unfit to be policemen and must be terminated -- involuntarily "retired" -- because they have reached the age of 50. Although we have called the right to work "of the very essence of the personal freedom and opportunity that it was the purpose of the [Fourteenth] Amendment to secure," Truax v. Raich, 239 U. S. 33, 239 U. S. 41 (1915), the Court finds that the right to work is not a fundamental right. And, while agreeing that "the treatment of the aged in this Nation has not been wholly free of discrimination," ante at 427 U. S. 313, the Court holds that the elderly are not a suspect class. Accordingly, the Court undertakes the scrutiny mandated by the bottom tier of its two-tier equal protection framework, finds the challenged legislation not to be "wholly unrelated" to its objective, and holds, therefore, that it survives equal protection attack. I respectfully dissent.

I

Although there are signs that its grasp on the law is weakening, the rigid two-tier model still holds sway as the Court's articulated description of the equal protection test. Again, I must object to its perpetuation. The model's two fixed modes of analysis, strict scrutiny and mere rationality, simply do not describe the inquiry the Court has undertaken -- or should undertake in equal protection cases. Rather, the inquiry has been much more sophisticated, and the Court should admit as much. It has focused upon the character of the classification in question, the relative importance to individuals in the class discriminated against of the governmental benefits that they do not receive, and the state interests asserted in support of the classification. Marshall v. United States, 414 U. S. 417, 414 U. S. 432-433 (1974) (MARSHALL, J., dissenting); San Antonio School District v. Rodriguez, 411 U. S. 1, 411 U. S. 98-110 (1973) (MARSHALL, J., dissenting); Richardson v. Belcher, 404 U. S. 78, 404 U. S. 90-91 (1971) (MARSHALL, J., dissenting); Dandridge v. Williams, 397 U. S. 471, 397 U. S. 519-530 (1970) (MARSHALL, J., dissenting). See also City of Charlotte v. Firefighters, 426 U. S. 283, 426 U. S. 286 (1976); Memorial Hospital v. Maricopa County, 415 U. S. 250, 415 U. S. 253-254 (1974); Dunn v. Blumstein, 405 U. S. 330, 405 U. S. 335 (1972); Kramer v. Union School Dist., 395 U. S. 621, 395 U. S. 626 (1969); Williams v. Rhodes, 393 U. S. 23, 393 U. S. 30 (1968).

Although the Court outwardly adheres to the two-tier model, it has apparently lost interest in recognizing further "fundamental" rights and "suspect" classes. See San Antonio School District v. Rodriguez, supra, (rejecting education as a fundamental right); Frontiero v. Richardson, 411 U. S. 677 (1973) (declining to treat women as a suspect class). In my view, this result is the natural consequence of the limitations of the Court's traditional equal protection analysis. If a statute invades a "fundamental" right or discriminates against a "suspect" class, it is subject to strict scrutiny. If a statute is subject to strict scrutiny, the statute always, or nearly always, see Korematsu v. United States, 323 U. S. 214 (1944), is struck down. Quite obviously, the only critical decision is whether strict scrutiny should be invoked at all. It should be no surprise, then, that the Court is hesitant to expand the number of categories of rights and classes subject to strict scrutiny, when each expansion involves the invalidation of virtually every classification bearing upon a newly covered category. [1]

But however understandable the Court's hesitancy to invoke strict scrutiny, all remaining legislation should not drop into the bottom tier, and be measured by the mere rationality test. For that test, too, when applied as articulated, leaves little doubt about the outcome; the challenged legislation is always upheld. See New Orleans v. Dukes, ante p. 427 U. S. 297 (overruling Morey v. Doud, 354 U. S. 457 (1957), the only modern case in which this Court has struck down an economic classification as irrational). It cannot be gainsaid that there remain rights, not now classified as "fundamental," that remain vital to the flourishing of a free society, and classes, not now classified as "suspect," that are unfairly burdened by invidious discrimination unrelated to the individual worth of their members. Whatever we call these rights and classes, we simply cannot forgo all judicial protection against discriminatory legislation bearing upon them, but for the rare instances when the legislative choice can be termed "wholly irrelevant" to the legislative goal. McGowan v. Maryland, 366 U. S. 420, 366 U. S. 425 (1961).

While the Court's traditional articulation of the rational basis test does suggest just such an abdication, happily, the Court's deeds have not matched its words. Time and again, met with cases touching upon the prized rights and burdened classes of our society, the Court has acted only after a reasonably probing look at the legislative goals and means, and at the significance of the personal rights and interests invaded. Stanton v. Stanton, 421 U. S. 7 (1975); Weinberger v. Wiesenfeld, 420 U. S. 636 (1975); United States Dept. of Agriculture v. Moreno, 413 U. S. 528 (1973); Frontiero v. Richardson, 411 U. S. at 411 U. S. 691 (POWELL, J., concurring in judgment); James v. Strange, 407 U. S. 128 (1972); Weber v. Aetna Casualty & Surety Co., 406 U. S. 164 (1972); Eisenstadt v. Baird, 405 U. S. 438 (1972); Reed v. Reed, 404 U. S. 71 (1971). See San Antonio School District v. Rodriguez, supra at 411 U. S. 98-110 (MARSHALL, J., dissenting). [2]

These cases make clear that the Court has rejected, albeit sub silentio, its most deferential statements of the rationality standard in assessing the validity under the Equal Protection Clause of much noneconomic legislation.

But there are problems with deciding cases based on factors not encompassed by the applicable standards. First, the approach is rudderless, affording no notice to interested parties of the standards governing particular cases and giving no firm guidance to judges who, as a consequence, must assess the constitutionality of legislation before them on an ad hoc basis. Second, and not unrelatedly, the approach is unpredictable and requires holding this Court to standards it has never publicly adopted. Thus, the approach presents the danger that, as I suggest has happened here, relevant factors will be misapplied or ignored. All interests not "fundamental" and all classes not "suspect" are not the same; and it is time for the Court to drop the pretense that, for purposes of the Equal Protection Clause, they are.

II

The danger of the Court's verbal adherence to the rigid two-tier test, despite its effective repudiation of that test in the cases, is demonstrated by its efforts here. There is simply no reason why a statute that tells able-bodied police officers, ready and willing to work, that they no longer have the right to earn a living in their chosen profession merely because they are 50 years old should be judged by the same minimal standards of rationality that we use to test economic legislation that discriminates against business interests. See New Orleans v. Dukes, supra; Williamson v. Lee Optical Co., 348 U. S. 483 (1955). Yet, the Court today not only invokes the minimal level of scrutiny, it wrongly adheres to it. Analysis of the three factors I have identified above -- the importance of the governmental benefits denied, the character of the class, and the asserted state interests -- demonstrates the Court's error.

Whether "fundamental" or not, "the right of the individual . . . to engage in any of the common occupations of life'" has been repeatedly recognized by this Court as falling within the concept of liberty guaranteed by the Fourteenth Amendment. Board of Regents v. Roth, 408 U. S. 564, 408 U. S. 572 (1972), quoting Meyer v. Nebraska, 262 U. S. 390, 262 U. S. 399 (1923). As long ago as Butchers' Union Co. v. Crescent City Co., 111 U. S. 746 (1884), Mr. Justice Bradley wrote that this right

"is an inalienable right; it was formulated as such under the phrase 'pursuit of happiness' in the Declaration of Independence. . . . This right is a large ingredient in the civil liberty of the citizen."

Id. at 111 U. S. 762 (concurring opinion). And in Smith v. Texas, 233 U. S. 630 (1914), in invalidating a law that criminally penalized anyone who served as a freight train conductor without having previously served as a brakeman, and that thereby excluded numerous equally qualified employees from that position, the Court recognized that "all men are entitled to the equal protection of the law in their right to work for the support of themselves and families." Id. at 233 U. S. 641.

"Insofar as a man is deprived of the right to labor his liberty is restricted, his capacity to earn wages and acquire property is lessened, and he is denied the protection which the law affords those who are permitted to work. Liberty means more than freedom from servitude, and the constitutional guarantee is an assurance that the citizen shall be protected in the right to use his powers of mind and body in any lawful calling."

Id. at 233 U. S. 636. See also Arnett v. Kennedy, 416 U. S. 134 (1974); Perry v. Sindermann, 408 U. S. 593 (1972); Bell v. Burson, 402 U.S. 535 (1971); Keyshian v. Board of Regents, 385 U. S. 589, 385 U. S. 605-606 (1967); Schware v. Board of Bar Examiners, 353 U. S. 232, 353 U. S. 238-239 (1957); Slochower v. Board of Higher Education, 350 U. S. 551 (1956); Wieman v. Upderaff, 344 U. S. 183 (1952); Truax v. Raich, 239 U.S. at 239 U. S. 41. Even if the right to earn a living does not include the right to work for the government, [3] it is settled that, because of the importance of the interest involved, we have always carefully looked at the reasons asserted for depriving a government employee of his job.

While depriving any government employee of his job is a significant deprivation, it is particularly burdensome when the person deprived is an older citizen. Once terminated, the elderly cannot readily find alternative employment. The lack of work is not only economically damaging, but emotionally and physically draining. Deprived of his status in the community and of the opportunity for meaningful activity, fearful of becoming dependent on others for his support, and lonely in his new-found isolation, the involuntarily retired person is susceptible to physical and emotional ailments as a direct consequence of his enforced idleness. Ample clinical evidence supports the conclusion that mandatory retirement poses a direct threat to the health and life expectancy of the retired person, [4] and these consequences of termination for age are not disputed by appellants.

Thus, an older person deprived of his job by the government loses not only his right to earn a living, but, too often, his health as well, in sad contradiction of Browning's promise: "The best is yet to be,/The last of life, for which the first was made." [5]

Not only are the elderly denied important benefits when they are terminated on the basis of age, but the classification of older workers is itself one that merits judicial attention. Whether older workers constitute a "suspect" class or not, it cannot be disputed that they constitute a class subject to repeated and arbitrary discrimination in employment. See United States Department of Labor, The Older American Worker: Age Discrimination in Employment (1965); M. Barron, The Aging American 55-68 (1961). As Congress found in passing the Age Discrimination in Employment Act of 1967:

"[I]n the face of rising productivity and affluence, older workers find themselves disadvantaged in their efforts to retain employment, and especially to regain employment when displaced from jobs[.]"

"[T]he setting of arbitrary age limits regardless of potential for job performance has become a common practice, and certain otherwise desirable practices may work to the disadvantage of older persons[.]"

"[T]he incidence of unemployment, especially long-term unemployment with resultant deterioration of skill, morale, and employer acceptability is, relative to the younger ages, high among older workers; their numbers are great and growing; and their employment problems grave[.]"

81 Stat. 602, 29 U.S.C. § 621(a) (subsection numbers omitted). See also ante at 317 n. 11.

Of course, the Court is quite right in suggesting that distinctions exist between the elderly and traditional suspect classes such as Negroes, and between the elderly and "quasi-suspect" classes such as women or illegitimates. The elderly are protected not only by certain anti-discrimination legislation, but by legislation that provides them with positive benefits not enjoyed by the public at large. Moreover, the elderly are not isolated in society, and discrimination against them is not pervasive but is centered primarily in employment. The advantage of a flexible equal protection standard, however, is that it can readily accommodate such variables. The elderly are undoubtedly discriminated against, and when legislation denies them an important benefit -- employment -- I conclude that, to sustain the legislation, appellants must show a reasonably substantial interest and a scheme reasonably closely tailored to achieving that interest. Cf. San Antonio School District v. Rodriguez, 411 U.S. at 411 U. S. 124-126 (MARSHALL, J., dissenting). This inquiry, ultimately, is not markedly different from that undertaken by the Court in Reed v. Reed, 404 U. S. 71 (1971).

Turning, then, to appellants' arguments, I agree that the purpose of the mandatory retirement law is legitimate, and indeed compelling. The Commonwealth has every reason to assure that its state police officers are of sufficient physical strength and health to perform their jobs. In my view, however, the means chosen, the forced retirement of officers at age 50, is so overinclusive that it must fall.

All potential officers must pass a rigorous physical examination. Until age 40, this same examination must be passed every two years -- when the officer reenlists -- and, after age 40, every year. Appellants have conceded that

"[w]hen a member passes his reenlistment or annual physical, he is found to be qualified to perform all of the duties of the Uniformed Branch of the Massachusetts State Police."

App. 43. See id. at 52. If a member fails the examination, he is immediately terminated or refused reenlistment. Thus, the only members of the state police still on the force at age 50 are those who have been determined -- repeatedly -- by the Commonwealth to be physically fit for the job. Yet all of these physically fit officers are automatically terminated at age 50. Appellants do not seriously assert that their testing is no longer effective at age 50, [6] nor do they claim that continued testing would serve no purpose because officers over 50 are no longer physically able to perform their jobs. [7] Thus, the Commonwealth is in the position of already individually testing its police officers for physical fitness, conceding that such testing is adequate to determine the physical ability of an officer to continue on the job, and conceding that that ability may continue after age 50. In these circumstances, I see no reason at all for automatically terminating those officers who reach the age of 50; indeed, that action seems the height of irrationality.

Accordingly, I conclude that the Commonwealth's mandatory retirement law cannot stand when measured against the significant deprivation the Commonwealth's action works upon the terminated employees. I would affirm the judgment of the District Court. [8]

Notes

[1] Some classifications are so invidious that they should be struck down automatically absent the most compelling state interest, and by suggesting the limitations of strict scrutiny analysis I do not mean to imply otherwise. The analysis should be accomplished, however, not by stratified notions of "suspect" classes and "fundamental" rights, but by individualized assessments of the particular classes and rights involved in each case. Of course, the traditional suspect classes and fundamental rights would still rank at the top of the list of protected categories, so that in cases involving those

categories analysis would be functionally equivalent to strict scrutiny. Thus, the advantages of the approach I favor do not appear in such cases, but rather emerge in those dealing with traditionally less protected classes and rights. See infra at 427 U. S. 321-327.

[2] See also Gunther, The Supreme Court, 1971 Term, Foreword: In Search of Evolving Doctrine on a Changing Court: A Model for a Newer Equal Protection, 86 Harv.L.Rev. 1 (1972).

[3] See Board of Regents v. Roth, 408 U. S. 564, 408 U. S. 587 (1972) (MARSHALL, J., dissenting). Appellee makes no such claim; nor does he allege that procedural due process requires that he be afforded a hearing prior to termination.

[4] See American Medical Association, Committee on Aging, Retirement, A Medical Philosophy and Approach; M. Barron, The Aging American 76-86, and sources cited (1961). Because, as one former AMA president bluntly put it, "[d]eath comes at retirement," quoted in M. Barron, id. at 76, the AMA has formally taken a position against involuntary retirement and has submitted an amicus brief in this case to inform us of the medical consequences of the practice.

[5] R. Browning, Rabbi Ben Ezra, stanza 1.

[6] There may be an age at which passing a physical examination provides no substantial guarantee that the officer is fit for service for the coming year. In that case, the test has lost its predictive ability. There is no showing that age 50 marks such a line -- although appellants ask us to hypothesize that it does -- and indeed the evidence seems contrary to that supposition. First, among officers aged 40-49, who undergo yearly examinations, there is no general trend of increasing rejections with age, nor any suggestion that those who passed the examination served in less than a satisfactory manner. 376 F.Supp. 753, 756 (Mass.1974).

This evidence presents no reason to assume that testing suddenly loses its predictive ability after age 50. The only relevant studies presented are contrary to appellants' assumption. These studies support the conclusion that airline pilots should be terminated at age 60 because, after that age, medical examinations lose their predictive ability. See Air Line Pilots Assn., Int'l v. Quesada, 276 F.2d 892 (CA2 1960).

The suggestion that age 50 is not the critical point for predictive ability is also supported by the national experience. Appellee has produced a study of the laws of the 50 States that shows that Massachusetts' age-50 retirement law prescribes the earliest retirement age in the Nation, and that no other State requires its state police to retire before age 55. Brief for Appellee 37 n. 14.

In short, I refuse to hypothesize that testing after age 50 loses its predictive ability when the appellants have introduced absolutely nothing that supports this position.

[7] Indeed, the appellants have conceded that

"[a]ny individual member of the Uniformed Branch . . . whose age is fifty years or more may be capable of performing the physical activity required of the Uniformed

Branch . . . depending upon his individual physical condition."

App. 44. See id. at 52.

[8] The Court's conclusion today does not imply that all mandatory retirement laws are constitutionally valid. Here the primary state interest is in maintaining a physically fit police force, not a mentally alert or manually dexterous workforce. That the Court concludes it is rational to legislate on the assumption that physical strength and wellbeing decrease significantly with age does not imply that it will reach the same conclusion with respect to legislation based on assumptions about mental or manual ability. Accordingly, a mandatory retirement law for all government employees would stand in a posture different from the law before us today.

Shouldn't inventory contents of car to be impounded without warrant: Justice Marshall's dissent in South Dakota v. Opperman (July 6, 1976)

MR. JUSTICE MARSHALL, with whom MR. JUSTICE BRENNAN and MR. JUSTICE STEWART join, dissenting.

The Court today holds that the Fourth Amendment permits a routine police inventory search of the closed glove compartment of a locked automobile impounded for ordinary traffic violations. Under the Court's holding, such a search may be made without attempting to secure the consent of the owner and without any particular reason to believe the impounded automobile contains contraband, evidence, or valuables, or presents any danger to its custodians or the public. [1] Because I believe this holding to be contrary to sound elaboration of established Fourth Amendment principles, I dissent.

As MR. JUSTICE POWELL recognizes, the requirement of a warrant aside, resolution of the question whether an inventory search of closed compartments inside a locked automobile can ever be justified as a constitutionally "reasonable" search [2] depends upon a reconciliation of the owner's constitutionally protected privacy interests against governmental intrusion, and legitimate governmental interests furthered by securing the car and its contents. Terry v. Ohio, 392 U. S. 1, 392 U. S. 20-21 (1968); Camara v. Municipal Court, 387 U. S. 523, 387 U. S. 534-535, 387 U. S. 536-537 (1967). The Court fails clearly to articulate the reasons for its reconciliation of these interests in this case, but it is at least clear to me that the considerations alluded to by the Court, and further discussed by MR. JUSTICE POWELL, are insufficient to justify the Court's result in this case.

To begin with, the Court appears to suggest by reference to a "diminished" expectation of privacy, ante at 428 U. S. 368, that a person's constitutional interest in protecting the integrity of closed compartments of his locked automobile may routinely be sacrificed to governmental interests requiring interference with that privacy that are less compelling than would be necessary to justify a search of similar scope of the person's home or office. This has never been the law. The Court correctly observes that some prior cases have drawn distinctions between automobiles and homes or offices in Fourth Amendment cases; but even as the Court's discussion makes clear, the reasons for distinction in those cases are not present here. Thus, Chambers v. Maroney, 399 U. S. 42 (1970), and Carroll v. United States, 267 U. S. 132 (1925), permitted certain probable cause searches to be carried out without warrants in view of the exigencies created by the mobility of automobiles, but both decisions reaffirmed that the standard of probable cause necessary to authorize such a search was no less than the standard applicable to search of a home or office. Chambers, supra at 399 U. S. 51; Carroll, supra at 267 U. S. 155-156. [3] In other contexts, the Court has recognized that automobile travel sacrifices some privacy interests to the publicity of plain view, e.g., Cardwell v. Lewis, 417 U. S. 583, 417 U. S. 590 (1974) (plurality opinion); cf. Harris v. United States, 390 U. S. 234 (1968). But this recognition, too, is inapposite here, for there is no question of plain view in this case. [4] Nor does this case concern intrusions of the scope that the Court apparently assumes would ordinarily be permissible in order to insure the running safety of a car. While it may be that privacy expectations associated with automobile travel are in some regards less than those associated with a home or office, see United States v. Martinez-Fuerte, post at 428 U. S. 561-52, it is equally clear that "[t]he word automobile' is not a talisman in whose presence the Fourth Amendment fades away . . .," Coolidge v. New Hampshire, 403 U. S. 443, 403 U. S. 461 (1971). [5] Thus, we have recognized that "[a] search, even of an automobile, is a substantial invasion of privacy," United States v. Ortiz, 422 U. S. 891, 422 U. S. 896 (1975) (emphasis added), and, accordingly, our cases have consistently recognized that the nature and substantiality of interest required to justify a search of private areas of an automobile is no less than that necessary to justify an intrusion of similar scope into a home or office. See, e.g., United States v. Ortiz, supra; Almeida-Sanchez v. United States, 413 U. S. 266, 413 U. S. 269-270 (1973); Coolidge, supra; Dyke v. Taylor Implement Mfg. Co., 391 U. S. 216, 391 U. S. 221-222 (1968); Preston v. United States, 376 U. S. 364 (1964). [6]

The Court's opinion appears to suggest that its result may, in any event, be justified because the inventory search procedure is a "reasonable" response to

"three distinct needs: the protection of the owner's property while it remains in police custody . . .; the protection of the police against claims or disputes over lost or stolen property . . .; and the protection of the police from potential danger."

Ante at 428 U. S. 369. [7] This suggestion is flagrantly misleading, however, because the record of this case explicitly belies any relevance of the last two concerns. In any event, it is my view that none of these "needs," separately or together, can suffice to justify the inventory search procedure approved by the Court.

First, this search cannot be justified in any way as a safety measure, for -- though the Court ignores it -- the sole purpose given by the State for the Vermillion police's inventory procedure was to secure valuables, Record 75, 98. Nor is there any indication that the officer's search in this case was tailored in any way to safety concerns, or that ordinarily it is so circumscribed. Even aside from the actual basis for the police practice in this case, however, I do not believe that any blanket safety argument could justify a program of routine searches of the scope permitted here. As MR. JUSTICE POWELL recognizes, ordinarily "there is little danger associated with impounding unsearched automobiles," ante at 428 U. S. 378. [8] Thus, while the safety rationale may not be entirely discounted when it is actually relied upon, it surely cannot justify the search of every car upon the basis of undifferentiated possibility of harm; on the contrary, such an intrusion could ordinarily be justified only in those individual cases where the officer's inspection was prompted by specific circumstances indicating the possibility of a particular danger. See Terry v. Ohio, 392 U.S. at 392 U. S. 21, 392 U. S. 27; cf. Cady v. Dombrowski, 413 U. S. 433, 413 U. S. 448 (1973)

Second, the Court suggests that the search for valuables in the closed glove compartment might be justified as a measure to protect the police against lost property claims. Again, this suggestion is belied by the record, since -- although the Court declines to discuss it -- the South Dakota Supreme Court's interpretation of state law explicitly absolves the police, as "gratuitous depositors," from any obligation beyond inventorying objects in plain view and locking the car. 89 S.D. ____, 228 N.W.2d 152, 159 (1975). [9] Moreover, as MR. JUSTICE POWELL notes, ante at 428 U. S. 378-379, it may well be doubted that an inventory procedure would, in any event, work significantly to minimize the frustrations of false claims. [10]

Finally, the Court suggests that the public interest in protecting valuables that may be found inside a closed compartment of an impounded car may justify the inventory procedure. I recognize the genuineness of this governmental interest in protecting property from pilferage. But even if I assume that the posting of a guard would be fiscally impossible as an alternative means to the same protective end, [11] I cannot agree with the Court's conclusion. The Court's result authorizes -- indeed it appears to require -- the routine search of nearly every [12] car impounded. [13] In my view, the Constitution does not permit such searches as a matter of routine; absent specific consent, such a search is permissible only in exceptional circumstances of particular necessity.

It is at least clear that any owner might prohibit the police from executing a protective search of his impounded car, since, by hypothesis, the inventory is conducted for the owner's benefit. Moreover, it is obvious that not everyone whose car is impounded would want it to be searched. Respondent himself proves this; but one need not carry contraband to prefer that the police not examine one's private possessions. Indeed, that preference is the premise of the Fourth Amendment. Nevertheless, according to the Court's result, the law may presume that each owner in respondent's position consents to the search. I cannot agree. In my view, the Court's approach is squarely contrary to the law of consent; [14] it ignores the duty, in the absence of consent, to analyze in each individual case whether there is a need to search a particular car for the protection of its owner which is sufficient to outweigh the particular invasion. It is clear to me under established principles that, in order to override the absence of explicit consent, such a search must at least be conditioned upon the fulfillment of two requirements. [15] First, there must be specific cause to believe that a search of the scope to be undertaken is necessary in order to preserve the integrity of particular valuable property threatened by the impoundment:

"[I]n justifying the particular intrusion, the police officer must be able to point to specific and articulable facts which . . reasonably warrant that intrusion."

Terry v. Ohio, 392 U.S. at 392 U. S. 21. Such a requirement of

"specificity in the information upon which police action is predicated is the central teaching of this Court's Fourth Amendment jurisprudence,"

id. at 392 U. S. 21 n. 18, for

"[t]he basic purpose of this Amendment, as recognized in countless decisions of this Court, is to safeguard the privacy and security of individuals against arbitrary invasions by governmental officials."

Camara v. Municipal Court, 387 U.S. at 387 U. S. 528. Cf. United States v. Brignoni-Ponce, 422 U. S. 873, 422 U. S. 883-884 (1975); Cady v. Dombrowski, 413 U.S. at 413 U. S. 448; Terry v. Ohio, supra at 392 U. S. 27. Second, even where a search might be appropriate, such an intrusion may only follow the exhaustion and failure of reasonable efforts under the circumstances to identify and reach the owner of the property in order to facilitate alternative means of security or to obtain his consent to the search, for in this context the right to refuse the search remains with the owner. Cf. Bumper v. North Carolina, 391 U. S. 543 (1968). [16]

Because the record in this case shows that the procedures followed by the Vermillion police in searching respondent's car fall far short of these standards, in my view, the search was impermissible, and its fruits must be suppressed. First, so far as the record shows, the police in this case had no reason to believe that the glove compartment of the impounded car contained particular property of any substantial value. Moreover, the owner had apparently thought it adequate to protect whatever he left in the car overnight on the street in a business area simply to lock the car, and there is nothing in the record to show that the impoundment lot would prove a less secure location against pilferage, [17] cf. Mozzetti v. Superior Court, 4 Cal.2d 699, 707, 484 P.2d 84, 89 (1971), particularly when it would seem likely that the owner would claim his car and its contents promptly, at least if it contained valuables worth protecting. [18] Even if the police had cause to believe that the impounded car's glove compartment contained particular valuables, however, they made no effort to secure the owner's consent to the search. Although the Court relies, as it must, upon the fact that respondent was not present to make other arrangements for the care of his belongings, ante at 428 U. S. 375, in my view, that is not the end of the inquiry. Here, the police readily ascertained the ownership of the vehicle, Record 98-99, yet they searched it immediately without taking any steps to locate respondent and procure his consent to the inventory or advise him to make alternative arrangements to safeguard his property, id. at 32, 72, 73, 79. Such a failure is inconsistent with the rationale that the inventory procedure is carried out for the benefit of the owner.

The Court's result in this case elevates the conservation of property interests --

indeed mere possibilities of property interests -- above the privacy and security interests protected by the Fourth Amendment. For this reason, I dissent. On the remand, it should be clear in any event that this Court's holding does not preclude a contrary resolution of this case or others involving the same issues under any applicable state law. See Oregon v. Hass, 420 U. S. 714, 420 U. S. 726 (1975) (MARSHALL, J., dissenting).

Notes

[1] The Court does not consider, however, whether the police might open and search the glove compartment if it is locked, or whether the police might search a locked trunk or other compartment.

[2] I agree with MR. JUSTICE POWELL's conclusion, ante at 428 U. S. 377 n. 1, that, as petitioner conceded, Tr. of Oral Arg. 5, the examination of the closed glove compartment in this case is a "search." See Camara v. Municipal Court, 387 U. S. 523, 387 U. S. 530 (1967):

"It is surely anomalous to say that the individual and his private property are fully protected by the Fourth Amendment only when the individual is suspected of criminal behavior."

See also Cooper v. California, 386 U. S. 58, 386 U. S. 61 (1967), quoted in n. 5, infra. Indeed, the Court recognized in Harris v. United States, 390 U. S. 234, 390 U. S. 236 (1968), that the procedure invoked here would constitute a search for Fourth Amendment purposes.

[3] This is, of course, "probable cause in the sense of specific knowledge about a particular automobile." Almeida-Sanchez v. United States, 413 U. S. 266, 413 U. S. 281 (1973) (POWELL, J., concurring).

[4] In its opinion below, the Supreme Court of South Dakota stated that, in its view, the police were constitutionally justified in entering the car to remove, list, and secure objects in plain view from the outside of the car. 89 S.D. ___, ___, 228 N.W.2d 152, 158-159 (1975). This issue is not presented on certiorari here.

Contrary to the Court's assertion, however, ante at 428 U. S. 375-376, the search of respondent's car was not in any way "prompted by the presence in plain view of a number of valuables inside the car." In fact, the record plainly states that every vehicle taken to the city impound lot was inventoried, Record 33, 74, 75, and that, as a matter of "standard procedure," "every inventory search" would involve entry into the car's closed glove compartment. Id. at 43, 44. See also Tr. of Oral Arg. 7. In any case, as MR. JUSTICE POWELL recognizes, ante at 428 U. S. 377-378, n. 2, entry to remove plain view articles from the car could not justify a further search into the car's closed areas. Cf. Chimel v. California, 395 U. S. 752, 395 U. S. 763, 395 U. S. 764-768 (1969). Despite the Court's confusion on this point -- further reflected by its discussion of Mozzetti v. Superior Court, 4 Cal.3d 699, 484 P.2d 84 (1971), ante at 428 U. S. 371, and its reliance on state and lower federal court cases approving nothing more than inventorying of plain view items, e.g., Barker v. Johnson, 484 F.2d 941 (CA6 1973); United States v. Mitchell, 458 F.2d 960'

(CA9 1972); United States v. Fuller, 277 F.Supp. 97 (DC 1967), conviction aff'd, 139 U.S.App.D.C. 375, 433 F.2d 533 (1970); State v. Tully, 166 Conn.126, 348 A.2d 603 (1974); State v. Achter, 512 S.W.2d 894 (Mo.Ct.App. 1974); State v. All, 17 N.C.App. 284, 193 S.E.2d 770, cert. denied, 414 U.S. 866 (1973) -- I must conclude that the Court's holding also permits the intrusion into a car and its console even in the absence of articles in plain view.

[5] Moreover, as the Court observed in Cooper v. California, supra at 386 U. S. 61: "[L]awful custody of an automobile does not, of itself, dispense with constitutional requirements of searches thereafter made of it.'"

[6] It would be wholly unrealistic to say that there is no reasonable and actual expectation in maintaining the privacy of closed compartments of a locked automobile when it is customary for people in this day to carry their most personal and private papers and effects in their automobiles from time to time. Cf. Katz v. United States, 389 U. S. 347, 389 U. S. 352 (1967) (opinion of the Court); id. at 389 U. S. 361 (Harlan, J., concurring). Indeed, this fact is implicit in the very basis of the Court's holding -- that such compartments may contain valuables in need of safeguarding.

MR. JUSTICE POWELL observes, ante at 428 U. S. 380, and n. 7, that the police would not be justified in sifting through papers secured under the procedure employed here. I agree with this, and I note that the Court's opinion does not authorize the inspection of suitcases, boxes, or other containers which might themselves be sealed, removed, and secured without further intrusion. See, e.g., United States v.Lawson, 487 F.2d 468 (CA8 1973); State v. McDougal, 68 Wis.2d 399, 228 N.W.2d 671 (1975); Mozzetti v. Superior Court, supra. But this limitation does not remedy the Fourth Amendment intrusion when the simple inventorying of closed areas discloses tokens, literature, medicines, or other things which on their face may "reveal much about a person's activities, associations, and beliefs," California Bankers Assn. v. Shultz, 416 U. S. 21, 416 U. S. 78-79 (1974) (POWELL, J., concurring).

[7] The Court also observes that, "[i]n addition, police frequently attempt to determine whether a vehicle has been stolen and thereafter abandoned." Ante at 428 U. S. 369. The Court places no reliance on this concern in this case, however, nor could it. There is no suggestion that the police suspected that respondent's car was stolen, or that their search was directed at, or stopped with, a determination of the car's ownership. Indeed, although the police readily identified the car as respondent's, Record 98-99, the record does not show that they ever sought to contact him.

[8] The very premise of the State's chief argument, that the cars must be searched in order to protect valuables because no guard is posted around the vehicles, itself belies the argument that they must be searched at the city lot in order to protect the police there. These circumstances alone suffice to distinguish the dicta from Cooper v. California, 386 U.S. at 386 U. S. 61-62, recited by the Court, ante at 428 U. S. 373.

The Court suggests a further "crucial" justification for the search in this case: "protection of the public from vandals who might find a firearm, Cady v. Dombrowski,

[413 U.S. 433 (1973)], or as here, contraband drugs" (emphasis added). Ante at 428 U. S. 376 n. 10. This rationale, too, is absolutely without support in this record. There is simply no indication the police were looking for dangerous items. Indeed, even though the police found shotgun shells in the interior of the car, they never opened the trunk to determine whether it might contain a shotgun. Cf. Cady, supra. Aside from this, the suggestion is simply untenable as a matter of law. If this asserted rationale justifies search of all impounded automobiles, it must logically also justify the search of all automobiles, whether impounded or not, located in a similar area, for the argument is not based upon the custodial role of the police. See also Cooper v. California, supra at 386 U. S. 61, quoted in n. 5, supra. But this Court has never permitted the search of any car or home on the mere undifferentiated assumption that it might be vandalized and the vandals might find dangerous weapons or substances. Certainly Cady v. Dombrowski, permitting a limited search of a wrecked automobile where, inter alia, the police had a reasonable belief that the car contained a specific firearm, 413 U.S. at 413 U. S. 448, does not so hold.

[9] Even were the State to impose a higher standard of custodial responsibility upon the police, however, it is equally clear that such a requirement must be read in light of the Fourth Amendment's preeminence to require protective measures other than interior examination of closed areas.

[10] Indeed, if such claims can be deterred at all, they might more effectively be deterred by sealing the doors and trunk of the car, so that an unbroken seal would certify that the car had not been opened during custody. See Cabbler v. Superintendent, 374 F.Supp. 690, 700 (ED Va.1974), rev'd, 528 F.2d 1142 (CA4 1975), cert. pending, No. 75-1463.

[11] I do not believe, however, that the Court is entitled to make this assumption, there being no such indication in the record. Cf. Cady v. Dombrowski, supra at 413 U. S. 447.

[12] The Court makes clear, ante at 428 U. S. 375, that the police may not proceed to search an impounded car if the owner is able to make other arrangements for the safekeeping of his belongings. Additionally, while the Court does not require consent before a search, it does not hold that the police may proceed with such a search in the face of the owner's denial of permission. In my view, if the owner of the vehicle is in police custody or otherwise in communication with the police, his consent to the inventory is prerequisite to an inventory search. See Cabbler v. Superintendent, supra at 700; cf. State v. McDougal, 68 Wis.2d at 413, 228 N.W.2d at 678; Mozzetti v. Superior Court, 4 Cal.3d at 708, 484 P.2d at 89.

[13] In so requiring, the Court appears to recognize that a search of some, but not all, cars which there is no specific cause to believe contain valuables would itself belie any asserted property-securing purpose.

The Court makes much of the fact that the search here was a routine procedure, and attempts to analogize Cady v. Dombrowski. But it is quite clear that the routine in Cady was only to search where there was a reasonable belief that the car contained a dangerous weapon, 413 U.S. at 413 U. S. 443; see Dombrowski v. Cady, 319 F.Supp. 530, 532 (ED Wis.1970), not, as here, to search every car in custody without particular cause.

[14] Even if it may be true that many persons would ordinarily consent to a protective inventory of their car upon its impoundment, this fact is not dispositive since even a majority lacks authority to consent to the search of all cars in order to assure the search of theirs. Cf. United States v. Matlock, 415 U. S. 164, 415 U. S. 171 (1974); Stoner v. California, 376 U. S. 483 (1964).

[15] I need not consider here whether a warrant would be required in such a case.

[16] Additionally, although not relevant on this record, since the inventory procedure is premised upon benefit to the owner, it cannot be executed in any case in which there is reason to believe the owner would prefer to forgo it. This principle, which is fully consistent with the Court's result today, requires, for example, that, when the police harbor suspicions (amounting to less than probable cause) that evidence or contraband may be found inside the automobile, they may not inventory it, for they must presume that the owner would refuse to permit the search.

[17] While evidence at the suppression hearing suggested that the inventory procedures were prompted by past thefts at the impound lot, the testimony refers to only two such thefts, see ante at 428 U. S. 366 n. 1, over an undisclosed period of time. There is no reason on this record to believe that the likelihood of pilferage at the lot was higher or lower than that on the street where respondent left his car with valuables in plain view inside. Moreover, the failure of the police to secure such frequently stolen items as the car's battery, suggests that the risk of loss from the impoundment was not, in fact, thought severe.

[18] In fact respondent claimed his possessions about five hours after his car was removed from the street. Record 39, 93.

Discrimination not yet eliminated: Justice Marshall's dissent in Pasadena City Board of Education v. Spangler (June 28, 1976)

Mr. Justice MARSHALL, with whom Mr. Justice BRENNAN joins, dissenting.

I cannot agree with the Court that the District Court's refusal to modify the "no majority of any minority" provision of its order was erroneous. Because at the time of the refusal "racial discrimination through official action," Swann v. Board of Education, 402 U.S. 1, 32, 91 S.Ct. 1267, 1284, 28 L.Ed.2d 554 (1971), had apparently not yet been eliminated from the Pasadena school system, it is my view that the District Court did not abuse its discretion in refusing to dissolve a major part of its order.

In dying petitioners' motion for modification of the 1970 desegregation order, the District Court described a 3-year pattern of opposition by a number of the members of the Board of Education to both the spirit and letter of the Pasadena Plan. It found that "the Pasadena Plan has not had the cooperation from the Board that permits a realistic measurement of its educational success or failure." 375 F.Supp. 1304, 1308 (CD Cal. 1974) (footnote omitted). Moreover, the 1974 Board of Education submitted to the District Court an alternative to the Pasadena Plan, which, at least in the mind of one member of the Court of Appeals, "would very likely result in rapid resegregation." 519 F.2d 430, 435 (CA9 1975). I agree with Judge Ely that there is "abundant evidence upon which the district judge, in the reasonable exercise of his discretion, could rightly determine that the 'dangers' which induced the original determination of constitutional infringements in Pasadena have not diminished sufficiently to require modification or dissolution of the original Order." Id., at 434.

The Court's conclusion that modification of the District Court's order is mandated is apparently largely founded on the fact that during the Pasadena Plan's first year, its implementation did result in no school's having a majority of minority students. According to the Court, it follows from our decision in Swann, supra, that as soon as the school attendance zone scheme had been successful, even for a very short period, in fulfilling its objectives, the District Court should have relaxed its supervision over that aspect of the desegregation plan. It is irrelevant to the Court that the system may not have achieved " 'unitary' status in all other respects such as the hiring and promoting of teachers and administrators." Ante, at 2705 n. 5.

In my view, the Court, in so ruling, has unwarrantedly extended our statement in Swann that "(n)either school authorities nor district courts are constitutionally required to make year-by-year adjustments of the racial composition of student bodies Once the affirmative duty to desegregate has been accomplished and racial discrimination through official action is eliminated from the system." 402 U.S., at 31-32, 91 S.Ct. at 1284 (emphasis added). That statement recognizes on the one hand that a fully desegregated school system may not be compelled to adjust its attendance zones to conform to changing demographic patterns. But on the other hand, it also appears to recognize that Until such a unitary system is established, a district court may act with broad discretion discretion which includes the adjustment of attendance zones so that the goal of a wholly unitary system might be sooner achieved.

In insisting that the District Court largely abandon its scrutiny of attendance patterns, the Court might well be insuring that a unitary school system in which segregation has been eliminated "root and branch," Green v. County School Board, 391 U.S. 430, 438, 88 S.Ct. 1689, 1694, 20 L.Ed.2d 716 (1968), will never be achieved in Pasadena. For at the point that the Pasadena system is in compliance with the aspects of the plan specifying procedures for hiring and promoting teachers and administrators, it may be that the attendance patterns within the system will be such as to once again manifest substantial aspects of a segregated system. It seems to me singularly unwise for the Court to risk such a result.

We have held that "(o)nce a right and a violation have been shown, the scope of a district court's equitable powers to remedy past wrongs is broad, for breadth and flexibility are inherent in equitable remedies." Swann v. Board of Education, supra, 402

U.S., at 15, 91 S.Ct., at 1276. As the Court recognizes, Ante, at 432, there is no issue before us as to the validity of the District Court's original judgment that unconstitutional segregation existed in the Pasadena school system. Thus, there is no question as to there being both a "right and a violation." Moreover, at least as of the time that the District Court acted on the request for modification, the violation had not yet been entirely remedied. Particularly, given the breadth of discretion normally accorded a district court in fashioning equitable remedies, I see no reason to require the District Court in a case such as this to modify its order prior to the time that it is clear that the entire violation has been remedied and a unitary system has been achieved. 1 We should not compel the District Court to modify its order unless conditions have changed so much that "dangers, once substantial, have become attenuated to a shadow." United States v. Swift & Co., 2 286 U.S. 106, 119, 52 S.Ct. 460, 464, 76 L.Ed. 999 (1932). I, for one, cannot say that the District Court was in error in determining that such attenuation had not yet taken place and that modification of the order would "surely be to sign the death warrant of the Pasadena Plan and its objectives." 375 F.Supp., at 1309. Accordingly, I dissent.

Notes

1. In the course of final argument, the District Judge did make the spontaneous statement that the 1970 order "meant to me that at least during my lifetime there would be no majority of any minority in any school in Pasadena." As did the Court of Appeals, I disapprove the statement to the extent that it suggests that continuous redistricting can be required "even After the court has determined that its plan has been effectively implemented and Racial discrimination (has been) eliminated from the system." 519 F.2d, at 438 (emphasis added).

2. While I dissent from the Court's opinion, I do acknowledge the narrowness of its holding. Ante, at 435. For instance, the Court intimates that it would view this case differently if the demographic changes were themselves a product of a desegregation order. Ibid. Moreover, as the Court observes, this case does not involve an attendance-zone requirement calling "for defendants to submit 'step at a time' plans by definition incomplete at inception." Ibid.

What is perhaps most striking about the Rosebud Acts is the absence of any express provision disestablishing the Reservation: Justice Marshall's dissent in Rosebud Sioux Tribe v. Kneip (April 4, 1977)

MR. JUSTICE MARSHALL, with whom MR. JUSTICE BRENNAN and MR. JUSTICE STEWART join, dissenting.

The Court holds today that, in 1904, 1907, and 1910, Congress broke solemn promises it had made to the Rosebud Sioux Tribe and took from them, without any guarantee of compensation, three-quarters of their reservation. Although it was suggested at argument, Tr. of Oral Arg. 120, that the only consequence of such a holding would be to preclude the Tribe from continuing to exercise the jurisdiction granted to it by its approved constitution and bylaws, [1] in fact, much more is at stake. This case involves not just the rights of the Tribe, but also the rights of approximately 2,000 Indians living in the disputed area, and the right of the United States to continue to administer the disputed area as part of the Rosebud Reservation. [2] See 430 U. S. infra. In addition, the ramifications of today's decision may extend to a large number of other reservations throughout the Nation. See ibid. I therefore feel constrained to explain at length why the decision is, in my view, wholly unjustifiable.

Until today, the effect on reservation boundaries of Acts disposing of surplus reservation land was well settled. The general rule, entitled to "the broadest possible scope," is that, in interpreting these Acts, "legal ambiguities are resolved to the benefit of the Indians." DeCoteau v. District County Court, 420 U. S. 425, 420 U. S. 447 (1975). Congressional intent therefore must be "clear" before this Court will find that a reservation established by Congress (or the Executive) was disestablished. Mattz v. Arnett, 412 U. S. 481, 412 U. S. 505 (1973). Applying these principles, the Court has found disestablishment when Congress ratified a treaty by which Indians agreed to sell all interest in part or all of a reservation, DeCoteau v. District County Court, supra, or when Congress employed express words of termination, Mattz v. Arnett, supra at 412 U. S. 504 n. 22 (dictum). But when, as here, Congress merely "opened" a reservation -- that is, made reservation land available to non-Indians and acted as a sales agent on behalf of the Indians -- the reservation boundaries have been held to be unaffected. Mattz v. Arnett, supra; Seymour v. Superintendent, 368 U. S. 351 (1962). In DeCoteau, the Court clearly distinguished the two situations, observing:

"[A purchase-and-sale Act] is not a unilateral action by Congress, but the ratification of a previously negotiated agreement, to which a tribal majority consented. [It] does not merely open lands to settlement; it also appropriates and vests in the tribe a sum certain . . . in payment for the express cession and relinquishment of 'all' of the tribe's 'claim, right, title, and interest' in the unallotted lands. The statute in Mattz, by contrast, benefited the tribe only indirectly, by establishing a fund dependent on uncertain future sales of its land to settlers."

420 U.S. at 420 U. S. 448. Today, however, the Court obliterates this distinction, and, by holding against the Tribe when the evidence concerning congressional intent is palpably ambiguous, erodes the general principles for interpreting Indian statutes.

I

What is perhaps most striking about the Rosebud Acts, in light of the interpretation the Court places upon them, is the absence of any express provision disestablishing the Reservation. As we observed in Mattz: "Congress has used clear language of express termination when that result is desired." 412 U.S. at 412 U. S. 504 n. 22. We cited three examples in Mattz: 15 Stat. 221, which stated that "the Smith River reservation is hereby discontinued"; 27 Stat. 63, which stated that "a portion of the Colville Indian Reservation . . . is hereby, vacated and restored to the public domain"; and

33 Stat. 218, enacted just two days before the first of the Rosebud Acts, which stated that "the reservation lines of the said Ponca and Otoe and Missouria Indian reservations . . . are hereby abolished." The very Act that created the Rosebud Reservation provides yet another example, for, in that Act, Congress expressly "restored to the public domain" part of the Great Sioux Reservation.Act of Mar. 2, 1889, § 21, 25 Stat. 896. And other examples abound. [3]

The Acts in question contain no similar language. The Act of April 23, 1904, 33 Stat. 254, is a peculiarly drafted statute. In substance, it is no different from the statutes considered in Mattz and Seymour; it opens lands on the Reservation to white settlers, guarantees to the Indians the proceeds from the sale of the lands, but does not commit the United States to purchasing the land. [4] In form, however, the Act "amended and modified," and then "ratified," the 1901 Agreement between Inspector McLaughlin and the Rosebud Sioux in which the Tribe agreed to sell the lands in question to the United States for a lump sum; this Agreement had been rejected by the Congress in 1902. The "amendments" which Congress unilaterally inserted obviously were substantial, since they transformed the transaction from a DeCoteau-type purchase to a Mattz-type "opening." But because the ratification format was used, the 1904 Act contains language from the 1901 Agreement which provided that the

"Indians belonging on the Rosebud Reservation, South Dakota, for the consideration hereinafter named, do hereby cede, surrender, grant, and convey to the United States all their claim, right, title, and interest"

in the unallotted lands in Gregory County.

In DeCoteau, we stated that this language, when contained in an agreement approved by the Indians and ratified by Congress, is "precisely suited," 420 U.S. at 420 U. S. 445, to terminating a reservation. But I cannot agree with the Court, ante at 430 U. S. 597, that the language is equally well suited to disestablish the Reservation here. Its usage may simply mean that Congress found that working from an earlier document -- in this case the 1901 Agreement -- was easier than drafting a new law. Whereas, in DeCoteau, the key phrase expressed the Indians' understanding of what they were surrendering and the Government's understanding of what it was acquiring, here, the Indians had not agreed to this transaction, and the Government disclaimed any intent to purchase anything other than school lands, see n 4, supra. Indeed, as the Court concedes, ante at 430 U. S. 597, as a matter of English usage, the words "cede, surrender, grant, and convey," make no sense in the context of an "agreement" to which the seller has not assented. Thus the Court ultimately rests its decision on an asserted ability to "see what [Congress is] driving at,'" even though Congress has "`not said it.'" Ibid.

The 1907 and 1910 Acts are far simpler for present purposes. They contain neither words of cession nor words of termination. They simply "authorized and directed" the Secretary of the Interior "to sell or dispose of" the specified lands "under the general provisions of the homestead and town-site laws of the United States." Act of Mar. 2, 1907, §§ 1, 2, 34 Stat. 1230; Act of May 30, 1910, §§ 1, 2, c. 260, 36 Stat. 448. These statutes are virtually identical to the law construed in Seymour v. Superintendent, which also "authorized and directed" the Secretary "to sell or dispose of" specified lands "under the provisions of the homestead laws." Act of Mar. 22, 1906, §§ 1, 3, c. 1126, 34 Stat. 80-81. They are quite similar to the Act at issue in Mattz, which "declared" specified lands

"to be subject to settlement, entry, and purchase under the laws of the United States granting homestead rights and authorizing the sale of mineral, stone, and timber lands."

Act of June 17, 1892, 27 Stat. 52. They bear no resemblance, however, to the statutes cited in Mattz as examples of "clear language of express termination."

II

Since congressional intent must be unambiguous before we can conclude that Congress terminated part of an Indian reservation, the absence of any express provision to this effect in the Rosebud Acts strongly militates against the interpretation the Court places on those Acts. But I need not rely on congressional silence alone -- eloquent as it may be -- to reject the Court's interpretation. For both the text of the Acts and the circumstances surrounding their enactment affirmatively point to the opposite conclusion.

A

The text of the Acts provides numerous indications that Congress did not intend to remove the opened areas from the Reservation. First, the Acts granted the Indians a variety of rights in those areas. All three Acts, for example, permitted Indians with allotments in the counties to be opened to retain their allotments, [5] and the 1907 and 1910 Acts also allowed certain Indians without allotments in these counties to secure allotments there. [6] All three Acts also granted the Indians a beneficial interest in all the opened lands, since the Acts simply made the United States "trustee for [the] Indians to dispose of said lands." [7] And the 1904 and 1910 Acts authorized the Executive, before opening the counties to settlers, to reserve some lands for Indian schools, religious missions, and service agencies. [8] Of course, it is possible that Congress intended to remove the opened counties from the Reservation while leaving the Indians with a host of rights in the counties. But this interpretation of the statutes is surely strained, especially since nothing in the legislative history indicates that such an anomalous result was desired. Thus, it is far more sensible to view these grants to the Indians as evidence that Congress did not intend to terminate the Reservation immediately.

This interpretation is supported by other provisions in the Acts as well. In the 1907 and 1910 Acts, for example, Congress directed that payments received from sale of the lands to be opened were to be deposited "to the credit of the Indians belonging and having tribal rights on the Rosebud Reservation." [9] If the Rosebud Acts also removed the opened counties from the Reservation, then the members of the Tribe living in Gregory County, opened in 1904, were not entitled to share in the proceeds of the 1907 or 1910 sales, and the members of the Tribe living in Tripp County, opened by the Act of 1907, were not entitled to the 1910 proceeds, at the very least. [10] Again, it is possible that Congress intended this result. But, absent contrary evidence, it is far more reasonable to assume that Congress meant for all members of the Tribe living on the original Reservation to profit from the sales, since, prior to the Rosebud Acts, they all had equal rights in the opened lands. Thus, the manner in which Congress defined the class of beneficiaries in the 1907 and 1910 Acts indicates that Congress believed that the Indians living in the opened counties still "belonged" to the Reservation after the lands were opened.

Finally, all the statutes contain an important guide to interpretation that the Court ignores. Each Act states, in almost identical terms, that

"nothing in this 'agreement shall be construed to deprive the . . . Indians of the Rosebud Reservation, South Dakota, of any benefits to which they are entitled under existing treaties or agreements, not inconsistent with the provisions of this agreement.' [11]"

These provisions constitute clear congressional commands to interpret the Rosebud Acts so as to minimize conflicts with the Treaty of 1889. Yet the Court ignores these provisions, and maximizes the conflict, by construing the Acts to limit not just the Rosebud Sioux's land use, but also their jurisdiction. [12]

B

The Court's construction of the Rosebud Acts is also untenable when the Acts are placed in historical context. Just as we held in Mattz that the statute at issue there was to be interpreted "from the overview of the earlier General Allotment Act of 187, 24 Stat. 388," 412 U.S. at 412 U. S. 496, so, too, must the Rosebud Acts be construed from this perspective. As we observed in Mattz:

"[The policy of the General Allotment Act] was to continue the reservation system and the trust status of Indian lands, but to allot tracts to individual Indians for agriculture and grazing. When all the lands had been allotted and the trust expired, the reservation could be abolished. Unallotted lands were made available to non-Indians with the purpose, in part, of promoting interaction between the races and of encouraging Indians to adopt white ways."

Ibid. (footnote omitted). This policy reflected Congress' attempt "to reconcile the Government's responsibility for the Indians' welfare with the desire of non-Indians to settle upon reservation lands." DeCoteau v. District County Court, 420 U.S. at 420 U. S. 432. Because the "familiar forces," id. at 420 U. S. 431, at work on Congress demanded land for settlers, Congress opened the reservations. But because these forces were not overly concerned with the niceties of reservation boundaries, the reservation status of the opened areas was preserved until the trust period expired, to insure federal protection of the Indians while they were being "civilized" through contacts with white settlers. Thus, to interpret the Rosebud Acts as terminating three-fourths of the Rosebud Reservation is to set them at war with Congress' general policy toward Indians at the time the Acts were approved.

III

The Court ultimately rests its construction of the Acts on an analysis of their legislative history. While there may be occasional passages in the history that suggest an intent to terminate, [13] I cannot agree that such an intent is established with anything approaching the requisite clarity.

In the first place, the legislative history of the Rosebud Acts is extraordinarily sparse. The 1904 Act, which the Court properly regards as the crucial Act, was introduced by Representative Burke of South Dakota on January 19, 1904, 38 Cong.Rec. 902-903; was reported out of the Committee on Indian Affairs, which Mr. Burke chaired, two days later, id. at 1010; and passed the House on February 1, id. at 1469, after a debate that consumes only six pages in the Congressional Record, id. at 1423-1429. [14] The bill was transmitted to the Senate the same day; was reported out of the Committee chaired by Senator Gamble of South Dakota three days later, id. at 1601; and was called up, amended, and approved by the Senate without debate on April 18, id. at 4988. [15] The House concurred in the Senate amendments the following day without any discussion. Id. at 5155. The 1907 Act received even less congressional attention. It was approved within one month after it was introduced without any debate in the Senate, 41 Cong.Rec. 3323 (1907), and with a debate in the House that occupies only one page in the Record, id. at 3104. [16] Only the 1910 Act was seriously debated by Congress, and these debates focused almost exclusively on the method by which the opened lands would be distributed to white settlers. 45 Cong.Rec. 1066-1071, 5456-5473 (1910).

In light of the brevity of the debates, it is not surprising that there is a paucity of relevant materials. The Court finds just two quotations from the debates, ante at 430 U. S. 596, 430 U. S. 608, and three quotations from the Committee Reports, ante at 430 U. S. 595, 430 U. S. 611, 430 U. S. 612, that directly bear on the disestablishment issue. [17] What the Court cannot find, however, is particularly telling. Unlike the debates in Mattz, which revealed that "the establishment of the reservation . . . was viewed as a mistake and an injustice," 412 U.S. at 412 U. S. 500, there were no expressions of hostility toward the existence or size of the Rosebud Reservation. Nor were there any statements indicating that Congress intended to deviate from its general policy of preserving reservations or to abandon its role as guardian of the Indians living in the opened counties. Indeed, although Congress was aware that the Rosebud Acts initiated a new policy toward surplus lands [18] -- one which removed the Government from the role of buyer and the Indians from the role of seller -- at no point in the debates did anyone discuss the consequences of this change on Reservation boundaries.

The poverty of the Court's analysis is best revealed by its treatment of the history of the crucial 1904 Act. The Court begins with

"the undisputed fact that the 1901 Agreement, had it been ratified by Congress, would have disestablished that portion of the Rosebud Reservation which lay in Gregory County."

Ante at 430 U. S. 591. Its review of the legislative history then leads it to conclude that "there is no indication that Congress intended to change anything other than the form of, and responsibility for, payment." Ante at 430 U. S. 594-595. But the fact that Congress did not expressly repudiate all of the consequences of an Agreement to which it was not a party and which it had refused to ratify hardly establishes that Congress affirmatively intended those consequences to result from the very different transaction it devised in 1904. [19] It is at least equally plausible that Congress did not explain the effect of the 1904 Act because it assumed that the Act would have precisely the same effect as earlier nonpurchase surplus land Acts such as those considered in Mattz: the lands would be opened and the reservations preserved. Nor is the fact that Congress adopted the format of the 1901 Agreement especially probative, since this may have been done simply out of convenience.

Ultimately, what the legislative history demonstrates, as co-counsel for the State has aptly concluded, is that Congress manifested an "almost complete lack of . . . concern with the boundary issue." [20] The issue was of no great importance in the early 1900's, as it was commonly assumed that all reservations would be abolished when the trust period on allotted lands expired. There was no pressure on Congress to accelerate this timetable, so long as settlers could acquire unused land. Accordingly, Congress simply did not focus on the boundary question. Its indifference is perhaps best manifested by the fact that, in legislation concerning the Reservation enacted immediately subsequent to the Rosebud Acts, Congress at times referred to the opened counties as part of the Reservation, and at times referred to them as no longer part of the Reservation. [21] For the Court to find in this confusion and indifference a "clear" congressional intent to disestablish the Reservation is incomprehensible.

IV

The most obvious and immediate consequence of today's decision is jurisdictional. Even though the people of South Dakota have expressly declined to assume jurisdiction over Indian country, [22] from now on, crimes (or torts) committed by the Indians on nontrust land in the opened counties will be within the jurisdiction of the State. This will create an "impractical pattern of checkerboard jurisdiction," in which

"law enforcement officers . . . will find it necessary to search tract books in order to determine whether criminal jurisdiction over each particular offense . . . is in the State or Federal Government."

Seymour v. Superintendent, 368 U.S. at 368 U. S. 358. In addition, even while on their trust lands, the almost 2,000 enrolled Indians in the opened counties will be generally subject to "state law otherwise applicable to all citizens of the State," Mescalero Apache Tribe v. Jones, 411 U. S. 145, 411 U. S. 149 (1973), even if the same law could not be applied to Reservation Indians because it would "interfere with reservation self-government or would impair a right granted or reserved by federal law," id..at 411 U. S. 148. This is reason enough to be troubled by today's decision.

But beyond these jurisdictional consequences, the holding today places a grave cloud over the property rights of both the Tribe and the Indians living off the newly contracted Reservation. With respect to the Tribe, 4,600 acres in the opened counties were returned to it pursuant to the Indian Reorganization Act of 1934, 48 Stat. 984, after the Secretary found, in the words of § 3 of the Act, that these were "the remaining surplus lands of [an] Indian reservation" opened before June 18, 1934. But if the opened counties were not part of the Reservation, then the Secretary's right to return the land to the Tribe is at least open to question. [23] More seriously, the Indians living on trust lands in the opened counties have assumed that § 2 of the Reorganization Act, which extended the trust period on "Indian lands," applied to their property. But if these counties were not part of a reservation, this assumption is dubious, at best, since § 8 of the Act states that the Act shall not

"be construed to relate to Indian holdings of allotments . . . upon the public domain outside of the geographic boundaries of any Indian reservation now existing. . . ."

Should it be determined that the trust period was not extended, the State of South Dakota could claim crushing amounts of back taxes.

Finally, today's decision may result in a sharp reduction in the federal aid available to members of the Rosebud Tribe living off the Reservation. The Bureau of Indian Affairs has been administering the opened counties as part of the Reservation, see n 2, supra, and, in requesting appropriations for the Reservation Indians, has included Indians living in the opened counties, Brief for United States as Amicus Curiae 37-38. In addition, we have been advised by the Association on American Indian Affairs et al., as amici curiae, that the Rosebud Tribe has received a large amount of federal aid pursuant to a variety of federal programs. Brief 31-39. The Association reports that, in the past, the Tribe has been able to expend these monies for programs in the opened, as well as the closed, counties because the federal agencies have viewed all the counties as part of the Reservation. Ibid. But in light of today's decision, the Tribe's ability to use federal funds to benefit tribal members living in these counties is in serious doubt. [24]

Nor are these potential consequences limited to the Rosebud Reservation. The Rosebud Acts were described by their sponsors as the beginning of a new policy with respect to surplus lands. See n 18, supra. During the decade following the enactment of the first Rosebud Act, Congress passed 21 other statutes that opened surplus reservation lands to settlers. [25] If the Rosebud Acts diminished the Rosebud Reservation, then the boundaries of more than a score of other reservations must be in doubt.

Because I can find no principled justification for inflicting manifold injuries on the Rosebud Sioux Indians and for jeopardizing the rights of numerous other tribes, I respectfully dissent.

Notes

[1] The constitution of the Rosebud Sioux Tribe, approved by the Secretary of the Interior in 1935, App. 1396-1397, states in Art. I that

"[t]he jurisdiction of the Rosebud Sioux Tribe . . . shall extend to the territory within the original confines of the Rosebud Reservation boundaries as established by the act of March 2, 1889. . . ."

There is some confusion in the record concerning the jurisdictional history of the disputed area. At the conclusion of his lengthy opinion, the District Judge stated that

"the State of South Dakota has treated the [disputed] counties . . . as portions of the state over which the State of South Dakota can exercise jurisdiction since the passage of [the] acts."

375 F.Supp. 1065, 1083 (SD 1974). But contrary to the Court's suggestion, ante at 430 U. S. 604-605, n. 27, this statement is hotly disputed insofar as it implies that the Tribe has conceded jurisdiction. The Tribe claims it "has consistently exercised jurisdiction over Indians on all parts of the reservation." Reply Brief for Petitioner 2b. The United States agrees, Brief for United States as Amicus Curiae 32 n. 22, and has provided a number of examples, id. at 23a-32a.

[2] The United States reports that it has treated the disputed areas as part of the Reservation, and that it maintains or funds child welfare programs, burial assistance, outpatient clinics, and housing in these areas. Id. at 37-38. See also Letter from the Acting Area Director, Aberdeen, S.D. Bureau of Indian Affairs, to Neil Proto, Dept. of Justice, Aug. 23, 1974, App. 1405-1409, detailing these services.

[3] The National Indian Law Library's compilation of Allotment/Cession Statutes, Doc. No. 002279, contains 11 additional examples, taken from statutes enacted between 1888-1913.

[4] The United States did agree, in § 4 of the Act, to purchase sections 16 and 36 of Gregory County and to grant these sections to the State for school purposes. The significance of this grant is discussed in n. 12, infra.

[5] 1904 Act, § 1, Art. I; 1907 Act, § 1; 1910 Act, § 1.

[6] The 1907 Act provided in § 2 that, before opening the lands, the Secretary of the Interior

"may permit Indians who have an allotment within the Rosebud Reservation to relinquish such allotment and to receive in lieu thereof an allotment anywhere within said reservation, and he shall also allot one hundred and sixty acres of land to leach child . . . belonging on the Rosebud Reservation who has not heretofore received an allotment."

The fact that these allotments were to be made before the county was opened to settlers indicates that they could be taken from the lands to be opened. See also H.R.Rep. No. 7613, 59th Cong., 2d Sess., 3 (1907) ("The bill further provides that . . . the Indians within the reservation may relinquish allotments and select allotments in any other portion of the reservation, including the tract affected by this bill"). (Emphasis added.) The 1910 Act is even clearer in this regard; it excludes from the opened county lands that "have been or may be hereafter allotted to Indians." (Emphasis added.)

Significantly, the 1901 Agreement, which, if ratified, would have partially terminated the Reservation, did not contain any provision for new or in-lieu allotments in the tract to be ceded.

[7] 1904 Act, § 6; 1907 Act, § 8; 1910 Act, § 11. See also United States v. Brindle, 110 U. S. 688, 110 U. S. 693 (1884). Although as the Court notes, ante at 430 U. S. 596-

597, n. 18, Congress did attempt to assure that the beneficial interest eventually would be extinguished, the Acts contain no guarantee. Indeed, the Indians retained an interest in 4,600 acres until 1938, when these lands were restored to the Tribe.

[8] 1904 Act, § 2; 1910 Act, § 1 (second proviso). The 1910 Act, in § 1, also reserved timberland to the Indians, although there was a dispute in Congress as to whether any such land existed. Compare 45 Cong.Rec. 5471 (1910) (remarks of Rep. Burke) with S.Rep. No. 68, 61st Cong., 2d Sess., 3 (1910). The provision in the 1904 Act reserving these lands was not contained in the original Agreement.

[9] 1907 Act, § 5; 1910 Act, § 7.

[10] If the Rosebud Acts disestablished the Reservation, then arguably the Indians in Tripp County were not entitled to share in the 1907 proceeds either. By the time those proceeds were deposited "to the credit of the Indians belonging and having tribal rights on the Rosebud Reservation," Tripp County had already been opened -- and therefore, under the Court's view, removed from the Reservation -- by Act and Presidential Proclamation. Under this view, the Indians living in Mellette County, opened in 1910, would not have been entitled to the proceeds from the 1910 sales.

[11] 1904 Act, § 1, Art. V; 1907 Act, § 8; 1910 Act, § 11.

[12] The Court concludes that two other provisions in the Acts support its interpretation. First, it notes, ante at 430 U. S. 599-601, 430 U. S. 608, that, in all three Acts, Congress agreed to purchase two sections of the opened counties for school purposes. See n. 4, supra. Under the enabling Act admitting the Dakotas to the United States, Act of Feb. 22, 1889, § 10, 25 Stat. 679, Congress granted these sections to the State when a reservation was to be "extinguished and such lands [are] restored to, and becom[e] a part of, the public domain." Based on ambiguous statements in the legislative history, e.g., H.R.Rep. No. 443, 58th Cong., 2d Sess., 2 (1904) (the school provisions are "in conformity with . . . the enabling act"), the Court concludes that the grants in the Rosebud Acts were included "to implement the grant in the enabling act and for no other reason.'" Ante at 430 U. S. 600. But if that were true, the provisions in question would have been unnecessary, since the grant in the enabling Act was self-executing. Minnesota v. Hitchcock, 185 U. S. 373, 185 U. S. 392-393 (1902). Indeed, in 1902, the House Committee on Indian Affairs had reached this conclusion with respect to the proposed bill ratifying the 1901 Agreement, and, accordingly, it had deleted the school provisions from the Senate version of the bill. H.R.Rep. No. 2099, 57th Cong., 1st Sess., 1 (1902). Since the Committee included school provisions in the subsequent Rosebud Acts, e.g., H.R.Rep. No. 443, supra at 2, it apparently believed that the change in the nature of the transaction meant that Congress was no longer extinguishing the Reservation and restoring the land to the public domain. Nothing in the legislative history suggests, as the Court seems to imply, ante at 430 U. S. 601 n. 24, that Congress thought it was accomplishing the former, but not the latter.

Second, the Court notes, ante at 430 U. S. 613-615, that § 10 of the 1910 Act subjected the opened lands "to all the laws of the United States prohibiting the introduction of intoxicants into the Indian country.'" The Court reasons that, if Congress believed the Reservation would remain intact this provision was unnecessary, since the Act of July 23, 1892, 27 Stat. 260, already prohibited the introduction of intoxicants into "Indian country." Ante at 430 U. S. 614 n. 47. But, in 1910, the definition of "Indian country" was unsettled, and Congress may have feared that patented land within a reservation was nevertheless not Indian country under Bates v. Clark, 95 U. S. 204 (1877), because Indian title had been extinguished. Nothing in Dick v. United States, 208 U. S. 340 (1908), on which the Court relies, ante at 430 U. S. 614 n. 47, is to the contrary, as Dick involved ceded lands as to which the United States and the Indians had agreed federal laws would be applicable.

[13] The statements that most clearly suggest an intent to terminate are fully intelligible only to those with a knowledge of the geography of the Reservation. For example, in the House Committee Report on the 1904 Act, the Committee stated:

"There is no question but what the Indians have no use for the land that is proposed to be ceded by this bill; that the tract is only a very small portion of the Rosebud Reservation, and is really only a corner of the Reservation, which will be left compact and in a square tract. . . ."

By consulting a map, one discovers that, without Gregory County -- the tract in question -- the Rosebud Reservation would be "compact" and "square." See also 41 Cong.Rec. 3104 (1907) (remarks of Rep. Burke: "They will have left, after this land is disposed of, a reservation that is substantially 50 miles square"); S.Rep. No. 68, 61st Cong., 2d Sess., 2 (1910) ("The present area of the Rosebud Indian Reservation aggregates about 1,800,000 acres"); H.R.Rep. No. 332, 61st Cong., 2d Sess., 2 (1910) ("There will still be left a reservation containing about 1,000,000 acres, and . . . there is no occasion for continuing a reservation larger than it will be when Mellette County is disposed of.").

[14] In the preceding session of Congress, Representative Burke had introduced an identical bill, 36 Cong.Rec. 2409 (1903), which was approved by his Committee two days later, id. at 2473, but never reached the House floor.

[15] Senator Gamble had introduced a similar bill the preceding year, id. at 2434, had obtained Committee approval in two days, id. at 2498; and Senate approval, without debate six days later, id. at 2747-2748. He reintroduced the bill on January 25, 1904, 38 Cong.Rec. 1100, but the House bill was approved before the Senate could act on Senator Gamble's bill. See id. at 1877.

[16] Representative Burke and Senator Gamble each had introduced similar bills in December, 1906, 41 Cong. Rec 15, 50-51. After an agreement was reached between the Tribe and Inspector McLaughlin on January 21, 1907, Representative Burke introduced a new bill, id. at 1782. On February 14, 1907, the Office of Indian Affairs recommended that the agreement be approved (even though the Indians had not assented), and the bill was reported out of the House Committee that same day, id. at 3004. Two days later, it passed the House. Id. at 3105.

On February 18, the Senate Committee sent to the Senate a substitute version of the 1906 Gamble bill. Id. at 3207. By that time, however, the House had already approved the second Burke bill, and the Senate amended and approved that bill on February 19, id. at 3323.

[17] The Court also quotes some discussions bearing on the school lands and liquor law provisions. See n. 12, supra.

[18] See, e.g., H.R.Rep. No. 443, 58th Cong., 2d Sess., 2 (1904) ("[T]hese bills present a new idea . . ., and . . . will establish a new policy and be a departure from the policy that has long since prevailed").

[19] Although the Court states that the "problem in the Congress [with respect to the 1901 Agreement] was not jurisdiction, title, or boundaries. It was, simply put, money,'" ante at 430 U. S. 591 n. 10, the historical evidence is not nearly so clear. In the Senate, the concern with the 1901 Agreement was not with the fact that the United States was expending money to acquire the lands, but with its failure to obtain reimbursement from settlers. After much debate, however, the Senate ultimately rejected an amendment that would have required settlers to purchase the opened lands from the United States, 35 Cong.Rec. 4971 (1902), and approved the agreement, id. at 5024. The House, on the other hand, never even debated the ratification bill, and thus we have no first-hand knowledge of the basis for the opposition in that body. All of the statements that the Court relies on were made by proponents of the 1901 Agreement in connection with the 1903 and 1904 bills. Ante at 430 U. S. 591, and n. 10. Moreover, the fact that the House apparently was unwilling to authorize the United States to purchase the lands and recoup the costs from the settlers suggests that money was not the sole concern.

[20] Comment, New Town et al.: The Future of an Illusion, 18 S.D.L.Rev. 85, 117 (1973).

[21] For example, in 1909, Congress appropriated funds for a mission "[o]n the Rosebud Reservation," and included within this category a mission in Gregory County. 35 Stat. 809. On the other hand, a 1905 Act extending the time for settling in Gregory County referred to the lands as "heretofore a part of the Rosebud Indian Reservation." C. 545, 33 Stat. 700. The modern statutes appear to be more consistent in labeling the opened counties as part of the Reservation. See 77 Stat. 349 (1963); 78 Stat. 560 (1964); 89 Stat. 577 (1975).

The subsequent treatment of the disputed counties by the Interior Department reflects a similar confusion as to the status of the counties. Each side has presented to this Court a number of instances in which the counties were referred to by Department personnel in terms favorable to their case. Compare Brief for United States as Amicus Curiae 33-38, 33a-41a, with Brief for Respondents 106-120. In the two instances in which Department officials have addressed the question directly, however, they have concluded that the opened counties are part of the Reservation. 54 I.D. 559 (1934) (opinion of Commissioner of Indian Affairs on Restoration of Lands Formerly Indian to Tribal Ownership); App. 1398-1404 (memorandum of Field Solicitor, Aberdeen, S.D. Apr. 6,

1972).

[22] At oral argument, we were informed that, in 1962, the people of South Dakota rejected by a referendum an Act of the legislature that would have granted the State jurisdiction over Indian country pursuant to §§ 6, 7, 67 Stat. 590 (1953). Tr. of Oral Arg. 10.

[23] Arguably, the Secretary acted properly so long as the lands were part of the Reservation at the time they were opened. See 56 I.D. 330 (1938). This was not the theory on which the Secretary proceeded, however, in ordering restoration. 54 I.D. 559 (1934).

[24] For example, according to the United States, the Department of Housing and Urban Development, which has been making grants to the Tribe, will no longer be able to approve projects in the opened counties, since with respect to those counties the Tribe will no longer be a "governmental entity" or "public body" under 42 U.S.C. § 1460(h). Brief for United States as Amicus Curiae 38. The Department of Agriculture has already ruled, in light of the Court of Appeals decision, that money made available to the Tribe to acquire lands pursuant to 25 U.S.C. § 488 cannot be used in the opened counties. Brief for Association on American Indian Affairs et al. as Amici Curiae 36.

Of course, in holding that the opened counties are outside the Reservation, the Court does not necessarily preclude the Government or the Tribe from providing any aid to Indians in those counties. Cf. Morton v. Ruiz, 415 U. S. 199 (1974).

[25] National Indian Law Library, Allotment/Cession Statutes, Doc. No. 002279. Of these statutes, five were passed with the consent of the affected Indians; these five were enacted within a year after the first Rosebud Act.

In addition to the 21 post-Rosebud Act statutes, there are at least five pre-Rosebud Act laws which also opened surplus reservation land to settlers without Indian consent. There are also at least 15 pre-Rosebud Act laws which opened surplus land with consent.

The Immigration and Nationality Act of 1952 shouldn't discriminate between natural mother and natural father: Justice Marshall's dissent in Fiallo v. Bell (April 26, 1977)

MR. JUSTICE MARSHALL, with whom MR. JUSTICE BRENNAN joins, dissenting.

Until today, I thought it clear that, when Congress grants benefits to some citizens, but not to others, it is our duty to insure that the decision comports with Fifth Amendment principles of due process and equal protection. Today, however, the Court appears to hold that discrimination among citizens, however invidious and irrational, must be tolerated if it occurs in the context of the immigration laws. Since I cannot agree that Congress has license to deny fundamental rights to citizens according to the most disfavored criteria simply because the Immigration and Nationality Act is involved, I dissent.

I

The Immigration and Nationality Act of 1952 (INA), 8 U.S.C. § 1101 et seq., establishes the terms and conditions for entry into the United States. Among its various conditions, the Act requires that an alien seeking to enter the United States as a legal permanent resident must come within a restrictive numerical quota and must satisfy certain labor certification requirements. INA §§ 201, 202, 212(a)(14), 8 U.S.C. §§ 1151, 1152, 1182(a)(14) (1976 ed.), as amended by the Immigration and Nationality Act Amendments of 1976, 90 Stat. 2703 (hereinafter 1976 Amendments). In recognition of the fact that such requirements frequently separate families, Congress has provided that American citizens may petition to have the requirements waived for their immediate families -- spouse, parents, children. INA §§ 201(a), (b), 212(a)(14), 8 U.S.C. §§ 1151(a), (b), 1182(a)(14). [1]

The privilege is accorded only to those parents and children who satisfy the statute's definitions. Under INA § 101(b)(1), a "child" is defined as an unmarried person under 21 years of age who is a legitimate or legitimated child, a stepchild, an adopted child, or an illegitimate child by whom or on whose behalf a privilege is sought by virtue of the relationship of the child to its biological mother. 8 U.S.C. § 1101(b)(1). [2] A "parent" is defined under INA § 101(b)(2) solely on the basis of the individual's relationship with a "child" as defined by § 101(b)(1). 8 U.S.C. § 1101(b)(2). [3] The definitions cover virtually all parent-child relationships except that of biological father-illegitimate child. Thus, while all American citizens are entitled to bring in their alien children without regard to either the numerical quota or the labor certification requirement, fathers are denied this privilege with respect to their illegitimate children. Similarly, all citizens are allowed to have their parents enter without regard to the labor certification requirement, and, if the citizen is over 21, also without regard to the quota. Illegitimate children, however, are denied such preferences for their fathers.

The unfortunate consequences of these omissions are graphically illustrated by the case of appellant Cleophus Warner. [4]

Mr. Warner is a naturalized citizen of the United States who, pursuant to 8 U.S.C. § 1154, [5] petitioned the Attorney General for an immigrant visa for his illegitimate son Serge, a citizen of the French West Indies. Despite the fact that Mr. Warner acknowledged his paternity and registered as Serge's father shortly after his birth, has his name on Serge's birth certificate, and has supported and maintained Serge since birth, the special dispensation from the quota and labor certification requirements was denied because Serge was not a "child" under the statute. It matters not that, as the Government concedes, Tr. of Oral Arg. 226, Serge's mother has abandoned Serge to his father and has, by marrying another man, apparently rendered impossible, under French West Indies law, Mr. Warner's ever legitimating Serge. Mr. Warner is simply not Serge's "parent."

II

The Government contends that this legislation is not subject to judicial review.

Pointing to the fact that aliens have no constitutional right to immigrate to the United States and to a long line of cases that recognize that policies pertaining to the entry of aliens and their right to remain here are peculiarly concerned with the political conduct of government, the Government concludes that "[t]he congressional decision whether or to whom to extend such a valuable privilege . . . is not a subject of judicial concern." Brief for Appellees 22.

The Court rightly rejects this expansive claim and recognizes that

"[o]ur cases reflect acceptance of a limited judicial responsibility . . . even with respect to the power of Congress to regulate the admission and exclusion of aliens."

Ante at 430 U. S. 793 n. 5. It points out, however, that the scrutiny is circumscribed. Congress has "broad power to determine which classes of aliens may lawfully enter the country" and its political judgments warrant deference. Ante at 430 U. S. 794-796.

I wholeheartedly agree with the Court's rejection of the Government's claim of unreviewable discretion. Indeed, as I observed in Kleindienst v. Mandel, 408 U. S. 753, 408 U. S. 781 (1972) (dissenting opinion), the old immigration cases that reflect an absolute "hands-off" approach by this Court "are not the strongest precedents in the United States Reports." I am pleased to see the Court reveal once again a "reluctance to rely on them completely." Ibid. I also have no quarrel with the principle that the essentially political judgments by Congress as to which foreigners may enter and which may not deserve deference from the judiciary.

My disagreement with the Court arises from its application of the principle in this case. The review the majority purports to require turns out to be completely "toothless." Cf. Trimble v. Gordon, ante at 430 U. S. 767. After observing the effects of the denial of preferential status to appellants, the majority concludes: "[B]ut the decision nonetheless remains one solely for the responsibility of the Congress and wholly outside the power of this Court to control.'" Ante at 799. Such "review" reflects more than due deference; it is abdication. [6]

Assuming, arguendo, that such deference might be appropriate in some situations -- a supposition I find difficult to accept -- it is particularly inappropriate in this case.

This case, unlike most immigration cases that come before the Court, directly involves the rights of citizens, not aliens. "[C]oncerned with the problem of keeping families of United States citizens and immigrants united," H.R.Rep. No. 1199, 85th Cong., 1st Sess., 7 (1957), Congress extended to American citizens the right to choose to be reunited in the United States with their immediate families. The focus was on citizens and their need for relief from the hardships occasioned by the immigration laws. The right to seek such relief was given only to the citizen, not the alien. 8 U.S.C. § 1154. [7] If the citizen does not petition the Attorney General for the special "immediate relative" status for his parent or child, the alien, despite his relationship, can receive no preference. 8 U.S.C. § 1153(d). It is irrelevant that aliens have no constitutional right to immigrate and that Americans have no constitutional right to compel the admission of their families. The essential fact here is that Congress did choose to extend such privileges to American citizens, but then denied them to a small class of citizens. When Congress draws such lines among citizens, the Constitution requires that the decision comport with Fifth Amendment principles of equal protection and due process. The simple fact that the discrimination is set in immigration legislation cannot insulate from scrutiny the invidious abridgment of citizens' fundamental interests.

The majority responds that, in Kleindienst v. Mandel, supra, the Court recognized that First Amendment rights of citizens were "implicated," but refused to engage in the close scrutiny usually required in First Amendment cases. Therefore, it argues, no more exacting standard is required here. In that case, Mandel, a Belgian "revolutionary Marxist," could visit this country only if the Attorney General waived the statutory prohibition of visas to "[a]liens who advocate the economic, international, and governmental doctrines of World communism." 8 U.S.C. § 1182(a)(28)(D). The Attorney General denied the waiver, and suit was brought by Mandel and several citizens who claimed their First Amendment right to hear Mandel in person was abridged by the denial. Rejecting the Government's contention that it had "unfettered discretion, and any reason or no reason [for denying a waiver] may be given," the Court upheld the denial only after finding that it was based on a "legitimate and bona fide" reason -- Mandel's abuses of visa privileges on a prior visit. 408 U.S. at 408 U. S. 769. At the same time, however, the Court chose not to scrutinize more closely and accepted the reason without weighing against it the claimed First Amendment interest. It feared becoming embroiled in the "dangerous and undesirable" task of considering, every time an alien was denied a waiver, such factors as the projected number of people wishing to speak with the alien and the probity of his ideas. Id. at 408 U. S. 769.

Whatever the merits of the Court's fears in Mandel, cf. id. at 408 U. S. 774 (MARSHALL, J., dissenting), the present case is clearly distinguishable in two essential respects. First, in Mandel, Congress had not focused on citizens and their need for relief. Rather, the governmental action was concerned with keeping out "undesirables." The impact on the citizens' right to hear was an incidental and unavoidable consequence of that political judgment. The present case presents a qualitatively different situation. Here, the purpose of the legislation is to accord rights not to aliens, but to United States citizens. In so doing, Congress deliberately chose, for reasons unrelated to foreign policy concerns or threats to national security, to deny those rights to a class of citizens traditionally subject to discrimination. [8] Second, in Mandel, unlike the present case, appellees conceded the ability of Congress to enact legislation broadly prohibiting the entry of all aliens with Mandel's beliefs. [9] Their concern was directed instead to the exercise of the discretion granted the Attorney General to waive the prohibition. In the present case, by contrast, we are asked to engage in the traditional task of reviewing the validity of a general Act of Congress challenged as unconstitutional on its face. Totally absent therefore is the specter of involving the courts in second-guessing countless individual determinations by the Attorney General as to the merits of a particular alien's entrance.

III

A

Once it is established that this discrimination among citizens cannot escape traditional constitutional scrutiny simply because it occurs in the context of immigration legislation, the result is virtually foreordained. One can hardly imagine a more vulnerable statute.

The class of citizens denied the special privilege of reunification in this country is defined on the basis of two traditionally disfavored classifications -- gender and legitimacy. Fathers cannot obtain preferred status for their illegitimate children; mothers can. Conversely, every child except the illegitimate -- legitimate, legitimated, step-, adopted -- can obtain preferred status for his or her alien father. The Court has little tolerance for either form of discrimination. We require that gender-based classifications "serve important governmental objectives, and . . . be substantially related to achievement of those objectives." Califano v. Webster, ante at 430 U. S. 317; Califano v. Goldfarb, ante at 430 U. S. 210-211; Craig v. Boren, 429 U. S. 190, 429 U. S. 197 (1976); see also Weinberger v. Wiesenfeld, 420 U. S. 636 (1975); Stanton v Stanton, 421 U. S. 7 (1975); Taylor v. Louisiana, 419 U. S. 522 (1975); Frontiero v. Richardson, 411 U. S. 677 (1973); Reed v. Reed, 404 U. S. 71 (1971). We are similarly hostile to legislation excluding illegitimates from governmental beneficence, finding it "illogical and unjust" to deprive a child "simply because its natural father has not married its mother." Gomez v. Perez, 409 U. S. 535, 409 U. S. 538 (1973). See also Trimble v. Gordon, ante p. 430 U. S. 762; Jimenez v. Weinberger, 417 U. S. 628 (1974); Beaty v. Weinberger, 478 F.2d 300 (CA5 1973), summarily aff'd, 418 U.S. 901 (1974); New Jersey Welfare Rights Org. v. Cahill, 411 U. S. 619 (1973); Weber v. Aetna Casualty & Surety Co., 406 U. S. 164 (1972); Davis v. Richardson, 342 F.Supp. 58 (Conn., 1972), summarily aff'd, 409 U.S. 1069 (1972); Griffin v. Richardson, 346 F.Supp. 1226 (Md.), summarily aff'd, 409 U.S. 1069 (1972); Glona v. American Guarantee & Liability Ins Co., 391 U. S. 73 (1968); Levy v. Louisiana, 391 U. S. 68 (1968); cf. Mathews v. Lucas, 427 U. S. 495 (1976). But see Labine v. Vincent, 401 U. S. 532 (1971).

But it is not simply the invidious classifications that make the statute so vulnerable to constitutional attack. In addition, the statute interferes with the fundamental "freedom of personal choice in matters of marriage and family life." Cleveland Board of Education v. LaFleur, 414 U. S. 632, 414 U. S. 639-640 (1974); see also Roe v. Wade, 410 U. S. 113, 410 U. S. 152=153 (1973); Wisconsin v. Yoder, 406 U. S. 205, 406 U. S. 231-233 (1972); Stanley v. Illinois, 405 U. S. 645, 405 U. S. 651 (1972); Ginsberg v. New York, 390 U. S. 629, 390 U. S. 639 (1968); Griswold v. Connecticut, 381 U. S. 479 (1965); id. at 381 U. S. 495-496 (Goldberg, J., concurring); id. at 381 U. S. 502-503 (WHITE J., concurring); Poe v. Ullman, 367 U. S. 497, 367 U. S. 542-544, 367 U. S. 549-553 (Harlan, J., dissenting). The right to live together as a family belongs to both the child who seeks to bring in his or her father and the father who seeks the entrance of his child.

"It is no less important for a child to be cared for by its . . . parent when that parent is male, rather than female. And a father, no less than a mother, has a constitutionally protected right to the 'companionship, care, custody, and management' of 'the children he has sired and raised . . .' Stanley v. Illinois, 405 U. S. 645, 405 U. S. 651 (1972)."

Weinberger v. Wiesenfeld, supra at 420 U. S. 652. In view of the legislation's denial of this right to these classes, it is clear that, whatever the verbal formula, the Government bears a substantial burden to justify the statute.

B

There is no dispute that the purpose of these special preference provisions is to reunify families separated by the immigration laws. As Congress itself declared,

"[t]he legislative history of the Immigration and Nationality Act clearly indicates that the Congress intended [in these provisions] to provide for a liberal treatment of children, and was concerned with the problem of keeping families of United States citizens and immigrants united."

H.R.Rep. No. 1199, 85th Cong., 1st Sess., 7 (1957). It is also clear that, when Congress extended the privilege to cover the illegitimate child-mother relationship in 1957, it did so to alleviate hardships it found in several cases denying preferential status to illegitimate children and their mothers. Id. at 7-8. Accord, S.Rep. No. 1057, 86th Cong., 1st Sess., 4 (1957).

The legislative history, however, gives no indication of why these privileges were absolutely denied illegitimate children and their fathers. [10] The Government suggests that Congress may have believed that "such persons are unlikely to have maintained a close personal relationship with their offspring." Brief for Appellees 17. If so, Congress' chosen shorthand for "closeness" is obviously overinclusive. No one can dispute that there are legitimate, legitimated, step-, and adoptive parent-child relationships and mother-illegitimate child relationships that are not close, and yet are accorded the preferential status. Indeed, the most dramatic illustration of the overinclusiveness is the fact that, while Mr. Warner can never be deemed a "parent" of Serge, nevertheless, if he should marry, his wife could qualify as a step-parent, entitled to obtain for Serge the preferential status that Mr. Warner cannot obtain. Andrade v. Esperdy, 270 F.Supp. 516 (SDNY 1967); Nation v. Esperdy, 239 F.Supp. 531 (SDNY 1965). [11] Similarly, a man who, in an adulterous affair, fathers a child outside his marriage cannot be the "parent" of that child, but his wife may petition as step-parent. Matter of Stultz, 15 I. & N.Dec. (1975).

That the statute is underinclusive is also undisputed. Brief for Appellees 17; Tr. of Oral Arg. 21. Indeed, the Government could not dispute it in view of the close relationships exhibited in appellants' cases, recognized in our previous cases, see, e.g., Trimble v. Gordon, ante p. 430 U. S. 762; Weber v. Aetna Casualty & Surety Co., supra at 406 U. S. 169; Stanley v. Illinois, supra, and established in numerous studies. [12]

The Government suggests that Congress may have decided to accept the inaccurate classifications of this statute because they considered a case-by-case assessment of closeness and paternity not worth the administrative costs. This attempted justification is plainly inadequate. In Stanley v. Illinois, supra, we expressed our low regard for the use of "administrative convenience" as the rationale for interfering with a father's right to care for his illegitimate child.

"Procedure by presumption is always cheaper and easier than individualized determination. But when, as here, the procedure forecloses the determinative issues of competence and care, when it explicitly disdains present realities in deference to past formalities, it needlessly risks running roughshod over the important interests of both parent and child. It therefore cannot stand."

405 U.S. at 405 U. S. 656-657. See also Glona v. American Guarantee & Liability Ins. Co., supra.

This Court has been equally intolerant of the rationale when it is used to deny rights to the illegitimate child. While we are sensitive to "the lurking problems with respect to proof of paternity,'" Trimble v Gordon, ante at 430 U. S. 771, quoting Gomez v. Perez, 409 U. S. 535, 409 U. S. 538 (1973), we are careful not to allow them to be "`made into an impenetrable barrier that works to shield otherwise invidious discrimination.'" Trimble, ante at 430 U. S. 771. We require, at a minimum, that the "`statute [be] carefully tuned to alternative considerations,'" ante at 430 U. S. 772, quoting Mathews v. Lucas, 427 U.S. at 427 U. S. 513, and not exclude all illegitimates simply because some situations involve difficulties of proof. Ibid.

Given such hostility to the administrative convenience argument when invidious classifications and fundamental rights are involved, it is apparent that the rationale is inadequate in the present case. As I observed earlier, since Congress gave no indication that administrative costs were its concern, we should scrutinize the hypothesis closely. The likelihood of such a rationale is diminished considerably by the comprehensive and elaborate administrative procedures already established and employed by the INS in passing on claims of the existence of a parent-child relationship. All petitions are handled on a case-by-case basis, with the petitioner bearing the burden of proof. Moreover, the INS is no stranger to cases requiring proof of paternity. When, for example, a citizen stepmother petitions for the entrance of her husband's illegitimate child, she must necessarily prove that her husband is the child's father. [13] Indeed, it is ironic that, if Mr. Warner marries and his wife petitions for Serge, her proof will, in fact, be one step more complex than his would be -- not only must she prove his paternity, but she must also prove their marriage. Nevertheless, she would be entitled to an opportunity to prove those facts; he is not.

Nor is a fear of involvement with foreign laws and records a persuasive explanation of the omission. In administering the Act with respect to legitimated children, for example, the critical issue is whether the steps undertaken are adequate under local law to render the child legitimate, and the INS has become expert in such matters. [14] I note, in this connection, that, where a child was born in a country in which all children are legitimate, [15] proof of paternity is the critical issue, and the proof problems are identical to those involved with an illegitimate child.

Given the existence of these procedures and expertise, it is difficult indeed to give much weight to the hypothesized administrative convenience rationale. Moreover, as noted previously, this Court will not allow concerns with proof to justify "an impenetrable barrier that works to shield otherwise invidious discrimination." Gomez, supra at 409 U. S. 538. As the facts of this case conclusively demonstrate, Congress has "failed to consider the possibility of a middle ground between the extremes of complete exclusion and case-by-case determination of paternity." Trimble, ante at 430 U. S. 770-771. Mr. Warner is a classic example of someone who can readily prove both paternity and closeness. Appellees concede this. Tr. of Oral Arg. 21-22. The fact that he is denied the opportunity demonstrates beyond peradventure that Congress has failed to "carefully tun[e] [the statute] to alternative considerations.'" Trimble, ante at 430 U. S. 772, quoting Mathews v. Lucas, 427 U.S. at 427 U. S. 513. That failure is fatal to the statute. Trimble, ante at 430 U. S. 772-773. [16]

IV

When Congress grants a fundamental right to all but an invidiously selected class of citizens, and it is abundantly clear that such discrimination would be intolerable in any context but immigration, it is our duty to strike the legislation down. Because the Court condones the invidious discrimination in this case simply because it is embedded in the immigration laws, I must dissent.

MR JUSTICE WHITE also dissents, substantially for the reasons stated by MR. JUSTICE MARSHALL in his dissenting opinion.

Notes

[1] Title 8 U.S.C. §§ 1151(a) and (b) provide:

"§ 1151. Numerical limitations on total lawful admissions."

"(a) Quarterly and yearly limitations."

"Exclusive of special immigrants defined in section 1101(a)(27) of this title, and of the immediate relatives of United States citizens specified in subsection (b) of this section, the number of aliens who may be issued immigrant visas or who may otherwise acquire the status of an alien lawfully admitted to the United States for permanent residence, or who may, pursuant to section 1153(a)(7) of this title enter conditionally, (i) shall not in any of the first three quarters of any fiscal year exceed a total of 45,000 and (ii) shall not in any fiscal year exceed a total of 170,000."

"(b) Immediate relatives defined."

"The 'immediate relatives' referred to in subsection (a) of this section shall mean the children, spouses, and parents of a citizen of the United States: Provided, That in the case of parents, such citizen must be at least twenty-one years of age. The immediate relatives specified in this subsection who are otherwise qualified for admission as immigrants shall be admitted as such, without regard to the numerical limitations in this chapter."

(Emphasis added.) The changes made by the 1976 Amendments were not material to this case.

Title 8 U.S.C. § 1182(a)(14) provides:

"§ 1182. Excludable aliens."

"(a) General classes."

"Except as otherwise provided in this chapter, the following class of aliens shall be ineligible to receive visas and shall be excluded from admission into the United States:"

"* * * *"

"(14) Aliens seeking to enter the United States for the purpose of performing skilled or unskilled labor, unless the Secretary of Labor has determined and certified to the Secretary of State and to the Attorney General that (A) there are not sufficient workers in the United States who are able, willing, qualified, and available at the time of application for a visa and admission to the United States and at the place to which the alien is destined to perform such skilled or unskilled labor, and (b) the employment of such aliens will not adversely affect the wages and working conditions of the workers in the United States similarly employed. The exclusion of aliens under this paragraph shall apply to special immigrants defined in section 1101(a)(27)(A) of this title (other than the parents, spouses, or children of United States citizens or of aliens lawfully admitted to the United States for permanent residence), to preference immigrant aliens described in sections 1153(a)(3) and 1153(a)(6) of this title, and to nonpreference immigrant aliens described in section 1153(a)(8) of this title."

(Emphasis added.) For the significance of the 1976 Amendments on this section, see n. 4, infra.

[2] Title 8 U.S.C. § 1101(b)(1) provides:

"(1) The term 'child' means an unmarried person under twenty-one years of age who is -- "

"(A) a legitimate child; or"

"(B) a stepchild, whether or not born out of wedlock, provided the child had not reached the age of eighteen years at the time the marriage creating the status of stepchild occurred; or"

"(C) a child legitimated under the law of the child's residence or domicile, or under the law of the father's residence or domicile, whether in or outside the United States, if such legitimation takes place before the child reaches the age of eighteen years and the child is in the legal custody of the legitimating parent or parents at the time of such legitimation"

"(D) an illegitimate child, by, through whom, or on whose behalf a status, privilege, or benefit is sought by virtue of the relationship of the child to its natural mother;"

"(E) a child adopted while under the age of fourteen years if the child has thereafter been in the legal custody of, and has resided with, the adopting parent or parents for at least two years: Provided, That no natural parent of any such adopted child shall thereafter, by virtue of such parentage, be accorded any right, privilege, or status under this chapter."

"(F) a child, under the age of fourteen at the time a petition is filed in his behalf to accord a classification as an immediate relative under section 1151(b) of this title, who is an orphan because of the death or disappearance of, abandonment or desertion by, or separation or loss from, both parents, or for whom the sole or surviving parent is incapable of providing the proper care which will be provided the child if admitted to the United States and who has in writing irrevocably released the child for emigration and adoption; who has been adopted abroad by a United States citizen and his spouse who personally saw and observed the child prior to or during the adoption proceedings; or who is coming to the United States for adoption by a United States citizen and spouse who have complied with the preadoption requirements, if any, of the child's proposed residence: Provided, That no natural parent or prior adoptive parent of any such child shall thereafter, by virtue of such parentage, be accorded any right, privilege, or status under this chapter."

[3] Title 8 U.S.C. § 1101(b)(2) provides:

"The terms 'parent,' 'father,' or 'mother' mean a parent, father, or mother only where the relationship exists by reason of any of the circumstances set forth in subdivision (1) of this subsection."

[4] Instituting this suit with Warner were Ramon Fiallo, and Trevor and Earl Wilson. Both Fiallo, a five-year-old American citizen, and the Wilsons, teen-aged permanent resident aliens, sought the waiver of the labor certification requirements for their respective fathers. Although the 1976 Amendments removed the exemptions from the labor certification requirement for the parent-child relationship, nevertheless, their cases are not moot. There is a saving clause providing:

"The amendments made by this Act shall not operate to affect the entitlement to immigrant status or the order of consideration for issuance of an immigrant visa of an alien entitled to a preference status, under section 203(a) of the Immigration and Nationality Act, as in effect on the day before the effective date of this Act, on the basis of a petition filed with the Attorney General prior to such effective date."

1976 Amendments § 9. Since these situations cannot recur, however, I will focus on Mr. Warner, whose plight, unfortunately, can be repeated.

[5] The citizen seeking "immediate relative" status for his or her spouse, parent, or child must file a so-called Form I-130 petition with the Attorney General. See text accompanying n. 7, infra for a description of the procedure.

[6] The majority does not even engage in the modest degree of scrutiny required by Kleindienst v. Mandel, 408 U. S. 753 (1972). See discussion infra at 430 U. S. 807-808. That failure, I submit, is due to the fact that the statute could not even pass that standard

of review. See 430 U. S. infra.

[7] Under 8 U.S.C. § 1154(a),

"[a]ny citizen of the United States claiming that an alien is entitled to . . . an immediate relative status under section 1151(b) of this title . . . may file a petition with the Attorney General for such classification."

(Emphasis added.) Title 8 U.S.C. § 1154(b) prescribes the procedure after a petition is filed:

"(b) Investigation; consultation; approval; authorization to grant preference status"

"After an investigation of the facts in each case, and after consultation with the Secretary of Labor with respect to petitions to accord a status under section 1153(a)(3) or 1153(a)(6) of this title, the Attorney General shall, if he determines that the facts stated in the petition are true and that the alien in behalf of whom the petition is made is an immediate relative specified in section 1151(b) of this title, or is eligible for a preference status under section 1153(a) of this title, approve the petition and forward one copy thereof to the Department of State. The Secretary of State shall then authorize the consular officer concerned to grant the preference status."

Title 8 U.S.C. § 1153(d) precludes a consular officer from granting preferential status as an "immediate relative" "until he has been authorized to do so as provided by section 1154."

[8] Indeed, the majority concedes, ante at 430 U. S. 795 n. 6, that, if it is true that Congress has granted a right to citizens and not to aliens, my position is "persuasive." It then attempts to show that the premise is inaccurate. The effort, however, is doomed. There is no way to avoid the facts that, as the majority agrees, Congress was concerned with the problem of separating United States citizens from their families, and that, as the majority ignores, it specifically gave to citizens the right to seek special dispensation from the immigration restrictions for their immediate families. See discussion supra at 430 U. S. 806-807.

[9] The Court noted:

"[Appellees] concede that Congress could enact a blanket prohibition against entry of all aliens falling into the class defined by §§ 212(a)(28)(D) and (G)(v), and that First Amendment rights could not override that decision."

408 U.S. at 408 U. S. 767. But see id. at 408 U. S. 779 n. 4 (MARSHALL, J., dissenting).

[10] This absence should alert us to the danger, ever-present in legislation denying rights along gender and legitimacy lines, that it was very likely "habit, rather than analysis or actual reflection," Califano v. Goldfarb, ante at 430 U. S. 222 (STEVENS, J., concurring), that led Congress to assume that only mothers are close to their illegitimate children.

[11] The Immigration and Naturalization Service (INS) seeks to add a gloss in such cases requiring, in addition to the marriage between the petitioner and the father of

the illegitimate, some indicia of a "close family unit." Matter of Harris, 15 I. & N.Dec. ____ (1970). The phrase has not been defined, but we know that it includes a situation where the father, stepmother, and child have lived together at some time, Matter of The, 11 I. & N.Dec. 449 (1965), and excludes the case where neither father nor stepmother ever lived with or cared for the child. Matter of Harris, supra; Matter of Amado and Monteiro, 13 I. & N.Dec. 179 (1969); Matter of Soares, 12 I. & N.Dec. 653 (1968); Matter of Morris, 11 I. & N.Dec. 537 (1966). The only court to review this interpretation has rejected the added gloss. The fact of the marriage is sufficient to categorize the wife a "stepmother." Andrade v. Esperdy, 270 F.Supp. 516 (SDNY 1967).

[12] Chaskel, Changing Patterns of Services for Unmarried Parents, 49 Social Casework 3 (1968); Chaskel, The Unmarried Mother: Is She Different? 46 Child Welfare 65, 72 (1967); Herzog, Some Notes About Unmarried Fathers, 45 Child Welfare 194 (April 1966); Knight, Conferences for Pregnant Unwed Teen-Agers, 65 American Journal of Nursing 123, 126 (1965); Sauber, The Role of the Unmarried Father, 4 Welfare in Review 15, 16 (Nov.1966); Wessel, A Physician Looks at Services for Unmarried Parents, 49 Social Casework 11 (1968).

[13] The easiest proof is a birth certificate that names the father. Review of Immigration Problems: Hearings on H.R. 10993 before the Subcommittee on Immigration, Citizenship, and International Law of the House Committee on the Judiciary, 94th Cong., 1st and 2d Sess., 150-151, 154 (1975-1976). Alternatively, the INS obtains affidavits from the natural mother or other people familiar with the relationship, looks at school documents which may name the father, and considers facts of custody or support. Ibid. The INS also relies on local judicial determinations if they exist, but it does not require them, because

"alternative administrative recognition procedures . . . normally available to the natural father . . . are less cumbersome and time-consuming, and are regarded by consular officers as equally reliable with court determinations in eliminating fraudulent claims to the paternal relationship."

Id. at 151.

[14] The variations are many. In some countries, legitimation may be accomplished only by marriage of the natural parents, Matter of Blancapor, 14 I. & N.Dec. 427 (1973) (Philippines); Matter of F, 7 I. & N.Dec. 448 (1957) (Portugal); Matter of W, 9 I. & N.Dec. 223 (1961) (Surinam); Matter of J, 9 I. & N.Dec. 246 (1961) (British Guiana); Matter of C, 9 I. & N.Dec. 597 (1962) (Spain); by court decree, Matter of J and Y, 3 I. & N.Dec. 657 (1949); Matter of Duncan, 15 I. & N.Dec. ____ (I.D. 2373, 1975) (Liberia); or by formal recognition, Matter of K, 8 I. & N.Dec. 73 (1958) (Poland); Matter of Jancar, 11 I. & N.Dec. 365 (1965) (Yugoslavia); Matter of G, 9 I. & N.Dec. 518 (1961) (Hungary); Matter of Peters, 11 I. & N.Dec. 691 (1966) (Virginia Islands); Matter of Sinclair, 13 I. & N.Dec. 613 (1970) (Panama); Matter of Kubicka, 14 I. & N.Dec. 303 (1972) (Poland); Matter of Coker, 14 I. & N.Dec. 521 (1974) (Nigeria); Matter of Kim, 14 I. & N.Dec. 561 (1974) (Korea). In some countries, a child born out of wedlock is deemed the legitimate

child of both parents, Matter of G, supra; cf. Matter of Lo, 14 I. & N.Dec. 379 (1973) (People's Republic of China).

[15] See, e.g., Matter of G, supra; Matter of Lo, supra.

[16] Since resident aliens are also not to be arbitrarily denied privilege on the basis of gender and legitimacy, Hampton v. Mow Sun Wong, 426 U. S. 88 (1976); Sugarman v. Dougall, 413 U. S. 634 (1973); Graham v. Richardson, 403 U. S. 365 (1971), it is clear that appellants Earl and Trevor Wilson, if they meet the terms of the saving clause of the 1976 Amendments, should also be entitled to relief. See n. 5, supra.

Welfare programs should fund non-therapeutic abortions: Justice Marshall's dissent in Beal v. Doe (June 20, 1977)

MR. JUSTICE MARSHALL, dissenting. [*]

It is all too obvious that the governmental actions in these cases, ostensibly taken to "encourage" women to carry pregnancies to term, are in reality intended to impose a moral viewpoint that no State may constitutionally enforce. Roe v. Wade, 410 U.S. 113 (1973); Doe v. Bolton, 410 U.S. 179 (1973). Since efforts to overturn those decisions have been unsuccessful, the opponents of abortion have attempted every imaginable means to circumvent the commands of the Constitution and impose their moral choices upon the rest of society. See, e.g., Planned Parenthood of Missouri v. Danforth, 428 U.S. 52 (1976); Singleton v. Wulff, 428 U.S. 106 (1976); Bellotti v. Baird, 428 U.S. 132 (1976). The present cases involve the most vicious attacks yet devised. The impact of the regulations here falls tragically upon those among us least able to help or defend themselves. As the Court well knows, these regulations inevitably will have the practical effect of preventing nearly all poor women from obtaining safe and legal abortions. [n1]

The enactments challenged here brutally coerce poor women to bear children whom society will scorn for every day of their lives. Many thousands of unwanted minority and mixed-race children now spend blighted lives in foster homes, orphanages, and "reform" schools; cf. Smith v. Organization of Foster Families, 431 U.S. 816 (1977). Many children of the poor, sadly, will attend second-rate segregated schools. Cf. Milliken v. Bradley, 418 U.S. 717 (1974). And opposition remains strong against increasing Aid to Families With Dependent Children benefits for impoverished mothers and children, so that there is little chance for the children to grow up in a decent environment. Cf. Dandridge v. Williams, 397 U.S. 471 (1970). I am appalled at the ethical bankruptcy of those who preach a "right to life" that means, under present social policies, a bare existence in utter misery for so many poor women and their children.

I

The Court's insensitivity to the human dimension of these decisions is particularly obvious in its cursory discussion of appellees' equal protection claims in Maher v. Roe. That case points up once again the need for this Court to repudiate its outdated and intellectually disingenuous "two-tier" equal protection analysis. See generally Massachusetts Bd. of Retirement v. Murgia, 427 U.S. 307, 317 (1976) (MARSHALL, J., dissenting). As I have suggested before, this

model's two fixed modes of analysis, strict scrutiny and mere rationality, simply do not describe the inquiry the Court has undertaken -- or should undertake in equal protection cases.

Id. at 318. In the present case, in its evident desire to avoid strict scrutiny -- or indeed any meaningful scrutiny -- of the challenged legislation, which would almost surely result in its invalidation, see id. at 319, the Court pulls from thin air a distinction between laws that absolutely prevent exercise of the fundamental right to abortion and those that "merely" make its exercise difficult for some people. See Maher v. Roe, post at 471-474. MR. JUSTICE BRENNAN demonstrates that our cases support no such distinction, post at 485-489, and I have argued above that the challenged regulations are little different from a total prohibition from the viewpoint of the poor. But the Court's legal legerdemain has produced the desired result: a fundamental right is no longer at stake, and mere rationality becomes the appropriate mode of analysis. To no one's surprise, application of that test -- combined with misreading of Roe v. Wade to generate a "strong" state interest in "potential life" during the first trimester of pregnancy, see infra at 460; Maher v. Roe, post at 489-490 (BRENNAN, J., dissenting); post at 462 (BLACKMUN, J., dissenting) -- "leaves little doubt about the outcome; the challenged legislation is [as] always upheld." Massachusetts Bd. of Retirement v. Murgia, supra at 319. And once again, "relevant factors [are] misapplied or ignored," 427 U.S. at 321, while the Court "forgo[es] all judicial protection against discriminatory legislation bearing upon" a right "vital to the flourishing of a free society" and a class "unfairly burdened by invidious discrimination unrelated to the individual worth of [its] members." Id. at 320.

As I have argued before, an equal protection analysis far more in keeping with the actions, rather than the words, of the Court, see id. at 320-321, carefully weighs three factors -- "the importance of the governmental benefits denied, the character of the class, and the asserted state interests," id. at 322. Application of this standard would invalidate the challenged regulations.

The governmental benefits at issue here, while perhaps not representing large amounts of money for any individual, are nevertheless of absolutely vital importance in the lives of the recipients. The right of every woman to choose whether to bear a child is, as Roe v. Wade held, of fundamental importance. An unwanted child may be disruptive and destructive of the life of any woman, but the impact is felt most by those too poor to ameliorate those effects. If funds for an abortion are unavailable, a poor woman may feel that she is forced to obtain an illegal abortion that poses a serious threat to her health and even her life. See n. 1, supra. If she refuses to take this risk, and undergoes the pain and danger of state-financed pregnancy and childbirth, she may well give up all chance of escaping the cycle of poverty. Absent day-care facilities, she will be forced into full-time child care for years to come; she will be unable to work so that her family can break out of the welfare system or the lowest income brackets. If she already has children, another infant to feed and clothe may well stretch the budget past the breaking point. All chance to control the direction of her own life will have been lost.

I have already adverted to some of the characteristics of the class burdened by these regulations. While poverty alone does not entitle a class to claim government benefits, it is surely a relevant factor in the present inquiry. See San Antonio School Dist. v. Rodriguez, 411 U.S. 1, 70, 117-124 (1973) (MARSHALL, J., dissenting). Indeed, it was in the San Antonio case that MR. JUSTICE POWELL for the Court stated a test for analyzing discrimination on the basis of wealth that would, if fairly applied here, strike down the regulations. The Court there held that a wealth discrimination claim is made out by persons who share

two distinguishing characteristics: because of their impecunity, they [are] completely unable to pay for some desired benefit, and as a consequence, they sustai[n] an absolute deprivation of a meaningful opportunity to enjoy that benefit.

Id. at 20. Medicaid recipients are, almost by definition, "completely unable to pay for" abortions, and are thereby completely denied "a meaningful opportunity" to obtain them. [n2]

It is no less disturbing that the effect of the challenged regulations will fall with great disparity upon women of minority races. Nonwhite women now obtain abortions at nearly twice the rate of whites [n3] and it appears that almost 40% of minority women -- more than five times the proportion of whites -- are dependent upon Medicaid for their health care. [n4] Even if this strongly disparate racial impact does not alone violate the Equal Protection Clause, see Washington v. Davis, 426 U.S. 229 (1976); Jefferson v. Hackney, 406 U.S. 535 (1972), "at some point, a showing that state action has a devastating impact on the lives of minority racial groups must be relevant." Id. at 558, 575-576 (MARSHALL, J., dissenting).

Against the brutal effect that the challenged laws will have must be weighed the asserted state interest. The Court describes this as a "strong interest in protecting the potential life of the fetus." Maher v. Roe, post at 478. Yet in Doe v. Bolton, supra, the Court expressly held that any state interest during the first trimester of pregnancy, when 86% of all abortions occur, CDC Surveillance 3, was wholly insufficient to justify state interference with the right to abortion. 410 U.S. at 192-200. [n5] If a State's interest in potential human life before the point of viability is insufficient to justify requiring several physicians' concurrence for an abortion, ibid., I cannot comprehend how it magically becomes adequate to allow the present infringement on rights of disfavored classes. If there is any state interest in potential life before the point of viability, it certainly does not outweigh the deprivation or serious discouragement of a vital constitutional right of especial importance to poor and minority women. [n6]

Thus, taking account of all relevant factors under the flexible standard of equal protection review, I would hold the Connecticut and Pennsylvania Medicaid regulations and the St. Louis public hospital policy violative of the Fourteenth Amendment.

II

When this Court decided Roe v. Wade and Doe v. Bolton, it properly embarked on a course of constitutional adjudication no less controversial than that begun by Brown v. Board of Education, 347 U.S. 483 (1954). The abortion decisions are sound law and undoubtedly good policy. T hey have never been questioned by the Court, and we are told that today's cases "signa[l] no retreat from Roe or the cases applying it." Maher v. Roe, post at 475. The logic of those cases inexorably requires invalidation of the present enactments. Yet I fear that the Court's decisions will be an invitation to public officials, already under extraordinary pressure from well financed and carefully orchestrated lobbying campaigns, to approve more such restrictions. The effect will be to relegate millions of people to lives of poverty and despair. When elected leaders cower before public pressure, this Court, more than ever, must not shirk its duty to enforce the Constitution for the benefit of the poor and powerless.

*

[This opinion applies also to No . 75-1440, Maher, Commissioner of Social Services of Connecticut v. Roe et al., post, p. 464, and No. 75-442, Poelker, Mayor of St. Louis, et al. v. Doe, post, p. 519.]

Notes

1. Although an abortion performed during the first trimester of pregnancy is a relatively inexpensive surgical procedure, usually costing under $200, even this modest sum is far beyond the means of most Medicaid recipients. And "if one does not have it and is unable to get it, the fee might as well be" one hundred times as great. Smith v. Bennett, 365 U.S. 708, 712 (1961).

Even before today's decisions, a major reason that perhaps as much as one-third of the annual need for an estimated 1.8 million abortions went unmet was the fact that 8 out of 10 American counties did not have a single abortion provider. Sullivan, Tietze, & Dryfoos, Legal Abortion in the United States, 1975-1976, 9 Family Planning Perspectives 116-117, 121, 129 (1977). In 1975, 83,000 women had to travel from their home States to obtain abortions (there were 100 abortions performed in West Virginia and 310 in Mississippi), and about 300,000 more, or a total of nearly 40% of abortion patients, had to seek help outside their home counties. Id. at 116, 121, 124. In addition, only 18% of the public hospitals in the Nation performed even a single abortion in 1975, and, in 10 States, not one public hospital provided abortion services. Id. at 121, 128.

Given the political realities, it seems inevitable that the number and geographical distribution of abortion providers will diminish as a result of today's decisions. It is regrettable but likely that fewer public hospitals will provide the service and if Medicaid payments are unavailable, other hospitals, clinics, and physicians will be unable to do so. Since most Medicaid and public hospital patients probably do not have the money, the time, or the familiarity with the medical delivery system to travel to distant States or cities where abortions are available, today's decisions will put safe and legal abortions beyond their reach. The inevitable human tragedy that will result is reflected in a Government report:

[F]or some women, the lack of public funding for legal abortion acted as a deterrent to their obtaining the safer procedures. The following case history [of a death which occurred during 1975] exemplifies such a situation:

. . . A 41-year-old married woman with a history of 6 previous pregnancies, 5 living children, and 1 previous abortion sought an illegal abortion from a local dietician. Her stated reason for seeking an illegal procedure was financial, since Medicaid in her state of residence would not pay for her abortion. The illegal procedure cost $30, compared with an estimated $150 for a legal procedure. . . . Allegedly the operation was performed by inserting a metal rod to dilate the cervix. . . . [The woman died of cardiac arrest after two weeks of intensive hospital care and two operations.]

U.S. Dept. of Health, Education, and Welfare, Center for Disease Control, Abortion Surveillance, 1975, p. 9 (1977) (hereafter CDC Surveillance).

2. If public funds and facilities for abortions are sharply reduced, private charities, hospitals, clinics, and doctors willing to perform abortions for far less than the prevailing fee will, I trust, accommodate some of the need. But since abortion services are inadequately available even now, see n. 1, supra, such private generosity is unlikely to give many poor women "a meaningful opportunity" to obtain abortions.

3. Blacks and other nonwhite groups are heavily overrepresented among both abortion patients and Medicaid recipients. In 1975, about 13.1% of the population was nonwhite, Statistical Abstract of the United States, 1976, p. 25, yet 31% of women obtaining abortions were of a minority race. CDC Surveillance 2 and 24, Table 8. Furthermore, nonwhites secured abortions at the rate of 476 per 1,000 live births, while the corresponding figure for whites was only 277. Id. at 2, and Tables 8, 9. Abortion is thus a family planning method of considerably more significance for minority groups than for whites.

4. Although complete statistics are unavailable (three States, Puerto Rico, and the Virginia Islands having furnished no racial breakdown, and eight States giving incomplete data), nonwhites accounted for some 43.4% of Medicaid recipients during fiscal year 1974 in jurisdictions reporting. U.S. Dept. of HEW, National Center for Social Statistics, Medicaid Recipient Characteristics and Units of Selected Medical Services, Fiscal Year 1974, p. 2 (Feb.1977). Extrapolating this percentage to cover the entire Medicaid caseload of over 17.6 million, minority racial groups would account for 7,656,000 recipients. Assuming comparability of the HEW and census figures, this amounts to 27.4% of the Nation's nonwhite population. See Statistical Abstract, supra, n. 3, at 25. Since there are 1.8 female Medicaid recipients for every male, see Medicaid Recipient Characteristics, supra, the proportion of nonwhite women who must rely upon Medicaid is probably far higher, about 38.5%. The comparable figure for white women appears to be about 7%.

5. Requirements that the abortion be performed by a physician exercising his best

clinical judgment, and in a facility meeting narrowly tailored health standards, are allowable. Doe v. Bolton, 410 U.S. at 192-200.

6. Application of the flexible equal protection standard would allow the Court to strike down the regulations in these cases without calling into question laws funding public education or English language teaching in public schools. See Maher v. Roe, post at 476-477. By permitting a court to weigh all relevant factors, the flexible standard does not logically require acceptance of any equal protection claim that is "identical in principle" under the traditional approach to those advanced here. See Maher, post at 477.

Indian tribes enjoy the right to try and punish: Justice Marshall's dissent in Oliphant v. Suquamish Indian Tribe (March 6, 1978)

MR. JUSTICE MARSHALL, with whom THE CHIEF JUSTICE joins, dissenting.

I agree with the court below that the "power to preserve order on the reservation . . . is a sine qua non of the sovereignty that the Suquamish originally possessed." Oliphant v. Schlie, 544 F.2d 1007, 1009 (CA9 1976). In the absence of affirmative withdrawal by treaty or statute, I am of the view that Indian tribes enjoy, as a necessary aspect of their retained sovereignty, the right to try and punish all persons who commit offenses against tribal law within the reservation. Accordingly, I dissent.

Shouldn't exclude aliens from public employment as state troopers: Justice Marshall's dissent in Foley v. Connelie (March 22, 1978)

Mr. Justice MARSHALL, with whom Mr. Justice BRENNAN and Mr. Justice STEVENS joins, dissenting.

Almost a century ago, in the landmark case of Yick Wo v. Hopkins, 118 U.S. 356, 369, 6 S.Ct. 1064, 1070, 30 L.Ed. 220 (1886), this Court recognized that aliens are "persons" within the meaning of the Fourteenth Amendment. Eighty-five years later, in Graham v. Richardson, 403 U.S. 365, 91 S.Ct. 1848, 29 L.Ed.2d 534 (1971), the Court concluded that aliens constitute a " 'discrete and insular' minority," and that laws singling them out for unfavorable treatment "are therefore subject to strict judicial scrutiny." Id. at 372, 376, 91 S.Ct., at 1854. During the ensuing six Terms, we have invalidated state laws discriminating against aliens on four separate occasions, finding that such discrimination could not survive strict scrutiny. Sugarman v. Dougall, 413 U.S. 634, 93 S.Ct. 2842, 37 L.Ed.2d 853 (1973) (competitive civil service); In re Griffiths, 413 U.S. 717, 93 S.Ct. 2851, 37 L.Ed.2d 910 (1973) (attorneys); Examining Board v. Flores de Otero, 426 U.S. 572, 96 S.Ct. 2264, 49 L.Ed.2d 65 (1976) (civil engineers); Nyquist v. Mauclet, 432 U.S. 1, 97 S.Ct. 2120, 53 L.Ed.2d 63 (1977) (financial assistance for higher education).

Today the Court upholds a law excluding aliens from public employment as state troopers. It bases its decision largely on dictum from Sugarman v. Dougall, supra, to the effect that aliens may be barred from holding "state elective or important nonelective executive, legislative, and judicial positions," because persons in these positions "participate directly in the formulation, execution, or review of broad public policy." 413 U.S., at 647, 93 S.Ct., at 2850. 1 I do not agree with the Court that state troopers perform functions placing them within this "narrow . . . exception," Nyquist v. Mauclet, supra, at 11, 97 S.Ct., at 2126, to our usual rule that discrimination against aliens is presumptively unconstitutional. Accordingly I dissent.

In one sense, of course, it is true that state troopers participate in the execution of public policy. Just as firefighters execute the public policy that fires should be extinguished, and sanitation workers execute the public policy that streets should be kept clean, state troopers execute the public policy that persons believed to have committed crimes should be arrested. But this fact simply demonstrates that the Sugarman exception, if read without regard to its context, "would swallow the rule." Nyquist, supra, at 11, 97 S.Ct. at 2127. Although every state employee is charged with the "execution" of public policy, Sugarman unambiguously holds that a blanket exclusion of aliens from state jobs is unconstitutional.

Thus the phrase "execution of broad public policy" in Sugarman cannot be read to mean simply the carrying out of government programs, but rather must be interpreted to include responsibility for actually setting government policy pursuant to a delegation of substantial authority from the legislature. The head of an executive agency for example, charged with promulgating complex regulations under a statute, executes broad public policy in a sense that file clerks in the agency clearly do not. In short, as Sugarman indicates, those "elective or important nonelective" positions that involve broad policymaking responsibilities are the only state jobs from which aliens as a group may constitutionally be excluded. 413 U.S., at 647, 93 S.Ct., at 2850. In my view, the job of state trooper is not one of those positions.

There is a vast difference between the formulation and execution of broad public policy and the application of that policy to specific factual settings. While the Court is correct the "the exercise of police authority calls for a very high degree of judgment and discretion," ante, at 298, the judgments required are factual in nature; the policy judgments that govern an officer's conduct are contained in the Federal and State Constitutions, statutes, and regulations. 2 The officer responding to a particular situation is only applying the basic policy choices—which he has no role in shaping—to the facts as he perceives them. 3 We have previously recognized this distinction between the broad policy responsibilities exercised by high executive officials and the more limited responsibilities of police officers and found it relevant in defining the scope of immunity afforded under 42 U.S.C. 1983:

"When a court evaluates police conduct relating to an arrest its guideline is 'good faith and probable cause.' In the case of higher officers of the executive branch, however, the inquiry is far more complex since the range of decisions and choices—whether the formulation of policy, of legislation, of budgets, or of day-to-day decisions—is virtually infinite. . . . Since the options which a chief executive and his principal subordinates must consider are far broader and far more subtle than those made by officials with less responsibility, the range of discretion must be comparably broad." Scheuer v. Rhodes, 416 U.S. 232, 245-247, 94 S.Ct. 1683, 1691, 40 L.Ed.2d 90 (1974) (citation omitted).

The Court places great reliance on the fact that policemen make arrests and perform searches, often "without prior judicial authority." Ante, at 298. I certainly agree that "an arrest is a serious matter," ibid., and that we should be concerned about all "intrusions on the privacy of the individual." Ibid. But these concerns do not in any way make it "anomalous" for citizens to be arrested and searched by "noncitizen police officers," ante, at 299, at least not in New York State. By statute, New York authorizes "any person" to arrest another who has actually committed a felony or who has committed any other offense in the arresting person's presence. N.Y.Crim.Proc.Law § 140.30 (McKinney 1971). Moreover, a person making an arrest pursuant to this statute is authorized to make a search incident to the arrest. 4 While law enforcement is primarily the responsibility of state troopers, it is nevertheless difficult to understand how the Court can imply that the troopers' arrest and search authority justifies excluding aliens from the police force when the State has given all private persons, including aliens, such authority.

In Griffiths we held that the State could not limit the practice of law to citizens, "despite a recognition of the vital public and political role of attorneys," Nyquist v. Mauclet, 432 U.S., at 11, 97 S.Ct., at 2126. It is similarly not a denigration of the important public role of the state trooper—who, as the Court notes, ante, at 297, operates "in the most sensitive areas of daily life"—to find that his law enforcement responsibilities do not "make him a formulator of government policy." In re Griffiths, 413 U.S., at 729, 93 S.Ct., at 2858. Since no other rational reason, let alone a compelling state interest, has been advanced in support of the statute here at issue, 5 I would hold that the statute's xclusion of aliens from state trooper positions violates the Equal Protection Clause of the Fourteenth Amendment.

Notes

1. It is worth reiterating that "one need not be a citizen in order to take in good conscience an oath to support the Constitution. See In re Griffiths, 413 U.S., at 726 n. 18, 93 S.Ct. 2851." Hampton v. Mow Sun Wong, 426 U.S. 88, 111 n.43, 96 S.Ct. 1895, 1909, 48 L.Ed.2d 495.

2. "In its historical context, the assumption that only citizens would be employed in the federal service is easily understood. The new system of merit appointment, based on competitive examination, was replacing a patronage system in which appointment had often been treated as a method of rewarding support at the polls; since such rewards were presumably reserved for voters (or members of their families) who would necessarily be citizens, citizenship must have characterized most, if not all, federal employees at that

time. The assumption that such a requirement would survive the enactment of the new statute is by no means equivalent to a considered judgment that it should do so." Id., at 107, 96 S.Ct., at 1907.

3. "A second interest advanced in support of patronage is the need for political loyalty of employees, not to the end that effectiveness and efficiency be insured, but to the end that representative government not be undercut by tactics obstructing the implementation of policies of the new administration, policies presumably sanctioned by the electorate. The justification is not without force, but is nevertheless inadequate to validate patronage wholesale. Limiting patronage dismissals to policymaking positions is sufficient to achieve this governmental end." Elrod v. Burns, 427 U.S., at 367, 96 S.Ct., at 2687.

4. As the Court eloquently points out:

"The act of becoming a citizen is more than a ritual with no content beyond the fanfare of ceremony. A new citizen has become a member of a Nation, part of a people distinct from others. Cf. Worcester v. Georgia, 6 Pet. 515, 559, 8 L.Ed. 483 (1832). The individual, at that point, belongs to the polity and is entitled to participate in the processes of democratic decisionmaking. Accordingly, we have recognized 'a State's historical power to exclude aliens from participation in its democratic political institutions.' Dougall, supra, 413 U.S. at 648, 93 S.Ct. at 2850, as part of the sovereign's obligation 'to preserve the basic conception of a political community.' 413 U.S., at 647, 93 S.Ct., at 2125." Ante, at 295-296.

5. The Court has squarely held that a State may not treat employment as a scarce resource to be reserved for its own citizens. Sugarman v. Dougall, 413 U.S. 634, 641-645, 93 S.Ct. 2842, 2847-2849, 37 L.Ed.2d 853. Nor may a State impose special burdens on aliens to pro ide them with an incentive to become naturalized citizens. Nyquist v. Mauclet, 432 U.S. 1, 9-11, 97 S.Ct. 2120, 2126-2127, 53 L.Ed.2d 63. For it is the Federal Government that exercises plenary control over naturalization and immigration. Hampton v. Mow Sun Wong, 426 U.S., at 100-101, 96 S.Ct., at 1904. The Court's understanding that "most States expressly confine the employment of police officers to citizens," ante, at 299, is not persuasive. Most of the statutes cited to support that understanding were enacted before the Court had decided Sugarman. Some of the cited statutes are patently invalid as a result of Sugarman, and there is no evidence that most of the States referred to by the Court have decided to continue enforcement of their citizenship requirement for police officers after deliberate consideration of Sugarman's teaching that only policymaking officials would be unaffected by the holding.

I do not agree that the presumption should be deemed overcome in this case: Justice Marshall's concurrence and dissent in City of Los Angeles Department of Water and Power v. Manhart (April 25, 1978)

MR. JUSTICE MARSHALL, concurring in part and dissenting in part.

I agree that Title VII of the Civil Rights Act of 1964, as amended, forbids petitioners' practice of requiring female employees to make larger contributions to a pension fund than do male employees. I therefore join all of the Court's opinion except Part IV.

I also agree with the Court's statement in Part IV that, once a Title VII violation is found, Albemarle Paper Co. v. Moody, 422 U.S. 405 (1975), establishes a "presumption in favor of retroactive liability," and that this presumption "can seldom be overcome." Ante at 719. But I do not agree that the presumption should be deemed overcome in this case, especially since the relief was granted by the District Court in the exercise of its discretion, and was upheld by the Court of Appeals. I would affirm the decision below and therefore cannot join Part IV of the Court's opinion or the Court's judgment.

In Albemarle Paper Co. v. Moody, supra, this Court made clear that, subject to the presumption in favor of retroactive relief, the District Court retains its "traditional" equitable discretion "to locate 'a just result,'" with appellate review limited to determining "whether the District Court was 'clearly erroneous' in its factual findings and whether it 'abused' its . . . discretion." 422 U.S. at 424. See also Fed.Rule Civ.Proc. 52(a) (district court findings "shall not be set aside unless clearly erroneous"); Zenith Radio Corp. v. Hazeltine Research, Inc., 395 U.S. 100, 123 (199). The Court here does not assert that any findings of the District Court were clearly erroneous, nor does it conclude that there was any abuse of discretion. Instead, it states merely that the District Court gave "insufficient attention" to certain factors in striking the equitable balance. Ante at 719.

The first such factor mentioned by the Court relates to the "complexity" of the issue presented here, which may have led some pension fund administrators to assume that "a program like the Department's was entirely lawful," and that the alternative of equal contributions was perhaps unlawful because of a perceived "unfair[ness]" to men. Ante at 720. The District Court found, however, that petitioners "should have been placed on notice" of the illegality of requiring larger contributions from women on April 5, 1972, when the Equal Employment Opportunity Commission amended its regulations to make this illegality clear. [n1] The retrocative relief ordered by the District Court ran from April 5, 1972, through December 31, 1974, after which date petitioners changed to an equal contribution program. See ante at 706. Even if the April, 1972, beginning date were too early, a the Court contends, ante at 719 n. 36, [n2] during the nearly three-year period involved, there surely was some point at which "conscientious and intelligent administrators," ante at 720, should have responded to the EEOC's guidelines. Yet the Court today denies all retroactive relief, without even knowing whether petitioners made any efforts to ascertain their particular plan's legality.

The other major factor relied on by the Court involves "the potential impact . . . on the economy" that might result from retroactive changes in "the rules" applying to pension and insurance funds. According to the Court, such changes could "jeopardiz[e] [an] insurer's solvency and, ultimately, the insureds' benefits." Ante at 721. As with the first factor, however, little reference is made by the Court to the situation in this case. No claim is made by either petitioners or the Court that the relief granted here would in any way have threatened the plan's solvency, or indeed that risks of this nature were not "foresee[n]," and thus "included in the calculation of liability" and reflected in "the rates or contributions charged," ibid. [n3] No one has suggested, moreover, that the relatively modest award at issue -- involving a small percentage of the amounts withheld from respondents' paychecks for pension purposes over a 33-month period, see 553 F.2d 581, 592 (CA9 1976) -- could in any way be considered "devastating," ante at 722. And if a "devastating" award were made in some future case, this Court would have ample opportunity to strike it down at that time.

The necessarily speculative character of the Court's analysis in Part IV is underscored by its suggestion that the retroactive relief in this case would have led to a reduction in the benefits paid to retirees or an increase in the contributions paid by current employees. Ante at 722-723. It states that taking the award out of the pension fund was "apparently contemplated" by the courts below, ante at 723, but the District Court gave no indication of where it thought the recovery would come from. The Court of Appeals listed a number of ultimate sources of the money here involved, including increased employer contributions to the fund or one lump-sum payment from the Department 553 F.2d at 592. Indeed, the Department itself contemplated that the money for the award would come from city revenues, Pet. for Cert. 331, with the Department thereby paying for this Title VII award in the same way that it would have to pay any ordinary backpay award arising from its discriminatory practices. Hence the possibility of "harm" falling on "innocent" retirees or employees, ante at 723, is here largely chimerical.

There are thus several factors mentioned by the Court that might be important in some other case, but that appear to provide little cause for concern in the case presently before us. To the extent that the Court believes that these factors were not adequately considered when the award of retroactive relief was made, moreover, surely the proper course would be a remand to the District Court for further findings and a new equitable assessment of the appropriate remedy. When the District Court was found to have abused its discretion by denying backpay in Albemarle, this Court did not take it upon itself to formulate an award; it remanded to the District Court for this purpose. 422 U.S. at 424, 436. There is no more reason for the Court here to deny all retroactive relief on its own; once the relevant legal considerations are established, the task of finding the facts and applying the law to those facts is best left to the District Court, particularly when an equitable search for a "'just result'" is involved, id. at 424.

In this case, however, I do not believe that a remand is necessary. The District Court considered the question of when petitioners could be charged with knowledge of the state of the law, see supra at 729-730, and petitioners do not challenge the particular date selected or claim that they needed time to adjust their plan. As discussed above, moreover, no claim is made that the Department's or the plan's solvency would have been threatened, and it appears unlikely that either retirees or employees would have paid any part of the award. There is every indication, in short, that the factors which the Court thinks might be important in some hypothetical case are of no concern to the petitioners who would have had to pay the award in this case.

The Court today reaffirms "the force of the Albemarle presumption in favor of retroactive relief," ante at 723, yet fails to give effect to the principal reason why the presumption exists. In Albemarle, we emphasized that a "central" purpose of Title VII is "making persons whole for injuries suffered through past discrimination." 422 U.S. at 421; see id. at 418, 422. Respondents in this case cannot be "made whole" unless they receive a refund of the money that was illegally withheld from their paychecks by petitioners. Their claim to these funds is more compelling than is the claim in many backpay situations, where the person discriminated against receives payment for a period when he or she was not working. Here, as the Court of Appeals observed, respondents "actually earned the amount in question, but then had it taken from them in violation of Title VII." 553 F.2d at 592. In view of the strength of respondents' "restitution"-like claim, ibid., and in view of the statute's "central" make-whole purpose, Albemarle, 422 U.S. at 421, I would affirm the judgment of the Court of Appeals.

Notes

1. The District Court quoted the following from EEOC regulations:

"It shall not be a defense under Title [VII] to a charge of sex discrimination in benefits that the cost of such benefits is greater with respect to one sex than the other." 29 CFR § 1604.9(e).

387 F.Supp. 980, 981 (CD Cal.1975). See also 29 CFR § 1604.9(b) (1977) (employer may not "discriminate between men and women with regard to fringe benefits") (also adopted Apr. 5, 1972); § 1604.9(f) (employer's pension plan may not "differentiat[e] in benefits on the basis of sex") (adopted Apr. 5, 1972).

2. The Court also contends that respondents were not entitled to a refund of the full difference between the contributions that they made and the contributions made by similarly situated men, but rather only to the difference between their contributions "and the contributions they would have made under an actuarially sound and nondiscriminatory plan." Ante at 720 n. 36. This point, like the question of the appropriate date discussed in text, was not raised by petitioners, and would, in any event, argue for some reduction in the retroactive relief awarded, not for a complete denial of such relief. On its merits, moreover, the District Court's decision to place the women employees on an equal footing with their male coworkers surely was not unreasonable; the alternative suggested by the Court would still have left the women with higher pension payments than similarly situated men for the relevant period.

3. When respondents filed their charge with the EEOC in June, 1973, petitioners were put on notice of the possibility of retroactive relief being awarded. At that point, they could have -- and, for all we know, may have -- acted to ensure that the outcome of the litigation did not affect the viability of the plan by, for example, escrowing amounts to cover the contingency of losing to respondents. A prudent pension plan administrator, however certain of his legal position, could not reasonably have ignored such a contingency.

Thus, while the Court is correct that years of litigation may ensue after a charge is filed with the EEOC, this fact is largely irrelevant to the Court's concern about "major unforeseen contingencies," such as an award of retroactive relief adversely affecting the financial integrity of the pension plan. Ante at 721, 722 n. 42. And it is hardly likely that a retroactive award for the period prior to the filing of the EEOC charge would be "devastating" for the plan, since, as the Court recognizes, this period could not, in any case, be longer than two years. Ante at 722, and n. 42; see 42 U.S.C. § 2000e-5(g) (1970 ed., Supp. V). In the instant case, the period from when the award began to run until the charge was filed with the EEOC was just over one year, from April, 1972, to June, 1973. Even the liability for this period, moreover, at most would have involved only a small percentage of the contributions made by women employees, as discussed in text infra.

The Court demonstrates an attitude of callous indifference to the poor: Justice Marshall's dissent in Flagg Bros., Inc. v. Brooks (May 15, 1978)

MR. JUSTICE MARSHALL, dissenting.

Although I join my Brother STEVENS' dissenting opinion, I write separately to emphasize certain aspects of the majority opinion that I find particularly disturbing.

I cannot remain silent as the Court demonstrates, not for the first time, an attitude of callous indifference to the realities of life for the poor. See, e.g., Beal v. Doe, 432 U. S. 438, 432 U. S. 455-457 (1977) (MARSHALL, J., dissenting); United States v. Kras, 409 U. S. 434, 409 U. S. 458-460 (1973) (MARSHALL, J., dissenting). It blandly asserts that "respondent Jones . . . could have sought to replevy her goods at any time under state law." Ante at 436 U. S. 160. In order to obtain replevin in New York, however, respondent Jones would first have had to present to a sheriff an "undertaking" from a surety by which the latter would be bound to pay "not less than twice the value" of the goods involved and perhaps substantially more, depending in part on the size of the potential judgment against the debtor. N.Y.Civ.Prac.Law § 7102(e) (McKinney Supp. 19177). Sureties do not provide such bonds without receiving both a substantial payment in advance and some assurance of the debtor's ability to pay any judgment awarded.

Respondent Jones, according to her complaint, took home $87 per week from her job, had been evicted from her apartment, and faced a potential liability to the warehouseman of at least $335, an amount she could not afford. App. 44a-46a. The

Court's assumption that respondent would have been able to obtain a bond, and thus secure return of her household goods, must, under the circumstances, be regarded as highly questionable.* While the Court is technically correct that respondent "could have sought" replevin, it is also true that, given adequate funds, respondent could have paid her rent and remained in her apartment, thereby avoiding eviction and the seizure of her household goods by the warehouseman. But we cannot close our eyes to the realities that led to this litigation. Just as respondent lacked the funds to prevent eviction, it seems clear that, once her goods were seized, she had no practical choice but to leave them with the warehouseman, where they were subject to forced sale for nonpayment of storage charges.

I am also troubled by the Court's cavalier treatment of the place of historical factors in the "state action" inquiry. While we are, of course, not bound by what occurred centuries ago in England, see ante at 436 U. S. 163 n. 13, the test adopted by the Court itself requires us to decide what functions have been "traditionally exclusively reserved to the State," Jackson v. Metropolitan Edison Co., 419 U. S. 345, 419 U. S. 352 (1974) (emphasis added). Such an issue plainly cannot be resolved in a historical vacuum. New York's highest court has stated that, "[i]n [New York,] the execution of a lien . . . traditionally has been the function of the Sheriff." Blye v. Globe-Wernicke Realty Co., 33 N.Y.2d 15, 20, 300 N.E.2d 710, 713-714 (1973). Numerous other courts, in New York and elsewhere, have reached a similar conclusion. See, e.g., Sharrock v. Dell Buick-Cadillac, Inc., 56 App.Div.2d 446, 455, 393 N.Y.S.2d 166, 171 (1977) ("[T]he garageman, in executing his lien . . ., is performing the traditional function of the Sheriff, and is clothed with the authority of State law"); Parks v. "Mr. Ford," 556 F.2d 132, 141 (CA3 1977) (en banc) ("Pennsylvania has quite literally delegated to private individuals, [forced-sale] powers traditionally exclusively reserved' to sheriffs and constables"); Cox Bakeries, Inc. v. Timm Moving & Storage, Inc., 554 F.2d 356, 358 (CA8 1977) (Clark, J.) (by giving a warehouseman forced sale powers, "the state has delegated the traditional roles of judge, jury and sheriff"); Hall v. Garson, 430 F.2d 430, 439 (CA5 1970) ("The execution of a lien . . . has, in Texas, traditionally been the function of the Sheriff or constable").

By ignoring this history, the Court approaches the question before us as if it can be decided without reference to the role that the State has always played in lien execution by forced sale. In so doing, the Court treats the State as if it were, to use the Court's words, "a monolithic, abstract concept hovering in the legal stratosphere." Ante at 436 U. S. 160 n. 10. The state action doctrine, as developed in our past cases, requires that we come down to earth and decide the issue here with careful attention to the State's traditional role.

I dissent.

* New York's replevin statutes have been challenged by poor persons on the ground that they violated equal protection because the poor could not obtain the required "undertaking." See Laprease v. Raymours Furniture Co., 315 F.Supp. 716 (NDNY 1970) (three-judge court); Tamburro v. Trama, 59 Misc.2d 488, 299 N.Y.S.2d 528 (1969).

Racial quotas constitutional: Justice Marshall's concurrence and dissent in Regents of the University of California v. Bakke (June 28, 1978)

MR. JUSTICE MARSHALL.

I agree with the judgment of the Court only insofar as it permits a university to consider the race of an applicant in making admissions decisions. I do not agree that petitioner's admissions program violates the Constitution. For it must be remembered that, during most of the past 200 years, the Constitution, as interpreted by this Court, did not prohibit the most ingenious and pervasive forms of discrimination against the Negro. Now, when a State acts to remedy the effects of that legacy of discrimination, I cannot believe that this same Constitution stands as a barrier.

I

A

Three hundred and fifty years ago, the Negro was dragged to this country in chains to be sold into slavery. Uprooted from his homeland and thrust into bondage for forced labor, the slave was deprived of all legal rights. It was unlawful to teach him to read; he could be sold away from his family and friends at the whim of his master; and killing or maiming him was not a crime. The system of slavery brutalized and dehumanized both master and slave. [n1]

The denial of human rights was etched into the American Colonies' first attempts at establishing self-government. When the colonists determined to seek their independence from England, they drafted a unique document cataloguing their grievances against the King and proclaiming as "self-evident" that "all men are created equal" and are endowed "with certain unalienable Rights," including those to "Life, Liberty and the pursuit of Happiness." The self-evident truths and the unalienable rights were intended, however, to apply only to white men. An earlier draft of the Declaration of Independence, submitted by Thomas Jefferson to the Continental Congress, had included among the charges against the King that

[h]e has waged cruel war against human nature itself, violating its most sacred rights of life and liberty in the persons of a distant people who never offended him, captivating and carrying them into slavery in another hemisphere, or to incur miserable death in their transportation thither.

Franklin 88. The Southern delegation insisted that the charge be deleted; the colonists themselves were implicated in the slave trade, and inclusion of this claim might have made it more difficult to justify the continuation of slavery once the ties to England were severed. Thus, even as the colonists embarked on a course to secure their own freedom and equality, they ensured perpetuation of the system that deprived a whole race of those rights.

The implicit protection of slavery embodied in the Declaration of Independence was made explicit in the Constitution, which treated a slave as being equivalent to three-fifths of a person for purposes of apportioning representatives and taxes among the States. Art. I, § 2. The Constitution also contained a clause ensuring that the "Migration or Importation" of slaves into the existing States would be legal until at least 1808, Art. I, § 9, and a fugitive slave clause requiring that, when a slave escaped to another State, he must be returned on the claim of the master, Art. IV, § 2. In their declaration of the principles that were to provide the cornerstone of the new Nation, therefore, the Framers made it plain that "we the people," for whose protection the Constitution was designed, did not include those whose skins were the wrong color. As Professor John Hope Franklin has observed, Americans

> proudly accepted the challenge and responsibility of their new political freedom by establishing the machinery and safeguards that insured the continued enslavement of blacks.

Franklin 100.

The individual States likewise established the machinery to protect the system of slavery through the promulgation of the Slave Codes, which were designed primarily to defend the property interest of the owner in his slave. The position of the Negro slave as mere property was confirmed by this Court in Dred Scott v. Sandford, 19 How. 393 (1857), holding that the Missouri Compromise -- which prohibited slavery in the portion of the Louisiana Purchase Territory north of Missouri -- was unconstitutional because it deprived slave owners of their property without due process. The Court declared that, under the Constitution, a slave was property, and "[t]he right to traffic in it, like an ordinary article of merchandise and property, was guarantied to the citizens of the United States. . . ." Id. at 451. The Court further concluded that Negroes were not intended to be included as citizens under the Constitution, but were

> regarded as beings of an inferior order . . . altogether unfit to associate with the white race, either in social or political relations; and so far inferior that they had no rights which the white man was bound to respect . . . .

Id. at 407.

B

The status of the Negro as property was officially erased by his emancipation at the end of the Civil War. But the long-awaited emancipation, while freeing the Negro from slavery, did not bring him citizenship or equality in any meaningful way. Slavery was replaced by a system of

> laws which imposed upon the colored race onerous disabilities and burdens, and curtailed their rights in the pursuit of life, liberty, and property to such an extent that their freedom was of little value.

Slaughter-House Cases, 16 Wall. 36, 70 (1873). Despite the passage of the Thirteenth, Fourteenth, and Fifteenth Amendments, the Negro was systematically denied the rights those Amendments were supposed to secure. The combined actions and inactions of the State and Federal Governments maintained Negroes in a position of legal inferiority for another century after the Civil War.

The Southern States took the first steps to reenslave the Negroes. Immediately following the end of the Civil War, many of the provisional legislatures passed Black Codes, similar to the Slave Codes, which, among other things, limited the rights of Negroes to own or rent property and permitted imprisonment for breach of employment contracts. Over the next several decades, the South managed to disenfranchise the Negroes in spite of the Fifteenth Amendment by various techniques, including poll taxes, deliberately complicated balloting processes, property and literacy qualifications, and, finally, the white primary.

Congress responded to the legal disabilities being imposed in the Southern States by passing the Reconstruction Acts and the Civil Rights Acts. Congress also responded to the needs of the Negroes at the end of the Civil War by establishing the Bureau of Refugees, Freedmen, and Abandoned Lands, better known as the Freedmen's Bureau, to supply food, hospitals, land, and education to the newly freed slaves. Thus, for a time, it seemed as if the Negro might be protected from the continued denial of his civil rights, and might be relieved of the disabilities that prevented him from taking his place as a free and equal citizen.

That time, however, was short-lived. Reconstruction came to a close, and, with the assistance of this Court, the Negro was rapidly stripped of his new civil rights. In the words of C. Vann Woodward:

By narrow and ingenious interpretation [the Supreme Court's] decisions over a period of years had whittled away a great part of the authority presumably given the government for protection of civil rights.

Woodward 139.

The Court began by interpreting the Civil War Amendments in a manner that sharply curtailed their substantive protections. See, e.g., Slaughter-House Cases, supra; United States v. Reese, 92 U.S. 214 (1876); United States v. Cruikshank, 92 U.S. 542 (1876). Then, in the notorious Civil Rights Cases, 109 U.S. 3 (1883), the Court strangled Congress' efforts to use its power to promote racial equality. In those cases, the Court invalidated sections of the Civil Rights Act of 1875 that made it a crime to deny equal access to "inns, public conveyances, theatres and other places of public amusement." Id. at 10. According to the Court, the Fourteenth Amendment gave Congress the power to proscribe only discriminatory action by the State. The Court ruled that the Negroes who were excluded from public places suffered only an invasion of their social rights at the hands of private individuals, and Congress had no power to remedy that. Id. at 24-25.

When a man has emerged from slavery, and, by the aid of beneficent legislation, has shaken off the inseparable concomitants of that state,

the Court concluded,

there must be some stage in the progress of his elevation when he takes the rank of a mere citizen, and ceases to be the special favorite of the laws. . . .

Id. at 25. As Mr. Justice Harlan noted in dissent, however, the Civil War

Amendments and Civil Rights Acts did not make the Negroes the "special favorite" of the laws, but instead

sought to accomplish in reference to that race . . . . -- what had already been done in every State of the Union for the white race -- to secure and protect rights belonging to them as freemen and citizens; nothing more.

Id. at 61.

The Court's ultimate blow to the Civil War Amendments and to the equality of Negroes came in Plessy v. Ferguson, 163 U.S. 537 (1896). In upholding a Louisiana law that required railway companies to provide "equal but separate" accommodations for whites and Negroes, the Court held that the Fourteenth Amendment was not intended

to abolish distinctions based upon color, or to enforce social, as distinguished from political, equality, or a commingling of the two races upon terms unsatisfactory to either.

Id. at 544. Ignoring totally the realities of the positions of the two races, the Court remarked:

We consider the underlying fallacy of the plaintiff's argument to consist in the assumption that the enforced separation of the two races stamps the colored race with a badge of inferiority. If this be so, it is not by reason of anything found in the act, but solely because the colored race chooses to put that construction upon it.

Id. at 551.

Mr. Justice Harlan's dissenting opinion recognized the bankruptcy of the Court's reasoning. He noted that the "real meaning" of the legislation was "that colored citizens are so inferior and degraded that they cannot be allowed to sit in public coaches occupied by white citizens." Id. at 560. He expressed his fear that, if like laws were enacted in other States, "the effect would be in the highest degree mischievous." Id. at 563. Although slavery would have disappeared, the States would retain the power

to interfere with the full enjoyment of the blessings of freedom; to regulate civil rights, common to all citizens, upon the basis of race; and to place in a condition of legal inferiority a large body of American citizens. . . .

Ibid.

The fears of Mr. Justice Harlan were soon to be realized. In the wake of Plessy, many States expanded their Jim Crow laws, which had, up until that time, been limited primarily to passenger trains and schools. The segregation of the races was extended to residential areas, parks, hospitals, theaters, waiting rooms, and bathrooms. There were even statutes and ordinances which authorized separate phone booths for Negroes and whites, which required that textbooks used by children of one race be kept separate from those used by the other, and which required that Negro and white prostitutes be kept in separate districts. In 1898, after Plessy, the Charlestown News and Courier printed a parody of Jim Crow laws:

"If there must be Jim Crow cars on the railroads, there should be Jim Crow cars on the street railways. Also on all passenger boats. . . . If there are to be Jim Crow cars, moreover, there should be Jim Crow waiting saloons at all stations, and Jim Crow eating houses. . . . There should be Jim Crow sections of the jury box, and a separate Jim Crow dock and witness stand in every court -- and a Jim Crow Bible for colored witnesses to kiss."

Woodward 68. The irony is that, before many years had passed, with the exception of the Jim Crow witness stand,

all the improbable applications of the principle suggested by the editor in derision had been put into practice -- down to and including the Jim Crow Bible.

Id. at 69.

Nor were the laws restricting the rights of Negroes limited solely to the Southern States. In many of the Northern States, the Negro was denied the right to vote, prevented from serving on juries, and excluded from theaters, restaurants, hotels, and inns. Under President Wilson, the Federal Government began to require segregation in Government buildings; desks of Negro employees were curtained off; separate bathrooms and separate tables in the cafeterias were provided; and even the galleries of the Congress were segregated. When his segregationist policies were attacked, President Wilson responded that segregation was "'not humiliating, but a benefit,'" and that he was "'rendering [the Negroes] more safe in their possession of office, and less likely to be discriminated against.'" Kluger 91.

The enforced segregation of the races continued into the middle of the 20th century. In both World Wars, Negroes were, for the most part, confined to separate military units; it was not until 1948 that an end to segregation in the military was ordered by President Truman. And the history of the exclusion of Negro children from white public schools is too well known and recent to require repeating here. That Negroes were deliberately excluded from public graduate and professional schools -- and thereby denied the opportunity to become doctors, lawyers, engineers, and the like is also well established. It is, of course, true that some of the Jim Crow laws (which the decisions of this Court had helped to foster) were struck down by this Court in a series of decisions leading up to Brown v. Board of Education, 347 U.S. 483 (1954). See, e.g., Morgan v. Virginia, 328 U.S. 373 (1946); Sweatt v. Painter, 339 U.S. 629 (1950); McLaurin v. Oklahoma State Regents, 339 U.S. 637 (1950). Those decisions, however, did not automatically end segregation, nor did they move Negroes from a position of legal inferiority to one of equality. The legacy of years of slavery and of years of second-class citizenship in the wake of emancipation could not be so easily eliminated.

II

The position of the Negro today in America is the tragic but inevitable consequence of centuries of unequal treatment. Measured by any benchmark of comfort or achievement, meaningful equality remains a distant dream for the Negro.

A Negro child today has a life expectancy which is shorter by more than five years than that of a white child. [n2] The Negro child's mother is over three times more likely to die of complications in childbirth, [n3] and the infant mortality rate for Negroes is nearly twice that for whites. [n4] The median income of the Negro family is only 60% that of the median of a white family, [n5] and the percentage of Negroes who live in families with incomes below the poverty line is nearly four times greater than that of whites. [n6]

When the Negro child reaches working age, he finds that America offers him significantly less than it offers his white counterpart. For Negro adults, the unemployment rate is twice that of whites, [n7] and the unemployment rate for Negro teenagers is nearly three times that of white teenagers. [n8] A Negro male who completes four years of college can expect a median annual income of merely $110 more than a white male who has only a high school diploma. [n9] Although Negroes represent 11.5% of the population, [n10] they are only 1.2% of the lawyers and judges, 2% of the physicians, 2.3% of the dentists, 1.1% of the engineers and 2.6% of the college and university professors. [n11]

The relationship between those figures and the history of unequal treatment afforded to the Negro cannot be denied. At every point from birth to death, the impact of the past is reflected in the still disfavored position of the Negro.

In light of the sorry history of discrimination and its devastating impact on the lives of Negroes, bringing the Negro into the mainstream of American life should be a state interest of the highest order. To fail to do so is to ensure that America will forever remain a divided society.

III

I do not believe that the Fourteenth Amendment requires us to accept that fate. Neither its history nor our past cases lend any support to the conclusion that a university may not remedy the cumulative effects of society's discrimination by giving consideration to race in an effort to increase the number and percentage of Negro doctors.

A

This Court long ago remarked that

in any fair and just construction of any section or phrase of these [Civil War] amendments, it is necessary to look to the purpose which we have said was the pervading spirit of them all, the evil which they were designed to remedy. . . .

Slaughter-House Cases, 16 Wall. at 72. It is plain that the Fourteenth Amendment was not intended to prohibit measures designed to remedy the effects of the Nation's past treatment of Negroes. The Congress that passed the Fourteenth Amendment is the same Congress that passed the 1866 Freedmen's Bureau Act, an Act that provided many of its benefits only to Negroes. Act of July 16, 1866, ch. 200, 14 Stat. 173; see supra at 391. Although the Freedmen's Bureau legislation provided aid for refugees, thereby including white persons within some of the relief measures, 14 Stat. 174; see also Act of Mar. 3, 1865, ch. 90, 13 Stat. 507, the bill was regarded, to the dismay of many Congressmen, as "solely and entirely for the freedmen, and to the exclusion of all other persons. . . ." Cong.Globe, 39th Cong., 1st Sess., 544 (1866) (remarks of Rep. Taylor). See also id. at 634-635 (remarks of Rep. Ritter); id. at App. 78, 80-81 (remarks of Rep. Chandler). Indeed, the bill was bitterly opposed on the ground that it "undertakes to make the negro in some respects . . . superior . . ., and gives them favors that the poor white boy in the North cannot get." Id. at 401 (remarks of Sen. McDougall). See also id. at 319 (remarks of Sen. Hendricks); id. at 362 (remarks of Sen. Saulsbury); id. at 397 (remarks of Sen. Willey); id. at 544 (remarks of Rep. Taylor). The bill's supporters defended it not by rebutting the claim of special treatment, but by pointing to the need for such treatment:

The very discrimination it makes between "destitute and suffering" negroes and destitute and suffering white paupers proceeds upon the distinction that, in the omitted case, civil rights and immunities are already sufficiently protected by the possession of political power, the absence of which in the case provided for necessitates governmental protection.

Id. at App. 75 (remarks of Rep. Phelps).

Despite the objection to the special treatment the bill would provide for Negroes, it was passed by Congress. Id. at 421, 688. President Johnson vetoed this bill, and also a subsequent bill that contained some modifications; one of his principal objections to both bills was that they gave special benefits to Negroes. 8 Messages and Papers of the Presidents 3596, 3599, 3620, 3623 (1897). Rejecting the concerns of the President and the bill's opponents, Congress overrode the President's second veto. Cong.Globe, 39th Cong., 1st Sess., 3842, 3850 (1866).

Since the Congress that considered and rejected the objections to the 1866 Freedmen's Bureau Act concerning special relief to Negroes also proposed the Fourteenth Amendment, it is inconceivable that the Fourteenth Amendment was intended to prohibit all race-conscious relief measures. It

would be a distortion of the policy manifested in that amendment, which was adopted to prevent state legislation designed to perpetuate discrimination on the basis of race or color,

Railway Mail Assn. v. Corsi, 326 U.S. 88, 94 (1945), to hold that it barred state action to remedy the effects of that discrimination. Such a result would pervert the intent of the Framers by substituting abstract equality for the genuine equality the Amendment was intended to achieve.

B

As has been demonstrated in our joint opinion, this Court's past cases establish the constitutionality of race-conscious remedial measures. Beginning with the school desegregation cases, we recognized that, even absent a judicial or legislative finding of constitutional violation, a school board constitutionally could consider the race of students in making school assignment decisions. See Swann v. Charlotte-Mecklenburg Board of Education, 402 U.S. 1, 16 (1971); McDaniel v. Barresi, 402 U.S. 39, 41 (1971). We noted, moreover, that a

flat prohibition against assignment of students for the purpose of creating a racial balance must inevitably conflict with the duty of school authorities to disestablish dual school systems. As we have held in Swann, the Constitution does not compel any particular degree of racial balance or mixing, but when past and continuing constitutional violations are found, some ratios are likely to be useful as starting points in shaping a remedy. An absolute prohibition against use of such a device -- even as a starting point -- contravenes the implicit command of Green v. County School Board, 391 U.S. 430 (1968), that all reasonable methods be available to formulate an effective remedy.

Board of Education v. Swann, 402 U.S. 43, 46 (1971). As we have observed, "[a]ny other approach would freeze the status quo that is the very target of all desegregation processes." McDaniel v. Barresi, supra at 41.

Only last Term, in United Jewish Organizations v. Carey, 430 U.S. 144 (1977), we upheld a New York reapportionment plan that was deliberately drawn on the basis of race to enhance the electoral power of Negroes and Puerto Ricans; the plan had the effect of diluting the electoral strength of the Hasidic Jewish community. We were willing in UJO to sanction the remedial use of a racial classification even though it disadvantaged otherwise "innocent" individuals. In another case last Term, Califano v. Webster, 430 U.S. 313 (1977), the Court upheld a provision in the Social Security laws that discriminated against men because its purpose was "'the permissible one of redressing our society's longstanding disparate treatment of women.'" Id. at 317, quoting Califano v. Goldfarb, 430 U.S. 199, 209 n. 8 (1977) (plurality opinion). We thus recognized the permissibility of remedying past societal discrimination through the use of otherwise disfavored classifications.

Nothing in those cases suggests that a university cannot similarly act to remedy past discrimination. [n12] It is true that, in both UJO and Webster, the use of the disfavored classification was predicated on legislative or administrative action, but in neither case had those bodies made findings that there had been constitutional violations or that the specific individuals to be benefited had actually been the victims of discrimination. Rather, the classification in each of those cases was based on a determination that the group was in need of the remedy because of some type of past discrimination. There is thus ample support for the conclusion that a university can employ race-conscious measures to remedy past societal discrimination without the need for a finding that those benefited were actually victims of that discrimination.

IV

While I applaud the judgment of the Court that a university may consider race in its admissions process, it is more than a little ironic that, after several hundred years of class-based discrimination against Negroes, the Court is unwilling to hold that a class-based remedy for that discrimination is permissible. In declining to so hold, today's judgment ignores the fact that. for several hundred years, Negroes have been discriminated against not as individuals, but rather solely because of the color of their skins. It is unnecessary in 20th-century America to have individual Negroes demonstrate that they have been victims of racial discrimination; the racism of our society has been so pervasive that none, regardless of wealth or position, has managed to escape its impact. The experience of Negroes in America has been different in kind, not just in degree, from that of other ethnic groups. It is not merely the history of slavery alone, but also that a whole people were marked as inferior by the law. And that mark has endured. The dream of America as the great melting pot has not been realized for the Negro; because of his skin color, he never even made it into the pot.

These differences in the experience of the Negro make it difficult for me to accept that Negroes cannot be afforded greater protection under the Fourteenth Amendment where it is necessary to remedy the effects of past discrimination. In the Civil Rights Cases, supra, the Court wrote that the Negro emerging from slavery must cease "to be the special favorite of the laws." 109 U.S. at 25; see supra at 392. We cannot, in light of the history of the last century, yield to that view. Had the Court, in that decision and others, been willing to

do for human liberty and the fundamental rights of American citizenship what it did . . . for the protection of slavery and the rights of the masters of fugitive slaves,

109 U.S. at 53 (Harlan, J., dissenting), we would not need now to permit the recognition of any "special wards."

Most importantly, had the Court been willing in 1896, in Plessy v. Ferguson, to hold that the Equal Protection Clause forbids differences in treatment based on race, we would not be faced with this dilemma in 1978. We must remember, however, that the principle that the "Constitution is colorblind" appeared only in the opinion of the lone dissenter. 163 U.S. at 559. The majority of the Court rejected the principle of color blindness, and for the next 60 years, from Plessy to Brown v. Board of Education, ours was a Nation where, by law, an individual could be given "special" treatment based on the color of his skin.

It is because of a legacy of unequal treatment that we now must permit the institutions of this society to give consideration to race in making decisions about who will hold the positions of influence, affluence, and prestige in America. For far too long, the doors to those positions have been shut to Negroes. If we are ever to become a fully integrated society, one in which the color of a person's skin will not determine the opportunities available to him or her, we must be willing to take steps to open those doors. I do not believe that anyone can truly look into America's past and still find that a remedy for the effects of that past is impermissible.

It has been said that this case involves only the individual, Bakke, and this University. I doubt, however, that there is a computer capable of determining the number of persons and institutions that may be affected by the decision in this case. For example, we are told by the Attorney General of the United States that at least 27 federal agencies have adopted regulations requiring recipients of federal funds to take

"affirmative action to overcome the effects of conditions which resulted in limiting participation . . . by persons of a particular race, color, or national origin."

Supplemental Brief for United States as Amicus Curiae 16 (emphasis added). I cannot even guess the number of state and local governments that have set up affirmative action programs, which may be affected by today's decision.

I fear that we have come full circle. After the Civil War, our Government started several "affirmative action" programs. This Court, in the Civil Rights Cases and Plessy v. Ferguson, destroyed the movement toward complete equality. For almost a century, no action was taken, and this nonaction was with the tacit approval of the courts. Then we had Brown v. Board of Education and the Civil Rights Acts of Congress, followed by numerous affirmative action programs. Now, we have this Court again stepping in, this time to stop affirmative action programs of the type used by the University of California.

Notes

1. The history recounted here is perhaps too well known to require documentation. But I must acknowledge the authorities on which I rely in retelling it. J. Franklin, From Slavery to Freedom (4th ed.1974) (hereinafter Franklin); R. Kluger, Simple Justice (1975) (hereinafter Kluger); C. Woodward, The Strange Career of Jim Crow (3d ed.1974) (hereinafter Woodward).

2. U.S. Dept. of Commerce, Bureau of the Census, Statistical Abstract of the United States 65 (1977) (Table 94).

3. Id. at 70 (Table 102).

4. Ibid.

5. U.S. Dept. of Commerce, Bureau of the Census, Current Population Reports, Series P-60, No. 107, p. 7 (1977) (Table 1).

6. Id. at 20 (Table 14).

7. U.S. Dept. of Labor, Bureau of Labor Statistics, Employment and Earnings, January, 1978, p. 170 (Table 44).

8. Ibid.

9. U.S. Dept. of Commerce, Bureau of the Census, Current Population Reports, Series P-60, No. 105, p. 198 (1977) (Table 47).

10. U.S. Dept. of Commerce, Bureau of the Census, Statistical Abstract, supra, at 25 (Table 24).

11. Id. at 407-408 (Table 662) (based on 1970 census).

12. Indeed, the action of the University finds support in the regulations promulgated under Title VI by the Department of Health, Education, and Welfare and approved by the President, which authorize a federally funded institution to take affirmative steps to overcome past discrimination against groups even where the institution was not guilty of prior discrimination. 45 CFR § 80.3(b)(6)(ii) (1977).

Evidence obtained in patent violation of agency procedures shouldn't be admissible in a criminal prosecution: Justice Marshall's dissent in United States v. Caceres (April 2, 1979)

MR. JUSTICE MARSHALL, with whom MR. JUSTICE BRENNAN joins, dissenting.

The Court today holds that evidence obtained in patent violation of agency procedures is admissible in a criminal prosecution. In so ruling, the majority determines both that the Internal Revenue Service's failure to comply with its own mandatory regulations implicates no due process interest, and that the exclusionary rule is an inappropriate sanction for such noncompliance. Because I can subscribe to neither proposition, and because the Court's decision must inevitably erode respect for law among those charged with its administration, I respectfully dissent.

I

In a long line of cases beginning with Bridges v. Wixon, 326 U. S. 135, 326 U. S. 152-153 (1945), this Court has held that "one under investigation . . . is legally entitled to insist upon the observance of rules" promulgated by an executive or legislative body for his protection. See United States v. Nixon, 418 U. S. 683, 418 U. S. 695-696 (1974); Morton v. Ruiz, 415 U. S. 199, 415 U. S. 235 (1974); Yellin v. United States, 374 U. S. 109 (1963); Vitarelli v. Seaton, 359 U. S. 535 (1959); Service v. Dulles, 354 U. S. 363 (1957); United States ex rel. Accardi v. Shaughnessy, 347 U. S. 260 (1954). Underlying thee decisions is a judgment, central to our concept of due process, that government officials, no less than private citizens, are bound by rules of law. [1] Where individual interests are implicated, the Due Process Clause requires that an executive agency adhere to the standards by which it professes its action to be judged. See Vitarelli v. Seaton, supra, at 359 U. S. 547 (Frankfurter, J., concurring in part and dissenting in part).

Despite these well established precedents and the IRS's conceded failure to abide by mandatory investigative regulations, the Court finds no due process violation on the facts of this case. In reaching its conclusion, the majority relies on the absence of constitutional or statutory underpinnings for the regulations and on respondent's inability to establish prejudice from their circumvention. This approach draws support neither from our prior holdings nor from the principles on which the Due Process Clause is founded.

This Court has consistently demanded governmental compliance with regulations designed to safeguard individual interests even when the rules were not mandated by the Constitution or federal statute. In United States ex rel. Accardi v. Shaughnessy, supra, the Court granted a writ of habeas corpus where the Attorney General had disregarded applicable procedures for the Board of Immigration Appeals' suspension of deportation orders. Although the Attorney General had final power to deport the petitioner and had no statutory or constitutional obligation to provide for intermediate action by the Board, this Court held that while suspension procedures were in effect, "the Attorney General denies himself the right to sidestep the Board or dictate its decision." 347 U.S. at 347 U. S. 267. On similar reasoning, the Court, in Service v. Dulles, vacated a Foreign Service officer's national security discharge. While acknowledging that the Secretary of State was not obligated to adopt "rigorous substantive and procedural safeguards," the Court nonetheless held that "having done so he could not, so long as the Regulations remained unchanged, proceed without regard to them." 354 U.S. at 354 U. S. 388. Similarly, in

Vitarelli v. Seaton, we demanded adherence to Department of the Interior employee discharge procedures that were "generous beyond the requirements that bind [the] agency." 359 U.S. at 359 U. S. 547 (Frankfurter, J., concurring in part and dissenting in part). And most recently, in Morton v. Ruiz, we declined to permit the Bureau of Indian Affairs to depart from internal rules for establishing assistance eligibility requirements although the procedures were "more rigorous than otherwise would be required." 415 U.S. at 415 U. S. 235. See also United States v. Nixon, supra; Yellin v. United States, supra; 326 U. S. Wixon, 326 U. S. 135 (1945). [2] Thus, where internal regulations do not merely facilitate internal agency housekeeping, cf. American Farm Lines v. Black Ball Freight Service, 397 U. S. 532, 397 U. S. 538 (1970), [3] but rather afford significant procedural protections, we have insisted on compliance.

That the IRS regulations at issue here extend such protections is beyond dispute. As this Court recognized in Berger v. New York, 388 U. S. 41, 388 U. S. 63 (1967), "[f]ew threats to liberty exist which are greater than that posed by the use of eavesdropping devices." An agency's self-imposed constraints on the use of these devices, no less than limitations mandated by statute or by the Fourth Amendment, operate to preserve a "measure of privacy and a sense of personal security" for individuals potentially subject to surveillance. See United States v. White, 401 U. S. 745, 401 U. S. 790 (1971) (Harlan, J., dissenting).

Moreover, the history of the IRS authorization requirements clearly establishes that they were intended to protect privacy interests. The regulations were an outgrowth of investigations in 1965 and 1966 by a Subcommittee of the Senate Judiciary Committee concerning surveillance techniques of federal agencies. Testimony at Subcommittee hearings revealed that IRS agents had made extensive unauthorized use of a wide variety of eavesdropping techniques.

Hearings on S.Res. 9 before the Subcommittee on Administrative Practice and Procedure of the Senate Committee on the Judiciary, 89th Cong., 1st and 2d Sess., 1206-1208, 1762-1763, 1774-1777, 1828-1830, 1923-1935, 1999-2003 (1965-1966) (hereinafter S.Res. 39 Hearings). [4] Among the agency practices that the Subcommittee found offensive was the monitoring of certain conversations between taxpayers and IRS agents wired for sound. See, e.g., id. at 2017, 2078. Of more general concern was the agency's total failure to detect or disapprove violations of its own internal rules. Evidence before the Subcommittee indicated that supervisory personnel had condoned the use of illegal wiretaps, see id. 1517, 1546-1548, while upper level officials had remained ignorant of widespread departures from prescribed policies. See id. 1118, 1124-1128, 2005.

In response to that congressional investigation, the IRS convened a special Board of Inquiry to review agency surveillance practices and to recommend new procedures. Both the scope of the new regulations and the IRS Commissioner's representations to the Senate Subcommittee demonstrate that the agency was concerned not only with preventing "violation[s] of a person's constitutional or statutory rights," but also with "carefully control[ling]" certain investigatory techniques which, "although legal, nevertheless tend to be offensive to the public conscience." Id. at 1122 (testimony of Commissioner Cohen). The Commissioner further assured the Subcommittee that detailed regulations adopted by the agency in 1967 would guarantee such control. Id. at 1122-1126; CCH [1967] Stand.Fed.Tax Rep. � 6711, p. 71,756. Those regulations, recodified without substantial modification, are the basis of the instant proceedings. Compare Internal Revenue Service Manual � 652.22 (Sept.1975) with Internal Revenue Service Manual Supplement, Wiretapping and Electronic Eavesdropping, No. 93G-70 (July 10, 1967).

Against this historical backdrop, it is inarguable that these IRS regulations affect substantial individual interests. Indeed, the Court does not suggest otherwise. Rather, it places weight on respondent's failure to establish prejudice from agency illegality. Because Caceres cannot demonstrate that he "reasonably relied" on the regulations, ante at 440 U. S. 752, or that the failure to obtain proper authorization had any "discernible effect" on the IRS's decision to monitor his conversations with Agent Yee, ibid., the Court concludes that the agency's action implicates no due process interest. Such an approach is fundamentally misconceived. By assessing respondent's claim in terms of prejudice, the Court disregards not only its prior holdings, but also the principles of governmental regularity on which they rest.

To make subjective reliance controlling in due process analysis deflects inquiry from the relevant constitutional issue, the legitimacy of government conduct. If an individual is entitled only to the process that he subjectively believes is due, an agency could disregard its investigative rules with impunity provided it did so with consistency. For no person could "reasonably rely," ibid., on rules that were generally ignored. And to the extent that the majority views reliance as critical in an investigative context, it effectively reduces mandatory regulations to hortatory policies. Presumably the only persons with occasion to discover breaches of investigative rules will be those facing criminal prosecution. Such individuals will rarely, if ever, be able to establish that they planned their conduct with internal agency regulations in view. [5]

Moreover, the Court's focus on subjective reliance is inconsistent with our prior decisions enforcing due process guarantees. In Bridges v. Wixon, 326 U. S. 135 (1945), we vacated a deportation order because the Immigration and Naturalization Service had failed to observe regulations requiring that witness statements be made under oath, even though the petitioner's statements were not involved and he had not invoked the regulations at his deportation hearing. So too, in Yellin v. United States, 374 U. S. 109 (1963), this Court overturned the defendant's contempt conviction for refusal to testify before Congress where the House Committee on Un-American Activities had ignored rules requiring it to consider formally the injuries to a witness' reputation that might attend public hearings. Yet, as the dissent in Yellin pointed out, the defendant had predicated his refusal to testify on First Amendment grounds, not on the public nature of the proceedings, and had in "no way indicated that an executive session would have made any difference in his willingness to answer questions." Id. at 374 U. S. 141 (WHITE, J., dissenting).

Nor has this Court required, as it does today, that procedural irregularity affect the outcome of the governmental action at issue. For example, there was no suggestion in Yellin that, had the Committee formally considered the injury to the defendant's reputation, it would have convened an executive session. Indeed, the Committee Chairman had testified that this was precisely the kind of case where a public hearing was appropriate. Id. at 374 U. S. 117-118, n. 6. Nonetheless, the Court, even as it expressed doubt that procedural compliance would have made a difference, insisted that the defendant was entitled to no less. Id. at 374 U. S. 121. [6]

Similarly, the petitioner in Vitarelli v Seaton, 359 U. S. 535 (1959), was in no meaningful sense prejudiced by the Department of the Interior's departure from regulations governing employee discharges for national security reasons. After the petitioner filed suit, he received a revised notice of dismissal which complied with all applicable regulations. Despite the petitioner's inability to demonstrate that adherence to agency regulations would have affected the decision to discharge him, this Court ordered reinstatement.

Implicit in these decisions, [7] and in the Due Process Clause itself, is the premise that regulations bind with equal force whether or not they are outcome determinative. As its very terms make manifest, the Due Process Clause is, first and foremost, a guarantor of process. It embodies a commitment to procedural regularity independent of result. To focus on the conduct of individual defendants, rather than on that of the government, necessarily qualifies this commitment. If prejudice becomes critical in measuring due process obligations, individual officials may simply dispense with whatever procedures are unlikely to prove dispositive in a given case. Thus, the majority's analysis invites the very kind of capricious and unfettered decisionmaking that the Due Process Clause in general and these regulations in particular were designed to prevent.

Any fair application of our prior holdings mandates a different result. When the Government engages to protect individual interests, it may not constitutionally abrogate that commitment at its own convenience. I would hold the IRS to its surveillance authorization procedures regardless of whether a litigant can establish prejudice from their circumvention.

II

Having found a due process violation, I would require that the fruits of that illegality be suppressed in respondent's criminal prosecution. Mapp v. Ohio, 367 U. S. 643 (1961). Accordingly, under my analysis, it would be unnecessary to consider the scope of our supervisory powers, discussed in 440 U. S. Because, however, the Court addresses that issue, I must register my profound disagreement with both its reasoning and ultimate conclusion.

In determining that the exclusionary rule is an unwarranted sanction for the agency misconduct here, the Court attaches great significance to the agents' ostensible "good faith" in construing their own regulations to permit "emergency" surveillance of respondent in January and February, 1975. Ante at 440 U. S. 757, 440 U. S. 756. The record does not admit of such a charitable characterization. IRS Agent Yee alleged that respondent first attempted to bribe him in March, 1974. The IRS recorded a conversation between Caceres and Yee that same month. No further contact with Caceres concerning the bribe occurred until January, 1975, and no reasons have been offered for Agent Yee's failure to initiate surveillance during that 10-month hiatus. Nor does the record reflect any justification for the agency's failure to obtain approval for monitoring between the January 27 and January 31 meetings, to schedule meetings so as to permit timely authorization requests, or to process the January 31 authorization request expeditiously. In positing that the agents had a colorable basis for believing that the January 31 and February 6 meetings constituted "emergency situation[s]," see ante at 440 U. S. 756-757, the Court simply ignores the findings below that Agent Yee had absolute control over the scheduling of those conversations, and that any exigency was solely of the Government's own making. [8] This is plainly not an instance in which law enforcement officers have failed to grasp the nuances of constitutional doctrine in an area where the Court itself is sharply divided. Cf. Bivens v. Six Unknown Fed. Narcotics Agents, 403 U. S. 388, 403 U. S. 417 (1971) (BURGER, C.J., dissenting); Stone v. Powell, 428 U. S. 465, 428 U. S. 538-540 (1976) (WHITE, J., dissenting). Rather, the record demonstrates a breach of unambiguous and unquestionably applicable procedures.

Moreover, even assuming the good faith which the agency has failed to demonstrate, that consideration should not figure in our present analysis. Restricting application of the exclusionary rule to instances of bad faith would invite law enforcement officials to gamble that courts would grant absolution for all but the most egregious conduct. Since judges do not lightly cast aspersions on the motives of government officials, the suppression doctrine would be relegated to those rare circumstances where a litigant can prove insolent or calculated indifference to agency regulations. As we have noted in the context of Fourth Amendment violations, "[i]f subjective good faith alone were the test, . . . the people would be secure . . .' only in the discretion of the police." Beck v. Ohio, 379 U. S. 89, 379 U. S. 97 (1964). Just as intent has not been determinative in Fourth Amendment cases, see, e.g., Mincey v. Arizona, 437 U. S. 385 (1978); United States v. Brignoni-Ponce, 422 U. S. 873 (1975); Almeida-Sanchez v. United States, 413 U. S. 266 (1973), it should not be material here.

The Court next suggests that suppression is unnecessary in this case because "the Executive itself has provided for internal sanctions in cases of knowing violations of the electronic-surveillance regulations." Ante at 440 U. S. 756 (footnote omitted). Significantly, however, the Court does not assert that the sanctions which exist in theory are effectively employed in practice. While "[s]elf-scrutiny is a lofty ideal," Wolf v. Colorado, 338 U. S. 25, 338 U. S. 42 (1949) (Murphy, J., dissenting), nothing in the record before us indicates why IRS disciplinary procedures should enjoy the Court's special confidence. Quite the contrary, the circumstances surrounding the conception and continued operation of IRS authorization requirements illustrate a persistent indifference toward enforcement. [9] And abdication by the courts is unlikely to increase the agency's vigilance in disciplining or even discovering violations. To remove a defendant's incentive for exposing evasions or disingenuous constructions of applicable rules will inevitably diminish the agency's interest in self-monitoring. [10]

Finally, the Court declines to order suppression because

"a rigid application of an exclusionary rule to every regulatory violation could have a serious deterrent impact on the formulation of additional standards to govern prosecutorial and police procedures."

Ante at 440 U. S. 755-756. No support is offered for that speculation. In fact, all available evidence is to the contrary. Since 1967, the IRS has retained regulations requiring agents to give Miranda warnings in noncustodial settings despite Court of Appeals decisions suppressing statements taken in violation of those rules. United States v. Sourapas, 515 F.2d 295, 298 (CA9 1975); United States v. Leahey, 434 F.2d 7 (CA1 1970); United States v. Heffner, 420 F.2d 809 (CA4 1969). Significantly, the Court points to no instance in which an agency has withdrawn the procedural protections made meaningful by decisions such as Bridges v. Wixon, 326 U. S. 135 (1945), United States ex rel. Accardi v. Shaughnessy, 347 U. S. 260 (1954), Service v. Dulles, 354 U. S. 363 (1957), and Vitarelli v. Seaton, 359 U. S. 535 (1959).

Even if the majority's concern about inhibiting agency self-regulation were more solidly grounded, it could not justify the result in this case. Under today's decision, regulations largely unenforced by the IRS will be unenforceable by the courts. [11] I cannot share the Court's apparent conviction that much would be lost if the agency were to withdraw such rules in protest against judicial enforcement. Presumably Congress, which has been repeatedly dissuaded by the IRS from legislating in the area, [12] would then step into the breach. In the event of congressional action, this Court could not so cavalierly tolerate unauthorized electronic surveillance. See Miller v. United States, 357 U. S. 301 (1958). [13] Particularly where, as here, agency regulations were designed to stand in the place of legislative action, we should not hesitate to give them similar force and effect.

In my judgment, the Court has utterly failed to demonstrate why the exclusionary rule is inappropriate under the circumstances presented here. Equally disturbing is the majority's refusal even to acknowledge countervailing considerations. Quite apart from specific deterrence, there are significant values served by a rule that excludes evidence secured by lawless enforcement of the law. Denying an agency the fruits of noncompliance gives credibility to the due process and privacy interests implicated by its conduct. [14] Also, and perhaps more significantly, exclusion reaffirms the Judiciary's commitment to those values. Preservation of judicial integrity demands that unlawful intrusions on privacy should "find no sanction in the judgments of the courts." Weeks v. United States, 232 U. S. 383, 232 U. S. 392 (1914). See Elkins v. United States, 364 U. S. 206, 364 U. S. 222-223 (1960). Today's holding necessarily confers upon the Judiciary a "taint of partnership in official lawlessness." United States v. Calandra, 414 U. S. 338, 414

U. S. 357 (1974) (BRENNAN, J., dissenting). I decline to participate in that venture. I would affirm the judgment of the court below.

Notes

[1] Although not always expressly predicated on the Due Process Clause, these decisions are explicable in no other terms. The complaints in only two of the cases, Vitarelli v. Seaton, 359 U. S. 535 (1959), and Service v. Dulles, 354 U. S. 363 (1957), invoked the Administrative Procedure Act, see ante at 440 U. S. 754 n.19. In neither of these cases was the Act even mentioned in the Court's opinions. Rather, Vitarelli followed Service, see 359 U.S. at 359 U. S. 539-540, which, in turn, had relied on United States ex rel. Accardi v. Shaughnessy, 347 U. S. 260 (1954). See 354 U.S. at 354 U. S. 373, 354 U. S. 386-387. Both Accardi and its predecessor, Bridges v. Wixon, 326 U. S. 135 (1945), were habeas corpus cases. And Yellin v. United States, 374 U. S. 109 (1963), which involved criminal contempt sanctions, followed Accardi. Thus, it is clear that this line of precedent cannot be dismissed as federal administrative law. Cf. Board of Curators, Univ. of Mo. v. Horowitz, 435 U. S. 78, 435 U. S. 92 n. 8 (1978) (dictum). To the contrary, these decisions have been uniformly, and I believe properly, interpreted as resting on due process foundations. See United States v. Sourapas, 515 F.2d 295, 298 (CA9 1975); Konn v. Laird, 460 F.2d 1318 (CA7 1972); Antonuk v. United States, 445 F.2d 592, 595 (CA6 1971); Hollingsworth v. Balcom, 441 F.2d 419, 421 (CA6 1971); United States v. Leahey, 434 F.2d 7, 9 (CA1 1970); United States v. Lloyd, 431 F.2d 160, 171 (CA9 1970); Government of Canal Zone v. Brooks, 427 F.2d 346, 347 (CA5 1970); United States v. Heffner, 420 F.2d 809, 811-812 (CA4 1969); cf. Schatten v. United States, 419 F.2d 187, 191 (CA6 1969). See generally Berger, Do Regulations Really Bind Regulators, 62 Nw.U.L.Rev. 137 (1967).

[2] At issue in Bridges were regulations requiring that witness statements be made under oath and signed in order to be admissible in deportation hearings. As the Court correctly points out, ante at 440 U. S. 749, those rules were designed as "safeguards against essentially unfair procedures." 326 U.S. at 326 U. S. 153. However, there is no basis in precedent or in the language of Bridges itself for the majority's further intimation that the Due Process Clause "mandated" such protective regulations. Ante at 440 U. S. 749.

[3] American Farm Lines v. Black Ball Freight Service involved rules promulgated to assist an agency in compiling information for internal decisionmaking. As the American Farm Court noted in distinguishing Vitarelli v. Seaton, supra, these rules were not "intended primarily to confer important procedural benefits upon individuals in the face of otherwise unfettered discretion. . . ." 397 U.S. at 397 U. S. 538-539.

[4] As summarized by Senator Morse:

"The record reveals that illegal wiretapping by the Internal Revenue Service is not an occasional action of an overzealous agent, but is the logical and reasonable consequence of a well defined program. . . ."

Hearings on S.Res. 928 before the Subcommittee on Administrative Practice and

Procedure of the Senate Committee on the Judiciary, 90th Cong., 1st Sess., 29 (1967).

[5] Just as we do not expect defendants in Fourth Amendment cases to demonstrate that, but for the warrant requirement, they would have acted otherwise, we should not demand that those in respondent's position establish that they predicated their action on the existence of internal regulations. In both contexts, the rationale for mandating government compliance with procedural safeguards is the same: to prevent law enforcement officials from exercising unchecked discretion where substantial privacy interests are involved. And in neither case is a requirement of subjective reliance consistent with that objective.

[6] The Yellin Court, 374 U.S. at 374 U. S. 121, was equally dubious that agency adherence to its regulations would have affected the Attorney General's ultimate decision to deport in United States ex rel. Accardi v. Shaughnessy, 347 U.S. at 347 U. S. 267.

[7] In part, these decisions also reflect a prudent reluctance to speculate how another branch of government would have acted under different circumstances. Because the Court has so little apparent difficulty in hypothesizing that compliance would not have mattered in this case, see ante at 440 U. S. 752-753, 440 U. S. 757, it has adopted an approach that may well prove problematic in the next. Not all circumstances affecting agency decisions will so readily lend themselves to counterfactual analysis.

[8] See 545 F.2d 1182, 1187 (CA9 1976). For example, when Agent Yee proposed a meeting for the following day, Caceres responded: "I'll arrange my schedule to your convenience." App. 15.

[9] With respect to IRS officials' enthusiasm for self-discipline before and during the Senate investigation, Senator Long stated that "generally speaking, they have found wrongdoing only when the subcommittee has pointed directly and explicitly to it." S.Res. 39 Hearings 1118.

Since that investigation, the agency's performance has remained less than exemplary. In 1974, an internal audit of electronic surveillance within the IRS Intelligence Division revealed that 18 agents had engaged in 35 to 40 "instances" of improper monitoring within the previous year, with an "instance" defined to include as many as 15 different phone calls. Oversight Hearings into the Operations of the IRS before a Subcommittee of the House Committee on Government Operations, 94th Cong., 1st Sess., 42431, 450 (1975) (hereinafter Oversight Hearings). None of these employees were dismissed or demoted. In only one case did violations even actuate suspension. There, an employee who monitored his home telephone for "personal reasons completely unrelated to his official duties" was suspended for five days. Id. at 451; Reply Brief for United States 17, and n. 9. Four other employees received written reprimands. Eight received oral admonitions, three of which were confirmed in writing and none of which became part of the agents' personnel folders. Oversight Hearings 451, 453. The Service took no action in five cases. Id. at 451.

Such nominal sanctions hardly justify the Court's faith in agency self-restraint, particularly given the Government's failure to identify a single instance of internal disciplinary action by the IRS since 1974. See Reply Brief for United States 117.

[10] Professor Amsterdam, whom the majority cites for the proposition that regulations governing investigatory conduct

"may well provide more valuable protection to the public at large than the deterrence flowing from the occasional exclusion of items of evidence,"

ante at 440 U. S. 755, and n. 23, submits in the same article that federal review of compliance with such regulations through the exclusionary rule "remains essential." Amsterdam, Perspectives on the Fourth Amendment, 58 Minn.L.Rev. 349, 429 (1974). As he maintains, the suppression doctrine provides the "necessary occasions" for review of administrative problems and circumventions, and affords the "only available incentive" for law enforcement officials to make internal rules clear and incorporate them in personnel training. Ibid.

[11] See n 9, supra. Significantly, the Court does not suggest APA litigation as a plausible alternative means of enforcing investigative regulations. Unless a criminal prosecution is initiated, an individual is unlikely to discover that he was subject to unauthorized surveillance. And it strains credulity to suppose that an individual under criminal indictment would assume the expense, not to mention the risks of antagonizing government officials, that would attend APA proceedings. Cf. Amsterdam, The Supreme Court and the Rights of Suspects in Criminal Cases, 45 N.Y.U.L.Rev. 785, 787 (1970).

[12] See S.Res. 39 Hearings 1122-1124, 1144 (testimony of Commissioner Cohen); Oversight Hearings 401 (testimony of Commissioner Alexander); id. at 448 (testimony of Assistant Commissioner for Compliance Wolfe).

[13] In Miller, the Court suppressed evidence obtained after District of Columbia police forcibly entered an apartment without announcing their authority and purpose as required by a federal statute made applicable in the District by a ruling.

[14] See Oaks, Studying the Exclusionary Rule in Search and Seizure, 37 U.Chi.L.Rev. 665, 756 (1970) (by demonstrating that society attaches serious consequences to unlawful infringement of privacy interests, "the exclusionary rule invokes and magnifies the moral and educative force of the law. Over the long-term this may integrate some fourth amendment ideals into the value system or norms of behavior of law enforcement agencies").

Some constraints on pretrial discovery are essential to ensure free speech: Justice Marshall's dissent in Herbert v. Lando (April 18, 1979)

MR. JUSTICE MARSHALL, dissenting.

Although professing to maintain the accommodation of interests struck in New York Times Co. v. Sullivan, 376 U.S. 254 (1964), the Court today is unresponsive to the constitutional considerations underlying that opinion. Because I believe that some constraints on pretrial discovery are essential to ensure the "uninhibited [and] robust" debate on public issues which Sullivan contemplated, id., at 270, I respectfully dissent.

I

At issue in this case are competing interests of familiar dimension. States undeniably have an interest in affording individuals some measure of protection from unwarranted defamatory attacks. Libel actions serve that end, not only by assuring a forum in which reputations can be publicly vindicated and dignitary injuries compensated, but also by creating incentives for the press to exercise considered judgment before publishing material that compromises personal integrity. See Gertz v. Robert Welch, Inc., 418 U.S. 323, 341 -342 (1974); Rosenblatt v. Baer, 383 U.S. 75, 86 (1966).

Against these objectives must be balanced society's interest in promoting unfettered debate on matters of public importance. As this Court recognized in Sullivan, error is inevitable in such debate, and, if forced to guarantee the truth of all assertions, potential critics might suppress statements believed to be accurate "because of doubt whether [truthfulness] can be proved in court or fear of the expense of having to do so." 376 U.S., at 279 . Such self-censorship would be incompatible with the tenets on which the First Amendment and our democratic institutions are founded. Under a representative system of government, and informed electorate is a precondition of responsive decisionmaking. See Associated Press v. United States, 326 U.S. 1, 20 (1945); Grosjean v. American Press Co., 297 U.S. 233, 250 (1936); A. Meiklejohn, Free Speech and its Relation to Self-Government 88-89 (1948). To secure public exposure to the widest possible range of information and insights, some margin of error must be tolerated. Thus, absent knowing falsity or reckless disregard for the truth, the press is shielded from liability for defamatory statements regarding public figures. Curtis Publishing Co. v. Butts, 388 U.S. 130 (1967); New York Times Co. v. Sullivan, supra.

Yet this standard of liability cannot of itself accomplish the ends for which it was conceived. Insulating the press from ultimate liability is unlikely to avert self-censorship so long as any plaintiff with a deep pocket and a facially sufficient complaint is afforded unconstrained discovery of the editorial process. If the substantive balance of interests struck in Sullivan is to remain viable, it must be reassessed in light of the procedural realities under which libel actions are conducted.

II

The potential for abuse of liberal discovery procedures is of particular concern in the defamation context. As members of the bench and bar have increasingly noted, rules designed to facilitate expeditious resolution of civil disputes have too often proved tools for harassment and delay. 1 Capitalizing on this Court's broad mandate in Hickman v. Taylor, 329 U.S. 495, 507 (1947), reaffirmed in Schlagenhauf v. Holder, 379 U.S. 104, 114 -115 (1964), that discovery rules be accorded a "broad and liberal" scope, litigants have on occasion transformed Fed. Rule Civ. Proc. 26 devices into tactics of attrition. The possibility of such abuse is enhanced in libel litigation, for many self-perceived victims of defamation are animated by something more than a rational calculus of their chances of recovery. 2 Given the circumstances under which libel actions arise, plaintiffs' pretrial maneuvers may be fashioned more with an eye to deterrence or retaliation than to unearthing germane material.

Not only is the risk of in terrorem discovery particularly pronounced in the defamation context, but the societal consequences attending such abuse are of special magnitude. Rather than submit to the intrusiveness and expense of protracted discovery, even editors confident of their ability to prevail at trial or on a motion for summary judgment may find it prudent to "`steer far wid[e]' of the unlawful zone' thereby keeping protected discussion from public cognizance." Rosenbloom v. Metromedia, Inc., 403 U.S. 29, 53 (1971) (plurality opinion; citation omitted). Faced with the prospect of escalating attorney's fees, diversion of time from journalistic endeavors, and exposure of potentially sensitive information, editors may well make publication judgments that reflect less the risk of liability than the expense of vindication. 3

Although acknowledging a problem of discovery abuse, the Court suggests that the remedy lies elsewhere, in "major changes in the present Rules of Civil Procedure." Ante, at 177. And somewhat inconsistently, the Court asserts further that district judges already have "in fact and in law . . . ample powers . . . to prevent abuse." Ibid. I cannot agree. Where First Amendment rights are critically implicated, it is incumbent on this Court to safeguard their effective exercise. By leaving the directives of Hickman and Schlagenhauf unqualified with respect to libel litigation, the Court has abdicated that responsibility. 4

In my judgment, the same constitutional concerns that impelled us in Sullivan to confine the circumstances under which defamation liability could attach also mandate some constraints on roving discovery. I would hold that the broad discovery principles enunciated in Hickman and Schlagenhauf are inapposite in defamation cases. More specifically, I would require that district courts superintend pretrial disclosure in such litigation so as to protect the press from unnecessarily protracted or tangential inquiry. To that end, discovery requests should be measured against a strict standard of relevance. Further, because the threat of disclosure may intrude with special force on certain aspects of the editorial process, I believe some additional protection in the form of an evidentiary privilege is warranted.

III

The Court of Appeals extended a privilege subsuming essentially two kinds of discovery requests. The first included questions concerning the state of mind of an individual journalist, principally his conclusions and bases for conclusions as to the accuracy of information compiled during investigation. The second encompassed communications between journalists about matter to be included in the broadcast. 568 F.2d 974, 978 (CA2 1977). Reasoning that discovery of both forms of material would be intrusive, that the intrusion would be inhibiting, and that such inhibition would be inconsistent with the editorial autonomy recognized in Miami Herald Publishing Co. v. Tornillo, 418 U.S. 241 (1974), and Columbia Broadcasting System, Inc. v. Democratic

National Committee, 412 U.S. 94 (1973), the Court of Appeals concluded that a privilege from disclosure was essential. 568 F.2d, at 975.

With respect to state-of-mind inquiry, that syllogism cannot withstand analysis. For although discovery may well be intrusive, it is unclear how journalists faced with the possibility of such questions can be "chilled in the very process of thought." Id., at 984. Regardless of whether strictures are placed on discovery, reporters and editors must continue to think, and to form opinions and conclusions about the veracity of their sources and the accuracy of their information. At best, it can be argued only that failure to insulate the press from this form of disclosure will inhibit not the editing process but the final product - that the specter of questions concerning opinion and belief will induce journalists to refrain from publishing material thought to be accurate. But as my Brother BRENNAN notes, ante, at 192-193, this inhibition would emanate principally from Sullivan's substantive standard, not from the incremental effect of such discovery. So long as Sullivan makes state of mind dispositive, some inquiry as to the manner in which editorial decisions are made is inevitable. And it is simply implausible to suppose that asking a reporter why certain material was or was not included in a given publication will be more likely to stifle incisive journalism than compelling disclosure of other objective evidence regarding that decision. 5

I do not mean to suggest, as did the District Court here, that Tornillo and Columbia Broadcasting have "nothing to do" with this case. 73 F. R. D. 387, 396 (SDNY 1977). To the contrary, the values of editorial autonomy given recognition in those decisions should inform district courts as they monitor the discovery phase of defamation cases. But assuming that a trial judge has discharged his obligation to prevent unduly protracted or inessential disclosure, see supra, at 206, I am unpersuaded that the impact of state-of-mind inquiry will of itself threaten journalistic endeavor beyond the threshold contemplated by Sullivan.

External evidence of editorial decisionmaking, however, stands on a different footing. For here the concern is not simply that the ultimate product may be inhibited, but that the process itself will be chilled. Journalists cannot stop forming tentative hypotheses, but they can cease articulating them openly. If prepublication dialogue is freely discoverable, editors and reporters may well prove reluctant to air their reservations or to explore other means of presenting information and comment. The threat of unchecked discovery may well stifle the collegial discussion essential to sound editorial dynamics. As we recognized in United States v. Nixon, 418 U.S. 683, 705 (1974): "[T]hose who expect public dissemination of their remarks may well temper candor with a concern for appearances . . . to the detriment of the decisionmaking process." (Footnote omitted.) Cf. NLRB v. Sears, Roebuck & Co., 421 U.S. 132, 151 (1975). Society's interest in enhancing the accuracy of coverage of public events is ill-served by procedures tending to muffle expression of uncertainty. To preserve a climate of free interchange among journalists, the confidentiality of their conversation must be guaranteed.

It is not enough, I believe, to accord a discovery privilege that would yield before any plaintiff who can make a prima facie showing of falsity. See ante, at 197-198 (opinion of BRENNAN, J.). Unless a journalist knows with some certitude that his misgivings will enjoy protection, they may remain unexpressed. See 568 F.2d, at 994 (Oakes, J., concurring). If full disclosure is available whenever a plaintiff can establish that the press erred in some particular, editorial communication would not be demonstrably less inhibited than under the Court's approach. And by hypothesis, it is precisely those instances in which the risk of error is significant that frank discussion is most valuable.

Accordingly, I would foreclose discovery in defamation cases as to the substance of editorial conversation. 6 Shielding this limited category of evidence from disclosure would be unlikely to preclude recovery by plaintiffs with valid defamation claims. For there are a variety of other means to establish deliberate or reckless disregard for the truth, such as absence of verification, inherent implausibility, obvious reasons to doubt the veracity or accuracy of information, and concessions or inconsistent statements by the defendant. See St. Amant v. Thompson, 390 U.S. 727, 732 (1968). To the extent that such a limited privilege might deny recovery in some marginal cases, it is, in my view, an acceptable price to pay for preserving a climate conducive to considered editorial judgment.

I would therefore direct the Court of Appeals to remand this case to the District Court for determination first, whether the questions concerning Lando's state of mind satisfy the criteria set forth in Part II of this opinion, and second, whether respondents waived the privilege defined in Part III for prepublication discussions.

Notes

[1] See Bell, The Pound Conference Follow-up: A Response from the United States Department of Justice, 76 F. R. D. 320, 328-329 (1978); Erikson, The Pound Conference Recommendations: A Blueprint for the Justice System in the Twenty-First Century, 76 F. R. D. 277, 288-290 (1978); Lasker, The Court Crunch: A View from the Bench, 76 F. R. D. 245, 252 (1978); A. B. A. Litigation Section, Report of the Special Committee for the Study of Discovery Abuse (Oct. 1977); Stanley, President's Page, 62 A. B. A. J. 1375 (1976); Burger, Agenda for 2000 A. D. - A Need for Systematic Anticipation, 70 F. R. D. 83, 95-96 (1976); 4 J. Moore, Federal Practice § 26.02 3. (2d ed. 1976).

[2] See Anderson, Libel and Press Self-Censorship, 53 Texas L. Rev. 422, 435 (1975).

[3] As the facts of the instant case illustrate, that expense can be considerable. The deposition of Lando alone consumed 26 days and close to 3,000 pages of transcript. See 568 F.2d 974, 982 (CA2 1977).

[4] Although the separate opinions of my Brothers POWELL and STEWART display greater solicitude for First Amendment values than does the opinion for the Court, I believe that they too elide the critical issue presented by this case. Under the "broad and liberal" standard of Hickman, surely disclosure of what was known to a journalist but "was not published," ante, at 200 (opinion of STEWART, J.), will often be

germane to whether that individual proceeded with deliberate or reckless disregard for the truth. And admonishing district courts to monitor discovery in the "interest of justice," ante, at 180 (opinion of POWELL, J.) or to prevent "undue burden or expense," ibid., adds little to the guidance already afforded by Rule 26 and cannot adequately mitigate the burdens on the press so long as Hickman's directive remains in force. Moreover, neither opinion is directly responsive to the effect of discovery on editorial discussion. See infra, at 208-209.

[5] Respondents in this case produced a considerable amount of evidence regarding preparation of the broadcast:

"Lando answered innumerable questions about what he knew, or had seen; whom he interviewed; intimate details of his discussions with interviewees; and the form and frequency of his communications with sources. The exhibits produced included transcripts of his interviews; volumes of reporters notes; videotapes of interviews; and a series of drafts of the `60 Minutes' telecast. Herbert also discovered the contents of pre-telecast conversations between Lando and Wallace as well as reactions to documents considered by both." 568 F.2d, at 982 (footnote omitted).

As an abstract proposition, it is not self-evident why disclosure of this material, for which no privilege was sought, would be less likely to inhibit the final publication than state-of-mind inquiries, which in most cases would presumably elicit self-serving responses. Indeed, as the Court acknowledges, plaintiffs may "rarely be successful in proving awareness of falsehood from the mouth of the defendant himself." Ante, at 170.

Thus, I seriously doubt that state-of-mind questions will substantially "increase the likelihood of large damages judgments in libel actions." Ante, at 191 (opinion of BRENNAN, J.). But neither can it be disputed that such questions might on occasion generate answers useful to plaintiffs in defamation suits. See, e. g., Davis v. Schuchat, 166 U.S. App. D.C. 351, 355-356, 510 F.2d 731, 735-736 (1975); Goldwater v. Ginzburg, 414 F.2d 324, 334-335 (CA2 1969), cert. denied, 396 U.S. 1049 (1970); Varnish v. Best Medium Publishing Co., 405 F.2d 608, 612 (CA2 1968), cert. denied, 394 U.S. 987 (1969).

[6] Contrary to the Court's intimation, ante, at 165, 169-170, this would not be the first instance in which protection apart from the Sullivan malice standard has been extended to safeguard the constitutional interests implicated in libel suits. For example, lower courts have displayed sensitivity to First Amendment values in assessing motions to compel disclosure of confidential sources, see Cervantes v. Time, Inc., 464 F.2d 986, 992-994 (CA8 1972), cert. denied, 409 U.S. 1125 (1973), and motions by defendants for summary judgment. See Washington Post Co. v. Keogh, 125 U.S. App. D.C. 32, 34-35, 365 F.2d 965, 967-968 (1966), cert. denied, 385 U.S. 1011 (1967).

Different considerations would, of course, obtain if a privilege for editorial communications were sought in conjunction with criminal proceedings. Cf. New York Times Co. v. Jascalevich, 439 U.S. 1331 (1978) (MARSHALL, J., in chambers); United States v. Nixon, 418 U.S. 683, 712 -713 (1974); Branzburg v. Hayes, 408 U.S. 665 (1972); id., at 741-743 (STEWART, J., dissenting).

Limit to burdens on pretrial detainee inmates: Justice Marshall's dissent in Bell v. Wolfish (May 14, 1979)

MR. JUSTICE MARSHALL, dissenting.

The Court holds that the Government may burden pretrial detainees with almost any restriction, provided detention officials do not proclaim a punitive intent or impose conditions that are "arbitrary or purposeless." Ante, at 539. As if this standard were not sufficiently ineffectual, the Court dilutes it further by according virtually unlimited deference to detention officials' justifications for particular impositions. Conspicuously lacking from this analysis is any meaningful consideration of the most relevant factor, the impact that restrictions may have on inmates. Such an approach is unsupportable, given that all of these detainees are presumptively innocent and many are confined solely because they cannot afford bail. 1

In my view, the Court's holding departs from the precedent it purports to follow and precludes effective judicial review of the conditions of pretrial confinement. More fundamentally, I believe the proper inquiry in this context is not whether a particular restraint can be labeled "punishment." Rather, as with other due process challenges, the inquiry should be whether the governmental interests served by any given restriction outweigh the individual deprivations suffered.

I

The premise of the Court's analysis is that detainees, unlike prisoners, may not be "punished." To determine when a particular disability imposed during pretrial detention is punishment, the Court invokes the factors enunciated in Kennedy v. Mendoza-Martinez, 372 U.S. 144, 168 -169 (1963), quoted ante, at 537-538 (footnotes omitted):

"Whether the sanction involves an affirmative disability or restraint, whether it has historically been regarded as a punishment, whether it comes into play only on a finding of scienter, whether its operation will promote the traditional aims of punishment - retribution and deterrence, whether the behavior to which it applies is already a crime, whether an alternative purpose to which it may rationally be connected is assignable for it, and whether it appears excessive in relation to the alternative purpose assigned are all relevant to the inquiry, and may often point in differing directions."

A number of the factors enunciated above focus on the nature and severity of the impositions at issue. Thus, if weight were given to all its elements, I believe the Mendoza-Martinez inquiry could be responsive to the impact of the deprivations imposed on detainees. However, within a few lines after quoting Mendoza-Martinez, the Court restates the standard as whether there is an expressed punitive intent on the part of detention officials, and, if not, whether the restriction is rationally related to some nonpunitive purpose or appears excessive in relation to that purpose. Ante, at 538-539 Absent from the reformulation is any appraisal of whether the sanction constitutes an affirmative disability or restraint and whether it has historically been regarded as punishment. Moreover, when the Court applies this standard, it loses interest in the inquiry concerning excessiveness, and, indeed, eschews consideration of less restrictive alternatives, practices in other detention facilities, and the recommendations of the Justice Department and professional organizations. See ante, at 542-543, n. 25, 543-544, n. 27, 554. By this process of elimination, the Court contracts a broad standard, sensitive to the deprivations imposed on detainees, into one that seeks merely to sanitize official motives and prohibit irrational behavior. As thus reformulated, the test lacks any real content.

A

To make detention officials' intent the critical factor in assessing the constitutionality of impositions on detainees is unrealistic in the extreme. The cases on which the Court relies to justify this narrow focus all involve legislative Acts, not day-to-day administrative decisions. See Kennedy v. Mendoza-Martinez, supra (Nationality Act of 1940 and Immigration and Nationality Act of 1952); Flemming v. Nestor, 363 U.S. 603 (1960) (Social Security Act); De Veau v. Braisted, 363 U.S. 144 (1960) (New York Waterfront Commission Act). In discerning the intent behind a statutory enactment, courts engage in a familiar judicial function, usually with the benefit of a legislative history that preceded passage of the statute. The motivation for policies in detention facilities, however, will frequently not be a matter of public record. Detainees challenging these policies will therefore bear the substantial burden of establishing punitive intent on the basis of circumstantial evidence or retrospective explanations by detention officials, which frequently may be self-serving. Particularly since the Court seems unwilling to look behind any justification based on security, 2 that burden will usually prove insurmountable.

In any event, it will often be the case that officials believe, erroneously but in good faith, that a specific restriction is necessary for institutional security. As the District Court noted, "zeal for security is among the most common varieties of official excess," United States ex rel. Wolfish v. Levi, 439 F. Supp. 114, 141 (SDNY 1977), and the litigation in this area corroborates that conclusion. 3 A standard that focuses on punitive intent cannot effectively eliminate this excess. Indeed, the Court does not even attempt to "detail the precise extent of the legitimate governmental interests that may justify conditions or restrictions of pretrial detention." Ante, at 540. Rather, it is content merely to recognize that "the effective management of the detention facility . . . is a valid objective that may justify imposition of conditions and restrictions of pretrial detention and dispel any inference that such restrictions are intended as punishment." Ibid.

Moreover, even if the inquiry the Court pursues were more productive, it simply is not the one the Constitution mandates here. By its terms, the Due Process Clause focuses on the nature of deprivations, not on the persons inflicting them. If this concern is to be vindicated, it is the effect of conditions of confinement, not the intent behind them, that must be the focal point of constitutional analysis.

B

Although the Court professes to go beyond the direct inquiry regarding intent and to determine whether a particular imposition is rationally related to a nonpunitive purposes, this exercise is at best a formality. Almost any restriction on detainees, including, as the Court concedes, chains and shackles, ante, at 539 n. 20, can be found to have some rational relation to institutional security, or more broadly, to "the effective management of the detention facility." Ante, at 540. See Feeley v. Sampson, 570 F.2d 364, 380 (CA1 1977) (Coffin, C. J., dissenting). Yet this toothless standard applies irrespective of the excessiveness of the restraint or the nature of the rights infringed. 4

Moreover, the Court has not in fact reviewed the rationality of detention officials' decisions, as Mendoza-Martinez requires Instead, the majority affords "wide-ranging" deference to those officials "in the adoption and execution of policies and practices that in their judgment are needed to preserve internal order and discipline and to maintain institutional security." Ante, at 547. 5 Reasoning that security considerations in jails are little different than in prisons, the Court concludes that cases requiring substantial deference to prison administrators' determinations on security-related issues are equally applicable in the present context. Ante, at 546-547, nn. 28, 29.

Yet as the Court implicitly acknowledges, ante, at 545, the rights of detainees, who have not been adjudicated guilty of a crime, are necessarily more extensive than those of prisoners "who have been found to have violated one or more of the criminal laws established by society for its orderly governance." Jones v. North Carolina Prisoners' Union, 433 U.S. 119, 129 (1977). See Campbell v. McGruder, 188 U.S. App. D.C. 258, 264 n. 9, 580 F.2d 521, 527 n. 9 (1978). Judicial tolerance of substantial impositions on detainees must be concomitantly less. However, by blindly deferring to administrative judgments on the rational basis for particular restrictions, the Court effectively delegates to detention officials the decision whether pretrial detainees have been punished. This, in my view, is an abdication of an unquestionably judicial function.

II

Even had the Court properly applied the punishment test, I could not agree to its use in this context. It simply does not advance analysis to determine whether a given deprivation imposed on detainees constitutes "punishment." For in terms of the nature of the imposition and the impact on detainees, pretrial incarceration, although necessary to secure defendants' presence at trial, is essentially indistinguishable from punishment. 6 The detainee is involuntarily confined and deprived of the freedom "to be with his family and friends and to form the other enduring attachments of normal life," Morrissey v. Brewer, 408 U.S. 471, 482 (1972). Indeed, this Court has previously recognized that incarceration is an "infamous punishment." Flemming v. Nestor, 363 U.S., at 617; see also Wong Wing v. United States, 163 U.S. 228, 233 -234 (1896); Ingraham v. Wright, 430 U.S. 651, 669 (1977). And if the effect of incarceration itself is inevitably punitive, so too must be the cumulative impact of those restraints incident to that restraint. 7

A test that balances the deprivations involved against the state interests assertedly served 8 would be more consistent with the import of the Due Process Clause. Such an approach would be sensitive to the tangible physical and psychological harm that a particular disability inflicts on detainees and to the nature of the less tangible, but significant, individual interests at stake. The greater the imposition on detainees, the heavier the burden of justification the Government would bear. See Bates v. Little Rock, 361 U.S. 516, 524 (1960); Shapiro v. Thompson, 394 U.S. 618, 634 (1969); Kusper v. Pontikes, 414 U.S. 51, 58 -59 (1973).

When assessing the restrictions on detainees, we must consider the cumulative impact of restraints imposed during confinement. Incarceration of itself clearly represents a profound infringement of liberty, and each additional imposition increases the severity of that initial deprivation. Since any restraint thus has a serious effect on detainees, I believe the Government must bear a more rigorous burden of justification than the rational-basis standard mandates. See supra, at 567. At a minimum, I would require a showing that a restriction is substantially necessary to jail administration. Where the imposition is of particular gravity, that is, where it implicates interests of fundamental importance 9 or inflicts significant harms, the Government should demonstrate that the restriction serves a compelling necessity of jail administration. 10

In presenting its justifications, the Government could adduce evidence of the security and administrative needs of the institution as well as the fiscal constraints under which it operates. And, of course, considerations of competence and comity require some measure of deference to the judgments of detention officials. Their estimation of institutional needs and the administrative consequences of particular acts is entitled to weight. But as the Court has repeatedly held in the prison context, judicial restraint "cannot encompass any failure to take cognizance of valid constitutional claims." Procunier v. Martinez, 416 U.S. 396, 405 (1974); Bounds v. Smith, 430 U.S. 817, 832 (1977). Even more so here, with the rights of presumptively innocent individuals at stake, we cannot abdicate our judicial responsibility to evaluate independently the Government's asserted justifications for particular deprivations. In undertaking this evaluation, courts should thus examine evidence of practices in other detention and penal facilities. To be sure, conditions of detention should not survive constitutional challenge merely because they are no worse than circumstances in prisons. But this evidence can assist courts in evaluating justifications based on security, administrative convenience, and fiscal constraints.

Simply stated, the approach I advocate here weighs the detainees' interests implicated by a particular restriction against the governmental interests the restriction serves. As the substantiality of the intrusion on detainees' rights increases, so must the significance of the countervailing governmental objectives.

III

A

Applying this standard to the facts of this case, I believe a remand is necessary on the issue of double-bunking at the MCC. The courts below determined only whether double-bunking was justified by a compelling necessity, excluding fiscal and administrative considerations. Since it was readily ascertainable that the Government could not prevail under that test, detailed inquiry was unnecessary. Thus, the District Court granted summary judgment, without a full record on the psychological and physical harms caused by overcrowding. 11 To conclude, as the Court does here, that double-bunking has not inflicted "genuine privations and hardship over an extended period of time," ante, at 542, is inappropriate where respondents have not had an adequate opportunity to produce evidence suggesting otherwise. Moreover, that the District Court discerned no disputed issues of material fact, see ante, at 541 n. 24, is no justification for avoiding a remand, since what is material necessarily varies with the standard applied. Rather than pronouncing overbroad aphorisms about the principles "lurking in the Due Process Clause," ante, at 542, I would leave to the District Court in the first instance the sensitive balancing inquiry that the Due Process Clause dictates. 12

B

Although the constitutionality of the MCC's rule limiting the sources of hardback books was also decided on summary judgment, I believe a remand is unnecessary. 13 That individuals have a fundamental First Amendment right to receive information and ideas is beyond dispute. See Martin v. Struthers, 319 U.S. 141, 143 (1943); Stanley v. Georgia, 394 U.S. 557, 565 (1969); Red Lion Broadcasting Co. v. FCC, 395 U.S. 367, 390 (1969); see also Brandenburg v. Ohio, 395 U.S. 444, 448 (1969). Under the balancing test elaborated above, the Government must therefore demonstrate that its rule infringing on that interest serves a compelling necessity. As the courts below found, the Government failed to make such a showing. 14

In support of its restriction, the Government presented the affidavit of the MCC warden, who averred without elaboration that a proper and thorough search of incoming hardback books might require removal of the covers. Further, the warden asserted, "in the case of all books and magazines," it would be necessary to leaf through every page to ascertain that there was no contraband. App. 24. The warden offered no reasons why the institution could not place reasonable limitations on the number of books inmates could receive or use electronic devices and fluoroscopes to detect contraband rather than requiring inmates to purchase hardback books directly from publishers or stores. 15 As the Court of Appeals noted, "other institutions have not recorded untoward experiences with far less restrictive rules." Wolfish v. Levi, 573 F.2d 118, 130 (1978).

The limitation on receipt of hardback books may well be one rational response to the legitimate security concerns of the institution, concerns which I in no way intend to deprecate. But our precedents, as the courts below apparently recognized, United States ex rel. Wolfish v. United States, 428 F. Supp. 333, 341 (SDNY 1977); 573 F.2d, at 130, require some consideration of less restrictive alternatives, see, e. g., Shelton v. Tucker, 364 U.S. 479, 488 -490 (1960); Keyishian v. Board of Regents, 385 U.S. 589, 602 -604 (1967). There is no basis for relaxing this requirement when the rights of presumptively innocent detainees are implicated.

C

The District Court did conduct a trial on the constitutionality of the MCC package rule and room-search practices. Although the courts below applied a different standard, the record is sufficient to permit resolution of these issues here. And since this Court decides the questions, I think it appropriate to suggest the results that would obtain on this record under my standard.

Denial of the right to possess property is surely of heightened concern when viewed with the other indignities of detainment. See App. 73. As the District Court observed, it is a severe discomfort to do without personal items such as a watch or cosmetics, and things to eat, smoke, or chew. Indeed, the court noted, "[t]he strong dependence upon material things . . . gives rise to one of the deepest miseries of incarceration - the deprivation of familiar possessions." 439 F. Supp., at 150. Given this impact on detainees, the appropriate inquiry is whether the package restriction is substantially necessary to prison administration.

The Government's justification for such a broad rule cannot meet this burden. The asserted interest in ameliorating sanitation and storage problems and avoiding thefts, gambling, and inmate conflicts over personal property is belied, as the Court seems to recognize, ante, at 553, by the policy of permitting inmate purchases of up to $15 a week from the prison commissary. Detention officials doubtless have a legitimate interest in preventing introduction of drugs or weapons into the facility. But as both the District Court and the Court of Appeals observed, other detention institutions have adopted much less restrictive regulations than the MCC's governing receipt of packages. See, e. g., Miller v. Carson, 401 F. Supp. 835, 885 (MD Fla. 1975), aff'd, 563 F.2d 741 (CA5 1977); Giampetruzzi v. Malcolm, 406 F. Supp. 836, 842 (SDNY 1975). Inmates in New York state institutions, for example, may receive a 35-pound package each month, as well as clothing and magazines. See 439 F. Supp., at 152. 16

To be sure, practices in other institutions do not necessarily demarcate the constitutional minimum. See ante, at 554. But such evidence does cast doubt upon the Government's justifications based on institutional security and administrative convenience. The District Court held that the Government was obligated to dispel these doubts. The court thus required a reasoned showing why "there must be deprivations at the MCC so much harsher than deemed necessary in other institutions." 439 F. Supp., at 152. Absent such a showing, the court concluded that the MCC's rule swept too broadly and ordered detention officials to formulate a suitable alternative, at least with respect to items available from the commissary. Id., at 153. This holding seems an appropriate accommodation of the competing interests and a minimal intrusion on administrative prerogatives.

I would also affirm the ruling of the courts below that inmates must be permitted to observe searches of their cells. Routine searches such as those at issue here may be an unavoidable incident of incarceration. Nonetheless, the protections of the Fourth Amendment do not lapse at the jail-house door, Bonner v. Coughlin, 517 F.2d 1311, 1316-

1317 (CA7 1975) (Stevens, J.); United States v. Lilly, 576 F.2d 1240, 1244-1245 (CA5 1978). Detention officials must therefore conduct such searches in a reasonable manner, avoiding needless intrusions on inmates' privacy. Because unobserved searches may invite official disrespect for detainees' few possessions and generate fears that guards will steal personal property or plant contraband, see 439 F. Supp., at 148-149, the inmates' interests are significant.

The Government argues that allowing detainees to observe official searches would lead to violent confrontations and enable inmates to remove or conceal contraband. However, the District Court found that the Government had not substantiated these security concerns and that there were less intrusive means available to accomplish the institution's objectives. Ibid. Thus, this record does not establish that unobserved searches are substantially necessary to jail administration.

D

In my view, the body-cavity searches of MCC inmates represent one of the most grievous offenses against personal dignity and common decency. After every contact visit with someone from outside the facility, including defense attorneys, an inmate must remove all of his or her clothing, bend over, spread the buttocks, and display the anal cavity for inspection by a correctional officer. Women inmates must assume a suitable posture for vaginal inspection, while men must raise their genitals. And, as the Court neglects to note, because of time pressures, this humiliating spectacle is frequently conducted in the presence of other inmates. App. 77.

The District Court found that the stripping was "unpleasant, embarrassing, and humiliating." 439 F. Supp., at 146. A psychiatrist testified that the practice placed inmates in the most degrading position possible, App. 48, a conclusion amply corroborated by the testimony of the inmates themselves. Id., at 36-37, 41. 17 There was evidence, moreover, that these searches engendered among detainees fears of sexual assault, id., at 49, were the occasion for actual threats of physical abuse by guards, and caused some inmates to forgo personal visits. 439 F. Supp., at 147.

Not surprisingly, the Government asserts a security justification for such inspections. These searches are necessary, it argues, to prevent inmates from smuggling contraband into the facility. In crediting this justification despite the contrary findings of the two courts below, the Court overlooks the critical facts. As respondents point out, inmates are required to wear one-piece jumpsuits with zippers in the front. To insert an object into the vaginal or anal cavity, an inmate would have to remove the jumpsuit, at least from the upper torso. App. 45; Joint App. in Nos. 77-2035, 77-2135 (CA2), p. 925 (hereinafter Joint App.). Since contact visits occur in a glass-enclosed room and are continuously monitored by corrections officers, see 439 F. Supp., at 140, 147; Joint App. 144, 1208-1209, 18 such a feat would seem extraordinarily difficult. There was medical testimony, moreover, that inserting an object into the rectum is painful and "would require time and opportunity which is not available in the visiting areas," App. 49-50, and that visual inspection would probably not detect an object once inserted. Id., at 50.

Additionally, before entering the visiting room, visitors and their packages are searched thoroughly by a metal detector, fluoroscope, and by hand. Id., at 93; Joint App. 601, 1077. Correction officers may require that visitors leave packages or handbags with guards until the visit is over. Joint App. 1077-1078. Only by blinding itself to the facts presented on this record can the Court accept the Government's security rationale.

Without question, these searches are an imposition of sufficient gravity to invoke the compelling-necessity standard. It is equally indisputable that they cannot meet that standard. Indeed, the procedure is so unnecessarily degrading that it "shocks the conscience." Rochin v. California, 342 U.S. 165, 172 (1952). Even in Rochin, the police had reason to believe that the petitioner had swallowed contraband. Here, the searches are employed absent any suspicion of wrongdoing. It was this aspect of the MCC practice that the Court of Appeals redressed, requiring that searches be conducted only when there is probable cause to believe that the inmate is concealing contraband. The Due Process Clause, on any principled reading, dictates no less.

That the Court can uphold these indiscriminate searches highlights the bankruptcy of its basic analysis. Under the test adopted today, the rights of detainees apparently extend only so far as detention officials decide that cost and security will permit. Such unthinking deference to administrative convenience cannot be justified where the interests at stake are those of presumptively innocent individuals, many of whose only proven offense is the inability to afford bail. I dissent.

Notes

[1] The Bail Reform Act, 18 U.S.C. 3146, to which the Court adverts ante, at 524, provides that bail be set in an amount that will "reasonably assure" the defendant's presence at trial. In fact, studies indicate that bail determinations frequently do not focus on the individual defendant but only on the nature of the crime charged and that, as administered, the system penalizes indigent defendants. See, e. g., ABA Project on Standards for Criminal Justice, Pretrial Release 1-2 (1968); W. Thomas, Bail Reform in America 11-19 (1976). See also National Advisory Commission on Criminal Justice Standards and Goals, Corrections 102-103 (1973); National Association of Pretrial Service Agencies, Performance Standards and Goals for Pretrial Release and Diversion 1-3 (1978).

[2] Indeed, the Court glosses over the Government's statement in its posttrial memorandum that for inmates serving sentences, "the restrictions on the possession of personal property also serve the legitimate purpose of punishment." United States ex rel. Wolfish v. Levi, 439 F. Supp. 114, 153 (SDNY 1977); Post-trial Memorandum for Respondents in No. 75 Civ. 6000 (SDNY) 212 n., quoted ante, at 561 n. 43. This statement provides at least some indication that a similar motive may underlie application of the same rules to detainees. The Court's treatment of this point illustrates the indifference with which it pursues the intent inquiry.

[3] Thus, for example, lower courts have held a variety of security restrictions unconstitutional. E. g., Collins v. Schoonfield, 344 F. Supp. 257, 283 (Md. 1972) (warden

censored newspaper articles critical of his administration of jail); id., at 278 (mentally disturbed detainees shackled in jail infirmary); Inmates of Milwaukee County Jail v. Petersen, 353 F. Supp. 1157, 1164 (ED Wis. 1973) (detainees limited to two pages per letter; notice to relatives and friends of the time and place of detainee's next court appearance deleted on security grounds); United States ex rel. Manicone v. Corso, 365 F. Supp. 576 (EDNY 1973) (newspapers banned because they might disrupt prisoners and create a fire hazard); Miller v. Carson, 401 F. Supp. 835, 878 (MD Fla. 1975), aff'd, 563 F.2d 741 (CA5 1977) (detainees in hospital kept continuously chained to bed); O'Bryan v. County of Saginaw, 437 F. Supp. 582 (ED Mich. 1977) (detainees with bail of more than $500 prevented from attending religious services); Vest v. Lubbock County Commissioners Court, 444 F. Supp. 824 (ND Tex. 1977) (detainees limited to three pages per letter and six incoming and outgoing letters per week to facilitate censorship; guards authorized to refuse to mail or deliver letters containing "abusive" language).

[4] The Court does concede that "loading a detainee with chains and shackles and throwing him in a dungeon," ante, at 539 n. 20, would create an inference of punitive intent and hence would be impermissible. I am indeed heartened by this concession, but I do not think it sufficient to give force to the Court's standard.

[5] Indeed, lest the point escape the reader, the majority reiterates it 12 times in the course of the opinion. Ante, at 531, 540-541, n. 23, 544, 546-548, and nn. 29 and 30, 551, 554, 557 n. 38, 562.

[6] As Chief Judge Coffin has stated, "[i]t would be impossible, without playing fast and loose with the English language, for a court to examine the conditions of confinement under which detainees are incarcerated . . . and conclude that their custody was not punitive in effect if not in intent." Feeley v. Sampson, 570 F.2d 364, 380 (CA1 1978) (dissenting opinion). Accord, Campbell v. McGruder, 188 U.S. App. D.C. 258, 267, 580 F.2d 521, 530 (1978).

[7] If a particular imposition could be termed "punishment" under the Mendoza-Martinez criteria, I would, of course, agree that it violates the Due Process Clause. My criticism is that, in this context, determining whether a given restraint constitutes punishment is an empty semantic exercise. For pretrial incarceration is in many respects no different from the sanctions society imposes on convicted criminals. To argue over a question of characterization can only obscure what is in fact the appropriate inquiry, the actual nature of the impositions balanced against the Government's justifications.

[8] See New Motor Vehicle Board v. Orrin W. Fox Co., 439 U.S. 96, 112 -113 (1978) (MARSHALL, J., concurring); Poe v. Ullman, 367 U.S. 497, 542 (1961) (Harlan, J., dissenting); Moore v. East Cleveland, 431 U.S. 494, 499 (1977); Roe v. Wade, 410 U.S. 113, 115 (1973).

[9] See, e. g., Brandenburg v. Ohio, 395 U.S. 444, 448 (1969) (free speech); Bounds v. Smith, 430 U.S. 817 (1977) (access to the courts).

[10] Blackstone observed over 200 years ago:

"Upon the whole, if the offence be not bailable, or the party cannot find bail, he is to be committed to the county goal by the mittimus of the justice . . .; there to abide till delivered by due course of law. . . . But this imprisonment, as has been said, is only for safe custody, and not for punishment: therefore, in his dubious interval between the commitment and trial, a prisoner ought to be used with the utmost humanity; and neither be loaded with needless fetters, or subjected to other hardships than such as are absolutely requisite for the purpose of confinement only. . . ." 4 W. Blackstone, Commentaries *300.

[11] Other courts have found that in the circumstances before them overcrowding inflicted mental and physical damage on inmates. See, e.g., Detainees of Brooklyn House of Detention v. Malcolm, 520 F.2d 392, 396, and n. 4 (CA2 1975) (testimony of correctional experts that double-bunking is "psychologically destructive and increases homosexual impulses, tensions and aggressive tendencies"); Battle v. Anderson, 564 F.2d 388, 398 (CA10 1977); Campbell v. McGruder, 188 U.S. App. D.C., at 273, 580 F.2d, at 536 (overcrowding likely "to impair the mental and physical health" of detainees); Chapman v. Rhodes, 434 F. Supp. 1007, 1020 (SD Ohio 1977).

[12] The MCC has a single-bed capacity of 449 inmates. Under the Court's analysis, what is to be done if the inmate population grows suddenly to 600, or 900? The Court simply ignores the rated capacity of the institution. Yet this figure is surely relevant in assessing whether overcrowding inflicts harms of constitutional magnitude.

[13] The Court of Appeals' rulings on what this Court broadly designates "security restrictions" applied both to detainees and convicted prisoners. I believe impositions on these groups must be measured under different standards. See supra, at 568-571. I would remand to the District Court for a determination whether there is a continuing controversy with respect to convicted inmates. If the issues were contested, the body-cavity searches, at the least, would presumably be invalid. Cf.infra, at 576-578, and United States v. Lilly, 576 F.2d 1240 (CA5 1978).

[14] Nor can the Court's attempt to denominate the publisher-only rule as a reasonable "time, place and manner regulatio[n]," ante, at 552, substitute for such a showing. In each of the cases cited by the Court for this proposition, the private individuals had the ability to alter the time, place, or manner of exercising their First Amendment rights. Grayned v. City of Rockford, 408 U.S. 104 (1972) (ordinance prohibiting demonstration within 150 feet of a school at certain times of the day); Cox v. New Hampshire, 312 U.S. 569 (1941) (permissible to require license for parade); Cox v. Louisiana, 379 U.S. 536, 554 -555 (1965) (city could prohibit parades during rush hour); Adderley v. Florida, 385 U.S. 39 (1966) (public demonstration on premises of county jail). It is not clear that the detainees here possess the same freedom to alter the time, place, or manner of exercising their First Amendment rights. Indeed, as the Government acknowledges, Tr. of Oral Arg. 18, an unspecified number of detainees at the MCC are incarcerated because they cannot afford bail. For these persons, the option of purchasing hardback books from publishers or bookstores will frequently be unavailable. And it is hardly consistent with established First Amendment precepts to restrict inmates to

library selections made by detention officials.

[15] The MCC already uses such electronic equipment to search packages carried by visitors. See infra, at 578.

[16] In addition, the Justice Department's Draft Federal Standards for Corrections discourage limitations on the volume or content of inmate mail, including packages. Dept. of Justice, Federal Corrections Policy Task Force, Federal Standards for Corrections 63 (Draft, June 1978).

[17] While the Government presented psychiatric testimony that the procedures were not likely to create lasting emotional trauma, the District Court intimated some doubt as to the credibility of this testimony, and found that the injury was of constitutional dimension even if it did not require psychiatric treatment or leave permanent psychological scars. 439 F. Supp., at 150.

[18] To facilitate this monitoring, MCC officials limited to 25 the number of people in the visiting room at one time. Joint App. 1208. Inmates were forbidden to use the locked lavatories, and visitors could use them only by requesting a key from a correctional officer. App. 93; see Wolfish v. Levi, 573 F.2d 118, 125 (1978). The lavatories, as well, contain a built-in window for observation. Brief for Respondents 57.

Liberty-interest in parole: Justice Marshall's dissent in Greenholtz v. Inmates of Nebraska Penal and Correctional Complex (May 29, 1979)

MR. JUSTICE MARSHALL, with whom MR. JUSTICE BRENNAN and MR. JUSTICE STEVENS join, dissenting in part.

My disagreement with the Court's opinion extends to both its analysis of respondents' liberty interest and its delineation of the procedures constitutionally required in parole release proceedings. Although it ultimately holds that the Nebraska statutes create a constitutionally protected "expectation of parole," the Court nonetheless rejects the argument that criminal offenders have such an interest whenever a State establishes the possibility of parole. This gratuitous commentary reflects a misapplication of our prior decisions, and an unduly narrow view of the liberty protected by the Fourteenth Amendment. Since the Court chooses to address the issue, I must register my opinion that all prisoners potentially eligible for parole have a liberty interest of which they may not be deprived without due process, regardless of the particular statutory language that implements the parole system.

The Court further determines that the Nebraska Board of Parole already provides all the process that is constitutionally due. In my view, the Court departs from the analysis adopted in Morrissey v. Brewer, 408 U. S. 471 (1972), and Mathews v. Eldridge, 424 U. S. 319, 424 U. S. 335 (1976), and disregards considerations that militate for greater procedural protection. To supplement existing procedures, I would require that the Parole Board give each inmate reasonable notice of hearing dates and the factors to be considered, as well as a written statement of reasons and the essential facts underlying adverse decisions.

I

A

It is self-evident that all individuals possess a liberty interest in being free from physical restraint. Upon conviction for a crime, of course, an individual may be deprived of this liberty to the extent authorized by penal statutes. [1] But when a State enacts a parole system, and creates the possibility of release from incarceration upon satisfaction of certain conditions, it necessarily qualifies that initial deprivation. In my judgment, it is the existence of this system which allows prison inmates to retain their protected interest in securing freedoms available outside prison. [2] Because parole release proceedings clearly implicate this retained liberty interest, the Fourteenth Amendment requires that due process be observed, irrespective of the specific provisions in the applicable parole statute.

This Court's prior decisions fully support the conclusion that criminal offenders have a liberty interest in securing parole release. In Morrissey v. Brewer, supra, the Court held that all persons released on parole possess such an interest in remaining free from incarceration. Writing for the Court, MR. CHIEF JUSTICE BURGER stated that the applicability of due process protections turns "on the extent to which an individual will be condemned to suffer grievous loss,'" citing Joint Anti-Fascist Refugee Committee v. McGrath, 341 U. S. 123, 341 U. S. 168 (1951) (Frankfurter, J., concurring), and on the "nature of the interest." 408 U.S. at 408 U. S. 481. In assessing the gravity and nature of the loss caused by parole revocation, Morrissey relied on the general proposition that parole release enables an individual "to do a wide range of things open to persons who have never been convicted of any crime." Id. at 408 U. S. 482. [3] Following Morrissey, Gagnon v. Scarpelli, 411 U. S. 778 (1973), held that individuals on probation also retain a liberty interest which cannot be terminated without due process of law. Nowhere in either opinion did the Court even intimate that the weight or nature of the criminal offender's interest in maintaining his parole release or probation depends upon the specific terms of any statute, for in both cases the Court disregarded the applicable statutory language. [4] Rather, this liberty interest derived solely from the existence of a system that permitted criminal offenders to serve their sentences on probation or parole.

Wolff v. McDonnell, 418 U. S. 539 (1974), adopted a similar approach. There, the Court concluded that abrogation of a prisoner's good-time credits implicates his interest in subsequently obtaining release from incarceration. Although the Court recognized that Nebraska was not constitutionally obligated to establish a credit system, by creating "a right to a shortened prison sentence through the accumulation of credits for good behavior," id. at 418 U. S. 557, the State had allowed inmates to retain a liberty interest that could be terminated only for "serious misbehavior." This liberty interest derived from the existence of a credit system, not from the specific language of the implementing statute, see id. at 418 U. S. 555-558, as decisions applying Wolff have consistently recognized. [5]

B

A criminal offender's interest in securing release on parole is therefore directly comparable to the liberty interests we recognized in Morrissey, Scarpelli, and Wolff. However, because the Court discerns two distinctions between "parole release and parole revocation," ante at 442 U. S. 9, it refuses to follow these cases here. In my view, the proffered distinctions do not support this departure from precedent.

First, the Court finds a difference of constitutional dimension between a deprivation of liberty one has and a denial of liberty one desires. Ibid. While there is obviously some difference, it is not one relevant to the established constitutional inquiry. Whether an individual currently enjoys a particular freedom has no bearing on whether he possesses a protected interest in securing and maintaining that liberty. The Court acknowledged as much in Wolff v. McDonnell, supra, when it held that the loss of good-time credits implicates a liberty interest even though the forfeiture only deprived the prisoner of freedom he expected to obtain sometime hence. See Drayton v. McCall, 584 F.2d 1208, 1219 (CA2 1978). And in other contexts as well, this Court has repeatedly concluded that the Due Process Clause protects liberty interests that individuals do not currently enjoy. [6]

The Court's distinction is equally unrelated to the nature or gravity of the interest affected in parole release proceedings. The nature of a criminal offender's interest depends on the range of freedoms available by virtue of the parole system's existence. On that basis, Morrissey afforded constitutional recognition to a parolee's interest because his freedom on parole includes "many of the core values of unqualified liberty." 408 U.S. at 408 U. S. 482. This proposition is true regardless of whether the inmate is presently on parole or seeking parole release. As the Court of Appeals for the Second Circuit has recognized, "[w]hether the immediate issue be release or revocation, the stakes are the same: conditional freedom versus incarceration." United States ex rel. Johnson v. Chairman of New York State Board of Parole, 500 F.2d 925, 928, vacated as moot sub nom. Regan v. Johnson, 419 U.S. 1015 (1974).

The Court's second justification for distinguishing between parole release and parole revocation is based on the "nature of the decision that must be made in each case." Ante at 442 U. S. 9. The majority apparently believes that the interest affected by parole release proceedings is somehow diminished if the administrative decision may turn on "subjective evaluations." Yet the Court nowhere explains why the nature of the decisional process has even the slightest bearing in assessing the nature of the interest that this process may terminate. [7] Indeed, the Court's reasoning here is flatly inconsistent with its subsequent holding that respondents do have a protected liberty interest under Nebraska's parole statutes, which require a decision that is "subjective in part and predictive in part." Ante at 442 U. S. 13. For despite the Parole Board's argument that such an interest exists "only if the statutory conditions for [denying parole are] essentially factual, as in Wolff and Morrissey, rather than predictive," ante at 442 U. S. 12, the Court nonetheless concludes that respondents' interest is sufficient to merit constitutional protection.

But even assuming the subjective nature of the decisionmaking process were relevant to due process analysis in general, this consideration does not adequately distinguish the processes of granting and revoking parole. See Morrissey v. Brewer, 408 U. S. at 408 U. S. 477-480; Gagnon v. Scarpelli, 411 U.S. at 411 U. S. 781-782. Contrary to the Court's assertion that the decision to revoke parole is predominantly a "retrospective factual question,'" ante at 442 U. S. 9, Morrissey recognized that only the first step in the revocation decision can be so characterized. And once it is

"determined that the parolee did violate the conditions [of parole, a] second question arise[s]: should the parolee be recommitted to prison, or should other steps be taken to protect society and improve chances of rehabilitation? The first step is relatively simple; the second is more complex. The second question involves the application of expertise by the parole authority in making a prediction as to the ability of the individual to live in society without committing antisocial acts. . . . [T]his second step, deciding what to do about the violation once it is identified, is not purely factual, but also predictive and discretionary."

408 U.S. at 408 U. S. 479-480 (emphasis added). Morrissey thus makes clear that the parole revocation decision includes a decisive subjective component. Moreover, to the extent parole release proceedings hinge on predictive determinations, those assessments are necessarily predicated on findings of fact. [8] Accordingly, the presence of subjective considerations is a completely untenable basis for distinguishing the interests at stake here from the liberty interest recognized in Morrissey.

C

The Court also concludes that the existence of a parole system, by itself, creates "no more than a mere hope that the benefit will be obtained," ante at 442 U. S. 11, and thus does not give rise to a liberty interest. This conclusion appears somewhat gratuitous, given the Court's ultimate holding that the Nebraska statutes do generate a "legitimate expectation of [parole] release" which is protected by the Due Process Clause. Ante at 442 U. S. 12. Moreover, it is unclear what purpose can be served by the Court's endeavor to depreciate the expectations arising solely from the existence of a parole system. The parole statutes in many jurisdictions embody the same standards used in the Model Penal Code, upon which both the Nebraska and federal provisions are patterned, and the Court's analysis of the Nebraska statutes would therefore suggest that the other statutes must also create protectible expectations of release. [9]

Furthermore, in light of the role that parole has assumed in the sentencing process, I believe the Court misapplies its own test, see ante at 442 U. S. 11-12, by refusing to acknowledge that inmates have a legitimate expectation of release whenever the government establishes a parole system. As the Court observed in Morrissey:

"During the past 60 years, the practice of releasing prisoners on parole before the end of their sentences has become an integral part of the penological system. . . . Rather than being an ad hoc exercise of clemency, parole is an established variation on imprisonment of convicted criminals."

408 U.S. at 408 U. S. 477. Indeed, the available evidence belies the majority's broad assumptions concerning inmate expectations, at least with respect to the federal system, and there is no suggestion that experience in other jurisdictions is significantly different. [10]

Government statistics reveal that substantially less than one-third of all first-time federal offenders are held in prison until mandatory release. [11] In addition, 88% of the judges responding to a recent survey stated that they considered the availability of parole when imposing sentence, and 47% acknowledged their expectation that defendants would be released on parole after serving one-third of their sentences. [12] In accord with these views, the Administrative Conference of the United States has advised Congress that courts set maximum sentences anticipating "that a prisoner who demonstrates his desire for rehabilitation will not serve the maximum term or anything approaching the maximum." [13] And in discussing the sentencing provisions of the proposed revision of the Federal Criminal Code, S. 1437, the Senate Judiciary Committee observed:

"A federal judge who today believes that an offender should serve four years in prison may impose a sentence in the vicinity of ten years, knowing that the offender is eligible for parole release after one third of the sentence."

S.Rep. No. 95-605, p. 1169 (1977).

Thus, experience in the federal system has led both judges and legislators to expect that inmates will be paroled substantially before their sentences expire. Insofar as it is critical under the Court's due process analysis, this understanding would certainly justify a similar expectation on the part of the federal inmates. Hence, I believe it is unrealistic for this Court to speculate that the existence of a parole system provides prisoners "no more than a mere hope" of release. Ante at 442 U. S. 11.

II

A

I also cannot subscribe to the Court's assessment of the procedures necessary to safeguard respondents' liberty interest. Although the majority purports to rely on Morrissey v. Brewer and the test enunciated in Mathews v. Eldridge, 424 U. S. 319 (1976), its application of these standards is fundamentally deficient in several respects.

To begin with, the Court focuses almost exclusively on the likelihood that a particular procedure will significantly reduce the risk of error in parole release proceedings. Ante at 442 U. S. 14-16. Yet Mathews advances three factors to be considered in determining the specific dictates of due process:

"First, the private interest that will be affected by the official action; second, the risk of an erroneous deprivation of such interest through the procedures used, and the probable value, if any, of additional or substitute procedural safeguards; and finally, the Government's interest, including the function involved and the fiscal and administrative burdens that the additional or substitute procedural requirement would entail."

424 U.S. at 424 U. S. 335. By ignoring the other two factors set forth in Mathews, the Court skews the inquiry in favor of the Board. For example, the Court does not identify any justification for the Parole Board's refusal to provide inmates with specific advance notice of the hearing date or with a list of factors that may be considered. Nor does the Board demonstrate that it would be unduly burdensome to provide a brief summary of the evidence justifying the denial of parole. To be sure, these measures may cause some inconvenience, but "the Constitution recognizes higher values than speed and efficiency." Stanley v. Illinois, 405 U. S. 645, 405 U. S. 656 (1972); accord, Frontiero v. Richardson, 411 U. S. 677, 411 U. S. 690 (1973); Bell v. Burson, 402 U. S. 535, 402 U. S. 540-541 (1971). Similarly lacking in the Court's analysis is any recognition of the private interest affected by the Board's action. Certainly the interest in being released from incarceration is of sufficient magnitude to have some bearing on the process due. [14]

The second fundamental flaw in the Court's analysis is that it incorrectly evaluates the only factor actually discussed. The contribution that additional safeguards will make to reaching an accurate decision necessarily depends on the risk of error inherent in existing procedures. See Mathews v. Eldridge, supra, at 424 U. S. 334-335, 424 U. S. 343-347. Here, the Court finds supplemental procedures to be inappropriate because it assumes existing procedures adequately reduce the likelihood that an inmate's files will contain incorrect information which could lead to an erroneous decision. No support is cited for this assumption, and the record affords none. In fact, researchers and courts have discovered many substantial inaccuracies in inmate files, and evidence in the instant case revealed similar errors. [15] Both the District Court and the Court of Appeals found additional procedures necessary to decrease the margin of error in Nebraska's parole release proceedings. Particularly since the Nebraska statutes tie the parole decision to a number of highly specific factual inquiries, see ante at 442 U. S. 16-18, I see no basis in the record for rejecting the lower courts' conclusion.

Finally, apart from avoiding the risk of actual error, this Court has stressed the importance of adopting procedures that preserve the appearance of fairness and the confidence of inmates in the decisionmaking process. THE CHIEF JUSTICE recognized in Morrissey that "fair treatment in parole revocations will enhance the chance of rehabilitation by avoiding reactions to arbitrariness," 408 U.S. at 408 U. S. 484 (citation omitted), a view shared by legislators, courts, the American Bar Association, and other commentators. [16] This consideration is equally significant whether liberty interests are extinguished in parole release or parole revocation proceedings. As Mr. Justice Frankfurter argued in Joint Arti-Fascist Refugee Committee v. McGrath, 341 U.S. at 341 U. S. 171-172 (concurring opinion):

"The validity and moral authority of a conclusion largely depend on the mode by which it was reached. Secrecy is not congenial to truthseeking, and self-righteousness gives too slender an assurance of rightness. No better instrument has been devised for arriving at truth than to give a person in jeopardy of serious loss notice of the case against him and opportunity to meet it. Nor has a better way been found for generating the feeling, so important to a popular government, that justice has been done."

In my judgment, the need to assure the appearance, as well as the existence, of fairness supports a requirement that the Parole Board advise inmates of the specific dates for their hearings, the criteria to be applied, and the reasons and essential facts underlying adverse decisions. For

"'[o]ne can imagine nothing more cruel, inhuman, and frustrating than serving a prison term without knowledge of what will be measured and the rules determining whether one is ready for release.'"

K. Davis, Discretionary Justice: A Preliminary Inquiry 132 (1969).

B

Applying the analysis of Morrissey and Mathews, I believe substantially more procedural protection is necessary in parole release proceedings than the Court requires. The types of safeguards that should be addressed here, however, are limited by the posture of this case. [17] Thus, only three specific issues need be considered.

While the question is close, I agree with the majority that a formal hearing is not always required when an inmate first becomes eligible for discretionary parole. Ante at 442 U. S. 14-15. The Parole Board conducts an initial parole review hearing once a year for every inmate, even before the inmate is eligible for release. Although the scope of this hearing is limited, inmates are allowed to appear and present letters or statements supporting their case. If the Board concludes that an eligible inmate is a good candidate for release, it schedules a final and substantially more formal hearing.

The Court of Appeals directed the Parole Board to conduct such a formal hearing as soon as an inmate becomes eligible for parole, even where the likelihood of a favorable decision is negligible, but the court required no hearing thereafter. 576 F.2d 1274, 1285 (CA8 1978). From a practical standpoint, this relief offers no appreciable advantage to the inmates. If the Board would not have conducted a final hearing under current procedures, inmates gain little from a requirement that such a hearing be held, since the evidence almost certainly would be insufficient to justify granting release. And because the Court of Appeals required the Board to conduct only one hearing, inmates risk losing the right to a formal proceeding at the very point additional safeguards may have a beneficial impact. The inmates' interest in this modification of the Board's procedures is thus relatively slight. [18] Yet the burden imposed on the Parole Board by the additional formal hearings would be substantial. Accordingly, I believe the Board's current practice of combining both formal and informal hearings is constitutionally sufficient.

However, a different conclusion is warranted with respect to the hearing notices given inmates. The Board currently informs inmates only that it will conduct an initial review or final parole hearing during a particular month within the next year. The notice does not specify the day or hour of the hearing. Instead, inmates must check a designated bulletin board each morning to see if their hearing is scheduled for that day. In addition, the Board refuses to advise inmates of the criteria relevant in parole release proceedings, despite a state statute expressly listing 14 factors the Board must consider and 4 permissible reasons for denying parole. See Neb.Rev.Stat. § 83-1, 114 (1976), quoted ante at 442 U. S. 11, 442 U. S. 16-18.

Finding these procedures insufficient, the District Court and the Court of Appeals ordered that each inmate receive written advance notice of the time set for his hearing, along with a list of factors the Board may consider. 576 F.2d at 1285. [19] Although the Board has proffered no justification for refusing to institute these procedures, id. at 1283, the Court sets aside the relief ordered below on the ground that

"[t]here is no claim that either the timing of the notice or its substance seriously prejudices the inmate's ability to prepare adequately for the hearing."

Ante at 442 U. S. 14, n. 6. But respondents plainly have contended throughout this litigation that reasonable advance notice is necessary to enable them to organize their evidence, call the witnesses permitted by the Board, and notify private counsel allowed to participate in the hearing, see Brief for Respondents 5-66; Answer Brief for Appellee Inmates in No. 77-1889 (CA8), pp. 6, 9, 25, 28; Trial Brief for Inmates in Civ. 72-L-335(Neb.), pp. 17-18; and the courts below obviously agreed. See 576 F.2d at 1283; Mem.Op. in Civ. 72-335 (Neb., Oct. 21, 1977), App. to Pet. for Cert. 25, 39, 457. Given the significant private interests at stake, and the importance of reasonable notice in preserving the appearance of fairness, I see no reason to depart here from this Court's longstanding recognition that adequate notice is a fundamental requirement of due process, e.g., Memphis Light, Gas & Water Division v. Craft, 436 U. S. 1, 436 U. S. 13 (1978); Mullane v. Central Hanover Trust Co., 339 U. S. 306, 339 U. S. 314 (1950), a principle heretofore found equally applicable in the present context. Wolff v. McDonnell, 418 U.S. at 418 U. S. 563-564; Gagnon v. Scarpelli, 411 U.S. at 411 U. S. 786; Morrissey v. Brewer, 408 U.S. at 408 U. S. 486-487, 408 U. S. 489.

Finally, I would require the Board to provide a statement of the crucial evidence on which it relies in denying parole. [20] At present, the Parole Board merely uses a form letter noting the general reasons for its decision. In ordering the Board to furnish as well a summary of the essential facts underlying the denial, the Court of Appeals made clear that "detailed findings of fact are not required.'" 576 F.2d at 1284. The majority here, however, believes even this relief to be unwarranted, because it might render parole proceedings more adversary and equate unfavorable decisions with a determination of guilt. Ante at 442 U. S. 15-16.

The Court nowhere explains how these particular considerations are relevant to the inquiry required by Morrissey and Mathews. Moreover, it is difficult to believe that subsequently disclosing the factual justification for a decision will render the proceeding more adversary, especially when the Board already provides a general statement of reasons. [21] And to the extent unfavorable parole decisions resemble a determination of guilt, the Board has no legitimate interest in concealing from an inmate the conduct or failings of which he purportedly is guilty.

While requiring a summation of the essential evidence might entail some administrative inconvenience, in neither Morrissey v. Brewer, supra at 408 U. S. 489;

Gagnon v. Scarpelli, supra at 411 U. S. 786; nor Wolff v. McDonnell, supra, at 418 U. S. 563, 418 U. S. 564-565, did the Court find that this factor justified denying a written statement of the essential evidence and the reasons underlying a decision. It simply is not unduly

"burdensome to give reasons when reasons exist. Whenever an application . . . is denied . . ., there should be some reason for the decision. It can scarcely be argued that government would be crippled by a requirement that the reason be communicated to the person most directly affected by the government's action."

Board of Regents v. Roth, 408 U. S. 564, 408 U. S. 591 (1972) (MARSHALL, J., dissenting). See Mathews v. Eldridge, 424 U.S. at 424 U. S. 345-346; SEC v. Chenery Corp., 318 U. S. 80 (1943). And an inability to provide any reason suggests that the decision is, in fact, arbitrary. [22]

Moreover, considerations identified in Morrissey and Mathews militate in favor of requiring a statement of the essential evidence. Such a requirement would direct the Board's focus to the relevant statutory criteria and promote more careful consideration of the evidence. It would also enable inmates to detect and correct inaccuracies that could have a decisive impact. [23] And the obligation to justify a decision publicly would provide the assurance, critical to the appearance of fairness, that the Board's decision is not capricious. Finally, imposition of this obligation would afford inmates instruction on the measures needed to improve their prison behavior and prospects for parole, a consequence surely consistent with rehabilitative goals. [24] Balancing these considerations against the Board's minimal interest in avoiding this procedure, I am convinced that the Fourteenth Amendment requires the Parole Board to provide inmates a statement of the essential evidence, as well as a meaningful explanation of the reasons for denying parole release. [25]

Because the Court's opinion both depreciates inmates' fundamental liberty interest in securing parole release and sanctions denial of the most rudimentary due process protection, I respectfully dissent.

Notes

[1] A criminal conviction cannot, however, terminate all liberty interests. Wolff v. McDonnell, 418 U. S. 539, 418 U. S. 555-556 (1974); see, e.g., Procunier v. Navarette, 434 U. S. 555 (1978); Bounds v. Smith, 430 U. S. 817 (1977); Pell v. Procunier, 417 U. S. 817, 417 U. S. 822 (1974); Cruz v. Beto, 405 U. S. 319 (1972); Wilwording v. Swenson, 404 U. S. 249 (1971); Cooper v. Pate, 378 U. S. 546 (1964); Ex parte Hull, 312 U. S. 546 (1941); Weems v. United States, 217 U. S. 349 (1910). See also Carmona v. Ward, 439 U. S. 1091 (1979) (MARSHALL, J., dissenting).

[2] See Bell v. Wolfish, 441 U. S. 520, 441 U. S. 568-571 (1979) (MARSHALL, J., dissenting); id. at 441 U. S. 580-584 (STEVENS, J., dissenting); Leis v. Flynt, 439 U. S. 438, 439 U. S. 448-453 (1979) (STEVENS, J., dissenting); Meachum v. Fano, 427 U. S. 215, 427 U. S. 230 (1976) (STEVENS, J., dissenting); cf. Bell v. Wolfish, supra at 441 U. S.

535-536, 441 U. S. 545. See generally Smith v. Organization of Foster Families, 431 U. S. 816, 431 U. S. 842-847 (1977).

[3] Because parolees' enjoyment of these freedoms was subject to a number of restrictions, the Court characterized their liberty interest as "conditional." See 408 U.S. at 408 U. S. 480. The risk that violation of those conditions could lead to termination of parole status, however, did not diminish the significance of the parolees' interest, since the Due Process Clause anticipates that most liberty interests may be abrogated under proper circumstances. So too, here, respondents' interest does not forfeit constitutional protection simply because their freedom would also be subject to conditions or because of the possibility that the Nebraska Parole Board will deny release after providing due process of law.

[4] The state law in Morrissey, quoted only in the dissenting opinion, provided that "[a]ll paroled prisoners . . . shall be subject, at any time, to be taken into custody and returned to the institution. . . .'" 408 U.S. at 408 U. S. 493 n. 2 (Douglas, J., dissenting in part). The statute specified no other criteria for parole revocation. Thus, had the Court relied solely on particular statutory language, it could not have held that parolees possess a constitutionally protected interest in continuing their status. In Scarpelli, the Court completely ignored the pertinent statutory language. See 411 U.S. at 411 U. S. 781-782.

[5] Cf. Baxter v. Palmigiano, 425 U. S. 308, 425 U. S. 323-324 (1976). Lower courts have understood Wolff to require due process safeguards whenever good-time credits are revoked, and have not focused on the language of various statutory provisions. See, e.g., Franklin v. Shields, 569 F.2d 784, 788-790, 800-801 (CA4) (en banc), cert. denied, 435 U. S. 1003 (1978); United States ex rel. Larkins v. Oswald, 510 F.2d 583 (CA2 1975); Gomes v. Travisono, 510 F.2d 537 (CA1 1974); Willis v. Ciccone, 506 F.2d 1011, 1017 (CA8 1974); Workman v. Mitchell, 502 F.2d 1201 (CA9 1974). See also United States ex rel. Miller v. Twomey, 479 F.2d 701, 712-713 (CA7 1973) (Stevens, J.), cert. denied sub nom. Gutierrez v. Department of Public Safety of Ill., 414 U.S. 1146 (1974).

Meachum v. Fano, 427 U. S. 215 (1976), signals no departure from the basic principles recognized in Morrissey, Gagnon, and Wolff. While the majority in Meachum concluded that the prisoners did not have a protected liberty interest in avoiding transfers between penal institutions, the Court's opinion rested on the absence of any limitation on such transfers, rather than on particular statutory language. 427 U.S. at 427 U. S. 225-228. See Tracy v. Salamack, 572 F.2d 393, 395 n. 9 (CA2 1978); Four Certain Unnamed Inmates v. Hall, 550 F.2d 1291, 1292 (CA1 1977).

[6] See, e.g., Willner v. Committee on Character and Fitness, 373 U. S. 96 (1963); Speiser v. Randall, 357 U. S. 513 (1958); Konigsberg v. State Bar, 353 U. S. 252 (1957); Schware v. Board of Bar Examiners, 353 U. S. 232 (1957); Simmons v. United States, 348 U. S. 397 (1955); Goldsmith v. Board of Tax Appeals, 270 U. S. 117 (1926).

The Second Circuit has characterized the attempt to differentiate between a liberty interest currently enjoyed but subject to termination and an interest that can be enjoyed in the future following an administrative proceeding as actually "nothing more than a reincarnation of the right-privilege dichotomy in a not-too-deceptive disguise." United States ex rel. Johnson v. Chairman of New York State Board of Parole, 500 F.2d 925, 927-928, n. 2, vacated as moot sub nom. Regan v. Johnson, 419 U.S. 1015 (1974), construing United States ex rel. Bey v. Connecticut Board of Parole, 443 F.2d 1079, 1086 (CA2 1971), which the Court quotes ante at 442 U. S. 10; see Comment, The Parole System, 120 U.Pa.L.Rev. 282, 363 (1971).

[7] Government decisionmakers do not gain a "license for arbitrary procedure" when legislators confer a "substantial degree of discretion" regarding the assessment of subjective considerations. Kent v. United States, 383 U. S. 541, 383 U. S. 553 (1966); see Thorpe v. Housing Authority of City of Durham, 386 U. S. 670, 386 U. S. 678 (1967) (Douglas, J., concurring).

[8] See Franklin v. Shields, 569 F.2d at 791; Dawson, The Decision to Grant or Deny Parole: A Study of Parole Criteria in Law and Practice 1966 Wash.U.L.Q. 243, 248-285; cf. Morrissey v. Brewer, 408 U.S. at 408 U. S. 479-480. The Nebraska statutes, in particular, demonstrate the factual nature of the parole release inquiry. One provision, quoted ante at 442 U. S. 118, enumerates factual considerations such as the inmate's intelligence, family status, and employment history, which bear upon the four predictive determinations underlying the ultimate parole decision. See ante at 442 U. S. 11.

[9] The parole statutes of 47 States establish particular standards, criteria, or factors to be applied in parole release determinations. A list of these statutes is set out in the Brief for Jerome N. Frank Legal Services Organization et al. as Amici Curiae 30-31, 23a-26a. These criteria presumably will be a significant source of inmates' "legitimate expectations" regarding the availability of parole. Expectations would also be shaped by the role that parole actually assumes in a jurisdiction's penological system, see infra at 442 U. S. 30-31. It is in these respects that most parole statutes are similar. While there are some differences in statutory language among jurisdictions, it is unrealistic to believe that variations such as the use of "may," rather than "shall," see ante at 442 U. S. 11-12, could negate the expectations derived from experience with a parole system and the enumerated criteria for granting release.

[10] The New York State Parole Board, for example, granted parole in 75.4% of the cases it considered during 1972. See United States ex rel. Johnson v. Chairman of New York State Board of Parole, 500 F.2d at 928. In addition, recent studies show that parole is the method of release for approximately 70% of all criminal offenders returned each year to the community. Uniform Parole Reports, Parole in the United States: 1976 and 1977, p. 55 (1978). In some States, the figure is as high as 97%. See Kastenmeier & Eglit, Parole Release Decision-Making: Rehabilitation, Expertise, and the Demise of Mythology, 22 Am.U.L.Rev. 477, 481-482 (1973).

[11] See Brief for United States in United States v. Addonizio, O.T. 1978, No. 78-156, p. 55 n. 47.

[12] Project, Parole Release Decisionmaking and the Sentencing Process, 84 Yale L.J. 810, 882 n. 361 (1975).

[13] Hearings on H.R. 1598 and Identical Bills before the Subcommittee on Courts, Civil Liberties, and the Administration of Justice of the House Committee on the Judiciary, 93d Cong., 1st Sess., 163-164, 193 (1973) (testimony and statement of Antonin Scalia, Chairman of the Administrative Conference of the United States).

[14] While the severity of a loss does not, of itself, establish that an interest deserves constitutional protection, this factor does weigh heavily in determining the procedural safeguards mandated by the Fourteenth Amendment. See Goss v. Lopez, 419 U. S. 565, 419 U. S. 575-576 (1975); Board of Regents v. Roth, 408 U. S. 564 (1972).

[15] In this case, for example, the form notifying one inmate that parole had been denied indicated that the Board believed he should enlist in a self-improvement program at the prison. But in fact, the inmate was already participating in all such programs available. Tr. 38-39. Such errors in parole files are not unusual. E.g., Kohlman v. Norton, 380 F.Supp. 1073 (Conn.1974) (parole denied because file erroneously indicated that applicant had used gun in committing robbery); Leonard v. Mississippi State Probation and Parole Board, 373 F.Supp. 699 (ND Miss.1974), rev'd, 509 F.2d 820 (CA5), cert. denied, 423 U.S. 998 (1975) (prisoner denied parole on basis of illegal disciplinary action); In re Rodriguez, 14 Cal.3d 639, 537 P.2d 384 (1975) (factually incorrect material in file led parole officers to believe that prisoner had violent tendencies and that his "family reject[ed] him"); State v. Pohlabel, 61 N.J.Super. 242, 160 A.2d 647 (1960) (files erroneously showed that prisoner was under a life sentence in another jurisdiction); Hearings on H.R. 13118 et al. before Subcommittee No. 3 of the House Judiciary Committee, 92d Cong., 2d Sess., pt. VII-A, p. 451 (1972) (testimony of Dr. Willard Gaylin: "I have seen black men listed as white and Harvard graduates listed with borderline IQ's"); S. Singer D. Gottfredson, Development of a Data Base for Parole Decision-Making 2-5 (NCCD Research Center, Supp. Report 1, 1973) (information provided by FBI often lists same charge six or seven times without showing a final disposition).

[16] See, e.g., S.Rep. No. 94-369, p. 19 (1975) ("It is essential, then, that parole has both the fact and appearance of fairness to all. Nothing less is necessary for the maintenance of the integrity of our criminal justice institutions"); United States ex rel. Johnson v. Chairman of New York State Board of Parole, 500 F.2d at 928; Phillips v. Williams, 583 P.2d 488, 490 (Okla.1978), cert. pending, No. 78-1282; ABA, Standards Relating to the Legal Status of Prisoners (Tent. Draft 1977), in 14 Am.Crim.L.Rev. 377, 598 (1977); K. Davis, Discretionary Justice: A Preliminary Inquiry 126-133 (1969); Official Report of the New York State Special Commission on Attica 97, 98 (Bantam ed.1972).

[17] In accordance with the majority opinion, ante at 442 U. S. 16, n. 8, I do not address whether the Court of Appeals was correct in holding that the Nebraska Parole Board may not abandon the procedures it already provides. These safeguards include permitting inmates to appear and present documentary support at hearings, and providing a statement of reasons when parole is denied or deferred. Because the inmates failed to seek review of the Court of Appeals' decision, I also express no view on whether

it correctly held that the Board's practice of allowing inmates to present witnesses and retain counsel for final parole hearings was not constitutionally compelled. Finally, it would be inappropriate to consider the suggestion advanced here for the first time that inmates should be allowed access to their files in order to correct factual inaccuracies. Cf. ante at 442 U. S. 15, n. 7.

Nevertheless, the range of protections currently afforded does affect whether additional procedures are constitutionally compelled. The specific dictates of due process, of course, depend on what a particular situation demands. See Cafeteria & Restaurant Workers v. McElroy, 367 U. S. 886, 367 U. S. 895 (1961). Nebraska's use of formal hearings when the possibility of granting parole is substantial and informal hearings in other cases, for example, combined with provision of a statement of reasons for adverse decisions, obviously reduces the need for supplemental procedures.

[18] Although a formal hearing at the point of initial eligibility would reduce the risk of error and enhance the appearance of fairness, providing a summary of essential evidence and reasons, see n. 25, infra, together with allowing inmates to appear at informal hearings, decreases the justification for requiring the Board to conduct formal hearings in every case. See n. 17, supra.

[19] The courts below found that 72 hours' advance notice ordinarily would enable prisoners to prepare for their appearances. 576 F.2d at 1283. The Court of Appeals further determined that the statutory criteria were sufficiently specific that the Board need only include a list of those criteria with the hearing notices or post such a list in public areas throughout the institution. Ibid.

[20] Every other Court of Appeals holding the Due Process Clause applicable to parole release proceedings has also concluded that the parole board must advise the inmates in writing of the reasons for denying parole. See Franklin v. Shields, 569 F.2d at 800-801 (en banc); United States ex rel. Richerson v. Wolff, 525 F.2d 797 (CA7 1975), cert. denied, 425 U.S. 914 (1976); Childs v. United States Board of Parole, 167 U.S.App.D.C. 268, 511 F.2d 1270 (1974); United States ex rel. Johnson v. Chairman of New York State Board of Parole, 500 F.2d 925 (CA2), vacated as moot, 419 U.S. 1015 (1974). The parties to Franklin v. Shields did not request that the Parole Board also be required to provide a summary of the essential facts, see 569 F.2d at 787, 797, and the Fourth Circuit did not address the issue. The Second Circuit in Johnson expressly held that the statement of reasons must be supplemented by a summary of the "essential facts upon which the Board's inferences are based." 500 F.2d at 934. Richerson and Childs also indicated that the notice of reasons should include a description of the crucial facts. See 525 F.2d at 804; 511 F.2d at 1281-1284, aff'g 371 F.Supp. 1246, 1247 (1973).

[21] Contrary to its supposition here, in Wolff v. McDonnell, 418 U.S. at 418 U. S. 565, the Court could perceive no "prospect of prison disruption that can flow from the requirement of these statements."

[22] See Hirschkop & Millemann, The Unconstitutionality of Prison Life, 55 Va.L.Rev. 795, 811-812, 839 (1969).

[23] The preprinted list of reasons for denying parole is unlikely to disclose these types of factual errors. Out of 375 inmates denied parole during a 6-month period, the only reason given 285 of them was:

"Your continued correctional treatment, vocational, educational, or job assignment in the facility will substantially enhance your capacity to lead a law-abiding life when released at a later date."

App. 40-42. Although the denial forms also include a list of six "[r]ecommendations for correcting deficiencies," such as "[e]xhibit some responsibility and maturity," the evidence at trial showed that all six items were checked on 370 of the 375 forms, regardless of the facts of the particular case. App. 42; Tr. 38-39, 45-46.

[24] See, e.g., cases cited in n. 20, supra; Candarini v. Attorney General of United States, 369 F.Supp. 1132, 1137 (EDNY 1974); Monks v. New Jersey State Parole Board, 58 N.J. 238, 249, 277 A.2d 193, 199 (1971); K. Davis, Discretionary Justice: A Preliminary Inquiry 126-133 (1969); M. Frankel, Criminal Sentences 40-41 (1972); Dawson, The Decision to Grant or Deny Parole: A Study of Parole Criteria in Law and Practice, 1966 Wash.U.L.Q. 243, 302; Comment, 6 St. Mary's L.J. 478, 487 (1974).

[25] This statement of reasons and the summary of essential evidence should be provided to all inmates actually eligible for parole, whether the adverse decision is rendered following an initial review or a final parole hearing.

Minors should get due process, like a lawyer during questioning: Justice Marshall's dissent in Fare v. Michael C. (June 20, 1979)

MR. JUSTICE MARSHALL, with whom MR. JUSTICE BRENNAN and MR. JUSTICE STEVENS join, dissenting.

In Miranda v. Arizona, 384 U.S. 436 (1966), this Court sought to ensure that the inherently coercive pressures of custodial interrogation would not vitiate a suspect's privilege against self-incrimination. Nothing that these pressures "can operate very quickly to overbear the will of one merely made aware of his privilege," id., at 469, the Court held:

"If [a suspect in custody] indicates in any manner, at any time prior to or during questioning, that he wishes to remain silent, the interrogation must cease. At this point he has shown that he intends to exercise his Fifth Amendment privilege; any statement taken after the person invokes his privilege cannot be other than the product of compulsion, subtle or otherwise. . . . If the individual states that he wants an attorney, the interrogation must cease until an attorney is present." Id., at 473-474 (footnote omitted).

See also id., at 444-445.

As this Court has consistently recognized, the coerciveness of the custodial setting is of heightened concern where, as here, a juvenile is under investigation. In Haley v. Ohio, 332 U.S. 596 (1948), the plurality reasoned that because a 15 1/2-year-old minor was particularly susceptible to overbearing interrogation tactics, the voluntariness of his confession could not "be judged by the more exacting standards of maturity." Id., at 599. The Court reiterated this point in Gallegos v. Colorado, 370 U.S. 49, 54 (1962), observing that a 14-year-old suspect could not "be compared with an adult in full possession of his senses and knowledgeable of the consequences of his admissions." The juvenile defendant, in the Court's view, required

"the aid of more mature judgment as to the steps he should take in the predicament in which he found himself. A lawyer or an adult relative or friend could have given the petitioner the protection which his own immaturity could not." Ibid.

And, in In re Gault, 387 U.S. 1, 55 (1967), the Court admonished that "the greatest care must be taken to assure that [a minor's] admission was voluntary."

It is therefore critical in the present context that we construe Miranda's prophylactic requirements broadly to accomplish their intended purpose - "dispel[ling] the compulsion inherent in custodial surroundings." 384 U.S., at 458 . To effectuate this purpose, the Court must ensure that the "protective device" of legal counsel, id., at 465-466, 469, be readily available, and that any intimation of a desire to preclude questioning be scrupulously honored. Thus, I believe Miranda requires that interrogation cease whenever a juvenile requests an adult who is obligated to represent his interests. Such a request, in my judgment, constitutes both an attempt to obtain advice and a general invocation of the right to silence. For, as the California Supreme Court recognized, "`[i]t is fatuous to assume that a minor in custody will be in a position to call an attorney for assistance,'" 21 Cal. 3d 471, 475-476, 579 P.2d 7, 9 (1978), quoting People v. Burton, 6 Cal. 3d 375, 382, 491 P.2d 793, 797 (1971), or that he will trust the police to obtain a lawyer for him. 1 A juvenile in these circumstances will likely turn to his parents, or another adult responsible for his welfare, as the only means of securing legal counsel. Moreover, a request for such adult assistance is surely inconsistent with a present desire to speak freely. Requiring a strict verbal formula to invoke the protections of Miranda would "protect the knowledgeable accused from stationhouse coercion while abandoning the young person who knows no more than to ask for the . . . person he trusts." Chaney v. Wainwright, 561 F.2d 1129, 1134 (CA5 1977) (Goldberg, J., dissenting).

On my reading of Miranda, a California juvenile's request for his probation officer should be treated as a per se assertion of Fifth Amendment rights. The California Supreme Court determined that probation officers have a statutory duty to represent minors' interests and, indeed, are "trusted guardian figure[s]" to whom a juvenile would likely turn for assistance. 21 Cal. 3d, at 476, 579 P.2d, at 10. In addition, the court found, probation officers are particularly well suited to assist a juvenile "on such matters as to whether or not he should obtain an attorney" and "how to conduct himself with police." Id., at 476, 477, 579 P.2d, at 10. Hence, a juvenile's request for a probation officer may frequently be an attempt to secure protection from the coercive aspects of custodial questioning. 2

This Court concludes, however, that because a probation officer has law enforcement duties, juveniles generally would not call upon him to represent their interests, and if they did, would not be well served. Ante, at 721-722. But that conclusion ignores the California Supreme Court's express determination that the officer's responsibility to initiate juvenile proceedings did not negate his function as personal adviser to his wards. 3 I decline to second-guess that court's assessment of state law. See Murdock v. Memphis, 20 Wall. 590, 626 (1875); General Trading Co. v. State Tax Comm'n, 322 U.S. 335, 337 (1944); Scripto, Inc. v. Carson, 362 U.S. 207, 210 (1960). 4 Further, although the majority here speculates that probation officers have a duty to advise cooperation with the police, ante, at 721 - a proposition suggested only in the concurring opinion of two justices below, 21 Cal. 3d, at 479, 579 P.2d, at 11-12 (Mosk, J., joined by Bird, C. J., concurring) - respondent's probation officer instructed all his charges "not to go and admit openly to an offense, [but rather] to get some type of advice from . . . parents or a lawyer." App. 30. Absent an explicit statutory provision or judicial holding, the officer's assessment of the obligations imposed by state law is entitled to deference by this Court.

Thus, given the role of probation officers under California law, a juvenile's request to see his officer may reflect a desire for precisely the kind of assistance Miranda guarantees an accused before he waives his Fifth Amendment rights. At the very least, such a request signals a desire to remain silent until contact with the officer is made. Because the Court's contrary determination withdraws the safeguards of Miranda from those most in need of protection, I respectfully dissent.

Notes

[1] The facts of the instant case are illustrative. When the police offered to obtain an attorney for respondent, he replied: "How I know you guys won't pull no police officer in and tell me he's an attorney?" Ante, at 710. Significantly, the police made no attempt to allay that concern. See 21 Cal. 3d, at 476 n. 3, 579 P.2d, at 10 n. 3.

[2] The Court intimates that construing a request for a probation officer as an invocation of the Fifth Amendment privilege would undermine the specificity of Miranda's prophylactic rules. Ante, at 718. Yet the Court concedes that the statutory duty to "advise and care for the juvenile defendant," 21 Cal. 3d, at 477, 579 P.2d, at 10, distinguishes probation officers from other adults, such as coaches and clergymen. Ante, at 723. Since law enforcement officials should be on notice of such legal relationships, they would presumably have no difficulty determining whether a suspect has asserted his Fifth Amendment rights.

Although I agree with my Brother POWELL that, on the facts here, respondent was not "subjected to a fair interrogation free from inherently coercive circumstances," post, at 734, I do not believe a case-by-case approach provides police sufficient guidance, or affords juveniles adequate protection.

[3] In filing the petition and performing the other functions enumerated ante, at 720-721, n. 5, the probation officer must act in the best interests of the minor. See In re Steven C., 9 Cal. App. 3d 255, 264-265, 88 Cal. Rptr. 97, 101-102 (1970).

[4] One thing is certain. The California Supreme Court is more familiar with the duties and performance of its probation officers than we are.

Of course, "[i]t is peculiarly within the competence of the highest court of a State to determine that in its jurisdiction the police should be subject to more stringent rules than are required as a federal constitutional minimum." Oregon v. Hass, 420 U.S. 714, 728 (1975) (MARSHALL, J., dissenting). See also People v. Disbrow, 16 Cal. 3d 101, 545 P.2d 272 (1976) (refusing to follow Harris v. New York, 401 U.S. 222 (1971)); Brennan, State Constitutions and the Protection of Individual Rights, 90 Harv. L. Rev. 489 (1977).

Should need warrant for telephone numbers: Justice Marshall's dissent in Smith v. Maryland (June 20, 1979)

Mr. Justice MARSHALL, with whom Mr. Justice BRENNAN joins, dissenting.

The Court concludes that because individuals have no actual or legitimate expectation of privacy in information they voluntarily relinquish to telephone companies, the use of pen registers by government agents is immune from Fourth Amendment scrutiny. Since I remain convinced that constitutional protections are not abrogated whenever a person apprises another of facts valuable in criminal investigations, see, e. g., United States v. White, 401 U.S. 745, 786-790, 91 S.Ct. 1122, 1143-1145, 28 L.Ed.2d 453 (1971) (Harlan, J., dissenting); id., at 795-796, 91 S.Ct., at 1147-1148 (MARSHALL, J., dissenting); California Bankers Assn. v. Shultz, 416 U.S. 21, 95-96, 94 S.Ct. 1494, 1534, 39 L.Ed.2d 812 (1974) (MARSHALL, J., dissenting); United States v. Miller, 425 U.S. 435, 455-456, 96 S.Ct. 1619, 1629-1630, 48 L.Ed.2d 71 (1976) (MARSHALL, J., dissenting), I respectfully dissent.

Applying the standards set forth in Katz v. United States, 389 U.S. 347, 361, 88 S.Ct. 507, 516, 19 L.Ed.2d 576 (1967) (Harlan, J., concurring), the Court first determines that telephone subscribers have no subjective expectations of privacy concerning the numbers they dial. To reach this conclusion, the Court posits that individuals somehow infer from the long-distance listings on their phone bills, and from the cryptic assurances of "help" in tracing obscene calls included in "most" phone books, that pen registers are regularly used for recording local calls. See ante, at 742-743. But even assuming, as I do not, that individuals "typically know" that a phone company monitors calls for internal reasons, ante, at 743, 1 it does not follow that they expect this information to be made available to the public in general or the government in particular. Privacy is not a discrete commodity, possessed absolutely or not at all. Those who disclose certain facts to a bank or phone company for a limited business purpose need not assume that this information will be released to other persons for other purposes. See California Bankers Assn. v. Shultz, supra, 416 U.S., at 95-96, 94 S.Ct., at 1534 (MARSHALL, J., dissenting).

The crux of the Court's holding, however, is that whatever expectation of privacy petitioner may in fact have entertained regarding his calls, it is not one "society is prepared to recognize as 'reasonable'." Ante, at 743. In so ruling, the Court determines that individuals who convey information to third parties have "assumed the risk" of disclosure to the government. Ante, at 744,745. This analysis is misconceived in two critical respects.

Implicit in the concept of assumption of risk is some notion of choice. At least in the third-party consensual surveillance cases, which first incorporated risk analysis into Fourth Amendment doctrine, the defendant presumably had exercised some discretion in deciding who should enjoy his confidential communications. See, e. g., Lopez v. United States, 373 U.S. 427, 439, 83 S.Ct. 1381, 1388, 10 L.Ed.2d 462 (1963); Hoffa v. United States, 385 U.S. 293, 302-303, 87 S.Ct. 408, 413-414, 17 L.Ed.2d 374 (1966); United States v. White, supra, 401 U.S., at 751-752, 91 S.Ct., at 1125-1126 (plurality opinion). By contrast here, unless a person is prepared to forgo use of what for many has become a personal or professional necessity, he cannot help but accept the risk of surveillance. Cf. Lopez v. United States, supra, 373 U.S., at 465-466, 83 S.Ct., at 1401-1402 (BRENNAN, J., dissenting). It is idle to speak of "assuming" risks in contexts where, as a practical matter, individuals have no realistic alternative.

More fundamentally, to make risk analysis dispositive in assessing the reasonableness of privacy expectations would allow the government to define the scope of Fourth Amendment protections. For example, law enforcement officials, simply by announcing their intent to monitor the content of random samples of first-class mail or private phone conversations, could put the public on notice of the risks they would thereafter assume in such communications. See Amsterdam, Perspectives on the Fourth Amendment, 58 Minn.L.Rev. 349, 384, 407 (1974). Yet, although acknowledging this implication of its analysis, the Court is willing to concede only that, in some circumstances, a further "normative inquiry would be proper." Ante, at 740-741 n. 5. No meaningful effort is made to explain what those circumstances might be, or why this case is not among them.

In my view, whether privacy expectations are legitimate within the meaning of Katz depends not on the risks an individual can be presumed to accept when imparting information to third parties, but on the risks he should be forced to assume in a free and open society. By its terms, the constitutional prohibition of unreasonable searches and seizures assigns to the judiciary some prescriptive responsibility. As Mr. Justice Harlan, who formulated the standard the Court applies today, himself recognized: "since it is the task of the law to form and project, as well as mirror and reflect, we should not . . . merely recite . . . risks without examining the desirability of saddling them upon society." United States v. White, supra, 401 U.S., at 786, 91 S.Ct., at 1143 (dissenting opinion). In making this assessment, courts must evaluate the "intrinsic character" of investigative practices with reference to the basic values underlying the Fourth Amendment. California Bankers Assn. v. Shultz, 416 U.S., at 95, 94 S.Ct., at 1534 (MARSHALL, J., dissenting). And for those "extensive intrusions that significantly jeopardize individuals' sense of security . . . . more than self-restraint by law enforcement officials is required." United States v. White, supra, 401 U.S., at 786, 91 S.Ct., at 1143 (Harlan, J., dissenting).

The use of pen registers, I believe, constitutes such an extensive intrusion. To hold otherwise ignores the vital role telephonic communication plays in our personal and professional relationships, see Katz v. United States, 389 U.S., at 352, 88 S.Ct., at 511, as well as the First and Fourth Amendment interests implicated by unfettered official surveillance. Privacy in placing calls is of value not only to those engaged in criminal activity. The prospect of unregulated governmental monitoring will undoubtedly prove disturbing even to those with nothing illicit to hide. Many individuals, including members of unpopular political organizations or journalists with confidential sources, may legitimately wish to avoid disclosure of their personal contacts. See NAACP v. Alabama, 357 U.S. 449, 463, 78 S.Ct. 1163, 1172, 2 L.Ed.2d 1488 (1958); Branzburg v. Hayes, 408 U.S. 665, 695, 92 S.Ct. 2646, 2663, 33 L.Ed.2d 626 (1972); id., at 728-734, 92 S.Ct., at 2673-2676 (STEWART, J., dissenting). Permitting governmental access to telephone records on less than probable cause may thus impede certain forms of political affiliation and journalistic endeavor that are the hallmark of a truly free society. Particularly given the Government's previous reliance on warrantless telephonic surveillance to trace reporters' sources and monitor protected political activity, 2 I am unwilling to insulate use of pen registers from independent judicial review.

Just as one who enters a public telephone booth is "entitled to assume that the words he utters into the mouthpiece will not be broadcast to the world," Katz v. United States, supra, 389 U.S., at 352, 88 S.Ct., at 512, so too, he should be entitled to assume that the numbers he dials in the privacy of his home will be recorded, if at all, solely for the phone company's business purposes. Accordingly, I would require law enforcement officials to obtain a warrant before they enlist telephone companies to secure information otherwise beyond the government's reach.

1 Lacking the Court's apparently exhaustive knowledge of this Nation's telephone books and the reading habits of telephone subscribers, see ante, at 742-743, I decline to assume general public awareness of how obscene phone calls are traced. Nor am I persuaded that the scope of Fourth Amendment protection should turn on the concededly "esoteric functions" of pen registers in corporate billing, ante, at 742, functions with which subscribers are unlikely to have intimate familiarity.

2 See, e. g., Reporters Committee For Freedom of Press v. American Tel. & Tel. Co., 192 U.S.App.D.C. 376, 593 F.2d 1030 (1978), cert. denied, 440 U.S. 949, 99 S.Ct. 1431, 59 L.Ed.2d 639 (1979); Halperin v. Kissinger, 434 F.Supp. 1193 (DC 1977); Socialist Workers Party v. Attorney General, 463 F.Supp. 515 (SDNY 1978).

No preferences for veterans: Justice Marshall's dissent in Personnel Administrator of Massachusetts v. Feeney (June 5, 1979)

MR. JUSTICE MARSHALL, with whom MR. JUSTICE BRENNAN joins,

dissenting.

Although acknowledging that, in some circumstances, discriminatory intent may be inferred from the inevitable or foreseeable impact of a statute, ante at 442 U. S. 279 n. 25, the Court concludes that no such intent has been established here. I cannot agree. In my judgment, Massachusetts' choice of an absolute veterans' preference system evinces purposeful gender-based discrimination. And because the statutory scheme bears no substantial relationship to a legitimate governmental objective, it cannot withstand scrutiny under the Equal Protection Clause.

I

The District Court found that the "prime objective" of the Massachusetts veterans' preference statute, Mass.Gen.Laws Ann., ch. 31, § 23, was to benefit individuals with prior military service. Anthony v. Commonwealth, 415 F.Supp. 485, 497 (Mass.1976). See Feeney v. Massachusetts, 451 F.Supp. 143, 145 (Mass.1978). Under the Court's analysis, this factual determination

"necessarily compels the conclusion that the State intended nothing more than to prefer 'veterans.' Given this finding, simple logic suggests than an intent to exclude women from significant public jobs was not at work in this law."

Ante at 442 U. S. 277. I find the Court's logic neither simple nor compelling.

That a legislature seeks to advantage one group does not, as a matter of logic or of common sense, exclude the possibility that it also intends to disadvantage another. Individuals in general, and lawmakers in particular, frequently act for a variety of reasons. As this Court recognized in Arlington Heights v. Metropolitan Housing Dev. Corp., 429 U. S. 252, 429 U. S. 265 (1977),

"[r]arely can it be said that a legislature or administrative body operating under a broad mandate made a decision motivated solely by a single concern."

Absent an omniscience not commonly attributed to the judiciary, it will often be impossible to ascertain the sole or even dominant purpose of a given statute. See McGinnis v. Royster, 410 U. S. 263, 410 U. S. 276-277 (1973); Ely, Legislative and Administrative Motivation in Constitutional Law, 79 Yale L.J. 1205, 1214 (1970). Thus, the critical constitutional inquiry is not whether an illicit consideration was the primary or but-for cause of a decision, but rather whether it had an appreciable role in shaping a given legislative enactment. Where there is "proof that a discriminatory purpose has been a motivating factor in the decision, . . . judicial deference is no longer justified." Arlington Heights v. Metropolitan Housing Dev. Corp., supra at 429 U. S. 265-266 (emphasis added).

Moreover, since reliable evidence of subjective intentions is seldom obtainable, resort to inference based on objective factors is generally unavoidable. See Beer v. United States, 425 U. S. 130, 425 U. S. 148-149, n. 4 (1976) (MARSHALL, J., dissenting); cf. Palmer v. Thompson, 403 U. S. 217, 403 U. S. 224-225 (1971); United States v. O'Brien, 391 U. S. 367, 391 U. S. 383-384 (1968). To discern the purposes underlying facially neutral policies, this Court has therefore considered the degree, inevitability, and foreseeability of any disproportionate impact, as well as the alternatives reasonably available. See Monroe v. Board of Commissioners, 391 U. S. 450, 391 U. S. 459 (1968); Goss v. Board of Education, 373 U. S. 683, 373 U. S. 688-689 (1963); Gomillion v. Lightfoot, 364 U. S. 339 (1960); Griffin v. Illinois, 351 U. S. 12, 351 U. S. 17 n. 11 (1956). Cf. Albemarle Paper Co. v. Moody, 422 U. S. 405, 422 U. S. 425 (1975).

In the instant case, the impact of the Massachusetts statute on women is undisputed. Any veteran with a passing grade on the civil service exam must be placed ahead of a nonveteran, regardless of their respective scores. The District Court found that, as a practical matter, this preference supplants test results as the determinant of upper level civil service appointments. 415 F.Supp. at 488-489. Because less than 2% of the women in Massachusetts are veterans, the absolute preference formula has rendered desirable state civil service employment an almost exclusively male prerogative. 451 F.Supp. at 151 (Campbell, J., concurring).

As the District Court recognized, this consequence follows foreseeably, indeed inexorably, from the long history of policies severely limiting women's participation in the military. [1]

Although neutral in form, the statute is anything but neutral in application. It inescapably reserves a major sector of public employment to "an already established class which, as a matter of historical fact, is 98% male." Ibid. Where the foreseeable impact of a facially neutral policy is so disproportionate, the burden should rest on the State to establish that sex-based considerations played no part in the choice of the particular legislative scheme. Cf. Castaneda v. Partida, 430 U. S. 482 (1977); Washington v. Davis, 426 U. S. 229, 426 U. S. 241 (1976); Alexander v. Louisiana, 405 U. S. 625, 405 U. S. 632 (1972); see generally Brest, Palmer v. Thompson: An Approach to the Problem of Unconstitutional Legislative Motive, 1971 Sup.Ct.Rev. 95, 123.

Clearly, that burden was not sustained here. The legislative history of the statute reflects the Commonwealth's patent appreciation of the impact the preference system would have on women, and an equally evident desire to mitigate that impact only with respect to certain traditionally female occupations. Until 1971, the statute and implementing civil service regulations exempted from operation of the preference any job requisitions "especially calling for women." 1954 Mass. Acts, ch. 627, § 5. See also 1896 Mass. Acts, ch. 517, § 6; 1919 Mass. Acts, ch. 150, § 2; 1945 Mass. Acts, ch. 725, § 2(e); 1965 Mass. Acts, ch. 53; ante at 442 U. S. 266 nn. 13, 14. In practice, this exemption, coupled with the absolute preference for veterans, has created a gender-based civil service hierarchy, with women occupying low-grade clerical and secretarial jobs and men holding more responsible and remunerative positions. See 415 F.Supp. at 488; 451 F.Supp. at 148 n. 9.

Thus, for over 70 years, the Commonwealth has maintained, as an integral part of its veterans' preference system, an exemption relegating female civil service applicants to occupations traditionally filled by women. Such a statutory scheme both reflects and perpetuates precisely the kind of archaic assumptions about women's roles which we have previously held invalid. See Orr v. Orr, 440 U. S. 268 (1979); Califano v. Goldfarb, 430 U. S. 199, 430 U. S. 210-211 (1977); Stanton v. Stanton, 421 U. S. 7, 421 U. S. 14 (1975); Weinberger v. Wiesenfeld, 420 U. S. 636, 420 U. S. 645 (1975). Particularly when viewed against the range of less discriminatory alternatives available to assist veterans, [2] Massachusetts' choice of a formula that so severely restricts public employment opportunities for women cannot reasonably be thought gender-neutral. Cf. Albemarle Paper Co. v. Moody, supra, at 422 U. S. 425. The Court's conclusion to the contrary -- that "nothing in the record" evinces a "collateral goal of keeping women in a stereotypic and predefined place in the Massachusetts Civil Service," ante at 442 U. S. 279 -- displays a singularly myopic view of the facts established below. [3]

II

To survive challenge under the Equal Protection Clause, statutes reflecting gender-based discrimination must be substantially related to the achievement of important governmental objectives. See Califano v. Webster, 430 U. S. 313, 430 U. S. 316-317 (1977); Craig v. Boren, 429 U. S. 190, 429 U. S. 197 (1976); Reed v. Reed, 404 U. S. 71, 404 U. S. 76 (1971). Appellants here advance three interests in support of the absolute preference system: (1) assisting veterans in their readjustment to civilian life; (2) encouraging military enlistment; and (3) rewarding those who have served their country. Brief for Appellants 24. Although each of those goals is unquestionably legitimate, the "mere recitation of a benign, compensatory purpose" cannot, of itself, insulate legislative classifications from constitutional scrutiny. Weinberger v. Wiesenfeld, supra at 420 U. S. 648. And in this case, the Commonwealth has failed to establish a sufficient relationship between its objectives and the means chosen to effectuate them.

With respect to the first interest, facilitating veterans' transition to civilian status, the statute is plainly overinclusive. Cf. Trimble v. Gordon, 430 U. S. 762, 430 U. S. 770-772 (1977); Jimenez v. Weinberger, 417 U. S. 628, 417 U. S. 637 (1974). By conferring a permanent preference, the legislation allows veterans to invoke their advantage repeatedly, without regard to their date of discharge. As the record demonstrates, a substantial majority of those currently enjoying the benefits of the system are not recently discharged veterans in need of readjustment assistance. [4]

Nor is the Commonwealth's second asserted interest, encouraging military service, a plausible justification for this legislative scheme. In its original and subsequent reenactments, the statute extended benefits retroactively to veterans who had served during a prior specified period. See ante at 442 U. S. 265-267. If the Commonwealth's "actual purpose" is to induce enlistment, this legislative design is hardly well suited to that end. See Califano v. Webster, supra at 430 U. S. 317; Weinberger v. Wiesenfeld, supra at 420 U. S. 648. For I am unwilling to assume what appellants made no effort to prove, that the possibility of obtaining an ex post facto civil service preference significantly influenced the enlistment decisions of Massachusetts residents. Moreover, even if such influence could be presumed, the statute is still grossly overinclusive, in that it bestows benefits on men drafted as well as those who volunteered.

Finally, the Commonwealth's third interest, rewarding veterans, does not "adequately justify the salient features" of this preference system. Craig v. Boren, supra at 429 U. S. 202-203. See Orr v. Orr, supra at 440 U. S. 281. Where a particular statutory scheme visits substantial hardship on a class long subject to discrimination, the legislation cannot be sustained unless "carefully tuned to alternative considerations.'" Trimble v. Gordon, supra at 430 U. S. 772. See Caban v. Mohammed, 441 U. S. 380, 441 U. S. 392-393, n. 13 (1979); Mathews v. Lucas, 427 U. S. 495 (1976). Here, there are a wide variety of less discriminatory means by which Massachusetts could effect its compensatory purposes. For example, a point preference system, such as that maintained by many States and the Federal Government, see n. 2, supra, or an absolute preference for a limited duration, would reward veterans without excluding all qualified women from upper level civil service positions. Apart from public employment, the Commonwealth, can, and does, afford assistance to veterans in various ways, including tax abatements, educational subsidies, and special programs for needy veterans. See Mass.Gen.Laws Ann., ch. 59, § 5, Fifth (West Supp. 1979); Mass.Gen.Laws Ann., ch. 69, §§ 7, 7B (West Supp. 1979); and Mass.Gen.Laws Ann., chs. 115, 115A (West 1969 and Supp. 1978). Unlike these and similar benefits, the costs of which are distributed across the taxpaying public generally, the Massachusetts statute exacts a substantial price from a discrete group of individuals who have long been subject to employment discrimination, [5] and who, "because of circumstances totally beyond their control, have [had] little if any chance of becoming members of the preferred class." 415 F.Supp. at 499. See n. 1, supra.

In its present unqualified form, the veterans' preference statute precludes all but a small fraction of Massachusetts women from obtaining any civil service position also of interest to men. See 451 F.Supp. at 151 (Campbell, J., concurring). Given the range of alternatives available, this degree of preference is not constitutionally permissible.

I would affirm the judgment of the court below.

Notes

[1] See Anthony v. Massachusetts, 415 F.Supp. 485, 490, 495-499 (Mass. 1976); Feeney v. Massachusetts, 451 F.Supp. 143, 145, 148 (Mass. 1978). In addition to the 2% quota on women's participation in the Armed Forces, see ante at 442 U. S. 270 n. 21, enlistment and appointment requirements have been more stringent for females than males with respect to age, mental and physical aptitude, parental consent, and educational attainment. M. Binkin & S. Bach, Women and the Military (1977) (hereinafter Binkin and Bach); Note, The Equal Rights Amendment and the Military, 82 Yale L.J. 1533, 1539 (1973). Until the 1970's, the Armed Forces precluded enlistment and appointment of women, but not men, who were married or had dependent children. See 415 F.Supp. at 490; App. 85; Exs. 98, 99, 103, 104. Sex-based restrictions on advancement and training opportunities also diminished the incentives for qualified women to enlist. See Binkin and Bach 117, Beans, Sex Discrimination in the Military, 67 Mil.L.Rev.19, 59-83 (1975). Cf. Schlesinger v. Ballard, 419 U. S. 498, 419 U. S. 508 (1975).

Thus, unlike the employment examination in Washington v. Davis, 426 U. S. 229 (1976), which the Court found to be demonstrably job-related, the Massachusetts preference statute incorporates the results of sex-based military policies irrelevant to women's current fitness for civilian public employment. See 415 F.Supp. at 498-499.

[2] Only four States afford a preference comparable in scope to that of Massachusetts. See Fleming & Shanor, Veterans' Preferences and Public Employment: Unconstitutional Gender Discrimination?, 26 Emory L.J. 13, 17 n. 13 (1977) (citing statutes). Other States and the Federal Government grant point or tie-breaking preferences that do not foreclose opportunities for women. See id. at 13, and nn. 12, 14; ante at 442 U. S. 261 n. 7; Hearings on Veterans' Preference Oversight before the Subcommittee on Civil Service of the House Committee on Post Office and Civil Service, 95th Cong., 1st Sess., 4 (1977) (statement of Alan Campbell, Chairman, United States Civil Service Commission).

[3] Although it is relevant that the preference statute also disadvantages a substantial group of men, see ante at 442 U. S. 281 (STEVENS, J., concurring), it is equally pertinent that 47% of Massachusetts men over 18 are veterans, as compared to 0.8% of Massachusetts women. App. 83. Given this disparity, and the indicia of intent noted supra at 442 U. S. 284-285, the absolute number of men denied preference cannot be dispositive, especially since they have not faced the barriers to achieving veteran status confronted by women. See n. 1, supra.

[4] The eligibility lists for the positions Ms. Feeney sought included 95 veterans for whom discharge information was available. Of those 95 males, 64 (67%) were discharged prior to 1960. App. 106, 150-151, 169-170.

[5] See Frontiero v. Richardson, 411 U. S. 677, 411 U. S. 689 n. 23 (1973), Kahn v. Shevin, 416 U. S. 351, 416 U. S. 353-354 (1974); United States Bureau of t,he Census, Current Population Reports, No. 107, Money Income and Poverty Status of Families and Persons in the United States: 1976 (Advance Report) (Table 7) (Sept.1977).

Racially discriminatory motivation isn't necessary ingredient of a Fifteenth Amendment violation: Justice Marshall's dissent in City of Mobile v. Bolden (April 22, 1980)

MR. JUSTICE MARSHALL, dissenting. [*]

The American ideal of political equality, conceived in the earliest days of our colonial existence and fostered by the egalitarian language of the Declaration of Independence, could not forever tolerate the limitation of the right to vote to white propertied males. Our Constitution has been amended six times in the movement toward a democracy for more than the few, [n1] and this Court has interpreted the Fourteenth Amendment to provide that "a citizen has a constitutionally protected right to participate in elections on an equal basis with other citizens in the jurisdiction," Dunn v. Blumstein,

405 U.S. 330, 336 (1972). The Court's decision today is in a different spirit. Indeed, a plurality of the Court concludes that, in the absence of proof of intentional discrimination by the State, the right to vote provides the politically powerless with nothing more than the right to cast meaningless ballots. The District Court in both of these cases found that the challenged multimember districting schemes unconstitutionally diluted the Negro vote. These factual findings were upheld by the Court of Appeals, and the plurality does not question them. Instead, the plurality concludes that districting schemes do not violate the Equal Protection Clause unless it is proved that they were enacted or maintained for the purpose of minimizing or canceling out the voting potential of a racial minority. The plurality would require plaintiffs in vote-dilution cases to meet the stringent burden of establishing discriminatory intent within the meaning of Washington v. Davis, 426 U.S. 229 (1976); Arlington Heights v. Metropolitan Housing Dev. Corp., 429 U.S. 252 (1977); and Personnel Administrator of Mass. v. Feeney, 442 U.S. 256 (1979). In my view, our vote dilution decisions require only a showing of discriminatory impact to justify the invalidation of a multimember districting scheme, and, because they are premised on the fundamental interest in voting protected by the Fourteenth Amendment, the discriminatory impact standard adopted by them is unaffected by Washington v. Davis, supra, and its progeny. Furthermore, an intent requirement is inconsistent with the protection against denial or abridgment of the vote on account of race embodied in the Fifteenth Amendment and in § 2 of the Voting Rights Act of 1965, 79 Stat. 437, as amended, 42 U.S.C. § 1973. [n2] Even if, however, proof of discriminatory intent were necessary to support a vote-dilution claim, I would impose upon the plaintiffs a standard of proof less rigid than that provided by Personnel Administrator of Mass. v. Feeney, supra.

I

The Court does not dispute the proposition that multimember districting can have the effect of submerging electoral minorities and over-representing electoral majorities. [n3] It is for this reason that we developed a strong preference for single-member districting in court-ordered reapportionment plans. See ante at 66, n. 12. Furthermore, and more important for present purposes, we decided a series of vote-dilution cases under the Fourteenth Amendment that were designed to protect electoral minorities from precisely the combination of electoral laws and historical and social factors found in the present cases. [n4] In my view, the plurality's treatment of these cases is fanciful. Although we have held that multimember districts are not unconstitutional per se, see ante at 66, there is simply no basis for the plurality's conclusion that, under our prior cases, proof of discriminatory intent is a necessary condition for the invalidation of multimember districting.

A

In Fortson v. Dorsey, 379 U.S. 433 (1965), the first vote-dilution case to reach this Court, we stated explicitly that such a claim could rest on either discriminatory purpose or effect:

It might well be that, designedly or otherwise, a multimember constituency apportionment scheme, under the circumstances of a particular case, would operate to minimize or cancel out the voting strength of racial or political elements of the voting population.

Id. at 439 (emphasis added). We reiterated these words in Burns v. Richardson, 384 U.S. 73 (1966), interpreted them as the correct test to apply to vote-dilution claims, and described the standard as one involving "invidious effect," id. at 88. We then held that the plaintiffs had failed to meet their burden of proof:

[T]he demonstration that a particular multi-member scheme effects an invidious result must appear from evidence in the record. . . . That demonstration was not made here. In relying on conjecture as to the effects of multi-member districting, rather than demonstrated fact, the court acted in a manner more appropriate to the body responsible for drawing up the districting plan. Speculations do not supply evidence that the multi-member districting was designed to have, or had, the invidious effect necessary to a judgment of the unconstitutionality of the districting.

Id. at 88-89 (emphasis added) (footnote omitted). It could not be plainer that the Court in Burns considered discriminatory effect a sufficient condition for invalidating a multimember districting plan.

In Whitcomb v. Chavis, 403 U.S. 124 (1971),we again repeated and applied the Fortson standard, 403 U.S. at 143, 144, but determined that the Negro community's lack of success at the polls was the result of partisan politics, not racial vote dilution. Id. at 150-155. The Court stressed that both the Democratic and Republican Parties had nominated Negroes, and several had been elected. Negro candidates lost only when their entire party slate went down to defeat. Id. at 150, nn. 29-30, 152-153. In addition, the Court was impressed that there was no finding that officials had been unresponsive to Negro concerns. Id. at 152, n. 32, 155. [n5]

More recently, in White v. Regester, 412 U.S. 755 (1973), we invalidated the challenged multimember districting plans because their characteristics, when combined with historical and social factors, had the discriminatory effect of denying the plaintiff Negroes and Mexican-Americans equal access to the political process. Id. at 765-770. We stated that

it is not enough that the racial group allegedly discriminated against has not had legislative seats in proportion to its voting potential. The plaintiffs' burden is to produce evidence to support findings that the political processes leading to nomination and election were not equally open to participation by the group in question -- that its members had less opportunity than did other residents in the district to participate in the political processes and to elect legislators of their choice.

Id. at 765-766. We held that the three-judge District Court had properly applied this standard in invalidating the multimember districting schemes in the Texas counties of Dallas and Bexar. The District Court had determined that the characteristics of the challenged electoral systems -- multimember districts, a majority vote requirement for nomination in a primary election, and a rule mandating that a candidate running for a position in a multimember district must run for a specified "place" on the ticket -- though "neither in themselves improper nor invidious," reduced the electoral influence of Negroes and Mexican-Americans. Id. at 766. [n6] The District Court identified a number of social and historical factors that, when combined with the Texas electoral structure, resulted in vote dilution: (1) a history of official racial discrimination in Texas, including discrimination inhibiting the registration, casting of ballots, and political participation of Negroes; (2) proof that minorities were still suffering the effects of past discrimination; (3) a history of gross underrepresentation of minority interests; (4) proof of official insensitivity to the needs of minority citizens, whose votes were not needed by those in power; (5) the recent use of racial campaign tactics; and (6) a cultural and language barrier inhibiting the participation of Mexican-Americans. Id. at 766-770. Based "on the totality of the circumstances," we affirmed the District Court's conclusion that the use of multimember districts excluded the plaintiffs "from effective participation in political life." Id. at 769. [n7]

It is apparent that a showing of discriminatory intent in the creation or maintenance of multimember districts is as unnecessary after White as it was under our earlier vote-dilution decisions. Under this line of cases, an electoral districting plan is invalid if it has the effect of affording an electoral minority "less opportunity than . . . other residents in the district to participate in the political processes and to elect legislators of their choice," id. at 766. It is also apparent that the Court in White considered equal access to the political process as meaning more than merely allowing the minority the opportunity to vote. White stands for the proposition that an electoral system may not relegate an electoral minority to political impotence by diminishing the importance of its vote. The plurality's approach requiring proof of discriminatory purpose in the present cases is, then, squarely contrary to White and its predecessors. [n8]

B

The plurality fails to apply the discriminatory effect standard of White v. Regester because that approach conflicts with what the plurality takes to be an elementary principle of law. "[O]nly if there is purposeful discrimination," announces the plurality, "can there be a violation of the Equal Protection Clause of the Fourteenth Amendment." Ante at 66. That proposition is plainly overbroad. It fails to distinguish between two distinct lines of equal protection decisions: those involving suspect classifications, and those involving fundamental rights.

We have long recognized that, under the Equal Protection Clause, classifications based on race are "constitutionally suspect," Bolling v. Sharpe, 347 U.S. 497"] 347 U.S. 497, 499 (1954), and are subject to the "most rigid scrutiny," 347 U.S. 497, 499 (1954), and are subject to the "most rigid scrutiny," Korematsu v. United States, 323 U.S. 214"] 323 U.S. 214, 216 (1944), regardless of whether they infringe on an independently protected constitutional right. Cf. University of California Regents v. Bakke, 438 U.S. 265 (1978). Under 323 U.S. 214, 216 (1944), regardless of whether they infringe on an independently protected constitutional right. Cf. University of California Regents v. Bakke, 438 U.S. 265 (1978). Under Washington v. Davis, 426 U.S. 229 (1976), a showing of discriminatory purpose is necessary to impose strict scrutiny on facially neutral classifications having a racially discriminatory impact. Perhaps because the plaintiffs in the present cases are Negro, the plurality assumes that their vote-dilution claims are premised on the suspect-classification branch of our equal protection cases, and that, under Washington v. Davis, supra, they are required to prove discriminatory intent. That assumption fails to recognize that our vote-dilution decisions are rooted in a different strand of equal protection jurisprudence.

Under the Equal Protection Clause, if a classification "impinges upon a fundamental right explicitly or implicitly protected by the Constitution, . . . strict judicial scrutiny" is required, San Antonio Independent School Dist. v. Rodriguez, 411 U.S. 1, 17 (1973), regardless of whether the infringement was intentional. [n9] As I will explain, our cases recognize a fundamental right to equal electoral participation that encompasses protection against vote dilution. Proof of discriminatory purpose is, therefore, not required to support a claim of vote dilution. [n10] The plurality's erroneous conclusion to the contrary is the result of a failure to recognize the central distinction between White v. Regester, 412 U.S. 755 (1973), and Washington v. Davis, supra: the former involved an infringement of a constitutionally protected right, while the latter dealt with a claim of racially discriminatory distribution of an interest to which no citizen has a constitutional entitlement. [n11]

Nearly a century ago, the Court recognized the elementary proposition upon which our structure of civil rights is based: "[T]he political franchise of voting is . . . a fundamental political right, because preservative of all rights." Yick Wo v. Hopkins, 118 U.S. 356"] 118 U.S. 356, 370 (1886). We reiterated that theme in our landmark decision in 118 U.S. 356, 370 (1886). We reiterated that theme in our landmark decision in Reynolds v. Sims, 377 U.S. 533, 561-562 (1964), and stated that, because

the right of suffrage is a fundamental matter in a free and democratic society[,] . . . any alleged infringement of the right of citizens to vote must be carefully and meticulously scrutinized.

Ibid. We realized that

the right of suffrage can be denied by a debasement or dilution of the weight of a citizen's vote just as effectively as by wholly prohibiting the free exercise of the franchise.

Id. at 555. Accordingly, we recognized that the Equal Protection Clause protects "[t]he right of a citizen to equal representation and to have his vote weighted equally with those of all other citizens." Id. at 576. See also Wesberry v. Sanders, 376 U.S. 1, 17 (1964); Gray v. Sanders, 372 U.S. 368, 379-380 (1963). [n12]

Reynolds v. Sims and its progeny [n13] focused solely on the discriminatory effects of malapportionment. They recognize that, when population figures for the representational districts of a legislature are not similar, the votes of citizens in larger districts do not carry as much weight in the legislature as do votes cast by citizens in smaller districts. The equal protection problem attacked by the "one person, one vote" principle is, then, one of vote dilution: under Reynolds, each citizen must have an "equally effective voice" in the election of representatives. Reynolds v. Sims, supra at 565. In the present cases, the alleged vote dilution, though caused by the combined effects of the electoral structure and social and historical factors, rather than by unequal population distribution, is analytically the same concept: the unjustified abridgment of a fundamental right. [n14] It follows, then, that a showing of discriminatory intent is just as unnecessary under the vote-dilution approach adopted in Fortson v. Dorsey, 379 U.S. 433 (1965), and applied in White v. Regester, supra, as it is under our reapportionment cases. [n15]

Indeed, our vote-dilution cases have explicitly acknowledged that they are premised on the infringement of a fundamental right, not on the Equal Protection Clause's prohibition of racial discrimination. Our first vote-dilution decision, Fortson v. Dorsey, supra, involved a 1962 Georgia reapportionment statute that allocated the 54 seats of the Georgia Senate among the State's 159 counties. Thirty-three of the senatorial districts were made up of from one to eight counties each, and were single-member districts. The remaining 21 districts were allotted among the 7 most populous counties, with each county containing at least 2 districts and electing all of its senators by county-wide vote. The plaintiffs, who were registered voters residing in two of the multidistrict counties, [n16] argued that the apportionment plan, on its face, violated the Equal Protection Clause because county-wide voting in the seven multidistrict counties denied their residents a vote equal to that of voters residing in single-member constituencies. [n17] We were unconvinced that the plan operated to dilute any Georgian's vote, and therefore upheld the facial validity of the scheme. We cautioned, however, that the Equal Protection Clause would not tolerate a multimember districting plan that, "designedly or otherwise, . . operate[d] to minimize or cancel out the voting strength of racial or political elements of the voting population." 379 U.S. at 439 (emphasis added).

The approach to vote dilution adopted in Fortson plainly consisted of a fundamental rights analysis. If the Court had believed that the equal protection problem with alleged vote dilution was one of racial discrimination, and not abridgment of the right to vote, it would not have accorded standing to the plaintiffs, who were simply registered voters of Georgia alleging that the state apportionment plan, as a theoretical matter, diluted their voting strength because of where they lived. To the contrary, we did not question their standing, and held against them solely because we found unpersuasive their claim on the merits. The Court did not reach this result by inadvertence; rather, we explicitly recognized that we had adopted a fundamental rights approach when we stated that the Equal Protection Clause protected the voting strength of political, as well as racial, groups.

Until today, this Court had never deviated from this principle. We reiterated that our vote-dilution doctrine protects political groups in addition to racial groups in Burns v. Richardson, 384 U.S. at 88, where we allowed a general class of qualified voters to assert such a vote-dilution claim. In Whitcomb v. Chavis, 403 U.S. 124 (1971), we again explicitly recognized that political groups could raise such claims, id. at 143, 144. In White v. Regester, 412 U.S. 755 (1973), the plaintiffs were Negroes and Mexican-Americans, and accordingly the Court had no reason to discuss whether nonminority plaintiffs could assert claims of vote dilution. [n18] In a companion case to White, however, we again recognized that "political elements" were protected against vote dilution. Gaffney v. Cummings, 412 U.S. 735, 751 (1973). Two years later, in Dallas County v. Reese, 421 U.S. 477 (1975) (per curiam), we accorded standing to urban dwellers alleging vote dilution as to the election of the county commission and stated that multimember districting is unconstitutional if it "in fact operates impermissibly to dilute the voting strength of an identifiable element of the voting population." Id. at 480 (emphasis added). And in United Jewish Organizations v. Carey, 430 U.S. 144 (1977), the plurality opinion of MR JUSTICE WHITE stated that districting plans were subject to attack if they diluted the vote of "racial or political groups." Id. at 167 (emphasis in original). [n19]

Our vote-dilution decisions, then, involve the fundamental interest branch, rather than the antidiscrimination branch, of our jurisprudence under the Equal Protection Clause. They recognize a substantive constitutional right to participate on an equal basis in the electoral process that cannot be denied or diminished for any reason, racial or otherwise, lacking quite substantial justification. They are premised on a rationale wholly apart from that underlying Washington v. Davis, 426 U.S. 229 (1976). That decision involved application of a different equal protection principle, the prohibition on racial discrimination in the governmental distribution of interests to which citizens have no constitutional entitlement. [n20] Whatever may be the merits of applying motivational analysis to the allocation of constitutionally gratuitous benefits, that approach is completely misplaced where, as here, it is applied to the distribution of a constitutionally protected interest. [n21]

Washington v. Davis, then, in no way alters the discriminatory impact test developed in Fortson v. Dorsey, 379 U.S. 433 (1965), and applied in White v. Regester, supra, to evaluate claims of dilution of the fundamental right to vote. In my view, that test is now, and always has been, the proper method of safeguarding against inequitable distribution of political influence.

The plurality's response is that my approach amounts to nothing less than a constitutional requirement of proportional representation for groups. See ante at 75-80. That assertion amounts to nothing more than a red herring: I explicitly reject the notion that the Constitution contains any such requirement. See n. 7, supra. The constitutional protection against vote dilution found in our prior cases does not extend to those situations in which a group has merely failed to elect representatives in proportion to its share of the population. To prove unconstitutional vote dilution, the group is also required to carry the far more onerous burden of demonstrating that it has been effectively fenced out of the political process. See ibid. Typical of the plurality's mischaracterization of my position is its assertion that I would provide protection against vote dilution for "every 'political group,' or at least every such group that is in the minority." Ante at 75. The vote-dilution doctrine can logically apply only to groups whose electoral discreteness and insularity allow dominant political factions to ignore them. See nn. 7 and 19, supra. In short, the distinction between a requirement of proportional representation and the discriminatory effect test I espouse is by no means a difficult one, and it is hard for me to understand why the plurality insists on ignoring it.

The plaintiffs in No. 77-1844 proved that no Negro had ever been elected to the Mobile City Commission, despite the fact that Negroes constitute about one-third of the electorate, and that the persistence of severe racial bloc voting made it highly unlikely that any Negro could be elected at large in the foreseeable future. 423 F.Supp. 384, 387-389 (SD Ala 1976). Contrary to the plurality's contention, see ante at 75-76, however, I do not find unconstitutional vote dilution in this case simply because of that showing. The plaintiffs convinced the District Court that Mobile Negroes were unable to use alternative avenues of political influence. They showed that Mobile Negroes still suffered pervasive present effects of massive historical official and private discrimination, and that the City Commission had been quite unresponsive to the needs of the minority community. The City of Mobile has been guilty of such pervasive racial discrimination in hiring employees that extensive intervention by the Federal District Court has been required. 423 F.Supp. at 389, 400. Negroes are grossly underrepresented on city boards and committees. Id. at 389-390. The city's distribution of public services is racially discriminatory. Id. at 390-391. City officials and police were largely unmoved by Negro complaints about police brutality and a "mock lynching." Id. at 392. The District Court concluded that

[t]his sluggish and timid response is another manifestation of the low priority given to the needs of the black citizens and of the [commissioners'] political fear of a white backlash vote when black citizens' needs are at stake.

Ibid. See also the dissenting opinion of my Brother WHITE, ante p. 94.

A requirement of proportional representation would indeed transform this Court into a "super-legislature," ante at 76, and would create the risk that some groups would receive an undeserved windfall of political influence. In contrast, the protection against vote dilution recognized by our prior cases serves as a minimally intrusive guarantee of political survival for a discrete political minority that is effectively locked out of governmental decisionmaking processes. [n22] So understood, the doctrine hardly "'create[s] substantive constitutional rights in the name of guaranteeing equal protection of the laws,'" ibid., quoting San Antonio Independent School Dist. v. Rodriguez, 411 U.S. at 33. Rather, the doctrine is a simple reflection of the basic principle that the Equal Protection Clause protects "[t]he right of a citizen to equal representation and to have his vote weighted equally with those of all other citizens." Reynolds v. Sims, 377 U.S. at 576. [n23]

II

Section 1 of the Fifteenth Amendment provides:

The right of citizens of the United States to vote shall not be denied or abridged by the United States or by any State on account of race, color, or previous condition of servitude.

Today the plurality gives short shrift to the argument that proof of discriminatory intent is not a necessary condition to relief under this Amendment. See ante at 61-65. [n24] I have examined this issue in another context and reached the contrary result. Beer v. United States, 425 U.S. 130, 146-149, and nn. 3-5 (1976) (dissenting opinion). I continue to believe that "a showing of purpose or of effect is alone sufficient to demonstrate unconstitutionality," id. at 149, n. 5, and wish to explicate further why I find this standard appropriate for Fifteenth Amendment claims. First, however, it is necessary to address the plurality's apparent suggestion that the Fifteenth Amendment protects against only denial, and not dilution, of the vote. [n25]

A

The Fifteenth Amendment does not confer an absolute right to vote. See ante at 62. By providing that the right to vote cannot be discriminatorily "denied or abridged," however, the Amendment assuredly strikes down the diminution, as well as the outright denial, of the exercise of the franchise. An interpretation holding that the Amendment reaches only complete abrogation of the vote would render the Amendment essentially useless, since it is no difficult task to imagine schemes in which the Negro's marking of the ballot is a meaningless exercise.

The Court has long understood that the right to vote encompasses protection against vote dilution. "[T]he right to have one's vote counted" is of the same importance as "the right to put a ballot in a box." United States v. Mosley, 238 U.S. 383, 386 (1915). See United States v. Classic, 313 U.S. 299 (1941); Swafford v. Templeton, 185 U.S. 487 (1902); Wiley v. Sinkler, 179 U.S. 58 (1900); Ex parte Yarbrough, 110 U.S. 651 (1884). The right to vote is protected against the diluting effect of ballot-box stuffing. United States v. Saylor, 322 U.S. 385 (1944); Ex parte Siebold, 100 U.S. 371 (1880). Indeed, this Court has explicitly recognized that the Fifteenth Amendment protects against vote dilution. In Terry v. Adams, 345 U.S. 461 (1953), and Smith v. Allwright, 321 U.S. 649 (1944), the Negro plaintiffs did not question their access to the ballot for general elections. Instead, they argued, and the Court recognized, that the value of their votes had been diluted by their exclusion from participation in primary elections and in the slating of candidates by political parties. The Court's struggles with the concept of "state action" in those decisions were necessarily premised on the understanding that vote dilution was a claim cognizable under the Fifteenth Amendment.

Wright v. Rockefeller, 376 U.S. 52 (1964), recognized that an allegation of vote dilution resulting from the drawing of district lines stated a claim under the Fifteenth Amendment. The plaintiffs in that case argued that congressional districting in New York violated the Fifteenth Amendment because district lines had been drawn in a racially discriminatory fashion. Each plaintiff had access to the ballot; their complaint was that, because of intentional discrimination they resided in a district with population characteristics that had the effect of diluting the weight of their votes. The Court treated this claim as cognizable under the Fifteenth Amendment. More recently, in United Jewish Organizations v. Carey, 430 U.S. 144 (1977), we again treated an allegation of vote dilution arising from a redistricting scheme as stating a claim under the Fifteenth Amendment. See id. at 155, 161-162, 165-168 (opinion of WHITE, J.). Indeed, in that case, MR. JUSTICE STEWART found no Fifteenth Amendment violation, in part, because the plaintiffs had failed to prove

that the redistricting scheme was employed . . . to minimize or cancel out the voting strength of a minority class or interest; or otherwise to impair or burden the opportunity of affected persons to participate in the political process.

Id. at 179 (STEWART, J., joined by POWELL, J., concurring in judgment) (citing, e.g., White v. Regester, 412 U.S. 755 (1973); Fortson v. Dorsey, 379 U.S. 433 (1965); Wright v. Rockefeller, supra). See also Gomillion v. Lightfoot, 364 U.S. 339 (1960). It is plain, then, that the Fifteenth Amendment shares the concept of vote dilution developed in such Fourteenth Amendment decisions as Reynolds v. Sims, 377 U.S. 533 (1964), and Fortson v. Dorsey, supra. In fact, under the Court's unified view of the protections of the right to vote accorded by disparate portions of the Constitution, the concept of vote dilution is a core principle of the Seventeenth and Nineteenth Amendments, as well as the Fourteenth and Fifteenth:

The Fifteenth Amendment prohibits a State from denying or abridging a Negro's right to vote. The Nineteenth Amendment does the same for women. If a State in a state-wide election weighted the male vote more heavily than the female vote, or the white vote more heavily than the Negro vote, none could successfully contend that that discrimination was allowable. See Terry v. Adams, 345 U.S. 461. . . . Once the geographical unit for which a representative is to be chosen is designated, all who participate in the election are to have an equal vote -- whatever their race, whatever their sex, whatever their occupation, whatever their income, and wherever their home may be in that geographical unit. This is required by the Equal Protection Clause of the Fourteenth Amendment.

* * * *

The conception of political equality from the Declaration of Independence, to Lincoln's Gettysburg Address, to the Fifteenth, Seventeenth, and Nineteenth Amendments can mean only one thing -- one person, one vote.

Gray v. Sanders, 372 U.S. at 379, 381.

The plurality's suggestion that the Fifteenth Amendment reaches only outright denial of the ballot is wholly inconsistent not only with our prior decisions, but also with the gloss the plurality would place upon the Fourteenth Amendment's protection against vote dilution. As I explained in Part I, supra, I strongly disagree with the plurality's conclusion that our Fourteenth Amendment vote-dilution decisions have been based upon the Equal Protection Clause's prohibition of racial discrimination. Be that as it may, the plurality, at least, does not dispute that the Fourteenth Amendment's language -- that "[n]o State shall . . . deny to any person within its jurisdiction the equal protection of the laws" -- protects against dilution, as well as outright denial, of the right to vote on racial grounds, even though the Amendment does not mention any right to vote, and speaks only of the denial, and not the diminution, of rights. Yet when the plurality construes the language of the Fifteenth Amendment -- which explicitly acknowledges the right to vote and prohibits its denial or abridgment on account of race -- it seemingly would accord protection against only the absolute abrogation of the ballot.

An interpretation of the Fifteenth Amendment limiting its prohibitions to the outright denial of the ballot would convert the words of the Amendment into language illusory in symbol, and hollow in substance. Surely today's decision should not be read as endorsing that interpretation. [n26]

B

The plurality concludes that our prior decisions establish the principle that proof of discriminatory intent is a necessary element of a Fifteenth Amendment claim. [n27] In contrast, I continue to adhere to my conclusion in Beer v. United States, 425 U.S. at 148, n. 4 (dissenting opinion), that

[t]he Court's decisions relating to the relevance of purpose and/or effect analysis in testing the constitutionality of legislative enactments are somewhat less than a seamless web.

As I there explained, at various times, the Court's decisions have seemed to adopt three inconsistent approaches: (1) that purpose alone is the test for unconstitutionality; (2) that effect alone is the test; and (3) that purpose or effect, either alone or in combination, is sufficient to show unconstitutionality. Ibid. In my view, our Fifteenth Amendment jurisprudence on the necessity of proof of discriminatory purpose is no less unsettled than was our approach to the importance of such proof in Fourteenth Amendment racial discrimination cases prior to Washington v. Davis, 426 U.S. 229 (1976). What is called for in the present cases is a fresh consideration -- similar to our inquiry in Washington v. Davis, supra, with regard to Fourteenth Amendment discrimination claims -- of whether proof of discriminatory purpose is necessary to establish a claim under the Fifteenth Amendment. I will first justify my conclusion that our Fifteenth Amendment precedents do not control the outcome of this issue, and then turn to an examination of how the question should be resolved.

1

The plurality cites Guinn v. United States, 238 U.S. 347 (1915); Gomillion v. Lightfoot, 364 U.S. 339 (1960); Wright v. Rockefeller, 376 U.S. 52 (1964); Lassiter v. Northampton Election Bd., 360 U.S. 45 (1959); and Lane v. Wilson, 307 U.S. 268 (1939), as holding that proof of discriminatory purpose is necessary to support a Fifteenth Amendment claim. To me, these decisions indicate confusion, not resolution of this issue. As the plurality suggests, ante at 62, the Court in Guinn v. United States, supra, did examine the purpose of a "grandfather clause" in the course of invalidating it. Yet, 24 years later, in Lane v. Wilson, supra at 277, the Court struck down a more sophisticated exclusionary scheme because it "operated unfairly" against Negroes. In accord with the prevailing doctrine of the time, see Arizona v. California, 283 U.S. 423, 455, and n. 7 (1931), the Court in Lane seemingly did not question the motives of public officials.

In upholding the use of a literacy test for voters in Lassiter v. Northampton Election Bd., supra, the Court apparently concluded that the plaintiff had failed to prove either discriminatory purpose or effect. Gomillion v. Lightfoot, supra, can be read as turning on proof of discriminatory motive, but the Court also stressed that the challenged redrawing of municipal boundaries had the "essential inevitable effect" of removing Negro voters from the city, 364 U.S. at 341, and that

the inescapable human effect of this essay in geometry and geography is to despoil colored citizens, and only colored citizens, of their theretofore enjoyed voting rights,

id. at 347. Finally, in Wright v. Rockefeller, supra, the plaintiffs alleged only purposeful discriminatory redistricting, and therefore the Court had no reason to consider whether proof of discriminatory effect would satisfy the Fifteenth Amendment. [n28]

The plurality ignores cases suggesting that discriminatory purpose is not necessary to support a Fifteenth Amendment claim. In Terry v. Adams, 345 U.S. 461 (1953), a case in which no majority opinion was issued, three Justices approvingly discussed two decisions of the United States Court of Appeals for the Fourth Circuit [n29] holding

that no election machinery could be sustained if its purpose or effect was to deny Negroes on account of their race an effective voice in the governmental affairs of their country, state, or community.

Id. at 466 (opinion of Black, J., joined by Douglas and Burton, JJ.) (emphasis added). More recently, in rejecting a First Amendment challenge to a federal statute providing criminal penalties for knowing destruction of a Selective Service registration certificate, the Court, in United States v. O'Brien, 391 U.S. 367, 383 (1968), stated that

[i]t is a familiar principle of constitutional law that this Court will not strike down an otherwise constitutional statute on the basis of an alleged illicit legislative motive.

The Court in O'Brien, supra at 385, interpreted Gomillion v. Lightfoot, supra, as turning on the discriminatory effect, and not the alleged discriminatory purpose, of the challenged redrawing of municipal boundaries. Three years later, in Palmer v. Thompson, 403 U.S. 217, 224-225 (1971), the Court relied on O'Brien to support its refusal to inquire whether a city had closed its swimming pools to avoid racial integration. As in O'Brien, the Court in Palmer, supra at 225, interpreted Gomillion v. Lightfoot as focusing "on the actual effect" of the municipal boundary change, and not upon what motivated the city to redraw its borders. See also Wright v. Council of City of Emporia, 407 U.S. 451, 461-462 (1972).

In holding that racial discrimination claims under the Equal Protection Clause must be supported by proof of discriminatory intent, the Court in Washington v. Davis, supra, signaled some movement away from the doctrine that such proof is irrelevant to constitutional adjudication. Although the Court, 426 U.S. at 242-244, and n. 11, attempted mightily to distinguish Palmer v. Thompson, supra, its decision was, in fact, based upon a judgment that, in light of modern circumstances, the Equal Protection Clause's ban on racial discrimination in the distribution of constitutional gratuities should be interpreted as prohibiting only intentional official discrimination. [n30]

These vacillations in our approach to the relevance of discriminatory purpose belie the plurality's determination that our prior decisions require such proof to support Fifteenth Amendment claims. To the contrary, the Court today is in the same unsettled position with regard to the Fifteenth Amendment as it was four years ago in Washington v. Davis, supra, regarding the Fourteenth Amendment's prohibition of racial discrimination. The absence of old answers mandates a new inquiry.

2

The Court in Washington v. Davis required a showing of discriminatory purpose to support racial discrimination claims largely because it feared that a standard based solely on disproportionate impact would unduly interfere with the far-ranging governmental distribution of constitutional gratuities. [n31] Underlying the Court's decision was a determination that, since the Constitution does not entitle any person to such governmental benefits, courts should accord discretion to those officials who decide how the government shall allocate its scarce resources. If the plaintiff proved only that governmental distribution of constitutional gratuities had a disproportionate effect on a racial minority, the Court was willing to presume that the officials who approved the allocation scheme either had made an honest error or had foreseen that the decision would have a discriminatory impact, and had found persuasive, legitimate reasons for imposing it nonetheless. These assumptions about the good faith of officials allowed the Court to conclude that, standing alone, a showing that a governmental policy had a racially discriminatory impact did not indicate that the affected minority had suffered the stigma, frustration, and unjust treatment prohibited under the suspect classification branch of our equal protection jurisprudence.

Such judicial deference to official decisionmaking has no place under the Fifteenth Amendment. Section 1 of that Amendment differs from the Fourteenth Amendment's prohibition on racial discrimination in two crucial respects: it explicitly recognizes the right to vote free of hindrances related to race, and it sweeps no further. In my view, these distinctions justify the conclusion that proof of racially discriminatory impact should be sufficient to support a claim under the Fifteenth Amendment. The right to vote is of such fundamental importance in the constitutional scheme that the Fifteenth Amendment's command that it shall not be "abridged" on account of race must be interpreted as providing that the votes of citizens of all races shall be of substantially equal weight. Furthermore, a disproportionate impact test under the Fifteenth Amendment would not lead to constant judicial intrusion into the process of official decisionmaking. Rather, the standard would reach only those decisions having a discriminatory effect upon the minority's vote. The Fifteenth Amendment cannot tolerate that kind of decision, even if made in good faith, because the Amendment grants racial minorities the full enjoyment of the right to vote, not simply protection against the unfairness of intentional vote dilution along racial lines. [n32]

In addition, it is beyond dispute that a standard based solely upon the motives of official decisionmakers creates significant problems of proof for plaintiffs and forces the inquiring court to undertake an unguided, tortuous look into the minds of officials in the hope of guessing why certain policies were adopted and others rejected. See Palmer v. Thompson, 403 U.S. at 224-225; United States v. O'Brien, 391 U.S. at 382-386; cf. Keyes v. School District No. 1, Denver, Colo., 413 U.S. 189, 224, 227 (1973) (POWELL, J., concurring in part and dissenting in part). An approach based on motivation creates the risk that officials will be able to adopt policies that are the products of discriminatory intent so long as they sufficiently mask their motives through the use of subtlety and illusion. Washington v. Davis is premised on the notion that this risk is insufficient to overcome the deference the judiciary must accord to governmental decisions about the distribution of constitutional gratuities. That risk becomes intolerable, however, when the precious right to vote protected by the Fifteenth Amendment is concerned.

I continue to believe, then, that under the Fifteenth Amendment, an

[e]valuation of the purpose of a legislative enactment is just too ambiguous a task to be the sole tool of constitutional analysis. . . . [A] demonstration of effect ordinarily should suffice. If, of course, purpose may conclusively be shown, it too should be sufficient to demonstrate a statute's unconstitutionality.

Beer v. United States, 425 U.S. at 149-150, n. 5 (MARSHALL, J., dissenting). The plurality's refusal in this case even to consider this approach bespeaks an indifference to the plight of minorities who, through no fault of their own, have suffered diminution of the right preservative of all other rights. [n33]

III

If it is assumed that proof of discriminatory intent is necessary to support the vote-dilution claims in these cases, the question becomes what evidence will satisfy this requirement. [n34]

The plurality assumes, without any analysis, that these cases are appropriate for the application of the rigid test developed in Personnel Administrator of Mass. v. Feeney, 442 U.S. at 279, requiring that

the decisionmaker . . . selected or reaffirmed particular course of action at least in part "because of," not merely "in spite of," its adverse effects upon an identifiable group.

In my view, the Feeney standard creates a burden of proof far too extreme to apply in vote-dilution cases. [n35]

This Court has acknowledged that the evidentiary inquiry involving discriminatory intent must necessarily vary depending upon the factual context. See Arlington Heights v. Metropolitan Housing Dev. Corp., 429 U.S. at 264-268; Washington v. Davis, 426 U.S. at 253 (STEVENS, J., concurring). One useful evidentiary tool, long recognized by the common law, is the presumption that "[e]very man must be taken to contemplate the probable consequences of the act he does." Townsend v. Wathen, 9 East. 277, 280, 103 Eng.Rep. 579, 580-581 (K.B. 1808). The Court in Feeney, supra, at 279, n. 25, acknowledged that proof of foreseeability of discriminatory consequences could raise a "strong inference that the adverse effects were desired," but refused to treat this presumption as conclusive in cases alleging discriminatory distribution of constitutional gratuities.

I would apply the common law foreseeability presumption to the present cases. The plaintiffs surely proved that maintenance of the challenged multimember districting would have the foreseeable effect of perpetuating the submerged electoral influence of Negroes, and that this discriminatory effect could be corrected by implementation of a single-member districting plan. [n36] Because the foreseeable disproportionate impact was so severe, the burden of proof should have shifted to the defendants, and they should have been required to show that they refused to modify the districting schemes in spite of, not because of, their severe discriminatory effect. See Feeney, supra at 284 (MARSHALL, J., dissenting). Reallocation of the burden of proof is especially appropriate in these cases, where the challenged state action infringes the exercise of a fundamental right. The defendants would carry their burden of proof only if they showed that they considered submergence of the Negro vote a detriment, not a benefit, of the multimember systems, that they accorded minority citizens the same respect given to whites, and that they nevertheless decided to maintain the systems for legitimate reasons. Cf. Mt. Healthy City Board of Ed. v. Doyle, 429 U.S. 274, 287 (1977); Arlington Heights v. Metropolitan Housing Dev. Corp., supra at 270-271, n. 21.

This approach recognizes that

[f]requently the most probative evidence of intent will be objective evidence of what actually happened, rather than evidence describing the subjective state of mind of the actor. For normally the actor is presumed to have intended the natural consequences of his deeds. This is particularly true in the case of governmental action which is frequently the product of compromise, of collective decisionmaking, and of mixed motivation.

Washington v. Davis, supra at 253 (STEVENS, J., concurring). Furthermore, if proof of discriminatory purpose is to be required in these cases, this standard would comport with my view that the degree to which the government must justify a decision depends upon the importance of the interests infringed by it. See San Antonio Independent School Dist. v. Rodriguez, 411 U.S. at 109-110 (MARSHALL, J., dissenting). [n37]

The plurality also fails to recognize that the maintenance of multimember districts in the face of foreseeable discriminatory consequences strongly suggests that officials are blinded by "racially selective sympathy and indifference." [n38] Like outright racial hostility, selective racial indifference reflects a belief that the concerns of the minority are not worthy of the same degree of attention paid to problems perceived by whites. When an interest as fundamental as voting is diminished along racial lines, a requirement that discriminatory purpose must be proved should be satisfied by a showing that official action was produced by this type of pervasive bias. In the present cases, the plaintiffs presented strong evidence of such bias: they showed that Mobile officials historically discriminated against Negroes, that there are pervasive present effects of this past discrimination, and that officials have not been responsive to the needs of the minority community. It takes only the smallest of inferential leaps to conclude that the decisions to maintain multimember districting having obvious discriminatory effects represent, at the very least, selective racial sympathy and indifference resulting in the frustration of minority desires, the stigmatization of the minority as second-class citizens, and the perpetuation of inhumanity. [n39]

IV

The American approach to government is premised on the theory that, when citizens have the unfettered right to vote, public officials will make decisions by the democratic accommodation of competing beliefs, not by deference to the mandates of the powerful. The American approach to civil rights is premised on the complementary theory that the unfettered right to vote is preservative of all other rights. The theoretical foundations for these approaches are shattered where, as in the present cases, the right to vote is granted in form, but denied in substance.

It is time to realize that manipulating doctrines and drawing improper distinctions under the Fourteenth and Fifteenth Amendments, as well as under Congress' remedial legislation enforcing those Amendments, make this Court an accessory to the perpetuation of racial discrimination. The plurality's requirement of proof of intentional discrimination, so inappropriate in today's cases, may represent an attempt to bury the legitimate concerns of the minority beneath the soil of a doctrine almost as impermeable as it is serious. If so, the superficial tranquility created by such measures can be but short-lived. If this Court refuses to honor our long-recognized principle that the Constitution "nullifies sophisticated, as well as simple-minded, modes of discrimination," Lane v. Wilson, 307 U.S. at 275, it cannot expect the victims of discrimination to respect political channels of seeking redress. I dissent.

*

This opinion applies also to No. 78-357, Williams et al. v. Brown et al., post, p. 236.

Notes

1. U.S.Const., Amdts. 15, 17, 19, 23, 24, 26.

2. I agree with the plurality, see ante at 60-61, that the prohibition on denial or infringement of the right to vote contained in § 2 of the Voting Rights Act, 42 U.S.C. § 1973 contains the same standard as the Fifteenth Amendment. I disagree with the plurality's construction of that Amendment, however. See Part II, infra.

3. The Court does not quarrel with the generalization that, in many instances, an electoral minority will fare worse under multimember districting than under single-

member districting. Multimember districting greatly enhances the opportunity of the majority political faction to elect all representatives of the district. In contrast, if the multimember district is divided into several single-member districts, an electoral minority will have a better chance to elect a candidate of its choice, or at least to exert greater political influence. It is obvious that the greater the degree to which the electoral minority is homogeneous and insular, and the greater the degree that bloc voting occurs along majority-minority lines, the greater will be the extent to which the minority's voting power is diluted by multimember districting. See E. Banfield & J. Wilson, City Politics 91-96, 303-308 (1963); R. Dixon, Jr., Democratic Representation 12, 476-484, 503-527 (1968); Bonapfel, Minority Challenges to At-Large Elections : The Dilution Problem, 10 Ga.L.Rev. 353, 35860 (1976); Derfner, Racial Discrimination and the Right to Vote, 26 Vand.L.Rev. 523, 553-555 (1973); Comment, Effective Representation and Multimember Districts, 68 Mich.L.Rev. 1577, 1577-1579 (170). Recent empirical studies have documented the validity of this generalization. See Berry & Dye, The Discriminatory Effects of At-Large Elections, 7 Fla.St.U.L.Rev. 85, 113-122 (1979); Jones, The Impact of Local Election Systems on Black Political Representation, 11 Urb.Aff.Q. 345 (1976); Karnig, Black Resources and City Council Representation, 41 J.Pol. 134 (1979); Karnig, Black Representation on City Councils: The Impact of District Elections and Socioeconomic Factors, 12 Urb.Aff.Q. 223 (1976); Sloan, "Good Government" and the Politics of Race, 17 Soc.Prob. 161 (1969); The Impact of Municipal Reformism: A Symposium, 59 Soc.Sci.Q. 117 (1978).

The electoral schemes in these cases involve majority-vote, numbered-post, and staggered-term requirements. See Bolden v. City of Mobile, 423 F.Supp. 384, 386-387 (SD Ala.1976); Brown v. Moore, 428 F.Supp. 1123, 1126-1127 (SD Ala.1976). These electoral rules exacerbate the vote-dilutive effects of multimember districting. A requirement that a candidate must win by a majority of the vote forces a minority candidate who wins a plurality of votes in the general election to engage in a runoff election with his nearest competitor. If the competitor is a member of the dominant political faction, the minority candidate stands little chance of winning in the second election. A requirement that each candidate must run for a particular "place" or "post" creates head-to-head contests that minority candidates cannot survive. When a number of positions on a governmental body are to be chosen in the same election, members of a minority will increase the likelihood of election of a favorite candidate by voting only for him. If the remainder of the electorate splits its votes among the other candidates, the minority's candidate might well be elected by the minority's "single-shot voting." If the terms of the officeholders are staggered, the opportunity for single-shot voting is decreased. See City of Rome v. United States, post, p. 156; Zimmer v. McKeithen, 485 F.2d 1297, 1305 (CA5 1973) (en banc), aff'd on other grounds sub nom. East Carroll Parish School Bd. v. Marshall 424 U.S. 636 (1976) (per curiam); Bonapfel, supra; Derfner, supra.

4. The plurality notes that at-large elections were instituted in cities as a reform

measure to correct corruption and inefficiency in municipal government, and suggests that it "may be a rash assumption" to apply vote-dilution concepts to a municipal government elected in that fashion. See ante at 70, and n. 15. To the contrary, local governments are not exempt from the constitutional requirement to adopt representational districting ensuring that the votes of each citizen will have equal weight. Avery v. Midland County, 390 U.S. 474 (1968). Indeed, in Beer v. United States, 425 U.S. 130, 142, n. 14 (1976), and Abate v. Mundt, 403 U.S. 182, 184, n. 2 (1971), we assumed that our vote-dilution doctrine applied to local governments.

Furthermore, though municipalities must be accorded some discretion in arranging their affairs, see Abate v. Mundt, supra, there is all the more reason to scrutinize assertions that municipal, rather than state, multimember districting dilutes the vote of an electoral minority:

In statewide elections, it is possible that a large minority group in one multi-member district will be unable to elect any legislators, while in another multi-member district where the same group is a slight majority, they will elect the entire slate of legislators. Thus, the multi-member electoral system may hinder a group in one district, but prove an advantage in another. In at-large elections in cities, this is not possible. There is no way to balance out the discrimination against a particular minority group, because the entire city is one huge election district. The minority's loss is absolute.

Berry & Dye, supra, n. 3, at 87. That at-large elections were instituted as part of a "reform" movement in no way ameliorates these harsh effects. Moreover, in some instances, the efficiency and breadth of perspective supposedly resulting from a reform structure of municipal government are achieved at a high cost. In a white-majority city in which severe racial bloc voting is common, the city-wide view allegedly inculcated in city commissioners by at-large elections need not extend beyond the white community, and the efficiency of the commission form of government can be achieved simply by ignoring the concerns of the powerless minority.

It would be a mistake, then, to conclude that municipal at-large elections provide an inherently superior representational scheme. See also n. 3, supra; Chapman v. Meier, 372 F.Supp. 371, 388-392 (ND 1974) (three-judge court) (Bright, J., dissenting), rev'd, 420 U.S. 1 (1975). It goes without saying that a municipality has the freedom to design its own governance system. When that system is subjected to constitutional attack, however, the question is whether it was enacted or maintained with a discriminatory purpose or has a discriminatory effect, not whether it comports with one or another of the competing notions about "good government."

5. As the plurality notes, see ante at 66, we indicated in Whitcomb v. Chavis, 403 U.S. at 149, that multimember districts were unconstitutional if they were "conceived or operated as purposeful devices to further racial or economic discrimination." The Court in Whitcomb did not, however, suggest that discriminatory purpose was a necessary condition for the invalidation of multimember districting. Our decision in Whitcomb, supra at 143, acknowledged the continuing validity of the discriminatory impact test

adopted in Fortson v. Dorsey, 379 U.S. 433, 439 (1965), and restated it as requiring plaintiffs to prove that "multi-member districts unconstitutionally operate to dilute or cancel the voting strength of racial or political elements." Whitcomb, supra at 144 (emphasis added).

Abate v. Mundt, supra, decided the same day as Whitcomb, provides further evidence that Whitcomb did not alter the discriminatory effects standard developed in earlier cases. In Abate, supra at 184, n. 2, we rejected the argument that a multimember districting scheme had a vote-dilutive effect because

[pletitioners] . . . have not shown that these multimember districts, by themselves, operate to impair the voting strength of particular racial or political elements . . ., see Burns v. Richardson, 384 U.S. 73, 88 (1966).

6. See n. 3, supra.

7. White v. Regester makes clear the distinction between the concepts of vote dilution and proportional representation. We have held that, in order to prove an allegation of vote dilution, the plaintiffs must show more than simply that they have been unable to elect candidates of their choice. See 412 U.S. at 765-766; Whitcomb v. Chavis, supra at 149-150, 153. The Constitution, therefore, does not contain any requirement of proportional representation. Cf. United Jewish Organizations v. Carey, 430 U.S. 144 (1977); Gaffney v. Cummings, 412 U.S. 735 (1973). When all that is proved is mere lack of success at the polls, the Court will not presume that members of a political minority have suffered an impermissible dilution of political power. Rather, it is assumed that these persons have means available to them through which they can have some effect on governmental decisionmaking. For example, many of these persons might belong to a variety of other political, social, and economic groups that have some impact on officials. In the absence of evidence to the contrary, it may be assumed that officials will not be improperly influenced by such factors as the race or place of residence of persons seeking governmental action. Furthermore, political factions out of office often serve as watchdogs on the performance of the government, bind together into coalitions having enhanced influence, and have the respectability necessary to affect public policy.

Unconstitutional vote dilution occurs only when a discrete political minority whose voting strength is diminished by a districting scheme proves that historical and social factors render it largely incapable of effectively utilizing alternative avenues of influencing public policy. See n.19, infra. In these circumstances, the only means of breaking down the barriers encasing the political arena is to structure the electoral districting so that the minority has a fair opportunity to elect candidates of its choice.

The test for unconstitutional vote dilution, then, looks only to the discriminatory effects of the combination of an electoral structure and historical and social factors. At the same time, it requires electoral minorities to prove far more than mere lack of success at the polls.

We have also spoken of dilution of voting power in cases arising under the Voting Rights Act of 1965, 42 U.S.C. § 1973 et seq. Under § 5 of that Act, 42 U.S.C. § 1973c a state or local government covered by the Act may not enact new electoral procedures having the purpose or effect of denying or abridging the right to vote on account of race or color. We have interpreted this provision as prohibiting any retrogression in Negro voting power. Beer v. United States, 425 U.S. 130, 141 (1976). In some cases, we have labeled such retrogression a "dilution" of the minority vote. See, e.g., City of Rome v. United States, post, p. 156. Vote dilution under § 5, then, involves a standard different from that applied in cases such as White v. Regester, supra, in which diminution of the vote violating the Fourteenth or Fifteenth Amendment is alleged.

8. The plurality's approach is also inconsistent with our statement in Dallas County v. Reese, 421 U.S. 477, 480 (1975) (per curiam), that multimember districting violates the Equal Protection Clause if it "in fact operates impermissibly to dilute the voting strength of an identifiable element of the voting population." See also Chapman v. Meier, 420 U.S. at 17.

9. See Shapiro v. Thompson, 394 U.S. 618 (1969) (right to travel); Reynolds v. Sims, 377 U.S. 533 (1964) (right to vote); Douglas v. California, 372 U.S. 353 (1963); and Griffin v. Illinois, 351 U.S. 12 (1956) (right to fair access to criminal process). Under the rubric of the fundamental right of privacy, we have recognized that individuals have freedom from unjustified governmental interference with personal decisions involving marriage, Zablocki v. Redhail, 434 U.S. 374 (1978); Loving v. Virginia, 388 U.S. 1 (1967); procreation, Skinner v. Oklahoma ex rel. Williamson, 316 U.S. 535 (1942); contraception, Carey v. Population Services International, 431 U.S. 678 (1977); Eisenstadt v. Baird, 405 U.S. 438 (1972); Griswold v. Connecticut, 381 U.S. 479 (1965); abortion, Roe v. Wade, 410 U.S. 113 (1973); family relationships, Prince v. Massachusetts, 321 U.S. 158 (1944); and childrearing and education, Pierce v. Society of Sisters, 268 U.S. 510 (1925); Meyer v. Nebraska, 262 U.S. 390 (1923). See also Moore v. East Cleveland, 431 U.S. 494 (1977).

10. As the present cases illustrate, a requirement of proof of discriminatory intent seriously jeopardizes the free exercise of the fundamental right to vote. Although the right to vote is indistinguishable for present purposes from the other fundamental rights our cases have recognized, see n. 9, supra, surely the plurality would not require proof of discriminatory purpose in those cases. The plurality fails to articulate why the right to vote should receive such singular treatment. Furthermore, the plurality refuses to recognize the disutility of requiring proof of discriminatory purpose in fundamental rights cases. For example, it would make no sense to require such a showing when the question is whether a state statute regulating abortion violates the right of personal choice recognized in Roe v. Wade, supra. The only logical inquiry is whether, regardless of the legislature's motive, the statute has the effect of infringing that right. See, e.g., Planned Parenthood of Central Missouri v. Danforth, 428 U.S. 52 (1976).

11. Judge Wisdom of the Court of Appeals below recognized this distinction in a companion case, see Nevett v. Sides, 571 F.2d 209, 231-234 (CA5 1978) (specially concurring opinion). See also Comment, Proof of Racially Discriminatory Purpose Under the Equal Protection Clause: Washington v. Davis, Arlington Heights, Mt. Healthy, and

Williamsburgh, 12 Harv.Civ.Rights-Civ.Lib.L.Rev. 725, 758, n. 175 (1977); Note, Racial Vote Dilution in Multimember Districts: The Constitutional Standard After Washington v. Davis, 76 Mich.L.Rev. 694, 722-726 (1978); Comment, Constitutional Challenges to Gerrymanders, 45 U.Chi.L.Rev. 845, 869-877 (1978).

Washington v. Davis, 426 U.S. 229 (1976), involved alleged racial discrimination in public employment. By describing interests such as public employment as constitutional gratuities, I do not, of course, mean to suggest that their deprivation is immune from constitutional scrutiny. Indeed, our decisions have referred to the importance of employment, see Hampton v. Mow Sun Wong, 426 U.S. 88, 116 (1976); Meyer v. Nebraska, supra at 399; Truax v. Raich, 239 U.S. 33, 41 (1915), and we have explicitly recognized that, in some circumstances, public employment falls within the categories of liberty and property protected by the Fifth and Fourteenth Amendments, see, e.g., Arnett v. Kennedy, 416 U.S. 134 (1974); Perry v. Sindermann, 408 U.S. 593 (1972). The Court has not held, however, that a citizen has a constitutional right to public employment.

12. We have not, however, held that the Fourteenth Amendment contains an absolute right to vote. As we explained in Dunn v. Blumstein, 405 U.S. 330 (1972):

In decision after decision, this Court has made clear that a citizen has a constitutionally protected right to participate in elections on an equal basis with other citizens in the jurisdiction. [Citing cases.] This "equal right to vote" . . . is not absolute; the States have the power to impose voter qualifications, and to regulate access to the franchise in other ways. . . . But as a general matter,

before that right [to vote] can be restricted, the purpose of the restriction and the assertedly overriding interests served by it must meet close constitutional scrutiny.

Id. at 336 (quoting Evans v. Cornman, 398 U.S. 419, 426, 422 (1970)).

13. Avery v. Midland County, 390 U.S. 474 (1968), applied the equal representation standard of Reynolds v. Sims to local governments. See also e.g., Connor v. Finch, 431 U.S. 407 (1977); Lockport v. Citizens for Community Action, 430 U.S. 259 (1977); Hadley v. Junior College Dist., 397 U.S. 50 (1970).

14. In attempting to limit Reynolds v. Sims to its facts, see ante at 77-79, the plurality confuses the nature of the constitutional right recognized in that decision with the means by which that right can be violated. Reynolds held that, under the Equal Protection Clause, each citizen must be accorded an essentially equal voice in the election of representatives. The Court determined that unequal population distribution in a multidistrict representational scheme was one readily ascertainable means by which this right was abridged. The Court certainly did not suggest, however, that violations of the right to effective political participation mattered only if they were caused by malapportionment. The plurality's assertion to the contrary in this case apparently would require it to read Reynolds as recognizing fair apportionment as an end in itself, rather than as simply a means to protect against vote dilution.

15. Proof of discriminatory purpose has been equally unnecessary in our

decisions assessing whether various impediments to electoral participation are inconsistent with the fundamental interest in voting. In the seminal case, Harper v. Virginia Bd. of Elections, 383 U.S. 663 (1966), we invalidated a $1.50 poll tax imposed as a precondition to voting. Relying on our decision two years earlier in Reynolds v. Sims, see Harper, supra at 667-668, 670, we determined that "the right to vote is too precious, too fundamental to be so burdened or conditioned," 383 U.S. at 670. We analyzed the right to vote under the familiar standard that,

where fundamental rights and liberties are asserted under the Equal Protection Clause, classifications which might invade or restrain them must be closely scrutinized and carefully confined.

Ibid. In accord with Harper, we have applied heightened scrutiny in assessing the imposition of filing fees, e.g., Lubin v. Panish, 415 U.S. 709 (1974); limitations on who may participate in elections involving specialized governmental entities, e.g., Kramer v. Union School District, 395 U.S. 621 (1969); durational residency requirements, e.g., Dunn v. Blumstein, supra; enrollment time limitations for voting in party primary elections, e.g., Kusper v. Pontikes, 414 U.S. 51 (1973); and restrictions on candidate access to the ballot, e.g., Illinois Elections Bd v. Socialist Workers Party, 440 U.S. 173 (1979).

To be sure, we have approved some limitations on the right to vote. Compare, e.g., Salyer Land Co. v. Tulare Water District, 410 U.S. 719 (1973), with Kramer v. Union School District, supra. We have never, however, required a showing of discriminatory purpose to support a claim of infringement of this fundamental interest. To the contrary, the Court has accepted at face value the purposes articulated for a qualification of this right, and has invalidated such a limitation under the Equal Protection Clause only if its purpose either lacked sufficient substantiality when compared to the individual interests affected or could have been achieved by less restrictive means. See, e.g., Dunn v. Blumstein, supra at 335, 337, 343-360.

The approach adopted in this line of cases has been synthesized with the one-person, one-vote doctrine of Reynolds v. Sims in the following fashion:

It has been established in recent years that the Equal Protection Clause confers the substantive right to participate on an equal basis with other qualified voters whenever the State has adopted an electoral process for determining who will represent any segment of the State's population.

San Antonio Independent School Dist. v. Rodriguez, 411 U.S. 1"] 411 U.S. 1, 59, n. 2 (1973) (STEWART, J., concurring) (citing 411 U.S. 1, 59, n. 2 (1973) (STEWART, J., concurring) (citing Reynolds v. Sims, 377 U.S. 533 (1964); Kramer v. Union School District, supra; Dunn v. Blumstein, supra). It is plain that this standard requires no showing of discriminatory purpose to trigger strict scrutiny of state interference with the right to vote.

16. See Dorsey v. Fortson, 228 F.Supp. 259, 261 (ND Ga.1964) (three-judge court), rev'd, 379 U.S. 433 (1965).

17. Specifically, the plaintiffs contended that county-wide voting in the

multidistrict counties could, as a matter of mathematics, result in the nullification of the unanimous choice of the voters of one district. Fortson v. Dorsey, 379 U.S. at 436-437.

18. The same is true of our most recent case discussing vote dilution, Wise v. Lipscomb, 437 U.S. 535 (1978).

19. In contrast to a racial group, however, a political group will bear a rather substantial burden of showing that it is sufficiently discrete to suffer vote dilution. See Dallas County v. Reese, 421 U.S. 477 (1975) (per curiam) (allowing city dwellers to attack a county-wide multimember district). See generally Comment, Effective Representation and Multimember Districts, 68 Mich.L.Rev. 1577, 1594-1596 (1970).

20. The dispute in Washington v. Davis concerned alleged racial discrimination in public employment, an interest to which no one has a constitutional right, see n. 11, supra. In that decision, the Court held only that "the invidious quality of a law claimed to be racially discriminatory must ultimately be traced to a racially discriminatory purpose." 426 U.S. at 240 (emphasis added). The Court's decisions following Washington v. Davis have also involved alleged discrimination in the allocation of interests falling short of constitutional rights. Personnel Administrator of Mass. v. Feeney, 442 U.S. 256 (1979) (alleged sex discrimination in public employment); Arlington Heights v. Metropolitan Housing Dev. Corp., 429 U.S. 252 (1977) (alleged racial discrimination in zoning). As explained in Feeney, supra,

[w]hen some other independent right is not at stake . . . and when there is no "reason to infer antipathy," . . . it is presumed that "even improvident decisions will eventually be rectified by the democratic process."

442 U.S. at 272 (quoting Vance v. Bradley, 440 U.S. 93, 97 (1979)).

21. Professor Ely has recognized this distinction:

The danger I see is . . . that the Court, in its new-found enthusiasm for motivation analysis, will seek to export it to fields where it has no business. It therefore cannot be emphasized too strongly that analysis of motivation is appropriate only to claims of improper discrimination in the distribution of goods that are constitutionally gratuitous (that is, benefits to which people are not entitled as a matter of substantive constitutional right). . . . However, where what is denied is something to which the complainant has a substantive constitutional right -- either because it is granted by the terms of the Constitution or because it is essential to the effective functioning of a democratic government -- the reasons it was denied are irrelevant. It may become important in court what justifications counsel for the state can articulate in support of its denial or nonprovision, but the reasons that actually inspired the denial never can: to have a right to something is to have a claim on it irrespective of why it is denied. It would be a tragedy of the first order were the Court to expand its burgeoning awareness of the relevance of motivation into the thoroughly mistaken notion that a denial of a constitutional right does not count as such unless it was intentional.

Ely, The Centrality and Limits of Motivation Analysis, 15 San Diego L.Rev. 1155, 1160-1161 (1978) (emphasis in original) (footnotes omitted).

22. It is at this point that my view most diverges from the position expressed by my Brother STEVENS, ante. p. 83. He would strictly scrutinize state action having an adverse impact on an individual's right to vote. In contrast, he would apply a less stringent standard to state action diluting the political influence of a group. See ante at 83-85. The facts of the present cases, however, demonstrate that severe and persistent racial bloc voting, when coupled with the inability of the minority effectively to participate in the political arena by alternative means, can effectively disable the individual Negro, as well as the minority community as a whole. In these circumstances, MR. JUSTICE STEVENS' distinction between the rights of individuals and the political strength of groups becomes illusory.

23. The foregoing disposes of any contention that, merely by citing Wright v. Rockefeller, 376 U.S. 52 (1964), the Court in Washington v. Davis, 426 U.S. at 240, and Arlington Heights v. Metropolitan Housing Dev. Corp., 429 U.S. at 264, intended to bring vote-dilution cases within the discriminatory purpose requirement. Wright v. Rockefeller, supra, was a racial gerrymander case, and the plaintiffs had alleged only that they were the victims of an intentional scheme to draw districting lines discriminatorily. In focusing solely on whether the plaintiffs had proved intentional discrimination, the Court in Wright v. Rockefeller was merely limiting the scope of its inquiry to the issue raised by the plaintiffs. If Wright v. Rockefeller had been brought after this Court had decided our vote-dilution decisions, the plaintiffs perhaps would have recognized that, in addition to a claim of intentional racial gerrymandering, they could allege an equally sufficient cause of action under the Equal Protection Clause -- that the districting lines had the effect of diluting their vote.

Wright v. Rockefeller, then, treated proof of discriminatory purpose as a sufficient condition to trigger strict scrutiny of a districting scheme, but had no occasion to consider whether such proof was necessary to invoke that standard. Its citations in Washington v. Davis, supra, and Arlington Heights; supra, were useful to show the relevancy, but not the necessity, of evidence of discriminatory intent. These citations are in no way inconsistent with my view that proof of discriminatory purpose is not a necessary condition to the invalidation of multimember districts that dilute the vote of racial or political elements.

In addition, any argument that, merely by citing Wright v. Rockefeller, the Court in Washington v. Davis and Arlington Heights intended to apply the discriminatory intent requirement to vote-dilution claims is premised on two unpalatable assumptions. First, because the discussion of Wright v. Rockefeller was unnecessary to the resolution of the issues in both of those decisions, the argument assumes that the Court in both cases decided important issues in brief dicta. Second, the argument assumes that the Court twice intended covertly to overrule the discriminatory effects test applied in White v. Regester, 412 U.S. 755 (1973), without even citing White. Neither assumption is tenable.

24. It is important to recognize that only the four Members of the plurality are committed to this view. In addition to my Brother BRENNAN and myself, my Brother

STEVENS expressly states that proof of discriminatory effect can be a sufficient condition to support the invalidation of districting, see ante at 90. My Brother WHITE finds the proof of discriminatory purpose in these cases sufficient to support the decisions of the Courts of Appeals, and, accordingly, he does not reach the issue whether proof of discriminatory impact, standing alone, would suffice under the Fifteenth Amendment. My Brother BLACKMUN also expresses no view on this issue, since he too finds the proof of discriminatory intent sufficient to support the findings of violations of the Constitution.

25. The plurality states that,

[h]aving found that Negroes in Mobile "register and vote without hindrance," the District Court and Court of Appeals were in error in believing that the appellants invaded the protection of that Amendment in the present case.

Ante at 65.

26. Indeed, five Members of the Court decline the opportunity to ascribe to this view. In addition to my Brother BRENNAN and myself, my Brother STEVENS expressly states that the Fifteenth Amendment protects against diminution as well as denial of the ballot, see ante at 84, and n. 3. The dissenting opinion of my Brother WHITE and the separate opinion of my Brother BLACKMUN indicate that they share this view.

27. The plurality does not attempt to support this proposition by relying on the history surrounding the adoption of the Fifteenth Amendment. I agree that we should resolve the issue of the relevancy of proof of discriminatory purpose and effect by examining our prior decisions and by considering the appropriateness of alternative standards in light of contemporary circumstances. That was, of course, the approach used in Washington v. Davis, 426 U.S. 229 (1976), to evaluate that issue with regard to Fourteenth Amendment racial discrimination claims.

28. See n. 23, supra.

29. Rice v. Elmore, 165 F.2d 387 (1947), cert. denied, 333 U.S. 875 (1948), and Boskin v. Brown, 174 F.2d 391 (1949).

30. See nn. 20, 21, supra, and accompanying text.

31. The Court stated

A rule that a statute designed to serve neutral ends is nevertheless invalid, absent compelling justification, if in practice it benefits or burdens one race more than another would be far-reaching, and would raise serious questions about, and perhaps invalidate, a whole range of tax, welfare, public service, regulatory, and licensing statutes that may be more burdensome to the poor and to the average black than to the more affluent white.

426 U.S. at 248. See n. 20, supra.

32. Even if a municipal policy is shown to dilute the right to vote, however, the policy will not be struck down if the city shows that it serves highly important local interests and is closely tailored to effectuate only those interests. See Dunn v. Blumstein, 405 U.S. 330 (1972). Cf. Abate v. Mundt, 403 U.S. 182 (1971).

33. In my view, the standard of White v. Regester, 412 U.S. 755 (1973), see n. 7,

supra, and accompanying text, is the proper test under both the Fourteenth and Fifteenth Amendments for determining whether a districting scheme has the unconstitutional effect of diluting the Negro vote. It is plain that the District Court in both of the cases before us made the "intensely local appraisal" necessary under White, supra at 769, and correctly decided that the at-large electoral schemes for the Mobile City Commission and County School Board violated the White standard. As I earlier note with respect to No. 77-1844, see supra at 122-123, the District Court determined: (1) that Mobile Negroes still suffered pervasive present effects of massive historical official and private discrimination; (2) that the City Commission and County School Board had been quite unresponsive to the needs of the minority community; (3) that no Negro had ever been elected to either body, despite the fact that Negroes constitute about one-third of the electorate; (4) that the persistence of severe racial bloc voting made it highly unlikely that any Negro could be elected at large to either body in the foreseeable future; and (5) that no state policy favored at-large elections, and the local preference for that scheme was outweighed by the fact that the unconstitutional vote dilution could be corrected only by the imposition of single-member districts. Bolden v. City of Mobile, 423 F.Supp. 384 (SD Ala.1976); Brown v. Moore, 428 F.Supp. 1123 (SD Ala.1976). The Court of Appeals affirmed these findings in all respects. Bolden v. City of Mobile, 571 F.2d 238 (CA5 1978); Brown v. Moore, 575 F.2d 298 (CA5 1978). See also the dissenting opinion of my Brother WHITE, ante p. 94.

34. The statutes providing for at-large election of the members of the two governmental bodies involved in these cases, see n. 33, supra, have been in effect since the days when Mobile Negroes were totally disenfranchised by the Alabama Constitution of 1901. The District Court in both cases found, therefore, that the at-large schemes could not have been adopted for discriminatory purposes. Bolden v. City of Mobile, 423 F.Supp. at 386, 397; Brown v. Moore, 428 F.Supp. at 1126-1127, 1138. The issue is, then, whether officials have maintained these electoral systems for discriminatory purposes. Cf. Arlington Heights v. Metropolitan Housing Dev. Corp., 429 U.S. at 257-258, 267-271, and n. 17.

35. As the dissenting opinion of my Brother WHITE demonstrates, however, the facts of these cases compel a finding of unconstitutional vote dilution even under the plurality's standard.

36. Indeed, the District Court in the present cases concluded that the evidence supported the plaintiffs' position that unconstitutional vote dilution was the natural and foreseeable consequence of the maintenance of the challenged multimember districting. Brown v. Moore, 428 F.Supp. at 1138; Bolden v. City of Mobile, 423 F.Supp. at 397-398.

37. MR. JUSTICE STEVENS acknowledges that both discriminatory intent and discriminatory effect are present in No. 77-1844. See ante at 92-94. Nonetheless, he finds no constitutional violation, apparently because he believes that the electoral structure of Mobile conforms to a commonly used scheme, the discriminatory impact is, in his view, not extraordinary, and the structure is supported by sufficient noninvidious justifications so that it is neither wholly irrational nor entirely motivated by discriminatory animus. To

him, racially motivated decisions in this setting are an inherent part of the political process, and do not involve invidious discrimination.

The facts of the present cases, however, indicate that, in Mobile, considerations of race are far more powerful and pernicious than are considerations of other divisive aspects of the electorate. See supra at 446 U.S. 122"]122-123. In Mobile, as elsewhere, "the experience of Negroes . . . has been different in kind, not just in degree, from that of other ethnic groups." 122-123. In Mobile, as elsewhere, "the experience of Negroes . . . has been different in kind, not just in degree, from that of other ethnic groups." University of California Regents v. Bakke, 438 U.S. 265, 400 (1978) (opinion of MARSHALL, J.). An approach that accepts intentional discrimination against Negroes as merely an aspect of "politics as usual" strikes at the very hearts of the Fourteenth and Fifteenth Amendments.

38. Brest, The Supreme Court, 1975 Term -- Foreword: In Defense of the Antidiscrimination Principle, 90 Harv.L.Rev. 1, 7 (1976). See also Note, Racial Vote Dilution in Multimember Districts: The Constitutional Standard After Washington v. Davis, 76 Mich.L.Rev. 694, 716-719 (1978).

39. The plurality, ante at 74-75, n. 21, indicates that, on remand, the lower courts are to examine the evidence in these cases under the discriminatory intent standard of Personnel Administrator of Mass. v. Feeney, 442 U.S. 256 (1979), and may conclude that this test is met by proof of the refusal of Mobile's state legislative delegation to stimulate the passage of legislation changing Mobile's city government into a mayor-council system in which council members are elected from single-member districts. The plurality concludes, then, only that the District Court and the Court of Appeals in each of the present cases evaluated the evidence under an improper legal standard, and not that the evidence fails to support a claim under Feeney, supra. When the lower courts examine these cases under the Feeney standard, they should, of course, recognize the relevancy of the plaintiffs' evidence that vote dilution was a foreseeable and natural consequence of the maintenance of the challenged multimember districting, and that officials have apparently exhibited selective racial sympathy and indifference. Cf. Dayton Board of Education v. Brinkman, 443 U.S. 526 (1979); Columbus Board of Education v. Penick, 443 U.S. 449 (1979).

Finally, it is important not to confuse the differing views the plurality and I have on the elements of proving unconstitutional vote dilution. The plurality concludes that proof of intentional discrimination, as defined in Feeney, supra, is necessary to support such a claim. The plurality finds this requirement consistent with the statement in White v. Regester, 412 U.S. at 766, that unconstitutional vote dilution does not occur simply because a minority has not been able to elect representatives in proportion to its voting potential. The extra necessary element, according to the plurality, is a showing of discriminatory intent. In the plurality's view, the evidence presented in White going beyond mere proof of underrepresentation of the minority properly supported an inference that the multimember districting scheme in question was tainted with a discriminatory purpose.

The plurality's approach should be satisfied, then, by proof that an electoral scheme enacted with a discriminatory purpose effected a retrogression in the minority's voting power. Cf. Beer v. United States, 425 U.S. 130, 141 (1976). The standard should also be satisfied by proof that a scheme maintained for a discriminatory purpose has the effect of submerging minority electoral influence below the level it would have under a reasonable alternative scheme.

The plurality does not address the question whether proof of discriminatory effect is necessary to support a vote-dilution claim. It is clear from the above, however, that, if the Court at some point creates such a requirement, it would be satisfied by proof of mere disproportionate impact. Such a requirement would be far less stringent than the burden of proof required under the rather rigid discriminatory effects test I find in White v. Regester, supra. See n. 7, supra, and accompanying text.

Speech on private property: Justice Marshall's concurrence in Pruneyard Shopping Center v. Robins (June 9, 1980)

MR. JUSTICE MARSHALL, concurring.

I join the opinion of the Court, but write separately to make a few additional points.

I

In Food Employees v. Logan Valley Plaza, 391 U.S. 308 (1968), this Court held that the First and Fourteenth Amendments prevented a state court from relying on its law of trespass to enjoin the peaceful picketing of a business enterprise located within a shopping center. The Court concluded that, because the shopping center "serves as the community business block" and is open to the general public,

the State may not delegate the power, through the use of its trespass laws, wholly to exclude those members of the public wishing to exercise their First Amendment rights on the premises.

Id. at 319. The Court rejected the suggestion that such an abrogation of the state law of trespass would intrude on the constitutionally protected property rights of shopping center owners. And it emphasized that the shopping center was open to the public, and that reasonable restrictions on the exercise of communicative activity would be permitted.

[N]o meaningful claim to protection of a right of privacy can be advanced by respondents here. Nor on the facts of the case can any significant claim to protection of the normal business operation of the property be raised. Naked title is essentially all that is at issue.

Id. at 324.

The Court in Logan Valley emphasized that, if the property rights of shopping center owners were permitted to overcome the First Amendment rights of prospective petitioners, a significant intrusion on communicative activity would result. Because "[t]he large-scale movement of this country's population from the cities to the suburbs has been accompanied by the advent of the suburban shopping center," a contrary decision would have

> substantial consequences for workers seeking to challenge substandard working conditions, consumers protesting shoddy or overpriced merchandise, and minority groups seeking nondiscriminatory hiring policies.

Ibid. In light of these realities, we concluded that the First and Fourteenth Amendments prohibited the State from using its trespass laws to prevent the exercise of expressive activities on privately owned shopping centers, at least when those activities were related to the operations of the store at which they were directed.

In Lloyd Corp. v. Tanner, 407 U.S. 551"] 407 U.S. 551 (1972), the Court confined Logan Valley to its facts, holding that the First and Fourteenth Amendments were not violated when a State prohibited petitioning that was not designed to convey information with respect to the operation of the store that was being picketed. The Court indicated that a contrary result would constitute "an unwarranted infringement of property rights." 407 U.S. at 567. And in 407 U.S. 551 (1972), the Court confined Logan Valley to its facts, holding that the First and Fourteenth Amendments were not violated when a State prohibited petitioning that was not designed to convey information with respect to the operation of the store that was being picketed. The Court indicated that a contrary result would constitute "an unwarranted infringement of property rights." 407 U.S. at 567. And in Hudgens v. NLRB, 424 U.S. 507 (1976), the Court concluded that Lloyd had in fact overruled Logan Valley.

I continue to believe that Logan Valley was rightly decided, and that both Lloyd and Hudgens were incorrect interpretations of the First and Fourteenth Amendments. State action was present in all three cases. In all of them, the shopping center owners had opened their centers to the public at large, effectively replacing the State with respect to such traditional First Amendment forums as streets, sidewalks, and parks. The State had, in turn, made its laws of trespass available to shopping center owners, enabling them to exclude those who wished to engage in expressive activity on their premises. [n1] Rights of free expression become illusory when a State has operated in such a way as to shut off effective channels of communication. I continue to believe, then, that

> the Court's rejection of any role for the First Amendment in the privately owned shopping center complex stems . . . from an overly formalistic view of the relationship between the institution of private ownership of property and the First Amendment's guarantee of freedom of speech.

Hudgens v. NLRB, supra at 542 (dissenting opinion).

II

In the litigation now before the Court, the Supreme Court of California construed the California Constitution to protect precisely those rights of communication and expression that were at stake in Logan Valley, Lloyd, and Hudgens. The California court concluded that its State "[C]onstitution broadly proclaims speech and petition rights. Shopping centers to which the public is invited can provide an essential and invaluable forum for exercising those rights." 23 Cal.3d 899, 910, 592 P.2d 341, 347 (1979). Like the Court in Logan Valley, the California court found that access to shopping centers was crucial to the exercise of rights of free expression. And like the Court in Logan Valley, the California court rejected the suggestion that the Fourteenth Amendment barred the intrusion on the property rights of the shopping center owners. I applaud the court's decision, which is a part of a very healthy trend of affording state constitutional provisions a more expansive interpretation than this Court has given to the Federal Constitution. See Brennan State Constitutions and the Protection of Individual Rights, 90 Harv.L.Rev. 489 (1977).

Appellants, of course, take a different view. They contend that the decision below amounts to a constitutional "taking" or a deprivation of their property without due process of law. Lloyd, they claim, did not merely overrule Logan Valley's First Amendment holding; it overruled its due process ruling as well, recognizing a federally protected right on the part of shopping center owners to enforce the preexisting state law of trespass by excluding those who engage in communicative activity on their property. In my view, the issue appellants present is largely a restatement of the question of whether and to what extent a State may abrogate or modify common law rights. Although the cases in this Court do not definitively resolve the question, they demonstrate that appellants' claim has no merit.

Earlier this Term, in Martinez v. California, 444 U.S. 277 (1980), the Court was also confronted with a claim that the abolition of a cause of action previously conferred by state law was an impermissible taking of "property." We responded that, even if a preexisting state law remedy

is a species of "property" protected by the Due Process Clause, . . . it would remain true that the State's interest in fashioning its own rules of tort law is paramount to any discernible federal interest, except perhaps an interest in protecting the individual citizen from state action that is wholly arbitrary or irrational.

Id. at 281-282. Similarly, in the context of a claim that a guest statute impermissibly abrogated common law rights of tort, the Court observed that the Due Process Clause does not forbid the "creation of new rights, or the abolition of old ones recognized by the common law, to attain a permissible legislative object." Silver v. Silver, 280 U.S. 117, 122 (1929). And in Munn v. Illinois, 94 U.S. 113 (1877), the Court upheld a statute limiting the permissible rate for the warehousing of grain.

A person has no property, no vested interest, in any rule of the common law. . . . Rights of property which have been created by the common law cannot be taken away without due process; but the law itself, as a rule of conduct, may be changed at the will . . . of the legislature, unless prevented by constitutional limitations. Indeed, the great office of statutes is to remedy defects in the common law as they are developed, and to adapt it to the changes of time and circumstances.

Id. at 134. See also Second Employers' Liability Cases, 223 U.S. 1, 50 (1912); Crowell v. Benson, 285 U.S. 22, 41 (1932).

Appellants' claim in this case amounts to no less than a suggestion that the common law of trespass is not subject to revision by the State, notwithstanding the California Supreme Court's finding that state-created rights of expressive activity would be severely hindered if shopping centers were closed to expressive activities by members of the public. If accepted, that claim would represent a return to the era of Lochner v. New York, 198 U.S. 45 (1905), when common law rights were also found immune from revision by State or Federal Government. Such an approach would freeze the common law as it has been constructed by the courts, perhaps at its 19th-century state of development. It would allow no room for change in response to changes in circumstance. The Due Process Clause does not require such a result.

On the other hand, I do not understand the Court to suggest that rights of property are to be defined solely by state law, or that there is no federal constitutional barrier to the abrogation of common law rights by Congress or a state government. The constitutional terms "life, liberty, and property" do not derive their meaning solely from the provisions of positive law. They have a normative dimension as well, establishing a sphere of private autonomy which government is bound to respect. [n2] Quite serious constitutional questions might be raised if a legislature attempted to abolish certain categories of common law rights in some general way. Indeed, our cases demonstrate that there are limits on governmental authority to abolish "core" common law rights, including rights against trespass, at least without a compelling showing of necessity or a provision for a reasonable alternative remedy. [n3]

That "core" has not been approached in this case. The California Supreme Court's decision is limited to shopping centers, which are already open to the general public. The owners are permitted to impose reasonable restrictions on expressive activity. There has been no showing of interference with appellants' normal business operations. The California court has not permitted an invasion of any personal sanctuary. Cf. Stanley v. Georgia, 394 U.S. 557 (1969). No rights of privacy are implicated. In these circumstances, there is no basis for strictly scrutinizing the intrusion authorized by the California Supreme Court.

I join the opinion of the Court.

Notes

1. In this respect, the cases resembled Shelley v. Kraemer, 334 U.S. 1"] 334 U.S. 1 (1948), and 334 U.S. 1 (1948), and New York Times Co. v. Sullivan, 376 U.S. 254 (1964), in which the common law rules of contract and tort were held to constitute state action for Fourteenth Amendment purposes.

2. This understanding is embodied in cases in the procedural due process area holding that at least some "grievous losses" amount to deprivation of "liberty" or "property" within the meaning of the Due Process Clause, even if those losses are not

protected by statutory or common law. See Vitek v. Jones, 445 U.S. 480, 488-489 (1980), and cases cited; Mathews v. Eldridge, 424 U.S. 319, 333 (1976). See also Meachum v. Fano, 427 U.S. 215, 229 (1976) (STEVENS, J., dissenting).

3. For example, in Ingraham v. Wright, 430 U.S. 651 (1977), the Court found a constitutional liberty interest in freedom from corporal punishment, in large part on the ground that that interest was protected at common law. The Court stated that the

Due Process Clause . . . was intended to give Americans at least the protection against governmental power that they had enjoyed as Englishmen against the power of the Crown. The liberty preserved from deprivation without due process included the right "generally to enjoy those privileges long recognized at common law as essential to the orderly pursuit of happiness by free men."

Id. at 672-673 (citation omitted). In Duke Power Co. v. Carolina Environmental Study Group, 438 U.S. 59, 88 (1978), the Court reserved the question whether, in creating a compensation scheme for victims of nuclear accidents, Congress was constitutionally obliged to "provide a reasonable substitute remedy" for the abrogation of common law rights of tort. Similarly, in New York Central R. Co. v. White, 243 U.S. 188, 201 (1917), the Court expressed uncertainty as to whether

a State might, without violence to the constitutional guaranty of "due process of law," suddenly set aside all common law rules respecting liability as between employer and employee, without providing a reasonably just substitute,

and

doubted whether the State could abolish all rights of action on the one hand, or all defenses on the other, without setting up something adequate in their stead.

Medicaid should fund abortions: Justice Marshall's dissent in Harris v. McRae (June 30, 1980)

MR. JUSTICE MARSHALL, dissenting. [*]

Three years ago, in Maher v. Roe, 432 U.S. 464 (1977), the Court upheld a state program that excluded nontherapeutic abortions from a welfare program that generally subsidized the medical expenses incidental to pregnancy and childbirth. At that time, I expressed my fear

that the Court's decisions will be an invitation to public officials, already under extraordinary pressure from well-financed and carefully orchestrated lobbying campaigns, to approve more such restrictions

on governmental funding for abortion. Id. at 462 (dissenting both in Maher v. Roe, supra, and in Beal v. Doe, 432 U.S. 438 (1977), and Poelker v. Doe, 432 U.S. 519 (1977)).

That fear has proved justified. Under the Hyde Amendment, federal funding is denied for abortions that are medically necessary and that are necessary to avert severe and permanent damage to the health of the mother. The Court's opinion studiously avoids recognizing the undeniable fact that, for women eligible for Medicaid -- poor women -- denial of a Medicaid-funded abortion is equivalent to denial of legal abortion altogether. By definition, these women do not have the money to pay for an abortion themselves. If abortion is medically necessary and a funded abortion is unavailable, they must resort to back-alley butchers, attempt to induce an abortion themselves by crude and dangerous methods, or suffer the serious medical consequences of attempting to carry the fetus to term. Because legal abortion is not a realistic option for such women, the predictable result of the Hyde Amendment will be a significant increase in the number of poor women who will die or suffer significant health damage because of an inability to procure necessary medical services.

The legislation before us is the product of an effort to deny to the poor the constitutional right recognized in Roe v. Wade, 410 U.S. 113 (1973), even though the cost may be serious and long-lasting health damage. As my Brother STEVENS has demonstrated, see post, p. 349 (dissenting opinion), the premise underlying the Hyde Amendment was repudiated in Roe v. Wade, where the Court made clear that the state interest in protecting fetal life cannot justify jeopardizing the life or health of the mother. The denial of Medicaid benefits to individuals who meet all the statutory criteria for eligibility, solely because the treatment that is medically necessary involves the exercise of the fundamental right to chose abortion, is a form of discrimination repugnant to the equal protection of the laws guaranteed by the Constitution. The Court's decision today marks a retreat from Roe v. Wade and represents a cruel blow to the most powerless members of our society. I dissent.

I

In its present form, the Hyde Amendment restricts federal funding for abortion to cases in which "the life of the mother would be endangered if the fetus were carried to term" and "for such medical procedures necessary for the victims of rape or incest when such rape or incest has been reported promptly to a law enforcement agency or public health service." See ante at 302. Federal funding is thus unavailable even when severe and long-lasting health damage to the mother is a virtual certainty. Nor are federal funds available when severe health damage, or even death, will result to the fetus if it is carried to term.

The record developed below reveals that the standards set forth in the Hyde Amendment exclude the majority of cases in which the medical profession would recommend abortion as medically necessary. Indeed, in States that have adopted a standard more restrictive than the "medically necessary" test of the Medicaid Act, the number of funded abortions has decreased by over 98%. App. 289.

The impact of the Hyde Amendment on indigent women falls into four major categories. First, the Hyde Amendment prohibits federal funding for abortions that are necessary in order to protect the health and sometimes the life of the mother. Numerous conditions -- such as cancer, rheumatic fever, diabetes, malnutrition, phlebitis, sickle cell anemia, and heart disease -- substantially increase the risks associated with pregnancy or are themselves aggravated by pregnancy. Such conditions may make an abortion medically necessary in the judgment of a physician, but cannot be funded under the Hyde Amendment. Further, the health risks of undergoing an abortion increase dramatically as pregnancy becomes more advanced. By the time a pregnancy has progressed to the point where a physician is able to certify that it endangers the life of the mother, it is in many cases too late to prevent her death, because abortion is no longer safe. There are also instances in which a woman's life will not be immediately threatened by carrying the pregnancy to term, but aggravation of another medical condition will significantly shorten her life expectancy. These cases as well are not fundable under the Hyde Amendment.

Second, federal funding is denied in cases in which severe mental disturbances will be created by unwanted pregnancies. The result of such psychological disturbances may be suicide, attempts at self-abortion, or child abuse. The Hyde Amendment makes no provision for funding in such cases.

Third, the Hyde Amendment denies funding for the majority of women whose pregnancies have been caused by rape or incest. The prerequisite of a report within 60 days serves to exclude those who are afraid of recounting what has happened or are in fear of unsympathetic treatment by the authorities. Such a requirement is, of course, especially burdensome for the indigent, who may be least likely to be aware that a rapid report to the authorities is indispensable in order for them to be able to obtain an abortion.

Finally, federal funding is unavailable in cases in which it is known that the fetus itself will be unable to survive. In a number of situations, it is possible to determine in advance that the fetus will suffer an early death if carried to term. The Hyde Amendment, purportedly designed to safeguard "the legitimate governmental objective of protecting potential life," ante at 325, excludes federal funding in such cases.

An optimistic estimate indicates that as many as 100 excess deaths may occur each year as a result of the Hyde Amendment. [n1] The record contains no estimate of the health damage that may occur to poor women, but it shows that it will be considerable. [n2]

II

The Court resolves the equal protection issue in this case through a relentlessly formalistic catechism. Adhering to its "two-tiered" approach to equal protection, the Court first decides that so-called strict scrutiny is not required because the Hyde Amendment does not violate the Due Process Clause and is not predicated on a constitutionally suspect classification. Therefore,

the validity of classification must be sustained unless "the classification rests on grounds wholly irrelevant to the achievement of [any legitimate governmental] objective."

Ante at 322 (bracketed material in original), quoting McGowan v. Maryland, 366 U.S. 420, 425 (1961). Observing that previous cases have recognized "the legitimate governmental objective of protecting potential life," ante at 325, the Court concludes that the Hyde Amendment "establishe[s] incentives that make childbirth a more attractive alternative than abortion for persons eligible for Medicaid," ibid., and is therefore rationally related to that governmental interest.

I continue to believe that the rigid "two-tiered" approach is inappropriate, and that the Constitution requires a more exacting standard of review than mere rationality in cases such as this one. Further, in my judgment, the Hyde Amendment cannot pass constitutional muster even under the rational basis standard of review.

A

This case is perhaps the most dramatic illustration to date of the deficiencies in the Court's obsolete "two-tiered" approach to the Equal Protection Clause. See San Antonio Independent School Dist. v. Rodriguez, 411 U.S. 1, 98-110 (1973) (MARSHALL, J., dissenting); Massachusetts Bd. of Retirement v. Murgia, 427 U.S. 307, 318-321 (1976) (MARSHALL, J., dissenting); Maher v. Roe, 432 U.S. at 457-458 (MARSHALL, J., dissenting); Vance v. Bradley, 440 U.S. 93, 113-115 (1979) (MARSHALL, J., dissenting). [n3] With all deference, I am unable to understand how the Court can afford the same level of scrutiny to the legislation involved here -- whose cruel impact falls exclusively on indigent pregnant women -- that it has given to legislation distinguishing opticians from ophthalmologists, or to other legislation that males distinctions between economic interests more than able to protect themselves in the political process. See ante at 326, citing Williamson v. Lee Optical Co., 348 U.S. 483 (1955). Heightened scrutiny of legislative classifications has always been designed to protect groups

saddled with such disabilities, or subjected to such a history of purposeful unequal treatment, or relegated to such a position of political powerlessness as to command extraordinary protection from the majoritarian political process.

San Antonio Independent School Dist. v. Rodriguez, supra at 28. [n4] And while it is now clear that traditional "strict scrutiny" is unavailable to protect the poor against classifications that disfavor them, Dandridge v. Williams, 397 U.S. 471 (1970), I do not believe that legislation that imposes a crushing burden on indigent women can be treated with the same deference given to legislation distinguishing among business interests.

B

The Hyde Amendment, of course, distinguishes between medically necessary abortions and other medically necessary expenses. [n5] As I explained in Maher v. Roe, supra, such classifications must be assessed by weighing "'the importance of the governmental benefits denied, the character of the class, and the asserted state interests,'" id. at 458, quoting Massachusetts Bd. of Retirement v. Murgia, supra at 322. Under that approach, the Hyde Amendment is clearly invalid. [n6]

As in Maher, the governmental benefits at issue here are "of absolutely vital importance in the lives of the recipients." Maher v. Roe, supra at 458 (MARSHALL, J., dissenting). An indigent woman denied governmental funding for a medically necessary abortion is confronted with two grotesque choices. First, she may seek to obtain "an illegal abortion that poses a serious threat to her health and even her life." 432 U.S. at 458. Alternatively, she may attempt to bear the child, a course that may both significantly threaten her health and eliminate any chance she might have had "to control the direction of her own life," id. at 459.

The class burdened by the Hyde Amendment consists of indigent women, a substantial proportion of whom are members of minority races. As I observed in Maher, nonwhite women obtain abortions at nearly double the rate of whites, ibid. In my view, the fact that the burden of the Hyde Amendment falls exclusively on financially destitute women suggests

a special condition, which tends seriously to curtail the operation of those political processes ordinarily to be relied upon to protect minorities, and which may call for a correspondingly more searching judicial inquiry.

United States v. Carolene Products Co., 304 U.S. 144, 153, n. 4 (1938). For this reason, I continue to believe that "a showing that state action has a devastating impact on the lives of minority racial groups must be relevant" for purposes of equal protection analysis. Jefferson v. Hackney, 406 U.S. 535, 575-576 (1972) (MARSHALL, J., dissenting).

As I explained in Maher, the asserted state interest in protecting potential life is insufficient to "outweigh the deprivation or serious discouragement of a vital constitutional right of especial importance to poor and minority women." 432 U.S. at 461. In Maher, the Court found a permissible state interest in encouraging normal childbirth. Id. at 477-479. The governmental interest in the present case is substantially weaker than in Maher, for under the Hyde Amendment, funding is refused even in cases in which normal childbirth will not result: one can scarcely speak of "normal childbirth" in cases where the fetus will die shortly after birth, or in which the mother's life will be shortened or her health otherwise gravely impaired by the birth. Nevertheless, the Hyde Amendment denies funding even in such cases. In these circumstances, I am unable to see how even a minimally rational legislature could conclude that the interest in fetal life outweighs the brutal effect of the Hyde Amendment on indigent women. Moreover, both the legislation in Maher and the Hyde Amendment were designed to deprive poor and minority women of the constitutional right to choose abortion. That purpose is not constitutionally permitted under Roe v. Wade.

C

Although I would abandon the strict scrutiny/rational basis dichotomy in equal protection analysis, it is by no means necessary to reject that traditional approach to conclude, as I do, that the Hyde Amendment is a denial of equal protection. My Brother BRENNAN has demonstrated that the Amendment is unconstitutional because it impermissibly infringes upon the individual's constitutional right to decide whether to terminate a pregnancy. See ante at 332-334 (dissenting opinion). And as my Brother STEVENS demonstrates, see post at 350-352 (dissenting opinion), the Government's interest in protecting fetal life is not a legitimate one when it is in conflict with "the preservation of the life or health of the mother," Roe v. Wade, 410 U.S. at 165, and when the Government's effort to make serious health damage to the mother "a more attractive alternative than abortion," ante at 325, does not rationally promote the governmental interest in encouraging normal childbirth.

The Court treats this case as though it were controlled by Maher. To the contrary, this case is the mirror image of Maher. The result in Maher turned on the fact that the legislation there under consideration discouraged only nontherapeutic, or medically unnecessary, abortions. In the Court's view, denial of Medicaid funding for nontherapeutic abortions was not a denial of equal protection, because Medicaid funds were available only for medically necessary procedures. Thus the plaintiffs were seeking benefits which were not available to others similarly situated. I continue to believe that Maher was wrongly decided. But it is apparent that, while the plaintiffs in Maher were seeking a benefit not available to others similarly situated, appellees are protesting their exclusion from a benefit that is available to all others similarly situated. This, it need hardly be said, is a crucial difference for equal protection purposes.

Under Title XIX and the Hyde Amendment, funding is available for essentially all necessary medical treatment for the poor. Appellees have met the statutory requirements for eligibility, but they are excluded because the treatment that is medically necessary involves the exercise of a fundamental right, the right to choose an abortion. In short, these appellees have been deprived of a governmental benefit for which they are otherwise eligible, solely because they have attempted to exercise a constitutional right. The interest asserted by the Government, the protection of fetal life, has been declared constitutionally subordinate to appellees' interest in preserving their lives and health by obtaining medically necessary treatment. Roe v. Wade, supra. And finally, the purpose of the legislation was to discourage the exercise of the fundamental right. In such circumstances, the Hyde Amendment must be invalidated, because it does not meet even the rational basis standard of review.

III

The consequences of today's opinion -- consequences to which the Court seems oblivious -- are not difficult to predict. Pregnant women denied the funding necessary to procure abortions will be restricted to two alternatives. First, they can carry the fetus to term -- even though that route may result in severe injury or death to the mother, the fetus, or both. If that course appears intolerable, they can resort to self-induced abortions or attempt to obtain illegal abortions -- not because bearing a child would be inconvenient, but because it is necessary in order to protect their health. [n7] The result will not be to protect what the Court describes as "the legitimate governmental objective of protecting potential life," ante at 325, but to ensure the destruction of both fetal and maternal life. "There is another world 'out there,' the existence of which the Court . . . either chooses to ignore or fears to recognize." Beal v. Doe, 432 U.S. at 463 (BLACKMUN, J., dissenting). In my view, it is only by blinding itself to that other world that the Court can reach the result it announces today.

Ultimately, the result reached today may be traced to the Court's unwillingness to apply the constraints of the Constitution to decisions involving the expenditure of governmental funds. In today's decision, as in Maher v. Roe, the Court suggests that a withholding of funding imposes no real obstacle to a woman deciding whether to exercise her constitutionally protected procreative choice, even though the Government is prepared to fund all other medically necessary expenses, including the expenses of childbirth. The Court perceives this result as simply a distinction between a "limitation on governmental power" and "an affirmative funding obligation." Ante at 318. For a poor person attempting to exercise her "right" to freedom of choice, the difference is imperceptible. As my Brother BRENNAN has shown, see ante at 332-334 (dissenting opinion), the differential distribution of incentives -- which the Court concedes is present here, see ante at 325 -- can have precisely the same effect as an outright prohibition. It is no more sufficient an answer here than it was in Roe v. Wade to say that "'the appropriate forum'" for the resolution of sensitive policy choices is the legislature. See ante at 326, quoting Maher v. Roe at 479.

More than 35 years ago, Mr. Justice Jackson observed that the

task of translating the majestic generalities of the Bill of Rights . . . into concrete restraints on officials dealing with the problems of the twentieth century is one to disturb self-confidence.

West Virginia State Bd. of Education v. Barnette, 319 U.S. 624, 639 (1943). These constitutional principles, he observed for the Court,

grew in soil which also produced a philosophy that the individual['s] . . . liberty was attainable through mere absence of governmental restraints.

Ibid. Those principles must be

transplant[ed] . . . to a soil in which the laissez-faire concept or principle of noninterference has withered at least as to economic affairs, and social advancements are increasingly sought through closer integration of society and through expanded and strengthened governmental controls.

Id. at 640.

In this case, the Federal Government has taken upon itself the burden of financing practically all medically necessary expenditures. One category of medically necessary expenditure has been singled out for exclusion, and the sole basis for the exclusion is a premise repudiated for purposes of constitutional law in Roe v. Wade. The consequence is a devastating impact on the lives and health of poor women. I do not believe that a Constitution committed to the equal protection of the laws can tolerate this result. I dissent.

*

[This opinion applies also to No. 79-4, Williams et al. v. Zbaraz et al., No. 79-5, Miller, Acting Director, Illinois Department of Public Aid, et al. v. Zbaraz et al., and No. 79-491, United States v. Zbaraz et al., post p. 358.]

Notes

1. See App. 294-296.

2. For example, the number of serious complications deriving from abortions was estimated to be about 100 times the number of deaths from abortions. See id. at 200.

3. A number of individual Justices have expressed discomfort with the two-tiered approach, and I am pleased to observe that its hold on the law may be waning. See Craig v. Boren, 429 U.S. 190, 210-211, and n. * (1976) (POWELL, J., concurring); id. at 211-212 (STEVENS, J., concurring); post at 352, n. 4 (STEVENS, J., dissenting). Further, the Court has adopted an "intermediate" level of scrutiny for a variety of classifications. See Trimble v. Gordon, 430 U.S. 762 (1977) (illegitimacy); Craig v. Boren, supra, (sex discrimination); Foley v. Connelie, 435 U.S. 291 (1978) (alienage). Cf. University of California Regents v. Bakke, 438 U.S. 265, 324 (1978) (opinion of BRENNAN, WHITE, MARSHALL, and BLACKMUN, JJ.) (affirmative action).

4. For this reason, the Court has on occasion suggested that classifications discriminating against the poor are subject to special scrutiny under the Fifth and Fourteenth Amendments. See McDonald v. Board of Election, 394 U.S. 802, 807 (1969); Harper v. Virginia Bd. of Elections, 383 U.S. 663, 668 (1966).

5. As my Brother STEVENS suggests, see post at 355, n. 8 (dissenting opinion), the denial of funding for those few medically necessary services that are excluded from the Medicaid program is based on a desire to conserve federal funds, not on a desire to penalize those who suffer the excluded disabilities.

6. In practical effect, my approach is not in this context dissimilar to that taken in Craig v. Boren, supra at 197, where the Court referred to an intermediate standard of review requiring that classifications "must serve important governmental objectives and must be substantially related to achievement of those objectives."

7. Of course, some poor women will attempt to raise the funds necessary to obtain a lawful abortion. A court recently found that those who were fortunate enough to do so had to resort to

> not paying rent or utility bills, pawning household goods, diverting food and clothing money, or journeying to another state to obtain lower rates or fraudulently use a relative's insurance policy. . . . [S]ome patients were driven to theft.

Women's Health Services, Inc. v. Maher, 482 F.Supp. 725, 731, n. 9.

Minors should be able to have abortions without their parents or anyone else knowing: Justice Marshall's dissent in H.L. v. Matheson (March 23, 1981)

JUSTICE MARSHALL, with whom JUSTICE BRENNAN and JUSTICE BLACKMUN join, dissenting.

The decision of the Court is narrow. It finds shortcomings in appellant's complaint and therefore denies relief. Thus, the Court sends out a clear signal that more carefully drafted pleadings could secure both a plaintiff's standing to challenge the overbreadth of Utah Code Ann. 76-7-304 (2) (1978), and success on the merits. 1

Nonetheless, I dissent. I believe that even if the complaint is defective, the majority's legal analysis is incorrect and it yields an improper disposition here. More important, I cannot agree with the majority's view of the complaint, or its standing analysis. I therefore would reverse the judgment of the Supreme Court of Utah.

I

The Court finds appellant's complaint defective because it fails to allege that she is mature or emancipated, and neglects to specify her reasons for wishing to avoid notifying her parents about her abortion decision. As a result, the Court reasons, appellant lacks standing to challenge the overbreadth of the Utah parental notification statute. 2

The majority's standing analysis rests on prudential concerns and not on the constitutional limitations set by Art. III. See Gladstone, Realtors v. Village of Bellwood, 441 U.S. 91, 99 -100 (1979); Warth v. Seldin, 422 U.S. 490, 498 -499, 517-518 (1975). For the Court does not question that appellant's injury due to the statute's requirement falls within the legally protected ambit of her privacy interest, and that the relief requested would remedy the harm. See ante, at 407-409 (majority opinion); ante, at 418-419 (opinion of POWELL, J.). The Court decides only that appellant cannot challenge the blanket nature of the statute because she neglected to allege that by her personal characteristics, she is a member of particular groups that undoubtedly deserve exemption from a parental notice requirement. 3 Thus, the Court seems to apply the familiar prudential principle that an individual should not be heard to raise the rights of other persons. This principle, of course, has not precluded standing in other instances where, as here, the party has established the requisite and legally protected interest capable of redress through the relief requested. 4 See, e. g., Duke Power Co. v. Carolina Environmental Study Group, 438 U.S. 59, 80 -81 (1978); Singleton v. Wulff, 428 U.S. 106, 113 -118 (1976) (plurality opinion of BLACKMUN, J.); Doe v. Bolton, 410 U.S. 179, 188 - 189 (1973); Griswold v. Connecticut, 381 U.S. 479, 481 (1965); NAACP v. Alabama ex rel. Patterson, 357 U.S. 449, 459 -460 (1958); Barrows v. Jackson, 346 U.S. 249, 259 (1953).

I do not believe that prudential considerations should bar standing here, for I am persuaded that appellant's complaint establishes a claim that notifying her parents would not be in her best interests. 5 She alleged that she "believes that it is in her best interest that her parents not be informed of her [pregnant] condition," Complaint § 6, App. 4, and that after consulting with her physician, attorney, and social worker, "she understands what is involved in her decision" to seek an abortion, Complaint § 9, App. 4. 6 This claim was further supported, albeit without detail, at the evidentiary hearing. There appellant testified she did not feel she could discuss the abortion decision with her parents even after she consulted a social worker on the issue. Tr. 8, App. 26. 7 In my judgment, appellant has adequately asserted that she has persistently held reasons for believing parental notice would not be in her best interests. This provides a sufficient basis for standing to raise the challenge in her complaint. Appellant seeks to challenge a state statute, construed definitively by the highest court of that State to permit no exception to the notice requirement on the basis of any reasons offered by the minor. 604 P.2d 907, 913 (Utah 1979). As standing is a jurisdictional issue, separate and distinct from the merits, a court need not evaluate the persuasiveness of her reasons for opposing parental notice to conclude that appellant has a concrete interest in determining whether the parental notice statute is valid. 8

Yet even if the Court's view of appellant's complaint is correct, and even if prudence calls for denying her standing to raise the overbreadth claim, the Court erroneously concludes that the class represented by appellant suffers the identical standing disability. In so doing, the Court is apparently indifferent to the federalism or comity issues arising when this Court presumes to supervise the procedural determinations made by a state trial court under state law. Even if application of federal law governing class actions were appropriate in this case, the majority misapplies federal law by disturbing the class definition as approved by the trial court. The Court acknowledges, ante, at 401, 404 (BURGER, C. J.); ante, at 417, n. 6 (POWELL, J.), that the trial court granted appellant's motion to represent a class, and it is undisputed that this class includes all "minor women who are suffering unwanted pregnancies and desire to terminate the pregnancies but may not do so inasmuch as their physicians will not perform an abortion upon them without compliance with the provisions of Section 76-7-304 (2)." Complaint § 10, App. 5. This class by definition includes all minor women, self-supporting or dependent, sophisticated or naive, as long as the Utah statute interferes with the ability of these women to decide with their physicians to obtain abortions. If the Court is correct that appellant cannot raise challenges based on the interest of emancipated or mature minors, or others whose best interests call for avoiding parental notification, the proper disposition under federal law would be a remand. This remand would protect such class members by permitting the trial court to determine whether appellant is a proper and adequate class representative, and whether her claims are sufficiently similar to the class to warrant the class action. 9   Since the trial court enjoys considerable latitude in approving class actions, such a remand is appropriate only on those rare occasions where the reviewing court discerns an abuse of discretion. 10 But where an abuse of discretion is clear from the record, remand should ensue, and could result in redefinition or dismissal of the class, addition of other named plaintiffs to represent interests appellant cannot advance, or creation of subclasses with additional representative parties. 11 In contrast, it is improper to assume appellant adequately represents the entire class as defined by the trial court, but redefine the class appellant is deemed to represent, and deny relief on that basis. 12 Nonetheless, that is exactly the course selected by the majority today.

I instead assume that appellant adequately represents the class which the trial judge concluded she represents - all minor women seeking an abortion but finding the parental notice requirement an obstacle. I then would find that their rights and interests can be raised here by appellant in support of a facial challenge to the Utah statute, and conduct the appropriate review of appellant's claims.

II

Because the Court's treatment is so cursory, I review appellant's claims with due attention to our precedents.

Our cases have established that a pregnant woman has a fundamental right to choose whether to obtain an abortion or carry the pregnancy to term. Roe v. Wade, 410 U.S. 113 (1973); Doe v. Bolton, 410 U.S. 179 (1973). 13 Her choice, like the deeply intimate decisions to marry, 14 to procreate, 15 and to use contraceptives, 16 is guarded from unwarranted state intervention by the right to privacy. 17 Grounded in the Due Process Clause of the Fourteenth Amendment, the right to privacy 18 protects both the woman's "interest in independence in making certain kinds of important decisions" and her "individual interest in avoiding disclosure of personal matters." Whalen v. Roe, 429 U.S. 589, 599 -600 (1977).

In the abortion context, we have held that the right to privacy shields the woman from undue state intrusion in, and external scrutiny of, her very personal choice. Thus, in Roe v. Wade, supra, at 164, we held that during the first trimester of the pregnancy, the State's interest in protecting maternal health or the potential life of the fetus could not override the right of the pregnant woman and the attending physician to make the abortion decision through private, unfettered consultation. We further emphasized the restricted scope of permissible state action in this area when, in Doe v. Bolton, supra, at 198-200, we struck down state-imposed procedural requirements that subjected the woman's private decision with her physician to review by other physicians and a hospital committee.

It is also settled that the right to privacy, like many constitutional rights, 19 extends to minors. Planned Parenthood of Central Mo. v. Danforth, 428 U.S. 52 (1976); Bellotti v. Baird, 443 U.S. 622, 639 (1979) (Bellotti II) (POWELL, J.); id., at 653 (STEVENS, J.); T. H. v. Jones, 425 F. Supp. 873, 881 (Utah 1975), summarily aff'd on other grounds, 425 U.S. 986 (1976). Indeed, because an unwanted pregnancy is probably more of a crisis for a minor than for an adult, as the abortion decision cannot be postponed until her majority, "there are few situations in which denying a minor the right to make an important decision will have consequences so grave and indelible." Bellotti II, supra, at 646 (POWELL, J.). 20 Thus, for both the adult and the minor woman, state-imposed burdens on the abortion decision can be justified only upon a showing that the restrictions advance "important state interests." Roe v. Wade, 410 U.S., at 154; accord, Planned Parenthood of Central Mo. v. Danforth, supra, at 61. Before examining the state interests asserted here, it is necessary first to consider Utah's claim that its statute does not "imping[e] on a woman's decision to have an abortion" or "plac[e] obstacles in the path of effectuating such a decision." Brief for Appellees 9. This requires an examination of whether the parental notice requirement of the Utah statute imposes any burden on the abortion decision.

The ideal of a supportive family so pervades our culture that it may seem incongruous to examine "burdens" imposed by a statute requiring parental notice of a minor daughter's decision to terminate her pregnancy. 21 This Court has long deferred to the bonds which join family members for mutual sustenance. See Pierce v. Society of Sisters, 268 U.S. 510, 534 -535 (1925); May v. Anderson, 345 U.S. 528, 533 (1953); Griswold v. Connecticut, 381 U.S., at 486; Stanley v. Illinois, 405 U.S. 645, 651 (1972); Moore v. East Cleveland, 431 U.S. 494, 504 -505 (1977) (plurality opinion of POWELL, J.). Especially in times of adversity, the relationships within a family can offer the security of constant caring and aid. See id., at 505. Ideally, a minor facing an important decision will naturally seek advice and support from her parents, and they in turn will respond with comfort and wisdom. 22 If the pregnant minor herself confides in her family, she plainly relinquishes her right to avoid telling or involving them. For a minor in that circumstance, the statutory requirement of parental notice hardly imposes a burden.

Realistically, however, many families do not conform to this ideal. Many minors, like appellant, oppose parental notice and seek instead to preserve the fundamental, personal right to privacy. It is for these minors that the parental notification requirement creates a problem. In this context, involving the minor's parents against her wishes 23 effectively cancels her right to avoid disclosure of her personal choice. See Whalen v. Roe, 429 U.S., at 599 -600. Moreover, the absolute notice requirement publicizes her private consultation with her doctor and interjects additional parties in the very conference held confidential in Roe v. Wade, supra, at 164. Besides revealing a confidential decision, the parental notice requirement may limit "access to the means of effectuating that decision." Carey v. Population Services International, 431 U.S. 678, 688 (1977). Many minor women will encounter interference from their parents after the state-imposed notification. 24 In addition to parental disappointment and disapproval, the minor may confront physical or emotional abuse, withdrawal of financial support, or actual obstruction of the abortion decision. Furthermore, the threat of parental notice may cause some minor women to delay past the first trimester of pregnancy, after which the health risks increase significantly. 25 Other pregnant minors may attempt to self-abort or to obtain an illegal abortion rather than risk parental notification. 26 Still others may foresake an abortion and bear an unwanted child, which, given the minor's "probable education, employment skills, financial resources and emotional maturity. . . . may be exceptionally burdensome." Bellotti II, 443 U.S., at 642 (POWELL, J.). The possibility that such problems may not occur in particular cases does not alter the hardship created by the notice requirement on its face. 27 And that hardship is not a mere disincentive created by the State, 28 but is instead an actual state-imposed obstacle to the exercise of the minor woman's free choice. 29 For the class of pregnant minors represented by appellant, this obstacle is so onerous as to bar the desired abortions. 30 Significantly, the interference sanctioned by the statute does not operate in a neutral fashion. No notice is required for other pregnancy-related medical care, 31 so only the minor women who wish to abort encounter the burden imposed by the notification statute. Because the Utah requirement of mandatory parental notice unquestionably burdens the minor's privacy right, the proper analysis turns next to the State's proffered justifications for the infringements posed by the statute.

III

As established by this Court in Planned Parenthood of Central Mo. v. Danforth, the statute cannot survive appellant's challenge unless it is justified by a "significant state interest." 32 Further, the State must demonstrate that the means it selected are closely tailored to serve that interest. 33 Where regulations burden the rights of pregnant adults, we have held that the State legitimately may be concerned with "protection of health, medical standards, and prenatal life." Roe v. Wade, 410 U.S., at 155 . We concluded, however, that during the first trimester of pregnancy none of these interests sufficiently justifies state interference with the decision reached by the pregnant woman and her physician. Id., at 162-163. Nonetheless, appellees assert here that the parental notice requirement advances additional state interests not implicated by a pregnant adult's decision to abort. Specifically, appellees contend that the notice requirement improves the physician's medical judgment about a pregnant minor in two ways: it permits the parents to provide additional information to the physician, and it encourages consultation between the parents and the minor woman. Appellees also advance an independent state interest in preserving parental rights and family autonomy. I consider each of these asserted interests in turn. 34

A

In upholding the statute, the Utah Supreme Court concluded that the notification provision might encourage parental transmission of "additional information, which might prove invaluable to the physician in exercising his `best medical judgment.'" 35 Yet neither the Utah courts nor the statute itself specifies the kind of information contemplated for this purpose, nor why it is available to the parents but not to the minor woman herself. Most parents lack the medical expertise necessary to supplement the physician's medical judgment, and at best could provide facts about the patient's medical history. It seems doubtful that a minor mature enough to become pregnant and to seek medical advice on her own initiative would be unable or unwilling to provide her physician with information crucial to the abortion decision. In addition, by law the physician already is obligated to obtain all information necessary to form his best medical judgment, 36 and nothing bars consultation with the parents should the physician find it necessary.

Even if mandatory parental notice serves a substantial state purpose in this regard, the Utah statute fails to implement it. Simply put, the statute on its face does not require or even encourage the transfer of information; it does not even call for a conversation between the physician and the parents. A letter from the physician to the parents would satisfy the statute, as would a brief telephone call made moments before the abortion. 37 Moreover, the statute is patently underinclusive if its aim is the transfer of information known to the parents but unavailable from the minor woman herself. The statute specifically excludes married minors from the parental notice requirement; only her husband need be told of the planned abortion, Utah Code Ann. 76-7-304 (2) (1978), and Utah makes no claim that he possesses any information valuable to the physician's judgment but unavailable from the pregnant woman. Furthermore, no notice is required for other pregnancy-related care sought by the minor. See Utah Code Ann. 78-14-5 (4) (f) (1977) (authorizing woman of any age to consent to pregnancy-related medical care). The minor woman may consent to surgical removal and analysis of amniotic fluid, caesarian delivery, and other medical care related to pregnancy. The physician's decisions concerning such procedures would be enhanced by parental information as much as would the abortion decision, yet only the abortion decision triggers the parental notice requirement. This result is especially anomalous given the comparatively lesser health risks associated with abortion as contrasted with other pregnancy-related medical care. 38 Thus, the statute not only fails to promote the transfer of information as is claimed, it does not apply to other closely related contexts in which such exchange of information would be no less important. The goal of promoting consultation between the physician and the parents of the pregnant minor cannot sustain a statute that is so ill-fitted to serve it. 39

B

Appellees also claim the statute serves the legitimate purpose of improving the minor's decision by encouraging consultation between the minor woman and her parents. Appellees do not dispute that the State cannot legally or practically require such consultation. 40 Nor do appellees contest the fact that the decision is ultimately the minor's to make. 41 Nonetheless, the State seeks through the notice requirement to give parents the opportunity to contribute to the minor woman's abortion decision.

Ideally, facilitation of supportive conversation would assist the pregnant minor during an undoubtedly difficult experience. Again, however, when measured against the rationality of the means employed, the Utah statute simply fails to advance this asserted goal. The statute imposes no requirement that the notice be sufficiently timely to permit any discussion between the pregnant minor and the parents. Moreover, appellant's claims require us to examine the statute's purpose in relation to the parents who the minor believes are likely to respond with hostility or opposition. In this light, the statute is plainly overbroad. Parental consultation hardly seems a legitimate state purpose where the minor's pregnancy resulted from incest, where a hostile or abusive parental response is assured, or where the minor's fears of such a response deter her from the abortion she desires. The absolute nature of the statutory requirement, with exception permitted only if the parents are physically unavailable, violates the requirement that regulations in this fundamentally personal area be carefully tailored to serve a significant state interest. 42 "The need to preserve the constitutional right and the unique nature of the abortion decision, especially when made by a minor, require a State to act with particular sensitivity when it legislates to foster parental involvement in this matter." Bellotti II, 443 U.S., at 642 (POWELL, J.). Because Utah's absolute notice requirement demonstrates no such sensitivity, I cannot approve its interference with the minor's private consultation with the physician during the first trimester of her pregnancy.

C

Finally, appellees assert a state interest in protecting parental authority and family integrity. 43 This Court, of course, has recognized that the "primary role of the parents in the upbringing of their children is now established beyond debate as an enduring American tradition." Wisconsin v. Yoder, 406 U.S. 205, 232 (1972). See Prince v. Massachusetts, 321 U.S. 158 (1944); Meyer v. Nebraska, 262 U.S. 390 (1923). Indeed, "those who nurture [the child] and direct his destiny have the right, coupled with the high duty, to recognize and prepare him for additional obligations." Pierce v. Society of Sisters, 268 U.S., at 535 . Similarly, our decisions "have respected the private realm of family life which the state cannot enter." Prince v. Massachusetts, supra, at 166. See also Moore v. East Cleveland, 431 U.S., at 505 .

The critical thrust of these decisions has been to protect the privacy of individual families from unwarranted state intrusion. 44 Ironically, appellees invoke these decisions in seeking to justify state interference in the normal functioning of the family. Through its notice requirement, the State in fact enters the private realm of the family rather than leaving unaltered the pattern of interactions chosen by the family. Whatever its motive, state intervention is hardly likely to resurrect parental authority that the parents themselves are unable to preserve. 45 In rejecting a statute permitting parental veto of the minor woman's abortion decision in Planned Parenthood of Central Mo. v. Danforth, 428 U.S., at 75, we found it difficult to conclude that

"providing a parent with absolute power to overrule a determination, made by the physician and his minor patient, to terminate the patient's pregnancy will serve to strengthen the family unit. Neither is it likely that such veto power will enhance parental authority or control where the minor and the nonconsenting parent are so fundamentally in conflict and the very existence of the pregnancy already has fractured the family structure."

More recently, in Bellotti II, supra, at 638, JUSTICE POWELL observed that efforts to guide the social and moral development of young people are "in large part . . . beyond the competence of impersonal political institutions."

Appellees maintain, however, that Utah's statute "merely safeguards a reserved right which parents have to know of the important activities of their children by attempting to prevent a denial of the parental rights through deception." Brief for Appellees 3. Casting its purpose this way does not salvage the statute. For when the threat to parental authority originates not from the State but from the minor child, invocation of "reserved" rights of parents cannot sustain blanket state intrusion into family life such as that mandated by the Utah statute. Such a result not only runs counter to the private domain of the family which the State may not breach; it also conflicts with the limits traditionally placed on parental authority. Parental authority is never absolute, and has been denied legal protection when its exercise threatens the health or safety of the minor children. E. g., Prince v. Massachusetts, supra, at 169-170. Indeed, legal protection for parental rights is frequently tempered if not replaced by concern for the child's interest. 46 Whatever its importance elsewhere, parental authority deserves de minimis legal reinforcement where the minor's exercise of a fundamental right is burdened.

To decide this case, there is no need to determine whether parental rights never deserve legal protection when their assertion conflicts with the minor's rights and interests. 47 I conclude that this statute cannot be defended as a mere reinforcement of existing parental rights, for the statute reaches beyond the legal limits of those rights. The statute applies, without exception, to emancipated minors, 48 mature minors, 49 and minors with emergency health care needs, 50 all of whom, as Utah recognizes, by law have long been entitled to medical care unencumbered by parental involvement. Most relevant to appellant's own claim, the statutory restriction applies even where the minor's best interests - as evaluated by her physician - call for an abortion. The Utah trial court found as a fact that appellant's physician "believed along with her that she should be aborted and that he felt it was in her best medical interest to do so but he could not and would not perform an abortion upon her without informing her parents prior to aborting her because it was required of him by that statute and he was unwilling to perform an abortion upon her without complying with the provisions of the statute even though he believed it was best to do so." Civ. No. C-78-2719 (Dec. 26, 1978) (Findings of Fact § 7). Even if further review by adults other than her physician, counselor, and attorney were necessary to assess the minor's best interests, see Bellotti II, 443 U.S., at 640 -641, 643-644 (opinion of POWELL, J.), Utah's rejection of any exception to the notice requirement for a pregnant minor is plainly overbroad. In Bellotti II, we were unwilling to cut a pregnant minor off from any avenue to obtain help beyond her parents, and yet the Utah statute does just that.

In this area, I believe this Court must join the state courts and legislatures which have acknowledged the undoubted social reality: some minors, in some circumstances, have the capacity and need to determine their health care needs without involving their parents. As we recognized in Planned Parenthood of Central Mo. v. Danforth, 428 U.S., at 75, "[a]ny independent interest the parent may have in the termination of the minor daughter's pregnancy is no more weighty than the right of privacy of the competent minor mature enough to have become pregnant." 51 Utah itself has allocated pregnancy-related health care decisions entirely to the pregnant minor. 52 Where the physician has cause to doubt the minor's actual ability to understand and consent, by law he must pursue the requisites of the State's informed consent procedures. 53 The State cannot have a legitimate interest in adding to this scheme mandatory parental notice of the minor's abortion decision. This conclusion does not affect parents' traditional responsibility to guide their children's development, especially in personal and moral concerns. I am persuaded that the Utah notice requirement is not necessary to assure parents this traditional child-rearing role, and that it burdens the minor's fundamental right to choose with her physician whether to terminate her pregnancy. 54

IV

In its eagerness to avoid the clear application of our precedents, the Court today relies on a mistaken view of class-action law and prudential standing requirements. The Court's avoidance of the issue presented by the complaint nonetheless leaves our precedents intact. Under those precedents, I have no doubt that the challenged statute infringes upon the constitutional right to privacy attached to a minor woman's decision to complete or terminate her pregnancy. None of the reasons offered by the State justifies this intrusion, for the statute is not tailored to serve them. Rather than serving to enhance the physician's judgment, in cases such as appellant's the statute prevents implementation of the physician's medical recommendation. Rather than promoting the transfer of information held by parents to the minor's physician, the statute neglects to require anything more than a communication from the physician moments before the abortion. Rather than respecting the private realm of family life, the statute invokes the criminal justice machinery of the State in an attempt to influence the interactions within the family. Accordingly, I would reverse the judgment of the Supreme Court of Utah insofar as it upheld the statute against constitutional attack.

Notes

[1] Under the majority's view, to assure standing, the plaintiff pregnant minor simply need allege her desire to obtain an abortion, her inability to do so because of the statute, and her view that she is emancipated, mature, or that it is in her best interests to have an abortion performed without notifying her parents. The majority finds no standing problem where the complaint alleges that the plaintiff is emancipated or mature, and thus reaffirms the standing analysis employed in Bellotti v. Baird, 443 U.S. 622 (1979) (Bellotti II). See ante, at 406, n. 12. In addition, the Court relies in part on a decision by the Federal District Court in Utah, which enjoined application of the same Utah statute involved here to emancipated minors. L. R. v. Hansen, Civil No. C-80-0078J (Feb. 8, 1980). The Court apparently contemplates that similar challenges will meet with success in the future. For example, the District Court in L. R. v. Hansen also accorded intervenor status and awarded preliminary relief to a minor woman who, like appellant, is under 17 years old and is dependent upon a parent with whom she resides. The only difference between the allegations of the instant appellant and those of that intervenor is the latter's express allegation that parental notice would result in her expulsion from home and destruction of her relationship with her parent. L. R. v. Hansen, Civil No. C-80-0078J (Findings of Fact and Conclusions of Law § 4) (Oct. 24, 1980). Finally, the Court today does not question our prior decision upholding the standing of physicians to challenge abortion restrictions. See n. 4, infra.

[2] In essence, the Court concludes that because appellant neglected to make specific allegations about herself and her situation, she "lacks `the personal stake in the controversy needed to confer standing' to advance the overbreadth argument," ante, at 406 (quoting Harris v. McRae, 448 U.S. 297, 320 (1980)). The majority thus assumes that

a plaintiff raising an overbreadth challenge to an abortion statute must allege that she herself falls within the statute's overbroad reach. The quotation from Harris actually refers to an entirely different kind of standing issue: there the plaintiffs lacked standing because they failed to allege that they were in a position either to seek abortions or to receive Medicaid, and thus they lacked the concrete adverseness necessary to advance their challenge to the Medicaid limit on abortion funding. None of the cases cited for this point in Harris apply to the instant appeal. See O'Shea v. Littleton, 414 U.S. 488 (1974) (plaintiffs lack standing because of failure to allege specific injury); Bailey v. Patterson, 369 U.S. 31, 32 (1962) (petitioners "lack standing to enjoin criminal prosecutions under Mississippi's breach-of-peace statutes, since they do not allege that they have been prosecuted or threatened with prosecution under them").

A standing limitation on overbreadth challenges to an abortion statute has roots in a context hardly analogous to the instant case. For while we have frequently ruled that criminal defendants lack standing to challenge a statute's overbreadth when their conduct indisputably falls within the statute's legitimate core, e. g., United States v. National Dairy Products Corp., 372 U.S. 29 (1963); United States v. Harriss, 347 U.S. 612 (1954); Williams v. United States, 341 U.S. 97 (1951), these rulings bear little relationship to appellant's challenge to a State's restriction of her exercise of a fundamental right. See Planned Parenthood of Central Mo. v. Danforth, 428 U.S. 52 (1976); Doe v. Bolton, 410 U.S. 179 (1973). More relevant, I believe, is our analysis of standing to claim that a statute's overbreadth affects fundamental liberties, primarily those guaranteed by the First Amendment. Because of the risk that exercise of personal freedoms may be chilled by broad regulation, we permit facial overbreadth challenges without a showing that the moving party's conduct falls within the protected core. Gooding v. Wilson, 405 U.S. 518 (1972); Coates v. Cincinnati, 402 U.S. 611 (1971); United States v. Robel, 389 U.S. 258 (1967); Shuttlesworth v. City of Birmingham, 394 U.S. 147 (1969); Cox v. Louisiana, 379 U.S. 536 (1965); Aptheker v. Secretary of State, 378 U.S. 500 (1964); Kunz v. New York, 340 U.S. 290 (1951). See also United States v. Reese, 92 U.S. 214 (1876) (facial challenge under Fifteenth Amendment).

[3] See n. 1, supra. The Court does not question that exceptions from a parental notice requirement are necessary for minors emancipated from the custody or control of their parents, see n. 48, infra, and for minors able to demonstrate their maturity for the purpose of choosing to have an abortion, ante, at 406-407. See also Bellotti II, 443 U.S., at 651 (POWELL, J.); id., at 653 (STEVENS, J.). Nor does the Court depart from the view, made explicit in JUSTICE POWELL'S opinion in Bellotti II, supra, at 651, that a State cannot require parental notice when it would not be in the minor's best interests to do so. This position is articulated anew today by JUSTICE POWELL, ante, at 420, and bolstered by the majority, which acknowledges the need for exception where parental notification interferes with emergency medical treatment, ante, at 407, n. 14, and which leaves open the possibility of relief where the minor makes a "claim or showing as to . . . her relations with her parents," ante, at 407, or demonstrates a "hostile home situatio[n]," ante, at 407,

n. 14. See also L. R. v. Hansen, Civil No. C-80-0078J (Utah, Feb. 8, 1980, and Oct. 24, 1980).

[4] It is especially noteworthy that we have not refrained from according to physicians, threatened with the personal risk of prosecution, standing to challenge abortion restrictions by asserting the rights of any of their patients. E. g., Planned Parenthood of Central Mo. v. Danforth, supra, at 62; Doe v. Bolton, supra; Griswold v. Connecticut, 381 U.S. 479 (1965).

[5] In the instant case, application of the prudential rule causes undue commingling of jurisdictional and merits issues. For here, the third-party interests do not even come into play until appellant wishes to rebut the State's interests, which themselves are asserted only after appellant has established a burden on her protected interests. First, the appellant must satisfy a court that, on the merits, her fundamental right to privacy in consulting her physician about an abortion is burdened by the Utah statute. Only then need the State assert its countervailing state interests, which here include promoting family autonomy and parental authority. And only in rebuttal would appellant next challenge as overbroad the means employed by the State, for the absolute ban regulates the abortion decision of emancipated and mature minors, and others whose best interests call for an abortion without parental notice. Thus, in the name of prudence, the majority's standing analysis depends upon its evaluation of the complicated merits.

[6] Appellant's consultation with three professionals casts substantial doubt on JUSTICE POWELL'S suggestion, see ante, at 418, that appellant "desires not to explain to anyone her reasons either for wanting the abortion or for not wanting to notify her parents."

[7] This portion of the transcript is set out in full ante, at 402-403, n. 6, 403, n. 7.

JUSTICE POWELL correctly reports, ante, at 416-417, that the in-chambers hearing elicited from appellant statements essentially identical to her complaint. And it is also true that counsel for appellant objected to inquiries by the appellees and the trial judge regarding appellant's exact reasons for not wanting to talk with her parents about her pregnancy or other matters. What JUSTICE POWELL neglects to note, however, is that counsel's objections stemmed from the trial court's own ruling that any facts specific to appellant's situation would be irrelevant to the physician's duty under the statute to notify her parents of an abortion decision. Because the trial judge ruled that the statute and its sanctions would apply regardless of the pregnant minor's personal reasons for opposing parental notification, the judge sustained the objections to questions about appellant's particular reasons. Tr. 14-20, App. 31-36. It is this ruling that is the legal basis for the decision below, and not the trial judge's preliminary comments cited by the majority, ante, at 403, n. 8.

[8] I also doubt the wisdom in pinning a minor's success in challenging a blanket parental notice requirement to consideration of her particular situation by judges, as opposed to others who are more regularly involved in the counselling of adolescents. Cf. Bellotti II, 443 U.S., at 655 -656 (STEVENS, J.).

[9] As the Court observed in Eisen v. Carlisle & Jacquelin, 417 U.S. 156, 176 (1974), the federal class action procedure "was intended to insure that the judgment, whether favorable or not, would bind all class members who did not request exclusion from the suit." The binding effect of the class action's disposition poses serious due process concerns where the interests of class members are not properly represented. 7A C. Wright & A. Miller, Federal Practice and Procedure 1765 (1972).

Where review of the claims asserted is impaired by an obvious lack of homogeneity in the class approved by the trial court, the reviewing court must remand "for reconsideration of the class definition," Kremens v. Bartley, 431 U.S. 119, 134 -135 (1977), and for a determination whether the named plaintiff is a proper representative of the class, Martin v. Thompson Tractor Co., 486 F.2d 510, 511 (CA5 1973).

[10] E. g., Bogus v. American Speech & Hearing Assn., 582 F.2d 277 (CA3 1978); Dellums v. Powell, 184 U.S. App. D.C. 275, 566 F.2d 167 (1977), cert. denied, 438 U.S. 916 (1978); Barnett v. W. T. Grant Co., 518 F.2d 543 (CA4 1975); Arkansas Ed. Assn. v. Board of Ed. of Portland, Arkansas School Dist., 446 F.2d 763 (CA8 1971); Gold Strike Stamp Co. v. Christensen, 436 F.2d 791 (CA10 1970).

It is difficult to conclude that the trial judge below in fact abused his discretion in approving the class. Other courts have approved similar classes represented by similar named plaintiffs, e. g., Gary-Northwest Indiana Women's Services v. Bowen, 421 F. Supp. 734 (ND Ind. 1976) (unmarried pregnant 16-year-old proper representative for class of unmarried pregnant minors under 18 challenging abortion restriction), summarily aff'd, 429 U.S. 1067 (1977). Conflict within the class, moreover, seems unlikely, for "it is difficult to imagine why any person in the class appellant represents would have an interest in seeing [the challenged statute] upheld." Sosna v. Iowa, 419 U.S. 393, 403, n. 13 (1975).

[11] A class may need to be redefined, e. g., Gesicki v. Oswald, 336 F. Supp. 371, 374 (SDNY 1971) (three-judge court), divided into subclasses, e. g., Francis v. Davidson, 340 F. Supp. 351 (Md. 1972) (three-judge court), or otherwise modified, to adequately protect its members' interests. See generally 7 Wright & Miller, supra, 1758-1771 (1972 and Supp. 1980).

The majority mistakenly assumes, ante, at 406, n. 13, that it is free to rewrite the class as approved by the trial court because that court based its class definition on submissions from the plaintiff. This assumption runs counter to the general practice in both state and federal courts whereby the party seeking class certification proposes a class definition which is then subject to challenge by the opposing party. See 1 H. Newberg, Class Actions 644 (1977); 5 id., at 1376, 1403. Appellees challenged the class without success, and the State Supreme Court never questioned the trial court's approval of appellant's class.

[12] See ante, at 420-421 (opinion of STEVENS, J.). JUSTICE POWELL reasons, ante, at 417, n. 6, that the class members cannot raise the overbreadth claims because the record fails to disclose that they wish to raise such claims. In my view, the record is quite

to the contrary. The class members, through their class representative, unequivocally raised in the complaint the overbreadth challenge to the Utah statute. Complaint § 17, App. 6. This claim, along with the other allegations in the complaint, provided the context in which the trial judge approved appellant as class representative. In so approving, the trial court was obliged to ensure that appellant's allegations would adequately protect the interests of the class members, who would be bound by the judgment. If a reviewing court subsequently alters the claims that can be asserted by the named plaintiff, protection of the class interests requires a remand for reconsideration of the adequacy of the named plaintiff as class representative.

[13] See also Carey v. Population Services International, 431 U.S. 678, 684 -685 (1977); Griswold v. Connecticut, 381 U.S., at 482 -485.

[14] Zablocki v. Redhail, 434 U.S. 374, 384 -386 (1978); Loving v. Virginia, 388 U.S. 1, 12 (1967).

[15] Skinner v. Oklahoma ex rel. Williamson, 316 U.S. 535 (1942). See also Cleveland Board of Education v. La Fleur, 414 U.S. 632 (1974).

[16] Eisenstadt v. Baird, 405 U.S. 438, 453 (1972); Griswold v. Connecticut, supra; Carey v. Population Services International, supra; Poe v. Ullman, 367 U.S. 497, 539 (1961) (Harlan, J., dissenting) (ban on contraception is "intolerable and unjustifiable invasion of privacy in the conduct of the most intimate concerns of an individual's personal life").

[17] See also Union Pacific R. Co. v. Botsford, 141 U.S. 250, 251 (1891) ("No right is held more sacred, or is more carefully guarded, by the common law, than the right of every individual to the possession and control of his own person, free from all restraint or interference of others, unless by clear and unquestionable authority of law").

[18] The right has often been termed "the right to be let alone." See Olmstead v. United States, 277 U.S. 438, 478 (1928) (Brandeis, J., dissenting) (quoted with approval in Stanley v. Georgia, 394 U.S. 557, 564 (1969), and Eisenstadt v. Baird, supra, at 453-454, n. 10). Defining the spheres within which the government may not act without sufficient justification, the notion of privacy "emanates from the totality of the constitutional scheme under which we live." Poe v. Ullman, supra, at 521 (Douglas, J., dissenting).

[19] "Constitutional rights do not mature and come into being magically only when one attains the state-defined age of majority. Minors, as well as adults, are protected by the Constitution and possess constitutional rights. See, e. g., Breed v. Jones, 421 U.S. 519 (1975); Goss v. Lopez, 419 U.S. 565 (1975); Tinker v. Des Moines School Dist., 393 U.S. 503 (1969); In re Gault, 387 U.S. 1 (1967). The Court indeed, however, long has recognized that the State has somewhat broader authority to regulate the activities of children than of adults. Prince v. Massachusetts, 321 U.S., at 170; Ginsberg v. New York, 390 U.S. 629 (1968)." Planned Parenthood of Central Mo. v. Danforth, 428 U.S., at 74 -75.

See also Brown v. Board of Education, 347 U.S. 483 (1954) (children entitled to equal protection in schools).

The privacy right does not necessarily guarantee that "every minor, regardless of age or maturity, may give effective consent for termination of her pregnancy." Planned Parenthood of Central Mo. v. Danforth, supra, at 75. Utah, however, assigns this consent authority to a woman of any age who seeks pregnancy-related medical care, Utah Code Ann. 78-14-5 (4) (f) (1977), subject to the State's informed consent requirements, see Utah Code Ann. 76-7-305 (1978); 78-14-5 (1977). This appeal does not present the broad issue of when may a State require parental consent for a surgical procedure on a minor child, 604 P.2d 907, 910, n. 5 (Utah 1979). At issue here is only the scope of the minor's constitutional privacy right in the face of a statutory parental notice requirement.

[20] In striking down a related Utah prohibition against family planning assistance for minors absent parental consent, a Federal District Court reasoned that the "financial, psychological and social problems arising from teenage pregnancy and motherhood argue for our recognition of the right of minors to privacy as being equal to that of adults." T. H. v. Jones, 425 F. Supp. 873, 881 (Utah 1975), summarily aff'd on other grounds, 425 U.S. 986 (1976).

[21] Appellees also argue that "[i]t is difficult to contemplate a relationship where the right of privacy as formulated in the abortion context could be less relevant than in the confines of the nuclear family." Brief for Appellees 22. This view, however, was expressly rejected in Planned Parenthood of Central Mo. v. Danforth, supra, at 75.

[22] Realization of this ideal, however, must depend on the quality of emotional attachments within the family, and not on legal patterns imposed by the State. See Quilloin v. Walcott, 434 U.S. 246, 255 (1978); Moore v. East Cleveland, 431 U.S., at 506 .

[23] Nothing prevents the physician from encouraging the minor to consult her parents; only the minor who strenuously objects will remain burdened by the notice requirement.

[24] The record here contains little about appellant's situation because the trial judge excluded any such evidence as irrelevant to the facial challenge to the mandatory notice requirement. In light of her claim that the notice requirement inhibits the exercise of her right to choose an abortion, however, we may surmise that appellant expects family conflict over the abortion decision. Indeed, the transcript of the evidentiary hearing, quoted ante, at 402-403, n. 6, 403, n. 7 (opinion of BURGER, C. J.), demonstrates that consultation with her social worker, her physician, and her lawyer did not alter appellant's steadfast belief that she could not discuss the issue with her parents.

The records in other cases are also instructive as to the interference posed by some parents to the exercise of some minor's privacy right. See L. R. v. Hansen, Civil No. C-80-0078J (Utah, Oct. 24, 1980) (preliminary relief awarded to minor alleging parent expelled from home minor sister who disclosed facts of pregnancy and abortion); see Women's Community Health Center, Inc. v. Cohen, 477 F. Supp. 542, 548 (Me. 1979) (expert affidavits that some parents "will pressure the minor, causing great emotional distress and otherwise disrupting the family relationship"); Baird v. Bellotti, 450 F. Supp.

997, 1001 (Mass. 1978) (uncontested evidence some parents "would insist on an undesired marriage, or on continuance of the pregnancy as punishment" or even physically harm the minor); Wynn v. Carey, 582 F.2d 1375, 1388, n. 24 (CA7 1978) (suggesting same problems); In re Diane, 318 A. 2d 629, 630 (Del. Ch. 1974) (father opposes minor's abortion on religious grounds); State v. Koome, 84 Wash. 2d 901, 908, 530 P.2d 260, 265 (1975) (parent thinks forcing daughter to bear child will deter her future pregnancies). See Margaret S. v. Edwards, 488 F. Supp. 181 (ED La. 1980). Parents also may oppose a minor's decision not to abort. E. g., In re Smith, 16 Md. App. 209, 295 A. 2d 238 (1972). See generally F. Furstenberg, Unplanned Parenthood: The Social Consequences of Teenage Childbearing 54 (1976); Jolly, Young, Female, and Outside the Law, in Teenage Women in the Juvenile Justice System: Changing Values 97, 102 (1979) ("When a young girl becomes pregnant, many families refuse to allow her back into their home"); Osofsky & Osofsky, Teenage Pregnancy: Psychosocial Considerations, 21 Clin. Obstet. Gynecol. 1161, 1164-1165 (1978). See also J. Bedger, Teenage Pregnancy 123-124 (1980) (large majority of sampled pregnant minors predict parental opposition to their abortions).

[25] Women's Community Health Center, Inc. v. Cohen, supra, at 548 (affidavits showing parental notice "may cause an adolescent to delay seeking assistance with her pregnancy, increasing the hazardousness of an abortion should she choose one"); Cates, Adolescent Abortions in the United States, 1 J. Adolescent Health Care 18, 24 (1980); Bracken & Kasl, Delay in Seeking Induced Abortion: A Review and Theoretical Analysis, 121 Am. J. Obstet. Gynecol. 1008, 1013 (1975); Hofmann, Consent and Confidentiality and Their Legal and Ethical Implications for Adolescent Medicine, in Medical Care of the Adolescent 42, 51 (J. Gallagher, F. Heald & D. Garell eds., 3d ed. 1976).

If she decides to abort after the first trimester of pregnancy, the minor faces more serious health risks. Roe v. Wade, 410 U.S. 113, 163 (1973); Benditt, Second-Trimester Abortion in the United States, 11 Family Planning Perspectives 358 (1979); Cates, Schulz, Crimes, & Tyler, The Effect of Delay and Method Choice on the Risk of Abortion Morbidity, 9 Family Planning Perspectives 266 (1977). If she decides to bear the child, her health risks are also greater than if she had a first trimester abortion. Cates, 1 J. Adolescent Health Care, supra, at 24; Cates & Tietze, Standardized Mortality Rates Associated with Legal Abortion: United States 1972-1975, 10 Family Planning Perspectives 109 (1978) (abortion within first 16 weeks of pregnancy safer than carrying pregnancy to term); "The Earlier the Safer" Applies to all Abortions, 10 Family Planning Perspectives 243 (1978). See also Zackler, Andelman, & Bauer, The Young Adolescent as an Obstetric Risk, 103 Am. J. Obstet. Gynecol. 305 (1969) (complications associated with childbirth by minors).

[26] Women's Community Health Center, Inc. v. Cohen, supra, at 548 (affidavits that minor may turn to illegal abortion rather than have parents notified). See also Kahan, Baker, & Freeman, The Effect of Legalized Abortion on Morbidity Resulting from Criminal Abortion, 121 Am. J. Obstet. Gynecol. 114 (1975) (illegal abortion rate drops

when legal abortion available). The minor may also seek to abort herself, Alice v. Department of Social Welfare, 55 Cal. App. 3d 1039, 1044, 128 Cal. Rptr. 374, 377 (1976); A. Holder, Legal Issues in Pediatrics and Adolescent Medicine 285 (1977); or even commit suicide, see Teicher, A Solution to the Chronic Problem of Living: Adolescent Attempted Suicide, in Current Issues in Adolescent Psychiatry 129, 136 (J. Schoolar ed. 1973) (study showing that approximately one-fourth of female minors who attempt suicide do so because they are or believe they are pregnant).

[27] It is the presence of the notice requirement, and not merely its implementation in a particular case, that signifies the intrusion. Cf. Planned Parenthood of Central Mo. v. Danforth, 428 U.S. 52 (1976) (availability of veto, not exercise of veto, found unconstitutional).

Despite the Court's objection today that we have in the past "expressly declined to equate notice requirements with consent requirements," ante, at 411, n. 17, in Bellotti II the Court rejected a statute authorizing judicial review of a minor's abortion decision - as an alternative to parental consent - precisely because a parent notified of the court action might interfere. Thus, JUSTICE POWELL wrote for four Members of the Court: "[A]s the District Court recognized, `there are parents who would obstruct, and perhaps altogether prevent, the minor's right to go to court.' . . . There is no reason to believe that this would be so in the majority of cases where consent is withheld. But many parents hold strong views on the subject of abortion, and young pregnant minors, especially those living at home, are particularly vulnerable to their parents' efforts to obstruct both an abortion and their access to court." 443 U.S., at 647 .

[28] Thus, the notice requirement produces not only predictable disincentives to choose to abort, Harris v. McRae, 448 U.S., at 338 (MARSHALL, J., dissenting); id., at 330 (BRENNAN, J., dissenting); but also "`direct state interference with a protected activity,'" id., at 315 (quoting with approval Maher v. Roe, 432 U.S. 464, 475 (1977)).

[29] See Doe v. Bolton, 410 U.S. 179 (1973) (invalidating procedural restrictions on availability of abortions); Carey v. Population Services International, 431 U.S., at 687 - 689 (partial restrictions on access to contraceptives subject to constitutional challenge). Regardless of the personal views each of us may hold, the privacy right by definition secures latitude of choice for the pregnant minor without state approval of one decision over another. Thus, JUSTICE STEVENS improperly inverts the reasoning of our decisions when he reiterates his previous view that the importance of the abortion decision points to a "`State's interest in maximizing the probability that the decision be made correctly and with full understanding of the consequences of either alternative,'" ante, at 422 (emphasis added).

[30] See text accompanying n. 8 and see nn. 20, 24, 25, supra.

[31] Utah permits pregnant minors to consent to any medical procedure in connection with pregnancy and childbirth, but requires parental notice only before an abortion. Compare Utah Code Ann. 78-14-5 (4) (f) (1977) with 76-7-304 (2) (1978).

[32] 428 U.S., at 75 . Cf. Zablocki v. Redhail, 434 U.S., at 388; NAACP v. Button,

371 U.S. 415, 438 (1963). In Roe v. Wade, this Court concluded that the woman's privacy right may be tempered by "important [state] interests," 410 U.S., at 154, but the Court ultimately applied the "compelling state interest" test commonly used in reviewing state burdens on fundamental rights. Id., at 155. Although it may seem that the minor's privacy right is somehow less fundamental because it may be overcome by a "significant state interest," the more sensible view is that state interests inapplicable to adults may justify burdening the minor's right. Planned Parenthood of Central Mo. v. Danforth, supra, at 74-75.

[33] E. g., Roe v. Wade, supra, at 155; Griswold v. Connecticut, 381 U.S., at 485 .

[34] Appellees also argue that the notice requirement furthers legitimate state interests in enforcing Utah's criminal laws against statutory rape, fornication, adultery, and incest. Brief for Appellees 28-30. These interests were not asserted below, and are too tenuous to be considered seriously here.

[35] 604 P.2d, at 909-910.

[36] Section 76-7-304 (1) requires the physician to

"Consider all factors relevant to the well-being of the woman upon whom the abortion is to be performed including, but not limited to,

"(a) Her physical, emotional and psychological health and safety,

"(b) Her age,

"(c) Her familial situation."

Violations of this requirement are punishable by a year's imprisonment and $1,000 fine. Utah Code Ann. 76-3-204 (1), 76-3-301 (3), 76-7-314 (3) (1978). Criminal sanctions also apply if the physician neglects to obtain the minor's informed written consent, and such consent can be secured only after the physician has notified the patient:

"(a) Of the names and addresses of two licensed adoption agencies in the state of Utah and the services that can be performed by those agencies, and nonagency adoption may be legally arranged; and

"(b) Of the details of development of unborn children and abortion procedures, including any foreseeable complications, risks, and the nature of the post-operative recuperation period; and

"(c) Of any other factors he deems relevant to a voluntary and informed consent." Utah Code Ann. 76-7-305 (2) (1978).

The risk of malpractice suits also ensures that the physician will acquire whatever information he finds necessary before performing the abortion. See Utah Code Ann. 78-14-5 (1977).

Moreover, "[i]f a physician is licensed by the State, he is recognized by the State as capable of exercising acceptable clinical judgment. If he fails in this, professional censure and deprivation of his license are available remedies." Doe v. Bolton, 410 U.S., at 199 .

[37] The parties conceded as much at oral argument. Tr. of Oral Arg. 18-19, 29,

48.

[38] I am baffled by the majority's statement today that "[i]f the pregnant girl elects to carry her child to term, the medical decisions to be made entail few - perhaps none - of the potentially grave and emotional and psychological consequences of the decision to abort," ante, at 412-413. Choosing to participate in diagnostic tests involves risks to both mother and child, and also may burden the pregnant woman with knowledge that the child will be handicapped. See 3 National Institutes of Health, Prevention of Embryonic, Fetal, and Perinatal Disease 347-352 (R. Brent & M. Harris eds. 1976); Risks in the Practice of Modern Obstetrics 59-81, 369-370 (S. Aladjem ed. 1975). The decision to undergo surgery to save the child's life certainly carries as serious "emotional and psychological consequences" for the pregnant adolescent as does the decision to abort; in both instances, the minor confronts the task of calculating not only medical risks, but also all the issues involved in giving birth to a child. See id., at 59-81. For an unwed adolescent, these issues include her future educational and job opportunities, as well as the more immediate problems of finding financial and emotional support for offspring dependent entirely on her. Michael M. v. Sonoma County Superior Court, post, at 470, and nn. 3 and 4 (REHNQUIST, J.) (plurality opinion). When surgery to save the child's life poses greater risks to the mother's life, the emotional and ethical dimensions of the medical care decision assume crisis proportion. Of course, for minors, the mere fact of pregnancy and the experience of childbirth can produce psychological upheaval.

[39] More flexible regulations which defer to the physician's judgment but provide for parental notice in emergencies have been proposed. E. g., IJA-ABA Standards for Juvenile Justice, Rights of Minors 4.2, 4.6, 4.8 (1980) (minor can consent to pregnancy-related medical care; physician should seek to obtain minor's permission to notify parent, and notify parent over minor's objection only if failure to inform "could seriously jeopardize the health of the minor").

[40] 604 P.2d, at 912 ("the State has a special interest in encouraging (but does not require) an unmarried pregnant minor to seek the advice of her parents in making the important decision as to whether or not to bear a child").

[41] Ibid. (notification statute "does not per se impose any restriction on the minor as to her decision to terminate her pregnancy"). Cf. Utah Code Ann. 78-14-5 (4) (f) (1977) (woman of any age can consent to any medical care related to pregnancy). See generally Planned Parenthood of Central Mo. v. Danforth, 428 U.S., at 74 (State may not delegate absolute veto authority to parents of pregnant minor seeking abortion).

[42] State-sponsored counseling services, in contrast, could promote family dialogue and also improve the minor's decisionmaking process. Appellant H. L., for example, consulted with a counselor who supported her decision. The role of counselors can be significant in facilitating the pregnant woman's adjustment to decisions related to her pregnancy. See Smith, A Follow-Up Study of Women Who Request Abortion, 43 Am. J. Orthopsychiatry 574, 583-585 (1973).

[43] This interest, although not discussed by the state courts below, was the subject of appellees' most vigorous argument before this Court. The challenged provision does fall within the "Offenses Against the Family" chapter of the Utah Criminal Code, ante, at 400 (opinion of BURGER, C. J.), which also provides criminal sanctions for bigamy, Utah Code Ann. 76-7-101, incest, 76-7-102, adultery, 76-7-103, fornication, 76-7-104, and nonsupport and sale of children, 76-7-201 to 76-7-203 (1978).

[44] Wynn v. Carey, 582 F.2d, at 1385-1386; Note, The Minor's Right of Privacy: Limitations on State Action after Danforth and Carey, 77 Colum. L. Rev 1216, 1224 (1977).

[45] "The fact that the minor became pregnant and sought an abortion contrary to the parents' wishes indicates that whatever control the parent once had over the minor has diminished, if not evaporated entirely. And we believe that enforcing a single, albeit important, parental decision - at a time when the minor is near to majority status - by an instrument as blunt as a state statute is extremely unlikely to restore parental control." Poe v. Gerstein, 517 F.2d 787, 793-794 (CA5 1975), summarily aff'd, 428 U.S. 901 (1976).

[46] Thus, in Prince v. Massachusetts, this Court held that even parental rights protected by the First Amendment could be limited by the State's interest in prohibiting child labor. See Wisconsin v. Yoder, 406 U.S. 205, 233 -234 (1972) (discussing Prince). The State traditionally exercises a parens patriae function in protecting those who cannot take care of themselves. See Ginsberg v. New York, 390 U.S. 629, 641 (1968). Some of the earliest applications of parens patriae protected children against their "objectionable" parents. E. g., Wellesley v. Wellesley, 2 Bli. N. S. 124, 133-134, 4 Eng. Rep. 1078, 1082 (H. L. 1828). See generally Kleinfeld, The Balance of Power Among Infants, Their Parents and the State, Part III, 5 Family L. Q. 64, 66-71 (1971). Every State has enacted legislation to defend children from parental abuse. Wilcox, Child Abuse Laws: Past, Present, and Future, 21 J. Forensic Sciences 71, 72 (1976).

[47] The contexts in which this issue may arise are too varied to support any general rule. Appellees cite our recent decision in Parham v. J. R., 442 U.S. 584 (1979), to support their claim that parents should be presumed competent to be involved in their minor daughter's abortion decision. That decision is inapposite to this case in several respects. First, the minor child in Parham who was committed to a mental hospital was presumed incompetent to make the commitment decision himself. Id., at 623 (STEWART, J., concurring in judgment). In contrast, appellant by statute is presumed competent to make the decision about whether to complete or abort her pregnancy. Furthermore, in Parham, the Court placed critical reliance on the ultimately determinative, independent review of the commitment decision by medical experts. Here, the physician's independent medical judgment - that an abortion was in appellant's best medical interest - not only was not ultimate, it was defeated by the notice requirement. Finally, as JUSTICE STEWART emphasized in his opinion concurring in the judgment in Parham, the pregnant minor has a "personal substantive . . . right" to decide on an abortion. Id., at 623-624, n. 6.

[48] Most States through their legislature or courts have adopted the common-

law principle that a minor may become freed of the disabilities of that status - and at the same time release his parents from their parental obligations - prior to the actual date of his majority. Certain acts, in and of themselves, may occasion emancipation. See, e. g., Cal. Civ. Code Ann. 62 (West 1954 and Supp. 1981) (emancipation upon marriage or entry in Armed Services); Utah Code Ann. 15-2-1 (Supp. 1979) (emancipation upon marriage); Crook v. Crook, 80 Ariz. 275, 296 P.2d 951 (1956) (same). A minor may become partially emancipated if he is partially self-supporting, but still entitled to some parental assistance. See Katz, Schroeder, & Sidman, Emancipating Our Children - Coming of Legal Age in America, 7 Fam. L. Q. 211, 215 (1973). Several States by statute permit emancipation for a specific purpose, such as obtaining medical care without parental consent, e. g., Cal. Civ. Code Ann. 34.6 (West Supp. 1981); Mont. Code Ann. 41-1-402 (1979) (woman of any age may consent to pregnancy-related medical care); Utah Code Ann. 78-14-5 (4) (f) (1977) (same), 26-6-39.1 (1976) (minor can consent to medical treatment for venereal disease); Tex. Rev. Civ. Stat. Ann., Art. 4447i (Vernon 1976) (person at least 13 years old may consent to medical treatment for drug dependency). See Pilpel, Minors' Rights to Medical Care, 36 Albany L. Rev. 462 (1972). Several States provide for emancipation once the individual becomes a parent. E. g., Ky. Rev. Stat. 214-185 (2) (1977). In Utah, minors who become parents are authorized to make all medical care decisions for their offspring. Utah Code Ann. 78-14-5 (4) (a) (1977). See generally Cohen v. Delaware, L. & W. R. Co., 150 Misc. 450, 453-457, 269 N. Y. S. 667, 671-676 (1934); L. R. v. Hansen, No. C-80-0078J (Utah, Feb. 8, 1980) (self-supporting minor seeking abortion is emancipated and mature); Goldstein, Medical Care for the Child at Risk: On State Supervention of Parental Autonomy, 86 Yale L. J. 645, 663 (1977) (recommending objective criteria to avoid case-by-case determination of emancipation).

[49] The "mature minor" doctrine permits a child to consent to medical treatment if he is capable of appreciating its nature and consequences. E. g., L. R. v. Hansen, supra (this mature minor "is capable of understanding her condition and making an informed decision which she has done after carefully considering the alternatives available to her and consulting the persons with whom she felt she should consult" prior to abortion decision); Ark. Stat. Ann. 82-363 (g) (1976). See Lacey v. Laird, 166 Ohio St. 12, 139 N. E. 2d 25 (1956) (physician not liable for battery after acting with minor's consent); Smith v. Seibly, 72 Wash. 2d 16, 21-22, 431 P.2d 719, 723 (1967); Younts v. St. Francis Hosp. & School of Nursing, Inc., 205 Kan. 292, 300-301, 469 P.2d 330, 337 (1970).

Four Members of this Court embraced the "mature minor" concept in striking down a statute requiring parental notice and consent to a minor's abortion, regardless of her own maturity. Bellotti II, 443 U.S., at 643 -644, and nn. 22 and 23. In Bellotti II, JUSTICE POWELL's opinion for four Members of this Court suggested that a statute could withstand constitutional attack if it permitted case-by-case administrative or judicial determination of a pregnant minor's capacity to make an abortion decision with her physician and independent of her parents. Ibid. Because this view was expressed in a case not involving such a statute, and because it would expose the minor to the arduous and public rigors of administrative or judicial process, four other Members of this Court rejected it as advisory and at odds with the privacy interest at stake. Id., at 654-656, and n. 4 (STEVENS, J., joined by BRENNAN, MARSHALL, and BLACKMUN, JJ.). Nonetheless, even under JUSTICE POWELL's reasoning in Bellotti II, the instant statute is unconstitutional. Not only does it preclude case-by-case consideration of the maturity of the minor, it also prevents individualized review to determine whether parental notice would be harmful to the minor.

[50] E. g., Ky. Rev. Stat. 214.185 (3) (1977); Utah Code Ann. 26-31-8 (1976); 1979 Utah Laws, ch. 98, 7. The need for emergency medical care may even overcome the religious objections of the parents. E. g., In re Clark, 21 Ohio Op. 2d 86, 89-90, 185 N. E. 2d 128, 131-132 (Com. Pl., Lucas County 1962); In re Sampson, 65 Misc. 2d 658, 317 N. Y. S. 2d 641 (Family Ct.), aff'd, 37 App. Div. 2d 668, 323 N. Y. S. 2d 253 (1970); Mass. Gen. Laws. Ann., ch. 112, 12F (West Supp. 1981); Miss. Code Ann. 41-41-7 (1972). Delay in treating nonemergency health needs may, of course, produce an emergency, and for that reason, this Court found statutory provision for emergency but not nonemergency care illogical. Memorial Hospital v. Maricopa County, 415 U.S. 250, 261, 265 (1974). In asserting that the Utah statute would not apply to minors with emergency health care needs, the Court fails to point to anything in the statute, the record, or Utah case law to the contrary. The Supreme Court of Utah addressed only one kind of emergency: where the parents cannot be physically located in sufficient time to permit performance of the abortion. 604 P.2d, at 913. The court rejected any other emergency situation as an exception to the statute when it declined to afford a broad interpretation of the phrase, "if possible," which modifies the notice requirement. Even where the emergency is simply that the parents cannot be reached, the statute applies; the physician subject to its sanction merely has been granted an affirmative defense that he exercised "reasonable diligence" in attempting to locate and notify the parents. Ibid. The majority purports to draw support for its view of the Utah statute on this point from a Massachusetts statute, construed by the Massachusetts Supreme Judicial Court, see ante, at 407, n. 14.

[51] As one medical authority observed: "One can well argue that an adolescent old enough to make the decision to be sexually active . . ., and who is then responsible enough to seek professional assistance for his or her problem, is ipso facto mature enough to consent to his own health care." Hofmann, supra n. 25, at 51. See Goldstein, 86 Yale L. J., at 633.

[52] Utah Code Ann. 78-14-5 (4) (f) (1977).

[53] Utah Code Ann. 76-7-305 (1978) requires voluntary and informed written consent. See n. 36, supra.

[54] Cf. Wynn v. Carey, 582 F.2d, at 1388.

The Commission may be obliged to hold a hearing: Justice Marshall's dissent in Federal Communications Commission v. WNCN Listeners Guild (March 24, 1981)

JUSTICE MARSHALL, with whom JUSTICE BRENNAN joins, dissenting.

Under §§ 309(a) and 310(d) of the Communications Act of 1934, 48 Stat. 1064, as amended, 47 U.S.C. § 151 et seq. (Act), the Federal Communications Commission (Commission) may not approve an application for a radio license transfer, assignment, or renewal unless it finds that such change will serve "the public interest, convenience, and necessity." [1] Any party in interest may petition the Commission to deny the application, § 309(d)(1), and the Commission must hold hearing if "a substantial and material question of fact is presented," § 309(d)(2). In my judgment, the Court of Appeals correctly held that, in certain limited circumstances, the Commission may be obliged to hold a hearing to consider whether a proposed change in a licensee's entertainment program format is in the "public interest." [2] Accordingly, I would affirm the Judgment of the Court of Appeals insofar as it vacated the Commission's "Policy Statement." [3]

I

At the outset, I should point out that my understanding of the Court of Appeals' format cases is very different from the Commission's. [4] Both in its Policy Statement and in its brief before this Court, the Commission has insisted that the format doctrine espoused by the Court of Appeals "favor[s] a system of pervasive governmental regulation," [5] requiring "comprehensive, discriminating, and continuing state surveillance.'" [6]

The Commission further contends that enforcement of the format doctrine would impose "common carrier" obligations on broadcasters and substitute for "the imperfect system of free competition . . . a system of broadcast programming by government decree." [7] Were this an accurate description of the format doctrine, I would join the Court in reversing the judgment below. [8] However, I agree with the Court of Appeals that "the actual features of [its format doctrine] are scarcely visible in [the Commission's] highly colored portrait." 197 U.S.App.D.C. 319, 332, 610 F.2d 838, 851 (1979).

In fact, the Court of Appeals accepted the Commission's conclusion that entertainment program formats should ordinarily be left to competitive forces. The court emphasized that the format doctrine "was not intended as an alternative to format allocation by market forces," and "fully recognized that market forces do generally provide diversification of formats." Ibid. (Emphasis in original.) It explained that

"the Commission's obligation to consider format issues arises only when there is strong prima facie evidence that the market has, in fact, broken down,"

ibid., and suggested that a breakdown in the market may be inferred when notice of a format change "precipitate[s] an outpouring of protest," id. at 323, 610 F.2d at 842, or "significant public grumbling," ibid. The Court of Appeals further stated that

"[n]o public interest issue is raised if (1) there is an adequate substitute in the service area for the format being abandoned, (2) there dissenting is no substantial support for the endangered format as evidenced by an outcry of public protest, (3) the devotees of the endangered format are too few to be served by the available frequencies, or (4) the format is not financially viable."

Id. at 332, 610 F.2d at 851. Finally, the Court of Appeals indicated that the Commission's obligation to hold an evidentiary hearing is limited to those situations in which the record presents substantial questions of material fact. Id. at 324, 610 F.2d at 843. The Court of Appeals thus made clear that the format doctrine comes into play only in a few limited situations. Consequently, the issue presented by these cases is not whether the Commission may adopt a general policy of relying on licensee discretion and market forces to ensure diversity in entertainment programming formats. Rather, the question before us is whether the Commission may apply its general policy on format changes indiscriminately, and without regard to the effect in particular cases.

II

Although the Act does not define "public interest, convenience, and necessity," it is difficult to quarrel with the basic premise of the Court of Appeals' format cases that the term includes "a concern for diverse entertainment programming." Id. at 323, 610 F.2d at 842. [9] This Court has indicated that one of the Act's goals is "to secure the maximum benefits of radio to all the people of the United States." National Broadcasting Co. v. United States, 319 U. S. 190, 319 U. S. 217 (1943). [10]

And we have recognized "the long-established regulatory goals of . . . diversification of programming." FCC v. Midwest Video Corp., 440 U. S. 689, 440 U. S. 699 (1979). At the same time, our cases have acknowledged that the Commission enjoys broad discretion in determining how best to accomplish this goal. See FCC v. National Citizens Committee for Broadcasting, 436 U. S. 775 (1978); National Broadcasting Co. v. United States, supra. The Commission has concluded that a general policy of relying on market forces is the best method for promoting diversity in entertainment programming formats. As the majority notes, ante at 450 U. S. 595, this determination largely rests on the Commission's predictions about licensee behavior and the functioning of the radio broadcasting market.

I agree with the majority that predictions of this sort are within the Commission's institutional competence. I am also willing to assume that a general policy of disregarding format changes in making the "public interest" determination required by the Act is not inconsistent with the Commission's statutory obligation to give individualized consideration to each application. The Commission has broad rulemaking powers under the Act, [11] and we have approved efforts by the Commission to implement the Act's "public interest" requirement through rules and policies of general application. See, e.g., FCC v. National Citizens Committee for Broadcasting, supra; United States v. Storer Broadcasting Co., 351 U. S. 192 (1956); National Broadcasting Co. v. United States, supra.

The problem with the particular Policy Statement challenged here, however, is that it lacks the flexibility we have required of such general regulations and policies. See, e.g., United States v. Storer Broadcasting Co., supra; National Broadcasting Co. v. United States, supra. The Act imposes an affirmative duty on the Commission to make a particularized "public interest" determination for each application that comes before it. As we explained in National Broadcasting Co. v. United States, supra at 319 U. S. 225, the Commission must, in each case, "exercise an ultimate judgment whether the grant of a license would serve the public interest, convenience, or necessity.'" The Policy Statement completely forecloses any possibility that the Commission will reexamine the validity of its general policy on format changes as it applies to particular situations. Thus, even when it can be conclusively demonstrated that a particular radio market does not function in the manner predicted by the Commission, the Policy Statement indicates that the Commission will blindly assume that a proposed format change is in the "public interest." This result would occur even where reliance on the market to ensure format diversity is shown to be misplaced, and where it thus appears that action by the Commission is necessary to promote the public interest in diversity. This outcome is not consistent with the Commission's statutory responsibilities.

Moreover, our cases have indicated that an agency's discretion to proceed in complex areas through general rules is intimately connected to the existence of a "safety valve" procedure that allows the agency to consider applications for exemptions based on special circumstances. See E. I. du Pont de Nemours Co. v. Train, 430 U. S. 112, 430 U. S. 128 (1977); Permian Basin Area Rate Cases, 390 U. S. 747, 390 U. S. 771-772 (1968); FPC v. Texaco Inc., 377 U. S. 33, 377 U. S. 40-41 (1964); United States v. Storer Broadcasting Co., supra at 351 U. S. 204-205; National Broadcasting Co. v. United States, supra at 319 U. S. 207, 319 U. S. 225. See also WAIT Radio v. FCC, 135 U.S.App.D.C. 317, 321, 418 F.2d 1153, 1157 (1969); American Airlines v. CAB, 123 U.S.App. D C. 310, 359 F.2d 624 (en banc), cert. denied, 385 U.S. 843 (1966); WBEN, Inc. v. United States, 396 F.2d 601, 618 (CA2), cert. denied, 393 U.S. 914 (1968).

For example, in National Broadcasting Co. v. United States, supra, we upheld the Commission's Chain Broadcasting Regulations, but we emphasized the need for flexibility in administering the rules. We noted that the

"Commission provided that 'networks will be given full opportunity, on proper application . . . to call our attention to any reasons why the principle should be modified or held inapplicable.'"

Id. at 319 U. S. 207. And we concluded:

"The Commission therefore did not bind itself inflexibly to the licensing policies expressed in the regulations. In each case that comes before it, the Commission must still exercise an ultimate judgment whether the grant of a license would serve the 'public interest, convenience, or necessity.' If time and changing circumstances reveal that the 'public interest' is not served by application of the Regulations, it must be assumed that the Commission will act in accordance with its statutory obligations."

Id. at 319 U. S. 225. Similarly, in upholding the Commission's Multiple Ownership Rules in United States v. Storer Broadcasting Co., supra, we noted that the regulations allowed an opportunity for a "full hearing" for applicants "that set out adequate reasons why the Rules should be waived or amended." Id. at 205. [12]

This "safety valve" feature is particularly essential where, as here, the agency's decision that a general policy promotes the public interest is based on predictions and forecasts that, by definition, lack complete factual support. As the Court of Appeals admonished the Commission in a related context:

"the Commission is charged with administration in the 'public interest.' That an agency may discharge its responsibilities by promulgating rules of general application which, in the overall perspective, establish the 'public interest' for a broad range of situations, does not relieve it of an obligation to seek out the 'public interest' in particular, individualized cases. A general rule implies that a commission need not re-study the entire problem de novo and reconsider policy every time it receives an application for a waiver of the rule. On the other hand, a general rule, deemed valid because its overall objectives are in the public interest, may not be in the 'public interest' if extended to an applicant who proposes a new service that will not undermine the policy, served by the rule, that has been adjudged in the public interest."

WAIT Radio v. FCC, supra at 321, 418 F.2d at 1157.

In my judgment, this requirement of flexibility compels the Commission to provide a procedure through which listeners can attempt to show that a particular radio market differs from the Commission's paradigm, and thereby persuade the Commission to give particularized consideration to a proposed format change. Indeed, until the Policy Statement was published, the Commission had resolved to

"take an extra hard look at the reasonableness of any proposal which would deprive a community of its only source of a particular type of programming. [13]"

As I see it, the Court of Appeals' format doctrine was merely an attempt by that court to delineate the circumstances in which the Commission must temper its general policy in view of special circumstances. Perhaps the court would have been better advised to leave the task of defining these situations to the Commission. [14] But one need not endorse every feature of the Court of Appeals' approach to conclude that the court correctly invalidated the Commission's Policy Statement because of its omission of a "safety valve" procedure.

This omission is not only a departure from legal precedents; it is also a departure both from the Commission's consistent policies and its admissions here. For the Commission concedes that the radio market is an imperfect reflection of listener preferences, [15] and that listeners have programming interests that may not be reflected in the marketplace. The Commission has long recognized its obligation to examine program formats in making the "public interest" determination required by the Act. As early as 1929, the Commission's predecessor, the Federal Radio Commission, adopted the position that licensees were expected to provide a balanced program schedule designed to serve all substantial groups in their communities. Great Lakes Broadcasting Co., 3 F.R.C.Ann.Rep. 32, 34, rev'd on other grounds, 37 F.2d 993, cert. dism'd, 281 U.S. 706

(1929). The Commission's famous "Blue Book," [16] published in 1946, reaffirmed the emphasis on a well-balanced program structure and declared that the Commission has "an affirmative duty, in its public interest determinations, to give full consideration to program service." [17] As the Commission explained:

"It has long been an established policy of broadcasters themselves and of the Commission that the American system of broadcasting must serve significant minorities among our population, and the less dominant needs and tastes which most listeners have from time to time. [18]"

This theme was reiterated in the Commission's 1960 Program Statement, [19] which set forth 14 specific categories of programming that were deemed "major elements usually necessary to meet the public interest, needs and desires of the community," [20] and which emphasized the necessity of each broadcaster's programming serving the "tastes and needs" of its local community. [21] To ensure that licensee programming serves the needs of the community, the Commission has, for example, decreed that licensees have a special obligation to provide programs for children, even going so far as to declare that licensees must provide "a reasonable amount of [children's] programming which is designed to educate and inform -- and not simply to entertain." [22]

Moreover, in examining renewal applications, the Commission has considered claims that a licensee does not provide adequate children's programming, [23] or programming for women and children, [24] or for a substantial Spanish-American community, [25] or that the licensee has ignored issues of significance to the Negro community [26] or has not provided programming of specific interest to residents of a particular area. [27] In each case, the Commission reviewed submissions ranging from general summaries to transcripts of programs, to determine whether the licensee's programming met the public interest standard.

There is an obvious inconsistency between the Commission's recognition that the "public interest" standard requires it to consider licensee programming in the situations described above and its Policy Statement on review of entertainment program formats. Indeed, the sole instance in which the Commission will not consider listener complaints about programming is when they pertain to proposed changes in entertainment program formats. The Policy Statement attempts to explain this exceptional treatment of format changes by drawing a distinction between entertainment and nonentertainment programming. The Policy Statement suggests that the Commission reviews only nonentertainment programming, and, even then, only in special circumstances. Thus, the Policy Statement argues that the fairness doctrine and political broadcasting rules issued pursuant to § 315, 47 U.S.C. § 315, allow the Commission to exercise direct control of programming. In these areas, reasons the Statement, the Commission's role

"is limited to directing the licensee to broadcast some additional material so as not to completely ignore the viewpoints of others in the community. [28]"

This "limited involvement in licensee decisionmaking in the area of news and public affairs" [29] is contrasted, in the Commission's view, to "the pervasive, censorial nature of the involvement in format regulation." [30] The majority presumably concludes that the Commission has provided a rational explanation for distinguishing between entertainment and nonentertainment programming. With all due respect, I disagree.

In the first place, the distinction the Commission tries to draw between entertainment and nonentertainment programming is questionable. It is not immediately apparent, for example, why children's programming necessarily falls on the "nonentertainment" side of the spectrum, and the Commission has provided no explanation of how it decides the category to which particular programming belongs. Second, I see no reason why the Commission's review of entertainment programming cannot be as limited as its review of nonentertainment programming. Nothing prevents the Commission from limiting its role in reviewing format changes to "directing the licensee to broadcast additional material," thereby ensuring that the viewpoints of listeners who complain about a proposed format change are not completely ignored. Third, and most important, neither the fairness doctrine nor the political broadcasting rules have anything to do with the various situations described above in which the Commission has not hesitated to consider program formats in making the "public interest" determination. The fairness doctrine imposes an obligation on licensees to devote a "reasonable percentage" of broadcast time to controversial issues of public importance, and it requires that the coverage be fair in that it accurately reflect the opposing views. See Red Lion Broadcasting Co. v. FCC, 395 U. S. 367 (1069). The political broadcasting rules regulate broadcasts by candidates for federal and nonfederal public office. See The Law of Political Broadcasting and Cablecasting, 69 F.C.C.2d 2209 (1978). The Commission's examination of whether a broadcaster's format includes programming directed at women or at residents of the local community, or its requirement that licensees provide programming designed to serve the unique needs of children, simply has nothing to do with either the fairness doctrine or the political broadcasting rules. Thus, the Commission's purported justification for its inconsistency is no explanation at all, and I am puzzled by the majority's apparent conclusion that it provides a rational basis for the Commission's policy.

The majority attempts to minimize the inconsistency in the Commission's treatment of entertainment and nonentertainment programming by postulating that the difference "is not as pronounced as it may seem," ante at 450 U. S. 602. This observation, even if accurate, is simply beside the point. What is germane is the Commission's failure to consider listener complaints about entertainment programming to the same extent and in the same manner as it reviews complaints about nonentertainment programming. Thus, whereas the Commission will hold an evidentiary hearing to review complaints about nonentertainment programming where "it appears that the licensee has . . . act[ed] unreasonably or in bad faith,'" ibid. (quoting Mississippi Authority for Educational TV, 71 F.C.C.2d 1296, 1308 (1979)), the Commission will not consider an identical complaint about a licensee's change in its entertainment programming. As I have indicated, see supra at 450 U. S. 614-616, neither the Commission nor the majority is able to offer a satisfactory explanation for this inconsistency.

Nor can the Commission find refuge in its claim that,

"'[e]ven after all relevant facts [h]ad been fully explored in an evidentiary hearing, [the Commission] would have no assurance that a decision finally reached by [the Commission] would contribute more to listener satisfaction than the result favored by station management.'"

Policy Statement, 60 F.C.C.2d 858, 865 (1976), quoting Notice of Inquiry, 57 F.C.C.2d 580, 586 (1976). The same must be true of the decisions the Commission makes after reviewing listener complaints about nonentertainment programming, and I do not see why the Commission finds this result acceptable in one situation but not in the other. Much the same can be said for the majority's suggestion that the Commission should be spared the burden of "presuming to grasp, measure and weigh . . . elusive and difficult factors" such as determining the number of listeners who favor a particular change and measuring the intensity of their preferences, ante at 450 U. S. 601. But insofar as the Commission confronts these same "elusive and difficult factors" in reviewing nonentertainment programming, it need only apply the expertise it has acquired in dealing with these problems to review of entertainment programming.

III

Since I agree with the Court of Appeals that there may be situations in which the Commission is obliged to consider format changes in making the "public interest" determination mandated by the Act, it seems appropriate to comment briefly on the Commission's claim that the "acute practical problem[s]' inherent in format regulation render entirely speculative any benefits that such regulation might produce." [31] One of the principal reasons given in the Policy Statement for rejecting entertainment format regulation is that it would be "administratively a fearful and comprehensive nightmare" [32] that would impose "enormous costs on the participants and the Commission alike." [33] But at oral argument before the Court of Appeals, Commission counsel conceded that the "'administrative nightmare'" argument was an "'exaggeration'" which was not "'very significant at all'" to the Commission's ultimate conclusion. 197 U.S.App.D.C. at 330, 610 F.2d at 849. The Commission's reliance on claims that its own counsel later concedes to lack merit hardly strengthens one's belief in the rationality of its decisionmaking.

Although it has abandoned the "administrative nightmare" argument before this Court, the Commission nonetheless finds other "intractable" administrative problems in format regulation. For example, it insists that meaningful classification of radio broadcasts into format types is impractical, and that it is impossible to determine whether a proposed format change is in the public interest because the intensity of listener preferences cannot be measured. [34] Moreover, the Commission argues that format regulation will discourage licensee innovation and experimentation with formats, and that its effect on format diversity will therefore be counterproductive.

None of these claims has merit. Broadcasters have operated under the format doctrine during the past 10 years, yet the Commission is unable to show that there has been no innovation and experimentation with formats during this period. Indeed, a Commission staff study on the effectiveness of market allocation of formats indicates that licensees have been aggressive in developing diverse entertainment formats under the format doctrine regime. [35] This "evidence" -- a welcome contrast to the Commission's speculation -- undermines the Commission's claim that format regulation will disserve the "public interest" because it will inhibit format diversity.

The Commission's claim that it is impossible to classify formats, is largely overcome by the Court of Appeals' suggestion that the Commission could develop "a format taxonomy which, even if imprecise at the margins, would be sustainable so long as not irrational." [36] 197 U.S.App.D.C. at 334, 610 F.2d at 853. Even more telling is the staff study relied on by the Commission to show that there is broad format diversity in major radio markets, for the study used a format classification based on industry practice. [37] As the Court of Appeals noted, it is somewhat ironic that the Commission had no trouble "endorsing the validity of a study largely premised on classifications it claims are impossible to make." Ibid. [38] To be sure, courts do not sit to second-guess the assessments of specialized agencies like the Commission. But where, as here, the agency's position rests on speculations that are refuted by the agency's own administrative record, I am not persuaded that deference is due. [39]

IV

The Commission's Policy Statement is defective because it lacks a "safety valve" procedure that would allow the necessary flexibility in the application of the Commission's general policy on format changes to particular cases. In my judgment, the Court of Appeals' format doctrine was a permissible attempt by that court to provide the Commission with some guidance regarding the types of situations in which a reexamination of general policy might be necessary. Even if one were to conclude that the Court of Appeals described these situations too specifically, a view I do not share, I still think that the Court of Appeals correctly held that the Commission's Policy Statement must be vacated.

I respectfully dissent.

Notes

[1] The pertinent portions of 47 U.S.C. §§ 309(a) and 310(d) are quoted in the majority opinion, ante at 450 U. S. 584-585, n. 2.

[2] I will follow the majority, see ante at 450 U. S. 586, n. 4, in referring to a broadcaster' change in entertainment programming as a format change.

[3] Memorandum Opinion and Order, 60 F.C.C.2d 858 (1976) (Policy Statement), reconsideration denied, 66 F.C.C.2d 78 (1977) (Denial of Reconsideration).

[4] The opinion of the Court traces the development of the Court of Appeals' "format doctrine" and the Commission's "Policy Statement," see ante at 450 U. S. 586-593. I will not repeat that discussion here.

[5] Notice of Inquiry, Development of Policy Re: Changes in the Entertainment Formats of Broadcast Stations, 57 F.C.C.2d 580, 582 (1976) (Notice of Inquiry).

[6] Policy Statement, supra at 865 (quoting Lemon v. Kurtzman, 403 U. S. 602, 403 U. S. 619-620 (1971)).

[7] Denial of Reconsideration, supra at 81.

[8] Even the Court of Appeals agreed that

"[t]here would no doubt be severe statutory and constitutional difficulties with any system that required intrusive governmental surveillance, dictated programming choices, forced broad access obligations, or imposed an obligation to continue in service under any and all circumstances."

197 U.S.App.D.C. 319, 331-332, 610 F.2d 838, 850-851 (1979).

[9] See D. Ginsburg, Regulation of Radio Broadcasting 294 (1979) ("An argument against the desirability of diversity' in broadcast programming is difficult to imagine"). See generally Note, A Regulatory Approach to Diversifying Commercial Television Entertainment, 89 Yale L.J. 694 (1980).

[10] Section 303(g) of the Act, 47 U.S.C. § 303(g), directs the Commission to "encourage the larger and more effective use of radio in the public interest."

[11] The Commission is authorized to promulgate "such rules and regulations . . . not inconsistent with law, as may be necessary to carry out the provisions of [the Act]." 47 U.S.C. § 303(r).

[12] The majority argues, ante at 450 U. S. 601, n. 44, that although the Court considered the presence of a "safety valve" procedure in upholding the rules challenged in National Broadcasting Co. v. United States and United States v. Storer Broadcasting Co., the Court "did not hold that the Commission may never adopt a rule that lacks a waiver provision." Since this general question was not before the Court in those cases, it is hardly surprising that it did not render an advisory opinion to this effect. What is instructive, however, is the majority's inability to explain why a waiver provision was necessary in those cases, but is not required in the instant situation. As the cases cited in text make clear, this Court and the lower federal courts have insisted on a "safety valve" feature in upholding general rules promulgated by a variety of agencies. I believe it is incumbent on those who would depart from this practice to explain their reasoning.

[13] Zenith Radio Corp., 40 F.C.C.2d 223, 231 (1973) (additional views of Chairman Burch) (joined by a majority of the Commissioners).

[14] Confronted as it was by the Commission's resistance to its format doctrine, it is easy to understand why the Court of Appeals felt compelled to undertake this task.

[15] Policy Statement, 60 F.C.C.2d at 863.

[16] Public Service Responsibility of Broadcast Licensees (1946).

[17] Id. at 12.

[18] Id. at 15.

[19] En Banc Programming Inquiry, 44 F.C.C. 2303 (1960).

[20] Id. at 2314

[21] Id. at 2312.

[22] Children's Television Report and Policy Statement, 50 F.C.C.2d 1, 6 (1974).

[23] Channel 20, Inc., 70 F.C.C.2d 1770 (1979).

[24] Community Television of Southern California, 72 F.C.C.2d 349 (1979)

[25] Central California Communications Corp., 70 F.C.C.2d 1947 (1979).

[26] Mississippi Authority for Educational TV, 71 F.C.C.2d 1296 (1979); Alabama Educational Television Comm'n, 33 F.C.C.2d 495 (1971), renewal denied, 50 F.C.C.2d 461 (1975).

[27] Educational Broadcasting Corp., 70 F.C.C.2d 2204 (1979).

As the majority notes, ante at 450 U. S. 602-603, the Commission recently voted to reduce its role in regulating several aspects of commercial radio broadcasting, including regulation of nonentertainment programming. Thus, the Commission has announced its intention of eliminating its current guideline on the amounts of nonentertainment programming that radio stations should air. And the Commission has indicated that petitions to deny license renewals based on only the quantity of a licensee's nonentertainment programming will no longer be sufficient to support a challenge. For example, a petitioner would have to show that a licensee is doing little or no programming responsive to community issues in order to successfully challenge renewal of the license. Nonetheless, the Commission reiterated that nonentertainment programming is still a relevant issue for petitions to deny, that licensees have an obligation to offer nonentertainment programming addressing issues facing the community, and that the Commission will continue to inquire into the reasonableness of licensee programming decisions. See Deregulation of Radio, 46 Fed.Reg. 13888, 13890-13897 (1981) (to be codified at 47 CFR Parts 0 and 73).

[28] Denial of Reconsideration, 66 F.C.C.2d at 83 (emphasis in original).

[29] Ibid.

[30] Ibid.

[31] Brief for Federal Communications Commission and United States 35.

[32] Policy Statement, 60 F.C.C.2d at 856.

[33] Id. at 84.

[34] The Commission also insists that any findings about the financial viability of a particular format would be entirely speculative.

[35] See Policy Statement, supra at 873-881.

[36] There have been a number of comments and suggestions about how the Commission might best accomplish this task. See, e.g., 57 F.C.C.2d at 587-589 (concurring statement of Commissioner Hooks); D. Ginsburg, supra, n. 9, at 316; Note, Judicial Review of FCC Program Diversity Regulation, 75 Colum.L.Rev. 401, 436-437 (1975).

The Court of Appeals suggested that the Commission could consider an alternative approach of

"dispensing altogether with the need for classifying formats by simply taking the existence of significant and bona fide listener protest as sufficient evidence that the station's endangered programming has certain unique features for which there are no ready substitutes."

197 U.S.App.D.C. at 334, n. 47, 610 F.2d at 853, n. 47. The court indicated that

"this approach would focus attention on the essentials of the format doctrine, namely, that, when a significant sector of the populace is aggrieved by a planned programming change, this fact raises a legitimate question as to whether the proposed change is in the public interest."

Id. at 334-335, n. 47, 610 F.2d at 853-854, n. 47.

[37] See Policy Statement, supra at 875-880.

[38] Nor do I find merit in the Commission's claim that there are serious First Amendment problems with format regulation. In the first place, I see no reason to find constitutional defect in limited review of entertainment formats when no such defect arises with review of nonentertainment programming. In Red Lion Broadcasting Co. v. FCC, 395 U. S. 367, 395 U. S. 395 (1969), we held that the Commission does not transgress the First Amendment "in interesting itself in general program format and the kinds of programs broadcast by licensees." Indeed, First Amendment principles, if anything, would support format review as requested by listeners, for, as we indicated in Red Lion, "[i]t is the [First Amendment] right of the viewers and listeners, not the right of the broadcasters, which is paramount." Id. at 395 U. S. 390.

[39] All this suggests that the "practical difficulties" the Commission has identified are not intractable, and that these problems could be solved if the Commission channelled as much energy into devising workable standards as it has devoted to mischaracterizing the Court of Appeals' format doctrine.

Double-celling can be cruel and unusual punishment: Justice Marshall's dissent in Rhodes v. Chapman (June 15, 1981)

JUSTICE MARSHALL, dissenting.

From reading the Court's opinion in this case, one would surely conclude that the Southern Ohio Correctional Facility (SOCF) is a safe, spacious prison that happens to include many two-inmate cells because the State has determined that that is the best way to run the prison. But the facility described by the majority is not the one involved in this case. SOCF is overcrowded, unhealthful, and dangerous. None of those conditions results from a considered policy judgment on the part of the State. Until the Court's opinion today, absolutely no one - certainly not the "state legislatures" or "prison officials" to whom the majority suggests, see ante, at 352, that we defer in analyzing constitutional questions - had suggested that forcing long-term inmates to share tiny cells designed to hold only one individual might be a good thing. On the contrary, as the District Court noted, "everybody" is in agreement that double celling is undesirable. 1 No one argued at trial and no one has contended here that double celling was a legislative policy judgment. No one has asserted that prison officials imposed it as a disciplinary or a security matter. And no one has claimed that the practice has anything whatsoever to do with "punish[ing] justly," "deter[ring] future crime," or "return[ing] imprisoned persons to society with an improved chance of being useful, law-abiding citizens." See ante, at 352. The evidence and the District Court's findings clearly demonstrate that the only reason double celling was imposed on inmates at SOCF was that more individuals were sent there than the prison was ever designed to hold. 2

I do not dispute that the state legislature indeed made policy judgments when it built SOCF. It decided that Ohio needed a maximum-security prison that would house some 1,600 inmates. In keeping with prevailing expert opinion, the legislature made the further judgments that each inmate would have his own cell and that each cell would have approximately 63 square feet of floor space. But because of prison overcrowding. hundreds of the cells are shared, or "doubled," which is hardly what the legislature intended.

In a doubled cell, each inmate has only some 30-35 square feet of floor space. 3 Most of the windows in the Supreme Court building are larger than that. The conclusion of every expert who testified at trial and of every serious study of which I am aware is that a long-term inmate must have to himself, at the very least, 50 square feet of floor space - an area smaller than that occupied by a good-sized automobile - in order to avoid serious mental, emotional, and physical deterioration. 4 The District Court found that as a fact. 434 F. Supp. 1007, 1020-1021 (SD Ohio 1977). Even petitioners, in their brief in this Court, concede that double celling as practiced at SOCF is "less than desirable." Brief for Petitioners 17.

The Eighth Amendment "embodies `broad and idealistic concepts of dignity, civilized standards, humanity, and decency,'" against which conditions of confinement must be judged. Estelle v. Gamble, 429 U.S. 97, 102 (1976), quoting Jackson v. Bishop, 404 F.2d 571, 579 (CA8 1968). Thus the State cannot impose punishment that violates "the evolving standards of decency that mark the progress of a maturing society." Trop v. Dulles, 356 U.S. 86, 101 (1958) (plurality opinion). For me, the legislative judgment and the consistent conclusions by those who have studied the problem provide considerable evidence that those standards condemn imprisonment in conditions so crowded that serious harm will result. The record amply demonstrates that those conditions are present here. It is surely not disputed that SOCF is severely overcrowded. The prison is operating at 38% above its design capacity. 5 It is also significant that some two-thirds of the inmates at SOCF are serving lengthy or life sentences, for, as we have said elsewhere, "the length of confinement cannot be ignored in deciding whether the confinement meets constitutional standards." Hutto v. Finney, 437 U.S. 678, 686 (1978). Nor is double celling a short-term response to a temporary problem. The trial court found, and it is not contested, that double celling, if not enjoined, will continue for the foreseeable future. The trial court also found that most of the double-celled inmates spend most of their time in their cells. 6

It is simply not true, as the majority asserts, that "there is no evidence that double celling under these circumstances either inflicts unnecessary or wanton pain or is grossly disproportionate to the severity of crimes warranting imprisonment." Ante, at 348. The District Court concluded from the record before it that long exposure to these conditions will "necessarily" involve "excess limitation of general movement as well as physical and mental injury . . . ." 434 F. Supp., at 1020 (emphasis added). 7 And of course, of all the judges who have been involved in this case, the trial judge is the only one who has actually visited the prison. That is simply an additional reason to give in this case the deference we have always accorded to the careful conclusions of the finder of fact. There is not a shred of evidence to suggest that anyone who has given the matter serious thought has ever approved, as the majority does today, conditions of confinement such as those present at SOCF. I see no reason to set aside the concurrent conclusions of two courts that the overcrowding and double celling here in issue are sufficiently severe that they will, if left unchecked, cause deterioration in respondents' mental and physical health. These conditions in my view go well beyond contemporary standards of decency and therefore violate the Eighth and Fourteenth Amendments. I would affirm the judgment of the Court of Appeals.

If the majority did no more than state its disagreement with the courts below over the proper reading of the record, I would end my opinion here. But the Court goes further, adding some unfortunate dicta that may be read as a warning to federal courts against interference with a State's operation of its prisons. If taken too literally, the majority's admonitions might eviscerate the federal courts' traditional role of preventing a State from imposing cruel and unusual punishment through its conditions of confinement.

The majority concedes that federal courts "certainly have a responsibility to scrutinize claims of cruel and unusual confinement," ante, at 352, but adds an apparent caveat:

"In discharging this oversight responsibility, however, courts cannot assume that state legislatures and prison officials are insensitive to the requirements of the Constitution or to the perplexing sociological problems of how best to achieve the goals of the penal function in the criminal justice system: to punish justly, to deter future crime, and to return imprisoned persons to society with an improved chance of being useful, law-abiding citizens." Ibid.

As I suggested at the outset, none of this has anything to do with this case, because no one contends that the State had those goals in mind when it permitted SOCF to become overcrowded. This dictum, moreover, takes far too limited a view of the proper role of a federal court in an Eighth Amendment proceeding and, I add with some regret, far too sanguine a view of the motivations of state legislators and prison officials. Too often, state governments truly are "insensitive to the requirements of the Eighth Amendment," as is evidenced by the repeated need for federal intervention to protect the rights of inmates. See, e. g., Hutto v. Finney, 437 U.S. 678 (1978) (lengthy periods of punitive isolation); Estelle v. Gamble, 429 U.S. 97 (1976) (failure to treat inmate's medical needs); Battle v. Anderson, 564 F.2d 388 (CA10 1977) (severe overcrowding); Gates v. Collier, 501 F.2d 1291 (CA5 1974) (overcrowding and poor housing conditions); Holt v. Sarver, 442 F.2d 304 (CA8 1971) (unsafe conditions and inmate abuse); Pugh v. Locke, 406 F. Supp. 318 (MD Ala. 1976) (constant fear of violence and physical harm), aff'd, 559 F.2d 283 (CA5 1977), rev'd in part on other grounds, 438 U.S. 781 (1978) (per curiam). See also ante, at 353-361 (BRENNAN, J., concurring in judgment). 8

A society must punish those who transgress its rules. When the offense is severe, the punishment should be of proportionate severity. But the punishment must always be administered within the limitations set down by the Constitution. With the rising crime rates of recent years, there has been an alarming tendency toward a simplistic penological philosophy that if we lock the prison doors and throw away the keys, our streets will somehow be safe. In the current climate, it is unrealistic to expect legislators to care whether the prisons are overcrowded or harmful to inmate health. It is at that point - when conditions are deplorable and the political process offers no redress - that the federal courts are required by the Constitution to play a role. I believe that this vital duty was properly discharged by the District Court and the Court of Appeals in this case. The majority today takes a step toward abandoning that role altogether. I dissent.

Notes

[1] "The experts were all in agreement - as is everybody - that single celling is desirable." 434 F. Supp. 1007, 1016 (SD Ohio 1977).

[2] See id., at 1010-1011.

[3] The bed alone, which is bunk-style in the doubled cells, takes up approximately 20 square feet. Thus the actual amount of floor space per inmate, without making allowance for any other furniture in the room, is some 20-24 square feet, an area about the size of a typical door.

[4] See, e. g., American Public Health Assn., Standard for Health Services in Correctional Institutions 62 (1976) ("a minimum of 60 sq. ft."); Commission on Accreditation for Corrections, Manual of Standards for Adult Correctional Institutions 27 (1977) ("a floor area of at least 60 square feet"; "[i]n no case should the present use of the facility exceed designed use standards"); 3 National Institute of Justice, American Prisons and Jails 85, n. 6 (1980) ("80 square feet of floor space in long-term institutions"); National Sheriffs' Assn., A Handbook on Jail Architecture 63 (1975) ("[s]ingle occupancy detention rooms should average 70 to 80 square feet in area"); U.S. Dept. of Justice, Federal Standards for Prisons and Jails 17 (1980) ("at least 60 square feet of floor space"); National Council on Crime and Delinquency, Model Act for the Protection of Rights of Prisoners, 18 Crime & Delinquency 4, 10 (1972) ("not less than fifty square feet of floor space in any confined sleeping area"). Most of these studies recommend even more space for inmates who must spend more than 10 hours per day in their cells. One expert

witness, a former warden of Rikers Island, testified from his experience that the double celling, if continued over "an awful long stretch of time," could be expected to lead to "assault behavior" and "homosexual occurrences." Tr. 48. He added that "skid row bums" in Bowery flophouses tend to live in healthier surroundings than do double-celled inmates. Id., at 55. As will become apparent, the majority and I disagree over the weight to be given these studies and the expert testimony. But I emphasize that the majority has not pointed to a single witness or study refuting or even contradicting the conclusion of panel after panel of experts that an inmate needs as an absolute minimum 50 square feet of floor space to himself to avoid deterioration of his health.

[5] In my dissenting opinion in Bell v. Wolfish, 441 U.S. 520, 572, n. 12 (1979), I pointed out that the majority ignored "the rated capacity of the institution" in determining whether the challenged overcrowding was unconstitutional. In its opinion today, the Court at least mentions that SOCF is operating at 38% above its rated capacity, but it dismisses that rating as "[p]erhaps" reflecting "an aspiration toward an ideal environment for long-term confinement." Ante, at 349. "The question before us," the majority adds, "is not whether the designer of SOCF guessed incorrectly about future prison population, but whether the actual conditions of confinement at SOCF are cruel and unusual." Ante, at 350-351, n. 15. Rated capacity, the majority argues, is irrelevant because of the numerous factors that influence prison population. Actually, it is the factors that influence prison population that are irrelevant. By definition, rated capacity represents "the number of inmates that a confinement unit, facility, or entire correctional agency can hold." 3 National Institute of Justice, American Prisons and Jails 41-42 (1980). If prison population, for whatever reason, exceeds rated capacity, then the prison must accommodate more people than it is designed to hold - in short, it is overcrowded. And the greater the proportion by which prison population exceeds rated capacity, the more severe the overcrowding. I certainly do not suggest that rated capacity is the only factor to be considered in determining whether a prison is unconstitutionally overcrowded, but I fail to understand why the majority feels free to dismiss it entirely.

[6] Although the majority suggests, ante, at 344, n. 8, that this finding lacks a clear basis, the trial court also found as a fact that most inmates are out of their cells only 10 hours each day. 434 F. Supp., at 1013. This leaves 14 hours per day inside the cell. The trial court also found that a "substantial number" of inmates are out of their cells for no more than four to six hours per week. Id., at 1021.

The majority assumes, ante, at 350, n. 15, that the trial court's finding that most inmates are out of their cells only 10 hours each day is "flatly inconsistent" with its finding that regulations permit most inmates to be out of their cells up to 14 hours each day. The majority goes on to reject the first finding in favor of the second. A more reasonable course would be to read these two findings in such a way as to give meaning to both. Thus I read the District Court's opinion as finding that although most inmates are permitted to be out of their cells up to 14 hours each day, conditions in the prison are such that many choose not to do so.

The majority also attaches importance to the fact that the inmates who are locked in their cells for all but four to six hours a week are in a "restrictive classification." Ibid. It is not clear to me why this matters. The inmates who are out of their cells only four to six hours each week are in three categories: "receiving," a category in which new inmates are placed for "a couple of weeks"; "voluntarily idle," which presumably means what it says; and "limited activity," for those inmates who have requested, but have not received, protective custody. It is not immediately apparent why classification in any of these categories justifies imposition of otherwise cruel and unusual punishment. In particular, the State surely lacks authority to force an individual to choose between possibility of rape or other physical harm (the presumed reason for the request for protective custody) and unconstitutionally cramped quarters. The majority asserts, incorrectly, that some of these inmates have committed rule infractions. Ibid. In fact, inmates who commit infractions are out of their cells only two hours each week. 434 F. Supp., at 1013. Although this dissent has not addressed their particular plight, it is beyond question that if punishment is cruel and unusual, then the mere fact that an individual prisoner has committed a rule infraction does not warrant its imposition. See Hutto v. Finney, 437 U.S. 678, 685 -688 (1978).

[7] In its findings, the District Court credited expert testimony that "close quarters" would likely increase the incidence of schizophrenia and other mental disorders and that the double celling imposed in this case had led to increases in tension and in "aggressive and anti-social characteristics." 434 F. Supp., at 1017. There is no dispute that the prison was violent even before it became overcrowded, and that it has become more so. Contrary to the contention by the majority, ante, at 349-350, n. 15, I do not assert that violence has increased due to double celling. I accept the finding of the District Court that violence has increased due to overcrowding. See 434 F. Supp., at 1018. Plainly, this case involves much more than just the constitutionality of double celling per se. Other federal courts faced with overcrowded conditions have reached similar conclusions. See, e. g., Campbell v. McGruder, 188 U.S. App. D.C. 258, 273, 580 F.2d 521, 536 (1978); Battle v. Anderson, 564 F.2d 388, 399-401 (CA10 1977); Detainees of Brooklyn House of Detention v. Malcolm, 520 F.2d 392, 396, 399 (CA2 1975).

[8] The majority's treatment of the expert evidence in this case also calls for some comment. The Court asserts that expert opinions as to what is desirable in a prison "may be helpful and relevant with respect to some questions" but "`simply do not establish the constitutional minima; rather, they establish goals recommended by the organization in question.'" Ante, at 348, n. 13, quoting Bell v. Wolfish, 441 U.S., at 543 - 544, n. 27. That is more or less a truism, but it plainly does not advance analysis. No one would suggest that a study, no matter how competent, could ever establish a constitutional rule. But once the rule is established, it is surely the case that expert evidence can shed light on whether the rule is violated. Cf. Brown v. Board of Education, 347 U.S. 483, 494, n. 11 (1954) (using psychological studies to show harm from segregation). Thus even if it is true, as the majority asserts, that the Eighth Amendment

forbids only a punishment that "either inflicts unnecessary or wanton pain or is grossly disproportionate to the severity of crimes warranting imprisonment," ante, at 348, surely a court faced with a claim of unconstitutionality would want to know whether anyone had in fact studied the effect of the punishment in issue. Deciding whether that effect was of unconstitutional proportions, and, indeed, whether the study was competently done, would naturally remain the court's function. Here, the trial court deemed the expert opinion presented to it worthy of considerable weight in its assessment of the conditions at SOCF. The majority, however, casts it aside without even a token evaluation of the methodology, content, or results of any of the studies on which the District Court relied. If expert opinion is of as little value as the majority implies, then even plaintiffs with meritorious claims that their conditions of confinement violate the Eighth Amendment will have tremendous difficulty in proving their cases.

If men have to sign up for the draft, so do women: Justice Marshall's dissent in Rostker v. Goldberg (June 25, 1981)

JUSTICE MARSHALL, with whom JUSTICE BRENNAN joins, dissenting.

The Court today places its imprimatur on one of the most potent remaining public expressions of "ancient canards about the proper role of women," Phillips v. Martin Marietta Corp., 400 U.S. 542, 545 (1971) (MARSHALL, J., concurring). It upholds a statute that requires males, but not females, to register for the draft, and which thereby categorically excludes women from a fundamental civic obligation. Because I believe the Court's decision is inconsistent with the Constitution's guarantee of equal protection of the laws, I dissent.

I

A

The background to this litigation is set out in the opinion of the Court, ante at 59-64, and I will not repeat that discussion here. It bears emphasis, however, that the only question presented by this case is whether the exclusion of women from registration under the Military Selective Service Act, 50 U.S.C.App. § 451 et seq. (1976 ed. and Supp. III) (MSSA), contravenes the equal protection component of the Due Process Clause of the Fifth Amendment. Although the purpose of registration is to assist preparations for drafting civilians into the military, we are not asked to rule on the constitutionality of a statute governing conscription. [n1] With the advent of the All-Volunteer Armed Forces, the MSSA was specifically amended to preclude conscription as of July l, 1973, Pub.L. 92-129, § 101(a)(35), 85 Stat. 353, 50 U.S.C.App. § 467 (c), and reactivation of the draft would therefore require a legislative amendment. See S.Rep. No. 9826, p. 155 (1980). Consequently, we are not called upon to decide whether either men or women can be drafted at all, whether they must be drafted in equal numbers, in what order they should be drafted, or, once inducted, how they are to be trained for their respective functions. In addition, this case does not involve a challenge to the statutes or policies that prohibit female members of the Armed Forces from serving in combat. [n2] It is with this understanding that I turn to the task at hand.

B

By now it should be clear that statutes like the MSSA, which discriminate on the basis of gender, must be examined under the "heightened" scrutiny mandated by Craig v. Boren, 429 U.S. 190 (1976). [n3] Under this test, a gender-based classification cannot withstand constitutional challenge unless the classification is substantially related to the achievement of an important governmental objective. Kirchberg v. Feenstra, 450 U.S. 455, 459, 459-460 (1981); Wengler v. Druggist Mutual Ins. Co., 446 U.S. 142, 150 (1980); Califano v. Westcott, 443 U.S. 76, 84 (1979); Orr v. Orr, 440 U.S. 268, 278 (1979); Craig v. Boren, supra, at 197. This test applies whether the classification discriminates against males or females. Caban v. Mohammed, 441 U.S. 380, 391 (1979), Orr v. Orr, supra, at 278-279; Craig v. Boren, supra, at 204. [n4] The party defending the challenged classification carries the burden of demonstrating both the importance of the governmental objective it serves and the substantial relationship between the discriminatory means and the asserted end. See Wengler v. Druggist Mutual Ins. Co., supra, at 151; Caban v. Mohammed, supra, at 393; Craig v. Boren, supra, at 204. Consequently, before we can sustain the MSSA, the Government must demonstrate that the gender-based classification it employs bears "a close and substantial relationship to [the achievement of] important governmental objectives," Personnel Administrator of Massachusetts v. Feeney, 442 U.S. 256, 273 (1979).

C

The MSSA states that "an adequate armed strength must be achieved and maintained to insure the security of this Nation." 50 U.S.C.App. § 451 (b). I agree with the majority, ante at 70, that "[n]o one could deny that . . . the Government's interest in raising and supporting armies is an 'important governmental interest.'" Consequently, the first part of the Craig v. Boren test is satisfied. But the question remains whether the discriminatory means employed itself substantially serves the statutory end. In concluding that it does, the Court correctly notes that Congress enacted (and reactivated) the MSSA pursuant to its constitutional authority to raise and maintain armies. [n5] The majority also notes, ante at 64, that "the Court accords 'great weight to the decisions of Congress,'" quoting Columbia Broadcasting System, Inc. v. Democratic National Committee, 412 U.S. 94, 12 (1973), and that the Court has accorded particular deference to decisions arising in the context of Congress' authority over military affairs. I have no particular quarrel with these sentiments in the majority opinion. I simply add that even in the area of military affairs, deference to congressional judgments cannot be allowed to shade into an abdication of this Court's ultimate responsibility to decide constitutional questions. As the Court has pointed out:

[T]he phrase "war power" cannot be invoked as a talismanic incantation to support any exercise of congressional power which can be brought within its ambit.

"[E]ven the war power does not remove constitutional limitations safeguarding essential liberties."

United States v. Robel, 389 U.S. 258, 263-264 (1967), quoting Home Bldg. & Loan Assn. v. Blaisdell, 290 U.S. 398, 426 (1934). See United States v. L. Cohen Grocery Co., 255 U.S. 81, 88-89 (1921); Hamilton v. Kentucky Distilleries & Warehouse Co., 251 U.S. 146, 156 (1919); Ex parte Milligan, 4 Wall. 2, 121-127 (1866).

One such "safeguar[d] [of] essential liberties" is the Fifth Amendment's guarantee of equal protection of the laws. [n6] When, as here, a federal law that classifies on the basis of gender is challenged as violating this constitutional guarantee, it is ultimately for this Court, not Congress, to decide whether there exists the constitutionally required "close and substantial relationship" between the discriminatory means employed and the asserted governmental objective. See Powell v. McCormack, 395 U.S. 486"] 395 U.S. 486, 549 (1969); 395 U.S. 486, 549 (1969); Baker v. Carr, 369 U.S. 186, 211 (1962). In my judgment, there simply is no basis for concluding in this case that excluding women from registration is substantially related to the achievement of a concededly important governmental interest in maintaining an effective defense. The Court reaches a contrary conclusion only by using an "[a]nnounced degre[e] of 'deference' to legislative judgmen[t]" as a "facile abstractio[n] . . . to justify a result." Ante at 69, 70.

II

A

The Government does not defend the exclusion of women from registration on the ground that preventing women from serving in the military is substantially related to the effectiveness of the Armed Forces. Indeed, the successful experience of women serving in all branches of the Armed Services would belie any such claim. Some 150,000 women volunteers are presently on active service in the military, [n7] and their number is expected to increase to over 250,000 by 1985. See Department of Defense Authorization for Appropriations for Fiscal Year 1981: Hearings on S. 2294 before the Senate Committee on Armed Services, 96th Cong., 2d Sess., 1657, 1683 (1980) (1980 Senate Hearings); Women in the Military: Hearings before the Military Personnel Subcommittee of the House Committee on Armed Services, 96th Cong., 1st and 2d Sess., 13-23 (1979 and 1980) (Women in the Military Hearings). At the congressional hearings, representatives of both the Department of Defense and the Armed Services testified that the participation of women in the All-Volunteer Armed Forces has contributed substantially to military effectiveness. See, e.g., 1980 Senate Hearings, at 1389 (Lt. Gen. Yerks), 1682 (Principal Deputy Assistant Secretary of Defense Danzig); Women in the Military Hearings, at 123 (Assistant Secretary of Defense Pirie). Congress has never disagreed with the judgment of the military experts that women have made significant contributions to the effectiveness of the military. On the contrary, Congress has repeatedly praised the performance of female members of the Armed Forces, and has approved efforts by the Armed Services to expand their role. Just last year, the Senate Armed Services Committee declared:

Women now volunteer for military service and are assigned to most military specialties. These volunteers now make an important contribution to our Armed Forces. The number of women in the military has increased significantly in the past few years, and is expected to continue to increase.

S.Rep. No. 96-826, p. 157 (1980). Accord, S.Rep. No. 96-226, p. 8 (1979). [n8] These statements thus make clear that Congress' decision to exclude women from registration -- and therefore from a draft drawing on the pool of registrants -- cannot rest on a supposed need to prevent women from serving in the Armed Forces. The justification for the MSSA's gender-based discrimination must therefore be found in considerations that are peculiar to the objectives of registration.

The most authoritative discussion of Congress' reasons for declining to require registration of women is contained in the Report prepared by the Senate Armed Services Committee on the Fiscal Year 1981 Defense Authorization Bill. S.Rep. No. 96-826, supra, at 156-161. The Report's findings were endorsed by the House-Senate Conferees on the Authorization Bill. See S.Conf.Rep. No. 96-895, p. 100 (1980). Both Houses of Congress subsequently adopted the findings by passing the Conference Report. 126 Cong.Rec. 23126, 23261 (1980). As the majority notes, ante at 74, the Report's "findings are in effect findings of the entire Congress." The Senate Report sets out the objectives Congress sought to accomplish by excluding women from registration, see S.Rep. No. 96-826, supra, at 157-161, and this Court may appropriately look to the Report in evaluating the justification for the discrimination.

B

According to the Senate Report "[t]he policy precluding the use of women in combat is . . . the most important reason for not including women in a registration system." S.Rep. No. 96-826, supra, at 157; see also S.Rep. No. 96-226, supra, at 9. In reaffirming the combat restrictions, the Report declared:

Registering women for assignment to combat or assigning women to combat positions in peacetime then would leave the actual performance of sexually mixed units as an experiment to be conducted in war with unknown risk -- a risk that the committee finds militarily unwarranted and dangerous. Moreover, the committee feels that any attempt to assign women to combat positions could affect the national resolve at the time of mobilization, a time of great strain on all aspects of the Nation's resources.

S.Rep. No. 96-826, supra, at 157. Had appellees raised a constitutional challenge to the prohibition against assignment of women to combat, this discussion in the Senate Report might well provide persuasive reasons for upholding the restrictions. But the validity of the combat restrictions is not an issue we need decide in this case. [n9] Moreover, since the combat restrictions on women have already been accomplished through statutes and policies that remain in force whether or not women are required to register or to be drafted, including women in registration and draft plans will not result in their being assigned to combat roles. Thus, even assuming that precluding the use of women in combat is an important governmental interest in its own right, there can be no suggestion that the exclusion of women from registration and a draft is substantially related to the achievement of this goal.

The Court's opinion offers a different, though related, explanation of the relationship between the combat restrictions and Congress' decision not to require registration of women. The majority states that "Congress . . . clearly linked the need for renewed registration with its views of the character of a subsequent draft." Ante at 75. The Court also states that

Congress determined that any future draft, which would be facilitated by the registration scheme, would be characterized by a need for combat troops.

Ante at 76. The Court then reasons that, since women are not eligible for assignment to combat, Congress' decision to exclude them from registration is not unconstitutional discrimination, inasmuch as

[m]en and women, because of the combat restrictions on women, are simply not similarly situated for purposes of a draft or registration for a draft.

Ante at 78. There is a certain logic to this reasoning, but the Court's approach is fundamentally flawed.

In the first place, although the Court purports to apply the Craig v. Boren test, the "similarly situated" analysis the Court employs is in fact significantly different from the Craig v. Boren approach. Compare Kirchberg v. Feenstra, 450 U.S. at 459-460 (employing Craig v. Boren test), with id. at 463 (STEWART, J., concurring in result) (employing "similarly situated" analysis). The Court essentially reasons that the gender classification employed by the MSSA is constitutionally permissible because nondiscrimination is not necessary to achieve the purpose of registration to prepare for a draft of combat troops. In other words, the majority concludes that women may be excluded from registration because they will not be needed in the event of a draft. [n10]

This analysis, however, focuses on the wrong question. The relevant inquiry under the Craig v. Boren test is not whether a gender-neutral classification would substantially advance important governmental interests. Rather, the question is whether the gender-based classification is itself substantially related to the achievement of the asserted governmental interest. Thus, the Government's task in this case is to demonstrate that excluding women from registration substantially furthers the goal of preparing for a draft of combat troops. Or to put it another way, the Government must show that registering women would substantially impede its efforts to prepare for such a draft. Under our precedents, the Government cannot meet this burden without showing that a gender-neutral statute would be a less effective means of attaining this end. See Wengler v. Druggists Mutual Ins. Co., 446 U.S. at 151. As the Court explained in Orr v. Orr, 440 U.S. at 283 (emphasis added):

Legislative classifications which distribute benefits and burdens on the basis of gender carry the inherent risk of reinforcing sexual stereotypes about the "proper place" of women and their need for special protection. . . . Where, as here, the [Government's] . . . purposes are as well served by a gender-neutral classification as one that gender classifies, and therefore carries with it the baggage of sexual stereotypes, the

[Government] cannot be permitted to classify on the basis of sex.

In this case, the Government makes no claim that preparing for a draft of combat troops cannot be accomplished just as effectively by registering both men and women but drafting only men if only men turn out to be needed. [n11] Nor can the Government argue that this alternative entails the additional cost and administrative inconvenience of registering women. This Court has repeatedly stated that the administrative convenience of employing a gender classification is not an adequate constitutional justification under the Craig v. Boren test. See, e.g., Craig v. Boren, 429 U.S. at 198; Frontiero v. Richardson, 411 U.S. 677, 690-691 (1973).

The fact that registering women in no way obstructs the governmental interest in preparing for a draft of combat troops points up a second flaw in the Court's analysis. The Court essentially reduces the question of the constitutionality of male-only registration to the validity of a hypothetical program for conscripting only men. The Court posits a draft in which all conscripts are either assigned to those specific combat posts presently closed to women or must be available for rotation into such positions. By so doing, the Court is able to conclude that registering women would be no more than a "gestur[e] of superficial equality," ante at 79, since women are necessarily ineligible for every position to be filled in its hypothetical draft. If it could indeed be guaranteed in advance that conscription would be reimposed by Congress only in circumstances where, and in a form under which, all conscripts would have to be trained for and assigned to combat or combat rotation positions from which women are categorically excluded, then it could be argued that registration of women would be pointless.

But, of course, no such guarantee is possible. Certainly, nothing about the MSSA limits Congress to reinstituting the draft only in such circumstances. For example, Congress may decide that the All-Volunteer Armed Forces are inadequate to meet the Nation's defense needs even in times of peace, and reinstitute peacetime conscription. In that event, the hypothetical draft the Court relied on to sustain the MSSA's gender-based classification would presumably be of little relevance, and the Court could then be forced to declare the male-only registration program unconstitutional. This difficulty comes about because both Congress [n12] and the Court have lost sight of the important distinction between registration and conscription. Registration provides "an inventory of what the available strength is within the military qualified pool in this country." Reinstitution of Procedures for Registration Under the Military Selective Service Act: Hearing before the Subcommittee on Manpower and Personnel of the Senate Armed Services Committee, 96th Cong., 1st Sess., 10 (1979) (Selective Service Hearings) (statement of Gen. Rogers). Conscription supplies the military with the personnel needed to respond to a particular exigency. The fact that registration is a first step in the conscription process does not mean that a registration law expressly discriminating between men and women may be justified by a valid conscription program which would, in retrospect, make the current discrimination appear functionally related to the program that emerged.

But even addressing the Court's reasoning on its own terms, its analysis is flawed because the entire argument rests on a premise that is demonstrably false. As noted, the majority simply assumes that registration prepares for a draft in which every draftee must be available for assignment to combat. But the majority's draft scenario finds no support in either the testimony before Congress, or more importantly, in the findings of the Senate Report. Indeed, the scenario appears to exist only in the Court's imagination, for even the Government represents only that, "in the event of mobilization, approximately two-thirds of the demand on the induction system would be for combat skills." Brief for Appellant 29 (emphasis added). For my part, rather than join the Court in imagining hypothetical drafts, I prefer to examine the findings in the Senate Report and the testimony presented to Congress.

C

Nothing in the Senate Report supports the Court's intimation that women must be excluded from registration because combat eligibility is a prerequisite for all the positions that would need to be filled in the event of a draft. The Senate Report concluded only that "[i]f mobilization were to be ordered in a wartime scenario, the primary manpower need would be for combat replacements." S.Rep. No. 96-826, p. 160 (1980) (emphasis added). This conclusion was in keeping with the testimony presented at the congressional hearings. The Department of Defense indicated that, in the event of a mobilization requiring reinstitution of the draft, the primary manpower requirement would be for combat troops and support personnel who can readily be deployed into combat. See 1980 Senate Hearings, at 1395 (Principal Deputy Assistant Secretary of the Army Clark), 1390 (Lt. Gen. Yerks). But the Department indicated that conscripts would also be needed to staff a variety of support positions having no prerequisite of combat eligibility, and which therefore could be filled by women. Assistant Secretary of Defense (Manpower, Reserve Affairs, and Logistics) Pirie explained:

Not only will we need to expand combat arms, and as I said, that is the most pressing need, but we also will need to expand the support establishment at the same time to allow the combat arms to carry out their function successfully. The support establishment now uses women very effectively, and, in wartime, I think the same would be true.

Registration of Women: Hearing on H.R. 6569 before the Subcommittee on Military Personnel of the House Committee on Armed Services, 96th Cong., 2d Sess., 17 (1980) (1980 House Hearings). In testifying about the Defense Department's reasons for concluding that women should be included in registration plans, Pirie stated:

It is in the interest of national security that, in an emergency requiring the conscription for military service of the Nation's youth, the best qualified people for a wide variety of tasks in our Armed Forces be available. The performance of women in our Armed Forces today strongly supports the conclusion that many of the best qualified people for some military jobs in the 18-26 age category will be women.

Id. at 7. See 1980 Senate Hearings, at 171 (Secretary of the Army Alexander), 182

(Secretary of the Navy Claytor). [n13] The Defense Department also concluded that there are no military reasons that would justify excluding women from registration. The Department's position was described to Congress in these terms:

Our conclusion is that there are good reasons for registering [women]. Our conclusion is even more strongly that there are not good reasons for refusing to register them.

Id. at 1667-1668 (Principal Deputy Assistant Secretary of Defense Danzig) (emphasis added). All four Service Chiefs agreed that there are no military reasons for refusing to register women, and uniformly advocated requiring registration of women. The military's position on the issue was summarized by then Army Chief of Staff General Rogers:

[W]omen should be required to register for the reason that [Marine Corps Commandant] General Wilson mentioned, which is in order for us to have an inventory of what the available strength is within the military qualified pool in this country.

Selective Service Hearings, at 10; see id. at 10-11 (Adm. Hayward, Chief of Naval Operations; Gen. Allen, Air Force Chief of Staff; Gen. Wilson, Commandant, Marine Corps).

Against this background, the testimony at the congressional hearings focused on projections of manpower needs in the event of an emergency requiring reinstitution of the draft, and, in particular, on the role of women in such a draft. To make the discussion concrete, the testimony examined a draft scenario dealing with personnel requirements during the first six months of mobilization in response to a major war in Europe. The Defense Department indicated three constraints on the maximum number of women the Armed Services could use in the event of such a mobilization:

(1) legislative prohibitions against the use of women in certain military positions, (2) the policy to reserve certain assignments, such as ground combat roles, for men only, and (3) the need to reserve a substantial number of noncombat positions for men in order to provide a pool of ready replacements for ground combat positions.

1980 House Hearings at 6 (Assistant Secretary Pirie). After allowing for these constraints, the Defense Department reached the following conclusion about the number of female draftees that could be absorbed:

If we had a mobilization, our present best projection is that we could use women in some 80,000 of the jobs that we would be inducting 650,000 people for. The reason for that is because some 80,000 of those jobs, indeed, more than 80,000 of those jobs, are support related and not combat related.

We think women could fill those jobs quite well.

1980 Senate Hearings, at 1688 (Principal Deputy Assistant Secretary of Defense Danzig). See id. at 1661, 1665, 1828; 1980 House Hearings, at 6, 16-17 (Assistant Secretary of Defense Pirie). [n14] Finally, the Department of Defense acknowledged that amending the MSSA to authorize registration and induction of women did not necessarily mean that women would be drafted in the same numbers as men. Assistant Secretary

Pirie explained:

> If women were subject to the draft, the Department of Defense would determine the maximum number of women that could be used in the Armed Forces, subject to existing constraints and the needs of the Military Services to provide close combat fillers and replacements quickly. We estimate that this might require at least 80,000 additional women over the first six months. If there were not enough women volunteers, a separate draft call for women would be issued.

Id. at 6. See 1980 Senate Hearings at 1661 (Principal Deputy Assistant Secretary of Defense Danzig).

This review of the findings contained in the Senate Report and the testimony presented at the congressional hearings demonstrates that there is no basis for the Court's representation that women are ineligible for all the positions that would need to be filled in the event of a draft. Testimony about personnel requirements in the event of a draft established that women could fill at least 80,000 of the 650,000 positions for which conscripts would be inducted. Thus, with respect to these 80,000 or more positions, the statutes and policies barring women from combat do not provide a reason for distinguishing between male and female potential conscripts; the two groups are, in the majority's parlance, "similarly situated." As such, the combat restrictions cannot by themselves supply the constitutionally required justification for the MSSA's gender-based classification. Since the classification precludes women from being drafted to fill positions for which they would be qualified and useful, the Government must demonstrate that excluding women from those positions is substantially related to the achievement of an important governmental objective.

III

The Government argues, however, that the "consistent testimony before Congress was to the effect that there is no military need to draft women." Brief for Appellant 31 (emphasis in original). And the Government points to a statement in the Senate Report that

> [b]oth the civilian and military leadership agreed that there was no military need to draft women. . . . The argument for registration and induction of women . . . is not based on military necessity, but on considerations of equity.

S.Rep. No. 96-826, p. 158 (1980). In accepting the Government's contention, the Court asserts that the President's decision to seek authority to register women was based on "equity," and concludes that

> Congress was certainly entitled, in the exercise of its constitutional powers to raise and regulate armies and navies, to focus on the question of military need, rather than "equity."

Ante at 80. In my view, a more careful examination of the concepts of "equity" and "military need" is required.

As previously noted, the Defense Department's recommendation that women be included in registration plans was based on its conclusion that drafting a limited number of women is consistent with, and could contribute to, military effectiveness. See supra at 97-102. It was against this background that the military experts concluded that "equity" favored registration of women. Assistant Secretary Pirie explained:

Since women have proven that they can serve successfully as volunteers in the Armed Forces, equity suggests that they be liable to serve as draftees if conscription is reinstated.

1980 House Hearings at 7. By "considerations of equity," the military experts acknowledged that female conscripts can perform as well as male conscripts in certain positions, and that there is therefore no reason why one group should be totally excluded from registration and a draft. Thus, what the majority so blithely dismisses as "equity" is nothing less than the Fifth Amendment's guarantee of equal protection of the laws, which "requires that Congress treat similarly situated persons similarly," ante at 79. Moreover, whether Congress could subsume this constitutional requirement to "military need" in part depends on precisely what the Senate Report meant by "military need."

The Report stated that "[b]oth the civilian and military leadership agreed that there was no military need to draft women." S.Rep. No. 96-826, supra, at 158. An examination of what the "civilian and military leadership" meant by "military need" should therefore provide an insight into the Report's use of the term. Several witnesses testified that, because personnel requirements in the event of a mobilization could be met by drafting men, including women in draft plans is not a military necessity. For example, Assistant Secretary of Defense Pirie stated:

It is doubtful that a female draft can be justified on the argument that wartime personnel requirements cannot be met without them. The pool of draft eligible men . . . is sufficiently large to meet projected wartime requirements.

1980 House Hearings, at 6. See 1980 Senate Hearings at 1665 (Principal Deputy Assistant Secretary of Defense Danzig). Similarly, Army Chief of Staff General Meyer testified:

I do not believe there is a need to draft women in peacetime. In wartime, because there are such large numbers of young men available, approximately 2 million males in each year group of the draft age population, there would be no military necessity to draft females except, possibly, doctors, and other health professionals if there are insufficient volunteers from people with those skills.

Id. at 749. To be sure, there is no "military need" to draft women in the sense that a war could be waged without their participation. [n15] This fact is, however, irrelevant to resolving the constitutional issue. [n16] As previously noted, see supra at 94-95, it is not appellees' burden to prove that registration of women substantially furthers the objectives of the MSSA. [n17] Rather, because eligibility for combat is not a requirement for some of the positions to be filled in the event of a draft, it is incumbent on the Government to show that excluding women from a draft to fill those positions substantially furthers an important governmental objective.

It may be, however, that the Senate Report's allusion to "military need" is meant to convey Congress' expectation that women volunteers will make it unnecessary to draft any women. The majority apparently accepts this meaning when it states:

Congress also concluded that, whatever the need for women for noncombat roles during mobilization, whether 80,000 or less, it could be met by volunteers.

Ante at 81. But since the purpose of registration is to protect against unanticipated shortages of volunteers, it is difficult to see how excluding women from registration can be justified by conjectures about the expected number of female volunteers. [n18] I fail to see why the exclusion of a pool of persons who would be conscripted only if needed can be justified by reference to the current supply of volunteers. In any event, the Defense Department's best estimate is that, in the event of a mobilization requiring reinstitution of the draft, there will not be enough women volunteers to fill the positions for which women would be eligible. The Department told Congress:

If we had a mobilization, our present best projection is that we could use women in some 80,000 of the jobs we would be inducting 650,000 people for.

1980 Senate Hearings, at 1688 (Principal Deputy Assistant Secretary of Defense Danzig) (emphasis added). [n19] Thus, however the "military need" statement in the Senate Report is understood, it does not provide the constitutionally required justification for the total exclusion of women from registration and draft plans.

IV

Recognizing the need to go beyond the "military need" argument, the Court asserts that

Congress determined that staffing noncombat positions with women during a mobilization would be positively detrimental to the important goal of military flexibility.

Ante at 81-82. None would deny that preserving "military flexibility" is an important governmental interest. But to justify the exclusion of women from registration and the draft on this ground, there must be a further showing that staffing even a limited number of noncombat positions with women would impede military flexibility. I find nothing in the Senate Report to provide any basis for the Court's representation that Congress believed this to be the case.

The Senate Report concluded that "military reasons . . . preclude very large numbers of women from serving." S.Rep. No. 9826, p. 158 (1980) (emphasis added). The Report went on to explain:

Military flexibility requires that a commander be able to move units or ships quickly. Units or ships not located at the front or not previously scheduled for the front nevertheless must be able to move into action if necessary. In peace and war, significant rotation of personnel is necessary. We should not divide the military into two groups -- one in permanent combat and one in permanent support. Large numbers of non-combat positions must be available to which combat troops can return for duty before being redeployed.

Ibid. This discussion confirms the Report's conclusion that drafting "very large numbers of women" would hinder military flexibility. The discussion does not, however, address the different question whether drafting only a limited number of women would similarly impede military flexibility. The testimony on this issue at the congressional hearings was that drafting a limited number of women is quite compatible with the military's need for flexibility. In concluding that the Armed Services could usefully employ at least 80,000 women conscripts out of a total of 650,000 draftees that would be needed in the event of a major European war, the Defense Department took into account both the need for rotation of combat personnel and the possibility that some support personnel might have to be sent into combat. As Assistant Secretary Pirie testified:

If women were subject to the draft, the Department of Defense would determine the maximum number of women that could be used in the Armed Forces, subject to existing constraints and the needs of the Military Services to provide close combat fillers and replacements quickly. We estimate that this might require at least 80,000 additional women over the first 6 months.

1980 House Hearings, at 6 (emphasis added). See App. 278 (deposition of Principal Deputy Assistant Secretary of Defense Danzig). [n20]

Similarly, there is no reason why induction of a limited number of female draftees should any more divide the military into "permanent combat" and "permanent support" groups than is presently the case with the All-Volunteer Armed Forces. The combat restrictions that would prevent a female draftee from serving in a combat or combat rotation position also apply to the 150,000-250,000 women volunteers in the Armed Services. If the presence of increasing but controlled numbers of female volunteers has not unacceptably "divide[d] the military into two groups," it is difficult to see how the induction of a similarly limited additional number of women could accomplish this result. In these circumstances, I cannot agree with the Court's attempt to "interpret" the Senate Report's conclusion that drafting very large numbers of women would impair military flexibility, as proof that Congress reached the entirely different conclusion that drafting a limited number of women would adversely affect military flexibility.

V

The Senate Report itself recognized that the "military flexibility" objective speaks only to the question whether "very large numbers" of women should be drafted. For the Report went on to state:

It has been suggested that all women be registered, but only a handful actually be inducted in an emergency. The committee finds this a confused and ultimately unsatisfactory solution.

S.Rep. No. 96-826, p. 158 (1980). The Report found the proposal "confused" and "unsatisfactory" for two reasons.

First, the President's proposal [to require registration of women] does not include any change in section 5(a)(1) of the [MSSA], which requires that the draft be conducted impartially among those eligible. Administration witnesses admitted that the current language of the law probably precludes induction of women and men on any but a random basis, which should produce roughly equal numbers of men and women. Second, it is conceivable that the courts, faced with a congressional decision to register men and women equally because of equity considerations, will find insufficient justification for then inducting only a token number of women into the Services in an emergency.

Id. at 158-159 (emphasis in original). The Report thus assumed that, if women are registered, any subsequent draft would require simultaneous induction of equal numbers of male and female conscripts. The Report concluded that such a draft would be unacceptable:

It would create monumental strains on the training system, would clog the personnel administration and support systems needlessly, and would impede our defense preparations at a time of great national need.

Other administrative problems such as housing and different treatment with regard to dependency, hardship and physical standards would also exist.

Id. at 159. [n21] See also S.Rep. No. 96-226, p. 9 (1979). Relying on these statements, the majority asserts that, even

assuming that a small number of women could be drafted for noncombat roles, Congress simply did not consider it worth the added burdens of including women in draft and registration plans.

Ante at 81. In actual fact, the conclusion the Senate Report reached is significantly different from the one the Court seeks to attribute to it.

The specific finding by the Senate Report was that,

[i]f the law required women to be drafted in equal numbers with men, mobilization would be severely impaired because of strains on training facilities and administrative systems.

S.Rep. No. 9826, supra, at 160 (emphasis added). There was, however, no suggestion at the congressional hearings that simultaneous induction of equal numbers of males and female conscripts was either necessary or desirable. The Defense Department recommended that women be included in registration and draft plans, with the number of female draftees and the timing of their induction to be determined by the military's personnel requirements. See supra at 100-101. [n22] In endorsing this plan, the Department gave no indication that such a draft would place any strains on training and administrative facilities. Moreover. the Director of the Selective Service System testified that a registration and induction process including both males and females would present no administrative problems. See 1980 Senate Hearings at 1679 (Bernard Rostker); App. 247-248 (deposition of Bernard Rostker),

The Senate Report simply failed to consider the possibility that a limited number of women could be drafted because of its conclusion that § 5(a)(1) of the MSSA does not authorize drafting different numbers of men and women and its speculation on judicial reaction to a decision to register women. But since Congress was free to amend § 5(a)(1), and indeed would have to undertake new legislation to authorize any draft, the matter cannot end there. Furthermore, the Senate Report's speculation that a statute authorizing differential induction of male and female draftees would be vulnerable to constitutional challenge is unfounded. The unchallenged restrictions on the assignment of women to combat, the need to preserve military flexibility, and the other factors discussed in the Senate Report provide more than ample grounds for concluding that the discriminatory means employed by such a statute would be substantially related to the achievement of important governmental objectives. Since Congress could have amended § 5(a)(1) to authorize differential induction of men and women based on the military's personnel requirements, the Senate Report's discussion about "added burdens" that would result from drafting equal numbers of male and female draftees provides no basis for concluding that the total exclusion of women from registration and draft plans is substantially related to the achievement of important governmental objectives.

In sum, neither the Senate Report itself nor the testimony presented at the congressional hearings provides any support for the conclusion the Court seeks to attribute to the Report -- that drafting a limited number of women, with the number and the timing of their induction and training determined by the military's personnel requirements, would burden training and administrative facilities.

VI

After reviewing the discussion and findings contained in the Senate Report, the most I am able to say of the Report is that it demonstrates that drafting very large numbers of women would frustrate the achievement of a number of important governmental objectives that relate to the ultimate goal of maintaining "an adequate armed strength . . . to insure the security of this Nation," 50 U.S.C.App. § 451(b). Or to put it another way, the Senate Report establishes that induction of a large number of men, but only a limited number of women, as determined by the military's personnel requirements, would be substantially related to important governmental interests. But the discussion and findings in the Senate Report do not enable the Government to carry its burden of demonstrating that completely excluding women from the draft by excluding them from registration substantially furthers important governmental objectives.

In concluding that the Government has carried its burden in this case, the Court adopts "an appropriately deferential examination of Congress' evaluation of the evidence," ante at 83 (emphasis in original). The majority then proceeds to supplement Congress' actual findings with those the Court apparently believes Congress could (and should) have made. Beyond that, the Court substitutes hollow shibboleths about "deference to legislative decisions" for constitutional analysis. It is as if the majority has lost sight of the fact that "it is the responsibility of this Court to act as the ultimate interpreter of the Constitution." Powell v. McCormack, 395 U.S. at 549. See Baker v. Carr, 369 U.S. at 211. Congressional enactments in the area of military affairs must, like all other laws, be judged by the standards of the Constitution. For the Constitution is the supreme law of the land, and all legislation must conform to the principles it lays down.

As the Court has pointed out,

the phrase "war power" cannot be invoked as a talismanic incantation to support any exercise of congressional power which can be brought within its ambit.

United States v. Robel, 389 U.S. at 263-264.

Furthermore,

[w]hen it appears that an Act of Congress conflicts with [a constitutional] provisio[n], we have no choice but to enforce the paramount commands of the Constitution. We are sworn to do no less. We cannot push back the limits of the Constitution merely to accommodate challenged legislation.

Trop v. Dulles, 356 U.S. 86, 104 (1958) (plurality opinion). In some 106 instances since this Court was established, it has determined that congressional action exceeded the bounds of the Constitution. I believe the same is true of this statute. In an attempt to avoid its constitutional obligation, the Court today "pushes back the limits of the Constitution" to accommodate an Act of Congress.

I would affirm the judgment of the District Court.

Notes

1. Given the Court's lengthy discourse on the background to this litigation, it is interesting that the Court chooses to bury its sole reference to this fact in a footnote. See ante at 60, n. 1.

2. By statute, female members of the Air Force and the Navy may not be assigned to vessels or aircraft engaged in combat missions. See 10 U.S.C. § 6015 (1976 ed., Supp III), § 8549. Although there are no statutory restrictions on the assignment of women to combat in the Army and the Marine Corps, both services have established policies that preclude such assignment.

Appellees do not concede the constitutional validity of these restrictions on women in combat, but they have taken the position that their validity is irrelevant for purposes of this case.

3. I join the Court, see ante at 69, in rejecting the Solicitor General's suggestion that the gender-based classification employed by the MSSA should be scrutinized under the "rational relationship" test used in reviewing challenges to certain types of social and economic legislation. See, e.g., Schweiker v. Wilson, 450 U.S. 221 (1981); United States Railroad Retirement Bd. v. Fritz, 449 U.S. 166 (1980).

4. Consequently, it is of no moment that the constitutional challenge in this case is pressed by men who claim that the MSSA's gender classification discriminates against them.

5. The Constitution grants Congress the power "To raise and support Armies," "To Provide and maintain a Navy," and "To make Rules for the Government and Regulation of the land and naval Forces." U.S.Const., Art. I, § 8, cls. 12-14.

6. Although the Fifth Amendment contains no Equal Protection Clause, this Court has held that "the Fifth Amendment's Due Process Clause prohibits the Federal

Government from engaging in discrimination that is 'so unjustifiable as to be violative of due process.'" Schlesinger v. Ballard, 419 U.S. 498, 500, n. 3 (1975), quoting Bolling v. Sharpe, 347 U.S. 497, 499 (1954)

7. With the repeal in 1967 of a statute limiting the number of female members of the Armed Forces to 2% of total enlisted strength, the number of women in the military has risen steadily both in absolute terms and as a percentage of total active military personnel. The percentage has risen from 0.78% in 1966, to over 5% in 1976, and is expected to rise to 12% by 1985. See U.S. Dept. of Defense, Use of Women in the Military 5-6 (2d ed.1978), reprinted at App. 98, 111-113; M. Binkin & S. Bach, Women and the Military 13-21 (1977).

8. In summarizing the testimony presented at the congressional hearings, Senator Cohen stated:

[B]asically, the evidence has come before this committee that participation of women in the All-Volunteer Force has worked well, has been praised by every military officer who has testified before the committee, and that the jobs are being performed with the same, if not, in some cases, with superior skill.

1980 Senate Hearings, at 1678.

9. As noted, see n. 2, supra, appellees elected not to challenge the constitutionality of the combat restrictions.

10. I would have thought the logical conclusion from this reasoning is that there is, in fact, no discrimination against women, in which case one must wonder why the Court feels compelled to pledge its purported fealty to the Craig v. Boren test.

11. Alternatively, the Government could employ a classification that is related to the statutory objective but is not based on gender, for example, combat eligibility. Under the current scheme, large subgroups of the male population who are ineligible for combat because of physical handicaps or conscientious objector status are nonetheless required to register.

12. The Court quotes Senator Warner's comment: "'I equate registration with the draft,'" ante at 75. The whole of Senator Warner's statement merits quotation, because it explains why Congress refused to acknowledge the distinction between registration and the draft. Senator Warner stated:

Frankly, I equate registration with the draft because there is no way you can establish a registration law on a coequal basis and then turn right around and establish a draft law on a nonequal basis. I think the court would knock that down right away.

1980 Senate Hearings at 1197.

13. Pirie explained the reasoning behind the Defense Department's conclusion in these terms:

Large numbers of military women work in occupations such as electronics, communications, navigation, radar repair, jet engine mechanics, drafting, surveying, ordnance, transportation, and meteorology, and do so very effectively, as has been shown by numerous DOD studies and tests. The work women in the Armed Forces do today is essential to the readiness and capability of the forces. In case of war that would still be true, and the number of women doing similar work would inevitably expand beyond our peacetime number of 250,000.

Women have traditionally held the vast majority of jobs in fields such as administrative/clerical and health care/medical. An advantage of registration for women is that a pool of trained personnel in these traditionally female jobs would exist in the event that sufficient volunteers were not available. It would make far greater sense to include women in a draft call, and thereby gain many of these skills, than to draft only males who would not only require training in these fields but would be drafted for employment in jobs traditionally held by females. A further advantage would be to release males currently holding noncombatant jobs for reassignment to combat jobs.

1980 House Hearings at 6.

14. The Defense Department arrived at this number after it surveyed the military services, and asked them how many women they could use [in the event of a mobilization of] 650,000, and received answers suggesting that they could use about 80,000.

1980 Senate Hearings at 1665 (Principal Deputy Assistant Secretary of Defense Danzig).

15. A colloquy between Senator Jepsen and Principal Deputy Assistant Secretary of Defense Danzig reveals that some Members of Congress understood "military need" in this sense.

Mr. DANZIG. . . .

We surveyed the military services, and asked them how many women they could use among those 650,000, and received answers suggesting that they could use 80,000.

Let me indicate when I say they could use[,] I do not mean to imply that they would have to use women. Our Department of Defense view is that women would be useful in a mobilization scenario. If women were not available, I do not think the republic would crumble. Men could be used instead.

Senator JEPSEN. So there is no explicit military requirement involved?

* * * *

Mr. DANZIG. My problem, Senator, and I don't mean to be semantic about it, is with the use of the words, "explicit requirement." If you said to me, for example, does the military require people with brown eyes to serve, I would tell you no, because people with blue eyes, et cetera, could do the job.

On the other hand, I wouldn't deny that they could do the job and that we would find them useful.

1980 Senate Hearings, at 1665; see id. at 1853-1856.

16. Deputy Assistant Attorney General Simms explained as much to Congress in his testimony at the hearings. He stated:

[T]he question of military necessity for drafting women is irrelevant to the constitutional issue, which is whether or not there is sufficient justification by whatever test the courts may apply for not registering women.

Id. at 1667.

17. If we were to assign appellees this burden, then all of the Court's prior "mid-level" scrutiny equal protection decisions would be drawn into question. For the Court would be announcing a new approach under which the party challenging a gender-based classification has the burden of showing that elimination of the classification substantially furthers an important governmental interest.

18. As Assistant Secretary of Defense Pirie explained:

Perhaps sufficient women volunteers would come forward to meet this need, perhaps not. Having our young women register in advance would put us in a position to call women if they do not volunteer in sufficient numbers,

quoted at 126 Cong.Rec. 13885-13886 (1980). See 1980 Senate Hearings at 1828 (Principal Deputy Assistant Secretary of Defense Danzig).

Past wartime recruitment experience does not bear out the Court's sanguine view. With the advent of the Korean War, an unsuccessful effort was made to recruit some 100,000 women to meet the rapidly expanding manpower requirements. See Use of Women in the Military. supra, n. 7, at 5, App. 111.

19. A colloquy between Representative Hillis and Assistant Secretary of Defense Pirie at the House Hearings makes clear that the 80,000 number is in addition to the number of women serving in the All-Volunteer Armed Forces.

Mr. PIRIE. Mr. Hillis, we estimate that we would need 650,000 individuals to be inducted over the first six months.

Mr. HILLIS. How many of those would be women?

Mr. PIRIE. At least 80,000 of these individuals would be women, Mr. Hillis.

Mr. HILLIS. That is, even if we had the 250,000 [women in active service expected by 1985], you are talking about another 80,000, which projects into about 330,000.

Mr. PIRIE. Yes, sir.

1980 House Hearings at 22.

20. Senator Warner questioned the Service Chiefs about the "impact on your service as a consequence of a draft, which would be based on a total provision of equality between male and female." Selective Service Hearings, at 15 (emphasis added). Two of the Service Chiefs answered Senator Warner's question about the effect of a draft of equal numbers of men and women. Their answers merit quotation.

General ALLEN [Air Force]. It would not have any unfavorable effect on the Air Force. We would have no objection to such a draft.

Ibid.

General WILSON [Marine Corps]. . . .

* * * *

. . . [W]e would be perfectly happy to have women drafted. That is up to the 5 percent goal which I believe we can handle in the Marine Corps.

Ibid.

21. The Report further explained:

If the Congress were to mandate equal registration of men and women, therefore, we might well be faced with a situation in which the combat replacements needed in the first 60 days -- say 100,000 men -- would have to be accompanied by 100,000 women. Faced with this hypothetical, the military witnesses stated that such a situation would be intolerable.

S.Rep. No. 96-826 at 159.

22. As stated in the Senate Report

Selective Service Plans provide[d] for drafting only men during the first 60 days, and only a small number of women would be included in the total drafted for the first 180 day.

Id. at 158.

Statute criminalizing placement of hand-delivered civic association notices in letterboxes fails this test: Justice Marshall's dissent in United States Postal Service v. Council of Greenburgh Civic Associations (June 25, 1981)

JUSTICE MARSHALL, dissenting.

When the Framers of the Constitution granted Congress the authority "[t]o establish Post Offices and Post Roads," Art. I, 8, cl. 7, they placed the powers of the Federal Government behind a national communication service. Protecting the economic viability and efficiency of that service remains a legitimate and important congressional objective. This case involves a statute defended on that ground, but I believe it is unnecessary for achieving that purpose and inconsistent with the underlying commitment to communication.

The challenged statute, 18 U.S.C. 1725, prohibits anyone from knowingly placing unstamped "mailable matter" in any box approved by the United States Postal Service for receiving or depositing material carried by the Postal Service. Violators may be punished with fines of up to $300 for each offense. In this case, appellee civic associations claimed, and the District Court agreed, that this criminal statute unreasonable restricts their First Amendment right of free expression.

The Court today upholds the statute on the theory that its focus - the letterbox situated on residential property - is not a public forum to which the First Amendment guarantees access. I take exception to the result, the analysis, and the premise that private persons lose their prerogatives over the letterboxes they own and supply for mail service.

First, I disagree with the Court's assumption that if no public forum is involved, the only First Amendment challenges to be considered are whether the regulation is content-based, see ante, at 132-133, and reasonable, ante, at 131, n. 7. Even if the Postal Service were not a public forum, which, as I later suggest, I do not accept, the statute advanced in its aid is a law challenged as an abridgment of free expression. Appellees seek to carry their own circulars and to deposit them in letterboxes owned by private persons who use them to receive mail, and challenge the criminal statute forbidding this use of private letterboxes. The question, then, is whether this statute burdens any First Amendment rights enjoyed by appellees. If so, it must be determined whether this burden is justified by a significant governmental interest substantially advanced by the statute. See Consolidated Edison Co. v. Public Service Comm'n, 447 U.S. 530, 540 (1980); Grayned v. City of Rockford, 408 U.S. 104, 115 (1972); Cameron v. Johnson, 390 U.S. 611, 616 -617 (1968); Thornhill v. Alabama, 310 U.S. 88, 96, 104-105 (1940).

That appellee civic associations enjoy the First Amendment right of free expression cannot be doubted; both their purposes and their practices fall within the core of the First Amendment's protections. We have long recognized the constitutional rights of groups which seek, as appellees do, to "communicate ideas, positions on local issues, and civic information to their constituents" 1 through written handouts and thereby to promote the free discussion of governmental affairs so central to our democracy. See, e. g., Martin v. City of Struthers, 319 U.S. 141, 146 -147 (1943); Schneider v. State, 308 U.S. 147 (1939); Lovell v. Griffin, 303 U.S. 444 (1938). By traveling door to door to hand-deliver their messages to the homes of community members, appellees employ the method of written expression most accessible to those who are not powerful, established, or well financed. "Door to door distribution of circulars is essential to the poorly financed causes of little people." Martin v. City of Struthers, supra, at 146. See Schneider v. State, supra, at 164. Moreover, "[f]reedom of speech, freedom of the press, freedom of religion are available to all, not merely to those who can pay their own way." Murdock v. Pennsylvania, 319 U.S. 105, 111 (1943). And such freedoms depend on liberty to circulate; "`indeed, without circulation, the publication would be of little value.'" Talley v. California, 362 U.S. 60, 64 (1960), quoting Lovell v. Griffin, supra, at 452.

Countervailing public interests, such as protection against fraud and preservation of privacy, may warrant some limitation on door-to-door solicitation and canvassing. But we have consistently held that nay such restrictions, to be valid, must be narrowly drawn "`in such a manner as not to intrude upon the rights of free speech.'" Hynes v. Mayor and Council of Borough of Oradell, 425 U.S. 610, 616 (1976), quoting Thomas v. Collins, 323 U.S. 516, 540 -541 (1945). Consequently, I cannot agree with the Court's conclusion, ante, at 132-133, that we need not ask whether the ban against placing such messages in letterboxes is a restriction on appellees' free expression rights. Once appellees are at the doorstep, only 1725 restricts them from placing their circulars in the box provided by the resident. The District Court determined after an evidentiary hearing that only by placing their circulars in the letterboxes may appellees be certain that their messages will be secure from wind, rain, or snow, and at the same time will alert the attention of the residents without notifying would-be burglars that no one has returned home to remove items from doorways or stoops. 490 F. Supp. 157, 160-163 (1980). The court concluded that the costs and delays of mail service put the mails out of appellees' reach, and that other alternatives, such as placing their circulars in doorways, are "much less satisfactory." Id., at 160. 2 We have in the past similarly recognized the burden placed on First Amendment rights when the alternative channels of communication involve more cost, less autonomy, and reduced likelihood of reaching the intended audience. Linmark Associates, Inc. v. Willingboro, 431 U.S. 85, 93 (1977).

I see no ground to disturb these factual determinations of the trier of fact. And, given these facts, the Postal Service bears a heavy burden to show that its interests are legitimate and substantially served by the restriction of appellees' freedom of expression. See, e. g., Hynes v. Mayor and Council of the Borough of Oradell, supra, at 617-618; Konigsberg v. State Bar of California, 366 U.S. 36, 49 -51 (1961); Marsh v. Alabama, 326 U.S. 501, 509 (1946). Although the majority does not rule that the trial court's findings were clearly erroneous, as would be required to set them aside, the Court finds persuasive the interests asserted by the Postal Service in defense of the statute. Those interests - "protect[ing] mail revenues while at the same time facilitating the secure and efficient delivery of the mails," ante, at 129 - are indeed both legitimate and important. But mere assertion of an important, legitimate interest does not satisfy the requirement that the challenged restriction specifically and precisely serve that end. See Hynes v. Mayor and Council of the Borough of Oradell, supra. See also Cox v. Louisiana, 379 U.S. 536, 557 - 558 (1965) (restriction must be applied uniformly and nondiscriminatorily).

Here, the District Court concluded that the Postal Service "has not shown that failure to enforce the statute as to [appellees] would result in a substantial loss of revenue, or a significant reduction in the government's ability to protect the mails by investigating and prosecuting mail theft, mail fraud, or unauthorized private mail delivery service." 490 F. Supp., at 163. 3 In light of this failure of proof, I cannot join the Court's conclusion that the Federal Government may thus curtail appellees' ability to inform community residents about local civic matters. That decision, I fear, threatens a departure from this Court's belief that free expression, as "the matrix, the indispensable condition, of nearly every other form of freedom," Palko v. Connecticut, 302 U.S. 319, 327 (1937), must not yield unnecessarily before such governmental interests as economy or efficiency. Certainly, free expression should not have to yield here, where the intruding statute has seldom been enforced. 4 As the exceptions created by the Postal Service itself demonstrate, 5 the statute's asserted purposes easily could be advanced by less intrusive alternatives, such as a nondiscriminatory permit requirement for depositing unstamped circulars in letterboxes. 6 Therefore, I would find 18 U.S.C. 1725 constitutionally defective.

Even apart from the result in this case, I must differ with the Court's use of the public forum concept to avoid application of the First Amendment. Rather than a threshold barrier that must be surmounted before reaching the terrain of the First Amendment, the concept of a public forum has more properly been used to open varied governmental locations to equal public access for free expression, subject to the constraints on time, place, or manner necessary to preserve the governmental function. E.

g., Grayned v. City of Rockford, 408 U.S., at 115 -117 (area around public school); Chicago Area Military Project v. Chicago, 508 F.2d 921 (CA7) (city airport), cert. denied, 421 U.S. 992 (1975); Albany Welfare Rights Organization v. Wyman, 493 F.2d 1319 (CA2) (welfare office waiting room), cert. denied sub nom. Lavine v. Albany Welfare Rights Organization, 419 U.S. 838 (1974); Wolin v. Port of New York Authority, 392 F.2d 83 (CA2) (port authority), cert. denied, 393 U.S. 940 (1968); Reilly v. Noel, 384 F. Supp. 741 (RI 1974) (rotunda of courthouse). See generally Lehman v. City of Shaker Heights, 418 U.S. 298, 303 (1974); Stone, Fora Americana: Speech in Public Places, S. Ct. Rev. 233, 251-252 (1974). These decisions apply the public forum concept to secure the First Amendment's commitment to expression unfettered by governmental designation of its proper scope, audience, or occasion.

I believe these precedents support my conclusion that appellees should prevail in their First Amendment claim. The traditional function of the mails led this Court to embrace Justice Holmes' statement that "`[t]he United States may give up the Post Office when it sees fit, but while it carries it on the use of the mails is as much a part of free speech as the right to use our tongues . . . .'" Lamont v. Postmaster General, 381 U.S. 301, 305 (1965), quoting United States ex rel. Milwaukee Social Democratic Pub. Co. v. Burleson, 255 U.S. 407, 437 (1921) (Holmes, J., dissenting). Given its pervasive and traditional use as purveyor of written communication, the Postal Service, I believe, may properly be viewed as a public forum. The Court relies on easily distinguishable cases in reaching the contrary conclusion. For the Postal Service's very purpose is to facilitate communication, which surely differentiates it from the military bases, jails, and mass transportation discussed in cases relied on by the Court, ante, at 129-130. 7 Cf. Tinker v. Des Moines Independent School Dist., 393 U.S. 503, 512 (1969). Drawing from the exceptional cases, where speech has been limited for special reasons, does not strike me as commendable analysis.

The inquiry in our public forum cases has instead asked whether "the manner of expression is basically incompatible with the normal activity of a particular place at a particular time." Grayned v. City of Rockford, 408 U.S., at 116 . Compare Grayned v. City of Rockford (restriction on speech permissible near school while in session) with Tinker v. Des Moines Independent School Dist., supra (symbolic speech protected even during school hours); Cameron v. Johnson, 390 U.S. 611 (1968) (restriction on picketing permitted where limited to entrance of courthouse), with Brown v. Louisiana, 383 U.S. 131 (1966) (silent protest in library protected); Adderley v. Florida, 385 U.S. 39 (1966) (protest near jailyard inconsistent with jail purposes), with Edwards v. South Carolina, 372 U.S. 229 (1963) (protest permitted on state capitol grounds). Assuming for the moment that the letterboxes, as "authorized depositories," are under governmental control and thus part of the governmental enterprise, their purpose is hardly incompatible with appellees' use. For the letterboxes are intended to receive written communication directed to the residents and to protect such materials from the weather or the intruding eyes of would-be burglars.

Reluctance to treat the letterboxes as public forums might stem not from the Postal Service's approval of their form but instead from the fact that their ownership and use remain in the hands of private individuals. 8 Even that hesitation, I should think, would be misguided, for those owners necessarily retain the right to receive information as a counterpart of the right of speakers to speak. Kleindienst v. Mandel, 408 U.S. 753, 762 -765 (1972); Red Lion Broadcasting Co. v. FCC, 395 U.S. 367, 389 -390 (1969); Lamont v. Postmaster General, supra, at 307; Martin v. City of Struthers, 319 U.S., at 143 . Cf. Procunier v. Martinez, 416 U.S. 396, 408 (1974) (communication by letter depends on receipt by addressee). On that basis alone, I would doubt the validity of 18 U.S.C. 1725, for it deprives residents of the information which civic groups or individuals may wish to deliver to these private receptacles. 9

I remain troubled by the Court's effort to transform the letterboxes entirely into components of the governmental enterprise despite their private ownership. Under the Court's reasoning, the Postal Service could decline to deliver mail unless the recipients agreed to open their doors to the letter carrier - and then the doorway, or even the room inside could fall within Postal Service control. 10 Instead of starting with the scope of governmental control, I would adhere to our usual analysis which looks to whether the exercise of a First Amendment right is burdened by the challenged governmental action, and then upholds that action only where it is necessary to advance a substantial and legitimate governmental interest. In my view, the statute criminalizing the placement of hand-delivered civic association notices in letterboxes fails this test. The brute force of the criminal sanction and other powers of the Government, I believe, may be deployed to restrict free expression only with greater justification. I dissent.

Notes

[1] 490 F. Supp. 157, 162 (1980).

[2] Indeed, the record in this litigation indicates that appellees circulated less information when inhibited from using the letterboxes. Plaintiffs' Answer to Written Interrogatories, Record, Doc. No. 23, § 8, pp. 6-7. The practical effect of applying the statute in residential communities would preclude Girl Scouts, Boy Scouts, charities, neighbors, and others from leaving invitations or notes in the place residents most likely check for messages.

[3] The Government's interest in ensuring the security of the mails is advanced more directly by 18 U.S.C. 1341, 1708. To the extent that the security and efficiency problems are attributed to overcrowding in letterboxes, the problem could be resolved simply by requiring larger boxes.

As for protection of mail revenues, it is significant that the District Court found the cost of using the mails prohibitive, given appellees' budgets, and the delays in mail delivery too great to make it useful for appellees' needs. 490 F. Supp., at 160. Apparently, appellees' compliance with 18 U.S.C. 1725 would not increase mail revenues. Although protection of the Postal Service obviously must take the form of national regulation, having broad application, a statute's nondiscriminatory terms may not save it where infringement of speech is demonstrated. Murdock v. Pennsylvania, 319 U.S. 105, 115 (1943).

[4] Appellant conceded at oral argument that the Postal Service knew of no convictions and only one attempted prosecution under the statute. Tr. of Oral Arg. 15. That unsuccessful prosecution was dismissed because the District Court found impermissibly vague the prohibition on depositing unstamped "mailable matter such as statements of account, circulars, sales bills, or other like matter." United States v. Rogers, Cr. No. 72-87 (MD La. Feb. 16, 1973) (emphasis added). Apparently, no prosecutions have since been attempted, although the statute may be used to support the efforts of local postal offices in collecting unpaid postage. Tr. of Oral Arg. 15.

[5] The Postal Service has interpreted the statute to exempt mailslots, id., at 8, and to provide exception for certain kinds of deliveries, Domestic Mail Manual (DMM) 156.58 (newspapers, normally mailed but delivered on Sunday or holidays); 39 CFR 310.6 (1979) (letters dispatched within 50 miles of destination and same-day delivery). And by applying only to "mailable matter," the statute excludes pornography and other items not lawfully carried by the Postal Service. The Service thus has itself acknowledged that the statute sweeps more broadly than necessary.

[6] Such a permit requirement could accomplish the central purpose of the statute - to restrain commercial enterprises from avoiding postal fees by employing their own delivery services. See ante, at 125.

[7] Rather than supporting the conclusion that the Postal Service letterbox is not a public forum, the cases cited by the majority, ante, at 129-130, in fact point in the other direction. The Court resolved two First Amendment issues in Jones v. North Carolina Prisoners' Union, 433 U.S. 119 (1977): the scope of associational rights retained by convicted prisoners, and their right, if any, to bulk mail rates. The Court analyzed both issues under the principle that while in prison, "an inmate does not retain those First Amendment rights that are `inconsistent with his status as a prisoner or with the legitimate penological objectives of the corrections system.'" Id., at 129, quoting Pell v. Procunier, 417 U.S. 817, 822 (1974). No such principle applies to appellees. Furthermore, the public forum analysis in Jones asked whether exercise of the First Amendment rights would be incompatible with the purposes of the governmental facility, a question answerable in the negative in this case.

In Greer v. Spock, 424 U.S. 828, 838 (1976), the Court concluded that Fort Dix was not a public forum due to its military purpose and the power of "'the commanding officer summarily to exclude civilians from the area of his command'" (quoting Cafeteria Workers v. McElroy, 367 U.S. 886, 893 (1961)). At the same time, the Court emphasized that political campaign literature could still be distributed at the base unless it posed a clear danger to troop discipline and loyalty, 424 U.S., at 840 . Thus, the base remained a "public forum" at least for written communication. A plurality of the Court in Lehman v. City of Shaker Heights, 418 U.S. 298, 303 -304 (1974), found the city transit system not a public forum because its advertising space was incidental to its primary commercial transportation purpose. The plurality nevertheless recognized that the state action present necessitated a balancing analysis of the First Amendment interests of those seeking advertising space and the interests of the government and the users of the transit system. Further, both the plurality and Justice Douglas, in his separate opinion concurring in the result, relied on an analogy to the mass media which has no obligation under the First Amendment to broadcast or print any particular story or advertisement. Id., at 303 (opinion of BLACKMUN, J.); id., at 306 (opinion of Douglas, J.). In contrast, the Postal Service is obliged to accept all mailable matter. Finally, in Adderley v. Florida, 385 U.S. 39 (1966), the security needs of the jail were critical to the Court's conclusion that trespassers on the jail grounds could properly be prosecuted. Adderley itself noted that spaces more traditionally used by the public would more likely be public forums, id., at 41-42, and this treatment is appropriate here, given the traditional public use of the Postal Service. The determinative question in each of these cases was not whether the government owned or controlled the property, but whether the nature of the governmental interests warranted the restrictions on expression. That is the question properly asked in this case.

[8] But see Marsh v. Alabama, 326 U.S. 501 (1946).

[9] The Court announced the First Amendment rights of recipients in Lamont v. Postmaster General, 381 U.S. 301 (1965). There, the Court struck down a postal regulation denying delivery of Communist propaganda sent from outside the country, even though the regulation permitted such delivery to recipients who notified the Postal Service in writing that they wished to receive the material. Untenable, in the Court's view, was the fact that under the regulatory scheme, "[t]he addressee carries an affirmative obligation which we do not think the Government may impose on him." Id., at 307. The concern for the addressee's First Amendment rights should govern here.

[10] Appellant suggests no First Amendment problem is presented because residents would not erect letterboxes but for the Postal Service, and the First Amendment did not compel the creation of the Service. Brief for Appellant 18-19. This argument obviously proves too much, because the First Amendment did not ordain the establishment of schools or libraries, and yet we have held that once established, these public facilities must be managed consistently with the First Amendment. Tinker v. Des Moines Independent School Dist., 393 U.S. 503 (1969); Brown v. Louisiana, 383 U.S. 131 (1966).

Williams' conduct is clearly prohibited by the statute: Justice Marshall's dissent in Williams v. United States (June 29, 1982)

JUSTICE MARSHALL, with whom THE CHIEF JUSTICE, JUSTICE BRENNAN, and JUSTICE WHITE join, dissenting.

The majority, after developing an overly technical "definition" of the meaning of a check - a definition which will come as quite a surprise to banks and businesses that accept checks in exchange for goods, services, or cash on the representation that the drawer has sufficient funds to cover the check - concludes that the question whether petitioner Williams' check-kiting scheme is covered by 18 U.S.C. 1014 is ambiguous. The majority then applies its version of the rule of lenity, and decides that Williams cannot be convicted for violating this statute. Because I believe that the majority misapplies the rule of lenity, and because Williams' conduct is clearly prohibited by the statute, I respectfully dissent.

I

Before addressing the application of 1014 to Williams' conduct, I think that it is helpful to set forth clearly what is not involved here. This is not a case in which a defendant, through careless bookkeeping, wrote checks on accounts with insufficient funds. Nor is this a case in which a defendant wrote a check on an account containing insufficient funds with the good-faith intention to deposit in that account an amount that would cover the check before it cleared in the normal course of business. Rather, this case clearly involves fraudulent conduct. Petitioner Williams engaged in an intentional check-kiting scheme. He misled the first bank into honoring his worthless, or virtually worthless, check and extending him immediate credit. This extension of credit enabled him to "play the float" and cover that check by misleading another bank into extending him credit on an equally worthless check. In effect, Williams was able to obtain interest-free extensions of credit. Williams, who was a bank president, does not, nor can he, make any credible argument that he was unaware that his conduct was wrongful. With this in mind, I turn to the question whether Williams' conduct constitutes a violation of 18 U.S.C. 1014.

Section 1014 is a comprehensive statute designed to protect the assets of federally insured lending institutions. The Government establishes a violation of this statute by proving that the defendant "knowingly [made] any false statement or . . . willfully overvalue[d] any . . . property or security, for the purpose of influencing in any way the action of [any federally insured bank] upon any . . . advance, . . . commitment, or loan." 18 U.S.C. 1014 (emphasis added). Just last Term, we reiterated that "[i]n determining the scope of a statute, we look first to its language. If the statutory language is unambiguous, in the absence of a `clearly expressed legislative intent to the contrary, that language must ordinarily be regarded as conclusive.'" United States v. Turkette, 452 U.S. 576, 580 (1981) (quoting Consumer Product Safety Comm'n v. GTE Sylvania, Inc., 447 U.S. 102, 108 (1980)). In my view, the plain language of 1014 covers the check-kiting scheme practiced by Williams, and nothing in the legislative history of the statute indicates that Congress intended to exclude this type of scheme from the coverage of the statute.

A

The language of 1014 is sweeping. It embraces numerous entities in which the Federal Government has a financial interest. It proscribes, in the disjunctive, a wide variety of deceptive schemes that might impair the financial stability of these institutions. Cf. United States v. Naftalin, 441 U.S. 768, 774 (1979) (disjunctive prohibitions intended to "cover additional kinds of illegalities - not to narrow the reach of the prior sections"). The statute refers broadly to "any false statement or report," and to overvaluations of "any" property or security. The list of transactions to which the statute applies is equally expansive - it covers "any application, advance, discount, purchase, purchase agreement, repurchase agreement, commitment, or loan, or any change or extension of any of the same, by renewal, deferment of action or otherwise, or the acceptance, release, or substitution of security therefor." 18 U.S.C. 1014.

The broad statutory language clearly evinces its legislative purpose - Congress hoped to protect federally insured institutions from losses stemming from false statements or misrepresentations that mislead the institutions into making financial commitments, advances, or loans. The statute was intended to be broad enough "to maintain the vitality of the FDIC insurance program . . . and `to cover all undertakings which might subject the FDIC insured bank to risk of loss.'" United States v. Pinto, 646 F.2d 833, 838 (CA3) (quoting United States v. Stoddart, 574 F.2d 1050, 1053 (CA10 1978)), cert. denied, 454 U.S. 816 (1981). This broad language does not lend itself to the restrictive interpretation endorsed by the Court today. Cf. United States v. Culbert, 435 U.S. 371 (1978).

Nothing on the face of 1014 "suggests a congressional intent to limit its coverage" to a particular kind of transaction. United States v. Culbert, supra, at 373. Check kiting, which threatens the assets of federally insured banks in precisely the same way as a misrepresentation in a loan application, should not be excluded from the reach of the statute simply because the terms of the statute and its legislative history do not specifically identify check kiting by name or precise description. This method of statutory construction was rejected recently in Harrison v. PPG Industries, Inc., 446 U.S. 578, 592 (1980):

"[I]t would be a strange canon of statutory construction that would require Congress to state in committee reports or elsewhere in its deliberations that which is obvious on the face of a statute. In ascertaining the meaning of a statute, a court cannot, in the manner of Sherlock Holmes, pursue the theory of the dog that did not bark."

Unfortunately, in my view, the Court's approach to interpreting 1014 comes dangerously close to the method we rejected in Harrison. Unless one accepts the Court's overly restrictive and technical "definition" of a check, check-kiting schemes clearly fall within the broad language of that statute.

B

As the majority recognizes, a violation of 1014 is established when the Government proves two elements: that the defendant either made a "false statement or report," or "willfully overvalue[d] any . . . property or security;" and that the defendant did so "for the purpose of influencing in any way the action of [a federally insured institution] upon any application, advance, . . . commitment, or loan." After recognizing this, however, the majority's analysis jumps the track. The majority concludes that when a drawer presents a kited check to a bank with the knowledge that he does not have sufficient funds, and with the intent not to cover that check with anything other than another virtually worthless kited check, he has not made "any false statement or report," or "willfully overvalue[d] any . . . property or security" within the meaning of the statute. In my view, neither of these conclusions withstands analysis.

(1)

The basis for the Court's conclusion that Williams did not make a "false statement or report" is concededly technical and "simple": "a check is not a factual assertion at all, and therefore cannot be characterized as `true' or `false.'" Ante, at 284. This argument proves too much: it would apply equally to material omissions or failures to disclose in connection with loan applications. However, the Courts of Appeals have held that the failure to disclose material information needed to avoid deception in connection with loan transactions covered by 1014 constitutes a "false statement or report," and thus violates the statute. See, e. g., United States v. Greene, 578 F.2d 648, 657 (CA5 1978), cert. denied, 439 U.S. 1133 (1979). I assume that the majority would not disagree with this analysis, which is based on established contract principles. I am at a loss as to why the majority does not apply the same analysis to the transactions at issue in this case.

The majority's description of a check as an "`unconditional promise or order to pay a sum certain in money,'" ante, at 285 (quoting the Uniform Commercial Code 3-104(1)(b), 2 U. L. A. 17 (1977)), is unexceptionable as a conclusory description of "black-letter" law. However, this oversimplified description fails to look behind the bare technical definition of a check. Moreover, this description is not at all inconsistent with the necessary implications that a check carries. "In giving a check, the drawer impliedly represents that he has on deposit with the drawee banks funds equivalent to the face amount of the check." F. Whitney, The Law of Modern Commercial Practices 341 (2d ed. 1965). 1 Despite the majority's equivocation on this point, those who write or accept checks in exchange for goods, services, or cash undoubtedly understand that this implicit representation has been made. 2 A check is accepted with the expectation that it will be paid in the normal course of collection. A banker who knew that the drawer did not have funds on deposit would not credit the check to the drawer's account or reduce it to cash. Regardless of any contractual breach also involved in check kiting, a person who writes a series of checks knowing that there are no funds to cover them has made intentional false representations within the reach of 1014.

Any other view, including that endorsed by the Court today, would interfere with the manner in which a major portion of commercial transactions are conducted in our society today. Williams was charged with, and the jury convicted him of, making a false representation (or, more precisely, a material omission) when he presented his check to the bank with the knowledge that he did not have sufficient funds to cover the check, and with the further intent not to cover that check before it cleared with anything other than another worthless kited check. See n. 2, supra. Therefore, his conviction under 1014 should stand.

(2)

In addition to violating 1014 by intentionally making a false statement to a federally insured bank for the purpose of obtaining credit, Williams also violated the statute for a separate and independent reason. Although Williams presented to the bank for immediate credit a check which on its face represented an amount exceeding $50,000, he well knew that in fact the check was virtually worthless. In so doing, he "willfully overvalue[d] . . . property or security" for the purpose of obtaining credit. 3 The Court's rejection of the Government's argument with respect to this issue is startling in both its brevity and its concededly technical and "literal" interpretation of the legal value of a check which completely ignores the meaning attributed to checks in the real world.

The very essence of a check-kiting scheme is the successful overvaluation of a security or property which misleads a bank into issuing immediate credit on the assumption that the security or property is in fact valued at the amount represented on its face. A check-kiting scheme is successful only when the bank to which the check is presented assumes that the check is supported by adequate funds in the account upon which it is drawn, and that the face amount of the check is in fact its value. See supra, at 296-298; United States v. Payne, 602 F.2d 1215, 1217-1218 (CA5 1979). If the bank does not accept the valuation on the face of the check, and instead either inquires into the status of the account on which the check is drawn or waits until the check clears before paying the face amount of the check, the scheme will collapse. Of course, it would be more prudent for a bank to take such precautions just as it would be prudent for banks to inquire carefully into the accuracy of all representations made concerning the value of collateral pledged as security for conventional loans. However, this more prudent course is not always practicable. Moreover, the bank may not believe that such precautions are necessary where, as here, the person presenting the check is the president of another bank presumed to know the illegality, and the drastic adverse consequences to a bank, of a check-kiting scheme. In any event, a bank's failure to take all possible precautions does not bar prosecution under 1014, which places the burden of avoiding false representations, at the risk of criminal prosecution, upon the person who seeks the funds of the federally insured bank. Section 1014 forbids a person seeking such funds to make "any" false statement or to "willfully overvalue" any security or property to obtain use of the bank's funds. A kited check is "willfully overvalued" within the meaning of the statute, just as worthless securities presented as collateral for a loan are "willfully overvalued." See United States v. Calandrella, 605 F.2d 236 (CA6), cert. denied sub nom. Kaye v. United States, 444 U.S. 991 (1979).

(3)

The Court does not question that the second element of a 1014 violation - that Williams presented his kited check for the purpose of influencing the bank to extend him credit in the form of a loan or an advance - is satisfied in this case. Clearly, Williams' conduct was directed at misleading a bank into extending immediate credit. Indeed, the whole purpose of Williams' kiting scheme was to obtain an immediate extension of credit by depositing a check purportedly supported by adequate funds. The banks that extended funds on the basis of Williams' worthless, and not yet collected, checks made an "advance," a "loan," and a "commitment" within the ordinary meaning of these terms. See, e. g., United States v. Payne, supra, at 1218 (check kiting has effect of inducing a credit, a loan, or an advance); United States v. Street, 529 F.2d 226, 229 (CA6 1976) (check kiting is the obtaining of "forced credit"); J. White & R. Summers, Uniform Commercial Code 558 (2d ed. 1980); F. Whitney, supra n. 1, 310, pp. 451-452.

If a worthless check is submitted to a bank for reasons other than to obtain an extension of credit, the conduct simply is not check kiting in the ordinary sense of the term, and would not fall within the prohibition of 1014. 4 However, if a properly instructed jury concludes that a worthless check was submitted in order to obtain immediate credit from a bank, there is no reason to regard the conduct as falling outside the reach of 1014. The jury that convicted Williams was so instructed, see n. 2, supra, and found that Williams' conduct constituted a "false representation" designed to influence the banks into extending him immediate credit.

C

The unambiguous language of 1014 clearly proscribes conduct commonly referred to as check kiting. This language should be given effect in the absence of clear indications in the legislative history that Congress did not intend to proscribe this conduct. See United States v. Turkette, 452 U.S., at 580 . There are no such indications in the legislative history. To the contrary, the legislative history makes clear that the statute was not limited to borrowers or to loan applications. See S. Rep. No. 1078, 88th Cong., 2d Sess., 4 (1964); H. R. Conf. Rep. No. 91-1784, p. 66 (1970).

The Court finds no indication that Congress intended to exclude check-kiting schemes from the scope of the statute. The Court's brief review of the legislative history to 1014 does suggest that the primary purpose of the statute is to prohibit misrepresentations in connection with conventional loan applications. However, neither this fact, nor the fact that most convictions under the statute involve such transactions, compels the Court to ignore the broad language and purposes of the statute by interpreting it to cover only these transactions. In the past, we have consistently rejected the argument that a criminal statute must be given its narrowest meaning by limiting its scope to effectuate only its primary purpose. See, e. g., United States v. Turkette, supra; United States v. Naftalin, 441 U.S. 768 (1979); United States v. Moore, 423 U.S. 122 (1975).

II

In light of the broad protection Congress intended to accord federally insured institutions against fraudulent or deceptive conduct intended to mislead these institutions into extending credit and the broad, unrestricted statutory language embodied in 1014, I marvel at the Court's method of interpreting this statute. Indeed, today's decision is utterly incompatible with a number of prior decisions of this Court in which we addressed similar arguments raised by persons convicted under broad federal statutes. See, e. g., United States v. Turkette, supra; Rubin v. United States, 449 U.S. 424 (1981); United States v. Naftalin, supra; United States v. Culbert, 435 U.S. 371 (1978). In these decisions, we have consistently looked first to the statutory language to determine the scope and purpose of the statute. If it were evident from the face of the statute that the statute was written broadly in order to prohibit certain kinds of conduct which entail specific risks or dangers deemed by the legislators to be sufficiently unacceptable to warrant criminal sanction, we do not frustrate this purpose by distorting either the statutory language employed or the conduct of the accused in the name of the "rule of lenity." See, e. g., United States v. Turkette, supra; Rubin v. United States, supra.

In contrast with this established approach, the majority today interprets 1014 without acknowledging the broad statutory language chosen by Congress. This error is compounded by the Court's failure to address the fact that this broad language was intended to proscribe, in generic and disjunctive terms, precisely the type of conduct of which Williams was found guilty - intentionally misleading the bank into extending him credit - and to protect federally insured institutions from precisely the risk of loss to which Williams' conduct subjected them. Ignoring these factors, the majority begins its analysis by employing an oversimplified, concededly technical and literal interpretation of the "legal definition" of a check. In then observes that Congress never explicitly stated that it intended the statute to cover check-kiting schemes. It concludes that in the absence of such an express statement, the rule of lenity requires that the statute not cover these schemes.

The majority's approach to the question of statutory construction is a prime example of what this Court has time and again said the rule of lenity does not entail:

"The canon in favor of strict construction is not an inexorable command to override common sense and evident statutory purpose. It does not require magnified emphasis upon a single ambiguous word in order to give it a meaning contradictory to the fair import of the whole remaining language. As was said in United States v. Gaskin, 320 U.S. 527, 530, the canon `does not require distortion or nullification of the evident meaning and purpose of the legislation.' Nor does it demand that a statute be given the `narrowest meaning'; it is satisfied if the words are given their fair meaning in accord with the manifest intent of the lawmakers." United States v. Brown, 333 U.S. 18, 25 -26 (1948) (quoted in United States v. Turkette, supra, at 588, n. 10, and United States v. Moore, supra, at 145).

If the broad language and evident purpose of the statute had been given effect, there would have been no need to parse the legislative history for affirmative evidence that Congress "demand[ed] a broader reading of the statute." Ante, at 288. Holding that 1014 reaches check kiting does not produce an absurd result, render the statute internally contradictory, or diverge from legislative policy. To the contrary, Congress' policy, manifest in 1014 and elsewhere throughout Title 18 of the United States Code, is that federal criminal sanctions are necessary to provide federally insured banking institutions with comprehensive protection against practices that cause risk of loss. The Court's construction of 1014, on the other hand, results in a large loophole in the protection afforded these institutions by limiting the statute's application to formal loan transactions. After today's decision, a bank's protection against false statements intended to influence credit transactions depends not upon whether a misrepresentation was made in connection with a loan, advance, or commitment, but rather upon whether a court concluded that the transaction was "traditional" or that Congress specified that transaction by name in a committee report.

It is worth observing that in this case, none of the general justifications for applying the rule of lenity are present. In Huddleston v. United States, 415 U.S. 814, 831 (1974), this Court explained that the rule of lenity "is rooted in the concern of the law for individual rights, and in the belief that fair warning should be accorded as to what conduct is criminal and punishable by deprivation of liberty or property." There is no question that Williams, a bank president, knew that his check-kiting scheme was wrongful. The majority's attempt to buttress its decision by arguing that check kiting has traditionally been regulated by the States, and that federal enforcement might interfere with this regulation, is completely unjustified. 5 The Federal Government, which provides deposit insurance, has a paramount interest in safeguarding the financial integrity of federally insured banking institutions. The Courts of Appeals have been virtually unanimous in holding that check kiting is subject to federal prosecution under the mail and wire fraud statutes, see, e. g., United States v. Giordano, 489 F.2d 327 (CA2 1973); United States v. Constant, 501 F.2d 1284 (CA5 1974), cert. denied, 420 U.S. 910 (1975), and the majority apparently does not question these decisions. Therefore, a check-kiting prosecution under 1014, which by its terms applies only to federally insured institutions, results in no new inroad upon state criminal jurisdiction.

Under the version of the rule of lenity adopted today, conduct which falls within the literal terms of a broad statute, which proscribes in disjunctive and generic terms the type of conduct at issue, and which is designed to protect against the very risk created by such conduct, escapes the reach of the statute unless Congress specifies that conduct by name in the statute or describes it in detail in the statute's legislative history. In order to find Williams' conduct outside the scope of 1014, the majority ignores the function of a check in today's society. The rule of lenity has never been interpreted to require this kind of result. I am at a loss to explain why the Court adopts this approach today and consequently turns the rule of lenity on its head. Accordingly, I dissent.

Notes

[1] The Court's facile conclusion that Williams made no false statement or misrepresentation when he presented his check to a bank for immediate credit, knowing that the check was not supported by sufficient funds and that he was not going to cover the check before it cleared with anything other than another kited check, is contrary to

the theory underlying most prosecutions under state bad check laws. These laws are not based upon the defendant's breach of a contractual promise that he will pay a sum certain upon demand, but upon the fact that in knowingly presenting a bad check the defendant has committed fraud and misrepresentation and can be punished for committing a crime. Brief for United States 20; Brief for Petitioner 28-29, and n. 17. See also F. Whitney, The Law of Modern Commercial Practices 341 (2d ed. 1965). The Court attempts to avoid the obvious problem this fact presents to its method of statutory interpretation by stating that the federal statute does not apply "in terms" to check kiting, while some state laws do. See ante, at 285, n. 6. This reasoning is circular. The reason why 1014 does not "in terms" reach a check-kiting scheme, while certain state laws do, is because the Court ipse dixit totally discredits the theory upon which the state laws are premised and refuses to read the terms of the statute in the only manner that is consistent with this theory.

[2] The manner in which the Court manufactures "confusion" over the common understanding of a check is difficult to comprehend. See ante, at 286, n. 7. Most of it is totally irrelevant because each of the majority's "common understandings" of the meaning of a check are entirely consistent with prosecuting a check-kiting scheme under 1014. The majority suggests that the "common understanding" of a check is only that sufficient funds will be present by the time the check clears or that the drawer will make good the payment of the face amount of the check if the bank refuses payment. Even if the majority is correct, prosecuting a check-kiting scheme under 1014 would be justified because the jury found that Williams had intentionally acted inconsistently with each of these understandings. The jury was specifically instructed that it could not convict unless it found that Williams "made the false statement with fraudulent intent to influence the [bank] to extend [him] credit." App. 37. The judge added that a statement is "false" if it "relates to a material fact and is untrue and is then known to be untrue by the person making it." Id., at 38. The judge further instructed the jury that "[t]he crucial question in check-kiting is whether the defendant intended to write checks which he could not reasonably expect to cover and thereby defraud the bank, or whether he was genuinely involved in the process of depositing funds and then making legitimate withdrawals against them. Hence, proof that the checks were eventually paid might well be pertinent to defendant's initial intent, that is, whether he intended to deceive the bank." Ibid. Therefore, the jury was clearly instructed to acquit Williams if he had shared with the Court even its most lenient and unrealistic interpretation of the implied representation made when one presents a check. The jury had to find that Williams had given the bank the kited check with the express intent not to actually cover the check, but only to receive this extension of credit for as long as the check-kiting scheme continued.

[3] Section 1014 applies to the willful overvaluation of "any . . . property, or security." Again, this element of the statute is cast in broad rather than restrictive terms. Congress plainly intended to proscribe the willful overvaluation of anything of value given to a lending institution. There is no suggestion that the broad generic terms "any . . . property or security" were meant to exclude items such as checks presented to obtain a

temporary extension of credit. There is no reason to interpret this language to exclude checks. A check is plainly a form of property under even the majority's most restrictive definition - it is a demand to a drawee to pay a sum certain of money, which is backed by a promise of the drawer to make payment in the event of default. Furthermore, as evidenced by other provisions of Title 18, including the general definitional section, 18 U.S.C. 8, a check is a type of "security." See, e. g., 18 U.S.C. 2311.

[4] The Court's fears that holding a check-kiting scheme to be covered by 1014 would entail broad implications, see ante, at 286-287, are misguided. If there was no intent on the part of the check kiter to defraud the bank into extending credit, there would be no 1014 violation. The fact that the Government brought separate counts for each check in the check-kiting scheme does not alter the fact that it was essential to conviction under the jury instructions for the jury to find that petitioner was involved in a check-kiting scheme intentionally designed to defraud the banks.

[5] In Title 18, Congress has provided comprehensive criminal sanctions to protect federally insured institutions. See, e. g., 18 U.S.C. 212, 213 (loans or gratuities offered to bank examiners by bank officials; acceptance of same by examiners); 18 U.S.C. 493 (forging, counterfeiting, or passing bonds and obligations); 18 U.S.C. 656 (theft from banks by bank examiners); 18 U.S.C. 709 (1976 ed. and Supp. IV) (false advertising that bank deposits are insured by Federal Deposit Insurance Corporation). Congress has sought to protect fully the integrity of the federal insurance program, and the protection against check kiting afforded by 1014 is consistent with this scheme. See, e. g., United States v. Bush, 599 F.2d 72, 75 (CA5 1979); United States v. Pinto, 646 F.2d 833, 838 (CA3), cert. denied, 454 U.S. 816 (1981); United States v. Stoddart, 574 F.2d 1050, 1053 (CA10 1978). Construing 1014 to cover check kiting does not displace the authority of the States. Rather, it complements state law enforcement in an area where the federal interest is substantial. See United States v. Turkette, 452 U.S. 576, 586, n. 9 (1981) (interpreting the Racketeer Influenced and Corrupt Organizations statute) ("[T]he States remain free to exercise their police powers to the fullest constitutional extent in defining and prosecuting crimes within their respective jurisdictions. That some of those crimes may also constitute [violations of federal law], is no restriction on the separate administration of criminal justice by the States").

Standing: Justice Marshall's dissent in City of Los Angeles v. Lyons (April 20, 1983)

JUSTICE MARSHALL, with whom JUSTICE BRENNAN, JUSTICE BLACKMUN, and JUSTICE STEVENS join, dissenting.

The District Court found that the city of Los Angeles authorizes its police officers to apply life-threatening chokeholds to citizens who pose no threat of violence, and that respondent, Adolph Lyons, was subjected to such a chokehold. The Court today holds that a federal court is without power to enjoin the enforcement of the city's policy, no matter how flagrantly unconstitutional it may be. Since no one can show that he will be choked in the future, no one -- not even a person who, like Lyons, has almost been choked to death -- has standing to challenge the continuation of the policy. The city is free to continue the policy indefinitely, as long as it is willing to pay damages for the injuries and deaths that result. I dissent from this unprecedented and unwarranted approach to standing.

There is plainly a "case or controversy" concerning the constitutionality of the city's chokehold policy. The constitutionality of that policy is directly implicated by Lyons' claim for damages against the city. The complaint clearly alleges that the officer who choked Lyons was carrying out an official policy, and a municipality is liable under 42 U.S.C. § 1983 for the conduct of its employees only if they acted pursuant to such a policy. Monell v. New York City Dept. of Social Services, 436 U. S. 658, 436 U. S. 694 (1978). Lyons therefore has standing to challenge the city's chokehold policy and to obtain whatever relief a court may ultimately deem appropriate. None of our prior decisions suggests that his requests for particular forms of relief raise any additional issues concerning his standing. Standing has always depended on whether a plaintiff has a "personal stake in the outcome of the controversy," Baker v. Carr, 369 U. S. 186, 369 U. S. 204 (1962), not on the "precise nature of the relief sought." Jenkins v. McKeithen, 395 U. S. 411, 395 U. S. 423 (1969) (opinion of MARSHALL, J., joined by Warren, C.J., and BRENNAN, J.).

I

A

Respondent Adolph Lyons is a 24-year-old Negro male who resides in Los Angeles. According to the uncontradicted evidence in the record, [1] at about 2 a.m. on October 6, 1976, Lyons was pulled over to the curb by two officers of the Los Angeles Police Department (LAPD) for a traffic infraction because one of his tail-lights was burned out. The officers greeted him with drawn revolvers as he exited from his car. Lyons was told to face his car and spread his legs. He did so. He was then ordered to clasp his hands and put them on top of his head. He again complied. After one of the officers completed a patdown search, Lyons dropped his hands, but was ordered to place them back above his head, and one of the officers grabbed Lyons' hands and slammed them onto his head. Lyons complained about the pain caused by the ring of keys he was holding in his hand. Within 5 to 10 seconds, the officer began to choke Lyons by applying a forearm against his throat. As Lyons struggled for air, the officer handcuffed him, but continued to apply the chokehold until he blacked out. When Lyons regained consciousness, he was lying face down on the ground, choking, gasping for air, and spitting up blood and dirt. He had urinated and defecated. He was issued a traffic citation and released.

On February 7, 1977, Lyons commenced this action under 42 U.S.C. § 1983 against the individual officers and the city, alleging violations of his rights under the

Fourth, Eighth, and Fourteenth Amendments to the Constitution and seeking damages and declaratory and injunctive relief. He claimed that he was subjected to a chokehold without justification, and that defendant officers were "carrying out the official policies, customs and practices of the Los Angeles Police Department and the City of Los Angeles." Count II, 13. [2] These allegations were included or incorporated in each of the Counts in which the city was named as a defendant. See Counts II through VI. Lyons alleged that the city authorizes the use of chokeholds "in innumerable situations where [the police] are not threatened by the use of any deadly force whatsoever." Count V, ◆ 22.

Although the city instructs its officers that use of a chokehold does not constitute deadly force, since 1975, no less than 16 persons have died following the use of a chokehold by an LAPD police officer. Twelve have been Negro males. [3] The evidence submitted to the District Court [4] established that, for many years, it has been the official policy of the city to permit police officers to employ chokeholds in a variety of situations where they face no threat of violence. In reported "altercations" between LAPD officers and citizens, the chokeholds are used more frequently than any other means of physical restraint. [5] Between February, 1975, and July, 1980, LAPD officers applied chokeholds on at least 975 occasions, which represented more than three-quarters of the reported altercations. [6]

It is undisputed that chokeholds pose a high and unpredictable risk of serious injury or death. Chokeholds are intended to bring a subject under control by causing pain and rendering him unconscious. Depending on the position of the officer's arm and the force applied, the victim's voluntary or involuntary reaction, and his state of health, an officer may inadvertently crush the victim's larynx, trachea, or hyoid. The result may be death caused by either cardiac arrest or asphyxiation. [7] An LAPD officer described the reaction of a person to being choked as "do[ing] the chicken," Exh. 44, p. 93, in reference apparently to the reactions of a chicken when its neck is wrung. The victim experiences extreme pain. His face turns blue as he is deprived of oxygen, he goes into spasmodic convulsions, his eyes roll back, his body wriggles, his feet kick up and down, and his arms move about wildly.

Although there has been no occasion to determine the precise contours of the city's chokehold policy, the evidence submitted to the District Court provides some indications. LAPD Training Officer Terry Speer testified that an officer is authorized to deploy a chokehold whenever he "feels that there's about to be a bodily attack made on him." App. 31 (emphasis added). A training bulletin states that "[c]ontrol holds . . . allow officers to subdue any resistance by the suspects." Exh. 47, p. 1 (emphasis added). In the proceedings below, the city characterized its own policy as authorizing the use of chokeholds "to gain control of a suspect who is violently resisting the officer or trying to escape,'" to "subdue any resistance by the suspects," [8] and to permit an officer, "where . . . resisted, but not necessarily threatened with serious bodily harm or death, . . . to subdue a suspect who forcibly resists an officer." (Emphasis added.) [9]

The training given LAPD officers provides additional revealing evidence of the city's chokehold policy. Officer Speer testified that, in instructing officers concerning the use of force, the LAPD does not distinguish between felony and misdemeanor suspects. App. 379. Moreover, the officers are taught to maintain the chokehold until the suspect goes limp, id. at 387; App. to Pet. for Cert. 51a, despite substantial evidence that the application of a chokehold invariably induces a "flight or flee" syndrome, producing an involuntary struggle by the victim which can easily be misinterpreted by the officer as willful resistance that must be overcome by prolonging the chokehold and increasing the force applied. See n. 7, supra. In addition, officers are instructed that the chokeholds can be safely deployed for up to three or four minutes. App. 387-388; App. to Pet. for Cert. 48. Robert Jarvis, the city's expert who has taught at the Los Angeles Police Academy for the past 12 years, admitted that officers are never told that the bar-arm control can cause death if applied for just two seconds. App. 388. Of the nine deaths for which evidence was submitted to the District Court, the average duration of the choke where specified was approximately 40 seconds.

C

In determining the appropriateness of a preliminary injunction, the District Court recognized that the city's policy is subject to the constraints imposed by the Due Process Clause of the Fourteenth Amendment. The court found that,

"[d]uring the course of this confrontation, said officers, without provocation or legal justification, applied a Department-authorized chokehold, which resulted in injuries to plaintiff."

(Emphasis added.) The court found that the

"City of Los Angeles and the Department authorize the use of these holds under circumstances where no one is threatened by death or grievous bodily harm."

The court concluded that the use of the chokeholds constitutes "deadly force," and that the city may not constitutionally authorize the use of such force "in situations where death or serious bodily harm is not threatened." On the basis of this conclusion, the District Court entered a preliminary injunction enjoining "the use of both the carotid artery and bar arm holds under circumstances which do not threaten death or serious bodily injury." [10] As the Court of Appeals noted,

"[a]ll the trial judge has done, so far, is to tell the city that its police officers may not apply life-threatening strangleholds to persons stopped in routine police work unless the application of such force is necessary to prevent serious bodily harm to an officer."

656 F.2d 417, 418 (1981).

II

At the outset, it is important to emphasize that Lyons' entitlement to injunctive relief and his entitlement to an award of damages both depend upon whether he can show that the city's chokehold policy violates the Constitution. An indispensable prerequisite of municipal liability under 42 U.S.C. § 1983 is proof that the conduct complained of is attributable to an unconstitutional official policy or custom. Polk County v. Dodson, 454 U. S. 312, 454 U. S. 326 (1981); Monell v. New York City Dept. of Social Services, 436 U.S.

at 436 U. S. 694. It is not enough for a § 1983 plaintiff to show that the employees or agents of a municipality have violated or will violate the Constitution, for a municipality will not be held liable solely on a theory of respondeat superior. See Monell, supra, at 436 U. S. 694.

The Court errs in suggesting that Lyons' prayer for injunctive relief in Count V of his first amended complaint concerns a policy that was not responsible for his injuries, and that therefore could not support an award of damages. Ante at 461 U. S. 106-107, n. 7. Paragraph 8 of the complaint alleges that Lyons was choked "without provocation, legal justification or excuse."

Paragraph 13 expressly alleges that

"[t]he Defendant Officers were carrying out the official policies, customs and practices of the Los Angeles Police Department and the City of Los Angeles,"

and that, "by virtue thereof, defendant City is liable for the actions" of the officers. (Emphasis added.) These allegations are incorporated in each of the Counts against the city, including Count V.

There is no basis for the Court's assertion that Lyons has failed to allege "that the City either orders or authorizes application of the chokeholds where there is no resistance or other provocation." Ante at 461 U. S. 106, n. 7. I am completely at a loss to understand how paragraphs 8 and 13 can be deemed insufficient to allege that the city's policy authorizes the use of chokeholds without provocation. The Court apparently finds Lyons' complaint wanting because, although it alleges that he was choked without provocation and that the officers acted pursuant to an official policy, it fails to allege in haec verba that the city's policy authorizes the choking of suspects without provocation. I am aware of no case decided since the abolition of the old common law forms of action, and the Court cites none, that in any way supports this crabbed construction of the complaint. A federal court is capable of concluding for itself that two plus two equals four. [11]

The Court also errs in asserting that, even if the complaint sufficiently alleges that the city's policy authorizes the use of chokeholds without provocation, such an allegation is, in any event, "belied by the record made on the application for preliminary injunction." Ibid. This conclusion flatly contradicts the District Court's express factual finding, which was left undisturbed by the Court of Appeals, that the officers applied a "Department-authorized chokehold which resulted in injuries to plaintiff." (Emphasis added.) The city does not contend that this factual finding is clearly erroneous. [12]

In sum, it is absolutely clear that Lyons' requests for damages and for injunctive relief call into question the constitutionality of the city's policy concerning the use of chokeholds. If he does not show that that policy is unconstitutional, he will be no more entitled to damages than to an injunction.

III

Since Lyons' claim for damages plainly gives him standing, and since the success of that claim depends upon a demonstration that the city's chokehold policy is unconstitutional, it is beyond dispute that Lyons has properly invoked the District Court's authority to adjudicate the constitutionality of the city's chokehold policy. The dispute concerning the constitutionality of that policy plainly presents a "case or controversy" under Art. III. The Court nevertheless holds that a federal court has no power under Art. III to adjudicate Lyons' request, in the same lawsuit, for injunctive relief with respect to that very policy. This anomalous result is not supported either by precedent or by the fundamental concern underlying the standing requirement. Moreover, by fragmenting a single claim into multiple claims for particular types of relief and requiring a separate showing of standing for each form of relief, the decision today departs from this Court's traditional conception of standing and of the remedial powers of the federal courts.

A

It is simply disingenuous for the Court to assert that its decision requires "[n]o extension" of O'Shea v. Littleton, 414 U. S. 488 (1974), and Rizzo v. Goode, 423 U. S. 362 (1976). Ante at 461 U. S. 105. In contrast to this case O'Shea and Rizzo involved disputes focusing solely on the threat of future injury which the plaintiffs in those cases alleged they faced. In O'Shea, the plaintiffs did not allege past injury and did not seek compensatory relief. [13] In Rizzo, the plaintiffs sought only declaratory and injunctive relief, and alleged past instances of police misconduct only in an attempt to establish the substantiality of the threat of future injury. There was similarly no claim for damages based on past injuries in Ashcroft v. Mattis, 431 U. S. 171 (1977), or Golden v. Zwickler, 394 U. S. 103 (1969), [14] on which the Court also relies.

These decisions do not support the Court's holding today. As the Court recognized in O'Shea, standing under Art. III is established by an allegation of "threatened or actual injury.'" 414 U.S. at 414 U. S. 493, quoting Linda R. S. v. Richard D., 410 U. S. 614, 410 U. S. 617 (1973) (emphasis added). See also 414 U.S. at 414 U. S. 493, n. 2. Because the plaintiffs in O'Shea, Rizzo, Mattis, and Zwickler did not seek to redress past injury, their standing to sue depended entirely on the risk of future injury they faced. Apart from the desire to eliminate the possibility of future injury, the plaintiffs in those cases had no other personal stake in the outcome of the controversies.

By contrast, Lyons' request for prospective relief is coupled with his claim for damages based on past injury. In addition to the risk that he will be subjected to a chokehold in the future, Lyons has suffered past injury. [15] Because he has a live claim for damages, he need not rely solely on the threat of future injury to establish his personal stake in the outcome of the controversy. [16] In the cases relied on by the majority, the Court simply had no occasion to decide whether a plaintiff who has standing to litigate a dispute must clear a separate standing hurdle with respect to each form of relief sought. [17]

B

The Court's decision likewise finds no support in the fundamental policy underlying the Art. III standing requirement -- the concern that a federal court not decide a legal issue if the plaintiff lacks a sufficient

"personal stake in the outcome of the controversy as to assure that concrete adverseness which sharpens the presentation of issues upon which the court so largely depends for illumination of difficult . . . questions."

    Baker v. Carr, 369 U.S. at 369 U. S. 204. As this Court stated in Flast v. Cohen, 392 U. S. 83, 392 U. S. 101 (1968),

    "the question of standing is related only to whether the dispute sought to be adjudicated will be presented in an adversary context and in a form historically viewed as capable of judicial resolution."

    See also Valley Forge Christian College v. Americans United for Separation of Church and State, 454 U. S. 464, 454 U. S. 472 (1982) (standing requirement ensures that "the legal questions presented to the court will be resolved, not in the rarified atmosphere of a debating society, but in a concrete factual context conducive to a realistic appreciation of the consequences of judicial action").

    Because Lyons has a claim for damages against the city, and because he cannot prevail on that claim unless he demonstrates that the city's chokehold policy violates the Constitution, his personal stake in the outcome of the controversy adequately assures an adversary presentation of his challenge to the constitutionality of the policy. [18] Moreover, the resolution of this challenge will be largely dispositive of his requests for declaratory and injunctive relief. No doubt the requests for injunctive relief may raise additional questions. But these questions involve familiar issues relating to the appropriateness of particular forms of relief, and have never been thought to implicate a litigant's standing to sue. The denial of standing separately to seek injunctive relief therefore cannot be justified by the basic concern underlying the Art. III standing requirement. [19]

    C

    By fragmenting the standing inquiry and imposing a separate standing hurdle with respect to each form of relief sought, the decision today departs significantly from this Court's traditional conception of the standing requirement and of the remedial powers of the federal courts. We have never required more than that a plaintiff have standing to litigate a claim. Whether he will be entitled to obtain particular forms of relief should he prevail has never been understood to be an issue of standing. In determining whether a plaintiff has standing, we have always focused on his personal stake in the outcome of the controversy, not on the issues sought to be litigated, Flast v. Cohen, supra, at 392 U. S. 99, or the "precise nature of the relief sought." Jenkins v. McKeithen, 395 U.S. at 395 U. S. 423 (opinion of MARSHALL, J., joined by Warren, C.J., and BRENNAN, J.).

    1

    Our cases uniformly state that the touchstone of the Art. III standing requirement is the plaintiff's personal stake in the underlying dispute, not in the particular types of relief sought. Once a plaintiff establishes a personal stake in a dispute, he has done all that is necessary to "invok[e] the court's authority . . . to challenge the action sought to be adjudicated." Valley Forge Christian College v. Americans United for Separation of

Church and State, supra, at 454 U. S. 471-472. See, e.g., Flast v. Cohen, 392 U.S. at 392 U. S. 101 (stake in "the dispute to be adjudicated in the lawsuit"); Eisenstadt v. Baird, 405 U. S. 438, 405 U. S. 443 (1972) (plaintiff must have "sufficient interest in challenging the statute's validity").

The personal stake of a litigant depends, in turn, on whether he has alleged a legally redressable injury. In determining whether a plaintiff has a sufficient personal stake in the outcome of a controversy, this Court has asked whether he "personally has suffered some actual or threatened injury," Gladstone, Realtors v. Village of Bellwood, 441 U. S. 91, 441 U. S. 99 (1979) (emphasis added), whether the injury "fairly can be traced to the challenged action," Simon v. Eastern Kentucky Welfare Rights Org., 426 U. S. 26, 426 U. S. 41 (1976), and whether plaintiff's injury "is likely to be redressed by a favorable decision." Id. at 426 U. S. 38. See also Duke Power Co. v. Carolina Environmental Study Group, Inc., 438 U. S. 59, 438 U. S. 74 (1978); Warth v. Seldin, 422 U. S. 490, 422 U. S. 508 (1975). These well-accepted criteria for determining whether a plaintiff has established the requisite personal stake do not fragment the standing inquiry into a series of discrete questions about the plaintiff's stake in each of the particular types of relief sought. Quite the contrary, they ask simply whether the plaintiff has a sufficient stake in seeking a judicial resolution of the controversy.

Lyons has alleged past injury and a risk of future injury and has linked both to the city's chokehold policy. Under established principles, the only additional question in determining standing under Art. III is whether the injuries he has alleged can be remedied or prevented by some form of judicial relief. Satisfaction of this requirement ensures that the lawsuit does not entail the issuance of an advisory opinion without the possibility of any judicial relief, and that the exercise of a court's remedial powers will actually redress the alleged injury. [20] Therefore, Lyons needs to demonstrate only that, should he prevail on the merits, "the exercise of the Court's remedial powers would redress the claimed injuries." Duke Power Co., supra, at 438 U. S. 74. See also Warth v. Seldin, supra, at 422 U. S. 508; Simon, supra, at 426 U. S. 38. Lyons has easily made this showing here, for monetary relief would plainly provide redress for his past injury, and prospective relief would reduce the likelihood of any future injury. Nothing more has ever been required to establish standing.

The Court's decision turns these well-accepted principles on their heads by requiring a separate standing inquiry with respect to each request for relief. Until now, questions concerning remedy were relevant to the threshold issue of standing only in the limited sense that some relief must be possible. The approach adopted today drastically alters the inquiry into remedy that must be made to determine standing.

2

The Court's fragmentation of the standing inquiry is also inconsistent with the way the federal courts have treated remedial issues since the merger of law and equity. The federal practice has been to reserve consideration of the appropriate relief until after a determination of the merits, not to foreclose certain forms of relief by a ruling on the pleadings. The prayer for relief is no part of the plaintiff's cause of action. See 2A J. Moore & J. Lucas, Moore's Federal Practice 118.18, p. 8-216, and n. 13 (1983) (Moore), and cases cited therein; C. Wright, A. Miller, & M. Kane, Federal Practice and Procedure § 2664 (1983) (Wright, Miller, & Kane). Rather,

"[the usual rule is] that, where legal rights have been invaded and a federal statute provides for a general right to sue for such invasion, federal courts may use any available remedy to make good the wrong done."

Bell v. Hood, 327 U. S. 678, 327 U. S. 684 (1946) (footnote omitted).

Rule 54(c) of the Federal Rules of Civil Procedure specifically provides that

"every final judgment shall grant the relief to which the party in whose favor it is rendered is entitled, even if the party has not demanded such relief in his pleadings."

The question whether a plaintiff has stated a claim turns not on "whether [he] has asked for the proper remedy, but whether he is entitled to any remedy." (Emphasis added.) Wright, Miller, & Kane § 2664. This is fully consistent with the approach taken in our standing cases. Supra at 461 U. S. 128-129 and this page, and n. 20.

The Court provides no justification for departing from the traditional treatment of remedial issues and demanding a separate threshold inquiry into each form of relief a plaintiff seeks. It is anomalous to require a plaintiff to demonstrate "standing" to seek each particular form of relief requested in the complaint when, under Rule 54(c), the remedy to which a party may be entitled need not even be demanded in the complaint. [21] See Holt Civic Club v. Tuscaloosa, 439 U. S. 60, 439 U. S. 65-66 (1978); Albemarle Paper Co. v. Moody, 422 U. S. 405, 422 U. S. 424 (1975). The traditional federal practice is a sound one. Even if it appears highly unlikely at the outset of a lawsuit that a plaintiff will establish that he is entitled to a particular remedy, there are dangers inherent in any doctrine that permits a court to foreclose any consideration of that remedy by ruling on the pleadings that the plaintiff lacks standing to seek it. A court has broad discretion to grant appropriate equitable relief to protect a party who has been injured by unlawful conduct, as well as members of the class, from future injury that may occur if the wrongdoer is permitted to continue his unlawful actions. Where, as here, a plaintiff alleges both past injury and a risk of future injury and presents a concededly substantial claim that a defendant is implementing an unlawful policy, it will rarely be easy to decide with any certainty at the outset of a lawsuit that no equitable relief would be appropriate under any conceivable set of facts that he might establish in support of his claim.

In sum, the Court's approach to standing is wholly inconsistent with well-established standing principles, and clashes with our longstanding conception of the remedial powers of a court and what is necessary to invoke the authority of a court to resolve a particular dispute.

IV

Apart from the question of standing, the only remaining question presented in the petition for certiorari is whether the preliminary injunction issued by the District Court must be set aside because it "constitute[s] a substantial interference in the operation of a municipal police department." Pet. for Cert. i. [22] In my view, it does not.

In the portion of its brief concerning this second question, the city argues that the District Court ignored the principles of federalism set forth in Rizzo v. Goode, 423 U. S. 362 (1976). Brief for Petitioner 40-47. The city's reliance on Rizzo is misplaced. That case involved an injunction which "significantly revis[ed] the internal procedures of the Philadelphia police department." 423 U.S. at 423 U. S. 379. The injunction required the police department to adopt "a comprehensive program for dealing adequately with civilian complaints,'" to be formulated in accordance with extensive "guidelines" established by the District Court. Id. at 423 U. S. 369, quoting Council of Organizations on Phila. Police A. & R. v. Rizzo, 357 F.Supp. 1289, 1321 (1973). Those guidelines specified detailed revisions of police manuals and rules of procedure, as well as the adoption of specific procedures for processing, screening, investigating, and adjudicating citizen complaints. In addition, the District Court supervised the implementation of the comprehensive program, issuing detailed orders concerning the posting and distribution of the revised police procedures and the drawing up of a "Citizen's Complaint Report" in a format designated by the court. The District Court also reserved jurisdiction to review the progress of the police department. 423 U.S. at 423 U. S. 365, n. 2. This Court concluded that the sweeping nature of the injunctive relief was inconsistent with "the principles of federalism." Id. at 423 U. S. 380.

The principles of federalism simply do not preclude the limited preliminary injunction issued in this case. Unlike the permanent injunction at issue in Rizzo, the preliminary injunction involved here entails no federal supervision of the LAPD's activities. The preliminary injunction merely forbids the use of chokeholds absent the threat of deadly force, permitting their continued use where such a threat does exist. This limited ban takes the form of a preventive injunction, which has traditionally been regarded as the least intrusive form of equitable relief. Moreover, the city can remove the ban by obtaining approval of a training plan. Although the preliminary injunction also requires the city to provide records of the uses of chokeholds to respondent and to allow the court access to such records, this requirement is hardly onerous, since the LAPD already maintains records concerning the use of chokeholds.

A district court should be mindful that "federal court intervention in the daily operation of a large city's police department . . . is undesirable, and to be avoided if at all possible." Rizzo, supra, at 423 U. S. 381 (BLACKMUN, J., dissenting). [23] The modest interlocutory relief granted in this case differs markedly, however, from the intrusive injunction involved in Rizzo, and simply does not implicate the federalism concerns that arise when a federal court undertakes to "supervise the functioning of the police department." 423 U.S. at 423 U. S. 380.

V

Apparently because it is unwilling to rely solely on its unprecedented rule of standing, the Court goes on to conclude that, even if Lyons has standing, "[t]he equitable remedy is unavailable." Ante at 461 U. S. 111. The Court's reliance on this alternative ground is puzzling for two reasons.

If, as the Court says, Lyons lacks standing under Art. III, the federal courts have no power to decide his entitlement to equitable relief on the merits. Under the Court's own view of Art. III, the Court's discussion in 461 U. S.

In addition, the question whether injunctive relief is available under equitable principles is simply not before us. We granted certiorari only to determine whether Lyons has standing, and whether, if so, the preliminary injunction must be set aside because it constitutes an impermissible interference in the operation of a municipal police department. We did not grant certiorari to consider whether Lyons satisfies the traditional prerequisites for equitable relief. See n. 22, supra.

Even if the issue had been properly raised, I could not agree with the Court's disposition of it. With the single exception of Rizzo v. Goode, supra, [24] all of the cases relied on by the Court concerned injunctions against state criminal proceedings. The rule of Younger v. Harris, 401 U. S. 37 (1971), that such injunctions can be issued only in extraordinary circumstances in which the threat of injury is "great and immediate," id. at 401 U. S. 46, reflects the venerable rule that equity will not enjoin a criminal prosecution, the fact that constitutional defenses can be raised in such a state prosecution, and an appreciation of the friction that injunctions against state judicial proceedings may produce. See ibid.; Steffel v. Thompson, 415 U. S. 452, 415 U. S. 462 (1974); 28 U.S.C. § 2283.

Our prior decisions have repeatedly emphasized that where an injunction is not directed against a state criminal or quasi-criminal proceeding, "the relevant principles of equity, comity, and federalism" that underlie the Younger doctrine "have little force." Steffel v. Thompson, supra, at 415 U. S. 462, citing Lake Carriers' Assn. v. MacMullan, 406 U. S. 498, 406 U. S. 509 (1972). Outside the special context in which the Younger doctrine applies, we have held that the appropriateness of injunctive relief is governed by traditional equitable considerations. See Doran v. Salem Inn, Inc., 422 U. S. 922, 422 U. S. 930 (1975). Whatever the precise scope of the Younger doctrine may be, the concerns of comity and federalism that counsel restraint when a federal court is asked to enjoin a state criminal proceeding simply do not apply to an injunction directed solely at a police department.

If the preliminary injunction granted by the District Court is analyzed under general equitable principles, rather than the more stringent standards of Younger v. Harris, it becomes apparent that there is no rule of law that precludes equitable relief and requires that the preliminary injunction be set aside. "In reviewing such interlocutory relief, this Court may only consider whether issuance of the injunction constituted an abuse of discretion." Brown v. Chote, 411 U. S. 452, 411 U. S. 47 (1973).

The District Court concluded, on the basis of the facts before it, that Lyons was choked without provocation pursuant to an unconstitutional city policy. Supra at 461 U. S. 119. Given the necessarily preliminary nature of its inquiry, there was no way for the District Court to know the precise contours of the city's policy or to ascertain the risk that

Lyons, who had alleged that the policy was being applied in a discriminatory manner, might again be subjected to a chokehold. But in view of the Court's conclusion that the unprovoked choking of Lyons was pursuant to a city policy, Lyons has satisfied "the usual basis for injunctive relief, that there exists some cognizable danger of recurrent violation.'" Rondeau v. Mosinee Paper Corp., 422 U. S. 49, 422 U. S. 59 (1975), quoting United States v. W. T. Grant Co., 345 U. S. 629, 345 U. S. 633 (1953). The risk of serious injuries and deaths to other citizens also supported the decision to grant a preliminary injunction. Courts of equity have much greater latitude in granting injunctive relief "in furtherance of the public interest than . . . when only private interests are involved." Virginian R. Co. v. Railway Employees, 300 U. S. 515, 300 U. S. 552 (1937). See Wright, Miller, & Kane § 2948; 7 Moore ◆ 65.04[1]. In this case, we know that the District Court would have been amply justified in considering the risk to the public, for after the preliminary injunction was stayed, five additional deaths occurred prior to the adoption of a moratorium. See n. 3, supra. Under these circumstances, I do not believe that the District Court abused its discretion.

Indeed, this Court has approved of a decision that directed issuance of a permanent injunction in a similar situation. See Lankford v. Gelston, 364 F.2d 197 (CA4 1966), cited with approval in Allee v. Medrano, 416 U. S. 802, 416 U. S. 816, n. 9 (1974). See n. 15, supra. In Lankford, citizens whose houses had been searched solely on the basis of uncorroborated, anonymous tips sought injunctive relief. The Fourth Circuit, sitting en banc, held that the plaintiffs were entitled to an injunction against enforcement of the police department policy authorizing such searches, even though there was no evidence that their homes would be searched in the future. Lyons is no less entitled to seek injunctive relief. To hold otherwise is to vitiate

"one of the most valuable features of equity jurisdiction, to anticipate and prevent a threatened injury, where the damages would be insufficient or irreparable."

Vicksburg Waterworks Co. v. Vicksburg, 185 U. S. 65, 185 U. S. 82 (1902).

Here it is unnecessary to consider the propriety of a permanent injunction. The District Court has simply sought to protect Lyons and other citizens of Los Angeles pending a disposition of the merits. It will be time enough to consider the propriety of a permanent injunction when and if the District Court grants such relief.

VI

The Court's decision removes an entire class of constitutional violations from the equitable powers of a federal court. It immunizes from prospective equitable relief any policy that authorizes persistent deprivations of constitutional rights as long as no individual can establish with substantial certainty that he will be injured, or injured again, in the future. THE CHIEF JUSTICE asked in Bivens v. Six Unknown Fed. Narcotics Agents, 403 U. S. 388, 403 U. S. 419 (1971) (dissenting opinion), "what would be the judicial response to a police order authorizing shoot to kill' with respect to every fugitive"? His answer was that it would be "easy to predict our collective wrath and outrage." Ibid. We now learn that wrath and outrage cannot be translated into an order to cease the unconstitutional practice, but only an award of damages to those who are victimized by the practice and live to sue, and to the survivors of those who are not so fortunate. Under the view expressed by the majority today, if the police adopt a policy of "shoot to kill," or a policy of shooting 1 out of 10 suspects, the federal courts will be powerless to enjoin its continuation. Cf. Linda R. S. v. Richard D., 410 U.S. at 410 U. S. 621 (WHITE, J., dissenting). The federal judicial power is now limited to levying a toll for such a systematic constitutional violation.

Notes

[1] The following summary of the evidence is taken from Lyons' deposition and his "Notice of Application and Application for Preliminary Injunction and Declaratory Relief; Points and Authorities," pp. 3-1. Although petitioner's answer contains a general denial of the allegations set forth in the complaint, petitioner has never presented any evidence to challenge Lyons' account. Brief for Petitioner 8.

[2] Count I of the first amended complaint also stated a claim against the individual officers for damages. � 8.

[3] Thus, in a city where Negro males constitute 9% of the population, they have accounted for 75% of the deaths resulting from the use of chokeholds. In addition to his other allegations, Lyons alleged racial discrimination in violation of the Equal Protection Clause of the Fourteenth Amendment. �� 10, 15, 23, 24, 25, 30.

Of the 16 deaths, 10 occurred prior to the District Court's issuance of the preliminary injunction, although at that time the parties and the court were aware of only 9. On December 24, 1980, the Court of Appeals stayed the preliminary injunction pending appeal. Four additional deaths occurred during the period prior to the grant of a further stay pending filing and disposition of a petition for certiorari, 453 U. S. 1308 (1981) (REHNQUIST, J., in chambers), and two more deaths occurred thereafter.

[4] Lyons' motion for a preliminary injunction was heard on affidavits, depositions, and government records.

[5] Statement of Officer Pascal K. Dionne (officer-in-charge of the Physical Training and Self-Defense Unit of the LAPD), App. 240-241.

[6] Statement of Officer Pascal K. Dionne, id. at 259. These figures undoubtedly understate the frequency of the use of chokeholds, since, as Officer Dionne, a witness for the city, testified, the figures compiled do not include all altercations between police officers and citizens. Id. at 241. Officer Dionne's statement does not define "altercation," and does not indicate when "altercation reports" must be filed by an officer.

The city does not maintain a record of injuries to suspects.

[7] The physiological effects of the chokeholds were described as follows by Dr. A. Griswold, an expert in pathology (id. at 364-367):

"From a medical point of view, the bar arm control is extremely dangerous in an unpredictable fashion. Pressure from a locked forearm across the neck sufficient to compress and close the trachea, applied for a sufficient period of time to cause unconsciousness from asphyxia must, to an anatomical certainty, also result in . . . a very high risk of a fractured hyoid bone or crushed larynx. The risk is substantial, but at the same time, unpredictable."

"It depends, for one thing, on which vertical portion of the neck the forearm pressure is exerted. . . ."

"Another factor contributing to unpredictability is the reaction of the victim. . . . [The] pressure exerted in a bar arm control . . . can result in a laryngeal spasm or seizure which simply shuts off the trachial air passage, leading to death by asphyxiation. Also, it must result in transmission to the brain of nerve messages that there is immediate, acute danger of death. This transmission immediately sets up a flight or flee' syndrome wherein the body reacts violently to save itself or escape. Adrenalin output increases enormously; blood oxygen is switched to muscles, and strong, violent struggle ensues which is to a great extent involuntary. From a medical point of view, there would be no way to distinguish this involuntary death struggle from a willful, voluntary resistance. Thus, an instruction to cease applying the hold when "resistance ceases" is meaningless."

"This violent struggle . . . increases the risk of permanent injury or death to the victim. This reserve may already be in a state of reduction by reason of cardiac, respiratory or other disease."

"The LAPD [operates under a] misconception . . . that the length of time for applying the hold is the sole measure of risk. This is simply not true. If sufficient force is applied, the larynx can be crushed or hyoid fractured, with death ensuing, in seconds. An irreversible laryngeal spasm can also occur in seconds."

"From a medical point of view, the carotid control is extremely dangerous in a manner that is at least as equally unpredictable as the bar arm control."

". . . When applied with sufficient pressure, this control will crush the carotid sheath against the bony structure of the neck, foreseeably shutting down the supply of oxygenated blood to the brain and leading to unconsciousness in approximately 10 to 15 seconds."

"However, pressure on both carotid sheaths also results in pressure, if inadvertent or unintended, on both of the vagus nerves. The vagus nerves (right and left) arise in the brain and are composed of both sensory and motor fibers. . . . Stimulation of these nerves by pressure can activate reflexes within the vagus system that can result in immediate heart stoppage (cardiac arrest). . . . There is also evidence that cardiac arrest can result from simultaneous pressure on both vagus nerves, regardless of the intensity or duration of the pressure."

[8] City's Opposition to Application for Preliminary Injunction, No. 770420 (CD Cal.), pp. 26, 30.

[9] Brief in Opposition to Motion to Stay, in No. A-230 (CD Cal.), p. 4.

[10] The preliminary injunction provided that the city itself could lift the injunction by obtaining court approval of a training program, and also required the city to keep records of all uses of chokeholds and to make those records available.

The District Court refrained from determining the precise nature of the city's policy, given the limited nature of its inquiry at the preliminary injunction stage. Brown v. Chote, 411 U. S. 452, 411 U. S. 456 (1973).

[11] Contrary to the Court's suggestion, ante at 461 U. S. 106-107, n. 7, there is clearly no inconsistency between the allegation in paragraph 8 of the complaint that Lyons was choked "without provocation, legal justification or excuse" and the allegations that the city authorizes chokeholds "in situations where [officers] are threatened by far less than deadly force." �� 20, 23.

[12] Even if the issue were properly before us, I could not agree that this Court should substitute its judgment for that of the District Court. One of the city's own training officers testified that an officer is authorized to use a chokehold whenever he "feels that there's about to be a bodily attack made on him." App. 381. This testimony indicates that an officer is authorized to use a chokehold whenever he subjectively perceives a threat, regardless of whether the suspect has done anything to provide an objective basis for such a perception. The District Court's finding is not refuted by the statement of the city's policy which is set forth in an LAPD manual, ante at 461 U. S. 110, for municipal liability under § 1983 may be predicated on proof of an official custom whether or not that custom is embodied in a formal policy. Monell v. New York City Dept. of Social Services, 436 U. S. 658, 436 U. S. 694 (1978).

[13] Although counsel for the plaintiffs in O'Shea suggested at oral argument that certain plaintiffs had been exposed to illegal conduct in the past, in fact,

"[n]o damages were sought against the petitioners . . . , nor were any specific instances involving the individually named respondents set forth in the claim against these judicial officers."

414 U.S. at 414 U. S. 492. The Court referred to the absence of past injury repeatedly. See id. at 414 U. S. 492, 414 U. S. 495, and n. 3.

[14] The plaintiff in Mattis did originally seek damages, but after the District Court found that the defendant officers were shielded by the good faith immunity, he pursued only prospective relief. Although we held that the case had been mooted by the elimination of the damages claim, we in no way suggested that the plaintiff's requests for declaratory and injunctive relief could not have been entertained had his damages claim remained viable. We held only that, where a plaintiff's

"primary claim of a present interest in the controversy is that he will obtain emotional satisfaction from a ruling that his son's death was wrongful,"

431 U.S. at 431 U. S. 172 (footnote omitted), he does not have the personal stake in the outcome required by Art. III. In Zwickler, the plaintiff did not even allege that he would or might run for office again; he merely asserted that he "can be a candidate for Congress again." 394 U.S. at 394 U. S. 109. We held that this mere logical possibility was insufficient to present an actual controversy.

[15] In Lankford v. Gelston, 364 F.2d 197 (1966) (en banc), which we cited with approval in Allee v. Medrano, 416 U. S. 802, 416 U. S. 816, n. 9 (1974), the Fourth Circuit

found standing on facts indistinguishable from this case. In Lankford, the Court of Appeals held that four Negro families who had been subjected to an illegal house search were entitled to seek injunctive relief against the Baltimore Police Department's policy of conducting wholesale searches based only on uncorroborated anonymous tips, even though the plaintiffs there did not claim that they were more likely than other Negro residents of the city to be subjected to an illegal search in the future.

[16] In O'Shea itself, the Court suggested that the absence of a damages claim was highly pertinent to its conclusion that the plaintiff had no standing. The Court noted that plaintiffs' "claim for relief against the State's Attorney[,] where specific instances of misconduct with respect to particular individuals are alleged," 414 U.S. at 414 U. S. 495 (emphasis added), stood in "sharp contrast" to their claim for relief against the magistrate and judge, which did not contain similar allegations. The plaintiffs did seek damages against the State's Attorney. See Spomer v. Littleton, 414 U. S. 514, 414 U. S. 518 n. 5 (1974). Like the claims against the State's Attorney in O'Shea, Lyons' claims against the city allege both past injury and the risk of future injury. Whereas, in O'Shea, the Court acknowledged the significance for standing purposes of past injury, the Court today inexplicably treats Lyons' past injury for which he is seeking redress as wholly irrelevant to the standing inquiry before us.

[17] The Court's reliance on Rizzo is misplaced for another reason. In Rizzo, the Court concluded that the evidence presented at trial failed to establish an

"affirmative link between the occurrence of the various incidents of police misconduct and the adoption of any plan or policy by [defendants]."

423 U.S. at 423 U. S. 371. Because the misconduct being challenged was, in the Court's view, the result of the behavior of unidentified officials not named as defendants, rather than any policy of the named defendants -- the City Managing Director, and the Police Commissioner, id. at 423 U. S. 372 -- the Court had "serious doubts" whether a case or controversy existed between the plaintiffs and those defendants. Here, by contrast, Lyons has clearly established a case or controversy between himself and the city concerning the constitutionality of the city's policy. See supra at 461 U. S. 120-122. In Rizzo, the Court specifically distinguished those cases where a case or controversy was found to exist because of the existence of an official policy responsible for the past or threatened constitutional deprivations. 423 U.S. at 423 U. S. 373-374, distinguishing Hague v. CIO, 307 U. S. 496 (1939); Allee v. Medrano, 416 U. S. 802 (1974); Lankford v. Gelston, supra.

[18] It is irrelevant that the District Court has severed Lyons' claim for damages from his claim for injunctive relief. Ante at 461 U. S. 105, n. 6. If the District Court, in deciding whether to issue an injunction, upholds the city's policy against constitutional attack, this ruling will be res judicata with respect to Lyons' claim for damages. The severance of the claims therefore does not diminish Lyons' incentive to establish the unconstitutionality of the policy.

It is unnecessary to decide here whether the standing of a plaintiff who alleges past injury that is legally redressable depends on whether he specifically seek damages. See Lankford v. Gelston, supra, (plaintiffs who did not seek damages permitted to seek injunctive relief based on past injury). See n. 15, supra.

[19] The Court errs in asserting that Lyons has no standing to seek injunctive relief because the injunction prayed for in Count V reaches suspects who, unlike Lyons, offer resistance or attempt to escape. Ante at 461 U. S. 106-107, n. 7. Even if a separate inquiry into Lyons' standing to seek injunctive relief, as opposed to damages, were appropriate, and even if he had no standing to seek the entire injunction he requests, it would not follow that he had no standing to seek any injunctive relief. Even under the Court's view, Lyons presumably would have standing to seek to enjoin the use of chokeholds without provocation. There would therefore be no justification for reversing the judgment below in its entirety.

The Court's reliance on the precise terms of the injunction sought in Count V is also misplaced for a more fundamental reason. Whatever may be said for the Court's novel rule that a separate showing of standing must be made for each form of relief requested, the Court is simply wrong in assuming that the scope of the injunction prayed for raises a question of standing. A litigant is entitled to advance any substantive legal theory which would entitle him to relief. Lyons' entitlement to relief may ultimately rest on the principle that a municipality may not authorize the use of chokeholds absent a threat of deadly force. This principle, which the District Court tentatively embraced in issuing the preliminary injunction, would support the entire injunction sought in Count V. Alternatively, Lyons' entitlement to relief may rest on some narrower theory. If Lyons prevails, the appropriateness of the injunction prayed for in Count V will depend on the legal principle upon which the District Court predicates its decision. It may well be judicious for the District Court, in the exercise of its discretion, to rest its decision on a theory that would not support the full scope of the injunction that Lyons requests. But this has nothing whatsoever to do with Lyons' standing.

[20] This limited inquiry into remedy, which addresses two jurisdictional concerns, provides no support for the Court's requirement that standing be separately demonstrated with respect to each particular form of relief sought. First, a court must have the power to fashion some appropriate remedy. This concern, an aspect of the more general case-or-controversy requirement, reflects the view that the adjudication of rights which a court is powerless to enforce is tantamount to an advisory opinion. See Aetna Life Ins. Co. v. Haworth, 300 U. S. 227, 300 U. S. 241 (1937) ("[The controversy] must be a real and substantial [one] admitting of specific relief through a decree of a conclusive character, as distinguished from an opinion advising what the law would be upon a hypothetical state of facts") (emphasis added). Second, a court must determine that there is an available remedy which will have a "substantial probability," Warth v. Seldin, 422 U. S. 490, 422 U. S. 508 (1975), of redressing the plaintiff's injury. This latter concern is merely a recasting of the causal nexus, supra at 461 U. S. 128, that must exist between the alleged injury and the action being challenged, and ensures that the granting of judicial

relief will not be an exercise in futility. See Duke Power Co. v. Carolina Environmental Study Group, 438 U. S. 59, 438 U. S. 74 (1978). These considerations are summarized by the requirement that a plaintiff need only allege an injury that is "legally redressable." Jenkins v. McKeithen, 395 U. S. 411, 395 U. S. 424 (1969) (emphasis added).

[21] It is not clear from the Court's opinion whether the District Court is wholly precluded from granting any form of declaratory or injunctive relief, even if it ultimately holds that Lyons should prevail on his claim for damages against the city on the ground that the city's chokehold policy is unconstitutional and is responsible for his injury.

[22] Question 1 of the petition raised the question of Lyons' standing. Question 2 of the petition states:

"Does a federal court order constitute a substantial interference in the operation of a municipal police department where it (a) modifies policies concerning use of force and (b) takes control of such department's training and reporting systems relative to a particular force technique?"

[23] Of course, municipalities may be enjoined under § 1983, Monell v. New York City Dept. of Social Service, 436 U. S. 658 (1978), and this Court has approved of the issuance of injunctions by federal courts against state or municipal police departments where necessary to prevent the continued enforcement of unconstitutional official policies. See, e.g., Allee v. Medrano, 416 U. S. 802 (1974); Hague v. CIO, 307 U. S. 496 (1939); Lankford v. Gelton, 364 F.2d 197 (CA4 1966) (en banc), cited with approval in Allee, supra, at 416 U. S. 816. Although federalism concerns are relevant in fashioning an appropriate relief, we have stated repeatedly that a federal court retains the power to order any available remedy necessary to afford full relief for the invasion of legal rights. See, e.g., Swann v. Charlotte-Mecklenburg Board of Education, 402 U. S. 1, 402 U. S. 14 (1971); Bell v. Hood, 327 U. S. 678, 327 U. S. 684 (1946).

[24] As explained above, Rizzo v. Goode does not support a decision barring Lyons from obtaining any injunctive relief, for that case involved an injunction which entailed judicial supervision of the workings of a municipal police department, not simply the sort of preventive injunction that Lyons seeks. Supra at 461 U. S. 132-133.

Murphy's failure to claim his privilege against self-incrimination did not result in the forfeiture of his rights: Justice Marshall's dissent in Minnesota v. Murphy (February 22, 1984)

JUSTICE MARSHALL, with whom JUSTICE STEVENS joins, and with whom JUSTICE BRENNAN joins except as to Part II-A, dissenting.

The opinion of the Court helpfully clarifies the scope of the privilege against self-incrimination that may be asserted by a probationer when asked questions by an officer of the State. As the majority points out, two principles shape the probationer's constitutional rights. First, because probation revocation proceedings are not criminal in nature, Gagnon v. Scarpelli, 411 U.S. 778, 782 (1973), and because the Fifth Amendment ban on compelled self-incrimination applies only to criminal proceedings, the possibility that a truthful answer to a question might result in the revocation of his probation does not accord the probationer a constitutional right to refuse to respond. Ante, at 435-436, n. 7. Second, a probationer retains the privilege enjoyed by all citizens to refuse "to answer official questions put to him in any . . . proceeding, civil or criminal, formal or informal, where the answers might incriminate him in future criminal proceedings," Lefkowitz v. Turley, 414 U.S. 70, 77 (1973). Ante, at 426.

From the foregoing propositions, it follows that the power of a State to compel a probationer to answer a given question varies depending upon the manner in which the probationer's answer might incriminate him. If a truthful response might reveal that he has violated a condition of his probation but would not subject him to criminal prosecution, the State may insist that he respond and may penalize him for refusing to do so. 1 See ante, at 435-436, n. 7. By contrast, if there is a chance that a truthful answer to a given question would expose the probationer to liability for a crime different from the crime for which he has already been convicted, he has a right to refuse to answer and the State may not attempt to coerce him to forgo that right. 2 See ante, at 435. As the majority points out, if the answer to a question might lead both to criminal sanctions and to probation revocation, the State has the option of insisting that the probationer respond, in return for an express guarantee of immunity from criminal liability. 3 Ante, at 436, n. 7. Unless it exercises that option, however, the State may not interfere with the probationer's right "to remain silent unless he chooses to speak in the unfettered exercise of his own will," Malloy v. Hogan, 378 U.S. 1, 8 (1964).

The flaw in the opinion of the Court lies not in its analysis of the constitutional rights available to a probationer, but in its finding that those rights were not violated in this case. The majority concludes that, "since Murphy revealed incriminating information instead of timely asserting his Fifth Amendment privilege, his disclosures were not compelled incriminations." Ante, at 440. In my view, that conclusion is inconsistent with our prior cases dealing with invocations of the Fifth Amendment. For two independent reasons, Murphy's failure to claim his privilege against self-incrimination before responding to his probation officer's inquiry regarding his participation in the 1974 murder did not result in the forfeiture of his right to object to the use of his admissions in a subsequent criminal prosecution. First, the State of Minnesota had threatened Murphy with a penalty for refusing to respond to questions; our decisions make clear that such a threat relieves its target of the duty to claim the benefit of the Fifth Amendment. Second, under the circumstances of this case, the State was obliged to prove that Murphy was aware of his constitutional rights and freely waived them; by showing nothing more than that Murphy failed to assert his privilege before answering, the State failed to carry its burden.

I

As the majority acknowledges, if an officer of a State asks a person a question under circumstances that deprive him of a "`free choice to admit, to deny, or to refuse to answer,'" and he answers the question without attempting to assert his privilege against self-incrimination, his response will be deemed to have been "compelled" and will be inadmissible as evidence against him. Garner v. United States, 424 U.S. 648, 656 -657 (1976) (quoting Lisenba v. California, 314 U.S. 219, 241 (1941)); see ante, at 429. Our cases make clear that the State will be found to have deprived the person of such a "free choice" if it threatens him with a substantial sanction if he refuses to respond. Lefkowitz v. Turley, 414 U.S., at 82 -83. Two rules flow from the foregoing principle: If the State presents a person with the "Hobson's choice" of incriminating himself or suffering a penalty, and he nevertheless refuses to respond, the State cannot constitutionally make good on its threat to penalize him. Id., at 77; Sanitation Men v. Commissioner of Sanitation, 392 U.S. 280, 284 (1968); Gardner v. Broderick, 392 U.S. 273, 277 -278 (1968). Conversely, if the threatened person decides to talk instead of asserting his privilege, the State cannot use his admissions against him in a subsequent criminal prosecution. Garrity v. New Jersey, 385 U.S. 493, 500 (1967).

It might appear that these two rules would defeat one another. A person presented with what appears to be a Hobson's choice could be charged with the knowledge that, under this Court's precedents, he may choose either option with impunity. His awareness that the State can use neither his silence nor his confessions against him would seem to eliminate the "compulsion" supposedly inherent in the situation. 4 More specifically, it might be argued that, because it is now settled that a person cannot be penalized for asserting his Fifth Amendment privilege, if he decides to talk rather than assert his constitutional right to remain silent, his statements should be deemed voluntary.

This Court has consistently refused to allow the two rules to undercut each other in this way. 5 Our refusal derives from two considerations. First, many - probably most - of the persons threatened with sanctions if they refuse to answer official questions lack sufficient knowledge of this Court's decisions to be aware that the State's threat is idle. Second, the State's attempt to coerce self-incriminating statements by promising to penalize silence is itself constitutionally offensive, and the mere possibility that the State profited from the attempt is sufficient to forbid it to make use of the admissions it elicited. See Gardner v. Broderick, supra, at 279.

For similar reasons, when a person who has been threatened with a penalty makes self-incriminating statements, we have declined to inquire whether his decision to speak was the proximate result of the threat. In most cases, it would be difficult for the person to prove that, but for the threat, he would have held his peace and that no other intervening causes (such as pangs of conscience) induced him to confess. 6 The State, having exerted pressures repugnant to the Constitution, should not be allowed to profit from the uncertainty whether those pressures had their intended effect. Sensitivity to the foregoing concerns is reflected in our decision in Garrity v. New Jersey, supra. The petitioners in that case had never argued that their confessions were in fact induced by the State's warning that they might be fired if they refused to answer, and the lower courts had not so found. 7 Nevertheless, the Court concluded that the petitioners' statements "were infected by the coercion inherent in this scheme of questioning and cannot be sustained as voluntary." Id., at 497-498 (footnote omitted).

In sum, the majority errs when it suggests that, to claim the benefit of the Fifth Amendment, a person who made self-incriminating statements after being threatened with a penalty if he remained silent must show that his apprehension that the State would carry out its promise was objectively "reasonable," ante, at 438. Our decisions make clear that the threat alone is sufficient to render all subsequent testimony "compelled." See supra, at 443-444. 8 Likewise, the majority errs when it implies that a defendant has a duty to prove that the State's threat, and not some other motivation, prompted his confession, see ante, at 437-438. Under our precedents, the defendant need only prove that the State presented him with a constitutionally impermissible choice and that he thereupon incriminated himself. See supra, at 444-445.

When the foregoing principles are applied to this case, it becomes clear that Murphy's confession to the 1974 murder must be deemed to have been "compelled." When Murphy was placed on probation, he was given a letter setting forth the conditions under which he was discharged. The pertinent portions of the letter provide:

"For the present you are only conditionally released. If you comply with the conditions of your probation you may expect to be discharged at the expiration of the period stated. If you fail to comply with the requirements you may be returned to Court at any time for further hearing or commitment. . . .

"It will be necessary for you to obey strictly the following conditions:

"BE TRUTHFUL to your Probation Officer in all matters." App. to Pet. for Cert. C-33 - C-34 (emphasis in original).

Murphy was required to sign the letter, attesting that he had read and understood the instructions. Id., at C-35.

The majority contends that the foregoing passages merely required Murphy to answer nonincriminating questions and forbade him to make false statements to his probation officer. Ante, at 437. The majority's interpretation, which is essential to its result, is simply incredible. A reasonable layman would interpret the imperative, "be truthful . . . in all matters," as a command to answer honestly all questions presented. Any ambiguity inherent in the language of the directive is dispelled by its context. The duty to be truthful in dealings with the probation officer is listed as the first term of the conditions of probation. The critical phrase is capitalized. And the injunction is immediately preceded by an instruction "to obey strictly the following conditions." 9

In short, the State of Minnesota presented Murphy with a set of official instructions that a reasonable man would have interpreted to require him, upon pain of the revocation of his probation, to answer truthfully all questions asked by his probation officer. 10 Probation revocation surely constitutes a "substantial sanction." 11 Under our precedents, therefore, by threatening Murphy with that sanction if he refused to answer,

Minnesota deprived itself of constitutional authority to use Murphy's subsequent answers in a criminal prosecution against him.

The majority's efforts to avoid that conclusion are unpersuasive. First, the majority faults Murphy for failing to ask his probation officer for a "clarification" of the terms of his probation. Ante, at 437. The letter by which the State informed Murphy of the terms of his probation contained no suggestion that he was entitled to such a "clarification"; on the contrary, the letter informed Murphy that he was required to "obey strictly" the conditions enumerated and that failure to do so might result in his "commitment." More importantly, as indicated above, our decisions establish that a person told by the State that he may be penalized for refusing to answer does not bear the responsibility to determine whether the State would or could make good on its threat. See supra, at 443-444. Second, the majority relies on the absence of "direct evidence that Murphy confessed because he feared that his probation would be revoked if he remained silent." Ante, at 437. Under our precedents, no such "direct evidence" of a causal link between the threat and the response is required in order to prevent the use in a criminal prosecution of Murphy's confession. See supra, at 444-445.

In conclusion, because the terms of Murphy's probation deprived him of "a free choice to admit, to deny, or to refuse to answer" when his probation officer confronted him with the allegation that he had committed the 1974 murder, our decisions forbid the introduction into evidence against him of his confession.

II

Even if Minnesota had not impaired Murphy's freedom to respond or to refuse to respond to incriminating questions regarding the 1974 murder, I would hold his confession inadmissible because, in view of the circumstances under which he was interrogated, the State had a duty to prove that Murphy waived his privilege against self-incrimination, and it has not made such a showing.

A

It is now settled that, in most contexts, the privilege against self-incrimination is not self-executing. "[I]n the ordinary case," if a person questioned by an officer of the State makes damaging disclosures instead of asserting his privilege, he forfeits his right to object to subsequent use of his admissions against him. Garner v. United States, 424 U.S., at 654 . This forfeiture occurs even if the person is subject to a general legal duty to respond to the officer's questions. See United States v. Washington, 431 U.S. 181 (1977); ante, at 427. And it occurs regardless of whether the person's failure to claim the privilege was founded upon a knowing and intelligent decision to waive his constitutional right not to answer those questions that might incriminate him. Garner v. United States, supra, at 654, n. 9; see also ante, at 427-428.

At first blush, this harsh doctrine seems incompatible with our repeated assertions of the importance of the Fifth Amendment privilege in our constitutional scheme. Twenty years ago, we observed:

"[T]he American system of criminal prosecution is accusatorial, not inquisitorial, and . . . the Fifth Amendment privilege is its essential mainstay. . . . Governments, state and federal, are thus constitutionally compelled to establish guilt by evidence independently and freely secured, and may not by coercion prove a charge against an accused out of his own mouth." Malloy v. Hogan, 378 U.S., at 7 -8 (citation omitted).

In view of our continued adherence to the foregoing principles, 12 it appears anomalous that, in most contexts, we allow governments to take advantage of witnesses' failure, sometimes as a result of ignorance or momentary inattention, to claim the benefit of the privilege in a "timely" fashion.

The explanation for our seemingly callous willingness to countenance forfeitures of Fifth Amendment rights must be sought in a combination of three factors. First and most importantly, we presume that most people are aware that they need not answer an official question when a truthful answer might expose them to criminal prosecution. "At this point in our history virtually every schoolboy is familiar with the concept, if not the language," of the constitutional ban on compelled self-incrimination. Michigan v. Tucker, 417 U.S. 433, 439 (1974). We thus take for granted that, in most instances, when a person discloses damaging information in response to an official inquiry, he has made an intelligent decision to waive his Fifth Amendment rights.

Second, in the vast majority of situations in which an officer of the State asks a citizen a question, the officer has no reason to know that a truthful response would reveal that the citizen has committed a crime. Under such circumstances, one of the central principles underlying the Fifth Amendment - that governments should not "deliberately see[k] to avoid the burdens of independent investigation by compelling self-incriminating disclosures" - has little relevance. Garner v. United States, supra, at 655-656. Thus, in the ordinary case, few constitutional values are threatened when the government fails to preface an inquiry with an explicit reminder that a response is not required if it might expose the respondent to prosecution.

Third, a general requirement that government officials preface all questions with such reminders would be highly burdensome. Our concern with the protection of constitutional rights should not blind us to the fact that, in general, governments have the right to everyone's testimony. E. g., Branzburg v. Hayes, 408 U.S. 665, 688 (1972). A rule requiring officials, before asking citizens for information, to tell them that they need not reveal incriminating evidence would unduly impede the capacity of government to gather the data it needs to function effectively. 13

In sum, a general rule requiring the prosecution, before introducing a confession, to prove that the defendant intelligently and voluntarily waived his right not to incriminate himself would protect few persons (because most know their legal rights), would do little to promote the values that underlie the Fifth Amendment, and would substantially impair the information-gathering capacity of government. 14

It should be apparent that these considerations do not apply with equal force in all contexts. Until today, the Court has been sensitive to variations in their relevance and strength. Accordingly, we have adhered to the general principle that a defendant forfeits his privilege if he fails to assert it before making incriminating statements only in situations implicating several of the factors that support the principle. More specifically, we have applied the principle only in cases in which at least two of the following statements have been true: (a) At the time the damaging disclosures were made, the defendant's constitutional right not to make them was clearly established. (b) The defendant was given sufficient warning that he would be asked potentially incriminating questions to be able to secure legal advice and to reflect upon how he would respond. (c) The environment in which the questions were asked did not impair the defendant's ability intelligently to exercise his rights. (d) The questioner had no reason to assume that truthful responses would be self-incriminating.

A review of a few of the leading cases should suffice to establish the point. 15 In United States v. Kordel, 397 U.S. 1 (1970), the Government submitted interrogatories to the defendant in a civil suit. Though the defendant (a corporate officer) was aware that the Government was planning to bring a criminal action against him, he answered the questions instead of asserting his privilege against self-incrimination. The Court ruled that his answers could be admitted in the ensuing prosecution. In so holding, the Court emphasized the facts that established law made clear that the defendant had a constitutional right to refuse to answer the interrogatories, that he was free to consult with counsel before responding, and that nothing in the circumstances under which the questions were presented impaired the defendant's ability to appreciate the consequences of his actions. Id., at 7, 9-10.

The defendant in Garner v. United States, 424 U.S. 648 (1976), was a professional gambler who made incriminating disclosures on his Form 1040 income tax returns. The Court held that he could be prosecuted partly on the basis of his admissions. Though the defendant's constitutional right to refuse to provide the requested information was perhaps less clear and straightforward than the right of the usual defendant, the Court stressed that other factors rendered inexcusable his failure to learn and assert his entitlements. Thus, the Court pointed out that the defendant was free to consult with a lawyer and could fill out the tax return at his leisure in an environment of his choosing. Id., at 658. Moreover, every taxpayer is required to fill out a Form 1040; the Government, in imposing that duty, has no reason to assume that any given taxpayer's responses will be self-incriminating. 16 Thus, the United States in Garner could not be faulted for requesting the information that the defendant provided.

Finally, in United States v. Washington, 431 U.S. 181 (1977), the Court confirmed the proposition that a witness called to testify before a grand jury must claim the benefit of the privilege or forfeit it. 17 The Court acknowledged that "the grand jury room engenders an atmosphere conducive to truthtelling" and thus might have exerted some pressure on the defendant not to assert his rights. Id., at 187. In addition, the Court recognized that the Government was not blameless insofar as a criminal investigation had focused on the defendant and thus the questioners had ample reason to believe that truthful answers by the defendant would be self-incriminating. 18 But, the Court reasoned, the situation contained other safeguards that warranted adherence to the principle that a privilege not asserted is lost. First, the defendant's right to refuse to respond had been perfectly clear; indeed, at the outset of the proceeding, the defendant had been explicitly warned of his right not to answer questions if his responses might incriminate him. Id., at 186, 188. 19 Second, not only had the defendant been afforded an opportunity before appearing to seek legal advice, but also, at the start of the hearing, he was told that a lawyer would be provided for him if he wished and could not afford one. Id., at 183-184. Under those circumstances, the Court concluded that it was inconceivable that the defendant's decision not to assert his privilege was uninformed or involuntary. 20

By contrast, in cases in which only one of the statements enumerated above, see supra, at 452-453, has been true, the Court has refused to adhere to the general rule that a privilege not claimed is lost, and instead has insisted upon a showing that the defendant made a knowing and intelligent decision to forgo his constitutional right not to incriminate himself. The classic situation of this sort is custodial interrogation. In Miranda v. Arizona, 384 U.S. 436 (1966), the Court acknowledged that the right of a suspect in police custody not to answer questions is well established. However, we stressed that other aspects of the situation impair the ability of the suspect to exercise his rights and threaten the values underlying the Fifth Amendment: the suspect is unable to consult with counsel regarding how he should respond to questions; the environment in which the questions are presented (the police station, from which the suspect is forbidden to leave) "work[s] to undermine the individual's will to resist and to compel him to speak where he would not otherwise do so freely," id., at 467; and the interrogators are well aware that truthful answers to their questions are likely to incriminate the suspect. In short, only one of the four circumstances favoring application of the general principle exist in the context of custodial interrogation. To mitigate the risk that suspects would ignorantly or involuntarily fail to claim their privilege against self-incrimination under these circumstances, the Court in Miranda imposed a requirement that they be shown to have freely waived their rights after being fully apprised of them. Id., at 475-479. 21

B

If we remain sensitive to the concerns implicit in the foregoing pattern of cases, we should insist that the State, in the instant case, demonstrate that Murphy intelligently waived his right to remain silent. None of the four conditions that favor application of the principle that a defendant forfeits his privilege if he fails to claim it before confessing can be found in the circumstances under which Murphy was interrogated. First, the existence and scope of Murphy's constitutional right to refuse to testify were at best unclear when he appeared in the probation officer's office. It is undisputed that the conditions of Murphy's probation imposed on him a duty to answer all questions presented by his probation officer except those implicating his Fifth Amendment rights. 22 What exactly those rights were was far from apparent. The majority opinion in this case constitutes the first authoritative analysis of the privilege against self-incrimination available to a probationer. The ambiguity of scope of that privilege prior to today is suggested by the fact the Solicitor General, appearing for the United States as amicus curiae, seriously misconceived the rights that might have been asserted by Murphy when examined by his probation officer. 23 If, after being afforded substantial opportunity for research and reflection, the lawyers who represent the Nation err in their explication of the relevant constitutional principles, Murphy surely cannot be charged with knowledge of his entitlements. 24

Second, contrary to the suggestion of the majority, ante, at 432, Murphy was given no warning that he would be asked potentially incriminating questions. The letter in which Murphy's probation officer instructed him to make an appointment informed him that the purpose of the meeting was "[t]o further discuss a treatment plan for the remainder of [his] probation." App. to Pet. for Cert. C-36. In view of the fact that Murphy remained under a legal obligation to attend treatment sessions, 25 there was no reason why he should have assumed from the letter that the officer planned to question him regarding prior criminal activity. 26 In short, prior to the moment he was asked whether he had committed the murder, Murphy had no reason to suspect that he would be obliged to respond to incriminating questions. He thus had no opportunity to consult a lawyer, or even to consider how he should proceed.

Third, the environment in which the questioning occurred impaired Murphy's ability to recognize and claim his constitutional rights. It is true, as the majority points out, that the discussion between a probation officer and a probationer is likely to be less coercive and intimidating than a discussion between a police officer and a suspect in custody. Ante, at 433. But it is precisely in that fact that the danger lies. In contrast to the inherently adversarial relationship between a suspect and a policeman, the relationship between a probationer and the officer to whom he reports is likely to incorporate elements of confidentiality, even friendship. Indeed, many probation officers deliberately cultivate such bonds with their charges. 27 The point should not be overstated; undoubtedly, few probationers are entirely blind to the fact that their probation officers are "peace officer[s], . . . allied, to a greater or lesser extent, with [their] fellow peace officers." Fare v. Michael C., 442 U.S. 707, 720 (1979). On the other hand, many probationers develop "relationship[s] of trust and cooperation" with their officers. Id., at 722. 28 Through abuse of that trust, a probation officer can elicit admissions from a probationer that the probationer would be unlikely to make to a hostile police interrogator.

The instant case aptly illustrates the danger. Before she sent her letter to Murphy asking him to make an appointment, the probation officer had decided to try to induce him to confess to the 1974 killing and to turn over that information to the police. She was aware that, if she were successful, Murphy would soon be arrested and tried for murder. 29 There was thus no prospect whatsoever that the information she elicited would be used to design a treatment program to be followed by Murphy during the remainder of his probation. Yet, in her letter, she described the purpose of the meeting as that of "discuss[ing] a treatment plan." When Murphy arrived at the meeting, she persisted in the deceit; instead of informing him at once what she intended to do with his anticipated confession to the 1974 murder, she told him that "her main concern was to talk to him about the relationship of the prior crime and the one of which he was convicted and about his need for treatment under the circumstances." 324 N. W. 2d 340, 341 (Minn. 1982). That Murphy succumbed to the deception is apparent from the sequence of his responses. Instead of denying responsibility for the 1974 killing, he admitted his guilt but sought to explain that extenuating circumstances accounted for that crime. Because those circumstances no longer existed, he argued, he had no need for further treatment. Only after Murphy had made his confession did the officer inform him of her intent to transmit that information to the police. In short, the environment in which the interview was conducted afforded the probation officer opportunities to reinforce and capitalize on Murphy's ignorance that he had a right to refuse to answer incriminating questions, and the officer deliberately and effectively exploited those opportunities.

Finally, it is indisputable that the probation officer had reason to know that truthful responses to her questions would expose Murphy to criminal liability. This case does not arise out of a spontaneous confession to a routine question innocently asked by a government official. Rather, it originates in precisely the sort of situation the Fifth Amendment was designed to prevent - in which a government, instead of establishing a defendant's guilt through independent investigation, seeks to induce him, against his will, to convict himself out of his own mouth.

In sum, none of the factors that, in most contexts, justify application of the principle that a defendant loses his Fifth Amendment privilege unless he claims it in a timely fashion are present in this case. Accordingly, the State should be obliged to demonstrate that Murphy knew of his constitutional rights and freely waived them. Because the State has made no such showing, I would hold his confession inadmissible.

III

The criminal justice system contains safeguards that should minimize the damage done by the Court's decision today. In the future, responsible criminal defense attorneys whose clients are given probation will inform those clients, in their final interviews, that they may disregard probation conditions insofar as those conditions are inconsistent with probationers' Fifth Amendment rights. The attorneys will then carefully instruct their clients on the nuances of those rights as we have now explicated them. 30 Armed with this knowledge, few probationers will succumb to the sort of pressure and deceit that overwhelmed Murphy.

Because Murphy himself had the benefit of none of the safeguards just described, I would affirm the judgment of the Supreme Court of Minnesota that the admission into evidence of the disclosures he made to his probation officer violated the Constitution.

I respectfully dissent.

Notes

[1] This is not to suggest that a State must or should organize its probation system in a fashion that compels probationers to respond under these circumstances, only that a State is not prevented by the Federal Constitution from doing so.

[2] It makes no difference whether the criminal conduct that the probationer might reveal was committed before or after the crime for which he was convicted or before or after the conviction itself.

[3] JUSTICE BRENNAN and I remain persuaded that "the Fifth Amendment's privilege against self-incrimination requires that any jurisdiction that compels a man to incriminate himself grant him absolute immunity under its laws from prosecution for any transaction revealed in that testimony." Piccirillo v. New York, 400 U.S. 548, 562 (1971) (BRENNAN, J., joined by MARSHALL, J., dissenting). A majority of the Court, however, adheres to the view that the constitutional prohibition is not violated as long as the witness is accorded immunity against the use, in a criminal prosecution, of his testimony or the fruits thereof. See, e. g., Lefkowitz v.Turley, 414 U.S. 70, 84 (1973).

[4] See Friendly, The Fifth Amendment Tomorrow: The Case for Constitutional Change, 37 U. Cin. L. Rev. 671, 708 (1968); Spevak v. Klein, 385 U.S. 511, 531 (1967) (WHITE, J., dissenting).

[5] Thus, in Lefkowitz v. Turley, supra, the Court described its prior decision in Gardner v. Broderick, 392 U.S. 273 (1968), in the following terms: "Although under Garrity any waiver executed may have been invalid and any answers elicited inadmissible in evidence, the State did not purport to recognize as much and instead attempted to coerce a waiver on the penalty of loss of employment. . . . Hence, the State's statutory provision requiring [appellant's] dismissal for his refusal to waive immunity could not stand." 414 U.S., at 80 -81. In the same opinion, the Court acknowledged that the rule announced in Garrity itself remained good law. See 414 U.S., at 79 -80, 82. The Court today does not question the vitality of either the line of cases originating in Gardner or the line originating in Garrity.

[6] Such proof would be especially difficult in cases in which the defendant has confessed to a serious crime, thereby subjecting himself to a penalty - in the form of protracted incarceration - far more severe than the penalty that the State threatened to impose if he refused to answer. Despite the implausibility, under such circumstances, of an allegation that the State's threat induced the confession, we have never suggested that the defendant would be unable to avail himself of the doctrine enunciated in Garrity. Indeed, the situation presented in Garrity itself fits the scenario just described.

[7] As Justice Harlan observed in dissent: "All of the petitioners consented to give statements, none displayed any significant hesitation, and none suggested that the decision to offer information was motivated by the possibility of discharge." 385 U.S., at 505. The majority did not question Justice Harlan's description of the case.

[8] Cf. Escobedo v. Illinois, 378 U.S. 478, 499 (1964) (WHITE, J., dissenting) ("If an accused is told he must answer and does not know better, it would be very doubtful

that the resulting admissions could be used against him"). A similar principle obtains in the Fourth Amendment context. It is well established that a "consent" to a search that consists of nothing more than submission to the "presumed authority" of a colorably valid search warrant is invalid. E. g., Lo-Ji Sales, Inc. v. New York, 442 U.S. 319, 329 (1979); Bumper v. North Carolina, 391 U.S. 543, 548 -549 (1968).

[9] The Solicitor General observes: "Citizens are often required to be truthful in their dealings with the government; any person commits a crime if, for example, he makes a false statement to a federal law enforcement officer in connection with a matter within the officer's jurisdiction. 18 U.S.C. 1001." Brief for United States as Amicus Curiae 19. It is precisely because such proscriptions on lying to government officials are so common that the emphatic injunction contained in Murphy's probation conditions must be interpreted to impose on him more extensive obligations.

[10] At the time Murphy made his confession, no Minnesota court had authoritatively interpreted either the probation condition at issue or the Minnesota statute from which it derives. Nor can a definitive construction of these crucial aspects of state law be found in the opinions of either the trial court of the Minnesota Supreme Court in this case. After cataloging the considerations on which it founded its ruling that Murphy's confession was admissible, the trial court observed: "Against these factors is the fact that a condition of his probation was that he be honest with his probation officer, and that he was there ostensibly to discuss further treatment in regard to his current probation. Failure to follow through with either of these could have resulted in revocation of the probation and potential imprisonment." App. to Pet. for Cert. B-14. The foregoing passage suggests that the trial court assumed that Murphy was under a duty to answer all questions presented by his probation officer, but is too ambiguous to be fairly relied upon as an "interpretation" of the probation condition. Because the State Supreme Court held Murphy's confession inadmissible for different reasons, it did not have occasion to decide whether a refusal to answer the questions asked by his probation officer would have exposed Murphy to revocation of his probation. The majority professes to be "hesitant," "[w]ithout the benefit of an authoritative state-court construction of the condition," to construe it to impose upon Murphy a duty to answer in addition to a duty not to lie. Ante, at 437. For the reasons indicated in the text, I do not share the majority's hesitation; it seems to me clear that a reasonable man would have interpreted the letter to require him to answer all questions. But even if I agreed that the import of the crucial phrase is not apparent, I would object to the majority's disposition of the case. The proper course would be to remand to the Minnesota Supreme Court to allow it to provide an "authoritative construction" of the provisions of state law around which the dispute revolves.

[11] Even the critics of the line of cases forbidding use of statements made after a State threatened a witness with an economic sanction acknowledge that a State may not threaten to put a person in jail for refusing to answer questions. See Friendly, 37 U. Cin. L. Rev., at 676; Greenawalt, Silence as a Moral and Constitutional Right, 23 Wm. & Mary

L. Rev. 15, 66-68 (1981).

[12] See, e. g., Garner v. United States, 424 U.S., at 655 -656.

[13] It might be argued that no such general rule would be required to ensure that persons did not incriminate themselves without first making intelligent decisions to waive their constitutional rights. All that would be necessary would be a rule forbidding the State to make any use of a self-incriminating disclosure in a prosecution against its maker unless he had been reminded of his privilege before making the statement. The police (and other officials) would be free to ask questions without accompanying warnings. If a person questioned made damaging disclosures, the State could not use his statements against him, but the State would thereby be in no worse a position than if the questions had not been asked at all. The police would simply be obliged thereupon to conduct an independent investigation, and to secure a conviction on the basis of "evidence independently and freely secured," see Malloy v. Hogan, 378 U.S. 1, 8 (1964). The response to the foregoing argument is that, in a situation of the sort just described, the State would indeed be in a significantly worse position than if the questions had not been asked. The reason is that, in a subsequent prosecution, the State would bear the burden of proving that it made no use whatever of the incriminating disclosures. See Kastigar v. United States, 406 U.S. 441, 460 (1972). The difficulty of sustaining that burden would often be such as wholly to frustrate prosecution. See Westen & Mandell, To Talk, To Balk, or To Lie: The Emerging Fifth Amendment Doctrine of the "Preferred Response," 19 Am. Crim. L. Rev. 521, 531-532 (1982). Desire to avoid such situations would induce government officials either to preface their questions with warnings or to refrain from asking them at all. The net effect would be to reduce the capacity of government to obtain needed information.

[14] Cf. Schneckloth v. Bustamonte, 412 U.S. 218, 227 -234, 242 (1973) (refusing, for similar reasons, to adopt a waiver standard for testing the voluntariness of consents to searches).

[15] I do not renounce the views I expressed in concurrence or dissent in several of the cases discussed below. My purpose in canvassing the relevant decisions is simply to demonstrate that, even under the analysis adopted by the majorities in those cases, the result reached by the Court today is wrong.

[16] Cf. United States v. Oliver, 505 F.2d 301, 306-308 (CA7 1974) (Stevens, J.) (distinguishing, for Fifth Amendment purposes, income reporting statutes "designed to procure incriminating disclosures from a select group of persons engaged in criminal conduct" and reporting statutes "applicable to the public at large, . . . [whose] demands for information are neutral in the sense that they apply evenly to the few who have illegal earnings and the many who do not").

[17] Prior to Washington, that proposition had frequently been advanced in dictum. See, e. g., United States v. Mandujano, 425 U.S. 564, 574 -575 (1976) (dictum); Rogers v. United States, 340 U.S. 367, 370 (1951) (alternative holding); United States v. Monia, 317 U.S. 424, 427 (1943) (dictum).

[18] JUSTICE BRENNAN and I remain convinced that the fact that a criminal investigation has focused on a grand jury witness is sufficient to tip the constitutional balance in favor of a requirement that the prosecution prove that any damaging disclosures made by the witness were founded upon a knowing and intelligent waiver of the witness' rights. See 431 U.S., at 191 (BRENNAN, J., joined by MARSHALL, J., dissenting); United States v. Mandujano, supra, at 596-602 (BRENNAN, J., joined by MARSHALL, J., concurring in judgment). However, the argument advanced in the text does not depend upon that conviction.

[19] The Court declined, however, to decide whether such warnings were constitutionally required. 431 U.S., at 186, 190.

[20] See also United States ex rel. Vajtauer v. Commissioner of Immigration, 273 U.S. 103, 113 (1927) (defendant who made incriminating disclosures when questioned by an immigration inspector deemed (in dictum) to have waived his privilege when his right to refuse to answer was clear, he had been given adequate notice of the sort of questions he would be asked, and he was represented by counsel at the hearing); United States v. Murdock, 284 U.S. 141, 148 (1931) (when defendant was summoned to appear before revenue agent, consulted with counsel just prior to the interview, and clearly had a right not to incriminate himself, his failure to invoke the Fifth Amendment as a justification for his refusal to answer resulted in a waiver of his privilege) (dictum); Beckwith v. United States, 425 U.S. 341 (1976) (incriminating disclosures made by taxpayer who was interviewed in his home and place of business by Internal Revenue agents after being reminded of his Fifth Amendment rights held admissible in a prosecution against him); Oregon v. Mathiason, 429 U.S. 492 (1977) (per curiam) (parolee's confession to a police officer held admissible where parolee was not in custody at the time of the questioning, parolee had ample warning that he would be asked incriminating questions, and parolee was clearly entitled to refuse to respond); Roberts v. United States, 445 U.S. 552, 559 (1980) (in a case in which the Government had "no substantial reason to believe that the requested disclosures [were] likely to be incriminating," and the defendant clearly had a right not to incriminate himself, the defendant's refusal to answer without asserting his privilege held properly used against him in the determination of his sentence). The presence of two of the four safeguards likewise legitimates the settled principle that a citizen not in custody who is asked potentially incriminating questions by a police officer must claim the benefit of the Fifth Amendment instead of answering if he wishes to retain his privilege. Miranda v. Arizona, 384 U.S. 436, 477 -478 (1966). Under such circumstances, not only does the citizen have a well-established right to refuse to answer, but also the environment is not such as to discourage or frustrate the assertion of his right. See id., at 478.

[21] A less well-known situation involving a similar paucity of safeguards against inadvertent or uninformed abandonment of constitutional rights is that presented in Smith v. United States, 337 U.S. 137 (1949), and Emspak v. United States, 349 U.S. 190 (1955). In each case, the defendant was summoned to testify before an official body,

appeared, and early in the proceeding invoked his privilege against self-incrimination. Questioning continued (in one case under a grant of immunity, in the other on unrelated topics). Later in the proceeding, the defendant was asked whether he wished to claim the privilege with regard to a specific substantive question. In each case, three factors reduced the defendant's ability, at that point, intelligently to exercise his constitutional rights and rendered the activities of his interrogators constitutionally suspect: the defendant's right to refuse to answer the question at issue was unclear; the environment in which the questions were presented was moderately coercive; and the nature of the proceeding as well as the defendant's prior assertion of his privilege against self-incrimination alerted the questioner to the likelihood that a truthful answer to the crucial question would expose the defendant to criminal liability. In both cases, the Court held that the defendant could be prosecuted on the basis of his answer to the decisive question only if the Government were able to demonstrate that he had made a sufficiently unequivocal and intelligent waiver of his Fifth Amendment rights to satisfy the standard enunciated in Johnson v. Zerbst, 304 U.S. 458, 464 (1938) ("an intentional relinquishment or abandonment of a known right or privilege"). In both instances, the Court concluded that the Government had failed to make such a showing, and therefore reversed the defendant's conviction.

[22] The majority construes Murphy's probation conditions to impose on him a general duty to respond to questions, but to contain an exemption for questions that impinged upon his Fifth Amendment rights. Ante, at 436-437. The State of Minnesota, in its brief in this case, adopts the same interpretation. See Brief for Petitioner 36-38 (arguing that probationers in Minnesota are obliged to answer all questions asked by their probation officers except those to which they may assert "valid" claims of privilege). Though I find that construction implausible, see Part I, supra, I assume it for present purposes. The point made here is simply that, at the time Murphy was interrogated, the scope of his Fifth Amendment rights - and therefore the scope of the hypothesized exemption from the general duty to answer - was ambiguous.

[23] The Solicitor General argued in the alternative that, "[w]hen a person has been convicted of a crime, his constitutional rights can be limited to the extent reasonably necessary to accommodate the government's penal and rehabilitative interests," and therefore that the government may constitutionally exert upon a probationer pressures to incriminate himself that it could not exert upon a citizen who had not been convicted of a crime. Brief for United States as Amicus Curiae 8; see id., at 27-32. That proposition is rejected by the Court today.

[24] Cf. Maness v. Meyers, 419 U.S. 449, 466 (1975) ("A layman may not be aware of the precise scope, the nuances, and boundaries of his Fifth Amendment privilege").

[25] Contrary to the majority's suggestion, ante, at 432, nothing in the record indicates that the probation officer had "excused" Murphy from the condition of probation that required him "to pursue . . . Alpha treatment," App. to Pet. for Cert. C-35;

the Minnesota Supreme Court found merely that she had agreed not to seek revocation of his probation because of his breach of that condition, see 324 N. W. 2d 340, 341 (1982).

[26] Indeed, for reasons discussed infra, at 460, it appears that the letter was shrewdly designed to prevent Murphy from discerning in advance the true purpose of the meeting.

[27] See A. Smith & L. Berlin, Introduction to Probation and Parole 116-119 (1979); Mangrum, The Humanity of Probation Officers, 36 Fed. Probation 47 (June 1972); Note, Observations on the Administration of Parole, 79 Yale L. J. 698, 704-708 (1970); People v. Parker, 82 App. Div. 2d 661, 667, 442 N. Y. S. 2d 803, 807 (1981), aff'd, 57 N. Y. 2d 815, 441 N. E. 2d 1118 (1982).

[28] The relationship at issue in Fare was that between a probation officer and a juvenile probationer. But many of the Court's observations can be extended to the relationship between an officer and an adult probationer. See n. 27, supra.

[29] Indeed, when Murphy refused to turn himself in, it was his probation officer who secured the order for his arrest.

[30] It is to be hoped, moreover, that persons currently on probation who are no longer represented by counsel will somehow be informed of the central principle established by the Court's decision: that a probationer has a right to refuse to respond to a question the answer to which might expose him to criminal liability unless he is granted immunity from the use of his answer against him in a subsequent criminal prosecution.

Police should need warrant to search private land with no trespassing sign: Justice Marshall's dissent in Oliver v. United States (April 17, 1984)

JUSTICE MARSHALL, with whom JUSTICE BRENNAN and JUSTICE STEVENS join, dissenting.

In each of these consolidated cases, police officers, ignoring clearly visible "No Trespassing" signs, entered upon private land in search of evidence of a crime. At a spot that could not be seen from any vantage point accessible to the public, the police discovered contraband, which was subsequently used to incriminate the owner of the land. In neither case did the police have a warrant authorizing their activities.

The Court holds that police conduct of this sort does not constitute an "unreasonable search" within the meaning of the Fourth Amendment. The Court reaches that startling conclusion by two independent analytical routes. First, the Court argues that, because the Fourth Amendment, by its terms, renders people secure in their "persons, houses, papers, and effects," it is inapplicable to trespasses upon land not lying within the curtilage of a dwelling. Ante at 466 U. S. 176-177. Second, the Court contends that "an individual may not legitimately demand privacy for activities conducted out of doors in fields, except in the area immediately surrounding the home." Ante at 466 U. S. 178. Because I cannot agree with either of these propositions, I dissent.

I

The first ground on which the Court rests its decision is that the Fourth Amendment "indicates with some precision the places and things encompassed by its protections," and that real property is not included in the list of protected spaces and possessions. Ante at 466 U. S. 176. This line of argument has several flaws. Most obviously, it is inconsistent with the results of many of our previous decisions, none of which the Court purports to overrule. For example, neither a public telephone booth nor a conversation conducted therein can fairly be described as a person, house, paper, or effect, [1] yet we have held that the Fourth Amendment forbids the police without a warrant to eavesdrop on such a conversation. Katz v. United States, 389 U. S. 347 (1967). Nor can it plausibly be argued that an office or commercial establishment is covered by the plain language of the Amendment; yet we have held that such premises are entitled to constitutional protection if they are marked in a fashion that alerts the public to the fact that they are private. Marshall v. Barlow's, Inc., 436 U. S. 307, 436 U. S. 311 (1978); G. M. Leasing Corp. v. United States, 429 U. S. 338, 429 U. S. 358-359 (1977). [2]

Indeed, the Court's reading of the plain language of the Fourth Amendment is incapable of explaining even its own holding in this case. The Court rules that the curtilage, a zone of real property surrounding a dwelling, is entitled to constitutional protection. Ante at 466 U. S. 180. We are not told, however, whether the curtilage is a "house" or an "effect" -- or why, if the curtilage can be incorporated into the list of things and spaces shielded by the Amendment, a field cannot.

The Court's inability to reconcile its parsimonious reading of the phrase "persons, houses, papers, and effects" with our prior decisions, or even its own holding, is a symptom of a more fundamental infirmity in the Court's reasoning. The Fourth Amendment, like the other central provisions of the Bill of Rights that loom large in our modern jurisprudence, was designed not to prescribe with "precision" permissible and impermissible activities, but to identify a fundamental human liberty that should be shielded forever from government intrusion. [3] We do not construe constitutional provisions of this sort the way we do statutes, whose drafters can be expected to indicate with some comprehensiveness and exactitude the conduct they wish to forbid or control and to change those prescriptions when they become obsolete. [4] Rather, we strive, when interpreting these seminal constitutional provisions, to effectuate their purposes -- to lend them meanings that ensure that the liberties the Framers sought to protect are not undermined by the changing activities of government officials. [5]

The liberty shielded by the Fourth Amendment, as we have often acknowledged, is freedom "from unreasonable government intrusions into . . . legitimate expectations of privacy." United States v. Chaduck, 433 U. S. 1, 433 U. S. 7 (1977). That freedom would be incompletely protected if only government conduct that impinged upon a person, house, paper, or effect were subject to constitutional scrutiny. Accordingly, we have repudiated the proposition that the Fourth Amendment applies only to a limited set of locales or kinds of property. In Katz v. United States, we expressly rejected a proffered locational theory of the coverage of the Amendment, holding that it "protects people, not places." 389 U.S. at 389 U. S. 351. Since that time, we have consistently adhered to the view that the applicability of the provision depends solely upon

"whether the person invoking its protection can claim a 'justifiable,' a 'reasonable,' or a 'legitimate expectation of privacy' that has been invaded by government action."

Smith v. Maryland, 442 U. S. 735, 442 U. S. 740 (1979). [6] The Court's contention that, because a field is not a house or effect, it is not covered by the Fourth Amendment is inconsistent with this line of cases, and with the understanding of the nature of constitutional adjudication from which it derives. [7]

II

The second ground for the Court's decision is its contention that any interest a landowner might have in the privacy of his woods and fields is not one that "society is prepared to recognize as reasonable.'" Ante at 466 U. S. 177 (quoting Katz v. United States, 389 U.S. at 389 U. S. 361 (Harlan, J., concurring)).

The mode of analysis that underlies this assertion is certainly more consistent with our prior decisions than that discussed above. But the Court's conclusion cannot withstand scrutiny.

As the Court acknowledges, we have traditionally looked to a variety of factors in determining whether an expectation of privacy asserted in a physical space is "reasonable." Ante at 466 U. S. 177-178. Though those factors do not lend themselves to precise taxonomy, they may be roughly grouped into three categories. First, we consider whether the expectation at issue is rooted in entitlements defined by positive law. Second, we consider the nature of the uses to which spaces of the sort in question can be put. Third, we consider whether the person claiming a privacy interest manifested that interest to the public in a way that most people would understand and respect. [8] When the expectations of privacy asserted by petitioner Oliver and respondent Thornton [9] are examined through these lenses, it becomes clear that those expectations are entitled to constitutional protection.

A

We have frequently acknowledged that privacy interests are not coterminous with property rights. E.g., United States v. Salvucci, 448 U. S. 83, 448 U. S. 91 (1980). However, because

"property rights reflect society's explicit recognition of a person's authority to act as he wishes in certain areas, [they] should be considered in determining whether an individual's expectations of privacy are reasonable."

Rakas v. Illinois, 439 U. S. 128, 439 U. S. 153 (1978) (POWELL, J., concurring). [10] Indeed, the Court has suggested that, insofar as

"[o]ne of the main rights attaching to property is the right to exclude others, . . . one who owns or lawfully possesses or controls property will, in all likelihood, have a legitimate expectation of privacy by virtue of this right to exclude."

Id. at 439 U. S. 144, n. 12 (opinion of the Court). [11]

It is undisputed that Oliver and Thornton each owned the land into which the police intruded. That fact alone provides considerable support for their assertion of legitimate privacy interests in their woods and fields. But even more telling is the nature of the sanctions that Oliver and Thornton could invoke, under local law, for violation of their property rights. In Kentucky, a knowing entry upon fenced or otherwise enclosed land, or upon unenclosed land conspicuously posted with signs excluding the public, constitutes criminal trespass. Ky.Rev.Stat. §§ 511.070(1), 511.080, 511.090(4) (1975). The law in Maine is similar. An intrusion into

"any place from which [the intruder] may lawfully be excluded and which is posted in a manner prescribed by law or in a manner reasonably likely to come to the attention of intruders or which is fenced or otherwise enclosed"

is a crime. Me.Rev.Stat.Ann., Tit. 17A, § 402(1)(C) (1964). [12] Thus, positive law not only recognizes the legitimacy of Oliver's and Thornton's insistence that strangers keep off their land, but subjects those who refuse to respect their wishes to the most severe of penalties -- criminal liability. Under these circumstances, it is hard to credit the Court's assertion that Oliver's and Thornton's expectations of privacy were not of a sort that society is prepared to recognize as reasonable.

B

The uses to which a place is put are highly relevant to the assessment of a privacy interest asserted therein. Rakas v. Illinois, supra, at 439 U. S. 153 (POWELL, J., concurring). If, in light of our shared sensibilities, those activities are of a kind in which people should be able to engage without fear of intrusion by private persons or government officials, we extend the protection of the Fourth Amendment to the space in question, even in the absence of any entitlement derived from positive law. E.g., Katz v. United States, 389 U.S. at 389 U. S. 352-353. [13]

Privately owned woods and fields that are not exposed to public view regularly are employed in a variety of ways that society acknowledges deserve privacy. Many landowners like to take solitary walks on their property, confident that they will not be confronted in their rambles by strangers or policemen. Others conduct agricultural businesses on their property. [14] Some landowners use their secluded spaces to meet lovers, others to gather together with fellow worshippers, still others to engage in sustained creative endeavor. Private land is sometimes used as a refuge for wildlife, where flora and fauna are protected from human intervention of any kind. [15] Our respect for the freedom of landowners to use their posted "open fields" in ways such as these partially explains the seriousness with which the positive law regards deliberate invasions of such spaces, see supra at 466 U. S. 190-191, and substantially reinforces the landowners' contention that their expectations of privacy are "reasonable."

C

Whether a person "took normal precautions to maintain his privacy" in a given space affects whether his interest is one protected by the Fourth Amendment. Rawlings v.

Kentucky, 448 U. S. 98, 448 U. S. 105 (1980). [16] The reason why such precautions are relevant is that we do not insist that a person who has a right to exclude others exercise that right. A claim to privacy is therefore strengthened by the fact that the claimant somehow manifested to other people his desire that they keep their distance.

Certain spaces are so presumptively private that signals of this sort are unnecessary; a homeowner need not post a "Do Not Enter" sign on his door in order to deny entrance to uninvited guests. [17] Privacy interests in other spaces are more ambiguous, and the taking of precautions is consequently more important; placing a lock on one's footlocker strengthens one's claim that an examination of its contents is impermissible. See United States v. Chaduck, 433 U.S. at 433 U. S. 11. Still other spaces are, by positive law and social convention, presumed accessible to members of the public unless the owner manifests his intention to exclude them.

Undeveloped land falls into the last-mentioned category. If a person has not marked the boundaries of his fields or woods in a way that informs passersby that they are not welcome, he cannot object if members of the public enter onto the property. There is no reason why he should have any greater rights as against government officials. Accordingly, we have held that an official may, without a warrant, enter private land from which the public is not excluded and make observations from that vantage point. Air Pollution Variance Board v. Western Alfalfa Corp., 416 U. S. 861, 416 U. S. 865 (1974). Fairly read, the case on which the majority so heavily relies, Hester v. United States, 265 U. S. 57 (1924), affirms little more than the foregoing unremarkable proposition. From aught that appears in the opinion in that case, the defendants, fleeing from revenue agents who had observed them committing a crime, abandoned incriminating evidence on private land from which the public had not been excluded. Under such circumstances, it is not surprising that the Court was unpersuaded by the defendants' argument that the entry onto their fields by the agents violated the Fourth Amendment. [18]

A very different case is presented when the owner of undeveloped land has taken precautions to exclude the public. As indicated above, a deliberate entry by a private citizen onto private property marked with "No Trespassing" signs will expose him to criminal liability. I see no reason why a government official should not be obliged to respect such unequivocal and universally understood manifestations of a landowner's desire for privacy. [19]

In sum, examination of the three principal criteria we have traditionally used for assessing the reasonableness of a person's expectation that a given space would remain private indicates that interests of the sort asserted by Oliver and Thornton are entitled to constitutional protection. An owner's right to insist that others stay off his posted land is firmly grounded in positive law. Many of the uses to which such land may be put deserve privacy. And, by marking the boundaries of the land with warnings that the public should not intrude, the owner has dispelled any ambiguity as to his desires.

The police in these cases proffered no justification for their invasions of Oliver's and Thornton's privacy interests; in neither case was the entry legitimated by a warrant or by one of the established exceptions to the warrant requirement. I conclude, therefore, that the searches of their land violated the Fourth Amendment, and the evidence obtained in the course of those searches should have been suppressed.

III

A clear, easily administrable rule emerges from the analysis set forth above: private land marked in a fashion sufficient to render entry thereon a criminal trespass under the law of the State in which the land lies is protected by the Fourth Amendment's proscription of unreasonable searches and seizures. One of the advantages of the foregoing rule is that it draws upon a doctrine already familiar to both citizens and government officials. In each jurisdiction, a substantial body of statutory and case law defines the precautions a landowner must take in order to avail himself of the sanctions of the criminal law. The police know that body of law, because they are entrusted with responsibility for enforcing it against the public; it therefore would not be difficult for the police to abide by it themselves.

By contrast, the doctrine announced by the Court today is incapable of determinate application. Police officers, making warrantless entries upon private land, will be obliged in the future to make on-the-spot judgments as to how far the curtilage extends, and to stay outside that zone. [20] In addition, we may expect to see a spate of litigation over the question of how much improvement is necessary to remove private land from the category of "unoccupied or undeveloped area" to which the "open fields exception" is now deemed applicable. See ante at 466 U. S. 180, n. 11.

The Court's holding not only ill-serves the need to make constitutional doctrine "workable for application by rank-and-file, trained police officers," Illinois v. Andreas, 463 U. S. 765, 463 U. S. 772 (1983), it withdraws the shield of the Fourth Amendment from privacy interests that clearly deserve protection. By exempting from the coverage of the Amendment large areas of private land, the Court opens the way to investigative activities we would all find repugnant. Cf., e.g., United States v. Lace, 669 F.2d 46, 54 (CA2 1982) (Newman, J., concurring in result) ("[W]hen police officers execute military maneuvers on residential property for three weeks of round-the-clock surveillance, can that be called reasonable'?"); State v. Brady, 406 So. 2d 1093, 1094-1095 (Fla. 1981) ("In order to position surveillance groups around the ranch's airfield, deputies were forced to cross a dike, ram through one gate and cut the chain lock on another, cut or cross posted fences, and proceed several hundred yards to their hiding places"), cert. granted, 456 U.S. 988, supplemental memoranda ordered and oral argument postponed, 459 U.S. 986 (1982). [21]

The Fourth Amendment, properly construed, embodies and gives effect to our collective sense of the degree to which men and women, in civilized society, are entitled "to be let alone" by their governments. Olmstead v. United States, 277 U. S. 438, 277 U. S. 478 (1928) (Brandeis, J., dissenting); cf. Smith v. Maryland, 442 U.S. at 442 U. S. 750 (MARSHALL, J., dissenting). The Court's opinion bespeaks and will help to promote an impoverished vision of that fundamental right.

I dissent.

Notes

[1] The Court informs us that the Framers would have understood the term "effects" to encompass only personal property. Ante at 466 U. S. 177, n. 7. Such a construction of the term would exclude both a public phone booth and spoken words.

[2] On the other hand, an automobile surely does constitute an "effect." Under the Court's theory, cars should therefore stand on the same constitutional footing as houses. Our cases establish, however, that car owners' diminished expectations that their cars will remain free from prying eyes warrants a corresponding reduction in the constitutional protection accorded cars. E.g., United States v. Martinez-Fuerte, 428 U. S. 543, 428 U. S. 561 (1976).

[3] By their terms, the provisions of the Bill of Rights curtail only activities by the Federal Government, See Barron v. Mayor and City Council of Baltimore, 7 Pet. 243 (1833), but the Fourteenth Amendment subjects state and local governments to the most important of those restrictions, see, e.g., Cantwell v. Connecticut, 310 U. S. 296 (1940) (First Amendment); Wolf v. Colorado, 338 U. S. 25 (1949) (Fourth Amendment).

[4] Cf. 17 U. S. Maryland, 4 Wheat. 316, 17 U. S. 407 (1819) ("[W]e must never forget, that it is a constitution we are expounding." Such a document cannot be as detailed as a "legal code"; "[i]ts nature . . . requires, that only its great outlines should be marked, its important objects designated, and the minor ingredients which compose those objects be deduced from the nature of the objects themselves") (emphasis in original).

[5] Our rejection of the mode of interpretation appropriate for statutes is perhaps clearest in our treatment of the First Amendment. That Amendment provides, in pertinent part, that "Congress shall make no law . . . abridging the freedom of speech, or of the press," but says nothing, for example, about restrictions on expressive behavior or about access to the courts. Yet, to give effect to the purpose of the Amendment, we have applied it to regulations of conduct designed to convey a message, e.g., Edwards v. South Carolina, 372 U. S. 229 (1963), and have accorded constitutional protection to the public's "right of access to criminal trials," Globe Newspaper Co. v. Superior Court, 457 U. S. 596, 457 U. S. 604-605 (1982).

[6] See also United States v. Chadwick, 433 U. S. 1, 433 U. S. 7, 11 (1977) (disagreeing with the suggestion that the Fourth Amendment "protects only dwellings and other specifically designated locales"; asserting instead that the purpose of the Amendment "is to safeguard individuals from unreasonable government invasions of legitimate privacy interests"); Rakas v. Illinois, 439 U. S. 128, 439 U. S. 143 (1978) (holding that the determinative question is "whether the person who claims the protection of the Amendment has a legitimate expectation of privacy in the invaded place").

Our most recent decisions continue to rely on the conception of the purpose and scope of the Fourth Amendment that we enunciated in Katz. See, e.g., United States v. Jacobsen, ante at 466 U. S. 113-118; Michigan v. Clifford, 464 U. S. 287, 464 U. S. 292-293 (1984); Illinois v. Andreas, 463 U. S. 765, 463 U. S. 771 (1983); United States v. Place, 462 U. S. 696, 462 U. S. 706-707 (1983); Texas v. Brown, 460 U. S. 730, 460 U. S. 738-740 (1983) (plurality opinion); United States v. Knotts, 460 U. S. 276, 460 U. S. 280-281 (1983).

[7] Sensitive to the weakness of its argument that the "persons or things" mentioned in the Fourth Amendment exhaust the coverage of the provision, the Court goes on to analyze at length the privacy interests that might legitimately be asserted in "open fields." The inclusion of Parts 466 U. S. S. 182|>IV in the opinion, coupled with the Court's reaffirmation of Katz and its progeny, ante at 466 U. S. 177, strongly suggests that the plain language theory sketched in 466 U. S.

[8] The privacy interests protected by the Fourth Amendment are not limited to expectations that physical areas will remain free from public and government intrusion. See supra at 466 U. S. 187-188. The factors relevant to the assessment of the reasonableness of a nonspatial privacy interest may well be different from the three considerations discussed here. See, e.g., Smith v. Maryland, 442 U. S. 735, 442 U. S. 747-748 (1979) (Stewart, J., dissenting); id. at 442 U. S. 750-752 (MARSHALL, J., dissenting).

[9] The Court does not dispute that Oliver and Thornton had subjective expectations of privacy, nor could it in view of the lower courts' findings on that issue. See United States v. Oliver, No. CR80-00005-01-BG (WD Ky., Nov. 14, 1980), App. to Pet. for Cert. in No. 82-15, pp.19-20; Maine v. Thornton, No. CR82-10 (Me.Super.Ct., Apr. 16, 1982), App. to Pet. for Cert. in No. 82-1273, pp. B-4 - B-5.

[10] The Court today seeks to evade the force of this principle by contending that the law of property is designed to serve various "prophylactic" and "economic" purposes unrelated to the protection of privacy. Ante at 466 U. S. 183-184, and n. 15. Such efforts to rationalize the distribution of entitlements under state law are interesting and may have some explanatory power, but cannot support the weight the Court seeks to place upon them. The Court surely must concede that one of the purposes of the law of real property (and specifically the law of criminal trespass, see infra, this page and 466 U. S. 191, and n. 12) is to define and enforce privacy interests -- to empower some people to make whatever use they wish of certain tracts of land without fear that other people will intrude upon their activities. The views of commentators, old and new, as to other functions served by positive law are thus insufficient to support the Court's sweeping assertion that, "in the case of open fields, the general rights of property . . . have little or no relevance to the applicability of the Fourth Amendment," ante at 466 U. S. 183-184.

[11] See also Rawlings v. Kentucky, 448 U. S. 98, 448 U. S. 112 (1980) (BLACKMUN, J., concurring).

[12] Cf. Comment to ALI, Model Penal Code § 221.2, p. 87 (1980) ("The common thread running through these provisions [a sample of state criminal trespass laws] is the element of unwanted intrusion, usually coupled with some sort of notice to would-be

intruders that they may not enter. Most people do not object to strangers tramping through woodland or over pasture or open range. On the other hand, intrusions into buildings, onto property fenced in a manner manifestly designed to exclude intruders, or onto any private property in defiance of actual notice to keep away is generally considered objectionable, and under some circumstances frightening").

[13] In most circumstances, this inquiry requires analysis of the sorts of uses to which a given space is susceptible, not the manner in which the person asserting an expectation of privacy in the space was in fact employing it. See, e.g., United States v. Chadwick, 433 U.S. at 433 U. S. 13. We make exceptions to this principle and evaluate uses on a case-by-case basis in only two contexts: when called upon to assess (what formerly was called) the "standing" of a particular person to challenge an intrusion by government officials into a area over which that person lacked primary control, see, e.g., Rakas v. Illinois, 439 U.S. at 439 U. S. 148-149; Jones v. United States, 362 U. S. 257, 362 U. S. 265-266 (1960), and when it is possible to ascertain how a person is using a particular space without violating the very privacy interest he is asserting, see, e.g., Katz v. United States, 389 U.S. at 389 U. S. 352. (In cases of the latter sort, the inquiries described in this Part and in 466 U. S. infra, are coextensive). Neither of these exceptions is applicable here. Thus, the majority's contention that, because the cultivation of marihuana is not an activity that society wishes to protect, Oliver and Thornton had no legitimate privacy interest in their fields, ante at 466 U. S. 182-183, and n. 13, reflects a misunderstanding of the level of generality on which the constitutional analysis must proceed.

[14] We accord constitutional protection to businesses conducted in office buildings, see supra at 466 U. S. 185-186; it is not apparent why businesses conducted in fields that are not open to the public are less deserving of the benefit of the Fourth Amendment.

[15] This last-mentioned use implicates a kind of privacy interest somewhat different from those to which we are accustomed. It involves neither a person's interest in immunity from observation nor a person's interest in shielding from scrutiny the residues and manifestations of his personal life. Cf. Weinreb, Generalities of the Fourth Amendment, 42 U.Chi.L.Rev. 47, 52-54 (1974). It derives, rather, from a person's desire to preserve inviolate a portion of his world. The idiosyncracy of this interest does not, however, render it less deserving of constitutional protection.

[16] See also Rakas v. Illinois, supra, at 439 U. S. 152 (POWELL, J., concurring); United States v. Chadwick, supra, at 433 U. S. 11; Katz v. United States, supra, at 389 U. S. 352.

[17] However, if the homeowner acts affirmatively to invite someone into his abode, he cannot later insist that his privacy interests have been violated. Lewis v. United States, 385 U. S. 206 (1966).

[18] An argument supportive of the position taken by the Court today might be constructed on the basis of an examination of the record in Hester. It appears that, in his

approach to the house, one of the agents crossed a pasture fence. See Tr. of Record in Hester v. United States, O.T. 1923, No. 243, p. 16. However, the Court, in its opinion, placed no weight upon -- indeed, did not even mention -- that circumstance.

In any event, to the extent that Hester may be read to support a rule any broader than that stated in Air Pollution Variance Board v. Western Alfalfa Corp., 416 U. S. 861 (1974), it is undercut by our decision in Katz, which repudiated the locational theory of the coverage of the Fourth Amendment enunciated in Olmstead v. United States, 277 U. S. 438 (1928), and by the line of decisions originating in Katz, see supra at 466 U. S. 187-188, and n. 6.

[19] Indeed, important practical considerations suggest that the police should not be empowered to invade land closed to the public. In many parts of the country, landowners feel entitled to use self-help in expelling trespassers from their posted property. There is thus a serious risk that police officers, making unannounced, warrantless searches of "open fields," will become involved in violent confrontations with irate landowners, with potentially tragic results. Cf. McDonald v. United States, 335 U. S. 451, 335 U. S. 460-461 (1948) (Jackson, J., concurring).

[20] The likelihood that the police will err in making such judgments is suggested by the difficulty experienced by courts when trying to define the curtilage of dwellings. See, e.g., United States v. Berrong, 712 F.2d 1370, 1374, and n. 7 (CA11 1983), cert. pending, No. 83-988, United States v. Van Dyke, 643 F.2d 992, 993-994 (CA4 1981).

[21] Perhaps the most serious danger in the decision today is that, if the police are permitted routinely to engage in such behavior, it will gradually become less offensive to us all. As Justice Brandeis once observed:

"Our Government is the potent, the omnipresent teacher. For good or for ill, it teaches the whole people by its example. Crime is contagious. If the Government becomes a lawbreaker, it breeds contempt for law. . . ."

Olmstead v. United States, 277 U.S. at 277 U. S. 485 (dissenting opinion). See also Solem v. Stumes, 465 U. S. 638, 465 U. S. 667 (1984) (STEVENS, J., dissenting).

Right to counsel should be right to effective counsel: Justice Marshall's dissent in Strickland v. Washington (May 14, 1984)

JUSTICE MARSHALL, dissenting.

The Sixth and Fourteenth Amendments guarantee a person accused of a crime the right to the aid of a lawyer in preparing and presenting his defense. It has long been settled that "the right to counsel is the right to the effective assistance of counsel." McMann v. Richardson, 397 U. S. 759, 397 U. S. 771, n. 14 (1970). The state and lower federal courts have developed standards for distinguishing effective from inadequate assistance. [1] Today, for the first time, this Court attempts to synthesize and clarify those standards. For the most part, the majority's efforts are unhelpful. Neither of its two principal holdings seems to me likely to improve the adjudication of Sixth Amendment claims. And, in its zeal to survey comprehensively this field of doctrine, the majority makes many other generalizations and suggestions that I find unacceptable. Most importantly, the majority fails to take adequate account of the fact that the locus of this case is a capital sentencing proceeding. Accordingly, I join neither the Court's opinion nor its judgment.

I

The opinion of the Court revolves around two holdings. First, the majority ties the constitutional minima of attorney performance to a simple "standard of reasonableness." Ante at 466 U. S. 688. Second, the majority holds that only an error of counsel that has sufficient impact on a trial to "undermine confidence in the outcome" is grounds for overturning a conviction. Ante at 466 U. S. 694. I disagree with both of these rulings.

A

My objection to the performance standard adopted by the Court is that it is so malleable that, in practice, it will either have no grip at all or will yield excessive variation in the manner in which the Sixth Amendment is interpreted and applied by different courts. To tell lawyers and the lower courts that counsel for a criminal defendant must behave "reasonably" and must act like "a reasonably competent attorney," ante at 466 U. S. 687, is to tell them almost nothing. In essence, the majority has instructed judges called upon to assess claims of ineffective assistance of counsel to advert to their own intuitions regarding what constitutes "professional" representation, and has discouraged them from trying to develop more detailed standards governing the performance of defense counsel. In my view, the Court has thereby not only abdicated its own responsibility to interpret the Constitution, but also impaired the ability of the lower courts to exercise theirs.

The debilitating ambiguity of an "objective standard of reasonableness" in this context is illustrated by the majority's failure to address important issues concerning the quality of representation mandated by the Constitution. It is an unfortunate but undeniable fact that a person of means, by selecting a lawyer and paying him enough to ensure he prepares thoroughly, usually can obtain better representation than that available to an indigent defendant, who must rely on appointed counsel, who, in turn, has limited time and resources to devote to a given case. Is a "reasonably competent attorney" a reasonably competent adequately paid retained lawyer or a reasonably competent appointed attorney? It is also a fact that the quality of representation available to ordinary defendants in different parts of the country varies significantly. Should the standard of performance mandated by the Sixth Amendment vary by locale? [2] The majority offers no clues as to the proper responses to these questions.

The majority defends its refusal to adopt more specific standards primarily on the ground that

"[n]o particular set of detailed rules for counsel's conduct can satisfactorily take account of the variety of circumstances faced by defense counsel or the range of legitimate decisions regarding how best to represent a criminal defendant."

Ante at 466 U. S. 688-689. I agree that counsel must be afforded "wide latitude" when making "tactical decisions" regarding trial strategy, see ante at 466 U. S. 689; cf. infra, at 466 U. S. 712, 466 U. S. 713, but many aspects of the job of a criminal defense attorney are more amenable to judicial oversight. For example, much of the work involved in preparing for a trial, applying for bail, conferring with one's client, making timely objections to significant, arguably erroneous rulings of the trial judge, and filing a notice of appeal if there are colorable grounds therefor could profitably be made the subject of uniform standards.

The opinion of the Court of Appeals in this case represents one sound attempt to develop particularized standards designed to ensure that all defendants receive effective legal assistance. See 693 F.2d 1243, 1251-1258 (CA5 1982) (en banc). For other, generally consistent efforts, see United States v. Decoster, 159 U.S.App.D.C. 326, 333-334, 487 F.2d 1197, 1203-1204 (1973), disapproved on rehearing, 199 U.S.App.D.C. 359, 624 F.2d 196 (en banc), cert. denied, 444 U.S. 944 (1979); Coles v. Peyton, 389 F.2d 224, 226 (CA4), cert. denied, 393 U.S. 849 (1968); People v. Pope, 23 Cal.3d 412, 424-425, 590 P.2d 859, 866 (1979); State v. Harper, 57 Wis.2d 543, 550-557, 205 N.W.2d 1, 6-9 (1973). [3] By refusing to address the merits of these proposals, and indeed suggesting that no such effort is worthwhile, the opinion of the Court, I fear, will stunt the development of constitutional doctrine in this area.

B

I object to the prejudice standard adopted by the Court for two independent reasons. First, it is often very difficult to tell whether a defendant convicted after a trial in which he was ineffectively represented would have fared better if his lawyer had been competent. Seemingly impregnable cases can sometimes be dismantled by good defense counsel. On the basis of a cold record, it may be impossible for a reviewing court confidently to ascertain how the government's evidence and arguments would have stood up against rebuttal and cross-examination by a shrewd, well-prepared lawyer. The difficulties of estimating prejudice after the fact are exacerbated by the possibility that evidence of injury to the defendant may be missing from the record precisely because of the incompetence of defense counsel. [4] In view of all these impediments to a fair evaluation of the probability that the outcome of a trial was affected by ineffectiveness of counsel, it seems to me senseless to impose on a defendant whose lawyer has been shown to have been incompetent the burden of demonstrating prejudice.

Second and more fundamentally, the assumption on which the Court's holding rests is that the only purpose of the constitutional guarantee of effective assistance of counsel is to reduce the chance that innocent persons will be convicted. In my view, the guarantee also functions to ensure that convictions are obtained only through fundamentally fair procedures. [5] The majority contends that the Sixth Amendment is not violated when a manifestly guilty defendant is convicted after a trial in which he was represented by a manifestly ineffective attorney. I cannot agree. Every defendant is entitled to a trial in which his interests are vigorously and conscientiously advocated by an able lawyer. A proceeding in which the defendant does not receive meaningful assistance in meeting the forces of the State does not, in my opinion, constitute due process.

In Chapman v. California, 386 U. S. 18, 386 U. S. 23 (1967), we acknowledged that certain constitutional rights are "so basic to a fair trial that their infraction can never be treated as harmless error." Among these rights is the right to the assistance of counsel at trial. Id. at 386 U. S. 23, n. 8; see Gideon v. Wainwright, 372 U. S. 335 (1963). [6] In my view, the right to effective assistance of counsel is entailed by the right to counsel, and abridgment of the former is equivalent to abridgment of the latter. [7] I would thus hold that a showing that the performance of a defendant's lawyer departed from constitutionally prescribed standards requires a new trial regardless of whether the defendant suffered demonstrable prejudice thereby.

II

Even if I were inclined to join the majority's two central holdings, I could not abide the manner in which the majority elaborates upon its rulings. Particularly regrettable are the majority's discussion of the "presumption" of reasonableness to be accorded lawyers' decisions and its attempt to prejudge the merits of claims previously rejected by lower courts using different legal standards.

A

In defining the standard of attorney performance required by the Constitution, the majority appropriately notes that many problems confronting criminal defense attorneys admit of "a range of legitimate" responses. Ante at 466 U. S. 689. And the majority properly cautions courts, when reviewing a lawyer's selection amongst a set of options, to avoid the hubris of hindsight. Ibid. The majority goes on, however, to suggest that reviewing courts should "indulge a strong presumption that counsel's conduct" was constitutionally acceptable, ibid.; see ante at 466 U. S. 690, 466 U. S. 696, and should "appl[y] a heavy measure of deference to counsel's judgments," ante at 466 U. S. 691.

I am not sure what these phrases mean, and I doubt that they will be self-explanatory to lower courts. If they denote nothing more than that a defendant claiming he was denied effective assistance of counsel has the burden of proof, I would agree. See United States v. Cronic, ante at 466 U. S. 658. But the adjectives "strong" and "heavy" might be read as imposing upon defendants an unusually weighty burden of persuasion. If that is the majority's intent, I must respectfully dissent. The range of acceptable behavior defined by "prevailing professional norms," ante at 466 U. S. 688, seems to me sufficiently broad to allow defense counsel the flexibility they need in responding to novel problems of trial strategy. To afford attorneys more latitude, by "strongly presuming" that their behavior will fall within the zone of reasonableness, is covertly to legitimate convictions and sentences obtained on the basis of incompetent conduct by defense counsel.

The only justification the majority itself provides for its proposed presumption is that undue receptivity to claims of ineffective assistance of counsel would encourage too many defendants to raise such claims, and thereby would clog the courts with frivolous suits and "dampen the ardor" of defense counsel. See ante at 466 U. S. 690. I have more confidence than the majority in the ability of state and federal courts expeditiously to dispose of meritless arguments and to ensure that responsible, innovative lawyering is not inhibited. In my view, little will be gained and much may be lost by instructing the lower courts to proceed on the assumption that a defendant's challenge to his lawyer's performance will be insubstantial.

B

For many years, the lower courts have been debating the meaning of "effective" assistance of counsel. Different courts have developed different standards. On the issue of the level of performance required by the Constitution, some courts have adopted the forgiving "farce-and-mockery" standard, [8] while others have adopted various versions of the "reasonable competence" standard. [9] On the issue of the level of prejudice necessary to compel a new trial, the courts have taken a wide variety of positions, ranging from the stringent "outcome-determinative" test [10] to the rule that a showing of incompetence on the part of defense counsel automatically requires reversal of the conviction regardless of the injury to the defendant. [11]

The Court today substantially resolves these disputes. The majority holds that the Constitution is violated when defense counsel's representation falls below the level expected of reasonably competent defense counsel, ante at 466 U. S. 687-691, and so affects the trial that there is a "reasonable probability" that, absent counsel's error, the outcome would have been different, ante at 466 U. S. 691-696.

Curiously, though, the Court discounts the significance of its rulings, suggesting that its choice of standards matters little, and that few if any cases would have been decided differently if the lower courts had always applied the tests announced today. See ante at 466 U. S. 696-697. Surely the judges in the state and lower federal courts will be surprised to learn that the distinctions they have so fiercely debated for many years are, in fact, unimportant.

The majority's comments on this point seem to be prompted principally by a reluctance to acknowledge that today's decision will require a reassessment of many previously rejected ineffective assistance of counsel claims. The majority's unhappiness on this score is understandable, but its efforts to mitigate the perceived problem will be ineffectual. Nothing the majority says can relieve lower courts that hitherto have been using standards more tolerant of ineffectual advocacy of their obligation to scrutinize all claims, old as well as new, under the principles laid down today.

III

The majority suggests that, "[f]or purposes of describing counsel's duties," a capital sentencing proceeding "need not be distinguished from an ordinary trial." Ante at 466 U. S. 687. I cannot agree.

The Court has repeatedly acknowledged that the Constitution requires stricter adherence to procedural safeguards in a capital case than in other cases.

"[T]he penalty of death is qualitatively different from a sentence of imprisonment, however long. Death, in its finality, differs more from life imprisonment than a 100-year prison term differs from one of only a year or two. Because of that qualitative difference, there is a corresponding difference in the need for reliability in the determination that death is the appropriate punishment in a specific case."

Woodson v. North Carolina, 428 U. S. 280, 428 U. S. 305 (1976) (plurality opinion) (footnote omitted). [12]

The performance of defense counsel is a crucial component of the system of protections designed to ensure that capital punishment is administered with some degree of rationality. "Reliability" in the imposition of the death sentence can be approximated only if the sentencer is fully informed of "all possible relevant information about the individual defendant whose fate it must determine." Jurek v. Texas, 428 U. S. 262, 428 U. S. 276 (1976) (opinion of Stewart, POWELL, and STEVENS, JJ.). The job of amassing that information and presenting it in an organized and persuasive manner to the sentencer is entrusted principally to the defendant's lawyer. The importance to the process of counsel's efforts, [13] combined with the severity and irrevocability of the sanction at stake, require that the standards for determining what constitutes "effective assistance" be applied especially stringently in capital sentencing proceedings. [14]

It matters little whether strict scrutiny of a claim that ineffectiveness of counsel resulted in a death sentence is achieved through modification of the Sixth Amendment standards or through especially careful application of those standards. JUSTICE BRENNAN suggests that the necessary adjustment of the level of performance required of counsel in capital sentencing proceedings can be effected simply by construing the phrase, "reasonableness under prevailing professional norms," in a manner that takes into account the nature of the impending penalty. Ante at 466 U. S. 704-706. Though I would prefer a more specific iteration of counsel's duties in this special context, [15] I can accept that proposal. However, when instructing lower courts regarding the probability of impact upon the outcome that requires a resentencing, I think the Court would do best explicitly to modify the legal standard itself. [16] In my view, a person on death row, whose counsel's performance fell below constitutionally acceptable levels, should not be compelled to demonstrate a "reasonable probability" that he would have been given a life sentence if his lawyer had been competent, see ante at 466 U. S. 694; if the defendant can establish a significant chance that the outcome would have been different, he surely should be entitled to a redetermination of his fate. Cf. United States v. Agurs, 427 U. S. 97, 427 U. S. 121-122 (1976) (MARSHALL, J., dissenting). [17]

IV

The views expressed in the preceding section oblige me to dissent from the majority's disposition of the case before us. [18] It is undisputed that respondent's trial counsel made virtually no investigation of the possibility of obtaining testimony from respondent's relatives, friends, or former employers pertaining to respondent's character or background. Had counsel done so, he would have found several persons willing and able to testify that, in their experience, respondent was a responsible, nonviolent man, devoted to his family, and active in the affairs of his church. See App. 338-365. Respondent contends that his lawyer could have and should have used that testimony to "humanize" respondent, to counteract the impression conveyed by the trial that he was little more than a cold-blooded killer. Had this evidence been admitted, respondent argues, his chances of obtaining a life sentence would have been significantly better.

Measured against the standards outlined above, respondent's contentions are substantial. Experienced members of the death penalty bar have long recognized the crucial importance of adducing evidence at a sentencing proceeding that establishes the defendant's social and familial connections. See Goodpaster, The Trial for Life: Effective Assistance of Counsel in Death Penalty Cases, 58 N.Y.U.L.Rev. 299, 300-303, 334-335 (1983). The State makes a colorable -- though, in my view, not compelling -- argument that defense counsel in this case might have made a reasonable "strategic" decision not to present such evidence at the sentencing hearing on the assumption that an unadorned acknowledgment of respondent's responsibility for his crimes would be more likely to appeal to the trial judge, who was reputed to respect persons who accepted responsibility for their actions. [19] But however justifiable such a choice might have been after counsel had fairly assessed the potential strength of the mitigating evidence available to him, counsel's failure to make any significant effort to find out what evidence might be garnered from respondent's relatives and acquaintances surely cannot be described as "reasonable." Counsel's failure to investigate is particularly suspicious in light of his candid admission that respondent's confessions and conduct in the course of the trial gave him a feeling of "hopelessness" regarding the possibility of saving respondent's life, see App. 383-384, 400-401.

That the aggravating circumstances implicated by respondent's criminal conduct were substantial, see ante at 466 U. S. 700, does not vitiate respondent's constitutional claim; judges and juries in cases involving behavior at least as egregious have shown mercy, particularly when afforded an opportunity to see other facets of the defendant's personality and life. [20] Nor is respondent's contention defeated by the possibility that the material his counsel turned up might not have been sufficient to establish a statutory mitigating circumstance under Florida law; Florida sentencing judges and the Florida Supreme Court sometimes refuse to impose death sentences in cases

"in which, even though statutory mitigating circumstances do not outweigh statutory aggravating circumstances, the addition of nonstatutory mitigating circumstances tips the scales in favor of life imprisonment."

Barclay v. Florida, 463 U. S. 939, 463 U. S. 964 (1983) (STEVENS, J., concurring in judgment) (emphasis in original).

If counsel had investigated the availability of mitigating evidence, he might well have decided to present some such material at the hearing. If he had done so, there is a significant chance that respondent would have been given a life sentence. In my view, those possibilities, conjoined with the unreasonableness of counsel's failure to investigate, are more than sufficient to establish a violation of the Sixth Amendment and to entitle respondent to a new sentencing proceeding.

I respectfully dissent.

Notes

[1] See Note, Identifying and Remedying Ineffective Assistance of Criminal Defense Counsel: A New Look After United States v. Decoster, 93 Harv.L.Rev. 752, 756-758 (1980); Note, Effective Assistance of Counsel: The Sixth Amendment and the Fair Trial Guarantee, 50 U.Chi.L.Rev. 1380, 1386-1387, 1399-1401, 1408-1410 (1983).

[2] Cf., e.g., Moore v. United States, 432 F.2d 730, 736 (CA3 1970) (defining the constitutionally required level of performance as "the exercise of the customary skill and knowledge which normally prevails at the time and place").

[3] For a review of other decisions attempting to develop guidelines for assessment of ineffective assistance of counsel claims, see Erickson, Standards of Competency for Defense Counsel in a Criminal Case, 17 Am.Crim.L.Rev. 233, 242-248 (1979). Many of these decisions rely heavily on the standards developed by the American Bar Association. See ABA Standards for Criminal Justice 4-1.1 - 4-8.6 (2d ed.1980).

[4] Cf. United States v. Ellison, 557 F.2d 128, 131 (CA7 1977). In discussing the related problem of measuring injury caused by joint representation of conflicting interests, we observed:

"[T]he evil . . . is in what the advocate finds himself compelled to refrain from doing, not only at trial, but also as to possible pretrial plea negotiations and in the sentencing process. It may be possible in some cases to identify from the record the prejudice resulting from an attorney's failure to undertake certain trial tasks, but even with a record of the sentencing hearing available, it would be difficult to judge intelligently the impact of a conflict on the attorney's representation of a client. And to assess the impact of a conflict of interests on the attorney's options, tactics, and decisions in plea negotiations would be virtually impossible. Thus, an inquiry into a claim of harmless error here would require, unlike most cases, unguided speculation."

Holloway v. Arkansas, 435 U. S. 475, 436 U. S. 490-491 (1978) (emphasis in original). When defense counsel fails to take certain actions, not because he is "compelled" to do so, but because he is incompetent, it is often equally difficult to ascertain the prejudice consequent upon his omissions.

[5] See United States v. Decoster, 199 U.S.App.D.C. 369, 464-457, 624 F.2d 196, 291-294 (en banc) (Bazelon, J., dissenting), cert. denied, 444 U.S. 944 (1979); Note, 93 Harv.L.Rev. at 767-770.

[6] In cases in which the government acted in a way that prevented defense counsel from functioning effectively, we have refused to require the defendant, in order to obtain a new trial, to demonstrate that he was injured. In Glasser v. United States, 315 U.

S. 60, 315 U. S. 76-76 (1942), for example, we held:

"To determine the precise degree of prejudice sustained by [a defendant] as a result of the court's appointment of [the same counsel for two codefendants with conflicting interests] is at once difficult and unnecessary. The right to have the assistance of counsel is too fundamental and absolute to allow courts to indulge in nice calculations as to the amount of prejudice arising from its denial."

As the Court today acknowledges, United State v. Cronic, ante at 466 U. S. 662, n. 31, whether the government or counsel himself is to blame for the inadequacy of the legal assistance received by a defendant should make no difference in deciding whether the defendant must prove prejudice.

[7] See United States v. Yelardy, 567 F.2d 863, 865, n. 1 (CA6), cert. denied, 439 U.S. 842 (1978); Beasley v. United States, 491 F.2d 687, 696 (CA6 1974); Commonwealth v. Badger, 482 Pa. 240, 243-244, 393 A.2d 642, 644 (1978).

[8] See, e.g., State v. Pacheco, 121 Ariz. 88, 91, 588 P.2d 830, 833 (1978); Hoover v. State, 270 Ark. 978, 980, 606 S.W.2d 749, 761 (1980); Line v. State, 272 Ind. 353, 354-355, 397 N.E.2d 975, 976 (1979).

[9] See, e.g., Trapnell v. United States, 725 F.2d 149, 155 (CA2 1983); Cooper v. Fitzharris, 586 F.2d 1325, 1328-1330 (CA9 1978) (en banc), cert. denied, 440 U.S. 974 (1979).

[10] See, e.g., United States v. Decoster, 199 U.S.App.D.C. at 370, and n. 74, 624 F.2d at 208, and n. 74 (plurality opinion); Knight v. State, 394 So.2d 997, 1001 (Fla.1981).

[11] See n. 7, supra.

[12] See also Zant v. Stephens, 462 U. S. 862, 462 U. S. 884-885 (1983); Eddings v. Oklahoma, 455 U. S. 104, 455 U. S. 110-112 (1982); Lockett v. Ohio, 438 U. S. 586, 438 U. S. 604 (1978) (plurality opinion).

[13] See Goodpaster, The Trial for Life: Effective Assistance of Counsel in Death Penalty Cases, 58 N.Y.U.L.Rev. 299, 303 (1983).

[14] As JUSTICE BRENNAN points out, ante at 466 U. S. 704, an additional reason for examining especially carefully a Sixth Amendment challenge when it pertains to a capital sentencing proceeding is that the result of finding a constitutional violation in that context is less disruptive than a finding that counsel was incompetent in the liability phase of a trial.

[15] See 466 U. S. supra. For a sensible effort to formulate guidelines for the conduct of defense counsel in capital sentencing proceedings, see Goodpaster, supra, at 343-345, 360-362.

[16] For the purposes of this and the succeeding section, I assume, solely for the sake of argument, that some showing of prejudice is necessary to state a violation of the Sixth Amendment. But cf. 466 U. S. supra.

[17] As I read the opinion of the Court, it does not preclude this kind of adjustment of the legal standard. The majority defines "reasonable probability" as "a probability sufficient to undermine confidence in the outcome." Ante at 466 U. S. 694. In

view of the nature of the sanction at issue, and the difficulty of determining how a sentencer would have responded if presented with a different set of facts, it could be argued that a lower estimate of the likelihood that the outcome of a capital sentencing proceeding was influenced by attorney error is sufficient to "undermine confidence" in that outcome than would be true in an ordinary criminal case.

[18] Adhering to my view that the death penalty is unconstitutional under all circumstances, Gregg v. Georgia, 428 U. S. 153, 428 U. S. 231 (1976) (MARSHALL J., dissenting), I would vote to vacate respondent's sentence even if he had not presented a substantial Sixth Amendment claim.

[19] Two considerations undercut the State's explanation of counsel's decision. First, it is not apparent why adducement of evidence pertaining to respondent's character and familial connections would have been inconsistent with respondent's acknowledgment that he was responsible for his behavior. Second, the Florida Supreme Court possesses -- and frequently exercises -- the power to overturn death sentences it deems unwarranted by the facts of a case. See State v. Dixon, 283 So.2d 1, 10 (1973). Even if counsel's decision not to try to humanize respondent for the benefit of the trial judge were deemed reasonable, counsel's failure to create a record for the benefit of the State Supreme Court might well be deemed unreasonable.

[20] See, e.g., Farmer & Kinard, The Trial of the Penalty Phase (1976), reprinted in 2 California State Public Defender, California Death Penalty Manual N-33, N-45 (1980).

Preventive detention of a juvenile pursuant to 320.5(3)(b) violates the Due Process Clause: Justice Marshall's dissent in Schall v. Martin (June 4, 1984)

JUSTICE MARSHALL, with whom JUSTICE BRENNAN and JUSTICE STEVENS join, dissenting.

The New York Family Court Act governs the treatment of persons between 7 and 16 years of age who are alleged to have committed acts that, if committed by adults, would constitute crimes. 1 The Act contains two provisions that authorize the detention of juveniles arrested for offenses covered by the Act [2] for up to 17 days pending adjudication of their guilt. 3 Section 320.5(3)(a) empowers a judge of the New York Family Court to order detention of a juvenile if he finds "there is a substantial probability that [the juvenile] will not appear in court on the return date." Section 320.5(3)(b), the provision at issue in these cases, authorizes detention if the judge finds "there is a serious risk [the juvenile] may before the return date commit an act which if committed by an adult would constitute a crime." 4

There are few limitations on 320.5(3)(b). Detention need not be predicated on a finding that there is probable cause to believe the child committed the offense for which he was arrested. The provision applies to all juveniles, regardless of their prior records or the severity of the offenses of which they are accused. The provision is not limited to the prevention of dangerous crimes; a prediction that a juvenile if released may commit a minor misdemeanor is sufficient to justify his detention. Aside from the reference to "serious risk," the requisite likelihood that the juvenile will misbehave before his trial is not specified by the statute.

The Court today holds that preventive detention of a juvenile pursuant to 320.5(3)(b) does not violate the Due Process Clause. Two rulings are essential to the Court's decision: that the provision promotes legitimate government objectives important enough to justify the abridgment of the detained juveniles' liberty interests, ante, at 274; and that the provision incorporates procedural safeguards sufficient to prevent unnecessary or arbitrary impairment of constitutionally protected rights, ante, at 277, 279-280. Because I disagree with both of those rulings, I dissent.

I

The District Court made detailed findings, which the Court of Appeals left undisturbed, regarding the manner in which 320.5(3)(b) is applied in practice. Unless clearly erroneous, those findings are binding upon us, see Fed. Rule Civ. Proc. 52(a), and must guide our analysis of the constitutional questions presented by these cases.

The first step in the process that leads to detention under 320.5(3)(b) is known as "probation intake." A juvenile may arrive at intake by one of three routes: he may be brought there directly by an arresting officer; he may be detained for a brief period after his arrest and then taken to intake; he may be released upon arrest and directed to appear at a designated time. United States ex rel. Martin v. Strasburg, 513 F. Supp. 691, 701 (SDNY 1981). The heart of the intake procedure is a 10-to-40-minute interview of the juvenile, the arresting officer, and sometimes the juvenile's parent or guardian. The objectives of the probation officer conducting the interview are to determine the nature of the offense the child may have committed and to obtain some background information on him. Ibid.

On the basis of the information derived from the interview and from an examination of the juvenile's record, the probation officer decides whether the case should be disposed of informally ("adjusted") or whether it should be referred to the Family Court. If the latter, the officer makes an additional recommendation regarding whether the juvenile should be detained. "There do not appear to be any governing criteria which must be followed by the probation officer in choosing between proposing detention and parole . . . ." Ibid.

The actual decision whether to detain a juvenile under 320.5(3)(b) is made by a Family Court judge at what is called an "initial appearance" - a brief hearing resembling an arraignment. 5 Id., at 702. The information on which the judge makes his determination is very limited. He has before him a "petition for delinquency" prepared by a state agency, charging the juvenile with an offense, accompanied with one or more affidavits attesting to the juvenile's involvement. Ordinarily the judge has in addition the written report and recommendation of the probation officer. However, the probation officer who prepared the report rarely attends the hearing. Ibid. Nor is the complainant likely to appear. Consequently, "[o]ften there is no one present with personal knowledge of what happened." Ibid.

In the typical case, the judge appoints counsel for the juvenile at the time his case is called. Thus, the lawyer has no opportunity to make an independent inquiry into the juvenile's background or character, and has only a few minutes to prepare arguments on the child's behalf. Id., at 702, 708. The judge ordinarily does not interview the juvenile, id., at 708, makes no inquiry into the truth of allegations in the petition, id., at 702, and does not determine whether there is probable cause to believe the juvenile committed the offense. 6 The typical hearing lasts between 5 and 15 minutes, and the judge renders his decision immediately afterward. Ibid.

Neither the statute nor any other body of rules guides the efforts of the judge to determine whether a given juvenile is likely to commit a crime before his trial. In making detention decisions, "each judge must rely on his own subjective judgment, based on the limited information available to him at court intake and whatever personal standards he himself has developed in exercising his discretionary authority under the statute." Ibid. Family Court judges are not provided information regarding the behavior of juveniles over whose cases they have presided, so a judge has no way of refining the standards he employs in making detention decisions. Id., at 712.

After examining a study of a sample of 34 cases in which juveniles were detained under 320.5(3)(b) 7 along with various statistical studies of pretrial detention of juveniles in New York, 8 the District Court made findings regarding the circumstances in which the provision habitually is invoked. Three of those findings are especially germane to appellees' challenge to the statute. First, a substantial number of "first offenders" are detained pursuant to 320.5(3)(b). For example, at least 5 of the 34 juveniles in the sample had no prior contact with the Family Court before being detained and at least 16 had no prior adjudications of delinquency. Id., at 695-700. 9 Second, many juveniles are released - for periods ranging from five days to several weeks - after their arrests and are then detained under 320.5(3)(b), despite the absence of any evidence of misconduct during the time between their arrests and "initial appearances." Sixteen of the thirty-four cases in the sample fit this pattern. Id., at 705, 713-714. Third, "the overwhelming majority" of the juveniles detained under 320.5(3)(b) are released either before or immediately after their trials, either unconditionally or on parole. Id., at 705. At least 23 of the juveniles in the sample fell into this category. Martin v. Strasburg, 689 F.2d 365, 369, n. 19 (CA2 1982); see 513 F. Supp., at 695-700.

Finally, the District Court made a few significant findings concerning the conditions associated with "secure detention" pursuant to 320.5(3)(b). 10 In a "secure facility," "[t]he juveniles are subjected to strip-searches, wear institutional clothing and follow institutional regimen. At Spofford [Juvenile Detention Center], which is a secure facility, some juveniles who have had dispositional determinations and were awaiting placement (long term care) commingle with those in pretrial detention (short term care)."

Id., at 695, n. 5.

It is against the backdrop of these findings that the contentions of the parties must be examined.

II

A

As the majority concedes, ante, at 263, the fact that 320.5(3)(b) applies only to juveniles does not insulate the provision from review under the Due Process Clause. "[N]either the Fourteenth Amendment nor the Bill of Rights is for adults alone." In re Gault, 387 U.S. 1, 13 (1967). Examination of the provision must of course be informed by a recognition that juveniles have different needs and capacities than adults, see McKeiver v. Pennsylvania, 403 U.S. 528, 550 (1971), but the provision still "must measure up to the essentials of due process and fair treatment," Kent v. United States, 383 U.S. 541, 562 (1966).

To comport with "fundamental fairness," 320.5(3)(b) must satisfy two requirements. First, it must advance goals commensurate with the burdens it imposes on constitutionally protected interests. Second, it must not punish the juveniles to whom it applies.

The majority only grudgingly and incompletely acknowledges the applicability of the first of these tests, but its grip on the cases before us is undeniable. It is manifest that 320.5(3)(b) impinges upon fundamental rights. If the "liberty" protected by the Due Process Clause means anything, it means freedom from physical restraint. Ingraham v. Wright, 430 U.S. 651, 673 -674 (1977); Board of Regents v. Roth, 408 U.S. 564, 572 (1972). Only a very important government interest can justify deprivation of liberty in this basic sense. 11

The majority seeks to evade the force of this principle by discounting the impact on a child of incarceration pursuant to 320.5(3)(b). The curtailment of liberty consequent upon detention of a juvenile, the majority contends, is mitigated by the fact that "juvenile, unlike adults, are always in some form of custody." Ante, at 265. In any event, the majority argues, the conditions of confinement associated with "secure detention" under 320.5(3)(b) are not unduly burdensome. Ante, at 271. These contentions enable the majority to suggest that 320.5(3)(b) need only advance a "legitimate state objective" to satisfy the strictures of the Due Process Clause. Ante, at 256-257, 263-264, 274. 12

The majority's arguments do not survive scrutiny. Its characterization of preventive detention as merely a transfer of custody from a parent or guardian to the State is difficult to take seriously. Surely there is a qualitative difference between imprisonment and the condition of being subject to the supervision and control of an adult who has one's best interests at heart. And the majority's depiction of the nature of confinement under 320.5(3)(b) is insupportable on this record. As noted above, the District Court found that secure detention entails incarceration in a facility closely resembling a jail and that pretrial detainees are sometimes mixed with juveniles who have been found to be delinquent. Supra, at 287-288. Evidence adduced at trial reinforces these findings. For example, Judge Quinones, a Family Court Judge with eight years of experience, described the conditions of detention as follows:

"Then again, Juvenile Center, as much as we might try, is not the most pleasant place in the world. If you put them in detention, you are liable to be exposing these youngsters to all sorts of things. They are liable to be exposed to assault, they are liable to be exposed to sexual assaults. You are taking the risk of putting them together with a youngster that might be much worse than they, possibly might be, and it might have a bad effect in that respect." App. 270.

Many other observers of the circumstances of juvenile detention in New York have come to similar conclusions. 13

In short, fairly viewed, pretrial detention of a juvenile pursuant to 320.5(3)(b) gives rise to injuries comparable to those associated with imprisonment of an adult. In both situations, the detainee suffers stigmatization and severe limitation of his freedom of movement. See In re Winship, 397 U.S. 358, 367 (1970); In re Gault, 387 U.S., at 27 . Indeed, the impressionability of juveniles may make the experience of incarceration more injurious to them than to adults; all too quickly juveniles subjected to preventive detention come to see society at large as hostile and oppressive and to regard themselves as irremediably "delinquent." 14 Such serious injuries to presumptively innocent persons - encompassing the curtailment of their constitutional rights to liberty - can be justified only by a weighty public interest that is substantially advanced by the statute. 15

The applicability of the second of the two tests is admitted even by the majority. In Bell v. Wolfish, 441 U.S. 520, 535 (1979), the Court held that an adult may not be punished prior to determination that he is guilty of a crime. 16 The majority concedes, as it must, that this principle applies to juveniles. Ante, at 264, 269. Thus, if the only purpose substantially advanced by 320.5(3)(b) is punishment, the provision must be struck down.

For related reasons, 320.5(3)(b) cannot satisfy either of the requirements discussed above that together define "fundamental fairness" in the context of pretrial detention.

B

Appellants and the majority contend that 320.5(3)(b) advances a pair of intertwined government objectives: "protecting the community from crime," ante, at 264, and "protecting a juvenile from the consequences of his criminal activity," ante, at 266. More specifically, the majority argues that detaining a juvenile for a period of up to 17 days prior to his trial has two desirable effects: it protects society at large from the crimes he might have committed during that period if released; and it protects the juvenile himself "both from potential physical injury which may be suffered when a victim fights back or a policeman attempts to make an arrest and from the downward spiral of criminal activity into which peer pressure may lead the child." Ante, at 264-266.

Appellees and some amici argue that public purposes of this sort can never justify incarceration of a person who has not been adjudicated guilty of a crime, at least in the absence of a determination that there exists probable cause to believe he committed a criminal offense. 17 We need not reach that categorial argument in these cases because, even if the purposes identified by the majority are conceded to be compelling, they are not sufficiently promoted by detention pursuant to 320.5(3)(b) to justify the concomitant impairment of the juveniles' liberty interests. 18 To state the case more precisely, two circumstances in combination render 320.5(3)(b) invalid in toto: in the large majority of cases in which the provision is invoked, its asserted objectives are either not advanced at all or are only minimally promoted; and, as the provision is written and administered by the state courts, the cases in which its asserted ends are significantly advanced cannot practically be distinguished from the cases in which they are not.

1

Both of the courts below concluded that only occasionally and accidentally does pretrial detention of a juvenile under 320.5(3)(b) prevent the commission of a crime. Three subsidiary findings undergird that conclusion. First, Family Court judges are incapable of determining which of the juveniles who appear before them would commit offenses before their trials if left at large and which would not. In part, this incapacity derives from the limitations of current knowledge concerning the dynamics of human behavior. On the basis of evidence adduced at trial, supplemented by a thorough review of the secondary literature, see 513 F. Supp., at 708-712, and nn. 31-32, the District Court found that "no diagnostic tools have as yet been devised which enable even the most highly trained criminologists to predict reliably which juveniles will engage in violent crime." Id., at 708. The evidence supportive of this finding is overwhelming. 19 An independent impediment to identification of the defendants who would misbehave if released is the paucity of data available at an initial appearance. The judge must make his decision whether to detain a juvenile on the basis of a set of allegations regarding the child's alleged offense, a cursory review of his background and criminal record, and the recommendation of a probation officer who, in the typical case, has seen the child only once. Id., at 712. In view of this scarcity of relevant information, the District Court credited the testimony of appellees' expert witness, who "stated that he would be surprised if recommendations based on intake interviews were better than chance and assessed the judge's subjective prognosis about the probability of future crime as only 4% better than chance - virtually wholly unpredictable." Id., at 708. 20

Second, 320.5(3)(b) is not limited to classes of juveniles whose past conduct suggests that they are substantially more likely than average juveniles to misbehave in the immediate future. The provision authorizes the detention of persons arrested for trivial offenses 21 and persons without any prior contacts with juvenile court. Even a finding that there is probable cause to believe a juvenile committed the offense with which he was charged is not a prerequisite to his detention. See supra, at 285, and n. 6. 22

Third, the courts below concluded that circumstances surrounding most of the cases in which 320.5(3)(b) has been invoked strongly suggest that the detainee would not have committed a crime during the period before his trial if he had been released. In a significant proportion of the cases, the juvenile had been released after his arrest and had not committed any reported crimes while at large, see supra, at 287; it is not apparent why a juvenile would be more likely to misbehave between his initial appearance and his trial than between his arrest and initial appearance. Even more telling is the fact that "the vast majority" of persons detained under 320.5(3)(b) are released either before or immediately after their trials. 698 F.2d, at 369; see 513 F. Supp., at 705. The inference is powerful that most detainees, when examined more carefully than at their initial appearances, are deemed insufficiently dangerous to warrant further incarceration. 23

The rarity with which invocation of 320.5(3)(b) results in detention of a juvenile who otherwise would have committed a crime fatally undercuts the two public purposes assigned to the statute by the State and the majority. The argument that 320.5(3)(b) serves "the State's `parens patriae interest in preserving and promoting the welfare of the child,'" ante, at 265 (citation omitted), now appears particularly hollow. Most juveniles detained pursuant to the provision are not benefited thereby, because they would not have committed crimes if left to their own devices (and thus would not have been exposed to the risk of physical injury or the perils of the cycle of recidivism, see ante, at 266). On the contrary, these juveniles suffer several serious harms: deprivation of liberty and stigmatization as "delinquent" or "dangerous," as well as impairment of their ability to prepare their legal defenses. 24 The benefits even to those few juveniles who would have committed crimes if released are not unalloyed; the gains to them are partially offset by the aforementioned injuries. In view of this configuration of benefits and harms, it is not surprising that Judge Quinones repudiated the suggestion that detention under 320.5(3)(b) serves the interests of the detainees. App. 269-270.

The argument that 320.5(3)(b) protects the welfare of the community fares little better. Certainly the public reaps no benefit from incarceration of the majority of the detainees who would not have committed any crimes had they been released. Prevention of the minor offenses that would have been committed by a small proportion of the persons detained confers only a slight benefit on the community. 25 Only in occasional cases does incarceration of a juvenile pending his trial serve to prevent a crime of violence and thereby significantly promote the public interest. Such an infrequent and haphazard gain is insufficient to justify curtailment of the liberty interests of all the presumptively innocent juveniles who would have obeyed the law pending their trials had they been given the chance. 26

2

The majority seeks to deflect appellees' attack on the constitutionality of 320.5(3)(b) by contending that they have framed their argument too broadly. It is possible, the majority acknowledges, that "in some circumstances detention of a juvenile [pursuant to 320.5(3)(b)] would not pass constitutional muster. But the validity of those detentions must be determined on a case-by-case basis." Ante, at 273; see ante, at 268-269, n. 18. The majority thus implies that, even if the Due Process Clause is violated by most detentions under 320.5(3)(b) because those detainees would not have committed crimes if released, the statute nevertheless is not invalid "on its face" because detention of those persons who would have committed a serious crime comports with the Constitution. Separation of the properly detained juveniles from the improperly detained juveniles must be achieved through "case-by-case" adjudication.

There are some obvious practical impediments to adoption of the majority's proposal. Because a juvenile may not be incarcerated under 320.5(3)(b) for more than 17 days, it would be impracticable for a particular detainee to secure his freedom by challenging the constitutional basis of his detention; by the time the suit could be considered, it would have been rendered moot by the juvenile's release or long-term detention pursuant to a delinquency adjudication. 27 Nor could an individual detainee avoid the problem of mootness by filing a suit for damages or for injunctive relief. This Court's declaration that 320.5(3)(b) is not unconstitutional on its face would almost certainly preclude a finding that detention of a juvenile pursuant to the statute violated any clearly established constitutional rights; in the absence of such a finding all state officials would be immune from liability in damages, see Harlow v. Fitzgerald, 457 U.S. 800 (1982). And, under current doctrine pertaining to the standing of an individual victim of allegedly unconstitutional conduct to obtain an injunction against repetition of that behavior, it is far from clear that an individual detainee would be able to obtain an equitable remedy. Compare INS v. Delgado, 466 U.S. 210, 217, n. 4 (1984), with Los Angeles v. Lyons, 461 U.S. 95, 105 -106 (1983).

But even if these practical difficulties could be surmounted, the majority's proposal would be inadequate. Precisely because of the unreliability of any determination whether a particular juvenile is likely to commit a crime between his arrest and trial, see supra, at 293-294, no individual detainee would be able to demonstrate that he would have abided by the law had he been released. In other words, no configuration of circumstances would enable a juvenile to establish that he fell into the category of persons unconstitutionally detained rather than the category constitutionally detained. 28 Thus, to protect the rights of the majority of juveniles whose incarceration advances no legitimate state interest, 320.5(3)(b) must be held unconstitutional "on its face."

C

The findings reviewed in the preceding section lend credence to the conclusion reached by the courts below: 320.5(3)(b) "is utilized principally, not for preventive purposes, but to impose punishment for unadjudicated criminal acts." 689 F.2d, at 372; see 513 F. Supp., at 715-717.

The majority contends that, of the many factors we have considered in trying to determine whether a particular sanction constitutes "punishment," see Kennedy v. Mendoza-Martinez, 372 U.S. 144, 168 -169 (1963), the most useful are "whether an alternative purpose to which [the sanction] may rationally be connected is assignable for it, and whether it appears excessive in relation to the alternative purpose assigned," ibid. (footnotes omitted). See ante, at 269. Assuming, arguendo, that this test is appropriate, but cf. Bell v. Wolfish, 441 U.S., at 564 -565 (MARSHALL, J., dissenting), it requires affirmance in these case. The alternative purpose assigned by the State to 320.5(3)(b) is the prevention of crime by the detained juveniles. But, as has been shown, that objective is advanced at best sporadically by the provision. Moreover, 320.5(3)(b) frequently is invoked under circumstances in which it is extremely unlikely that the juvenile in question would commit a crime while awaiting trial. The most striking of these cases involve juveniles who have been at large without mishap for a substantial period of time prior to their initial appearances, see supra, at 287, and detainees who are adjudged delinquent and are nevertheless released into the community. In short, 320.5(3)(b) as administered by the New York courts surely "appears excessive in relation to" the putatively legitimate objectives assigned to it.

The inference that 320.5(3)(b) is punitive in nature is supported by additional materials in the record. For example, Judge Quinones and even appellants' counsel acknowledged that one of the reasons juveniles detained pursuant to 320.5(3)(b) usually are released after the determination of their guilt is that the judge decides that their pretrial detention constitutes sufficient punishment. 689 F.2d, at 370-371, and nn. 27-28. Another Family Court Judge admitted using "preventive detention" to punish one of the juveniles in the sample. 513 F. Supp., at 708. 29

In summary, application of the litmus test the Court recently has used to identify punitive sanctions supports the finding of the lower courts that preventive detention under 320.5(3)(b) constitutes punishment. Because punishment of juveniles before adjudication of their guilt violates the Due Process Clause, see supra, at 291-292, the provision cannot stand.

III

If the record did not establish the impossibility, on the basis of the evidence available to a Family Court judge at a 320.5(3)(b) hearing, of reliably predicting whether a given juvenile would commit a crime before his trial, and if the purposes relied upon by the State were promoted sufficiently to justify the deprivations of liberty effected by the provision, I would nevertheless still strike down 320.5(3)(b) because of the absence of procedural safeguards in the provision. As Judge Newman, concurring in the Court of Appeals observed, "New York's statute is unconstitutional because it permits liberty to be denied, prior to adjudication of guilt, in the exercise of unfettered discretion as to an issue of considerable uncertainty - likelihood of future criminal behavior." 689 F.2d, at 375.

Appellees point out that 320.5(3)(b) lacks two crucial procedural constraints. First, a New York Family Court judge is given no guidance regarding what kinds of evidence he should consider or what weight he should accord different sorts of material in deciding whether to detain a juvenile. 30 For example, there is no requirement in the statute that the judge take into account the juvenile's background or current living situation. Nor is a judge obliged to attach significance to the nature of a juvenile's criminal record or the severity of the crime for which he was arrested. 31 Second, 320.5(3)(b) does not specify how likely it must be that a juvenile will commit a crime before his trial to warrant his detention. The provision indicates only that there must be a "serious risk" that he will commit an offense and does not prescribe the standard of proof that should govern the judge's determination of that issue. 32

Not surprisingly, in view of the lack of directions provided by the statute, different judges have adopted different ways of estimating the chances whether a juvenile will misbehave in the near future. "Each judge follows his own individual approach to [the detention] determination." 513 F. Supp., at 702; see App. 265 (testimony of Judge Quinones). This discretion exercised by Family Court judges in making detention decisions gives rise to two related constitutional problems. First, it creates an excessive risk that juveniles will be detained "erroneously" - i. e., under circumstances in which no public interest would be served by their incarceration. Second, it fosters arbitrariness and inequality in a decisionmaking process that impinges upon fundamental rights.

A

One of the purposes of imposing procedural constraints on decisions affecting life, liberty, or property is to reduce the incidence of error. See Fuentes v. Shevin, 407 U.S. 67, 80 -81 (1972). In Mathews v. Eldridge, 424 U.S. 319 (1976), the Court identified a complex of considerations that has proved helpful in determining what protections are constitutionally required in particular contexts to achieve that end:

"[I]dentification of the specific dictates of due process generally requires consideration of three distinct factors: First, the private interest that will be affected by the official action; second, the risk of an erroneous deprivation of such interest through the procedures used, and the probable value, if any, of additional or substitute procedural safeguards; and finally, the Government's interest, including the function involved and the fiscal and administrative burdens that the additional or substitute procedural requirement would entail." Id., at 335.

As Judge Newman recognized, 689 F.2d, at 375-376, a review of these three factors in the context of New York's preventive-detention scheme compels the conclusion that the Due Process Clause is violated by 320.5(3)(b) in its present form. First, the private interest affected by a decision to detain a juvenile is personal liberty. Unnecessary abridgment of such a fundamental right, see supra, at 288, should be avoided if at all possible.

Second, there can be no dispute that there is a serious risk under the present statute that a juvenile will be detained erroneously - i. e., despite the fact that he would not commit a crime if released. The findings of fact reviewed in the preceding sections make it apparent that the vast majority of detentions pursuant to 320.5(3)(b) advance no state interest; only rarely does the statute operate to prevent crime. See supra, at 297-298. This high incidence of demonstrated error should induce a reviewing court to exercise utmost care in ensuring that no procedures could be devised that would improve the accuracy of the decisionmaking process. Opportunities for improvement in the extant regime are apparent even to a casual observer. Most obviously, some measure of guidance to Family Court judges regarding the evidence they should consider and the standard of proof they should use in making their determinations would surely contribute to the quality of their detention determinations. 33

The majority purports to see no value in such additional safeguards, contending that activity of estimating the likelihood that a given juvenile will commit a crime in the near future involves subtle assessment of a host of variables, the precise weight of which cannot be determined in advance. Ante, at 279. A review of the hearings that resulted in the detention of the juveniles included in the sample of 34 cases reveals the majority's depiction of the decisionmaking process to be hopelessly idealized. For example, the operative portion of the initial appearance of Tyrone Parson, the three-card monte player, 34 consisted of the following:

"COURT OFFICER: Will you identify yourself.

. . . . .

"TYRONE PARSON: Tyrone Parson, Age 15.

"THE COURT: Miss Brown, how many times has Tyrone been known to the Court?

. . . . .

"MISS BROWN: Seven times.

"THE COURT: Remand the respondent." Petitioners' Exhibit 18a. 35

This kind of parody of reasoned decisionmaking would be less likely to occur if judges were given more specific and mandatory instructions regarding the information they should consider and the manner in which they should assess it.

Third and finally, the imposition of such constraints on the deliberations of the Family Court judges would have no adverse effect on the State's interest in detaining dangerous juveniles and would give rise to insubstantial administrative burdens. For example, a simple directive to Family Court judges to state on the record the significance they give to the seriousness of the offense of which a juvenile is accused and to the nature of the juvenile's background would contribute materially to the quality of the decisionmaking process without significantly increasing the duration of initial appearances.

In summary, the three factors enumerated in Mathews in combination incline overwhelmingly in favor of imposition of more stringent constraints on detention determinations under 320.5(3)(b). Especially in view of the impracticability of correcting erroneous decisions through judicial review, see supra, at 298-300, the absence of meaningful procedural safeguards in the provision renders it invalid. See Santosky v. Kramer, 455 U.S. 745, 757, and n. 9 (1982).

B

A principle underlying many of our prior decisions in various doctrinal settings is that government officials may not be accorded unfettered discretion in making decisions that impinge upon fundamental rights. Two concerns underlie this principle: excessive discretion fosters inequality in the distribution of entitlements and harms, inequality which is especially troublesome when those benefits and burdens are great; and discretion can mask the use by officials of illegitimate criteria in allocating important goods and rights.

So, in striking down on vagueness grounds a vagrancy ordinance, we emphasized the "unfettered discretion it places in the hands of the . . . police." Papachristou v. City of Jacksonville, 405 U.S. 156, 168 (1972). Such flexibility was deemed constitutionally offensive because it "permits and encourages an arbitrary and discriminatory enforcement of the law." Id., at 170. Partly for similar reasons, we have consistently held violative of the First Amendment ordinances which make the ability to engage in constitutionally protected speech "contingent upon the uncontrolled will of an official - as by requiring a permit or license which may be granted or withheld in the discretion of such official." Staub v. City of Baxley, 355 U.S. 313, 322 (1958); accord, Shuttlesworth v. City of Birmingham, 394 U.S. 147, 151, 153 (1969). Analogous considerations inform our understanding of the dictates of the Due Process Clause. Concurring in the judgment in Zablocki v. Redhail, 434 U.S. 374 (1978), striking down a statute that conditioned the right to marry upon the satisfaction of child-support obligations, JUSTICE POWELL aptly observed:

"Quite apart from any impact on the truly indigent, the statute appears to `confer upon [the judge] a license for arbitrary procedure,' in the determination of whether an applicant's children are `likely thereafter to become public charges.' A serious question of procedural due process is raised by this feature of standardless discretion, particularly in light of the hazards of prediction in this area." Id., at 402, n. 4 (quoting Kent v. United States, 383 U.S., at 553).

The concerns that powered these decisions are strongly implicated by New York's preventive-detention scheme. The effect of the lack of procedural safeguards constraining detention decisions under 320.5(3)(b) is that the liberty of a juvenile arrested even for a petty crime is dependent upon the "caprice" of a Family Court judge. See 513 F. Supp., at 707. The absence of meaningful guidelines creates opportunities for judges to use illegitimate criteria when deciding whether juveniles should be incarcerated pending their trials - for example, to detain children for the express purpose of punishing them. 36 Even the judges who strive conscientiously to apply the law have little choice but to assess juveniles' dangerousness on the basis of whatever standards they deem appropriate. 37 The resultant variation in detention decisions gives rise to a level of inequality in the deprivation of a fundamental right too great to be countenanced under the Constitution.

IV

The majority acknowledges - indeed, founds much of its argument upon - the principle that a State has both the power and the responsibility to protect the interests of the children within its jurisdiction. See Santosky v. Kramer, supra, at 766. Yet the majority today upholds a statute whose net impact on the juveniles who come within its purview is overwhelmingly detrimental. Most persons detained under the provision reap no benefit and suffer serious injuries thereby. The welfare of only a minority of the detainees is even arguably enhanced. The inequity of this regime, combined with the arbitrariness with which it is administered, is bound to disillusion its victims regarding the virtues of our system of criminal justice. I can see - and the majority has pointed to - no public purpose advanced by the statute sufficient to justify the harm it works.

I respectfully dissent.

Notes

[1] N. Y. Jud. Law 301.2(1), 302.1(1) (McKinney 1983) (hereinafter Family Court Act or FCA). Children aged 13 or over accused of murder and children aged 14 or over accused of kidnaping, arson, rape, or a few other serious crimes are exempted from the coverage of the Act and instead are prosecuted as "juvenile offenders" in the adult criminal courts. N. Y. Penal Law 10.00(18), 30.00(2) (McKinney Supp. 1983-1984). For the sake of simplicity, offenses covered by the Family Court Act, as well as the more serious offenses enumerated above, hereinafter will be referred to generically as crimes.

[2] Ironically, juveniles arrested for very serious offenses, see n. 1, supra, are not subject to preventive detention under this or any other provision.

[3] Strictly speaking, "guilt" is never adjudicated under the Act; nor is the juvenile ever given a trial. Rather, whether the juvenile committed the offense is ascertained in a "factfinding hearing." In most respects, however, such a hearing is the functional equivalent of an ordinary criminal trial. For example, the juvenile is entitled to counsel and the State bears the burden of demonstrating beyond a reasonable doubt that the juvenile committed the offense of which he is accused. See FCA 341.2(1), 342.2(2); cf. In re Winship, 397 U.S. 358 (1970); In re Gault, 387 U.S. 1 (1967) (establishing constitutional limitations on the form of such proceedings in recognition of the severity of their impact upon juveniles). For convenience, the ensuing discussion will use the terminology associated with adult criminal proceedings when describing the treatment of juveniles in New York.

[4] At the time appellees first brought their suit, the pertinent portions of FCA 320.5(3) were embodied in FCA 739(a). I agree with the majority that the reenactment of the crucial provision under a different numerical heading does not render the case moot. See ante, at 256, n. 2.

[5] If the juvenile is detained upon arrest, this hearing must be held on the next court day or within 72 hours, whichever comes first. FCA 307.3(4).

[6] The majority admits that "the Family Court judge is not required to make a finding of probable cause at the initial appearance," but contends that the juvenile has the option to challenge the sufficiency of the petition for delinquency on the ground that it fails to establish probable cause. Ante, at 276. None of the courts that have considered the constitutionality of New York's preventive-detention system has suggested that a juvenile has a statutory right to a probable-cause determination before he is detained. The provisions cited by the majority for its novel reading of the statute provide only shaky support for its contention. FCA 315.1, which empowers the juvenile to move to dismiss a petition lacking allegations sufficient to satisfy 311.2, provides that "[a] motion to dismiss under this section must be made within the time provided for in section 332.2." Section

332.2, in turn, provides that pretrial motions shall be made within 30 days after the initial appearance and before the factfinding hearing. If the juvenile has been detained, the judge is instructed to "hear and determine pre-trial motions on an expedited basis," 332.2(4), but is not required to rule upon such motions peremptorily. In sum, the statutory scheme seems to contemplate that a motion to dismiss a petition for lack of probable cause, accompanied with "supporting affidavits, exhibits and memoranda of law," 332.2(2), would be filed sometime after the juvenile is detained under 320.5(3)(b). And there is no reason to expect that the ruling on such a motion would be rendered before the juvenile would in any event be entitled to a probable-cause hearing under 325.1(2). That counsel for a juvenile ordinarily is not even appointed until a few minutes prior to the initial appearance, see supra, at 284 and this page, confirms this interpretation. The lesson of this foray into the tangled provisions of the New York Family Court Act is that the majority ought to adhere to our usual policy of relying whenever possible for interpretation of a state statute upon courts better acquainted with its terms and applications.

[7] The majority refuses to consider the circumstances of these 34 cases, dismissing them as unrepresentative, ante, at 272, n. 21, and focuses instead on the lurid facts associated with the cases of the three named appellees. I cannot agree that the sample is entitled to so little weight. There was uncontested testimony at trial to the effect that the 34 cases were typical. App. 128 (testimony of Steven Hiltz, an attorney with 8 1/2 years of experience before the Family Court). At no point in this litigation have appellants offered an alternative selection of instances in which 320.5(3)(b) has been invoked. And most importantly, despite the fact that the District Court relied heavily on the sample when assessing the manner in which the statute is applied, see 513 F. Supp., at 695-700, appellants did not dispute before the Court of Appeals the representativeness of the 34 cases, see Martin v. Strasburg, 689 F.2d 365, 369, n. 19 (CA2 1982). When the defendants in a plaintiff class action challenge on appeal neither the certification of the class, see ante, at 261, n. 10, nor the plaintiffs' depiction of the character of the class, we ought to analyze the case as it comes to us and not try to construct a new version of the facts on the basis of an independent and selective review of the record.

[8] As the Court of Appeals acknowledged, 689 F.2d, at 369, n. 18, there are defects in all of the available statistical studies. Most importantly, none of the studies distinguishes persons detained under 320.5(3)(a) from persons detained under 320.5(3)(b). However, these flaws did not disable the courts below from making meaningful - albeit rough - generalizations regarding the incidence of detention under the latter provision. Especially when conjoined with the sample of 34 cases submitted by appellees, see n. 7, supra, the studies are sufficient to support the three findings enumerated in the text. Even the majority, though it chastises appellees for failing to assemble better data, ante, at 272, and n. 21, does not suggest that those findings are clearly erroneous.

[9] The figures in the text are taken from the District Court's summary of the 34

cases in the sample. Review of the transcripts of the hearings in those cases reveals the actual number to be 9 and 23, respectively. See Petitioners' Exhibits 6a, 11a, 12a, 14a, 15a, 16a, 19a, 24a, 35a.

[10] The state director of detention services testified that, in 1978, approximately six times as many juveniles were admitted to "secure facilities" as to "non-secure facilities." See 513 F. Supp., at 703, n. 8. These figures are not broken down as to persons detained under 320.5(3)(a) and persons detained under 320.5(3)(b). There seems no dispute, however, that most of the juveniles held under the latter provision are subjected to "secure detention."

[11] This principle underlies prior decisions of the Court involving various constitutional provisions as they relate to pretrial detention. In Gerstein v. Pugh, 420 U.S. 103, 113 -114 (1975), we relied in part on the severity of "[t]he consequences of prolonged detention" in construing the Fourth Amendment to forbid pretrial incarceration of a suspect for an extended period of time without "a judicial determination of probable cause." In Stack v. Boyle, 342 U.S. 1, 4 -5 (1951), we stressed the importance of a person's right to freedom until proved guilty in construing the Eighth Amendment to proscribe the setting of bail "at a figure higher than an amount reasonably calculated to" assure the presence of the accused at trial. Cf. Baker v. McCollan, 443 U.S. 137, 149 -150, 153 (1979) (STEVENS, J., dissenting).

[12] The phrase "legitimate governmental objective" appears at several points in the opinion of the Court in Bell v. Wolfish, 441 U.S. 520 (1979), e. g., id., at 538-539, and the majority may be relying implicitly on that decision for the standard it applies in these cases. If so, the reliance is misplaced. Wolfish was exclusively concerned with the constitutionality of conditions of pretrial incarceration under circumstances in which the legitimacy of the incarceration itself was undisputed; the Court avoided any discussion of the showing a State must make in order to justify pretrial detention in the first instance. See id., at 533-534, and n. 15. The standard employed by the Court in Wolfish thus has no bearing on the problem before us.

[13] All of the 34 juveniles in the sample were detained in Spofford Juvenile Center, the detention facility for New York City. Numerous studies of that facility have attested to its unsavory characteristics. See, e. g., Citizens' Committee for Children of New York, Inc., Juvenile Detention Problems in New York City 3-4 (1970); J. Stone, R. Ruskin, & D. Goff, An Inquiry into the Juvenile Centers Operated by the Office of Probation 25-27, 52-54, 79-80 (1971). Conditions in Spofford have been successfully challenged on constitutional grounds (by a group of inmates of a different type), see Martarella v. Kelley, 359 F. Supp. 478 (SDNY 1973), but nevertheless remain grim, see Mayor's Task Force on Spofford: First Report v, viii-ix, 20-21 (June 1978). Not surprisingly, a former New York City Deputy Mayor for Criminal Justice has averred that "Spofford is, in many ways, indistinguishable from a prison." Petitioners' Exhibit 30, § 6 (affidavit of Herbert Sturz, June 29, 1978).

[14] Cf. Aubry, The Nature, Scope and Significance of Pre-Trial Detention of

Juveniles in California, 1 Black L. J. 160, 164 (1971).

[15] This standard might be refined in one of two ways. First, it might be argued that, because 320.5(3)(b) impinges upon "[l]iberty from bodily restraint," which has long been "recognized as the core of the liberty protected by the Due Process Clause," Greenholtz v. Nebraska Penal Inmates, 442 U.S. 1, 18 (1979) (POWELL, J., concurring in part and dissenting in part), the provision can pass constitutional muster only if it promotes a "compelling" government interest. See People ex rel. Wayburn v. Schupf, 39 N. Y. 2d 682, 687, 350 N. E. 2d 906, 908 (1976) (requiring a showing of a "compelling State interest" to uphold 320.5(3)(b)); cf. Shapiro v. Thompson, 394 U.S. 618, 634 (1969). Alternatively, it might be argued that the comparatively brief period of incarceration permissible under the provision warrants a slight lowering of the constitutional bar. Applying the principle that the strength of the state interest needed to legitimate a statute depends upon the degree to which the statute encroaches upon fundamental rights, see Williams v. Illinois, 399 U.S. 235, 259 -260, 262-263 (1970) (Harlan, J., concurring in result), it might be held that an important - but not quite "compelling" - objective is necessary to sustain 320.5(3)(b). In the present context, there is no need to choose between these doctrinal options, because 320.5(3)(b) would fail either test.

[16] See also Ingraham v. Wright, 430 U.S. 651, 671 -672, and n. 40, 673-674 (1977); Gregory v. Chicago, 394 U.S. 111, 112 (1969); Thompson v. Louisville, 362 U.S. 199, 206 (1960).

[17] Cf. Sellers v. United States, 89 S. Ct. 36, 38, 21 L. Ed. 2d 64, 67 (1968) (Black, J., in chambers) (questioning whether a defendant's dangerousness can ever justify denial of bail).

[18] An additional reason for not reaching appellees' categorical objection to the purposes relied upon by the State is that the Court of Appeals did not pass upon the validity of those objectives. See 689 F.2d, at 372. We are generally chary of deciding important constitutional questions not reached by a lower court.

[19] See, e. g., American Psychiatric Association, Clinical Aspects of the Violent Individual 27-28 (1974); Cocozza & Steadman, The Failure of Psychiatric Predictions of Dangerousness: Clear and Convincing Evidence, 29 Rutgers L. Rev. 1084, 1094-1101 (1976); Diamond, The Psychiatric Prediction of Dangerousness, 123 U. Pa. L. Rev. 439 (1974); Ennis & Litwack, Psychiatry and the Presumption of Expertise: Flipping Coins In the Courtroom, 62 Calif. L. Rev. 693 (1974); Schlesinger, The Prediction of Dangerousness in Juveniles: A Replication, 24 Crime & Delinquency 40, 47 (1978); Steadman & Cocozza, Psychiatry, Dangerousness and the Repetitively Violent Offender, 69 J. Crim. L. & C. 226, 229-231 (1978); Wenk, Robison, & Smith, Can Violence Be Predicted?, 18 Crime & Delinquency 393, 401 (1972); Preventive Detention: An Empirical Analysis, 6 Harv. Civ. Rights - Civ. Lib. L. Rev. 289 (1971).

[20] The majority brushes aside the District Court's findings on this issue with the remark that "a prediction of future criminal conduct . . . forms an important element in many decisions, and we have specifically rejected the contention . . . `that it is

impossible to predict future behavior and that the question is so vague as to be meaningless.'" Ante, at 278-279 (footnote and citation omitted). Whatever the merits of the decisions upon which the majority relies, but cf., e. g., Barefoot v. Estelle, 463 U.S. 880, 909 (1983) (MARSHALL, J., dissenting), they do not control the problem before us. In each of the cases in which the Court has countenanced reliance upon a prediction of future conduct in a decisionmaking process impinging upon life or liberty, the affected person had already been convicted of a crime. See Greenholtz v. Nebraska Penal Inmates, 442 U.S. 1 (1979) (grant of parole); Jurek v. Texas, 428 U.S. 262 (1976) (death sentence); Morrissey v. Brewer, 408 U.S. 471 (1972) (parole revocation). The constitutional limitations upon the kinds of factors that may be relied on in making such decisions are significantly looser than those upon decisionmaking processes that abridge the liberty of presumptively innocent persons. Cf. United States v. Tucker, 404 U.S. 443, 446 (1972) ("[A] trial judge in the federal judicial system generally has wide discretion in determining what sentence to impose. . . . [B]efore making that determination, a judge may appropriately conduct an inquiry broad in scope, largely unlimited either as to the kind of information he may consider, or the source from which it may come").

[21] For example, Tyrone Parson, aged 15, one of the members of the sample, was arrested for enticing others to play three-card monte. Petitioners' Exhibit 18b. After being detained for five days under 320.5(3)(b), the petition against him was dismissed on the ground that "the offense alleged did not come within the provisions of the penal law." 513 F. Supp., at 698-699.

In contrast to the breadth of the coverage of the Family Court Act, the District of Columbia adult preventive-detention statute that was upheld in United States v. Edwards, 430 A. 2d 1321 (D.C. 1981), cert. denied, 455 U.S. 1022 (1982), authorizes detention only of persons charged with one of a prescribed set of "dangerous crime[s]" or "crime[s] of violence." D.C. Code 23-1322(a)(1), (2) (1981).

Prediction whether a given person will commit a crime in the future is especially difficult when he has committed only minor crimes in the past. Cf. Baldasar v. Illinois, 446 U.S. 222, 231 (1980) (POWELL, J., dissenting) ("No court can predict with confidence whether a misdemeanor defendant is likely to become a recidivist").

[22] By contrast, under the District of Columbia statute, see n. 21, supra, the judge is obliged before ordering detention to find, inter alia, a "substantial probability" that the defendant committed the serious crime for which he was arrested. D.C. Code 23-1322(b)(2)(C) (1981).

[23] Both courts below made this inference. See 689 F.2d, at 372; 513 F. Supp., at 705. Indeed, the New York Court of Appeals, in upholding the statute, did not disagree with this explanation of the incidence of its application. People ex rel. Wayburn v. Schupf, 39 N. Y. 2d, at 690, 350 N. E. 2d, at 910.

Release (before or after trial) of some of the juveniles detained under 320.5(3)(b) may well be due to a different factor: the evidence against them may be insufficient to support a finding of guilt. It is conceivable that some of those persons are so crime-prone that they would have committed an offense if not detained. But even the majority does not suggest that persons who could not be convicted of any crimes may nevertheless be imprisoned for the protection of themselves and the public.

[24] See testimony of Steven Hiltz, App. 130-134 (describing the detrimental effects of pretrial detention of a juvenile upon the preparation and presentation of his defense); cf. Barker v. Wingo, 407 U.S. 514, 533 (1972); Bitter v. United States, 389 U.S. 15, 16 -17 (1967) (per curiam); Stack v. Boyle, 342 U.S., at 8; Miller, Preventive Detention - A Guide to the Eradication of Individual Rights, 16 How. L. J. 1, 15 (1970).

[25] Cf. Tribe, An Ounce of Detention: Preventive Justice in the World of John Mitchell, 56 Va. L. Rev. 371, 381 (1970) ("[Under a statute proposed by the Attorney General,] trivial property offenses may be deemed sufficiently threatening to warrant preventive imprisonment. No tenable concept of due process could condone a balance that gives so little weight to the accused's interest in pretrial liberty").

[26] Some amici contend that a preventive-detention statute that, unlike 320.5(3)(b), covered only specific categories of juveniles and embodied stringent procedural safeguards would result in incarceration only of juveniles very likely to commit crimes of violence in the near future. E. g., Brief for American Bar Association as Amicus Curiae 9-14. It could be argued that, even though such a statute would unavoidably result in detention of some juveniles who would not have committed any offenses if released (because of the impossibility of reliably predicting the behavior of individual persons, see supra, at 293-294), the gains consequent upon the detention of the large proportion who would have committed crimes would be sufficient to justify the injuries to the other detainees. To decide the cases before us, we need not consider either the feasibility of such a scheme or its constitutionality.

[27] The District Court, whose knowledge of New York procedural law surely exceeds ours, concluded that "[t]he short span of pretrial detention makes effective review impossible." 513 F. Supp., at 708, n. 29. The majority dismisses this finding, along with a comparable finding by the Court of Appeals, see 689 F.2d, at 373, as "mistaken." Ante, at 280. But neither of the circumstances relied upon by the majority supports its confident judgment on this point. That the New York courts suspended their usual rules of mootness in order to consider an attack on the constitutionality of the statute as a whole, see People ex rel. Wayburn v. Schupf, 39 N. Y. 2d, at 686, 350 N. E. 2d, at 907-908, in no way suggests that they would be willing to do so if an individual detainee challenged the constitutionality of 320.5(3)(b) as applied to him. The majority cites one case in which a detainee did obtain his release by securing a writ of habeas corpus. However, that case involved a juvenile who was not given a probable-cause hearing within six days of his detention - a patent violation of the state statute. See 513 F. Supp., at 708. That a writ of habeas corpus could be obtained on short notice to remedy a glaring statutory violation provides no support for the majority's suggestion that individual detainees could effectively petition for release by challenging the constitutionality of their detentions.

[28] This problem is exacerbated by the fact that Family Court judges, when making findings justifying a detention pursuant to 320.5(3)(b), do not specify whether there is a risk that the juvenile would commit a serious crime or whether there is a risk that he would commit a petty offense. A finding of the latter sort should not be sufficient under the Due Process Clause to justify a juvenile's detention. See supra, at 297-298, and n. 25. But a particular detainee has no way of ascertaining the grounds for his incarceration.

[29] See transcript of the initial appearance of Ramon Ramos, # 1356/80, Judge Heller presiding, Petitioners' Exhibit 42, p. 11:

"This business now of being able to get guns, is now completely out of proportion. We are living in a jungle. We are living in a jungle, and it is time that these youths that are brought before the Court, know that they are in a Court, and that if these allegations are true, that they are going to pay the penalty.

"As for the reasons I just state[d] on the record, . . . I am remand[ing] the respondent to the Commissioner of Juvenile Justice, secure detention."

[30] The absence of any limitations on the sorts of reasons that may support a determination that a child is likely to commit a crime if released means that the statutory requirement that the judge state "reasons" on the record, see ante, at 276, does not meaningfully constrain the decisionmaking process.

[31] See 513 F. Supp., at 713:

"Whether the juvenile was a first offender with no prior conduct, whether the court was advised that the juvenile was an obedient son or was needed at home, whether probation intake recommended parole, the case histories in this record disclose that it was not unusual for the court to discount these considerations and order remand based on a 5 to 15 minute evaluation."

[32] Cf. Addington v. Texas, 441 U.S. 418, 431 -433 (1979) ("clear and convincing" proof constitutionally required to justify civil commitment to mental hospital).

[33] Judge Newman, concurring below, pointed to three other protections lacking in 320.5(3)(b): "the statute places no limits on the crimes for which the person subject to detention has been arrested . . ., the judge ordering detention is not required to make any evaluation of the degree of likelihood that the person committed the crime of which he is accused[,] . . . [and] the statute places no limits on the type of crimes that the judge believes the detained juvenile might commit if released." 689 F.2d, at 377. In my view, the absence of these constraints is most relevant to the question whether the ends served by the statute can justify its broad reach, see Part II-B, supra. However, as Judge Newman observed, they could also be considered procedural flaws. Certainly, a narrowing of the categories of persons covered by 320.5(3)(b), along the lines sketched by Judge Newman, would reduce the incidence of error in the application of the provision.

[34] See n. 21, supra.

[35] Parson's case is not unique. The hearings accorded Juan Santiago and

Daniel Nelson, for example, though somewhat longer in duration, were nearly as cavalier and undiscriminating. See Petitioners' Exhibits 13a, 22a.

[36] See n. 29, supra.

[37] See 513 F. Supp., at 708:

"It is clear that the judge decides on pretrial detention for a variety of reasons - as a means of protecting the community, as the policy of the judge to remand, as an express punitive device, or because of the serious nature of the charge[,] among others" (citations omitted).

Should be no "public safety" exception for Miranda warning: Justice Marshall's dissent in New York v. Quarles (June 12, 1984)

Justice MARSHALL, with whom Justice BRENNAN and Justice STEVENS join, dissenting.

The police in this case arrested a man suspected of possessing a firearm in violation of New York law. Once the suspect was in custody and found to be unarmed, the arresting officer initiated an interrogation. Without being advised of his right not to respond, the suspect incriminated himself by locating the gun. The majority concludes that the State may rely on this incriminating statement to convict the suspect of possessing a weapon. I disagree. The arresting officers had no legitimate reason to interrogate the suspect without advising him of his rights to remain silent and to obtain assistance of counsel. By finding on these facts justification for unconsented interrogation, the majority abandons the clear guidelines enunciated in Miranda v. Arizona, 384 U.S. 436, 86 S.Ct. 1602, 16 L.Ed.2d 694 (1966), and condemns the American judiciary to a new era of post hoc inquiry into the propriety of custodial interrogations. More significantly and in direct conflict with this Court's longstanding interpretation of the Fifth Amendment, the majority has endorsed the introduction of coerced self-incriminating statements in criminal prosecutions. I dissent.

* Shortly after midnight on September 11, 1980, Officer Kraft and three other policemen entered an A & P supermarket in search of respondent Quarles, a rape suspect who was reportedly armed. After a brief chase, the officers cornered Quarles in the back of the store. As the other officers trained their guns on the suspect, Officer Kraft frisked Quarles and discovered an empty shoulder holster. Officer Kraft then handcuffed Quarles, and the other officers holstered their guns. With Quarles' hands manacled behind his back and the other officers standing close by, Officer Kraft questioned Quarles: "Where is the gun?" Gesturing towards a stack of liquid-soap cartons a few feet away, Quarles responded: "The gun is over there." Behind the cartons, the police found a loaded revolver. The State of New York subsequently failed to prosecute the alleged rape, and charged Quarles on a solitary count of criminal possession of a weapon in the third degree. 1 As proof of the critical element of the offense, the State sought to introduce

Quarles' response to Officer Kraft's question as well as the revolver found behind the cartons. The Criminal Term of the Supreme Court of the State of New York ordered both Quarles' statement and the gun suppressed. The suppression order was affirmed first by the Appellate Division, 85 App.Div.2d 936, 447 N.Y.S.2d 84 (1981), and again by the New York Court of Appeals, 58 N.Y.2d 664, 458 N.Y.S.2d 520, 444 N.E.2d 984 (1982) (mem.).

The majority's entire analysis rests on the factual assumption that the public was at risk during Quarles' interrogation. This assumption is completely in conflict with the facts as found by New York's highest court. Before the interrogation began, Quarles had been "reduced to a condition of physical powerlessness." Id., at 667, 458 N.Y.S.2d, at 522, 444 N.E.2d, at 986. Contrary to the majority's speculations, ante, at 657, Quarles was not believed to have, nor did he in fact have, an accomplice to come to his rescue. When the questioning began, the arresting officers were sufficiently confident of their safety to put away their guns. As Officer Kraft acknowledged at the suppression hearing, "the situation was under control." App. 35a. Based on Officer Kraft's own testimony, the New York Court of Appeals found: "Nothing suggests that any of the officers was by that time concerned for his own physical safety." 58 N.Y.2d, at 666, 458 N.Y.S.2d, at 521, 444 N.E.2d, at 985. The Court of Appeals also determined that there was no evidence that the interrogation was prompted by the arresting officers' concern for the public's safety. Ibid.

The majority attempts to slip away from these unambiguous findings of New York's highest court by proposing that danger be measured by objective facts rather than the subjective intentions of arresting officers. Ante, at 655-656. Though clever, this ploy was anticipated by the New York Court of Appeals: "There is no evidence in the record before us that there were exigent circumstances posing a risk to the public safety. . . ." 58 N.Y.2d, at 666, 458 N.Y.S.2d, at 521, 444 N.E.2d, at 985.

The New York court's conclusion that neither Quarles nor his missing gun posed a threat to the public's safety is amply supported by the evidence presented at the suppression hearing. Again contrary to the majority's intimations, ante, at 657, no customers or employees were wandering about the store in danger of coming across Quarles' discarded weapon. Although the supermarket was open to the public, Quarles' arrest took place during the middle of the night when the store was apparently deserted except for the clerks at the checkout counter. The police could easily have cordoned off the store and searched for the missing gun. Had they done so, they would have found the gun forthwith. The police were well aware that Quarles had discarded his weapon somewhere near the scene of the arrest. As the State acknowledged before the New York Court of Appeals: "After Officer Kraft had handcuffed and frisked the defendant in the supermarket, he knew with a high degree of certainty that the defendant's gun was within the immediate vicinity of the encounter. He undoubtedly would have searched for it in the carton a few feet away without the defendant having looked in that direction and saying that it was there." Brief for Appellant in No. 2512/80 (N.Y.Ct.App.), p. 11 (emphasis added).

Earlier this Term, four Members of the majority joined an opinion stating:

"Questions of historical fact . . . must be determined, in the first instance, by state courts and deferred to, in the absence of 'convincing evidence' to the contrary, by the federal courts." Rushen v. Spain, 464 U.S. 114, 120, 104 S.Ct. 453, 456, 78 L.Ed.2d 267 (1983) (per curiam). In this case, there was convincing, indeed almost overwhelming, evidence to support the New York court's conclusion that Quarles' hidden weapon did not pose a risk either to the arresting officers or to the public. The majority ignores this evidence and sets aside the factual findings of the New York Court of Appeals. More cynical observers might well conclude that a state court's findings of fact "deserve a 'high measure of deference,' " ibid. (quoting Sumner v. Mata, 455 U.S. 591, 598, 102 S.Ct. 1303, 1307, 71 L.Ed.2d 480 (1982)), only when deference works against the interests of a criminal defendant.

II

The majority's treatment of the legal issues presented in this case is no less troubling than its abuse of the facts. Before today's opinion, the Court had twice concluded that, under Miranda v. Arizona, 384 U.S. 436, 86 S.Ct. 1602, 16 L.Ed.2d 694 (1966), police officers conducting custodial interrogations must advise suspects of their rights before any questions concerning the whereabouts of incriminating weapons can be asked. Rhode Island v. Innis, 446 U.S. 291, 298-302, 100 S.Ct. 1682, 1688-1690, 64 L.Ed.2d 297 (1980) (dicta); Orozco v. Texas, 394 U.S. 324, 89 S.Ct. 1095, 22 L.Ed.2d 311 (1969) (holding). 2 Now the majority departs from these cases and rules that police may withhold Miranda warnings whenever custodial interrogations concern matters of public safety. 3

The majority contends that the law, as it currently stands, places police officers in a dilemma whenever they interrogate a suspect who appears to know of some threat to the public's safety. Ante, at 657. If the police interrogate the suspect without advising him of his rights, the suspect may reveal information that the authorities can use to defuse the threat, but the suspect's statements will be inadmissible at trial. If, on the other hand, the police advise the suspect of his rights, the suspect may be deterred from responding to the police's questions, and the risk to the public may continue unabated. According to the majority, the police must now choose between establishing the suspect's guilt and safeguarding the public from danger.

The majority proposes to eliminate this dilemma by creating an exception to Miranda v. Arizona for custodial interrogations concerning matters of public safety. Ante, at 658-659. Under the majority's exception, police would be permitted to interrogate suspects about such matters before the suspects have been advised of their constitutional rights. Without being "deterred" by the knowledge that they have a constitutional right not to respond, these suspects will be likely to answer the questions. Should the answers also be incriminating, the State would be free to introduce them as evidence in a criminal prosecution. Through this "narrow exception to the Miranda rule," ante, at 658, the majority proposes to protect the public's safety without jeopardizing the prosecution of criminal defendants. I find in this reasoning an unwise and unprincipled departure from our Fifth Amendment precedents.

Before today's opinion, the procedures established in Miranda v. Arizona had "the virtue of informing police and prosecutors with specificity as to what they may do in conducting custodial interrogation, and of informing courts under what circumstances statements obtained during such interrogation are not admissible." Fare v. Michael C., 442 U.S. 707, 718, 99 S.Ct. 2560, 2568, 61 L.Ed.2d 197 (1979); see Harryman v. Estelle, 616 F.2d 870, 873-874 (CA5 1980) (en banc), cert. denied, 449 U.S. 860, 101 S.Ct. 161, 66 L.Ed.2d 76 (1980). In a chimerical quest for public safety, the majority has abandoned the rule that brought 18 years of doctrinal tranquility to the field of custodial interrogations. As the majority candidly concedes, ante, at 658, a public-safety exception destroys forever the clarity of Miranda for both law enforcement officers and members of the judiciary. The Court's candor cannot mask what a serious loss the administration of justice has incurred.

This case is illustrative of the chaos the "public-safety" exception will unlease. The circumstances of Quarles' arrest have never been in dispute. After the benefit of briefing and oral argument, the New York Court of Appeals, as previously noted, concluded that there was "no evidence in the record before us that there were exigent circumstances posing a risk to the public safety." 58 N.Y.2d, at 666, 458 N.Y.S.2d, at 521, 444 N.E.2d, at 985. Upon reviewing the same facts and hearing the same arguments, a majority of this Court has come to precisely the opposite conclusion: "So long as the gun was concealed somewhere in the supermarket, with its actual whereabouts unknown, it obviously posed more than one danger to the public safety. . . ." Ante, at 657.

If after plenary review two appellate courts so fundamentally differ over the threat to public safety presented by the simple and uncontested facts of this case, one must seriously question how law enforcement officers will respond to the majority's new rule in the confusion and haste of the real world. As THE CHIEF JUSTICE wrote in a similar context: "Few, if any, police officers are competent to make the kind of evaluation seemingly contemplated. . . ." Rhode Island v. Innis, 446 U.S., at 304, 100 S.Ct., at 1691 (concurring in judgment). Not only will police officers have to decide whether the objective facts of an arrest justify an unconsented custodial interrogation; they will also have to remember to interrupt the interrogation and read the suspect his Miranda warnings once the focus of the inquiry shifts from protecting the public's safety to ascertaining the suspect's guilt. Disagreements of the scope of the "public-safety" exception and mistakes in its application are inevitable. 4

The end result, as Justice O'CONNOR predicts, will be "a finespun new doctrine on public safety exigencies incident to custodial interrogation, complete with the hairsplitting distinctions that currently plague our Fourth Amendment jurisprudence." Ante, at 663-664. In the meantime, the courts will have to dedicate themselves to spinning this new web of doctrines, and the country's law enforcement agencies will have to suffer patiently through the frustations of another period of constitutional uncertainty.

III

Though unfortunate, the difficulty of administering the "public-safety" exception is not the most profound flaw in the majority's decision. The majority has lost sight of the fact that Miranda v. Arizona and our earlier custodial-interrogation cases all implemented a constitutional privilege against self-incrimination. The rules established in these cases were designed to protect criminal defendants against prosecutions based on coerced self-incriminating statements. The majority today turns its back on these constitutional considerations, and invites the government to prosecute through the use of what necessarily are coerced statements.

The majority's error stems from a serious misunderstanding of Miranda v. Arizona and of the Fifth Amendment upon which that decision was based. The majority implies that Miranda consisted of no more than a judicial balancing act in which the benefits of "enlarged protection for the Fifth Amendment privilege" were weighed against "the cost to society in terms of fewer convictions of guilty suspects." Ante, at 2632. Supposedly because the scales tipped in favor of the privilege against self-incrimination, the Miranda Court erected a prophylactic barrier around statements made during custodial interrogations. The majority now proposes to return to the scales of social utility to calculate whether Miranda's prophylactic rule remains cost-effective when threats to the public's safety are added to the balance. The results of the majority's "test" are announced with pseudoscientific precision:

"We conclude that the need for answers to questions in a situation posing a threat to the public safety outweighs the need for the prophylactic rule protecting the Fifth Amendment's privilege against self-incrimination." Ante, at 657.

The majority misreads Miranda. Though the Miranda dissent prophesized dire consequences, see 384 U.S., at 504, 516-517, 86 S.Ct., at 1643, 1649-1650 (Harlan, J., dissenting), the Miranda Court refused to allow such concerns to weaken the protections of the Constitution:

"A recurrent argument made in these cases is that society's need for interrogation outweighs the privilege. This argument is not unfamiliar to this Court. The whole thrust of our foregoing discussion demonstrates that the Constitution has prescribed the rights of the individual when confronted with the power of government when it provided in the Fifth Amendment that an individual cannot be compelled to be a witness against himself. That right cannot be abridged." Id., at 479, 86 S.Ct., at 1630 (citation omitted).

Whether society would be better off if the police warned suspects of their rights before beginning an interrogation or whether the advantages of giving such warnings would outweigh their costs did not inform the Miranda decision. On the contrary, the Miranda Court was concerned with the proscriptions of the Fifth Amendment, and, in particular, whether the Self-Incrimination Clause permits the government to prosecute individuals based on statements made in the course of custodial interrogations.

Miranda v. Arizona was the culmination of a century-long inquiry into how this Court should deal with confessions made during custodial interrogations. Long before Miranda, the Court had recognized that the Federal Government was prohibited from introducing at criminal trials compelled confessions, including confessions compelled in the course of custodial interrogations. In 1924, Justice Brandeis was reciting settled law when he wrote: "A confession obtained by compulsion must be excluded whatever may have been the character of the compulsion, and whether the compulsion was applied in a judicial proceeding or otherwise." Wan v. United States, 266 U.S. 1, 14-15, 45 S.Ct. 1, 3-4, 69 L.Ed. 131 (citing Bram v. United States, 168 U.S. 532, 18 S.Ct. 183, 42 L.Ed. 568 (1897)).

Prosecutors in state courts were subject to similar constitutional restrictions. Even before Malloy v. Hogan, 378 U.S. 1, 84 S.Ct. 1489, 12 L.Ed.2d 653 (1964), formally applied the Self-Incrimination Clause of the Fifth Amendment to the States, the Due Process Clause constrained the States from extorting confessions from criminal defendants. Chambers v. Florida, 309 U.S. 227, 60 S.Ct. 472, 84 L.Ed. 716 (1940); Brown v. Mississippi, 297 U.S. 278, 56 S.Ct. 461, 80 L.Ed. 682 (1936). Indeed, by the time of Malloy, the constraints of the Due Process Clause were almost as stringent as the requirements of the Fifth Amendment itself. 378 U.S., at 6-7, 84 S.Ct., at 1492-1493; see, e.g., Haynes v. Washington, 373 U.S. 503, 83 S.Ct. 1336, 10 L.Ed.2d 513 (1963).

When Miranda reached this Court, it was undisputed that both the States and the Federal Government were constitutionally prohibited from prosecuting defendants with confessions coerced during custodial interrogations. 5 As a theoretical matter, the law was clear. In practice, however, the courts found it exceedingly difficult to determine whether a given confession had been coerced. Difficulties of proof and subtleties of interrogation technique made it impossible in most cases for the judiciary to decide with confidence whether the defendant had voluntarily confessed his guilt or whether his testimony had been unconstitutionally compelled. Courts around the country were spending countless hours reviewing the facts of individual custodial interrogations. See Note, Developments in the Law Confessions, 79 Harv.L.Rev. 935 (1966).

Miranda dealt with these practical problems. After a detailed examination of police practices and a review of its previous decisions in the area, the Court in Miranda determined that custodial interrogations are inherently coercive. The Court therefore created a constitutional presumption that statements made during custodial interrogations are compelled in violation of the Fifth Amendment and are thus inadmissible in criminal prosecutions. As a result of the Court's decision in Miranda, a statement made during a custodial interrogation may be introduced as proof of a defendant's guilt only if the prosecution demonstrates that the defendant knowingly and intelligently waived his constitutional rights before making the statement. 6 The now-familiar Miranda warnings offer law enforcement authorities a clear, easily administered device for ensuring that criminal suspects understand their constitutional rights well enough to waive them and to engage in consensual custodial interrogation.

In fashioning its "public-safety" exception to Miranda, the majority makes no attempt to deal with the constitutional presumption established by that case. The majority does not argue that police questioning about issues of public safety is any less coercive than custodial interrogations into other matters. The majority's only contention is that police officers could more easily protect the public if Miranda did not apply to custodial interrogations concerning the public's safety. 7 But Miranda was not a decision about public safety; it was a decision about coerced confessions. Without establishing that interrogations concerning the public's safety are less likely to be coercive than other interrogations, the majority cannot endorse the "public-safety" exception and remain faithful to the logic of Miranda v. Arizona.

B

The majority's avoidance of the issue of coercion may not have been inadvertent. It would strain credulity to contend that Officer Kraft's questioning of respondent Quarles was not coercive. 8 In the middle of the night and in the back of an empty supermarket, Quarles was surrounded by four armed police officers. His hands were handcuffed behind his back. The first words out of the mouth of the arresting officer were: "Where is the gun?" In the majority's phrase, the situation was "kaleidoscopic." Ante, at 656. Police and suspect were acting on instinct. Officer Kraft's abrupt and pointed question pressured Quarles in precisely the way that the Miranda Court feared the custodial interrogations would coerce self-incriminating testimony.

That the application of the "public-safety" exception in this case entailed coercion is no happenstance. The majority's ratio decidendi is that interrogating suspects about matters of public safety will be coercive. In its cost-benefit analysis, the Court's strongest argument in favor of a "public-safety" exception to Miranda is that the police would be better able to protect the public's safety if they were not always required to give suspects their Miranda warnings. The crux of this argument is that, by deliberately withholding Miranda warnings, the police can get information out of suspects who would refuse to respond to police questioning were they advised of their constitutional rights. The "public-safety" exception is efficacious precisely because it permits police officers to coerce criminal defendants into making involuntary statements.

Indeed, in the efficacy of the "public-safety" exception lies a fundamental and constitutional defect. Until today, this Court could truthfully state that the Fifth Amendment is given "broad scope" "where there has been genuine compulsion of testimony." Michigan v. Tucker, 417 U.S. 433, 440, 94 S.Ct. 2357, 2362, 41 L.Ed.2d 182 (1974). Coerced confessions were simply inadmissible in criminal prosecutions. The "public-safety" exception departs from this principle by expressly inviting police officers to coerce defendants into making incriminating statements, and then permitting prosecutors to introduce those statements at trial. Though the majority's opinion is cloaked in the beguiling language of utilitarianism, the Court has sanctioned sub silentio criminal prosecutions based on compelled self-incriminating statements. I find this result in direct conflict with the Fifth Amendment's dictate that "no person . . . shall be compelled in any criminal case to be a witness against himself."

The irony of the majority's decision is that the public's safety can be perfectly well protected without abridging the Fifth Amendment. If a bomb is about to explode or the public is otherwise imminently imperiled, the police are free to interrogate suspects without advising them of their constitutional rights. Such unconsented questioning may take place not only when police officers act on instinct but also when higher faculties lead them to believe that advising a suspect of his constitutional rights might decrease the likelihood that the suspect would reveal life-saving information. If trickery is necessary to protect the public, then the police may trick a suspect into confessing. While the Fourteenth Amendment sets limits on such behavior, nothing in the Fifth Amendment or our decision in Miranda v. Arizona proscribes this sort of emergency questioning. All the Fifth Amendment forbids is the introduction of coerced statements at trial. Cf. Weatherford v. Bursey, 429 U.S. 545, 97 S.Ct. 837, 51 L.Ed.2d 30 (1977) (Sixth Amendment violated only if trial affected).

To a limited degree, the majority is correct that there is a cost associated with the Fifth Amendment's ban on introducing coerced self-incriminating statements at trial. Without a "public-safety" exception, there would be occasions when a defendant incriminated himself by revealing a threat to the public, and the State was unable to prosecute because the defendant retracted his statement after consulting with counsel and the police cannot find independent proof of guilt. Such occasions would not, however, be common. The prosecution does not always lose the use of incriminating information revealed in these situations. After consulting with counsel, a suspect may well volunteer to repeat his statement in hopes of gaining a favorable plea bargain or more lenient sentence. The majority thus overstates its case when it suggests that a police officer must necessarily choose between public safety and admissibility. 9

But however frequently or infrequently such cases arise, their regularity is irrelevant. The Fifth Amendment prohibits compelled self-incrimination. 10 As the Court has explained on numerous occasions, this prohibition is the mainstay of our adversarial system of criminal justice. Not only does it protect us against the inherent unreliability of compelled testimony, but it also ensures that criminal investigations will be conducted with integrity and that the judiciary will avoid the taint of official lawlessness. See Murphy v. Waterfront Comm'n, 378 U.S. 52, 55, 84 S.Ct. 1594, 1596, 12 L.Ed.2d 678 (1964). The policies underlying the Fifth Amendment's privilege against self-incrimination are not diminished simply because testimony is compelled to protect the public's safety. The majority should not be permitted to elude the Amendment's absolute prohibition simply by calculating special costs that arise when the public's safety is at issue. Indeed, were constitutional adjudication always conducted in such an ad hoc manner, the Bill of Rights would be a most unreliable protector of individual liberties.

IV

Having determined that the Fifth Amendment renders inadmissible Quarles' response to Officer Kraft's questioning, I have no doubt that our precedents require that the gun discovered as a direct result of Quarles' statement must be presumed inadmissible as well. The gun was the direct product of a coercive custodial interrogation. In Silverthorne Lumber Co. v. United States, 251 U.S. 385, 40 S.Ct. 182, 64 L.Ed. 319

(1920), and Wong Sun v. United States, 371 U.S. 471, 83 S.Ct. 407, 9 L.Ed.2d 441 (1963), this Court held that the Government may not introduce incriminating evidence derived from an illegally obtained source. This Court recently explained the extent of the Wong Sun rule:

"Although Silverthorne and Wong Sun involved violations of the Fourth Amendment, the 'fruit of the poisonous tree' doctrine has not been limited to cases in which there has been a Fourth Amendment violation. The Court has applied the doctrine where the violations were of the Sixth Amendment, see United States v. Wade, 388 U.S. 218 87 S.Ct. 1926, 18 L.Ed.2d 1149 (1967), as well as of the Fifth Amendment." Nix v. Williams, 467 U.S. 431, 442, 104 S.Ct. 2501, 2508, 81 L.Ed.2d 377 (footnote omitted).

Accord United States v. Crews, 445 U.S. 463, 470, 100 S.Ct. 1244, 1249, 63 L.Ed.2d 537 (1980). 11 When they ruled on the issue, the New York courts were entirely correct in deciding that Quarles' gun was the tainted fruit of a nonconsensual interrogation and therefore was inadmissible under our precedents.

However, since the New York Court of Appeals issued its opinion, the scope of the Wong Sun doctrine has changed. In Nix v. Williams, supra, this Court construed Wong Sun to permit the introduction into evidence of constitutionally tainted "fruits" that inevitably would have been discovered by the government. In its briefs before this Court and before the New York courts, petitioner has argued that the "inevitable-discovery" rule, if applied to this case, would permit the admission of Quarles' gun. Although I have not joined the Court's opinion in Nix, and although I am not wholly persuaded that New York law would permit the application of the "inevitable-discovery" rule to this case, 12 I believe that the proper disposition of the matter is to vacate the order of the New York Court of Appeals to the extent that it suppressed Quarles' gun and remand the matter to the New York Court of Appeals for further consideration in light of Nix v. Williams.

Accordingly, I would affirm the order of the Court of Appeals to the extent that it found Quarles' incriminating statement inadmissible under the Fifth Amendment, would vacate the order to the extent that it suppressed Quarles' gun, and would remand the matter for reconsideration in light of Nix v. Williams.

Notes

1. Under New York law, any person who possesses a loaded firearm outside of his home or place of business is guilty of criminal possession of a weapon in the third degree. N.Y. Penal Law § 265.02(4) (McKinney 1980).

2. The majority attempts to distinguish Orozco by stressing the fact that the interrogation in this case immediately followed Quarles' arrest whereas the interrogation in Orozco occurred some four hours after the crime and was investigatory. Ante, at 655, n. 8. I fail to comprehend the distinction. In both cases, a group of police officers had taken a suspect into custody and questioned the suspect about the location of a missing gun. In both cases a dangerous weapon was missing, and in neither case was there any direct evidence where the weapon was hidden.

3. Although the majority stresses the exigencies of Quarles' arrest, it is undisputed that Quarles was in custody when Officer Kraft's questioning began, ante, at 655, and there is nothing in the majority's rationale—save the instincts of police officers—to prevent it from applying to all custodial interrogations.

4. One of the peculiarities of the majority's decision is its suggestion that police officers can "distinguish almost instinctively" questions tied to public safety and questions designed to elicit testimonial evidence. Ante, at 658. Obviously, these distinctions are extraordinarily difficult to draw. In many cases—like this one—custodial questioning may serve both purposes. It is therefore wishful thinking for the majority to suggest that the intuitions of police officers will render its decision self-executing.

5. There was, of course, still considerable confusion over whether the Sixth Amendment or the Fifth Amendment provided the basis for this prohibition. See Escobedo v. Illinois, 378 U.S. 478, 84 S.Ct. 1758, 12 L.Ed.2d 977 (1964). But the matter was undeniably of constitutional magnitude.

6. Until today, the Court has consistently adhered to Miranda's holding that, absent informed waiver, statements made during a custodial interrogation cannot be used to prove a defendant's guilt. Admittedly, in Harris v. New York, 401 U.S. 222, 91 S.Ct. 643, 28 L.Ed.2d 1 (1971), the Court permitted such statements to be introduced to impeach a defendant, but their introduction was tolerated only because the jury had been instructed to consider the statements "only in passing on [the defendant's] credibility and not as evidence of guilt." Id., at 223, 91 S.Ct., at 644.

7. The majority elsewhere attempts to disguise its decision as an effort to cut back on the overbreadth of Miranda's prophylactic standard. Ante, at 654-655. The disguise is transparent. Although Miranda was overbroad in that its application excludes some statements made during custodial interrogations that are not in fact coercive, the majority is not dealing with a class of cases affected by Miranda's overbreadth. The majority is exempting from Miranda's prophylactic rule incriminating statements that were elicited to safeguard the public's safety. As is discussed below, see infra, at 685-686, the majority supports the "public-safety" exception because "public-safety" interrogations can be coercive. In this respect, the Court's decision differs greatly from Michigan v. Tucker, 417 U.S. 433, 94 S.Ct. 2357, 41 L.Ed.2d 182 (1974), in which the Court sanctioned the admission of the fruits of a Miranda violation, but only because the violation was technical and the interrogation itself noncoercive.

8. The majority's reliance on respondent's failure to claim that his testimony was compelled by police conduct can only be disingenuous. Before today's opinion, respondent had no need to claim actual compulsion. Heretofore, it was sufficient to demonstrate that the police had conducted nonconsensual custodial interrogation. But now that the law has changed, it is only fair to examine the facts of the case to determine whether coercion probably was involved.

9. I also seriously question how often a statement linking a suspect to the threat to the public ends up being the crucial and otherwise unprovable element of a criminal

prosecution. The facts of the current case illustrate this point. The police arrested respondent Quarles not because he was suspected of carrying a gun, but because he was alleged to have committed rape. Ante, at 651-652. Had the State elected to prosecute on the rape count alone, respondent's incriminating statement about the gun would have had no role in the prosecution. Only because the State dropped the rape count and chose to proceed to trial solely on the criminal-possession charge did respondent's answer to Officer Kraft's question become critical.

10. In this sense, the Fifth Amendment differs fundamentally from the Fourth Amendment, which only prohibits unreasonable searches and seizures. See Fisher v. United States, 425 U.S. 391, 400, 96 S.Ct. 1569, 1575, 48 L.Ed.2d 39 (1976). Accordingly, the various exceptions to the Fourth Amendment permitting warrantless searches under various circumstances should have no analogy in the Fifth Amendment context. Curiously, the majority accepts this point, see, ante, at 652, n. 2, but persists in limiting the protections of the Fifth Amendment.

11. As our decisions in Nix and Crews reveal, the treatment of derivative evidence proposed in Justice O'CONNOR's opinion concurring in the judgment in part and dissenting in part, ante, p. 660, represents a much more radical departure from precedent than that opinion acknowledges. Although I have serious doubts about the wisdom of her proposal, I will not discuss them here. Petitioner never raised this novel theory of federal constitutional law before any New York court, see Brief for Appellant in No. 2512/80 (N.Y.Ct.App.); Brief for Appellant in No. 2512-80 (N.Y.App.Div.), and no New York court considered the theory sua sponte. The matter was therefore "not pressed or passed on in the courts below." McGoldrick v. Compagnie Generale Transatlantique, 309 U.S. 430, 434, 60 S.Ct. 670, 672, 84 L.Ed. 849 (1940). Since petitioner's derivative-evidence theory is of considerable constitutional importance,

it would be inconsistent with our precedents to permit petitioner to raise it for the first time now. See Illinois v. Gates, 462 U.S. 213, 217-223, 103 S.Ct. 2317, 2321-2324, 76 L.Ed.2d 527 (1983). An independent reason for declining to rule on petitioner's derivative-evidence theory is that petitioner may have been barred by New York procedures from raising this theory before the New York Court of Appeals. See n. 12, infra. Even if the claim were properly presented, it would be injudicious for the Court to embark on a new theory of derivative evidence when the gun in question might be admissible under the construction of Wong Sun just enunciated by the Court in Nix v. Williams. See, infra, this page and 690.

12. At least two procedural hurdles could prevent petitioner from making use of the "inevitable-discovery" exception on remand. First, petitioner did not claim inevitable discovery at the suppression hearing. This case therefore contains no record on the issue, and it is unclear whether the question is preserved under New York's procedural law. People v. Martin, 50 N.Y.2d 1029, 431 N.Y.S.2d 689, 409 N.E.2d 1363 (1980); People v. Tutt, 38 N.Y.2d 1011, 384 N.Y.S.2d 444, 348 N.E.2d 920 (1976). Second, the New York Rules of Criminal Procedure have codified the "fruit-of-the-poisonous-tree" doctrine.

N.Y.Crim.Proc.Law § 710.20(4) (McKinney 1980 and Supp. 1983-1984). Even after Nix v. Williams, Quarles' gun may still be suppressed under state law. These issues, of course, are matters of New York law, which could be disposed of by the New York courts on remand.

Sleeping outside in winter in a highly public place for the purpose of protesting homelessness is protected speech: Justice Marshall's dissent in Clark v. Community for Creative Nonviolence (June 29, 1984)

JUSTICE MARSHALL, with whom JUSTICE BRENNAN joins, dissenting.

The Court's disposition of this case is marked by two related failings. First, the majority is either unwilling or unable to take seriously the First Amendment claims advanced by respondents. Contrary to the impression given by the majority, respondents are not supplicants seeking to wheedle an undeserved favor from the Government. They are citizens raising issues of profound public importance who have properly turned to the courts for the vindication of their constitutional rights. Second, the majority misapplies the test for ascertaining whether a restraint on speech qualifies as a reasonable time, place, and manner regulation. In determining what constitutes a sustainable regulation, the majority fails to subject the alleged interests of the Government to the degree of scrutiny required to ensure that expressive activity protected by the First Amendment remains free of unnecessary limitations.

I

The proper starting point for analysis of this case is a recognition that the activity in which respondents seek to engage -- sleeping in a highly public place, outside, in the winter for the purpose of protesting homelessness -- is symbolic speech protected by the First Amendment. The majority assumes, without deciding, that the respondents' conduct is entitled to constitutional protection. Ante at 293. The problem with this assumption is that the Court thereby avoids examining closely the reality of respondents' planned expression. The majority's approach denatures respondents' asserted right, and thus makes all too easy identification of a Government interest sufficient to warrant its abridgment. A realistic appraisal of the competing interests at stake in this case requires a closer look at the nature of the expressive conduct at issue and the context in which that conduct would be displayed.

In late autumn of 1982, respondents sought permission to conduct a round-the-clock demonstration in Lafayette Park and on the Mall. Part of the demonstration would include homeless persons sleeping outside in tents without any other amenities. [n1] Respondents sought to begin their demonstration on a date full of ominous meaning to any homeless person: the first day of winter. Respondents were similarly purposeful in choosing demonstration sites. The Court portrays these sites -- the Mall and Lafayette Park -- in a peculiar fashion. According to the Court:

Lafayette Park and the Mall . . . are unique resources that the Federal Government holds in trust for the American people. Lafayette Park is a roughly 7-acre square located across Pennsylvania Avenue from the White House. Although originally part of the White House grounds, President Jefferson set it aside as a park for the use of residents and visitors. It is a "garden park with a . . . formal landscaping of flowers and trees, with fountains, walks and benches." . . . The Mall is a stretch of land running westward from the Capitol to the Lincoln Memorial some two miles away. It includes the Washington Monument, a series of reflecting pools, trees, lawns, and other greenery. It is bordered by, inter alia, the Smithsonian Institution and the National Gallery of Art. Both the Park and the Mall were included in Major Pierre L'Enfant's original plan for the Capital. Both are visited by vast numbers of visitors from around the country, as well as by large numbers of residents of the Washington metropolitan area.

Ante at 290. Missing from the majority's description is any inkling that Lafayette Park and the Mall have served as the sites for some of the most rousing political demonstrations in the Nation's history. It is interesting to learn, I suppose, that Lafayette Park and the Mall were both part of Major Pierre L'Enfant's original plan for the Capital. Far more pertinent, however, is that these areas constitute, in the Government's words, "a fitting and powerful forum for political expression and political protest." Brief for Petitioners 11. [n2]

The primary [n3] purpose for making sleep an integral part of the demonstration was "to reenact the central reality of homelessness," Brief for Respondents 2, and to impress upon public consciousness, in as dramatic a way as possible, that homelessness is a widespread problem, often ignored, that confronts its victims with life-threatening deprivations. [n4] As one of the homeless men seeking to demonstrate explained:

Sleeping in Lafayette Park or on the Mall, for me, is to show people that conditions are so poor for the homeless and poor in this city that we would actually sleep outside in the winter to get the point across.

Id. at 3.

In a long line of cases, this Court has afforded First Amendment protection to expressive conduct that qualifies as symbolic speech. See, e.g., Tinker v. Des Moines School Dist., 393 U.S. 503"] 393 U.S. 503 (1969) (black armband worn by students in public school as protest against United States policy in Vietnam war); Brown v. Louisiana, 383 U.S. 131 (1966) (sit-in by Negro students in "whites only" library to protest segregation); Stromberg v. California, 283 U.S. 359 (1931) (flying red flag as gesture of support for communism). In light of the surrounding context, respondents' proposed activity meets the qualifications. The Court has previously acknowledged the importance of context in determining whether an act can properly be denominated as "speech" for First Amendment purposes and has provided guidance concerning the way in which courts should "read" a context in making this determination. The leading case is 393 U.S. 503 (1969) (black armband worn by students in public school as protest against United States policy in Vietnam war); Brown v. Louisiana, 383 U.S. 131 (1966) (sit-in by Negro students in "whites only" library to protest segregation); Stromberg v. California, 283 U.S. 359 (1931) (flying red flag as gesture of support for communism). In light of the surrounding context, respondents' proposed activity meets the qualifications. The Court has previously acknowledged the importance of context in determining whether an act can properly be denominated as "speech" for First Amendment purposes and has provided guidance concerning the way in which courts should "read" a context in making this determination. The leading case is Spence v. Washington, 418 U.S. 405 (1974), where this Court held that displaying a United States flag with a peace symbol attached to it was conduct protected by the First Amendment. The Court looked first to the intent of the speaker -- whether there was an "intent to convey a particularized message" -- and second to the perception of the audience -- whether "the likelihood was great that the message would be understood by those who viewed it." Id. at 410-411. Here, respondents clearly intended to protest the reality of homelessness by sleeping outdoors in the winter in the near vicinity of the magisterial residence of the President of the United States. In addition to accentuating the political character of their protest by their choice of location and mode of communication, respondents also intended to underline the meaning of their protest by giving their demonstration satirical names. Respondents planned to name the demonstration on the Mall "Congressional Village," and the demonstration in Lafayette Park, "Reaganville II." App. 13.

Nor can there be any doubt that in the surrounding circumstances the likelihood was great that the political significance of sleeping in the parks would be understood by those who viewed it. Certainly the news media understood the significance of respondents' proposed activity; newspapers and magazines from around the Nation reported their previous sleep-in and their planned display. [n5] Ordinary citizens, too, would likely understand the political message intended by respondents. This likelihood stems from the remarkably apt fit between the activity in which respondents seek to engage and the social problem they seek to highlight. By using sleep as an integral part of their mode of protest, respondents

can express with their bodies the poignancy of their plight. They can physically demonstrate the neglect from which they suffer with an articulateness even Dickens could not match.

Community for Creative Non-Violence v. Watt, 227 U.S.App.D.C.19, 34, 703 F.2d 586, 601 (1983) (Edwards, J. concurring).

It is true that we all go to sleep as part of our daily regimen, and that, for the most part, sleep represents a physical necessity, and not a vehicle for expression. But these characteristics need not prevent an activity that is normally devoid of expressive purpose from being used as a novel mode of communication. Sitting or standing in a library is a commonplace activity necessary to facilitate ends usually having nothing to do with making a statement. Moreover, sitting or standing is not conduct that an observer would normally construe as expressive conduct. However, for Negroes to stand or sit in a "whites only" library in Louisiana in 1965 was powerfully expressive; in that particular context, those acts became "monuments of protest" against segregation. Brown v. Louisiana, supra, at 139.

The Government contends that a foreseeable difficulty of administration counsels against recognizing sleep as a mode of expression protected by the First Amendment. The predicament the Government envisions can be termed "the imposter problem": the problem of distinguishing bona fide protesters from imposters whose requests for permission to sleep in Lafayette Park or the Mall on First Amendment grounds would mask ulterior designs -- the simple desire, for example, to avoid the expense of hotel lodgings. The Government maintains that such distinctions cannot be made without inquiring into the sincerity of demonstrators, and that such an inquiry would, itself, pose dangers to First Amendment values, because it would necessarily be content-sensitive. I find this argument unpersuasive. First, a variety of circumstances already require government agencies to engage in the delicate task of inquiring into the sincerity of claimants asserting First Amendment rights. See, e.g., Wisconsin v. Yoder, 406 U.S. 205, 215-216 (1972) (exception of members of religious group from compulsory education statute justified by group's adherence to deep religious conviction, rather than subjective secular values); Welsh v. United States, 398 U.S. 333, 343-344 (1970) (eligibility for exemption from military service as conscientious objector status justified by sincere religious beliefs). It is thus incorrect to imply that any scrutiny of the asserted purpose of persons seeking a permit to display sleeping as a form of symbolic speech would import something altogether new and disturbing into our First Amendment jurisprudence. Second, the administrative difficulty the Government envisions is now nothing more than a vague apprehension. If permitting sleep to be used as a form of protected First Amendment activity actually created the administrative problems the Government now envisions, there would emerge a clear factual basis upon which to establish the necessity for the limitation the Government advocates.

The Government's final argument against granting respondents' proposed activity any degree of First Amendment protection is that the contextual analysis upon which respondents rely is fatally flawed by overinclusiveness. The Government contends that the Spence approach is overinclusive because it accords First Amendment status to a wide variety of acts that, although expressive, are obviously subject to prohibition. As the Government notes,

[a]ctions such as assassination of political figures and the bombing of government buildings can fairly be characterized as intended to convey a message that is readily perceived by the public.

Brief for Petitioners 24, n. 18. The Government's argument would pose a difficult problem were the determination whether an act constitutes "speech" the end of First Amendment analysis. But such a determination is not the end. If an act is defined as speech, it must still be balanced against countervailing government interests. The balancing which the First Amendment requires would doom any argument seeking to protect antisocial acts such as assassination or destruction of government property from government interference, because compelling interests would outweigh the expressive value of such conduct.

II

Although sleep in the context of this case is symbolic speech protected by the First Amendment, it is nonetheless subject to reasonable time, place, and manner restrictions. I agree with the standard enunciated by the majority:

[R]estrictions of this kind are valid provided that they are justified without reference to the content of the regulated speech, that they are narrowly tailored to serve a significant governmental interest, and that they leave open ample alternative channels for communication of the information.

Ante at 293 (citations omitted). [n6] I conclude, however, that the regulations at issue in this case, as applied to respondents, fail to satisfy this standard.

According to the majority, the significant Government interest advanced by denying respondents' request to engage in sleep-speech is the interest in

maintaining the parks in the heart of our Capital in an attractive and intact condition, readily available to the millions of people who wish to see and enjoy them by their presence.

Ante at 296. That interest is indeed significant. However, neither the Government nor the majority adequately explains how prohibiting respondents' planned activity will substantially further that interest.

The majority's attempted explanation begins with the curious statement that it seriously doubts that the First Amendment requires the Park Service to permit a demonstration in Lafayette Park and the Mall involving a 24-hour vigil and the erection of tents to accommodate 150 people. Ante at 296. I cannot perceive why the Court should have "serious doubts" regarding this matter, and it provides no explanation for its uncertainty. Furthermore, even if the majority's doubts were well founded, I cannot see how such doubts relate to the problem at hand. The issue posed by this case is not whether the Government is constitutionally compelled to permit the erection of tents and the staging of a continuous 24-hour vigil; rather, the issue is whether any substantial Government interest is served by banning sleep that is part of a political demonstration.

What the Court may be suggesting is that, if the tents and the 24-hour vigil are permitted, but not constitutionally required to be permitted, then respondents have no constitutional right to engage in expressive conduct that supplements these activities. Put in arithmetical terms, the Court appears to contend that, if X is permitted by grace, rather than by constitutional compulsion, X 1 can be denied without regard to the requirements the Government must normally satisfy in order to restrain protected activity. This notion, however, represents a misguided conception of the First Amendment. The First Amendment requires the Government to justify every instance of abridgment. That requirement stems from our oft-stated recognition that the First Amendment was designed to secure "the widest possible dissemination of information from diverse and antagonistic sources," Associated Press v. United States, 326 U.S. 1, 20 (1945), and "to assure unfettered interchange of ideas for the bringing about of political and social changes desired by the people." Roth v. United States, 354 U.S. 476, 484 (1957). See also Buckley v. Valeo, 424 U.S. 1, 49 (1976); New York Times Co. v. Sullivan, 376 U.S. 254, 266 (1964); Whitney v. California, 274 U.S. 357, 375-378 (1927) (Brandeis, J., concurring). Moreover, the stringency of that requirement is not diminished simply because the activity the Government seeks to restrain is supplemental to other activity that the Government may have permitted out of grace, but was not constitutionally compelled to allow. If the Government cannot adequately justify abridgment of protected expression, there is no reason why citizens should be prevented from exercising the first of the rights safeguarded by our Bill of Rights.

The majority's second argument is comprised of the suggestion that, although sleeping contains an element of expression, "its major value to [respondents'] demonstration would have been facilitative." Ante at 296. While this observation does provide a hint of the weight the Court attached to respondents' First Amendment claims, [n7] it is utterly irrelevant to whether the Government's ban on sleeping advances a substantial Government interest.

The majority's third argument is based upon two claims. The first is that the ban on sleeping relieves the Government of an administrative burden because, without the flat ban, the process of issuing and denying permits to other demonstrators asserting First Amendment rights to sleep in the parks "would present difficult problems for the Park Service." Ante at 297. The second is that the ban on sleeping will increase the probability that

some around-the-clock demonstrations for days on end will not materialize, [that] others will be limited in size and duration, and that the purpose of the regulation will thus be materially served,

ante at 297, that purpose being "to limit the wear and tear on park properties." Ante at 299.

The flaw in these two contentions is that neither is supported by a factual showing that evinces a real, as opposed to a merely speculative, problem. The majority fails to offer any evidence indicating that the absence of an absolute ban on sleeping would present administrative problems to the Park Service that are substantially more difficult than those it ordinarily confronts. A mere apprehension of difficulties should not be enough to overcome the right to free expression. See United States v. Grace, 461 U.S. 171, 182 (1983); Tinker v. Des Moines School Dist., 393 U.S. at 508. Moreover, if the Government's interest in avoiding administrative difficulties were truly "substantial," one would expect the agency most involved in administering the parks at least to allude to such an interest. Here, however, the perceived difficulty of administering requests from other demonstrators seeking to convey messages through sleeping was not among the reasons underlying the Park Service regulations. [n8] Nor was it mentioned by the Park Service in its rejection of respondents' particular request. [n9]

The Court's erroneous application of the standard for ascertaining a reasonable time, place, and manner restriction is also revealed by the majority's conclusion that a substantial governmental interest is served by the sleeping ban because it will discourage "around-the-clock demonstrations for days," and thus further the regulation's purpose "to limit wear and tear on park properties." Ante at 299. The majority cites no evidence indicating that sleeping engaged in as symbolic speech will cause substantial wear and tear on park property. Furthermore, the Government's application of the sleeping ban in the circumstances of this case is strikingly underinclusive. The majority acknowledges that a proper time, place, and manner restriction must be "narrowly tailored." Here, however, the tailoring requirement is virtually forsaken, inasmuch as the Government offers no justification for applying its absolute ban on sleeping, yet is willing to allow respondents to engage in activities -- such as feigned sleeping -- that is no less burdensome.

In short, there are no substantial Government interests advanced by the Government's regulations as applied to respondents. All that the Court's decision advances are the prerogatives of a bureaucracy that over the years has shown an implacable hostility toward citizens' exercise of First Amendment rights. [n10]

III

The disposition of this case impels me to make two additional observations. First, in this case, as in some others involving time, place, and manner restrictions, [n11] the Court has dramatically lowered its scrutiny of governmental regulations once it has determined that such regulations are content-neutral. The result has been the creation of a two-tiered approach to First Amendment cases: while regulations that turn on the content of the expression are subjected to a strict form of judicial review, [n12] regulations that are aimed at matters other than expression receive only a minimal level of scrutiny. The minimal scrutiny prong of this two-tiered approach has led to an unfortunate diminution of First Amendment protection. By narrowly limiting its concern to whether a given regulation creates a content-based distinction, the Court has seemingly overlooked the fact that content-neutral restrictions are also capable of unnecessarily restricting protected expressive activity. [n13] To be sure, the general prohibition against content-based regulations is an essential tool of First Amendment analysis. It helps to put into operation the well-established principle that

government may not grant the use of a forum to people whose views it finds acceptable, but deny use to those wishing to express less favored or more controversial views.

Police Department of Chicago v. Mosley, 408 U.S. 92, 95-96 (1972). The Court, however, has transformed the ban against content distinctions from a floor that offers all persons at least equal liberty under the First Amendment into a ceiling that restricts persons to the protection of First Amendment equality -- but nothing more. [n14] The consistent imposition of silence upon all may fulfill the dictates of an evenhanded content-neutrality. But it offends our "profound national commitment to the principle that debate on public issues should be uninhibited, robust, and wide-open." New York

Times Co. v. Sullivan, 376 U.S. at 270. [n15]

Second, the disposition of this case reveals a mistaken assumption regarding the motives and behavior of Government officials who create and administer content-neutral regulations. The Court's salutary skepticism of governmental decisionmaking in First Amendment matters suddenly dissipates once it determines that a restriction is not content-based. The Court evidently assumes that the balance struck by officials is deserving of deference so long as it does not appear to be tainted by content discrimination. What the Court fails to recognize is that public officials have strong incentives to over-regulate even in the absence of an intent to censor particular views. This incentive stems from the fact that of the two groups whose interests officials must accommodate -- on the one hand, the interests of the general public and, on the other, the interests of those who seek to use a particular forum for First Amendment activity -- the political power of the former is likely to be far greater than that of the latter. [n16]

The political dynamics likely to lead officials to a disproportionate sensitivity to regulatory, as opposed to First Amendment, interests can be discerned in the background of this case. Although the Park Service appears to have applied the revised regulations consistently, there are facts in the record of this case that raise a substantial possibility that the impetus behind the revision may have derived less from concerns about administrative difficulties and wear and tear on the park facilities than from other, more "political," concerns. The alleged need for more restrictive regulations stemmed from a court decision favoring the same First Amendment claimants that are parties to this case. See n. 1, supra. Moreover, in response both to the Park Service's announcement that it was considering changing its rules and the respondents' expressive activities, at least one powerful group urged the Service to tighten its regulations. [n17] The point of these observations is not to impugn the integrity of the National Park Service. Rather, my intention is to illustrate concretely that government agencies, by their very nature, are driven to over-regulate public forums to the detriment of First Amendment rights, that facial viewpoint-neutrality is no shield against unnecessary restrictions on unpopular ideas or modes of expression, and that, in this case in particular, there was evidence readily available that should have impelled the Court to subject the Government's restrictive policy to something more than minimal scrutiny. For the foregoing reasons, I respectfully dissent.

Notes

1. The previous winter, respondents had held a similar demonstration after courts ruled that the Park Service regulations then in effect did not extend to respondents' proposed activities. Community for Creative Non-Violence v. Watt, 216 U.S.App.D.C. 394, 670 F.2d 1213 (1982) (CCNV I). Those activities consisted of setting up and sleeping in nine tents in Lafayette Park. The regulations at issue in this case were promulgated in direct response to CCNV I. 47 Fed.Reg. 24299 (1982).

2. At oral argument, the Government informed the Court "that, on any given day,

there will be an average of three or so demonstrations going on" in the Mall-Lafayette Park area. Tr. of Oral Arg. 3-4. Respondents accurately describe Lafayette Park "as the American analogue to 'speaker's Corner' in Hyde Park." Brief for Respondents 16, n. 25.

3. Another purpose for making sleep part of the demonstration was to enable participants to weather the rigors of the round-the-clock vigil and to encourage other homeless persons to participate in the demonstration. As respondents stated in their application for a demonstration permit:

If there was ever any question as to whether sleeping was a necessary element in this demonstration, it should be answered by now [in light of the previous year's demonstration]. No matter how hard we tried to get [homeless persons] to come to Reaganville [the name given to the demonstration by respondents], they simply would not come until sleeping was permitted.

App. 14.

4. Estimates on the number of homeless persons in the United States range from two to three million. See Brief for National Coalition for the Homeless as Amicus Curiae 3. Though numerically significant, the homeless are politically powerless, inasmuch as they lack the financial resources necessary to obtain access to many of the most effective means of persuasion. Moreover, homeless persons are likely to be denied access to the vote, since the lack of a mailing address or other proof of residence within a State disqualifies an otherwise eligible citizen from registering to vote. Id. at 5.

The detrimental effects of homelessness are manifold, and include psychic trauma, circulatory difficulties, infections that refuse to heal, lice infestations, and hypothermia. Id. at 14-15. In the extreme, exposure to the elements can lead to death; over the 1983 Christmas weekend in New York City, 14 homeless persons perished from the cold. See N.Y. Times, Dec. 27, 1983, p. A1., col. 1.

5. See articles appended to Declaration of Mary Ellen Hombs, Record, Vol. 1.

6. I also agree with the majority that no substantial difference distinguishes the test applicable to time, place, and manner restrictions and the test articulated in United States v. O'Brien, 391 U.S. 367 (1968). See ante at 298-299, n. 8.

7. The facilitative purpose of the sleep-in takes away nothing from its independent status as symbolic speech. Moreover, facilitative conduct that is closely related to expressive activity is itself protected by First Amendment considerations. I therefore find myself in agreement with Judge Ginsburg, who noted that

the personal noncommunicative aspect of sleeping in symbolic tents at a demonstration site bears a close, functional relationship to an activity that is commonly comprehended as "free speech."

Community for Creative Non-Violence v. Watt, 227 U.S.App.D.C. 19, 40, 703 F.2d 586, 607 (1983).

[S]leeping in the tents, rather than simply standing or sitting down in them, allows the demonstrator to sustain his or her protest without stopping short of the officially-granted round-the-clock permission.

Ibid. For me, as for Judge Ginsburg, that linkage itself

suffices to require a genuine effort to balance the demonstrators' interests against other concerns for which the government bears responsibility.

Ibid. .

8. See 47 Fed.Reg. 24301 (1982).

9. App. 16-17.

10. At oral argument, the Government suggested that the ban on sleeping should not be invalidated as applied to respondents simply because the Government is willing to allow respondents to engage in other nonverbal acts of expression that may also trench upon the Government interests served by the ban. Tr. of Oral Arg. 15, 23. The Government maintains that such a result makes the Government a victim of its own generosity. However the Government's characterization of itself as an unstinting provider of opportunities for protected expression is thoroughly discredited by a long line of decisions compelling the National Park Service to allow the expressive conduct it now claims to permit as a matter of grace. See, e.g., Women Strike for Peace v. Morton, 153 U.S.App.D.C.198, 472 F.2d 1273 (1972); A Quaker Action Group v. Morton, 170 U.S.App.D.C. 124, 516 F.2d 717 (1975); United States v. Abney, 175 U.S.App.D.C. 247, 534 F.2d 984 (1976).

11. See, e.g., City Council of Los Angeles v. Taxpayers for Vincent, 466 U.S. 789 (1984); Heffron v. International Society for Krishna Consciousness, Inc., 452 U.S. 640 (1981). But see United States v. Grace, 461 U.S. 171 (1983); Tinker v. Des Moines School Dist., 393 U.S. 503 (1969); Brown v. Louisiana, 383 U.S. 131 (1966).

12. See, e.g., Landmark Communications, Inc. v. Virginia, 435 U.S. 829 (1978). It should be noted, however, that there is a context in which regulations that are facially content-neutral are nonetheless subjected to strict scrutiny. This situation arises when a regulation vests standardless discretion in officials empowered to dispense permits for the use of public forums. See, e.g., Lovell v. City of Griffin, 303 U.S. 444 (1938); Hague v. CIO, 307 U.S. 496 (1939); Shuttlesworth v. City of Birmingham, 394 U.S. 147 (1969).

13. See Redish, The Content Distinction in First Amendment Analysis, 34 Stan.L.Rev. 113 (1981).

14. Furthermore, a content-neutral regulation does not necessarily fall with random or equal force upon different groups or different points of view. A content-neutral regulation that restricts an inexpensive mode of communication will fall most heavily upon relatively poor speakers and the points of view that such speakers typically espouse. See, e.g., City Council of Los Angeles v. Taxpayers for Vincent, supra, at 812-813, n. 30. This sort of latent inequality is very much in evidence in this case, for respondents lack the financial means necessary to buy access to more conventional modes of persuasion.

A disquieting feature about the disposition of this case is that it lends credence to the charge that judicial administration of the First Amendment, in conjunction with a social order marked by large disparities in wealth and other sources of power, tends systematically to discriminate against efforts by the relatively disadvantaged to convey their political ideas. In the past, this Court has taken such considerations into account in adjudicating the First Amendment rights of those among us who are financially deprived. See, e.g., Martin v. Struthers, 319 U.S. 141, 146 (1943) (striking down ban on door-to-door distribution of circulars in part because this mode of distribution is "essential to the poorly financed causes of little people"); Marsh v. Alabama, 326 U.S. 501 (1946) (State cannot impose criminal sanction on person for distributing literature on sidewalk of town owned by private corporation). Such solicitude is noticeably absent from the majority's opinion, continuing a trend that has not escaped the attention of commentators. See, e.g., Dorsen & Gora, Free Speech, Property, and The Burger Court: Old Values, New Balances, 1982 S.Ct.Rev.195; Van Alstyne, The Recrudescence of Property Rights as the Foremost Principle of Civil Liberties: The First Decade of the Burger Court, 43 Law & Contemp. Prob. 66 (summer 1980).

15. For a critique of the limits of the equality principle in First Amendment analysis see Redish, supra, at 134-139.

16. See Goldberger, Judicial Scrutiny in Public Forum Cases: Misplaced Trust in the Judgment of Public Officials, 32 Buffalo L.Rev. 175, 208 (1983).

17. See Declaration of Mary Ellen Hombs, Exhibit 1kk, Record, Vol. 1.

Blanket prohibition on contact visits unreasonable: Justice Marshall's dissent in Block v. Rutherford (July 3, 1984)

JUSTICE MARSHALL, with whom JUSTICE BRENNAN and JUSTICE STEVENS join, dissenting.

This case marks the fourth time in recent years that the Court has turned a deaf ear to inmates' claims that the conditions of their confinement violate the Federal Constitution. See Rhodes v. Chapman, 452 U.S. 337 (1981); Bell v. Wolfish, 441 U.S. 520 (1979); Hudson v. Palmer, ante, p. 517. Guided by an unwarranted confidence in the good faith and "expertise" of prison administrators and by a pinched conception of the meaning of the Due Process Clauses and the Eighth Amendment, a majority of the Court increasingly appears willing to sanction any prison condition for which the majority can imagine a colorable rationale, no matter how oppressive or ill-justified that condition is in fact. So, here, the Court upholds two policies in force at the Los Angeles County Central Jail. Under one, a pretrial detainee is not permitted any physical contact with members of his family, regardless of how long he is incarcerated pending his trial or how slight is the risk that he will abuse a visitation privilege. Under the other, detainees are not allowed to observe searches of their cells, despite the fact that such searches frequently result in arbitrary destruction or confiscation of the detainees' property. In my view, neither of these policies comports with the Constitution.

I

In Bell v. Wolfish, supra, the Court established a set of principles defining constitutionally permissible treatment of incarcerated persons who have not been convicted of crimes. In the years since Wolfish, I have not abandoned my view that the Court's decision in that case was fundamentally misconceived. See 441 U.S., at 563 -579 (MARSHALL, J., dissenting). However, even if I thought the doctrine enunciated in Wolfish was defensible, I could not abide the manner in which the majority construes and applies that doctrine to dispose of respondents' challenge to the jail's rule against contact visitation.

One of the premises of the principal holding in Wolfish was that the plaintiffs' claims did not implicate any "fundamental liberty interests" such as those "delineated in . . . Roe v. Wade, 410 U.S. 113 (1973); Eisenstadt v. Baird, 405 U.S. 438 (1972); Stanley v. Illinois, 405 U.S. 645 (1972); Griswold v. Connecticut, 381 U.S. 479 (1965); [and] Meyer v. Nebraska, 262 U.S. 390 (1923)." Id., at 534-535. Aside from the right not to be punished prior to adjudication of guilt, the only general interest that could be asserted by the plaintiffs in Wolfish, the Court contended, was a "desire to be free from discomfort." Id., at 534. 1 The comparatively unimportant nature of that interest made it possible for the Court to adopt a deferential legal standard: "[A] particular condition or restriction of pretrial detention" passes muster under the Due Process Clause as long as it "is reasonably related to a legitimate governmental objective," id., at 539.

The Court today reiterates and relies on the foregoing test. Ante, at 586. In so doing, however, the Court ignores a crucial difference between the interests at stake in Wolfish and in this case. Unlike the Wolfish plaintiffs, respondents can and do point to a fundamental right abridged by the jail's policy - namely, their freedom to engage in and prevent the deterioration of their relationships with their families.

The importance of the right asserted by respondents was acknowledged by the District Court. "[T]he ability of a man to embrace his wife and his children from time to time during the weeks or months while he is awaiting trial," the court found, "is a matter of great importance to him." Rutherford v. Pitchess, 457 F. Supp. 104, 110 (1978). 2 Denial of contact visitation, the court concluded, is "very traumatic treatment." App. to Pet. for Cert. 25. Substantial evidence in the record supports the District Court's findings. William Nagel, an expert in the field of corrections, testified that contact visitation was crucial in allowing prisoners to maintain their familial bonds. Tr. 4174-4175. Similarly, Dr. Terry Kupers, a psychiatrist, testified that denial of contact visitation contributes to the breakup of prisoners' marriages and generally threatens their mental health. Id., at 4647-4651. The secondary literature buttresses these assertions, 3 as do the conclusions reached by other courts. 4

The significant injury to familial relations wrought by the jail's policy of denying contact visitation means that that policy must be tested against a legal standard more constraining than the rule announced in Wolfish. Our cases leave no doubt that persons' freedom to enter into, maintain, and cultivate familial relations is entitled to constitutional protection. E. g., Santosky v. Kramer, 455 U.S. 745, 753 (1982). Among the relationships that we have expressly shielded from state interference are bonds between spouses, see Zablocki v. Redhail, 434 U.S. 374 (1978), and between parents and their children, see Wisconsin v. Yoder, 406 U.S. 205 (1972); Stanley v. Illinois, supra. The special status of these relationships in our constitutional scheme derives from several considerations: the fact that traditionally they have been regarded as sacrosanct, 5 the important role they have played in fostering diversity and pluralism in our culture, 6 and their centrality to the emotional life of many persons. 7

Determination of exactly how the doctrine established in the aforementioned cases bears upon a ban on contact visitation by pretrial detainees would be difficult. On the one hand, it could be argued that the "withdrawal or limitation of many privileges and rights" that necessarily accompanies incarceration, Price v. Johnston, 334 U.S. 266, 285 (1948), combined with the fact that the inmates' familial bonds are not altogether severed by such a ban, means that something less than a "compelling" government interest would suffice to legitimate the impairment of the inmates' rights. 8 On the other hand, two factors suggest that only a very important public purpose could sustain the policy. First, even persons lawfully incarcerated after being convicted of crimes retain important constitutional rights; 9 presumptively innocent persons surely are entitled to no less. 10 Second, we have previously insisted upon very persuasive justifications for government regulations that significantly, but not prohibitively, interfered with the exercise of familial rights; 11 arguably, a similarly stringent test should control here. However, a sensitive balancing of these competing considerations is unnecessary to resolve the case before us. At a minimum, petitioners, to prevail, should be required to show that the jail's policy materially advances a substantial government interest. Petitioners have not made and, on this record, could not make such a demonstration. 12

It should be emphasized that what petitioners must defend is not their reluctance to allow unlimited contact visitation, but rather their refusal to adopt the specific reforms ordered by the lower courts. The District Court's order, it should be recalled, was carefully circumscribed:

"Commencing not more than ninety days following the date of this order, the defendants will make available a contact visit once each week to each pretrial detainee that has been held in the jail for one month or more, and concerning whom there is no indication of drug or escape propensities; provided, however, that no more than fifteen hundred such visits need be allowed in any one week. In the event that the number of requested visits in any week exceeds fifteen hundred, or such higher number as the Sheriff voluntarily undertakes to accommodate, a reasonable system of rotation or other priorities may be maintained. The lengths of such visits shall remain in the discretion of the Sheriff." App. to Pet. for Cert. 38.

Petitioners object to this order, and defend their current rule prohibiting all contact between inmates and their families, on two main grounds. Neither of the proffered justifications survives scrutiny.

First, petitioners contend that a ban on contact visitation is necessary to prevent the introduction into the jail of drugs and weapons. It must be admitted that this is a legitimate and important goal. However, petitioners fail to show that its realization would be materially impaired by adoption of the reforms ordered by the District Court. Indeed, evidence adduced at trial establishes the contrary. Several witnesses testified that security procedures could be implemented that would make importation of contraband very difficult. Among the precautions effectively used at other institutions are: searches of prisoners before and after visits; dressing of prisoners in special clothes for visitation; examination of prisoners and visitors with metal detectors and fluoroscopes; exclusion of parcels from the visiting area; rejection of visitors who do not comply with visiting rules; and continuous observation of the visiting area by guards. E. g., Tr. 4164-4166, 4232, 4576-4577. 13 Mr. Nagel testified that these procedures would "prevent everything except the most extreme methods of introducing drugs into the institution." Id., at 4170. Further protection against the transmission of contraband from visitors to inmates is provided by the District Court's restriction of its order to inmates who have been classified as low risk. In short, there is no reason to think that compliance with the lower courts' directive would result in more than a negligible increase in the flow of drugs or weapons into the jail. 14

Second, petitioners contend that allowance of contact visitation would endanger innocent visitors who are placed in near proximity to dangerous detainees. Again, though the importance of the objective is apparent, the nexus between it and the jail's current policy is not. As indicated above, the District Court's order applies only to detainees who are unlikely to try to escape. And security measures could be employed by petitioners that would make it very difficult for inmates to hurt or take advantage of visitors. See supra, at 602. Finally, the administrators of other institutions that have long permitted contact visits between inmates and their families testified at trial that violent incidents resulting from such visitation are rare, apparently because inmates value their visitation privileges so highly. 15

The majority seeks to shore up petitioners' two arguments with miscellaneous subsidiary claims. In an effort to discredit the limitations on the District Court's order, the majority argues that determination of which inmates have a sufficiently low propensity to misbehave would be difficult and time-consuming, especially in light of "the brevity of detention and the constantly changing nature of the inmate population." Ante, at 587. This contention is rebutted by the District Court's finding that, after an inmate has been incarcerated for a month, jail officials have considerable information regarding his background and behavior patterns, and by evidence in the record that the jail already has a classification system that, with some modification and improvement, could be used to evaluate detainees' propensities for escape and drug abuse. App. to Pet. for Cert. 33. 16 Next, the majority contends that compliance with the District Court's order would be expensive. Ante, at 588, n. 9. Again, the District Court's findings are decisive; the court found that only "modest" changes in the jail facilities would be required. App. to Pet. for Cert. 33. More fundamentally, a desire to run a jail as cheaply as possible is not a legitimate reason for abridging the constitutional rights of its occupants. Finally, the majority suggests that the District Court's order might cause some dissension in the jail, because inmates denied visitation privileges would resent those granted such privileges. Ante, at 587. There is no evidence whatsoever in the record to support this speculative observation.

In sum, neither petitioners nor the majority have shown that permitting low-risk pretrial detainees who have been incarcerated for more than a month occasionally to have contact visits with their spouses and children would frustrate the achievement of any substantial state interest. 17 Because such visitation would significantly alleviate the adverse impact of the jail's current policies upon respondents' familial rights, its deprivation violates the Due Process Clause.

II

The majority brusquely rejects respondents' challenge to the jail's policy of refusing to permit detainees to observe searches of their cells on the ground that respondents' claim is foreclosed by the decision in Wolfish. If respondents' claim were indeed identical to that presented by the Wolfish plaintiffs, I would vote to affirm on this issue for the reasons stated in my dissenting opinion in Wolfish. See 441 U.S., at 576 . In fact, however, the two cases differ in a crucial respect, and that difference provides an independent ground for sustaining the judgment below.

The Court in Wolfish held that the policy adopted by the Metropolitan Correctional Center of not allowing pretrial detainees to observe searches of their cells did not violate the Fourth Amendment and did not constitute punishment violative of the Due Process Clause. Id., at 556-557, 560-561. Respondents in this case make a quite different claim. They assert that the Central Jail's policy of searching cells and confiscating or destroying personal possessions found therein, without allowing inmates to observe those searches, deprives inmates of property without due process of law. On the record before us, I think respondents' claim is meritorious.

One of the purposes of the Due Process Clause is to reduce the incidence of error in deprivations of life, liberty, or property. See Fuentes v. Shevin, 407 U.S. 67, 80 -81 (1972). One of the ways such error can be reduced, in turn, is by allowing persons whose interests may be affected adversely by government decisions to participate in those decisions. In Mathews v. Eldridge, 424 U.S. 319 (1976), the Court identified a complex of considerations that are helpful in determining whether the Constitution mandates such participation in particular contexts:

"[I]dentification of the specific dictates of due process generally requires consideration of three distinct factors: First, the private interest that will be affected by the official action; second, the risk of an erroneous deprivation of such interest through the procedures used, and the probable value, if any, of additional or substitute procedural safeguards; and finally, the Government's interest, including the function involved and the fiscal and administrative burdens that the additional or substitute procedural requirement would entail." Id., at 335.

Application of these factors to the facts of the instant case provides strong support for the judgment of the courts below. As the District Court aptly observed, the private interests affected by the jail's cell-search procedure are important. "The possessions that a man is allowed to keep in his cell are meager indeed, being limited to things like a few pictures, magazines, cigarettes, candy bars, and perhaps an extra pair of socks. Nonetheless, these items are cherished by the inmates." App. to Pet. for Cert. 27-28. 18 Next, the District Court found that the risk, under the jail's current policy, that inmates' possessions will be destroyed unnecessarily is substantial. Unannounced shakedown searches inevitably are somewhat hasty, and the officers conducting them have significant discretion in deciding what to leave and what to confiscate. Id., at 28. If allowed to observe the process, inmates can persuade the officers to preserve possessions that would otherwise be destroyed. Ibid. 19 Finally, to allow detainees to witness searches of their cells would impose only slight burdens on the jail officials. In response to the District Court's original order, petitioners developed alternative methods of conducting shakedown searches, each of which made it possible for inmates to be present. One of those procedures, known as "Method C," proved to be no less effectual, no more time-consuming, and only slightly more expensive than the practice challenged by respondents. 20 The demonstrated feasibility 21 and minor cost of this option renders indefensible, in my view, petitioners' insistence that detainees not be permitted to observe cell searches.

In sum, this seems a classic instance in which an "established state procedure," as distinguished from "a random and unauthorized act by a state employee," has the effect of causing unnecessary deprivations of private property. Compare Logan v. Zimmerman Brush Co., 455 U.S. 422, 435 -436 (1982), with Hudson v. Palmer, ante, p. 517, and Parratt v. Taylor, 451 U.S. 527, 541 (1981). In view of the ease with which petitioners could implement an alternative procedure that would reduce the incidence of wanton destruction of inmates' possessions, I would affirm the judgment of the courts below that the jail's current practice violates the Due Process Clause. 22

I respectfully dissent.

Notes

[1] The Wolfish plaintiffs did assert various other rights in challenging specific conditions in their prison. See, e. g., 441 U.S., at 548 -552 (First Amendment); id., at 555-557 (Fourth Amendment). But the Court did not consider those particular interests in formulating its general standard (on which the Court relies today) for determining the constitutionality, under the Due Process Clause, of the treatment of pretrial detainees. See id., at 530, 534-535.

[2] It should be stressed that, while most of the jail inmates are detained for only brief periods of time (and thus are not covered by the District Court's order), some are detained for very substantial periods. For example, plaintiffs Rutherford and Taylor were held in the jail pending their trials for 38 months and 32 months, respectively. App. 53.

[3] See, e. g., Zemans & Cavan, Marital Relationships of Prisoners, 49 J. Crim. L., C. & P. S. 50 (1958); Note, On Prisoners and Parenting: Preserving the Tie that Binds, 87 Yale L. J. 1408, 1416, 1424 (1978).

[4] See Jones v. Diamond, 636 F.2d 1364, 1377 (CA5), cert. granted sub nom. Ledbetter v. Jones, 452 U.S. 959, cert. dism'd, 453 U.S. 950 (1981); Boudin v. Thomas, 533 F. Supp. 786, 792-793 (SDNY 1982) (pointing out, inter alia, that, when an inmate's child is too young to talk, denial of contact visitation is the equivalent of denial of any visitation whatsoever); Rhem v. Malcolm, 371 F. Supp. 594, 602-603 (SDNY), aff'd, 507 F.2d 333 (CA2 1974).

[5] See Bellotti v. Baird, 443 U.S. 622, 638 (1979) (plurality opinion); Meyer v. Nebraska, 262 U.S. 390, 402 (1923).

[6] See Moore v. East Cleveland, 431 U.S. 494, 506 (1977) (plurality opinion); Pierce v. Society of Sisters, 268 U.S. 510, 535 (1925).

[7] See Smith v. Organization of Foster Families, 431 U.S. 816, 844 (1977); Stanley v. Illinois, 405 U.S. 645, 652 (1972).

[8] Cf. Schall v. Martin, 467 U.S. 253, 291, n. 15 (1984) (MARSHALL, J., dissenting) (suggesting a test under which "the strength of the state interest needed to legitimate a statute [would depend] upon the degree to which the statute encroaches upon fundamental rights") (emphasis in original; citation omitted); Bell v. Wolfish, 441 U.S. 520, 569 -571 (1979) (MARSHALL, J., dissenting).

[9] See, e. g., Procunier v. Martinez, 416 U.S. 396 (1974) (freedom of speech); Lee v. Washington, 390 U.S. 333 (1968) (per curiam) (equal protection of the laws); cf. Wolff v. McDonnell, 418 U.S. 539, 555 -556 (1974) ("There is no iron curtain drawn between the Constitution and the prisons of this country").

[10] Cf. Bell v. Wolfish, supra, at 535, n. 16 (pretrial detainees, unlike sentenced inmates, may not be punished).

[11] See, e. g., Zablocki v. Redhail, 434 U.S. 374, 387 (1978) (invalidating a statute that, as applied to most persons, seriously intruded upon, but did not abrogate, the right to marry); Cleveland Board of Education v. LaFleur, 414 U.S. 632, 640 (1974) (striking down administrative regulations that imposed a "heavy burden" on teachers' right to have children).

[12] Respondents contend that, even if this case were controlled by the standard enunciated in Wolfish, they should prevail, because petitioners have not advanced even a "legitimate governmental objective" in support of the jail's policy. Because of the manner in which I approach the case, I need not address respondents' argument on this score.

[13] The majority implies that the intrusiveness of some of these measures provides an additional justification for petitioners' refusal to allow any contact visitation. See ante, at 588, n. 9. It is possible that some inmates or visitors might decide to forgo visitation rather than submit to such procedures, but surely the choice should be left to them.

[14] It should be pointed out that drugs and weapons enter the jail in significant

quantities through several other routes. See Tr. 3307, 4526-4527; cf. id., at 4589-4590, 4624-4625 (describing similar problems at other institutions). It would thus be a mistake to think that the jail is currently free of contraband, and that the small amounts that might enter the facility through contact visitation would infect the facility for the first time.

[15] For example, Arnett Gaston, Warden of the New York City Men's House of Detention (Riker's Island), testified that significant physical confrontations have been largely absent from his facility. Id., at 4368. Lloyd Patterson, Superintendent of Deuel Vocational Institution for 10 years, testified that he could recall only three or four incidents during that period. Id., at 4589. Mr. Nagel, drawing on his 11 years of experience in the New Jersey prison system and visits to more than 350 other institutions, corroborated those observations. Id., at 4167-4168.

[16] Lieutenant Thomas Lonergan testified at trial that, at present, the identities and backgrounds of 70% of the inmates are ascertained within three weeks of their admission. Id., at 4450-4451.

[17] The feasibility of the limited contact visitation program ordered by the District Court is further suggested by the number of other institutions that have similar programs. Approximately 80% of the inmates in the California prison system are permitted contact visitation. Id., at 4587. It appears that the current policy of the Federal Bureau of Prisons is to allow visitation privileges to both convicted inmates and pretrial detainees. See id., at 1955. In New York City, all except identifiably dangerous pretrial detainees are permitted contact visits with their families. Id., at 4339, 4362. (Indeed, the agency that oversees the operation of the city's detention facilities has filed a brief contending that contact visitation is feasible and that its denial must be deemed punitive. Brief for New York City Board of Correction as Amicus Curiae 9-29.)

[18] Cf. Hudson v. Palmer, ante, at 542 (STEVENS, J., concurring in part and dissenting in part) ("Personal letters, snapshots of family members, a souvenir, a deck of cards, a hobby kit, perhaps a diary or a training manual for an apprentice in a new trade, or even a Bible - a variety of inexpensive items may enable a prisoner to maintain contact with some part of his past and an eye to the possibility of a better future").

[19] This last finding is based in part on the District Court Judge's visit to the jail:

"My own limited observation, as is mentioned in my memorandum of February 15, 1979, revealed an instance upon which the opportunity for a prisoner to make a plea or an explanation on his own behalf resulted in saving his property from confiscation. It was obvious that this fact meant a good deal to him, and I believe that the incident justifies a significant generalization." App. to Pet. for Cert. 28; see id., at 36.

[20] The District Court described this procedure, and compared it with the jail's present policy, as follows:

"Method A involved searching all of the cells in a row while the inmates remained in the day room, which is the manner in which searches currently are conducted. In Method C, the men occupying a particular cell were brought from the day room and stood outside their cell while it was being searched. When such search was completed, the men were locked in their cell and the remaining cells were searched successively in the same manner. Methods B and D are so unsatisfactory and expensive that no further comment concerning them is indicated.

"According to the statistics reported by the defendants, Methods A and C take substantially the same amount of time, and C is slightly more expensive, due to the need to utilize a few more deputies to escort the prisoners and to insure against assault upon the deputies that are engaged in searching the cell." Id., at 35-36; see Tr. 4122-4143 (testimony of Deputy Sheriff Lombardi).

[21] In their brief, petitioners object to Method C on one ground they did not press below. Relying on a single comment made at trial by Deputy Sheriff Lombardi, petitioners contend that detainees, if allowed to observe cell searches, would learn where they could hide contraband with impunity. Id., at 4116. Deputy Lombardi offered no substantiation for her prediction and indeed, when summarizing petitioners' objections to Method C, did not consider this point important enough even to mention. See id., at 4132-4133. Especially in the absence of any finding on this issue by the District Court, petitioners' bald contention seems to me entitled to little weight.

[22] Cf. Hudson v. Palmer, ante, at 541, n. 4 (STEVENS, J., concurring in part and dissenting in part) (observing that the holding of the Court in Hudson does not cover "cases in which it is contended that the established prison procedures themselves create an unreasonable risk that prisoners will be unjustifiably deprived of their property").

Mandatory registration for military service violates self-incrimination and equal protection: Justice Marshall's dissent in Selective Service System v. Minnesota Public Interest Research Group (July 5, 1984)

JUSTICE MARSHALL, dissenting.

In 1980, after a 5-year suspension, the United States Government reinstituted registration for military service. By Presidential Proclamation, all men born after January 1, 1960, were required to register with the Selective Service System within 30 days of their 18th birthday. [1] The issue in this case is not whether Congress has authority to implement the law, but whether the method it has chosen to do so offends constitutional guarantees of individual rights. I conclude that § 12(f) fails to pass constitutional muster on two grounds. First, it compels self-incrimination, in violation of the Fifth Amendment. Second, it violates the right to equal protection of the laws guaranteed under the Due Process Clause of that Amendment.

I

At the time of the enactment of the statute before the Court today, Congress understood that, of the draft-eligible population of 9,039,000 men, some 674,000 had failed to register, and many more registrants had failed to provide current mailing addresses. [2] Explanations for this widespread dereliction of legal duty have been as varied as the proposals to obtain full compliance. Testifying at oversight hearings, Government officials have told Congress that most nonregistrants are "uninformed of the requirement or are unaware of the importance of registration," [3] while only "a relatively small number of nonregistrants have knowingly' neglected their duty." [4] Private organizations have testified that noncompliance with the Selective Service law "is grounded in registration's violation of individual conscience and its infringement of religious freedom"; [5] that they oppose draft registration as a "massive government surveillance system" in which the Government collects, stores, and exchanges data on individuals in violation of constitutional and statutory rights; [6] and that many cannot register as a matter of conscience because current regulations prohibit them from adjudicating their conscientious objector status prior to induction. [7]

Both the agency and Congress have crafted strategies to increase compliance with the law, such as increasing publicity programs, declaring a grace period when nonregistrants could comply without fear of prosecution, and posting lists of registrants in their local post offices. [8] To identify and locate nonregistrants, Selective Service has collected Social Security numbers on draft registration forms, and located nonregistrants through computer data bank sharing with the Department of Health and Human Services and through mail forwarding by the Internal Revenue Service. [9] Several persons have been prosecuted for their failure to register, and the names of others have been forwarded to the Department of Justice for investigation and possible prosecution; the attendant publicity is seen by the agency as an effective method of communicating the duty to register and the seriousness of the failure to do so. [10]

It is in this context that Congress considered and adopted the statute before the Court, which was introduced on the floor by Representative Solomon and Senator Hayakawa as a rider to the Department of Defense Authorization Act of 1983. Section 1113(a) added a new subsection to the "Offenses and Penalties" section of the Military Selective Service Act. 50 U.S.C.App. 462(f). The statute creates ineligibility for any form of assistance or benefit provided under Title IV of the Higher Education Act of 1965 (20 U.S.C. § 1070 et seq.) for any person required to register who fails to do so, 50 U.S.C.App. § 462(f)(1), and requires those persons to file with their post-secondary institution a "statement of compliance" with the draft registration requirement, 50 U.S.C.App. § 453. § 462(f)(2). As the Court holds today, the purpose of this statute was not to penalize nonregistrants, but to encourage compliance with the legal duty to provide information to the Selective Service System.

It is tempting to succumb to the comfortable conclusions the majority draws after its glancing review of this legislation. After all, the Government has an explicit constitutional duty to provide for the common defense. "[I]n a free society," as Congress has declared,

"the obligations and privileges of serving in the armed forces and the reserve components thereof should be shared generally, in accordance with a system of selection which is fair and just. . . ."

§ 451(c). The statute at issue has something to do with promoting full compliance with the registration law, which in turn promotes fairness in allocating burdens in the event of reinstitution of involuntary induction. Much of the legislative rhetoric promoting § 12(f) seems unexceptional: youth should accept the obligations as well as the privileges of a democracy. [11] Nevertheless, mindful that "[i]t is the duty of courts to be watchful for the constitutional rights of the citizen, and against any stealthy encroachments thereon," Boyd v. United States, 116 U. S. 616, 116 U. S. 634-635 (1886), I must dissent.

II

I do not have to disagree with the majority that § 12(f) does not violate the constitutional prohibition against bills of attainder. That holding depends on construing the statute to permit late registration, ante at 468 U. S. 849-851, which in turn depends on construing Congress' intent as encouragement of compliance with the Selective Service registration requirement. Ante at 468 U. S. 854. The majority emphasizes the "nonpunitive spirit" of the legislation implicit in the fact that Congress "allowed all nonregistrants to qualify for Title IV aid simply by registering late." Ante at 468 U. S. 855. Congress did not, however, grant immunity from criminal prosecution for that act of late registration. Absent such a grant, § 12(f) must be struck because it compels self-incrimination.

The Fifth Amendment privilege against coerced self-incrimination extends to every means of government information gathering. Lefkowitz v. Turley, 414 U. S. 70, 414 U. S. 77 (1973); Murphy v. Waterfront Comm'n, 378 U. S. 52, 378 U. S. 90 (1964) (WHITE, J., concurring); Counselman v. Hitchcock, 142 U. S. 547, 142 U. S. 562 (1892). In our regulatory state, the line between permissible conditioning of the Government's taxing and spending power and impermissible Government coercion of information that presents a real threat of self-incrimination is not easy to identify. But I am confident the line has been crossed here. [12]

I do not take issue with the majority's conclusion, ante at 468 U. S. 856-857, that the Title IV application process itself does not require a student to divulge incriminating information to the educational institution. [13] The neutrality of this compliance verification system is central to the majority's acceptance of the permissible, regulatory purpose of the statute. However, our inquiry cannot stop there. Although § 12(f) does not coerce an admission of nonregistration, it does coerce registration with the Selective Service System, and hence individual reporting of self-incriminatory information directly to the Federal Government.

If appellees were to register with Selective Service now so that they could submit statements of compliance to obtain financial aid for their schooling, they would still be in violation of federal law, for, by registering late, they would not have submitted to registration "in accordance with any proclamation" issued under § 3 of the Military Selective Service Act, 50 U.S.C.App. § 453. § 462(f)(1). Failure to comply with Selective

Service registration requirements within 30 days of one's 18th birthday is a felony, punishable by imprisonment for up to five years and/or a fine of up to $10,000. 50 U.S.C.App. § 462(a).

A student who registers late provides the Government with two crucial links in the chain of evidence necessary to prosecute him criminally. Cf. Marchetti v. United States, 390 U. S. 39, 390 U. S. 48, and n. 9 (1968). First, he supplies the Government with proof of two elements of a violation: his birth date and date of registration. Second, and perhaps more importantly, he calls attention to the fact that he is one of the 674,000 young men in technical violation of the Military Selective Service Act. Armed with these data, the Government need prove only that the student "knowingly" failed to register at the time prescribed by law in order to obtain a conviction. 50 U.S.C.App. § 462(a). When students, such as appellees in this case, have acknowledged their awareness of their legal duty to register, App. 11-12, 24-25, the Government could prosecute the commission of a felony.

There can be little doubt that a late registration creates a "real and appreciable" hazard of incrimination and prosecution, and that the risk is not "so improbable that no reasonable man would suffer it to influence his conduct." Brown v. Walker, 161 U. S. 591, 161 U. S. 599-600 (1896). In their brief to this Court, for example, the appellants explicitly acknowledge that, although

"failure to register within [30 days of one's 18th birthday] does not disqualify the registrant for Title IV aid, it is a criminal offense punishable under 50 U.S.C.App. (& Supp. V) 462."

Brief for Appellants 17, n. 7. The Government thus appears to reserve the right to use information obtained by the leverage of withholding education aid as a basis for criminal prosecution. Communications with registering men convey the same message. For example, both the "Registration Form," SSS Form 1, and the "Acknowledgement Letter," SSS Form 3A, which is mailed to men as legal proof of compliance with Selective Service registration requirements, advise registrants that the information they have provided

"may be furnished to the . . . Department of Justice -- for review and processing of suspected violations of the Military Selective Service Act . . . [and to the] Federal Bureau of Investigation -- for location of an individual when suspected of violation of the Military Selective Service Act."

Finally, recent Government actions have acknowledged the realistic potential for prosecution. For example, President Reagan declared a "grace period" in the first months of 1982, in which men could register without penalty. [14] The obvious implication of this declaration is that, once the grace period expires, late registrants will be prosecuted. All of these governmental actions confirm the serious risk of self-incrimination and prosecution inherent in the act of late registration. [15]

Having established that late registration is an incriminating act, the question to be asked is whether the Government has exercised its powers in a way that deprives appellees of the freedom to refrain from self-incrimination through late registration. Garrity v. New Jersey, 385 U. S. 493, 385 U. S. 496 (1967); Malloy v. Hogan, 378 U. S. 1, 378 U. S. 8 (1964). When the Government extracts incriminating information by the leverage of the threat of penalties, including the "threat of substantial economic sanction," Lefkowitz v. Turley, 414 U.S. at 414 U. S. 82-83, the information is not volunteered. Thus, our cases have found coercion in statutes that extracted information through the threat of termination of state employment, Garrity v. New Jersey, supra; Uniformed Sanitation Men Assn., Inc. v. Commissioner of Sanitation, 392 U. S. 280 (1968); Gardner v. Broderick, 392 U. S. 273 (1968), through the threat of exclusion of a person from a profession, Spevack v. Klein, 385 U. S. 511 (1967), or through the threat of exclusion from participation in government contracts, Lefkowitz v. Turley, supra.

The threat of the denial of student aid is substantial economic coercion, and falls within the ambit of these cases. For students who had received federal education aid before enactment of § 12(f), termination of aid is coercive, because it could force these students to curtail their studies, thereby forfeiting their investment in prior education and abandoning their hopes for obtaining a degree. Five of the six appellees in these cases fall into this category. App. 11-12, 24-25. Students who have not previously received federal aid may also be coerced by § 12(f). All students understand that entry into most professions and technical trades requires post-secondary education. For students who cannot otherwise afford this education, compliance with § 12(f) is coerced by the threat of foreclosing future employment opportunities. All of the appellees have stated that their own career plans require them to complete a college education. Ibid.; see also id. at 16, 29.

By withholding federal aid and the opportunity to obtain post-secondary education, § 12(f) levies a substantial burden on students who have failed to register with the Selective Service System. This statutory provision coerces students into incriminating themselves by filing late registration forms. As the Court noted in Garrity v. New Jersey, supra, at 385 U. S. 497, the

"option to lose their means of livelihood or to pay the penalty of self-incrimination is the antithesis of free choice to speak out or to remain silent."

I therefore completely agree with appellees that this enforcement mechanism violates the Fifth Amendment's proscription against self-incrimination as interpreted in our previous cases, and would strike the provision down on this ground alone. [16]

Moreover, I do not understand the Court today to dispute that § 12(f) raises serious Fifth Amendment problems. The Court concedes that it would be incriminating for appellees to register with the Selective Service now. Ante at 468 U. S. 857. The Court furthermore strongly suggests that appellees could exercise their Fifth Amendment rights if they did register, cf. Garner v. United States, 424 U. S. 648 (1976), and that the Government could not compel their answers at that point without immunization. Ante at 468 U. S. 858. [17] The majority incorrectly assumes, however, that appellees must claim their privilege against self-incrimination before they can raise a Fifth Amendment claim in this lawsuit. What the majority fails to recognize is that it would be just as incriminating for appellees to exercise their privilege against self-incrimination when they registered as it would be to fill out the form without exercising the privilege. [18] The barrier to prosecuting Military Selective Service Act violators is not so much the Government's inability to discover a birth date or date of registration as the difficulty in identifying the 674,000 nonregistrants. The late registrant who "takes the Fifth" on SSS Form 1 calls attention to himself as much as, if not more than, a late registrant who marks down his birth date and date of registration.

In Marchetti v. United States, 390 U. S. 39 (1968), and the related case of Grosso v. United States, 390 U. S. 62 (1968), the Court faced a similar situation, in which complying with a federal registration requirement was the practical equivalent of confessing to a crime. In those cases, federal law required persons engaged in the business of accepting wagers to register and pay an occupational and excise tax. Compliance did not exempt the gambler from any penalties for conducting his business, which was widely prohibited under federal and state law, and the information obtained if he did comply was readily available to assist the authorities in enforcing those penalties. Petitioners failed to file the required forms because they feared that they would be prosecuted for gambling if they revealed their activities to the Federal Government; they were convicted of willful failure to do so. The Court reversed the convictions, holding invalid a "statutory system . . . utilized to pierce the anonymity of citizens engaged in criminal activity." Grosso v. United States, supra, at 390 U. S. 76 (BRENNAN, J., concurring). The Court recognized that, by filing an incomplete form or explicitly invoking their Fifth Amendment privilege on the form itself, petitioners would incriminate themselves by informing the Government that they were involved in illegal gambling activities. The Court therefore ruled that petitioners could exercise their Fifth Amendment rights by making "a claim' by silence," Garner v. United States, supra, at 424 U. S. 659, n. 11, and refraining from filing the required forms.

The Marchetti-Grosso Court based its holding in part on the fact that the information-gathering scheme was directed at those "inherently suspect of criminal activities." Marchetti v. United States, supra, at 390 U. S. 47. Here, it is fair to say that the Government does not expect that most registrants will be in violation of the Selective Service laws. At first blush, the required information might therefore seem less like the Marchetti-Grosso inquiries and more like income tax returns, "neutral on their face and directed at the public at large." Albertson v. Subversive Activities Control Board, 382 U. S. 70, 382 U. S. 79 (1965). In Garner v. United States, supra, at 424 U. S. 661, the Court noted that the great majority of persons who file income tax returns do not incriminate themselves by disclosing the information required by the Government. Because the Government has no reason to anticipate incriminating responses when requiring citizens' self-reporting of answers to neutral regulatory inquiries, our cases put the burden of asserting a Fifth Amendment privilege on the speaker, and the right to make a claim by silence is not available.

To adopt this analogy, however, is to ignore the actual case or controversy before the Court. When Congress passed § 12(f), its focus was assuredly not prospective. As the majority explains, Congress forged the link between education aid and Selective Service registration in order to bring into compliance with the law the 674,000 existing nonregistrants, including the six appellees in these cases. Ante at 468 U. S. 849-850, and n. 4. Although, as a general matter, it is correct to say that registration is like an income tax return (neutral on its face and directed to the (male) population at large), § 12(f)-compelled late registration is directed to a group inherently suspect of criminal activity, squarely presenting a Marchetti issue.

In my view, therefore, young men who have failed to register with Selective Service, and at whom § 12(f) was substantially aimed, are entitled to the same "claim by silence" as Marchetti and Grosso. But these students are compelled to forgo that right under this statutory scheme. The defect in § 12(f) is that it denies students seeking federal aid the freedom to withhold their identities from the Federal Government. If appellees assert their Fifth Amendment privilege by their silence, they are penalized for exercising a constitutional right by the withholding of education aid. If they succumb to the economic coercion either by registering, or by registering but claiming the privilege as to particular disclosures, they have incriminated themselves.

Thus, I cannot accept the majority's view that appellees' Fifth Amendment claims are not ripe for review. If the Court is suggesting that appellees must wait until they are prosecuted for late registration before adjudication of their claim, that

"is, in effect, to contend that they should be denied the protection of the Fifth Amendment privilege intended to relieve claimants of the necessity of making a choice between incriminating themselves and risking serious punishments for refusing to do so."

Albertson v. Subversive Activities Control Board, supra, at 367 U. S. 76. As in Albertson, where a federal statute required members of the Communist Party to register, appellees are put to the choice of registering, without a decision on the merits of their constitutional privilege claim, or not registering and suffering a penalty. A nonregistrant's most efficacious opportunity to exercise his privilege against self-incrimination without simultaneously compromising that privilege is to challenge § 12(f) anonymously, as appellees have done in this case.

In sum, appellees correctly state that this law coerces them into self-incrimination in the face of a substantial risk of prosecution. That risk should be cured by a statutory grant of immunity. See Minnesota v. Murphy, 465 U. S. 420, 465 U. S. 429, and 465 U. S. 435-436, n. 7 (1984) (opinion of the Court); id. at 465 U. S. 442 (MARSHALL, J., dissenting). The grant would confirm that Congress' intent in passing § 12(f) was not to punish nonregistrants, but to promote compliance with the registration requirement. The Government

"may validly insist on answers to even incriminating questions . . . as long as it recognizes that the required answers may not be used in a criminal proceeding, and thus eliminates the threat of incrimination."

Minnesota v. Murphy, supra, at 465 U. S. 436, n. 7, and cases cited therein. See also Counselman v. Hitchcock, 142 U.S. at 142 U. S. 564-565, 585-586. The Government has a substantial interest in obtaining information to assure complete and accurate Selective Service registration, but obtaining it under the compulsion of § 12(f), which is "capable of forcing the self-incrimination which the Amendment forbids," Lefkowitz v. Cunningham, 431 U. S. 801, 431 U. S. 806 (1977), is unconstitutional in the absence of immunity for the compelled disclosures. If Congress enacted § 12(f) to encourage compliance with registration requirements, and not to identify and punish late registrants, the constitutional legislative purpose would be fulfilled without implicating students' Fifth Amendment privilege against self-incrimination.

III

The aspect of the law that compels self-incrimination is doubly troubling because a discrete subgroup of nonregistrants bears the brunt of the statute. The Federal Government has a duty under the Due Process Clause of the Fifth Amendment to guarantee to all its citizens the equal protection of the laws. Rostker v. Goldberg, 453 U. S. 57 (1981); Bolling v. Sharpe, 347 U. S. 497 (1954). Section 12(f), in my view, violates that constitutional duty.

The majority's superficial, indeed cavalier, rejection of appellees' equal protection argument, ante at 468 U. S. 858, n. 16, demonstrates once again a "callous indifference to the realities of life for the poor," Flagg Bros., Inc. v. Brooks, 436 U. S. 149, 436 U. S. 166 (1978) (MARSHALL, J., dissenting), and the inadequacy of the Court's analytical structure in this area of law. We should look to

"the character of the classification in question, the relative importance to individuals in the class discriminated against of the governmental benefits that they do not receive, and the asserted state [or federal] interests in support of the classification."

Dandridge v. Williams, 397 U. S. 471, 397 U. S. 521 (1970) (MARSHALL, J., dissenting). See also San Antonio Independent School District v. Rodriguez, 411 U. S. 1, 411 U. S. 98-99 (1973) (MARSHALL, J., dissenting). As a majority of the Court has noted,

"the courts are called upon to decide whether Congress, acting under an explicit constitutional grant of authority, has by that action transgressed an explicit guarantee of individual rights which limits the authority so conferred,"

and labels "may all too readily become facile abstractions used to justify a result." Rostker v. Goldberg, supra, at 453 U. S. 70.

The majority is factually incorrect when it states that the statute at issue in this case treats all nonregistrants alike. "Only low-income and middle-income students will be caught in this trap," as was pointed out in floor debate on § 12(f). 128 Cong.Rec. 18356 (1982) (remarks of Rep. Moffett).

Title IV education aid is awarded on the basis of need. See 20 U.S.C. § 1089 (need analysis) and accompanying regulations. Although federal education aid is significant for a large segment of post-secondary students, more than three out of four post-secondary students dependent on family incomes under $6,000 are receiving Title IV aid. U.S. Dept.

of Education, Office of Student Financial Assistance, OSFA Program Book 18 (July 1981) (hereinafter OSFA Program Book). [19] In contrast, only 8% of students dependent on families with incomes over $30,000 receive any Department of Education-funded financial aid. Ibid. In the Basic Educational Opportunity Grant Program (now known as Pell Grants), 83.1% of the recipients are dependent on families with incomes of less than $12,000. Id. at 27. In the State Student Incentive Program, 69.4% of the recipients are in this category. Id. at 78 (figures for fiscal year 1977). It is therefore absurd to state that § 12(f) "treats all nonregistrants alike, denying aid to both the poor and the wealthy." Ante at 468 U. S. 859, n. 17. The wealthy do not require, are not applying for, and do not receive federal education assistance, and therefore are not subject to the requirement that they file statements that they have complied with the Selective Service registration requirement, nor to the economic compulsion to provide incriminating facts to the Government in the act of late registration. [20] Yet the obligation to comply with the law, and the failure to do so, know no economic distinction.

As appellees argued in the District Court and in their brief to this Court, by linking draft compliance with education aid, Congress has created a de facto classification based on wealth, [21] and has laid an unequal hand on those who have committed precisely the same offense of failing to register with the Selective Service within 30 days of their 18th birthday. Cf. Yick Wo v. Hopkins, 118 U. S. 356, 118 U. S. 373-374 (1886). Further, § 12(f) clearly burdens these individuals' interest in access to education, which "provides the basic tools by which individuals might lead economically productive lives to the benefit of us all." Plyler v. Doe, 457 U. S. 202, 457 U. S. 221 (1982). Many of our cases have stressed the extraordinary nature of the individual's interest in education. See, e.g., Plyler v. Doe, supra, at 457 U. S. 234, 457 U. S. 236 (BLACKMUN, J., concurring); Vlandis v. Kline, 412 U. S. 441, 412 U. S. 459 (1973) (WHITE, J., concurring in judgment). I continue to believe that interest to be fundamental because of the relationship education bears to our most basic constitutional values. See, e.g., Martinez v. Bynum, 461 U. S. 321, 461 U. S. 346 (1983) (dissenting opinion); Plyler v. Doe, supra, at 457 U. S. 230-231 (concurring opinion). I have written at length to explain my position, San Antonio Independent School District v. Rodriguez, 411 U.S. at 411 U. S. 110-117, and need not repeat the analysis here. [22]

Declining to look at how § 12(f) actually works, the majority is satisfied not only that the statute does not disfavor any classification, but also that it

"is rationally related to the legitimate Government objectives of encouraging registration and fairly allocating scarce federal resources."

Ante at 468 U. S. 859, n. 17. But can Congress' admittedly important interest in enforcing the Military Selective Service Act justify unleashing a dual system for its enforcement? While all nonregistrants are subject to imprisonment and fine, only those nonregistrants who qualify for education aid based on need are subjected both to that criminal process and to the economic compulsion imposed by the loss of financial aid. Federal courts cannot overlook the fact that Congress' "understandable indignation" at nonregistrants, ante at 468 U. S. 856, n. 15, focused on a discrete subgroup.

If we accept that the purpose of § 12(f) is to promote compliance with Selective Service registration, then we must also consider the fit between the law and its object. The universe of nonregistrants at the time of this legislation was understood to be more than half a million men. The majority does not offer any support for its statement that "[t]hose who fail to register . . . are a significant part of the class to which Title IV assistance is otherwise offered." Ante at 468 U. S. 854, n. 13. See Tr. of Oral Arg. 11 (Government has no information on number of nonregistrants who are receiving financial aid).

We should reject the suggestion that the putative age-group overlap between the group required to register with Selective Service and the group pursuing post-secondary education is sufficient justification for this law. While it is true that the Equal Protection Clause does not require that legislatures resolve either all or none of a problem, Railway Express Agency, Inc. v. New York, 336 U. S. 106, 336 U. S. 110 (1949), it is also true that

"nothing opens the door to arbitrary action so effectively as to allow . . . officials to pick and choose only a few to whom they will apply legislation, and thus to escape the political retribution that might be visited upon them if larger numbers were affected."

Id. at 336 U. S. 112-113 (Jackson, J., concurring). When the law lays an unequal hand on those who have committed precisely the same offense, the discrimination is invidious. Cf. Skinner v. Oklahoma ex rel. Williamson, 316 U. S. 535, 316 U. S. 541 (1942). Further, the adverse consequences of § 12(f) on an identifiable group are inevitable, creating a strong inference that the adverse consequences were desired. Cf. Personnel Administrator of Massachusetts v. Feeney, 442 U. S. 256, 442 U. S. 279, n. 25 (1979).

The floor debate provides support for that inference. The House sponsor of § 12(f), Representative Solomon, acknowledged criticism that the amendment singled out the disadvantaged.

"Now, maybe we are discriminating against the poor. And if we are, I guarantee I am going to come back with legislation on this floor tomorrow and the next day and the next day and every day of this session with amendments that will prohibit any funds from being used for the Job Training Act if they are not registered, for any unemployment compensation insurance if they are not registered, and for any kind of taxpayers' money if they are not registered."

128 Cong.Rec. 18366 (1982). [23] "They" are the poor -- a discrete subgroup of persons who receive financial benefits from their Government. This animus cannot be rationalized away by the argument that Congress has an important interest in the fair allocation of scarce resources. Entitlement programs of far greater scope than education aid -- for example, farm price supports -- confer benefits to a broader spectrum of economic interests, while much of our tax law -- oil depletion allowances, accelerated depreciation, capital gains, property owners' deductions -- favors the more advantaged. We can well imagine the effective political resistance that would follow Congress' conditioning rich persons' Government benefits and entitlements. I can think of no constitutionally valid purpose that would justify singling out the less advantaged for

special law enforcement attention.

Congress has enacted other, constitutional means to enforce the Selective Service registration laws, means that do not involve invidious discrimination among subclasses of lawbreakers. The right to an education is too basic, and the governmental need to discriminate among nonregistrants is too tenuous for this Court to hide behind the screen of a rational relationship test to permit the misuse of nondiscriminatory education policy to meet the unrelated goals of military service.

IV

As the District Court noted, the issue before us "turns not on whether the registration law should be enforced, but in what manner." Doe v. Selective Service System, 557 F.Supp. 937, 950 (1983). For the reasons stated above, I find § 12(f) of the Military Selective Service Act violative of the Fifth Amendment, both because it compels self-incrimination and because it violates due process by denying persons the equal protection of the laws. I respectfully dissent.

Notes

[1] Registration consists of completing SSS Form 1, available at any post office. The form requires the registrant to provide date of birth, sex, Social Security number, name, current and permanent mailing address, current telephone number, affirmation that the information provided is true, and date of that affirmation. A postal clerk date-stamps and initials the form, indicating whether the registrant produced identification. The registrant is under a continuing duty to notify Selective Service of changes in these data.

[2] Oversight Hearing on Selective Service Prosecutions before the Subcommittee on Courts, Civil Liberties, and the Administration of Justice of the House Committee on the Judiciary, 97th Cong., 2d Sess., 10 (1982) (hereinafter Oversight Hearing) (statement of Director of Selective Service, Maj. Gen. Thomas Turnage (Ret.)) (hereinafter Turnage); Attachment 17, id. at 95-105 (Report of General Accounting Office). On the floor of the House the same day, Representative Solomon estimated 93% compliance and 700,000 nonregistrants. 128 Cong.Rec. 18355-18356 (1982).

[3] Oversight Hearing, at 11 (statement of Turnage); see also id. at 7 (statement of Kenneth J. Coffey, Associate Director, (Military) Federal Personnel and Compensation Division, U.S. General Accounting Office).

[4] Id. at 10 (statement of Turnage).

[5] Id. at 47 (statement of Delton Franz for the National Interreligious Service Board for Conscientious Objectors). This group understands registration to be an integral part of conscription for war. Oversight Hearing, at 47-48. Cf. Rostker v. Goldberg, 453 U.S. 57, 453 U.S. 68 (1981) ("Congress specifically linked its consideration of registration to induction, see, e.g., S.Rep. No. 96-826, pp. 156, 160 (1980). Congressional judgments concerning registration and the draft are based on judgments concerning military operations and [combat] needs . . .").

[6] Oversight Hearing, at 35 (statement of David Landau, Legislative Counsel, American Civil Liberties Union, Washington, D.C.) (expressing concern that data collected for, e.g., tax and Social Security purposes, upon a promise of confidentiality, are being used for enforcement purposes, by exemptions from the Privacy Act of 1974, which generally prohibits data-matching among Government agencies). See also n. 9, infra.

[7] Oversight Hearing, at 34-35 (statement of Landau) (contrasting regulations under prior draft, permitting application for conscientious objector status immediately after registration, and current regulations, presumptively classifying all registrants as available for induction, and permitting application for other status only within the 10-day period after receipt of a notice of induction). See 32 CFR §§ 1624.5(a), 1633.2(h), 1633.3 (1983). See also Oversight Hearing, at 42-43 (testimony of Rev. Barry Lynn, President, Draft Action).

[8] Id. at 81-82 (statement of Turnage).

[9] After a class action successfully challenged agency practice as a violation of the Privacy Act of 1974, § 2, note following 5 U.S.C. § 552a (statutory authorization required to collect Social Security numbers), Congress amended the Military Selective Service Act to require registrants to provide Social Security numbers. Department of Defense Authorization Act of 1982, Pub.L. 97-86, § 916, 95 Stat. 1129, 50 U.S.C.App. § 453. See Wolman v. United States, 542 F.Supp. 84 (DC 1982). Pub.L. 97-86 also authorized the President to require the Secretary of Health and Human Services to furnish the Director of Selective Service, for enforcement purposes, the name, date of birth, Social Security number, and address of any person required to register for the draft. 50 U.S.C.App. § 462(e).

The agency also has considered cooperation with nonfederal data systems, such as state drivers' licenses, and private data systems on a fee basis. Oversight Hearing, at 84.

[10] Id. at 13-14 (statement of Lawrence Lippe, Criminal Division, Department of Justice) (159 persons, self-identified nonregistrants or reported by others, referred to United States Attorneys for possible prosecution; Department "keeping in close touch" with Selective Service as it begins active enforcement program through use of Social Security and other records). The Court has granted certiorari in Wayte v. United States, 467 U.S. 1214 (1984), to consider the First Amendment challenge to the Government's program of investigating and prosecuting persons identified through their vocal opposition to draft registration.

[11] See 128 Cong.Rec. 9665 (1982) (remarks of Sen. Hayakawa).

[12] Of course, there are other "rights of constitutional stature whose exercise [government] may not condition by the exaction of a price," Garrity v. New Jersey, 385 U.S. 493, 385 U.S. 500 (1967), such as the exercise of rights guaranteed by the First Amendment, but the posture of this appeal presents only a challenge to the burdens the legislation places on the exercise of Fifth Amendment rights.

[13] The compliance form does not require the student to state either the date of

his birth or the date of his registration. The verification of registration, SSS Form 3A, required of all students after July 1, 1985, contains a "Date of Record," which would appear not to be the date of registration. 34 CFR §§ 668.26(b), (d)(1) (1983).

[14] Registration Under the Military Selective Service Act, 18 Weekly Comp. of Pres. Doc. 8 (1982). The grace period extended from January 7 through February 28, 1982. N.Y. Times, Jan. 21, 1982, p. 14, col. 3. The Director of Selective Service, General Turnage, noted the correlation between extending immunity and encouraging registration compliance. Oversight Hearing, at 80-81 ("we have run clear off the chart"). See also id. at 5-6 (400,000 registered as a result of 2-month grace period).

[15] Appellants' contention that the threat of incrimination is speculative, and that therefore the Fifth Amendment is not implicated, rests entirely on the assertion that, under current (but concededly not "immutable") policy, prosecution for late registration is unlikely. Reply Brief for Appellants 15-16; Tr. of Oral Arg. 14. Just this Term, we acknowledged that "policy choices are made by one administration, and often reevaluated by another administration." United States v. Mendoza, 464 U. S. 154, 464 U. S. 161 (1984). Considering that the statute of limitations for Selective Service registration violations is five years from the date of compliance with the law, or, for nonregistrants, age 31, 50 U.S.C.App. § 462(d), as well as the unpredictability and wide range of public and political responses to the act of noncooperation with military service over the course of our history, a nonregistrant reasonably expects immunity for his compelled disclosures, not merely references to current policy. The hard fact is that the penalty for late registration is precisely the same as the penalty for nonregistration: a possible prison term of five years and/or a possible fine of $10,000.

[16] Of course, the general rule that a person must affirmatively assert the Fifth Amendment privilege or be deemed to have waived it, see, e.g., United States v. Kordel, 397 U. S. 1, 397 U. S. 7-10 (1970), is simply inapplicable in "the classic penalty situation [which excuses] the failure to assert the privilege." Minnesota v. Murphy, 465 U. S. 420, 465 U. S. 435, and n. 7 (1984); see also id. at 465 U. S. 443-446 (MARSHALL, J., dissenting).

[17] Appellees would have two choices: complete the registration form or note the Fifth Amendment privilege on the incomplete form. In either case, should appellees be prosecuted, they would argue that the card could not be introduced in evidence, and that the Government has the burden of proving that it made no use whatever of the incriminating disclosures. Counselman v. Hitchcock, 142 U. S. 547, 142 U. S. 585-586 (1982). They might also argue that, having claimed the Fifth Amendment on their registration card, they can in good faith certify to the educational institution that they have complied with the Selective Service requirement, and receive Title IV aid. A statutory grant of immunity would far better promote Congress' aims.

[18] Of course, the Government can always draw an incriminating inference when a person claims a Fifth Amendment privilege. In the usual case, however, the Government has, for example, subpoenaed a witness to testify, and thus has already

identified him. Whether he chooses not to appear, or appears but invokes the privilege, the Government knows of his refusal to cooperate. The appellees and other nonregistrants are not known to the Government. Therefore, invocation of the Fifth Amendment by appellees gives the Government a different quality of information.

[19] Although the OSFA Program Book is published annually, we cite to the 1981 edition because it contains the most recent statistics for distribution of federal education aid by income and ethnic group. Unless otherwise noted, the figures reported in the 1981 OSFA Program Book are for the 1978-1979 academic year.

[20] Students who are members of ethnic minority groups are especially reliant on federal assistance to obtain training beyond high school. 56.7% of Basic Educational Opportunity Grant recipients, 52.1% of Student Educational Opportunity Grant recipients, and 46.4% of Work Study grants recipients are ethnic minorities, OSFA Program Book 27, 65, 74, although these students are still a small percentage of the post-secondary student body. For example, only 14.3% of the college students in 1982 were minorities. U.S. Dept. of Commerce, Statistical Abstract of the United States 161, Table 258 (1984). Section 12(f) also penalizes only male students. In Rostker v. Goldberg, 453 U. S. 57 (1981), the Court held that gender differences influence combat roles and military needs, and therefore justify male-only draft registration. While I disagreed with that conclusion, noting that the statute "thereby categorically excludes women from a fundamental civic obligation," id. at 453 U. S. 86, even had I joined the Court, I would protest the extension of this gender classification into the area of federal education assistance, an area in which gender is irrelevant and any classification based on gender is constitutionally objectionable. Men and women are similarly situated for purposes of the allocation of education funds. That principle should not be undermined by co-opting education law to enforce criminal laws.

[21] The defects of the wealth classification are heightened because the classification is also based on youth. We would ignore our responsibility if we failed to give the statute before us most careful scrutiny. The young persons affected by this statute are in the very process of forging a means to establish their independence. Although enfranchised, they are less able to exercise their vote because of their transience and, frequently, state laws burdening student voter registration. See, e.g., N.Y. Elec.Law § 5-104 (McKinney 1978). To my mind, they are "relegated to such a position of political powerlessness as to command extraordinary protection from the majoritarian political process." San Antonio Independent School District v. Rodriguez, 411 U. S. 1, 411 U. S. 28 (1973) (opinion of the Court); United States v. Carolene Products Co., 304 U. S. 144, 304 U. S. 152, n. 4 (1938).

[22] Where our prior cases have focused particularly on the extraordinary importance to the individual of elementary and secondary education, our concern that burdening access to education creates permanent class distinctions and political disadvantage is equally relevant here. Post-secondary education is the necessary prerequisite to pursuit of countless vocations, both professional and technical.

Deprivation of a livelihood is too great a price to pay for the assertion of the Fifth Amendment privilege. Spevack v. Klein, 385 U. S. 511 (1967).

[23] See also Job Training Partnership Act, Pub.L. 97-300, § 504, 96 Stat. 1399, 29 U.S.C. § 1504. The Act is a

"new job training program for the drop-out youth who are not prepared for employment, for welfare recipients who need training to escape from dependency, [and] for the economically disadvantaged who cannot compete in the labor market without help,"

as well as for dislocated workers. S.Rep. No. 97-469, p. 1 (1982). Title 29 U.S.C. 1504 requires the Secretary of Labor to

"insure that each individual participating in any program established under this Act . . . has not violated section 3 of the Military Selective Service Act"

by not registering. See also Oversight Hearing, at 85 (remarks of Turnage) (positing linking compliance requirement with federal employment, unemployment compensation, Veterans' Administration dependency benefits, Social Security survivor's benefits, and Comprehensive Employment and Training Act programs).

His occupation is maritime employment: Justice Marshall's dissent in Herb's Welding, Inc. v. Gray (March 18, 1985)

JUSTICE MARSHALL, with whom JUSTICE BRENNAN, JUSTICE BLACKMUN, and JUSTICE O'CONNOR join, dissenting.

Today the Court holds that a marine petroleum worker is not covered by the Longshoremen's and Harbor Workers' Compensation Act (LHWCA or Act), 44 Stat. 1424, as amended, 33 U.S.C. § 901 et seq., when pursuing his occupation on a fixed offshore rig within the 3-mile limit of a State's territorial waters. Although such an individual routinely travels over water as an essential part of his job and performs the rest of his job adjacent to and surrounded by water, he is not covered because, in the Court's view, his occupation is not "maritime employment." See § 2(3), 33 U.S.C. § 902(3). The Court reaches this conclusion even though a worker of the same occupation, working in the same industry, and performing the same tasks on a rig located in the same place, would be covered if that rig were one that was capable of floating. [1] Neither the Court nor any of the parties have identified any reason why Congress might have desired this distinction. To the contrary, a principal congressional goal behind the 1972 Amendments was to rid the Act of just such arbitrary distinctions derived from traditional admiralty jurisprudence. Because the coverage pattern that the Court adopts is at odds with the Act's 1972 Amendments, and because the accident here meets the Amendments' status and situs tests, I respectfully dissent.

I

At the outset, it is useful to examine the LHWCA's general coverage pattern, and, in particular, the purposes of its 1972 Amendments. Before 1972, LHWCA coverage was determined largely by the traditional "locality" test of maritime tort jurisdiction. Under that test, if an accident occurred on the navigable waters (which usually meant on a vessel), the worker was covered, no matter how close the accident may have been to the adjoining land or pier; in contrast, if an accident occurred on adjoining land, a pier, or a wharf, there was only state coverage, no matter how close the accident may have been to the water's edge. See Nacirema Operating Co. v. Johnson, 396 U. S. 212 (1969). Cf. Victory Carriers v. Law, 404 U. S. 202 (1971). A longshoreman moving cargo from ship to pier was thus covered for injuries incurred on board the ship, but not for any injuries incurred after stepping onto the pier. Nacirema Operating Co., supra. See also P. C. Pfeiffer Co. v. Ford, 444 U. S. 69, 444 U. S. 72 (1979) ("A single situs requirement . . . governed the scope of [the Act's] coverage").

Behind this system of "checkered coverage" stood the reality that federal and state workers' compensation schemes usually had very different benefit levels, the state benefit levels often being inadequate. See n. 2, infra. Thus, those workers whose professional lives might require that they move back and forth between water and adjoining land -- "amphibious workers" -- and whose protection was the principal goal of the LHWCA, had to rely for workers' compensation on an imperfect amalgam of federal and state workers' compensation laws. As critics noted, the system's adequacy in any given case was a function of the pure fortuity of a work-related accident's exact location. [2]

In 1972, Congress amended the Act, expanding coverage landward as a means of rationalizing the coverage pattern. This case involves two of the principal Amendments. First, Congress expanded the situs of coverage to include those areas immediately adjacent to the water, in which maritime workers would be likely to spend a large part of their working lives. The Act would now cover

"disability or death result[ing] from an injury occurring upon the navigable waters of the United States (including any adjoining pier, wharf, dry dock, terminal, building way, marine railway, or other adjoining area customarily used by an employer in loading, unloading, repairing, or building a vessel). . . ."

§ 3(a), 33 U.S.C. § 903(a) (emphasis added). Congress thus broke with the tradition of applying the strict locality test of admiralty tort jurisdiction to limit LHWCA's coverage.

But if only the situs of coverage had been altered, a new problem would have been created. Expanding the situs landward would not only have brought uniform coverage to those occupations previously covered in part, it would also have brought within the covered situs large numbers of occupations whose members had never before been covered at all. Workers such as truckdrivers or clericals, though present on a pier at certain times as part of their employment, are engaging in purely land-bound, rather than amphibious, occupations. See Northeast Marine Terminal Co. v. Caputo, 432 U. S. 249, 432 U. S. 267 (1977); S.Rep. 13; H.R.Rep. 10-11. To expand coverage to these workers, whose work lives take them back and forth between newly covered "adjoining area[s]" and uncovered inland locations would create a serious demarcation line problem, and would also obviously recreate, and even enlarge, the problem of "checkered coverage" based on the fortuity of the exact location of a particular injury. Thus, Congress adopted a "status" test for coverage to exclude members of these land-bound occupations.

"The 1972 Amendments thus changed what had been essentially only a 'situs' test of eligibility for compensation to one looking to both the 'situs' of the injury and the 'status' of the injured."

See Caputo, supra, at 432 U. S. 264-265.

Under the "status" test, coverage was limited to those "engaged in maritime employment." § 2(3), 33 U.S.C. § 902(3):

"The term 'employee' means any person engaged in maritime employment, including any longshoreman or other person engaged in longshoring operations, and any harborworker including a ship repairman, shipbuilder, and shipbreaker. . . . [3]"

Both changes together were part of an effort to rationalize the Act's coverage pattern. Congress wanted a system that did not depend on the "fortuitous circumstance of whether the injury occurred on land or over water," S.Rep. 13; H.R.Rep. 10-11, and it wanted a "uniform compensation system to apply to employees who would otherwise be covered . . . for part of their activity." Ibid. Analyzing this case in terms of Congress' stated goals and in terms of this Court's prior efforts to give meaning to the 1972 Amendments makes clear that the Act applies to marine petroleum workers such as Gray.

Workers on fixed offshore rigs are "amphibious workers" who spend almost their entire worklife either traveling on the navigable waters or laboring on statutorily covered pier-like areas immediately adjacent thereto. They are exposed on a daily basis to hazards associated with maritime employment. And most important, given the fact that workers on floating rigs are covered by the Act, the Court's result recreates exactly the type of "incongruous" coverage distinctions that Congress specifically sought to eliminate in 1972.

II

The Court analyzes only the "maritime employment" status test, finding that that issue disposes of the case, and makes unnecessary any discussion of "situs." Although the Court starts its analysis from the premise that "[t]he Act does not define the term maritime employment,'" ante at 470 U. S. 421, its own analysis of the term is quite conclusory and inadequate. The Court focuses on traditional admiralty law's treatment of fixed petroleum platforms, as found in a 1969 admiralty decision of this Court and a 1953 statute. It thus ignores that it was precisely the desire to break with traditional admiralty law's rigid locality-based distinctions that motivated Congress' passage of the 1972 LHWCA Amendments. Although the pre-1972 law cited by the Court was specifically based on those distinctions, the Court concludes that that law "foreclose[s]" the possibility that these workers might be engaged in "maritime employment." Ibid. The Court thus offers a conclusion that comports neither with the structure of the 1972

Amendments nor with our prior cases interpreting the Amendments' purposes. Instead, it derives its conclusion from straightforward pre-1972 applications of the very admiralty law concept that the 1972 Amendments were intended to eliminate as a limit on LHWCA coverage the concept that coverage should stop at the water's edge.

A

The Court constructs its interpretation of "maritime employment" around the premise that the 1972 Congress had no desire to alter the law of Rodrigue v. Aetna Casualty & Surety Co., 395 U. S. 352 (1969), a pre-1972 admiralty case that had nothing to do with the LHWCA. In Rodrigue, wrongful-death actions were brought in admiralty under the Death on the High Seas Act, 41 Stat. 537, 46 U.S.C. § 761 et seq., when two petroleum workers were killed on fixed offshore platforms on the Outer Continental Shelf. One worker was killed using a crane on a platform to unload a barge, the other fell from a derrick high above a platform. Rodrigue presented the issue of whether admiralty jurisdiction existed with regard to these accidents, either by its own force or by force of the 1953 Outer Continental Shelf Lands Act (Lands Act), 67 Stat. 462, 43 U.S.C. § 1331 et seq. (prescribing choice of law to govern the Outer Continental Shelf). We unanimously held that traditional admiralty jurisdiction did not reach the situs of a fixed offshore rig, and that Congress, in passing the Lands Act, did not desire to alter this result.

The Rodrigue Court's reasoning as to admiralty law's inapplicability was straightforward, and is best found in a statement that has substantial irony, given the current Court's insistence that Rodrigue tells us what Congress meant in the 1972 LHWCA Amendments: the Rodrigue Court declared that

"[a]dmiralty jurisdiction has not been construed to extend to accidents on piers, jetties, bridges, or even ramps or railways running into the sea."

395 U.S. at 395 U. S. 360. Rodrigue concluded, as the Court now emphasizes, that drilling platforms have "no more connection with the ordinary stuff of admiralty than do accidents on piers.'" Ante at 470 U. S. 421-422 (quoting 395 U.S. at 395 U. S. 360). This may be so, but it is clear that the 1972 LHWCA Amendments were intended to expand LHWCA coverage well beyond the bounds of traditional admiralty law. Most obviously, they were meant to reach accidents on the very piers that Rodrigue had analogized to fixed oil platforms. § 3(a), 33 U.S.C. § 903(a). Rodrigue correctly stated that fixed platforms (like piers), are localities unconnected with "the ordinary stuff of admiralty." 395 U.S. at 395 U. S. 360. However, it is just as clear that the very purpose of the 1972 Amendments was to expand LHWCA coverage beyond the "ordinary stuff " of traditional admiralty jurisprudence. [4]

That Rodrigue's holding was based on the application of admiralty's traditional locality test cannot be doubted, and it would likely have been so understood by Congress in 1972. For example, just prior to the 1972 LHWCA Amendments' passage, this Court cited Rodrigue as one of more than 40 cases following the traditional view that,"[i]n regard to torts . . ., the jurisdiction of the admiralty is exclusively dependent upon the locality of the act." [5] Given this basis of Rodrigue, there is simply no necessary relation between that case and the meaning of the "maritime employment" status test under the post-1972 LHWCA. Rather than mandate a result in the instant case, Rodrigue is irrelevant to its disposition. [6]

B

The Court also focuses on the legislative history of the 1953 Lands Act, as discussed in Rodrigue, to show that, long before the 1972 Amendments, Congress had determined that workers on fixed platforms were not "engaged in maritime activity." Ante at 470 U. S. 422-423. But the 1953 determination was simply to provide law for the Outer Continental Shelf without altering the traditional locality test of admiralty coverage. There is no reason to assume that that decision governs the meaning of a 1972 statute that had nothing to do with the Outer Continental Shelf and was otherwise explicitly meant to alter this very admiralty rule. In that sense, the congressional intent behind the Lands Act might be as irrelevant to this case as is Rodrigue's discussion of traditional admiralty tort locality.

The irrelevance of Rodrigue's Lands Act analysis can best be seen by examining the point in the legislative history that Rodrigue most emphasized: The Lands Act Congress chose not to adopt admiralty law as the exclusive law for Outer Continental Shelf fixed platform workers because of those workers' close ties to shore communities. 395 U.S. at 395 U. S. 361-365. Those ties gave offshore workers and shore communities a shared interest in those workers' continued access to state protective legislation. Id. at 395 U. S. 362. Because of this, the Lands Act Congress viewed "maritime law [as] inapposite to . . . fixed structures," id. at 395 U. S. 363; but that supports no inference that in 1972 Congress desired to exclude these workers from the LHWCA definition of "maritime employment. "

In 1972, Congress clearly did not seek to limit LHWCA coverage according to a worker's connection to the shoreside community, and indeed, it is hard to argue that that was ever a factor limiting LHWCA coverage. First, the principal targets of both the 1972 expansion of coverage and the initial 1927 Act were longshoremen and harborworkers; both are groups significantly more closely tied to their shoreside communities than are offshore petroleum workers. [7] Second, Congress was well aware that workers on floating rigs had a long history of coverage under the LHWCA, see n. 1, supra, and yet they are not argued to be less "connected" to the shore communities than are those on fixed platforms. Third, and most important, Congress provided that post-1972 LHWCA coverage -- unlike traditional admiralty law coverage -- would not deprive a worker of access to state remedies. "[T]he 1972 extension of federal jurisdiction supplements, rather than supplants, state compensation law." Sun Ship, Inc. v. Pennsylvania, 447 U. S. 715, 447 U. S. 720 (1980). Congress thus made clear that there would be no incompatibility between "maritime" status and a close connection to the shoreside State.

In general, a close connection between an arguably "maritime" occupation and the shoreside community may very well form the basis of a decision not to exclusively apply admiralty law coverage to the affairs of that occupation. Indeed, that is just the rationale Rodrigue attributed to the Congress that passed the Lands Act. But, as is shown by the above factors, the same rationale cannot explain the coverage of the post-1972 LHWCA. [8]

Although Rodrigue's analysis of the Lands Act is largely irrelevant to the issues in the instant case, a closer examination of the Lands Act as a whole reveals that its authors held views which actually support coverage in this case. In a number of instances unrelated to the Rodrigue case, the Lands Act evidences a congressional understanding that work on fixed offshore platforms has maritime attributes. Even though the Lands Act did not generally apply admiralty law to fixed rigs on the Outer Continental Shelf, it also did not leave the law of worker safety in the exclusive hands of the States. First, it explicitly provided for LHWCA coverage of Outer Continental Shelf fixed platform workers. See 43 U.S.C. § 1333(b). While application of the LHWCA to a locale does not necessarily indicate a congressional determination that the locale's activities are in some sense "maritime," [9] the Lands Act goes substantially beyond this in indicating that there is a "maritime" component to worker safety problems on fixed oil rigs. In particular, Congress chose to vest authority for general safety regulation of fixed or floating platforms on the Outer Continental Shelf in the Coast Guard, "the agency traditionally charged with regulation and enforcement of maritime matters." Pure Oil Co. v. Snipes, 293 F.2d 60, 66 (CA5 1961). See 43 U.S.C. § 1333(d). In accordance with that authorization, the Coast Guard promptly promulgated a code of safety regulations that reflected the existence of the same sort of hazards on these rigs as one would associate with "maritime" environments. See 21 Fed.Reg. 900 (1956). [10] Thus Congress and the Coast Guard have recognized that the offshore locality of platform workers' work significantly affects their working conditions.

C

The Court's analysis in the instant case is flawed not only because it uses particularly irrelevant pre-1972 decisions to define the outer boundaries of "maritime employment," but also because its premise, that Congress understood "maritime employment" to be a clear pre-1972 concept, is itself highly suspect. In Director, OWCP v. Perini North River Associates, 459 U. S. 297 (1983), we emphasized that "maritime status" was a concept with little if any history in the LHWCA before the 1972 Amendments. See id. at 459 U. S. 307, n. 17. Its only appearance was in the requirement that an employee, to be covered, had to be employed by an employer

"any of whose employees [were] employed in maritime employment, in whole or in part, upon the navigable waters of the United States (including any dry dock)."

§ 2(4), 33 U.S.C. § 902(4) (1970 ed.). Despite this language,

"there was little litigation concerning whether an employee was in 'maritime employment' for purposes of being the employee of a statutory employer."

Perini, supra, at 459 U. S. 309-310. As a leading treatise describes the pre-1972 situation:

"Workers who are not seamen, but who nevertheless suffer injury on navigable waters, are no doubt (or so the courts have been willing to assume) engaged in 'maritime employment.' . . . [N]o one seems to have doubted that they could recover under [LHWCA], provided only that the proof satisfied the 'navigable waters' test."

G. Gilmore & C. Black, Law of Admiralty 428-430 (2d ed.1975). Thus, in 1972, there was no well-defined occupational status concept of "maritime employment" within LHWCA jurisprudence. To the extent the concept had any preexisting meaning, it implied very wide coverage of workers whose occupations required any regular presence on navigable waters. Cf. Perini, supra. [11]

III

After erroneously determining that its decision in this case is mandated by Rodrigue and the legislative history of the Lands Act, the Court turns to its formulation of a "test" for "maritime employment." Its discussion of the statutory language, legislative history, and prior Court interpretations of the "maritime employment" provision of § 2(3) is quite brief. Much of it is little more than a determination that, in our prior cases and in the legislative history, offshore drilling work was never specifically stated to be covered by the statute. See ante at 470 U. S. 423-424. Of course, none of these sources had ever purported to offer an exclusive list of covered occupations, and as the Court agrees, we have previously read the "maritime employment" concept as "not limited to the occupations specifically mentioned in § 2(3)." Ante at 470 U. S. 423. Nevertheless, the Court's analysis presumes there is little coverage outside the specific occupations listed.

The only "test" that the Court comes close to announcing seems to involve an inquiry into whether an occupation is sufficiently related to maritime commerce (which seems to be confined to ship construction and cargo moving, ante at 470 U. S. 423-424) for it to be within a class of tasks "inherently maritime." Ante at 470 U. S. 425. The Court offers no justification for why the category should be so limited, nor does it seriously evaluate whether fixed offshore rig workers could fall into the category of "maritime commerce." The content of such a category is not as self-evident as the Court assumes, [12] nor would all agree that offshore rig workers are self-evidently "nonmaritime." [13]

This "test" is adopted in spite of the fact that no prior decisions of this Court have held the status test to be so limited. Caputo and P. C. Pfeiffer Co., which the Court cites as if they had established those limits, ante at 470 U. S. 423-424, were decisions that analyzed the concept of occupational status as it applied to different aspects of longshoring operations. Although those decisions contain important discussions concerning the structure and history of the Act, the only discussions on the limits of "maritime employment" were within the particular factual setting of those cases, that is, the decisions only sought to distinguish among those occupations normally found on a pier during the loading and unloading of a ship. The decisions did not purport to limit the Act's coverage to that particular setting, nor did they try to define any precise limits for the occupational status test outside that setting.

In Perini, we held that a construction worker injured while working on a barge during the construction of a riverside sewage treatment plant was "engaged in maritime employment." Although Perini's precise holding concerned only the occupational status of a worker injured while required to be on the actual navigable waters, the necessary implications of that holding are of course not limited to the facts of that case. The Court reads Perini as having no importance to an understanding of what the term "maritime employment" might mean outside the situation where a worker is injured on the actual navigable waters. Ante at 470 U. S. 424-425, n. 10. But the statute applies the term "maritime employment" to all coverage situations, with no hint that its meaning should radically change depending on an injury's exact situs. See P. C. Pfeiffer Co., 444 U.S. at 444 U. S. 78-79. Nor does the Act's structure or language allow for an interpretation that, in effect, exempts workers injured on the actual navigable waters from the requirement that they be "engaged in maritime employment." Perini declined to rest on a rationale that focused only on the situs of the injury. It instead saw location as significant principally because an occupation's location is an aspect of the occupation's status.

"[W]e emphasize that we in no way hold that Congress meant for such employees to receive LHWCA coverage merely by meeting the situs test, and without any regard to the 'maritime employment' language. . . . We consider those employees to be 'engaged in maritime employment' not simply because they are injured in a historically maritime locale, but because they are required to perform their employment duties upon navigable waters."

459 U.S. at 459 U. S. 323-324.

Although, in the instant case, the particular injury did not occur on the actual navigable waters, and in Perini it did, Gray's work did involve his repeated and required presence on the navigable waters. Perini and its approach to the status test are thus highly relevant.

Perini is also relevant because it repeatedly refused to rest its holding on any inquiry into whether the claimant's work had a "direct" or "substantial relation" to navigation or traditional notions of maritime commerce. See Perini, 459 U.S. at 459 U. S. 311, n. 21, 459 U. S. 315, 459 U. S. 318. Such a test was urged on the Court as a test that would deny coverage to the claimant, and Perini, after extensively discussing the Act's history, see n. 11, supra, firmly concluded that the 1972 Congress did not mean to incorporate such an inquiry into the analysis of occupational status. The Court today offers an analysis quite close to that which Perini explicitly rejected.

IV

To determine whether an offshore fixed platform worker is "engaged in maritime employment," the Court should have turned to three principles that we have previously applied to such questions. First, prior cases make clear that we must interpret coverage in light of the overall purposes of the Act. A major purpose of the 1972 Amendments was to eliminate those aspects of the prior system that made coverage depend on the "fortuitous circumstance of whether the injury occurred on land or over water," S.Rep. at 13; H.R.Rep. at 10, and to provide workers with a "uniform compensation system to apply to employees who would otherwise be covered by this Act for part of their activity." Id. at 10-

11. Cf. Sun Ship, 447 U.S. at 447 U. S. 725-726 ("The legislative policy animating the LHWCA's landward shift was remedial [and] the amendments' framers acted out of solicitude for the workers").

Second, we have said that Congress' concerns in extending coverage went beyond a concern for the exact locations of any particular worker's work routine, and in that sense "maritime employment" is an "occupational, rather than a geographic, concept." P. C. Pfeiffer Co., supra, at 444 U. S. 79.

Third, we have said that a major factor in the determination of "maritime employment" is whether the members of an occupation are "required to perform their employment duties upon navigable waters." Perini, supra, at 459 U. S. 323-324.

A

In applying these principles to this case, it becomes clear that offshore fixed oil platform workers should be considered in "maritime employment." When viewed from an occupational perspective, it is a glaring fact that, unless classified as Jones Act seamen, see n. 3, supra, all offshore oil rig workers who work on floating rigs are engaged in maritime employment for LHWCA purposes, for they all must work "on the actual navigable waters." See Perini, supra, at 459 U. S. 323. See also n. 1, supra. Other than the fact that their rigs were a traditional admiralty situs, there is little to distinguish the job or location of a worker on a floating rig from those of a worker on a fixed rig. Physically, the structures may be quite similar. [14] For example, they are similarly small, [15] relatively isolated, and totally surrounded by the sea. The two types of structures are parts of similar enterprises and operations that are carried out in the same marine environment. Indeed, other than for the type of structure, the locations of the work are the same. Moreover, the work tasks are quite similar, as are the working conditions and hazards. [16] I can therefore see no reason to believe that Congress, in passing a measure designed to rationalize coverage patterns through an occupational test for coverage, would have wanted to treat these workers as belonging to two different occupations, one maritime and the other nonmaritime. [17]

In Perini we held that the fact that a worker is required to work over the actual navigable waters is weighty evidence of his or her maritime status. 459 U.S. at 459 U. S. 323-324. This holding clearly calls for the inclusion of fixed rig workers within the maritime employment classification. Here, Gray's job was to do welding, as needed, on oil rigs scattered over the Bay Marchand oil field. He was thus required to live on a rig and regularly travel back and forth over water among the rigs in the oil field. The argument that Gray performed work over the actual navigable waters is trivialized by the Court when it characterizes him as "a worker whose job is entirely land-based but who takes a boat to work." Ante at 470 U. S. 427, n. 13. This was not simply the life of a land-based commuter who chose to travel to work by boat; it is the life of someone required to live and work in a marine environment and to engage in ocean travel as an integral part of his job duties. When traveling among the rigs, he was no less at work than when he was on a rig doing welding jobs, so his job is one that requires his presence on the actual navigable waters.

The maritime nature of the occupation is even more apparent from examining its location in terms of the expanded situs coverage of the 1972 Amendments. Assuming that a fixed offshore platform is a covered situs under § 3(a), then fixed platform workers could not simply be termed "land-based" workers. Ibid. Unlike typical "land-based" workers, they would spend virtually their entire work lives within the statute's covered "maritime situs" -- that is, either on or immediately adjacent to the actual navigable waters. This is, in fact, the situation here, for a fixed offshore oil rig easily fits into § 3(a)'s situs test.

Section 3(a) provides that coverage extends to any

"pier, wharf, dry dock, terminal, building way, marine railway, or other . . . area [adjoining the navigable waters] customarily used by an employer in loading, unloading, repairing, or building a vessel."

33 U.S.C. § 903(a). This describes the typical fixed offshore oil rig. Since a fixed rig is of limited size and completely surrounded by water, all materials and workers on the rig are brought there and unloaded over water, and thus a customary use of the rig is the loading and unloading of cargo and people. One commentator has characterized the situation as follows:

"Worker transportation is one of the most basic problems associated with offshore operations. Transportation is accomplished either by boats or helicopters. High-speed crew boats transport work crews when time is available and the distance is less than about 50 miles. Helicopters transport crews and other personnel over long distances or when time is important. The transportation of equipment to offshore rigs is accomplished with work boats. These boats . . . are versatile, high powered, and essential to offshore operations. Thus, all platforms must be provided with mooring bits, bumpers, cranes, stairs, etc., for use with work boats and crew boats."

W. Graff, Introduction to Offshore Structures 3 (1981). The rig is thus an "area [adjoining the navigable waters] customarily used by an employer in loading [or] unloading . . . a vessel." § 3(a), 33 U.S.C. § 903(a).

Fixed rigs are also physically quite analogous to piers or wharves. They are of limited size, see n. 15, supra, so a worker almost anywhere on the deck would be aware of his close proximity to the water. Similarly, the decks are elevated over the water, built to provide access to the water, and situated so that working conditions are influenced by the surrounding marine environment. Given these factors, I have little problem classifying the whole of the platform as a covered situs, [18] either because it is an "other adjoining area customarily used by an employer in loading [or] unloading" or because it is analogous to a pier or wharf facility.

Given this determination, a fixed platform worker is quite distinct from the truckdriver or clerical worker who, in the legislative history, exemplifies the nonmaritime worker. See supra at 470 U. S. 430-431. Truckdrivers or clericals are land-bound workers whose work never takes them on the actual navigable waters, and only sporadically takes them on the pier-like areas brought under the LHWCA's coverage by the 1972 Amendments. The greatest part of their work is done in inland locales that are clearly beyond the coverage of the Act. Therefore, coverage of these workers under the Act could, at most, be "checkered" and "fortuitous." Avoiding such widespread "checkered coverage" was an envisioned function of the status test. See supra at 470 U. S. 430-432. Fixed rig workers, in contrast, are in a position to benefit from uniform coverage if classified as "maritime," for they are on a covered situs for the overwhelming part of their work. Classifying them as "maritime" in light of their constant and required presence on a covered situs conforms to Congress' desire for uniform coverage of those workers who would otherwise be partially covered. Under the Court's approach, they remain only partially covered.

A last reason for classifying these workers as maritime is that they face working conditions and hazards associated with their maritime location. This was clearly stated in the testimony of a high official of an offshore drilling company before a recent congressional hearing on offshore worker safety:

"Offshore work has a special set of concerns, because we are a hybrid industry. In one sense, we are an onshore industry that initially crept out over the water. But it is equally fair to characterize us as a maritime industry, the same as the merchant marine or any other."

"In point of fact, we share all of the concerns of both the drilling and maritime industries, plus a few uniquely ours. [19] "

The same sentiment is recognized in the delegation of regulatory authority to the Coast Guard and in the Coast Guard regulations, see n. 10, supra, and accompanying text, and has been noted by legal and occupational health authorities. [20] Clearly these workers do far more than just "breathe salt air." See ante at 470 U. S. 423.

B

The Court supports its conclusion that fixed offshore oil rig workers are nonmaritime by arguing that their work is similar to drilling work done on land. But this reasoning must fail for a number of reasons. First, it ignores that, while the work is similar to work done on land, it is virtually identical to work on floating oil rigs -- which is clearly maritime.

Second, the Court's reasoning ignores that many indisputably maritime occupations are quite analogous to nonmaritime occupations. A forklift or crane operator who moves cargo on a pier and a "checker" who inventories that cargo are considered longshoremen with maritime status, even though their work may be quite similar to that of inland workers in a warehousing operation. See Caputo, 432 U.S. at 432 U. S. 249 ("checker" was engaged in "maritime employment"); see also Perini, 459 U. S. 297 (1983) (construction worker may be engaged in "maritime employment"). The issue is not whether job duties are similar to those of nonmaritime workers, but whether the enterprise in question necessitates that work be done in a maritime environment. Longshoring work, regardless of its similarity to other jobs, must be done on or adjacent to the navigable waters. Similarly, the extraction of oil from beneath the ocean floor necessitates that certain tasks be done over and adjacent to the ocean.

Third, the Court's reasoning ignores that, whatever the similarities to land-based work, the work schedules, working conditions, and job hazards of offshore workers are in some ways quite different from their land-based counterparts. And most of the differences are the result of the offshore workers' proximity to the sea. See supra at 470 U. S. 448-449.

V

For the reasons discussed above, respondent Gray was "engaged in maritime employment" within the meaning of § 2(3) of the Act. It is also clear that a fixed offshore petroleum platform is a covered situs within the meaning of § 3(a) of the Act. I would thus affirm the Court of Appeals.

Notes

[1] "Floating" petroleum rigs are classified as vessels in admiralty jurisprudence, see Producers Drilling Co. v. Gray, 361 F.2d 432, 437 (CA5 1966), and as such have long been within the Act's coverage. Ante at 470 U. S. 416-417, n. 2. It must be emphasized, however, that, in admiralty law, the classification of a structure as "floating" turns only on its capacity to float, and not on the relevance of buoyancy to its typical use or its state at the time of an injury. Many "floating" offshore petroleum rigs are so classified because they are floated to their drilling sites; but once there, they are elevated above the water and supported by legs that rest on the ocean bottom. See Producers Drilling Co., supra, at 437 (classification includes "almost any structure that once floated or is capable of floating on navigable waters . . .' and . . . includes `special purpose structures not usually employed as a means of transport by water, but designed to float on water'") (quoting Offshore Co. v. Robison, 266 F.2d 769, 771 (CA5 1959)). See also n. 14, infra.

[2] As both the Senate and House Reports that accompanied the 1972 Amendments stated:

"[C]overage of the present Act stops at the water's edge; injuries occurring on land are covered by State Workmen's Compensation laws. The result is a disparity in benefits payable for death or disability for the same type of injury depending on which side of the water's edge and in which State the accident occurs."

"To make matters worse, most State Workmen's Compensation laws provide benefits which are inadequate. . . ."

S.Rep. No. 92-1125, pp. 12-13 (1972) (hereinafter cited as S.Rep.); H.R.Rep. No. 92-1441, pp. 10-11 (1972) (containing identical language) (hereinafter cited as H.R.Rep.).

[3] The term employee is further limited by the exclusion of

"[m]aster[s] or member[s] of a crew of any vessel, or any person engaged by the master to load or unload or repair any small vessel under eighteen tons net."

§ 2(3), 33 U.S.C. § 902(3). The exclusion corresponds to "seamen" who enjoy Jones Act coverage. See 46 U.S.C. § 688. This exception is irrelevant to this case.

[4] Indeed, we have explicitly refused to interpret the word "maritime" as used in the § 2(3)'s status test according to the limits that we have applied to the word's usage in the maritime jurisdictional statute. Director, OWCP v. Perini North River Associates, 459 U. S. 297, 459 U. S. 320, n. 29 (1983) ("Although the term maritime' occurs [in] both . . these are two different statutes `each with different legislative histories and jurisprudential interpretations over the course of decades'") (quoting Boudreaux v. American Workover, Inc., 680 F.2d 1034, 1049-1050 (CA5 1982)).

[5] Victory Carriers v. Law, 404 U. S. 202, 404 U. S. 205, and n. 2 (1971) (quoting Justice Story in Thomas v. Lane, 23 F.Cas. 957, 960 (No. 13,902) (CC Me. 1813)). See also Swaim, Yes, Virginia, There Is An Admiralty: The Rodrigue Case, 16 Loyola L.Rev. 43 (1969-1970) (criticizing Rodrigue as an example of a particularly narrow application of the traditional locality test). In Nacirema Operating Co. v. Johnson, 396 U. S. 212, 396 U. S. 215, n. 6 (1969), we stated that Rodrigue affirmed the "settled doctrine" that structures like piers were not within traditional admiralty situs. The 1972 Amendments, of course, explicitly overturned the application of this "settled doctrine" to the LHWCA.

[6] Rodrigue's irrelevance to the meaning of the post-1972 "maritime employment" test is illustrated by the fact that one of the Rodrigue decedents, Dore, was killed in an activity that would clearly have been within post-1972 LHWCA coverage, using a crane to unload a barge that was docked at the oil rig. 395 U.S. at 395 U. S. 353. Even under the analysis used by the Court today, such a worker would be "engaged in maritime employment." Yet in Rodrigue, Dore's unloading work and the other worker's oil derrick work were both viewed as equally beyond "the ordinary stuff of admiralty." Id. at 395 U. S. 360.

The Court defends Rodrigue's relevance to this case in a curious way. The Court asserts that Rodrigue had gone beyond simply analogizing drilling platforms to piers, and actually held that drilling platforms "are islands." Ante at 470 U. S. 422, n. 6. This is put forth as if to imply that Rodrigue's holding rested on something other than a simple analysis of traditional maritime tort locality. But relevant maritime law recognized no legal distinction between injuries on "piers" and injuries on "islands." Both were equally understood simply to be injuries on localities that were not "on the navigable waters." Rodrigue's additional metaphor equating drilling platforms with islands added no additional legal point to that decision. It is, to say the least, peculiar to now look back on that opinion's casual choice of metaphors as a basis for determining the contours of subsequently created legal rights in an unrelated statute.

[7] While longshoremen and harborworkers work and live in the shoreside communities, offshore petroleum workers may work on facilities located in the open sea, and may be required to live on these facilities for prolonged periods of time. In the Gulf of Mexico, for example, the prevailing practice is for offshore workers to live on the drilling rigs for seven days, followed by seven days away from the rigs. International Labour Office, Safety Problems in the Offshore Petroleum Industry 19 (1978). This obviously makes the work less "connected" to the shore community. Respondent Gray testified that

this was his schedule. Tr. in 77-LHCA-1308, before Administrative Law Judge, p. 31.

[8] It may be notable that, in 1972, Congress explicitly overturned Nacirema's holding that the LHWCA did not cover injuries on piers, but Congress has taken no action to overturn Victory Carriers' determination that workers on piers are not generally governed by admiralty law.

[9] Congress has used the LHWCA as a general worker's compensation statute in a variety of federal circumstances that have no maritime concerns. See Perini, 459 U.S. at 459 U. S. 326, n. 1 (STEVENS, J., dissenting) (listing statutes that apply LHWCA to defense bases, the District of Columbia, etc.).

[10] The Fifth Circuit found in these initial regulations a determination that

"whether . . . fixed or submersible, these oil well drilling structures located in the midst of the high seas present substantially all of the perils of the seas, and are therefore to be regulated as such."

Pure Oil Co. v. Snipes, 293 F.2d 60, 66-67 (1961). The Coast Guard continues to regulate occupational safety and health on these structures, see 46 Fed.Reg. 2199 (1981) (Memorandum of understanding between U.S. Geological Survey and U.S. Coast Guard), and the regulations still reflect a concern for maritime dangers. See 33 CFR pts. 144 and 146 (1983) (requiring that platforms be equipped with buoyant work vests, life preservers, lifefloats, emergency communications equipment, general alarm systems, sufficient handrails, and buoys). See generally 33 CFR Subchapter N (1983).

[11] A status-like doctrine called "maritime but local," which was quite similar to the Court's position today, was found in the early years of the LHWCA. This doctrine applied state, rather than federal, law to govern accidents on the waters if the worker's activities had no "direct relation" to navigation or commerce and if "the application of local law [would not] materially affect" the uniformity of maritime law. Grant Smith-Porter v. Rohde, 257 U. S. 469, 257 U. S. 477 (1922). See also Western Fuel Co. v. Garcia, 257 U. S. 233, 257 U. S. 242 (1921). Like the Court's approach, this concept was ill-defined, and it gave rise to "one of the most flourishing, as it was surely the most depressing, branches of federal jurisprudence." G. Gilmore & C. Black, Law of Admiralty 420 (2d ed.1975). See also Perini, supra, at 459 U. S. 307. This Court eventually established that the LHWCA did not incorporate the "maritime but local" doctrine. See Calbeck v. Travelers Insurance Co., 370 U. S. 114 (1962); cf. Davis v. Department of Labor, 317 U. S. 249 (1942); Parker v. Motor Boat Sales, 314 U. S. 244 (1941). More recently, this Court has explicitly held that the 1972 status requirement of § 2(3) did not reinsert in the Act this "concept that plagued maritime compensation law for more than 40 years." See Perini, supra, at 459 U. S. 322. Unfortunately, the Court today comes quite close to accomplishing just that reinsertion.

[12] For example, the Court accepts shipbuilding, which is included among § 2(3)'s enumerated occupations, as obviously "maritime." But contracts for shipbuilding were not traditionally considered within admiralty contract jurisdiction. See People's Ferry Co. v. Beers, 20 How. 393 (1858). See also Gilmore & Black, supra, at 16.

[13] For example, Gilmore and Black begin their treatise with a list of cases that are not within admiralty jurisdiction, but which might be considered intuitively "maritime." Rodrigue is among them. Gilmore & Black, supra, at 27. See also Alston, Admiralty Jurisdiction and Fixed Offshore Drilling Platforms: A Radical Plea Reconsidered, 28 Loyola L.Rev. 379 (1982) (urging admiralty coverage for workers on fixed platforms); Robertson, Injuries to Marine Petroleum Workers: A Plea for Radical Simplification, 55 Texas L.Rev. 973 (1977) (same). The Court's assertion that offshore oil workers are not engaged in "maritime commerce" is similarly conclusory. In contrast, the Court of Appeals concluded that extracting oil and gas from under the ocean floor and transporting it to the shore is a part of "maritime commerce." See 703 F.2d 176, 180 (CA5 1983); see also Pippen v. Shell Oil Co., 661 F.2d 378, 384 (CA5 1981). Leaving aside intuitions about what constitutes "maritime commerce," I would note that the enterprise here is the same as that carried out by floating rigs, which are classified as vessels, see n. 1, supra, and are thus presumably within almost any definition of "maritime commerce."

[14] See, e.g., International Labour Office, supra, n. 7, at 5 ("Jack-up rigs," which make up 42% of the world's floating rigs, are "self-elevating platforms equipped with legs which can be lowered until they reach the sea bed and support the main section of the drilling platform. Throughout the drilling process the platform is kept in the raised position above the water surface"). See also n. 1, supra.

[15] Although the record does not reflect the platform's size in this case, fixed and floating platforms are of similarly limited size. See Hearings on S.2318 et al. before the Subcommittee on Labor of the Senate Committee on Labor and Public Welfare, 92d Cong., 2d Sess., 836 (1972) (hereinafter cited as Hearings) (oil company document calling a fixed platform with a "150-foot-square deck" a "real giant"); id. at 834 (floating rig described as having a 200-foot-square deck).

[16] Counsel for petitioners went so far as to declare:

"The hazards are no different. . . . There are no differences at all. There is absolutely no difference between a person who is more or less permanently assigned to a vessel and drilling or a person who is more or less permanently assigned to a platform and drilling."

Tr. of Oral Arg. 6.

[17] Beyond the similarity of the two classifications, additional factors militate against treating them as distinct occupations. For example, some workers work on both fixed and floating rigs. See, e.g., Pippen v. Shell Oil Co., 661 F.2d at 383, n. 6 (75% of worker's time was on floating rigs and 25% on fixed rigs). Similarly, the distinction between "fixed" and "floating" rigs is not always a rigid one. Structures called "tender type platforms" include a fixed platform with floating "tender ships" moored adjacent thereto. See Hearings at 480; W. Graff, Introduction to Offshore Structures 3, 25 (1981). The drilling operation is divided between the platform and the tender ship, and the two are usually connected by walkways so workers can move back and forth between them. See Robertson, 55 Texas L.Rev. at 997-998. In both these contexts, the Court's approach

creates the same "walking in and out of coverage" situation that the 1972 Amendments sought to eliminate. Cf. id. at 992 ("Admiralty law is notable for the presence of fine and often intuitively questionable distinctions that involve devastating consequences. But even within the context of a system accustomed to such line-drawing, [the fixed-floating rig distinction] looks peculiar" (footnotes omitted)).

[18] In Northeast Marine Terminal Co. v. Caputo, 432 U. S. 249, 432 U. S. 279-280 (1977), we held that the whole of a facility adjoining the water was a covered situs where part of the facility was used for loading vessels. See G. Gilmore & C. Black, Law of Admiralty 424 (2d ed.1975) (urging a broad reading of the situs test to avoid unnecessary line-drawing problems).

[19] Hearing on the Safety of Life at Sea and Safety on Oil and Gas Rigs on the Outer Continental Shelf before the Subcommittee on Panama Canal/Outer Continental Shelf of the House Committee on Merchant Marine and Fisheries, 98th Cong., 1st Sess., 38 (1983) (testimony of T. S. McIntosh, executive vice-president and chief operating officer of the Zapata Corp. and president of the Zapata Off-Shore Co.).

[20] See Alston, 28 Loyola L.Rev. at 402-403; Robertson, 55 Texas L.Rev. at 994-996. See also International Labour Office, supra, n. 7, at 19 (exposure to weather); ibid. (extended isolation may lead to morale, alcoholism, and safety problems); id. at 21-23 (controlling fires and blow-outs may be more difficult because of inaccessibility of platform); id. at 24 (confined space and isolation makes excessive noise a much more serious problem in offshore oil operations than in onshore oil operations); id. at 27 (slipperiness, clutter, weather conditions, and danger of falling overboard can make transfer of supplies dangerous).

Distinguishing contributions from independent expenditures makes no sense: Justice Marshall's dissent in Federal Election Commission v. National Conservative Political Action Committee (March 18, 1985)

JUSTICE MARSHALL, dissenting.

In Buckley v. Valeo, 424 U. S. 1 (1976) (per curiam), this Court upheld congressional limitations on contributions to candidates for federal office, but struck down limitations on independent expenditures made on behalf of such candidates. In upholding the former, the Court stated that

"the weighty interests served by restricting the size of financial contributions to political candidates are sufficient to justify the limited effect upon First Amendment freedoms caused by the $1,000 contribution ceiling."

Id. at 424 U. S. 29. In striking down the latter, the Court noted that an expenditure limitation "fails to serve any substantial interest in stemming the reality or appearance of corruption in the electoral process," and that "it heavily burdens core First Amendment expression." Id. at 424 U. S. 47-48. Relying on Buckley, the Court today strikes down a limitation on expenditures by "political committees." Although I joined the portion of the Buckley per curiam that distinguished contributions from independent expenditures for First Amendment purposes, I now believe that the distinction has no constitutional significance.

The contribution/expenditure distinction in Buckley was grounded on two factors. First, the Court reasoned that independent expenditures offer significantly less potential for abuse than contributions:

"Unlike contributions, such independent expenditures may well provide little assistance to the candidate's campaign, and may indeed prove counterproductive. The absence of prearrangement and coordination of an expenditure with the candidate or his agent not only undermines the value of the expenditure to the candidate, but also alleviates the danger that expenditures will be given as a quid pro quo for improper commitments from the candidate."

Id. at 424 U. S. 47.

Undoubtedly, when an individual interested in obtaining the proverbial ambassadorship had the option of either contributing directly to a candidate's campaign or doing so indirectly through independent expenditures, he gave money directly. It does not take great imagination, however, to see that, when the possibility for direct financial assistance is severely limited, as it is in light of Buckley's decision to uphold the contribution limitation, such an individual will find other ways to financially benefit the candidate's campaign. It simply belies reality to say that a campaign will not reward massive financial assistance provided in the only way that is legally available. And the possibility of such a reward provides a powerful incentive to channel an independent expenditure into an area that a candidate will appreciate. Surely an eager supporter will be able to discern a candidate's needs and desires; similarly, a willing candidate will notice the supporter's efforts. To the extent that individuals are able to make independent expenditures as part of a quid pro quo, they succeed in undermining completely the first rationale for the distinction made in Buckley.

The second factor supporting the distinction between contributions and expenditures was the relative magnitude of the First Amendment interest at stake. The Court found that the constitutional interest implicated in the limitation on expenditures was the right to advocate the election or defeat of a particular candidate. This right, the Court reasoned,

"is no less entitled to protection under the First Amendment than the discussion of political policy generally or advocacy of the passage or defeat of legislation."

Id. at 424 U. S. 48. In contrast, the Court found that the limitation on contributions primarily implicated "the contributor's freedom of political association." Id. at 424 U. S. 24-25. Although the Court acknowledged that this right was a "fundamental" one, id. at 424 U. S. 25, it concluded that the expenditure ceiling imposed significantly more severe restrictions on political freedoms than the contribution limitation, id. at 424 U. S. 23.

I disagree that the limitations on contributions and expenditures have significantly different impacts on First Amendment freedoms. First, the underlying rights at issue -- freedom of speech and freedom of association -- are both core First Amendment rights. Second, in both cases, the regulation is of the same form: it concerns the amount of money that can be spent for political activity. Thus, I do not see how one interest can be deemed more compelling than the other.*

In summary, I am now unpersuaded by the distinction established in Buckley. I have come to believe that the limitations on independent expenditures challenged in that case and here are justified by the congressional interests in promoting "the reality and appearance of equal access to the political arena," id. at 424 U. S. 287 (opinion of MARSHALL, J.), and in eliminating political corruption and the appearance of such corruption. Therefore, I dissent, substantially for the reasons expressed in Parts 470 U. S. 470 U. S. and 470 U. S. from the Court's decision today to strike down § 9012(f)'s limitation on independent expenditures by "political committees."

Also, I join 470 U. S. which concerns the standing of the Democratic National Committee.

* At the time Buckley was decided, three of the eight Members who heard that case agreed that contributions and expenditures should be treated in the same manner for First Amendment purposes. See 424 U.S. at 424 U. S. 241 (opinion of BURGER, C.J.) ("For me, contributions and expenditures are two sides of the same First Amendment coin"); id. at 424 U. S. 261 (opinion of WHITE, J.) ("For constitutional purposes, it is difficult to see the difference between the two situations"); id. at 424 U. S. 290 (opinion of BLACKMUN, J.) ("I am not persuaded that the Court makes, or indeed is able to make, a principled constitutional distinction between the contribution limitations, on the one hand, and the expenditure limitations, on the other, that are involved here").

Court claims to be using rational-basis scrutiny, but that surely can't be the case and the court should be honest about that: Justice Marshall's dissent in City of Cleburne, Texas v. Cleburne Living Center, Inc. (July 1, 1985)

JUSTICE MARSHALL, with whom JUSTICE BRENNAN and JUSTICE BLACKMUN join, concurring in the judgment in part and dissenting in part.

The Court holds that all retarded individuals cannot be grouped together as the "feeble-minded" and deemed presumptively unfit to live in a community. Underlying this holding is the principle that mental retardation, per se, cannot be a proxy for depriving retarded people of their rights and interests without regard to variations in individual ability.

With this holding and principle I agree. The Equal Protection Clause requires attention to the capacities and needs of retarded people as individuals.

I cannot agree, however, with the way in which the Court reaches its result or with the narrow, as-applied remedy it provides for the city of Cleburne's equal protection violation. The Court holds the ordinance invalid on rational basis grounds, and disclaims that anything special, in the form of heightened scrutiny, is taking place. Yet Cleburne's ordinance surely would be valid under the traditional rational basis test applicable to economic and commercial regulation. In my view, it is important to articulate, as the Court does not, the facts and principles that justify subjecting this zoning ordinance to the searching review -- the heightened scrutiny -- that actually leads to its invalidation. Moreover, in invalidating Cleburne's exclusion of the "feeble-minded" only as applied to respondents, rather than on its face, the Court radically departs from our equal protection precedents. Because I dissent from this novel and truncated remedy, and because I cannot accept the Court's disclaimer that no "more exacting standard" than ordinary rational basis review is being applied, ante at 473 U. S. 442, I write separately.

I

At the outset, two curious and paradoxical aspects of the Court's opinion must be noted. First, because the Court invalidates Cleburne's zoning ordinance on rational basis grounds, the Court's wide-ranging discussion of heightened scrutiny is wholly superfluous to the decision of this case. This "two for the price of one" approach to constitutional decisionmaking -- rendering two constitutional rulings where one is enough to decide the case -- stands on their head traditional and deeply embedded principles governing exercise of the Court's Article III power. Just a few weeks ago, the Court

"call[ed] to mind two of the cardinal rules governing the federal courts: 'One, never to anticipate a question of constitutional law in advance of the necessity of deciding it; the other never to formulate a rule of constitutional law broader than is required by the precise facts to which it is to be applied.'"

Brockett v. Spokane Arcades, Inc., 472 U. S. 491, 472 U. S. 501 (1985) (WHITE, J.) (quoting Liverpool, New York & Philadelphia S.S. Co. v. Commissioners of Emigration, 113 U. S. 33, 113 U. S. 39 (1885)). [1] When a lower court correctly decides a case, albeit on what this Court concludes are unnecessary constitutional grounds, [2] "our usual custom" is not to compound the problem by following suit, but rather to affirm on the narrower, dispositive ground available. Alexander v. Louisiana, 405 U. S. 625, 405 U. S. 633 (1972). [3] The Court offers no principled justification for departing from these principles, nor, given our equal protection precedents, could it. See Mississippi University for Women v. Hogan, 458 U. S. 718, 458 U. S. 724, n. 9 (1982) (declining to address strict scrutiny when heightened scrutiny sufficient to invalidate action challenged); Stanton v. Stanton, 421 U. S. 7, 421 U. S. 13 (1975) (same); Hooper v. Bernalillo County Assessor, 472 U. S. 612, 472 U. S. 618 (1985) (declining to reach heightened scrutiny in review of residency-based classifications that fail rational basis test); Zobel v. Williams, 457 U. S. 55, 457 U. S. 60-61 (1982) (same); cf. Mitchell v. Forsyth, 472 U. S. 511, 472 U. S. 537-538 (1985) (O'CONNOR, J., concurring in part).

Second, the Court's heightened scrutiny discussion is even more puzzling given that Cleburne's ordinance is invalidated only after being subjected to precisely the sort of probing inquiry associated with heightened scrutiny. To be sure, the Court does not label its handiwork heightened scrutiny, and perhaps the method employed must hereafter be called "second order" rational basis review, rather than "heightened scrutiny." But however labeled, the rational basis test invoked today is most assuredly not the rational basis test of Williamson v. Lee Optical of Oklahoma, Inc., 348 U. S. 483 (1955); Allied Stores of Ohio, Inc. v. Bowers, 358 U. S. 522 (1959), and their progeny.

The Court, for example, concludes that legitimate concerns for fire hazards or the serenity of the neighborhood do not justify singling out respondents to bear the burdens of these concerns, for analogous permitted uses appear to pose similar threats. Yet under the traditional and most minimal version of the rational basis test, "reform may take one step at a time, addressing itself to the phase of the problem which seems most acute to the legislative mind." Williamson v. Lee Optical of Oklahoma, Inc., supra, at 348 U. S. 489; see American Federation of Labor v. American Sash Co., 335 U. S. 538 (1949); Semler v. Dental Examiners, 294 U. S. 608 (1935). The "record" is said not to support the ordinance's classifications, ante at 473 U. S. 448, 473 U. S. 450, but under the traditional standard, we do not sift through the record to determine whether policy decisions are squarely supported by a firm factual foundation. Exxon Corp. v. Eagerton, 462 U. S. 176, 462 U. S. 196 (1983); Minnesota v. Clover Leaf Creamery Co., 449 U. S. 456, 449 U. S. 461-462, 449 U. S. 464 (1981); Firemen v. Chicago, R. I. & P. R. Co., 393 U. S. 129, 393 U. S. 138-139 (1968). Finally, the Court further finds it "difficult to believe" that the retarded present different or special hazards inapplicable to other groups. In normal circumstances, the burden is not on the legislature to convince the Court that the lines it has drawn are sensible; legislation is presumptively constitutional, and a State "is not required to resort to close distinctions or to maintain a precise, scientific uniformity with reference" to its goals. Allied Stores of Ohio, Inc. v. Bowers, supra, at 358 U. S. 527; Metropolis Theatre Co. v. City of Chicago, 228 U. S. 61, 228 U. S. 68-70 (1913).

I share the Court's criticisms of the overly broad lines that Cleburne's zoning ordinance has drawn. But if the ordinance is to be invalidated for its imprecise classifications, it must be pursuant to more powerful scrutiny than the minimal rational basis test used to review classifications affecting only economic and commercial matters. The same imprecision in a similar ordinance that required opticians but not optometrists to be licensed to practice, see Williamson v. Lee Optical of Oklahoma, Inc., supra, or that excluded new but not old businesses from parts of a community, see New Orleans v. Dukes, supra, would hardly be fatal to the statutory scheme.

The refusal to acknowledge that something more than minimum rationality review is at work here is, in my view, unfortunate in at least two respects. [4] The suggestion that the traditional rational basis test allows this sort of searching inquiry creates precedent for this Court and lower courts to subject economic and commercial classifications to similar and searching "ordinary" rational basis review -- a small and regrettable step back toward the days of Lochner v. New York, 198 U. S. 45 (1905).

Moreover, by failing to articulate the factors that justify today's "second order" rational basis review, the Court provides no principled foundation for determining when more searching inquiry is to be invoked. Lower courts are thus left in the dark on this important question, and this Court remains unaccountable for its decisions employing, or refusing to employ, particularly searching scrutiny. Candor requires me to acknowledge the particular factors that justify invalidating Cleburne's zoning ordinance under the careful scrutiny it today receives.

II

I have long believed the level of scrutiny employed in an equal protection case should vary with

"the constitutional and societal importance of the interest adversely affected and the recognized invidiousness of the basis upon which the particular classification is drawn."

San Antonio Independent School District v. Rodriguez, 411 U. S. 1, 411 U. S. 99 (1973) (MARSHALL, J., dissenting). See also Plyler v. Doe, 457 U. S. 202, 457 U. S. 230-231 (1982) (MARSHALL, J., concurring); Dandridge v. Williams, 397 U. S. 471, 397 U. S. 508 (1970) (MARSHALL, J., dissenting). When a zoning ordinance works to exclude the retarded from all residential districts in a community, these two considerations require that the ordinance be convincingly justified as substantially furthering legitimate and important purposes. Plyler, supra; Mississippi University for Women v. Hogan, 458 U. S. 718 (1982); Frontiero v. Richardson, 411 U. S. 677 (1973); Mills v. Habluetzel, 456 U. S. 91 (1982); see also Buchanan v. Warley, 245 U. S. 60 (1917).

First, the interest of the retarded in establishing group homes is substantial. The right to "establish a home" has long been cherished as one of the fundamental liberties embraced by the Due Process Clause. See Meyer v. Nebraska, 262 U. S. 390, 262 U. S. 399 (1923). For retarded adults, this right means living together in group homes, for as deinstitutionalization has progressed, group homes have become the primary means by which retarded adults can enter life in the community. The District Court found as a matter of fact that

"[t]he availability of such a home in communities is an essential ingredient of normal living patterns for persons who are mentally retarded, and each factor that makes such group homes harder to establish operates to exclude persons who are mentally retarded from the community."

App. to Pet. for Cert. A-8. Excluding group homes deprives the retarded of much of what makes for human freedom and fulfillment -- the ability to form bonds and take part in the life of a community. [5]

Second, the mentally retarded have been subject to a "lengthy and tragic history," University of California Regents v. Bakke, 438 U. S. 265, 438 U. S. 303 (1978) (opinion of POWELL, J.), of segregation and discrimination that can only be called grotesque. During much of the 19th century, mental retardation was viewed as neither curable nor dangerous, and the retarded were largely left to their own devices. [6] By the latter part of the century and during the first decades of the new one, however, social views of the retarded underwent a radical transformation. Fueled by the rising tide of Social Darwinism, the "science" of eugenics, and the extreme xenophobia of those years, [7] leading medical authorities and others began to portray the "feeble-minded" as a "menace to society and civilization . . . responsible in a large degree for many, if not all, of our social problems." [8] A regime of state-mandated segregation and degradation soon emerged that, in its virulence and bigotry, rivaled, and indeed paralleled, the worst excesses of Jim Crow. Massive custodial institutions were built to warehouse the retarded for life; the aim was to halt reproduction of the retarded and "nearly extinguish their race." [9] Retarded children were categorically excluded from public schools, based on the false stereotype that all were ineducable and on the purported need to protect nonretarded children from them. [10] State laws deemed the retarded "unfit for citizenship." [11]

Segregation was accompanied by eugenic marriage and sterilization laws that extinguished for the retarded one of the "basic civil rights of man" -- the right to marry and procreate. Skinner v. Oklahoma ex rel. Williamson, 316 U. S. 535, 316 U. S. 541 (1942). Marriages of the retarded were made, and in some States continue to be, not only voidable but also often a criminal offense. [12] The purpose of such limitations, which frequently applied only to women of child-bearing age, was unabashedly eugenic: to prevent the retarded from propagating. [13] To assure this end, 29 States enacted compulsory eugenic sterilization laws between 1907 and 1931. J. Landman, Human Sterilization 302-303 (1932). See Buck v. Bell, 274 U. S. 200, 274 U. S. 207 (1927) (Holmes, J.); cf. 163 U. S. Ferguson, 163 U. S. 537 (1896); Bradwell v. Illinois, 16 Wall. 130, 83 U. S. 141 (1873) (Bradley, J., concurring in judgment).

Prejudice, once let loose, is not easily cabined. See University of California Regents v. Bakke, 438 U.S. at 435 U. S. 395 (opinion of MARSHALL, J.). As of 1979, most States still categorically disqualified "idiots" from voting, without regard to individual capacity and with discretion to exclude left in the hands of low-level election officials. [14] Not until Congress enacted the Education of the Handicapped Act, 84 Stat. 175, as amended, 20 U.S.C. § 1400 et seq., were "the door[s] of public education" opened wide to handicapped children. Hendrick Hudson District Board of Education v. Rowley, 458 U. S. 176, 458 U. S. 192 (1982). [15] But most important, lengthy and continuing isolation of the retarded has perpetuated the ignorance, irrational fears, and stereotyping that long have plagued them. [16]

In light of the importance of the interest at stake and the history of discrimination the retarded have suffered, the Equal Protection Clause requires us to do more than review the distinctions drawn by Cleburne's zoning ordinance as if they appeared in a taxing statute or in economic or commercial legislation. [17] The searching scrutiny I would give to restrictions on the ability of the retarded to establish community group homes leads me to conclude that Cleburne's vague generalizations for classifying the "feeble-minded" with drug addicts, alcoholics, and the insane, and excluding them where the elderly, the ill, the boarder, and the transient are allowed, are not substantial or important enough to overcome the suspicion that the ordinance rests on impermissible assumptions or outmoded and perhaps invidious stereotypes. See Plyler v. Doe, 457 U. S. 202 (1982); Roberts v. United States Jaycees, 468 U. S. 609 (1984); Mississippi University for Women v. Hogan, 458 U. S. 718 (1982); Mills v. Habluetzel, 456 U. S. 91 (1982).

III

In its effort to show that Cleburne's ordinance can be struck down under no "more exacting standard . . . than is normally accorded economic and social legislation," ante at 473 U. S. 442, the Court offers several justifications as to why the retarded do not warrant heightened judicial solicitude. These justifications, however, find no support in our heightened scrutiny precedents, and cannot withstand logical analysis.

The Court downplays the lengthy "history of purposeful unequal treatment" of the retarded, see San Antonio Independent School District v. Rodriguez, 411 U.S. at 411 U. S. 28, by pointing to recent legislative action that is said to "beli[e] a continuing antipathy or prejudice." Ante at 473 U. S. 443. Building on this point, the Court similarly concludes that the retarded are not "politically powerless," and deserve no greater judicial protection than "[a]ny minority" that wins some political battles and loses others. Ante at 473 U. S. 445. The import of these conclusions, it seems, is that the only discrimination courts may remedy is the discrimination they alone are perspicacious enough to see. Once society begins to recognize certain practices as discriminatory, in part because previously stigmatized groups have mobilized politically to lift this stigma, the Court would refrain from approaching such practices with the added skepticism of heightened scrutiny.

Courts, however, do not sit or act in a social vacuum. Moral philosophers may debate whether certain inequalities are absolute wrongs, but history makes clear that constitutional principles of equality, like constitutional principles of liberty, property, and due process, evolve over time; what once was a "natural" and "self-evident" ordering later comes to be seen as an artificial and invidious constraint on human potential and freedom. Compare Plessy v. Ferguson, 163 U. S. 537 (1896), and Bradwell v. Illinois, supra, at 83 U. S. 141 (Bradley, J., concurring in judgment), with Brown v. Board of Education, 347 U. S. 483 (1954), and Reed v. Reed, 404 U. S. 71 (1971). Shifting cultural, political, and social patterns at times come to make past practices appear inconsistent with fundamental principles upon which American society rests, an inconsistency legally cognizable under the Equal Protection Clause. It is natural that evolving standards of equality come to be embodied in legislation. When that occurs, courts should look to the fact of such change as a source of guidance on evolving principles of equality. In an analysis the Court today ignores, the Court reached this very conclusion when it extended heightened scrutiny to gender classifications and drew on parallel legislative developments to support that extension:

"[O]ver the past decade, Congress has itself manifested an increasing sensitivity to sex-based classifications [citing examples]. Thus, Congress itself has concluded that classifications based upon sex are inherently invidious, and this conclusion of a coequal branch of Government is not without significance to the question presently under consideration."

Frontiero v. Richardson, 411 U.S. at 411 U. S. 687. [18]

Moreover, even when judicial action has catalyzed legislative change, that change certainly does not eviscerate the underlying constitutional principle. The Court, for example, has never suggested that race-based classifications became any less suspect once extensive legislation had been enacted on the subject. See Palmore v. Sidoti, 466 U. S. 429 (1984).

For the retarded, just as for Negroes and women, much has changed in recent years, but much remains the same; outdated statutes are still on the books, and irrational fears or ignorance, traceable to the prolonged social and cultural isolation of the retarded, continue to stymie recognition of the dignity and individuality of retarded people. Heightened judicial scrutiny of action appearing to impose unnecessary barriers to the retarded is required in light of increasing recognition that such barriers are inconsistent with evolving principles of equality embedded in the Fourteenth Amendment.

The Court also offers a more general view of heightened scrutiny, a view focused primarily on when heightened scrutiny does not apply, as opposed to when it does apply. [19] Two principles appear central to the Court's theory. First, heightened scrutiny is said to be inapplicable where individuals in a group have distinguishing characteristics that legislatures properly may take into account in some circumstances. Ante at 473 U. S. 441-442. Heightened scrutiny is also purportedly inappropriate when many legislative classifications affecting the group are likely to be valid. We must, so the Court says,

"look to the likelihood that governmental action premised on a particular classification is valid as a general matter, not merely to the specifics of the case before us,"

in deciding whether to apply heightened scrutiny. Ante at 473 U. S. 446.

If the Court's first principle were sound, heightened scrutiny would have to await a day when people could be cut from a cookie mold. Women are hardly alike in all their characteristics, but heightened scrutiny applies to them because legislatures can rarely use gender itself as a proxy for these other characteristics. Permissible distinctions between persons must bear a reasonable relationship to their relevant characteristics, Zobel v. Williams, 457 U.S. at 457 U. S. 70 (BRENNAN, J., concurring), and gender per se is almost never relevant. Similarly, that some retarded people have reduced capacities in some areas does not justify using retardation as a proxy for reduced capacity in areas where relevant individual variations in capacity do exist.

The Court's second assertion -- that the standard of review must be fixed with reference to the number of classifications to which a characteristic would validly be relevant -- is similarly flawed. Certainly the assertion is not a logical one; that a characteristic may be relevant under some or even many circumstances does not suggest any reason to presume it relevant under other circumstances where there is reason to suspect it is not. A sign that says "men only" looks very different on a bathroom door than a courthouse door. But see 83 U. S. Illinois, 16 Wall. 130 (1873).

Our heightened-scrutiny precedents belie the claim that a characteristic must virtually always be irrelevant to warrant heightened scrutiny. Plyler, for example, held that the status of being an undocumented alien is not a "constitutional irrelevancy," and therefore declined to review with strict scrutiny classifications affecting undocumented aliens. 457 U.S. at 457 U. S. 219, n.19. While Frontiero stated that gender "frequently" and "often" bears no relation to legitimate legislative aims, it did not deem gender an impermissible basis of state action in all circumstances. 411 U.S. at 411 U. S. 686-687. Indeed, the Court has upheld some gender-based classifications. Rostker v. Goldberg, 453 U. S. 57 (1981); Michael M. v. Superior Court of Sonoma County, 450 U. S. 464 (1981). Heightened but not strict, scrutiny is considered appropriate in areas such as gender, illegitimacy, or alienage [20] because the Court views the trait as relevant under some circumstances, but not others. [21] That view -- indeed the very concept of heightened, as opposed to strict, scrutiny -- is flatly inconsistent with the notion that heightened scrutiny should not apply to the retarded because "mental retardation is a characteristic that the government may legitimately take into account in a wide range of decisions." Ante at 473 U. S. 446. Because the government also may not take this characteristic into account in many circumstances, such as those presented here, careful review is required to separate the permissible from the invalid in classifications relying on retardation.

The fact that retardation may be deemed a constitutional irrelevancy in some circumstances is enough, given the history of discrimination the retarded have suffered, to require careful judicial review of classifications singling out the retarded for special burdens. Although the Court acknowledges that many instances of invidious discrimination against the retarded still exist, the Court boldly asserts that, "in the vast majority of situations," special treatment of the retarded is "not only legitimate, but also desirable." Ante at 473 U. S. 444. That assertion suggests the Court would somehow have us calculate the percentage of "situations" in which a characteristic is validly and invalidly invoked before determining whether heightened scrutiny is appropriate. But heightened scrutiny has not been "triggered" in our past cases only after some undefined numerical threshold of invalid "situations" has been crossed. An inquiry into constitutional principle, not mathematics, determines whether heightened scrutiny is appropriate. Whenever evolving principles of equality, rooted in the Equal Protection Clause, require that certain classifications be viewed as potentially discriminatory, and when history reveals systemic unequal treatment, more searching judicial inquiry than minimum rationality becomes relevant.

Potentially discriminatory classifications exist only where some constitutional basis can be found for presuming that equal rights are required. Discrimination, in the Fourteenth Amendment sense, connotes a substantive constitutional judgment that two individuals or groups are entitled to be treated equally with respect to something. With regard to economic and commercial matters, no basis for such a conclusion exists, for as

Justice Holmes urged the Lochner Court, the Fourteenth Amendment was not "intended to embody a particular economic theory. . . ." Lochner v. New York, 198 U.S. at 198 U. S. 75 (dissenting). As a matter of substantive policy, therefore, government is free to move in any direction, or to change directions, [22] in the economic and commercial sphere. [23] The structure of economic and commercial life is a matter of political compromise, not constitutional principle, and no norm of equality requires that there be as many opticians as optometrists, see Williamson v. Lee Optical of Oklahoma, Inc., 348 U. S. 483 (1955), or new businesses as old, see New Orleans v. Dukes, 427 U. S. 297 (1976).

But the Fourteenth Amendment does prohibit other results under virtually all circumstances, such as castes created by law along racial or ethnic lines, see Palmore v. Sidoti, 466 U.S. at 466 U. S. 432-433; Loving v. Virginia, 388 U. S. 1 (1967); McLaughlin v. Florida, 379 U. S. 184 (1964); Shelley v. Kraemer, 334 U. S. 1, 334 U. S. 23 (1948); Hernandez v. Texas, 347 U. S. 475 (1954), and significantly constrains the range of permissible government choices where gender or illegitimacy, for example, are concerned. Where such constraints, derived from the Fourteenth Amendment, are present, and where history teaches that they have systemically been ignored, a "more searching judicial inquiry" is required. United States v. Carolene Products Co., 304 U. S. 144, 304 U. S. 153, n. 4 (1938).

That more searching inquiry, be it called heightened scrutiny or "second order" rational basis review, is a method of approaching certain classifications skeptically, with judgment suspended until the facts are in and the evidence considered. The government must establish that the classification is substantially related to important and legitimate objectives, see, e.g., Craig v. Boren, 429 U. S. 190 (1976), so that valid and sufficiently weighty policies actually justify the departure from equality. Heightened scrutiny does not allow courts to second-guess reasoned legislative or professional judgments tailored to the unique needs of a group like the retarded, but it does seek to assure that the hostility or thoughtlessness with which there is reason to be concerned has not carried the day. By invoking heightened scrutiny, the Court recognizes, and compels lower courts to recognize, that a group may well be the target of the sort of prejudiced, thoughtless, or stereotyped action that offends principles of equality found in the Fourteenth Amendment. Where classifications based on a particular characteristic have done so in the past, and the threat that they may do so remains, heightened scrutiny is appropriate. [24]

As the history of discrimination against the retarded and its continuing legacy amply attest, the mentally retarded have been, and in some areas may still be, the targets of action the Equal Protection Clause condemns. With respect to a liberty so valued as the right to establish a home in the community, and so likely to be denied on the basis of irrational fears and outright hostility, heightened scrutiny is surely appropriate.

IV

In light of the scrutiny that should be applied here, Cleburne's ordinance sweeps too broadly to dispel the suspicion that it rests on a bare desire to treat the retarded as outsiders, pariahs who do not belong in the community. The Court, while disclaiming that special scrutiny is necessary or warranted, reaches the same conclusion. Rather than striking the ordinance down, however, the Court invalidates it merely as applied to respondents. I must dissent from the novel proposition that "the preferred course of adjudication" is to leave standing a legislative Act resting on "irrational prejudice," ante at 473 U. S. 450, thereby forcing individuals in the group discriminated against to continue to run the Act's gauntlet.

The Court appears to act out of a belief that the ordinance might be "rational" as applied to some subgroup of the retarded under some circumstances, such as those utterly without the capacity to live in a community, and that the ordinance should not be invalidated in toto if it is capable of ever being validly applied. But the issue is not "whether the city may never insist on a special use permit for the mentally retarded in an R-3 zone." Ante at 473 U. S. 447. The issue is whether the city may require a permit pursuant to a blunderbuss ordinance drafted many years ago to exclude all the "feeble-minded," or whether the city must enact a new ordinance carefully tailored to the exclusion of some well-defined subgroup of retarded people in circumstances in which exclusion might reasonably further legitimate city purposes.

By leaving the sweeping exclusion of the "feebleminded" to be applied to other groups of the retarded, the Court has created peculiar problems for the future. The Court does not define the relevant characteristics of respondents or their proposed home that make it unlawful to require them to seek a special permit. Nor does the Court delineate any principle that defines to which, if any, set of retarded people the ordinance might validly be applied. Cleburne's City Council and retarded applicants are left without guidance as to the potentially valid, and invalid, applications of the ordinance. As a consequence, the Court's as-applied remedy relegates future retarded applicants to the standardless discretion of low-level officials who have already shown an all too willing readiness to be captured by the "vague, undifferentiated fears," ante at 473 U. S. 449, of ignorant or frightened residents.

Invalidating on its face the ordinance's special treatment of the "feeble-minded," in contrast, would place the responsibility for tailoring and updating Cleburne's unconstitutional ordinance where it belongs: with the legislative arm of the city of Cleburne. If Cleburne perceives a legitimate need for requiring a certain well-defined subgroup of the retarded to obtain special permits before establishing group homes, Cleburne will, after studying the problem and making the appropriate policy decisions, enact a new, more narrowly tailored ordinance. That ordinance might well look very different from the current one; it might separate group homes (presently treated nowhere in the ordinance) from hospitals, and it might define a narrow subclass of the retarded for whom even group homes could legitimately be excluded. Special treatment of the retarded might be ended altogether. But whatever the contours such an ordinance might take, the city should not be allowed to keep its ordinance on the books intact, and thereby shift to the courts the responsibility to confront the complex empirical and policy questions involved in updating statutes affecting the mentally retarded. A legislative solution would yield standards and provide the sort of certainty to retarded applicants and administrative officials that case-by-case judicial rulings cannot provide. Retarded applicants should not have to continue to attempt to surmount Cleburne's vastly overbroad ordinance.

The Court's as-applied approach might be more defensible under circumstances very different from those presented here. Were the ordinance capable of being cleanly severed, in one judicial cut, into its permissible and impermissible applications, the problems I have pointed out would be greatly reduced. Cf. United States v. Grace, 461 U. S. 171 (1983) (statute restricting speech and conduct in Supreme Court building and on its grounds invalid as applied to sidewalks); but cf. id. at 461 U. S. 184-188 (opinion concurring in part and dissenting in part). But no readily apparent construction appears, nor has the Court offered one, to define which group of retarded people the city might validly require a permit of, and which it might not, in the R-3 zone. The Court's as-applied holding is particularly inappropriate here, for nine-tenths of the group covered by the statute appears similarly situated to respondents, see ante at 473 U. S. 442, n. 9 -- a figure that makes the statutory presumption enormously overbroad. Cf. Stanley v. Illinois, 405 U. S. 645 (1972) (invalidating statutory presumption despite State's insistence that it validly applied to "most" of those covered).

To my knowledge, the Court has never before treated an equal protection challenge to a statute on an as-applied basis. When statutes rest on impermissibly overbroad generalizations, our cases have invalidated the presumption on its face. [25] We do not instead leave to the courts the task of redrafting the statute through an ongoing and cumbersome process of "as applied" constitutional rulings. In Cleveland Board of Education v. LaFleur, 414 U. S. 632 (1974), for example, we invalidated, inter alia, a maternity leave policy that required pregnant schoolteachers to take unpaid leave beginning five months before their expected due date. The school board argued that some teachers became physically incapable of performing adequately in the latter stages of their pregnancy, and we accepted this justification for purposes of our decision. Assuming the policy might validly be applied to some teachers, particularly in the last few weeks of their pregnancy, id. at 414 U. S. 647, n. 13, we nonetheless invalidated it in toto, rather than simply as applied to the particular plaintiff. The Court required school boards to employ "alternative administrative means" to achieve their legitimate health and safety goal, id. at 414 U. S. 647, or the legislature to enact a more carefully tailored statute, id. at 414 U. S. 647, n. 13.

Similarly, Caban v. Mohammed, 441 U. S. 380 (1979), invalidated a law that required parental consent to adoption from unwed mothers, but not from unwed fathers. This distinction was defended on the ground, inter alia, that unwed fathers were often more difficult to locate, particularly during a child's infancy. We suggested the legislature might make proof of abandonment easier or proof of paternity harder, but we required the legislature to draft a new statute tailored more precisely to the problem of locating unwed fathers. The statute was not left on the books by invalidating it only as applied to unwed fathers who actually proved they could be located. When a presumption is unconstitutionally overbroad, the preferred course of adjudication is to strike it down. See also United States Dept. of Agriculture v. Moreno, 413 U. S. 528 (1973); Stanley v. Illinois, supra; Vlandis v. Kline, 412 U. S. 441, 412 U. S. 453-454 (1973); Carrington v. Rash, 380 U. S. 89 (1965); Sugarman v. Dougall, 413 U. S. 634, 413 U. S. 646-649 (1973); Weber v. Aetna Casualty & Surety Co., 406 U. S. 164 (1972); Levy v. Louisiana, 391 U. S. 68 (1968).

In my view, the Court's remedial approach is both unprecedented in the equal protection area and unwise. This doctrinal change, of course, was not sought by the parties, suggested by the various amici, or discussed at oral argument. Moreover, the Court does not persuasively reason its way to its novel remedial holding nor reconsider our prior cases directly on point. Instead, the Court simply asserts that "this is the preferred course of adjudication." Given that this assertion emerges only from today's decision, one can only hope it will not become entrenched in the law without fuller consideration.

V

The Court's opinion approaches the task of principled equal protection adjudication in what I view as precisely the wrong way. The formal label under which an equal protection claim is reviewed is less important than careful identification of the interest at stake and the extent to which society recognizes the classification as an invidious one. Yet in focusing obsessively on the appropriate label to give its standard of review, the Court fails to identify the interests at stake or to articulate the principle that classifications based on mental retardation must be carefully examined to assure they do not rest on impermissible assumptions or false stereotypes regarding individual ability and need. No guidance is thereby given as to when the Court's free-wheeling, and potentially dangerous, "rational basis standard" is to be employed, nor is attention directed to the invidiousness of grouping all retarded individuals together. Moreover, the Court's narrow, as-applied remedy fails to deal adequately with the overbroad presumption that lies at the heart of this case. Rather than leaving future retarded individuals to run the gauntlet of this overbroad presumption, I would affirm the judgment of the Court of Appeals in its entirety, and would strike down on its face the provision at issue. I therefore concur in the judgment in part and dissent in part.

Notes

[1] See also Spector Motor Service, Inc. v. McLaughlin, 323 U. S. 101, 323 U. S. 105 (1944) ("If there is one doctrine more deeply rooted than any other in the process of constitutional adjudication, it is that we ought not to pass on questions of constitutionality . . . unless such adjudication is unavoidable"); Burton v. United States, 196 U. S. 283, 196 U. S. 295 (1905) ("It is not the habit of the court to decide questions of a constitutional nature unless absolutely necessary to a decision of the case"); see generally Ashwander v. TVA, 297 U. S. 288, 297 U. S. 346-348 (1936) (Brandeis, J.,

concurring).

Even today, the Court again "calls to mind" these principles, ante at 473 U. S. 447, but given the Court's lengthy dicta on heightened scrutiny, this call to principle must be read with some irony.

[2] I do not suggest the lower court erred in relying on heightened scrutiny, for I believe more searching inquiry than the traditional rational basis test is required to invalidate Cleburne's ordinance. See infra at 473 U. S. 458-460.

[3] See also Three Affiliated Tribes v. Wold Engineering, 467 U. S. 138, 467 U. S. 157-158 (1984); Leroy v. Great Western United Corp., 443 U. S. 173, 443 U. S. 181 (1979).

[4] The two cases the Court cites in its rational basis discussion, Zobel v. Williams, 457 U. S. 55 (1982), and United States Dept. of Agriculture v. Moreno, 413 U. S. 528 (1973), expose the special nature of the rational basis test employed today. As two of only a handful of modern equal protection cases striking down legislation under what purports to be a rational basis standard, these cases must be, and generally have been, viewed as intermediate review decisions masquerading in rational basis language. See, e.g., L. Tribe, American Constitutional Law § 16-31, p. 1090, n. 10 (1978) (discussing Moreno); see also Moreno, supra, at 413 U. S. 538 (Douglas, J., concurring); Zobel, supra, at 457 U. S. 65 (BRENNAN, J., concurring).

[5] Indeed, the group home in this case was specifically located near a park, a school, and a shopping center so that its residents would have full access to the community at large.

[6] S. Herr, Rights and Advocacy for Retarded People 18 (1983).

[7] On the role of these ideologies in this era, see K. Stampp, Era of Reconstruction, 1865-1877, pp. 18-22 (1965).

[8] H. Goddard, The Possibilities of Research as Applied to the Prevention of Feeblemindedness, Proceedings of the National Conference of Charities and Correction 307 (1915), cited in A. Deutsch, The Mentally Ill in America 360 (2d ed.1949). See also Fernald, The Burden of Feeblemindedness, 17 J. Psycho-Asthenics 87, 90 (1913) (the retarded "cause unutterable sorrow at home and are a menace and danger to the community"); Terman, Feeble-Minded Children in the Public Schools of California, 5 Schools & Society 161 (1917) ("[O]nly recently have we begun to recognize how serious a menace [feeblemindedness] is to the social, economic and moral welfare of the state. . . . [I]t is responsible . . . for the majority of cases of chronic and semi-chronic pauperism, and for much of our alcoholism, prostitution, and venereal diseases"). Books with titles such as "The Menace of the Feeble Minded in Connecticut" (1915), issued by the Connecticut School for Imbeciles, became commonplace. See C. Frazier, (Chairman, Executive Committee of Public Charities Assn. of Pennsylvania), The Menace of the Feeble-Minded In Pennsylvania (1913); W. Fernald, The Burden of Feeble-Mindedness (1912) (Mass.); Juvenile Protection Association of Cincinnati, The Feeble-Minded, Or the Hub to Our Wheel of Vice (1915) (Ohio). The resemblance to such works as R. Shufeldt, The Negro: A Menace to American Civilization (1907), is striking, and not coincidental.

[9] A. Moore, The Feeble-Minded in New York 3 (1911). This book was sponsored by the State Charities Aid Association. See also P. Tyor & L. Bell, Caring for the Retarded in America 71-104 (1984). The segregationist purpose of these laws was clear. See, e.g., Act of Mar. 22, 1915, ch. 90, 1915 Tex.Gen.Laws 143 (repealed 1955) (Act designed to relieve society of "the heavy economic and moral losses arising from the existence at large of these unfortunate persons").

[10] See Pennsylvania Assn. for Retarded Children v. Pennsylvania, 343 F.Supp. 279, 294-295 (ED Pa.1972); see generally S. Sarason & J. Doris, Educational Handicap, Public Policy, and Social History 271-272 (1979).

[11] Act of Apr. 3, 1920, ch. 210, § 17, 1920 Miss. Laws 288, 294.

[12] See, e.g., Act of Mar.19, 1928, ch. 156, 1928 Ky.Acts 534, remains in effect, Ky.Rev.Stat. § 402.990(2) (1984); Act of May 25, 1905, No. 136, § 1, 1905 Mich.Pub.Acts 185, 186, remains in effect; Mich.Comp.Laws § 551.6 (1979); Act of Apr. 3, 1920, ch. 210, § 29, 1920 Miss. Gen. Laws 288, 300, remains in effect with minor changes, Miss.Code Ann. § 41-21-45 (1972).

[13] See Chamberlain, Current Legislation -- Eugenics and Limitations of Marriage, 9 A.B.A.J. 429 (1923); Lau v. Lau, 81 N. H. 44, 122 A. 345, 346 (1923); State v. Wyman, 118 Conn. 501, 173 A. 155, 156 (1934). See generally Linn & Bowers, The Historical Fallacies Behind Legal Prohibitions of Marriages Involving Mentally Retarded Persons -- The Eternal Child Grows Up, 13 Gonz.L.Rev. 625 (1978); Shaman, Persons Who Are Mentally Retarded: Their Right to Marry and Have Children, 12 Family L. Q. 61 (1978); Note, The Right of the Mentally Disabled to Marry: A Statutory Evaluation, 15 J. Family L. 463 (1977).

[14] See Note, Mental Disability and the Right to Vote, 88 Yale L.J. 1644 (1979).

[15] Congress expressly found that most handicapped children, including the retarded, were simply shut out from the public school system. See 20 U.S.C. § 1400(b).

[16] See generally G. Allport, The Nature of Prejudice (1958) (separateness among groups exaggerates differences).

[17] This history of discrimination may well be directly relevant to the issue before the Court. Cleburne's current exclusion of the "feeble-minded" in its 1965 zoning ordinance appeared as a similar exclusion of the "feebleminded" in the city's 1947 ordinance, see Act of Sept. 26, 1947, § 5; the latter tracked word for word a similar exclusion in the 1929 comprehensive zoning ordinance for the nearby city of Dallas. See Dallas Ordinance, No. 2052, § 4, passed Sept. 11, 1929.

Although we have been presented with no legislative history for Cleburne's zoning ordinances, this genealogy strongly suggests that Cleburne's current exclusion of the "feeble-minded" was written in the darkest days of segregation and stigmatization of the retarded, and simply carried over to the current ordinance. Recently we held that extant laws originally motivated by a discriminatory purpose continue to violate the Equal Protection Clause, even if they would be permissible were they reenacted without a discriminatory motive. See Hunter v. Underwood, 471 U. S. 222, 471 U. S. 233 (1985). But in any event, the roots of a law that, by its terms, excludes from a community the "feebleminded" are clear. As the examples above attest, see n. 7, supra, "feebleminded" was the defining term for all retarded people in the era of overt and pervasive discrimination.

[18] Although Frontiero was a plurality opinion, it is now well established that gender classifications receive heightened scrutiny. See, e.g., Mississippi University for Women v. Hogan, 458 U. S. 718 (1982).

[19] For its general theories about heightened scrutiny, the Court relies heavily, indeed virtually exclusively, on the "lesson" of Massachusetts Board of Retirement v. Murgia, 427 U. S. 307 (1976). The brief per curiam in Murgia, however, was handed down in the days before the Court explicitly acknowledged the existence of heightened scrutiny. See Craig v. Boren, 429 U. S. 190 (1976); id. at 429 U. S. 210 (POWELL, J., concurring). Murgia explains why age-based distinctions do not trigger strict scrutiny, but says nothing about whether such distinctions warrant heightened scrutiny. Nor have subsequent cases addressed this issue. See Vance v. Bradley, 440 U. S. 93, 440 U. S. 97 (1979).

[20] Alienage classifications present a related variant, for strict scrutiny is applied to such classifications in the economic and social area, but only heightened scrutiny is applied when the classification relates to "political functions." Cabell v. Chavez-Salido, 454 U. S. 432, 454 U. S. 439 (1982); see also Bernal v. Fainter, 467 U. S. 216, 467 U. S. 220-222 (1984). Thus, characterization of the area to which an alienage classification applies is necessary to determine how strongly it must be justified.

[21] I express no view here as to whether strict scrutiny ought to be extended to these classifications.

[22] Constitutional provisions other than the Equal Protection Clause, such as the Contracts Clause, the Just Compensation Clause, or the Due Process Clause, may constrain the extent to which government can upset settled expectations when changing course and the process by which it must implement such changes.

[23] Only when it can be said that "Congress misapprehended what it was doing," United States Railroad Retirement Bd. v. Fritz, 449 U. S. 166, 449 U. S. 193 (1980) (BRENNAN, J., dissenting), will a classification fail the minimal rational basis standard. Even then, the classification fails not because of limits on the directions which substantive policy can take in the economic and commercial area, but because the classification reflects no underlying substantive policy -- it is simply arbitrary.

[24] No single talisman can define those groups likely to be the target of classifications offensive to the Fourteenth Amendment and therefore warranting heightened or strict scrutiny; experience, not abstract logic, must be the primary guide. The "political powerlessness" of a group may be relevant, San Antonio Independent School District v. Rodriguez, 411 U. S. 1, 411 U. S. 28 (1973), but that factor is neither necessary, as the gender cases demonstrate, nor sufficient, as the example of minors illustrates. Minors cannot vote and thus might be considered politically powerless to an

extreme degree. Nonetheless, we see few statutes reflecting prejudice or indifference to minors, and I am not aware of any suggestion that legislation affecting them be viewed with the suspicion of heightened scrutiny. Similarly, immutability of the trait at issue may be relevant, but many immutable characteristics, such as height or blindness, are valid bases of governmental action and classifications under a variety of circumstances. See ante at 473 U. S. 442-443, n. 10.

The political powerlessness of a group and the immutability of its defining trait are relevant insofar as they point to a social and cultural isolation that gives the majority little reason to respect or be concerned with that group's interests and needs. Statutes discriminating against the young have not been common nor need be feared because those who do vote and legislate were once themselves young, typically have children of their own, and certainly interact regularly with minors. Their social integration means that minors, unlike discrete and insular minorities, tend to be treated in legislative arenas with full concern and respect, despite their formal and complete exclusion from the electoral process.

The discreteness and insularity warranting a "more searching judicial inquiry," United States v. Carolene Products Co., 304 U. S. 144, 304 U. S. 153, n. 4 (1938), must therefore be viewed from a social and cultural perspective, as well as a political one. To this task judges are well suited, for the lessons of history and experience are surely the best guide as to when, and with respect to what interests, society is likely to stigmatize individuals as members of an inferior caste, or view them as not belonging to the community. Because prejudice spawns prejudice, and stereotypes produce limitations that confirm the stereotype on which they are based, a history of unequal treatment requires sensitivity to the prospect that its vestiges endure. In separating those groups that are discrete and insular from those that are not, as in many important legal distinctions, "a page of history is worth a volume of logic." New York Trust Co. v. Eisner, 256 U. S. 345, 256 U. S. 349 (1921) (Holmes, J.).

[25] The Court strongly suggests that the loose fit of the ordinance to its purported objectives signifies that the ordinance rests on "an irrational prejudice," ante at 473 U. S. 450, an unconstitutional legislative purpose. See Mississippi University for Women v. Hogan, 458 U.S. at 458 U. S. 725. In that event, recent precedent should make clear that the ordinance must, in its entirety, be invalidated. See Hunter v. Underwood, 471 U. S. 222 (1985). Hunter involved a 1902 constitutional provision disenfranchising various felons. Because that provision had been motivated, at least in part, by a desire to disenfranchise Negroes, we invalidated it on its face. In doing so, we did not suggest that felons could not be deprived of the vote through a statute motivated by some purpose other than racial discrimination. See Richardson v. Ramirez, 418 U. S. 24 (1974). Yet that possibility, or the possibility that the provision might have been only partly motivated by the desire to disenfranchise Negroes, did not suggest the provision should be invalidated only "as applied" to the particular plaintiffs in Hunter, or even as applied to Negroes more generally. Instead we concluded:

"Without deciding whether § 182 would be valid if enacted today without any impermissible motivation, we simply observe that its original enactment was motivated by a desire to discriminate against blacks on account of race, and the section continues to this day to have that effect. As such, it violates equal protection under Arlington Heights [v. Metropolitan Housing Development Corp., 429 U. S. 252 (1977)]."

471 U.S. at 471 U. S. 233. If a discriminatory purpose infects a legislative Act, the Act itself is inconsistent with the Equal Protection Clause, and cannot validly be applied to anyone.

Have to tell jury you bribed the witness to testify: Justice Marshall's dissent in United States v. Bagley (July 2, 1985)

JUSTICE MARSHALL, with whom JUSTICE BRENNAN joins, dissenting.

When the Government withholds from a defendant evidence that might impeach the prosecution's only witnesses, that failure to disclose cannot be deemed harmless error. Because that is precisely the nature of the undisclosed evidence in this case, I would affirm the judgment of the Court of Appeals, and would not remand for further proceedings.

I

The federal grand jury indicted the respondent, Hughes Anderson Bagley, on charges involving possession of firearms and controlled substances with intent to distribute. Following a bench trial, Bagley was found not guilty of the firearms charges, guilty of two counts of knowingly and intentionally distributing Valium, and guilty of several counts of a lesser included offense of possession of controlled substances. He was sentenced to six months' imprisonment and a special parole term of five years on the first count of distribution, and to three years of imprisonment, which were suspended, and five years' probation, on the second distribution count. He received a suspended sentence and five years' probation for the possession convictions.

The record plainly demonstrates that, on the two counts for which Bagley received sentences of imprisonment, the Government's entire case hinged on the testimony of two private security guards who aided the Bureau of Alcohol, Tobacco and Firearms (ATF) in its investigation of Bagley. In 1977, the two guards, O'Connor and Mitchell, worked for the Milwaukee Railroad; for about three years, they had been social acquaintances of Bagley, with whom they often shared coffee breaks. 7 Tr. 2-3; 8 Tr. 2a-3a. At trial, they testified that, on two separate occasions, they had visited Bagley at his home, where Bagley had responded to O'Connor's complaint that he was extremely anxious by giving him Valium pills. In total, Bagley received $8 from O'Connor, representing the cost of the pills. At trial, Bagley testified that he had a prescription for the Valium because he suffered from a bad back, 14 Tr. 963-964. No testimony to the contrary was introduced. O'Connor and Mitchell each testified that they had worn concealed transmitters and body recorders at these meetings, but the tape recordings were insufficiently clear to be admitted at trial and corroborate their testimony.

Before trial, counsel for Bagley had filed a detailed discovery motion requesting, among other things, "any deals, promises or inducements made to witnesses in exchange for their testimony." App. 17-19. In response to the discovery request, the Government had provided affidavits sworn by O'Connor and Mitchell that had been prepared during their investigation of Bagley. Each affidavit recounted in detail the dealings the witnesses had had with Bagley, and closed with the declaration,

"I made this statement freely and voluntarily without any threats or rewards, or promises of reward having been made to me in return for it."

Brief for United States 3, quoting Memorandum of Points and Authorities in Support of Pet. for Habeas Corpus, CV803592-RJK(M) (CD Cal.) Exhibits 1-9. Both of these agents testified at trial thereafter, and the Government did not disclose the existence of any deals, promises, or inducements. Counsel for Bagley asked O'Connor on cross-examination whether he was testifying in response to pressure or threats from the Government about his job, and O'Connor said he was not. 7 Tr. 89-90. In light of the affidavits, as well as the prosecutor's silence as to the existence of any promises, deals, or inducements, counsel did not pursue the issue of bias of either guard.

As it turns out, however, in May, 1977, seven months prior to trial, O'Connor and Mitchell each had signed an agreement providing that ATF would pay them for information they provided. The form was entitled "Contract for Purchase of Information and Payment of Lump Sum Therefor," and provided that the Bureau would,

"upon the accomplishment of the objective sought to be obtained . . . pay to said vendor a sum commensurate with services and information rendered."

App. 22-23. It further invited the Bureau's special agent in charge of the investigation, Agent Prins, to recommend an amount to be paid after the information received had proved "worthy of compensation." Agent Prins had personally presented these forms to O'Connor and Mitchell for their signatures. The two witnesses signed the last of their affidavits, which declared the absence of any promise of reward, the day after they signed the ATF forms. After trial, Agent Prins requested that O'Connor and Mitchell each be paid $500, but the Bureau reduced these "rewards" to $300 each. App. to Pet. for Cert. 14a. The District Court Judge concluded that

"it appears probable to the Court that O'Connor and Mitchell did expect to receive from the United States some kind of compensation, over and above their expenses, for their assistance, though perhaps not for their testimony."

Id. at 7a.

Upon discovering these ATF forms through a Freedom of Information Act request, Bagley sought relief from his conviction. The District Court Judge denied Bagley's motion to vacate his sentence, stating that, because he was the same judge who had been the original trier of fact, he was able to determine the effect the contracts would have had on his decision, more than four years earlier, to convict Bagley. The judge stated that, beyond a reasonable doubt, the contracts, if disclosed, would have had no effect upon the convictions:

"The Court has read in their entirety the transcripts of the testimony of James P. O'Connor and Donald E. Mitchell at the trial. . . . Almost all of the testimony of both of those witnesses was devoted to the firearm charges in the indictment. The Court found the defendant not guilty of those charges. With respect to the charges against the defendant of distributing controlled substances and possessing controlled substances with the intention of distributing them, the testimony of O'Connor and Mitchell was relatively very brief. With respect to the charges relating to controlled substances, cross-examination of those witnesses by defendant's counsel did not seek to discredit their testimony as to the facts of distribution, but rather sought to show that the controlled substances in question came from supplies which had been prescribed for defendant's own use. As to that aspect of their testimony, the testimony of O'Connor and Mitchell tended to be favorable to the defendant."

Id. at 8a.

The foregoing statement, as to which the Court remands for further consideration, is seriously flawed on its face. First, the testimony that the court describes was in fact the only inculpatory testimony in the case as to the two counts for which Bagley received a sentence of imprisonment. If, as the judge claimed, the testimony of the two information "vendors" was "very brief" and in part favorable to the defendant, that fact shows the weakness of the prosecutor's case, not the harmlessness of the error. If the testimony that might have been impeached is weak and also cumulative, corroborative, or tangential, the failure to disclose the impeachment evidence could conceivably be held harmless. But when the testimony is the start and finish of the prosecution's case, and is weak nonetheless, quite a different conclusion must necessarily be drawn.

Second, the court's statement that Bagley did not attempt to discredit the witnesses' testimony, as if to suggest that impeachment evidence would not have been used by the defense, ignores the realities of trial preparation and strategy, and is factually erroneous as well. Initially, the Government's failure to disclose the existence of any inducements to its witnesses, coupled with its disclosure of affidavits stating that no promises had been made, would lead all but the most careless lawyer to step wide and clear of questions about promises or inducements. The combination of nondisclosure and disclosure would simply lead any reasonable attorney to believe that the witness could not be impeached on that basis. Thus, a firm avowal that no payment is being received in return for assistance and testimony, if offered at trial by a witness who is not even a Government employee, could be devastating to the defense. A wise attorney would, of necessity, seek an alternative defense strategy.

Moreover, counsel for Bagley in fact did attempt to discredit O'Connor, by asking him whether two ATF agents had pressured him or had threatened that his job might be in jeopardy, in order to get him to cooperate. 7 Tr. 89-90. But when O'Connor answered in the negative, ibid., counsel stopped this line of questioning. In addition, counsel for

Bagley attempted to argue to the District Court, in his closing argument, that O'Connor and Mitchell had "fabricated" their accounts, 14 Tr. 1117, but the court rejected the proposition:

"Let me say this to you. I would find it hard to believe really that their testimony was fabricated. I think they might have been mistaken. You know, it is possible that they were mistaken. I really did not get the impression at all that either one or both of those men were trying at least in court here to make a case against the defendant."

Id. at 1117-1118. (Emphasis added.) The District Court, in so saying, of course had seen no evidence to suggest that the two witnesses might have any motive for "mak[ing] a case" against Bagley. Yet, as JUSTICE BLACKMUN points out, the possibility of a reward, the size of which is directly related to the Government's success at trial, gave the two witnesses a "personal stake" in the conviction and an "incentive to testify falsely in order to secure a conviction." Ante at 473 U. S. 683.

Nor is this case unique. Whenever the Government fails, in response to a request, to disclose impeachment evidence relating to the credibility of its key witnesses, the truthfinding process of trial is necessarily thrown askew. The failure to disclose evidence affecting the overall credibility of witnesses corrupts the process to some degree in all instances, see Giglio v. United States, 405 U. S. 150 (1972); Napue v. Illinois, 360 U. S. 264 (1959); United States v. Agurs, 427 U. S. 97, 427 U. S. 121 (1976) (MARSHALL, J., dissenting), but when "the reliability of a given witness may well be determinative of guilt or innocence,'" Giglio, supra, at 405 U. S. 154 (quoting Napue, supra, at 360 U. S. 269), and when "the Government's case depend[s] almost entirely on" the testimony of a certain witness, 405 U.S. at 405 U. S. 154, evidence of that witness' possible bias simply may not be said to be irrelevant, or its omission harmless. As THE CHIEF JUSTICE said in Giglio v. United States, in which the Court ordered a new trial in a case in which a promise to a key witness was not disclosed to the jury:

"[W]ithout [Taliento's testimony], there could have been no indictment and no evidence to carry the case to the jury. Taliento's credibility as a witness was therefore an important issue in the case, and evidence of any understanding or agreement as to a future prosecution would be relevant to his credibility, and the jury was entitled to know of it."

"For these reasons, the due process requirements enunciated in Napue and other cases cited earlier require a new trial."

Id. at 405 U. S. 154-155. Here, too, witnesses O'Connor and Mitchell were crucial to the Government's case. Here, too, their personal credibility was potentially dispositive, particularly since the allegedly corroborating tape recordings were not audible. It simply cannot be denied that the existence of a contract signed by those witnesses, promising a reward whose size would depend "on the Government's satisfaction with the end result," ante at 473 U. S. 683, might sway the trier of fact, or cast doubt on the truth of all that the witnesses allege. In such a case, the trier of fact is absolutely entitled to know of the contract, and the defense counsel is absolutely entitled to develop his case with an awareness of it. Whatever the applicable standard of materiality, see infra, in this instance, it undoubtedly is well met.

Indeed, Giglio essentially compels this result. The similarities between this case and that one are evident. In both cases, the triers of fact were left unaware of Government inducements to key witnesses. In both cases, the individual trial prosecutors acted in good faith when they failed to disclose the exculpatory evidence. See Giglio, supra, at 405 U. S. 151-153; App. to Pet. for Cert. 13a (Magistrate's finding that Bagley prosecutor would have disclosed information had he known of it). The sole difference between the two cases lies in the fact that, in Giglio, the prosecutor affirmatively stated to the trier of fact that no promises had been made. Here, silence in response to a defense request took the place of an affirmative error at trial -- although the prosecutor did make an affirmative misrepresentation to the defense in the affidavits. Thus, in each case, the trier of fact was left unaware of powerful reasons to question the credibility of the witnesses.

"[T]he truth-seeking process is corrupted by the withholding of evidence favorable to the defense, regardless of whether the evidence is directly contradictory to evidence offered by the prosecution."

Agurs, supra, at 427 U. S. 120 (MARSHALL, J., dissenting). In this case, as in Giglio, a new trial is in order, and the Court of Appeals correctly reversed the District Court's denial of such relief.

II

Instead of affirming, the Court today chooses to reverse and remand the case for application of its newly stated standard to the facts of this case. While I believe that the evidence at issue here, which remained undisclosed despite a particular request, undoubtedly was material under the Court's standard, I also have serious doubts whether the Court's definition of the constitutional right at issue adequately takes account of the interests this Court sought to protect in its decision in Brady v. Maryland, 373 U. S. 83 (1963).

A

I begin from the fundamental premise, which hardly bears repeating, that "[t]he purpose of a trial is as much the acquittal of an innocent person as it is the conviction of a guilty one." Application of Kapatos, 208 F.Supp. 883, 888 (SDNY 1962); see Giles v. Maryland, 386 U. S. 66, 386 U. S. 98 (1967) (Fortas, J., concurring in judgment) ("The State's obligation is not to convict, but to see that, so far as possible, truth emerges"). When evidence favorable to the defendant is known to exist, disclosure only enhances the quest for truth; it takes no direct toll on that inquiry. Moreover, the existence of any small piece of evidence favorable to the defense may, in a particular case, create just the doubt that prevents the jury from returning a verdict of guilty. The private whys and wherefores of jury deliberations pose an impenetrable barrier to our ability to know just which piece of information might make, or might have made, a difference.

When the state does not disclose information in its possession that might reasonably be considered favorable to the defense, it precludes the trier of fact from gaining access to such information, and thereby undermines the reliability of the verdict. Unlike a situation in which exculpatory evidence exists, but neither the defense nor the prosecutor has uncovered it, in this situation, the state already has, resting in its files, material that would be of assistance to the defendant. With a minimum of effort, the state could improve the real and apparent fairness of the trial enormously, by assuring that the defendant may place before the trier of fact favorable evidence known to the government. This proposition is not new. We have long recognized that, within the limit of the state's ability to identify so-called exculpatory information, the state's concern for a fair verdict precludes it from withholding from the defense evidence favorable to the defendant's case in the prosecutor's files. See, e.g., Pyle v. Kansas, 317 U. S. 213, 317 U. S. 215-216 (1942) (allegation that imprisonment resulted from perjured testimony and deliberate suppression by authorities of evidence favorable to him "charge a deprivation of rights guaranteed by the Federal Constitution"). [1]

This recognition no doubt stems in part from the frequently considerable imbalance in resources between most criminal defendants and most prosecutors' offices. Many, perhaps most, criminal defendants in the United States are represented by appointed counsel, who often are paid minimal wages and operate on shoestring budgets. In addition, unlike police, defense counsel generally is not present at the scene of the crime, or at the time of arrest, but instead comes into the case late. Moreover, unlike the government, defense counsel is not in the position to make deals with witnesses to gain evidence. Thus, an inexperienced, unskilled, or unaggressive attorney often is unable to amass the factual support necessary to a reasonable defense. When favorable evidence is in the hands of the prosecutor but not disclosed, the result may well be that the defendant is deprived of a fair chance before the trier of fact, and the trier of fact is deprived of the ingredients necessary to a fair decision. This grim reality, of course, poses a direct challenge to the traditional model of the adversary criminal process, [2] and perhaps because this reality so directly questions the fairness of our longstanding processes, change has been cautious and halting. Thus, the Court has not gone the full road and expressly required that the state provide to the defendant access to the prosecutor's complete files, or investigators who will assure that the defendant has an opportunity to discover every existing piece of helpful evidence. But cf. Ake v. Oklahoma, 470 U. S. 68 (1985) (access to assistance of psychiatrist constitutionally required on proper showing of need). Instead, in acknowledgment of the fact that important interests are served when potentially favorable evidence is disclosed, the Court has fashioned a compromise, requiring that the prosecution identify and disclose to the defendant favorable material that it possesses. This requirement is but a small, albeit important, step toward equality of justice. [3]

B

Brady v. Maryland, 373 U. S. 83 (1963), of course, established this requirement of disclosure as a fundamental element of a fair trial by holding that a defendant was denied due process if he was not given access to favorable evidence that is material either to guilt or punishment. Since Brady was decided, this Court has struggled, in a series of decisions, to define how best to effectuate the right recognized. To my mind, the Brady decision, the reasoning that underlay it, and the fundamental interest in a fair trial combine to give the criminal defendant the right to receive from the prosecutor, and the prosecutor the affirmative duty to turn over to the defendant, all information known to the government that might reasonably be considered favorable to the defendant's case. Formulation of this right, and imposition of this duty, are "the essence of due process of law. It is the State that tries a man, and it is the State that must insure that the trial is fair." Moore v. Illinois, 408 U. S. 786, 408 U. S. 809-810 (1972) (MARSHALL, J., concurring in part and dissenting in part). If that right is denied, or if that duty is shirked, however, I believe a reviewing court should not automatically reverse, but instead should apply the harmless error test the Court has developed for instances of error affecting constitutional rights. See Chapman v. California, 386 U. S. 18 (1967).

My view is based in significant part on the reality of criminal practice and on the consequently inadequate protection to the defendant that a different rule would offer. To implement Brady, courts must of course work within the confines of the criminal process. Our system of criminal justice is animated by two seemingly incompatible notions: the adversary model and the state's primary concern with justice, not convictions. Brady, of course, reflects the latter goal of justice, and is in some ways at odds with the competing model of a sporting event. Our goal, then, must be to integrate the Brady right into the harsh, daily reality of this apparently discordant criminal process.

At the trial level, the duty of the state to effectuate Brady devolves into the duty of the prosecutor; the dual role that the prosecutor must play poses a serious obstacle to implementing Brady. The prosecutor is by trade, if not necessity, a zealous advocate. He is a trained attorney who must aggressively seek convictions in court on behalf of a victimized public. At the same time, as a representative of the state, he must place foremost in his hierarchy of interests the determination of truth. Thus, for purposes of Brady, the prosecutor must abandon his role as an advocate and pore through his files, as objectively as possible, to identify the material that could undermine his case. Given this obviously unharmonious role, it is not surprising that these advocates oftentimes overlook or downplay potentially favorable evidence, often in cases in which there is no doubt that the failure to disclose was a result of absolute good faith. Indeed, one need only think of the Fourth Amendment's requirement of a neutral intermediary, who tests the strength of the policeman-advocate's facts, to recognize the curious status Brady imposes on a prosecutor. One telling example, offered by Judge Newman when he was a United States Attorney, suffices:

"I recently had occasion to discuss [Brady] at a PLI Conference in New York City before a large group of State prosecutors. . . . I put to them this case: You are prosecuting a bank robbery. You have talked to two or three of the tellers and one or two of the customers at the time of the robbery. They have all taken a look at your defendant in a line-up, and they have said, 'This is the man.' In the course of your investigation you also have found another customer who was in the bank that day, who viewed the suspect and came back and said, 'This is not the man.'"

"The question I put to these prosecutors was, do you believe you should disclose to the defense the name of the witness who, when he viewed the suspect, said 'that is not the man?' In a room of prosecutors not quite as large as this group, but almost as large, only two hands went up. There were only two prosecutors in that group who felt they should disclose or would disclose that information. Yet I was putting to them what I thought was the easiest case -- the clearest case for disclosure of exculpatory information!"

J. Newman, A Panel Discussion before the Judicial Conference of the Second Judicial Circuit (Sept. 8, 1967), reprinted in Discovery in Criminal Cases, 44 F.R.D. 481, 500-501 (1968) (hereafter Newman).

While familiarity with Brady no doubt has increased since 1967, the dual role that the prosecutor must play, and the very real pressures that role creates, have not changed.

The prosecutor surely greets the moment at which he must turn over Brady material with little enthusiasm. In perusing his files, he must make the often difficult decision as to whether evidence is favorable, and must decide on which side to err when faced with doubt. In his role as advocate, the answers are clear. In his role as representative of the state, the answers should be equally clear, and often to the contrary. Evidence that is of doubtful worth in the eyes of the prosecutor could be of inestimable value to the defense, and might make the difference to the trier of fact.

Once the prosecutor suspects that certain information might have favorable implications for the defense, either because it is potentially exculpatory or relevant to credibility, I see no reason why he should not be required to disclose it. After all, favorable evidence indisputably enhances the truthseeking process at trial. And it is the job of the defense, not the prosecution, to decide whether and in what way to use arguably favorable evidence. In addition, to require disclosure of all evidence that might reasonably be considered favorable to the defendant would have the precautionary effect of assuring that no information of potential consequence is mistakenly overlooked. By requiring full disclosure of favorable evidence in this way, courts could begin to assure that a possibly dispositive piece of information is not withheld from the trier of fact by a prosecutor who is torn between the two roles he must play. A clear rule of this kind, coupled with a presumption in favor of disclosure, also would facilitate the prosecutor's admittedly difficult task by removing a substantial amount of unguided discretion.

If a trial will thereby be more just, due process would seem to require such a rule absent a countervailing interest. I see little reason for the government to keep such information from the defendant. Its interest in nondisclosure at the trial stage is at best slight: the government apparently seeks to avoid the administrative hassle of disclosure, and to prevent disclosure of inculpatory evidence that might result in witness intimidation and manufactured rebuttal evidence. [4] Neither of these concerns, however, counsels in favor of a rule of nondisclosure in close or ambiguous cases. To the contrary, a rule simplifying the disclosure decision, by definition, does not make that decision more complex. Nor does disclosure of favorable evidence inevitably lead to disclosure of inculpatory evidence, as might an open file policy, or to the anticipated wrongdoings of defendants and their lawyers, if indeed such fears are warranted. We have other mechanisms for disciplining unscrupulous defense counsel; hamstringing their clients need not be one of them. I simply do not find any state interest that warrants withholding from a presumptively innocent defendant, whose liberty is at stake in the proceeding, information that bears on his case and that might enable him to defend himself.

Under the foregoing analysis, the prosecutor's duty is quite straightforward: he must divulge all evidence that reasonably appears favorable to the defendant, erring on the side of disclosure.

C

The Court, however, offers a complex alternative. It defines the right not by reference to the possible usefulness of the particular evidence in preparing and presenting the case, but retrospectively, by reference to the likely effect the evidence will have on the outcome of the trial. Thus, the Court holds that due process does not require the prosecutor to turn over evidence unless the evidence is "material," and the Court states that evidence is "material"

"only if there is a reasonable probability that, had the evidence been disclosed to the defense, the result of the proceeding would have been different."

Ante at 473 U. S. 682. Although this looks like a posttrial standard of review, see, e.g., Strickland v. Washington, 466 U. S. 668 (1984) (adopting this standard of review), it is not. Instead, the Court relies on this review standard to define the contours of the defendant's constitutional right to certain material prior to trial. By adhering to the view articulated in United States v. Agurs, 427 U. S. 97 (1976) -- that there is no constitutional duty to disclose evidence unless nondisclosure would have a certain impact on the trial -- the Court permits prosecutors to withhold with impunity large amounts of undeniably favorable evidence, and it imposes on prosecutors the burden to identify and disclose evidence pursuant to a pretrial standard that virtually defies definition.

The standard for disclosure that the Court articulates today enables prosecutors to avoid disclosing obviously exculpatory evidence while acting well within the bounds of their constitutional obligation. Numerous lower court cases provide examples of evidence that is undoubtedly favorable, but not necessarily "material" under the Court's definition, and that consequently would not have to be disclosed to the defendant under the Court's view. See, e.g., United States v. Sperling, 726 F.2d 69, 71-72 (CA2 1984) (prior statement disclosing motive of key Government witness to testify), cert. denied, 467 U.S. 1243 (1984); King v. Ponte, 717 F.2d 635 (CA1 1983) (prior inconsistent statements of Government witness); see also United States v. Oxman, 740 F.2d 1298, 1311 (CA3 1984) (addressing "disturbing" prosecutorial tendency to withhold information because of later opportunity to argue, with the benefit of hindsight, that information was not "material"), cert. pending sub nom. United States v. Pflaumer, No. 84-1033. The result is to veer sharply away from the basic notion that the fairness of a trial increases with the amount of existing favorable evidence to which the defendant has access, and to disavow the ideal of full disclosure.

The Court's definition poses other, serious problems. Besides legitimizing the nondisclosure of clearly favorable evidence, the standard set out by the Court also asks the prosecutor to predict what effect various pieces of evidence will have on the trial. He must evaluate his case and the case of the defendant -- of which he presumably knows very little -- and perform the impossible task of deciding whether a certain piece of information will have a significant impact on the trial, bearing in mind that a defendant will later shoulder the heavy burden of proving how it would have affected the outcome. At best, this standard places on the prosecutor a responsibility to speculate, at times without foundation, since the prosecutor will not normally know what strategy the defense will pursue or what evidence the defense will find useful. At worst, the standard invites a prosecutor, whose interests are conflicting, to gamble, to play the odds, and to take a chance that evidence will later turn out not to have been potentially dispositive. One Court of Appeals has recently vented its frustration at these unfortunate consequences:

"It seems clear that those tests [for materiality] have a tendency to encourage unilateral decisionmaking by prosecutors with respect to disclosure. . . . [T]he root of the problem is the prosecutor's tendency to adopt a retrospective view of materiality. Before trial, the prosecutor cannot know whether, after trial, particular evidence will prove to have been material. . . . Following their adversarial instincts, some prosecutors have determined unilaterally that evidence will not be material and, often in good faith, have disclosed it neither to defense counsel nor to the court. If and when the evidence emerges after trial, the prosecutor can always argue, with the benefit of hindsight, that it was not material."

United States v. Oxman, supra, at 1310.

The Court's standard also encourages the prosecutor to assume the role of the jury, and to decide whether certain evidence will make a difference. In our system of justice, that decision properly and wholly belongs to the jury. The prosecutor, convinced of the guilt of the defendant and of the truthfulness of his witnesses, may all too easily view as irrelevant or unpersuasive evidence that draws his own judgments into question. Accordingly he will decide the evidence need not be disclosed. But the ideally neutral trier of fact, who approaches the case from a wholly different perspective, is by the prosecutor's decision denied the opportunity to consider the evidence. The reviewing court, faced with a verdict of guilty, evidence to support that verdict, and pressures, again understandable, to finalize criminal judgments, is in little better position to review the withheld evidence than the prosecutor.

I simply cannot agree with the Court that the due process right to favorable evidence recognized in Brady was intended to become entangled in prosecutorial determinations of the likelihood that particular information would affect the outcome of trial. Almost a decade of lower court practice with Agurs convinces me that courts and prosecutors have come to pay

"too much deference to the federal common law policy of discouraging discovery in criminal cases, and too little regard to due process of law for defendants."

United States v. Oxman, supra, at 1310-1311. Apparently anxious to assure that reversals are handed out sparingly, the Court has defined a rigorous test of materiality. Eager to apply the "materiality" standard at the pretrial stage, as the Court permits them to do, prosecutors lose sight of the basic principles underlying the doctrine. I would return to the original theory and promise of Brady, and reassert the duty of the prosecutor to disclose all evidence in his files that might reasonably be considered favorable to the defendant's case. No prosecutor can know prior to trial whether such evidence will be of consequence at trial; the mere fact that it might be, however, suffices to mandate disclosure. [5]

D

In so saying, I recognize that a failure to divulge favorable information should not result in reversal in all cases. It may be that a conviction should be affirmed on appeal despite the prosecutor's failure to disclose evidence that reasonably might have been deemed potentially favorable prior to trial. The state's interest in nondisclosure at trial is minimal, and should therefore yield to the readily apparent benefit that full disclosure would convey to the search for truth. After trial, however, the benefits of disclosure may at times be tempered by the state's legitimate desire to avoid retrial when error has been harmless. However, in making the determination of harmlessness, I would apply our normal constitutional error test, and reverse unless it is clear beyond a reasonable doubt that the withheld evidence would not have affected the outcome of the trial. See Chapman v. California, 386 U. S. 18 (1967); see also Agurs, 427 U.S. at 427 U. S. 119-120 (MARSHALL, J., dissenting). [6]

Any rule other than automatic reversal, of course, dilutes the Brady right to some extent, and offers the prosecutor an incentive not to turn over all information. In practical effect, it might be argued, there is little difference between the rule I propose -- that a prosecutor must disclose all favorable evidence in his files, subject to harmless error review -- and the rule the Court adopts -- that the prosecutor must disclose only the favorable information that might affect the outcome of the trial. According to this argument, if a constitutional right to all favorable evidence leads to reversal only when the withheld evidence might have affected the outcome of the trial, the result will be the same as with a constitutional right only to evidence that will affect the trial outcome. See Capra, Access to Exculpatory Evidence: Avoiding the Agurs Problems of Prosecutorial Discretion and Retrospective Review, 53 Ford.L.Rev. 391, 409-410, n. 117 (1984). For several reasons, however, I disagree. First, I have faith that a prosecutor would treat a rule requiring disclosure of all information of a certain kind differently from a rule requiring disclosure only of some of that information. Second, persistent or egregious failure to comply with the constitutional duty could lead to disciplinary actions by the courts. Third, the standard of harmlessness I adopt is more protective of the defendant than that chosen by the Court, placing the burden on the prosecutor, rather than the defendant, to prove the harmlessness of his actions. It would be a foolish prosecutor who gambled too glibly with that standard of review. And finally, it is unrealistic to ignore the fact that, at the appellate stage, the state has an interest in avoiding retrial where the error is harmless beyond a reasonable doubt. That interest counsels against requiring a new trial in every case.

Thus, while I believe that some review for harmlessness is in order, I disagree with the Court's standard, even were it merely a standard for review, and not a definition of "materiality." First, I see no significant difference, for truthseeking purposes, between the Giglio situation and this one; for the same reasons I believe the result must therefore be the same here as in Giglio, see supra, at 473 U. S. 691-692, I also believe the standard for reversal should be the same. The defendant's entitlement to a new trial ought to be no different in the two cases, and the burden he faces on appeal should also be the same. Giglio remains the law for a class of cases, and I reaffirm my belief that the same standard applies to this case as well. See Agurs, supra, at 427 U. S. 119-120 (MARSHALL, J., dissenting).

Second, only a strict appellate standard, which places on the prosecutor a burden to defend his decisions, will remove the incentive to gamble on a finding of harmlessness. Any lesser standard, and especially one in which the defendant bears the burden of proof, provides the prosecutor with ample room to withhold favorable evidence, and provides a reviewing court with a simple means to affirm whenever, in its view, the correct result was reached. This is especially true given the speculative nature of retrospective review:

"The appellate court's review of 'what might have been' is extremely difficult in the context of an adversarial system. Evidence is not introduced in a vacuum; rather, it is built upon. The absence of certain evidence may thus affect the usefulness, and hence the use, of other evidence to which defense counsel does have access. Indeed, the absence of a piece of evidence may affect the entire trial strategy of defense counsel."

Capra, supra, at 412. As a consequence, the appellate court no less than the prosecutor must substitute its judgment for that of the trier of fact under an inherently slippery test. Given such factors as a reviewing court's natural inclination to affirm a judgment that appears "correct" and that court's obvious inability to know what a jury ever will do, only a strict and narrow test that places the burden of proof on the prosecutor will begin to prevent affirmances in cases in which the withheld evidence might have had an impact.

Even under the most protective standard of review, however, courts must be careful to focus on the nature of the evidence that was not made available to the defendant, and not simply on the quantity of the evidence against the defendant separate from the withheld evidence. Otherwise, as the Court today acknowledges, the reviewing court risks overlooking the fact that a failure to disclose has a direct effect on the entire course of trial.

Without doubt, defense counsel develops his trial strategy based on the available evidence. A missing piece of information may well preclude the attorney from pursuing a strategy that potentially would be effective. His client might consequently be convicted even though nondisclosed information might have offered an additional or alternative defense, if not pure exculpation. Under such circumstances, a reviewing court must be sure not to focus on the amount of evidence supporting the verdict to determine whether the trier of fact reasonably would reach the same conclusion. Instead, the court must decide whether the prosecution has shown beyond a reasonable doubt that the new evidence, if disclosed and developed by reasonably competent counsel, would not have affected the outcome of trial. [7]

In this case, it is readily apparent that the undisclosed information would have had an impact on the defense presented at trial, and perhaps on the judgment. Counsel for Bagley argued to the trial judge that the Government's two key witnesses had fabricated their accounts of the drug distributions, but the trial judge rejected the argument for lack of any evidence of motive. See supra at 473 U. S. 690. These key witnesses, it turned out, were each to receive monetary rewards whose size was contingent on the usefulness of their assistance. These rewards "served only to strengthen any incentive to testify falsely in order to secure a conviction." Ante at 473 U. S. 683. To my mind, no more need be said; this nondisclosure could not have been harmless. I would affirm the judgment of the Court of Appeals.

Notes

[1] As early as 1807, this Court made clear that, prior to trial, a defendant must have access to impeachment evidence in the Government's possession. Addressing defendant Aaron Burr's claim that he should have access to the letter of General Wilkinson, a key witness against Burr in his trial for treason, Chief Justice Marshall wrote:

"The application of that letter to the case is shown by the terms in which the communication was made. It is a statement of the conduct of the accused made by the person who is declared to be the essential witness against him. The order for producing this letter is opposed:"

"First, because it is not material to the defense. It is a principle, universally acknowledged, that a party has a right to oppose to the testimony of any witness against him, the declarations which that witness has made at other times on the same subject. If he possesses this right, he must bring forward proof of those declarations. This proof must be obtained before he knows positively what the witness will say; for if he waits until the witness has been heard at the trial, it is too late to meet him with his former declarations. Those former declarations, therefore, constitute a mass of testimony, which a party has a right to obtain by way of precaution, and the positive necessity of which can only be decided at the trial."

United States v. Burr, 25 F.Cas. 30, 36 (No. 14,692d) (CC Va. 1807).

[2] See Fortas, The Fifth Amendment: Nemo Tenetur Prodere Seipsum, 25 Clev.B.A.J. 91, 98 (1954) ("The state and [the defendant] could meet, as the law contemplates, in adversary trial, as equals -- strength against strength, resource against resource, argument against argument"); see also Babcock, Fair Play: Evidence Favorable to an Accused and Effective Assistance of Counsel, 34 Stan.L.Rev. 1133, 1142-1145 (1982) (discussing challenge Brady poses to traditional adversary model).

[3] Indeed, this Court's recent decision stating a stringent standard for demonstrating ineffective assistance of counsel makes an effective Brady right even more crucial. Without a real guarantee of effective counsel, the relative abilities of the state and the defendant become even more skewed, and the need for a minimal guarantee of access to potentially favorable information becomes significantly greater. See Strickland v. Washington, 466 U. S. 668 (1984); id. at 466 U. S. 712-715 (MARSHALL, J., dissenting); Babcock, supra, at 1163-1174 (discussing the interplay between the right to Brady material and the right to effective assistance of counsel).

[4] See Newman, 44 F.R.D. at 499 (describing the "serious" problem of witness intimidation that arises from prosecutor's disclosure of witnesses). But see Brennan, The Criminal Prosecution: Sporting Event or Quest for Truth?, 1963 Wash.U.L.Q. 279, 289-290 (disputing a similar argument).

[5] Brady not only stated the rule that suppression by the prosecution of evidence favorable to the defendant "violates due process where the evidence is material either to guilt or to punishment," 373 U.S. at 373 U. S. 87, but also observed that two decisions of the Court of Appeals for the Third Circuit "state the correct constitutional rule." Id. at 373 U. S. 86. Neither of those decisions limited the right only to evidence that is "material" within the meaning that the Court today articulates. Instead, they provide strong evidence that Brady might have used the word in its evidentiary sense, to mean, essentially, germane to the points at issue.

In United States ex rel. Almeida v. Baldi, 195 F.2d 815 (CA3 1952), cert. denied, 345 U.S. 904 (1953), the appeals court granted a petition for habeas corpus in a case in which the State had withheld from the defendant evidence that might have mitigated his punishment. After describing the withheld evidence as "relevant" and "pertinent," 195 F.2d at 819, the court concluded:

"We think that the conduct of the Commonwealth as outlined in the instant case is in conflict with our fundamental principles of liberty and justice. The suppression of evidence favorable to Almeida was a denial of due process."

Id. at 820. Similarly, in United States ex rel. Thompson v. Dye, 221 F.2d 763, 765 (CA3), cert. denied, 350 U.S. 875 (1955), the District Court had denied a petition for habeas corpus after finding that certain evidence of defendant's drunkenness at the time of the offense in question was not "vital" to the defense, and did not require disclosure. 123 F.Supp. 759, 762 (WD Pa.1954). The Court of Appeals reversed, observing that, whether or not the jury ultimately would credit the evidence at issue, the evidence was substantial, and the State's failure to disclose it cannot "be held as a matter of law to be unimportant to the defense here." 221 F.2d at 767.

It is clear that the term "material" has an evidentiary meaning quite distinct from that which the Court attributes to it. Judge Weinstein, for example, defines as synonymous the words "ultimate fact," "operative fact," "material fact," and "consequential fact," each of which, he states, means "a fact that is of consequence to the determination of the action.'" 1 J. Weinstein & M. Berger, Weinstein's Evidence � 401[03], n. 1 (1982) (quoting Fed.Rule Evid. 401). Similarly, another treatise on evidence explains that there are two components to relevance -- materiality and probative value.

"Materiality looks to the relation between the propositions for which the evidence is offered and the issues in the case. If the evidence is offered to help prove a proposition which is not a matter in issue, the evidence is immaterial."

E. Cleary, McCormick on Evidence § 185 (3d ed.1984). "Probative value" addresses the tendency of the evidence to establish a "material" proposition. Ibid. See also 1 J. Wigmore, Evidence § 2 (P. Tillers rev.1982). There is nothing in Brady to suggest that the Court intended anything other than a rule that favorable evidence need only relate to a proposition at issue in the case in order to merit disclosure.

Even if the Court did not use the term "material" simply to refer to favorable evidence that might be relevant, however, I still believe that due process requires that prosecutors have the duty to disclose all such evidence. The inherent difficulty in applying, prior to trial, a definition that relates to the outcome of the trial, and that is based on speculation and not knowledge, means that a considerable amount of potentially consequential material might slip through the Court's standard. Given the experience of the past decade with Agurs, and the practical problem that inevitably exists because the evidence must be disclosed prior to trial to be of any use, I can only conclude that all potentially favorable evidence must be disclosed. Of course, I agree with courts that have allowed exceptions to this rule on a showing of exigent circumstances based on security and law enforcement needs.

[6] In a case of deliberate prosecutorial misconduct, automatic reversal might well be proper. Certain kinds of constitutional error so infect the system of justice as to require reversal in all cases, such as discrimination in jury selection. See, e.g., Peters v. Kiff, 407 U. S. 493 (1972). A deliberate effort of the prosecutor to undermine the search for truth clearly is in the category of offenses antithetical to our most basic vision of the role of the state in the criminal process.

[7] For example, in United States ex rel. Butler v. Maroney, 319 F.2d 622 (CA3 1963), the defendant was convicted of first-degree murder. Trial counsel based his defense on temporary insanity at the time of the murder. During trial, testimony suggested that the shooting might have been the accidental result of a struggle, but defense counsel did not develop that defense. It later turned out that an eyewitness to the shooting had given police a statement that the victim and Butler had struggled prior to the murder. If defense counsel had known before trial what the eyewitness had seen, he might have relied on an additional defense, and he might have emphasized the struggle.

See Note, The Prosecutor's Constitutional Duty to Reveal Evidence to the Defendant, 74 Yale L.J. 136, 145 (1964). Unless the same information already was known to counsel before trial, the failure to disclose evidence of that kind simply cannot be harmless, because reasonably competent counsel might have utilized it to yield a different outcome. No matter how overwhelming the evidence that Butler committed the murder, he had a right to go before a trier of fact and present his best available defense.

Similarly, in Ashley v. Texas, 319 F.2d 80 (CA5), cert. denied, 375 U.S. 931 (1963), the defendant was sentenced to death for murder. The prosecutor disclosed to the defense a psychiatrist's report indicating that the defendant was sane, but he failed to disclose the reports of a psychiatrist and a psychologist indicating that the defendant was insane. The nondisclosed information did not relate to the trial defense of self-defense. But the failure to disclose the evidence clearly prevented defense counsel from developing the possibly dispositive defense that he might have developed through further psychiatric examinations and presentation at trial. The nondisclosed evidence obviously threw off the entire course of trial preparation, and a new trial was in order. In such a case, there simply is no need to consider -- in light of the evidence that actually was presented and the quantity of evidence to support the verdict returned -- the possible effect of the information on the particular jury that heard the case. Indeed, to make such an evaluation would be to substitute the reviewing court's judgment of the facts, including the previously undisclosed evidence, for that of the jury, and to do so without the benefit of competent counsel's development of the information.

See also Field, Assessing the Harmlessness of Federal Constitutional Error -- A Process in Need of a Rationale, 125 U.Pa.L.Rev. 15 (1976) (discussing application of harmless error test).

Klamath Tribe has special right to hunt and fish on certain lands: Justice Marshall's dissent in Oregon Department of Fish and Wildlife v. Klamath Indian Tribe (July 2, 1985)

JUSTICE MARSHALL, with whom JUSTICE BRENNAN joins, dissenting.

The Court today holds that the Klamath Tribe has no special right to hunt and fish on certain lands although it has done so undisturbed from time immemorial. Instead, the Tribe is determined to be subject to state regulation to the same extent as any other person in the State of Oregon. This Court has in the past recognized that Indian hunting and fishing rights -- even if nonexclusive, and even if existing apart from reservation lands -- are valuable property rights, not fully subject to state regulation and not to be deemed abrogated without explicit indication. [1] Although all agree that hunting and fishing have historically been vital to the continued prosperity of the Klamath, the Court today assumes that the Klamath Tribe silently gave up its rights to hunt and fish on these lands in a 1901 Agreement, approved by Congress in 1906, that had no purpose other than to benefit the Tribe for a previous injustice. It reaches this conclusion even though there is no historical evidence that any party to the Agreement envisioned it as having the effect of altering tribal hunting and fishing practices, and even though hunting and fishing practices did not in fact change as a result of the Agreement. Although I agree that the boilerplate language of the Agreement can be read as the Court does, I also believe that such a reading is not necessary, ignores the Agreement's historical context, and is not faithful to the well-established principles that Indian treaties are to be interpreted as they were likely understood by the tribe and that doubts concerning the meaning of a treaty should be resolved in favor of the tribe. [2] Accordingly, I dissent.

I

I will only briefly summarize the relevant history of the Klamath Reservation. As the Court explains, in 1864, the Klamath Tribe entered into a treaty with the United States whereby it agreed to settle on a reservation of 1.9 million acres in south central Oregon. Treaty of Oct. 14, 1864, 16 Stat. 707. This land was a small part of the 22 million acres of land to which the Klamath had held aboriginal title. As the Court points out:

"The 1864 Treaty also provided that the [Klamath Tribe] would have . . . 'the exclusive right of taking fish in the streams and lakes, included in said reservation, and of gathering edible roots, seeds, and berries within its limits.'"

Ante at 473 U. S. 755. Although the borders of the reservation soon became the subject of some dispute, the purposes of the Treaty have always been clear. These purposes, and the importance of Indian hunting and fishing rights to their accomplishment, were well stated in a report to Congress by a Commission appointed to study the later boundary dispute:

"It was evidently a principal object of the treaty to draw the Indians in from the large extent of territory over which they were roaming, subject to constant collisions with the steadily encroaching whites, and to concentrate them on an area much more limited, but which would still be ample to provide them with the means of subsistence."

"To attain this, the marked tendency of the treaty and the emphatic testimony of the Indians seek to make all the boundaries mountain ridges, a purpose of which the nature of the country renders easy of accomplishment on all sides except the north."

"There is no provision in the treaty, however, for the support of the Indians by the Government, and as the high altitude and the severity of the climate are unfavorable to the cultivation of cereals, their subsistence depended upon natural products, consisting principally of game, fish, wild roots, and seeds. These mountain barriers, therefore, must include a territory frequented by game, streams stocked with fish, and ground producing the roots and seeds which formed so large a portion of the subsistence of the Indians."

S. Doc. No. 93, 54th Cong., 2d Sess., 6-7 (1897) (Klamath Boundary Commission Report).

The boundaries of the reservation that was eventually established pursuant to the Treaty, however, contained only about two-thirds of the land promised the Klamath Tribe, and among the areas left outside the reservation were tribal hunting, fishing, and gathering grounds of substantial importance. These areas had been specifically included in the Treaty's definition of the planned reservation at the Tribe's insistence; but, as the result of an erroneous 1871 survey, over 617,000 acres of land promised to the Tribe were excluded from the newly established reservation. As a result of the erroneous survey and in violation of the Treaty, non-Indians began to enter on the land for stock grazing and, to a lesser extent, for settlement. See, e.g., S.Exec.Doc. No. 129, 53d Cong., 2d Sess., 4-6, 8-9, 11, 17 (1894) (various documents noting grazing uses and relatively light settlement); see also n. 5, infra. The Klamath vehemently and repeatedly protested these entrances, but nevertheless continued to hunt and fish on the excluded land. See S.Doc. No. 93, supra, at 11, 15-16, 18. The protests continued for decades, and eventually led to Congress' establishment of a Boundary Commission to determine the proper boundaries of the reservation and to determine the value of the erroneously excluded land. Act of June 10, 1896, ch. 398, 29 Stat. 321, 342.

The Boundary Commission went to the reservation and interviewed large numbers of Klamath. Tribal elders all insisted that they were sure that the disputed land was supposed to be in the reservation. They had explicitly demanded the land's inclusion in the 1864 Treaty, they explained, because of the land's traditional importance in the Tribe's essential hunting, fishing, and gathering activities. The Commissioners inspected the land and found a tribal fishing site upon which a stone dam had been constructed and maintained by the Tribe to aid in gathering large numbers of fish. The Commission concluded that the Klamath's complaints were largely justified, and deserving of redress. [3]

The Commission determined, pursuant to the Tribe's desires, that redress would take the form of officially ceding the excluded land back to the United States for compensation, leaving the border of the reservation where it had been erroneously set. As the Court notes, however, the Commission determined the value of the excluded land with no reference to its use for hunting, fishing, or gathering -- basing valuation on its use for timber and stock grazing. Yet the Commission knew the land's importance to the Tribe for hunting and fishing, since this was the basis of the Commission's finding that it had been erroneously excluded from the reservation. Similarly, during the course of the two years of negotiations toward an agreement, there was no reference to any cessation of hunting, fishing, or gathering activity on the land in question, nor, it is true, to the continuing of such activity. The issue was simply never mentioned, and there is certainly no specific evidence that anyone, whether Klamath or Government official, envisioned that the Agreement would compel the Tribe to in any way alter the important hunting and fishing activities that it had been engaged in since the initial establishment of the reservation. During that time, the Tribe had been forced to accept that others were entering and using the land, but the Tribe also had continued to fish and hunt as it always had done.

The Court is correct that the Tribe seemed fully satisfied with the possibility that the excluded land would be ceded to the United States for compensation, and there were no protests raised concerning loss of fishing, hunting, and gathering rights. Ante at 473 U. S. 759. But I cannot conclude from this silence that the Tribe understood and agreed to the extinguishing of hunting and fishing rights on the ceded land. Ante at 473 U. S. 770. Given the historical context of the 1901 Agreement, its proper interpretation is that, first, it compensated the Tribe for the fact that its position since the reservation's establishment had been less than the Tribe had been promised, and, second, it preserved the Tribe's position as it had actually existed since the erroneous survey. The Tribe's actual position between the erroneous survey and the 1901 Agreement included no ability to exercise exclusive possession of the erroneously excluded lands, although they had been promised that right in the 1864 Treaty; but the Tribe's position did include the ability to hunt and fish on those lands, and there is no reason to believe that a goal of the 1901 Agreement was to terminate such activities.

II

A

As the Court notes, the case focuses on two provisions of the 1901 Agreement. Article I of the Agreement contained a broad cession by the Tribe of "all their claim, right, title, and interest in and to" the excluded land. 34 Stat. 367. In contrast, Article IV of the Agreement broadly declared that

"nothing in [the] agreement shall be construed to deprive the said Klamath . . . of any benefits to which they are entitled under existing treaties, not inconsistent with the provisions of this agreement."

Respondent and the courts below argued that the language of Article IV can reasonably be interpreted as a reservation by the Indians of a nonexclusive right to hunt and fish on those parts of the ceded land not in private hands. [4]

The Court rejects this construction of Article IV because of its unexplained insistence that the 1901 Agreement must be understood in terms of the structure of the 1864 Treaty, which envisioned no nonexclusive or off-reservation hunting rights. Indeed, as the Court emphasizes, a provision of the 1864 Treaty obligated the Tribe's members to remain on the reservation established by its terms. 16 Stat. 708. Thus, in the Court's view, because the reservation was diminished by the 1901 Agreement, and because the 1864 Treaty envisioned that the Tribe would hunt and fish only on its reservation, the 1901 Agreement must also have diminished the area where hunting and fishing rights existed. To allow nonexclusive hunting and fishing rights on the ceded lands would, in the Court's view, create a "glaring inconsistency" with the 1864 Treaty, because to exercise such a right would have required the Tribe to leave the borders of its now-diminished reservation, in violation of the 1864 Treaty obligation to remain on reservation land. Ante at 473 U. S. 770.

B

This overly formal approach to treaty interpretation ignores the fundamental presumptions that Indian treaties are to be construed as the tribes would have understood them, Choctaw Nation v. Oklahoma, 397 U. S. 620, 397 U. S. 631 (1970), and that ambiguities should be resolved in favor of the tribe. Washington v. Washington Commercial Passenger Fishing Vessel Assn., 443 U. S. 658, 443 U. S. 675-676 (1979). I would have thought that an inquiry into the 1901 Agreement's meaning would focus, not primarily on the formal structure of the 1864 Treaty -- leaving both documents abstracted from their actual purposes and historical contexts -- but instead on the problems that arose since 1864 that gave rise to the need for the 1901 Agreement. Certainly, the latter approach is better suited to the goal of determining the purposes of the parties, and especially, to the goal of determining the understandings of the Tribe.

When looking at the 1901 Agreement in terms of its own historical setting, the evidence clearly supports two conclusions -- first, that the Tribe had no expectation that it was losing its ability to continue those fishing and hunting practices that it had been pursuing from time immemorial on the ceded lands, and second, that the United States had no particular interest in terminating such fishing and hunting activities.

(1)

The Tribe's perspective is not difficult to divine. At the time of the 1901 Agreement, as well as at the time of the 1906 Act of Congress which ratified this Agreement, "[h]unting, fishing, gathering and trapping [were] crucial to the survival of the Klamath Indians." App.19 (stipulated facts). The Tribe had received, under the 1864 Treaty, the right to hunt and fish on the specific lands that were ceded in the 1901 Agreement, and had received that right because it had insisted on the particular importance to the Tribe of its ability to hunt and fish on those specific lands. Although these lands had not been included within the erroneous borders of the original reservation, the Tribe nevertheless entered them to hunt and fish.

The 1864 Treaty had also granted the Tribe the exclusive right to possess the lands in question, and particularly prohibited the use of these lands by non-Indians. 16 Stat. 708. But the Tribe had never been able to exercise this right to exclude others. The erroneous boundaries had opened the lands to others; thus, the Tribe's ability to hunt and fish had become nonexclusive, and its ability to exercise exclusive possession had disappeared. This was what it had lost, and accordingly, tribal members' complaints had focused only on the presence of non-Indians on their lands. They never asserted an interference with their ability to hunt and fish. It is clear that the Tribe envisioned the 1901 Agreement only as providing compensation for the loss that the Tribe had suffered. And there is certainly nothing in the record to indicate that the Agreement in any way was working a further loss on the Tribe. In this context, Article IV makes clear that the Tribe was not to lose any benefits that it had actually possessed as it entered the 1901 Agreement.

(2)

The United States' purposes were similarly clear, as the 1901 Agreement was entirely a result of Indian demands for the redress of an unfortunate mistake. The United States fully understood that the land in question was ill-suited for agriculture and settlement, and the record reflects no other collateral purposes of Congress. Indeed, there is no evidence of any pressures on Congress from non-Indians urging the cession at issue. [5] There is simply no reason to believe that the United States -- acting as trustee and seeking to compensate the Tribe for an unjust and accidental diminishment of their reservation -- intended silently to effectuate a further diminution of tribal rights. We should not lightly assume that Congress, acting as a trustee of the Tribe's interests, wished to deprive the Tribe of access to food supplies that it might need and had always utilized.

It is likely that the United States' interests in 1901 had little to do with preserving the formal structure of the 1864 Treaty, an interest that the Court today assumes. Although the 1864 Treaty required the Tribe to stay on the land reserved to it by the Treaty, the alternative in 1864 was the Tribe's continued presence on over 22 million acres of land to which it held aboriginal title. The land on which the Tribe was to stay, although poor land for settlement, was known to contain game, fish, and vegetation in such quantities as to allow the Tribe to be self-sufficient, with no reason to wander. By 1901, there was no longer an issue as to whether the Tribe would ever again wander over the 22 million acres they had once held under aboriginal title -- the Klamath had fully accepted that they would remain on a much smaller area. But the issue of retaining the Tribe's self-sufficiency was still a concern.

In 1901, the Klamath were not viewed as hostile Indians, see n. 5, infra, and the surrounding land was minimally settled, at best. For the United States to prohibit all tribal access to the ceded areas would have served no interest that the United States ever publicly declared, and it would have compromised the Klamath's ability to remain self-sufficient. It is thus unreasonable to believe that the United States, while purporting to act for the benefit of the Indians, placed a high priority on assuring that the Klamath be strictly confined to the now-diminished area of their reservation, even if that would mean less access to food. The United States' interests would have been fully served by reading the 1864 Treaty to require only that the Tribe not leave the area that was initially specified as the reservation. Article IV of the 1901 Agreement can thus easily be seen as an effort to preserve the Tribe's right to travel, hunt, and fish on the full area of the original reservation, so long as those activities are consistent with the Tribe's loss of exclusive possessory rights in the ceded lands. So long as the ceded lands were not opened to significant settlement, this resolution would fully serve what interest there still was in containing the Klamath, and would not compromise the shared interest in continuing the Klamath's self-sufficiency.

(3)

This interpretation of the parties' perspectives fully conforms to what we know of the parties' subsequent behavior. [6] Congress never opened the ceded lands to settlement, and in fact, by the time it had ratified the 1901 Agreement, "[v]irtually all the land ceded by the Tribe was . . . closed to entry and placed in either national forests or parks." App. 13-14 (stipulated facts). No argument has been made that continued hunting and fishing by the Indians is incompatible with the land's uses. The Tribe's behavior is also fully consistent with its current interpretation of the Agreement. The parties have stipulated that the Tribe has in fact "continued to hunt, fish and trap on the excluded lands from the time of their cession to the present," id. at 14 (stipulated facts). Thus, no subsequent behavior of the United States or of the Tribe reflects an expectation that the Tribe would alter its hunting and fishing patterns as a result of the cession.

(4)

Last, the 1901 Agreement's treatment of the issue of compensation also provides evidence that the parties did not envision that the Agreement denied the Klamath continued access to these traditional hunting and fishing grounds. The parties have stipulated that the Commission in no way considered the land's value for hunting or fishing when it calculated the proper compensation to the Tribe. Id. at 12. Yet the Commission was well aware that the land was a hunting and fishing ground of some importance to the Tribe. Similarly, when the Indian Claims Commission reviewed and supplemented the compensation awarded the Klamath -- more than six decades after the ratification of the Agreement -- it never assigned any value to hunting or fishing rights. Id. at 14; see also Klamath and Modoc Tribes v. United States, 20 Ind.Cl.Comm'n 522 (1969). The silence of both these bodies is not surprising if one accepts that the cession did not envision that Indian hunting and fishing would cease. We do not normally assume that the United States, without providing compensation, intended to deprive a tribe of valued hunting and fishing rights. Menominee Tribe of Indians v. United States, 391 U. S. 404, 391 U. S. 413 (1968) (will not lightly assume that Congress meant to abrogate hunting and fishing rights without provision of compensation); cf. United States v. Sioux Nation of Indians, 448 U. S. 371, 448 U. S. 422-424 (1980) (will not assume that compensation designed to ensure Tribe's survival after it gave up traditional hunting activities was intended to cover both the taking of hunting rights and the taking of land). Nor should we lightly assume that the Tribe silently accepted the lack of specific compensation because its members understood that their valued hunting and fishing rights were merely incidental to land ownership. [7]

C

The analysis of the Agreement offered here is fully consistent with this Court's prior cases regarding Indian hunting and fishing rights. We have accepted that nonexclusive hunting and fishing rights have often existed independently from rights of exclusive possession of land. Thus, there have been many treaties in which Indians have explicitly reserved nonexclusive hunting and fishing rights while ceding the corresponding lands. See nn. 1 and 4, supra. Similarly, Congress has explicitly reserved to a Tribe continued hunting and fishing rights even after a reservation has been fully terminated. See, e.g., 25 U.S.C. § 564m(b) (fishing rights explicitly reserved upon termination of Klamath Reservation in 1954); see also Kimball v. Callahan, 590 F.2d 768, 772 (CA9), cert. denied, 444 U.S. 826 (1979). But most importantly, this Court has held that hunting and fishing rights can, by implication, survive the full termination of a reservation, even where the enactment terminating the reservation is written in broad language and makes no reference to those rights' survival. Menominee Tribe of Indians v. United States, supra.

In this case, as a result of the erroneous survey, there was a de facto separation of the Klamath's hunting and fishing rights from their rights of exclusive possession of the land. The former rights existed to the extent they could, consistent with the loss of the latter rights. In essence, the Tribe was left with off-reservation rights to hunt and fish on land from which it could not exclude others. The 1901 Agreement, which preserved to the Klamath all "benefits to which they are entitled under existing treaties, not inconsistent with the provisions of the [cession]," was not meant to take from them what was left of their right of access to their traditional hunting and fishing grounds.

III

In light of this Court's repeated statements that the abrogation of Indian rights should not be lightly inferred, and that treaties be interpreted as they would have been understood by the Indians, I find the Court's opinion today disturbing. Rather than follow the sort of historical inquiry that these canons should call for, the Court analyzes the case as one involving little more than the plain meaning of boilerplate language. It turns to history only to determine if its perceived "plain meaning" would be an impossible one. Ultimately, this produces a largely insensitive and conclusory historical inquiry that ignores how events almost certainly appeared to the Tribe.

The decision today represents another erroneous deprivation of the Klamath's tribal rights. The Court has offered no reason to believe the 1901 Agreement was designed to accomplish anything other than the redress of the wrong that had already been done to the Tribe. The Court has certainly offered no reason to believe that it was designed to effectuate a further diminution of the Klamath's rights.

I respectfully dissent.

Notes

[1] See, e.g., United States v. Sioux Nation of Indians, 448 U. S. 371, 448 U. S. 422-423 (1980); Menominee Tribe of Indians v. United States, 391 U. S. 404 (1968); Tulee v. Washington, 315 U. S. 681 (1942).

[2] See Washington v. Washington Commercial Passenger Fishing Vessel Assn., 443 U. S. 658, 443 U. S. 675-676 (1979); Choctaw Nation v. Oklahoma, 397 U. S. 620, 397 U. S. 631 (1970); see also Menominee Tribe of Indians v. United States, supra, at 391 U. S. 413 (the intention to abrogate treaty rights is not to be lightly imputed to Congress).

[3] The Boundary Commission concluded its report as follows:

"In conclusion, we respectfully submit that, during all this long period of thirty-two years, these Indians have exhibited a patient and unwavering confidence in the justice of the Government demanding the highest commendation."

"Believing themselves to be grievously wronged by the white settlements on land they considered secured to them by solemn pledge of the Government and from which their subsistence was largely drawn, they yet endured all the aggravating conditions of these years, resisting all the allurements of the adjacent and kindred tribes during the [recent war] and remained loyal and true."

S.Doc. No. 93, 54th Cong., 2d Sess., 11 (1897).

[4] As the Court notes, ante at 473 U. S. 764-765, n. 15, the Klamath claim a hunting and fishing right quite similar to the right of nonexclusive, off-reservation hunting and fishing expressly reserved by many of the Indians of the Pacific Northwest when they entered cession agreements. See Puyallup Tribe v. Department of Game of Washington, 391 U. S. 392 (1968); United States v. Winans, 198 U. S. 371 (1905). I would also agree with the Court that such a right is not an "absolute freedom from state regulation." See ante at 473 U. S. 765, n. 16. It should also be emphasized, however, that the right is nonetheless a valuable one, placing significant limits on permissible state regulation. See Antoine v. Washington, 420 U. S. 194, 420 U. S. 207 (1975) (State must demonstrate that its regulation is a reasonable and necessary conservation measure, and that its application to the Indians is necessary in the interest of conservation); see also Department of Game of Washington v. Puyallup Tribe, 414 U. S. 44 (1973); Tulee v. Washington, 315 U.S. at 315 U. S. 684.

[5] As the Court points out, see ante at 473 U. S. 759-760, n. 8, the United States' first negotiator considered the excluded land "practically worthless" and believed that Congress should restore to the reservation the unentered excluded acreage, rather than purchase it. The Tribe resisted this recommendation, preferring the compensated cession that was eventually accepted by Congress.

[6] This Court has accepted that subsequent history of Indian lands can give "additional clue[s] as to what Congress expected would happen [with respect to] land on a particular reservation." Solem v. Bartlett, 465 U. S. 463, 465 U. S. 472 (1984).

[7] The Court speculates that the right to hunt and fish was simply not viewed by the Indians as a right separate from the right to possess the land. But the Indians clearly did value the hunting and fishing, and both before and after the 1901 Agreement, the Indians continued to hunt and fish without interference even though, during both periods, they knew that they did not exercise exclusive possession of the land. I decline to assume that the Indians were simply consciously violating the law.

No successive prosecutions by different States: Justice Marshall's dissent in Heath v. Alabama (December 3, 1985)

JUSTICE MARSHALL, with whom JUSTICE BRENNAN joins, dissenting.

Seizing upon the suggestion in past cases that every "independent" sovereign government may prosecute violations of its laws even when the defendant has already been tried for the same crime in another jurisdiction, the Court today gives short shrift to the policies underlying those precedents. The "dual sovereignty" doctrine, heretofore used to permit federal and state prosecutions for the same offense, was born of the need to accommodate complementary state and federal concerns within our system of concurrent territorial jurisdictions. It cannot justify successive prosecutions by different States. Moreover, even were the dual sovereignty doctrine to support successive state prosecutions as a general matter, it simply could not legitimate the collusion between Georgia and Alabama in this case to ensure that petitioner is executed for his crime.

I

On August 31, 1981, the body of Rebecca Heath was discovered in an abandoned car in Troup County, Georgia. Because the deceased was a resident of Russell County, Alabama, members of the Russell County Sheriff's Department immediately joined Troup County authorities in investigating the causes and agents of her death. Tr. 359. This cooperative effort proved fruitful. On September 4, petitioner Larry Heath, the deceased's husband, was arrested and brought to the Georgia State Patrol barracks in Troup County, where he confessed to having hired other men to murder his wife. Shortly thereafter, petitioner was indicted by the grand jury of Troup County for malice murder. The prosecution's notice to petitioner that it was seeking the death penalty triggered the beginning of the Unified Appeals Procedure that Georgia requires in capital cases. But while these pretrial proceedings were still in progress, petitioner seized the prosecution's offer of a life sentence in exchange for a guilty plea. Upon entry of his plea in February, 1982, petitioner was sentenced in Troup County Superior Court to life imprisonment. His stay in the custody of Georgia authorities proved short, however. Three months later, a Russell County, Alabama, grand jury indicted him for the capital offense of murdering Rebecca Heath during the course of a kidnaping in the first degree.

The murder of Rebecca Heath must have been quite noteworthy in Russell County, Alabama. By petitioner's count, of the 82 prospective jurors questioned before trial during voir dire, all but 7 stated that they were aware that petitioner had pleaded guilty to the same crime in Georgia. Id. at 294. The voir dire responses of almost all of the remaining 75 veniremen can only be characterized as remarkable. When asked whether they could put aside their knowledge of the prior guilty plea in order to give petitioner a fair trial in Alabama, the vast majority answered in the affirmative. See, e.g., id. at 110, 112-113, 134, 254. These answers satisfied the trial judge, who denied petitioner's challenges for cause except as to those jurors who explicitly admitted that the Georgia proceedings would probably affect their assessment of petitioner's guilt.

With such a well-informed jury, the outcome of the trial was surely a foregone conclusion. Defense counsel could do little but attempt to elicit information from prosecution witnesses tending to show that the crime was committed exclusively in Georgia. The court having rejected petitioner's constitutional and jurisdictional claims, the defense was left to spend most of its summation arguing that Rebecca Heath may not actually have been kidnaped from Alabama before she was murdered, and that petitioner was already being punished for ordering that murder. Petitioner was convicted and, after sentencing hearings, was condemned to die. The conviction and sentence were upheld by the Alabama Court of Criminal Appeals, 455 So.2d 898 (1983), and the Alabama Supreme

Court. Ex parte Heath, 455 So.2d 905 (1984).

II

Had the Georgia authorities suddenly become dissatisfied with the life sentence petitioner received in their courts and reindicted petitioner in order to seek the death penalty once again, that indictment would without question be barred by the Double Jeopardy Clause of the Fifth Amendment, as applied to the States by the Fourteenth Amendment, Benton v. Maryland, 395 U. S. 784 (1969). Whether the second indictment repeated the charge of malice murder or instead charged murder in the course of a kidnaping, it would surely, under any reasonable constitutional standard, offend the bar to successive prosecutions for the same offense. See Brown v. Ohio, 432 U. S. 161, 432 U. S. 166 (1977); id. at 432 U. S. 170 (BRENNAN, J., concurring).

The only difference between this case and such a hypothetical volte-face by Georgia is that here Alabama, not Georgia, was offended by the notion that petitioner might not forfeit his life in punishment for his crime. The only reason the Court gives for permitting Alabama to go forward is that Georgia and Alabama are separate sovereigns.

A

The dual sovereignty theory posits that where the same act offends the laws of two sovereigns,

"It cannot be truly averred that the offender has been twice punished for the same offence; but only that by one act he has committed two offences, for each of which he is justly punishable."

Moore v. Illinois, 14 How. 13, 55 U. S. 20 (1852). Therefore,

"prosecutions under the laws of separate sovereigns do not, in the language of the Fifth Amendment, 'subject [the defendant] for the same offence to be twice put in jeopardy.'"

United States v. Wheeler, 435 U. S. 313, 435 U. S. 317 (1978). Mindful of the admonitions of Justice Black, we should recognize this exegesis of the Clause as, at best, a useful fiction and, at worst, a dangerous one. See Bartkus v. Illinois, 359 U. S. 121, 359 U. S. 158 (1959) (Black, J., dissenting). No evidence has ever been adduced to indicate that the Framers intended the word "offence" to have so restrictive a meaning. [1]

This strained reading of the Double Jeopardy Clause has survived and indeed flourished in this Court's cases not because of any inherent plausibility, but because it provides reassuring interpretivist support for a rule that accommodates the unique nature of our federal system. Before this rule is extended to cover a new class of cases, the reasons for its creation should therefore be made clear.

Under the constitutional scheme, the Federal Government has been given the exclusive power to vindicate certain of our Nation's sovereign interests, leaving the States to exercise complementary authority over matters of more local concern. The respective spheres of the Federal Government and the States may overlap at times, and even where they do not, different interests may be implicated by a single act. See, e.g., Abbate v. United States, 359 U. S. 187 (1959) (conspiracy to dynamite telephone company facilities entails both destruction of property and disruption of federal communications network). Yet were a prosecution by a State, however zealously pursued, allowed to preclude further prosecution by the Federal Government for the same crime, an entire range of national interests could be frustrated. The importance of those federal interests has thus quite properly been permitted to trump a defendant's interest in avoiding successive prosecutions or multiple punishments for the same crime. See Screws v. United States, 325 U. S. 91, 325 U. S. 108-110, and n. 10 (1945) (plurality opinion). Conversely, because "the States under our federal system have the principal responsibility for defining and prosecuting crimes," Abbate v. United States, supra, at 359 U. S. 195, it would be inappropriate -- in the absence of a specific congressional intent to preempt state action pursuant to the Supremacy Clause -- to allow a federal prosecution to preclude state authorities from vindicating "the historic right and obligation of the States to maintain peace and order within their confines," Bartkus v. Illinois, supra, at 359 U. S. 137.

The complementary nature of the sovereignty exercised by the Federal Government and the States places upon a defendant burdens commensurate with concomitant privileges. Past cases have recognized that the special ordeal suffered by a defendant prosecuted by both federal and state authorities is the price of living in a federal system, the cost of dual citizenship. Every citizen, the Court has noted,

"owes allegiance to the two departments, so to speak, and within their respective spheres must pay the penalties which each exacts for disobedience to its laws. In return, he can demand protection from each within its own jurisdiction."

United States v. Cruikshank, 92 U. S. 542, 92 U. S. 551 (1876). See Moore v. Illinois, supra, at 55 U. S. 20 ("Every citizen . . . may be said to owe allegiance to two sovereigns, and may be liable to punishment for an infraction of the laws of either").

B

Because all but one of the cases upholding the dual sovereignty doctrine have involved the unique relationship between the Federal Government and the States, [2] the question whether a similar rule should exempt successive prosecutions by two different States from the command of the Double Jeopardy Clause is one for which this Court's precedents provide all too little illumination. Only once before has the Court explicitly considered competing state prosecutorial interests. In that case, it observed that, where an act is prohibited by the laws of two States with concurrent jurisdiction over the locus of the offense,

"the one first acquiring jurisdiction of the person may prosecute the offense, and its judgment is a finality in both States, so that one convicted or acquitted in the courts of the one State cannot be prosecuted for the same offense in the courts of the other."

Nielsen v. Oregon, 212 U. S. 315, 212 U. S. 320 (1909).

Where two States seek to prosecute the same defendant for the same crime in two separate proceedings, the justifications found in the federal-state context for an exemption from double jeopardy constraints simply do not hold. Although the two States may have opted for different policies within their assigned territorial jurisdictions, the sovereign concerns with whose vindication each State has been charged are identical. Thus, in contrast to the federal-state context, barring the second prosecution would still permit one government to act upon the broad range of sovereign concerns that have been reserved to the States by the Constitution. The compelling need in the federal-state context to subordinate double jeopardy concerns is thus considerably diminished in cases involving successive prosecutions by different States. Moreover, from the defendant's perspective, the burden of successive prosecutions cannot be justified as the quid pro quo of dual citizenship.

To be sure, a refusal to extend the dual sovereignty rule to state-state prosecutions would preclude the State that has lost the "race to the courthouse" from vindicating legitimate policies distinct from those underlying its sister State's prosecution. But, as yet, I am not persuaded that a State's desire to further a particular policy should be permitted to deprive a defendant of his constitutionally protected right not to be brought to bar more than once to answer essentially the same charges.

III

Having expressed my doubts as to the Court's ill-considered resolution of the dual sovereignty question in this case, I must confess that my quarrel with the Court's disposition of this case is based less upon how this question was resolved than upon the fact that it was considered at all. Although, in granting Heath's petition for certiorari, this Court ordered the parties to focus upon the dual sovereignty issue, I believe the Court errs in refusing to consider the fundamental unfairness of the process by which petitioner stands condemned to die.

Even where the power of two sovereigns to pursue separate prosecutions for the same crime has been undisputed, this Court has barred both governments from combining to do together what each could not constitutionally do on its own. See Murphy v. Waterfront Comm'n, 378 U. S. 52 (1964); Elkins v. United States, 364 U. S. 206 (1960). [3] And just as the Constitution bars one sovereign from facilitating another's prosecution by delivering testimony coerced under promise of immunity or evidence illegally seized, I believe that it prohibits two sovereigns from combining forces to ensure that a defendant receives only the trappings of criminal process as he is sped along to execution.

While no one can doubt the propriety of two States cooperating to bring a criminal to justice, the cooperation between Georgia and Alabama in this case went far beyond their initial joint investigation. Georgia's efforts to secure petitioner's execution did not end with its acceptance of his guilty plea. Its law enforcement officials went on to play leading roles as prosecution witnesses in the Alabama trial. Indeed, had the Alabama trial judge not restricted the State to one assisting officer at the prosecution's table during trial, a Georgia officer would have shared the honors with an Alabama officer. Tr. 298. Although the record does not reveal the precise nature of the assurances made by Georgia authorities that induced petitioner to plead guilty in the first proceeding against him, I cannot believe he would have done so had he been aware that the officials whose forbearance he bought in Georgia with his plea would merely continue their efforts to secure his death in another jurisdiction. Cf. Santobello v. New York, 404 U. S. 257, 404 U. S. 262 (1971).

Even before the Fourteenth Amendment was held to incorporate the protections of the Double Jeopardy Clause, four Members of this Court registered their outrage at

"an instance of the prosecution's being allowed to harass the accused with repeated trials and convictions on the same evidence, until it achieve[d] its desired result of a capital verdict."

Ciucci v. Illinois, 356 U. S. 571, 356 U. S. 573 (1958). Such "relentless prosecutions," they asserted, constituted

"an unseemly and oppressive use of a criminal trial that violates the concept of due process contained in the Fourteenth Amendment, whatever its ultimate scope is taken to be."

Id. at 356 U. S. 575. The only differences between the facts in Ciucci and those in this case are that here the relentless effort was a cooperative one between two States and that petitioner sought to avoid trial by pleading guilty. Whether viewed as a violation of the Double Jeopardy Clause or simply as an affront to the due process guarantee of fundamental fairness, Alabama's prosecution of petitioner cannot survive constitutional scrutiny. I therefore must dissent.

Notes

[1] It is curious to note how reluctant the Court has always been to ascertain the intent of the Framers in this area. The furthest the Court has ever progressed on such an inquiry was to note:

"It has not been deemed relevant to discussion of our problem to consider dubious English precedents concerning the effect of foreign criminal judgments on the ability of English courts to try charges arising out of the same conduct. . . ."

Bartkus v. Illinois, 359 U.S. at 359 U. S. 128, n. 9. But see id. at 359 U. S. 156 (Black, J., dissenting); M. Friedland, Double Jeopardy 360-364 (1969).

[2] United States v. Wheeler, 435 U. S. 313 (1978), where the Court upheld successive prosecutions by Federal Government and Navajo tribal authorities, merely recognizes an analogous relationship between two governments with complementary concerns. While the Court noted that "Congress has plenary authority to legislate for the Indian tribes in all matters, including their form of government," id. at 435 U. S. 319, Congress has in fact wisely refrained from interfering in this sensitive area. The relationship between federal and tribal authorities is thus, in this respect, analogous to that between the Federal Government and the States.

[3] To be sure, Murphy, which bars a State from compelling a witness to give testimony that might be used against him in a federal prosecution, and Elkins, which bars the introduction in a federal prosecution of evidence illegally seized by state officers, do not necessarily undermine the basis of the rule allowing successive state and federal prosecutions. It is one thing to bar a sovereign from using certain evidence, and quite

another to bar it from prosecuting altogether. But these cases can be read to suggest that, despite the independent sovereign status of the Federal and State Governments, courts should not be blind to the impact of combined federal-state law enforcement on an accused's constitutional rights. See Note, Double Prosecution by State and Federal Governments: Another Exercise in Federalism, 80 Harv.L.Rev. 1538, 1647 (1967). Justice Harlan's belief that Murphy "abolished the two sovereignties' rule," Stevens v. Marks, 383 U. S. 234, 383 U. S. 250 (1966) (Harlan, J., concurring in part, dissenting in part), was thus well-founded.

Court misconceives role of the grand jury and the harmless error doctrine: Justice Marshall's dissent in United States v. Mechanik (February 25, 1986)

JUSTICE MARSHALL, dissenting.

The Court concedes that federal prosecutors violated Rule 6(d) of the Federal Rules of Criminal Procedure in presenting their case against defendants Mechanik and Lill to the grand jury. The Court holds, however, that, because defendants were ultimately convicted of some of the counts against them, "any error in the grand jury proceeding connected with the charging decision was harmless beyond a reasonable doubt." Ante at 475 U. S. 70. Because I believe that the majority's rule misconceives the role both of the grand jury and of the harmless error doctrine, I dissent.

I

The Court's decision today renders Rule 6(d) almost unenforceable. As the facts of this litigation demonstrate, Rule 6(d) violations are difficult for defendants to uncover. The grand jury conducts its investigation in secret, aided only by the prosecutors and witnesses. United States v. Calandra, 414 U. S. 338, 414 U. S. 343 (1974). Defendants are not entitled to grand jury transcripts before trial; due to the strictly enforced tradition of grand jury secrecy, defendants generally have access to no information whatsoever regarding the conduct of the grand jury proceedings. See M. Frankel & G. Naftalis, The Grand Jury 81-89 (1977). Requests by defendants pursuant to Rule 6(e)(3)(C)(ii) for disclosure of grand jury materials, "upon a showing that grounds may exist for a motion to dismiss the indictment because of matters occurring before the grand jury," are rarely granted; a defendant often can make the necessary showing only with the aid of the materials he seeks to discover. See 1 C. Wright, Federal Practice and Procedure § 108, pp. 263-265 (2d ed.1982). Defendants' only access to grand jury materials is likely to be through the medium of the Jencks Act, 18 U.S.C. § 3500, which requires the prosecutor, after direct examination of a Government witness, to produce the witness' prior statements. That disclosure, however, does not take place until after trial has begun, and then only on a piecemeal and incomplete basis.

There is thus little likelihood that a defendant can raise a substantial claim under Rule 6(d) before his trial begins. After the start of trial, overwork and the press of events may prevent the district judge from disposing of a newly raised Rule 6(d) claim. The most attractive course for the district judge will be to defer a ruling until the close of trial, the course ultimately followed in this case. Indeed, the district judge may not have the opportunity to rule until that time. Under today's decision, however, deferring a meritorious Rule 6(d) claim until the close of trial disposes of it permanently. If the movant is acquitted, then his Rule 6(d) motion is moot; if the movant is convicted, under the majority's reasoning, then any error was harmless. The Court's decision thus offers busy district judges a new and unique way to reduce their workload; one need not believe in a judicial conspiracy against the assertion of Rule 6(d) rights to suspect that district judges, faced with Rule 6(d) motions necessarily raised in the middle of trial, will follow the Court's invitation.

Should a district judge decide a Rule 6(d) motion during trial, the majority's scheme insulates that ruling from appellate review. Appeal before judgment is unlikely; the Court has never allowed immediate appeal of an order issued after the start of a criminal trial. See Flanagan v. United States, 465 U. S. 259, 465 U. S. 269 (1984). [1] And under the decision today, such rulings cannot be appealed after judgment. Enforcement of Rule 6(d) is thus left to the unreviewable largesse of the district court.

II

A

We have no reason to believe that Congress intended Rule 6(d) to have so little practical meaning. The legislative history of Rule 6, indeed, belies that approach. In 1933, Congress was faced with

"a conflict of legal decision as to the right, under existing law, to permit stenographers in grand jury rooms without invalidating the subsequent conviction of defendant."

S.Rep. No. 64, 73d Cong., 1st Sess., 1 (1933). It responded by adding a narrow clause to the harmless error statute, Rev.Stat. § 1025 (later codified as 18 U.S.C. § 556 (1946 ed.)), providing that no indictment should be found insufficient, or conviction be reversed, because of the presence of stenographers in the grand jury room. But Congress nowhere expressed disagreement with the general proposition that the presence of an unauthorized person in the grand jury room invalidates a subsequent conviction. E.g., United States v. Fall, 56 App.D.C. 83, 84, 10 F.2d 648, 649 (1925); Latham v. United States, 226 F. 420, 424 (CA5 1915).

More recently, Congress amended Rule 6 in 1972 to incorporate by reference the provisions of the Jury Selection and Service Act of 1968; it provided that a defendant may move to dismiss the indictment based on the Government's failure to comply with that Act in the selection of the grand jury array or of individual grand jurors. Fed.Rule Crim.Proc. 6(b)(2). The advisory notes expressly state that the district judge may rule on such a challenge to the grand jury either before or after the verdict. Advisory Committee Notes on Fed.Rule Crim.Proc. 6, 18 U.S.C.App. p. 568 (1972 amendment). There is no hint that Congress, in providing for a ruling after the verdict, intended that ruling to be a mere intellectual exercise.

B

The majority's opinion misconceives the role of harmless error analysis. We have recognized that harmless error doctrine, denying any remedy in cases of clear prosecutorial misconduct, "can work very unfair and mischievous results." Chapman v. California, 386 U. S. 18, 386 U. S. 22 (1967). Denying defendants relief for clear violations of their procedural rights reduces the law to "pretend-rules,'" United States v. Borello, 766 F.2d 46, 58 (CA2 1985), quoting United States v. Antonelli Fireworks Co., 155 F.2d 631, 661 (CA2) (Frank, J., dissenting), cert. denied, 329 U.S. 742 (1946); it means that prosecutors are free to engage in prohibited conduct subject only to "purely ceremonial" words of appellate displeasure. 155 F.2d at 661.

The Court's rule that all grand jury misconduct becomes harmless after conviction, however, is especially pernicious. Contrary to the majority's suggestion that reversal is too costly a remedy for grand jury misconduct, ante at 475 U. S. 72, it is the majority's refusal to reverse convictions for demonstrated grand jury misconduct that imposes unacceptable costs. There are few limitations on the conduct of the prosecutor before the grand jury. Those limitations are found only in Federal Rule of Criminal Procedure 6, the text of which takes up little more than a page in the official compilation of United States laws. Violations of even those isolated restrictions, in by far the majority of cases, will go undetected by defendants. The only way to allow even minimally effective enforcement of those rules is to reverse the convictions of defendants whose indictments were tainted by Rule 6 violations.

Such an approach would not hamper the enforcement of the criminal law. Violations of Rule 6(d) will be nonexistent if the prosecutor exercises proper control over access to the grand jury chambers. The substantive law is not onerous or ambiguous, and most violations are the product of the prosecutor's failure to adopt safeguards to ensure compliance. See 2 W. LaFave & J. Israel, Criminal Procedure § 15.6, p. 333 (1984). There is no danger of a prosecutor slipping into an inadvertent Rule 6(d) violation comparable to that, say, of making an ill-worded remark in the heat of trial. Courts would not often have cause to reverse convictions because of Rule 6(d) violations.

The majority's goal of upholding criminal convictions not marred by substantial defect does not justify reducing Congress' command regarding the proper conduct of grand jury proceedings to a mere form of words, without practical effect. Respect for the rule of law demands that improperly procured indictments be quashed even after conviction, because

"only by upsetting convictions so obtained can the ardor of prosecuting officials be kept within legal bounds and justice be secured; for in modern times, all prosecution is in the hands of officials."

United States v. Remington, 208 F.2d 567, 574 (CA2 1953) (L. Hand, J., dissenting). [2]

III

The opinion concurring in the judgment suggests that the Rule 6(d) violation in this litigation should be viewed as harmless on the theory that the grand jury would have returned the same indictment regardless of the prosecutor's misconduct. Under that approach, a district court faced with a Rule 6(d) violation should examine the grand jury transcripts in an attempt to divine the effect of the violation on the jury's charging decision, and allow the indictment or conviction to stand only if it finds that there was no such effect. Such a rule would be contrary to the traditional black-letter law that "[a]ny violation of Rule 6(d) is per se prejudicial to the defendant and will result in dismissal of the indictment," 8 J. Moore, Federal Practice � 6.04[7], p. 6-91 (2d ed.1985). [3] I believe that such an approach would be unworkable and would undermine the limits Congress imposed on the conduct of grand jury investigations.

Many of the reasons given above for rejecting the majority's view that grand jury impropriety is always harmless once a verdict is reached, apply in this context as well. Given defendants' difficulty in discovering Rule 6(d) violations, it is all the more important that dismissal of the indictment be certain when violations of the Rule are found. Only such a sanction can come close to providing prosecutors with an incentive to obey the Rule's commands. See United States v. Pignatiello, 582 F.Supp. 251, 255 (Colo.1984).

Such harmless error analysis, moreover, overlooks the practical impossibility of determining the effect of a Rule 6(d) violation. The prejudicial impact of the unauthorized presence of persons in the grand jury room will often be impossible to quantify, and may not be apparent from the grand jury transcript. As one court wrote:

"A change in expression, a pressure on the hand or a warning glance would not be shown upon the minutes, but might well influence, suppress or alter testimony to the prejudice of the defendant. There may have been prior expressions or conversations between the two witnesses which the one then giving testimony might well hesitate to repudiate or modify in the presence of the other. The District Attorney here contends . . . that defendant suffered no prejudice by the joint presence of the two sisters, but . . . '[t]he court cannot know that this suggestion represents the fact.' We think the practice offers too great a possibility for the exercise of undue influence to be condoned."

State v. Revere, 232 La. 184, 207, 94 So.2d 25, 34 (1957) (emphasis omitted; citations omitted; internal quotations omitted). Any case-by-case analysis to determine whether the defendant was actually prejudiced is simply too speculative to afford defendants meaningful protection, and imposes a difficult burden on the courts that outweighs the benefits to be derived. The distinction between the truly harmless error and the more dangerous one is not "such a pronounced one that the Court can cloak the one with the mantle of legality and yet recognize the dangers of the other and prohibit it." United States v. Carper, 116 F.Supp. 817, 821 (DC 1963).

That approach, finally, is likely to require a detailed inquiry that will frustrate and undermine the secrecy of grand jury inquiry. See United States v. Treadway, 445 F.Supp. 959 (ND Tex.1978). The district court may have to discuss the testimony of grand jury witnesses who did not appear at trial. The goals of grand jury secrecy, however, counsel that such analysis should not be spread across the public record. See United States v. Sells Engineering, Inc., 463 U. S. 418, 424-425 (1983). [4]

IV

This litigation illustrates the extent to which the Court is willing to reduce the substantive law to "pretend-rules," Borello, 766 F.2d at 58, in order to affirm a criminal conviction. But by denigrating Congress' commands and eviscerating enforcement of Rule 6(d), the Court creates "a greater danger to a free people than the escape of some criminals from punishment." United States v. Di Re, 332 U. S. 581, 332 U. S. 595 (1948). I believe that the District Court in this case should have reversed defendants' conspiracy convictions without inquiry into the prejudice done to defendants by the Rule 6(d) violation. I therefore would affirm the judgment of the Court of Appeals.

Notes

[1] Denial of a Rule 6(d) motion could conceivably be subject to interlocutory appeal under the collateral order doctrine of Cohen v. Beneficial Industrial Loan Corp., 337 U. S. 541 (1949). Such an order may be both collateral to the main action and, as a result of today's opinion, wholly unreviewable after final judgment. Cf. United States v. Hollywood Motor Car Co., 458 U. S. 263, 458 U. S. 267 (1982) (claim that indictment should be dismissed on grounds of prosecutorial vindictiveness not subject to interlocutory appeal because reviewable after conviction); United States v. Garner, 632 F.2d 758 (CA9 1980) (claim that indictment should be dismissed on grounds of grand jury irregularities not subject to interlocutory appeal because reviewable after conviction); United States v. Bird, 709 F.2d 388, 391, and n. 17 (CA5 1983) (collecting cases).

[2] Our case law, further, is inconsistent with the majority's broad holding that any error in the grand jury proceedings, no matter how egregious, is rendered harmless beyond a reasonable doubt by a petit jury's subsequent guilty verdict. Vasquez v. Hillery, 474 U. S. 254 (1986), involving the "grave constitutional trespass" of racial discrimination, id. at 262, belies that holding. The Court's assessment of the nature of the grand jury process refutes the rationale articulated by the majority today:

"Nor are we persuaded that discrimination in the grand jury has no effect on the fairness of the criminal trials that result from that grand jury's actions. The grand jury does not determine only that probable cause exists to believe that a defendant committed a crime, or that it does not. In the hands of the grand jury lies the power to charge a greater offense or a lesser offense; numerous counts or a single count; and perhaps most significant of all, a capital offense or a noncapital offense -- all on the basis of the same facts. Moreover, '[t]he grand jury is not bound to indict in every case where a conviction can be obtained.' United States v. Ciambrone, 601 F.2d 616, 629 (CA2 1979) (Friendly, J., dissenting). Thus, even if a grand jury's determination of probable cause is confirmed in hindsight by a conviction on the indicted offense, that confirmation in no way suggests that the discrimination did not impermissibly infect the framing of the indictment and, consequently, the nature or very existence of the proceedings to come."

Vasquez v. Hillery, supra, at 474 U. S. 263 (emphasis added).

[3] See also 2 W. LaFave &; J. Israel, Criminal Procedure §15.6, p. 332 (1984) ("Most federal courts . . . treat unauthorized presence as a per se ground for dismissal, requiring no showing of prejudice"). Cases cited by the Solicitor General as requiring harmless error analysis are distinguishable. Those cases involved only brief, inadvertent interruptions of the grand jury, during which the grand jury proceedings came to an immediate halt, United States v. Computer Sciences Corp., 689 F.2d 1181, 1185-1186 (CA4 1982), cert. denied, 459 U.S. 1105 (1983); United States v. Kahan & Lessin Co., 695 F.2d 1122, 1124 (CA9 1982); United States v. Rath, 406 F.2d 757 (CA6), cert. denied, 394 U.S. 920 (1969), or a "fleeting" appearance in the grand jury room by a person assisting in the movement of bulky documents, United States v. Condo, 741 F.2d 238, 239 (CA9 1984), cert. denied, 469 U.S. 1164 (1985). Indeed, the Fourth Circuit panel, whose reasoning was adopted by the en banc court, saw no inconsistency between Computer Sciences, supra, and the per se rule of the instant case. 735 F.2d 136, 139-140 (1984).

[4] JUSTICE O'CONNOR suggests, noting the reference to 18 U.S.C. § 556 (1946 ed.) in the Advisory Committee Notes to Rule 6, that the rulemakers intended violations of Rule 6(d) to be subject to the harmless error rule. Ante at 475 U. S. 75-76. The legislative history of former § 556 does not support that view. The section, as first enacted in 1872, provided that

"[n]o indictment . . . shall be deemed insufficient, nor shall the trial, judgment, or other proceeding thereon be affected by reason of any defect or imperfection in matter of form only, which shall not tend to the prejudice of the defendant."

Rev.Stat. § 1025 (emphasis added). There is no indication that this law was meant to disturb the settled law regarding unauthorized persons in the grand jury room, see United States v. Edgerton, 80 F. 374 (Mont. 1897); rather, it seems likely that the statute was directed at technical defects in the wording of the indictment, see, e.g., People v. St. Clair, 56 Cal.406 (1880) (reversing conviction because word "larceny" in indictment was misspelled); People v. Vice, 21 Cal.344 (1864) (reversing conviction because indictment, while alleging that defendant took certain property by threats and force, failed to allege that the property did not belong to defendant). See also supra at 475 U. S. 82.

No reason surviving divorced spouses who remarried could not receive the same survivor's benefits allowed to remarried widowed spouses: Justice Marshall's dissent in Bowen v. Owens (May 19, 1986)

JUSTICE MARSHALL, with whom JUSTICE BRENNAN joins, dissenting.

The Court demonstrates an enviable ability to discern rationality where there is none. But the majority's efforts to imagine plausible legislative scenarios cannot obscure the simple truth: there is absolutely no evidence that Congress had any rational basis for deciding in 1977 that surviving divorced spouses who remarried could not receive the same survivor's benefits allowed to remarried widowed spouses. Because I believe that such a distinction between two groups treated similarly in other respects cannot survive the scrutiny required by the equal protection component of the Fifth Amendment's Due Process Clause, I dissent.

I

In 1977, a Report of the House Committee on Ways and Means noted one drawback of the benefits scheme then in force:

"Present law provides, in general, that the marriage (or remarriage) of a worker's divorced or surviving spouse, parent, or child prevents or terminates entitlement to benefits based on the worker's social security earnings record. For example, a widow who remarries before age 60 cannot get benefits based on her first husband's earnings as long as she is married. If she remarries after age 60, the benefits based on the first husband's social security are reduced or terminated; the widow gets either a wife's benefit based on her first husband's earnings (which is less than the widow's benefit she was getting) or a wife's benefit based on her current husband's earnings (if he is a beneficiary), whichever is higher. Benefits are not payable to divorced spouses and young surviving spouses who are remarried."

"Your committee is especially concerned about the effect of these provisions on older surviving spouses (and divorced spouses). Accordingly, your committee has recommended changes in the law which would eliminate marriage or remarriage as a factor affecting entitlement to benefits or benefit amounts. Specifically, under your committee's bill, marriage or remarriage would not bar or terminate entitlement to benefits as a divorced spouse, surviving spouse . . . parent, or child, and remarriage would not cause any reduction in aged widow's or widower's insurance benefits."

H.R.Rep. No. 95-702, pt. 1, pp. 47-48 (1977).

The Senate version of this bill, however, did not address any of the House Committee's concerns. And a subsequent Report tersely records the result of discussions between conferees from both Houses on this issue:

"The Senate recedes, with an amendment that would retain only that part of the House-passed provisions that would prevent reduction in benefits for widows and widowers who remarry after age 60."

H.R.Conf.Rep. No. 95-837, p. 73 (1977). The compromise thus produced the Social Security provisions in effect between 1979 and 1983 that are the subject of this suit. Those provisions authorized payment of survivor's benefits to widowed spouses who remarried after age 60, but not to similarly situated divorced widowed spouses.

II

As a historical matter, I suspect that the Court is right to characterize the distinction drawn by the 1977 Act between widowed spouses and surviving divorced spouses as the product of Congress' decision to "take one step at a time," ante at 476 U. S.

347, toward a program that would reflect "the needs of today's society," H.R.Rep. No. 95-702, pt. 1, supra, at 4. However, under the Due Process Clause, even legislative classifications that result from compromise must bear at least a rational relationship to a legitimate governmental purpose. Had Congress accommodated the House's reform goals with the Senate's more conservative outlook in this area by passing a law giving benefits to only those remarried widowed spouses who had been born on odd-numbered days of the calendar, we would surely have to strike the provision down as irrational. The question here is thus whether Congress had any rational basis for taking the particular step that it chose to take in 1977.

Recognizing that it is not enough to label the 1977 provisions a waystation on the road to a sensible destination, the Court argues that the statutory distinction between surviving divorced spouses and widowed spouses was based upon a legislative judgment that widowed spouses were the more dependent of the two groups. The problem with the majority's rationalization is that Congress never expressed it, or even hinted at it. The relevant legislative history contains absolutely no evidence to support the assumption that a divorced survivor is any less dependent than a widowed survivor, or to indicate that, in 1977, Congress was at all motivated by that assumption.

The majority attempts to fill the gap by assuming that Congress must have perceived a distinction between divorced spouses and widowed spouses because it required that the former, but not the latter, be married to the wage-earner for 10 years in order to receive benefits. That distinction can perhaps be taken as evidence that Congress believed that a divorced spouse who had been married to the wage-earner for less than 10 years was not sufficiently dependent on the wage-earner's income to justify the extension of benefits. Yet it can hardly be taken as an indication that surviving divorced spouses who did satisfy the 10-year requirement were thought any less dependent than widowed spouses. Divorced spouses meeting that requirement were not treated differently from widowed spouses for any purpose other than the remarriage provisions, and there is no indication in the statute or legislative history that Congress ever attempted to articulate a difference between the two groups justifying different treatment.

"When a legislative purpose can be suggested only by the ingenuity of a government lawyer litigating the constitutionality of a statute, a reviewing court may be presented not so much with a legislative policy choice, as its absence."

Schweiker v. Wilson, 450 U. S. 221, 450 U. S. 244 (1981) (POWELL, J., dissenting); see United States Railroad Retirement Board v. Fritz, 449 U. S. 166, 449 U. S. 184 (1980) (BRENNAN, J., dissenting). While the absence of a clear statement of purposes need not doom a statute under rationality review, our task must always be to determine whether a particular rational purpose actually motivated the Legislature. See Fritz, supra, at 449 U. S. 188 (BRENNAN, J., dissenting). We have no indication in this case that Congress had any basis for drawing this line other than its desire to find a point of compromise between the two Houses. With the help of the Government's lawyers, the Court has tried hard to come up with a hypothetical justification for Congress' action. I do not think that is our job. I dissent.

Eligibility and benefit levels in the federal food stamp program may be determined on an individual basis rather than just a "household" basis: Justice Marshall's dissent in Lyng v. Castillo (June 27, 1986)

JUSTICE MARSHALL, dissenting.

This case demonstrates yet again the lack of vitality in this Court's recent equal protection jurisprudence. See, e.g., Cleburne v. Cleburne Living Center, 473 U. S. 432, 473 U. S. 455 (1985) (MARSHALL, J., concurring in judgment in part and dissenting in part); San Antonio Independent School Dist. v. Rodriguez, 411 U. S. 1, 411 U. S. 70 (1973) (MARSHALL, J., dissenting). In my view, when analyzing classifications affecting the receipt of governmental benefits, a court must consider

"the character of the classification in question, the relative importance to individuals in the class discriminated against of the governmental benefits that they do not receive, and the asserted state interests in support of the classification."

Dandridge v. Williams, 397 U. S. 471, 397 U. S. 521 (1970) (MARSHALL, J., dissenting). By contrast, the Court's rigid, bipolar approach, which purports to apply rational basis scrutiny unless a suspect classification is involved or the exercise of a fundamental right is impeded, see ante at 477 U. S. 638-639, puts legislative classifications impinging upon sensitive issues of family structure and survival on the same plane as a refusal to let a merchant hawk his wares on a particular street corner. I do not believe the equal protection component of the Due Process Clause could become such a blunt instrument.

The importance of the interests involved in this case can hardly be denied. The Court concludes that the challenged statute does not directly and substantially interfere with family living arrangements, cf. Moore v. East Cleveland, 431 U. S. 494 (1977) (plurality opinion), because it "does not order or prevent any group of persons from dining together, " ante at 477 U. S. 638. The Court relies, apparently, on the fact that the statute does not use criminal sanctions, but merely the loss of benefits, to influence family living decisions. It is a bit late in the day, however, to cut off due process analysis -- be it procedural or substantive -- by simply invoking such a distinction. See Goldberg v. Kelly, 397 U. S. 254, 397 U. S. 262 (1970); Shapiro v. Thompson, 394 U. S. 618, 394 U. S. 627 (1969).

The food stamp benefits at issue are necessary for the affected families' very survival, and the Federal Government denies that benefit to families who do not, by preparing their meals together, structure themselves in a manner that the Government believes will minimize unnecessary expenditures. The importance of that benefit belies any suggestion that the Government is not directly and substantially influencing the living arrangements of families whose resources are so low that they must rely on their relatives for shelter. The Government has thus chosen to intrude into the family dining room -- a place where I would have thought the right to privacy exists in its strongest form. What possible interest can the Government have in preventing members of a family from dining as they choose? It is simply none of the Government's business.

The challenged classifications amount to a conclusive presumption that related families living under the same roof do all of their cooking together. Thus, the regulation does not merely affect the important privacy interest in family living arrangements recognized in Moore, but the even more vital interest in survival. As Congress itself recognized, some separate families live in the same house, but cannot prepare meals together because of different work schedules. See S.Rep. No. 97-504, p. 26 (1982). Others may lack sufficient plates and utensils to accommodate more than a few persons at once, or may have only one burner on their stove. These extended families simply lack the option of cooking and eating together. For them, the legislative presumption in this case does far greater damage than merely prescribing with whom they must dine. By assuming that they realize economies of scale that they in fact cannot achieve, the regulation threatens their lives and health by denying them the minimal benefits provided to all other families of similar income and needs.

Balanced against these vital interests is Congress' undeniably legitimate desire to prevent fraud and waste in the food stamp program. The legislative presumption that Congress used, however, is related at best tenuously to the achievement of those goals. While I believe that our standard of review must take into consideration the importance of the individual interests affected, I have some doubt that the classification used here could pass even a rational basis test. In United States Dept. of Agriculture v. Moreno, 413 U. S. 528 (1973), we held that a definition of "household" that excluded any living group containing an individual unrelated to any other member of the group did not rationally further the Government's interest in preventing fraud in the food stamp program. Despite the Court's attempts to distinguish this case from Moreno, the critical fact in both cases is that the statute drew a distinction that bears no necessary relation to the prevention of fraud. See id. at 413 U. S. 535-536 ("denial of essential federal food assistance to all otherwise eligible households containing unrelated members" not rationally related to fraud prevention). In the present case, the Government has provided no justification for the conclusion that related individuals living together are more likely to lie about their living arrangements than are unrelated individuals. Nor has it demonstrated that fraudulent conduct by related households is more difficult to detect than similar abuses by unrelated households.

Congress stressed its desire to prevent fraud in the food stamp program, see H.R.Rep. No. 97-687, p. 25 (1982); H.R.Rep. No. 97-106, p. 50 (1981), and it classified the "household consolidation" provision as an antifraud measure. Nevertheless, the Committee Reports cite no hard evidence that related persons living together were in fact significant sources of fraud; the Committees merely determined that the Government could save money by "tighten[ing] the definition of an eligible food stamp household."

S.Rep. No. 97-504 at 24. The House did hypothesize, in the course of considering the 1981 amendments, that an 18-year-old child living with his parents could declare himself a separate household for food stamp purposes, H.R.Rep. No. 97-106, at 119. If indeed that abuse widely existed, the resulting legislation, which lumped together all nonelderly parents and their offspring living under one roof as a "household," provided a more than sufficient cure. Nevertheless, Congress proceeded to restrict eligibility even further the following year.

When it moved beyond the rule that merely grouped parents and children, and, in the 1982 amendments, grouped siblings together as well, Congress interfered substantially with the desires of demonstrably separate families to remain separate families. It did so, moreover, while recognizing that distinct families living together often are genuinely separate households, and that the food stamp program should permit separate families that are not related to live together, but maintain separate households. S.Rep. No. 97-504, at 25. Congress nevertheless assumed that related families are less likely to be genuinely separate households than are unrelated families, and failed even to provide related families a chance to rebut the legislative presumption. In view of the importance to the affected families of their family life and their very survival, the Court's extreme deference to this untested assumption is simply inappropriate. I respectfully dissent.

Shouldn't require students to pay for school-bus service: Justice Marshall's dissent in Kadrmas v. Dickinson Public Schools (June 24, 1988)

JUSTICE MARSHALL, with whom JUSTICE BRENNAN joins, dissenting.

In San Antonio Independent School Dist. v. Rodriguez, 411 U.S. 1 (1973), I wrote that the Court's holding was a "retreat from our historic commitment to equality of educational opportunity and [an] unsupportable acquiescence in a system which deprives children in their earliest years of the chance to reach their full potential." Id., at 71 (dissenting). Today, the Court continues the retreat from the promise of equal educational opportunity by holding that a school district's refusal to allow an indigent child who lives 16 miles from the nearest school to use a school-bus service without paying a fee does not violate the Fourteenth Amendment's Equal Protection Clause. Because I do not believe that this Court should sanction discrimination against the poor with respect to "perhaps the most important function of state and local governments," Brown v. Board of Education, 347 U.S. 483, 493 (1954), I dissent.

The Court's opinion suggests that this case does not concern state action that discriminates against the poor with regard to the provision of a basic education. The Court notes that the particular governmental action challenged in this case involves the provision of transportation, rather than the provision of educational services. See ante, at 459-460, 460-461. Moreover, the Court stresses that the denial of transportation to Sarita

Kadrmas did not in fact prevent her from receiving an education; notwithstanding the denial of bus service, Sarita's family ensured that she attended school each day. See ante, at 458, 460-461. 1 To the Court, then, this case presents no troublesome questions; indeed, the Court's facile analysis suggests some perplexity as to why this case ever reached this Court.

I believe the Court's approach forgets that the Constitution is concerned with "sophisticated as well as simple-minded modes of discrimination." Lane v. Wilson, 307 U.S. 268, 275 (1939). This case involves state action that places a special burden on poor families in their pursuit of education. Children living far from school can receive a public education only if they have access to transportation; as the state court noted in this case, "a child must reach the schoolhouse door as a prerequisite to receiving the educational opportunity offered therein." 402 N. W. 2d 897, 901 (N. D. 1987). Indeed, for children in Sarita's position, imposing a fee for transportation is no different in practical effect from imposing a fee directly for education. Moreover, the fee involved in this case discriminated against Sarita's family because it necessarily fell more heavily upon the poor than upon wealthier members of the community. 2 Cf. Bullock v. Carter, 405 U.S. 134, 144 (1972) (voting system based on flat fees "falls with unequal weight on voters, as well as candidates, according to their economic status"); Griffin v. Illinois, 351 U.S. 12, 17 . n. 11 (1956) (opinion of Black, J.) (state law imposing flat fee for trial transcript is "nondiscriminatory on its face," but "grossly discriminatory in its operation"). This case therefore presents the question whether a State may discriminate against the poor in providing access to education. I regard this question as one of great urgency.

As I have stated on prior occasions, proper analysis of equal protection claims depends less on choosing the "formal label" under which the claim should be reviewed than upon identifying and carefully analyzing the real interests at stake. Cleburne v. Cleburne Living Center, Inc., 473 U.S. 432, 478 (1985) (MARSHALL, J., dissenting); see Selective Service System v. Minnesota Public Interest Research Group, 468 U.S. 841, 876 (1984) (MARSHALL, J., dissenting). In particular, the Court should focus on "the character of the classification in question, the relative importance to individuals in the class discriminated against of the governmental benefits that they do not receive, and the asserted state interests in support of the classification." Dandridge v. Williams, 397 U.S. 471, 521 (1970) (MARSHALL, J., dissenting); see San Antonio Independent School Dist. v. Rodriguez, supra, at 98-99 (MARSHALL, J., dissenting). Viewed from this perspective, the discrimination inherent in the North Dakota statute fails to satisfy the dictates of the Equal Protection Clause.

The North Dakota statute discriminates on the basis of economic status. This Court has determined that classifications based on wealth are not automatically suspect. See, e. g., Maher v. Roe, 432 U.S. 464, 470 -471 (1977). Such classifications, however, have a measure of special constitutional significance. See, e. g., McDonald v. Board of Election Comm'rs of Chicago, 394 U.S. 802, 807 (1969) ("[A] careful examination on our part is especially warranted where lines are drawn on the basis of wealth . . ."); Harper v.

Virginia Bd. of Elections, 383 U.S. 663, 668 (1966) ("Lines drawn on the basis of wealth or property . . . are traditionally disfavored"). This Court repeatedly has invalidated statutes, on their face or as applied, that discriminated against the poor. See, e. g., Little v. Streater, 452 U.S. 1 (1981); Bullock v. Carter, supra; Harper v. Virginia Bd. of Elections, supra; Griffin v. Illinois, supra. The Court has proved most likely to take such action when the laws in question interfered with the access of the poor to the political and judicial processes. One source of these decisions, in my view, is a deep distrust of policies that specially burden the access of disadvantaged persons to the governmental institutions and processes that offer members of our society an opportunity to improve their status and better their lives. The intent of the Fourteenth Amendment was to abolish caste legislation. See Plyler v. Doe, 457 U.S. 202, 213 (1982). When state action has the predictable tendency to entrap the poor and create a permanent underclass, that intent is frustrated. See id., at 234 (BLACKMUN, J., concurring). Thus, to the extent that a law places discriminatory barriers between indigents and the basic tools and opportunities that might enable them to rise, exacting scrutiny should be applied.

The statute at issue here burdens a poor person's interest in an education. The extraordinary nature of this interest cannot be denied. This Court's most famous statement on the subject is contained in Brown v. Board of Education, 347 U.S., at 493 :

"[E]ducation is perhaps the most important function of state and local governments. Compulsory school attendance laws and the great expenditures for education both demonstrate our recognition of the importance of education to our democratic society. It is required in the performance of our most basic public responsibilities, even service in the armed forces. It is the very foundation of good citizenship. Today it is a principal instrument in awakening the child to cultural values, in preparing him for later professional training, and in helping him to adjust normally to his environment. In these days, it is doubtful that any child may reasonably be expected to succeed in life if he is denied the opportunity of an education."

Since Brown, we frequently have called attention to the vital role of education in our society. We have noted that "education is necessary to prepare citizens to participate effectively and intelligently in our open political system . . . ." Wisconsin v. Yoder, 406 U.S. 205, 221 (1972); see San Antonio Independent School Dist. v. Rodriguez, 411 U.S., at 112 -115 (MARSHALL, J., dissenting). We also have recognized that education prepares individuals to become self-reliant participants in our economy. See Plyler v. Doe, supra, at 221-222; Wisconsin v. Yoder, supra, at 221. A statute that erects special obstacles to education in the path of the poor naturally tends to consign such persons to their current disadvantaged status. By denying equal opportunity to exactly those who need it most, the law not only militates against the ability of each poor child to advance herself or himself, but also increases the likelihood of the creation of a discrete and permanent underclass. Such a statute is difficult to reconcile with the framework of equality embodied in the Equal Protection Clause.

This Court's decision in Plyler v. Doe, supra, supports these propositions. The

Court in Plyler upheld the right of the children of illegal aliens to receive the free public education that the State of Texas made available to other residents. The Court in that case engaged in some discussion of alienage, a classification not relevant here. The decision, however, did not rest upon this basis. Rather, the Court made clear that the infirmity of the Texas law stemmed from its differential treatment of a discrete and disadvantaged group of children with respect to the provision of education. The Court stated that education is not "merely some governmental `benefit' indistinguishable from other forms of social welfare legislation." Id., at 221. The Court further commented that the state law "poses an affront to one of the goals of the Equal Protection Clause: the abolition of governmental barriers presenting unreasonable obstacles to advancement on the basis of individual merit." Id., at 221-222. Finally, the Court called attention to the tendency of the Texas law to create a distinct underclass of impoverished illiterates who would be unable to participate in and contribute to society. See id., at 222-224. The Plyler Court's reasoning is fully applicable here. As in Plyler, the State in this case has acted to burden the educational opportunities of a disadvantaged group of children, who need an education to become full participants in society.

The State's rationale for this policy is based entirely on fiscal considerations. The State has allowed Dickinson and certain other school districts to charge a nonwaivable flat fee for bus service so that these districts may recoup part of the costs of the service. The money that Dickinson collects from applying the busing fee to indigent families, however, represents a minuscule proportion of the costs of the bus service. As the Court notes, ante, at 454, all of the fees collected by Dickinson amount to only 11% of the cost of providing the bus service, and the fees collected from poor families represent a small fraction of the total fees. Exempting indigent families from the busing fee therefore would not require Dickinson to make any significant adjustments in either the operation or the funding of the bus service. Indeed, as the Court states, most school districts in the State provide full bus service without charging any fees at all. See ante, at 465. The state interest involved in this case is therefore insubstantial; it does not begin to justify the discrimination challenged here.

The Court's decision to the contrary "demonstrates once again a `callous indifference to the realities of life for the poor.'" Selective Service System v. Minnesota Public Interest Research Group, 468 U.S., at 876 (MARSHALL, J., dissenting), quoting Flagg Bros., Inc. v. Brooks, 436 U.S. 149, 166 (1978) (MARSHALL, J., dissenting). These realities may not always be obvious from the Court's vantage point, but the Court fails in its constitutional duties when it refuses, as it does today, to make even the effort to see. For the poor, education is often the only route by which to become full participants in our society. In allowing a State to burden the access of poor persons to an education, the Court denies equal opportunity and discourages hope. I do not believe the Equal Protection Clause countenances such a result. I therefore dissent.

Notes

[1] The Court therefore does not address the question whether a State constitutionally could deny a child access to a minimally adequate education. In prior cases, this Court explicitly has left open the question whether such a deprivation of access would violate a fundamental constitutional right. See Papasan v. Allain, 478 U.S. 265, 284 (1986); San Antonio Independent School Dist. v. Rodriguez, 411 U.S. 1, 25, n. 60, 36-37 (1973). That question remains open today.

[2] There is no dispute that the Kadrmas family was indigent at the time relevant to this litigation. The family's annual income at the time of trial was at or near the poverty line. In addition, the family was heavily in debt, owing a total of $13,000.

The "independent source" exception to the exclusionary rule doesn't justify admitting "rediscovered" evidence: Justice Marshall's dissent in Murray v. United States (June 27, 1988)

JUSTICE MARSHALL, with whom JUSTICE STEVENS and JUSTICE O'CONNOR join, dissenting.

The Court today holds that the "independent source" exception to the exclusionary rule may justify admitting evidence discovered during an illegal warrantless search that is later "rediscovered" by the same team of investigators during a search pursuant to a warrant obtained immediately after the illegal search. I believe the Court's decision, by failing to provide sufficient guarantees that the subsequent search was, in fact, independent of the illegal search, emasculates the Warrant Clause and undermines the deterrence function of the exclusionary rule. I therefore dissent.

This Court has stated frequently that the exclusionary rule is principally designed to deter violations of the Fourth Amendment. See, e.g., United States v. Leon, 468 U. S. 897, 468 U. S. 906 (1984); Elkins v. United States, 364 U. S. 206, 364 U. S. 217 (1960). By excluding evidence discovered in violation of the Fourth Amendment, the rule

"compel[s] respect for the constitutional guaranty in the only effectively available way, by removing the incentive to disregard it."

Id. at 364 U. S. 217. The Court has crafted exceptions to the exclusionary rule when the purposes of the rule are not furthered by the exclusion. As the Court today recognizes, the independent source exception to the exclusionary rule "allows admission of evidence that has been discovered by means wholly independent of any constitutional violation." Nix v. Williams, 467 U. S. 431, 467 U. S. 443 (1984); see Silverthorne Lumber Co. v. United States, 251 U. S. 385, 251 U. S. 392 (1920). The independent source exception, like the inevitable discovery exception, is primarily based on a practical view that, under certain circumstances, the beneficial deterrent effect that exclusion will have on future constitutional violations is too slight to justify the social cost of excluding probative evidence from a criminal trial. See Nix v. Williams, supra, at 467 U. S. 444-446; cf. United States v. Leon, supra, 468 U. S. 906-909. When the seizure of the evidence at issue is "wholly independent of" the constitutional violation, then exclusion arguably will have no effect on a law enforcement officer's incentive to commit an unlawful search. [1]

Given the underlying justification for the independent source exception, any inquiry into the exception's application must keep sight of the practical effect admission will have on the incentives facing law enforcement officers to engage in unlawful conduct. The proper scope of the independent source exception, and guidelines for its application, cannot be divined in a factual vacuum; instead, they must be informed by the nature of the constitutional violation and the deterrent effect of exclusion in particular circumstances. In holding that the independent source exception may apply to the facts of these cases, I believe the Court loses sight of the practical moorings of the independent source exception and creates an affirmative incentive for unconstitutional searches. This holding can find no justification in the purposes underlying both the exclusionary rule and the independent source exception.

The factual setting of the instant case is straightforward. Federal Bureau of Investigation (FBI) and Drug Enforcement Agency (DEA) agents stopped two vehicles after they left a warehouse and discovered bales of marijuana. DEA Supervisor Garibotto and an assistant United States attorney then returned to the warehouse, which had been under surveillance for several hours. After demands that the warehouse door be opened went unanswered, Supervisor Garibotto forced open the door with a tire iron. A number of agents entered the warehouse. No persons were found inside, but the agents saw numerous bales of marijuana in plain view. Supervisor Garibotto then ordered everyone out of the warehouse. Agents did not reenter the warehouse until a warrant was obtained some eight hours later. The warehouse was kept under surveillance during the interim.

It is undisputed that the agents made no effort to obtain a warrant prior to the initial entry. The agents had not begun to prepare a warrant affidavit, and, according to FBI Agent Cleary, who supervised the FBI's involvement, they had not even engaged in any discussions of obtaining a warrant. App 52. The affidavit in support of the warrant obtained after the initial search was prepared by DEA Agent Keaney, who had tactical control over the DEA agents and who had participated in the initial search of the warehouse. The affidavit did not mention the warrantless search of the warehouse, nor did it cite information obtained from that search. In determining that the challenged evidence was admissible, the Court of Appeals assumed that the initial warrantless entry was not justified by exigent circumstances, and that the search therefore violated the Warrant Clause of the Fourth Amendment.

Under the circumstances of these cases, the admission of the evidence "reseized" during the second search severely undermines the the deterrence function of the exclusionary rule. Indeed, admission in these cases affirmatively encourages illegal searches. The incentives for such illegal conduct are clear. Obtaining a warrant is inconvenient and time consuming. Even when officers have probable cause to support a warrant application, therefore, they have an incentive first to determine whether it is worthwhile to obtain a warrant. Probable cause is much less than certainty, and many "confirmatory" searches will result in the discovery that no evidence is present, thus saving the police the time and trouble of getting a warrant. If contraband is discovered, however, the officers may later seek a warrant to shield the evidence from the taint of the illegal search. The police thus know in advance that they have little to lose and much to gain by forgoing the bother of obtaining a warrant and undertaking an illegal search.

The Court, however, "see[s] the incentives differently." Ante at 487 U. S. 540. Under the Court's view, today's decision does not provide an incentive for unlawful searches, because the officer undertaking the search would know that

"his action would add to the normal burden of convincing a magistrate that there is probable cause the much more onerous burden of convincing a trial court that no information gained from the illegal entry affected either the law enforcement officers' decision to seek a warrant or the magistrate's decision to grant it."

Ibid. The Court, however, provides no hint of why this risk would actually seem significant to the officers. Under the circumstances of these cases, the officers committing the illegal search have both knowledge and control of the factors central to the trial court's determination. First, it is a simple matter, as was done in these cases, to exclude from the warrant application any information gained from the initial entry, so that the magistrate's determination of probable cause is not influenced by the prior illegal search. Second, today's decision makes the application of the independent source exception turn entirely on an evaluation of the officers' intent. It normally will be difficult for the trial court to verify, or the defendant to rebut, an assertion by officers that they always intended to obtain a warrant, regardless of the results of the illegal search. [2] The testimony of the officers conducting the illegal search is the only direct evidence of intent, and the defendant will be relegated simply to arguing that the officers should not be believed. Under these circumstances, the litigation risk described by the Court seems hardly a risk at all; it does not significantly dampen the incentive to conduct the initial illegal search. [3]

The strong Fourth Amendment interest in eliminating these incentives for illegal entry should cause this Court to scrutinize closely the application of the independent source exception to evidence obtained under the circumstances of the instant cases; respect for the constitutional guaranty requires a rule that does not undermine the deterrence function of the exclusionary rule. When, as here, the same team of investigators is involved in both the first and second search, there is a significant danger that the "independence" of the source will in fact be illusory, and that the initial search will have affected the decision to obtain a warrant notwithstanding the officers' subsequent assertions to the contrary. It is therefore crucial that the factual premise of the exception -- complete independence -- be clearly established before the exception can justify admission of the evidence. I believe the Court's reliance on the intent of the law enforcement officers who conducted the warrantless search provides insufficient guarantees that the subsequent legal search was unaffected by the prior illegal search.

To ensure that the source of the evidence is genuinely independent, the basis for a finding that a search was untainted by a prior illegal search must focus, as with the inevitable discovery doctrine, on "demonstrated historical facts capable of ready verification or impeachment." Nix v. Williams, 467 U.S. at 467 U. S. 445, n. 5. In the instant cases, there are no "demonstrated historical facts" capable of supporting a finding that the subsequent warrant search was wholly unaffected by the prior illegal search. The same team of investigators was involved in both searches. The warrant was obtained immediately after the illegal search, and no effort was made to obtain a warrant prior to the discovery of the marijuana during the illegal search. The only evidence available that the warrant search was wholly independent is the testimony of the agents who conducted the illegal search. Under these circumstances, the threat that the subsequent search was tainted by the illegal search is too great to allow for the application of the independent source exception. [4] The Court's contrary holding lends itself to easy abuse, and offers an incentive to bypass the constitutional requirement that probable cause be assessed by a neutral and detached magistrate before the police invade an individual's privacy. [5]

The decision in Segura v. United States, 468 U. S. 796 (1984), is not to the contrary. In Segura, the Court expressly distinguished between evidence discovered during an initial warrantless entry and evidence that was not discovered until a subsequent legal search. The Court held that, under those circumstances, when no information from an illegal search was used in a subsequent warrant application, the warrant provided an independent source for the evidence first uncovered in the second, lawful search.

Segura is readily distinguished from the present cases. The admission of evidence first discovered during a legal search does not significantly lessen the deterrence facing the law enforcement officers contemplating an illegal entry so long as the evidence that is seen is excluded. This was clearly the view of Chief Justice Burger, joined by JUSTICE O'CONNOR, when he stated that the Court's ruling would not significantly detract from the deterrent effects of the exclusionary rule because

"officers who enter illegally will recognize that whatever evidence they discover as a direct result of the entry may be suppressed, as it was by the Court of Appeals in this case."

Id. at 468 U. S. 812. As I argue above, extending Segura to cover evidence discovered during an initial illegal search will eradicate this remaining deterrence to illegal entry. Moreover, there is less reason to believe that an initial illegal entry was prompted by a desire to determine whether to bother to get a warrant in the first place, and thus was not wholly independent of the second search, if officers understand that evidence they discover during the illegal search will be excluded even if they subsequently return with a warrant.

In sum, under circumstances as are presented in these cases, when the very law enforcement officers who participate in an illegal search immediately thereafter obtain a warrant to search the same premises, I believe the evidence discovered during the initial illegal entry must be suppressed. Any other result emasculates the Warrant Clause, and provides an intolerable incentive for warrantless searches. I respectfully dissent.

Notes

[1] The clearest case for the application of the independent source exception is when a wholly separate line of investigation, shielded from information gathered in an illegal search, turns up the same evidence through a separate, lawful search. Under these circumstances, there is little doubt that the lawful search was not connected to the constitutional violation. The exclusion of such evidence would not significantly add to the deterrence facing the law enforcement officers conducting the illegal search, because they would have little reason to anticipate the separate investigation leading to the same evidence.

[2] Such an intent-based rule is of dubious value for other reasons as well. First, the intent of the officers prior to the illegal entry often will be of little significance to the relevant question: whether, even if the initial entry uncovered no evidence, the officers' would return immediately with a warrant to conduct a second search. Officers who have probable cause to believe contraband is present genuinely might intend later to obtain a warrant, but after the illegal search uncovers no such contraband, those same officers might decide their time is better spent than to return with a warrant. In addition, such an intent rule will be difficult to apply. The Court fails to describe how a trial court will properly evaluate whether the law enforcement officers' fully intended to obtain a warrant regardless of what they discovered during the illegal search. The obvious question is whose intent is relevant? Intentions clearly may differ both among supervisory officers and among officers who initiate the illegal search.

[3] The litigation risk facing these law enforcement officers may be contrasted with the risk faced by the officer in Nix v. Williams, 467 U. S. 431 (1984). Nix involved an application of the inevitable discovery exception to the exclusionary rule. In that case, the Court stressed that an officer

"who is faced with the opportunity to obtain evidence illegally will rarely, if ever, be in a position to calculate whether the evidence sought would inevitably be discovered."

Id. at 467 U. S. 445. Unlike the officer in Nix, who had no way of knowing about the progress of a wholly separate line of investigation that already had begun at the time of his unconstitutional conduct, the officers in the instant cases, at least under the Court's analysis, have complete knowledge and control over the factors relevant to the determination of "independence."

[4] To conclude that the initial search had no effect on the decision to obtain a warrant, and thus that the warrant search was an "independent source" of the challenged evidence, one would have to assume that, even if the officers entered the premises and discovered no contraband, they nonetheless would have gone to the Magistrate, sworn that they had probable cause to believe that contraband was in the building, and then returned to conduct another search. Although such a scenario is possible, I believe it is more plausible to believe that the officers would not have chosen to return immediately to

the premises with a warrant to search for evidence had they not discovered evidence during the initial search.

[5] Given that the law enforcement officers in these cases made no movement to obtain a warrant prior to the illegal search, these cases do not present the more difficult issue whether, in light of the strong interest in deterring illegal warrantless searches, the evidence discovered during an illegal search ever may be admitted under the independent source exception when the second legal search is conducted by the same investigative team pursuing the same line of investigation.

Can't retry someone who's already started serving their sentence: Justice Marshall's dissent in Lockhart v. Nelson (November 14, 1988)

JUSTICE MARSHALL, with whom JUSTICE BRENNAN and JUSTICE BLACKMUN join, dissenting.

Under Arkansas law, a defendant who is convicted of a class B felony and "who has previously been convicted of . . . [or] found guilty of four 4. or more felonies" may be sentenced to an enhanced term of imprisonment ranging from 20 years to 40 years. Ark. Stat. Ann. 41-1001(2)(b) (1977) (current version at Ark. Code Ann. 5-4-501(b)(3) (1987)). At the March 1982 sentencing trial held after Johnny Lee Nelson pleaded guilty to the class B felony of burglary, 1 the State of Arkansas introduced evidence indicating that Nelson had four prior felony convictions. Nelson protested that he had received a gubernatorial pardon for one of the convictions. The prosecutor and the trial judge disbelieved Nelson's claim, however, and the jury sentenced him to 20 years in prison. Three and a half years later - during which time Nelson, from jail, persistently implored Arkansas courts to investigate his pardon claim - a Federal District Court finally ordered the State to check its records. Lo and behold, it turned out that Nelson had been pardoned - and Arkansas soon announced its intention to try Nelson, once again, as a habitual offender. 2

The majority holds today that, although Arkansas attempted once and failed to prove that Nelson had the four prior convictions required for habitual offender status, it does not violate the Double Jeopardy Clause for Arkansas to attempt again. I believe, however, that Nelson's retrial is squarely foreclosed by Burks v. United States, 437 U.S. 1 (1978), where we held that a State may not retry a defendant where it failed initially to present sufficient evidence of guilt. The majority rushes headlong past those facets of Nelson's case and of Arkansas law that reveal the prosecution's failure to present sufficient evidence of guilt in this case, in order to answer the open and narrow question of double jeopardy law on which the Court granted certiorari. By virtue of the majority's haste, Nelson now faces a new sentencing trial, and Arkansas will be able to augment the evidence it presented at Nelson's initial trial with evidence of prior convictions it opted not to introduce in the first place. Because this result embodies the classic double jeopardy evil of a State "honing its trial strategies and perfecting its evidence through successive attempts at conviction," Tibbs v. Florida, 457 U.S. 31, 41 (1982), I dissent.

I

The Double Jeopardy Clause is "designed to protect an individual from being subjected to the hazards of trial and possible conviction more than once for an alleged offense." Green v. United States, 355 U.S. 184, 187 (1957). Reflecting this principle, we held in Burks that the prohibition against double jeopardy prevents retrial where a State's evidence at trial is found insufficient. See also Hudson v. Louisiana, 450 U.S. 40 (1981); Greene v. Massey, 437 U.S. 19 (1978). The Burks rule is based on the time-honored notion that the State should be given only "one fair opportunity to offer whatever proof it [can] assemble." Burks, supra, at 16. Unlike a finding of reversible trial error, which traditionally has not barred retrial, see United States v. Tateo, 377 U.S. 463 (1964); United States v. Ball, 163 U.S. 662 (1896), reversal for evidentiary insufficiency "constitute[s] a decision to the effect that the government has failed to prove its case." Burks, supra, at 15.

This case is troubling in a number of respects, not the least of which is that no one in the Arkansas criminal justice system seems to have taken Nelson's pardon claim at all seriously. At bottom, however, this case is controlled by the Burks insufficiency principle. For under Arkansas' law of pardons, the State's evidence against Nelson in his sentencing trial was at all times insufficient to prove four valid prior convictions. The majority errs in treating this as a case of mere trial error, and in reaching the unsettled issue whether, after a trial error reversal based on the improper admission of evidence, a reviewing court should evaluate the sufficiency of the evidence by including, or excluding, the tainted evidence. See Greene v. Massey, supra, at 26, n. 9 (expressly reserving this question). This case has nothing to do with inadmissible evidence and everything to do with Arkansas' defective proof.

As the District Court noted in ruling for Nelson, Arkansas decisional law holds that pardoned convictions have no probative value in sentence enhancement proceedings. See 641 F. Supp. 174, 183 (ED Ark. 1986) (under Arkansas law: "[A] pardon renders the conviction a nullity. . . . [F]or purposes of the enhancement statute, a conviction which has been pardonned [sic] is not a conviction"). The District Court cited a 1973 decision of the Arkansas Supreme Court, Duncan v. State, 254 Ark. 449, 494 S. W. 2d 127 (1973), which held that a pardoned conviction cannot be counted toward the four prior convictions required under the State's sentence enhancement statute. The Duncan court, id., at 451, 494 S. W. 2d, at 129, quoted with approval this Court's decision in Ex parte Garland, 4 Wall. 333, 380 (1867), where we stated: "A pardon reaches both the punishment prescribed for the offense and the guilt of the offender; and when the pardon is full, it releases the punishment and blots out of existence the guilt, so that in the eye of the law the offender is as innocent as if he had never committed the offense." Drawing upon that state-court holding, the District Court in this case concluded: "The truth is that the state could not have provided any evidence to rebut the petitioner's contention because it did not exist." 641 F. Supp., at 184. 3

That Arkansas was not roused to investigate Nelson's pardon claim until long after his trial does not transform the State's failure of proof - fatal for double jeopardy purposes under Burks - into a mere failure of admissibility. As the District Court noted, Arkansas law establishes "that the prosecutor must carry the significant burden of ferreting out information regarding the validity of prior convictions whenever he seeks enhancement." 641 F. Supp., at 184 (citing Roach v. State, 255 Ark. 773, 503 S. W. 2d 467 (1973)). The delay in the discovery of Nelson's pardon does not change the essential fact that, as a matter of state law, the paper evidence of the disputed conviction presented by the prosecutor was devoid of probative value from the moment the conviction was expunged by the pardon. A pardon simply "blots out of existence" the conviction as if it had never happened. Duncan v. State, supra, at 451, 494 S. W. 2d, at 129. If, in seeking to prove Nelson's four prior convictions, the State had offered documented evidence to prove three valid prior convictions and a blank piece of paper to prove a fourth, no one would doubt that Arkansas had produced insufficient evidence and that the Double Jeopardy Clause barred retrial. There is no constitutionally significant difference between that hypothetical and this case. 4

In sum, Arkansas had "one fair opportunity to offer whatever proof it could assemble" that Nelson had four prior convictions, Burks, 437 U.S., at 16, but it "failed to prove its case." Id., at 15. In reversing both the District Court and the Court of Appeals to give Arkansas a second chance to sentence Nelson as a habitual offender, the majority pays no more than lipservice to the Burks insufficiency principle. I would therefore hold that the Double Jeopardy Clause prohibits Arkansas from subjecting Nelson to a new sentencing trial at which it can "supply evidence" of a fourth conviction "which it failed to muster in the first proceeding." Id., at 11.

II

Even if I did not regard this as a case of insufficient evidence controlled by Burks, I could not join my colleagues in the majority. The question whether a reviewing court, in evaluating insufficiency for double jeopardy purposes, should look to all the admitted evidence, or just the properly admitted evidence, is a complex one. It is worthy of the thoughtful consideration typically attending this Court's decisions concerning the Double Jeopardy Clause.

The majority instead resolves this issue as if it had already been decided. Ante, at 40-41. In the majority's view: "It is quite clear from our opinion in Burks that a reviewing court must consider all of the evidence admitted by the trial court in deciding whether retrial is permissible under the Double Jeopardy Clause." Ibid. Burks decided no such thing. At issue in Burks was whether a finding of initial insufficiency bars a defendant's retrial; we held that it did. Burks did not presume to decide the completely distinct issue, raised by this case, of by what measure a reviewing court evaluates insufficiency in cases where a piece of evidence which went to the jury is later ruled inadmissible. Indeed, had Burks settled or even logically foreclosed this issue, there would have been no reason for us specifically to reserve its resolution in Greene v. Massey, 437 U.S., at 26, n. 9 - a case decided the very same day as Burks. 5

It seems to me that the Court's analysis of this issue should begin with the recognition that, in deciding when the double jeopardy bar should apply, we are balancing two weighty interests: the defendant's interest in repose and society's interest in the orderly administration of justice. See, e. g., United States v. Tateo, 377 U.S., at 466 . The defendant's interest in avoiding successive trials on the same charge reflects the idea that the State

"should not be allowed to make repeated attempts to convict an individual for an alleged offense, thereby subjecting him to embarrassment, expense and ordeal and compelling him to live in a continuing state of anxiety and insecurity, as well as enhancing the possibility that even though innocent he may be found guilty." Green v. United States, 355 U.S., at 187 -188.

See also Burks, supra, at 11. Society's corresponding interest in the sound administration of justice reflects the fact that "[i]t would be a high price indeed for society to pay were every accused granted immunity from punishment because of any defect sufficient to constitute reversible error in the proceedings leading to conviction." United States v. Tateo, supra, at 466.

I do not intend in this dissenting opinion to settle what rule best accommodates these competing interests in cases where a reviewing court has determined that a portion of a State's proof was inadmissible. At first blush, it would seem that the defendant's interest is every bit as great in this situation as in the Burks situation. Society's interest, however, would appear to turn on a number of variables. The chief one is the likelihood that retrying the defendant will lead to conviction. See United States v. Tateo, supra, at 466 (noting society's interest "in punishing one whose guilt is clear"). In appraising this likelihood, one might inquire into whether prosecutors tend in close cases to hold back probative evidence of a defendant's guilt; if they do not, there would be scant societal interest in permitting retrial given that the State's remaining evidence is, by definition, insufficient. 6 Alternatively, one might inquire as to why the evidence at issue was deemed inadmissible. Where evidence was stricken for reasons having to do with its unreliability, it would seem curious to include it in the sufficiency calculus. Inadmissible hearsay evidence, for example, or evidence deemed defective or nonprobative as a matter of law thus might not be included. By contrast, evidence stricken in compliance with evidentiary rules grounded in other public policies - the policy of encouraging subsequent remedial measures embodied in Federal Rule of Evidence 407, for example, or the policy of deterring unconstitutional searches and seizures embodied in the exclusionary rule - might more justifiably be included in a double jeopardy sufficiency analysis. 7

The Court today should have enunciated rules of this type, rules calibrated to accommodate, as best as possible, the defendant's interest in repose with society's interest in punishing the guilty. Regrettably, the majority avoids such subtlety in its terse opinion. Instead, it opts for a declaration that our decision in Burks - although no one knew it at the time - was settling the issue on which we granted certiorari here. This is ipse dixit jurisprudence of the worst kind. I dissent.

Notes

[1] Nelson pleaded guilty to having taken $45.00 from a vending machine in 1979. See 641 F. Supp. 174, 175 (ED Ark. 1986).

[2] The conviction for which Nelson was pardoned was a 1960 conviction for assault with intent to rape. He was pardoned in 1964 by Arkansas Governor Orval E. Faubus. App. 6 (text of pardon).

The record in this case shows that Nelson attempted unsuccessfully both during and after his trial to alert state authorities to this pardon. During the trial, Nelson stated that after serving three years in jail, he "had the case investigated and the governor at the time Faubus which [sic] gave me a pardon for my sentence." Id., at 8 (abridged transcript of sentencing trial). He added: "[A]t my home I have documents of that pardon on that [sic]." Id., at 9. The prosecutor did not question Nelson about this claim. Instead, the prosecutor moved to strike Nelson's testimony on the ground that Nelson was "confused as to the meaning of the pardon and a commutation." Id., at 11. The prosecutor further stated: "I think the records are clear that are in the court . . . ." Id., at 11-12. Ultimately, the trial judge, and Nelson's own defense counsel - who like the prosecutor had never investigated Nelson's claim of pardon - accepted this account. Id., at 12.

After receiving the enhanced sentence, Nelson sought both on direct appeal and in state postconviction actions to have his claim investigated. Only after a Federal District Court ordered Arkansas to investigate Nelson's claim did Nelson's pardon finally come to light - in August 1985. Id., at 1-4.

[3] The Court of Appeals did not disturb this determination of the District Court. Rather, it focused upon, and rejected, Arkansas' separate contention that double jeopardy does not attach to sentence enhancement trials. See 828 F.2d 446, 449 (CA8 1987). That issue is not before this Court, Arkansas having conceded the validity of this aspect of the Court of Appeals' ruling. See ante, at 36-37, n. 4. The Court of Appeals also rejected as incorrect Arkansas' claim that, in cases of trial error, reviewing courts should not engage in any subsequent review for insufficiency, however measured. 828 F.2d, at 450.

[4] The majority offers its own analogy: the discovery of Nelson's pardon, it states, is like "newly discovered evidence." Ante, at 41, n. 7. The majority overlooks a critical distinction. The emergence of new evidence in no way strips the old evidence of all probative value; while new evidence may cast doubt on the persuasiveness of the old evidence, its emergence does not render once sufficient evidence "insufficient." Arkansas' law of pardons, by contrast, robs evidence of a pardoned conviction of all probative value. It was thus not the discovery of Nelson's pardon that stripped his prior conviction of evidentiary weight, but rather the fact of the pardon itself. The discovery of Nelson's pardon merely called the parties' attention to this critical fact.

[5] None of the numerous appellate court cases cited by the majority in support of its resolution of this issue, ante, at 41, n. 8, interpreted Burks as disposing of the sufficiency question before us. Rather, with varying degrees of analysis, these courts evaluated the ramifications of including or excluding tainted evidence in a sufficiency analysis upon the interests of the defendant and of society - precisely the analytic approach I urge in the succeeding paragraphs. See, e. g., United States v. Tranowski, 702 F.2d 668, 671 (CA7 1983) (concluding that policy arguments favor including tainted evidence in insufficiency analysis), cert. denied, 468 U.S. 1217 (1984); Bullard v. Estelle, 665 F.2d 1347, 1358-1361 (CA5 1982) (using similar interest analysis in case involving retrial for sentence enhancement and concluding that inadmissible evidence should not be included in insufficiency analysis).

[6] It is no answer to say that prosecutors who initially lacked sufficient admissible evidence may gather more before a retrial. Such conduct is precisely what the Double Jeopardy Clause was designed to guard against. See Tibbs v. Florida, 457 U.S. 31, 41 (1982).

[7] Arkansas suggests a "clear trial court ruling" test as a means of accommodating defense and societal interests. Under this test, where a trial court has affirmatively ruled that a piece of evidence is admissible, a State is entitled to rely on that ruling by counting this evidence in a subsequent insufficiency analysis - even if a reviewing court had ruled the evidence inadmissible. Brief for Petitioner 12. This test furthers a societal interest of which this Court took note in United States v. Tateo, 377 U.S. 463, 466 (1964): the interest in not deterring appellate courts from safeguarding defendants' rights. It is not at all clear, however, that Arkansas' test would authorize retrial in this case. Far from having refrained from introducing evidence of additional convictions in reliance on a trial court's determination that Nelson had not received a pardon, the prosecutor in this case seems to have done all he could to lead the trial court to believe that Nelson's pardon claim was meritless. See n. 2, supra.

Not unconstitutional for a city to allocate a portion of its contracting dollars for businesses owned or controlled only by members of minority groups: Justice Marshall's dissent in Richmond v. Croson (January 23, 1989)

JUSTICE MARSHALL, with whom JUSTICE BRENNAN and JUSTICE BLACKMUN join, dissenting.

It is a welcome symbol of racial progress when the former capital of the Confederacy acts forthrightly to confront the effects of racial discrimination in its midst. In my view, nothing in the Constitution can be construed to prevent Richmond, Virginia, from allocating a portion of its contracting dollars for businesses owned or controlled by members of minority groups. Indeed, Richmond's set-aside program is indistinguishable in all meaningful respects from - and in fact was patterned upon - the federal set-aside plan which this Court upheld in Fullilove v. Klutznick, 448 U.S. 448 (1980).

A majority of this Court holds today, however, that the Equal Protection Clause of the Fourteenth Amendment blocks Richmond's initiative. The essence of the majority's position 1 is that Richmond has failed to catalog adequate findings to prove that past discrimination has impeded minorities from joining or participating fully in Richmond's construction contracting industry. I find deep irony in second-guessing Richmond's judgment on this point. As much as any municipality in the United States, Richmond knows what racial discrimination is; a century of decisions by this and other federal courts has richly documented the city's disgraceful history of public and private racial discrimination. In any event, the Richmond City Council has supported its determination that minorities have been wrongly excluded from local construction contracting. Its proof includes statistics showing that minority-owned businesses have received virtually no city contracting dollars and rarely if ever belonged to area trade associations; testimony by municipal officials that discrimination has been widespread in the local construction industry; and the same exhaustive and widely publicized federal studies relied on in Fullilove, studies which showed that pervasive discrimination in the Nation's tight-knit construction industry had operated to exclude minorities from public contracting. These are precisely the types of statistical and testimonial evidence which, until today, this Court had credited in cases approving of race-conscious measures designed to remedy past discrimination.

More fundamentally, today's decision marks a deliberate and giant step backward in this Court's affirmative-action jurisprudence. Cynical of one municipality's attempt to redress the effects of past racial discrimination in a particular industry, the majority launches a grapeshot attack on race-conscious remedies in general. The majority's unnecessary pronouncements will inevitably discourage or prevent governmental entities, particularly States and localities, from acting to rectify the scourge of past discrimination. This is the harsh reality of the majority's decision, but it is not the Constitution's command.

I

As an initial matter, the majority takes an exceedingly myopic view of the factual predicate on which the Richmond City Council relied when it passed the Minority Business Utilization Plan. The majority analyzes Richmond's initiative as if it were based solely upon the facts about local construction and contracting practices adduced during the city council session at which the measure was enacted. Ante, at 479-481. In so doing, the majority downplays the fact that the city council had before it a rich trove of evidence that discrimination in the Nation's construction industry had seriously impaired the competitive position of businesses owned or controlled by members of minority groups. It is only against this backdrop of documented national discrimination, however, that the local evidence adduced by Richmond can be properly understood. The majority's refusal to recognize that Richmond has proved itself no exception to the dismaying pattern of national exclusion which Congress so painstakingly identified infects its entire analysis of this case.

Six years before Richmond acted, Congress passed, and the President signed, the Public Works Employment Act of 1977, Pub. L. 95-28, 91 Stat. 116, 42 U.S.C. 6701 et seq. (Act), a measure which appropriated $4 billion in federal grants to state and local governments for use in public works projects. Section 103(f)(2) of the Act was a minority business set-aside provision. It required state or local grantees to use 10% of their federal grants to procure services or supplies from businesses owned or controlled by members of statutorily identified minority groups, absent an administrative waiver. In 1980, in Fullilove, supra, this Court upheld the validity of this federal set-aside. Chief Justice Burger's principal opinion noted the importance of overcoming those "criteria, methods, or practices thought by Congress to have the effect of defeating, or substantially impairing, access by the minority business community to public funds made available by congressional appropriations." Fullilove, 448 U.S., at 480 . Finding the set-aside provision properly tailored to this goal, the Chief Justice concluded that the program was valid under either strict or intermediate scrutiny. Id., at 492.

The congressional program upheld in Fullilove was based upon an array of congressional and agency studies which documented the powerful influence of racially exclusionary practices in the business world. A 1975 Report by the House Committee on Small Business concluded:

"The effects of past inequities stemming from racial prejudice have not remained in the past. The Congress has recognized the reality that past discriminatory practices have, to some degree, adversely affected our present economic system.

"While minority persons comprise about 16 percent of the Nation's population, of the 13 million businesses in the United States, only 382,000, or approximately 3.0 percent, are owned by minority individuals. The most recent data from the Department of Commerce also indicates that the gross receipts of all businesses in this country totals about $2, 540.8 billion, and of this amount only $16.6 billion, or about 0.65 percent was realized by minority business concerns.

"These statistics are not the result of random chance. The presumption must be made that past discriminatory systems have resulted in present economic inequities." H. R. Rep. No. 94-468, pp. 1-2 (1975) (quoted in Fullilove, supra, at 465) (opinion of Burger, C. J.) (emphasis deleted and added).

A 1977 Report by the same Committee concluded:

"[O]ver the years, there has developed a business system which has traditionally excluded measurable minority participation. In the past more than the present, this system of conducting business transactions overtly precluded minority input. Currently, we more often encounter a business system which is racially neutral on its face, but because of past overt social and economic discrimination is presently operating, in effect, to perpetuate these past inequities. Minorities, until recently have not participated to any measurable extent, in our total business system generally, or in the construction industry in particular." H. R. Rep. No. 94-1791, p. 182 (1977), summarizing

H. R. Rep. No. 94-468, p. 17 (1976 (quoted in Fullilove, supra, at 466, n. 48).

Congress further found that minorities seeking initial public contracting assignments often faced immense entry barriers which did not confront experienced nonminority contractors. A report submitted to Congress in 1975 by the United States Commission on Civil Rights, for example, described the way in which fledgling minority-owned businesses were hampered by "deficiencies in working capital, inability to meet bonding requirements, disabilities caused by an inadequate `track record,' lack of awareness of bidding opportunities, unfamiliarity with bidding procedures, preselection before the formal advertising process, and the exercise of discretion by government procurement officers to disfavor minority businesses." Fullilove, supra, at 467 (summarizing United States Comm'n on Civil Rights, Minorities and Women as Government Contractors (May 1975)).

Thus, as of 1977, there was "abundant evidence" in the public domain "that minority businesses ha[d] been denied effective participation in public contracting opportunities by procurement practices that perpetuated the effects of prior discrimination." Fullilove, supra, at 477-478. 2 Significantly, this evidence demonstrated that discrimination had prevented existing or nascent minority-owned businesses from obtaining not only federal contracting assignments, but state and local ones as well. See Fullilove, supra, at 478. 3

The members of the Richmond City Council were well aware of these exhaustive congressional findings, a point the majority, tellingly, elides. The transcript of the session at which the council enacted the local set-aside initiative contains numerous references to the 6-year-old congressional set-aside program, to the evidence of nationwide discrimination barriers described above, and to the Fullilove decision itself. See, e. g., App. 14-16, 24 (remarks of City Attorney William H. Hefty); id., at 14-15 (remarks of Councilmember William J. Leidinger); id., at 18 (remarks of minority community task force president Freddie Ray); id., at 25, 41 (remarks of Councilmember Henry L. Marsh III); id., at 42 (remarks of City Manager Manuel Deese).

The city council's members also heard testimony that, although minority groups made up half of the city's population, only 0.67% of the $24.6 million which Richmond had dispensed in construction contracts during the five years ending in March 1983 had gone to minority-owned prime contractors. Id., at 43 (remarks of Councilmember Henry W. Richardson). They heard testimony that the major Richmond area construction trade associations had virtually no minorities among their hundreds of members. 4 Finally, they heard testimony from city officials as to the exclusionary history of the local construction industry. 5 As the District Court noted, not a single person who testified before the city council denied that discrimination in Richmond's construction industry had been widespread. Civ. Action No. 84-0021 (ED Va., Dec. 3, 1984) (reprinted in Supp. App. to Juris. Statement 164-165). 6 So long as one views Richmond's local evidence of discrimination against the backdrop of systematic nationwide racial discrimination which Congress had so painstakingly identified in this very industry, this case is readily resolved.

II

"Agreement upon a means for applying the Equal Protection Clause to an affirmative-action program has eluded this Court every time the issue has come before us." Wygant v. Jackson Bd. of Education, 476 U.S. 267, 301 (1986) (MARSHALL, J., dissenting). My view has long been that race-conscious classifications designed to further remedial goals "must serve important governmental objectives and must be substantially related to achievement of those objectives" in order to withstand constitutional scrutiny. University of California Regents v. Bakke, 438 U.S. 265, 359 (1978) (joint opinion of BRENNAN, WHITE, MARSHALL, and BLACKMUN, JJ.) (citations omitted); see also Wygant, supra, at 301-302 (MARSHALL, J., dissenting); Fullilove, 448 U.S., at 517 -519 (MARSHALL, J., concurring in judgment). Analyzed in terms of this two-pronged standard, Richmond's set-aside, like the federal program on which it was modeled, is "plainly constitutional." Fullilove, supra, at 519 (MARSHALL, J., concurring in judgment).

A

1

Turning first to the governmental interest inquiry, Richmond has two powerful interests in setting aside a portion of public contracting funds for minority-owned enterprises. The first is the city's interest in eradicating the effects of past racial discrimination. It is far too late in the day to doubt that remedying such discrimination is a compelling, let alone an important, interest. In Fullilove, six Members of this Court deemed this interest sufficient to support a race-conscious set-aside program governing federal contract procurement. The decision, in holding that the federal set-aside provision satisfied the equal protection principles under any level of scrutiny, recognized that the measure sought to remove "barriers to competitive access which had their roots in racial and ethnic discrimination, and which continue today, even absent any intentional discrimination or unlawful conduct." 448 U.S., at 478; see also id., at 502-506 (Powell, J., concurring); id., at 520 (MARSHALL, J., concurring in judgment). Indeed, we have repeatedly reaffirmed the government's interest in breaking down barriers erected by past racial discrimination in cases involving access to public education, McDaniel v. Barresi, 402 U.S. 39, 41 (1971); University of California Regents v. Bakke, 438 U.S., at 320 (opinion of Powell, J.); id., at 362-364 (joint opinion of BRENNAN, WHITE, MARSHALL, and BLACKMUN, JJ.), employment, United States v. Paradise, 480 U.S. 149, 167 (1987) (plurality opinion); id., at 186-189 (Powell, J., concurring), and valuable government contracts, Fullilove, 448 U.S., at 481 -484 (opinion of Burger, C. J.); id., at 496-497 (Powell, J., concurring); id., at 521 (MARSHALL, J., concurring in judgment).

Richmond has a second compelling interest in setting aside, where possible, a portion of its contracting dollars. That interest is the prospective one of preventing the city's own spending decisions from reinforcing and perpetuating the exclusionary effects of past discrimination. See Fullilove, 448 U.S., at 475 (noting Congress' conclusion that "the subcontracting practices of prime contractors could perpetuate the prevailing impaired access by minority businesses to public contracting opportunities"); id., at 503 (Powell, J., concurring).

The majority pays only lipservice to this additional governmental interest. See ante, at 491-493, 503-504. But our decisions have often emphasized the danger of the government tacitly adopting, encouraging, or furthering racial discrimination even by its own routine operations. In Shelley v. Kraemer, 334 U.S. 1 (1948), this Court recognized this interest as a constitutional command, holding unanimously that the Equal Protection Clause forbids courts to enforce racially restrictive covenants even where such covenants satisfied all requirements of state law and where the State harbored no discriminatory intent. Similarly, in Norwood v. Harrison, 413 U.S. 455 (1973), we invalidated a program in which a State purchased textbooks and loaned them to students in public and private schools, including private schools with racially discriminatory policies. We stated that the Constitution requires a State "to steer clear, not only of operating the old dual system of racially segregated schools, but also of giving significant aid to institutions that practice racial or other invidious discrimination." Id., at 467; see also Gilmore v. City of Montgomery, 417 U.S. 556 (1974) (upholding federal-court order forbidding city to allow private segregated schools which allegedly discriminated on the basis of race to use public parks).

The majority is wrong to trivialize the continuing impact of government acceptance or use of private institutions or structures once wrought by discrimination. When government channels all its contracting funds to a white-dominated community of established contractors whose racial homogeneity is the product of private discrimination, it does more than place its imprimatur on the practices which forged and which continue to define that community. It also provides a measurable boost to those economic entities that have thrived within it, while denying important economic benefits to those entities which, but for prior discrimination, might well be better qualified to receive valuable government contracts. In my view, the interest in ensuring that the government does not reflect and reinforce prior private discrimination in dispensing public contracts is every bit as strong as the interest in eliminating private discrimination - an interest which this Court has repeatedly deemed compelling. See, e. g., New York State Club Assn. v. New York City, 487 U.S. 1, 14, n. 5 (1988); Board of Directors of Rotary Int'l v. Rotary Club of Duarte, 481 U.S. 537, 549 (1987); Roberts v. United States Jaycees, 468 U.S. 609, 623 (1984); Bob Jones University v. United States, 461 U.S. 574, 604 (1983); Runyon v. McCrary, 427 U.S. 160, 179 (1976). The more government bestows its rewards on those persons or businesses that were positioned to thrive during a period of private racial discrimination, the tighter the deadhand grip of prior discrimination becomes on the present and future. Cities like Richmond may not be constitutionally required to adopt setaside plans. But see North Carolina Bd. of Education v. Swann, 402 U.S. 43, 46 (1971) (Constitution may require consideration of race in remedying state-sponsored school segregation); McDaniel, supra, at 41 (same, and stating that "[a]ny other approach would freeze the status quo that is the very target of all desegregation processes"). But there can be no doubt that when Richmond acted affirmatively to stem the perpetuation of patterns of discrimination through its own decisionmaking, it served an interest of the highest order.

2

The remaining question with respect to the "governmental interest" prong of equal protection analysis is whether Richmond has proffered satisfactory proof of past racial discrimination to support its twin interests in remediation and in governmental nonperpetuation. Although the Members of this Court have differed on the appropriate standard of review for race-conscious remedial measures, see United States v. Paradise, 480 U.S., at 166, and 166-167, n. 17 (plurality opinion); Sheet Metal Workers v. EEOC, 478 U.S. 421, 480 (1986) (plurality opinion), we have always regarded this factual inquiry as a practical one. Thus, the Court has eschewed rigid tests which require the provision of particular species of evidence, statistical or otherwise. At the same time we have required that government adduce evidence that, taken as a whole, is sufficient to support its claimed interest and to dispel the natural concern that it acted out of mere "paternalistic stereotyping, not on a careful consideration of modern social conditions." Fullilove v. Klutznick, supra, at 519 (MARSHALL, J., concurring in judgment).

The separate opinions issued in Wygant v. Jackson Bd. of Education, a case involving a school board's race-conscious layoff provision, reflect this shared understanding. Justice Powell's opinion for a plurality of four Justices stated that "the trial court must make a factual determination that the employer had a strong basis in evidence for its conclusion that remedial action was necessary." 476 U.S., at 277. JUSTICE O'CONNOR'S separate concurrence required "a firm basis for concluding that remedial action was appropriate." Id., at 293. The dissenting opinion I authored, joined by JUSTICES BRENNAN and BLACKMUN, required a government body to present a "legitimate factual predicate" and a reviewing court to "genuinely consider the circumstances of the provision at issue." Id., at 297, 303. Finally, JUSTICE STEVENS' separate dissent sought and found "a rational and unquestionably legitimate basis" for the school board's action. Id., at 315-316. Our unwillingness to go beyond these generalized standards to require specific types of proof in all circumstances reflects, in my view, an understanding that discrimination takes a myriad of "ingenious and pervasive forms." University of California Regents v. Bakke, 438 U.S., at 387 (separate opinion of MARSHALL, J.).

The varied body of evidence on which Richmond relied provides a "strong," "firm," and "unquestionably legitimate" basis upon which the city council could determine that the effects of past racial discrimination warranted a remedial and prophylactic governmental response. As I have noted, supra, at 530-534, Richmond acted against a backdrop of congressional and Executive Branch studies which demonstrated with such force the nationwide pervasiveness of prior discrimination that Congress presumed that "'present economic inequities'" in construction contracting resulted from "`past discriminatory systems.'" Supra, at 531 (quoting H. R. Rep. No. 94-468, pp. 1-2 (1975)). The city's local evidence confirmed that Richmond's construction industry did not deviate from this pernicious national pattern. The fact that just 0.67% of public construction expenditures over the previous five years had gone to minority-owned prime contractors, despite the city's racially mixed population, strongly suggests that construction contracting in the area was rife with "present economic inequities." To the extent this enormous disparity did not itself demonstrate that discrimination had occurred, the descriptive testimony of Richmond's elected and appointed leaders drew the necessary link between the pitifully small presence of minorities in construction contracting and past exclusionary practices. That no one who testified challenged this depiction of widespread racial discrimination in area construction contracting lent significant weight to these accounts. The fact that area trade associations had virtually no minority members dramatized the extent of present inequities and suggested the lasting power of past discriminatory systems. In sum, to suggest that the facts on which Richmond has relied do not provide a sound basis for its finding of past racial discrimination simply blinks credibility.

Richmond's reliance on localized, industry-specific findings is a far cry from the reliance on generalized "societal discrimination" which the majority decries as a basis for remedial action. Ante, at 496, 499, 505. But characterizing the plight of Richmond's minority contractors as mere "societal discrimination" is not the only respect in which the majority's critique shows an unwillingness to come to grips with why construction-contracting in Richmond is essentially a whites-only enterprise. The majority also takes the disingenuous approach of disaggregating Richmond's local evidence, attacking it piecemeal, and thereby concluding that no single piece of evidence adduced by the city, "standing alone," see, e. g., ante, at 503, suffices to prove past discrimination. But items of evidence do not, of course, "stan[d] alone" or exist in alien juxtaposition; they necessarily work together, reinforcing or contradicting each other.

In any event, the majority's criticisms of individual items of Richmond's evidence rest on flimsy foundations. The majority states, for example, that reliance on the disparity between the share of city contracts awarded to minority firms (0.67%) and the minority population of Richmond (approximately 50%) is "misplaced." Ante, at 501. It is true that, when the factual predicate needed to be proved is one of present discrimination, we have generally credited statistical contrasts between the racial composition of a work force and the general population as proving discrimination only where this contrast revealed "gross statistical disparities." Hazelwood School Dist. v. United States, 433 U.S. 299, 307 -308 (1977) (Title VII case); see also Teamsters v. United States, 431 U.S. 324, 339 (1977) (same). But this principle does not impugn Richmond's statistical contrast, for two reasons. First, considering how minuscule the share of Richmond public construction contracting dollars received by minority-owned businesses is, it is hardly unreasonable to conclude that this case involves a "gross statistical disparit[y]." Hazelwood School Dist., supra, at 307. There are roughly equal numbers of minorities and nonminorities in

Richmond - yet minority-owned businesses receive one-seventy-fifth of the public contracting funds that other businesses receive. See Teamsters, supra, at 342, n. 23 ("[F]ine tuning of the statistics could not have obscured the glaring absence of minority [bus] drivers. . . . [T]he company's inability to rebut the inference of discrimination came not from a misuse of statistics but from `the inexorable zero'") (citation omitted) (quoted in Johnson v. Transportation Agency, Santa Clara County, 480 U.S. 616, 656 -657 (1987) (O'CONNOR, J., concurring in judgment)).

Second, and more fundamentally, where the issue is not present discrimination but rather whether past discrimination has resulted in the continuing exclusion of minorities from a historically tight-knit industry, a contrast between population and work force is entirely appropriate to help gauge the degree of the exclusion. In Johnson v. Transportation Agency, Santa Clara County, supra, JUSTICE O'CONNOR specifically observed that, when it is alleged that discrimination has prevented blacks from "obtaining th[e] experience" needed to qualify for a position, the "relevant comparison" is not to the percentage of blacks in the pool of qualified candidates, but to "the total percentage of blacks in the labor force." Id., at 651; see also Steelworkers v. Weber, 443 U.S. 193, 198 - 199, and n. 1 (1979); Teamsters, supra, at 339, n. 20. This contrast is especially illuminating in cases like this, where a main avenue of introduction into the work force - here, membership in the trade associations whose members presumably train apprentices and help them procure subcontracting assignments - is itself grossly dominated by nonminorities. The majority's assertion that the city "does not even know how many MBE's in the relevant market are qualified," ante, at 502, is thus entirely beside the point. If Richmond indeed has a monochromatic contracting community - a conclusion reached by the District Court, see Civ. Action No. 84-0021 (ED Va. 1984) (reprinted in Supp. App. to Juris. Statement 164) - this most likely reflects the lingering power of past exclusionary practices. Certainly this is the explanation Congress has found persuasive at the national level. See Fullilove, 448 U.S., at 465 . The city's requirement that prime public contractors set aside 30% of their subcontracting assignments for minority-owned enterprises, subject to the ordinance's provision for waivers where minority-owned enterprises are unavailable or unwilling to participate, is designed precisely to ease minority contractors into the industry.

The majority's perfunctory dismissal of the testimony of Richmond's appointed and elected leaders is also deeply disturbing. These officials - including councilmembers, a former mayor, and the present city manager - asserted that race discrimination in area contracting had been widespread, and that the set-aside ordinance was a sincere and necessary attempt to eradicate the effects of this discrimination. The majority, however, states that where racial classifications are concerned, "simple legislative assurances of good intention cannot suffice." Ante, at 500. It similarly discounts as minimally probative the city council's designation of its setaside plan as remedial. "[B]lind judicial deference to legislative or executive pronouncements," the majority explains, "has no place in equal protection analysis." Ante, at 501.

No one, of course, advocates "blind judicial deference" to the findings of the city council or the testimony of city leaders. The majority's suggestion that wholesale deference is what Richmond seeks is a classic straw-man argument. But the majority's trivialization of the testimony of Richmond's leaders is dismaying in a far more serious respect. By disregarding the testimony of local leaders and the judgment of local government, the majority does violence to the very principles of comity within our federal system which this Court has long championed. Local officials, by virtue of their proximity to, and their expertise with, local affairs, are exceptionally well qualified to make determinations of public good "within their respective spheres of authority." Hawaii Housing Authority v. Midkiff, 467 U.S. 229, 244 (1984); see also FERC v. Mississippi, 456 U.S. 742, 777 -778 (1982) (O'CONNOR, J., concurring in judgment in part and dissenting in part). The majority, however, leaves any traces of comity behind in its headlong rush to strike down Richmond's race-conscious measure.

Had the majority paused for a moment on the facts of the Richmond experience, it would have discovered that the city's leadership is deeply familiar with what racial discrimination is. The members of the Richmond City Council have spent long years witnessing multifarious acts of discrimination, including, but not limited to, the deliberate diminution of black residents' voting rights, resistance to school desegregation, and publicly sanctioned housing discrimination. Numerous decisions of federal courts chronicle this disgraceful recent history. In Richmond v. United States, 422 U.S. 358 (1975), for example, this Court denounced Richmond's decision to annex part of an adjacent county at a time when the city's black population was nearing 50% because it was "infected by the impermissible purpose of denying the right to vote based on race through perpetuating white majority power to exclude Negroes from office." Id., at 373; see also id., at 382 (BRENNAN, J., dissenting) (describing Richmond's "flagrantly discriminatory purpose . . . to avert a transfer of political control to what was fast becoming a black-population majority") (citation omitted). 7

In Bradley v. School Bd. of Richmond, 462 F.2d 1058, 1060, n. 1 (CA4 1972), aff'd by an equally divided Court, 412 U.S. 92 (1973), the Court of Appeals for the Fourth Circuit, sitting en banc, reviewed in the context of a school desegregation case Richmond's long history of inadequate compliance with Brown v. Board of Education, 347 U.S. 483 (1954), and the cases implementing its holding. The dissenting judge elaborated:

"The sordid history of Virginia's, and Richmond's attempts to circumvent, defeat, and nullify the holding of Brown I has been recorded in the opinions of this and other courts, and need not be repeated in detail here. It suffices to say that there was massive resistance and every state resource, including the services of the legal officers of the state, the services of private counsel (costing the State hundreds of thousands of dollars), the State police, and the power and prestige of the Governor, was employed to defeat Brown I. In Richmond, as has been mentioned, not even freedom of choice became actually effective until 1966, twelve years after the decision of Brown I." 462 F.2d, at 1075

(Winter, J.) (emphasis in original) (footnotes and citations omitted).

The Court of Appeals majority in Bradley used equally pungent words in describing public and private housing discrimination in Richmond. Though rejecting the black plaintiffs' request that it consolidate Richmond's school district with those of two neighboring counties, the majority nonetheless agreed with the plaintiffs' assertion that "within the City of Richmond there has been state (also federal) action tending to perpetuate apartheid of the races in ghetto patterns throughout the city." Id., at 1065 (citing numerous public and private acts of discrimination). 8

When the legislatures and leaders of cities with histories of pervasive discrimination testify that past discrimination has infected one of their industries, armchair cynicism like that exercised by the majority has no place. It may well be that "the autonomy of a State is an essential component of federalism," Garcia v. San Antonio Metropolitan Transit Authority, 469 U.S. 528, 588 (1985) (O'CONNOR, J., dissenting), and that "each State is sovereign within its own domain, governing its citizens and providing for their general welfare," FERC v. Mississippi, supra, at 777 (O'CONNOR, J., dissenting), but apparently this is not the case when federal judges, with nothing but their impressions to go on, choose to disbelieve the explanations of these local governments and officials. Disbelief is particularly inappropriate here in light of the fact that appellee Croson, which had the burden of proving unconstitutionality at trial, Wygant, 476 U.S., at 277 -278 (plurality opinion), has at no point come forward with any direct evidence that the city council's motives were anything other than sincere. 9

Finally, I vehemently disagree with the majority's dismissal of the congressional and Executive Branch findings noted in Fullilove as having "extremely limited" probative value in this case. Ante, at 504. The majority concedes that Congress established nothing less than a "presumption" that minority contracting firms have been disadvantaged by prior discrimination. Ibid. The majority, inexplicably, would forbid Richmond to "share" in this information, and permit only Congress to take note of these ample findings. Ante, at 504-505. In thus requiring that Richmond's local evidence be severed from the context in which it was prepared, the majority would require cities seeking to eradicate the effects of past discrimination within their borders to reinvent the evidentiary wheel and engage in unnecessarily duplicative, costly, and time-consuming factfinding.

No principle of federalism or of federal power, however, forbids a state or local government to draw upon a nationally relevant historical record prepared by the Federal Government. See Renton v. Playtime Theatres, Inc., 475 U.S. 41, 51 -52 (1986) (city is "entitled to rely on the experiences of Seattle and other cities" in enacting an adult theater ordinance, as the First Amendment "does not require a city . . . to conduct new studies or produce evidence independent of that already generated by other cities, so long as whatever evidence the cities relies upon is reasonably believed to be relevant to the problem that the city addresses"); see also Steelworkers v. Weber, 443 U.S., at 198, n. 1 ("Judicial findings of exclusion from crafts on racial grounds are so numerous as to make such exclusion a proper subject for judicial notice"); cf. Wygant, supra, at 296

(MARSHALL, J., dissenting) ("No race-conscious provision that purports to serve a remedial purpose can be fairly assessed in a vacuum"). 10 Of course, Richmond could have built an even more compendious record of past discrimination, one including additional stark statistics and additional individual accounts of past discrimination. But nothing in the Fourteenth Amendment imposes such onerous documentary obligations upon States and localities once the reality of past discrimination is apparent. See infra, at 555-561.

     B

     In my judgment, Richmond's set-aside plan also comports with the second prong of the equal protection inquiry, for it is substantially related to the interests it seeks to serve in remedying past discrimination and in ensuring that municipal contract procurement does not perpetuate that discrimination. The most striking aspect of the city's ordinance is the similarity it bears to the "appropriately limited" federal set-aside provision upheld in Fullilove. 448 U.S., at 489 . Like the federal provision, Richmond's is limited to five years in duration, ibid., and was not renewed when it came up for reconsideration in 1988. Like the federal provision, Richmond's contains a waiver provision freeing from its subcontracting requirements those nonminority firms that demonstrate that they cannot comply with its provisions. Id., at 483-484. Like the federal provision, Richmond's has a minimal impact on innocent third parties. While the measure affects 30% of public contracting dollars, that translates to only 3% of overall Richmond area contracting. Brief for Appellant 44, n. 73 (recounting federal census figures on construction in Richmond); see Fullilove, supra, at 484 (burden shouldered by nonminority firms is "relatively light" compared to "overall construction contracting opportunities").

     Finally, like the federal provision, Richmond's does not interfere with any vested right of a contractor to a particular contract; instead it operates entirely prospectively. 448 U.S., at 484 . Richmond's initiative affects only future economic arrangements and imposes only a diffuse burden on nonminority competitors - here, businesses owned or controlled by nonminorities which seek subcontracting work on public construction projects. The plurality in Wygant emphasized the importance of not disrupting the settled and legitimate expectations of innocent parties. "While hiring goals impose a diffuse burden, often foreclosing only one of several opportunities, layoffs impose the entire burden of achieving racial equality on particular individuals, often resulting in serious disruption of their lives. That burden is too intrusive." Wygant, 476 U.S., at 283; see Steelworkers v. Weber, supra, at 208.

     These factors, far from "justify[ing] a preference of any size or duration," ante, at 505, are precisely the factors to which this Court looked in Fullilove. The majority takes issue, however, with two aspects of Richmond's tailoring: the city's refusal to explore the use of race-neutral measures to increase minority business participation in contracting, ante, at 507, and the selection of a 30% set-aside figure. Ante, at 507-508. The majority's first criticism is flawed in two respects. First, the majority overlooks the fact that since

1975, Richmond has barred both discrimination by the city in awarding public contracts and discrimination by public contractors. See Richmond, Va., City Code 17.1 et seq. (1985). The virtual absence of minority businesses from the city's contracting rolls, indicated by the fact that such businesses have received less than 1% of public contracting dollars, strongly suggests that this ban has not succeeded in redressing the impact of past discrimination or in preventing city contract procurement from reinforcing racial homogeneity. Second, the majority's suggestion that Richmond should have first undertaken such race-neutral measures as a program of city financing for small firms, ante, at 507, ignores the fact that such measures, while theoretically appealing, have been discredited by Congress as ineffectual in eradicating the effects of past discrimination in this very industry. For this reason, this Court in Fullilove refused to fault Congress for not undertaking race-neutral measures as precursors to its race-conscious set-aside. See Fullilove, 448 U.S., at 463 -467 (noting inadequacy of previous measures designed to give experience to minority businesses); see also id., at 511 (Powell, J., concurring) ("By the time Congress enacted [the federal set-aside] in 1977, it knew that other remedies had failed to ameliorate the effects of racial discrimination in the construction industry"). The Equal Protection Clause does not require Richmond to retrace Congress' steps when Congress has found that those steps lead nowhere. Given the well-exposed limitations of race-neutral measures, it was thus appropriate for a municipality like Richmond to conclude that, in the words of JUSTICE BLACKMUN, "[i]n order to get beyond racism, we must first take account of race. There is no other way." University of California Regents v. Bakke, 438 U.S., at 407 (separate opinion). 11

As for Richmond's 30% target, the majority states that this figure "cannot be said to be narrowly tailored to any goal, except perhaps outright racial balancing." Ante, at 507. The majority ignores two important facts. First, the set-aside measure affects only 3% of overall city contracting; thus, any imprecision in tailoring has far less impact than the majority suggests. But more important, the majority ignores the fact that Richmond's 30% figure was patterned directly on the Fullilove precedent. Congress' 10% figure fell "roughly halfway between the present percentage of minority contractors and the percentage of minority group members in the Nation." Fullilove, supra, at 513-514 (Powell, J., concurring). The Richmond City Council's 30% figure similarly falls roughly halfway between the present percentage of Richmond-based minority contractors (almost zero) and the percentage of minorities in Richmond (50%). In faulting Richmond for not presenting a different explanation for its choice of a set-aside figure, the majority honors Fullilove only in the breach.

III

I would ordinarily end my analysis at this point and conclude that Richmond's ordinance satisfies both the governmental interest and substantial relationship prongs of our Equal Protection Clause analysis. However, I am compelled to add more, for the majority has gone beyond the facts of this case to announce a set of principles which unnecessarily restricts the power of governmental entities to take race-conscious measures to redress the effects of prior discrimination.

A

Today, for the first time, a majority of this Court has adopted strict scrutiny as its standard of Equal Protection Clause review of race-conscious remedial measures. Ante, at 493-494; ante, at 520 (SCALIA, J., concurring in judgment). This is an unwelcome development. A profound difference separates governmental actions that themselves are racist, and governmental actions that seek to remedy the effects of prior racism or to prevent neutral governmental activity from perpetuating the effects of such racism. See, e. g., Wygant v. Jackson Bd. of Education, 476 U.S., at 301 -302 (MARSHALL, J., dissenting); Fullilove, supra, at 517-519 (MARSHALL, J., concurring in judgment); University of California Regents v. Bakke, 438 U.S., at 355 -362 (joint opinion of BRENNAN, WHITE, MARSHALL, and BLACKMUN, JJ.).

Racial classifications "drawn on the presumption that one race is inferior to another or because they put the weight of government behind racial hatred and separatism" warrant the strictest judicial scrutiny because of the very irrelevance of these rationales. Id., at 357-358. By contrast, racial classifications drawn for the purpose of remedying the effects of discrimination that itself was race based have a highly pertinent basis: the tragic and indelible fact that discrimination against blacks and other racial minorities in this Nation has pervaded our Nation's history and continues to scar our society. As I stated in Fullilove: "Because the consideration of race is relevant to remedying the continuing effects of past racial discrimination, and because governmental programs employing racial classifications for remedial purposes can be crafted to avoid stigmatization, . . . such programs should not be subjected to conventional `strict scrutiny' - scrutiny that is strict in theory, but fatal in fact." Fullilove, supra, at 518-519 (citation omitted).

In concluding that remedial classifications warrant no different standard of review under the Constitution than the most brutal and repugnant forms of state-sponsored racism, a majority of this Court signals that it regards racial discrimination as largely a phenomenon of the past, and that government bodies need no longer preoccupy themselves with rectifying racial injustice. I, however, do not believe this Nation is anywhere close to eradicating racial discrimination or its vestiges. In constitutionalizing its wishful thinking, the majority today does a grave disservice not only to those victims of past and present racial discrimination in this Nation whom government has sought to assist, but also to this Court's long tradition of approaching issues of race with the utmost sensitivity.

B

I am also troubled by the majority's assertion that, even if it did not believe generally in strict scrutiny of race-based remedial measures, "the circumstances of this case" require this Court to look upon the Richmond City Council's measure with the strictest scrutiny. Ante, at 495. The sole such circumstance which the majority cites, however, is the fact that blacks in Richmond are a "dominant racial grou[p]" in the city.

Ibid. In support of this characterization of dominance, the majority observes that "blacks constitute approximately 50% of the population of the city of Richmond" and that "[f]ive of the nine seats on the City Council are held by blacks." Ibid.

While I agree that the numerical and political supremacy of a given racial group is a factor bearing upon the level of scrutiny to be applied, this Court has never held that numerical inferiority, standing alone, makes a racial group "suspect" and thus entitled to strict scrutiny review. Rather, we have identified other "traditional indicia of suspectness": whether a group has been "saddled with such disabilities, or subjected to such a history of purposeful unequal treatment, or relegated to such a position of political powerlessness as to command extraordinary protection from the majoritarian political process." San Antonio Independent School Dist. v. Rodriguez, 411 U.S. 1, 28 (1973).

It cannot seriously be suggested that nonminorities in Richmond have any "history of purposeful unequal treatment." Ibid. Nor is there any indication that they have any of the disabilities that have characteristically afflicted those groups this Court has deemed suspect. Indeed, the numerical and political dominance of nonminorities within the State of Virginia and the Nation as a whole provides an enormous political check against the "simple racial politics" at the municipal level which the majority fears. Ante, at 493. If the majority really believes that groups like Richmond's nonminorities, which constitute approximately half the population but which are outnumbered even marginally in political fora, are deserving of suspect class status for these reasons alone, this Court's decisions denying suspect status to women, see Craig v. Boren, 429 U.S. 190, 197 (1976), and to persons with below-average incomes, see San Antonio Independent School Dist., supra, at 28, stand on extremely shaky ground. See Castaneda v. Partida, 430 U.S. 482, 504 (1977) (MARSHALL, J., concurring).

In my view, the "circumstances of this case," ante, at 495, underscore the importance of not subjecting to a strict scrutiny straitjacket the increasing number of cities which have recently come under minority leadership and are eager to rectify, or at least prevent the perpetuation of, past racial discrimination. In many cases, these cities will be the ones with the most in the way of prior discrimination to rectify. Richmond's leaders had just witnessed decades of publicly sanctioned racial discrimination in virtually all walks of life - discrimination amply documented in the decisions of the federal judiciary. See supra, at 544-546. This history of "purposefully unequal treatment" forced upon minorities, not imposed by them, should raise an inference that minorities in Richmond had much to remedy - and that the 1983 set-aside was undertaken with sincere remedial goals in mind, not "simple racial politics." Ante, at 493.

Richmond's own recent political history underscores the facile nature of the majority's assumption that elected officials' voting decisions are based on the color of their skins. In recent years, white and black councilmembers in Richmond have increasingly joined hands on controversial matters. When the Richmond City Council elected a black man mayor in 1982, for example, his victory was won with the support of the city council's four white members. Richmond Times-Dispatch, July 2, 1982, p. 1, col.

1. The vote on the set-aside plan a year later also was not purely along racial lines. Of the four white councilmembers, one voted for the measure and another abstained. App. 49. The majority's view that remedial measures undertaken by municipalities with black leadership must face a stiffer test of Equal Protection Clause scrutiny than remedial measures undertaken by municipalities with white leadership implies a lack of political maturity on the part of this Nation's elected minority officials that is totally unwarranted. Such insulting judgments have no place in constitutional jurisprudence.

C

Today's decision, finally, is particularly noteworthy for the daunting standard it imposes upon States and localities contemplating the use of race-conscious measures to eradicate the present effects of prior discrimination and prevent its perpetuation. The majority restricts the use of such measures to situations in which a State or locality can put forth "a prima facie case of a constitutional or statutory violation." Ante, at 500. In so doing, the majority calls into question the validity of the business set-asides which dozens of municipalities across this Nation have adopted on the authority of Fullilove.

Nothing in the Constitution or in the prior decisions of this Court supports limiting state authority to confront the effects of past discrimination to those situations in which a prima facie case of a constitutional or statutory violation can be made out. By its very terms, the majority's standard effectively cedes control of a large component of the content of that constitutional provision to Congress and to state legislatures. If an antecedent Virginia or Richmond law had defined as unlawful the award to nonminorities of an overwhelming share of a city's contracting dollars, for example, Richmond's subsequent set-aside initiative would then satisfy the majority's standard. But without such a law, the initiative might not withstand constitutional scrutiny. The meaning of "equal protection of the laws" thus turns on the happenstance of whether a state or local body has previously defined illegal discrimination. Indeed, given that racially discriminatory cities may be the ones least likely to have tough antidiscrimination laws on their books, the majority's constitutional incorporation of state and local statutes has the perverse effect of inhibiting those States or localities with the worst records of official racism from taking remedial action.

Similar flaws would inhere in the majority's standard even if it incorporated only federal antidiscrimination statutes. If Congress tomorrow dramatically expanded Title VII of the Civil Rights Act of 1964, 78 Stat. 253, as amended, 42 U.S.C. 2000e et seq. - or alternatively, if it repealed that legislation altogether - the meaning of equal protection would change precipitately along with it. Whatever the Framers of the Fourteenth Amendment had in mind in 1868, it certainly was not that the content of their Amendment would turn on the amendments to or the evolving interpretations of a federal statute passed nearly a century later. 12

To the degree that this parsimonious standard is grounded on a view that either 1 or 5 of the Fourteenth Amendment substantially disempowered States and localities from remedying past racial discrimination, ante, at 490-491, 504, the majority is seriously mistaken. With respect, first, to 5, our precedents have never suggested that this provision - or, for that matter, its companion federal-empowerment provisions in the Thirteenth and Fifteenth Amendments - was meant to pre-empt or limit state police power to undertake race-conscious remedial measures. To the contrary, in Katzenbach v. Morgan, 384 U.S. 641 (1966), we held that 5 "is a positive grant of legislative power authorizing Congress to exercise its discretion in determining whether and what legislation is needed to secure the guarantees of the Fourteenth Amendment." Id., at 651 (emphasis added); see id., at 653-656; South Carolina v. Katzenbach, 383 U.S. 301, 326 - 327 (1966) (interpreting similar provision of the Fifteenth Amendment to empower Congress to "implemen[t] the rights created" by its passage); see also City of Rome v. United States, 446 U.S. 156, 173 (1980) (same). Indeed, we have held that Congress has this authority even where no constitutional violation has been found. See Katzenbach v. Morgan, supra (upholding Voting Rights Act provision nullifying state English literacy requirement we had previously upheld against Equal Protection Clause challenge). Certainly Fullilove did not view 5 either as limiting the traditionally broad police powers of the States to fight discrimination, or as mandating a zero-sum game in which state power wanes as federal power waxes. On the contrary, the Fullilove plurality invoked 5 only because it provided specific and certain authorization for the Federal Government's attempt to impose a race-conscious condition on the dispensation of federal funds by state and local grantees. See Fullilove, 448 U.S., at 476 (basing decision on 5 because "[i]n certain contexts, there are limitations on the reach of the Commerce Power").

As for 1, it is too late in the day to assert seriously that the Equal Protection Clause prohibits States - or for that matter, the Federal Government, to whom the equal protection guarantee has largely been applied, see Bolling v. Sharpe, 347 U.S. 497 (1954) - from enacting race-conscious remedies. Our cases in the areas of school desegregation, voting rights, and affirmative action have demonstrated time and again that race is constitutionally germane, precisely because race remains dismayingly relevant in American life.

In adopting its prima facie standard for States and localities, the majority closes its eyes to this constitutional history and social reality. So, too, does JUSTICE SCALIA. He would further limit consideration of race to those cases in which States find it "necessary to eliminate their own maintenance of a system of unlawful racial classification" - a "distinction" which, he states, "explains our school desegregation cases." Ante, at 524 (SCALIA, J., concurring in judgment). But this Court's remedy-stage school desegregation decisions cannot so conveniently be cordoned off. These decisions (like those involving voting rights and affirmative action) stand for the same broad principles of equal protection which Richmond seeks to vindicate in this case: all persons have equal worth, and it is permissible, given a sufficient factual predicate and appropriate tailoring, for government to take account of race to eradicate the present effects of race-based subjugation denying that basic equality. JUSTICE SCALIA'S artful distinction allows him to avoid having to repudiate "our school desegregation cases," ibid., but, like the arbitrary limitation on race-conscious relief adopted by the majority, his approach "would freeze the status quo that is the very target" of the remedial actions of States and localities. McDaniel v. Barresi, 402 U.S., at 41; see also North Carolina Bd. of Education v. Swann, 402 U.S., at 46 (striking down State's flat prohibition on assignment of pupils on basis of race as impeding an "effective remedy"); United Jewish Organizations v. Carey, 430 U.S. 144, 159 -162 (1977) (upholding New York's use of racial criteria in drawing district lines so as to comply with 5 of the Voting Rights Act).

The fact is that Congress' concern in passing the Reconstruction Amendments, and particularly their congressional authorization provisions, was that States would not adequately respond to racial violence or discrimination against newly freed slaves. To interpret any aspect of these Amendments as proscribing state remedial responses to these very problems turns the Amendments on their heads. As four Justices, of whom I was one, stated in University of California Regents v. Bakke:

"[There is] no reason to conclude that the States cannot voluntarily accomplish under 1 of the Fourteenth Amendment what Congress under 5 of the Fourteenth Amendment validly may authorize or compel either the States or private persons to do. A contrary position would conflict with the traditional understanding recognizing the competence of the States to initiate measures consistent with federal policy in the absence of congressional pre-emption of the subject matter. Nothing whatever in the legislative history of either the Fourteenth Amendment or the Civil Rights Acts even remotely suggests that the States are foreclosed from furthering the fundamental purpose of equal opportunity to which the Amendment and those Acts are addressed. Indeed, voluntary initiatives by the States to achieve the national goal of equal opportunity have been recognized to be essential to its attainment. `To use the Fourteenth Amendment as a sword against such State power would stultify that Amendment.' Railway Mail Assn. v. Corsi, 326 U.S. 88, 98 (Frankfurter, J., concurring)." 438 U.S., at 368 (footnote omitted; emphasis added).

In short, there is simply no credible evidence that the Framers of the Fourteenth Amendment sought "to transfer the security and protection of all the civil rights . . . from the States to the Federal government." The Slaughter-House Cases, 16 Wall. 36, 77-78 (1873). 13 The three Reconstruction Amendments undeniably "worked a dramatic change in the balance between congressional and state power," ante, at 490: they forbade state-sanctioned slavery, forbade the state-sanctioned denial of the right to vote, and (until the content of the Equal Protection Clause was substantially applied to the Federal Government through the Due Process Clause of the Fifth Amendment) uniquely forbade States to deny equal protection. The Amendments also specifically empowered the Federal Government to combat discrimination at a time when the breadth of federal power under the Constitution was less apparent than it is today. But nothing in the Amendments themselves, or in our long history of interpreting or applying those momentous charters, suggests that States, exercising their police power, are in any way constitutionally inhibited from working alongside the Federal Government in the fight against discrimination and its effects.

IV

The majority today sounds a full-scale retreat from the Court's longstanding solicitude to race-conscious remedial efforts "directed toward deliverance of the century-old promise of equality of economic opportunity." Fullilove, 448 U.S., at 463 . The new and restrictive tests it applies scuttle one city's effort to surmount its discriminatory past, and imperil those of dozens more localities. I, however, profoundly disagree with the cramped vision of the Equal Protection Clause which the majority offers today and with its application of that vision to Richmond, Virginia's, laudable set-aside plan. The battle against pernicious racial discrimination or its effects is nowhere near won. I must dissent.

Notes

[1] In the interest of convenience, I refer to the opinion in this case authored by JUSTICE O'CONNOR as "the majority," recognizing that certain portions of that opinion have been joined by only a plurality of the Court.

[2] Other Reports indicating the dearth of minority-owned businesses include H. R. Rep. No. 92-1615, p. 3 (1972) (Report of the Subcommittee on Minority Small Business Enterprise, finding that the "long history of racial bias" has created "major problems" for minority businessmen); H. R. Doc. No. 92-194, p. 1 (1972) (text of message from President Nixon to Congress, describing federal efforts "to press open new doors of opportunity for millions of Americans to whom those doors had previously been barred, or only half-open"); H. R. Doc. No. 92-169, p. 1 (1971) (text of message from President Nixon to Congress, describing paucity of minority business ownership and federal efforts to give "every man an equal chance at the starting line").

[3] Numerous congressional studies undertaken after 1977 and issued before the Richmond City Council convened in April 1983 found that the exclusion of minorities had continued virtually unabated - and that, because of this legacy of discrimination, minority businesses across the Nation had still failed, as of 1983, to gain a real toehold in the business world. See, e. g., H. R. Rep. No. 95-949, pp. 2, 8 (1978) (Report of House Committee on Small Business, finding that minority businesses "are severely under-capitalized" and that many minorities are disadvantaged "because they are identified as members of certain racial categories"); S. Rep. No. 95-1070, pp. 14-15 (1978); (Report of Senate Select Committee on Small Business, finding that the federal effort "has fallen far short of its goal to develop strong and growing disadvantaged small businesses," and "recogniz[ing] the pattern of social and economic discrimination that continues to deprive racial and ethnic minorities, and others, of the opportunity to participate fully in the free enterprise system"); S. Rep. No. 96-31, pp. IX, 107 (1979) (Report of Senate Select Committee on Small Business, finding that many minorities have "suffered the effects of discriminatory practices or similar invidious circumstances over which they have no control"); S. Rep. No. 96-974, p. 3 (1980) (Report of Senate Select Committee on Small Business, finding that government aid must be "significantly increased" if minority-

owned businesses are to "have the maximum practical opportunity to develop into viable small businesses"); H. R. Rep. No. 97-956, p. 35 (1982) (Report of House Committee on Small Business, finding that federal programs to aid minority businesses have had "limited success" to date, but concluding that success could be "greatly expanded" with "appropriate corrective actions"); H. R. Rep. No. 98-3, p. 1 (1983) (Report of House Committee on Small Business, finding that "the small business share of Federal contracts continues to be inadequate").

[4] According to testimony by trade association representatives, the Associated General Contractors of Virginia had no blacks among its 130 Richmond-area members, App. 27-28 (remarks of Stephen Watts); the American Subcontractors Association had no blacks among its 80 Richmond members, id., at 36 (remarks of Patrick Murphy); the Professional Contractors Estimators Association had 1 black member among its 60 Richmond members, id., at 39 (remarks of Al Shuman); the Central Virginia Electrical Contractors Association had 1 black member among its 45 members, id., at 40 (remarks of Al Shuman); and the National Electrical Contractors Association had 2 black members among its 81 Virginia members. Id., at 34 (remarks of Mark Singer).

[5] Among those testifying to the discriminatory practices of Richmond's construction industry was Councilmember Henry Marsh, who had served as mayor of Richmond from 1977 to 1982. Marsh stated:

"I have been practicing law in this community since 1961, and I am familiar with the practices in the construction industry in this area, in the State, and around the nation. And I can say without equivocation, that the general conduct in the construction industry in this area, and the State and around the nation, is one in which race discrimination and exclusion on the basis of race is widespread.

"I think the situation involved in the City of Richmond is the same . . . . I think the question of whether or not remedial action is required is not open to question." Id., at 41.

Manuel Deese, who in his capacity as City Manager had oversight responsibility for city procurement matters, stated that he fully agreed with Marsh's analysis. Id., at 42.

[6] The representatives of several trade associations did, however, deny that their particular organizations engaged in discrimination. See, e. g., id., at 38 (remarks of Al Shuman, on behalf of the Central Virginia Electrical Contractors Association).

[7] For a disturbing description of the lengths to which some Richmond white officials went during recent decades to hold in check growing black political power, see J. Moeser & R. Dennis, The Politics of Annexation - Oligarchic Power in a Southern City 50-188 (1982).

[8] Again the dissenting judge - who would have consolidated the school districts - elaborated:

"[M]any other instances of state and private action contribut[ed] to the concentration of black citizens within Richmond and white citizens without. These were principally in the area of residential development. Racially restrictive convenants were freely employed. Racially discriminatory practices in the prospective purchase of county property by black purchasers were followed. Urban renewal, subsidized public housing and government-sponsored home mortgage insurance had been undertaken on a racially discriminatory basis. [The neighboring counties] provided schools, roads, zoning and development approval for the rapid growth of the white population in each county at the expense of the city, without making any attempt to assure that the development that they made possible was integrated. Superimposed on the pattern of government-aided residential segregation . . . had been a discriminatory policy of school construction, i. e., the selection of school construction sites in the center of racially identifiable neighborhoods manifestly to serve the educational needs of students of a single race.

"The majority does not question the accuracy of these facts." 462 F.2d, at 1075-1076 (Winter, J.) (emphasis in original) (footnote omitted).

[9] Cf. Fullilove v. Klutznick, 448 U.S. 448, 541 (1980) (STEVENS, J., dissenting) (noting statements of sponsors of federal set-aside that measure was designed to give their constituents "a piece of the action").

[10] Although the majority sharply criticizes Richmond for using data which it did not itself develop, it is noteworthy that the federal set-aside program upheld in Fullilove was adopted as a floor amendment "without any congressional hearings or investigation whatsoever." L. Tribe, American Constitutional Law 345 (2d ed. 1988). The principal opinion in Fullilove justified the set-aside by relying heavily on the aforementioned studies by agencies like the Small Business Administration and on legislative reports prepared in connection with prior, failed legislation. See Fullilove v. Klutznick, 448 U.S., at 478 (opinion of Burger, C. J.) ("Although the Act recites no preambulary `findings' on the subject, we are satisfied that Congress had abundant historical basis from which it could conclude that traditional procurement practices, when applied to minority businesses, could perpetuate the effects of prior discrimination"); see also id., at 549-550, and n. 25 (STEVENS, J., dissenting) (noting "perfunctory" consideration accorded the set-aside provision); Days, Fullilove, 96 Yale L. J. 453, 465 (1987) ("One can only marvel at the fact that the minority set-aside provision was enacted into law without hearings or committee reports, and with only token opposition") (citation and footnote omitted).

[11] The majority also faults Richmond's ordinance for including within its definition of "minority group members" not only black citizens, but also citizens who are "Spanish-speaking, Oriental, Indian, Eskimo, or Aleut persons." Ante, at 506. This is, of course, precisely the same definition Congress adopted in its set-aside legislation. Fullilove, supra, at 454. Even accepting the majority's view that Richmond's ordinance is overbroad because it includes groups, such as Eskimos or Aleuts, about whom no evidence of local discrimination has been proffered, it does not necessarily follow that the balance of Richmond's ordinance should be invalidated.

[12] Although the majority purports to "adher[e] to the standard of review employed in Wygant," ante, at 494, the "prima facie case" standard it adopts marks an

implicit rejection of the more generally framed "strong basis in evidence" test endorsed by the Wygant v. Jackson Bd. of Education, 476 U.S. 267 (1986) plurality, and the similar "firm basis" test endorsed by JUSTICE O'CONNOR in her separate concurrence in that case. See id., at 289; id., at 286. Under those tests, proving a prima facie violation of Title VII would appear to have been but one means of adducing sufficient proof to satisfy Equal Protection Clause analysis. See Johnson v. Transportation Agency, Santa Clara County, 480 U.S. 616, 632 (1987) (plurality opinion) (criticizing suggestion that race-conscious relief be conditioned on showing of a prima facie Title VII violation).

The rhetoric of today's majority opinion departs from Wygant in another significant respect. In Wygant, a majority of this Court rejected as unduly inhibiting and constitutionally unsupported a requirement that a municipality demonstrate that its remedial plan is designed only to benefit specific victims of discrimination. See 476 U.S., at 277 -278; id., at 286 (O'CONNOR, J., concurring in part and concurring in judgment); id., at 305 (MARSHALL, J., dissenting). JUSTICE O'CONNOR noted the Court's general agreement that a "remedial purpose need not be accompanied by contemporaneous findings of actual discrimination to be accepted as legitimate as long as the public actor has a firm basis for believing that remedial action is required. . . . [A] plan need not be limited to the remedying of specific instances of identified discrimination for it to be deemed sufficiently `narrowly tailored,' or `substantially related,' to the correction of prior discrimination by the state actor." Id., at 286-287. The majority's opinion today, however, hints that a "specific victims" proof requirement might be appropriate in equal protection cases. See, e. g., ante, at 504 (States and localities "must identify that discrimination . . . with some specificity"). Given that just three Terms ago this Court rejected the "specific victims" idea as untenable, I believe these references - and the majority's cryptic "identified discrimination" requirement - cannot be read to require States and localities to make such highly particularized showings. Rather, I take the majority's standard of "identified discrimination" merely to require some quantum of proof of discrimination within a given jurisdiction that exceeds the proof which Richmond has put forth here.

[13] Tellingly, the sole support the majority offers for its view that the Framers of the Fourteenth Amendment intended such a result are two law review articles analyzing this Court's recent affirmative-action decisions, and a Court of Appeals decision which relies upon statements by James Madison. Ante, at 491. Madison, of course, had been dead for 32 years when the Fourteenth Amendment was enacted.

No compulsory collection and chemical testing of railroad workers' blood and urine: Justice Marshall's dissent in Skinner v. Railway Labor Executives' Association (March 21, 1989)

JUSTICE MARSHALL, with whom JUSTICE BRENNAN joins, dissenting.

The issue in this case is not whether declaring a war on illegal drugs is good public policy. The importance of ridding our society of such drugs is, by now, apparent to all. Rather, the issue here is whether the Government's deployment in that war of a particularly draconian weapon -- the compulsory collection and chemical testing of railroad workers' blood and urine -- comports with the Fourth Amendment. Precisely because the need for action against the drug scourge is manifest, the need for vigilance against unconstitutional excess is great. History teaches that grave threats to liberty often come in times of urgency, when constitutional rights seem too extravagant to endure. The World War II relocation camp cases, Hirabayashi v. United States, 320 U.S. 81 (1943); Korematsu v. United States, 323 U.S. 214 (1944), and the Red scare and McCarthy-era internal subversion cases, Schenck v. United States, 249 U.S. 47 (1919); Dennis v. United States, 341 U.S. 494 (1951), are only the most extreme reminders that, when we allow fundamental freedoms to be sacrificed in the name of real or perceived exigency, we invariably come to regret it.

In permitting the Government to force entire railroad crews to submit to invasive blood and urine tests, even when it lacks any evidence of drug or alcohol use or other wrongdoing, the majority today joins those shortsighted courts which have allowed basic constitutional rights to fall prey to momentary emergencies. The majority holds that the need of the Federal Railroad Administration (FRA) to deter and diagnose train accidents outweighs any "minimal" intrusions on personal dignity and privacy posed by mass toxicological testing of persons who have given no indication whatsoever of impairment. Ante at 624. In reaching this result, the majority ignores the text and doctrinal history of the Fourth Amendment, which require that highly intrusive searches of this type be based on probable cause, not on the evanescent cost-benefit calculations of agencies or judges. But the majority errs even under its own utilitarian standards, trivializing the raw intrusiveness of, and overlooking serious conceptual and operational flaws in, the FRA's testing program. These flaws cast grave doubts on whether that program, though born of good intentions, will do more than ineffectually symbolize the Government's opposition to drug use.

The majority purports to limit its decision to post-accident testing of workers in "safety-sensitive" jobs, ante at 620, much as it limits its holding in the companion case to the testing of transferees to jobs involving drug interdiction or the use of firearms. National Treasury Employees Union v. Von Raab, post at 664. But the damage done to the Fourth Amendment is not so easily cabined. The majority's acceptance of dragnet blood and urine testing ensures that the first, and worst, casualty of the war on drugs will be the precious liberties of our citizens. I therefore dissent.

I

The Court today takes its longest step yet toward reading the probable cause requirement out of the Fourth Amendment. For the fourth time in as many years, a majority holds that a "'special nee[d], beyond the normal need for law enforcement,'" makes the "'requirement'" of probable cause "'impracticable.'" Ante at 619 (citations omitted). With the recognition of "[t]he Government's interest in regulating the conduct of railroad employees to ensure safety" as such a need, ante at 620, the Court has now permitted "special needs" to displace constitutional text in each of the four categories of searches enumerated in the Fourth Amendment: searches of "persons," ante at 613-614; "houses," Griffin v. Wisconsin, 483 U.S. 868 (1987); "papers," O'Connor v. Ortega, 480 U.S. 709 (1987); and "effects," New Jersey v. T.L.O., 469 U.S. 325 (1985).

The process by which a constitutional "requirement" can be dispensed with as "impracticable" is an elusive one to me. The Fourth Amendment provides that

[t]he right of the people to be secure in their persons, houses, papers, and effects, against unreasonable searches and seizures, shall not be violated; and no Warrants shall issue, but upon probable cause, supported by Oath or affirmation, and particularly describing the place to be searched, and the persons or things to be seized.

The majority's recitation of the Amendment, remarkably, leaves off after the word "violated," ante at 613, but the remainder of the Amendment -- the Warrant Clause -- is not so easily excised. As this Court has long recognized, the Framers intended the provisions of that Clause -- a warrant and probable cause -- to "provide the yardstick against which official searches and seizures are to be measured." T.L.O., supra, at 359-360 (opinion of BRENNAN, J.). Without the content which those provisions give to the Fourth Amendment's overarching command that searches and seizures be "reasonable," the Amendment lies virtually devoid of meaning, subject to whatever content shifting judicial majorities, concerned about the problems of the day, choose to give to that supple term. See Dunaway v. New York, 442 U.S. 200, 213 (1979) ("[T]he protections intended by the Framers could all too easily disappear in the consideration and balancing of the multifarious circumstances presented by different cases"). Constitutional requirements like probable cause are not fair-weather friends, present when advantageous, conveniently absent when "special needs" make them seem not.

Until recently, an unbroken line of cases had recognized probable cause as an indispensable prerequisite for a full-scale search, regardless of whether such a search was conducted pursuant to a warrant or under one of the recognized exceptions to the warrant requirement. T.L.O., supra, at 358 and 359, n. 3 (opinion of BRENNAN, J.); see also Chambers v. Maroney, 399 U.S. 42, 51 (1970). Only where the Government action in question had a "substantially less intrusive" impact on privacy, Dunaway, supra, at 210, and thus clearly fell short of a full-scale search, did we relax the probable cause standard. Id. at 214 ("For all but those narrowly defined intrusions, the requisite 'balancing' . . . is embodied in the principle that seizures are 'reasonable' only if supported by probable cause"); see also T.L.O., supra, at 360 (opinion of BRENNAN, J.). Even in this class of cases, we almost always required the Government to show some individualized suspicion to justify the search. [n1] The few searches which we upheld in the absence of individualized justification were routinized, fleeting, and nonintrusive encounters conducted pursuant to regulatory programs which entailed no contact with the person. [n2]

In the four years since this Court, in T.L.O., first began recognizing "special needs" exceptions to the Fourth Amendment, the clarity of Fourth Amendment doctrine has been badly distorted, as the Court has eclipsed the probable cause requirement in a patchwork quilt of settings: public school principals' searches of students' belongings, T.L.O.; public employers' searches of employees' desks, O'Connor; and probation officers' searches of probationers' homes, Griffin. [n3] Tellingly, each time the Court has found that "special needs" counseled ignoring the literal requirements of the Fourth Amendment for such full-scale searches in favor of a formless and unguided "reasonableness" balancing inquiry, it has concluded that the search in question satisfied that test. I have joined dissenting opinions in each of these cases, protesting the "jettison[ing of] . . . the only standard that finds support in the text of the Fourth Amendment" and predicting that the majority's "Rohrschach-like 'balancing test'" portended "a dangerous weakening of the purpose of the Fourth Amendment to protect the privacy and security of our citizens." T.L.O., supra, at 357-358 (opinion of BRENNAN, J.).

The majority's decision today bears out that prophecy. After determining that the Fourth Amendment applies to the FRA's testing regime, the majority embarks on an extended inquiry into whether that regime is "reasonable," an inquiry in which it balances "'all the circumstances surrounding the search or seizure and the nature of the search or seizure itself.'" Ante at 619, quoting United States v. Montoya de Hernandez, 473 U.S. 531, 537 (1985). The result is "special needs" balancing analysis' deepest incursion yet into the core protections of the Fourth Amendment. Until today, it was conceivable that, when a Government search was aimed at a person and not simply the person's possessions, balancing analysis had no place. No longer: with nary a word of explanation or acknowledgment of the novelty of its approach, the majority extends the "special needs" framework to a regulation involving compulsory blood withdrawal and urinary excretion, and chemical testing of the bodily fluids collected through these procedures. And until today, it was conceivable that a prerequisite for surviving "special needs" analysis was the existence of individualized suspicion. No longer: in contrast to the searches in T.L.O., O'Connor, and Griffin, which were supported by individualized evidence suggesting the culpability of the persons whose property was searched, [n4] the regulatory regime upheld today requires the post-accident collection and testing of the blood and urine of all covered employees -- even if every member of this group gives every indication of sobriety and attentiveness.

In widening the "special needs" exception to probable cause to authorize searches of the human body unsupported by any evidence of wrongdoing, the majority today completes the process begun in T.L.O. of eliminating altogether the probable cause requirement for civil searches -- those undertaken for reasons "beyond the normal need for law enforcement." Ante at 619 (citations omitted). In its place, the majority substitutes a manipulable balancing inquiry under which, upon the mere assertion of a "special need," even the deepest dignitary and privacy interests become vulnerable to governmental incursion. See ante at 619 (distinguishing criminal from civil searches). By its terms, however, the Fourth Amendment -- unlike the Fifth and Sixth -- does not confine its protections to either criminal or civil actions. Instead, it protects generally "[t]he right of the people to be secure." [n5]

The fact is that the malleable "special needs" balancing approach can be justified only on the basis of the policy results it allows the majority to reach. The majority's concern with the railroad safety problems caused by drug and alcohol abuse is laudable; its cavalier disregard for the text of the Constitution is not. There is no drug exception to the Constitution, any more than there is a communism exception or an exception for other real or imagined sources of domestic unrest. Coolidge v. New Hampshire, 403 U.S. 443, 455 (1971). Because abandoning the explicit protections of the Fourth Amendment seriously imperils "the right to be let alone -- the most comprehensive of rights and the right most valued by civilized men," Olmstead v. United States, 277 U.S. 438, 478 (1928) (Brandeis, J., dissenting), I reject the majority's "special needs" rationale as unprincipled and dangerous.

II

The proper way to evaluate the FRA's testing regime is to use the same analytic framework which we have traditionally used to appraise Fourth Amendment claims involving full-scale searches, at least until the recent "special needs" cases. Under that framework, we inquire, serially, whether a search has taken place, see, e.g., Katz v. United States, 389 U.S. 347, 350-353 (1967); whether the search was based on a valid warrant or undertaken pursuant to a recognized exception to the warrant requirement, see, e.g., Welsh v. Wisconsin, 466 U.S. 740, 748-750 (1984); whether the search was based on probable cause or validly based on lesser suspicion because it was minimally intrusive, see, e.g., Dunaway, 442 U.S. at 208-210; and, finally, whether the search was conducted in a reasonable manner, see, e.g., Winston v. Lee, 470 U.S. 753, 763-766 (1985). See also T.L.O., 469 U.S. at 354-355 (opinion of BRENNAN, J.) (summarizing analytic framework).

The majority's threshold determination that "covered" railroad employees have been searched under the FRA's testing program is certainly correct. Ante at 616-618. Who among us is not prepared to consider reasonable a person's expectation of privacy with respect to the extraction of his blood, the collection of his urine, or the chemical testing of these fluids? United States v. Jacobsen, 466 U.S. 109, 113 (1984). [n6] The majority's ensuing conclusion that the warrant requirement may be dispensed with, however, conveniently overlooks the fact that there are three distinct searches at issue. Although the importance of collecting blood and urine samples before drug or alcohol metabolites disappear justifies waiving the warrant requirement for those two searches under the narrow "exigent circumstances" exception, see Schmerber v. California, 384 U.S. 757, 770 (1966) ("[T]he delay necessary to obtain a warrant . . . threaten[s] 'the destruction of evidence'"), no such exigency prevents railroad officials from securing a warrant before chemically testing the samples they obtain. Blood and urine do not spoil if properly collected and preserved, and there is no reason to doubt the ability of railroad officials to grasp the relatively simple procedure of obtaining a warrant authorizing, where appropriate, chemical analysis of the extracted fluids. It is therefore wholly unjustified to dispense with the warrant requirement for this final search. See Chimel v. California, 395 U.S. 752, 761-764 (1969) (exigency exception permits warrantless searches only to the extent that exigency exists).

It is the probable cause requirement, however, that the FRA's testing regime most egregiously violates, a fact which explains the majority's ready acceptance and expansion of the countertextual "special needs" exception. By any measure, the FRA's highly intrusive collection and testing procedures qualify as full-scale personal searches. Under our precedents, a showing of probable cause is therefore clearly required. But even if these searches were viewed as entailing only minimal intrusions on the order, say, of a police stop-and-frisk, the FRA's program would still fail to pass constitutional muster, for we have, without exception, demanded that even minimally intrusive searches of the person be founded on individualized suspicion. See supra at 638, and n. 1. The federal parties concede it does not satisfy this standard. Brief for Federal Parties 18. Only if one construes the FRA's collection and testing procedures as akin to the routinized and fleeting regulatory interactions which we have permitted in the absence of individualized suspicion, see n. 2, supra, might these procedures survive constitutional scrutiny. Presumably for this reason, the majority likens this case to United States v. Martinez-Fuerte, 428 U.S. 543 (1976), which upheld brief automobile stops at the border to ascertain the validity of motorists' residence in the United States. Ante at 624. Case law and common sense reveal both the bankruptcy of this absurd analogy and the constitutional imperative of adhering to the textual standard of probable cause to evaluate the FRA's multifarious full-scale searches.

Compelling a person to submit to the piercing of his skin by a hypodermic needle so that his blood may be extracted significantly intrudes on the "personal privacy and dignity against unwarranted intrusion by the State" against which the Fourth Amendment protects. Schmerber, supra, at 767. As we emphasized in Terry:

Even a limited search of the outer clothing . . . constitutes a severe, though brief, intrusion upon cherished personal security, and it must surely be an annoying, frightening, and perhaps humiliating experience.

392 U.S. 24-25. We have similarly described the taking of a suspect's fingernail scrapings as a "'severe, though brief, intrusion upon cherished personal security.'" Cupp v. Murphy, 412 U.S. 291, 295 (1973) (quoting Terry, supra, at 24-25, and upholding this procedure upon a showing of probable cause). The government-compelled withdrawal of blood, involving as it does the added aspect of physical invasion, is surely no less an intrusion. The surrender of blood on demand is, furthermore, hardly a quotidian occurrence. Cf. Martinez-Fuerte, supra, at 557 (routine stops involve "quite limited" intrusion).

In recognition of the intrusiveness of this procedure, we specifically required in

Schmerber that police have evidence of a drunk-driving suspect's impairment before forcing him to endure a blood test:

> The interests in human dignity and privacy which the Fourth Amendment protects forbid any such intrusions on the mere chance that desired evidence might be obtained. In the absence of a clear indication that in fact such evidence will be found, these fundamental human interests require law officers to suffer the risk that such evidence may disappear. . . .

384 U.S. at 769-770. Schmerber strongly suggested that the "clear indication" needed to justify a compulsory blood test amounted to a showing of probable cause, which "plainly" existed in that case. Id. at 768. Although subsequent cases interpreting Schmerber have differed over whether a showing of individualized suspicion would have sufficed, compare Winston, 470 U.S. at 760 (Schmerber "noted the importance of probable cause"), with Montoya de Hernandez, 473 U.S. at 540 (Schmerber "indicate[d] the necessity for particularized suspicion"), by any reading, Schmerber clearly forbade compulsory blood tests on any lesser showing than individualized suspicion. Exactly why a blood test which, if conducted on one person, requires a showing of at least individualized suspicion may, if conducted on many persons, be based on no showing whatsoever, the majority does not -- and cannot -- explain. [n7]

Compelling a person to produce a urine sample on demand also intrudes deeply on privacy and bodily integrity. Urination is among the most private of activities. It is generally forbidden in public, eschewed as a matter of conversation, and performed in places designed to preserve this tradition of personal seclusion. Cf. Martinez-Fuerte, supra, at 560 (border-stop questioning involves no more than "some annoyance," and is neither "frightening" nor "offensive"). The FRA, however, gives scant regard to personal privacy, for its Field Manual instructs supervisors monitoring urination that railroad workers must provide urine samples "under direct observation by the physician/technician." Federal Railroad Administration, United States Dept. of Transportation, Field Manual: Control of Alcohol and Drug Use in Railroad Operations D-5 (1986) (emphasis added). [n8] That the privacy interests offended by compulsory and supervised urine collection are profound is the overwhelming judgment of the lower courts and commentators. As Professor -- later Solicitor General -- Charles Fried has written:

> [I]n our culture, the excretory functions are shielded by more or less absolute privacy, so much so that situations in which this privacy is violated are experienced as extremely distressing, as detracting from one's dignity and self esteem.

Privacy, 77 Yale L.J. 475, 487 (1968). [n9]

The majority's characterization of the privacy interests implicated by urine collection as "minimal," ante at 624, is nothing short of startling. This characterization is, furthermore, belied by the majority's own prior explanation of why compulsory urination constitutes a search for the purposes of the Fourth Amendment:

> "There are few activities in our society more personal or private than the passing

of urine. Most people describe it by euphemisms, if they talk about it at all. It is a function traditionally performed without public observation; indeed, its performance in public is generally prohibited by law as well as social custom."

Ante at 617, quoting National Treasury Employees Union v. Von Raab, 816 F.2d 170, 175 (CA5 1987). The fact that the majority can invoke this powerful passage in the context of deciding that a search has occurred, and then ignore it in deciding that the privacy interests this search implicates are "minimal," underscores the shameless manipulability of its balancing approach.

Finally, the chemical analysis the FRA performs upon the blood and urine samples implicates strong privacy interests apart from those intruded upon by the collection of bodily fluids. Technological advances have made it possible to uncover, through analysis of chemical compounds in these fluids, not only drug or alcohol use, but also medical disorders such as epilepsy, diabetes, and clinical depression. Cf. Martinez-Fuerte, 428 U.S. at 558, quoting United States v. Brignoni-Ponce, 422 U.S. 873, 880 (1975) (checkpoint inquiry involves only "'a brief question or two'" about motorist's residence). As the Court of Appeals for the District of Columbia has observed:

[S]uch tests may provide Government officials with a periscope through which they can peer into an individual's behavior in her private life, even in her own home.

Jones v. McKenzie, 266 U.S.App.D.C. 85, 89, 833 F.2d 335, 339 (1987); see also Capua v. Plainfield, 643 F.Supp. 1507, 1511 (NJ 1986) (urine testing is "form of surveillance" which "reports on a person's off-duty activities just as surely as someone had been present and watching"). The FRA's requirement that workers disclose the medications they have taken during the 30 days prior to chemical testing further impinges upon the confidentiality customarily attending personal health secrets.

By any reading of our precedents, the intrusiveness of these three searches demands that they -- like other full-scale searches -- be justified by probable cause. It is no answer to suggest, as does the majority, that railroad workers have relinquished the protection afforded them by this Fourth Amendment requirement, either by "participat[ing] in an industry that is regulated pervasively to ensure safety" or by undergoing periodic fitness tests pursuant to state law or to collective bargaining agreements. Ante at 627.

Our decisions in the regulatory search area refute the suggestion that the heavy regulation of the railroad industry eclipses workers' rights under the Fourth Amendment to insist upon a showing of probable cause when their bodily fluids are being extracted. This line of cases has exclusively involved searches of employer property, with respect to which

[c]ertain industries have such a history of government oversight that no reasonable expectation of privacy could exist for a proprietor over the stock of such an enterprise.

Marshall v. Barlow's, Inc., 436 U.S. 307, 313 (1978) (emphasis added; citation omitted), quoted in New York v. Burger, 482 U.S. 691, 700 (1987). Never have we intimated that regulatory searches reduce employees' rights of privacy in their persons. See Camara v. Municipal Court of San Francisco, 387 U.S. 523, 537 (1967) ("[T]he inspections are [not] personal in nature"); cf. Donovan v. Dewey, 452 U.S. 594, 598-599 (1981); Marshall, supra, at 313. As the Court pointed out in O'Connor, individuals do not lose Fourth Amendment rights at the workplace gate, 480 U.S. at 716-718; see also Oliver v. United States, 466 U.S. 170, 178, n. 8 (1984), any more than they relinquish these rights at the schoolhouse door, T.L.O., 469 U.S. at 333, or the hotel room threshold. Hoffa v. United States, 385 U.S. 293, 301 (1966). These rights mean little indeed if, having passed through these portals, an individual may remain subject to a suspicionless search of his person justified solely on the grounds that the Government already is permitted to conduct a search of the inanimate contents of the surrounding area. In holding that searches of persons may fall within the category of regulatory searches permitted in the absence of probable cause or even individualized suspicion, the majority sets a dangerous and ill-conceived precedent.

The majority's suggestion that railroad workers' privacy is only minimally invaded by the collection and testing of their bodily fluids because they undergo periodic fitness tests, ante at 624-625, is equally baseless. As an initial matter, even if participation in these fitness tests did render "minimal" an employee's "interest in bodily security," ante at 628, such minimally intrusive searches of the person require, under our precedents, a justificatory showing of individualized suspicion. See supra, at 637. More fundamentally, railroad employees are not routinely required to submit to blood or urine tests to gain or to maintain employment, and railroad employers do not ordinarily have access to employees' blood or urine, and certainly not for the purpose of ascertaining drug or alcohol usage. That railroad employees sometimes undergo tests of eyesight, hearing, skill, intelligence, and agility, ante at 627, n. 8, hardly prepares them for Government demands to submit to the extraction of blood, to excrete under supervision, or to have these bodily fluids tested for the physiological and psychological secrets they may contain. Surely employees who release basic information about their financial and personal history so that employers may ascertain their "ethical fitness" do not, by so doing, relinquish their expectations of privacy with respect to their personal letters and diaries, revealing though these papers may be of their character.

I recognize that invalidating the full-scale searches involved in the FRA's testing regime for failure to comport with the Fourth Amendment's command of probable cause may hinder the Government's attempts to make rail transit as safe as humanly possible. But constitutional rights have their consequences, and one is that efforts to maximize the public welfare, no matter how well-intentioned, must always be pursued within constitutional boundaries. Were the police freed from the constraints of the Fourth Amendment for just one day to seek out evidence of criminal wrongdoing, the resulting convictions and incarcerations would probably prevent thousands of fatalities. Our refusal to tolerate this spectre reflects our shared belief that even beneficent governmental power -- whether exercised to save money, save lives, or make the trains run on time -- must always yield to "a resolute loyalty to constitutional safeguards." Almeida-Sanchez v. United States, 413 U.S. 266, 273 (1973). The Constitution demands no less loyalty here.

III

Even accepting the majority's view that the FRA's collection and testing program is appropriately analyzed under a multifactor balancing test, and not under the literal terms of the Fourth Amendment, I would still find the program invalid. The benefits of suspicionless blood and urine testing are far outstripped by the costs imposed on personal liberty by such sweeping searches. Only by erroneously deriding as "minimal" the privacy and dignity interests at stake, and by uncritically inflating the likely efficacy of the FRA's testing program, does the majority strike a different balance.

For the reasons stated above, I find nothing minimal about the intrusion on individual liberty that occurs whenever the Government forcibly draws and analyzes a person's blood and urine. Several aspects of the FRA's testing program exacerbate the intrusiveness of these procedures. Most strikingly, the agency's regulations not only do not forbid, but, in fact, appear to invite criminal prosecutors to obtain the blood and urine samples drawn by the FRA and use them as the basis of criminal investigations and trials. See 49 CFR § 219.211(d) (1987) ("Each sample . . . may be made available to . . . a party in litigation upon service of appropriate compulsory process on the custodian of the sample . . ."). This is an unprecedented invitation, leaving open the possibility of criminal prosecutions based on suspicionless searches of the human body. Cf. National Treasury Employees Union, post at 666 (Customs Service drug-testing program prohibits use of test results in criminal prosecutions); Camara, 387 U.S. at 537.

To be sure, the majority acknowledges, in passing, the possibility of criminal prosecutions, ante at 621, n. 5, but it refuses to factor this possibility into its Fourth Amendment balancing process, stating that "the record does not disclose that [49 CFR § 219.211(d) (1987)] was intended to be, or actually has been, so used." Ibid. This demurrer is highly disingenuous. The federal parties concede that they find "no prohibition on the release of FRA testing results to prosecutors." Brief for Federal Parties 10, n. 15. The absence of prosecutions to date -- which is likely due to the fact that the FRA's regulations have been held invalid for much of their brief history -- hardly proves that prosecutors will not avail themselves of the FRA's invitation in the future. If the majority really views the impact of FRA testing on privacy interests as minimal even if these tests generate criminal prosecutions, it should say so. If the prospect of prosecutions would lead the majority to reassess the validity of the testing program with prosecutions as part of the balance, it should say so, too, or condition its approval of that program on the nonrelease of test results to prosecutors. In ducking this important issue, the majority gravely disserves both the values served by the Fourth Amendment and the rights of those persons whom the FRA searches. Furthermore, the majority's refusal to restrict the release of test results casts considerable doubt on the conceptual basis of its decision -- that the "special need" of railway safety is one "beyond the normal need for law enforcement." Ante at 619 (citations omitted). [n10]

The majority also overlooks needlessly intrusive aspects of the testing process itself. Although the FRA requires the collection and testing of both blood and urine, the agency concedes that mandatory urine tests -- unlike blood tests -- do not measure current impairment, and therefore cannot differentiate on-duty impairment from prior drug or alcohol use which has ceased to affect the user's behavior. See 49 CFR § 219.309(2) (1987) (urine test may reveal use of drugs or alcohol as much as 60 days prior to sampling). Given that the FRA's stated goal is to ascertain current impairment, and not to identify persons who have used substances in their spare time sufficiently in advance of their railroad duties to pose no risk of on-duty impairment, § 219.101(a), mandatory urine testing seems wholly excessive. At the very least, the FRA could limit its use of urinalysis to confirming findings of current impairment suggested by a person's blood tests. The additional invasion caused by automatically testing urine as well as blood hardly ensures that privacy interests "will be invaded no more than is necessary." T.L.O., 469 U.S. at 343.

The majority's trivialization of the intrusions on worker privacy posed by the FRA's testing program is matched at the other extreme by its blind acceptance of the Government's assertion that testing will "dete[r] employees engaged in safety-sensitive tasks from using controlled substances or alcohol," and "help railroads obtain invaluable information about the causes of major accidents." Ante at 629, 630. With respect, first, to deterrence, it is simply implausible that testing employees after major accidents occur, 49 CFR § 219.201(a)(1) (1987), will appreciably discourage them from using drugs or alcohol. As JUSTICE STEVENS observes in his concurring opinion:

Most people -- and I would think most railroad employees as well -- do not go to work with the expectation that they may be involved in a major accident, particularly one causing such catastrophic results as loss of life or the release of hazardous material requiring an evacuation. Moreover, even if they are conscious of the possibilities that such an accident might occur and that alcohol or drug use might be a contributing factor, if the risk of serious personal injury does not deter their use of these substances, it seems highly unlikely that the additional threat of loss of employment would have any effect on their behavior.

Ante at 634. Under the majority's deterrence rationale, people who skip school or work to spend a sunny day at the zoo will not taunt the lions because their truancy or absenteeism might be discovered in the event they are mauled. It is, of course, the fear of the accident, not the fear of a post-accident revelation, that deters. The majority's credulous acceptance of the FRA's deterrence rationale is made all the more suspect by the agency's failure to introduce, in an otherwise ample administrative record, any studies explaining or supporting its theory of accident deterrence.

The poverty of the majority's deterrence rationale leaves the Government's interest in diagnosing the causes of major accidents as the sole remaining justification for the FRA's testing program. I do not denigrate this interest, but it seems a slender thread from which to hang such an intrusive program, particularly given that the knowledge that one or more workers were impaired at the time of an accident falls far short of proving that substance abuse caused or exacerbated that accident. See 839 F.2d 575, 587 (CA9 1988). Some corroborative evidence is needed: witness or coworker accounts of a worker's misfeasance, or at least indications that the cause of the accident was within a worker's area of responsibility. Such particularized facts are, of course, the very essence of the individualized suspicion requirement which the respondent railroad workers urge, and which the Court of Appeals found to "pos[e] no insuperable burden on the government." Id. at 588. Furthermore, reliance on the importance of diagnosing the causes of an accident as a critical basis for upholding the FRA's testing plan is especially hard to square with our frequent admonition that the interest in ascertaining the causes of a criminal episode does not justify departure from the Fourth Amendment's requirements. "[T]his Court has never sustained a search upon the sole ground that officers reasonably expected to find evidence of a particular crime. . . ." Katz, 389 U.S. at 356. Nor should it here.

IV

In his first dissenting opinion as a Member of this Court, Oliver Wendell Holmes observed:

Great cases, like hard cases, make bad law. For great cases are called great, not by reason of their real importance in shaping the law of the future, but because of some accident of immediate overwhelming interest which appeals to the feelings and distorts the judgment. These immediate interests exercise a kind of hydraulic pressure which makes what previously was clear seem doubtful, and before which even well settled principles of law will bend.

Northern Securities Co. v. United States, 193 U.S. 197, 400-401 (1904).

A majority of this Court, swept away by society's obsession with stopping the scourge of illegal drugs, today succumbs to the popular pressures described by Justice Holmes. In upholding the FRA's plan for blood and urine testing, the majority bends time-honored and textually based principles of the Fourth Amendment -- principles the Framers of the Bill of Rights designed to ensure that the Government has a strong and individualized justification when it seeks to invade an individual's privacy. I believe the Framers would be appalled by the vision of mass governmental intrusions upon the integrity of the human body that the majority allows to become reality. The immediate victims of the majority's constitutional timorousness will be those railroad workers whose bodily fluids the Government may now forcibly collect and analyze. But ultimately, today's decision will reduce the privacy all citizens may enjoy, for, as Justice Holmes understood, principles of law, once bent, do not snap back easily. I dissent.

Notes

1. The first, and leading, case of a minimally intrusive search held valid when based on suspicion short of probable cause is Terry v. Ohio, 392 U.S. 1, 30 (1968), where we held that a police officer who observes unusual conduct suggesting criminal activity by

persons he reasonably suspects are armed and presently dangerous may "conduct a carefully limited search of the outer clothing of such persons." See also United States v. Hensley, 469 U.S. 221 (1985) (upholding brief stop of person described on wanted flyer while police ascertain if arrest warrant has been issued); Delaware v. Prouse, 440 U.S. 648 (1979) (invalidating discretionary stops of motorists to check licenses and registrations when not based on reasonable suspicion that the motorist is unlicensed, the automobile is unregistered, or that the vehicle or an occupant should otherwise be detained); Pennsylvania v. Mimms, 434 U.S. 106 (1977) (upholding limited search where officers who had lawfully stopped car saw a large bulge under the driver's jacket); United States v. Brignoni-Ponce, 422 U.S. 873 (1975) (upholding brief stops by roving border patrols where officers reasonably believe car may contain illegal aliens); Adams v. Williams, 407 U.S. 143 (1972) (upholding brief stop to interrogate suspicious individual believed to be carrying narcotics and gun).

2. See, e.g., United States v. Martinez-Fuerte, 428 U.S. 543 (1976) (brief interrogative stop at permanent border checkpoint to ascertain motorist's residence status); Camara v. Municipal Court of San Francisco, 387 U.S. 523 (1967) (routine annual inspection by city housing department).

3. The "special needs" the Court invoked to justify abrogating the probable cause requirement were, in New Jersey v. T.L.O., 469 U.S. 325, 341 (1985), "the substantial need of teachers and administrators for freedom to maintain order in the schools"; in O'Connor v. Ortega, 480 U.S. 709, 725 (1987), "the efficient and proper operation of the workplace"; and in Griffin v. Wisconsin, 483 U.S. 868, 878 (1987), the need to preserve "the deterrent effect of the supervisory arrangement" of probation.

4. See T.L.O., supra, at 346 (teacher's report that student had been smoking provided reasonable suspicion that purse contained cigarettes); O'Connor, supra, at 726 (charges of specific financial improprieties gave employer individualized suspicion of misconduct by employee); Griffin, supra, at 879-880 (tip to police officer that probationer was storing guns in his apartment provided reasonable suspicion).

5. That the Fourth Amendment applies equally to criminal and civil searches was emphasized, ironically enough, in the portion of T.L.O. holding the Fourth Amendment applicable to schoolhouse searches. 469 U.S. at 335. The malleability of "special needs" balancing thus could not be clearer: the majority endorses the applicability of the Fourth Amendment to civil searches in determining whether a search has taken place, but then wholly ignores it in the subsequent inquiry into the validity of that search.

6. The FRA's breath-testing procedures also constitute searches subject to constitutional safeguards. See ante at 616-617 (reaching same conclusion). I focus my discussion on the collection and testing of blood and urine because those more intrusive procedures better demonstrate the excesses of the FRA's scheme.

7. The majority, seeking to lessen the devastating ramifications of Schmerber v. California, 384 U.S. 757 (1966), and to back up its assertion that Government-imposed blood extraction does not "infringe significant privacy interests," ante at 625, emphasizes

Schmerber's observation that blood tests are commonplace, and can be performed with "'virtually no risk, trauma, or pain.'" Ibid., quoting 384 U.S. at 771. The majority, however, wrenches this statement out of context. The Schmerber Court made this statement only after it established that the blood test fell within the exigent circumstances exception to the warrant requirement, and that the test was supported by probable cause. Indeed, the statement was made only in the context of the separate inquiry into whether the compulsory blood test was conducted in a reasonable manner. 384 U.S. at 768-772; see also Winston v. Lee, 470 U.S. 753, 760-761 (1985) ("Schmerber recognized that the ordinary requirements of the Fourth Amendment would be the threshold requirements for conducting this kind of surgical search and seizure. . . . Beyond these standards, Schmerber's inquiry considered a number of other factors in determining the 'reasonableness' of the blood test") (emphasis added). The majority also cites South Dakota v. Neville, 459 U.S. 553 (1983), and Breithaupt v. Abram, 352 U.S. 432 (1957), for the proposition that blood tests are commonplace. Ante at 625. In both those cases, however, the police officers who attempted to impose blood tests on drunk-driving suspects had exceptionally strong evidence of the driver's inebriation. 459 U.S. at 554-556; 352 U.S. at 433.

8. The majority dismisses as nonexistent the intrusiveness of such "direct observation," on the ground that FRA regulations state that such observation is not "require[d]." 50 Fed.Reg. 31555 (1985), cited ante at 626. The majority's dismissal is too hasty, however, for the regulations -- in the very same sentence -- go on to state: "but observation is the most effective means of ensuring that the sample is that of the employee and has not been diluted." 50 Fed.Reg. 31555 (1985). Even if this were not the case, the majority's suggestion that officials monitoring urination will disregard the clear commands of the Field Manual with which they are provided is dubious, to say the least.

9. See, e.g., National Treasury Employees Union v. Von Raab, 816 F.2d 170, 175 (CA5 1987), aff'd in pertinent part, post, p. 656; Taylor v. O'Grady, 669 F.Supp. 1422, 1433-1434 (ND Ill.1987); Feliciano v. Cleveland, 661 F.Supp. 578, 586 (ND Ohio 1987); American Federation of Government Employees, AFL-CIO v. Weinberger, 651 F.Supp. 726, 732-733 (SD Ga.1986); Capua v. Plainfield, 643 F.Supp. 1507, 1514 (NJ 1986).

10. As a result of the majority's extension of the regulatory search doctrine to searches of the person, individuals the FRA finds to have used drugs may face criminal prosecution, even if their impairment had nothing to do with causing an accident. The majority observes that evidence of criminal behavior unearthed during an otherwise valid regulatory search is not excludible unless the search is shown to be a "pretext" for obtaining evidence for a criminal trial, ante at 621, n. 5, citing New York v. Burger, 482 U.S. 691, 716-717, n. 27 (1987) -- a defense the majority belittles but, mercifully, preserves for another day.

Can't deny prisoners visits from parents, spouses, children, clergy members, and close friends: Justice Marshall's dissent in Kentucky Department of Corrections v. Thompson (May 15, 1989)

Justice MARSHALL, with whom Justice BRENNAN and Justice STEVENS join, dissenting.

As a result of today's decision, correctional authorities at the Kentucky State Reformatory are free to deny prisoners visits from parents, spouses, children, clergy members, and close friends for any reason whatsoever, or for no reason at all. Prisoners will not even be entitled to learn the reason, if any, why a visitor has been turned away. In my view, the exercise of such unbridled governmental power over the basic human need to see family members and friends strikes at the heart of the liberty protected by the Due Process Clause of the Fourteenth Amendment. Recognizing a liberty interest in this case would not create a right to "unfettered visitation," ante, at 460, but would merely afford prisoners rudimentary procedural safeguards against retaliatory or arbitrary denials of visits. Because the majority refuses to take this small step, I dissent.

* The majority begins its analysis by conceding, as it must under our precedents, that prisoners do not shed their constitutioal rights at the prison gate, but instead retain a residuum of constitutionally protected liberty independent of any state laws or regulations. See ante, at 459-4611908. [1] In the balance of its opinion, however, the majority proceeds to prove the emptiness of this initial gesture. In concluding that prison visits implicate no retained liberty interest, the majority applies the following oft-cited test: " 'As long as the conditions or degree of confinement to which the prisoner is subjected is within the sentence imposed upon him and is not otherwise violative of the Constitution, the Due Process Clause does not in itself subject an inmate's treatment by prison authorities to judicial oversight.' " Ante, at 1908, quoting Montanye v. Haymes, 427 U.S. 236, 242, 96 S.Ct. 2543, 2547, 49 L.Ed.2d 466 (1976). On its face, the "within the sentence" test knows few rivals for vagueness and pliability, not the least because a typical prison sentence says little more than that the defendant must spend a specified period of time behind bars. As applied, this test offers prisoners scant more protection, for the Justices employing it have rarely scrutinized the actual conditions of confinement faced by the prisoners in the correctional institutions at issue. Under this approach, therefore, "a prisoner crosses into limbo when he enters into penal confinement." Hewitt v. Helms, 459 U.S. 460, 482, 103 S.Ct. 864, 877, 74 L.Ed.2d 675 (1983) (STEVENS, J., dissenting). In theory he retains some minimal interest in liberty protected by the Due Process Clause, but in practice this interest crystallizes only on those infrequent occasions when a majority of the Court happens to say so. [2]

I have previously stated that, when prison authorities alter a prisoner's conditions of confinement, the relevant question should be whether the prisoner has suffered "a sufficiently 'grievous loss' to trigger the protection of due process." Olim v. Wakinekona, 461 U.S. 238, 252, 103 S.Ct. 1741, 1749, 75 L.Ed.2d 813 (1983)

(MARSHALL, J., dissenting), quoting Vitek v. Jones, 445 U.S. 480, 488, 100 S.Ct. 1254, 1261, 63 L.Ed.2d 552 (1980); see also Morrissey v. Brewer, 408 U.S. 471, 481, 92 S.Ct. 2593, 2600, 33 L.Ed.2d 484 (1972). The answer depends not only on the nature and gravity of the change, but also on whether the prisoner has been singled out arbitrarily for disparate treatment. "For an essential attribute of the liberty protected by the Constitution is the right to the same kind of treatment as the State provides to other similarly situated persons. A convicted felon, though he is properly placed in a disfavored class, retains this essential right." Hewitt, supra, 459 U.S., at 485-486, 103 S.Ct., at 879 (STEVENS, J., dissenting) (footnote omitted); see also Olim, supra, 461 U.S., at 252, 103 S.Ct., at 1749 (MARSHALL, J., dissenting). Put another way, the retained liberty interest protected by the Constitution encompasses the right to be free from arbitrary governmental action affecting significant personal interests. See Wolff v. McDonnell, 418 U.S. 539, 571-572, n. 19, 94 S.Ct. 2963, 2982, n. 19, 41 L.Ed.2d 935 (1974).

Prison visits have long been recognized as critically important to inmates as well as to the communities to which the inmates ultimately will return. [3] Without visits, a prisoner "may be entirely cut off from his only contacts with the outside world." Olim, supra, 461 U.S., at 253, 103 S.Ct., at 1750 (MARSHALL, J., dissenting). Confinement without visitation

"brings alienation and the longer the confinement the greater the alienation. There is little, if any, disagreement that the opportunity to be visited by friends and relatives is more beneficial to the confined person than any other form of communication.

"Ample visitation rights are also important for the family and friends of the confined person. . . . Preservation of the family unit is important to the reintegration of the confined person and decreases the possibility of recidivism upon release. . . . [V]isitation has demonstrated positive effects on a confined person's ability to adjust to life while confined as well as his ability to adjust to life upon release. . . ." National Conference of Commissioners on Uniform State Laws, Model Sentencing and Corrections Act § 4-115, Comment (1979) (hereinafter NCCUSLA) (citations omitted). [4]

Consistent with this view, numerous governmental and private organizations which deal closely with correctional institutions have promulgated standards designed "to maximize visiting opportunities for inmates." U.S. Dept. of Justice, Federal Standards for Prisons and Jails, Standard 12.12 (1980). [5] Although the details vary, the standards uniformly provide that visitors should not be barred except for good cause shown. Kentucky itself, in its statewide Corrections Policies and Procedures (Commonwealth Procedures), recognizes that visits permit reformatory inmates such as Kenneth Bobbitt and Kevin Black "to maintain morale and contact with the community," and thus "are important to the inmate and his success within the community upon release." App. 98.

The majority intimates that the actions taken against prisoners Bobbitt and Black were based on good cause, see ante, at 458, but the very essence of these prisoners' factual allegations is that no such cause existed. Id., at 57-58, 61, 66-68, 70-71. If Bobbitt and Black are correct, they may well have suffered a "grievous loss" by being singled out arbitrarily for unjustifiably harsh treatment. No evidence whatsoever indicates that visitors to the reformatory have ever been barred for any reason except those enumerated as legitimate in the Commonwealth Procedures and the institution-specific Reformatory Procedures Memorandum (Reformatory Memorandum). See ante, at 456-458, nn. 1, 2. It is nowhere suggested, furthermore, that these prisoners' sentences contemplated denials of visits for nonenumerated reasons, or that such denials are " 'well within the terms of confinement ordinarily contemplated' " in the reformatory. Ante, at 461, quoting Hewitt, 459 U.S., at 468, 103 S.Ct., at 869. Under the majority's disposition, neither prisoner will ever have a right to contest the prison authorities' account. One need hardly be cynical about prison administrators to recognize that the distinct possibility of retaliatory or otherwise groundless deprivations of visits calls for a modicum of procedural protections to guard against such behavior.

Even if I believed that visit denials did not implicate a prisoner's retained liberty interest, I would nonetheless find that a liberty interest has been "created" by the Commonwealth's visitation regulations and policies. [6] As the majority notes, " 'a State creates a protected liberty interest by placing substantive limitations on official discretion.' " Ante, at 462, quoting Olim, 461 U.S., at 249, 103 S.Ct., 1747. I fully agree with the majority that "[t]he regulations and procedures at issue in this case do provide certain 'substantive predicates' to guide the decisionmaker." Ante, at 463. But I cannot agree that Kentucky's prison regulations do not create a liberty interest because they "lack the requisite relevant mandatory language." Ibid. As an initial matter, I fail to see why mandatory language always is an essential element of a state-created liberty interest. Once it is clear that a State has imposed substantive criteria in statutes or regulations to guide or limit official discretion, there is no reason to assume-as the majority does-that officials applying the statutes or regulations are likely to ignore the criteria if there is not some undefined quantity of the words "shall" or "must." Drafters of statutes or regulations do not ordinarily view the criteria they establish as mere surplusage. Absent concrete evidence that state officials routinely ignore substantive criteria set forth in statutes or regulations (and there is no such evidence here), it is only proper to assume that the criteria are regularly employed in practice, thereby creating legitimate expectations worthy of protection by the Due Process Clause. Common sense suggests that expectations stem from practice as well as from the language of statutes or re ulations. Vitek v. Jones, 445 U.S., at 489, 100 S.Ct., at 1261 (approving lower courts' reliance on "objective expectation, firmly fixed in state law and official Penal Complex practice"). [7] This point escapes the majority, which apparently harbors the "unrealistic [belief] that variations such as the use of 'may' rather than 'shall' could negate the expectations derived from experience with a [prison] system and . . . enumerated criteria. . . ." Greenholtz v. Nebraska Penal Inmates, 442 U.S. 1, 29-30, n. 9, 99 S.Ct. 2100, 2115 n. 9, 60 L.Ed.2d 668 (1979) (MARSHALL, J., dissenting) (citation omitted).

Even if I thought it proper to rely on the presence or absence of mandatory language, I would still disagree with the majority's determination that the regulations here lack such language. [8] The majority relies primarily on a statement in the Reformatory Memorandum that "administrative staff reserves the right to allow or disallow visits." It is important, however, to put this "caveat," ante, at 464, in proper context. The Reformatory Memorandum's section on visitation occupies 33 pages of the joint appendix. The caveat appears just once in a general, introductory paragraph which also includes the statement that "it is the policy of the Kentucky State Reformatory to respect the right of inmates to have visits." App. 106 (emphasis added). Over the next 20 pages, the Reformatory Memorandum lays out in great detail the mandatory "procedures to be enforced in regard to all types of visits." Ibid. (emphasis added). [9] It states, for example, that "[v]isits will be conducted seven (7) days a week," id., at 107 (emphasis added); that "[a]n inmate is allowed three (3) separate visits . . . per week," id., at 108 (emphasis added); that "[t]here will be no visit list maintained which specifies who may visit an inmate," ibid. (emphasis added); that "[a]n inmate is allowed to have . . . three (3) adult visitors . . . per visit," id., at 108-109 (emphasis added); that visits "will be one and one-half hours," id., at 109 (emphasis added); and that "[e]ach inmate will be allowed one (1) outdoor visit per week," id., at 125 (emphasis added).

Only then does the Reformatory Memorandum enumerate the very specific reasons for which a visitor may be excluded. Id., at 132-134, quoted ante, at 457-458, n. 2. The duty officer does not have unfettered discretion with respect to visitors. Rather, he "has the responsibility of denying a visit for the above [enumerated] reasons." App. 134 (emphasis added). When a visit is denied, the reasons "will be documented." Ibid. (emphasis added). Presumably this means that the duty officer must keep a record of which of "the above reasons" caused him to exclude the visitor. The Reformatory Memorandum also expressly references the American Correctional Association's visitation standards, which provide that "visits may be limited only by the institution's schedule, space, and personnel constraints, or when there are substantial reasons to justify such limitations." American Correctional Association, Standards for Adult Correctional Institutions, Standard 2-4381 (2d ed. 1981) (emphasis added), cited at App. 106. Nothing in these standards even remotely contemplates the arbitrary exclusion of visitors.

When these mandatory commands are read in conjunction with the detailed rules set forth in the Commonwealth Procedures, [10] it is inconceivable that prisoners in the reformatory would not "reasonably form an objective expectation that a visit would necessarily be allowed absent the occurrence of one of the listed conditions." Ante, at 465. The majority inexplicably ignores nearly all of these commands, despite claiming to have considered the "overall effect of the regulations," ibid., and despite the Commonwealth's striking concession that the regulations "repeatedly use 'will', 'shall', and similar directive or mandatory language" in an effort "to advise inmates and potential visitors what is expected." Brief for Petitioners 13, 30 (emphasis added); see also Tr. of Oral Arg. 5-6 ("[O]ur procedures are very limiting in the discretion of the officials"). [11] In light of these mandatory commands, the caveat, as well as any other language that could be taken to suggest that visitors need not "fall within one of the described categories in order to be excluded," ante, at 464, amount to nothing more than mere boilerplate. The Court should reject the view that "state laws which impose substantive limitations and elaborate procedural requirements on official conduct create no liberty interest solely because there remains the possibility that an official will act in an arbitrary manner at the end of the process." Olim, 461 U.S., at 258-259, 103 S.Ct., at 1752 (MARSHALL, J., dissenting) (discussing holding in Hewitt); see also 461 U.S., at 259, n. 13, 103 S.Ct., at 1752, n. 13 (discussing similar holding in Greenholtz v. Nebraska Penal Inmates, 442 U.S. 1, 99 S.Ct. 2100, 60 L.Ed.2d 668 (1979); cf. Brennan v. Cunningham, 813 F.2d 1, 8 (C.A.1 1987).

Finally, the majority's reliance on the fact that both the Commonwealth Procedures and the Reformatory Memorandum provide that a visitor "may" be excluded if he falls within one of the enumerated categories, ante, at 464, is misplaced. The word "may" in this context simply means that prison authorities possess the discretion to allow visits from persons who fall within one of the enumerated categories. Surely this possibility cannot defeat a prisoner's legitimate expectation that visitors will be denied only when they fall within one of those categories. In Hewitt, regulations regarding administrative segregation were deemed to have created a liberty interest even though they stated that a prisoner "may" be placed in segregation on the occurrence of specified substantive predicates. See 459 U.S., at 470, n. 6, 103 S.Ct., at 871, n. 6. Likewise, in Vitek, a prisoner had a state-created liberty interest in not being transferred to a mental hospital even though the applicable state statute provided that the director of correctional services "may" transfer a prisoner to such a hospital after certain medical findings are made. See 445 U.S., at 483, n. 1, 100 S.Ct., at 1259, n. 1. If the use of the word "may" could not defeat a liberty interest in Hewitt or Vitek, I fail to see how it could do so here.

The prisoners in this case do not seek a right to unfettered visitation. All they ask is that the Court recognize that visitation is sufficiently important to warrant procedural protections to ensure that visitors are not arbitrarily denied. The protections need not be extensive, but simply commensurate with the special "needs and exigencies of the institutional environment." Wolff, 418 U.S., at 555, 94 S.Ct., at 2974. In making the threshold determination that the denial of visits can never implicate a prisoner's liberty interest, the majority thus establishes that when visitors are turned away, no process, not even notice, is constitutionally due. I cannot accept such a parsimonious reading of the Due Process Clause, and therefore dissent.

Can't be required to produce a child to the court if such production would be self-incriminating: Justice Marshall's dissent in Baltimore Department of Social Services v. Bouknight (February 20, 1990)

JUSTICE MARSHALL, with whom JUSTICE BRENNAN joins, dissenting.
Although the Court assumes that respondent's act of producing her child would

be testimonial and could be incriminating, ante, at 555, it nonetheless concludes that she cannot invoke her privilege against self-incrimination and refuse to reveal her son's current location. Neither of the reasons the Court articulates to support its refusal to permit respondent to invoke her constitutional privilege justifies its decision. I therefore dissent.

I

The Court correctly assumes, ante, at 555, that Bouknight's production of her son to the Maryland court would be testimonial because it would amount to an admission of Bouknight's physical control over her son. See Fisher v. United States, 425 U.S. 391, 410 (1976) (acts of production are testimonial if they contain implicit statement of fact). Accord, United States v. Doe, 465 U.S. 605, 612 -613 (1984). The Court also assumes, ante, at 555, that Bouknight's act of production would be self-incriminating. I would not hesitate to hold explicitly that Bouknight's admission of possession or control presents a "'real and appreciable'" threat of self-incrimination. Marchetti v. United States, 390 U.S. 39, 48 (1968). Bouknight's ability to produce the child would conclusively establish her actual and present physical control over him, and thus might "prove a significant `link in a chain' of evidence tending to establish [her] guilt." Ibid. (footnote omitted).

Indeed, the stakes for Bouknight are much greater than the Court suggests. Not only could she face criminal abuse and neglect charges for her alleged mistreatment of Maurice, but she could also be charged with causing his death. The State acknowledges that it suspects that Maurice is dead, and the police are investigating his case as a possible homicide. In these circumstances, the potentially incriminating aspects to Bouknight's act of production are undoubtedly significant.

II

Notwithstanding the real threat of self-incrimination, the Court holds that "Bouknight may not invoke the privilege to resist the production order because she has assumed custodial duties related to production and because production is required as part of a noncriminal regulatory regime." Ante, at 555-556. In characterizing Bouknight as Maurice's "custodian," and in describing the relevant Maryland juvenile statutes as part of a noncriminal regulatory regime, the Court relies on two distinct lines of Fifth Amendment precedent, neither of which applies to this litigation.

A

The Court's first line of reasoning turns on its view that Bouknight has agreed to exercise on behalf of the State certain custodial obligations with respect to her son, obligations that the Court analogizes to those of a custodian of the records of a collective entity. See ante, at 558-559. This characterization is baffling, both because it is contrary to the facts of this case and because this Court has never relied on such a characterization to override the privilege against self-incrimination except in the context of a claim of privilege by an agent of a collective entity. 1

Jacqueline Bouknight is Maurice's mother; she is not, and in fact could not be, his "custodian" whose rights and duties are determined solely by the Maryland juvenile protection law. See Md. Cts. & Jud. Proc. Code Ann. 3-801(j) (Supp. 1989) (defining "custodian" as "person or agency to whom legal custody of a child has been given by order of the court, other than the child's parent or legal guardian"). Although Bouknight surrendered physical custody of her child during the pendency of the proceedings to determine whether Maurice was a "child in need of assistance" (CINA) within the meaning of the Maryland Code, 3-801(e), Maurice's placement in shelter care was only temporary and did not extinguish her legal right to custody of her son. See 3-801(r). When the CINA proceedings were settled, Bouknight regained physical custody of Maurice and entered into an agreement with the Baltimore City Department of Social Services (BCDSS). In that agreement, which was approved by the juvenile court, Bouknight promised, among other things, to "cooperate with BCDSS," App. 28, but she retained legal custody of Maurice.

A finding that a child is in need of assistance does not by itself divest a parent of legal or physical custody, nor does it transform such custody to something conferred by the State. See, e. g., In re Jertrude O., 56 Md. App. 83, 97-98, 466 A. 2d 885, 893 (1983) (proving a child is a CINA differs significantly from proving that the parent's rights to legal and physical custody should be terminated). Thus, the parent of a CINA continues to exercise custody because she is the child's parent, not because the State has delegated that responsibility to her. Although the State has obligations "[t]o provide for the care, protection, and wholesome mental and physical development of children" who are in need of assistance, Md. Cts. & Jud. Proc. Code Ann. 3-802(a)(1) (1984), these duties do not eliminate or override a parent's continuing legal obligations similarly to provide for her child.

In light of the statutory structure governing a parent's relationship to a CINA, Bouknight is not acting as a custodian in the traditional sense of that word because she is not acting on behalf of the State. In reality, she continues to exercise her parental duties, constrained by an agreement between her and the State. That agreement, which includes a stipulation that Maurice was a CINA, allows the State, in certain circumstances, to intercede in Bouknight's relationship with her child. It does not, however, confer custodial rights and obligations on Bouknight in the same way corporate law creates the custodial status of a corporate agent.

Moreover, the rationale for denying a corporate custodian Fifth Amendment protection for acts done in her representative capacity does not apply to this case. The rule for a custodian of corporate records rests on the well-established principle that a collective entity, unlike a natural person, has no Fifth Amendment privilege against self-incrimination. See Hale v. Henkel, 201 U.S. 43, 69 -70 (1906) (corporation has no privilege); United States v. White, 322 U.S. 694, 701 (1944) (labor union has no privilege). Because an artificial entity can act only through its agents, a custodian of such an entity's documents may not invoke her personal privilege to resist producing documents that may incriminate the entity, even if the documents may also incriminate the custodian. Wilson v. United States, 221 U.S. 361, 384 -385 (1911). As we explained in

White:

"[I]ndividuals, when acting as representatives of a collective group, cannot be said to be exercising their personal rights and duties nor to be entitled to their purely personal privileges. Rather they assume the rights, duties and privileges of the artificial entity or association of which they are agents or officers and they are bound by its obligations. . . . And the official records and documents of the organization that are held by them in a representative rather than in a personal capacity cannot be the subject of the personal privilege against self-incrimination, even though production of the papers might tend to incriminate them personally." 322 U.S., at 699 (citations omitted; emphasis added).

Jacqueline Bouknight is not the agent for an artificial entity that possesses no Fifth Amendment privilege. Her role as Maurice's parent is very different from the role of a corporate custodian who is merely the instrumentality through whom the corporation acts. I am unwilling to extend the collective entity doctrine into a context where it denies individuals, acting in their personal rather than representative capacities, their constitutional privilege against self-incrimination.

B

The Court's decision rests as well on cases holding that "the ability to invoke the privilege may be greatly diminished when invocation would interfere with the effective operation of a generally applicable, civil regulatory requirement." Ante, at 557. The cases the Court cites have two common features: they concern civil regulatory systems not primarily intended to facilitate criminal investigations, and they target the general public. See California v. Byers, 402 U.S. 424, 430 -431 (1971) (determining that a "hit and run" statute that required a driver involved in an accident to stop and give certain information was primarily civil). In contrast, regulatory regimes that are directed at a "`selective group inherently suspect of criminal activities,'" Marchetti, 390 U.S., at 57 (quoting Albertson v. Subversive Activities Control Board, 382 U.S. 70, 79 (1965)), do not result in a similar diminution of the Fifth Amendment privilege.

1

Applying the first feature to this case, the Court describes Maryland's juvenile protection scheme as "a broadly directed, noncriminal regulatory regime governing children cared for pursuant to custodial orders." Ante, at 559. The Court concludes that Bouknight cannot resist an order necessary for the functioning of that system. The Court's characterization of Maryland's system is dubious and highlights the flaws inherent in the Court's formulation of the appropriate Fifth Amendment inquiry. Virtually any civil regulatory scheme could be characterized as essentially noncriminal by looking narrowly or, as in this case, solely to the avowed noncriminal purpose of the regulations. If one focuses instead on the practical effects, the same scheme could be seen as facilitating criminal investigations. The fact that the Court holds Maryland's juvenile statute to be essentially noncriminal, notwithstanding the overlapping purposes underlying that statute and Maryland's criminal child abuse statutes, proves that the Court's test will never be used to find a relationship between the civil scheme and law enforcement goals significant enough to implicate the Fifth Amendment.

The regulations embodied in the juvenile welfare statute are intimately related to the enforcement of state criminal statutes prohibiting child abuse, Md. Ann. Code, Art. 27, 35A (1987). State criminal decisions suggest that information supporting criminal convictions is often obtained through civil proceedings and the subsequent protective oversight by BCDSS. See, e. g., Lee v. State, 62 Md. App. 341, 489 A. 2d 87 (1985). See also 3 Code of Md. Regs. 07.02.07.08(A)(1) and 07.02.07.08(C)(1)(b) (1988) (requiring Social Services Administration to maintain a Child Abuse Central Registry and allowing law enforcement officials access to the Registry). In this respect, Maryland's juvenile protection system resembles the revenue system at issue in Marchetti, which required persons engaged in the business of accepting wagers to provide certain information about their activities to the Federal Government. Focusing on the effects of the regulatory scheme, the Court held that this revenue system was not the sort of neutral civil regulatory scheme that could trump the Fifth Amendment privilege. Even though the Government's "principal interest [was] evidently the collection of revenue," 390 U.S., at 57, the information sought would increase the "likelihood that any past or present gambling offenses [would] be discovered and successfully prosecuted," id., at 52.

In contrast to Marchetti, the Court here disregards the practical implications of the civil scheme and holds that the juvenile protection system does not "'focu[s] almost exclusively on conduct which was criminal.'" Ante, at 560 (quoting Byers, supra, at 454 (Harlan, J., concurring in judgment). See also Byers, supra, at 430 (plurality opinion) (determining statute at issue to be "essentially regulatory, not criminal"). I cannot agree with this approach. The State's goal of protecting children from abusive environments through its juvenile welfare system cannot be separated from criminal provisions that serve the same goal. When the conduct at which a civil statute aims - here, child abuse and neglect - is frequently the same conduct subject to criminal sanction, it strikes me as deeply problematic to dismiss the Fifth Amendment concerns by characterizing the civil scheme as "unrelated to criminal law enforcement or investigation," ante, at 561. A civil scheme that inevitably intersects with criminal sanctions may not be used to coerce, on pain of contempt, a potential criminal defendant to furnish evidence crucial to the success of her own prosecution.

I would apply a different analysis, one that is more faithful to the concerns underlying the Fifth Amendment. This approach would target respondent's particular claim of privilege, the precise nature of the testimony sought, and the likelihood of self-incrimination caused by this respondent's compliance. "To sustain the privilege, it need only be evident from the implications of the question, in the setting in which it is asked, that a responsive answer to the question or an explanation of why it cannot be answered might be dangerous because injurious disclosure could result." Hoffman v. United States, 341 U.S. 479, 486 -487 (1951). Accord, Marchetti, supra, at 48; Malloy v. Hogan, 378 U.S. 1, 11 -12 (1964). This analysis unambiguously indicates that Bouknight's Fifth

Amendment privilege must be respected to protect her from the serious risk of self-incrimination. See supra, at 563-564.

An individualized inquiry is preferable to the Court's analysis because it allows the privilege to turn on the concrete facts of a particular case, rather than on abstract characterizations concerning the nature of a regulatory scheme. Moreover, this particularized analysis would not undermine any appropriate goals of civil regulatory schemes that may intersect with criminal prohibitions. Instead, the ability of a State to provide immunity from criminal prosecution permits it to gather information necessary for civil regulation, while also preserving the integrity of the privilege against self-incrimination. The fact that the State throws a wide net in seeking information does not mean that it can demand from the few persons whose Fifth Amendment rights are implicated that they participate in their own criminal prosecutions. Rather, when the State demands testimony from its citizens, it should do so with an explicit grant of immunity.

2

The Court's approach includes a second element; it holds that a civil regulatory scheme cannot override Fifth Amendment protection unless it is targeted at the general public. Such an analysis would not be necessary under the particularized approach I advocate. Even under the Court's test, however, Bouknight's right against self-incrimination should not be diminished because Maryland's juvenile welfare scheme clearly is not generally applicable. A child is considered in need of assistance because "[h]e is mentally handicapped or is not receiving ordinary and proper care and attention, and . . . [h]is parents . . . are unable or unwilling to give proper care and attention to the child and his problems." Md. Cts. & Jud. Proc. Code Ann. 3-801(e) (Supp. 1989). The juvenile court has jurisdiction only over children who are alleged to be in need of assistance, not over all children in the State. See 3-804(a). It thus has power to compel testimony only from those parents whose children are alleged to be CINA's. In other words, the regulatory scheme that the Court describes as "broadly directed," ante, at 559, is actually narrowly targeted at parents who through abuse or neglect deny their children the minimal reasonable level of care and attention. Not all such abuse or neglect rises to the level of criminal child abuse, but parents of children who have been so seriously neglected or abused as to warrant allegations that the children are in need of state assistance are clearly "a selective group inherently suspect of criminal activities." See supra, at 567.

III

In the end, neither line of precedents relied on by the Court justifies riding roughshod over Bouknight's constitutional privilege against self-incrimination. The Court cannot accurately characterize her as a "custodian" in the same sense as the Court has used that word in the past. Nor is she the State's "agent," whom the State may require to act on its behalf. Moreover, the regulatory scheme at issue here is closely intertwined with the criminal regime prohibiting child abuse and applies only to parents whose abuse or neglect is serious enough to warrant state intervention.

Although I am disturbed by the Court's willingness to apply inapposite precedent to deny Bouknight her constitutional right against self-incrimination, especially in light of the serious allegations of homicide that accompany this civil proceeding, I take some comfort in the Court's recognition that the State may be prohibited from using any testimony given by Bouknight in subsequent criminal proceedings. Ante, at 561 (leaving open the question of the "State's ability to use the testimonial aspects of Bouknight's act of production" in such criminal proceedings). 2 Because I am not content to deny Bouknight the constitutional protection required by the Fifth Amendment now in the hope that she will not be convicted later on the basis of her own testimony, I dissent.

Notes

[1] The Court claims that the principle espoused in the collective entity cases was "extend[ed] well beyond the corporate context" in Shapiro v. United States, 335 U.S. 1 (1948). Ante, at 558. Shapiro, however, did not rest on the existence of an agency relationship between a collective entity and the custodian of its records. Instead, the petitioner was denied the Fifth Amendment privilege because the records sought were kept as part of a generalized regulatory system that required all businesses, unincorporated as well as incorporated, to retain records of certain transactions. See 335 U.S., at 22 -23, 27, 33. Shapiro turned on the Court's view "that the privilege which exists as to private papers cannot be maintained in relation to `records required by law to be kept in order that there may be suitable information of transactions which are the appropriate subjects of governmental regulation and the enforcement of restrictions validly established.'" Id., at 33 (quoting Davis v. United States, 328 U.S. 582, 589 -590 (1946)). See also Marchetti v. United States, 390 U.S. 39, 57 (1968) (describing rationale in Shapiro); ante, at 558 (emphasizing that Shapiro had custody of "documents in which the Government had a direct and particular regulatory interest" (emphasis added)). Thus, Shapiro is properly analyzed with the cases concerning testimony required as a part of a noncriminal regulatory regime, rather than with the cases concerning testimony compelled from custodians of collective entities' records.

[2] I note, with both exasperation and skepticism about the bona fide nature of the State's intentions, that the State may be able to grant Bouknight use immunity under a recently enacted immunity statute, even though it has thus far failed to do so. See 1989 Md. Laws, ch. 288 (amending 9-123). Although the statute applies only to testimony "in a criminal prosecution or a proceeding before a grand jury of the State," Md. Cts. & Jud. Proc. Code Ann. 9-123(b)(1) (Supp. 1989), the State represented to this Court that "[a]s a matter of law, [granting limited use immunity for the testimonial aspects of Bouknight's compliance with the production order] would now be possible," Tr. of Oral Arg. 10. If such a grant of immunity has been possible since July 1989 and the State has refused to invoke it so that it can litigate Bouknight's claim of privilege, I have difficulty believing that the State is sincere in its protestations of concern for Maurice's well-being.

Evidence obtained in violation of a court ruling (like Payton v. New York) should be excluded: Justice Marshall's dissent in New York v. Harris (April 18, 1990)

JUSTICE MARSHALL, with whom JUSTICE BRENNAN, JUSTICE BLACKMUN, and JUSTICE STEVENS join, dissenting.

Police officers entered Bernard Harris' home and arrested him there. They did not have an arrest warrant, he did not consent to their entry, and exigent circumstances did not exist. An arrest in such circumstances violates the Fourth Amendment. See Payton v. New York, 445 U.S. 573 (1980); see also ante, at 16, 17. About an hour after his arrest, Harris made an incriminating statement, which the government subsequently used at his trial. The majority concedes that the fruits of that illegal entry must be suppressed. See ante, at 20. The sole question before us is whether Harris' statement falls within that category.

The majority answers this question by adopting a broad and unprecedented principle, holding that "where the police have probable cause to arrest a suspect, the exclusionary rule does not bar the State's use of a statement made by the defendant outside of his home, even though the statement is taken after an arrest made in the home in violation of Payton." Ante, this page. The majority's conclusion is wrong. Its reasoning amounts to nothing more than an analytical sleight of hand, resting on errors in logic, misreadings of our cases, and an apparent blindness to the incentives the Court's ruling creates for knowing and intentional constitutional violations by the police. I dissent.

I

In recent years, this Court has repeatedly stated that the principal purpose of the Fourth Amendment's exclusionary rule is to eliminate incentives for police officers to violate that Amendment. See, e. g., United States v. Leon, 468 U.S. 897, 906 (1984). A police officer who violates the Constitution usually does so to obtain evidence that he could not secure lawfully. The best way to deter him is to provide that any evidence so obtained will not be admitted at trial. Deterrence of constitutional violations thus requires the suppression not only of evidence seized during an unconstitutional search, but also of "derivative evidence, both tangible and testimonial, that is the product of the primary evidence, or that is otherwise acquired as an indirect result of the unlawful search." Murray v. United States, 487 U.S. 533, 536 -537 (1988) (citing Nardone v. United States, 308 U.S. 338, 341 (1939)); see also Wong Sun v. United States, 371 U.S. 471, 488 (1963). Not all evidence connected to a constitutional violation is suppressible, however. Rather, the Court has asked "`whether, granting establishment of the primary illegality, the evidence to which instant objection is made has been come at by exploitation of that illegality or instead by means sufficiently distinguishable to be purged of the primary taint.'" Ibid. (quoting J. Maguire, Evidence of Guilt 221 (1959)). Accord, Brown v. Illinois,

422 U.S. 590, 599 (1975); Dunaway v. New York, 442 U.S. 200, 217 -218 (1979); Taylor v. Alabama, 457 U.S. 687, 690 (1982).

Because deterrence is a principal purpose of the exclusionary rule, our attenuation analysis must be driven by an understanding of how extensive exclusion must be to deter violations of the Fourth Amendment. We have long held that where police have obtained a statement after violating the Fourth Amendment, the interest in deterrence does not disappear simply because the statement was voluntary, as required by the Fifth Amendment. See, e. g., Brown, supra, at 601-602; Dunaway, supra, at 216-217; Taylor, supra, at 690. Police officers are well aware that simply because a statement is "voluntary" does not mean that it was entirely unaffected by the Fourth Amendment violation. See Brown, supra, at 601-602. Indeed, if the Fourth Amendment required exclusion only of statements taken in violation of the Fifth Amendment, the Fourth Amendment would serve no independent purpose. A regime that suppresses only some fruits of constitutional violations is a regime that barely begins to eliminate the incentives to violate the Constitution.

When faced with a statement obtained after an illegal arrest, then, a court will have occasion to engage in the attenuation inquiry only if it first determines that the statement is "voluntary," for involuntary statements are suppressible in any event. Attenuation analysis assumes that the statement is "voluntary" and asks whether the connection between the illegal police conduct and the statement nevertheless requires suppression to deter Fourth Amendment violations. That question cannot be answered with a set of per se rules. An inquiry into whether a suspect's statement is properly treated as attributable to a Fourth Amendment violation or to the suspect's independent act of will has an irreducibly psychological aspect, and irrebuttable presumptions are peculiarly unhelpful in such a context. Accordingly, we have identified several factors as relevant to the issue of attenuation: the length of time between the arrest and the statement, the presence of intervening circumstances, and the "purpose and flagrancy" of the violation. See, e. g., Brown, supra, at 603-604.

We have identified the last factor as "particularly" important. 422 U.S., at 604 . When a police officer intentionally violates what he knows to be a constitutional command, exclusion is essential to conform police behavior to the law. Such a "flagrant" violation is in marked contrast to a violation that is the product of a good-faith misunderstanding of the relevant constitutional requirements. This Court has suggested that excluding evidence that is the product of the latter variety of violation may result in deterrence of legitimate law enforcement efforts. See Leon, supra, at 918-920. Underlying this view is the theory that officers fear that if their judgment as to the constitutionality of their conduct turns out to be wrong, the consequences of their misjudgments may be too costly to justify the possible law enforcement benefits. Any doubt concerning the constitutionality of a course of action will therefore be resolved against that course of action. Whatever the truth of that theory, 1 the concern that officers who act in good faith will be overdeterred is nonexistent when, based on a cynical calculus of the likely results of a suppression hearing, an officer intentionally decides to violate what he knows to be a constitutional command.

An application of the Brown factors to this case compels the conclusion that Harris' statement at the station house must be suppressed. About an hour elapsed between the illegal arrest and Harris' confession, without any intervening factor other than the warnings required by Miranda v. Arizona, 384 U.S. 436 (1966). This Court has held, however, that "Miranda warnings, alone and per se, . . . cannot assure in every case that the Fourth Amendment violation has not been unduly exploited." Brown, supra, at 603 (citing Westover v. United States, decided with Miranda v. Arizona, supra, at 496-497). See also supra, at 22-23. Indeed, in Brown, we held that a statement made almost two hours after an illegal arrest, and after Miranda warnings had been given, was not sufficiently removed from the violation so as to dissipate the taint. 422 U.S., at 604 .

As to the flagrancy of the violation, petitioner does not dispute that the officers were aware that the Fourth Amendment prohibited them from arresting Harris in his home without a warrant. Notwithstanding the officers' knowledge that a warrant is required for a routine arrest in the home,

"the police went to defendant's apartment to arrest him and, as the police conceded, if defendant refused to talk to them there they intended to take him into custody for questioning. Nevertheless, they made no attempt to obtain a warrant although five days had elapsed between the killing and the arrest and they had developed evidence of probable cause early in their investigation. Indeed, one of the officers testified that it was departmental policy not to get warrants before making arrests in the home. From this statement a reasonable inference can be drawn . . . that the department's policy was a device used to avoid restrictions on questioning a suspect until after the police had strengthened their case with a confession. Thus, the police illegality was knowing and intentional, in the language of Brown, it `had a quality of purposefulness,' and the linkage between the illegality and the confession is clearly established." 72 N. Y. 2d 614, 622, 532 N. E. 2d 1229, 1233-1234 (1988) (citation omitted). 2

In short, the officers decided, apparently consistent with a "departmental policy," to violate Harris' Fourth Amendment rights so they could get evidence that they could not otherwise obtain. As the trial court held, "No more clear violation of [Payton], in my view, could be established." App. 20. Where, as here, there is a particularly flagrant constitutional violation and little in the way of elapsed time or intervening circumstances, the statement in the police station must be suppressed.

II

Had the Court analyzed this case as our precedents dictate that it should, I could end my discussion here - the dispute would reduce to an application of the Brown factors to the constitutional wrong and the inculpatory statement that followed. But the majority chooses no such unremarkable battleground. Instead, the Court redrafts our cases in the service of conclusions they straightforwardly and explicitly reject. Specifically, the Court finds suppression unwarranted on the authority of its newly fashioned per se rule. In the majority's view, when police officers make a warrantless home arrest in violation of Payton, their physical exit from the suspect's home necessarily breaks the causal chain between the illegality and any subsequent statement by the suspect, such that the statement is admissible regardless of the Brown factors. 3

The Court purports to defend its new rule on the basis of the self-evident proposition that the Fourth Amendment does not necessarily require the police to release or to forgo the prosecution of a suspect arrested in violation of Payton. Ante, at 18. To the Court, it follows as a matter of course from this proposition that a Payton violation cannot in any way be the "cause" of a statement obtained from the suspect after he has been forced from his home and is being lawfully detained. Because an attenuation inquiry presupposes some connection between the illegality and the statement, the Court concludes that no such inquiry is necessary here. Ante, at 18. Neither logic nor precedent supports that conclusion.

A

Certainly, the police were not required to release Harris or forgo his prosecution simply because officers arrested him in violation of Payton. But it is a dramatic leap from that unexceptionable proposition to the suggestion that the Payton violation thus had no effect once the police took Harris from his home. The Court's view to the contrary appears to rest on a cramped understanding of the purposes underlying Payton. The home is a private place, more private than any other. An invasion into the home is therefore the worst kind of invasion of privacy. An intrusion into that sanctum is an assault on the individual's solitude and on the family's communal bonds. As we said in Payton:

"The Fourth Amendment protects the individual's privacy in a variety of settings. In none is the zone of privacy more clearly defined than when bounded by the unambiguous physical dimensions of an individual's home - a zone that finds its roots in clear and specific constitutional terms: `The right of the people to be secure in their . . . houses . . . shall not be violated.' That language unequivocally establishes the proposition that `[a]t the very core [of the Fourth Amendment] stands the right of a man to retreat into his own home and there be free from unreasonable governmental intrusion.'" 445 U.S., at 589 -590 (ellipses in original) (quoting Silverman v. United States, 365 U.S. 505, 511 (1961)).

See also California v. Ciraolo, 476 U.S. 207, 212 -213 (1986) ("The protection afforded the curtilage is essentially a protection of families and personal privacy in an area intimately linked to the home, both physically and psychologically, where privacy expectations are most heightened").

The majority's per se rule in this case fails to take account of our repeated holdings that violations of privacy in the home are especially invasive. Rather, its rule is necessarily premised on the proposition that the effect of a Payton violation magically vanishes once the suspect is dragged from his home. But the concerns that make a warrantless home arrest a violation of the Fourth Amendment are nothing so evanescent. A person who is forcibly separated from his family and home in the dark of night after uniformed officers have broken down his door, handcuffed him, and forced him at gunpoint to accompany them to a police station does not suddenly breathe a sigh of relief at the moment he is dragged across his doorstep. Rather, the suspect is likely to be so frightened and rattled that he will say something incriminating. These effects, of course, extend far beyond the moment the physical occupation of the home ends. The entire focus of the Brown factors is to fix the point at which those effects are sufficiently dissipated that deterrence is not meaningfully advanced by suppression. The majority's assertion, as though the proposition were axiomatic, that the effects of such an intrusion must end when the violation ends is both undefended and indefensible. The Court's saying it may make it law, but it does not make it true.

B

The majority's reading of our cases similarly lacks foundation. In the majority's view, our attenuation cases are not concerned with the lingering taint of an illegal arrest; rather, they focus solely on whether a subsequently obtained statement is made during an illegal detention of the suspect. Ante, at 18-19 (quoting 72 N. Y. 2d, at 625, 532 N. E. 2d, at 1235 (Titone, J., concurring)). In the Court's view, if (and only if) the detention is illegal at the moment the statement is made will it be suppressed. Unlike an arrest without probable cause, a Payton violation alone does not make the subsequent detention of the suspect illegal. Thus, the Court argues, no statement made after a Payton violation has ended is suppressible by reason of the Fourth Amendment violation as long as the police have probable cause. 4

The majority's theory lacks any support in our cases. In each case presenting issues similar to those here, we have asked the same question: whether the invasion of privacy occasioned by the illegal arrest taints a statement made after the violation has ended - stated another way, whether the arrest caused the statement. See, e. g., Wong Sun, 371 U.S., at 485 -488; Brown, 422 U.S., at 591 -592, 599, 603; Dunaway, 442 U.S., at 217, 218; Taylor, 457 U.S., at 690, 694. Never before today has this Court asked whether the illegality itself was continuing at the time the evidence was secured. See Leon, 468 U.S., at 911 (WHITE, J., for the Court) ("In short, the `dissipation of the taint' concept that the Court has applied in deciding whether exclusion is appropriate in a particular case `attempts to mark the point at which the detrimental consequences of illegal police action become so attenuated that the deterrent effect of the exclusionary rule no longer justifies its cost'") (citation omitted).

Indeed, such an approach would render irrelevant the first and second of the Brown factors, which focus, respectively, on the passage of time and the existence of intervening factors between the illegality and the subsequently obtained statement. If, as the majority claims, the Brown analysis does not even apply unless the illegality is ongoing at the time the evidence is secured, no time would ever pass and no circumstance would ever intervene between the illegality and the statement.

The only Supreme Court case in which the majority even attempts to find support is United States v. Crews, 445 U.S. 463 (1980). Crews, however, is inapposite. In that case, the defendant moved to suppress a witness's in-court identification of him on the ground that he had been illegally arrested. Crews' theory was that he was the fruit of his own illegal arrest - that he himself should have been "suppressed." Because no identification of him could have been made if he were not in the courtroom, his argument proceeded, that identification had to be suppressed in turn. The Court rejected Crews' argument:

"Insofar as [Crews] challenges his own presence at trial, he cannot claim immunity from prosecution simply because his appearance in court was precipitated by an unlawful arrest. An illegal arrest, without more, has never been viewed as a bar to subsequent prosecution, nor as a defense to a valid conviction. The exclusionary principle of Wong Sun and Silverthorne Lumber Co. [v. United States, 251 U.S. 385 (1920),] delimits what proof the Government may offer against the accused at trial, closing the courtroom door to evidence secured by official lawlessness. [Crews] is not himself a suppressible `fruit,' and the illegality of his detention cannot deprive the Government of the opportunity to prove his guilt through the introduction of evidence wholly untainted by the police misconduct." 445 U.S., at 474 (citations omitted; footnote omitted; emphases added).

Seen in context, the majority's misuse of Crews is apparent. As in Wong Sun, Brown, and Taylor, Harris seeks to suppress evidence - a statement he made one hour after his arrest. He does not contend that he cannot be tried because he was arrested illegally, nor does he in any way link his demand for suppression of his statement to a claim that his presence at trial, or anywhere else, should somehow be suppressed. Crews is therefore irrelevant. The only authority the majority cites that directly supports its novel view of Brown is a concurring opinion in the New York Court of Appeals, ante, at 19, which is hardly a sufficient basis on which to reject almost 30 years of cases.

C

Perhaps the most alarming aspect of the Court's ruling is its practical consequences for the deterrence of Payton violations. Imagine a police officer who has probable cause to arrest a suspect but lacks a warrant. The officer knows if he were to break into the home to make the arrest without first securing a warrant, he would violate the Fourth Amendment and any evidence he finds in the house would be suppressed. Of course, if he does not enter the house, he will not be able to use any evidence inside the house either, for the simple reason that he will never see it. The officer also knows, though, that waiting for the suspect to leave his house before arresting him could entail a lot of waiting, and the time he would spend getting a warrant would be better spent arresting criminals. The officer could leave the scene to obtain a warrant, thus avoiding some of the delay, but that would entail giving the suspect an opportunity to flee.

More important, the officer knows that if he breaks into the house without a warrant and drags the suspect outside, the suspect, shaken by the enormous invasion of privacy he has just undergone, may say something incriminating. Before today's decision, the government would only be able to use that evidence if the Court found that the taint of the arrest had been attenuated; after the decision, the evidence will be admissible regardless of whether it was the product of the unconstitutional arrest. 5 Thus, the officer envisions the following best-case scenario if he chooses to violate the Constitution: He avoids a major expenditure of time and effort, ensures that the suspect will not escape, and procures the most damaging evidence of all, a confession. His worst-case scenario is that he will avoid a major expenditure of effort, ensure that the suspect will not escape, and will see evidence in the house (which would have remained unknown absent the constitutional violation) that cannot be used in the prosecution's case in chief. The Court thus creates powerful incentives for police officers to violate the Fourth Amendment. In the context of our constitutional rights and the sanctity of our homes, we cannot afford to presume that officers will be entirely impervious to those incentives.

I dissent.

Notes

[1] This Court has never held that an officer's good-faith misunderstanding of the law justifies the admission of unconstitutionally seized evidence except in the limited context of the officer's good-faith and objectively reasonable reliance on a facially valid warrant issued by a neutral and detached magistrate. United States v. Leon, 468 U.S. 897, 925 -926 (1984). Even in that limited context, I think that suppression is required. See id., at 928-960 (BRENNAN, J., dissenting).

[2] The "restrictions on questioning" to which the court refers are restrictions imposed by New York law. New York law provides that an arrest warrant may not issue until an "accusatory instrument" has been filed against the suspect. N. Y. Crim. Proc. Law 120.20 (McKinney 1981). The New York courts have held that police officers may not question a suspect in the absence of an attorney once such an accusatory instrument has been filed. People v. Samuels, 49 N. Y. 2d 218, 400 N. E. 2d 1344 (1980). These two rules operate to prohibit police from questioning a suspect after arresting him in his home unless his lawyer is present. If the police comply with Payton, the suspect's lawyer will likely tell him not to say anything, and the police will get nothing. On the other hand, if they violate Payton by refusing to obtain a warrant, the suspect's right to counsel will not have attached at the time of the arrest, and the police may be able to question him without interference by a lawyer. The lower court's inference that a departmental policy of violating the Fourth Amendment existed was thus fully justified.

[3] The Court has a caveat of sorts. It holds that "where the police have probable cause to arrest a suspect, the exclusionary rule does not bar the State's use of a statement made by the defendant outside of his home, even though the statement is taken after an arrest made in the home in violation of Payton." Ante, at 21 (emphasis added). But the caveat adds nothing. As the Court concedes, it is unconstitutional for the police to hold a suspect without probable cause, and any statement made during a detention for which probable cause is lacking "is unquestionably the product of [the] illegal governmental activity - i. e., the wrongful detention." Ante, at 19. (internal quotation marks omitted;

citation omitted). Thus, the Court concedes that any statement taken from a suspect who is in custody without probable cause must be suppressed, irrespective of whether there was an antecedent Payton violation.

[4] The Court assures us that it does not hold "that a statement taken by the police while a suspect is in custody is always admissible as long as the suspect is in legal custody." Ante, at 20. Rather, such statements "would of course be inadmissible if, for example, they were the product of coercion, if Miranda warnings were not given, or if there was a violation of the rule of Edwards v. Arizona, 451 U.S. 477 (1981)." Ibid. As the majority is no doubt well aware, each of these examples constitutes a violation of the Fifth Amendment. But suppressing the consequences of a violation of the Fifth Amendment does nothing to deter violations of the Fourth. See, supra, at 23. The Court's disclaimer thus only serves to reinforce the conclusion that its ruling rests on the still-undefended premise that the effects of Payton violations end at the suspect's doorstep.

[5] Indeed, if the officer, as here, works in New York State, the Court's assertion that "[i]t is doubtful therefore that the desire to secure a statement from a criminal suspect would motivate the police to violate Payton," ante, at 21, takes on a singularly ironic cast. The court below found as a matter of fact that the officers in this case had intentionally violated Payton for precisely the reason the Court identifies as "doubtful." See n. 2, supra, and accompanying text.

Undercover agents should also have to give Miranda warnings: Justice Marshall's dissent in Illinois v. Perkins (June 4, 1990)

Justice MARSHALL, dissenting.

This Court clearly and simply stated its holding in Miranda v. Arizona, 384 U. S. 436 (1966):

"[T]he prosecution may not use statements, whether exculpatory or inculpatory, stemming from custodial interrogation of the defendant unless it demonstrates the use of procedural safeguards effective to secure the privilege against self-incrimination."

Id. at 384 U. S. 444. The conditions that require the police to apprise a defendant of his constitutional rights -- custodial interrogation conducted by an agent of the police -- were present in this case. Because Lloyd Perkins received no Miranda warnings before he was subjected to custodial interrogation, his confession was not admissible.

The Court reaches the contrary conclusion by fashioning an exception to the Miranda rule that applies whenever "an undercover law enforcement officer posing as a fellow inmate . . . ask[s] questions that may elicit an incriminating response" from an incarcerated suspect. Ante at 496 U. S. 300. This exception is inconsistent with the rationale supporting Miranda, and allows police officers intentionally to take advantage of suspects unaware of their constitutional rights. I therefore dissent.

The Court does not dispute that the police officer here conducted a custodial interrogation of a criminal suspect. Perkins was incarcerated in county jail during the questioning at issue here; under these circumstances, he was in custody as that term is defined in Miranda. 384 U.S. at 384 U. S. 444; Mathis v. United States, 391 U. S. 1, 391 U. S. 4-5 (1968) (holding that defendant incarcerated on charges different from the crime about which he is questioned was in custody for purposes of Miranda). The Solicitor General argues that Perkins was not in custody for purpose of Miranda because he was familiar with the custodial environment as a result of being in jail for two days and previously spending time in prison. Brief for United States 11. Perkins' familiarity with confinement, however, does not transform his incarceration into some sort of noncustodial arrangement. Cf. Orozco v. Texas, 394 U. S. 324 (1969) (holding that suspect who had been arrested in his home and then questioned in his bedroom was in custody, notwithstanding his familiarity with the surroundings).

While Perkins was confined, an undercover police officer, with the help of a police informant, questioned him about a serious crime. Although the Court does not dispute that Perkins was interrogated, it downplays the nature of the 35-minute questioning by disingenuously referring to it as a "conversatio[n]." Ante at 496 U. S. 295-296. The officer's narration of the "conversation" at Perkins' trial, however, reveals that it clearly was an interrogation.

"[Agent:] You ever do anyone?"

"[Perkins:] Yeah, once in East St. Louis, in a rich white neighborhood."

"Informant: I didn't know they had any rich white neighborhoods in East St. Louis."

"Perkins: It wasn't in East St. Louis, it was by a race track in Fairview Heights. . . . "

"[Agent]: You did a guy in Fairview Heights?"

"Perkins: Yeah, in a rich white section where most of the houses look the same."

"[Informant]: If all the houses look the same, how did you know you had the right house?"

"Perkins: Me and two guys cased the house for about a week. I knew exactly which house, the second house on the left from the corner."

"[Agent]: How long ago did this happen?"

"Perkins: Approximately about two years ago. I got paid $5,000 for that job."

"[Agent]: How did it go down?"

"Perkins: I walked up to . . . this guy['s] house with a sawed-off under my trenchcoat."

"[Agent]: What type gun[?]"

"Perkins: A .12 gauge Remmington [sic] Automatic Model 1100 sawed-off."

App. 49-50. The police officer continued the inquiry, asking a series of questions designed to elicit specific information about the victim, the crime scene, the weapon, Perkins' motive, and his actions during and after the shooting. Id. at 50-52. This interaction was not a "conversation"; Perkins, the officer, and the informant were not equal participants in a free-ranging discussion, with each man offering his views on different topics. Rather, it was an interrogation: Perkins was subjected to express questioning likely to evoke an incriminating response.

Rhode Island v. Innis, 446 U. S. 291, 446 U. S. 300-301 (1980).

Because Perkins was interrogated by police while he was in custody, Miranda required that the officer inform him of his rights. In rejecting that conclusion, the Court finds that "conversations" between undercover agents and suspects are devoid of the coercion inherent in stationhouse interrogations conducted by law enforcement officials who openly represent the State. Ante at 496 U. S. 296. Miranda was not, however, concerned solely with police coercion. It dealt with any police tactics that may operate to compel a suspect in custody to make incriminating statements without full awareness of his constitutional rights. See Miranda, supra, 384 U.S. at 384 U. S. 468 (referring to "inherent pressures of the interrogation atmosphere"); Estelle v. Smith, 451 U. S. 454, 451 U. S. 467 (1981) ("The purpose of [the Miranda] admonitions is to combat what the Court saw as inherently compelling pressures' at work on the person and to provide him with an awareness of the Fifth Amendment privilege and the consequences of forgoing it") (quoting Miranda, 384 U.S. at 384 U. S. 467). Thus, when a law enforcement agent structures a custodial interrogation so that a suspect feels compelled to reveal incriminating information, he must inform the suspect of his constitutional rights and give him an opportunity to decide whether or not to talk.

The compulsion proscribed by Miranda includes deception by the police. See Miranda, supra, 384 U.S. at 384 U. S. 453 (indicting police tactics "to induce a confession out of trickery," such as using fictitious witnesses or false accusations); Berkemer v. McCarty, 468 U. S. 420, 468 U. S. 433 (1984) ("The purposes of the safeguards prescribed by Miranda are to ensure that the police do not coerce or trick captive suspects into confessing") (emphasis deleted, emphasis added). Cf. Moran v. Burbine, 475 U. S. 412, 475 U. S. 421 (1986) ("[T]he relinquishment of the right [protected by the Miranda warnings] must have been voluntary in the sense that it was the product of a free and deliberate choice rather than intimidation, coercion, or deception") (emphasis added). Although the Court did not find trickery by itself sufficient to constitute compulsion in Hoffa v. United States, 385 U. S. 293 (1966), the defendant in that case was not in custody. Perkins, however, was interrogated while incarcerated. As the Court has acknowledged in the Sixth Amendment context:

"[T]he mere fact of custody imposes pressures on the accused; confinement may bring into play subtle influences that will make him particularly susceptible to the ploys of undercover Government agents."

United States v. Henry, 447 U. S. 264, 447 U. S. 274 (1980). See also Massiah v. United States, 377 U. S. 201, 377 U. S. 206 (1964) (holding, in the context of the Sixth Amendment, that defendant's constitutional privilege against self-incrimination was "more seriously imposed upon . . . because he did not even know that he was under interrogation by a government agent") (citation, internal quotation marks omitted).

Custody works to the State's advantage in obtaining incriminating information. The psychological pressures inherent in confinement increase the suspect's anxiety, making him likely to seek relief by talking with others. Dix, Undercover Investigations and Police Rulemaking, 53 Texas L.Rev. 203, 230 (1975). See also Gibbs, The First Cut is the Deepest: Psychological Breakdown and Survival in the Detention Setting, in The Pains of Imprisonment 97, 107 (R. Johnson & H. Toch eds. 1982); Hagel-Seymour, Environmental Sanctuaries for Susceptible Prisoners, in The Pains of Imprisonment, supra, at 267, 279; Chicago Tribune, Apr. 15, 1990, p. D3 (prosecutors have found that prisoners often talk freely with fellow inmates). The inmate is thus more susceptible to efforts by undercover agents to elicit information from him. Similarly, where the suspect is incarcerated, the constant threat of physical danger peculiar to the prison environment may make him demonstrate his toughness to other inmates by recounting or inventing past violent acts.

"Because the suspect's ability to select people with whom he can confide is completely within their control, the police have a unique opportunity to exploit the suspect's vulnerability. In short, the police can insure that if the pressures of confinement lead the suspect to confide in anyone, it will be a police agent."

White, Police Trickery in Inducing Confessions, 127 U.Pa.L.Rev. 581, 605 (1979). In this case, the police deceptively took advantage of Perkins' psychological vulnerability by including him in a sham escape plot, a situation in which he would feel compelled to demonstrate his willingness to shoot a prison guard by revealing his past involvement in a murder. See App. 49 (agent stressed that a killing might be necessary in the escape and then asked Perkins if he had ever murdered someone).

Thus, the pressures unique to custody allow the police to use deceptive interrogation tactics to compel a suspect to make an incriminating statement. The compulsion is not eliminated by the suspect's ignorance of his interrogator's true identity. The Court therefore need not inquire past the bare facts of custody and interrogation to determine whether Miranda warnings are required.

The Court's adoption of an exception to the Miranda doctrine is incompatible with the principle, consistently applied by this Court, that the doctrine should remain simple and clear. See, e.g., Miranda, supra, 384 U.S. at 384 U. S. 441-42 (noting that one reason certiorari was granted was "to give concrete constitutional guidelines for law enforcement agencies and courts to follow"); McCarty, supra, 468 U.S. at 468 U. S. 430 (noting that one of "the principal advantages of the [Miranda] doctrine . . . is the clarity of that rule"); Arizona v. Roberson, 486 U. S. 675, 486 U. S. 680 (1988) (same). See also New York v. Quarles, 467 U. S. 649, 467 U. S. 657-658 (1984) (recognizing need for clarity in Miranda doctrine and finding that narrow "public safety" exception would not significantly lessen clarity and would be easy for police to apply). We explained the benefits of a bright-line rule in Fare v. Michael C., 442 U. S. 707 (1979):

"Miranda's holding has the virtue of informing police and prosecutors with specificity as to what they may do in conducting custodial interrogation, and of informing courts under what circumstances statements obtained during such interrogation are not admissible."

Id. at 442 U. S. 718.

The Court's holding today complicates a previously clear and straightforward doctrine. The Court opines that

"[l]aw enforcement officers will have little difficulty putting into practice our holding that undercover agents need not give Miranda warnings to incarcerated suspects."

Ante at 496 U. S. 299-300. Perhaps this prediction is true with respect to fact patterns virtually identical to the one before the Court today. But the outer boundaries of the exception created by the Court are by no means clear. Would Miranda be violated, for instance, if an undercover police officer beat a confession out of a suspect, but the suspect thought the officer was another prisoner who wanted the information for his own purposes?

Even if Miranda, as interpreted by the Court, would not permit such obviously compelled confessions, the ramifications of today's opinion are still disturbing. The exception carved out of the Miranda doctrine today may well result in a proliferation of departmental policies to encourage police officers to conduct interrogations of confined suspects through undercover agents, thereby circumventing the need to administer Miranda warnings. Indeed, if Miranda now requires a police officer to issue warnings only in those situations in which the suspect might feel compelled "to speak by the fear of reprisal for remaining silent or in the hope of more lenient treatment should he confess," ante at 496 U. S. 296-297, presumably it allows custodial interrogation by an undercover officer posing as a member of the clergy or a suspect's defense attorney. Although such abhorrent tricks would play on a suspect's need to confide in a trusted adviser, neither would cause the suspect to "think that the listeners have official power over him," ante at 496 U. S. 297. The Court's adoption of the "undercover agent" exception to the Miranda rule thus is necessarily also the adoption of a substantial loophole in our jurisprudence protecting suspects' Fifth Amendment rights.

I dissent.

* As the case comes to us, it involves only the question whether Miranda applies to the questioning of an incarcerated suspect by an undercover agent. Nothing in the Court's opinion suggests that, had respondent previously invoked his Fifth Amendment right to counsel or right to silence, his statements would be admissible. If respondent had invoked either right, the inquiry would focus on whether he subsequently waived the particular right. See Edwards v. Arizona, 451 U. S. 477 (1981); Michigan v. Mosley, 423 U. S. 96, 423 U. S. 104 (1975). As the Court made clear in Moran v. Burbine, 475 U. S. 412, 475 U. S. 421 (1986), the waiver of Miranda rights "must [be] voluntary in the sense that it [must be] the product of a free and deliberate choice rather than intimidation, coercion or deception." (Emphasis added). Since respondent was in custody on an unrelated charge when he was questioned, he may be able to challenge the admission of these

statements if he previously had invoked his Miranda rights with respect to that charge. See Arizona v. Roberson, 486 U. S. 675 (1988); Mosley, supra, 423 U.S. at 423 U. S. 104. Similarly, if respondent had been formally charged on the unrelated charge and had invoked his Sixth Amendment right to counsel, he may have a Sixth Amendment challenge to the admissibility of these statements. See Michigan v. Jackson, 475 U. S. 625, 475 U. S. 629-636 (1986). Cf. Roberson, supra, 486 U.S. at 486 U. S. 683-85.

Third Parties shouldn't be able to give consent to enter: Justice Marshall's dissent in Illinois v. Rodriguez (June 21, 1990)

Justice Marshall, with whom Justice Brennan and Justice Stevens join, dissenting.

Dorothy Jackson summoned police officers to her house to report that her daughter Gail Fischer had been beaten. Fischer told police that Ed Rodriguez, her boyfriend, was her assaulter. During an interview with Fischer, one of the officers asked if Rodriguez dealt in narcotics. Fischer did not respond. Fischer did agree, however, to the officers' request to let them into Rodriguez's apartment so that they could arrest him for battery. The police, without a warrant and despite the absence of an exigency, entered Rodriguez's home to arrest him. As a result of their entry, the police discovered narcotics that the State subsequently sought to introduce in a drug prosecution against Rodriguez.

The majority agrees with the Illinois appellate court's determination that Fischer did not have authority to consent to the officers' entry of Rodriguez's apartment. Ante, at 4. The Court holds that the warrantless entry into Rodriguez's home was nonetheless valid if the officers reasonably believed that Fischer had authority to consent. Ante, at 11. The majority's defense of this position rests on a misconception of the basis for third-party consent searches. That such searches do not give rise to claims of constitutional violations rests not on the premise that they are "reasonable" under the Fourth Amendment, see ante, at 6, but on the premise that a person may voluntarily limit his expectation of privacy by allowing others to exercise authority over his possessions. Cf. Katz v. United States, 389 U.S. 347, 351 (1967) ("What a person knowingly exposes to the public, even in his home or office, is not a subject of Fourth Amendment protection"). Thus, an individual's decision to permit another "joint access [to] or control [over the property] for most purposes," United States v. Matlock, 415 U.S. 164, 171, n.7 (1974), limits that individual's reasonable expectation of privacy and to that extent limits his Fourth Amendment protections. Cf. Rakas v. Illinois, 439 U.S. 128, 148 (1978) (because passenger in car lacked "legitimate expectation of privacy in the glove compartment," Court did not decide whether search would violate Fourth Amendment rights of someone who had such expectation). If an individual has not so limited his expectation of privacy, the police may not dispense with the safeguards established by the Fourth Amendment.

The baseline for the reasonableness of a search or seizure in the home is the presence of a warrant. Skinner v. Railway Labor Executives Assn., 489 U.S. (1989). Indeed, "searches and seizures inside a home without a warrant are presumptively unreasonable." Payton v. New York, 445 U.S. 573, 586 (1980). Exceptions to the warrant requirement must therefore serve "compelling" law enforcement goals. Mincey v. Arizona, 437 U.S. 385, 394 (1978). Because the sole law enforcement purpose underlying third-party consent searches is avoiding the inconvenience of securing a warrant, a departure from the warrant requirement is not justified simply because an officer reasonably believes a third party has consented to a search of the defendant's home. In holding otherwise, the majority ignores our longstanding view that "the informed and deliberate determinations of magistrates ... as to what searches and seizures are permissible under the Constitution are to be preferred over the hurried action of officers and others who may happen to make arrests." United States v. Lefkowitz, 285 U.S. 452, 464 (1932).

I

The Fourth Amendment provides that "[t]he right of the people to be secure in their ... houses ... shall not be violated." We have recognized that the "physical entry of the home is the chief evil against which the wording of the Fourth Amendment is directed." United States v. United States District Court, 407 U.S. 297, 313 (1972). We have further held that "a search or seizure carried out on a suspect's premises without a warrant is per se unreasonable, unless the police can show that it falls within one of a carefully defined set of exceptions." Coolidge v. New Hampshire, 403 U.S. 443, 474 (1971). Those exceptions must be crafted in light of the warrant requirement's purposes. As this Court stated in McDonald v. United States, 335 U.S. 451 (1948):

"The presence of a search warrant serves a high function. Absent some grave emergency, the Fourth Amendment has interposed a magistrate between the citizen and the police. This was done not to shield criminals nor to make the home a safe haven for illegal activities. It was done so that an objective mind might weigh the need to invade that privacy in order to enforce the law. The right of privacy was deemed too precious to entrust to the discretion of those whose job is the detection of crime and the arrest of criminals." Id., at 455-456.

The Court has tolerated departures from the warrant requirement only when an exigency makes a warrantless search imperative to the safety of the police and of the community. See, e.g., id., at 456, ("We cannot be true to that constitutional requirement and excuse the absence of a search warrant without a showing by those who seek exemption from the constitutional mandate that the exigencies of the situation made that course imperative"); Warden v. Hayden, 387 U.S. 294 (1967) (hot pursuit); Chimel v. California, 395 U.S. 752 (1969) (interest in officers' safety justifies search incident to an arrest); Michigan v. Tyler, 436 U.S. 499, 509 (1978) ("compelling need for official action and no time to secure a warrant" justifies warrantless entry of burning building). The Court has often heard, and steadfastly rejected, the invitation to carve out further exceptions to the warrant requirement for searches of the home because of the burdens on police investigation and prosecution of crime. Our rejection of such claims is not due to a lack of appreciation of the difficulty and importance of effective law enforcement, but rather to our firm commitment to "the view of those who wrote the Bill of Rights that the privacy of a person's home and property may not be totally sacrificed in the name of maximum simplicity in enforcement of the criminal law." Mincey, supra, at 393 (citing United States v. Chadwick, 433 U.S. 1, 6-11 (1977)).

In the absence of an exigency, then, warrantless home searches and seizures are unreasonable under the Fourth Amendment. The weighty constitutional interest in preventing unauthorized intrusions into the home overrides any law enforcement interest in relying on the reasonable but potentially mistaken belief that a third party has authority to consent to such a search or seizure. Indeed, as the present case illustrates, only the minimal interest in avoiding the inconvenience of obtaining a warrant weighs in on the law enforcement side.

Against this law enforcement interest in expediting arrests is "the right of a man to retreat into his own home and there be free from unreasonable governmental intrusion." Silverman v. United States, 365 U.S. 505, 511 (1961). To be sure, in some cases in which police officers reasonably rely on a third party's consent, the consent will prove valid, no intrusion will result, and the police will have been spared the inconvenience of securing a warrant. But in other cases, such as this one, the authority claimed by the third party will be false. The reasonableness of police conduct must be measured in light of the possibility that the target has not consented. Where "[n]o reason is offered for not obtaining a search warrant except the inconvenience to the officers and some slight delay necessary to prepare papers and present the evidence to a magistrate," the Constitution demands that the warrant procedure be observed. Johnson v. United States, 333 U.S. 10, 15 (1948). The concerns of expediting police work and avoiding paperwork "are never very convincing reasons and, in these circumstances, certainly are not enough to by-pass the constitutional requirement." Ibid. In this case, as in Johnson, "[n]o suspect was fleeing or likely to take flight. The search was of permanent premises, not of a movable vehicle. No evidence or contraband was threatened with removal or destruction.... If the officers in this case were excused from their constitutional duty of presenting their evidence to a magistrate, it is difficult to think of a case in which it should be required." Ibid.

Unlike searches conducted pursuant to the recognized exceptions to the warrant requirement, see supra, at 191-192, third-party consent searches are not based on an exigency and therefore serve no compelling social goal. Police officers, when faced with the choice of relying on consent by a third party or securing a warrant, should secure a warrant, and must therefore accept the risk of error should they instead choose to rely on consent.

II

Our prior cases discussing searches based on third-party consent have never suggested that such searches are "reasonable." In United States v. Matlock, this Court upheld a warrantless search conducted pursuant to the consent of a third party who was living with the defendant. The Court rejected the defendant's challenge to the search, stating that a person who permits others to have "joint access or control for most purposes ... assume[s] the risk that [such persons] might permit the common area to be searched." 415 U.S., at 171, n.7; see also Frazier v. Cupp, 394 U.S. 731, 740 (1969) (holding that defendant who left a duffel bag at another's house and allowed joint use of the bag "assumed the risk that [the person] would allow someone else to look inside"). As the Court's assumption-of-risk analysis makes clear, third-party consent limits a person's ability to challenge the reasonableness of the search only because that person voluntarily has relinquished some of his expectation of privacy by sharing access or control over his property with another person.

A search conducted pursuant to an officer's reasonable but mistaken belief that a third party had authority to consent is thus on an entirely different constitutional footing from one based on the consent of a third party who in fact has such authority. Even if the officers reasonably believed that Fischer had authority to consent, she did not, and Rodriguez's expectation of privacy was therefore undiminished. Rodriguez accordingly can challenge the warrantless intrusion into his home as a violation of the Fourth Amendment. This conclusion flows directly from Stoner v. California, 376 U.S. 483 (1964). There, the Court required the suppression of evidence seized in reliance on a hotel clerk's consent to a warrantless search of a guest's room. The Court reasoned that the guest's right to be free of unwarranted intrusion "was a right ... which only [he] could waive by word or deed, either directly or through an agent." Id., at 489. Accordingly, the Court rejected resort to "unrealistic doctrines of 'apparent authority'" as a means of upholding the search to which the guest had not consented. Id., at 488. [n.1]

III

Acknowledging that the third party in this case lacked authority to consent, the majority seeks to rely on cases suggesting that reasonable but mistaken factual judgments by police will not invalidate otherwise reasonable searches. The majority reads these cases as establishing a "general rule" that "what is generally demanded of the many factual determinations that must regularly be made by agents of the government — whether the magistrate issuing a warrant, the police officer executing a warrant, or the police officer conducting a search or seizure under one of the exceptions to the warrant requirement — is not that they always be correct, but that they always be reasonable." Ante, at 8.

The majority's assertion, however, is premised on the erroneous assumption that third-party consent searches are generally reasonable. The cases the majority cites thus provide no support for its holding. In Brinegar v. United States, 338 U.S. 160 (1949), for example, the Court confirmed the unremarkable proposition that police need only probable cause, not absolute certainty, to justify the arrest of a suspect on a highway. As Brinegar makes clear, the possibility of factual error is built into the probable cause standard, and such a standard, by its very definition, will in some cases result in the arrest of a suspect who has not actually committed a crime. Because probable cause defines the reasonableness of searches and seizures outside of the home, a search is reasonable under the Fourth Amendment whenever that standard is met, notwithstanding the possibility of "mistakes" on the part of police. Id., at 176. In contrast, our cases have already struck the balance against warrantless home intrusions in the absence of an exigency. See supra, at 191-192. Because reasonable factual errors by law enforcement officers will not validate unreasonable searches, the reasonableness of the officer's mistaken belief that the third party had authority to consent is irrelevant. [n.2]

The majority's reliance on Maryland v. Garrison, 480 U.S. 79 (1987), is also misplaced. In Garrison, the police obtained a valid warrant for the search of the "third floor apartment" of a building whose third floor in fact housed two apartments. Id., at 80. Although the police had probable cause to search only one of the apartments, they entered both apartments because "[t]he objective facts available to the officers at the time suggested no distinction between [the apartment for which they legitimately had the warrant and the entire third floor]." Id., at 88. The Court held that the officers' reasonable mistake of fact did not render the search unconstitutional. Id., at 88-89. As in Brinegar, the Court's decision was premised on the general reasonableness of the type of police action involved. Because searches based on warrants are generally reasonable, the officers' reasonable mistake of fact did not render their search "unreasonable." This reasoning is evident in the Court's conclusion that little would be gained by adopting additional burdens "over and above the bedrock requirement that, with the exceptions we have traced in our cases, the police may conduct searches only pursuant to a reasonably detailed warrant." Garrison, supra, at 89, n.14.

Garrison, like Brinegar, thus tells us nothing about the reasonableness under the Fourth Amendment of a warrantless arrest in the home based on an officer's reasonable but mistaken belief that the third party consenting to the arrest was empowered to do so. The majority's glib assertion that "[i]t would be superfluous to multiply" its citations to cases like Brinegar, Hill, and Garrison, ante, at 8, is thus correct, but for a reason entirely different than the majority suggests. Those cases provide no illumination of the issue raised in this case, and further citation to like cases would be as superfluous as the discussion on which the majority's conclusion presently depends.

IV

Our cases demonstrate that third-party consent searches are free from constitutional challenge only to the extent that they rest on consent by a party empowered to do so. The majority's conclusion to the contrary ignores the legitimate expectations of privacy on which individuals are entitled to rely. That a person who allows another joint access over his property thereby limits his expectation of privacy does not justify trampling the rights of a person who has not similarly relinquished any of his privacy expectation.

Instead of judging the validity of consent searches, as we have in the past, based on whether a defendant has in fact limited his expectation of privacy, the Court today carves out an additional exception to the warrant requirement for third-party consent searches without pausing to consider whether "'the exigencies of the situation' make the needs of law enforcement so compelling that the warrantless search is objectively reasonable under the Fourth Amendment," Mincey, 437 U.S., at 394 (citations omitted). Where this free-floating creation of "reasonable" exceptions to the warrant requirement will end, now that the Court has departed from the balancing approach that has long been part of our Fourth Amendment jurisprudence, is unclear. But by allowing a person to be subjected to a warrantless search in his home without his consent and without exigency, the majority has taken away some of the liberty that the Fourth Amendment was designed to protect.

Notes

1 The majority insists that the rationale of Stoner is "ambiguous — and perhaps deliberately so" with respect to the permissibility of third-party searches where the suspect has not conferred actual authority on the third party. Ante, at 9. Stoner itself is clear, however; today's majority manufactures the ambiguity. When the Stoner Court stated that the Fourth Amendment is to not to be eroded "by unrealistic doctrines of 'apparent authority,'" 376 U.S., at 488, and that "only the petitioner could waive by word or deed" his freedom from a warrantless search, id., at 489, the Court rejected precisely the proposition that the majority today adopts.

The majority regards Stoner's rejection of "unrealistic doctrines of 'apparent authority'" as ambiguous on the theory that the Court might have been referring only to unreasonable applications of such doctrines, and not to the doctrines themselves. Ante, at 910. But Stoner's express description of apparent authority doctrines as unrealistic cannot be viewed as mere happenstance. The Court in fact used the word "applications" in the same sentence to refer to misapplications of the actual authority doctrine: "Our decisions make clear that the rights protected by the Fourth Amendment are not to be eroded by strained applications of the law of agency or by unrealistic doctrines of 'apparent authority.'" 376 U.S., at 488 (emphasis added). The full sentence thus unambiguously confirms that Stoner rejected any reliance on apparent authority doctrines.

Nor did the Stoner Court leave open the door for a police officer to rely on a reasonable but mistaken belief in a third party's authority to consent when it remarked that "there is nothing in the record to indicate that the police had any basis whatsoever to believe that the night clerk had been authorized by the petitioner to permit the police to search the petitioner's room." Id., at 489. Stating that a defendant must "by word or deed" waive his rights, ibid., is not inconsistent with noting that, in a particular case, the absence of actual waiver is confirmed by the police's inability to identify any basis for their contention that waiver had indeed occurred.

2 The same analysis applies to Hill v. California, 401 U.S. 797 (1971), where the Court upheld a search incident to an arrest in which officers reasonably but mistakenly

believed that the person arrested in the defendant's home was the defendant. The Court refused to disturb the state court's holding that "'[w]hen the police have probable cause to arrest one party, and when they reasonably mistake a second party for the first party, then the arrest of the second party is a valid arrest.'" Id., at 802 (brackets in original) (quoting People v. Hill, 69 Cal. 2d 550, 553, 446 P. 2d 521, 523 (1968)). Given that the Court decided Hill before the extension of the warrant requirement to arrests in the home, Payton v. New York, 445 U.S. 573 (1980), Hill should be understood no less than Brinegar as simply a gloss on the meaning of "probable cause." The holding in Hill rested on the fact that the police had probable cause to believe that Hill had committed a crime. In such circumstances, the reasonableness of the arrest for which the police had probable cause was not undermined by the officers' factual mistake regarding the identity of the person arrested.

Parental notification and 48-hour delay requirements for minors for abortions unconstitutional: Justice Marshall's concurrence and dissent in Hodgson v. Minnesota (June 25, 1990)

Justice Marshall, with whom Justice Brennan and Justice Blackmun join, concurring in part, concurring in the judgment in part, and dissenting in part.

I concur in Parts I, II, IV, and VII of Justice Stevens' opinion for the Court in No.881309. [1] Although I do not believe that the Constitution permits a State to require a minor to notify or consult with a parent before obtaining an abortion, compare ante, at 24, with infra, at 312, I am in substantial agreement with the remainder of the reasoning in Part V of the Court's opinion. For the reasons stated by Justice Stevens, ante, at 2834, Minnesota's two-parent notification requirement is not even reasonably related to a legitimate state interest. Therefore, that requirement surely would not pass the strict scrutiny applicable to restrictions on a woman's fundamental right to have an abortion.

I dissent from the judgment of the Court in No.891125, however, that the judicial bypass option renders the parental notification and 48-hour delay requirements constitutional. See post, at 34 (opinion of O'Connor, J.); post, at 1721 (opinion of Kennedy, J.). The bypass procedure cannot save those requirements because the bypass itself is unconstitutional both on its face and as applied. At the very least, this scheme substantially burdens a woman's right to privacy without advancing a compelling state interest. More significantly, in some instances it usurps a young woman's control over her own body by giving either a parent or a court the power effectively to veto her decision to have an abortion.

I

This Court has consistently held since Roe v. Wade, 410 U.S. 113 (1973), that the constitutional right of privacy "is broad enough to encompass a woman's decision whether or not to terminate her pregnancy." Id., at 153. We have also repeatedly stated that "[a] woman's right to make that choice freely is fundamental." Thornburgh v. American College of Obstetricians and Gynecologists, 476 U.S. 747, 772 (1986). Accord Akron v. Akron Center for Reproductive Health, Inc., 462 U.S. 416, 420, n.1 (1983); Roe, supra, at 155. As we reiterated in American College of Obstetricians and Gynecologists, supra, "Few decisions are more personal and intimate, more properly private, or more basic to individual dignity and autonomy, than a woman's decision with the guidance of her physician and within the limits specified in Roe whether to end her pregnancy." Id., at 772. Accordingly, we have subjected state laws limiting that right to the most exacting scrutiny, requiring a State to show that such a law is narrowly drawn to serve a compelling interest. Roe, supra, at 155; Akron Center for Reproductive Health, supra, at 427. Only such strict judicial scrutiny is sufficiently protective of a woman's right to make the intensely personal decision whether to terminate her pregnancy.

Roe remains the law of the land. See Webster v. Reproductive Health Services, 492 U.S., (1989) (plurality opinion); id., at (O'Connor, J., concurring in part and concurring in judgment); id., at (Blackmun, J., concurring in part and dissenting in part). Indeed, today's decision reaffirms the vitality of Roe, as five Justices have voted to strike down a state law restricting a woman's right to have an abortion. Accordingly, to be constitutional, state restrictions on abortion must meet the rigorous test set forth above.

II

I strongly disagree with the Court's conclusion that the State may constitutionally force a minor woman either to notify both parents (or in some cases only one parent [2]) and then wait 48 hours before proceeding with an abortion, or disclose her intimate affairs to a judge and ask that he grant her permission to have an abortion. See post, at 1721 (opinion of Kennedy, J.). Cf. ante, at 2728 (opinion of Stevens, J.) (finding that requiring minor to wait 48 hours after notifying one parent reasonably furthers legitimate state interest). First, the parental notification and delay requirements significantly restrict a young woman's right to reproductive choice. I base my conclusion not on my intuition about the needs and attitudes of young women, but on a sizable and impressive collection of empirical data documenting the effects of parental notification statutes and of delaying an abortion. Second, the burdensome restrictions are not narrowly tailored to serve any compelling state interest. Finally, for the reasons discussed in Part III, infra, the judicial bypass procedure does not save the notice and delay requirements.

A

Neither the scope of a woman's privacy right nor the magnitude of a law's burden is diminished because a woman is a minor. Bellotti v. Baird, 443 U.S. 622, 642 (1979) (Bellotti II) (plurality opinion); Planned Parenthood of Central Missouri v. Danforth, 428 U.S. 52, 74 (1976). Rather, a woman's minority status affects only the nature of the State's interests. Although the Court considers the burdens that the two-parent notification requirement imposes on a minor woman's exercise of her right to privacy, ante, at 2930, and n.36, it fails to recognize that forced notification of only one parent also significantly burdens a young woman's right to have an abortion, see post, at 23 (opinion of O'Connor,

J.); post, at 1217 (opinion of Kennedy, J.). Cf. ante, at 2728 (opinion of Stevens, J.).

A substantial proportion of pregnant minors voluntarily consult with a parent regardless of the existence of a notification requirement. See, e.g., Torres, Forrest, & Eisman, Telling Parents: Clinic Policies and Adolescents' Use of Family Planning and Abortion Services, 12 Family Planning Perspectives 284, 287, 288, 290 (1980) (51% of minors discussed abortion with parents in the absence of a parental consent or notification requirement). Minors 15 years old or younger are even more likely voluntarily to discuss the abortion decision with their parents. Id., at 290 (69% of such minors voluntarily discuss abortion with parents). For these women, the notification requirement by itself does not impose a significant burden. But for those young women who would choose not to inform their parents, the burden is evident: the notification requirement destroys their right to avoid disclosure of a deeply personal matter. Cf. Whalen v. Roe, 429 U.S. 589, 599-600 (1977).

A notification requirement can also have severe physical and psychological effects on a young woman. First, forced notification of one parent, like forced notification of both parents, can be extremely traumatic for a young woman, depending on the nature of her relationship with her parents. Cf. ante, at 2930, and n.36. The disclosure of a daughter's intention to have an abortion often leads to a family crisis, characterized by severe parental anger and rejection. Osofsky & Osofsky, Teenage Pregnancy: Psychosocial Considerations, 21 Clinical Obstetrics and Gynecology 1161, 1164-1165 (1978). The impact of any notification requirement is especially devastating for minors who live in fear of physical, psychological, or sexual abuse. See, e.g., Clary, Minor Women Obtaining Abortions: A Study of Parental Notification in a Metropolitan Area, 72 American J. of Pub. Health 283, 284 (1982) (finding that many minors chose not to inform parents voluntarily because of fear of negative consequences such as physical punishment or other retaliation). See also Tr. 911 (testimony of Dr. Elissa Benedek) (stating that usually minors accurately predict parental reaction to news about daughters' pregnancies). Cf. ante, at 1718, and n.25. Certainly, child abuse is not limited to families with two parents.

Second, the prospect of having to notify a parent causes many young women to delay their abortions, thereby increasing the health risks of the procedure. See Cates, Schulz, & Grimes, The Risks Associated with Teenage Abortion, 309 New England J. of Medicine 621, 623 (1983) (finding that for women 19 years old and younger, the number of deaths per 100,000 abortions was 0.2 for the first 8 weeks of pregnancy, 0.6 for weeks 912, 3.4 for weeks 1316, and 7.8 for week 17 and after). See also H.L. v. Matheson, 450 U.S. 398, 439 (1981) (Marshall, J., dissenting). The risks posed by this delay are especially significant because adolescents already delay seeking medical care until relatively late in their pregnancies, when risks are higher. See 1 National Research Council, Risking the Future: Adolescent Sexuality, Pregnancy, and Childbearing 114 (C.Hayes ed. 1987).

In addition, a notification requirement compels many minors seeking an abortion to travel to a State without such a requirement to avoid notifying a parent. Cartoof &

Klerman, Parental Consent for Abortion: Impact of the Massachusetts Law, 76 American J. of Pub. Health 397, 399 (1986) (finding that one-third of minors seeking abortions traveled outside of State to avoid Massachusetts' parental notice requirement). Other women may resort to the horrors of self-abortion or illegal abortion rather than tell a parent. Torres, Forrest, & Eisman, supra, at 288 (9" of minors attending family planning clinics said they would have a self-induced or illegal abortion rather then tell a parent); H.L. v. Matheson, supra, at 439, and n.26 (Marshall, J., dissenting). See also Greydanus & Railsback, Abortion in Adolescence, 1 Seminars in Adolescent Medicine 213, 214 (1985) (noting 100-times greater death rate for women who obtain illegal abortions than for those who obtain legal ones). [3] Still others would forgo an abortion entirely and carry the fetus to term, Torres, Forrest, & Eisman, supra, at 289, 291 (9" of minors in family planning clinics said they would carry fetus to term rather than inform parents of decision to abort), subjecting themselves to the much greater health risks of pregnancy and childbirth and to the physical, psychological, and financial hardships of unwanted motherhood. See Greydanus & Railsback, supra, at 214 (noting that minor's overall risk of dying from childbirth is over nine times greater than risk of dying from legal abortion); Lewis, Minors' Competence to Consent to Abortion, 42 American Psychologist 84, 87 (1987) ("[P]regnancy continuation poses far greater psychological, physical, and economic risks to the adolescent than does abortion") (citation omitted). See also Bellotti II, 443 U.S., at 642 (plurality opinion) ("[C]onsidering her probable education, employment skills, financial resources, and emotional maturity, unwanted motherhood may be exceptionally burdensome for a minor"). Clearly, then, requiring notification of one parent significantly burdens a young woman's right to terminate her pregnancy.

B

The 48-hour delay after notification further aggravates the harm caused by the pre-notification delay that may flow from a minor's fear of notifying a parent. Moreover, the 48-hour delay burdens the rights of all minors, including those who would voluntarily consult with one or both parents.[4] Justice Stevens' assertion that the 48-hour delay "imposes only a minimal burden," ante, at 449; see also post, at 496 (opinion of Kennedy, J.), ignores the increased health risks and costs that this delay entails. The District Court specifically found as a matter of fact that "[d]elay of any length in performing an abortion increases the statistical risk of mortality and morbidity." 648 F.Supp. 756, 765 (Minn 1986). Even a brief delay can have a particularly detrimental impact if it pushes the abortion into the second trimester, when the operation is substantially more risky and costly. Ibid. See also C. Tietze & S. Henshaw, Induced Abortion: A World Review 1986, pp. 103-104 (6th ed. 1986) (rate of major complications nearly doubles in the week following the end of the first trimester and increases significantly thereafter). Moreover, the District Court found that the 48-hour delay "frequently is compounded by scheduling factors such as clinic hours, transportation requirements, weather, a minor's school and work commitments, and sometimes a single parent's family and work commitments," often resulting in an effective delay of a week or more. 648 F. Supp., at 765.[5] The increased risk caused by a delay of that magnitude, the District Court found, is statistically significant at any point in the pregnancy. Ibid. Certainly no pregnant woman facing these heightened risks to her health would dismiss them as "minimal."[6]

C

Because the parental notification and delay requirements burden a young woman's right freely to decide whether to terminate her pregnancy, the State must show that these requirements are justified by a compelling state interest and are closely tailored to further that interest. The main purpose of the notification requirement is to "protect the well-being of minors by encouraging minors to discuss with their parents the decision whether to terminate their pregnancies" Id., at 766. The 48-hour delay, in turn, is designed to provide parents with adequate time to consult with their daughters. Ante, at 27 (opinion of Stevens, J.); post, at 17 (opinion of Kennedy, J.). As Justice Stevens states, such consultation is intended to ensure that the minor's decision is "knowing and intelligent." Ante, at 27. I need not determine whether the State's interest ultimately outweighs young women's privacy interests, however, because the strictures here are not closely tailored to further the State's asserted goal.

For the many young women who would voluntarily consult with a parent before having an abortion, see supra, at 4, the notification and delay requirements are superfluous, and so do not advance the State's interest. The requirements affect only those women who would not otherwise notify a parent. But compelled notification is unlikely to result in productive consultation in families in which a daughter does not feel comfortable consulting her parents about intimate or sexual matters. See Melton, Legal Regulation of Adolescent Abortion: Unintended Effects, 42 American Psychologist 79, 81 (1987) (stating that in many families, compelled parental notification is unlikely to result in meaningful discussion about the daughter's predicament); Tr. 13571358 (testimony of Dr. Steven Butzer) (stating that involuntary disclosure is disruptive to family and has "almost universally negative" effects, in accord with minor's expectations). Moreover, in those families with a history of child abuse, a pregnant minor forced to notify a parent is more likely to be greeted by physical assault or psychological harrassment than open and caring conversation about her predicament. See Tr. 316 (testimony of Dr. Lenore Walker) (stating that forced notification in dysfunctional families is likely to sever communication patterns and increase the risk of violence); H.L. v. Matheson, 450 U.S., at 446 (Marshall, J., dissenting). Forced notification in such situations would amount to punishing the daughter for the lack of a stable and communicative family environment, when the blame for that situation lies principally, if not entirely, with the parents. Parental notification in the less-than-ideal family, therefore, would not lead to an informed decision by the minor. [7]

The State also claims that the statute serves the interest of protecting parents' independent right "to shape the[ir] child[ren]'s values and lifestyle[s]" and "to determine and strive for what they believe to be best for their children." Brief for Petitioners in No.881309, p.26. If this is so, the statute is surely underinclusive, as it does not require parental notification where the minor seeks medical treatment for pregnancy, venereal disease, or alcohol and other drug abuse. See Minn. Stat. 144.343(1) (1988). Are we to believe that Minnesota parents have no interest in their children's well-being in these other contexts?

In any event, parents' right to direct their children's upbringing is a right against state interference with family matters. See, e.g., Prince v. Massachusetts, 321 U.S. 158, 166 (1944) (noting that this Court's decisions "have respected the private realm of family life which the state cannot enter"). See also Wisconsin v. Yoder, 406 U.S. 205, 232 (1972); Pierce v. Society of Sisters, 268 U.S. 510, 534535 (1925). Yet, ironically, the State's requirements here affirmatively interfere in family life by trying to force families to conform to the State's archetype of the ideal family. Cf. Moore v. East Cleveland, 431 U.S. 494, 506 (1977) ("[T]he Constitution prevents [the state] from standardizing its children and its adults by forcing all to live in certain narrowly defined family patterns"); ante, at 31. It is a strange constitutional alchemy that would transform a limitation on state power into a justification for governmental intrusion into family interactions. Moreover, as a practical matter, "state intervention is hardly likely to resurrect parental authority that the parents themselves are unable to preserve." H.L. v. Matheson, supra, at 448 (Marshall, J., dissenting). See also Planned Parenthood of Central Mo., 428 U.S., at 75 (finding it unlikely that parental veto power over abortion "will enhance parental authority or control where the minor and the nonconsenting parent are so fundamentally in conflict and the very existence of the pregnancy already has fractured the family structure").

Even if the State's interest is construed as merely the facilitation of the exercise of parental authority, the notification and delay requirements are not narrowly drawn. Parental authority is not limitless. Certainly where parental involvement threatens to harm the child, the parent's authority must yield. Prince v. Massachusetts, supra, at 169 170; H.L. v. Matheson, supra, at 449 (Marshall, J., dissenting). Yet the notification and delay requirements facilitate the exercise of parental authority even where it may physically or psychologically harm the child. See supra, at 910.

Furthermore, the exercise of parental authority in some instances will take the form of obstructing the minor's decision to have an abortion. A parent who objects to the abortion, once notified, can exert strong pressure on the minor in the form of stern disapproval, withdrawal of financial support, or physical or emotional abuse to block her from getting an abortion. See Bellotti II, 443 U.S., at 647 (plurality opinion) ("[M]any parents hold strong views on the subject of abortion, and young pregnant minors, especially those living at home, are particularly vulnerable to their parents' efforts to obstruct ... an abortion"). See also H.L. v. Matheson, 450 U.S., at 438439 (Marshall, J., dissenting). In such circumstances, the notification requirement becomes, in effect, a consent requirement. As discussed below, infra, at 13, the State may not permit any person, including a parent, to veto a woman's decision to terminate her pregnancy. Because the notification and delay requirements effectively give parents the opportunity to exercise an unconstitutional veto in some situations, those requirements are not narrowly tailored to the State's interest in facilitating legitimate exercises of parental authority.

III

The parental notification and 48-hour delay requirements, then, do not satisfy the strict scrutiny applicable to laws restricting a woman's constitutional right to have an abortion. The judicial bypass procedure cannot salvage those requirements because that procedure itself is unconstitutional.

A

The State argues that the bypass procedure saves the notification and delay requirements because it provides an alternative way to obtain a legal abortion for minors who would be harmed by those requirements. This Court has upheld a one-parent consent requirement where the State provided an alternative judicial procedure "'whereby a pregnant minor [could] demonstrate that she [was] sufficiently mature to make the abortion decision herself or that, despite her immaturity, an abortion would be in her best interests.'" Planned Parenthood Assn. of Kansas City, Inc. v. Ashcroft, 462 U.S. 476, 491 (1983) (opinion of Powell, J.) (quoting Akron Center for Reproductive Health, 462 U.S., at 439-440).

I continue to believe, however, that a judicial bypass procedure of this sort is itself unconstitutional because it effectively gives a judge "an absolute veto over the decision of the physician and his patient." Planned Parenthood Assn. of Kansas City, supra, at 504 (Blackmun, J., concurring in part and dissenting in part); see also Bellotti II, 443 U.S., at 655 (Stevens, J., concurring in judgment) ("The provision of an absolute veto to a judge ... is to me particularly troubling. ... It is inherent in the right to make the abortion decision that the right may be exercised without public scrutiny and in defiance of the contrary opinion of the sovereign or other third parties") (footnote omitted); Planned Parenthood of Central Mo., supra, at 74 ("[T]he State does not have the constitutional authority to give a third party an absolute, and possibly arbitrary, veto over the decision of the physician and his patient to terminate the patient's pregnancy, regardless of the reason for withholding the consent"). No person may veto any minor's decision, made in consultation with her physician, to terminate her pregnancy. An "immature" minor has no less right to make decisions regarding her own body than a mature adult.

Minnesota's bypass provision allows a judge to authorize an abortion if he determines either that a woman is sufficiently mature to make the decision on her own or, if she is not sufficiently mature, that an abortion without parental notification would serve her best interests. Minn. Stat. 144.343(6) (1988). Of course, if a judge refuses to authorize an abortion, a young woman can then reevaluate whether she wants to notify a parent. But many women will carry the fetus to term rather than notify a parent. See supra, at 6. Other women may decide to inform a parent but then confront parental pressure or abuse so severe as to obstruct the abortion. For these women, the judge's refusal to authorize an abortion effectively constitutes an absolute veto.

The constitutional defects in any provision allowing someone to veto a woman's abortion decision are exacerbated by the vagueness of the standards contained in this statute. The statute gives no guidance on how a judge is to determine whether a minor is sufficiently "mature" and "capable" to make the decision on her own. See Minn. Stat. 144.343(6)(c)(i) (1988) (judge shall authorize abortion if he "determines that the pregnant woman is mature and capable of giving informed consent to the proposed abortion"). Cf. Lewis, 42 American Psychologist, at 84, 87 (noting the absence of a judicial standard for assessing maturity). The statute similarly is silent as to how a judge is to determine whether an abortion without parental notification would serve an immature minor's "best interests." 144.343(6)(c)(i) (judge shall authorize abortion for immature minor without notification "if said judge concludes that the pregnant woman's best interests would be served thereby"). Is the judge expected to know more about the woman's medical needs or psychological makeup than her doctor? Should he consider the woman's financial and emotional status to determine the quality of life the woman and her future child would enjoy in this world? Neither the record nor the Court answers such questions. As Justice Stevens wrote in Bellotti II, the best interest standard "provides little real guidance to the judge, and his decision must necessarily reflect personal and societal values and mores whose enforcement upon the minor particularly when contrary to her own informed and reasonable decision is fundamentally at odds with privacy interests underlying the constitutional protection afforded to her decision." 443 U.S., at 655656 (Stevens, J., concurring in judgment). It is difficult to conceive of any reason, aside from a judge's personal opposition to abortion, that would justify a finding that an immature woman's best interests would be served by forcing her to endure pregnancy and childbirth against her will.

B

Even if I did not believe that a judicial bypass procedure was facially unconstitutional, the experience of Minnesota's procedure in operation demonstrates that the bypass provision before us cannot save the parental notification and delay requirements. This Court has addressed judicial bypass procedures only in the context of facial challenges. See Planned Parenthood Assn. of Kansas City, 462 U.S., at 490-493 (opinion of Powell, J.); Akron Center for Reproductive Health, 462 U.S., at 439-442; Bellotti II, 443 U.S., at 643-644 (plurality opinion). The Court has never considered the actual burdens a particular bypass provision imposes on a woman's right to choose an abortion. Such consideration establishes that, even if judges authorized every abortion sought by petitioning minors, Minnesota's judicial bypass is far too burdensome to remedy an otherwise unconstitutional statute.

The District Court found that the bypass procedure imposed significant burdens on minors. First, "scheduling practices in Minnesota courts typically require minors to wait two or three days between their first contact with the court and the hearing on their petitions. This delay may combine with other factors to result in a delay of a week or more. 648 F.Supp., at 763. As noted above, supra, at 467-468, a delay of only a few days can significantly increase the health risks to the minor; a week-long delay inevitably does. Furthermore, in several counties in Minnesota, no judge is willing to hear bypass petitions, forcing women in those areas to travel long distances to obtain a hearing. 648 F.Supp., at 763; Donovan, Judging Teenagers: How Minors Fare When They Seek Court-Authorized Abortions, 15 Family Planning Perspectives 259, 264 (1983) (50% of Minnesota minors utilizing bypass were not residents of city in which court was located); Melton, 42 American Psychologist, at 80 ("In Minnesota, where judges in rural counties have often recused themselves from participation in the abortion hearings, minors sometimes have to travel a round-trip of more than 500 miles for the hearing"). The burden of such travel, often requiring an overnight stay in a distant city, is particularly heavy for poor women from rural areas. Furthermore, a young woman's absence from home, school, or work during the time required for such travel and for the hearing itself can jeopardize the woman's confidentiality. See ibid.

The District Court also found that the bypass procedure can be extremely traumatic for young women.

"The experience of going to court for a judicial authorization produces fear and tension in many minors. Minors are apprehensive about the prospect of facing an authority figure who holds in his hands the power to veto their decision to proceed without notifying one or both parents. Many minors are angry and resentful at being required to justify their decision before complete strangers. Despite the confidentiality of the proceeding, many minors resent having to reveal intimate details of their personal and family lives to these strangers. Finally, many minors are left feeling guilty and ashamed about their lifestyle and their decision to terminate their pregnancy. Some mature minors and some minors in whose best interests it is to proceed without notifying their parents are so daunted by the judicial proceeding that they forego the bypass option and either notify their parents or carry to term.

"Some minors are so upset by the bypass proceeding that they consider it more difficult than the medical procedure itself. Indeed the anxiety resulting from the bypass proceeding may linger until the time of the medical procedure and thus render the latter more difficult than necessary." 648 F. Supp., at 763764. [8]

Yet, despite the substantial burdens imposed by these proceedings, the bypass is, in effect, a "rubber stamp," id., at 766 (testimony of Honorable William Sweeney); only an extremely small number of petitions are denied, id., at 765. See also Melton, supra, at 80 ("Available research indicates that judicial bypass proceedings are merely pro forma. Although they represent substantial intrusion on minors' privacy and take up significant amounts of court time, there is no evidence that they promote more reasoned decision making or screen out adolescents who may be particularly immature or vulnerable. ... The hearings typically last less than 15 minutes. ... Despite the complex issues involved (maturity and the best interests of the minor), experts are rarely if ever called to testify"). The judges who have adjudicated over 90% of the bypass petitions between 1981 and

1986 could not identify any positive effects of the bypass procedure. See 648 F. Supp., at 766; ante, at 20, and n.29. The large number of women who undergo the bypass process do not receive any sort of counseling from the court which is not surprising, given the court's limited role and lack of expertise in that area. The bypass process itself thus cannot serve the state interest of promoting informed decisionmaking by all minors. If the State truly were concerned about ensuring that all minors consult with a knowledgeable and caring adult, it would provide for some form of counseling rather than for a judicial procedure in which a judge merely gives or withholds his consent. [9]

Thus, regardless of one's view of the facial validity of a bypass procedure, Minnesota's procedure in practice imposes an excessive burden on young women's right to choose an abortion. Cf. Bellotti II, 443 U.S., at 655 (Stevens, J., concurring in judgment) ("[T]he need to commence judicial proceedings in order to obtain a legal abortion would impose a burden at least as great as, and probably greater than, that imposed on the minor child by the need to obtain the consent of a parent"). Furthermore, the process does not serve the State's interest of ensuring that minors' decisions are informed. Surely, then, a State could not require that all minor women seeking an abortion obtain judicial approval. [10] The Court's holding that the burdensome bypass procedure saves the State's burdensome notification and delay requirements thus strikes me as the equivalent of saying that two wrongs make a right. I cannot accept such a novel judicial calculus.

IV

A majority of the Court today strikes down an unreasonable and vastly overbroad requirement that a pregnant minor notify both her parents of her decision to obtain an abortion. With that decision I agree. At the same time, though, a different majority holds that a State may require a young woman to notify one or even both parents and then wait 48 hours before having an abortion, as long as the State provides a judicial bypass procedure. From that decision I vehemently dissent. This scheme forces a young woman in an already dire situation to choose between two fundamentally unacceptable alternatives: notifying a possibly dictatorial or even abusive parent and justifying her profoundly personal decision in an intimidating judicial proceeding to a black-robed stranger. For such a woman, this dilemma is more likely to result in trauma and pain than in an informed and voluntary decision.

Notes

1 I concur in Part VII on the understanding that the opinion does not dispute that a minor's liberty interest alone outweighs the interest of the second parent in shaping a child's values and lifestyles, regardless of the interest of the first parent. Cf. ante, at 3132.

2 The statute provides for one-parent notification where only one parent is living or where the second parent "cannot be located through reasonably diligent effort." Minn. Stat. 144.343(3) (1988).

3 Dr. Jane Hodgson testified before the District Court that one 14-year-old patient, in order to keep her pregnancy private, tried to induce an abortion with the help of her friends by inserting a metallic object into her vagina, thereby tearing her body, scarring her cervix, and causing bleeding. When that attempt failed to induce an abortion, the patient, then four or five months pregnant, finally went to an abortion clinic. Because of the damage to the patient's cervix, doctors had to perform a hysterotomy, meaning that that woman must have a Cesarean section to deliver a child in the future. App. 462.

4 As Justice Stevens notes, ante, at 449, the 48-hour delay does not apply if a parent or court consents to the abortion.

5 Although these other factors would constrain a young woman's ability to schedule an abortion even in the absence of the 48-hour delay requirement, the addition of the immutable statutory delay reduces both the woman's and the clinic's scheduling flexibility, and thus can exacerbate the effect of the other factors. For instance, a woman might contact a clinic on Monday and find that her schedule and the clinic's allow for only a Tuesday appointment for that week. Without the 48-hour delay requirement, the woman could be treated the next day; with the statutory delay, however, the woman would be forced to wait a week.

6 Justice Stevens concludes that the 48-hour delay requirement actually results in "little or no delay," because the statutory period "may run concurrently with the time necessary to make an appointment for the procedure." Ante, at 449. See also post, at 496 (opinion of Kennedy, J.) ("48-hour waiting period . . . results in little or no delay"); 853 F.2d 1452, 1465 (CA8 1988) (en banc). Justice Stevens bases this conclusion on the testimony of the co-administrator of one abortion clinic that a 1 or 2-day scheduling backlog was typical. Ante, at 449, n. 34. "One or two days" however, obviously means that the backlog is not necessarily 48 hours. Furthermore, that witness also stated that if "a woman says that she must be seen on a particular day, our policy is we will always see her." App. 147. But because of the mandated 48-hour delay, the clinic cannot honor a woman's request for an abortion until at least two full days have elapsed. The testimony therefore is hardly sufficient to justify ignoring the District Court's factual finding with regard to the effects of the delay requirement.

7 The State also asserts that the requirements permit parents to provide doctors with relevant information about their daughters' medical history and "to assist with ensuring that proper after-care procedures are followed." Brief of Petitioners in No.881309, pp.3436. See also ante, at 27 (opinion of Justice Stevens) (delay period "permits the parent to inquire into the competency of the doctor performing the abortion"). If these are actual state interests, it seems peculiar that the State does not try to facilitate similar parental involvement in minors' treatment for pregnancy and childbirth, see infra, at 10, which pose far greater risks to the minor's health than abortion, see supra, at 67. In any event, compelled notification is unlikely to result in helpful parental involvement in those families in which a parent reacts to the news of the daughter's predicament by rejecting or abusing the young woman. See supra, at 9.

8 Dr. Hodgson testified that some minors dread the court procedure so much that they become "wringing wet with perspiration" and frequently require a sedative beforehand. App. 468. One judge who has heard a significant number of bypass petitions testified that the court experience is "'very nervewracking'" for young women. 648 F. Supp., at 766. Another testified that pregnant minors' "'level of apprehension is twice what I normally see in court. ... You see all the typical things that you would see with somebody under incredible amounts of stress, answering monosyllabically, tone of voice, tenor of voice, shaky, wringing of hands, you know, one young lady had her hands were turning blue and it was warm in my office.'" Ibid.

9 Maine, for example, requires that a minor obtain the consent of a parent, guardian, or adult family member; undergo a judicial bypass; or receive counseling from the physician or a counselor according to specified criteria. See Me. Rev. Stat. Ann., Tit. 22, 1597A (Supp. 1989). Wisconsin requires abortion providers to encourage parental notification unless they determine that the minor has a valid reason for not notifying her parents. Wisc. Stat. 146.78 (19871988). In the latter situation, the provider must encourage but not require the minor to notify "another family member, close family friend, school counselor, social worker or other appropriate person." 146.78(5)(c). I express no opinion on the constitutionality or efficacy of these schemes, but raise them only as examples of alternatives that seem more closely related than a judicial bypass procedure to the goal of ensuring that the minor's decision is informed.

In any event, most abortion clinics already provide extensive counseling. See 1 National Research Council, Risking the Future: Adolescent Sexuality, Pregnancy, and Childbearing 191192 (C. Hayes ed. 1987) (90" of abortion clinics routinely provide counseling for all first-abortion patients, and all clinics make counseling available to all patients on request).

10 Indeed, the State conceded in oral argument before the Eighth Circuit, sitting en banc, that a judicial approval provision by itself would be unconstitutional. See 853 F. 2d, at 1469 (Lay, C.J., dissenting).

This cuts back on the principles that inform our selective-taxation precedents: Justice Marshall's dissent in Leathers v. Medlock (April 16, 1991)

Justice Marshall, with whom Justice Blackmun joins, dissenting.

This Court has long recognized that the freedom of the press prohibits government from using the tax power to discriminate against individual members of the media or against the media as a whole. See Grosjean v. American Press Co., 297 U.S. 233 (1936); Minneapolis Star & Tribune Co. v. Minnesota Comm'r of Revenue, 460 U.S. 575 (1983); Arkansas Writers' Project, Inc. v. Ragland, 481 U.S. 221 (1987). The Framers of the First Amendment, we have explained, specifically intended to prevent government from using disparate tax burdens to impair the untrammeled dissemination of information. We granted certiorari in this case to consider whether the obligation not to discriminate against individual members of the press prohibits the State from taxing one information medium — cable television — more heavily than others. The majority's answer to this question — that the State is free to discriminate between otherwise likesituated media so long as the more heavily taxed medium is not too "small" in number — is no answer at all, for it fails to explain which media actors are entitled to equal tax treatment. Indeed, the majority so adamantly proclaims the irrelevance of this problem that its analysis calls into question whether any general obligation to treat media actors evenhandedly survives today's decision. Because I believe the majority has unwisely cut back on the principles that inform our selective-taxation precedents, and because I believe that the First Amendment prohibits the State from singling out a particular information medium for heavier tax burdens than are borne by like-situated media, I dissent.

I

A

Our decisions on selective taxation establish a nondiscrimination principle for like-situated members of the press. Under this principle, "differential treatment, unless justified by some special characteristic of the press, . . . is presumptively unconstitutional," and must be struck down "unless the State asserts a counterbalancing interest of compelling importance that it cannot achieve without differential taxation." Minneapolis Star, supra, at 585.

The nondiscrimination principle is an instance of government's general First Amendment obligation not to interfere with the press as an institution. As the Court explained in Grosjean, the purpose of the Free Press Clause "was to preserve an untrammeled press as a vital source of public information." 297 U. S., at 250. Reviewing both the historical abuses associated with England's infamous " `taxes on knowledge' " and the debates surrounding ratification of the Constitution, see id., at 246-250; Minneapolis Star, 460 U. S., at 583-586, and nn. 6-7, our decisions have recognized that the Framers viewed selective taxation as a distinctively potent "means of abridging the freedom of the press," id., at 586, n. 7.

We previously have applied the nondiscrimination principle in two contexts. First, we have held that this principle prohibits the State from imposing on the media tax burdens not borne by like-situated nonmedia enterprises. Thus, in Minneapolis Star, we struck down a use tax that applied to the ink and paper used in newspaper production but not to any other item used as a component of a good to be sold at retail. See id., at 578, 581-582. Second, we have held that the nondiscrimination principle prohibits the State from taxing individual members of the press unequally. Thus, as an alternative ground in Minneapolis Star, we concluded that the State's use tax violated the First Amendment because it exempted the first $100,000 worth of ink and paper consumed and thus effectively singled out large publishers for a disproportionate tax burden. See id., at 591-592. Similarly, in Arkansas Writers' Project, we concluded that selective exemptions for certain periodicals rendered unconstitutional the application of a general sales tax to the remaining periodicals "because [the tax] [was] not evenly applied to all magazines." See 481 U. S., at 229 (emphasis added); see also Grosjean v. American Press Co., supra (tax applied only to newspapers that meet circulation threshold unconstitutionally discriminates against more widely circulated newspapers).

Before today, however, we had not addressed whether the nondiscrimination principle prohibits the State from singling out a particular information medium for tax burdens not borne by other media. Grosjean and Minneapolis Star both invalidated tax schemes that discriminated between different members of a single medium, namely, newspapers. Similarly, Arkansas Writers' Project invalidated a general sales tax because it "treat[ed] some magazines less favorably than others," 481 U. S., at 229, leaving open the question whether less favorable tax treatment of magazines than of newspapers furnished an additional ground for invalidating the scheme, see id., at 233. This case squarely presents the question whether the State may discriminate between distinct information media, for under Arkansas' general sales tax scheme, cable operators pay a sales tax on their subscription fees that is not paid by newspaper or magazine companies on their subscription fees or by television or radio broadcasters on their advertising revenues. [n.1] In my view, the principles that animate our selective-taxation cases clearly condemn this form of discrimination.

B

Although cable television transmits information by distinctive means, the information service provided by cable does not differ significantly from the information services provided by Arkansas' newspapers, magazines, television broadcasters, and radio stations. This Court has recognized that cable operators exercise the same core press function of "communication of ideas as do the traditional enterprises of newspaper and book publishers, public speakers, and pamphleteers," Los Angeles v. Preferred Communications, Inc., 476 U.S. 488, 494 (1986), and that "[c]able operators now share with broadcasters a significant amount of editorial discretion regarding what their programming will include," FCC v. Midwest Video Corp., 440 U.S. 689, 707 (1979). See also ante, at 4 (acknowledging that cable television is "part of the `press' "). In addition, the cable-service providers in this case put on extensive and unrebutted proof at trial designed to show that consumers regard the news, sports, and entertainment features provided by cable as largely interchangeable with the services provided by other members of the print and electronic media. See App. 81-85, 100-101, 108, 115, 133-137, 165-170. See generally Competition, Rate Deregulation and the Commission's Policies Relating to Provision of Cable Television Service, 5 FCC Record 4962, 4967 (1990) (discussing competition between cable and other forms of television).

Because cable competes with members of the print and electronic media in the larger information market, the power to discriminate between these media triggers the central concern underlying the nondiscrimination principle: the risk of covert censorship. The nondiscrimination principle protects the press from censorship prophylactically, condemning any selective-taxation scheme that presents the "potential for abuse" by the State, Minneapolis Star, 460 U. S., at 592 (emphasis added), independent of any actual "evidence of an improper censorial motive," Arkansas Writers' Project, supra, at 228; see Minneapolis Star, supra, at 592 ("Illicit legislative intent is not the sine qua non of a violation of the First Amendment"). The power to discriminate among likesituated media presents such a risk. By imposing tax burdens that disadvantage one information medium relative to another, the State can favor those media that it likes and punish those that it dislikes.

Inflicting a competitive disadvantage on a disfavored medium violates the First Amendment "command that the government . . . shall not impede the free flow of ideas." Associated Press v. United States, 326 U.S. 1, 20 (1945). We have previously recognized that differential taxation within an information medium distorts the marketplace of ideas by imposing on some speakers costs not borne by their competitors. See Grosjean, 297 U. S., at 241, 244-245 (noting competitive disadvantage arising from differential tax based on newspaper circulation). Differential taxation across different media likewise "limit[s] the circulation of information to which the public is entitled," id., at 250, where, as here, the relevant media compete in the same information market. By taxing cable television more heavily relative to its social cost than newspapers, magazines, broadcast television and radio, Arkansas distorts consumer preferences for particular information formats, and thereby impairs "the widest possible dissemination of information from diverse and antagonistic sources." Associated Press v. United States, supra, at 20.

Because the power selectively to tax cable operators triggers the concerns that underlie the nondiscrimination principle, the State bears the burden of demonstrating that "differential treatment" of cable television is justified by some "special characteristic" of that particular information medium or by some other "counterbalancing interest of compelling importance that [the State] cannot achieve without differential taxation." Minneapolis Star, supra, at 585 (footnote omitted). The State has failed to make such a showing in this case. As the Arkansas Supreme Court found, the amount collected from the cable operators pursuant to the state sales tax does not correspond to any social cost peculiar to cabletelevision service, see 301 Ark. 483, 485, 785 S. W. 2d 202, 203 (1990); indeed, cable operators in Arkansas must pay a franchise fee expressly designed to defray the cost associated with cable's unique exploitation of public rights of way. See ibid. The only justification that the State asserts for taxing cable operators more heavily than newspapers, magazines, television broadcasters and radio stations is its interest in raising revenue. See Brief for Respondents in No. 90-38, p. 9. This interest is not sufficiently compelling to overcome the presumption of unconstitutionality under the nondiscrimination principle. See Arkansas Writers' Project, 481 U. S., at 231-232; Minneapolis Star, supra, at 586. [n.2]

II

The majority is undisturbed by Arkansas' discriminatory tax regime. According to the majority, the power to single out cable for heavier tax burdens presents no realistic threat of governmental abuse. The majority also dismisses the notion that the State has any general obligation to treat members of the press evenhandedly. Neither of these conclusions is supportable.

A

The majority dismisses the risk of governmental abuse under the Arkansas tax scheme on the ground that the number of media actors exposed to the tax is "large." Ante, at 9. According to the majority, where a tax is generally applicable to nonmedia enterprises, the selective application of that tax to different segments of the media offends the First Amendment only if the tax is limited to "a small number of speakers," ante, at 8, for it is only under those circumstances that selective taxation "resembles a penalty for particular speakers or particular ideas," ante, at 9. The selective sales tax at issue in Arkansas Writers' Project, the majority points out, applied to no more than three magazines. See ante, at 8. The tax at issue here, "[i]n contrast," applies "uniformly to the approximately 100 cable systems" in operation in Arkansas. Ibid. (emphasis added). In my view, this analysis is overly simplistic and is unresponsive to the concerns that inform our selective-taxation precedents.

To start, the majority's approach provides no meaningful guidance on the intermedia scope of the nondiscrimination principle. From the majority's discussion, we can infer that three is a sufficiently "small" number of affected actors to trigger First Amendment problems and that one hundred is too "large" to do so. But the majority fails to pinpoint the magic number between three and one hundred actors above which discriminatory taxation can be accomplished with impunity. Would the result in this case be different if Arkansas had only 50 cable-service providers? Or 25? The suggestion that the First Amendment prohibits selective taxation that "resembles a penalty" is no more helpful. A test that turns on whether a selective tax "penalizes" a particular medium presupposes some baseline establishing that medium's entitlement to equality of treatment with other media. The majority never develops any theory of the State's obligation to treat like-situated media equally, except to say that the State must avoid discriminating against too "small" a number of media actors.

In addition, the majority's focus on absolute numbers fails to reflect the concerns that inform the nondiscrimination principle. The theory underlying the majority's "small versus large" test is that "a tax on the services provided by a large number of cable operators offering a wide variety of programming throughout the State," ante, at 9, poses no "risk of affecting only a limited range of views," ante, at 8. This assumption is unfounded. The record in this case furnishes ample support for the conclusion that the State's cable operators make unique contributions to the information market. See, e. g., App. 82 (testimony of cable operator that he offers "certain religious programming" that "people demand . . . because they otherwise could not have access to it"); id., at 138 (cable offers Spanish-language information network); id., at 150 (cable broadcast of local city council meetings). The majority offers no reason to believe that programs like these are duplicated by other media. Thus, to the extent that selective taxation makes it harder for

Arkansas' 100 cable operators to compete with Arkansas' 500 newspapers, magazines, and broadcast television and radio stations, see 1 Gale Directory of Publications and Broadcast Media 67-68 (123d ed. 1991), Arkansas' discriminatory tax does "risk . . . affecting only a limited range of views," and may well "distort the market for ideas" in a manner akin to direct "content-based regulation." Ante, at 8. [n.3]

The majority also mistakenly assesses the impact of Arkansas' discriminatory tax as if the State's 100 cable operators comprised 100 additional actors in a statewide information market. In fact, most communities are serviced by only a single cable operator. See generally 1 Gale Directory, supra, at 69-91. Thus, in any given locale, Arkansas' discriminatory tax may disadvantage a single actor, a "small" number even under the majority's calculus.

Even more important, the majority's focus on absolute numbers ignores the potential for abuse inherent in the State's power to discriminate based on medium identity. So long as the disproportionately taxed medium is sufficiently "large," nothing in the majority's test prevents the State from singling out a particular medium for higher taxes, either because the State does not like the character of the services that the medium provides or because the State simply wishes to confer an advantage upon the medium's competitors.

Indeed, the facts of this case highlight the potential for governmental abuse inherent in the power to discriminate among like-situated media based on their identities. Before this litigation began, most receipts generated by the media — including newspaper sales, certain magazine subscription fees, print and electronic media advertising revenues, and cable television and scrambled-satellite television subscription fees — were either expressly exempted from, or not expressly included in, the Arkansas sales tax. See Ark. Code. Ann. 84-1903, 84-1904(f), (j), (1947 and Supp. 1985); see also Arkansas Writers' Project, 481 U. S., at 224-225. Effective July 1, 1987, however, the legislature expanded the tax base to include cable television subscription fees. See App. to Pet. for Cert. in No. 90-38, p. 16a. Cable operators then filed this suit, protesting the discriminatory treatment in general and the absence of any tax on scrambled-satellite television — cable's closest rival — in particular. While the case was pending on appeal to the Arkansas Supreme Court, the Arkansas legislature again amended the sales tax, this time extending the tax to the subscription fees paid for scrambled satellite television. 301 Ark., at 484, 785 S. W. 2d, at 203. Of course, for all we know, the legislature's initial decision selectively to tax cable may have been prompted by a similar plea from traditional broadcast media to curtail competition from the emerging cable industry. If the legislature did indeed respond to such importunings, the tax would implicate government censorship as surely as if the government itself disapproved of the new competitors.

As I have noted, however, our precedents do not require "evidence of an improper censorial motive," Arkansas Writers' Project, supra, at 228, before we may find that a discriminatory tax violates the Free Press Clause; it is enough that the application of a tax offers the "potential for abuse," Minneapolis Star, 460 U. S., at 492 (emphasis added). That potential is surely present when the legislature may, at will, include or exclude various media sectors from a general tax.

B

The majority, however, does not flinch at the prospect of intermedia discrimination. Purporting to draw on Regan v. Taxation With Representation of Washington, 461 U.S. 540 (1983) — a decision dealing with the tax-deductibility of lobbying expenditures — the majority embraces "the proposition that a tax scheme that discriminates among speakers does not implicate the First Amendment unless it discriminates on the basis of ideas." Ante, at 9-10 (emphasis added). "[T]he power to discriminate in taxation," the majority insists, is "[i]nherent in the power to tax." Ante, at 11.

Read for all they are worth, these propositions would essentially annihilate the nondiscrimination principle, at least as it applies to tax differentials between individual members of the press. If Minneapolis Star, Arkansas Writers' Project, and Grosjean stand for anything, it is that the "power to tax" does not include "the power to discriminate" when the press is involved. Nor is it the case under these decisions that a tax regime that singles out individual members of the press implicates the First Amendment only when it is "directed at, or presents the danger of suppressing, particular ideas." Ante, at 13 (emphasis added). Even when structured in a manner that is content neutral, a scheme that imposes differential burdens on like-situated members of the press violates the First Amendment because it poses the risk that the State might abuse this power. See Minneapolis Star, supra, at 592.

At a minimum, the majority incorrectly conflates our cases on selective taxation of the press and our cases on the selective taxation (or subsidization) of speech generally. Regan holds that the government does not invariably violate the Free Speech Clause when it selectively subsidizes one group of speakers according to content-neutral criteria. This power, when exercised with appropriate restraint, inheres in government's legitimate authority to tap the energy of expressive activity to promote the public welfare. See Buckley v. Valeo, 424 U.S. 1, 90-97 (1976).

But our cases on the selective taxation of the press strike a different posture. Although the Free Press Clause does not guarantee the press a preferred position over other speakers, the Free Press Clause does "protec[t] [members of press] from invidious discrimination." L. Tribe, American Constitutional Law 12-20, p. 963 (2d ed. 1988). Selective taxation is precisely that. In light of the Framers' specific intent "to preserve an untrammeled press as a vital source of public information," Grosjean, 297 U. S., at 250; see Minneapolis Star, supra, at 585, n. 7, our precedents recognize that the Free Press Clause imposes a special obligation on government to avoid disrupting the integrity of the information market. As Justice Stewart explained:

"[T]he Free Press guarantee is, in essence, a structural provision of the Constitution. Most of the other provisions in the Bill of Rights protect specific liberties or specific rights of individuals: freedom of speech, freedom of worship, the right to counsel, the privilege against compulsory self-incrimination, to name a few. In contrast, the Free Press Clause extends protection to an institution." Stewart, "Or of the Press," 26 Hastings L. J. 631, 633 (1975) (emphasis in original).

Because they distort the competitive forces that animate this institution, tax differentials that fail to correspond to the social cost associated with different information media, and that are justified by nothing more than the State's desire for revenue, violate government's obligation of evenhandedness. Clearly, this is true of disproportionate taxation of cable television. Under the First Amendment, government simply has no business interfering with the process by which citizens' preferences for information formats evolve. [n.4]

Today's decision unwisely discards these teachings. I dissent.

Notes

1 Subject to various exemptions, Arkansas law imposes a 4% tax on the receipts from sales of all tangible personal property and of specified services. Ark. Code. Ann. 26-52-301, 26-52-302, 26-52-401 (1987 and Supp. 1989). Cable television service is expressly included in the tax. See 26-52-301(D)(i) (Supp. 1989). Proceeds from the sale of newspapers, 26-52-401(4) (Supp. 1989), and from the sale of magazines by subscription, 26-52-401(14) (Supp. 1989); Revenue Policy Statement 1988-1 (Mar. 10, 1988), reprinted in CCH Ark. Tax Rep. 69-415, are expressly exempted, as are the proceeds from the sale of advertising in newspapers and other publications, 26-52-401(13) (Supp. 1989). Proceeds from the sale of advertising for broadcast radio and television services are not included in the tax.

Insofar as the Arkansas Supreme Court found that cable and scrambled satellite television are a single medium, 301 Ark. 483, 487, 785 S. W. 2d 202, 204-205 (1990), this case also involves a straightforward application of Arkansas Writers' Project and Minneapolis Star in resolving the cable operators' constitutional challenge to the taxes that they paid prior to 1989, the year in which Arkansas amended its sales tax to include the subscription fees collected by scrambled-satellite television. I would affirm on that basis the Arkansas Supreme Court's conclusion that the pre-1989 version of the Arkansas sales tax violated the First Amendment by imposing on cable a tax burden not borne by its scrambled satellite television.

2 I need not consider what, if any, state interests might justify selective taxation of cable television, since the State has advanced no interest other than revenue enhancement. I also do not dispute that the unique characteristics of cable may justify special regulatory treatment of that medium. See Los Angeles v. Preferred Communications, Inc., 476 U.S. 488, 496 (1986) (Blackmun, J., concurring); cf. Red Lion Broadcasting Co. v. FCC, 395 U.S. 367, 386-401 (1969). I conclude only that the State is not free to burden cable with a selective tax absent a clear nexus between the tax and a "special characteristic" of cable television service or a "counter-balancing interest of

compelling importance." Minneapolis Star, 460 U. S., at 585.

3 Even if it did happen to apply neutrally across the range of viewpoints expressed in the Arkansas information market, Arkansas' discriminatory tax would still raise First Amendment problems. "It hardly answers one person's objection to a restriction on his speech that another person, outside his control, may speak for him." Regan v. Taxation with Representation of Washington, 461 U.S. 540, 553 (1983) (Blackmun, J., concurring).

4 The majority's reliance on Mabee v. White Plains Publishing Co., 327 U.S. 178 (1946), and Oklahoma Press Publishing Co. v. Walling, 327 U.S. 186 (1946), is also misplaced. At issue in those cases was a provision that exempted small newspapers with primarily local distribution from the Fair Labor Standards Act of 1938 (FLSA). In upholding the provision, the Court noted that the exemption promoted a legitimate interest in placing the exempted papers "on a parity with other small town enterprises" that also were not subject to regulation under the FLSA. Mabee, supra, at 184; see also Oklahoma Press, supra, at 194. In Minneapolis Star, we distinguished these cases on the ground that, unlike the FLSA exemption, Minnesota's discrimination between large and small newspapers did not derive from, or correspond to, any general state policy to benefit small businesses. See 460 U. S., at 592, and n. 16. Similarly, Arkansas' discrimination against cable operators derives not from any general, legitimate state policy unrelated to speech but rather from the simple decision of state officials to treat one information medium differently from all others. Thus, like the schemes in Arkansas Writers' Project and Minneapolis Star, but unlike the scheme at issue in Mabee and Oklahoma Press, the Arkansas tax scheme must be supported by a compelling interest to survive First Amendment scrutiny. Cf. United States v. O'Brien, 391 U.S. 367, 377 (1968).

The Court radically redefines the content of the "abuse of the writ" doctrine: Justice Marshall's dissent in McCleskey v. Zant (April 16, 1991)

Justice Marshall, with whom Justice Blackmun and Justice Stevens join, dissenting.

Today's decision departs drastically from the norms that inform the proper judicial function. Without even the most casual admission that it is discarding longstanding legal principles, the Court radically redefines the content of the "abuse of the writ" doctrine, substituting the strict-liability "cause and prejudice" standard of Wainwright v. Sykes, 433 U.S. 72 (1977), for the good-faith "deliberate abandonment" standard of Sanders v. United States, 373 U.S. 1 (1963). This doctrinal innovation, which repudiates a line of judicial decisions codified by Congress in the governing statute and procedural rules, was by no means foreseeable when the petitioner in this case filed his first federal habeas application. Indeed, the new rule announced and applied today was not even requested by respondent at any point in this litigation. Finally, rather than remand this case for reconsideration in light of its new standard, the majority performs an independent reconstruction of the record, disregarding the factual findings of the District Court and applying its new rule in a manner that encourages state officials to conceal evidence that would likely prompt a petitioner to raise a particular claim on habeas. Because I cannot acquiesce in this unjustifiable assault on the Great Writ, I dissent.

I

Disclaiming innovation, the majority depicts the "cause and prejudice" test as merely a clarification of existing law. Our decisions, the majority explains, have left "[m]uch confusion . . . on the standard for determining when a petitioner abuses the writ." Ante, at 8. But amidst this "confusion," the majority purports to discern a trend toward the causeand-prejudice standard and concludes that this is the rule that best comports with "our habeas corpus precedents," ante, at 21; see ante, at 26, and with the "complex and evolving body of equitable principles" that have traditionally defined the abuse-of-the-writ doctrine, id., at 20. This attempt to gloss over the break between today's decision and established precedents is completely unconvincing.

Drawing on the practice at common law in England, this Court long ago established that the power of a federal court to entertain a second or successive petition should turn not on "the inflexible doctrine of res judicata" but rather on the exercise of "sound judicial discretion guided and controlled by a consideration of whatever has a rational bearing on the subject." Wong Doo v. United States, 265 U.S. 239, 240-241 (1924); accord, Salinger v. Loisel, 265 U.S. 224, 230-232 (1924). Thus, in Wong Doo, the Court held that the District Court acted within its discretion in dismissing a petition premised on a ground that was raised but expressly abandoned in an earlier petition. "The petitioner had full opportunity," the Court explained, "to offer proof [of the abandoned ground] at the hearing on the first petition; and, if he was intending to rely on that ground, good faith required that he produce the proof then." 265 U. S., at 241. Noting that the evidence supporting the abandoned ground had been "accessible all the time," the Court inferred that petitioner, an alien seeking to forestall his imminent deportation, had split his claims in order to "postpone the execution of the [deportation] order." Ibid.

In Price v. Johnston, 334 U.S. 266 (1948), in contrast, the Court held that the District Court abused its discretion by summarily dismissing a petition that raised a claim not asserted in any of three previous petitions filed by the same prisoner. Whereas it had been clear from the record that the petitioner in Wong Doo had possessed access to the facts supporting his abandoned claim, the District Court in Price had no basis for assuming that the prisoner had "acquired no new or additional information since" the disposition of his earlier petitions. Id., at 290. "[E]ven if it [had been] found that petitioner did have prior knowledge of all the facts concerning the allegation in question," the Court added, the District Court should not have dismissed the petition before affording the prisoner an opportunity to articulate "some justifiable reason [why] he was previously unable to assert his rights or was unaware of the significance of relevant facts."

Id., at 291.

In Sanders v. United States, 373 U.S. 1 (1963), the Court crystallized the various factors bearing on a district court's discretion to entertain a successive petition. [n.1] The Court in Sanders distinguished successive petitions raising previously asserted grounds from those raising previously unasserted grounds. With regard to the former class of petitions, the Court explained, the district court may give "[c]ontrolling weight . . . to [the] denial of a prior application" unless "the ends of justice would . . . be served by reaching the merits of the subsequent application." Id., at 15. With regard to the latter, however, the district court must reach the merits of the petition unless "there has been an abuse of the writ . . . ." Id., at 17. In determining whether the omission of the claim from the previous petition constitutes an abuse of the writ, the judgment of the district court is to be guided chiefly by the " `[equitable] principle that a suitor's conduct in relation to the matter at hand may disentitle him to the relief he seeks.' " Ibid., quoting Fay v. Noia, 372 U.S. 391, 438 (1963).

"Thus, for example, if a prisoner deliberately withholds one of two grounds for federal collateral relief at the time of filing his first application, in the hope of being granted two hearings rather than one or for some other such reason, he may be deemed to have waived his right to a hearing on a second application presenting the withheld ground. The same may be true if, as in Wong Doo, the prisoner deliberately abandons one of his grounds at the first hearing. Nothing in the traditions of habeas corpus requires the federal courts to tolerate needless piecemeal litigation, or to entertain collateral proceedings whose only purpose is to vex, harass, or delay." 373 U. S., at 18.

What emerges from Sanders and its predecessors is essentially a good-faith standard. As illustrated by Wong Doo, the principal form of bad faith that the "abuse of the writ" doctrine is intended to deter is the deliberate abandonment of a claim the factual and legal basis of which are known to the petitioner (or his counsel) when he files his first petition. The Court in Sanders stressed this point by equating its analysis with that of Fay v. Noia, supra, which established the then-prevailing "deliberate bypass" test for the cognizability of claims on which a petitioner procedurally defaulted in state proceedings. See 373 U. S., at 18. A petitioner also abuses the writ under Sanders when he uses the writ to achieve some end other than expeditious relief from unlawful confinement — such as "to vex, harass, or delay." However, so long as the petitioner's previous application was based on a good-faith assessment of the claims available to him, see Price v. Johnston, supra, at 289; Wong Doo, supra, at 241; the denial of the application does not bar the petitioner from availing himself of "new or additional information," Price v. Johnston, supra, at 290, in support of a claim not previously raised. Accord, Advisory Committee's Note to Habeas Corpus Rule 9, 28 U. S. C., p. 427.

"Cause and prejudice" — the standard currently applicable to procedural defaults in state proceedings, see Wainwright v. Sykes, 433 U.S. 72 (1977) — imposes a much stricter test. As this Court's precedents make clear, a petitioner has cause for failing effectively to present his federal claim in state proceedings only when "some objective factor external to the defense impeded counsel's efforts to comply with the State's procedural rule . . . ." Murray v. Carrier, 477 U.S. 478, 488 (1986). Under this test, the state of mind of counsel is largely irrelevant. Indeed, this Court has held that even counsel's reasonable perception that a particular claim is without factual or legal foundation does not excuse the failure to raise that claim in the absence of an objective, external impediment to counsel's efforts. See Smith v. Murray, 477 U.S. 527, 535-536 (1986). In this sense, the cause component of the Wainwright v. Sykes test establishes a strict liability standard. [n.2]

Equally foreign to our abuse-of-the-writ jurisprudence is the requirement that a petitioner show "prejudice." Under Sanders, a petitioner who articulates a justifiable reason for failing to present a claim in a previous habeas application is not required in addition to demonstrate any particular degree of prejudice before the habeas court must consider his claim. If the petitioner demonstrates that his claim has merit, it is the State that must show that the resulting constitutional error was harmless beyond a reasonable doubt. See L. Yackle, Postconviction Remedies 133, p. 503 (1981). [n.3]

II

The real question posed by the majority's analysis is not whether the cause-and-prejudice test departs from the principles of Sanders — for it clearly does — but whether the majority has succeeded in justifying this departure as an exercise of this Court's common-lawmaking discretion. In my view, the majority does not come close to justifying its new standard.

A

Incorporation of the cause-and-prejudice test into the abuse-of-the-writ doctrine cannot be justified as an exercise of this Court's common-lawmaking discretion, because this Court has no discretion to exercise in this area. Congress has affirmatively ratified the Sanders good-faith standard in the governing statute and procedural rules, thereby insulating that standard from judicial repeal.

The abuse-of-the-writ doctrine is embodied in 28 U.S.C. 2244(b) and in Habeas Corpus Rule 9(b). Enacted three years after Sanders, 2244(b) recodified the statutory authority of a district court to dismiss a second or successive petition, amending the statutory language to incorporate the Sanders criteria:

"[A] subsequent application for a writ of habeas corpus . . . need not be entertained by a court . . . unless the application alleges and is predicated on a factual or other ground not adjudicated on the hearing of the earlier application for the writ, and unless the court . . . is satisfied that the applicant has not on the earlier application deliberately withheld the newly asserted ground or otherwise abused the writ." 28 U.S.C. 2244(b).

Consistent with Sanders, the purpose of the recodification was to spare a district court the obligation to entertain a petition "containing allegations identical to those asserted in a previous application that has been denied, or predicated upon grounds obviously well known to [the petitioner] when [he] filed the preceding application." S.

Rep. No. 1797, 89th Cong., 2d Sess., 2 (1966) (emphasis added). Rule 9(b) likewise adopts Sanders' terminology:

"A second or successive petition may be dismissed if the judge finds that it fails to allege new or different grounds for relief and the prior determination was on the merits or, if new and different grounds are alleged, the judge finds that the failure of the petitioner to assert those grounds in a prior petition constituted an abuse of the writ."

There can be no question that 2244(b) and Rule 9(b) codify Sanders. The legislative history of, and Advisory Committee's Notes to, Rule 9(b) expressly so indicate, see 28 U. S. C., pp. 426-427; H. R. Rep. No. 94-1471, pp. 5-6 (1976), and such has been the universal understanding of this Court, see Rose v. Lundy, 455 U.S. 509, 521 (1982), of the lower courts, see, e. g., Williams v. Lockhart, 862 F. 2d 155, 157 (CA8 1988); Neuschafer v. Whitley, 860 F. 2d 1470, 1474 (CA9 1988), cert. denied, sub nom. Demosthenes v. Neushafer, 493 U.S. 906 (1989); 860 F. 2d, at 1479 (Alarcon, J., concurring in result); Davis v. Dugger, 829 F. 2d 1513, 1518, n. 13 (CA11 1987); Passman v. Blackburn, 797 F. 2d 1335, 1341 (CA5 1986), cert. denied, 480 U.S. 948 (1987); United States v. Talk, 597 F. 2d 249, 250-251 (CA10 1979); United States ex rel. Fletcher v. Brierley, 460 F. 2d 444, 446, n. 4A (CA3), cert. denied, 409 U.S. 1044 (1972), and of commentators, see, e. g., 17A C. Wright, A. Miller & E. Cooper, Federal Practice and Procedure 4267, pp. 477478 (2d ed. 1988); L. Yackle, supra, 154. [n.4]

The majority concedes that 2244(b) and Rule 9(b) codify Sanders, see ante, at 19, but concludes nonetheless that Congress did "not answer" all of the "questions" concerning the abuse-of-the-writ doctrine, ante, at 18. The majority emphasizes that 2244(b) refers to second or successive petitions from petitioners who have "deliberately withheld the newly asserted ground or otherwise abused the writ" without exhaustively cataloging the ways in which the writ may "otherwise" be "abused." See ibid.; ante, at 21. From this "silenc[e]," the majority infers a congressional delegation of lawmaking power broad enough to encompass the engrafting of the cause-and-prejudice test onto the abuse-of-the-writ doctrine. Ante, at 18.

It is difficult to take this reasoning seriously. Because "cause" under Sykes makes the mental state of the petitioner (or his counsel) irrelevant, "cause" completely subsumes "deliberate abandonment." See Engle v. Isaac, 456 U.S. 107, 130, n. 36 (1982); see also Wainwright v. Sykes, 433 U. S., at 87. Thus, if merely failing to raise a claim without "cause" — that is, without some external impediment to raising it — necessarily constitutes an abuse of the writ, the statutory reference to deliberate withholding of a claim would be rendered superfluous. Insofar as Sanders was primarily concerned with limiting dismissal of a second or subsequent petition to instances in which the petitioner had deliberately abandoned the new claim, see 373 U. S., at 18, the suggestion that Congress invested courts with the discretion to read this language out of the statute is completely irreconcilable with the proposition that 2244(b) and Rule 9(b) codify Sanders.

To give content to "otherwise abus[e] the writ" as used in 2244(b), we must look to Sanders. As I have explained, the Court in Sanders identified two broad classes of bad-faith conduct that bar adjudication of a claim not raised in a previous habeas application: the deliberate abandonment or withholding of that claim from the first petition; and the filing of a petition aimed at some purpose other than expeditious relief from unlawful confinement, such as "to vex, harass, or delay." See ibid. By referring to second or successive applications from habeas petitioners who have "deliberately withheld the newly asserted ground or otherwise abused the writ," 2244(b) tracks this division. Congress may well have selected the phrase "otherwise abused the writ" with the expectation that courts would continue to elaborate upon the types of dilatory tactics that, in addition to deliberate abandonment of a known claim, constitute an abuse of the writ. But consistent with Congress' intent to codify Sanders' good-faith test, such elaborations must be confined to circumstances in which a petitioner's omission of an unknown claim is conjoined with his intentional filing of a petition for an improper purpose, such as "to vex, harass or delay."

The majority tacitly acknowledges this constraint on the Court's interpretive discretion by suggesting that "cause" is tantamount to "inexcusable neglect." This claim, too, is untenable. The majority exaggerates when it claims that the "inexcusable neglect" formulation — which this Court has never applied in an abuse-of-the-writ decision — functions as an independent standard for evaluating a petitioner's failure to raise a claim in a previous habeas application. It is true that Sanders compared its own analysis to the analysis in Townsend v. Sain, 372 U.S. 293 (1963), which established that a district court should deny an evidentiary hearing if the habeas petitioner inexcusably neglected to develop factual evidence in state proceedings. See id., at 317. Townsend, however, expressly equated "inexcusable neglect" with the "deliberate bypass" test of Fay v. Noia. See 372 U. S., at 317. [n.5] But even if "inexcusable neglect" does usefully describe a class of abuses separate from deliberate abandonment, the melding of "cause and prejudice" into the abuse-of-the-writ doctrine cannot be defended as a means of "giving content" to "inexcusable neglect." Ante, at 21. For under Sykes' strict-liability standard, mere attorney negligence is never excusable. See Murray v. Carrier, 477 U. S., at 488 ("So long as a defendant is represented by counsel whose performance is not constitutionally ineffective . . ., we discern no inequity in requiring him to bear the risk of attorney error that results in a procedural default").

Confirmation that the majority today exercises legislative power not properly belonging to this Court is supplied by Congress' own recent consideration and rejection of an amendment to 2244(b). It is axiomatic that this Court does not function as a backup legislature for the reconsideration of failed attempts to amend existing statutes. See Bowsher v. Merck & Co., 460 U.S. 824, 837, n. 12 (1983); FTC v. Ruberoid Co., 343 U.S. 470, 478-479 (1952); see also North Haven Bd. of Ed. v. Bell, 456 U.S. 512, 534-535 (1982). Yet that is exactly the effect of today's decision. As reported out of the House Committee on the Judiciary, 1303 of H. R. 5269, 101st Cong., 2d Sess. (1990), would have required dismissal of any second or subsequent application by a habeas petitioner under sentence of death unless the petitioner raised a new claim "the factual basis of [which] could not have been discovered by the exercise of reasonable diligence," H. R. Rep. No. 101-681, pt. 1, p. 29 (1990) (emphasis added). [n.6] The Committee Report accompanying this legislation explained that "courts have properly construed section 2244(b) and Rule 9(b) as codifications of the guidelines the [Supreme] Court itself prescribed in Sanders." Id., at 119 (citation omitted). The Report justified adoption of the tougher "reasonable diligence" standard on the ground that "[t]he Sanders guidelines have not . . . satisfactorily met concerns that death row prisoners may file second or successive habeas corpus applications as a means of extending litigation." Ibid. Unfazed by Congress' rejection of this legislation, the majority arrogates to itself the power to repeal Sanders and to replace it with a tougher standard. [n.7]

B

Even if the fusion of cause-and-prejudice into the abuse-of-the-writ doctrine were not foreclosed by the will of Congress, the majority fails to demonstrate that such a rule would be a wise or just exercise of the Court's common-lawmaking discretion. In fact, the majority's abrupt change in law subverts the policies underlying 2244(b) and unfairly prejudices the petitioner in this case.

The majority premises adoption of the cause-and-prejudice test almost entirely on the importance of "finality." See ante, at 22-24. At best, this is an insufficiently developed justification for cause-and-prejudice or any other possible conception of the abuse-of-the-writ doctrine. For the very essence of the Great Writ is our criminal justice system's commitment to suspending "[c]onventional notions of finality of litigation . . . where life or liberty is at stake and infringement of constitutional rights is alleged." Sanders, 373 U. S., at 8. To recognize this principle is not to make the straw-man claim that the writ must be accompanied by " `[a] procedural system which permits an endless repetition of inquiry into facts and law in a vain search for ultimate certitude.' " Ante, at 23, quoting Bator, Finality in Criminal Law and Federal Habeas Corpus for State Prisoners, 76 Harv. L. Rev. 441, 452 (1963). Rather, it is only to point out the plain fact that we may not, "[u]nder the guise of fashioning a procedural rule, . . . wip[e] out the practical efficacy of a jurisdiction conferred by Congress on the District Courts." Brown v. Allen, 344 U.S. 443, 498-499 (1953) (opinion of Frankfurter, J.).

The majority seeks to demonstrate that cause-and-prejudice strikes an acceptable balance between the state's interest in finality and the purposes of habeas corpus by analogizing the abuse-of-the-writ doctrine to the procedural-default doctrine. According to the majority, these two doctrines "implicate nearly identical concerns flowing from the significant costs of federal habeas corpus review." Ante, at 22. And because this Court has already deemed cause-and-prejudice to be an appropriate standard for assessing procedural defaults, the majority reasons, the same standard should be used for assessing the failure to raise a claim in a previous habeas petition. See ante, at 21-25.

This analysis does not withstand scrutiny. This Court's precedents on the procedural-default doctrine identify two purposes served by the cause-and-prejudice test. The first purpose is to promote respect for a State's legitimate procedural rules. See, e. g.,

Reed v. Ross, 468 U.S. 1, 14 (1984); Sykes, 433 U. S., at 87-90. As the Court has explained, the willingness of a habeas court to entertain a claim that a state court has deemed to be procedurally barred "undercut[s] the State's ability to enforce its procedural rules," Engle v. Isaac, 456 U. S., at 129, and may cause "state courts themselves [to be] less stringent in their enforcement," Sykes, supra, at 89. See generally Meltzer, State Court Forfeitures of Federal Rights, 99 Harv. L. Rev. 1128, 1150-1158 (1986). The second purpose of the cause-and-prejudice test is to preserve the connection between federal collateral review and the general "deterrent" function served by the Great Writ. " `[T]he threat of habeas serves as a necessary additional incentive for trial and appellate courts throughout the land to conduct their proceedings in a manner consistent with established constitutional standards.' " Teague v. Lane, 489 U.S. 288, 306 (1989) (plurality opinion), quoting Desist v. United States, 394 U.S. 244, 262-263 (1969) (Harlan, J., dissenting); see Rose v. Mitchell, 443 U.S. 545, 563 (1979). Obviously, this understanding of the disciplining effect of federal habeas corpus presupposes that a criminal defendant has given the state trial and appellate courts a fair opportunity to pass on his constitutional claims. See Murray v. Carrier, 477 U. S., at 487; Engle v. Isaac, supra, at 128-129. With regard to both of these purposes, the strictness of the cause-and-prejudice test has been justified on the ground that the defendant's procedural default is akin to an independent and adequate state-law ground for the judgment of conviction. See Sykes, supra, at 81-83.

Neither of these concerns is even remotely implicated in the abuse-of-the-writ setting. The abuse-of-the-writ doctrine clearly contemplates a situation in which a petitioner (as in this case) has complied with applicable state-procedural rules and effectively raised his constitutional claim in state proceedings; were it otherwise, the abuse-of-the-writ doctrine would not perform a screening function independent from that performed by the procedural-default doctrine and by the requirement that a habeas petitioner exhaust his state remedies, see 28 U.S.C. 2254(b), (c). Cf. ante, at 18. Because the abuse-of-the-writ doctrine presupposes that the petitioner has effectively raised his claim in state proceedings, a decision by the habeas court to entertain the claim notwithstanding its omission from an earlier habeas petition will neither breed disrespect for state-procedural rules nor unfairly subject state courts to federal collateral review in the absence of a state-court disposition of a federal claim. [n.8]

Because the abuse-of-the-writ doctrine addresses the situation in which a federal habeas court must determine whether to hear a claim withheld from another federal habeas court, the test for identifying an abuse must strike an appropriate balance between finality and review in that setting. Only when informed by Sanders does 2244(b) strike an efficient balance. A habeas petitioner's own interest in liberty furnishes a powerful incentive to assert in his first petition all claims that the petitioner (or his counsel) believes have a reasonable prospect for success. See Note, 83 Harv. L. Rev. 1038, 1153-1154 (1970); see also Rose v. Lundy, 455 U. S., at 520 ("The prisoner's principal interest, of course, is in obtaining speedy federal relief on his claims"). Sanders' bar on the later assertion of claims omitted in bad faith adequately fortifies this natural incentive. At the same time, however, the petitioner faces an effective disincentive to asserting any claim that he believes does not have a reasonable prospect for success: the adverse adjudication of such a claim will bar its reassertion under the successive-petition doctrine, see 28 U.S.C. 2244(b); Sanders, supra, at 17, whereas omission of the claim will not prevent the petitioner from asserting the claim for the first time in a later petition should the discovery of new evidence or the advent of intervening changes in law invest the claim with merit, S. Rep. No. 1797, at 2; Advisory Committee's Note to Habeas Corpus Rule 9, 28 U. S. C., p. 427.

The cause-and-prejudice test destroys this balance. By design, the cause-and-prejudice standard creates a nearirrebuttable presumption that omitted claims are permanently barred. This outcome not only conflicts with Congress' intent that a petitioner be free to avail himself of newly discovered evidence or intervening changes in law, S. Rep. No. 1797, at 2; Advisory Committee's Note to Habeas Corpus Rule 9, 28 U. S. C., p. 427, but also subverts the statutory disincentive to the assertion of frivolous claims. Rather than face the cause-and-prejudice bar, a petitioner will assert all conceivable claims, whether or not these claims reasonably appear to have merit. The possibility that these claims will be adversely adjudicated and thereafter be barred from relitigation under the successive-petition doctrine will not effectively discourage the petitioner from asserting them, for the petitioner will have virtually no expectation that any withheld claim could be revived should his assessment of its merit later prove mistaken. Far from promoting efficiency, the majority's rule thus invites the very type of "baseless claims," ante, at 24, that the majority seeks to avert.

The majority's adoption of the cause-and-prejudice test is not only unwise, but also manifestly unfair. The proclaimed purpose of the majority's new strict-liability standard is to increase to the maximum extent a petitioner's incentive to investigate all conceivable claims before filing his first petition. See ante, at 29. Whatever its merits, this was not the rule when the petitioner in this case filed his first petition. From the legislative history of 2244(b) and Rule 9(b) and from the universal agreement of courts and commentators, see supra, at 8, McCleskey's counsel could have reached no other conclusion but that his investigatory efforts in preparing his client's petition would be measured against the Sanders good-faith standard. There can be little question that his efforts satisfied that test; indeed, the District Court expressly concluded that McCleskey's counsel on his first habeas conducted a reasonable and competent investigation before concluding that a claim based on Massiah v. United States, 377 U.S. 201 (1964), would be without factual foundation. See App. 84-85; see also infra, at 21. Before today, that would have been enough. The Court's utter indifference to the injustice of retroactively applying its new, strict-liability standard to this habeas petitioner stands in marked contrast to this Court's eagerness to protect States from the unfair surprise of "new rules" that enforce the constitutional rights of citizens charged with criminal wrongdoing. See Butler v. McKellar, 494 U. S. —, — (1990); Saffle v. Parks, 494 U. S. —, — (1990); Teague v. Lane, 489 U. S., at 299-310 (plurality opinion).

This injustice is compounded by the Court's activism in fashioning its new rule. The applicability of Sykes' causeand-prejudice test was not litigated in either the District Court or the Court of Appeals. The additional question that we requested the parties to address reasonably could have been read to relate merely to the burden of proof under the abuse-of-the-writ doctrine; [n.9] it evidently did not put the parties on notice that this Court was contemplating a change in the governing legal standard, since respondent did not even mention Sykes or cause-and-prejudice in its brief or at oral argument, much less request the Court to adopt this standard. [n.10] In this respect, too, today's decision departs from norms that inform the proper judicial function. See Heckler v. Campbell, 461 U.S. 458, 468, n. 12 (1983) (Court will consider ground in support of judgment not raised below only in extraordinary case); accord, Granfinanciera, S. A. v. Nord berg, 492 U.S. 33, 39 (1989). It cannot be said that Mc Cleskey had a fair opportunity to challenge the reasoning that the majority today invokes to strip him of his Massiah claim.

III

The manner in which the majority applies its new rule is as objectionable as the manner in which the majority creates that rule. As even the majority acknowledges, see ante, at 1, the standard that it announces today is not the one employed by the Court of Appeals, which purported to rely on Sanders, see 890 F. 2d 342, 347 (CA 11 1989). See ante, at 1. Where, as here, application of a different standard from the one applied by the lower court requires an in-depth review of the record, the ordinary course is to remand so that the parties have a fair opportunity to address, and the lower court to consider, all of the relevant issues. See, e. g., Anderson v. Liberty Lobby, Inc., 477 U.S. 242, 257 (1986); Mandel v. Bradley, 432 U.S. 173, 179 (1977) (per curiam); see also United States v. Hasting, 461 U.S. 499, 515-518 (1983) (Stevens, J., concurring in judgment) (Court should not undertake record-review "function that can better be performed by other judges").

A remand would have been particularly appropriate in this case in view of the patent deficiencies in the reasoning of the Court of Appeals. The Court of Appeals concluded that McCleskey deliberately abandoned his Massiah claim because his counsel "made a knowing choice not to pursue the claim after having raised it" unsuccessfully on state collateral review. 890 F. 2d, at 349. This reasoning, which the majority declines to endorse, is obviously faulty. As I have explained, the abuse-of-the-writ doctrine is independent from the procedural-default and exhaustion doctrines; 2244(b) and Rule 9(b) contemplate a habeas petitioner who has effectively presented his claim in state proceedings but withheld that claim from a previous habeas application. Because 2244(b) and Rule 9(b) authorize the district court to consider such a claim under appropriate circumstances, it cannot be the case that a petitioner invariably abuses the writ by consciously failing to include in his first habeas petition a claim raised in state proceedings. Insofar as Congress intended that the district court excuse the withholding of a claim when the petitioner produces newly discovered evidence or intervening changes in law, S. Rep. No. 1797, at 2; Advisory Committee's Note to Habeas Corpus Rule

9, 28 U. S. C., p. 427, a petitioner cannot be deemed to have deliberately abandoned the claim in an earlier habeas proceeding unless the petitioner was aware then of the evidence and law that support the claim. See, e. g., Wong Doo, 265 U. S., at 241. If the Court of Appeals had properly applied Sanders, it would almost certainly have agreed with the District Court's conclusion that McCleskey was not aware of the evidence that supported his Massiah claim when he filed his first petition. In any case, because the Court of Appeals' reversal was based on an erroneous application of Sanders, the majority's decision not to remand cannot be justified on the ground that the Court of Appeals would necessarily have decided the case the same way under the cause-and-prejudice standard.

Undaunted by the difficulty of applying its new rule without the benefit of any lower court's preliminary consideration, the majority forges ahead to perform its own independent review of the record. The majority concludes that McCleskey had no cause to withhold his Massiah claim because all of the evidence supporting that claim was available before he filed his first habeas petition. The majority purports to accept the District Court's finding that Offie Evans' 21-page statement was, at that point, being held beyond McCleskey's reach. See ante, at 29-30, and n. *. [n.11] But the State's failure to produce this document, the majority explains, furnished no excuse for McCleskey's failure to assert his Massiah claim "because McCleskey participated in the conversations reported by Evans," and therefore "knew everything in the document that the District Court relied upon to establish the ab initio connection between Evans and the police." Ante, at 31. The majority also points out that no external force impeded McCleskey's discovery of the testimony of jailer Worthy. See ibid.

To appreciate the hollowness — and the dangerousness — of this reasoning, it is necessary to recall the District Court's central finding: that the State did covertly plant Evans in an adjoining cell for the purpose of eliciting incriminating statements that could be used against McCleskey at trial. See App. 83. Once this finding is credited, it follows that the State affirmatively misled McCleskey and his counsel throughout their unsuccessful pursuit of the Massiah claim in state collateral proceedings and their investigation of that claim in preparing for McCleskey's first federal habeas proceeding. McCleskey's counsel deposed or interviewed the assistant district attorney, various jailers, and other government officials responsible for Evans' confinement, all of whom denied any knowledge of an agreement between Evans and the State. See App. 25-28, 44-47, 79, 85.

Against this background of deceit, the State's withholding of Evans' 21-page statement assumes critical importance. The majority overstates McCleskey's and his counsel's awareness of the statement's contents. For example, the statement relates that state officials were present when Evans made a phone call at McCleskey's request to McCleskey's girlfriend, Plaintiff's Exh. 8, p. 14, a fact that McCleskey and his counsel had no reason to know and that strongly supports the District Court's finding of an ab initio relationship between Evans and the State. But in any event, the importance of the statement lay much less in what the statement said than in its simple existence. Without the statement, McCleskey's counsel had nothing more than his client's testimony to back up counsel's own suspicion of a possible Massiah violation; given the state officials' adamant denials of any arrangement with Evans, and given the state habeas court's rejection of the Massiah claim, counsel quite reasonably concluded that raising this claim in McCleskey's first habeas petition would be futile. All this changed once counsel finally obtained the statement, for at that point, there was credible, independent corroboration of counsel's suspicion. This additional evidence not only gave counsel the reasonable expectation of success that had previously been lacking, but also gave him a basis for conducting further investigation into the underlying claim. Indeed, it was by piecing together the circumstances under which the statement had been transcribed that McCleskey's counsel was able to find Worthy, a state official who was finally willing to admit that Evans had been planted in the cell adjoining McCleskey's. [n.12]

The majority's analysis of this case is dangerous precisely because it treats as irrelevant the effect that the State's disinformation strategy had on counsel's assessment of the reasonableness of pursing the Massiah claim. For the majority, all that matters is that no external obstacle barred McCleskey from finding Worthy. But obviously, counsel's decision even to look for evidence in support of a particular claim has to be informed by what counsel reasonably perceives to be the prospect that the claim may have merit; in this case, by withholding the 21-page statement and by affirmatively misleading counsel as to the State's involvement with Evans, state officials created a climate in which McCleskey's first habeas counsel was perfectly justified in focusing his attentions elsewhere. The sum and substance of the majority's analysis is that McCleskey had no "cause" for failing to assert the Massiah claim because he did not try hard enough to pierce the State's veil of deception. Because the majority excludes from its conception of cause any recognition of how state officials can distort a petitioner's reasonable perception of whether pursuit of a particular claim is worthwhile, the majority's conception of "cause" creates an incentive for state officials to engage in this very type of misconduct.

Although the majority finds it unnecessary to reach the question whether McCleskey was "prejudiced" by the Massiah violation in this case, I have no doubt that the admission of Evans' testimony at trial satisfies any fair conception of this prong of the Sykes test. No witness from the furniture store was able to identify which of the four robbers shot the off-duty police officer. The State did put on evidence that McCleskey had earlier stolen the pearl-handled pistol that was determined to be the likely murder weapon, but the significance of this testimony was clouded by a co-defendant's admission that he had been carrying this weapon for weeks at a time, App. 16, and by a prosecution witness' own prior statement that she had seen only the codefendant carry the pistol, id., at 11-14. See also id., at 89 (District Court finding that "the evidence on [McCleskey's] possession of the gun in question was conflicting"). Outside of the self-serving and easily impeachable testimony of the codefendant, the only evidence that directly supported the

State's identification of McCleskey as the triggerman was the testimony of Evans. As the District Court found, "Evans' testimony about the petitioner's incriminating statements was critical to the state's case." Id., at 89. Without it, the jury might very well have reached a different verdict.

Thus, as I read the record, McCleskey should be entitled to the consideration of his petition for habeas corpus even under the cause-and-prejudice test. The case is certainly close enough to warrant a remand so that the issues can be fully and fairly briefed.

IV

Ironically, the majority seeks to defend its doctrinal innovation on the ground that it will promote respect for the "rule of law." Ante, at 24. Obviously, respect for the rule of law must start with those who are responsible for pronouncing the law. The majority's invocation of " `the orderly administration of justice,' " ante, at 27, rings hollow when the majority itself tosses aside established precedents without explanation, disregards the will of Congress, fashions rules that defy the reasonable expectations of the persons who must conform their conduct to the law's dictates, and applies those rules in a way that rewards state misconduct and deceit. Whatever "abuse of the writ" today's decision is designed to avert pales in comparison with the majority's own abuse of the norms that inform the proper judicial function.

I dissent.

Notes

1 Although Sanders examined the abuse-of-the-writ question in the context of a motion for collateral review filed under 28 U.S.C. 2255 the Court made it clear that the same principles apply in the context of a petition for habeas corpus filed under 28 U.S.C. 2254. See 373 U. S., at 12-15.

2 Contrary to the majority's suggestion, this Court's more recent decisions on abuse of the writ by no means foreshadowed the shift to Sykes' strict-liability standard. The cases cited by the majority all involved eleventh-hour dispositions of capital stay applications, and the cursory analysis in each ruling suggests merely that the habeas petitioner failed to carry his burden of articulating a credible explanation for having failed to raise the claim in an earlier petition. See Advisory Committee's Note to Habeas Corpus Rule 9, 28 U. S. C., p. 427 ("[T]he petitioner has the burden of proving that he has not abused the writ"); accord, Price v. Johnston, 334 U.S. 266, 292 (1948); see also Sanders v. United States, 373 U.S. 1, 10 (1963) (Government merely has burden to plead abuse of the writ). Thus, in Woodard v. Hutchins, 464 U.S. 377 (1984) (per curiam), the five Justices concurring in the order concluded that the habeas petitioner had abused the writ because he "offer[ed] no explanation for having failed to raise [three new] claims in his first petition for habeas corpus." Id., at 379 (Powell, J., joined by Burger, C. J., Blackmun, Rehnquist, and O'Connor, JJ., concurring in order vacating stay) (emphasis added). A petitioner who gives no explanation for omitting his claims from a previous application

necessarily fails to carry his burden of justification. Similarly, in Antone v. Dugger, 465 U.S. 200 (1984) (per curiam), the Court rejected as "meritless" the petitioner's claim that the imminence of his execution prevented his counsel from identifying all of the claims that could be raised in the first petition, because the petitioner's execution had in fact been stayed during the pendency of the original habeas proceeding. Id., at 206, n. 4. Finally, in Delo v. Stokes, 495 U. S. — (1990) (per curiam), the Court in a five-sentence analysis concluded that the petitioner had abused the writ by raising a claim the legal basis of which was readily apparent at the time of the first petition. Id., at ---. The opinion says nothing about whether the petitioner offered any explanation to rebut the presumption that the petitioner had deliberately abandoned this claim. In short, the analysis in these decisions is as consistent with Sanders' deliberate-abandonment test as with Sykes' cause-and-prejudice test.

3 The majority is simply incorrect, moreover, when it claims that the "prejudice" component of the Sykes test is "[w]ell-defined in the case law." Ante, at 27. The Court in Sykes expressly declined to define this concept, see 433 U. S., at 91, and since then, the Court has elaborated upon "prejudice" only as it applies to nonconstitutional jury-instruction challenges, leaving the "the import of the term in other situations . . . an open question." United States v. Frady, 456 U.S. 152, 168 (1982). Thus, far from resolving "confusion" over the proper application of the abuse of the writ doctrine, today's decision creates it.

4 In this respect, the abuse-of-the-writ doctrine rests on a different foundation from the procedural-default doctrine. In Wainwright v. Sykes, 433 U.S. 72 (1977), the Court emphasized that the procedural-default rule set down in Fay v. Noia, 372 U.S. 391 (1963), derived only from "comity" considerations, 433 U. S., at 83, and explained that the content of this doctrine is therefore subject to the Court's traditional, common-law discretion "to overturn or modify its earlier views of the scope of the writ, even where the statutory language authorizing judicial action has remained unchanged," id., at 81. But unlike Fay v. Noia's "deliberate bypass" test for procedural defaults, the "deliberate abandonment" test of Sanders has been expressly ratified by Congress. This legislative action necessarily constrains the scope of this Court's common-lawmaking discretion.

5 Indeed, Congress expressly amended Rule 9(b) to eliminate language that would have established a standard similar to "inexcusable neglect." As initially submitted to Congress, Rule 9(b) would have authorized a district court to entertain a second or successive petition raising a previously unasserted ground unless the court "finds that the failure of the petitioner to assert th[at] groun[d] in a prior petition is not excusable." H. R. Rep. No. 94-1471, p. 8 (1976) (emphasis added). Explaining that "the `not excusable' language [would] creat[e] a new and undefined standard that [would] g[ive] a judge too broad a discretion to dismiss a second or successive petition," Congress substituted Sanders' "abuse of the writ" formulation. See id., at 5. This amendment was designed to "brin[g] Rule 9(b) into conformity with existing law." Ibid.

6 House bill 5269 was the House version of the legislation that became the Crime

Control Act of 1990, Pub. L. 101-647, 104 Stat. 4789 the final version of which left 2244(b) unamended.

7 Moreover, the rejected amendment to 2244(b) would have changed the standard only for second or subsequent petitions filed by petitioners under a sentence of death, leaving the Sanders standard intact for noncapital petitioners. The majority's decision today changes the standard for all habeas petitioners.

8 Insofar as the habeas court's entertainment of the petitioner's claim in these circumstances depends on the petitioner's articulation of a justifiable reason for having failed to raise the claim in the earlier federal petition, see Sanders, 373 U. S., at 17-18; Price v. Johnston, 334 U. S., at 291, the federal court may very well be considering the claim on the basis of evidence discovered after, or legal developments that postdate, the termination of the state proceedings. But the decision to permit a petitioner to avail himself of federal habeas relief under those conditions is one that Congress expressly made in authorizing district courts to entertain second or successive petitions under 2244(b) and Rule 9(b). See S. Rep. No. 1797, at 2 ("newly discovered evidence" is basis for second petition raising previously unasserted ground); Advisory Committee's Note to Habeas Corpus Rule 9, 28 U. S. C., p. 427 ("A retroactive change in the law and newly discovered evidence are examples" of "instances in which petitioner's failure to assert a ground in a prior petition is excusable").

9 The question reads: "Must the State demonstrate that a claim was deliberately abandoned in an earlier petition for a writ of habeas corpus in order to establish that inclusion of that claim in a subsequent habeas petition constitutes abuse of the writ?" 496 U. S. — (1990) (emphasis added).

10 Petitioner McCleskey addressed the applicability of the cause-and-prejudice test only in his reply brief and in response to arguments raised by amicus curiae Criminal Justice Legal Foundation. It is well established, however, that this Court will not consider an argument advanced by amicus when that argument was not raised or passed on below and was not advanced in this Court by the party on whose behalf the argument is being raised. See United Parcel Service, Inc. v. Mitchell, 451 U.S. 56, 60, n. 2 (1981); Bell v. Wolfish, 441 U.S. 520, 531, n. 13 (1979); Knetsch v. United States, 364 U.S. 361, 370 (1960).

11 Nonetheless, "for the sake of completeness," the majority feels constrained to express its opinion that "this finding is not free from substantial doubt." Ante, at 30, n. *. Pointing to certain vague clues arising at different points during the state proceedings at trial and on direct and collateral review, the majority asserts that "[t]he record . . . furnishes strong evidence that McCleskey knew or should have known of the Evans document before the first federal petition." Ibid. It is the majority's account, however, that is incomplete. Omitted is any mention of the State's evasions of counsel's repeated attempts to compel disclosure of any statement in the State's possession. In particular, the majority neglects to mention the withholding of the statement from a box of documents produced during discovery in McCleskey's state collateral-review action; these

documents were represented to counsel as comprising "a complete copy of the prosecutor's file resulting from the criminal prosecution of Warren McCleskey in Fulton County." App. 29 (emphasis added). McCleskey ultimately obtained the statement by filing a request under a state "open records" statute that was not construed to apply to police-investigative files until six years after McCleskey's first federal habeas proceeding. See generally Napper v. Georgia Television Co., 257 Ga. 156, 356 S. E. 2d 640 (1987). This fact, too, is missing from the majority's account.

12 The majority gratuitously characterizes Worthy's testimony as being contradictory on the facts essential to McCleskey's Massiah claim. See ante, at 6. According to the District Court — which is obviously in a better position to know than is the majority — "Worthy never wavered from the fact that someone, at some point, requested his permission to move Evans to be near McCleskey." App. 78; accord id., at 81 ("The fact that someone, at some point, requested his permission to move Evans is the one fact from which Worthy never wavered in his two days of direct and cross-examination. The state has introduced no affirmative evidence that Worthy is either lying or mistaken").

The court decides questions we didn't grant certiorari too, and doesn't even understand what the case is about (more than reputation): Justice Marshall's dissent in Siegert v. Gilley (May 23, 1991)

JUSTICE MARSHALL, with whom JUSTICE BLACKMUN joins, and with whom JUSTICE STEVENS joins as to Parts II and III, dissenting.

The majority today decides a question on which we did not grant certiorari. Moreover, in deciding that petitioner Siegert failed to allege a violation of a clearly established constitutional right, the majority completely mischaracterizes the nature of Siegert's claim. Siegert alleged significantly more than mere "damage [to] reputation" and "future employment prospects." Ante at 500 U. S. 234. Because the alleged defamation was "accompan[ied] [by a] loss of government employment," Paul v. Davis, 424 U. S. 693, 424 U. S. 706 (1976) (emphasis added), as well as a change in "legal status" occasioned by the effective foreclosure of any opportunity for hospital credentials, see id. at 424 U. S. 705, Siegert has alleged the deprivation of a cognizable liberty interest in reputation. Because I view the majority's disposition of this case as both procedurally and substantively unjustified, I dissent.

I

The majority incorrectly claims that

"[w]e granted certiorari in this case to determine whether the . . . Court of Appeals . . . properly directed dismissal of petitioner's Bivens claim on the grounds that he had not overcome respondent's claim of qualified immunity."

Ante at 500 U. S. 227. In fact, the two questions on which we granted certiorari were much more specific.

"1. In a claim for damages under Bivens v. Six Unknown Named Agents, 403 U. S. 388 (1971), in which malice has been alleged and where qualified immunity has been raised as a defense, whether a 'heightened pleading' standard which precludes limited discovery prior to disposition on a summary judgment motion violates applicable law?"

"2. In a Bivens claim for damages, whether a federal official can be qualifiedly immune from suit without regard to whether the challenged conduct was discretionary in nature?"

Pet. for Cert. i. According to this Court's Rule 14.1(a): "[O]nly the questions set forth in the petition [for writ of certiorari], or fairly included therein, will be considered by the Court." In my view, neither of the questions set forth in the petition is broad enough to subsume the issue that the majority contends is presented in this case. [1]

One would have thought from the questioning during oral argument that the Court was well aware that it was at least debatable whether the issue the majority now decides was within the grant of review. When counsel for Siegert addressed the question whether Siegert had stated a compensable injury to a protected liberty interest, she was admonished:

"[T]he first question presented in your petition for certiorari is the extent of discovery which you should be allowed where there's a defensive [sic] qualified immunity. That really has nothing to do with the merits of your case, I would think."

Tr. of Oral Arg. 5. When counsel raised the issue again, she was told: "You really haven't explicitly addressed either of the questions presented in your petition for certiorari. I suggest you do so." Id. at 12. Rather than attempting to explain why the issue the majority today reaches is subsumed by the grant of certiorari, the majority disingenuously recharacterizes the question presented.

"Absent unusual circumstances, we are chary of considering issues not presented in petitions for certiorari." Berkemer v. McCarty, 468 U. S. 420, 468 U. S. 443, n. 38 (1984) (citation omitted). The majority makes no attempt to show that this case presents "unusual circumstances." Moreover, the significance of the issue the majority decides -- the extent of a government employee's constitutional liberty interest in reputation -- militates even more heavily in favor of restraint. As the author of today's opinion once wrote:

"Where difficult issues of great public importance are involved, there are strong reasons to adhere scrupulously to the customary limitations on our discretion."

Illinois v. Gates, 462 U. S. 213, 462 U. S. 224 (1983). Adherence to "customary limitations on our discretion" is necessary not only to ensure that parties are not denied their "day in court" but also to ensure that we receive the full benefit of briefing and argument before deciding difficult and important legal issues. The issue that now has become central to the majority's disposition of this case received only scant briefing by the parties. See Brief for Petitioner 17-20; Brief for Respondent 26, n. 16. The majority's insistence on reaching this issue in this context disserves our adjudicative process and undermines public respect for our decisions.

II

I also disagree with the merits of the majority's holding. The majority concludes that Siegert has not alleged the violation of any "right," "clearly established" or otherwise. In my view, there can be no doubt that the conduct alleged deprived Siegert of a protected liberty interest, and that this right was clearly established at the time Gilley wrote his letter. Siegert's claim, therefore, should surmount Gilley's assertion of qualified immunity. See Harlow v. Fitzgerald, 457 U. S. 800, 457 U. S. 818 (1982). [2]

A

Paul v. Davis, 424 U. S. 693 (1976), holds that injury to reputation, standing alone, is not enough to demonstrate deprivation of a liberty interest. See id. at 424 U. S. 712. Paul also establishes, however, that injury to reputation does deprive a person of a liberty interest when the injury is combined with the impairment of "some more tangible" government benefit. Id. at 424 U. S. 701. It is enough, for example, if the plaintiff shows that the reputational injury causes the "loss of government employment," id. at 424 U. S. 706, or the imposition of a legal disability, such as the loss of "the right to purchase or obtain liquor in common with the rest of the citizenry," id. at 424 U. S. 708 (citing Wisconsin v. Constantineau, 400 U. S. 433 (1971)).

This standard is met here, because the injury to Siegert's reputation caused him to lose the benefit of eligibility for future government employment. A condition of Siegert's employment with the Army hospital in Bremerhaven was that he be "credentialed" to treat both children and adults. Siegert alleges (and we must accept as true) that Gilley's letter caused him not to be credentialed, and thus effectively foreclosed his eligibility for future Government employment. According to Siegert, after Gilley wrote the letter charging that Siegert was "inept and unethical, perhaps the least trustworthy individual I have supervised in . . . thirteen years," App. 6, Siegert was informed that the Army's credentials committee was recommending that he not be credentialed because reports about him were "extremely unfavorable," id. at 7. As a result, Siegert contends, he lost government employment as a psychologist at the Bremerhaven Army hospital, similar future employment at another Army hospital in Stuttgart, and any legitimate opportunity to be considered for like Government employment any time in the future. See id. at 6-9, 19-23. [3]

We have repeatedly recognized that an individual suffers the loss of a protected liberty interest

"'where government action has operated to bestow a badge of disloyalty or infamy, with an attendant foreclosure from other employment opportunity.'"

Paul v. Davis, supra, 424 U.S. at 424 U. S. 705, quoting Cafeteria Workers v. McElroy, 367 U. S. 886, 367 U. S. 898 (1961) (emphasis supplied by Paul v. Davis Court). Thus, although the at-will government employee in Board of Regents of State Colleges v. Roth, 408 U. S. 564 (1972), did not have a legal entitlement to retain his job, the Court recognized that a liberty interest would be deprived where "the State . . . imposed on [the plaintiff] a stigma or other disability that foreclosed his freedom to take advantage of other employment opportunities."

Id. at 408 U. S. 573. Accord, Paul, supra, 424 U.S. at 424 U. S. 709-710 (quoting Roth). [4] The same conclusion should apply here.

Citing Paul, the majority suggests that reputational injury deprives a person of liberty only when combined with loss of present employment, not future employment. See ante at 500 U. S. 234. This suggestion rests on a gross mischaracterization of Paul. The Paul Court rejected a private employee's generalized claim of loss of future employment prospects where the plaintiff made no showing of a loss of government employment or future opportunities for government employment; indeed no governmental benefit or entitlement was at risk in Paul. The plaintiff in Paul, who had been labeled by the government as a shoplifter, had merely been told by his supervisor that, although he would not be fired, he "had best not find himself in a similar situation'" in the future. Paul, supra, at 424 U. S. 696. Therefore, Paul truly was a case where the only interest the plaintiff was asserting was injury to his reputation.

Although Paul rejected a private employee's claim, it expressly reaffirmed Roth, McElroy, and other decisions recognizing that stigmatization deprives a person of liberty when it causes loss of present or future government employment. See Paul, supra, at 424 U. S. 702-710. Indeed, the Paul Court explained the decision in Joint Anti-Fascist Refugee Comm. v. McGrath, 341 U. S. 123 (1951) -- which held that the plaintiffs stated a cognizable claim against the Attorney General's designation of certain organizations as "Communist" on a list furnished to the Civil Service Commission -- primarily in terms of the deprivation this action would work on the present and future government employment opportunities of members of such organizations. See Paul, 424 U.S. at 424 U. S. 702-705; see also id. at 424 U. S. 704 ("To be deprived not only of present government employment but of future opportunity, for it certainly is no small injury when government employment so dominates the field of opportunity,'" quoting Joint Anti-Fascist Refugee Comm., supra, 341 U.S. at 341 U. S. 184-185 (Jackson, J., concurring)). Foreclosure of opportunity for future government employment clearly is within the ambit of the "more tangible interests" that, when coupled with reputation, create a protected liberty interest. See Paul, supra, 424 U.S. at 424 U. S. 701-702 (noting the Court's recognition of a liberty interest in United States v. Lovett, 328 U. S. 303 (1946), where congressional action stigmatized three Government employees and "`prohibit[ed] their ever holding a government job'").

B

It is also clear that Gilley should have known that his alleged conduct deprived Siegert of a liberty interest. If our case law left any doubt that reputational injury deprives a person of liberty when it causes loss of future government employment, that doubt was dispelled by the decisions of the Court of Appeals for the District of Columbia Circuit, the jurisdiction where Gilley worked. See, e.g., Davis v. Scherer, 468 U. S. 183, 468 U. S. 191-192 (1984) (for purposes of determining whether a constitutional right was clearly established, the Court may look to the law of the relevant circuit at the time of the conduct in question). [5] On numerous occasions prior to Gilley's challenged conduct, the District of Columbia Circuit reiterated the principle that a person is deprived of a protected liberty interest when stigmatizing charges "effectively foreclos[e] [his or her] freedom to take advantage of other Government employment opportunities." Old Dominion Dairy Products, Inc. v. Secretary of Defense, 203 U.S.App.D.C. 371, 382, 631 F.2d 953, 964 (1980). See also Conset Corp. v. Community Services Administration, 211 U.S.App.D.C. 61, 67, 655 F.2d 1291, 1297 (1981) (liberty deprived if "memorandum was effectively used to bar Conset from government contract work due to charges calling into question Conset's integrity, honesty or business reputation"); Mosrie v. Barry, 231 U.S.App.D.C. 113, 123, 718 F.2d 1151, 1161 (1983) (liberty deprived if government-imposed stigma "so severely impaired [the plaintiff's] ability to take advantage of a legal right, such as a right to be considered for government contracts or employment . . . that the government can be said to have 'foreclosed' one's ability to take advantage of it and thus extinguished the right"); Doe v. United States Department of Justice, 243 U.S.App.D.C. 354, 373, 753 F.2d 1092, 1111 (1985) (government defamation resulting in a "[l]oss of present or future government employment" implicates a liberty interest).

This established principle was applied by the District of Columbia Circuit in a case with facts strikingly similar to those that confront us here. In Bartel v. Federal Aviation Administration, 233 U.S.App.D.C. 297, 725 F.2d 1403 (1984), the plaintiff, Bartel, had once worked for the Federal Aviation Administration (FAA) as an air safety inspector, left its employ for a job in Canada, and then applied for reemployment with the FAA. An FAA official who learned that Bartel was seeking reemployment allegedly sent letters to other FAA officials stating his opinion that Bartel had violated the federal Privacy Act of 1974, 5 U.S.C. § 552a, during his previous tenure with the FAA. As a result, Bartel claimed the FAA informed him that he would not be hired for a job for which he had been determined to be "best qualified." Eventually Bartel secured a temporary GS-12 position, although a permanent GS-13 position for which he was qualified was available. See 223 U.S.App.D.C. at 299-300, 725 F.2d at 1405-1406. Bartel brought suit claiming, inter alia, a due process violation because he had been branded and denied employment without an opportunity to refute the charges in the letter. The District of Columbia Circuit agreed that Paul v. Davis was controlling, and found that Bartel had stated a cognizable liberty interest in reputation sufficient to survive a motion for summary judgment. See 233 U.S.App.D.C. at 309, 725 F.2d at 1415.

"The complaint states that Bartel was denied a specific job because of the [stigmatizing letter]. . . . The crux of the complaint, as we read it, is that Bartel was not considered for FAA employment on a basis equal with others of equivalent skill and experience -- i.e., that he was wrongfully denied the 'right to be considered for government [employment] in common with all other persons.' For an individual whose entire career revolved around aviation, this denial may have effectively abridged his freedom to take advantage of public employment."

Ibid. (citations omitted; emphasis add.) See also Doe v. United States Department of Justice, supra, at 373, n. 20, 753 F.2d at 1111 (noting that Bartel had "alleged a protected liberty interest because an FAA letter had accused him of Privacy Act violations and thus hampered his ability to seek government employment on an equal basis with others of similar skill and experience").

After the District of Columbia Circuit's holding in Bartel, it should have been abundantly clear to any reasonable governmental official that mailing stigmatizing letters in circumstances that would severely impair or effectively foreclose a government employee from obtaining similar government employment in the future would deprive the individual of a constitutionally protected liberty interest. Yet that is precisely what Siegert alleges Gilley did. [6]

C

Finally, there remains the primary question on which we granted certiorari: whether, in a Bivens action in which malice has been alleged and where qualified immunity has been raised as a defense, a "heightened pleading" standard must be met in order to allow limited discovery prior to disposition on a summary judgment motion. Under my understanding of Paul, I do not believe Siegert would have to prove malice in order to establish a constitutional violation. However, I believe the Court of Appeals erred in holding that a district court may not permit limited discovery in a case involving unconstitutional motive unless the plaintiff proffers direct evidence of the unconstitutional motive. See 282 U.S.App.D.C. 392, 398-399, 895 F.2d 797, 803-804 (1990). Because evidence of such intent is peculiarly within the control of the defendant, the "heightened pleading" rule employed by the Court of Appeals effectively precludes any Bivens action in which the defendant's state of mind is an element of the underlying claim. I find no warrant for such a rule as a matter of precedent or common sense.

This Court has stated that "bare allegations of malice should not suffice to subject government officials either to the costs of trial or to the burdens of broad-reaching discovery." Harlow v. Fitzgerald, 457 U.S. at 457 U. S. 817-818. Yet it also has recognized that, in some instances, limited discovery "tailored specifically to the question of . . . qualified immunity" may be necessary. Anderson v. Creighton, 483 U. S. 635, 483 U. S. 646-647, n. 6 (1987). In my view, a plaintiff pleading a Bivens claim that requires proof of the defendant's intent should be afforded such discovery whenever the plaintiff has gone beyond bare, conclusory allegations of unconstitutional purpose. Siegert has offered highly specific circumstantial evidence of unconstitutional motive. For this reason, I believe that the Court of Appeals erred in overturning the District Court's order permitting limited discovery.

III

It is a perverse jurisprudence that recognizes the loss of a "legal" right to buy liquor as a significant deprivation but fails to accord equal significance to the foreclosure of opportunities for government employment. The loss in Siegert's case is particularly tragic because his professional specialty appears to be one very difficult to practice outside of government institutions. The majority's callous disregard of the real interests at stake in this case is profoundly disturbing. I dissent.

Notes

[1] The question on which the majority claims the Court granted certiorari actually was presented in respondent Gilley's brief in opposition to certiorari. See Brief in Opposition I ("Whether the court of appeals correctly dismissed this Bivens action on grounds of qualified immunity"). However, our grant of certiorari did not purport to accept respondent's depiction of the question presented. See 498 U. S. 918 (1990). Indeed, in his brief on the merits, respondent urged that the very issue that the majority today resolves in his favor "is scarcely related to the questions on which the Court granted certiorari, [and] is not properly before the Court." Brief for Respondent 26, n. 16.

[2] The question whether Gilley's alleged conduct in this case was a discretionary function for which he would be entitled to raise the defense of qualified immunity was the second question presented in the petition for certiorari. See supra at 500 U. S. 237. The majority does not address this issue. Consequently, I will state only briefly my view that Gilley's function in responding to the credentials request form was inherently discretionary. The form requested that Gilley send "all information" on Siegert's "job performance and [hospital] privileges." App. to Pet. for Cert. 55a. Because the form did not prescribe any specific conduct and Siegert has not identified any other rules or restrictions which mandated a specific mode or manner of response, Gilley was called upon to exercise his judgment as to what information must be sent.

[3] Siegert contends that he had a legitimate expectation that he would be credentialed based upon his job performance at St. Elizabeth's. For his first five years at St. Elizabeth's, Siegert attests that he received exemplary job performance ratings from his supervisors and was rated "outstanding" for his performance in 1984. App. 20. Gilley became Siegert's supervisor in January, 1985. According to Siegert, professional and personal differences soon arose between the two because of Siegert's extensive medical leave due to a head injury and Siegert's resistance to Gilley's attempts to modify some aspects of a behavior modification program. Id. at 19-20. After Siegert had obtained his position with Bremerhaven, he was given advanced notice that he was going to be terminated by St. Elizabeth's. Siegert then worked out an agreement with St. Elizabeth's with the precise understanding that he would resign and his personnel file would not be tainted. Id. at 21. Approximately three weeks after Siegert resigned, Gilley sent the stigmatizing letter. See id. at 5-6.

[4] Notably, the concept of liberty under the Due Process Clause includes
"'the right of the individual to contract, to engage in any of the common occupations of life . . . and generally to enjoy those privileges long recognized . . . as essential to the orderly pursuit of happiness by free men.'"
Board of Regents v. Roth, 408 U. S. 564, 408 U. S. 572 (1972), quoting Meyer v. Nebraska, 262 U. S. 390, 262 U. S. 399 (1923).

[5] In Anderson v. Creighton, 483 U. S. 635 (1987), this Court explained that a right is "clearly established" when its "contours [are] sufficiently clear that a reasonable official would understand that what he is doing violates that right." Id. at 483 U. S. 640. Anderson stressed that a right may be "clearly established" even though "the very action in question" has not previously been held unlawful. Rather, it is enough "to say that, in the light of preexisting law, the unlawfulness [is] apparent." Ibid. Accord, Mitchell v. Forsyth, 472 U. S. 511, 472 U. S. 535, n. 12 (1985) ("We do not intend to suggest that an official is always immune from liability or suit for a warrantless search merely because the warrant requirement has never explicitly been held to apply to a search conducted in identical circumstances").

[6] The "Credential Information Request Form" specifically informed Gilley that Siegert was applying for hospital credentials in order to work as a clinical psychologist at an Army hospital and that information on Siegert's credentials and work history was needed in order to complete the process. See App. to Pet. for Cert. 55a. As an objective matter, in these circumstances, Gilley should have known that to send a letter charging that Siegert was "inept and unethical, perhaps the least trustworthy individual I have supervised in . . . thirteen years" would severely hamper, if not foreclose, Siegert's ability to gain credentials, particularly for working with children. Cf. Old Dominion Dairy Products, Inc. v. Secretary of Defense, 203 U.S.App.D.C. 371, 381 631 F.2d 953, 963 (1980) ("A determination was made that Old Dominion lacked integrity,' and that determination was communicated through official Government channels, and would likely continue to be communicated every time Old Dominion bid for a contract").

Consent to search car shouldn't include consent to open containers, should need another consent for that: Justice Marshall's dissent in Florida v. Luz Piedad Jimeno (May 23, 1991)

Justice Marshall, with whom Justice Stevens joins, dissenting.

The question in this case is whether an individual's general consent to a search of the interior of his car for narcotics should reasonably be understood as consent to a search of closed containers inside the car. Nothing in today's opinion dispels my belief that the two are not one and the same from the consenting individual's standpoint. Consequently, an individual's consent to a search of the interior of his car should not be understood to authorize a search of closed containers inside the car. I dissent.

In my view, analysis of this question must start by identifying the differing expectations of privacy that attach to cars and closed containers. It is well established that an individual has but a limited expectation of privacy in the interior of his car. A car ordinarily is not used as a residence or reposi- tory for one's personal effects, and its passengers and con- tents are generally exposed to public view. See Cardwell v. Lewis, 417 U. S. 583, 590 (1974) (plurality opinion). More- over, cars "are subjected to pervasive and continuing govern- mental regulation and controls," South Dakota v. Opperman, 428 U.S. 364, 368 (1976), and may be seized by the police when necessary to protect public safety or to facilitate the flow of traffic, see id., at 368-369.

In contrast, it is equally well established that an individual has a heightened expectation of privacy in the contents of a closed container. See, e. g., United States v. Chadwick, 433 U.S. 1, 13 (1977). Luggage, handbags, paper bags, and other containers are common repositories for one's papers and effects, and the protection of these items from state intrusion lies at the heart of the Fourth Amendment. U. S. Const., Amdt. 4 ("The right of the people to be secure in their . . . papers, and effects, against unreasonable searches and seizures, shall not be violated"). By placing his possessions inside a container, an individual manifests an intent that his possessions be "preserve[d] as private," United States v. Katz, 389 U.S. 347, 351 (1967), and thus kept "free from public examination," United States v. Chadwick, supra, at 11.

The distinct privacy expectations that a person has in a car as opposed to a closed container do not merge when the individual uses his car to transport the container. In this situation, the individual still retains a heightened expectation of privacy in the container. See Robbins v. California, 453 U.S. 420, 425 (1981) (plurality opinion); Arkansas v. Sanders, 442 U.S. 753, 763-764 (1979). Nor does an individual's heightened expectation of privacy turn on the type of container in which he stores his possessions. Notwithstanding the majority's suggestion to the contrary, see ante, at 3-4, this Court has soundly rejected any distinction between "worthy" containers, like locked briefcases, and "unworthy" containers, like paper bags.

"Even though such a distinction perhaps could evolve in a series of cases in which paper bags, locked trunks, lunch buckets, and orange crates were placed on one side of the line or the other, the central purpose of the Fourth Amendment forecloses such a distinction. For just as the most frail cottage in the kingdom is absolutely entitled to the same guarantees of privacy as the most majestic mansion, so also may a traveler who carries a toothbrush and a few articles of clothing in a paper bag or knotted scarf claim an equal right to conceal his possessions from official inspection as the sophisticated executive with the locked attachÀe case." United States v. Ross, 456 U.S. 798, 822 (1982) (footnotes omitted).

Because an individual's expectation of privacy in a container is distinct from, and far greater than, his expectation of privacy in the interior of his car, it follows that an individual's consent to a search of the interior of his car cannot necessarily be understood as extending to containers in the car. At the very least, general consent to search the car is ambiguous with respect to containers found inside the car. In my view, the independent and divisible nature of the privacy interests in cars and containers mandates that a police officer who wishes to search a suspicious container found during a consensual automobile search obtain additional consent to search the container. If the driver intended to authorize search of the container, he will say so; if not, then he will say no. [n.1] The only objection that the police could have to such a rule is that it would prevent them from exploiting the ignorance of a citizen who simply did not anticipate that his con- sent to search the car would be understood to authorize the police to rummage through his packages.

According to the majority, it nonetheless is reasonable for a police officer to construe generalized consent to search an automobile for narcotics as extending to closed containers, because "[a] reasonable person may be expected to know that narcotics are generally carried in some form of a container." Ante, at 3. This is an interesting contention. By the same logic a person who consents to a search of the car from the driver's seat could also be deemed to consent to a search of his person or indeed of his body cavities, since a reasonable person may be expected to know that drug couriers frequently store their contraband on their persons or in their body cavities. I suppose (and hope) that even the majority would reject this conclusion, for a person who consents to the search of his car for drugs certainly does not consent to a search of things other than his car for drugs. But this example illustrates that if there is a reason for not treating a closed container as something "other than" the car in which it sits, the reason cannot be based on intuitions about where people carry drugs. The majority, however, never identifies a reason for conflating the distinct privacy expectations that a person has in a car and in closed containers.

The majority also argues that the police should not be required to secure specific consent to search a closed container, because " `[t]he community has a real interest in encouraging consent.' " Ante, at 4, quoting Schneckloth v. Bustamonte, 412 U.S. 218, 243 (1973). I find this rationalization equally unsatisfactory. If anything, a rule that permits the police to construe a consent to search more broadly than it may have been intended would discourage individuals from consenting to searches of their cars. Apparently, the majority's real concern is that if the police were required to ask for additional consent to search a closed container found during the consensual search of an automobile, an individual who did not mean to authorize such additional searching would have an opportunity to say no. In essence, then, the majority is claiming that "the community has a real interest" not in encouraging citizens to consent to investigatory efforts of their law enforcement agents, but rather in encouraging individuals to be duped by them. This is not the community that the Fourth Amendment contemplates.

Almost 20 years ago, this Court held that an individual could validly "consent" to a search -- or, in other words, waive his right to be free from an otherwise unlawful search -- with- out being told that he had the right to withhold his consent. See Schneckloth v. Bustamonte, supra. In Schneckloth, as in this case, the Court cited the practical interests in efficacious law enforcement as the basis for not requiring the police to take meaningful steps to establish the basis of an individual's consent. I dissented in Schneckloth, and what I wrote in that case applies with equal force here.

"I must conclude, with some reluctance, that when the Court speaks of practicality, what it really is talking of is the continued ability of the police to capitalize on the ignorance of citizens so as to accomplish by subterfuge what they could not achieve by relying only on the knowing relinquishment of constitutional rights. Of course it would be "practical" for the police to ignore the commands of the Fourth Amendment, if by practicality we mean that more criminals will be apprehended, even though the constitutional rights of innocent people go by the board. But such a practical advantage is achieved only at the cost of permitting the police to disregard the limitations that the Constitution places on their behavior, a cost that a constitutional democracy cannot long absorb." 412 U. S., at 288.

I dissent.

Notes

1 Alternatively, the police could obtain such consent in advance by asking the individual for permission to search both the car and any closed containers found inside.

The suspicionless police sweep of buses violates privacy: Justice Marshall's dissent in Florida v. Bostick (June 20, 1991)

Justice Marshall, with whom Justice Blackmun and Justice Stevens join, dissenting.

Our Nation, we are told, is engaged in a "war on drugs." No one disputes that it is the job of law-enforcement officials to devise effective weapons for fighting this war. But the effectiveness of a law-enforcement technique is not proof of its constitutionality. The general warrant, for example, was certainly an effective means of law enforcement. Yet it was one of the primary aims of the Fourth Amendment to protect citizens from the tyranny of being singled out for search and seizure without particularized suspicion notwithstanding the effectiveness of this method. See Boyd v. United States, 116 U.S. 616, 625-630 (1886); see also Harris v. United States, 331 U.S. 145, 171 (1947) (Frankfurter, J., dissenting). In my view, the law-enforcement technique with which we are confronted in this case — the suspicionless police sweep of buses in intrastate or interstate travel — bears all of the indicia of coercion and unjustified intrusion associated with the general warrant. Because I believe that the bus sweep at issue in this case violates the core values of the Fourth Amendment, I dissent.

I

At issue in this case is a "new and increasingly common tactic in the war on drugs": the suspicionless police sweep of buses in interstate or intrastate travel. United States v. Lewis, — U. S. App. D. C. —, —, 921 F. 2d 1294, 1295 (1990); see United States v. Flowers, 912 F. 2d 707, 710 (CA4 1990) (describing technique in Charlotte, North Carolina); United States v. Madison, 744 F. Supp. 490, 492-493 (SDNY 1990) (describing technique in Port Authority terminal in New York City); United States v. Chandler, 744 F. Supp. 333, 335 (DC 1990) ("[I]t has become routine to subject interstate travelers to warrantless searches and intimidating interviews while sitting aboard a bus stopped for a short layover in the Capital"); 554 So. 2d 1153, 1156-1157 (Fla. 1989) (describing Florida police policy of " `working the buses' "); see also ante, at 1. Typically under this technique, a group of state or federal officers will board a bus while it is stopped at an intermediate point on its route. Often displaying badges, weapons or other indicia of authority, the officers identify themselves and announce their purpose to intercept drug traffickers. They proceed to approach individual passengers, requesting them to show identification, produce their tickets, and explain the purpose of their travels. Never do the officers advise the passengers that they are free not to speak with the officers. An "interview" of this type ordinarily culminates in a request for consent to search the passenger's luggage. See generally United States v. Lewis, supra, at —, 921 F. 2d, at 1296; United States v. Flowers, supra, at 708-709; United States v. Madison, supra, at 493; 554 So. 2d, at 1154.

These sweeps are conducted in "dragnet" style. The police admittedly act without an "articulable suspicion" in deciding which buses to board and which passengers to approach for interviewing. [n.1] By proceeding systematically in this fashion, the police are able to engage in a tremendously high volume of searches. See, e. g., Florida v. Kerwick, 512 So. 2d 347, 348-349 (Fla. App. 1987) (single officer employing sweep technique able to search over 3,000 bags in nine-month period). The percentage of successful drug interdictions is low. See United States v. Flowers, supra, at 710 (sweep of 100 buses resulted in seven arrests).

To put it mildly, these sweeps "are inconvenient, intrusive, and intimidating." United States v. Chandler, 744 F. Supp. at, 335. They occur within cramped confines, with officers typically placing themselves in between the passenger selected for an interview and the exit of the bus. See, e. g., id., at 336. Because the bus is only temporarily stationed at a point short of its destination, the passengers are in no position to leave as a means of evading the officers' questioning. Undoubtedly, such a sweep holds up the progress of the bus. See United States v. Fields, 909 F. 2d 470, 474 n. 2 (CA11 1990); cf. United States v. Rembert, 694 F. Supp. 163, 175 (WDNC 1988) (reporting testimony of officer that he makes " `every effort in the world not to delay the bus' " but that the driver does not leave terminal until sweep is complete). Thus, this "new and increasingly common tactic," United States v. Lewis, supra, at —, 921 F. 2d, at 1295, burdens the experience of traveling by bus with a degree of governmental interference to which, until now, our society has been proudly unaccustomed. See, e. g., State ex rel. Ekstrom v. Justice Court, 136 Ariz. 1, 6, 663 P. 2d 992, 997 (1983) (Feldman, J., concurring) ("The thought that an American can be compelled to `show his papers' before exercising his right to walk the streets, drive the highways or board the trains is repugnant to American institutions and ideals").

This aspect of the suspicionless sweep has not been lost on many of the lower courts called upon to review the constitutionality of this practice. Remarkably, the courts located at the heart of the "drug war" have been the most adamant in condemning this technique. As one Florida court put it:

" `[T]he evidence in this cause has evoked images of other days, under other flags, when no man traveled his nation's roads or railways without fear of unwarranted interruption, by individuals who held temporary power in the Government. The spectre of American citizens being asked, by badge-wielding police, for identification, travel papers — in short a raison d'etre — is foreign to any fair reading of the Constitution, and its guarantee of human liberties. This is not Hitler's Berlin, nor Stalin's Moscow, nor is it white supremacist South Africa. Yet in Broward County, Florida, these police officers approach every person on board buses and trains ("that time permits") and check identification [and] tickets, [and] ask to search luggage — all in the name of "voluntary cooperation" with law enforcement . . . .' " 554 So. 2d, at 1158, quoting State v. Kerwick, supra, at 348349 (quoting trial court order).

The District Court for the District of Columbia spoke in equally pointed words:

"It seems rather incongruous at this point in the world's history that we find totalitarian states becoming more like our free society while we in this nation are taking on their former trappings of suppressed liberties and freedoms."

"The random indiscriminate stopping and questioning of individuals on interstate busses seems to have gone too far. If this Court approves such `bus stops' and allows prosecutions to be based on evidence seized as a result of such `stops,' then we will have stripped our citizens of basic Constitutional protections. Such action would be inconsistent with what this nation has stood for during its 200 years of existence. If passengers on a bus passing through the Capital of this great nation cannot be free from police interference where there is absolutely no basis for the police officers to stop and question them, then the police will be free to accost people on our streets without any reason or cause. In this `anything goes' war on drugs, random knocks on the doors of our citizens' homes seeking `consent' to search for drugs cannot be far away. This is not America." United States v. Lewis, 728 F. Supp. 784, 788-789, rev'd, — U. S. App. D. C. —, 921 F. 2d 1294 (1990).

See also United States v. Alexander, 755 F. Supp. 448, 453 (DC 1991); United States v. Madison, 744 F. Supp., at 495-497; United States v. Chandler, supra, at, 335-336; United States v. Mark, 742 F. Supp. 17, 18-19 (DC 1990); United States v. Alston, 742 F. Supp. 13, 15 (DC 1990); United States v. Cothran, 729 F. Supp. 153, 156-158 (DC 1990), rev'd, — U. S. App. D. C. —, 921 F. 2d 1294 (1990); United States v. Felder, 732 F. Supp. 204, 209 (DC 1990).

The question for this Court, then, is whether the suspicion less, dragnet-style sweep of buses in intrastate and interstate travel is consistent with the Fourth Amendment. The majority suggests that this latest tactic in the drug war is perfectly compatible with the Constitution. I disagree.

II

I have no objection to the manner in which the majority frames the test for determining whether a suspicionless bus sweep amounts to a Fourth Amendment "seizure." I agree that the appropriate question is whether a passenger who is approached during such a sweep "would feel free to decline the officers' requests or otherwise terminate the encounter." Ante, at 7. What I cannot understand is how the majority can possibly suggest an affirmative answer to this question.

The majority reverses what it characterizes as the Florida Supreme Court's "per se rule" against suspicionless encounters between the police and bus passengers, see ante, at 3-4, 5-6, 10, suggesting only in dictum its "doubt" that a seizure occurred on the facts of this case, see ante, at 7. However, the notion that the Florida Supreme Court decided this case on the basis of any "per se rule" independent of the facts of this case is wholly a product of the majority's imagination. As the majority acknowledges, the Florida Supreme Court "stated explicitly the factual premise for its decision." Ante, at 1. This factual premise contained all of the details of the encounter between respondent and the police. See 554 So. 2d, at 1154; ante, at 2. The lower court's analysis of whether respondent was seized drew heavily on these facts, and the court repeatedly emphasized that its conclusion was based on "all the circumstances" of this case. 554 So. 2d, at 1157 (emphasis added); see ibid. ("Here, the circumstances indicate that the officers effectively `seized' [respondent]" (emphasis added)).

The majority's conclusion that the Florida Supreme Court, contrary to all appearances, ignored these facts is based solely on the failure of the lower court to expressly incorporate all of the facts into its reformulation of the certified question on which respondent took his appeal. See ante, at 3. [n.2] The majority never explains the basis of its implausible assumption that the Florida Supreme Court intended its phrasing of the certified question to trump its opinion's careful treatment of the facts in this case. Certainly, when this Court issues an opinion, it does not intend lower courts and parties to treat as irrelevant the analysis of facts that the parties neglected to cram into the question presented in the petition for certiorari. But in any case, because the issue whether a seizure has occurred in any given factual setting is a question of law, see United States v. Mendenhall, 446 U.S. 544, 554-555 (1980) (opinion of Stewart, J.); United States v. Maragh, 282 U. S. App. D. C. 256, 258-259, 894 F. 2d 415, 417-418 (CADC), cert. denied, — U. S. — (1990), nothing prevents this Court from deciding on its own whether a seizure occurred based on all of the facts of this case as they appear in the opinion of the Florida Supreme Court.

These facts exhibit all of the elements of coercion associated with a typical bus sweep. Two officers boarded the Greyhound bus on which respondent was a passenger while the bus, en route from Miami to Atlanta, was on a brief stop to pick up passengers in Fort Lauderdale. The officers made a visible display of their badges and wore bright green "raid" jackets bearing the insignia of the Broward County Sheriff's Department; one held a gun in a recognizable weapons pouch. See 554 So. 2d, at 1154, 1157. These facts alone constitute an intimidating "show of authority." See Michigan v. Chesternut, 486 U.S. 567, 575 (1988) (display of weapon contributes to coercive environment); United States v. Mendenhall, supra, at 554 (opinion of Stewart, J.) ("threatening presence of several officers" and "display of a weapon"); id., at 555 (uniformed attire). Once on board, the officers approached respondent, who was sitting in the back of the bus, identified themselves as narcotics officers and began to question him. See 554 So. 2d, at 1154. One officer stood in front of respondent's seat, partially blocking the narrow aisle through which respondent would have been required to pass to reach the exit of the bus. See id., at 1157.

As far as is revealed by facts on which the Florida Supreme Court premised its decision, the officers did not advise respondent that he was free to break off this "interview." Inexplicably, the majority repeatedly stresses the trial court's implicit finding that the police officers advised respondent that he was free to refuse permission to search his travel bag. See ante, at 2, 7-8. This aspect of the exchange between respondent and the police is completely irrelevant to the issue before us. For as the State concedes, and as the majority purports to "accept," id., at 4, if respondent was unlawfully seized when the officers approached him and initiated questioning, the resulting search was likewise unlawful no matter how well advised respondent was of his right to refuse it. See Florida v. Royer, 460 U.S. 491, 501, 507-508 (1983) (plurality opinion); Wong Sun v. United States, 371 U.S. 471 (1963). Consequently, the issue is not whether a passenger in respondent's position would have felt free to deny consent to the search of his bag, but whether such a passenger — without being apprised of his rights — would have felt free to terminate the antecedent encounter with the police.

Unlike the majority, I have no doubt that the answer to this question is no. Apart from trying to accommodate the officers, respondent had only two options. First, he could have remained seated while obstinately refusing to respond to the officers' questioning. But in light of the intimidating show of authority that the officers made upon boarding the bus, respondent reasonably could have believed that such behavior would only arouse the officers' suspicions and intensify their interrogation. Indeed, officers who carry out bus sweeps like the one at issue here frequently admit that this is the effect of a passenger's refusal to cooperate. See, e. g., United States v. Cothran, 729 F. Supp., at 156; United States v. Felder, 732 F. Supp., at 205. The majority's observation that a mere refusal to answer questions, "without more," does not give rise to a reasonable basis for seizing a passenger, ante, at 7, is utterly beside the point, because a passenger unadvised of his rights and otherwise unversed in constitutional law has no reason to know that the police cannot hold his refusal to cooperate against him.

Second, respondent could have tried to escape the officers' presence by leaving the bus altogether. But because doing so would have required respondent to squeeze past the gun-wielding inquisitor who was blocking the aisle of the bus, this hardly seems like a course that respondent reasonably would have viewed as available to him. [n.3] The majority lamely protests that nothing in the stipulated facts shows that the questioning officer "point[ed] [his] gu[n] at [respondent] or otherwise threatened him" with the weapon. Ante, at 8 (emphasis added). Our decisions recognize the obvious point, however, that the choice of the police to "display" their weapons during an encounter exerts significant coercive pressure on the confronted citizen. E. g., Michigan v. Chesternut, supra, at 575; United States v. Mendenhall, supra, at 554. We have never suggested that the police must go so far as to put a citizen in immediate apprehension of being shot before a court can take account of the intimidating effect of being questioned by an officer with weapon in hand.

Even if respondent had perceived that the officers would let him leave the bus, moreover, he could not reasonably have been expected to resort to this means of evading their intrusive questioning. For so far as respondent knew, the bus' departure from the terminal was imminent. Unlike a person approached by the police on the street, see Michigan v. Chesternut, supra, or at a bus or airport terminal after reaching his destination, see United States v. Mendenhall, supra, a passenger approached by the police at an intermediate point in a long bus journey cannot simply leave the scene and repair to a safe haven to avoid unwanted probing by law enforcement officials. The vulnerability that an intrastate or interstate traveler experiences when confronted by the police outside of his "own familiar territory" surely aggravates the coercive quality of such an encounter. See Schneckloth v. Bustamonte, 412 U.S. 218, 247 (1973).

The case on which the majority primarily relies, INS v. Delgado, 466 U.S. 210 (1984), is distinguishable in every relevant respect. In Delgado, this Court held that workers approached by law-enforcement officials inside of a factory were not "seized" for purposes of the Fourth Amendment. The Court was careful to point out, however, that the presence of the agents did not furnish the workers with a reasonable basis for believing that they were not free to leave the factory, as at least some of them did. See id., at 218-219, and n. 7. Unlike passengers confronted by law-enforcement officials on a bus stopped temporarily at an intermediate point in its journey, workers approached by law-enforcement officials at their workplace need not abandon personal belongings and venture into unfamiliar environs in order to avoid unwanted questioning. Moreover, the workers who did not leave the building in Delgado remained free to move about the entire factory, see id., at 218, a considerably less confining environment than a bus. Finally, contrary to the officer who confronted respondent, the law-enforcement officials in Delgado did not conduct their interviews with guns in hand. See id., at 212.

Rather than requiring the police to justify the coercive tactics employed here, the majority blames respondent for his own sensation of constraint. The majority concedes that respondent "did not feel free to leave the bus" as a means of breaking off the interrogation by the Broward County officers. Ante, at 6. But this experience of confinement, the majority explains, "was the natural result of his decision to take the bus." Ibid. (emphasis added). Thus, in the majority's view, because respondent's "freedom of movement was restricted by a factor independent of police conduct — i. e., by his being a passenger on a bus," ante, at 7, respondent was not seized for purposes of the Fourth Amendment.

This reasoning borders on sophism and trivializes the values that underlie the Fourth Amendment. Obviously, a person's "voluntary decision" to place himself in a room with only one exit does not authorize the police to force an encounter upon him by placing themselves in front of the exit. It is no more acceptable for the police to force an encounter on a person by exploiting his "voluntary decision" to expose himself to perfectly legitimate personal or social constraints. By consciously deciding to single out persons who have undertaken interstate or intrastate travel, officers who conduct suspicionless, dragnet-style sweeps put passengers to the choice of cooperating or of exiting their buses and possibly being stranded in unfamiliar locations. It is exactly because this "choice" is no "choice" at all that police engage this technique.

In my view, the Fourth Amendment clearly condemns the suspicionless, dragnet-style sweep of intrastate or interstate buses. Withdrawing this particular weapon from the government's drug-war arsenal would hardly leave the police without any means of combatting the use of buses as instrumentalities of the drug trade. The police would remain free, for example, to approach passengers whom they have a reasonable, articulable basis to suspect of criminal wrongdoing. [n.4] Alternatively, they could continue to confront passengers without suspicion so long as they took simple steps, like advising the passengers confronted of their right to decline to be questioned, to dispel the aura of coercion and intimidation that pervades such encounters. There is no reason to expect that such requirements would render the Nation's buses law enforcement-free zones.

III

The majority attempts to gloss over the violence that today's decision does to the Fourth Amendment with empty admonitions. "If th[e] [war on drugs] is to be fought," the majority intones, "those who fight it must respect the rights of individuals, whether or not those individuals are suspected of having committed a crime." Ante, at 9. The majority's actions, however, speak louder than its words.

I dissent.

Notes

1 That is to say, the police who conduct these sweeps decline to offer a reasonable, articulable suspicion of criminal wrongdoing sufficient to justify a warrantless "stop" or "seizure" of the confronted passenger. See Terry v. Ohio, 392 U.S. 1, 20-22, 30-31 (1968); Florida v. Royer, 460 U.S. 491, 498-499 (1983) (plurality opinion). It does not follow, however, that the approach of passengers during a sweep is completely random. Indeed, at least one officer who routinely confronts interstate travelers candidly admitted that race is a factor influencing his decision whom to approach. See United States v. Williams, No. 1:89CR0135 (ND Ohio, June 13, 1989), p. 3 ("Detective Zaller testified that the factors initiating the focus upon the three young black males in this case included: (1) that they were young and black . . . ."), aff'd, No. 89-4083 (CA6, Oct. 19, 1990), p. 7 (the officers "knew that the couriers, more often than not, were young black males"), vacated and remanded, 500 U. S. — (1991). Thus, the basis of the decision to single out particular passengers during a suspicion less sweep is less likely to be inarticulable than unspeakable.

2 As reformulated, this question read:

"Does an impermissible seizure result when police mount a drug search on buses during scheduled stops and question boarded passengers without articulable reasons for doing so, thereby obtaining consent to search the passengers' luggage?" 554 So. 2d, at 1154.

3 As the majority's discussion makes plain, see ante, at 2, 7-8, the officer questioning respondent clearly carried a weapons pouch during the interview. See also 554 So. 2d, at 1157.

4 Insisting that police officers explain their decision to single out a particular passenger for questioning would help prevent their reliance on impermissible criteria such as race. See n. 1, supra.

No victim-impact statements: Justice Marshall's dissent in Payne v. Tennessee (June 27, 1991)

Justice Marshall, with whom Justice Blackmun joins, dissenting.

Power, not reason, is the new currency of this Court's decisionmaking. Four Terms ago, a five-Justice majority of this Court held that "victim impact" evidence of the type at issue in this case could not constitutionally be introduced during the penalty phase of a capital trial. Booth v. Maryland, 482 U.S. 496 (1987). By another 5-4 vote, a majority of this Court rebuffed an attack upon this ruling just two Terms ago. South Carolina v. Gathers, 490 U.S. 805 (1989). Nevertheless, having expressly invited respondent to renew the attack, 498 U. S. — (1991), today's majority overrules Booth and Gathers and credits the dissenting views expressed in those cases. Neither the law nor the facts supporting Booth and Gathers underwent any change in the last four years. Only the personnel of this Court did.

In dispatching Booth and Gathers to their graves, today's majority ominously suggests that an even more extensive upheaval of this Court's precedents may be in store. Renouncing this Court's historical commitment to a conception of "the judiciary as a source of impersonal and reasoned judgments," Moragne v. States Marine Lines, 398 U.S. 375, 403 (1970), the majority declares itself free to discard any principle of constitutional liberty which was recognized or reaffirmed over the dissenting votes of four Justices and with which five or more Justices now disagree. The implications of this radical new exception to the doctrine of stare decisis are staggering. The majority today sends a clear signal that scores of established constitutional liberties are now ripe for reconsideration, thereby inviting the very type of open defiance of our precedents that the majority rewards in this case. Because I believe that this Court owes more to its constitutional precedents in general and to Booth and Gathers in particular, I dissent.

I

Speaking for the Court as then constituted, Justice Powell and Justice Brennan set out the rationale for excluding victim-impact evidence from the sentencing proceedings in a capital case. See Booth v. Maryland, supra, at 504-509; South Carolina v.

Gathers, supra, at 810-811. As the majorities in Booth and Gathers recognized, the core principle of this Court's capital jurisprudence is that the sentence of death must reflect an " `individualized determination' " of the defendant's " `personal responsibility and moral guilt' " and must be based upon factors that channel the jury's discretion " `so as to minimize the risk of wholly arbitrary and capricious action.' " Booth v. Maryland, supra, at 502, quoting Zant v. Stephens, 462 U.S. 862, 879 (1983); Enmund v. Florida, 458 U.S. 782, 801 (1982), and Gregg v. Georgia, 428 U.S. 153, 189 (1976) (joint opinion of Stewart, Powell, and Stevens, JJ.); accord, South Carolina v. Gathers, supra, at 810. The State's introduction of victim-impact evidence, Justice Powell and Justice Brennan explained, violates this fundamental principle. Where, as is ordinarily the case, the defendant was unaware of the personal circumstances of his victim, admitting evidence of the victim's character and the impact of the murder upon the victim's family predicates the sentencing determination on "factors . . . wholly unrelated to the blameworthiness of [the] particular defendant." Booth v. Maryland, supra, at 504; South Carolina v. Gathers, supra, 810. And even where the defendant was in a position to foresee the likely impact of his conduct, admission of victimimpact evidence creates an unacceptable risk of sentencing arbitrariness. As Justice Powell explained in Booth, the probative value of such evidence is always outweighed by its prejudicial effect because of its inherent capacity to draw the jury's attention away from the character of the defendant and the circumstances of the crime to such illicit considerations as the eloquence with which family members express their grief and the status of the victim in the community. See Booth v. Maryland, supra, at 505-507, and n. 8; South Carolina v. Gathers, supra, 810-811. I continue to find these considerations wholly persuasive, and I see no purpose in trying to improve upon Justice Powell's and Justice Brennan's exposition of them.

There is nothing new in the majority's discussion of the supposed deficiencies in Booth and Gathers. Every one of the arguments made by the majority can be found in the dissenting opinions filed in those two cases, and, as I show in the margin, each argument was convincingly answered by Justice Powell and Justice Brennan. [n.1]

But contrary to the impression that one might receive from reading the majority's lengthy rehearsing of the issues addressed in Booth and Gathers, the outcome of this case does not turn simply on who — the Booth and Gathers majorities or the Booth and Gathers dissenters — had the better of the argument. Justice Powell and Justice Brennan's position carried the day in those cases and became the law of the land. The real question, then, is whether today's majority has come forward with the type of extraordinary showing that this Court has historically demanded before overruling one of its precedents. In my view, the majority clearly has not made any such showing. Indeed, the striking feature of the majority's opinion is its radical assertion that it need not even try.

II

The overruling of one of this Court's precedents ought to be a matter of great moment and consequence. Although the doctrine of stare decisis is not an "inexorable command," Burnet v. Coronado Oil & Gas Co., 285 U.S. 393, 405 (1932) (Brandeis, J., dissenting), this Court has repeatedly stressed that fidelity to precedent is fundamental to "a society governed by the rule of law," Akron v. Akron Center for Reproductive Health, Inc., 462 U.S. 416, 420 (1983). See generally Patterson v. McLean Credit Union, 491 U.S. 164, 172 (1989) ("[I]t is indisputable that stare decisis is a basic self-governing principle within the Judicial Branch, which is entrusted with the sensitive and difficult task of fashioning and preserving a jurisprudential system that is not based upon `an arbitrary discretion.' The Federalist, No. 78, p. 490 (H. Lodge ed. 1888) (A. Hamilton)"); Appeal of Concerned Corporators of Portsmouth Savings Bank, 129 N. H. 183, 227, 525 A. 2d 671, 701 (1987) (Souter, J., dissenting) ("[S]tare decisis . . . `is essential if case-by-case judicial decision-making is to be reconciled with the principle of the rule of law, for when governing legal standards are open to revision in every case, deciding cases becomes a mere exercise of judicial will, with arbitrary and unpredictable results,' " quoting Thorn burgh v. American College of Obstetricians and Gynecologists, 476 U.S. 747, 786-787 (1986) (White, J., dissenting)).

Consequently, this Court has never departed from pre-cedent without "special justification." Arizona v. Rumsey, 467 U.S. 203, 212 (1984). Such justifications include the advent of "subsequent changes or development in the law" that undermine a decision's rationale, Patterson v. McLean Credit Union, supra, at 173; the need "to bring [a decision] into agreement with experience and with facts newly ascertained," Burnet v. Coronado Oil & Gas Co., supra, at 412 (Brandeis, J., dissenting); and a showing that a particular precedent has become a "detriment to coherence and consistency in the law," Patterson v. McLean Credit Union, supra, at 173.

The majority cannot seriously claim that any of these traditional bases for overruling a precedent applies to Booth or Gathers. The majority does not suggest that the legal rationale of these decisions has been undercut by changes or developments in doctrine during the last two years. Nor does the majority claim that experience over that period of time has discredited the principle that "any decision to impose the death sentence be, and appear to be, based on reason rather than caprice or emotion," Gardner v. Florida, 430 U.S. 349, 358 (1977) (plurality opinion), the larger postulate of political morality on which Booth and Gathers rest.

The majority does assert that Booth and Gathers "have defied consistent application by the lower courts," ante, at 19, but the evidence that the majority proffers is so feeble that the majority cannot sincerely expect anyone to believe this claim. To support its contention, the majority points to Justice O'Connor's dissent in Gathers, which noted a division among lower courts over whether Booth prohibited prosecutorial arguments relating to the victim's personal characteristics. See 490 U. S., at 813. That, of course, was the issue expressly considered and resolved in Gathers. The majority also cites The Chief Justice's dissent in Mills v. Maryland, 486 U.S. 367, 395-398 (1988). That opinion does not contain a single word about any supposed "[in]consistent application" of Booth in the lower courts. Finally, the majority refers to a divided Ohio Supreme Court decision disposing of an issue concerning victim-impact evidence. See State v. Huertas, 51 Ohio St. 3d 22, 553 N. E. 2d 1058 (1990), cert. dism'd as improvidently granted, 498 U. S. — (1991). Obviously, if a division among the members of a single lower court in a single case were sufficient to demonstrate that a particular precedent was a "detriment to coherence and consistency in the law," Patterson v. McLean Credit Union, supra, at 173, there would hardly be a decision in United States Reports that we would not be obliged to reconsider.

It takes little real detective work to discern just what has changed since this Court decided Booth and Gathers: this Court's own personnel. Indeed, the majority candidly explains why this particular contingency, which until now has been almost universally understood not to be sufficient to warrant overruling a precedent, see, e. g., Florida Dept. of Health and Rehabilitative Services v. Florida Nursing Home Assn., 450 U.S. 147, 153 (1981) (Stevens, J., concurring); Mitchell v. W. T. Grant Co., 416 U.S. 600, 636 (1974) (Stewart, J., dissenting); Mapp v. Ohio, 367 U.S. 643, 677 (1961) (Harlan, J., dissenting); but see South Carolina v. Gathers, supra, at 824 (Scalia, J., dissenting), is sufficient to justify overruling Booth and Gathers. "Considerations in favor of stare decisis are at their acme," the majority explains, "in cases involving property and contract rights, where reliance interests are involved[;] the opposite is true in cases such as the present one involving procedural and evidentiary rules." Ante, at 18 (citations omitted). In addition, the majority points out, "Booth and Gathers were decided by the narrowest of margins, over spirited dissents" and thereafter were "questioned by members of the Court." Ante, at 18-19. Taken together, these considerations make it legitimate, in the majority's view, to elevate the position of the Booth and Gathers dissenters into the law of the land.

This truncation of the Court's duty to stand by its own precedents is astonishing. By limiting full protection of the doctrine of stare decisis to "cases involving property and contract rights," ante, at 18, the majority sends a clear signal that essentially all decisions implementing the personal liberties protected by the Bill of Rights and the Fourteenth Amendment are open to reexamination. Taking into account the majority's additional criterion for overruling — that a case either was decided or reaffirmed by a 5-4 margin "over spirited dissen[t]," ante, at 19 — the continued vitality of literally scores of decisions must be understood to depend on nothing more than the proclivities of the individuals who now comprise a majority of this Court. See, e. g., Metro Broadcasting v. FCC, 497 U. S. — (1990) (authority of Federal government to set aside broadcast licenses for minority applicants); Grady v. Corbin, 495 U. S. — (1990) (right under Double Jeopardy Clause not to be subjected twice to prosecution for same criminal conduct); Mills v. Maryland, supra (Eighth Amendment right to jury instructions that do not preclude consideration of nonunanimous mitigating factors in capital sentencing); United States v. Paradise, 480 U.S. 149 (1987) (right to promotions as remedy for racial discrimination in government hiring); Ford v. Wainwright, 477 U.S. 399 (1986) (Eighth Amendment right not to be executed if insane); Thornburgh v. American College of Obstetricians and Gynecologists, 476 U.S. 747 (1986) (reaffirming right to abortion recognized in Roe v. Wade, 410 U.S.

113 (1973)); Aguilar v. Felton, 473 U.S. 402 (1985) (Establishment Clause bar on governmental financial assistance to parochial schools). [n.2]

In my view, this impoverished conception of stare decisis cannot possibly be reconciled with the values that inform the proper judicial function. Contrary to what the majority suggests, stare decisis is important not merely because individuals rely on precedent to structure their commercial activity but because fidelity to precedent is part and parcel of a conception of "the judiciary as a source of impersonal and reasoned judgments." Moragne v. States Marine Lines, 398 U. S., at 403. Indeed, this function of stare decisis is in many respects even more critical in adjudication involving constitutional liberties than in adjudication involving commercial entitlements. Because enforcement of the Bill of Rights and the Fourteenth Amendment frequently requires this Court to rein in the forces of democratic politics, this Court can legitimately lay claim to compliance with its directives only if the public understands the Court to be implementing "principles . . . founded in the law rather than in the proclivities of individuals." Vasquez v. Hillery, 474 U.S. 254, 265 (1986). [n.3] Thus, as Justice Stevens has explained, the "stron[g] presumption of validity" to which "recently decided cases" are entitled "is an essential thread in the mantle of protection that the law affords the individual. . . . It is the unpopular or beleaguered individual — not the man in power — who has the greatest stake in the integrity of the law." Florida Dept. of Health and Rehabilitative Services v. Florida Nursing Home Assn., 450 U. S., at 153154 (concurring opinion).

Carried to its logical conclusion, the majority's debilitated conception of stare decisis would destroy the Court's very capacity to resolve authoritatively the abiding conflicts between those with power and those without. If this Court shows so little respect for its own precedents, it can hardly expect them to be treated more respectfully by the state actors whom these decisions are supposed to bind. See Mitchell v. W. T. Grant Co., 416 U. S., at 634 (Stewart, J., dissenting). By signaling its willingness to give fresh consideration to any constitutional liberty recognized by a 5-4 vote "over spirited dissen[t]," ante, at 19, the majority invites state actors to renew the very policies deemed unconstitutional in the hope that this Court may now reverse course, even if it has only recently reaffirmed the constitutional liberty in question.

Indeed, the majority's disposition of this case nicely illustrates the rewards of such a strategy of defiance. The Tennessee Supreme Court did nothing in this case to disguise its contempt for this Court's decisions in Booth and Gathers. Summing up its reaction to those cases, it concluded:

"It is an affront to the civilized members of the human race to say that at sentencing in a capital case, a parade of witnesses may praise the background, character and good deeds of Defendant (as was done in this case), without limitation as to relevancy, but nothing may be said that bears upon the character of, or harm imposed, upon the victims." 791 S. W. 2d 10, 19 (1990).

Offering no explanation for how this case could possibly be distinguished from

Booth and Gathers — for obviously, there is none to offer — the court perfunctorily declared that the victim-impact evidence and the prosecutor's argument based on this evidence "did not violate either [of those decisions]." Ibid. It cannot be clearer that the court simply declined to be bound by this Court's precedents. [n.4]

Far from condemning this blatant disregard for the rule of law, the majority applauds it. In the Tennessee Supreme Court's denigration of Booth and Gathers as "an affront to the civilized members of the human race," the majority finds only confirmation of "the unfairness of the rule pronounced by" the majorities in those cases. Ante, at 16. It is hard to imagine a more complete abdication of this Court's historic commitment to defending the supremacy of its own pronouncements on issues of constitutional liberty. See Cooper v. Aaron, 358 U.S. 1 (1958); see also Hutto v. Davis, 454 U.S. 370, 375 (1982) (per curiam) ("[U]nless we wish anarchy to prevail within the federal judicial system, a precedent of this Court must be followed by the lower federal courts no matter how misguided the judges of those courts may think it to be"). In light of the cost that such abdication exacts on the authoritativeness of all of this Court's pronouncements, it is also hard to imagine a more short-sighted strategy for effecting change in our constitutional order.

III

Today's decision charts an unmistakable course. If the majority's radical reconstruction of the rules for overturning this Court's decisions is to be taken at face value — and the majority offers us no reason why it should not — then the overruling of Booth and Gathers is but a preview of an even broader and more far-reaching assault upon this Court's precedents. Cast aside today are those condemned to face society's ultimate penalty. Tomorrow's victims may be minorities, women, or the indigent. Inevitably, this campaign to resurrect yesterday's "spirited dissents" will squander the authority and the legitimacy of this Court as a protector of the powerless.

I dissent.

Notes

1 The majority's primary argument is that punishment in criminal law is frequently based on an "assessment of [the] harm caused by the defendant as a result of the crime charged." Ante, at 9. See also Booth v. Maryland, 482 U.S. 496, 516 (1987) (White, J., dissenting); id., at 519-520 (Scalia, J., dissenting); South Carolina v. Gathers, 490 U.S. 805, 818-819 (1989) (O'Connor, J., dissenting). Nothing in Booth or Gathers, however, conflicts with this unremarkable observation. These cases stand merely for the proposition that the State may not put on evidence of one particular species of harm — namely, that associated with the victim's personal characteristics independent of the circumstances of the offense — in the course of a capital murder proceeding. See Booth v. Maryland, supra, at 507, n. 10 (emphasizing that decision does not bar reliance on victim-impact evidence in capital sentencing so long as such evidence "relate[s] directly to the circumstances of the crime"); id., at 509, n. 12 (emphasizing that decision does not bar

reliance on victim-impact evidence in sentencing for noncapital crimes). It may be the case that such a rule departs from the latitude of sentencers in criminal law generally "[to] tak[e] into consideration the harm done by the defendant." Ante, at 15. But as the Booth Court pointed out, because this Court's capital-sentencing jurisprudence is founded on the premise that "death is a `punishment different from all other sanctions,' " it is completely unavailing to attempt to infer from sentencing considerations in noncapital settings the proper treatment of any particular sentencing issue in a capital case. 482 U. S., at 509, n. 12, quoting Woodson v. North Carolina, 428 U.S. 280, 303-304, 305 (1976) (opinion of Stewart, Powell, and Stevens, JJ.).

The majority also discounts Justice Powell's concern with the inherently prejudicial quality of victim-impact evidence. "[T]he mere fact that for tactical reasons it might not be prudent for the defense to rebut victim impact evidence," the majority protests, "makes the case no different than others in which a party is faced with this sort of a dilemma." Ante, 13. See also Booth v. Maryland, supra, at 518 (White, J., dissenting). Unsurprisingly, this tautology is completely unresponsive to Justice Powell's argument. The Booth Court established a rule excluding introduction of victim-impact evidence not merely because it is difficult to rebut — a feature of victim-impact evidence that may be "no different" from that of many varieties of relevant, legitimate evidence — but because the effect of this evidence in the sentencing proceeding is unfairly prejudicial: "The prospect of a `mini-trial' on the victim's character is more than simply unappealing; it could well distract the sentencing jury from its constitutionally required task — determining whether the death penalty is appropriate in light of the background and record of the accused and the particular circumstances of the crime." 482 U. S., at 507. The law is replete with per se prohibitions of types of evidence the probative effect of which is generally outweighed by its unfair prejudice. See, e. g., Fed. Rules Evid. 404, 407-412. There is nothing anomalous in the notion that the Eighth Amendment would similarly exclude evidence that has an undue capacity to undermine the regime of individualized sentencing that our capital jurisprudence demands.

Finally, the majority contends that the exclusion of victim-impact evidence "deprives the State of the full moral force of its evidence and may prevent the jury from having before it all the information necessary to determine the proper punishment for a first-degree murder." Ante, at 15. The majority's recycled contention, see Booth, supra, at 517 (White, J., dissenting); id., at 520 (Scalia, J., dissenting); Gathers, supra, at 817-818 (O'Connor, J., dissenting), begs the question. Before it is possible to conclude that the exclusion of victim-impact evidence prevents the State from making its case or the jury from considering relevant evidence, it is necessary to determine whether victim-impact evidence is consistent with the substantive standards that define the scope of permissible sentencing determinations under the Eighth Amendment. The majority offers no persuasive answer to Justice Powell and Justice Brennan's conclusion that victim-impact evidence is frequently irrelevant to any permissible sentencing consideration and that such evidence risks exerting illegitimate "moral force" by directing the jury's attention on illicit considerations such as the victim's standing in the community.

2 Based on the majority's new criteria for overruling, these decisions, too, must be included on the "endangered precedents" list: Rutan v. Republican Party of Illinois, 497 U. S. — (1990) (First Amendment right not to be denied public employment on the basis of party affiliation); Peel v. Attorney Registration and Disciplinary Comm'n, 496 U. S. — (1990) (First Amendment right to advertise legal specialization); Zinermon v. Burch, 494 U.S. 113 (1990) (due process right to procedural safeguards aimed at assuring voluntariness of decision to commit oneself to mental hospital); James v. Illinois, 493 U.S. 307 (1990) (Fourth Amendment right to exclusion of illegally obtained evidence introduced for impeachment of defense witness); Rankin v. McPherson, 483 U.S. 378 (1987) (First Amendment right of public employee to express views on matter of public importance); Rock v. Arkansas, 483 U.S. 44 (1987) (Fifth Amendment and Sixth Amendment right of criminal defendant to provide hypnotically refreshed testimony on his own behalf); Gray v. Mississippi, 481 U.S. 648 (1987) (rejecting applicability of harmless error analysis to Eighth Amendment right not to be sentenced to death by "death qualified" jury); Maine v. Moulton, 474 U.S. 159 (1985) (Sixth Amendment right to counsel violated by introduction of statements made to government informant-codefendant in course of preparing defense strategy); Garcia v. San Antonio Metropolitan Transit Auth., 469 U.S. 528 (1985) (rejecting theory that Tenth Amendment provides immunity to states from federal regulation); Pulliam v. Allen, 466 U.S. 522 (1984) (right to obtain injunctive relief from constitutional violations committed by judicial officials).

3 It does not answer this concern to suggest that Justices owe fidelity to the text of the Constitution rather than to the case law of this Court interpreting the Constitution. See, e. g., South Carolina v. Gathers, 490 U. S., at 825. (Scalia, J., dissenting). The text of the Constitution is rarely so plain as to be self-executing; invariably, this Court must develop mediating principles and doctrines in order to bring the text of constitutional provisions to bear on particular facts. Thus, to rebut the charge of personal lawmaking, Justices who would discard the mediating principles embodied in precedent must do more than state that they are following the "text" of the Constitution; they must explain why they are entitled to substitute their mediating principles for those that are already settled in the law. And such an explanation will be sufficient to legitimize the departure from precedent only if it measures up to the extraordinary standard necessary to justify overruling one of this Court's precedents. See generally Note, 103 Harv. L. Rev. 1344, 1351-1354 (1990).

4 Equally unsatisfactory is the Tennessee Supreme Court's purported finding that any error associated with the victim-impact evidence in this case was harmless. See 791 S. W. 2d, at 19. This finding was based on the court's conclusion that "the death penalty was the only rational punishment available" in light of the "inhuman brutality" evident in the circumstances of the murder. Ibid. It is well established that a State cannot make the death penalty mandatory for any class of aggravated murder; no matter how "brutal" the circumstances of the offense, the State must permit the sentencer discretion to impose a

sentence of less than death. See Roberts v. Louisiana 428 U.S. 325 (1976); Woodson v. North Carolina 428 U.S. 280 (1976). It follows that an appellate court cannot deem error to be automatically harmless based solely on the aggravated character of a murder without assessing the impact of the error on the sentencer's discretion. Cf. Clemons v. Mississippi, 494 U. S. —, — (1990).

To sentence petitioner to death, the jury was required to find that the mitigating circumstances shown by petitioner did not outweigh the aggravating circumstances. See App. 21-22. In what it tried to pass off as harmless error analysis, the Tennessee Supreme Court failed to address how the victim-impact evidence introduced during the sentencing proceedings in this case likely affected the jury's determination that the balance of aggravating and mitigating circumstances dictated a death sentence. Outside of a videotape of the crime scene, the State introduced no additional substantive evidence in the penalty phase other than the testimony of Mary Zvolanek, mother and grandmother of the murder victims. See 791 S. W. 2d, at 17. Under these circumstances, it is simply impossible to conclude that this victim-impact testimony, combined with the prosecutor's extrapolation from it in his closing argument, was harmless beyond a reasonable doubt.

Made in the USA
Middletown, DE
16 October 2017